learn

Sociology

Sociology

Edward Brent, PhD
Professor of Sociology
University of Missouri
Colombia, Missouri

J. Scott Lewis, PhD
Assistant Professor of Sociology
Penn State Harrisburg
Harrisburg, Pennsylvania

Contributions by:
Romana Pires, MA, MS
Assistant Professor, Sociology
San Bernardino Valley College
San Bernardino, California

JONES & BARTLETT
LEARNING

World Headquarters
Jones & Bartlett Learning
5 Wall Street
Burlington, MA 01803
978-443-5000
info@jblearning.com
www.jblearning.com

Jones & Bartlett Learning books and products are available through most bookstores and online booksellers. To contact Jones & Bartlett Learning directly, call 800-832-0034, fax 978-443-8000, or visit our website, www.jblearning.com.

Substantial discounts on bulk quantities of Jones & Bartlett Learning publications are available to corporations, professional associations, and other qualified organizations. For details and specific discount information, contact the special sales department at Jones & Bartlett Learning via the above contact information or send an email to specialsales@jblearning.com.

Production Credits

Chief Executive Officer: Ty Field
President: James Homer
Senior Vice President: Eve Howard
Senior Development Editor: William Wahlgren
Senior Editorial Assistant: Rainna Erikson
VP, Production and Design: Anne E. Spencer
Production Manager: Susan Schultz
Production Editor: Tina Chen
Production Assistant: Kristen Rogers
Director of Marketing: Alisha Weisman
Senior Marketing Manager: Andrea DeFronzo

Marketing Communications Manager: Katie Hennessy
VP, Manufacturing and Inventory Control: Therese Connell
Manufacturing and Inventory Control Supervisor: Amy Bacus
Composition: diacriTech
Text Design: Anne Spencer and Karen Leduc
Cover Design: Timothy Dziewit and Karen Leduc
Visual Overview Design: CoDesign, Boston
Director of Photo Research and Permissions: Amy Wrynn
Rights & Photo Research Assistant: Joseph Veiga
Rights & Photo Research Assistant: David Millar

Cover/Title Page Images: (clockwise from top left) © iofoto/Shutterstock, Inc.; © Ioannis Pantzi/Shutterstock, Inc.; © Andresr/Shutterstock, Inc.; © Rob Marmion/Shutterstock, Inc.; © Amos Morgan/Photodisc/Thinkstock; © Jupiter images/Pixland/Thinkstock; © Andresr/Shutterstock, Inc.; © Warren Goldswain/Shutterstock, Inc.; © mamahoohooba/Shutterstock, Inc.; © Blend Images/Shutterstock, Inc.; © Alena Ozerova/Shutterstock, Inc.; © vgstudio/Shutterstock, Inc.
Printing and Binding: Courier Companies
Cover Printing: Courier Companies

ISBN: 978-1-4496-7246-1

Library of Congress Cataloging-in-Publication Data
(Unavailable at time of printing)

6048

Printed in the United States of America
17 16 15 14 13   10 9 8 7 6 5 4 3 2 1

Brief Contents

Contents

© Ingram Publishing/Thinkstock

© Photos.com/Thinkstock

© Stockbyte/Thinkstock

© Heather Renee/Shutterstock, Inc.

© Nzgmw2788/Dreamstime.com

© iStockphoto/Thinkstock

© Ingram Publishing/Thinkstock

(Left and Right) © iStockphoto/Thinkstock

© altrendo images/Thinkstock

Contents

© iStockphoto/Thinkstock

Contents XV

© Wavebreak Media/Thistock

© Medioimages/Photodisc/Thinkstock

© Steven Greaves/Corbis

Welcome

Welcome to *Learn Sociology*! Our goal with *Learn Sociology* is to create content for introductory sociology that establishes a new paradigm for student-centered learning.

Learn Sociology is written with the 21st-century student in mind. We have developed a fresh presentation for introductory sociology that is highly interactive, compatible with digital applications, and cognizant of the challenges of an ever-evolving economic landscape. To us, the perfect textbook makes learners want to immerse themselves with the concepts and applications and presents everything they need to know in a reliably structured format. That's what we've done with *Learn Sociology*. We have drawn on the best practices of educational pedagogy with an approach that emphasizes "immersive learning;" that is, a learning experience that deeply engages students in the application of new knowledge and skills—an approach that pairs critical analysis of sociological concepts with examples from everyday life and allows readers to actively engage with the curriculum.

About The Learn Series

Learn Sociology is a publication of **The Learn Series**, a completely new course curriculum solution from Jones & Bartlett Learning that provides a fresh, integrated print and digital program solution for general education survey courses. **The Learn Series** is produced with today's "digitally native" students in mind by re-envisioning the learning experience and focusing not just on *what* students learn but also *how* students learn. **The Learn Series** is characterized by authoritative and notable authors; visual, modular design; student-centered pedagogy; and integrated formative and summative assessments that improve learning outcomes—features that allow instructors to easily customize and personalize course curriculum. **The Learn Series** provides the most interactive and advanced curriculum solution for today's student-centered learning environments by emphasizing the skills students need to thrive in the 21st-century knowledge-based economy.

For more information on additional titles in the series, please visit **www.TheLearnSeries.com**.

Skills for the 21st-Century Workforce

	Sample 21st-Century Addressable Workforce Skills			Supporting Pedagogy in The Learn Series
RESEARCH LITERACY	Able to determine the extent of information needed	Able to evaluate information and its sources critically	Can apply evidence to new problem solutions	Group and individual projects Online Writing Tutorial included in Navigate
INTERPERSONAL COMMUNICATION & PUBLIC SPEAKING	Can convey ideas and meaning through oral communication	Able to speak persuasively in a group	Can effectively work in a team structure to solve problems	Group and individual projects Discussion questions Instructor's Resource Curriculum Guide with additional group projects and activities
PROBLEM SOLVING & CRITICAL ANALYSIS	Able to analyze data; Able to synthesize different types of information	Able to evaluate source material for validity, etc.	Able to make decisions based on data	The Sociological Imagination, a critical thinking feature Short essay questions in Test Bank Interactive exercises in Navigate PAL: Learn Sociology

Continues

	Sample 21st-Century Addressable Workforce Skills			Supporting Pedagogy in The Learn Series
TECHNOLOGY LITERACY	Able to use the Internet critically	Able to retrieve and manage information via technology	Able to use basic word processing and spreadsheet software/tools	Navigate Learn Sociology Chapter Projects Online activities and assignments
WRITTEN COMMUNICATION	Able to organize and outline the main topics or thesis	Uses a variety of simple and complex sentences to create a fluid writing style	Able to write complete, grammatically correct sentences	Online Writing Tutorial included in Navigate Short essay questions in assessment banks

The Approach of *Learn Sociology*

Sociology, the scientific study of society and social life, is even more important today than it was in the past, as people seek to understand the dramatic changes occurring in the world and make decisions regarding controversial issues. Sociology helps students understand how their individual lives are influenced by social structures and historical circumstances that simultaneously limit their possible actions and provide opportunities. Throughout this text, we emphasize several recurring social issues: social structure, social control, social inequality, the social construction of reality, scientific knowledge, and social change. Each important in its own right, these issues inform our understanding of many other concerns. Each of these issues is the focus of one or more chapters and plays at least some role in every chapter. They are brought together by the sociological imagination, which constantly reminds us that to understand social life we must consider how individual problems reflect broader social issues and how the biography of each individual is played out in the broader context of social history.

Sociology is a broad discipline with diverse theoretical perspectives, a wide range of research methods, and includes an array of fascinating topics. Sociology addresses issues ranging from macro-scale issues of urban growth, the economy, population changes, and social movements; to mid-level issues including how people use networks to communicate and accomplish tasks, how organizations achieve efficiencies, and how social movements take shape; to micro-level issues of how groups work, how individuals are socialized to fit into society, and how people communicate and share meaning.

Learn Sociology integrates classic theories of sociology with contemporary empirically-grounded studies. Throughout we emphasize how sociology uses the methods of science to examine social issues and prepare students to understand the foundations of that knowledge as well as its limits.

The discipline of sociology is an ongoing conversation about social life written about, for, and by many different people. Sociology examines how people's lives are influenced by their social class, gender, race, ethnicity, age, sexual orientation, geographic location, and historical era. It is the story of you, the reader, and the story of all of us as we express our individuality, accommodate our differences, and celebrate our diversity. With this in mind, we have taken great pains to cover material of interest to students from diverse backgrounds and to raise questions relevant to each of us and to all of us.

The Structure of *Learn Sociology*

Learn Sociology helps optimize learning through enhanced coverage, study, testing, and review while emphasizing the "applying" that reinforces comprehension. Pedagogical features are designed to provide a preview of the material and ensure key concepts are well understood. Each chapter contains numbered sections, or modules, that address a major concept in the introductory sociology curriculum. These modules are self-contained key content units. Each module has associated learning objectives, a preview statement, illustrations, and a concept learning check assessment. This modular content unit structure informs the entire *Learn Sociology* program.

All of the content in *Learn Sociology* is highly visual, current, and easy to understand. Visual overviews play to dynamic learning and underscore important points. Our goal with *Learn Sociology* is to present accurate core content rooted in best-in-class pedagogy while avoiding distracting off-topic add-ons. The result is an introductory sociology curriculum that is engaging, consistent, and complete—and which helps students measure their progress at every step.

Learn Sociology is fully comprehensive and designed for cutting-edge coursework. By incorporating opportunities for immersive learning, *Learn Sociology* maximizes teaching productivity, enhances student learning, and addresses the challenges of teaching and learning introductory sociology in fresh, new ways.

Pedagogical Aids and Features

Learn Sociology is based on a modular concept format that provides a clear organization of the key topics pertaining to introductory sociology. With this modular format, digital versions of *Learn Sociology* are also fully customizable, allowing faculty full control over the desired curriculum. For more information on customization options, please visit the publisher website at www.jblearning.com.

This essential textbook covers more than 100 introductory sociology topics and divides them into modules linked with learning objectives, providing students with a structured road map for learning, reviewing, and self-assessment.

Every chapter in *Learn Sociology* is organized with the following structure to help learners engage with the concepts in the textbook as they read:

Chapter Sections

The modular format dictates that each chapter opens with a series of learning objectives, which reappear whenever a topic is repeated to help guide students' learning. Each chapter contains several numbered sections that address a major topic or concept; sections are largely self-contained units of content instruction. Any element or feature labeled with a section number reflects and is relevant to that section.

Chapter Overview

Content-specific chapter overviews provide a summary of key chapter concepts and serve as a "master plan" to visually show the scope and sequence of content covered. Students use the Chapter Overviews as a map, to guide them through critical concepts and keep them connected to learning objectives.

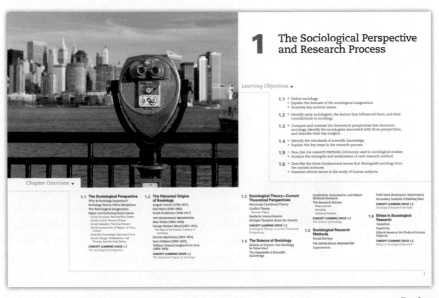

Section Preview Statement

Within each section, a preview statement summarizes the content of the section that follows. These preview statements prepare students for the content ahead, providing advance organization during reading.

3.1 Socialization through Societal Experience

Socialization is the process by which a person learns the beliefs, values, and behavior of his or her society.

▪ Discuss how societal experience impacts an individual's socialization.

Figures and Tables

Figures and tables underscore key points or present complex information. They provide an effective alternative mode of instruction, presented schematically to aid the reader visually and reinforce the text. References to figures in the text are in color to make it easier to locate the figure and pop right back into the reading.

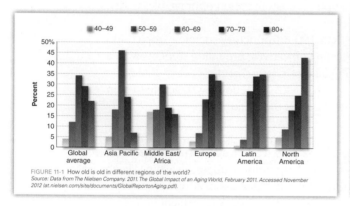

FIGURE 11-1 How old is old in different regions of the world?
Source: Data from The Nielsen Company. 2011. The Global Impact of an Aging World, February 2011. Accessed November 2012 (at.nielsen.com/site/documents/GlobalReportonAging.pdf).

TABLE 10-1 Male- and Female-Dominated Occupations

	Percent Female	
Predominantly Male Occupations	2004	2010
Engineers	13.8%	12.9%
Dentists	22.0	25.5
Physicians	29.4	32.3
Lawyers and judges—2010 just lawyers	29.4	31.5
Firefighters	5.1	3.6
Predominantly Female Occupations		
Elementary and middle school teachers	81.3	81.8
Librarians	83.2	82.8
Registered nurses	92.2	91.1
Receptionists	92.4	92.7
Secretaries	96.9	96.1
Restaurant servers	73.1	71.1

Source: U.S. Census Bureau. 2006. Statistical Abstract. Accessed May 2012 (http://www.census.gov/compendia/statab/2006/labor_force_employment_earnings/labor.pdf); U.S. Census Bureau. 2012. Statistical Abstract. Accessed May 2012 (http://www.census.gov/prod/2011pubs/12statab/labor.pdf).

Concept Learning Check

At the end of every section, a Concept Learning Check is presented to test mastery of the material in that section. These checks focus on familiar "pain points" for students and provide extra coaching on the key concepts in the chapter. This gives learners a chance to apply what they have studied in fresh examples, or to see the material applied from a different perspective.

CONCEPT LEARNING CHECK 10.3 Theoretical Perspectives on Sexuality

Match the following arguments with the theory most closely associated with them.

_____ 1. This theory argues against the bias against anyone who is not a heterosexual.

_____ 2. This theory argues the importance of legitimate births helps regulate sexual behavior to ensure that children will receive the support they need to grow up.

_____ 3. This theory argues that notions of what is right or wrong in terms of sexual behavior are formed through interactions among people and can vary from one society to the next or one time to the next.

_____ 4. This theory argues that women are viewed sexually as part of the domination of women by men.

A. Feminist theory
B. Queer theory
C. Symbolic interactionism
D. Structural-functional theory

The Sociological Imagination

The Sociological Imagination incorporates critical analysis of key concepts and applies a sociological orientation and lens. It replaces **The Learn Series'** usual Critical Thinking Application feature.

Chapter Key Terms

Key Terms appear in blue in the text at point of use and are defined in a way that doesn't interrupt the main idea of the sentence. Key terms are also provided in the margin with sharp definitions that can be used as flashcards. Key terms are also found as an alphabetical list at the very end of the chapter and in the final glossary.

THE SOCIOLOGICAL IMAGINATION Suicide: Individual Tragedy, Social Fact

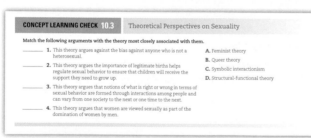

How could any "choice" by a person be more personal or individual than the decision to commit suicide? Yet Emile Durkheim (1858–1917) challenged this common conception and demonstrated the great promise of the new science of sociology in what was one of the first examples of research using empirical data to examine social issues. In a landmark study of suicide, Durkheim (1897) compared the suicide rates in several European countries. He found that suicide rates were relatively stable from year to year but differed substantially between categories of people. Durkheim found that Protestants kill themselves more often than Catholics, the wealthy more often than the poor, males more often than females, and the unmarried more often than people who are married. He concluded that suicide is not just a highly personal individual act but is also influenced by social factors. Durkheim reasoned that categories of people who were more likely to commit suicide all had fewer social bonds and attachments than people less likely to commit suicide. Single people have fewer social ties. The rich and men in the male-dominated societies of his day each had greater autonomy and hence fewer constraints on their behavior. Protestants were more individualistic and practiced fewer solidarity-enhancing rituals than Catholics and hence experienced fewer social ties and bonds to others or to their religious beliefs. Durkheim's study of suicide is an excellent example of quantitative sociological research identifying social facts that exist independently and are beyond the control of individuals. It is a testament to the lasting importance of the work of early sociologists like Emile Durkheim that today, more than 100 years after Durkheim's seminal work, suicide rates for different countries and different categories of people still vary dramatically.

EVALUATE

1. Using the sociological imagination, explain how Durkheim's study of suicide reflects a link between private troubles and public issues.

2. If Durkheim had found that there were no systematic patterns in suicide rates, what would that have implied about a possible link between private troubles and public issues?

3. Do you think the differences Durkheim found between men and women would continue to be found today? How have differences between men and women changed since then and how might that affect those results?

4. Do you think there are differences today in suicide rates among men and women? How might societal changes related to gender affect these results?

Durkheim reasoned that specific categories of people were more likely to commit suicide.
© Rob Hainer/Shutterstock

Visual Overview

The Visual Overview provides a dynamic visual diagram of one or more key concepts and helps to tie chapter themes and segments into a cohesive whole.

Visual Summary

The Visual Summary is located at the end of the chapter and recaps the main ideas in each section using brief, bulleted sentences that are highlighted with an image that refers back to the section content.

Chapter Review Test

The Chapter Review Test is a multiple-choice self-quiz covering the entire chapter. Headings correlate to chapter sections as well as objective statements. Answers that provide complete rationales are included.

Chapter Discussion Questions

Open-ended questions provoke thoughtful discussions in the classroom or in online discussion boards. These questions are carefully chosen to illuminate key concepts of the chapter and to create a constructive experience of discussion, evaluation, and comparison in order to solidify comprehension.

Chapter Projects

Potential projects for individuals, pairs, or small groups are suggested. These can be done either in class or outside of class. They focus on an issue related to students' lives and experience, real-world applications, or media depictions of sociological concepts.

Learn Sociology Digital Curriculum

Learn Sociology is a comprehensive and integrated print and digital solution for courses in introductory sociology. Instructors and students can use the following digital resources in part or in whole:

Navigate PAL: Learn Sociology is a powerful personalized adaptive learning (PAL) platform that uniquely combines a diagnostic to create a study plan, deploying personalized assessment and remediation, and student learning analytics tools all in one easy-to-use, online application. PAL helps students study more effectively so they can make the most of their study time.

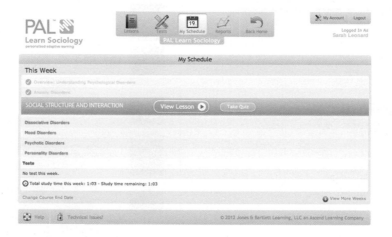

Navigate PAL: Learn Sociology is organized by chapter and chapter section with corresponding learning objectives. PAL allows your students to quiz and test themselves, then review using text pages, presentation coaching objects, and video tutorials on tough chapter content, and provides interactive assessments. PAL helps students prepare for mid-terms and finals and master the concepts of each chapter.

Navigate PAL also provides reports for the instructor providing information on the individual student, as well as the class in total and their mastery of core concepts and course learning objectives.

Key reports for the instructor:

Navigate PAL: Learn Sociology Reports (by Tab in PAL Instructor view)	Course Level	Student Level	Key Benefit	Comparison Data	How the data is exported and/or links to an LMS or grading system
Objective Reports	Course Objectives and class's proficiency	By objective: each individual student's proficiency for that objective	Isolates a student's and a class's knowledge gaps	Students see their individual proficiency in each objective in the course. Instructors see class average proficiency on each objective.	Instructors can export information into a CSV.
Test and Quizzes Reports	Class average scores on each quiz and test	By quiz or test: each individual student's score	Class mastery by quiz/test and student scores by quiz/test	Students see the number of correct answers provided and the percentage of correct answers. Instructors see class average score on test.	Instructors can export information into a CSV to use in a grade book.

Navigate PAL: Learn Sociology Reports (by Tab in PAL Instructor view)	Course Level	Student Level	Key Benefit	Comparison Data	How the data is exported and/or links to an LMS or grading system
Usage Reports	A graphical representation of class's PAL usage including Lesson Usage, Test and Quiz Usage, and System Usage (logins)	Compare individual user's PAL usage with other users in the course; including Lesson Usage, Test and Quiz Usage, and System Usage (logins)	Understand your class's usage of PAL	Students see their usage compared to other students in the course. Instructors see single class average compared to other classes.	N/A
Recent Activity Report	Class's recent activity on Quizzes, Tests, and Remediation Activities	Recent activity for users in the course	Review recent work		N/A
Per Student Report	N/A	N/A	Birds-eye view into each student's work		Instructors can export information into a CSV.

Navigate Learn Sociology is a simple-to-use and fully customizable online learning platform activating the core curriculum content by the text authors with interactive objects, tools, and assessments, and robust reporting and grading functionality.

Deploying digital content that extends the core text, organized by lesson, topic, and learning objectives, instructors can use Navigate Learn Sociology as part of an online or hybrid course offering within their campus learning management system, as desired, requiring little to no start-up time.

Flowable to any device, Navigate Learn Sociology is a course tailored to today's mobile student.

Digital Textbook Alternatives. For students who prefer electronic textbooks, *Learn Sociology* is also available in digital format from leading ebook retailers such as Coursesmart, Amazon, and Google.

Navigate Companion Website. Designed to accompany the *Learn Sociology* textbook, the Navigate Companion Website features numerous interactive activities including Chapter Quizzes, Flashcards, Crosswords, Glossary, and informative learning resources like our Video and Web Links. Activities concentrate on key parts of the text that gauge understanding and help students prepare for class and study more effectively. Lastly, this site includes PowerPoint slides, articles that correlate to The Sociological Imagination in the text, and information on PAL should students want additional resources to further study and master the course. For free access please go to http://sociology.jbpub.com/brent/learnsociologystudent.

Learn Sociology Instructor Resource Program

Every element in the Instructor Resource Program maps to chapter and section-level learning objectives. Student learning outcomes are developed by the main authors of the core text ensuring quality and consistency throughout, creating one of the largest and most comprehensive instructor packages on the market. For all these resources in one location, please see the Learn Sociology Instructor Place.

The comprehensive Instructor Resource Program includes:

- **Instructor Resource Curriculum Guide** features chapter overviews, chapter outlines, suggested lectures, discussion questions, projects, handouts, and media resources—all keyed to chapter section and learning objectives, when and where possible. We also include sample syllabi and correlation grids connecting learning objectives to the scope and sequence of the text, as well as to selected 21st-century workforce skills.
- **Learn Sociology Digital Resources** contains an up-to-date media list for the latest links to videos and animations compiled from around the Web and mapped to the content of *Learn Sociology*.
- **Brownstone's *Diploma* Testing Software** provides a comprehensive bank of test questions written by the main text authors. The complete bank includes over 150 Critical Thinking, Applied, and Factual questions per chapter, each tagged to chapter learning objectives and Bloom's Taxonomy. Questions can be sorted, selected, and edited based on level of difficulty or question type.
- **PowerPoint™ Presentation Slides** in multiple formats: includes PowerPoint with chapter images only; PowerPoint with chapter outlines and key narrative; and PowerPoint with outlines, key narrative, and images. All of the PowerPoint slide presentations contain detailed notes for instructor talking points and include references to support chapter learning objectives.
- **Learn Sociology Instructor Place** provides online access to PowerPoints, Instructor Resource Curriculum Guide, 21st-century workforce skills correlation grid, discussion questions, suggested student projects, video resources links, chapter-by-chapter media bibliography, sample syllabi—basically all of the *Learn Sociology* resources in a digital format.

For any of these resources, please contact your Jones & Bartlett Learning Account Representative at 1-800-832-0034.

More Free Resources for Students to Support Basic Writing Skills

A Writing Tutorial for College Students

The ability to organize and outline main topics and write complete, grammatically correct sentences is a critical skill for today's freshman-level student. Combining the best of English composition manuals and various open resources available online, *Learn Sociology* includes a specially developed free resource designed to help students improve basic writing skills, analyze resources on the web, and perform critical analysis of a topic. The website, www.AWritingTutorialforCollegeStudents.com, distills the essential skills of writing into eight succinct modules:

1. Introduction to College Writing
2. Structure and Thesis Statements
3. Mechanics and Grammar
4. Research, Citation, and Avoiding Plagiarism
5. Making an Argument
6. The Research Paper
7. The Writing Process
8. Elegance and Style

About the Authors

Dr. Antone Minard, PhD

Dr. Minard earned his PhD from the University of California, Los Angeles. He currently resides in Vancouver, British Columbia, where he teaches in the Humanities Department at Simon Fraser University and in the Department of Classical, Near Eastern, and Religious Studies at the University of British Columbia.

Dr. Amy Hale, PhD

Dr. Hale earned her PhD from the University of California, Los Angeles, and teaches introductory students in a variety of courses, disciplines, and delivery systems emphasizing writing projects and assignments.

Acknowledgments

There is an art to aiding in the creation of a textbook like this one. It is an effort that involves encouragement, opportunity, and collaboration. There are dozens of people who have mastered this art and who made the completion of this project possible. We want to start by thanking Eve Howard, senior vice president at Jones & Bartlett Learning. Eve's vision has been the essence of this project, and she provided wonderful motivational speeches, mentorship, understanding, and advice. We would also like to thank our editor, Bill Wahlgren, for his tireless guidance with the manuscript and for his patience and gentility. Without the help extended by each of them, we would not have developed the skills necessary to carry out this project, nor would we have as deep an appreciation of the meaning of collaboration. We would like to especially thank our chief marketing strategist, Alison Pendergast.

Romana Pires of San Bernardino Valley College expertly jumped in and assisted us with the discussion questions and projects at the end of the chapters, taking advantage of her experience with successful online class delivery, and with several of the ancillary elements of the *Learn Sociology* resources. Wendy Ludgewait also contributed to the development of the learning objectives and assessments and the lecture materials.

We also want to thank the reviewers of *Learn Sociology*, who took time out of their hectic schedules to pore over the drafts of the chapters. Your dedication, attention to detail, and expertise helped shape this text. We learned so much from each of you. Thank you!

In-Depth Sociology Faculty Reviewers

Rebecca S. Fahrlander, PhD, University of Nebraska at Omaha
Susan Wortmann, PhD, Nebraska Wesleyan University
Romana Pires, MA, MS, San Bernardino Valley College
Richard Mordi, PhD, Keiser University
Angie Henderson, PhD, University of Northern Colorado
Donice Brown, MS, LPC, Keiser University
James David Ballard, PhD, California State University, Northridge
Richard Sullivan, PhD, Illinois State University

In addition to the reviewers, special thanks to the many instructors who participated in our expanded review and market research, which aided us in rounding out the strategy for The Learn Series, as well as refining the pedagogy and chapters of *Learn Sociology*.

Sociology Faculty Analysts

Christobel Asiedu, Louisiana Tech University

Rebecca Fahrlander, University of Nebraska, Omaha

Tammi Gray, Collin College

Scot Hamilton, University of West Georgia

Caroline Kozojed, Bismarck State College

Danielle MacCartney, Webster University

Ryan Messatzzia, Wor-Wic Community College

Ken Muir, Appalachian State

Kendra Murphy, University of Memphis

Romana Pires, San Bernardino Valley College

Alan Rudy, Central Michigan University

Tracy Scott, Emory University

Craig Shumway, Mesa Community College

Donna Sullivan, Marshall University

Suzanne Sutphin, University of South Carolina

Sean Taylor, Des Moines Area Community College, Boone

Kathleen Tiemann, University of North Dakota

Michael Wise, Appalachian State University

About the Authors

Dr. Edward Brent received his PhD in sociology from the University of Minnesota, Twin Cities in 1976 followed by two postdoctoral fellowships, one in systematic studies of interaction at Minnesota and one in information systems at the University of Missouri. He has taught at the University of Missouri, Columbia since 1976, and in addition to sociology, has taught computer science, management, and health informatics. His investigations examine the intelligent application of computers in the areas of teaching and research. He is founder and president of Idea Works, Inc., which develops software for intelligent text analysis.

J. Scott Lewis is an assistant professor of sociology at Penn State Harrisburg. He received his PhD in sociology in 2006 from Bowling Green State University, where he specialized in social psychology and family studies. He currently publishes primarily in the area of biosociology, which explores how human evolution influences the way in which humans construct culture. He lives in Harrisburg, Pennsylvania with his wife and two children.

© iStockphoto/Thinkstock

Chapter Overview ▼

1 The Sociological Perspective and Research Process

Learning Objectives ▼

1.1
- Define sociology.
- Explain the features of the sociological imagination.
- Illustrate key societal issues.

1.2
- Identify early sociologists, the factors that influenced them, and their contributions to sociology.

1.3
- Compare and contrast the theoretical perspectives that dominate sociology, identify the sociologists associated with those perspectives, and describe their key insights.

1.4
- Identify the standards of scientific knowledge.
- Explain the key steps in the research process.

1.5
- Describe the research methods commonly used in sociological studies.
- Analyze the strengths and weaknesses of each research method.

1.6
- Describe the three fundamental issues that distinguish sociology from the natural sciences.
- Examine ethical issues in the study of human subjects.

An overheard phone conversation. Waiting to board my plane at the airport, I couldn't help but overhear the phone conversation of what appeared to be a college student.

. . . And how's dad? Good. I'm glad he's beginning to get over losing that job. It wasn't anything he did. They were "downsizing" and he was just one more unlucky victim. . . . I know you feel that way, Mom, but he feels badly enough without us blaming him for it . . . yeah, he was in the union, but they laid others off too, almost everyone except. . . . Well, OK, I don't want to argue about it. Perhaps he could have done something to prevent it. But I still think that was a lousy way to treat him after 23 years working for those slave drivers. . . . Yeah, I know. It's tough getting a new job when you're that age, even with a master's degree and experience. . . .

Huh? No, I'm not dating him any more. He's history. I thought I told . . . Yeah, I know you didn't think he was good enough for me anyway, ever since he dropped out of school. . . .

My classes? It's tough, like you'd expect for a good school. They're OK, except for French. I don't know why they make us. . . . Yes, I'm working at it. After all you taught me, you don't think I'd just blow it off, do you? No, they wouldn't let me drop it . . . some rule about the number of hours required to keep my financial aid. I must have argued with the person at the registration office for an hour before I gave up. She just wouldn't listen to reason.

Two other female students walk up to stand beside the first. They look impatient. One makes a show of glancing at her watch and whispers to the other, "Let's go on. Jessie can catch up later." The girl on the phone looks at them pleadingly and holds up her index finger. "OK," says the other student, "one minute."

. . . Yeah, Mom, I know partying too much is dangerous (the other two girls look at her in disbelief). *. . but I have to keep my mental health, too* (the other two girls display a big thumbs-up).

. . . So you'll put the money into my account tomorrow? Thanks, Mom. Yeah. I love you too. Yeah, Mom. I've got to go now. I have to study for the French test. Yeah, I love you too. Take care and say hello to Dad when he gets home. Bye.

The first student hangs up the phone, smiles at her friends, and says, "I can't believe I agreed to go home next weekend! What was I thinking?" as they walk off down the hall.

What is the meaning of this exchange? Most people familiar with modern American culture should quickly recognize that this is a college student talking on the phone to her family. She is borrowing money and discussing her grades in school and how things are at home. She is impatient to finish the conversation so she can go out with her friends. This "account" (this description and explanation of these events) demonstrates a reasonably good understanding of what has transpired. It is good enough to permit most of us, with no training other than growing up in America, to understand the conversation, classify it, and, if we so desire, participate in or respond to it. In fact, each of us, as someone who has to live in society, attempts to account for, explain, and predict what is happening around us in order to survive and function successfully in our everyday lives.

But this common-sense account does not begin to encompass all that is going on in this encounter. There is much more we need to understand. Even commonplace and seemingly trivial events in our everyday lives such as this phone conversation are reflections of fundamental social forces that shape our lives. Sociology gives us the theoretical perspectives, concepts, and methodological tools to understand social life on many levels. After finishing this chapter, you should be able to read this same passage and see it in a different light based on the sociological perspective. Underlying this interaction are issues of social structures, inequality, social change, globalization, and bureaucracies. Different sociological theories each help account for different aspects of the interaction. Finally, the methods of social research can be used to study such interactions to find underlying patterns and insights.

In this chapter we will introduce key themes, concepts, and sociological theories that can be used to understand social life. We will identify fundamental issues that recur throughout the book. We will examine the history of sociology, identifying some of the early sociologists who shaped this perspective, and consider the historical problems they faced in their times that shaped the sociological perspective. Then we will examine the three dominant theoretical views of sociology, showing how each of them contributes to the sociological imagination, and identify their essential concepts and the issues they address. Finally, we will examine common research methods and the standards of science that guide sociology. Let us begin by describing the sociological perspective.

1.1 The Sociological Perspective

Sociology helps us see the world from a new perspective through the sociological imagination and addresses several major and enduring societal issues.

- Define sociology.
- Explain the features of the sociological imagination.
- Illustrate key societal issues.

Why Is Sociology Important?

Sociology is the scientific study of social life. The sociological perspective looks at individual human behavior in the broader social context of the society in which people live, the times in which they find themselves, and the social position of the individual. To most people, sociology offers a new way of looking at the world. Much of the social discourse we encounter in our daily lives, in newspaper articles, in television or film dramas, and in political debates tends to focus on the individual with little or no sensitivity or understanding of how our individual lives are affected by the broader social circumstances in which they take place. Sociology helps us to see our world from a different perspective. The sociological perspective is very different from the way in which most people view social life, and it helps us to see the world from a new perspective, one called the sociological imagination.

Sociology The scientific study of social life.

Sociology Versus Other Disciplines

To better understand sociology, it helps to compare it to other disciplines. Obviously, as a social science, sociology differs from the natural sciences because they do not study people while sociology does. Sociology differs from the humanities by being a science and applying the standards and strategies of science. Sociology differs from applied fields like social work or psychiatry in that sociology is primarily focused on improving our understanding of social life, while fields like social work and psychiatry are primarily focused on applying knowledge to help individuals solve problems in their lives. It should be pointed out, however, that sociology does have a long history of sociologists who were very concerned with making a better world by applying sociological knowledge, and sociologists feel a social responsibility to make knowledge available to others to address important social issues.

Among the social sciences, sociology differs from psychology in that psychology emphasizes individuals while sociologists emphasize understanding individuals in the context of social forces that affect them. Sociology also tends to be broader than other social sciences, overlapping in many ways with economics and political science. Sociology considers the economy and political institutions as but two of the many kinds of social institutions that can be understood sociologically. So, while economists focus on economic exchange and political scientists focus on political institutions, sociologists study not only those but also other forms of social interaction and other institutions. Sociology and anthropology are, in many respects, similar in that they both study the full range of social institutions and forms of interaction, but anthropology places greater emphasis on studying other cultures and has a much stronger biological and archaeological component.

The Sociological Imagination

Sociological imagination The capacity for individuals to understand the relationship between their individual lives and broad social forces that influence them.

Social structure Enduring, relatively stable patterns of social behavior.

Sociologist C. Wright Mills first described the key features of the sociological perspective. According to Mills (1959), the **sociological imagination** is the capacity for individuals to understand the relationship between their individual lives and broad social forces that influence them. The sociological imagination is a dramatically different way of looking at the world from the way most of us may be accustomed. Instead of looking to individuals to explain events, the sociological imagination encourages us to consider the broader social forces that have affected those individuals. This is not to say that individuals are not responsible for their own behavior. Sociologists recognize that individuals have some choice in their lives and individuals should be held accountable for their actions. But individuals are influenced by social circumstances, and if we want to understand someone's beliefs and behaviors, we also must understand those social circumstances.

Mills argued that the sociological imagination helps us understand the intersection between history and biography (Mills 1959). By *history*, Mills means the broad historical events affecting society. The housing crisis and the financial crisis leading up to the Great Recession beginning in 2008 are examples of such broad historical circumstances. By *biography*, Mills means the significant events in an individual's life and the experiences that shape them. Losing a job in 2009 and having your home mortgage foreclosed in 2011 would be examples of individual biographical events in a person's life that are linked to broader historical trends. In other words, the sociological imagination helps us understand events in historical context. Those events were much more likely during that time period than they had been in the previous decades, during which most people enjoyed years of relative stability in jobs and those who bought houses usually saw their value increase.

Similarly, Mills argued, the sociological imagination helps us understand the link between private troubles (or successes) and public issues. Private troubles or successes could include events such as being the victim of a crime or having to drop out of college due to lack of funds. Public issues are common circumstances or trends in a society that affect many people. These could include a high crime rate or a high dropout rate among college students due to financial constraints. In this case, the sociological imagination helps us to see the general trends that are behind particular events. An individual is more likely to be the victim of crime in a neighborhood with a high crime rate or to run out of money while going to an expensive college in which many students experience the same problem.

Major and Enduring Social Issues

The sociological perspective leads to several enduring societal issues that will be visited and revisited throughout this text. These issues provide a framework for understanding many of the most important insights of sociology. Here, I will briefly identify these themes, illustrate some of the questions they raise, and point ahead to chapters in which each issue will play an important role.

- Social structure
- Social control
- Social inequality
- The social construction of reality
- Scientific knowledge
- Social change

Social Structure: Red and Blue States

During the 2012 US presidential election, both the Republican and Democratic parties campaigned extensively in states like Ohio, Florida, and Wisconsin FIGURE 1-1. Yet they ran few advertisements and gave very few campaign speeches in states like Oklahoma, Illinois, and Texas. Why? Because of social structure.

Social structures are enduring and relatively stable patterns of social life. Social life takes place within the context of social structures that simultaneously constrain our interactions and emerge from them. Some of the most important and most pervasive

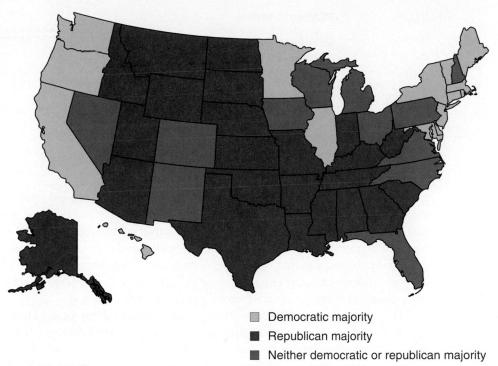

□ Democratic majority

■ Republican majority

■ Neither democratic or republican majority

FIGURE 1-1 Red, blue, and purple are often used to indicate states leaning toward Democrats (blue states) or Republicans (red states) in US elections; purple is used for states with no clear majority.
Source: Data from Barone, Michael. 2012. States Aren't Red or Blue Forever. The American. Retrieved January 2012 (http://www.american.com/archive/2012/march/states-arent-red-or-blue-forever).

social structures are components of culture. **Culture** is a combination of ideas, behaviors, and material objects that members of a society have created and adopted for carrying out necessary tasks of daily life and that are passed on from one generation to the next. Because the winner of the US presidential election is determined by votes in the Electoral College and most states cast all their votes for the candidate winning the majority in their state, there is little point in campaigning heavily in a state that traditionally votes for the party of your opponent. Understanding this social structure is essential for campaign politics. In general, we can no more understand social life without understanding social structures than we could drive across the country without a highway map.

Social structures include everything from social organizations such as a university to institutions such as the criminal justice system to regular patterns in household behavior such as rates of fast-food consumption. This book will explore questions such as "What are some of the important social structures?" "How do they constrain behavior?" "How have those social structures changed over time?"

Social structure plays a strong role in understanding regularities in how people interact, such as social statuses and roles, bureaucracies and social institutions such as the criminal justice system, the family, educational institutions, religious organizations, the political and economic systems, the healthcare system, and communities.

Social Control: Posture Photos

Would you let someone take nude pictures of you—no, not when you were a baby, but now, as an adult? Most people would say no to that question. Fewer than 5% of students say yes when asked in the author's classes. Yet thousands of otherwise sane students at some of the nation's most prestigious universities had such nude photos taken of themselves, including George H. W. Bush, Hillary Rodham Clinton, and many others. Years later, this became public knowledge when *The New York Times* published the details, labeling it "the posture photo scandal." Why did this happen? Social control.

Social control consists of efforts by society to regulate people's behavior and thoughts. There are many formal and informal methods by which societies exert social control, and they are surprisingly effective. Preposterous as it may seem now, over several decades, every student attending those colleges was required to have nude posture

Culture A combination of ideas, behaviors, and material objects that members of a society have created and adopted for carrying out necessary tasks of daily life and that are passed on from one generation to the next.

Social control Efforts by society to regulate people's behavior and thoughts.

FIGURE 1-2 There is growing inequality in which the top 1% of households in the United States holds an increasing share of income. *Source: Data from Shaw, H., and C. Stone. 2012. "Incomes at the Top Rebounded in First Full Year of Recovery, New Analysis of Tax Data Shows Top 1 Percent's Share of Income Starting to Rise Again." Center on Budget and Policy Priorities. Accessed October 2012 (http://www.cbpp.org/cms/index. cfm?fa=view&id=3697).*

1% of population   20% of income

photos taken as a matter of school policy. For decades, scientists believed a person's body shape could predict whether that person would become a criminal (Sheldon 1949). As part of that research, scientists persuaded those universities to require that all students have naked posture photos taken. But later research found criminals to include people of all body shapes, and that theory was abandoned. Even though the great majority of those students probably entered college believing they would never let others take nude photos of them, for decades virtually every student complied.

The issue of social control raises fundamental questions about society. How do societies survive and not break down into anarchy? How do societies distinguish acceptable behavior from unacceptable deviance? Who decides what is deviant behavior? How do individuals know what they should and should not do? How is unacceptable behavior punished and how is desirable behavior rewarded? How is social control exerted even when there is no one watching over each person at all times? Social control recurs in every chapter and is covered extensively in Chapter 6, *Deviance and Crime*, along with Chapter 17, *Collective Behavior, Social Movements, and Social Change*.

Social Inequality: The One Percent

In the fall of 2011, in response to the financial crisis that began in 2008, protests took place in over 95 cities across the United States and around the world in support of the Occupy movement (Thompson 2011). These protests ultimately included a diverse collection of people who joined the protest for different reasons. Despite the muddled message from so much diversity, these protests highlighted growing inequality in which the 1% (the top 1% of all households) holds an increasing share of income and wealth both in the United States and around the world. A 2012 report by the Center on Budget and Policy Priorities (Shaw and Stone 2012) indicates that the share of total income for the 1% in the United States rose to 19.8% in 2010 FIGURE 1-2 and is among the highest percentages since the late 1920s. Income of the 1% increased by nearly 12% from 2009 to 2010, while the income of the bottom 90% of households fell substantially during the recession of 2008 to 2009 and remained at its lowest level since 1983 in inflation-adjusted dollars (Shaw and Stone 2012).

Social stratification is the term used to describe patterns of inequality in a society. Income inequality and wealth inequality are only two of many forms of social inequality that, in the 21st century, is growing throughout the world. Why do we have inequality? Why is there so much inequality? What types of inequality exist? What causes inequality? What are the consequences of extreme inequality for those left behind and for the society as a whole? These are some of the many questions sociologists ask about social inequality. The social inequality theme is pervasive and can be found in every chapter in this text. It is particularly emphasized in Chapters 7 through 10, which examine class and stratification in the United States, global stratification, inequalities of race and ethnicity, and inequalities of gender.

Social Construction of Reality: Is This a Crime?

On November 2, 1995, Cambridge, Massachusetts, police arrested Toni Marie Angeli for taking photographs of her nude four-year-old son after police were called by photo shop employees who developed the film (*The New York Times* 1996). Yet many families

Social stratification Patterns of inequality in a society.

Income inequality and wealth inequality are only two of many forms of social inequality that in the 21st century is growing throughout the world.
© iStockphoto/Thinkstock

have nude photographs of young children taken in bathtubs, playing outside, and so on. Is this a crime? This example illustrates the importance of the social construction of reality—the view that the meaning of social life is negotiated as part of a social process among participants and that therefore reality is not directly experienced by individuals so much as it is socially constructed. Admittedly, the first time students hear this claim that reality is socially constructed, many of them object. After all, surely there is a reality out there that we all experience even if we disagree about it. Maybe not so much. Let us play the example forward and see where it takes us.

A photo shop employee saw the naked child in photographs with adults and was concerned that this might be evidence of child abuse or pornography. So he called the police, who confronted Ms. Angeli when she picked up the photographs. She explained that the child was her son. What is more, the photographs were for a photography class at Harvard University. This reveals how the social construction of reality operates, because the photo shop employee and Ms. Angeli were offering two very different views of the same "reality." The police and eventually the courts had to determine which view was "real." Regardless of what her intent was or whether abuse had occurred, if the court had decided it was child abuse, Ms. Angeli would have suffered the consequences. If the photographs were viewed as normal family pictures, she would not be punished. So the "reality" of the situation as measured by real consequences for participants is that constructed within the criminal justice system.

The social construction of reality is of fundamental importance for understanding how meaning gets assigned to cultural elements (Chapter 2), understanding how social interaction takes place (Chapter 4), deciding whether an act is deviance or a crime (Chapter 6), and resolving political debates and affecting outcomes of campaigns (Chapter 14). It also recurs in other chapters wherever contentious issues are considered.

Scientific Knowledge: Race and Crime

Blacks accused of a crime are treated more harshly than whites in the United States. Right? Some people might say this is just common sense and we do not need a science of sociology to determine whether it is true. Other people might disagree and argue that blacks and whites are treated fairly and equally by our criminal justice system when accused of a crime. However, one classic sociological study found that neither of these statements is entirely true. In a classic study, sociologist Gary LaFree (1980) studied 881 rape cases processed by the criminal justice system over a five-year period in a single city in the 1970s. He found that one-third of the rape suspects reported were whites and that proportion stayed virtually unchanged throughout the criminal justice process. This suggests that blacks and whites are treated nearly the same. However, when he looked at whether the victim was black or white, he found huge differences. The proportion of black suspects in rapes of black women dropped from 44.7% of reported rapes to only 16.7% imprisoned for six or more years, while the proportion of black suspects in rapes of white women increased from 23% of reported rapes to 50% imprisoned for six or more years. Black suspects accused of raping white women were nearly six times more likely to end up in prison than black suspects accused of raping black women and nearly three times as likely as white suspects accused of raping white women.

This study illustrates the importance of scientific knowledge. Sociology is not just common sense. In fact, much common sense is just plain wrong. Sociology also needs to distinguish itself from opinion. But how can scientific knowledge be separated from other forms of knowing? What standards must be met to be a science? What procedures are required to avoid potential biases? How can we assure ourselves that we are not just fooling others and ourselves?

This need for a science of sociology and the dependence of sociology on evidence-based studies is a theme that recurs throughout this text. It is particularly important in the last half of this chapter, where the standards of scientific knowledge and common procedures for conducting sociological research are discussed. In each of the other chapters, the results of scientific studies will be presented that are the basis for

Cell phones and social media have played and will continue to play a prominent role in movements for social change.

© arindambanerjee/Shutterstock, Inc.

Globalization Increasing interdependence throughout the world.

sociological knowledge. Information about how those studies were performed is provided so readers can have sufficient information about how those studies were performed and their validity can be judged.

Social Change: Globalization, Cell Phones, and the Arab Spring

The Arab Spring is the name given to a wave of demonstrations and protests that took place in the Arab world beginning in late 2010 and, by 2012, had forced rulers from power in Tunisia, Egypt, Libya, and Yemen, and led to major uprisings in many other Arab countries (Schillinger 2011). This is but one of many examples of social change.

All of this occurred in a region in which many of these rulers had held power for decades. Why did these dramatic changes occur after all those years? What causes social change to occur in some times and places and not others? What are the major forms of social change that are transforming our lives? What can we predict for the future? For thousands of years, civilization changed slowly or not at all, and the lives of children were much like those of their parents. Yet the past two centuries have seen increasingly rapid changes fundamentally transform social life. Societies have become urbanized, once-stable populations have ballooned in size, industrialization and bureaucratization transformed work and the economy, social and political movements reshaped global power structures and led to greater secularization throughout much of the past century, new technologies promise new capabilities but threaten old ways of doing things, and **globalization**—increasing interdependence throughout the world—affects nearly every aspect of our lives, from the cultural elements we adopt from other countries to the economic interdependence that comes from increased trade to the changing job situation as countries compete globally for markets.

These many different social changes are woven together. Social media, for example, had an important role in the Arab Spring helping protesters to organize activities and get word out to the press and the world, and cell phones made this possible while people were on the move. Today there are more than seven billion people in the world and more than six billion active cell phones (Farivar 2012). How is this new technology changing the world, not only in affluent high-income countries but also in poor countries? There are reportedly more cell phones in the world today than there are toothbrushes (Lazaro 2012). Social change is central to our understanding of collective behavior and social movements that seek to create social change (Chapter 17). It is also central to population and urbanization (Chapter 16), which are two of the fundamental social changes reshaping our lives. Social change is an important theme throughout this text. Every major topic has to include some consideration of how it is changing over time.

CONCEPT LEARNING CHECK 1.1   The Sociological Perspective

For each of the following, select the statement that best illustrates that issue.

_____ **1.** Social structure

_____ **2.** Social control

_____ **3.** Social inequality

_____ **4.** Social construction of reality

_____ **5.** Scientific knowledge

_____ **6.** Social change

A. India continues to see rapid growth in population every year.

B. There are several kinds of colleges and universities in the United States, including private schools, public schools, for-profit schools, and religious schools.

C. Council members debated for several hours before finally agreeing construction noise is a problem and creating a task force to propose a solution.

D. In the United States, the net worth of black households is less than a tenth that of white households.

E. After World War II, at the Nuremberg War Crimes Trial, many of the defendants accused of war crimes argued that they were ordered to perform the acts and hence should not be held accountable.

F. The study by LaFree (1980) examined data from rape cases in a Midwestern city, following accused rapists through the criminal justice system.

1.2 The Historical Origins of Sociology

Sociology as a discipline began in the late 19th century, arose during a time of social upheaval, and was shaped by several early sociologists.

- Identify early sociologists, the factors that influenced them, and their contributions to sociology.

Sociology is a relatively new discipline, beginning in the late 19th century and only taking clear shape during the early 20th century. Sociology arose during a time of great social upheaval. That historical context strongly influenced early sociologists, affecting the issues they addressed and shaping the approach to understanding the discipline that became sociology. The fundamental issues, perspectives, and concerns raised by these early sociologists continue to influence sociology a century later and will be revisited throughout this text.

The 19th century was a period of rapid and profound social change. The American and French revolutions of the late 18th century led people to call into question traditional aspects of social life. The French Revolution, for example, not only overthrew the aristocracy but also upset social order completely. Both revolutions led to new ideas, including the conviction that individuals possessed inalienable rights that should be respected by government. Rapid advances in astronomy, physics, and mathematics were transforming the way people viewed the natural world, and science provided a view of the world that began to challenge more traditional views based on religion.

The Industrial Revolution began around 1750 in England and spread throughout Europe and the United States. The **Industrial Revolution** was marked by a dramatic change in the nature of production in which machines replaced tools, steam and other energy sources replaced human or animal power, and skilled workers were replaced with mostly unskilled workers. This led to profound changes in social life as production was taken out of the homes to centralized factories where large machines could be run by steam engines. As the Industrial Revolution progressed, it spread to more and more areas of the economy, coming first in the textile industry, then mining, the steel industry, mass transportation, and eventually encompassing all aspects of the economy. By 1800, more British workers were employed in manufacturing than in agriculture, and Britain became the first industrialized country. The United States did not reach this stage until 70 years later (Lenski and Lenski 1982).

Along with the Industrial Revolution came urbanization as workers left farms to seek factory jobs in the rapidly expanding cities. Rapid technological change spurred by advances in science and the Industrial Revolution led to dramatic advances in steam ships and railroads, manufacturing, and communications. Great inequality developed as owners of the new factories, railroads, and mills became multimillionaires while people who once made a good living at crafts were forced to take factory jobs that barely offered a subsistence wage.

This historical overview helps make clear how early sociologists were influenced by the broad social changes that were occurring during their lifetimes. At the same time, we can assess the relevance of their ideas for today and tomorrow. It is instructive to look at their work as they tried to explain "modernity," since we are ourselves on the cusp of yet another transition—from modernity to postmodernity—and are trying to make sense of this equally rapid and no less profound social change.

> **Industrial Revolution** A dramatic change in the nature of production in which machines replaced tools, steam and other energy sources replaced human or animal power, and skilled workers were replaced with mostly unskilled workers.

Many workers were compelled to join together to form unions, sometimes using strikes or work stoppages, to negotiate better wages and working conditions.

© John Gress/Corbis

August Comte (1798–1857)

August Comte touched upon themes of scientific knowledge, social control, and social change. Comte was the first to propose applying the scientific method to social life and is often called the father of sociology. Born in a small town in France, Comte later moved to Paris. He was heavily influenced by the French Revolution (1789) that overthrew the aristocracy of France and threatened the entire social order. Comte was interested in how societies achieve social order ("social statics") and what causes a society to change ("social dynamics").

Comte (1975) argued there were three historical stages in the emergence of sociology as a scientific discipline. In the earliest theological stage, which lasted until the Renaissance, society was seen as an expression of the will of God, and understanding social life required theological explanations. The Renaissance ushered in a metaphysical stage in which nature was seen as the basis for explaining human behavior, as illustrated by philosopher Thomas Hobbes, who argued social life was the result of people acting in their own selfish interests. Comte believed sociology was ready for a third stage, the scientific stage. Comte was inspired by natural scientists such as the astronomers Copernicus and Galileo and physicist and mathematician Isaac Newton. He believed in scientific sociology, in which explanations of social life would be based on science. Comte called this scientific approach to sociology *positivism*. **Positivism** is an approach to sociology that assumes the methods of the natural sciences such as physics can be applied successfully to the study of social life and the scientific principles learned can be applied to solving social problems. Comte never actually conducted scientific investigations himself. Comte proposed this new science of social life be called sociology, from the Latin *socius* (being with others) and the Greek *logos* (study of).

Karl Marx (1818–1883)

Karl Marx emphasized the themes of inequality, social change, and scientific knowledge. Born and educated in Germany, Marx was expelled for advocating revolution and spent the last half of his life in abject poverty in London, where he studied in the library of the British Museum and wrote for radical newspapers but never held an academic position. Marx, a German social philosopher, greatly influenced sociology. Marx lived in England during the period when the effects of the Industrial Revolution and capitalism were dramatically transforming economic and social life. This was a period in which a few people who owned the new mills and factories were gaining great wealth while workers in those new factories were being paid bare subsistence wages. Marx was greatly influenced by the tremendous inequality he saw all around him, and his critique of capitalism based on class conflict was an effort to explain that inequality. Marx believed that human history was a history of class conflict, with each stage in history dominated by one class exploiting another. In his own time, Marx saw this conflict expressed as a continuing class struggle and argued that capitalism was based on class conflict. One class, the **bourgeoisie** or capitalists, own the **means of production**—the technologies and resources required for producing goods or services in an economy, such as factories, raw materials, and machines. The second class, the **proletariat**, or workers, sell their labor to capitalists for wages. Workers are paid less than the value of what they produce. The **surplus value** (the difference between what manufacturers are paid for goods or services and what they pay workers to produce them) becomes profit for the capitalist. The proletariat are exploited because they are paid only enough to survive, with the surplus value (the value they produce minus their wages) providing profit for the bourgeoisie. Marx argued workers would eventually realize how unfairly they were being treated and would unite in a workers' revolt. Capitalism would fall and would be replaced by a classless society in which individuals would work according to their ability and be rewarded according to their need (Marx, 1867; Marx and Engels, 1848). While many of Marx's predictions have not come true in the United States and most other developed societies, his work with Engels, *The Communist Manifesto*, is commonly regarded as one of the most influential political writings of all time. The conflict Marx saw in the workplace has been a continuing feature of modern life and promises to be a prominent feature of postmodern life in the 21st century. His explanation of social life as the result of fundamental conflict is the basis for conflict theory and has been applied to a wide range of issues well beyond economic ones. This approach has become the basis for conflict theory that has influenced many areas of sociology, including the sociology of knowledge and the sociology of religion.

Positivism An approach to sociology that assumes the methods of the natural sciences such as physics can be applied successfully to the study of social life and the scientific principles learned can be applied to solving social problems.

Bourgeoisie (capitalists) Those owning the means of production, including land, raw materials, forests, factories, and machines.

Means of production The technologies and resources required for producing goods or services in an economy, such as factories, raw materials, and machines.

Proletariat (workers) People who sell their labor to capitalists for wages.

Surplus value The difference between what manufacturers are paid for goods or services and what they pay workers to produce them.

Emile Durkheim (1858–1917)

Emile Durkheim emphasized the themes of social structure, social control, social change, and scientific knowledge. Born and raised in eastern France, educated in France and Germany, Emile Durkheim obtained the first academic appointment in sociology in France in 1877 at the University of Bordeaux and in 1906 moved to the Sorbonne. Durkheim was interested in the impact of social structures on individual behavior. He argued (Durkheim 1895) that **social facts**—regular patterns of behavior—exist independently of individuals and constrain individual behavior. At the same time, he argued, individuals internalize social facts as guidelines for behavior to the point where it may be difficult for individuals or people studying them to separate the ideas and values of the individual from those of the larger society that have influenced the individual.

> **Social facts** Regular patterns of behavior characterizing a society that exist independent of individuals and are beyond the control of individuals.

Like Comte before him, Durkheim was heavily influenced by the French Revolution and sought to understand the forces that hold society together. Durkheim was also influenced by the Industrial Revolution and the ongoing process of urbanization. Durkheim argued (Durkheim 1893) that the mechanical solidarity of small, traditional rural communities in which most people performed the same kind of work and had shared values and perspectives was being replaced in complex industrial societies by a new kind of solidarity. He called this new form of solidarity organic solidarity because it resembled biological organisms with their different organs, each of which performs a different role to keep the organism alive. The organic solidarity of modern industrial

---

THE SOCIOLOGICAL IMAGINATION   Suicide: Individual Tragedy, Social Fact

How could any "choice" by a person be more personal or individual than the decision to commit suicide? Yet Emile Durkheim (1858–1917) challenged this common conception and demonstrated the great promise of the new science of sociology in what was one of the first examples of research using empirical data to examine social issues. In a landmark study of suicide, Durkheim (1897) compared the suicide rates in several European countries. He found that suicide rates were relatively stable from year to year but differed substantially between categories of people. Durkheim found that Protestants kill themselves more often than Catholics, the wealthy more often than the poor, males more often than females, and the unmarried more often than people who are married. He concluded that suicide is not just a highly personal individual act but is also influenced by social factors. Durkheim reasoned that categories of people who were more likely to commit suicide all had fewer social bonds and attachments than people less likely to commit suicide. Single people have fewer social ties. The rich and men in the male-dominated societies of his day each had greater autonomy and hence fewer constraints on their behavior. Protestants were more individualistic and practiced fewer solidarity-enhancing rituals than Catholics and hence experienced fewer social ties and bonds to others or to their religious beliefs. Durkheim's study of suicide is an excellent example of quantitative sociological research identifying social facts that exist independently and are beyond the control of individuals. It is a testament to the lasting importance of the work of early sociologists like Emile Durkheim that today, more than 100 years after Durkheim's seminal work, suicide rates for different countries and different categories of people still vary dramatically.

EVALUATE

1. Using the sociological imagination, explain how Durkheim's study of suicide reflects a link between private troubles and public issues.

2. If Durkheim had found that there were no systematic patterns in suicide rates, what would this have implied about a possible link between private troubles and public issues?

3. Do you think the differences Durkheim found between men and women would continue to be found today? How have differences between men and women changed since then and how might that affect those results?

4. Do you think there are differences today in suicide rates among men and women? How might societal changes related to gender affect these results?

Durkheim reasoned that specific categories of people were more likely to commit suicide.

© Rob Hainer/Shutterstock, Inc.

societies was one based on increased specialization and a division of labor in which different people perform different tasks rather than everyone doing much the same thing. Durkheim also contributed to the sociology of religion (Durkheim 1912) and the sociology of education (Durkheim 1922).

Max Weber (1864–1920)

Max Weber's wide-ranging work addressed the themes of social change, scientific knowledge, social structures, the social construction of reality, and inequality. The eldest child of a successful Protestant entrepreneur, Max Weber (pronounced "VAY-ber") was born and lived in the Kaiser's Germany and held professorships in the new academic discipline of sociology. Unlike Durkheim, who emphasized the influence of social structures on individuals, Weber emphasized rational action by human actors based on their own subjective understanding (verstehen) anchored in a context of shared cultural ideas.

Weber (1904–1905) argued there was a connection between religious beliefs and the development of capitalism. In European nations where there were both Protestants and Catholics, Weber noted that an overwhelming number of business leaders, skilled workers, and capitalists were Protestant. He argued (Weber 1904) that the **Protestant work ethic** (a disciplined work ethic, rational approach to life, and an emphasis on this world) helped lead to the rise of capitalism among Protestants. This Protestant work ethic was heavily influenced by Calvinism. John Calvin was a leader in the Protestant Reformation who believed in predestination, with some people condemned from birth to eternal damnation while others were destined to receive salvation. Calvinists, desperate for confirmation that they were among the chosen ones, sought signs in this life that they would receive God's favor. Eventually, Calvinists came to rely heavily on economic success and wealth as signs of divine favor. The wealthier a person became, the more certain it was that he or she was favored by God. To Calvinists, wealth became the measure of both worldly and afterworldly success. Ironically, since the accumulation of wealth itself was the measure of God's favor, Calvinists typically did little to enjoy their wealth, living frugally and reinvesting their money to gain still further wealth. Nor were Calvinists inclined to share their wealth with the poor, who were viewed as people obviously not in God's favor. Thus, Calvinist beliefs were fertile ground for the development of capitalism, and countries with many Protestants who were influenced by such beliefs tended to adopt industrial capitalism earlier than other countries.

Weber also argued that social inequality in systems of stratification was based not just on economics but also on class, status, and power in complex causal relationships rather than the simple economic determinism of Marx. Weber developed a methodology of research that attempted to be value free, relying on causal explanations and ideal types such as his well-known types of authority and types of rationality.

Weber (1913) saw modern life as experiencing increasing rationality—human action in which goals are set and achieved in the most efficient manner. He argued that preindustrial societies were dominated by traditional values and beliefs handed down from generation to generation. In contrast, industrial societies, he argued, were becoming rationalized, where the **rationalization of society** is the transition from a society dominated by tradition to one dominated by reason and rationally calculable scientific criteria. Today's "big-box stores" like Wal-Mart exemplify rationality when they do everything they can to cut their costs and maximize their profits while still being able to sell items for less than the competition. For example, Wal-Mart discovered it could save a few pennies per item by putting bottles of shampoo and other beauty products on their shelves without a box. When millions of bottles are sold every year, that small change significantly increased Wal-Mart's profits. Nowhere is rationalization more evident than in the changing character of social organizations. Weber argued that traditional organizations based on custom and personal relationships were being superseded by **bureaucracies**—organizations based on rationality, having a clear division of labor, written rules and regulations, impersonality, hierarchical lines of authority, and selection and promotion based on competence (Weber 1913).

Protestant work ethic A disciplined work ethic, rational approach to life, and an emphasis on this world.

Rationalization of society The transition from a society dominated by tradition to one dominated by reason and rationally calculable scientific criteria.

Bureaucracy An organization based on rationality, having a clear division of labor, written rules and regulations, impersonality, hierarchical lines of authority, and selection and promotion based on competence.

George Herbert Mead (1863–1931)

George Herbert Mead's work addressed the themes of the social construction of reality and social control. The son of a New England minister, George Herbert Mead studied at Oberlin, Harvard, Leipzig, and Berlin. He was an instructor at the University of Michigan until he was invited by John Dewey to the new University of Chicago, where Mead taught until he died.

Mead is a cofounder of symbolic interactionism, a perspective emphasizing the importance of symbols and meanings for human interaction. Mead (whose papers were published posthumously in 1934) believed that to understand human behavior, we need to consider the person's concept of self. In his view, the self includes the "I" and the "me." The "I" is the self as subject who makes decisions and takes actions based on his or her desires, while the "**me**" is the self as object as the person is regarded by others. Thinking is an internal dialogue between the I and the me. Based on these ideas, Mead developed a theory of socialization in developmental stages. First, infants exist in the world before they understand it, mimicking the gestures of others but not understanding the meaning of those gestures for others. As individuals are socialized, they become able to **take the role of the other**—to understand how others view the situation and what it means from their perspective. For example, a teenager wishing to borrow his mother's car needs to understand her concern for his safety and whether he might get into trouble. Eventually, the mature individual would come to understand the **generalized other**—the collective attitudes of the entire community regarding how the individual is expected to behave. The generalized other provides a mechanism for the individual to internalize the norms and values of society.

"I" The self as subject who makes decisions and takes actions based on his or her desires.

"Me" The self as object as the person is regarded by others.

Take the role of the other To understand how others view the situation and what it means from their perspective.

Generalized other The collective attitudes of the entire community regarding how they are expected to behave.

The Rest of the Picture: Diversity in Sociology

Perhaps you noticed that all of the famous founders of sociology discussed above were white males. We have to keep in mind that sociology developed in times when the roles available for women or people of color in academic life were far more restricted than today. As a result, the early sociologists who had the greatest impact on the discipline were all white males. However, we do not have to look far to find examples of women and minorities who also made important contributions to the discipline—contributions that even today are often overlooked.

Harriet Martineau (1802–1876)

In a time when few women were able to obtain a formal education, Harriet Martineau, a native of England from a wealthy family, not only became educated but also went on to study social life in both England and the United States. She was interested in social reform, traveled widely, and was an active advocate for the abolition of slavery. An accomplished author of dozens of books, many articles, and more than 1,000 newspaper columns, her book, *Society in America,* published in 1837, provided an insightful examination of the family customs, religion, politics, and race and gender relations in the United States at that time. Unfortunately, like other early women sociologists, her work, which also examined sociological research methods and the British agricultural and political economy, has been largely ignored within sociology. While she is best known for translating Comte's work into English, some sociologists argue that the first woman sociologist deserves to be considered hand in hand with the discipline's better-known founders (Deegan 1991; Rossi 1973).

Jane Addams (1860–1935)

Many early North American sociologists combined their interest in sociology with the role of social reformer. Since women sociologists of the time were denied academic appointments, many of them redirected their efforts into social reform. Jane Addams epitomizes this approach. Although she came from a wealthy family, in 1889 she, along with Ellen G. Starr, founded Hull House, a center located in Chicago's slums, to provide assistance to immigrants. Her keen sociological insights into class differences and the assimilation of immigrants into society helped her work there be far more effective than it would otherwise have been. Sociologists at the nearby University of Chicago, at her invitation, often visited Hull House. Based on this work, she was cowinner of the Nobel Peace Prize in 1931—the only sociologist to be so recognized. She was also active in the women's suffrage movement and the peace movement.

William Edward Burghardt Du Bois (1868–1963)

The son of a poor Massachusetts family, W. E. B. Du Bois was the first African American to receive a PhD from Harvard. He authored more than 100 scholarly articles and 20 books on race and race relations. While employed by the University of Pennsylvania in Philadelphia, he authored a classic sociological work, *The Philadelphia Negro: A Social Study*, in 1899. In this book, he analyzed race relations in Philadelphia and found that some of the more successful African Americans in the community severed their ties with other African Americans to gain greater acceptance by whites. This weakened the African-American community. Du Bois sought to "put science into sociology" by studying "my own people, pointing out all the facts, both good and bad regarding the American Negro and his plight." Du Bois disagreed with the social Darwinism that dominated the times, arguing that African Americans were not inferior but were the victims of white prejudice and discrimination. Early in his life, he was optimistic that racial divisions could be overcome. However, during his lifetime, he was largely ignored by mainstream sociology. The *American Journal of Sociology*, for example, never even reviewed his landmark work, *The Philadelphia Negro*. By the age of 93, Du Bois was disillusioned with the lack of significant progress in race relations in the United States and emigrated to Ghana, where he died two years later.

CONCEPT LEARNING CHECK 1.2   The Historical Origins of Sociology

Match the phrase below with the correct author.

_____ **1.** The only sociologist to earn a Nobel prize.

_____ **2.** Inequality should be measured based on class, status, and power.

_____ **3.** The methods of the natural sciences can be applied successfully to a science of society.

_____ **4.** Author of *The Philadelphia Negro*.

_____ **5.** Developed the concept of the generalized other.

_____ **6.** Conducted one of the first examples of research using empirical data to examine social issues.

A. Emile Durkheim

B. Max Weber

C. Jane Addams

D. W. E. B. Du Bois

E. August Comte

F. George Herbert Mead

1.3 Sociological Theory—Current Theoretical Perspectives

Three theoretical perspectives express much of the variation in sociological thought: structural-functional theory, conflict theory, and symbolic interactionism.

- Compare and contrast the theoretical perspectives that dominate sociology, identify the sociologists associated with those perspectives, and describe their key insights.

Theory An organized set of concepts and relationships among those concepts offered as an explanation or account of some phenomenon.

Theory plays a crucial role in sociology. A **theory** is an organized set of concepts and relationships among those concepts offered as an explanation or account of some phenomenon. One of the features that distinguishes sociology from some other disciplines is its emphasis on developing a body of theories that can be generalized beyond particular times and places. Sociology as a discipline is unified through the sociological perspective, the viewpoint that humans are influenced and are a product of the social environment, including culture and the social structure. The theoretical perspectives, although seemingly different explanations, share common ground—the sociological perspective. There are several strong theoretical perspectives that have been applied to a wide range of social phenomena. We will provide a brief overview of these theories here. We will draw upon these theories throughout the text to account for empirical findings as we discuss various issues in sociology.

Structural-Functional Theory

A key theme of **structural-functional theory** is that society can be viewed as a system of parts, each of which contributes to the whole. Structural-functional theory grew out of Auguste Comte's concern for how society achieves order. Another early sociologist, Herbert Spencer, used a biological organism as an analogy for society, developing a view of society that became known as social Darwinism because of its similarity to Charles Darwin's argument regarding the evolution of species. Spencer (1873–1881) argued that, just as the various social structures of the human body such as the brain, heart, lungs and so on are interdependent and each contribute to the survival of the organism, social structures are also interdependent and contribute to the survival of society. The most effective social structures will persist over time while less effective ones disappear, a process of survival of the fittest. Hence, we can understand society by identifying social structures and determining their function for society.

So, what is a social structure? Societies do not have arms and legs. Instead, social structures are enduring, relatively stable patterns of social behavior. Social structures include expectations attached to positions and relationships, the distribution of people among social positions, and the distribution of social rewards. Examples of social structures include collectivities of people displaying various levels of organization, ranging from small groups to families to multibillion-dollar corporations such as IBM to the criminal justice system to societies and nation-states. But social structures also include less tangible examples such as a persistent pay gap between what men and women are paid for comparable work, the ways in which we expect parents to behave toward their children, and the fact that members of the Mormon Church are more likely to live in Utah while members of the Baptist Church are more likely to live in states that were part of the Confederacy.

A structural-functionalist explains social structures by identifying the functions they perform for the society as a whole. A **function** is the consequence or effect of a social structure for the society as a whole. The structural-functional argument is illustrated for families in FIGURE 1-3. Families, a social structure, are found in societies because

> **Structural-functional theory**
> The theory that society can be viewed as a system of parts, each of which contributes to the whole.

Social structures include collectivities of people displaying various levels of organization.

© Loskutnikov/Shutterstock, Inc.

> **Function** The consequence or effect of a social structure for the society as a whole.

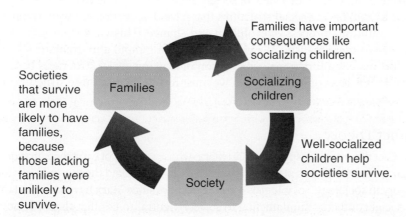

FIGURE 1-3 Structural-functional theory example: families.

Families have important consequences like socializing children.

Socializing children

Well-socialized children help societies survive.

Society

Societies that survive are more likely to have families, because those lacking families were unlikely to survive.

Families

they perform useful functions, such as socializing children. Successfully socialized children help societies survive by preparing children to take their place in society and leading to a stable or increasing population. Societies with effective families are likely to continue to persist, while societies without strong families may have existed in the past but are unlikely to have survived.

In the United States, by the 1950s, the structural-functional theory dominated American sociological work. Perhaps the best-known sociologist from this era is Talcott Parsons, who extended functional theory by dropping the organic analogy and viewing society as a social system (Parsons 1951). He elaborated this perspective by attempting to determine the basic tasks all societies must complete in order to survive and then identifying the social structures that help accomplish those tasks.

More recently, Robert Merton (1968) extended functional theory by arguing that we as individuals are not always aware of all the functions of a social structure. **Manifest functions** are the obvious and usually intended consequences of actions, while **latent functions** are the less obvious and often unintended consequences. The manifest function of the educational system, for example, is to educate young people so they can eventually take their place in and contribute to society. However, the educational system has a number of latent functions, providing adult supervision for young children and later providing the place where young people often meet the person they will eventually marry. Merton also pointed out that not all social structures have positive benefits for the society. **Dysfunctions** are the negative consequences of a social structure. A **latent dysfunction** is a negative consequence of a social structure that is not immediately obvious. Latent dysfunctions play a particularly important role in social life because policies designed to produce positive functions often also lead to latent functions that were not anticipated. For example, offering employees early retirement bonuses has the function of reducing the payroll for a corporation but also has the latent dysfunction of producing a temporary increase in expenses required to pay the additional benefits to people selecting early retirement.

The greatest contribution of the structural-functional view is that it is inherently social, focusing on **emergent properties** of societies—important characteristics that cannot be reduced to some simple combination of characteristics of individuals or other components of societies—and explaining the characteristics of social structures by their relationship to other structures and society. This view is clearly very sociological and not at all psychological or individualistic. But notice the role of the individual in this view—as object. Structural-functionalism has also been criticized for "taking people out of the equation" by emphasizing the effects of structures on individuals and ignoring **agency**—the capacity for people to act to change their own lives and to influence others. Functionalism has also been criticized on a number of other grounds. Structural-functional arguments sometimes appear teleological or circular because they explain a structural feature by its consequences. Others have charged that structural-functionalism is inherently conservative because it encourages us to think of societies as fixed systems needing to be preserved largely in their current state.

Modern functionalism as reflected in Merton's work takes an important shift in direction, moving from a view of society as fixed and stable to one that may still be in process, still having social structures that have dysfunctions as well as functions and in a continuing process of evolution and change. This view is far less conservative and seems more realistic in a world experiencing rapid and dramatic social change. Unfortunately, a functional explanation of existing social structures based on their functions is less compelling when we must recognize that those structures may have dysfunctions as well.

Conflict Theory

Conflict theory was inspired by Karl Marx, whose critique of capitalism first developed a theory of social life based upon conflict. This argument laid the groundwork for conflict theory in sociology. Sociologists over the decades since Marx have extended this notion of social conflict as fundamental to society. Central to conflict theory is **power**—the

Manifest functions The obvious and usually intended consequences of actions.

Latent functions The less obvious and often unintended consequences of actions.

Dysfunctions The negative consequences of a social structure.

Latent dysfunction A negative consequence of a social structure that is not immediately obvious.

Emergent properties Important characteristics that cannot be reduced to a simple combination of characteristics of individuals or other components.

Agency The capacity for people to act to change their own lives and to influence others.

Power The ability to influence others even in the face of resistance.

ability to influence others even in the face of resistance. Social power can derive from any or several different social resources, including financial wealth, the capacity to inflict violence on others, legitimate authority, knowledge, tradition, and expertise. Many sociologists regard C. Wright Mills as the founder of modern conflict theory. His 1956 book, *The Power Elite*, argued that much power in the United States rested with a **power elite** consisting of leaders of dominant institutions, including the military, corporations, and political institutions. The power elite monopolizes power in the United States and dominates other institutions and individuals.

Conflict theory can also be broadly applied in any area in which there are inherent conflicts between categories of people who compete for scarce resources. Beginning with W. E. B. Du Bois, a the conflict perspective has been applied to understanding race relations. It has also been applied to understanding relations between a variety of dominant and minority groups. A prominent example is feminist theory, which focuses on conflict between men and women.

The conflict Marx saw in the workplace has been a continuing feature of modern life and promises to be a prominent feature of postmodern life in the 21st century.

©i4lcocl2/Shutterstock, Inc.

Feminist Theory

Feminist theory criticizes traditional sociological work, arguing that it has been sexist as a result of the dominance of males in society in general and the preponderance of males within sociology. They argue traditional sociological research often ignores gender as an important variable, focuses on men's problems, overgeneralizes from men to both genders, takes the male point of reference, and takes for granted traditional gender roles (Reinharz 1992). For example, early sociological studies that looked at factors predicting the educational level and occupational prestige people would attain in life focused solely on men, assumed that these processes were important only for men, presumed that women would display similar results, and took for granted traditional gender roles by examining the impact of father's education and occupation on sons but ignoring the impact of mothers.

One variant of feminist theory, standpoint theory (Collins 1986; Smith 1987), argues that women, because of their subordinate position in society, are more aware of the inequalities of gender and the consequences of gender for various aspects of one's life. Hence, women are better able to raise these issues and address them in theory and research. This notion that oppressed minorities are better able to see the realities of social life than their oppressors has also been raised for blacks. "To be in someone else's power . . . induces doubts about the ordering of the universe, while those who have power can assume it is part of the natural order of things and invent or adopt ideas which justify their possession of it" (Albert Hourani, cited in Terkel 1992).

Conflict theory makes an important contribution to sociology by recognizing that there are sometimes inherent conflicts of interest between different categories of people. That conflict, whether based on social class, race, gender, or other social divisions, often leads to great inequality. However, critics point out that conflict is not inherent in every social situation, and in some cases, everyone benefits more from cooperation than from conflict. The activist role of conflict theorists who hope to change the world rather than merely interpret it also makes their motives suspect to others. Defenders of the conflict view argue that every theoretical perspective has its own political consequences, and having consequences neither can nor should be avoided.

Power elite Leaders of dominant institutions, including the military, corporations, and political institutions.

Symbols The words, gestures, and objects that communicate meaning between people.

Symbolic Interactionism

Symbolic interactionism was introduced to sociology by George Herbert Mead (Mead 1934), Cooley (1909), and W. I. Thomas (1931). Symbolic interactionism combines the importance of mutual interactions among people from Georg Simmel (1902–1917) with Max Weber's notion of verstehen and the importance of the self-concept (from William James 1890). For symbolic interactionists, it is **symbols**—the words, gestures, and objects that communicate meaning between people—that permit social interaction to go beyond that of other animals. It is only through symbols that we can define and distinguish various social relationships such as parent and child, and symbols permit coordinating our actions with others, passing culture on to future generations. Without symbols, we could not have books. Language would be limited to crude gestures and signs mimicking the things they stand for—like the "language" of other animals. Abstract thought would not be possible. Mathematics and everything that depends on mathematics, from engineering to architecture to accounting, would not be possible. In short, symbols are essential for social life as we know it.

The meaning of symbols can change in different contexts. Saying "yes" in answer to a question obviously has different meanings depending on the question. A fur coat may be worn to symbolize wealth or to demonstrate cultural pride of indigenous northern people. In everyday interaction, people often find themselves offering a "**definition of the situation**"—a statement or action that explicitly or implicitly suggests the meaning the actor would like others to attribute to his or her actions. Definitions of the situation have real consequences. As W. I. Thomas (Thomas and Thomas 1928) stated it in what has come to be known as the **Thomas theorem**, "if men define situations as real, they are real in their consequences." For example, offering money to a casual acquaintance may be intended as an offer of help. However, other actors may offer competing definitions of the situation. If the casual acquaintance offered money is a police officer who has just stopped you for a traffic violation, he might define your action as an attempt to bribe him.

Often, such competing definitions of the situation can be reconciled to produce a **negotiated order**—a shared meaning for the situation agreed upon by all participants. This process of negotiating the meaning of a situation raises another fundamental issue that will be revisited throughout this text—the **social construction of reality**. In this constructivist view, since the meaning of social life is negotiated in a social process among participants, reality is not directly experienced by individuals so much as it is socially constructed. An extreme version of this view would argue that there is no reality other than that which is socially constructed. A less extreme view might argue that even though there may be an objective reality out there somewhere, we as individuals do not directly experience it but are influenced in our perception of reality by social interaction and meanings other people attribute to that reality.

As people interact with others, they are shaped by perceptions of themselves by those others. Cooley (1902:152) referred to this as the **looking-glass self**—people mold themselves in response to how other people perceive them, and the individual's responses serve to reinforce the perspectives of other people. Robert Merton (1968:477) took this a step farther to describe a **self-fulfilling prophecy**—a prediction that leads, directly or indirectly, to becoming true. For example, if a child is disappointing to her parents and they begin to believe she will not succeed in school, the child may sense that they do not have faith in her abilities and quit trying, leading her to fail in school. Both of these are clarifications of how the social construction of reality helps to shape or even become reality.

One focus of symbolic interactionism is what many call the sociology of everyday life. This work examines mundane interactions from people's normal daily lives to understand how those people find and express meaning in their lives. Just because this work focuses on everyday occurrences should not lead us to think of it as trivial or inconsequential. In fact, just the opposite. Sociological research in the interactionist tradition is helping us to understand how everyday interaction reproduces the social structures of society (Giddens 1984). In this view, social structures arise from and persist only through continuing individual action. Social movements are organized efforts by people to change society. Social change often results from such individual and collective action. Perhaps even more important (and certainly more common) than the changes in social structures that result from collective social interaction is the continuity in social structures that is also the results of social interaction, as social structures are reproduced and maintained through daily actions of individuals. Without social interactions to implement policies, carry out necessary tasks, and enforce social control, social organizations and institutions could not survive.

Definition of the situation A statement or action that explicitly or implicitly suggests the meaning the actor would like others to attribute to his or her actions.

Thomas theorem "If men define situations as real, they are real in their consequences."

Negotiated order A shared meaning for the situation agreed upon by all participants.

Social construction of reality We as individuals do not directly experience reality but are influenced in our perception of it by social interaction and meanings other people attribute to that reality.

Looking-glass self People mold themselves in response to how other people perceive them, and the individual's responses serve to reinforce the perspectives of other people.

Self-fulfilling prophecy A prediction that leads, directly or indirectly, to becoming true.

Existing organizations, institutions, and cultures, then, are the result of the cumulative impact of individual actions over time. This is illustrated by the way most organizations honor founders and other individuals who have been instrumental in their development.

The greatest contribution of interactionist theories is the insight that social life is the product of individuals interacting with one another. This alerts us to the importance of both the meaning individuals attach to that interaction and the ways in which they employ interaction to reproduce existing social structures or change them. However, this approach is sometimes criticized for deemphasizing social structures.

Multiple Theories: Room for Growth

Together, these three theoretical perspectives provide a broad base for sociological analysis of social life. While each is sociological, they also have different emphases, different assumptions, and are often applied to different levels of analysis. Both structural-functionalism and conflict theory look at social life at the macro level. **Macro-level** studies focus on social structures that influence individuals, such as groups, organizations, cultures, or even societies. These include studies of structural changes in the jobs available in a society, the patterns of growth of cities, and studies of legislation affecting the criminal justice system. In contrast, the symbolic interactionist approach focuses on the micro level. **Micro-level** studies focus on individuals, thoughts, actions, and individual behaviors. Micro-level studies often focus on day-to-day activities and relations among people such as conflict within a group, patterns of talk in friendship groups, or how people select marriage partners. However, none of these theories are necessarily limited to a specific level of analysis, and some of the most interesting recent work in sociology attempts to bridge the gap between micro-level studies and macro-level studies by studies at the meso level. **Meso-level** studies either focus on intermediate level structures, such as the family or small organizations, or may try to bridge the micro and macro levels to show how one influences the other. Studies of classroom behavior or family dynamics are likely to be meso-level analyses, though they might also focus on micro-level aspects.

These different levels of analysis sometimes reflect important differences in how these sociologists view social life. Macro-level analyses tend to view individuals as passive objects acted upon by external forces. In contrast, micro- or meso-level analyses tend to view individuals as active actors who, though constrained by social circumstances, can make decisions and take actions that influence their own lives and those of others. This relates to the philosophical question of free will versus determinism—whether people have free will to affect their lives or have their lives determined by external forces beyond their control.

Each theory contributes fundamental insights into important issues facing societies as well as individuals. Yet each has limitations, and none of these perspectives alone provides a comprehensive view of social life. For this reason, we will draw upon insights from each of these perspectives throughout this text. While these theories have not been successfully integrated in a comprehensive manner and perhaps cannot be, this leaves a tension or dynamic in each chapter. In this important sense, the work of sociology is not yet done. While considering multiple theoretical perspectives helps us to identify important insights for each of the topics we will cover, there will remain, in each chapter, a number of questions and problems still unsolved that represent important issues for the sociologists of tomorrow. Perhaps some of the readers of this text will make important contributions to solving those problems.

Whatever else can be said about theories, they develop best when combined with empirical research. Theorizing alone (sometimes called "armchair theorizing") is not usually the pattern of work in sociology. Instead, sociologists working in each of these traditions are usually actively engaged in research in which they test these theories and refine them by examining social life. How do they do this? This is our next topic: the science of sociology.

Macro-level studies Studies that focus on social structures that influence individuals, such as groups, organizations, cultures, or even societies.

Micro-level studies Research focusing on individuals, thoughts, actions, and individual behaviors.

Meso-level studies Studies that either focus on intermediate-level structures, such as the family or small organizations, or may try to bridge the micro and macro levels to show how one influences the other.

CONCEPT LEARNING CHECK 1.3   Sociological Theory—Current Theoretical Perspectives

For each of these three theories, select a concept associated with the theory and the sociologist associated with that concept.

THEORY	CONCEPT	SOCIOLOGIST
_____ 1. Structural-functional theory	**A.** Social class	**i.** Robert Merton
_____ 2. Conflict theory	**B.** Verstehen	**ii.** Max Weber
_____ 3. Interactionist theory	**C.** Manifest function	**iii.** Karl Marx

1.4 The Science of Sociology

Sociology is a science. To be a science, it must meet the standards of scientific knowledge that apply to all sciences. These standards distinguish scientific knowledge from common sense and other forms of "knowing."

- Identify the standards of scientific knowledge.
- Explain the key steps in the research process.

Sociology has, from the beginning, been torn between reform and science—whether to seek to understand the world or to change it. This tension continues today. However, the "road map" for what sociology must do to be a science is clear, and sociologists use this as a set of standards and guidelines for conducting research.

Reform or Science: Can Sociology Be Value Free?

There is a tension within sociology between those who emphasize the science of sociology and those who seek to reform society. The reform perspective is illustrated by Jane Addams, whose work at the Hull House and her Nobel Peace Prize reflect efforts to make the world a better place. In fact, many of the earliest articles published in the first journal of the discipline—the *American Journal of Sociology*—seem from today's perspective to be a curious blend of science with reform and even a strong dose of religious fervor. This reform perspective is consistent in many ways with Marx as well. Marx and many other proponents of conflict theory argue the proper role of a social scientist should not be that of a disinterested, objective observer of social life but rather an active proponent of social change. This view is epitomized by Marx's famous statement, emblazoned on his tombstone, "The philosophers have only interpreted the world, in various ways; the point, however, is to change it." Sociologists working in the tradition of Karl Marx argue it is impossible to separate our values from our research. Instead, they suggest, researchers should make their values and basic assumptions known so that others can judge their work accordingly.

In contrast, the scientific perspective is reflected in Comte's early efforts to create sociology as the science of society. But how can sociologists distinguish their scientific approach to social life from the politicized and self-interested positions of other actors in social life? After all, critics could charge, the sociologists' view is merely one more opinion, no better and no worse than that of any other person. To help distinguish the science of sociology from other views, sociologists such as Max Weber have argued that sociological research should be value free. That is, the researcher should not permit her own values to influence the research. Research should be objective—beyond the influence of our own values, beliefs, and biases—and should provide an impartial and reasoned view of the issues. The scientific approach to sociology identifies a number of commonly accepted standards for scientific knowledge that together provide a process for developing and validating knowledge and that distinguish scientific knowledge from competing forms of knowledge.

The Standards of Scientific Knowledge

Sociology is a social science, a discipline that applies the principles of scientific inquiry to the social world. Sociology is not an ideology, not a political position, not a religion, and not a system of beliefs. Those play a legitimate role in public discourse and arguments over public policy. But those are not the same as scientific knowledge. Scientific knowledge must meet four standards: It must be empirically testable, falsifiable, reproducible, and generalizable. TABLE 1-1 lists these standards, defines each, and provides both an example and counterexample.

One hallmark of scientific knowledge is that it must be empirically testable. Surveys are one form of empirical data that can test many theories. However, philosophical questions such as "How many angels can dance on the head of a pin?" simply cannot be tested empirically and cannot be part of scientific knowledge.

Scientific knowledge should be falsifiable. Philosopher of science Karl Popper (1963) argued that it is impossible to prove a theory to be true. How, for example, could we prove even a simple statements like "all cities must have a central business district?" To prove this statement true, we would have to examine all cities now, in the past, and in the future. On the other hand, all it takes to disprove such a statement is a single case in which it is not true. Hence, Popper argues, scientific knowledge should be falsifiable. We should be able to deduce implications from it that can clearly be disproven if they are wrong. It is by conjecturing a theory and then refuting it that scientific progress is made. Predicting one candidate will win, for example, can be falsified if the other candidate wins the election. But vague predictions, such as a horoscope prediction that "you will meet a tall dark stranger," are so ambiguous that we could never falsify them. Someone, for example, could argue that that person was not the tall dark stranger after all.

Scientific knowledge should be reproducible. If you interview your classmates and ask who they will vote for in the next presidential election, someone else should be able to conduct a similar survey with the same questions and get virtually identical responses. If only you can produce some effect and everyone else who tries to reproduce your study fails to find the same effect, then people will begin to suspect there is something wrong with your knowledge claim. For example, in 1989, electrochemists Stanley Pons and Martin Fleischmann (Fleischmann and Pons 1989) reported a study in which their electrolysis of heavy water on a palladium electrode appeared to generate unaccounted-for heat and to give off small amounts of neutrons and other byproducts, suggesting they had produced cold fusion—a fusion reaction at near

TABLE 1-1 Standards of Science

Standard	Definition	Examples	Counterexamples
Empirically testable	Empirical data can be obtained that can show whether it is true or false.	Surveys are used to predict voting in election studies.	Some politicians predict elections based on "instinct" or a "gut feeling."
Falsifiable	It is possible to identify possible results that would show it is wrong.	If the predicted candidate fails to win, then the prediction is wrong.	This candidate will do better with your contribution; unfortunately we have no comparison.
Reproducible	Others should be able to perform similar studies and obtain similar results.	Other polls should show similar results.	A poll by the campaign gives their candidate a 5% advantage compared to all other polls.
Transferable	The same results should be likely to occur across different settings, different times, and for different people.	Older voters tend to be more conservative than younger voters consistently in many surveys.	Younger voters and minorities voted in higher percentages in the 2008 presidential election, but their percentages dropped back to "normal" in 2010.

room temperature. If so, this would have been a Nobel Prize–winning discovery. However, subsequent studies were unable to confirm it, and eventually cold fusion became widely discredited, attracting only a few researchers because it did not meet the standard of reproducibility.

Scientific knowledge should be transferable. It is **transferable** if the results are likely to apply in other settings and circumstances. For example, studies of voting in different times, different places, and for different issues usually find that older voters are more conservative than younger voters. However, your personal experience with service at a restaurant may not be similar to that of other customers. Similarly, the particular events leading to a specific revolution in one country may not occur in other revolutions. So an account of a specific revolution, while interesting and perhaps good history, may not be applied to revolutions in general.

Qualitative, Quantitative, and Mixed-Methods Research

Qualitative research is research emphasizing verbal descriptions and avoiding counting items or the use of mathematics. Qualitative research is often used for exploratory research studying a new area when the researcher does not know much about the area and wants to learn from the people being studied. Qualitative studies often include extensive verbal narratives with rich textual descriptions of events and people, often group people and actions into types, and attempt to understand what those types mean to the people being studied. For example, Michael Burawoy (1979) conducted qualitative research in which he worked as a machinist in a machine shop in the 1970s. He observed how workers and managers interacted and then wrote a book describing the patterns of behaviors he found and how those workers found meaning in their work.

Quantitative research emphasizes numerical descriptions of data, counting, and the use of mathematics and statistics to describe and analyze data. Studies in which many people are asked the same standard questions and then the results are counted and compared using statistics are examples of quantitative research. Often they compare how frequently things occur for people from different backgrounds based on things like age, race, and gender. They also often attempt to determine causal relationships. For example, the National Health and Social Life Survey (Michael et al. 1994) is a quantitative study that asked more than 3,000 people a set of standardized questions about health-related behaviors, then compared the frequency of various behaviors for people of different ages, sexes, races, and so on.

The qualitative and quantitative approaches to research have important differences, so it is important to understand how they are different. But they are not mutually exclusive. Many researchers conduct **mixed-methods research**—research that combines both qualitative and quantitative research in the same study. For example, Michael Burawoy's (1979) study of work in a machine shop is primarily qualitative, but it also includes a quantitative component. One common form of mixed-methods research uses qualitative research first to identify key issues of importance to the people being studied, then uses that information to construct a standardized questionnaire sent to many people and analyzed quantitatively. There are other ways these approaches are combined as well. The primary goal is to use each for the part of the research for which it is most appropriate.

The Research Process

The research process is a cycle consisting of eight steps that take place for each research project. This process is summarized in FIGURE 1-4, which is influenced by the work of sociologist Walter Wallace (1971). First we will summarize the overall process. Then we will examine the key steps in more detail below.

1. **Select a topic.** First researchers select a topic to research, such as expanding use of smart phones. This should be something that can fill in a gap about something important that we do not know. It could have practical importance such

---

Transferable If the results are likely to apply in other settings and circumstances.

Qualitative research Research emphasizing verbal descriptions and avoiding counting items or the use of mathematics.

Quantitative research Emphasizes numerical descriptions of data, counting, and the use of mathematics and statistics to describe and analyze data.

Mixed-methods research Research that combines both qualitative and quantitative research in the same study.

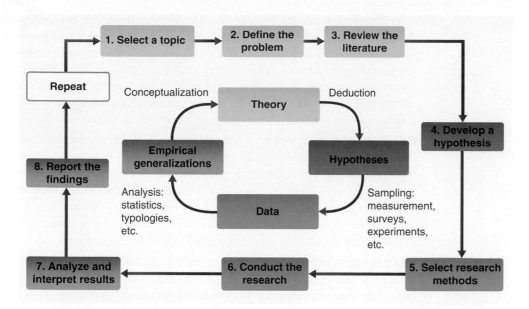

FIGURE 1-4 The research process.
Source: Adapted from Wallace, Walter L. 1971. The Logic of Science in Sociology. *Piscataway, NJ: Transaction Publishers.*

as influencing new laws about the use of smart phones, or it could just help us understand how people use them. Usually the initial topic is much too broad and needs to be narrowed. What is it about smart phones that seems most interesting and most important to study?

2. **Define the problem.** The literature review should help narrow the topic to a well-defined problem. In this case, you might decide to study how people use smart phones, and in particular you are interested in how young adults use them as opposed to older adults. You may develop a theory of how people use smart phones. A **theory** is an organized set of concepts and relationships among concepts that can be proposed to explain something of interest. For example, your theory might expect that people are more likely to have smart phones if they are more comfortable with new technology and are more likely to use them for tasks important to themselves. This is becoming a lot more specific, but it still needs to be narrowed by developing a hypothesis that you can actually test.

3. **Review the literature.** A review of the literature identifies what has already been discovered and published about this topic so you do not waste time duplicating earlier work. Often your initial research idea has already been studied, but there are important gaps that need to be examined. For example, there may be several studies of smart phones but very few studies of how they are used.

4. **Develop a hypothesis or research question.** In a theory, the concepts are related logically to one another, and logic can be used to deduce hypotheses. A **hypothesis** is a testable statement about the relationship between two or more concepts that is not known to be true but can be tested in research. You may argue that younger people are more comfortable with technology than older people, and younger people often travel and shop. From this you can deduce two hypotheses: (a) younger adults are more likely to have smart phones than older adults, and (b) younger adults are more likely to use smart phones to find their way in cities and to save money on major purchases. Not all studies have hypotheses. Often qualitative research is exploratory and not enough is known about what is being studied to make a prediction. For example, if we were not confident younger people are more comfortable with technology, then we could not deduce our hypotheses and, instead, we might have a research question such as "Are younger adults more comfortable using technology than middle-age and older adults?"

Theory An organized set of concepts and relationships among concepts that can be proposed to explain something of interest.

Hypothesis A testable statement about the relationship between two or more concepts that is not known to be true but can be tested in research.

5. **Select research methods.** Next you need to select methods that are appropriate for this topic to answer your research questions. Sociologists employ common research methods or designs. These include: (a) social surveys, (b) experiments, (c) field work (participant observation), (d) secondary analysis of existing data, and (e) content analysis. We will examine these in more detail below. For this example, you might choose to do a social survey in which you will ask people their age, whether they own a smart phone, and (if they have a smart phone) how they use the phone.

6. **Collect the data.** Next, you must collect **data**—empirically obtained information— to test the hypotheses of your theory. There are two key steps in this process: You must link the theory to observable data that can be used to test your hypotheses, and you must select which cases you will study for this test. These steps are called measurement and sampling, respectively. We examine both in detail below. For this example, let us imagine you choose to study people at your university (sample) and ask them to complete an online questionnaire (measurement).

7. **Analyze and interpret the results.** Once all the data are collected, you must summarize the findings. When you have hypotheses, you need to compare the data from your research with what you predicted you would find in your hypotheses. For example, we would look at the data to see if young adults are more likely to have a smartphone, as predicted. If you have a research question, then you need to try to answer the question with the data. When data and theory agree, the theory is supported, and when they disagree, the theory is not supported. Often computer programs are used to help with the analysis, allowing the researcher to do in minutes what would take days or even weeks to do by hand. For statistical analysis, a commonly used program is SPSS (Statistical Package for the Social Sciences). For qualitative analysis, one such program is Qualrus, and the Methodologist's Toolchest helps design research projects.

8. **Report the findings.** When the study is complete, the findings should be shared with others by publishing them in a **peer-reviewed scientific journal**—a journal in which other researchers who know the topic examine the article before it is published to make sure it meets the standards of science described earlier. The report shows how your findings fit in with what was known before and identify whatever unique contributions your study makes. It then becomes available for other researchers to read in their literature review. In this way, you contribute to the body of scientific knowledge.

These eight steps make up one research cycle. But the overall process of research never ends. After your study is completed, you or other researchers use the information you gathered in your study to suggest further studies. You may find that your theory is supported in some respects but not in others. That information is used to revise the theory, and then the process begins again. Scientific knowledge is developed in a never-ending process in which knowledge is continually refined but never final. Each study may answer some questions, but it often generates new ones.

This overview highlights the general process of research and points to the importance of three key steps in that process: (1) measurement, (2) sampling, and (3) analysis. To be able to understand sociological research, we need to know the basics of each of these elements of the research process. We turn to those now.

Measurement

Theoretical concepts are measured by empirical variables. A **concept** is an abstract idea or theoretical construct usually represented by a word or brief phrase summarizing some meaningful aspect of the real world. For example, concepts in this theory include ownership of smart phones, income, ease of navigation, and expenditures on major purchases. Operational definitions connect abstract theoretical concepts to measurable variables. An **operational definition** is a description of procedures used to measure a concept in sufficient detail so that someone else could perform the same procedure

---

Data Empirically obtained information.

Peer-reviewed scientific journal A journal in which other researchers who know the topic examine an article before it is published to make sure it meets the standards of science.

Concept An abstract idea or theoretical construct usually represented by a word or brief phrase summarizing some meaningful aspect of the real world.

Operational definition A description of procedures used to measure a concept in sufficient detail so that someone else could perform the same procedure and get a similar result.

and get a similar result. A **variable** is a measurable trait or characteristic that can vary and that is used to measure a concept. In this study, for example, the concept, income, may be measured with a specific question on a questionnaire: "What is your annual income (in thousands of dollars)?" The question measures a variable, and the answer to the question can take on a range of possible values (e.g., $50,000, $20,000, etc.).

Variables can be judged by how validly and reliably they measure a concept. **Reliability** is the extent to which a measure or scale produces consistent results for different times, different people, and different research methods. **Validity** is the extent to which a measure or scale measures what we think it measures. Reliability and validity can be illustrated with a dartboard. Reliability is measured by how consistently the darts are thrown, though they may all be off target. Validity is measured by how close the darts are on the average to the center of the target. A measure can be reliable but invalid (just as a person might consistently throw darts high and to the right) or valid but unreliable (if darts were evenly distributed around the bulls-eye).

Constructing reliable and valid measures can be surprisingly difficult. Even something as simple as the wording of a question can make a variable an unreliable or invalid measure of a concept. In social surveys, the questions asked of respondents tend to be answered with greater reliability and validity when they:

- Ask things respondents could reasonably be expected to know. Do not expect them to be able to tell you how they spent the last 24 hours in great detail or to accurately report how they felt in a situation that occurred years ago.

- Ask things respondents want to tell you correctly. Respondents are like the rest of us and are not eager to report behaviors or attitudes that may be embarrassing or may threaten their respectability. This is called a social desirability bias—respondents tend to answer questions in ways that make them appear to have socially desirable traits such as being truthful, smart, and fair.

- Ask things that are neither too difficult to answer nor consume too much time. Try to avoid asking questions that require respondents to look up records, perform complex calculations, or recall events long ago.

Reliability and validity apply to all kinds of measures, not just questions. For example, observations of people's behavior are more likely to be reliable and valid if the observer does not have to watch too many people at the same time, if events are not happening too quickly, or if it is possible to videotape the events and replay the tape repeatedly or in slow motion to get precise measurements.

Sampling

People are diverse. They have different attitudes, values, and understandings of the social world. Obviously, we cannot study just one or a very few people and expect that what is true of them will be true of all people. However, studying the entire **population**— everyone of interest—is usually much too expensive and time consuming. The United States Census surveys every household in the United States every 10 years, costing many millions of dollars every time it is done.

Most quantitative sociological research examines a **sample**—a subset of members of the population rather than the entire population—with the intention of generalizing the results to the broader population. Qualitative research has a similar goal of providing transferable knowledge that can be applied to other situations. Samples are much less costly to study than entire populations. However, the way we select the sample determines whether the sample can be generalized to the broader population. A sample is **biased** if it produces results that are systematically different from those of the population in a specific direction. For example, shortly before the 1936 presidential election, the *Literary Digest* (a popular news magazine of the day) conducted an election poll sampling more than two million people from telephone directories and automobile registration lists and predicted in bold headlines, "President Alf Landon wins over Franklin Roosevelt by a whopping 57% to 43% landslide." Two weeks later, Roosevelt won with 61% of the vote. A similar mistake occurred after World War II

Variable A measurable trait or characteristic that can vary and that is used to measure a concept.

Reliability The extent to which a measure or scale produces consistent results for different times, different people, and different research methods.

Validity The extent to which a measure or scale measures what we think it measures.

Population Everyone of interest for a study.

Sample A subset of members of the population rather than the entire population.

Biased Results that are systematically different from those of the population in a specific direction.

when a poll predicted presidential candidate Thomas Dewey would defeat incumbent President Harry Truman for election. What happened?

Despite the very large sample size, the sample was not representative of voters as a whole. In 1936, during the Great Depression, many voters did not own automobiles and did not have telephones. The sample overrepresented affluent people who were more likely to vote for the Republican, Alf Landon. During the same election, a young man named George Gallup conducted his own poll and correctly predicted not only that Roosevelt would win handily but also that the *Literary Digest* poll would be very inaccurate. After that early success, Gallup went on to create the Gallup Poll organization, which continues to this day to conduct scientific polls based on representative samples.

Probability sampling
Procedures for which each case in the population has some known probability of being included in the sample and all segments of the population are represented in the sample.

Theoretical sampling A procedure that selects new cases different from already sampled ones to provide a basis for comparison.

The best procedures for ensuring that the cases obtained for a sample are like cases in the general population is to use a probability sampling procedure and sample sizes of 100 or more for quantitative studies. **Probability sampling** procedures are procedures for which each case in the population has some known probability of being included in the sample and all segments of the population are represented in the sample. The simplest probability sample is a simple random sample in which every case in the population has the same chance of being selected. For example, a simple random sample of US senators currently in office might be obtained by tossing a coin into the air once for each senator. If the coin is heads, the senator is included in the sample. If the coin is tails, the senator is not included. If the coin is a fair one, landing heads half of the time and tails the other half, then this should be an unbiased sample of senators representative of the entire population of serving senators. For qualitative research, a common strategy to obtain a transferable sample that can be applied to other settings is to employ **theoretical sampling**—a procedure that selects new cases different from already sampled ones to provide a basis for comparison (Glaser and Strauss 1967).

If our study of smart phone usage is a quantitative study, a probability sample of phone users selected by randomly dialing telephone numbers is less likely to be biased than a survey given to students in an introductory sociology classroom at a college. College students do not reflect the full range of possible income, and their use of phones may be different than the use by middle-aged and older adults. If we were doing a qualitative study of smart phone usage, we would want to interview respondents having different characteristics, such as men and women, people of different race and ethnic groups, and people with different income levels and different ages. That would permit us to see how those groups might be different and could suggest variables to explore more in further research.

Statistical Analysis

After empirical data have been collected to test our hypotheses by measuring variables for a sample of cases, the next step is to analyze the results. Qualitative sociologists employ a number of strategies to summarize and make sense of their findings, most common of which is the ideal type (Weber 1903–1917). An ideal type is an abstract hypothetical concept based on characteristics of the phenomenon but not necessarily corresponding perfectly to any actual case.

Sociologist Wayne Brekhus (2003) provides an example of an analysis based on ideal types. Brekhus conducted in-depth interviews with gay men living in suburban areas and found three ideal types of identity management strategies. Peacocks (or gay life stylers) are men who are always on and out as gay 100% of the time and 100% intensity. They are comfortable with their gayness, and it is a fundamental aspect of who they are. Chameleons (or commuters) are men who are 100% gay but only 15% of the time. These men see themselves as adaptable. In the suburbs where they live and for most aspects of their lives, they are not noticeably gay, but in gay bars or urban areas where they feel free to enact their gay identity, they are 100% gay. The third type, centaurs (integrators) are 15% gay 100% of the time. For them, being gay is just one aspect of their lives and they feel no need to flaunt it.

Quantitative sociologists use statistics to summarize their findings in **empirical generalizations**—summary statements about the data that highlight important findings. **Statistics** are mathematical measures summarizing important characteristics found in data. Three common types of statistics will be encountered in this text. Descriptive statistics are used to summarize important characteristics of a population. Measures of association or correlation assess the extent to which two variables are related or can be predicted from one another. Tests of significance are used to determine whether observed results could have happened by chance.

Descriptive statistics. What is the average age of students in a sociology class? What is the average income for US citizens? Answers to questions like these are provided by descriptive statistics that that summarize the extent to which values of a single variable cluster around some values and not others. The three most commonly used statistics to measure average—the mean, median, and mode—are illustrated in FIGURE 1-5 for a discussion group of nine students in an introductory sociology class. Notice that the mean age of 22 is older than all but one of the students. This is due to the much higher age of a single student. The mean is like the balancing point for a teeter-totter, where extreme values have larger influence. Generally, sociologists prefer to use the statistic that takes advantage of the most information since it is likely to represent more completely the observed pattern. Of these three statistics, the mode uses the least information (only the most commonly occurring category), the median next (since it considers the order of every case), and the mean uses the most information (including both the order and the magnitude for each case). So sociologists would usually prefer to use the mean. However, the mean is not the best summary measure of central tendency when there are a few extreme scores that can dramatically distort the mean. The median is less influenced by extreme values, so it is generally a better measure of the average than the mean when variables are distributed very unevenly, such as wealth or income.

Reading tables. Tables are often used in sociology to examine relationships between variables. Most common are contingency tables that show the extent to which values of one variable are contingent on or predict values of another variable, as illustrated in **TABLE 1-2**. The first step in reading a table is to examine the title. The title identifies the topic of the table and the kind of data it contains. In this table, the title indicates that the data describe student grades as a function of effort. The row heading indicates the row variable (grade) and subheadings indicate the values (below average or above average). Similarly, the column heading indicates the column variable (effort) and the column sub-headings indicate the values (low or high). The cells of the table are labeled from a to d. In each cell are the frequencies of occurrence (the number of people with that combination of values) and the row percentage (the percentage of cases in that row falling into that cell). For example, a student who put forth low effort and received a below-average grade would fall in cell "a" in the top left of the four cells in this table. Someone who put forth high effort and achieved an above-average grade would be in cell "d" in the bottom right.

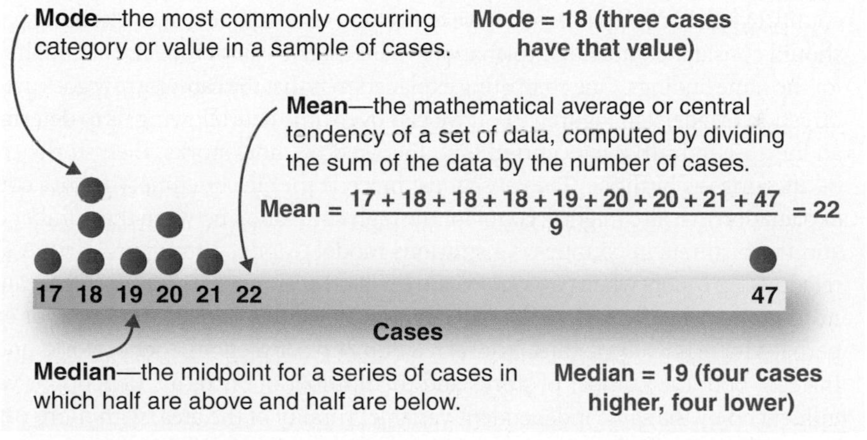

Empirical generalizations Summary statements about the data that highlight important findings.

Statistics Mathematical measures summarizing important characteristics found in data.

Mode—the most commonly occurring category or value in a sample of cases.

Mode = 18 (three cases have that value)

Mean—the mathematical average or central tendency of a set of data, computed by dividing the sum of the data by the number of cases.

$$\text{Mean} = \frac{17 + 18 + 18 + 18 + 19 + 20 + 20 + 21 + 47}{9} = 22$$

17 18 19 20 21 22   47

Cases

Median—the midpoint for a series of cases in which half are above and half are below.

Median = 19 (four cases higher, four lower)

FIGURE 1-5 Three ways to measure "average."

TABLE 1-2 Student Grade by Effort

Grade	Effort	
	Low	High
Below average	[a]**7** (70%)	[b]**20** (40%)
Above average	[c]**3** (30%)	[d]**30** (60%)

Associated When the values of one variable depend on or can be predicted from the values of the other variable.

Measures of association. Often, in tables like this, we are interested in examining the effects of one of the variables on the other variable. Two variables are **associated** when the values of one variable depend on or can be predicted from the values of the other variable. Here, we might expect that greater effort should lead to a better grade. If effort affects grades, then a larger percentage of students who put forth high effort should score above average than students who put forth low effort, and indeed, 60% of those with high effort score above average compared to only 30% of those with low effort. Students who worked hard were twice as likely to score above average as students who did not. A commonly used measure of association between two variables is the Pearson product-moment correlation coefficient. This correlation coefficient ranges from –1 to +1, with zero indicating no association between the variables and the departure of the statistic from zero indicating the magnitude of the association. Negative numbers indicate higher values of one variable are associated with lower values of the other, and positive numbers indicate higher values of one variable are associated with higher values of the other. The formula for computing this correlation is widely available in statistics texts and will not be discussed here. For these data, the correlation is +0.22—an association large enough to suggest it is worth studying to improve your grade.

Separating cause and association. It is tempting to think that if two variables are highly associated, then there must be a causal relationship between them FIGURE 1-6. If, as we saw above, people who study for a test are more likely to get a good grade than those who did not, then it is natural to suspect that studying affects grades. However, association is *not* the same as causation. It is possible for two variables to have a very strong association yet not have *any* direct causal relationship between them. This is illustrated by a curious finding reported by Wallis and Roberts (1956:79). A newspaper account noted a positive correlation between the number of storks' nests and the number of human births in various parts of northwestern Europe. The newspaper did not jump to conclusions but pointed out the correlation and humorously left it to the readers to make their own judgments.

The first and most obvious, but not necessarily the best, explanation for the correlation would be to assume that the number of storks causes or influences the birthrate in each county (Model 1 in Figure 1-6). However, before we conclude that storks bring babies, we should consider competing explanations—alternative causal models that might account for the same findings. One competing explanation is that the causal arrow goes in the other direction (Model 2 in Figure 1-6). If we had over-time data allowing us to determine that an increase in birth rate occurred first, followed by more storks, then storks could not be affecting the birthrate. The cause must precede the effect in time. Another competing explanation that also might account for the high correlation between the number of storks and the birthrate in counties is a spurious model (Model 3 in Figure 1-6). A spurious relationship occurs when two variables are related and appear to have a direct causal connection, but actually both of the variables are affected by a third variable. For example, perhaps there is really no direct causal relationship between number of storks and births. Instead, both the number of storks and the number of births are dependent variables, influenced by the same independent variable, rurality of the area, with more rural areas having fewer people and fewer nesting places for storks such as chimneys and houses.

FIGURE 1-6 Association vs. causality.

• Two variables are associated when the values of one variable depend on or can be predicted from the values of the other variable.
• Just because two variables are associated does not mean that one causes the other.

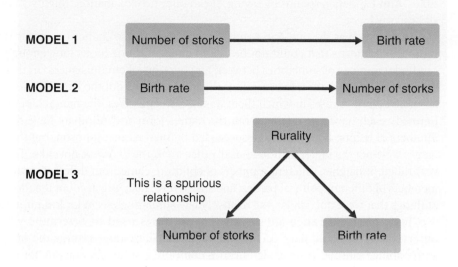

FIGURE 1-6 Association vs. causality.

How do we determine which of these causal models accounts for the data? The easiest way to distinguish between association and causal relationships is to conduct an experiment. Then you can see how changes in values of the independent variable affect the dependent variables when other variables are controlled (we will examine experiments in more detail later in this chapter). However, experiments are often impractical or unethical. When it is not possible to conduct experiments, sociologists instead use a statistical analysis strategy called "elaboration" (Blalock 1964) to examine the effect of one variable on another while controlling for other variables statistically. In this example, we can control for rurality, holding it constant, and see if the correlation between number of storks and the number of births is still found. If a simple causal model is true (either Model 1 or Model 2), the correlation should still be found. If the spurious model (Model 3) is true, then we should find no correlation between number of storks and the number of births when we control for rurality. In fact, when this was done, the association between the number of storks and the number of births in an area disappeared. Thus, both simple causal explanations for this result are ruled out and we can conclude that the relationship is a spurious one.

Tests of significance. A frequent concern in any science is whether observed regularities could have occurred by chance. Superstition, conspiracy theories, and astrological horoscopes are all examples of nonscientific knowledge that appear to explain no more than chance events. How can a social science like sociology avoid falling into the trap of thinking that there is a relationship between variables when the pattern is simply a chance occurrence? For example, if the average (median) income for females is 98% of that for males in similar jobs in a corporation, is this evidence of sexual discrimination? Could that difference have occurred due to chance or does it reflect a significant impact of gender on salary?

The problem of ruling out chance occurrence is illustrated by a column frequently rerun by newspaper columnist Ann Landers. This column quoted a letter from a writer who documents several similarities between John Kennedy and Abraham Lincoln, implying there must be some connection between their assassinations. The similarities include the following:

• Both were concerned with civil rights.

• Both were shot from behind and in the head.

- Both were succeeded by former senators from the South named Johnson.
- Andrew Johnson was born in 1808 and Lyndon Johnson in 1908.
- The names Lincoln and Kennedy each contain seven letters.

The writer ends by asking, "Can all the above be coincidental? It doesn't seem possible." Ann Landers responds by saying, "I can offer no explanation. Mighty strange is all I can say."

Letters such as the one Ann Landers describes confuse chance occurrences with significant patterns that could not be due to chance. If one looks long enough, one can find a number of similarities between any two sets of circumstances. In this case, there are a few similarities between Lincoln and Kennedy. But the letter overlooks the far more common cases in which there was no similarity. Yes, the names Lincoln and Kennedy each have seven letters, but the names John and Abraham have different numbers of letters. Both men were succeeded by men named Johnson, but their first names were not the same. In thousands of other ways, the two were not alike. They had very different heights, different numbers of children, came from different states, were members of different political parties, and so on. If we take into account the thousands of things that were not similar, the relatively few similarities seem far less impressive.

Tests of significance Statistical procedures used to determine whether observed results could have occurred by chance.

Tests of significance are statistical procedures used to determine whether observed results could have occurred by chance. These tests assume the sample is a probability sample. Tests of significance compute a summary statistic for a group of cases and compare that statistic to the range of possible values that might have occurred due to chance. Then, if the computed statistic is outside the range of likely values based on chance variation, it is concluded the results are statistically significant. On the other hand, if the computed statistic falls within the range of values likely to occur by chance, then the results are nonsignificant and we cannot rule out the possibility that they are due to chance. Results of tests of significance are often reported as significant if those results could have occurred by chance less than 5% of the time. There are many specific tests of significance, but what is important for this text is understanding the logic of significance tests.

CONCEPT LEARNING CHECK 1.4   The Science of Sociology

For each part of the description of the research project, identify the term that best describes it.

_____ 1. The researchers are interested in the optimism of college students about the future.

_____ 2. To do this, they will select 300 college students at random from a list of undergraduate students at their university.

_____ 3. They realize that students at this college might not be the same as college students in general.

_____ 4. They want to see whether men are more optimistic than women.

_____ 5. They will ask people to describe their optimism on a five-point scale by selecting the number closest to their view ([1] very pessimistic [2] pessimistic [3] not sure [4] optimistic [5] very optimistic).

_____ 6. They hope that if they were to ask people this same question now and 10 weeks from now, the responses would be the same both times.

_____ 7. They will compare the mean optimism of women students with that of men students to see if they are different.

A. Bias

B. Concept

C. Reliability

D. Sample

E. Operational definition

F. Hypothesis

G. Test of significance

1.5 Sociological Research Methods

There are several well-developed research methods commonly used in sociological research.

- Describe the research methods commonly used in sociological studies.
- Analyze the strengths and weaknesses of each research method.

Sociologists usually employ one of four common research designs or research methods. Each research method is a systematic approach to doing research, and those methods have different strengths and weaknesses that need to be understood in interpreting the research findings. In this section, we examine four research methods commonly used in sociological research: social surveys, participant observation (or field work), experiments, and analysis of existing data.

Social Surveys

Social surveys are a common method of social research gathering by asking people questions. A **respondent** is someone who answers questions in a social survey. Most of you have experienced surveys and heard of their results in political election polls, public opinion polls such as the Gallup Poll and the United States Census. Surveys allow many people to be studied quickly and inexpensively and are often used to provide a more representative sample than is possible with other research methods. Surveys with high **response rates**—the proportion of people asked to participate in the study who actually did so—are more likely to represent the broader population than surveys with low response rates.

Common forms of surveys are **interviews**, in which the researcher interacts in person with the respondent, asking him or her questions, or **questionnaires**, through which the respondent completes a mailed form or perhaps accesses it on the Internet. The questions may be about both objective factual information such as reported behaviors and subjective information such as attitudes and beliefs. **Closed-ended questions** require respondents to select from a list of available responses and are suitable when there are only a few well-known possible responses, such as

Race: [ ] White [ ] Black [ ] Asian [ ] Other

By forcing respondents to use those categories, the researcher standardizes results so he or she can compare them more easily. However, if important categories are not available (such as "Native American") or respondents are forced to select only a single response when several may apply (e.g., a person can be part white and part Native American), then the results can be biased and can miss important information. **Open-ended questions** permit people to use their own words to answer. For example, "What do you like most about this college?" permits a full range of possible responses, including those the researcher may not anticipate.

An illustration: The National Health and Social Life Survey. In 1987, when the AIDS epidemic was out of control and the number of infected people was growing exponentially, researchers first proposed conducting a national survey asking people about sexual practices with the intent of obtaining information that could be used to help control AIDS. This survey illustrates how social scientists design and conduct surveys that address important quality concerns that should be raised regarding any survey. How were the variables measured? How did they know the answers are valid and reliable? How many people responded? What was the response rate? Was there any reason to suspect the sample was biased? Did respondents appear to be telling the truth?

Questions for the survey were developed using standard procedures in the social sciences to avoid bias, subjected to scrutiny by other researchers, and pretested before being administered. Redundant questions were included to check the truthfulness of responses.

Respondent Someone who answers questions in a social survey.

Response rates The proportion of people asked to participate in the study who actually did so.

Interviews Surveys in which the researcher interacts in person with the respondent, asking him or her questions.

Questionnaires Surveys in which the respondent completes a form mailed to her or perhaps accessed on the Internet.

Closed-ended questions Questions that require respondents to select from a list of available responses.

Open-ended questions Questions that permit people to use their own words to answer.

Surveys allow many people to be studied quickly and inexpensively and are often used to provide a more representative sample than is possible with other research methods.

© Faiz Zaki/Shutterstock, Inc.

The researchers selected a probability sample of respondents using a multistage sampling process, first selecting geographic areas; then cities, towns, and rural areas within those areas; then neighborhoods within the chosen cities; then addresses in the selected neighborhoods; then residences within addresses (e.g., apartments within a high-rise building); and finally selecting at random adult members of the household. This sampling process ensures a representative unbiased sample of respondents, but it is very expensive.

Two hundred twenty interviewers were hired and flown to Chicago for training, and they eventually conducted 3,432 90-minute interviews about sexual behavior and other aspects of people's sex lives in face-to-face interviews at an average cost of $450 per interview. Nearly 80% of people contacted actually participated in the study (an 80% response rate), increasing our faith in the representativeness of the sample since so many people who were approached agreed to participate. The resulting sample was compared to the US population on various characteristics and found to be quite similar to the entire population. Finally, results were compared to those of similar high-quality rigorous scientific studies such as the General Social Survey and similar studies in other countries, and the results were found to be remarkably similar. All of these steps taken together help ensure the validity of the results.

This National Health and Social Life Survey found a number of results that challenged conventional wisdom about sexuality, contradicted key findings from earlier studies, and pointed to the need for this rigorous scientific survey. Despite popular

---

THE SOCIOLOGICAL IMAGINATION | Social Science Research and Politics

The National Health and Social Life Survey was conceived in 1987 as a way to gather useful data about sexual practices in the United States that could be used to help control AIDS. By identifying groups at risk due to their sexual behaviors, this study could help medical scientists target subpopulations for medical education to help reduce the spread of AIDS. But such a survey would only be useful if it asked rather explicit questions about sexual practices. Scientists and administrators at federal agencies, including the National Institute of Child Health and Human Development, the Centers for Disease Control and Prevention, and the National Institute of Mental Health, all supported conducting a survey of sexual practices. However, there was considerable pressure to narrow the survey, to reduce the questions asked, and to do such

things as quit asking questions of respondents once it was established the couple was monogamous. Finally, Senator Jesse Helms introduced an amendment to a bill funding the National Institutes of Health specifically prohibiting the Federal Government from paying for such a study. It passed by a vote of 66 to 34, and federal funding became impossible for the study. As a result, the researchers turned to private foundations to fund the study, and it was eventually funded, but it was a considerably smaller study with a sample of only 3,500 adults rather than the 20,000 originally planned. This meant that the number of cases of people falling into uncommon subcategories, such as homosexuals, was limited and less could be said about those groups (Michael et al. 1994:26–29).

EVALUATE

The sociological imagination encourages us to consider how the circumstances surrounding this survey reflect not just the private troubles of individuals diagnosed with HIV but also broad social problems in general. Consider how the historical development of this particular survey intersects with and reflects broader historical trends.

1. How might the reactions to discussions of sexual issues, reflected in opposition to this survey, reflect in the broader society? What are some other examples involving sexuality issues, in a public forum, that reflect the same broad issues?

2. Can this controversy also be seen as an example of a much broader issue of whether social research can be value free? Could we possibly expect to see similar controversy over surveys regarding major issues such as race relations or even political divisiveness?

3. Would federal funding and development of a survey about sexual practices or other controversial issues have been possible decades before 1987? Would they be more likely to occur and less controversial today? Do you think it will ever be easier to conduct such research without political interference in the future?

myths of love being the primary basis for selecting sexual partners and the notion that anyone can marry anyone as in *Cinderella*, the reality was more like Romeo and Juliet. That is, people are far more likely to choose sex partners similar to them in race, ethnicity, religion, age, and social class. Marital infidelity was much less common than many had thought. The number of homosexuals in the population was considerably less than once thought. And AIDS was still, to a very great extent, isolated to only some segments of the population.

Experiments

Experiments are empirical studies designed to test causal relationships between an **independent variable**—a variable expected to cause changes in a second variable—and the **dependent variable**—a variable thought to be influenced by an independent variable. The expected causal relationship is a **hypothesis**—a predicted relationship among variables. For example, in a classic sociological experiment, Bibb Latane and John Darley (Latane and Darley 1968) examined the effect of group inhibition on bystander intervention in emergencies. The hypothesis they tested was that **subjects** (people participating in the study), when confronted with a potential emergency, will intervene more quickly when they are alone than when in the presence of two other people. The independent variable was the number of people present (the subject alone, or the subject and two other people). The dependent variable was whether and how quickly the subject reported a problem.

To test a hypothesis, the researcher assigns some people at random (**random assignment**) to an **experimental group**—a group exposed to a treatment—then compares that group to a **control group** not exposed to the treatment. The control group should be as nearly identical as possible to the experimental group but lack the treatment. This study by Latane and Darley (1968) was a **laboratory experiment** (an experiment conducted in a controlled setting) as opposed to a **field experiment** (a study conducted in a natural setting such as a classroom where the researcher cannot control everything that happens). Subjects were asked to complete a questionnaire alone in a room (the control group) or in a room with two other subjects (the experimental group). While the subject completed the questionnaire, smoke began to puff into the room at irregular intervals from a wall vent. By the end of the experiment (six minutes later), smoke obscured vision in the room (this was the simulated emergency).

Three quarters of the 24 subjects in the "alone" condition reported the smoke before the experiment was ended, with a median delay of 2 minutes after first noticing it. Only one of the 10 subjects in the room with two other subjects reported the smoke during the six minutes the experiment was continued. The other nine continued working doggedly, coughed, rubbed smoke from their eyes, or opened the window but did not report the smoke. A statistical test of significance indicated this result could have happened by chance less than two times in one thousand ($p < .002$). They concluded their hypothesis was confirmed and the presence of other people in the room significantly inhibits bystander intervention in emergencies.

Field Work (Participant Observation)

In **participant observation** or **field work**, the researcher participates in and is directly involved in the lives of those he or she is studying. The observation usually occurs "in the field"—in a natural setting in which people are living and interacting rather than in an experimental laboratory. Participant observation research typically involves both observation and interviews with participants or informants. For example, Julius Roth is a sociologist who conducted participant observation while he was a patient in a tuberculosis clinic (Roth 1963). Erving Goffman (1967) acted as a card dealer to study casinos. Michael Burawoy (1979) worked as a machinist in a machine shop in the 1970s and compared his experiences with those from a similar study by Roy (1952) that took place in 1944 to 1945 in the same company.

Independent variable A variable expected to cause changes in a second variable.

Dependent variable A variable thought to be influenced by an independent variable.

Hypothesis A testable statement about the relationship between two or more concepts that is not known to be true but can be tested in research.

Subjects People participating in the study.

Random assignment Assigning people at random to different conditions to avoid bias and to make sure the conditions are comparable.

Experimental group A group exposed to a treatment.

Control group A group not exposed to the treatment.

Laboratory experiment An experiment conducted in a controlled setting.

Field experiment A study conducted in a natural setting such as a classroom where the researcher cannot control everything that happens.

Participant observation or field work Research in which the researcher participates in and is directly involved in the lives of those he or she is studying.

As a complete participant, Erving Goffman took a job as a card dealer to study gambling behavior without letting people know he was observing them.

© John Howard/DigitalVision/Thinkstock

Complete participant
Someone who participates in the setting fully and engages in unobtrusive research.

Unobtrusive research
Research in which those studied are not aware they are being studied.

Participant as observer
Research in which the researcher has a nonresearch reason for participating in the setting and decides to conduct research.

Observer as participant
Research in which the observer has only minimal participation in the setting and is not a natural or normal participant.

Complete observer Does not take part in the interaction at all and hence is less likely to cause the people studied to modify their actions.

Ethnography A typically detailed descriptive account summarizing and interpreting a culture or a collection of people studied.

Participant observers vary in the researcher role they take. Gold (1958) distinguished four categories:

1. The **complete participant** is someone who participates in the setting fully and engages in **unobtrusive research**—research in which those studied are not aware they are being studied. For example, Erving Goffman (1967) took a job as a dealer for the purpose of studying gambling behavior and casinos and conducted his observations without letting people know he was observing them.

2. The **participant as observer** is research in which the researcher has a nonresearch reason for participating in the setting and decides to conduct research. An example is Julius Roth (1963), who conducted his study of a clinic while he was confined there for several months as a tuberculosis patient.

3. The **observer as participant** is research in which the observer has only minimal participation in the setting and is not a natural or normal participant.

4. The **complete observer** does not take part in the interaction at all and hence is less likely to cause the people studied to modify their actions. An example of this would be a study in which people are observed from behind a one-way mirror or videotaped without knowing they are being watched.

The role taken by participant observers must balance ethical responsibilities to the subjects against concerns for how subjects might alter their behavior because they know they are being studied. Roles in which people know they are being observed can permit the researcher to ask questions that might seem inappropriate for a nonresearcher.

If participant observation is the description of the method of collecting data, "ethnography" is the description of the common result of such a study. An **ethnography** is a typically detailed descriptive account summarizing and interpreting a culture or a collection of people studied. What distinguishes ethnographies from other forms of research reports is that ethnographies are usually richly detailed, descriptive accounts of what went on and what the researcher experienced or observed, including many concrete events along with analysis. Where other research reports may appear dry, technical, and abstract, ethnographies often read like a novel or diary and give readers a sense of experiencing the events themselves.

For example, here is an account of Burawoy describing what happened one day when the parts he was working on were desperately needed to complete the assembly of engines at a manufacturing plant.

> I found myself encircled by the foreman, the night-shift superintendent, the foreman of inspectors, the scheduling man, the setup man, and, from time to time, a manager from some other department. Such royal attention had me flustered from the start. I couldn't even set up the balance properly. The superintendent became impatient and started ordering me to do this, that, and the other, all of which I knew to be wrong. It was futile to point that out. After all, who was I to contradict the superintendent? The most powerful thought to lodge in my head was to lift the pulley off the balance and hurl it at their feet. As the clay piled up on the plate, way beyond what was necessary to balance it, the superintendent began to panic. He obviously thought his neck was on the line, but he had little idea as to how the machine worked. He was an old-timer, unaccustomed to this new-fangled equipment. And so he followed the directions on the chart hanging from the machine—directions that Bill had instructed me to ignore because they were wrong. When the superintendent thought the plate was balanced, we started drilling holes in the pulley—more and more holes, until the surface was covered with them. Clearly something was wrong. I'd never seen such a mess of holes. But the superintendent was more concerned with getting the pulleys out of the department and onto the engines. He didn't dare ask me to turn the pulleys through 180 degrees to see if they were really balanced—the acid test. I knew they wouldn't balance out, and probably so did he. By the end of the shift I had managed to ruin twenty-three pulleys. (Burawoy 1979:69–70)

Gaining entry to the research site is often difficult in participant observation and can create suspicion and distrust among subjects. For example, Fetterman (1989:44) describes how gaining access to a library through power brokers caused lower-level library workers to mistrust him and made data collection extremely difficult. William Foot Whyte, a white Anglo-Saxon Harvard graduate student, found it extremely difficult at first to gain entry to a rundown neighborhood of Italian Americans in Boston to conduct his classic study, Street Corner Society (1981; orig. 1943). At one point, he was almost thrown out of a bar when he asked to join people at a table. At another time, his question to a group of gamblers about whether the cops had been paid off provoked vehement denials and great discomfort for both him and those he was studying. Ultimately, Whyte did what most participant observers must do to gain access: he found a key informant—someone with whom the researcher develops a trusting relationship, who knows the researcher is conducting research, and who gives the researcher an insider's view of the research setting. For Whyte, that key informant helped introduce him to others in the community, encouraged others to trust him, and advised Whyte when he was asking too many questions.

On the other hand, another danger for qualitative field researchers is not asking enough questions or not asking the right questions. For example, Richard Lee (1969) was studying bushmen in the Kalahari Desert and puzzled for days over what he had done to provoke their insults. It was only when he finally asked that he was told why they were treating him so badly. When Lee asked his informant why he had not told him this before and spared him the anguish of having to suffer the insults without knowing why, his informant's reply was, "because you never asked me."

Participant observation is particularly effective at helping researchers understand how people in the setting understand and make sense of their lives. However, participant observation usually requires months or years of work, so the researcher often only has time and resources to study one setting rather than many. Such studies of a single setting are often called **case studies**, and they typically constitute an intensive analysis of a single unit or case. In addition, the researcher usually spends the entire time in that setting in a single role. Are those experiences generalizable to other settings and other roles? How do we know, for example, that the machine shop studied by Burawoy is similar to other machine shops? How is it different from assembly lines and other forms of manufacturing? How is his view of that machine shop shaped by his employment as a machine operator rather than as foreman or manager or some other position?

> **Case studies** Participant observation studies of a single setting, usually constituting an intensive analysis of a single unit or case.

Secondary Analysis of Existing Data

Secondary analysis is the analysis of data for purposes other than the primary reason the information was originally collected. Collecting data for research is a very expensive, time-consuming process requiring considerable skill and access to subjects that can be difficult to obtain. Public opinion surveys, for example, often involve national surveys of thousands of respondents requiring hundreds of thousands of dollars to collect. Yet there are countless sources of already existing data that can be studied with less expense that would be impossible to collect solely for research purposes. Vast amounts of information are gathered as part of the ongoing activities of an organization (such as employment records of a company or student records in a school) or social process (such as licensure records, crime reports, or census records). Studies of large corporations, public policies, and the legislative process must rely upon secondary data generated by those organizations for their own uses. Those official documents, court records, legislations, personnel records, internal memos, manuals, brochures, and so on provide useful information that cannot be obtained in any other fashion.

> **Secondary analysis** The analysis of data for purposes other than the primary reason the information was originally collected.

Today there are literally thousands of large data sets available for secondary analysis, including crime statistics provided by the National Institute of Justice, political election polls from polling organizations such as the Gallup and Roper Polls, census data from the US Bureau of the Census, statistics on health and health-related behaviors from the National Center for Health Statistics, and hundreds of social and political surveys from federally sponsored research. Many of these data sets can be downloaded for analysis through the Internet. The Internet itself offers a rich and varied array of secondary data for possible analysis, ranging from biographical home pages of individuals to corporate documents to electronic mail messages.

Content analysis
A commonly used procedure for studying text by identifying specific characteristics of the text such as the frequency of occurrence of specific key words or phrases.

Historical-comparative research A study examining the ways in which social life changes across cultures and over time.

Documents make up a large portion of data available for secondary analysis. **Content analysis** is a commonly used procedure for studying text by identifying specific characteristics of the text such as the frequency of occurrence of specific key words or phrases. In addition to counting key words, computer programs for content analysis display key words in context (KWIC) as a means for helping to understand their meaning.

Another important example of secondary analysis is **historical-comparative research** examining the ways in which social life changes across cultures and over time. This research typically focuses on macro-level changes occurring over long periods of time or macro-level differences between cultures that influence and constrain individual behavior. There are many examples of historical-comparative research, both classical and contemporary, in sociology. Emile Durkheim's (1897) study of differences in suicide rates based on official suicide statistics from several European countries. Max Weber (1904–1905) *The Protestant Ethic and the Spirit of Capitalism* compared different societies (India, China, and European countries) to argue that Protestantism was a key historical factor encouraging the acceptance of rationality and the pursuit of material goods so important for the Industrial Revolution. More recently, Donald Granberg and Soren Holmberg (1988), in *The Political System Matters*, reanalyzed secondary data from dozens of preelection and postelection surveys in Sweden and the United States to show how the political systems in these two countries lead to different perceptions and behaviors by individuals.

Theda Skocpol (1979), in *States and Social Revolutions*, used a historical comparison of three different revolutions, the French Revolution of the late 1700s, the Russian Revolution of 1917, and the Chinese Revolution over the period between 1911 and the 1960s. In contrast to the dominant theories of revolution of the time that emphasized social-psychological mass states of mind or underlying economic processes, Skocpol emphasized social-structural explanations for revolution. Where other authors saw the French Revolution as a "bourgeois" revolution very different from the "socialist" revolutions in Russia and China, she argued all three revolutions shared themes of state breakdown, elite conflicts, and popular revolts leading to reconstitution of these states as more bureaucratic national states incorporating the masses. Her approach was consistent with the macroanalytic approach in which she tried to compare and contrast these different historical cases in order to establish the causes of social revolutions. Her structural approach downplayed and deromanticized the role of the great villains and heroes of other accounts. She characterized the Jacobins, the Bolsheviks, and the Maoists (the leaders of these three revolutions) as marginal elites building a new social order even as an old order was falling apart around them.

Scott (1990) suggests that historical documents should meet four criteria to be useful: they should be authentic, credible, and representative, and their meaning should be clear. A document is authentic only if it is an original or a faithful reproduction of an original document for which the true author can be established (that is, the document is not a forgery). A document is credible if the author was in a position to know the facts, competent to report them accurately, and the author's biases are not likely to have distorted the document or at least can be understood and taken into account. A document is representative if a wide range of documents were likely to have been preserved and survived over the years and to be made available to researchers. Finally, the document's meaning as intended by the author should be understood by the researcher. Skocpol's historical comparative study of revolutions also had to assess whether the different times and circumstances are comparable and whether the compared cases are actually independent of one another. Are Russian peasants comparable to Chinese peasants during these time periods? Is state breakdown in Russia in 1917 comparable to the state breakdown in China in 1949? Were the cases she compared actually independent of one another, or have they influenced each other through cultural diffusion, trade, or in some other manner so that it is not fair to think of them as independent tests of a theory? This is called Galton's problem, after the British anthropologist, Sir Francis Galton, who first raised the problem. For example, were events in China or Russia influenced by the earlier French Revolution? If so, does this damage her argument?

CONCEPT LEARNING CHECK 1.5   Sociological Research Methods

Match the following statements with the correct term or phrase that best describes them. There should be only one best answer.

_____ **1.** Researcher wants respondents to respond using standardized responses.

_____ **2.** We expect this new curriculum will increase student performance by 20%.

_____ **3.** These people are not exposed to the new educational tool for purposes of comparison.

_____ **4.** This study took place in a work setting.

_____ **5.** Researcher wants to study people's opinions but is not sure what things are important to them.

_____ **6.** This study examined data available on the Internet.

_____ **7.** This person was there during the time in question and knew most of the other participants.

A. Hypothesis

B. Field work

C. Credibility

D. Closed-ended questions

E. Open-ended questions

F. Secondary analysis

G. Control group

1.6 Ethics in Sociological Research

Because sociologists study humans, sociological research faces three fundamental issues that distinguish sociology from the natural sciences: verstehen (subjective experience), reactivity, and ethical issues.

- Describe the three fundamental issues that distinguish sociology from the natural sciences.
- Examine ethical issues in the study of human subjects.

Verstehen

First, people have a subjective experience that influences their behavior (what Max Weber called **verstehen**—German for "understanding"). This requires that people must be viewed as conscious actors, and our methods must go beyond a mere "social physics" to understand people's subjective experience, understanding, and motives in different situations. People interpret events and act according to the meaning they attribute to those events and their own motives. To understand why people act in a certain way, we must understand the meaning they attribute to events and their motives. For example, understanding the conflicts that occur between union workers and managers requires understanding their competing economic interests. To understand a harsh punishment for a student cheating on an examination, we must understand the core values of institutions of higher education. Standpoint theory (Smith 1987), a variant of feminist theory described earlier, emphasizes the different understanding of social life found among women and other oppressed minorities.

Verstehen The subjective understanding of individual participants anchored in a context of shared cultural ideas.

Reactivity

Most of us have at least occasionally felt self-conscious when we realized we were being watched or videotaped. This can lead us to change our behavior even if we try to "just act natural." Research involving human subjects must take into account the ways in which human actors may modify their behavior when they know they are being studied. **Reactivity** is the extent to which humans being studied "react" or respond to the research process or the researcher by changing their behavior, either unintentionally or intentionally.

A classic study that first documented the effects of reactivity on research subjects was the study by Elton Mayo and his colleagues of workers in Western Electric's Hawthorne Plant in the 1930s. In that study, researchers studied the effects of various changes on the productivity of a group of women who all worked together wiring electronic components in the bank wiring room FIGURE 1-7. The researchers varied seating arrangements, payment methods, lighting, and other factors. To their surprise, no matter what they changed, productivity increased. Ultimately, the researchers concluded that the key factor was paying attention to the workers by studying them. The women workers were motivated to work faster because someone was interested in their productivity. In the middle of the Great Depression, when this study took place, they may also have been motivated to keep their jobs. This effect has come to be called the Hawthorne effect after this famous study (Mayo 1933). The **Hawthorne effect** refers to the unintended effects on behavior produced when people are aware they are being studied.

Reactivity The extent to which humans being studied "react" or respond to the research process or the researcher by changing their behavior, either unintentionally or intentionally.

Hawthorne effect The unintended effects on behavior produced when people are aware they are being studied.

FIGURE 1-7 Hawthorne Plant, 1930s.

© National Geographic/Getty Images

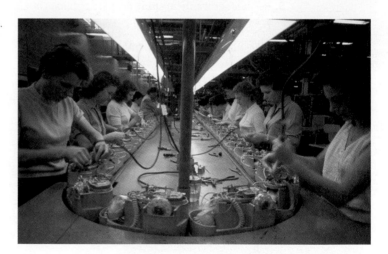

What does reactivity mean for sociological research today? It means that researchers studying people should be careful to minimize the effects of the research upon the observed behaviors of the subjects. Often this means designing research projects that minimize reactivity by not telling subjects they are being studied, or at least not telling subjects the specific goals of the research. However, researchers have to be careful when trying to minimize reactivity to keep in mind the third important issue that distinguishes social science research: ethical issues.

Ethical Issues in the Study of Human Subjects

When human subjects are studied in research, those people must be treated ethically. Shortly after World War II, the world was shocked by reports of abuses of war prisoners in biomedical experiments. In Japan, Japanese captors deliberately infected captured American and British prisoners of war with malaria and other fatal diseases. Reportedly, some prisoners were dissected while still alive to examine the physiological effects. In Germany, German captors exposed Allied prisoners of war to frigid waters until they died to see how long they could survive. By the 1960s, several research projects in the United States came to public attention that raised serious ethical concerns (though nowhere near as horrifying as those in World War II). The Tuskegee syphilis study examined the effects of untreated syphilis in black men for over 40 years even though a cure was discovered decades before the study ended. By the end of the study, at least 78 subjects had died as a direct result of advanced syphilitic lesions (Brandt 1978).

As a result of that and other studies, the federal government held a series of investigative hearings and eventually spelled out the ethical principles and guidelines for human subjects research in *The Belmont Report* (1979). That report led to federal regulations (Title 45, Code of Federal Regulations, Part 46, Revised June 18 1991:8–9) requiring that human subjects be protected in research. Those protections include the following:

a. Risks should be minimized and outweighed by potential benefits.

b. Subject privacy should be guaranteed by confidentiality or anonymity.

c. Subjects should be selected to share risks fairly.

d. Subjects should be informed fully about risks before agreeing to participate (informed consent).

The American Sociological Association—the professional association of sociologists—has its own code of ethics to which members are expected to agree that goes well beyond the Title 45 regulation noted above. This code is very detailed but is summarized based on five principles (ASA 2012):

1. Professional competence—members strive to maintain the highest levels of competence in their work and recognize their limitations.

2. Integrity—members must be honest, fair, and respectful to others.

3. Professional and scientific responsibility—members adhere to the highest scientific standards and accept responsibility for their work and have an ethical responsibility to share their findings with other researchers and the public.

4. Respect for people's rights—members respect the rights, dignity, and worth of all people and try to eliminate bias in their professional work.

5. Social responsibility—sociologists are aware of their scientific and professional responsibilities to communities in which they work.

All sociologists are expected to be aware of this code and to meet its standards.

Source: American Sociological Association (ASA). 2012. ASA Code of Ethics. Accessed November 2012 at http://www.asanet.org/about/ethics.cfm.

CONCEPT LEARNING CHECK 1.6   Ethics in Sociological Research

Consider each of the following studies and indicate the single feature below that most accurately describes each study. There is only one correct answer.

_____ 1. A gaming company secretly collected Social Security numbers from user accounts on the social media service through which the game is played and then hackers released names and Social Security numbers online.

_____ 2. The researcher sits on a bench in a mall and unobtrusively counts the number of young men walking by who are wearing sports-related t-shirts.

_____ 3. An anonymous online survey asks respondents their opinions about a border dispute between their country and a neighboring country.

_____ 4. Subjects are shown information regarding what will be done in the study and any potential risks, then are asked to indicate whether they would like to continue or exit.

_____ 5. A researcher spends two hours in the home of a family recording what they do and in which room.

A. Likely to have issues with reactivity

B. Not likely to have major problems with reactivity

C. Assesses verstehen

D. Exposes subjects to unnecessary risk

E. Has informed consent

Visual Overview Major Theoretical Perspectives

Here are some of the key features that distinguish the three major theoretical perspectives that dominate sociology. These three perspectives will be revisited in later chapters to show how they can be applied to the topics of each chapter.

Structural-Functional

Key concepts:
> Social structures
> Functions
> Latent functions
> Manifest functions
> Dysfunctions

Focus/themes:
> Social structures exist because of their function for society.
> Those social structures constrain individual behavior

Proponents:
> Emile Durkheim
> Herbert Spencer
> Talcott Parsons
> Robert Merton

Dominant level of analysis:
> Macro level: focusing on broad social patterns

Conflict

Key concepts:
> Inequality
> Power
> Conflict
> Social class
> Exploitation

Focus/themes:
> Inequality results from the scarce resources in which the rich and powerful use their power to maintain their power to maintain their privileged position.
> Conflict leads to social change.

Proponents:
> Karl Marx
> W. E. B. Du Bois
> Jane Addams

Dominant level of analysis:
> Macro level: focusing on broad social patterns

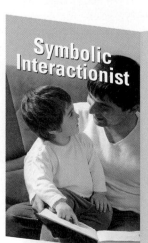

Symbolic Interactionist

Key concepts:
> Verstehen
> Definition of situation
> Negotiated order

Focus/themes:
> Social construction of reality.
> Social structures are reproduced through everyday interaction.

Proponents:
> Max Weber
> George Herbert Mead

Dominant level of analysis:
> Micro level: focusing on interactions among individuals

Visual Summary The Sociological Perspective and Research Process

1.1 The Sociological Perspective

- Sociology helps us see the world from a new perspective through the sociological imagination and addresses several major and enduring societal issues.

- Sociology is important because the sociological perspective looks at individual human behavior in the broader social context of the society and times in which people live, and the social position of the individual.

- Sociology should be distinguished from the natural sciences, the humanities, and other social sciences. Sociologists emphasize understanding individuals in the context of social forces that affect them.

- The sociological imagination is the capacity for individuals to understand the relationship between their individual lives and the social forces that influence them by relating personal biography to history and personal troubles to broader social issues.

- Major and enduring social issues addressed throughout this text include social structure, social control, social inequality, social construction of reality, scientific knowledge, and social change.

- Social structures are enduring and relatively stable patterns of social life that constrain our behavior yet also result from our behavior. An example would be the constitutional provisions for the electoral college electing the US President.

- Social control refers to efforts by society to regulate people's behavior and thought. It is surprisingly strong and pervasive and can lead to unexpected results.

- The amount of social inequality and the patterns of inequality found in the US stratification system as well as globally are a recurrent theme throughout the text.

- The meaning of social life is negotiated as part of a social process among participants, therefore reality is not directly experienced by individuals so much as it is socially constructed. This is illustrated when determining whether a particular event is a crime.

- What distinguishes scientific knowledge from common sense and politicized opinion is crucial for establishing the validity of sociology.

- Social life today is experiencing rapid social changes including urbanization, population changes, social and political movements, and technological change, all leading to globalization—increasing interdependence throughout the world.

1.2 The Historical Origins of Sociology

- Sociology as a discipline began in the late 19th century, during a time of social upheaval from major changes such as the French Revolution and the Industrial Revolution, and was shaped by several early sociologists.

- August Comte (1798–1857) proposed studying social life using scientific principles much like those used in the natural sciences (positivism) and coined the term "sociology."

- Karl Marx (1818–1883) developed the conflict perspective, arguing that human history was a history of class conflict with each stage, dominated by one class exploiting another.

- Emile Durkheim (1858–1917) was interested in the impact of social structures on individual behavior. He argued that social facts are regular patterns of behavior that exist independently of individuals and constrain individual behavior.

- Max Weber (1864–1920) made numerous contributions including recognizing a connection between the Protestant work ethic (a disciplined work ethic, a rational approach to life, and an emphasis on this world) and capitalism while also arguing that industrial societies were becoming rationalized.

- George Herbert Mead (1863–1931) was a cofounder of symbolic interactionism, a perspective emphasizing the importance of symbols and meanings for human interaction. He believed we needed to understand the person's concept of self and their ability to take the role of the other to understand both how people are socialized and how they interact with others.

- Harriet Martineau (1802–1876) was the first female sociologist, advocated for social reform and against slavery, and wrote *Society in America*, which examined American culture at the time.
- Jane Addams (1860–1935) co-founded Hull House in Chicago's slums to assist immigrants, influenced many of the academics at the University of Chicago

nearby, and was the only sociologist to be awarded a Nobel Peace Prize.
- William Edward Burghardt Du Bois (1868–1963) was the first African American to receive a PhD in any discipline from Harvard, taught at the University of Pennsylvania, and authored a classic study of race relations, *The Philadelphia Negro: A Social Study*.

1.3 Sociological Theory—Current Theoretical Perspectives

- Three theoretical perspectives express much of the variation in sociological thought: structural-functional theory, conflict theory, and symbolic interactionism.
- Structural-functional theory argues that societies have important social structures (enduring patterns) that lead to positive consequences (functions) for society, enabling them to survive. The theory was extended by Merton to distinguish manifest functions (those that are obvious and usually intended) from latent (those that are unintended and less obvious) functions, and to recognize that there can also be dysfunctions (negative consequences).
- Conflict theory grew out of the work by Karl Marx on class conflict and was modernized by C. Wright Mills in his study of the power elite. It has also been applied to race (e.g., W. E. B. Du Bois) and gender (feminist theory).
- Feminist theory criticizes traditional sociological work, arguing that it has

been sexist as a result of the dominance of males in society in general and the preponderance of males. Standpoint theory argues that because of their position of subservience, women are more aware of inequalities of gender.
- Symbolic interactionism was introduced by Mead (1934), Cooley (1909), and Thomas (1931) and emphasizes interactions among people, understanding life from their perspective (the verstehen of Max Weber), and the notion of self (Mead). It emphasizes symbols, defining the situation, and negotiated order. It also relates to the social construction of reality and the ways we are influenced by how others see us (the looking-glass self and self-fulfilling prophecies).
- Sociology has multiple theories at different levels (micro, macro, and meso) and while those theories differ, they each contribute understanding, share a broad sociological approach, and show that the sociological project is still a work in progress.

1.4 The Science of Sociology

- Sociology is a science. To be a science it must meet the standards of scientific knowledge that apply to all sciences. These standards distinguish scientific knowledge from common sense and other forms of knowing.
- Sociology has always had a tension between those who want to reform the world and those who want to understand it through science. This is reflected in concerns over whether sociology can be value-free.

- Sociology as a science can be judged by the extent to which it meets the standards of scientific knowledge. It must be empirically testable, falsifiable, reproducible, and generalizable.
- Sociological research is sometimes qualitative, sometimes quantitative, and in many cases employs both in mixed-methods research.
- The research process used in sociology and sciences in general typically involves eight steps: (1) select a topic,

(2) define the problem, (3) review the literature, (4) develop a hypothesis, (5) select research methods, (6) conduct the research, (7) analyze and interpret the results, and (8) report the findings. Research itself is a never-ending process; studies may answer some questions, but usually also raise new ones.

- Theoretical concepts are measured by empirical variables through operational definitions describing how they can be measured so that others can use similar procedures to obtain similar results with reliability (consistency) and validity (correctness).

- Because people are diverse, sociological research examines multiple people, but studying entire populations is usually too expensive and time-consuming. Most sociological research examines a sample (a subset of cases) from a population (all people or phenomena of interest).

- To avoid biased samples that mislead, sociologists often use probability sampling, in which every case has a known probability of being selected in quantitative studies, or theoretical sampling, in which cases are selected to permit comparisons in qualitative research.

- Statistical analysis computes mathematical summaries of data (statistics) to make empirical generalizations summarizing important findings. Three common types of statistics are: descriptive statistics (describing the distribution of a variable), measures of association (to assess whether two variables are related to one another), and tests of significance (to determine whether results could have occurred by chance).

- Descriptive statistics include the mean, median, and mode which differ in how much information is used and their appropriateness when a variable is unevenly distributed.

- Association between two variables does not always mean they are causally related, and competing causal models may account for the same observed association.

© Faiz Zaki/Shutterstock, Inc.

1.5 Sociological Research Methods

- There are several well-developed research methods commonly used in sociological research: social surveys, participant observation (field work), experiments, and analysis of existing data.

- Social surveys ask people questions in person, through questionnaires, or through phone interviews or online surveys. Questions can be very rigid, closed-ended questions with fixed options or open-ended questions that allow respondents to answer in their own words.

- Experiments manipulate an independent variable and then observe subjects (people in the study) to see how that influences dependent variables by comparing the experimental group (with one value of the independent variable) with the control group (having another value). In laboratory experiments subjects can often be randomly assigned to the two groups to minimize possible biases, while in field studies that take place in natural settings, researchers have less control.

- In participant observation, or field work, the researcher participates in and is directly involved in the lives of those he or she is studying. Researchers vary in the extent to which they participate in the activity they are studying. Results of such studies are often reported in ethnographies (detailed descriptive accounts).

- Secondary analysis is research that looks at existing data in a new way and includes content analysis to summarize important characteristics of texts and historical-comparative research, examining ways social life changes across cultures and over time.

45

© John Howard/DigitalVision/Thinkstock

1.6 Ethics in Sociological Research

- Because sociologists study humans, sociological research faces three fundamental issues that distinguish sociology from the natural sciences: verstehen (the subjective experience of the people being studied), reactivity (the tendency for people to change their behavior when they know they are being studied), and ethical issues.

- The federal government and research disciplines including sociology have developed standards for the ethical treatment of human subjects that include minimizing risks, guaranteeing privacy, spreading the risk fairly, and informing subjects fully about risks before they agree to participate (informed consent).

1.1 The Sociological Perspective

1. Charles was happy to graduate from college with his degree in education. However, it was still the middle of the Great Recession and jobs were scarce. So his first year was spent serving as a substitute teacher in two different school districts. What does this best illustrate?
   A. The intersection of history and biography
   B. Social inequality
   C. Social structure
   D. Social construction of reality

2. This church has a series of rituals that are performed routinely at every service. They provide a predictable framework for describing most services. What does this best illustrate?
   A. The intersection of history and biography
   B. Social inequality
   C. Social structure
   D. Social construction of reality

1.2 The Historical Origins of Sociology

3. Max Weber argued that the Catholic work ethic made countries that were predominantly Catholic more likely to be early participants in the Industrial Revolution.
   A. True
   B. False

4. Comte argued that Protestants were more individualistic and practiced fewer solidarity-enhancing rituals than Catholics and hence experienced fewer social ties and bonds to others or to their religious beliefs.
   A. True
   B. False

5. W. E. B. Du Bois believed that Spencerian social Darwinism helped explain differences between blacks and whites.
   A. True
   B. False

1.3 Sociological Theory—Current Theoretical Perspectives

6. A city council passed a new ordinance to fine someone for making too much noise in a residential neighborhood after 9 PM. However, the council was dismayed to see that teenagers and younger adults who used to have fairly safe but sometimes noisy parties in their homes were now much more often having wild, sometimes violent parties on the beach of a nearby lake. This is an example of:
   A. a dysfunction.
   B. a manifest function.
   C. negotiated order.
   D. a function.

7. Which two sociologists are associated with structural-functional theory?
   A. W. E. B. Du Bois and Emile Durkheim
   B. Robert Merton and Erving Goffman
   C. Max Weber and Talcott Parsons
   D. Herbert Spencer and Robert Merton

8. Which sociologist and concept are associated with the interactionist perspective?
   A. W. I. Thomas and social structures
   B. George Herbert Mead and the definition of the situation
   C. Max Weber and negotiated order
   D. Robert Merton and manifest function

1.4 The Science of Sociology

9. Lorena wants to know whether she should run for class president, so she asks several of her friends whether they would vote for her if she did. This is best described as:
   A. a biased population.
   B. a probabilistic sample.
   C. an empirical generalization.
   D. a biased sample.

10. Hans has a special horse. He can show him any number of items from 1 to 10 and ask him how many there are. Whenever Hans asks the horse, the horse always correctly taps its hoof the correct number of times. Unfortunately, when other people do it, the horse usually gets it wrong. Which standard of science does Hans's counting horse violate?
    A. Empirically testable
    B. Falsifiable
    C. Reproducible
    D. Generalizable

11. You collect anime (Japanese cartoons and computer animation) videos and you would like to know the average number of videos owned by your friends. You are a little uncertain which statistic to use because you know one of your friends has been doing this for years and has a much bigger collection than your other friends. Which statistic is best for this?
    A. Mean
    B. Mode
    C. Association
    D. Median

1.5 Sociological Research Methods

12. A response rate is:
    A. how quickly someone answers questions in a phone interview.
    B. how a respondent rates his or her experience.
    C. the proportion of responses that are accurate.
    D. the proportion of responses that are received.

13. A researcher is studying the effect of having lots of friends and family who help a person (social support) on how long the person lives (longevity), but only for males (gender) living in New York State (location). Which list below identifies the independent variable, dependent variable, and control variable in that order?
    A. Longevity, gender, social support
    B. Social support, location, longevity
    C. Longevity, social support, gender
    D. Social support, longevity, location

14. Which of the following were not identified by Scott as a criterion for deciding whether historical documents are useful for research?
    A. Authentic
    B. Credible
    C. Official
    D. Representative

1.6 Ethics in Sociological Research

15. Which of the following is *not* a protection of human subjects required by the federal regulation described in this chapter (Title 45, Code of Federal Regulations, Part 46, Revised June 18, 1991:8–9)?
    A. Risks should be minimized.
    B. Any risks should outweigh benefits.
    C. Subjects should be guaranteed confidentiality or anonymity.
    D. Subjects should be selected to share risks fairly.

16. A researcher observes students in a first-grade classroom as part of her study. She is worried that the students are acting differently because she is in the room. This would be an example of:
    A. verstehen.
    B. informed consent.
    C. confidentiality.
    D. reactivity.

CHAPTER ESSAY QUESTIONS

1. Given what Emile Durkheim said about suicide rates and social bonds, which group do you think he would predict to have higher suicide rates: college students in fraternities and sororities or college students living off campus? Why? Which of those do you think would have stronger social bonds?

2. Sociologists argue that families have a number of important social functions, including providing financial and moral support for children, regulating sexual behavior, socializing children to prepare them for social life as adults, and social placement, or helping them find a position in which they can be productive members of society. Are these functions evident in the opening vignette describing an overheard conversation? For each function, briefly quote a phrase from the conversation and indicate which function it illustrates.

3. The following description of a research project addresses many of the issues discussed in this chapter. However, the author was a student just starting to do research, and he did not use any of the technical terms usually used to describe the research. Unfortunately, this makes it much harder for others to read the study and understand what he did. Write a brief essay identifying at least four of the following concepts and giving a brief quotation from the study that illustrates it:

   A. Research method (e.g., experiment, survey, observation, etc.)
   B. Hypothesis
   C. Sample
   D. Reliability
   E. Validity
   F. Dependent variable

This research studied US college student opinions about gay marriage. We expected that students from rural areas would be more opposed to gay marriage than students from urban areas. For this research, we talked personally with 200 students randomly selected from a list of students at Central College. Each student was asked 20 questions about gay marriage and their personal characteristics, such as whether they were from a rural or urban area. Some of the students were spoken to a second time and the same questions were asked to see if the students responded the same way consistently at different times. We had a sociology professor look over the questions, and she agreed that they were good questions to assess opinions about gay marriage. After all data had been collected, we found the average opinion for rural students and compared it to that of urban students. We computed the averages by summing the scores for each student and dividing by the number of students. The difference was greater than what you would expect to occur by chance.

CHAPTER DISCUSSION QUESTIONS

1. Use the sociological imagination to discuss some of the common obstacles college students face that prevent them from graduating on time.

2. Based on your demographic characteristics such as sex, race, and social class, share with the class whether you would be attending college if you were the age you are now 50 years ago. Consider sociological concepts such as the social structure, social stratification, social construction of reality, and social change.

3. Use the structural-functional, conflict, feminist, and symbolic interactionism theories to explain why females generally have higher two-year and four-year college graduation rates than males do.

4. Discuss how a hypothesis might change depending on whether a sociologist chooses macro-level, meso-level, or micro-level analysis of a topic such as dating behaviors among college students.

5. What issues related to reliability and validity need to be considered when designing a research study using a probability sample to survey college students regarding their study behaviors?

6. Early sociologists were influenced by important events of their times, events that transformed society and called into question some of the things we often take for granted such as the stability of a society. What transforming events are taking place today or took place in the last few years that you think would influence sociologists today? Do those events relate to one or more of the major and enduring social issues? Which theoretical perspective (if any) do you think would best help us understand those events?

7. Review the opening vignette about the overheard phone conversation. Which of the three broad theoretical frameworks discussed in this chapter (conflict theory, structural-functional theory, and interactionist theory) do you think does the best job of explaining the most important issues reflected in that conversation? Justify why those issues are the most important and how that theory explains them.

8. Discuss the strengths and weaknesses of each of the following research methods: survey, experiment, participant observation, and secondary analysis.

CHAPTER PROJECTS

INDIVIDUAL PROJECTS

1. On the Internet, search for articles and Web pages about the Tuskegee Syphilis Study. Notice who wrote each article or Web page, how they approach the study, and what they say about it. Do you see differences in the published articles and the Web pages? Which do a better job of meeting the standards of scientific knowledge? (Of course, we should be careful about trying to generalize from a very small sample.)

2. In this chapter, we discussed the Hawthorne effect. This was a surprising finding from research in the 1930s that has been taken as one of the principles guiding social science research—the view that people may change their behavior when they know they are being studied. However, a relatively recent article in *The Economist* by Steven Levitt and John List further analyzes some of the key data from the Hawthorne studies, and they argue that other factors may be explain the findings. Read this article at http://www.economist.com/node/13788427?story_id =13788427&CFID=59507983&CFTOKEN=80637353. Do you think they made their case successfully? What standard of science are they claiming was not met in the original studies? Do you think we should ignore reactivity in sociological research? Write a brief essay presenting their case and your conclusions.

GROUP PROJECTS

1. Select one of the major and enduring issues discussed in this chapter. Then go online and look for recent news articles that relate to that issue. Explain how the issue helps you understand that article. Present your findings to the class.

2. Read an article in a sociology research journal (for example, *American Journal of Sociology, American Sociological Review*, or *Sociological Quarterly*). Look for what the article says about the major steps in the research process, such as theory, hypothesis, sample, measurement, data collection, or analysis. Each team member should pick one of the steps and contribute a clear summary of it in written or visual form. The team should then assemble the summaries as a coherent whole.

3. Consider the difference between the two sociological concepts: social facts and verstehen. Apply them to the topic of binge drinking among college students. Prepare a brief presentation of your findings.

Agency
Associated
Biased
Bourgeoisie (capitalists)
Bureaucracy
Case study
Closed-ended questions
Complete observer
Complete participant
Concept
Content analysis
Control group
Culture
Data
Definition of the situation
Dependent variable
Dysfunctions
Emergent properties
Empirical generalizations
Ethnography
Experimental group
Field experiment
Function
Generalized other
Globalization
Hawthorne effect
Historical-comparative research
Hypothesis
"I"
Independent variable
Industrial Revolution

Interviews
Laboratory experiment
Latent dysfunctions
Latent functions
Looking-glass self
Macro-level studies
Manifest functions
"Me"
Means of production
Meso-level studies
Micro-level studies
Mixed-methods research
Negotiated order
Observer as participant
Open-ended questions
Operational definition
Participant as observer
Participant observation or
   field work
Peer-reviewed scientific journal
Population
Positivism
Power
Power elite
Probability sampling
Proletariat (workers)
Protestant work ethic
Qualitative research
Quantitative research
Questionnaires
Random assignment

Rationalization of society
Reactivity
Reliability
Respondent
Response rates
Sample
Secondary analysis
Self-fulfilling prophecy
Social control
Social construction of reality
Social facts
Social stratification
Social structure
Sociological imagination
Sociology
Statistics
Structural-functional theory
Subjects
Surplus value
Symbols
Take the role of the other
Tests of significance
Theoretical sampling
Theory
Thomas theorem
Transferable
Unobtrusive research
Validity
Variable
Verstehen

1.1 The Sociological Perspective

1. Social structure [B. There are several kinds of colleges and universities in the United States, including private schools, public schools, for-profit schools, and religious schools.]

2. Social control [E. After World War II, at the Nuremberg War Crimes Trial, many of the defendants accused of war crimes argued that they were ordered to perform the acts and hence should not be held accountable.]

3. Social inequality [D. In the United States, the net worth of black households is less than a tenth that of white households.]

4. Social construction of reality [C. Council members debated for several hours before finally agreeing construction noise is a problem and creating a taskforce to propose a solution.]

5. Scientific knowledge [F. The study by LaFree (1980) examined data from rape cases in a Midwestern city, following accused rapists through the criminal justice system.]

6. Social change [A. India continues to see rapid growth in population every year.]

1.2 The Historical Origins of Sociology

1. The only sociologist to earn a Nobel prize [C. Jane Addams]

2. Inequality should be measured based on class, status, and power. [B. Max Weber]

3. The methods of the natural sciences can be applied successfully to a science of society. [E. August Comte]

4. Author of *The Philadelphia Negro* [D. W. E. B. Du Bois]

5. Developed the concept of the generalized other [F. George Herbert Mead]

6. Conducted one of the first examples of research using empirical data to examine social issues [A. Emile Durkheim]

1.3 Sociological Theory—Current Theoretical Perspectives

1. Structural-functional theory [C. Manifest function; i. Robert Merton]

2. Conflict theory [A. Social class; iii. Karl Marx]

3. Interactionist theory [B. Verstehen; ii. Max Weber]

1.4 The Science of Sociology

1. The researchers are interested in the optimism of college students about the future. [B. Concept]

2. To do this, they will select 300 college students at random from a list of undergraduate students at their university. [D. Sample]

3. They realize that students at this college might not be the same as college students in general. [A. Bias]

4. They want to see whether men are more optimistic than women. [F. Hypothesis]

5. They will ask people to describe their optimism on a five-point scale by selecting the number closest to their view. [E. Operational definition]

6. They hope that if they were to ask people this same question now and 10 weeks from now, the responses would be the same both times. [C. Reliability]

7. They will compare the mean optimism of women students with that of men students to see if the difference is greater than expected by chance. [G. Test of significance]

1.5 Sociological Research Methods

1. Researcher wants respondents to respond using standardized responses. [D. Closed-ended questions]

2. We expect this new curriculum will increase student performance by 20%. [A. Hypothesis]

3. These people are not exposed to the new educational tool for purposes of comparison. [G. Control group]

4. This study took place in a work setting. [B. Field work]

5. Researcher wants to study people's opinions but is not sure what things are important to them. [E. Open-ended questions]

6. This study examined data available on the Internet. [F. Secondary analysis]

7. This person was there during the time in question and knew most of the other participants. [C. Credibility]

1.6 Ethics in Sociological Research

1. A gaming company secretly collected Social Security numbers from user accounts on the social media service through which the game is played and then hackers released names and Social Security numbers online. [D. Exposes subjects to unnecessary risk]

2. The researcher sits on a bench in a mall and unobtrusively counts the number of young men walking by who are wearing sports-related t-shirts. [B. Not likely to have major problems with reactivity]

3. An anonymous online survey asks respondents their opinions about a border dispute between their country and a neighboring country. [C. Assesses verstehen]

4. Subjects are shown information regarding what will be done in the study and any potential risks, then are asked to indicate whether they would like to continue or exit. [E. Has informed consent]

5. A researcher spends two hours in the home of a family recording what they do and in which room. [A. Likely to have issues with reactivity]

ANSWERS TO CHAPTER REVIEW TEST

1.1 The Sociological Perspective

1. A. His career was affected by historical circumstances when he graduated.

2. C. Social structure is a regular pattern of behavior.

1.2 The Historical Origins of Sociology

3. B. False. It was the Protestant work ethic that encouraged the Industrial Revolution.

4. B. False. It was Max Weber who made this argument.

5. B. False. Du Bois disagreed with Spencer and argued blacks were the victims of racial discrimination and were not racially inferior.

1.3 Sociological Theory—Current Theoretical Perspectives

6. A. A dysfunction is a negative consequence.

7. D. Herbert Spencer and Robert Merton are both associated with structural-functional theory.

8. B. Mead developed the concept, definition of the situation, and the notion that this concept is associated with the interactionist perspective.

1.4 The Science of Sociology

9. D. It is biased because it includes only her friends. It is a sample because it is not all of her friends or all of the people who can vote.

10. C. It is not reproducible because other people cannot perform the same test and get the same result.

11. D. The median is the best choice because it is a descriptive statistic suitable for measuring the average, it uses more information than the mode, and unlike the mean, it is less affected by outliers.

1.5 Sociological Research Methods

12. D. A response rate is the proportion of people who were asked to respond who actually did respond.

13. D. The independent variable is social support, the dependent variable is longevity, and there are two control variables: location and gender.

14. C. Even unofficial documents can be useful, so long as they are known to be unofficial.

1.6 Ethics in Sociological Research.

15. B. Benefits should outweigh risks, not vice versa.

16. D. Reactivity occurs when people act differently when they know they are being studied.

ANSWERS TO CHAPTER ESSAY QUESTIONS

1. A good answer should indicate that higher rates of suicide would be predicted for people with fewer social bonds. College students living off campus typically have fewer friends and acquaintances than those in fraternities and sororities and may have weaker bonds as well.

2. A good answer should identify each function and match it with a quotation, such as those listed below:
- Financial and moral support—*So you'll put the money into my account tomorrow? Thanks, Mom. Yeah. I love you too.*
- Regulating sexual behavior—*Huh? No, I'm not dating him any more. He's history. I thought I told . . . Yeah, I know you didn't think he was good enough for me anyway, ever since he dropped out of school.*
- Socializing children to prepare them for life as an adult—*After all you taught me, you don't think I'd just blow it off, do you?*
- Social placement—*It's tough like you'd expect for such a good school.*

3. A good answer should identify at least four of these and link them to these quotations or a paraphrase of them.
- **A.** Research method (e.g., experiment, survey, observation, etc.)—They should indicate it used surveys or interviews and link to this phrase—*we talked personally with.*
- **B.** Hypothesis—*We expected that students from rural areas would be more opposed to gay marriage than students from urban areas.*
- **C.** Sample—*We talked personally with 200 students randomly selected from a list of students at Central College.*
- **D.** Reliability—*Some of the students were spoken to a second time and the same questions were asked to see if the students respond the same way consistently at different times.*
- **E.** Validity—*We had a sociology professor look over the questions, and she agreed that they were good questions to assess opinions about gay marriage.*

REFERENCES

American Sociological Association (ASA). 2012. *ASA Code of Ethics*. Accessed November 2012 at http://www.asanet.org/about/ethics.cfm.

The Belmont Report: Basic Ethical Principles and Their Applications. 1979. National Institutes of Health. Washington, DC: US Government Printing Office.

Blalock, H. 1964. *Causal Inferences in Nonexperimental Research*. Chapel Hill: University of North Carolina Press.

Brandt, Allan M. 1978. "Racism and Research: The Case of the Tuskegee Syphilis Study." *Hastings Center Report* 8 (6):21–29.

Brekhus, Wayne. 2003. *Peacocks, Chameleons, Centaurs: Gay Suburbia and the Grammar of Social Identity*. Chicago: University of Chicago Press.

Burawoy, Michael. 1979. *Manufacturing Consent: Changes in the Labor Process under Monopoly Capitalism*. Chicago: University of Chicago Press.

Code of Federal Regulations, Title 45, Part 46, Revised June 18, 1991, pp. 8–9.

Collins, Patricia Hill. 1986. "Learning from the Outside Within: The Sociological Significance of Black Feminist Thought." *Social Problems* 33:14–32.

Comte, Auguste. 1975. *Auguste Comte and Positivism: The Essential Writings*. Edited by Gertrude Lenzer. New York: Harper Torchbooks.

Cooley, Charles. 1909. *Social Organization: A Study of the Larger Mind*. New York: Charles Scribner's Sons.

Deegan, Mary Jo. (Editor). 1991. *Women in Sociology: A Biographical Sourcebook*. New York: Greenwood.

Du Bois, W. E. B. 1899. *The Philadelphia Negro: A Social Study*. New York: Schocken. Republished 1967.

Durkheim, Emile. 1893. *The Division of Labor in Society*. New York: Free Press. Republished 1964.

Durkheim, Emile. 1895. *The Rules of Sociological Method*. New York: Free Press. Republished 1964.

Durkheim, Emile. 1897. *Suicide*. New York: Free Press. Republished 1966.

Durkheim, Emile. 1912. *The Elementary Forms of Religious Life*. New York: Free Press.

Durkheim, Emile. 1922. *Education and Sociology*. Translated by Sherwood L. Fox. New York: Free Press. Republished 1956.

Farivar, C. 2012, October 11. "Talk Is Cheap: Cell Phones Hit Six Billion Worldwide." *Ars Technica*. Accessed October 2012 at http://arstechnica.com/business/2012/10/talk-is-cheap-six-billion-people-worldwide-have-cellphones/.

Fetterman, David M. 1989. *Ethnography: Step by Step*. Newbury Park, CA: Sage Publications.

Fleischmann, Martin, and Stanley Pons. 1989. "Electrochemically Induced Nuclear Fusion of Deuterium." *Journal of Electroanalytical Chemistry* 261(2A):301–308.

Giddens, Anthony. 1984. *The Constitution of Society*. Berkeley: University of California Press.

Glaser, Barney, and Anselm Strauss. 1967. *The Discovery of Grounded Theory: Strategies for Qualitative Research*. Chicago: Aldine.

Goffman, Erving. 1967. *Interaction Ritual: Essays on Face-to-Face Behavior*. Garden City, NY: Anchor Books.

Gold, R. 1958. "Roles in Sociological Field Observation." *Social Forces* 36: 217–213.

Granberg, Donald, and Soren Holmberg. 1988. *The Political System Matters: Social Psychology and Voting Behavior in Sweden and the United States*. Cambridge, UK: Cambridge University Press.

James, W. 1890. *The Principles of Psychology*. New York: Henry Holt (Reprinted Bristol: Thoemmes Press, 1999).

LaFree, Gary D. 1980. "The Effect of Sexual Stratification by Race on Official Reactions to Rape." *American Sociological Review* 45(10):842–848.

Latane, Bibb, and John M. Darley. 1968. "Group Inhibition of Bystander Intervention in Emergencies." *Journal of Personality and Social Psychology* 10:215–21.

Lazaro, F. 2012, September 25. "Helping Where 'There Are More Cell Phones than Toothbrushes.'" *PBS Newshour*. The Rundown. Accessed October 2012 at http://www.pbs.org/newshour/rundown/2012/09/helping.html.

Lee, Richard Borshay. 1969. "Eating Christmas in the Kalahari". *Natural History* 78(12):14–22.

Lenski, Gerhard, and Jean Lenski. 1982. *Human Societies: An Introduction to Macrosociology*. Fourth edition. New York: McGraw-Hill.

Martineau, Harriet. 1837. *Society in America*. London: Saunders and Otley. Reissued 2009 Cambridge, UK: Cambridge University Press.

Marx, Karl. 1867. *Capital*. Edited by Friedrich Engels. New York: International Publishers. Republished 1967.

Marx, Karl, and Friederich Engels. 1848. "The Communist Manifesto." pp. _____ in *Karl Marx: Selected Writings*, edited by David McClellan. New York: Oxford University Press. Republished 1977.

Mayo, Elton. 1933. *The Human Problems of an Industrial Civilization*. New York: McMillan.

Mead, George Herbert. 1934. *Mind, Self, and Society*. Chicago: University of Chicago Press.

Merton, Robert K. 1968. *Social Theory and Social Structure*. New York: Free Press.

Michael, Robert T., John H. Gagnon, Edward O. Laumann, and Gina Kolata. 1994. *Sex in America: A Definitive Survey*. Boston: Little, Brown & Company.

Mills, C. Wright. 1959. *The Sociological Imagination*. New York: Oxford University Press.

The New York Times. 1996, February 4. "Harvard Student Picks Jail in Dispute over Nude Photos of Son." *The New York Times*. Accessed October 2012 at http://www.nytimes.com/1996/02/04/us/harvard-student-picks-jail-in-dispute-over-nude-photos-of-son.html.

Parsons, Talcott. 1951. *The Social System*. England: Routledge & Kegan Paul Ltd.

Popper, Karl. 1963. *Conjectures and Refutations: The Growth of Scientific Knowledge* Reprinted edition. London: Routledge.

Reinharz, Shulamit. 1992. *Feminist Methods in Social Research*. New York: Oxford University Press.

Rossi, Alice. 1973. *The Feminist Papers*. New York: Bantam Books.

Rosenbaum, Ron. 1995. "The Great Ivy League Nude Posture Photo Scandal: How Scientists Coaxed America's Best and Brightest Out of Their Clothes." *The New York Times Magazine* Jan. 15.

Roth, Julius A. 1963. *Timetables; Structuring the Passage of Time in Hospital Treatment and Other Careers*. Indianapolis, IN: Bobbs-Merrill.

Roy, Donald. 1952. "Quota Restriction and Goldbricking in a Machine Shop." *American Journal of Sociology* 57:427–42.

Schillinger, R. 2011. "Social Media and the Arab Spring: What Have We Learned?" *Huffington Post*. Accessed October 2012 at http://www.huffington-post.com/raymond-schillinger/arab-spring-social-media_b_970165.html.

Skocpol, Theda. 1979. *States and Social Revolutions: A Comparative Analysis of France, Russia, and China*. New York: Cambridge University Press.

Shaw, H., and C. Stone. 2012. "Incomes at the Top Rebounded in First Full Year of Recovery, New Analysis of Tax Data Shows Top 1 Percent's Share of Income Starting to Rise Again." *Center on Budget and Policy Priorities*. Accessed October 2012 at http://www.cbpp.org/cms/index.cfm?fa=view&id=3697.

Sheldon, William H. 1949. *Varieties of Delinquent Youth*. New York: Harper & Bros.

Simmel, Georg. 1902–1917. *The Sociology of Georg Simmel*. Edited and Translated by Kurt H. Wolff. Glencoe, IL: Free Press. Individual papers first published between 1902 and 1917. Republished 1950.

Smith, Dorothy. 1987. *The Everyday World as Problematic*. Boston: Northeastern University Press.

Spencer, Herbert. 1873–1881. *Descriptive Sociology: or Groups of Sociological Facts*, parts 1–8, classified and arranged by Spencer, compiled and abstracted by David Duncan, Richard Schepping, and James Collier. London: Williams & Norgate.

REFERENCES, *continued*

Terkel, Studs. 1992. *Race: How Blacks and Whites Think and Feel about the American Obsession*. London: The Economist Intelligence Unit.

Thomas, W. I. 1931. *The Unadjusted Girl*. Boston: Little, Brown.

Thomas, W. I., and D. S. Thomas. 1928. *The Child in America: Behavior Problems and Programs*. New York: Knopf.

Thompson, D. 2011. "Occupy the World: The '99 Percent' Movement Goes Global." *The Atlantic*. Accessed October 2011 at http://www.theatlantic.com/business/archive/2011/10/occupy-the-world-the-99-percent-movement-goes-global/246757/.

Wallace, Walter L. 1971. *The Logic of Science in Sociology*. Piscataway, NJ: Transaction Publishers.

Wallis, A., and H. Roberts. 1956. *Statistics: A New Approach*. New York: Crowell-Collier Publishing.

Weber, Max. 1903–1917. *The Methodology of the Social Sciences*. Translated and edited by Edward A. Shils and Henry A. Finch. New York: Free Press.

Weber, Max. 1904–1905. *The Protestant Ethic and the Spirit of Capitalism*. New York: Scribner's. Republished 1958.

Weber, Max. 1913. *The Theory of Social and Economic Organization*. Translated by A. M. Henderson and Talcott Parsons. Edited by Talcott Parsons. Glencoe, IL: Free Press. Republished 1947.

Whyte, William Foote. 1943. *Street Corner Society: The Social Structure of an Italian Slum*. Chicago: University of Chicago Press. Republished 1981 (Third and expanded edition).

© Ingram Publishing/Thinkstock

Chapter Overview ▼

2 Culture

Learning Objectives ▼

2.1
- Define culture and discuss its significance for individuals and society.
- Describe cultural universals and cultural diversity.
- Explain ethnocentrism and cultural relativism.

2.2
- Illustrate key components of nonmaterial culture and discuss their importance.

2.3
- Describe the basic processes of discovery, invention, and diffusion in cultural change.
- Examine the use of technology in sociocultural evolution.

2.4
- Define high culture, popular culture, subcultures, and countercultures.
- Illustrate how each is related to social class and resistant to the dominant culture.
- Discuss the differences between multiculturalism and a global culture.

2.5
- Illustrate how the functional, conflict, and symbolic interaction theories provide different insights into culture.

© Corbis RF/Alamy

Bonn, Germany, June 13th. Arriving at the airport, I have to admit it was a little overwhelming rushing through, trying to follow all the signs in German. Thankfully, I was met outside by Mikael, who had invited me to consult with his German media firm to help them analyze news reports on the Internet. Later that morning, I was a little taken aback when I tried to make small talk with the head of the company and he seemed offended. When our meeting ended, he abruptly stood up, and it was clear that I was being dismissed. Worse yet, later I was taken to lunch with three of the company's employees, and by the time I returned, I was late for a major meeting with their senior officers. As I entered the room 15 minutes late, all eyes were upon me and they did not seem amused. Eventually things settled down, we had a productive meeting, and we agreed to work together on the project. But things certainly got off to a rough start. By the time I returned to the United States, I had a new appreciation for the sometimes subtle, sometimes not-so-subtle differences between the way people conduct business in the United States and Germany. Things that I had taken for granted before as natural and expected about my culture now look different as I recognize different ways they could be done.

Foreign travel is often one of the most effective ways to experience first-hand the importance of culture. My German trip illustrates some of the important aspects of culture to be addressed in this chapter. I am so used to the way we interact in business meetings in the United States (cultural immersion) that I don't even think about what kinds of behavior are appropriate or inappropriate. Feeling overwhelmed when first in a foreign culture is a common reaction and reflects culture shock. While I could count on Germany having means of transportation just as in the United States (a cultural universal), I didn't know in advance all the subtleties of finding bus routes and knowing how and where to purchase tickets (cultural variation). At that time, too, I hadn't yet had the good fortune to have read a little book by sociologists Edward Hall and Mildred Hall (1990) in which they describe some of the differences in culture between Germans and Americans, including the German emphasis on promptness and their tendency to view small talk about personal issues as inappropriate in a business setting.

2.1 Culture

Culture is all around us and so pervasive we are often unaware of it. We depend on it so much we sometimes have difficulty reacting to other cultures.

- Define culture and discuss its significance for individuals and society.
- Describe cultural universals and cultural diversity.
- Explain ethnocentrism and cultural relativism.

Growing up in a culture, it is easy to see things from the perspective of that culture but very hard to imagine how other cultures might do things differently without being exposed to those other cultures. Today, most people are exposed to other cultures through the Internet, television, and travel, to say nothing of films, books, and newspapers. This makes it easier to recognize there are often different ways to do things and to gain a tolerance or respect for other cultures. However, not everyone views other cultures as equal with their own, and some people view their own culture as the standard against which other cultures can be judged.

The Significance of Culture

Culture A combination of ideas, behaviors, and material objects that people have created and adopted for carrying out necessary tasks of daily life.

Culture is a combination of ideas, behaviors, and material objects that members of a society have created and adopted for carrying out necessary tasks of daily life and that are passed on from one generation to the next. These include ways of performing common tasks such as providing food and shelter, producing and caring for children, and solving disputes. A **society** consists of people living in a specific geographic region who share a common culture. Thus, societies and culture go hand in hand.

Culture is important for societies. In fact, culture is the foundation of human civilization. Where other animals rely on heredity as the fixed blueprint for life, humans have essentially written much of their own blueprint through their cultural heritage, what sociologist Ralph Linton called our "social heredity" and what Edmund Burke called "a contract between those who are living, those who are dead, and those who are yet to be born." The passing of culture from one generation to the next is called **cultural transmission**.

Culture is pervasive, influencing virtually every aspect of our lives. We depend on culture for directions as to how to behave, for shelter, food, work, and meaning in our lives. As Ruth Benedict (1938) said, "From the moment of his birth, the customs into which [an individual] is born shape his experience and behavior. By the time he can talk, he is the little creature of his culture." We are immersed so completely in our own culture that we sometimes lose sight of why we do things and how it might look to others. These taken-for-granted beliefs, behaviors, artifacts, and ideas become the lens through which we view life. It is often only when we find ourselves confronting another culture—such as when we travel—that we begin to see the arbitrariness of much of what we do.

As a result, foreign travelers and people who migrate to one country from another often initially experience a kind of **culture shock**—disorientation when first experiencing a new culture. You may have experienced a bit of culture shock yourself the first time you traveled to a foreign country. Almost everything about your life that you took for granted is suddenly replaced with something else. People are speaking a different language, the foods are strange and sometimes downright scary, the laws are different in often peculiar and unexpected ways, the customs seem odd, and beliefs of the locals may seem totally illogical.

Society People living in a specific geographic region who share a common culture.

Cultural transmission The passing of culture from one generation to the next.

Culture shock Disorientation when first experiencing a new culture.

Cultural universals Cultural elements found in all cultures.

Examples of cultural diversity from around the world.

(left to right) © JeremyRichards/ Shutterstock, Inc.; © iStockphoto/ Thinkstock; © Regien Paassen/ Shutterstock, Inc.; © Photos.com

Cultural Universals and Cultural Diversity

It is not hard to find a wide range of cultural variation when comparing people from different societies in everything from the foods they eat, to the clothes they wear, to modes of transportation, and to standards of beauty and rightness. A number of anthropologists, however, argue there are a number of cultural universals. **Cultural universals** are cultural elements found in all cultures. For example, in a classic work, Murdock (1945:124) examined hundreds of cultures and identified several dozen cultural elements he argued are cultural universals. Several of the items that he believed were cultural universals are shown in **TABLE 2-1**. Cultural universals reflect fundamental problems faced by every society, such as communication, government, socialization, coping with the environment, regulating reproduction, and assigning people roles (Aberle et al. 1950).

TABLE 2-1 Murdock's Cultural Universals

Food taboos	Games	Gestures
A calendar	Cooking	Dancing
Music	Myths	Religion
Sexual restrictions	Trade	Family
Housing	Language	

Source: Adapted from Murdock, George Peter. 1945. "The Common Denominator of Cultures," pp. 123–142 in Ralph Linton, ed., The Science of Man in the World Crisis. *New York: Columbia University Press.*

While anthropologists have found some version of these cultural elements in virtually every society, there is considerable cultural variation in the particular ways societies address those problems. For example, one of the sexual restrictions Murdock (1945) found was an incest taboo. While all societies may ban incest, they often differ in how incest is defined. In fact, they often define family differently, so who is a close relative varies from one culture to another. Similarly, while all societies may have some means of transportation, forms of transportation range from airplanes and sports cars to dog sleds and canoes. There also are extreme variations in culture, with behaviors that are taboo in some cultures being practiced widely in other cultures. Examples include premarital sex, cannibalism, public nudity, human sacrifice, infanticide, and slavery. This extreme variation, even in the way societies address common problems, raises questions of how we should respond to other cultures.

Ethnocentrism or Cultural Relativism

How do we, and how should we, understand those other cultures? Our immersion in our own culture often leads us not only to take it for granted but to also see it as the "right" way to do things. As a result, we tend to view other cultures from the standards of our own culture, sometimes failing to recognize the meaning of behaviors or the significance of elements of other cultures. This can be illustrated by first examining a description by anthropologist Horace Miner (1956) of the strange body rituals of a particularly intriguing culture, a North American tribe, the Nacirema.

A large part of their day, he notes, is spent in ritual activities often focused on the human body. For this purpose, each of their houses has one or more shrine rooms in which the rituals are performed in secret and in private. The focal point of the shrine is a box built into the wall where magic charms and potions are kept thought to be necessary for life and health. They keep so many such potions that they often forget their original purpose and, presumably, keep them in the belief their continued presence will somehow protect the family.

Among their daily rituals is what he calls the "revolting" practice of inserting a small bundle of hog hairs into their mouth, along with magical powders, then moving the bundle around in a series of highly formalized gestures. Male members also practice a daily rite in which they scrape and lacerate the surface of their face with a sharp instrument. Women members, on the other hand, practice a less frequent but equally bizarre ritual in which they "bake their heads in small ovens for about an hour."

Miner goes on to describe many other rituals of the Nacirema, concluding they are "a magic-ridden people. It is hard to understand how they have managed to exist so long under the burdens which they have imposed upon themselves."

If you have not already gotten Miner's point by now, you might consider what "Nacirema" spells backward. What are some of the cultural rituals and elements he was discussing? Miner's point is that many of the customs or cultural elements in our own lives that we do not even think about may appear arbitrary, illogical, and even offensive to someone from a different culture. These might include the foods you eat, personal hygiene behaviors, body piercings, or efforts to control how your body looks to others.

By briefly standing us on our heads to help us look at our own culture as though we were outsiders, Miner has helped us to understand ethnocentrism. **Ethnocentrism** is the view that your own culture is the standard against which other cultures can be judged right or wrong. As William Graham Sumner (1906:13) defined it, "ethnocentrism is the technical name for this view of things to which one's own group is the center of everything, and all others are scaled and rated with reference to it."

At the other extreme from ethnocentrism is cultural relativism. **Cultural relativism** is a view that judges other cultures not by standards of the observer's culture but by the standards of the other culture itself. An extreme variant of cultural relativism argues there is no universal right or wrong. However, it is difficult for most people to believe there was not something terribly wrong with Hitler's Germany or with countries where hundreds of thousands of people are massacred in open civil war such as between the Hutu and Tutsi in Rwanda in 1994 and again in 1996. The difficult task for all of us in a multicultural society and in a world growing ever more interdependent is to be able to tell the difference between universally legitimate moral standards and our own cultural biases.

Material and Nonmaterial Culture

Culture includes both material and nonmaterial components. The **material culture** includes all of the art, architecture, technological artifacts, and material objects created by a society. This includes the factories, highways, automobiles, computers, records, books, toys, skyscrapers, nuclear waste depositories, polluted rivers, and junkyards that are the products of modern societies. **Technology** consists of tools and the knowledge necessary to create and use them effectively. For example, technology includes both the knowledge of how to create and build computers but also the knowledge of how to use them to accomplish tasks. These tools and the products we create with them both help provide for basic survival needs of people and provide a mechanism for expressing differences. The houses in which we live, the cars we drive or the trains and buses we ride, and the foods we eat all not only provide basic functionality needed for survival but also permit us to express our own identities through variations in things such as the style of clothes we wear, the make of automobile we buy, and the size of our houses.

Ethnocentrism The view that your own culture is the standard against which other cultures can be judged right or wrong.

Cultural relativism A view that judges other cultures not by standards of the observer's culture but by the standards of the other culture itself.

Material culture All of the art, architecture, technological artifacts, and material objects created by a society.

Technology Tools and the knowledge necessary to create and use them effectively.

Nonmaterial culture Intangible creations of people expressing everything from fundamental religious beliefs to abstract scientific knowledge to proscriptions for behavior.

Examples of material culture, which includes all of the art, architecture, technological artifacts, and material objects created by a society.

(left to right) © AbleStock; © Hemera/Thinkstock; © Hemera/Thinkstock; © iStockphoto/Thinkstock

The **nonmaterial culture** consists of intangible creations of people expressing everything from fundamental religious beliefs to abstract scientific knowledge to proscriptions for behavior. The nonmaterial culture includes everything about culture that is not part of the material culture and includes symbols, values, beliefs, norms, attitudes, and language. We will discuss these elements in more detail in Section 2.2.

Match each of the numbered concepts below with a lettered statement that defines or reflects that concept.

_____ **1.** Cultural transmission

_____ **2.** Cultural universals

_____ **3.** Cultural relativism

_____ **4.** Material culture

A. The transfer of culture from one generation to the next

B. Judges cultures by the standards of that culture, not those of the observer

C. Cultural components that address common issues faced by all cultures and important for their survival, but the specific way they are addressed can vary considerably

D. The transfer of cultural components from one society to another

E. Judges other cultures relative to the standards of one's own culture

F. Buildings and roads

G. Cultural components that are nearly identical in every society

H. Religion

2.2 Components of Nonmaterial Culture

Nonmaterial culture includes a wide range of elements, including language, symbols, values, beliefs, and norms along with a curious gap between the ideal culture we claim and the real culture we actually practice.

■ Illustrate key components of nonmaterial culture and discuss their importance.

Nonmaterial culture includes cognitive elements, which express our thoughts, beliefs, and preferences, and normative elements, which express how we should behave. We begin with the cognitive elements—symbols, language, values, and beliefs—and then we finish with normative elements—norms, sanctions, and laws. FIGURE 2-1 diagrams the relations between and among the main components of culture.

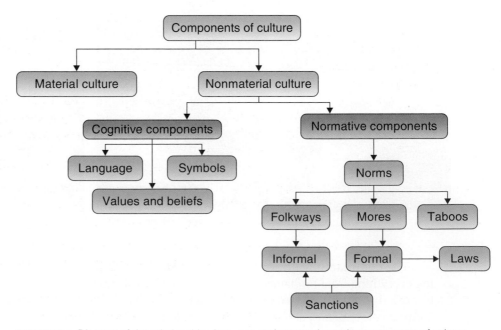

FIGURE 2-1 Diagram of the relationships between and among the main components of culture.

Symbols

Symbols are words, gestures, pictures, physical artifacts—in fact, anything that conveys meaning to people who share a culture. Examples of symbols include flags, distinctive haircuts, white coats worn by physicians, designer labels, trademarks and logos of companies, religious symbols like the Christian cross or the Muslim crescent, flags, swastikas, and nonverbal gestures such as salutes, waves, and hand signals conveying disrespect.

Symbols Words, gestures, pictures—in fact, anything that conveys meaning to people who share a culture.

Symbols surround us in our day-to-day lives as well as on special occasions.

(left to right) © Photodisc/Getty Images; © pixeldreams.eu/Shutterstock, Inc.; © Obvious/Shutterstock, Inc.

Symbols can be very important—important enough to fight for and even die for. People have been known to kill someone else for desecrating their nation's flag. During the Vietnam War era, demonstrators sometimes burned important symbols of the US society, including the flag, draft cards, and effigies of Uncle Sam, to express their anger and resistance to the war effort. Symbols are important in everyday life as well. If you do not believe symbols are important, then cut up all of your credit cards, throw away your university ID, burn your driver's license, and give away all of your dollar bills. After all, those are all merely symbols. Those symbols signify to others your creditworthiness, your status as a college student, your proven ability to operate a motor vehicle, and the willingness of the federal government to exchange certain green pieces of paper for something of value.

Symbols are arbitrary signs that stand for something. Because they are arbitrary, symbols can mean very different things in different contexts and cultures. The "V for victory" sign from World War II became a peace sign among hippies in the 1960s. The swastika employed as the official emblem of the Nazi party and the Third Reich had been used by a variety of cultures for thousands of years, including in China, Japan, India, and Native Americans, to represent various positive things, including life, sun, power, strength, or good luck (Rosenberg 2012).

Nonverbal gestures can have surprisingly different meanings in different cultures:

- Eating with one's left hand in Islamic societies is an insult because they reserve their left hand for unclean tasks.

- In Korea, letting someone see the bottom of your shoe is an insult.

- The "thumbs up" signal used in the United States to indicate approval has a very different meaning in Australia, Iraq, and some other countries, where it means "up yours!"

- The gesture in which a circle is made of the thumb and forefinger to indicate "OK" in the United States instead means in Germany a reference to what may be politely described as the hindquarters of a mule.

Various cultures have nonverbal gestures, all of which have meanings specific to each culture.

(left to right) © Thomas Northcut/Photodisc/ Thinkstock; © iStockphoto; © iStockphoto; © Ingram Publishing/Thinkstock

Language An abstract system of symbols and rules for their usage permitting people to represent abstract thoughts and experiences and communicate them to others.

Language

Language is an abstract system of symbols and rules for their usage permitting people to represent abstract thoughts and experiences and communicate them to others. Language is without a doubt one of the most important elements of culture. Language is crucial for the transmission of culture from one generation to another. Imagine how hard it would be to share the insights of a play by Shakespeare or a complex chemical process without language. All societies have a spoken language; most have a written language. However, the printed symbols used for written languages vary widely from collections of relatively few symbols making up an alphabet that can be combined to form words having meaning to languages consisting of thousands of unique symbols, such as Japanese or Chinese characters.

Languages provide a powerful mechanism for the sharing of culture from one generation to the next and from one society to another. Yet, ironically, language also provides one of the greatest barriers to the transmission of culture because of the substantial variation in languages and the difficulty of learning multiple languages. There are literally thousands of languages and dialects in use throughout the world. A striking fact is that roughly 6% (389) of the world's languages are each spoken by 1 million or more people and together are spoken by 94% of the world's population. The remaining 94% of languages are spoken by only 6% of the world's people. Some variant of Chinese is spoken by the most people (1.2 billion), followed by Spanish (329 million), English (328 million), and Japanese (221 million). The rest of the top 10 most common languages can be seen in FIGURE 2-2A (Lewis 2009). English is well on its way to becoming an unofficial global language since it is the most common second language in many parts of the world and (as can also be seen in FIGURE 2-2B) is the most commonly spoken language on the Internet, with Chinese a close second.

Language and Social Reality

Fire inspector Benjamin Whorf found a puzzling pattern when interviewing witnesses at fires that eventually led to a fundamental insight into one important cause of fires. At one fire, witnesses reported that "discarded pieces of metal" caught fire because they were wrapped in cardboard and wax. At another, witnesses reported that "empty gasoline drums" exploded when someone lit a match too near them.

From these clues, Whorf concluded that the ways in which people expressed their thoughts about a situation in language might have contributed to the occurrence of fires. What the people on the scene called "discarded pieces of metal" caught fire because they were wrapped in cardboard and wax. Because people called them "discarded pieces of metal" and thought of them as metal, they apparently overlooked the flammable nature of the wrapping and were careless. In a similar fashion, the "empty gasoline drums" exploded because they were not really "empty" but instead contained gasoline vapor. In both of these cases, he argued, language shaped thought.

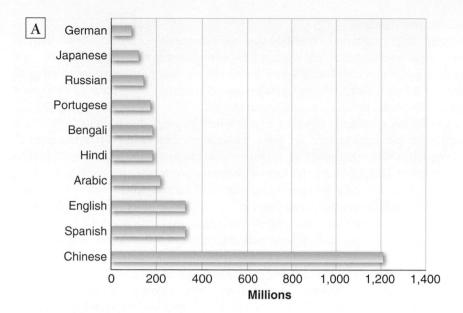

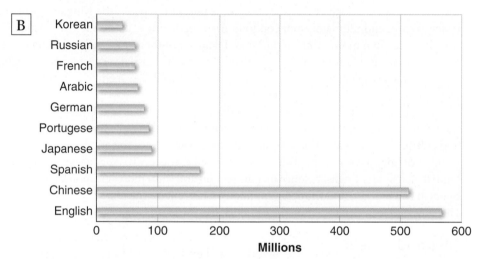

FIGURE 2-2 Top 10 most common languages used (A) in the world and (B) on the Internet.
*Source: (A) Data from Ethnologue Languages of the World. 2009. Table 3. Languages with at least
3 million first-language speakers. Retrieved November 2011 (http://www.ethnologue.com/ethno_docs/
distribution.asp?by=size). (B) Data from Internet World Stats, 2010. Retrieved November 2011
(http://www.internetworldstats.com/stats7.htm).*

Based on this and many other examples, Whorf, who was also a linguist, built on the earlier work of Edward Sapir to develop what has become known as the **Sapir-Whorf hypothesis** (Sapir 1929, 1949; Whorf 1956). This hypothesis argues that language shapes thought. Languages do not permit simple word-for-word conversions from one language to another. Instead, different languages have unique vocabularies representing different levels of refinement of concepts. As a result, some languages are better able to express some thoughts than others. That is, language shapes thought. This is a controversial hypothesis with far-reaching implications. For example, if it is true, then it may be difficult or even impossible for people who speak different languages to share the same thoughts and ideas completely and accurately. Language would restrict their conception of reality. Most researchers today believe language certainly influences thought and makes it easier to understand and think about some things and harder to understand and think about others. The importance of language for facilitating thinking is easily seen in the tendency for academic disciplines to develop their own extensive technical vocabulary, allowing them to express their detailed and specific knowledge. You have probably already noticed that much of your learning of sociology requires learning the vocabulary of sociological terms. The same is true of a chemistry class, English literature, biology, or any other discipline.

Sapir-Whorf hypothesis
Argues that language shapes thought.

Race, Class, and Gender

Language offers insight into some of the ways we intentionally or unintentionally express preconceptions about men and women, people of different races and ethnicities, and people in different social classes. We all know of far too many overtly negative terms for people of different races, religions, genders, and ethnicities. Those are used for explicit intentional ethnic, racial, class, and sexual slurs.

In addition, there are more subtle ways in which language disadvantages a particular group of people. For example, the English language includes terms that represent all people such as *human* and *mankind*, yet they include as part of the term *man* rather than *woman* (Basow 1992). Many terms carry with them a gender identity, such as *chairman*, *policeman*, *husband* and *wife*, *maid* and *janitor*, and *bachelor* and *spinster* (Miller and Swift 1991). Still others carry with them at least the expectation of the gender of the person, such as *secretary* or *nurse*. Words also sometimes have several meanings and may subtly connect race with negative connotations. Examples include *blackballed* for voting against someone, *blackmail* for forcing someone to do something by threatening exposure, or *black mark* for something that counts against someone.

Language dialects often distinguish between people from higher and lower social classes or from different races. In Oscar Wilde's play *Pygmalion*, a woman from London's lower class, with a distinct Cockney accent, is taught to speak "the King's English" in order to enter and ultimately fool London's aristocratic upper class. Such linguistic distinctions are often more subtle in the United States. But there are notable differences in language that affect how people are perceived. The use of a casual vernacular or distinctly ethnic or racial dialect in a business setting, for example, can seem inappropriate and jeopardize a person's chances for advancement (McWhorter 2000).

Language also provides a measure of the increasing racial and ethnic diversity of the United States. Different languages can pose a barrier as people from different ethnic and cultural heritages attempt to communicate. In FIGURE 2-3, the graph shows both the number of English vs. non-English speakers as well as the top 10 languages spoken in the United States, after English. Notice that the second and third most common languages are Spanish (28 million) and Chinese (2 million). This reflects the increasing population of Hispanic and Asian minorities in the United States (Modern Language Association 2011).

Values and Beliefs

Cultural **values** are standards of desirability, rightness, or importance in a society. They indicate whether something is good or bad, important or unimportant, attractive or unattractive. Values are *not* neutral. They are positive or negative. Personal values are values individuals hold on their own. They are not necessarily shared among all people in a society but instead vary from individual to individual. Personal values include preference for music, tastes in clothes, and so on. Other values are widely shared in a society and may reflect basic assumptions upon which that society is based. These widely shared cultural values can help us understand why people in that society react as they do to different events.

> **Values** Standards of desirability, rightness, or importance in a society.

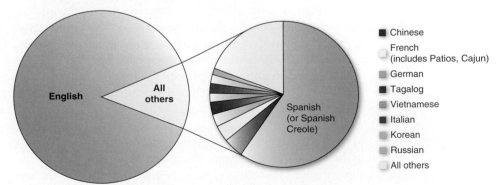

FIGURE 2-3 The top 10 languages spoken in the United States, after English.
Source: Data from Modern Language Association. 2011. Number of speakers per language in the United States. Retrieved November 2011 (http://arcgis.mla.org/mla/default.aspx).

US Cultural Values

In the United States, sociologist Robin Williams (1965) found several dominant values in American culture, including achievement and success, individualism, activity and work, efficiency and practicality, progress, material comfort, humanitarianism, science and technology, freedom, democracy, equal opportunity, and racism and group superiority.

For example, the **work ethic**—a respect for and appreciation of people who work hard and a sense that hard work should be rewarded—is illustrated by a quote from American inventor Thomas Alva Edison, who is often held up as a cultural icon the rest of us should emulate FIGURE 2-4.

> Yes, I am a hard worker. You know, when I am working on anything I keep at it night and day, sleeping a few hours with my clothes on. I sleep from 1:00 to 6:00 in the morning, and then I jump up and go to work again as fresh as a bird.
> — Thomas A. Edison, on hard work in America.

> **Work ethic** A respect for and appreciation of people who work hard and a sense that hard work should be rewarded.

Contradictions among Values

Notice that the last value found by Robin Williams was "racism and group superiority." Clearly that value can contradict values such as equal opportunity. Other values may also compete in particular instances. For example, when it comes to support for public assistance programs for the poor, our desire for material comfort, achievement, and success might lead us to want to reduce taxes. Yet our values of humanitarianism and equal opportunity might lead us to want to provide help. It is not uncommon for individuals to have some degree of imbalance among these sometimes competing values. For example, with regard to the issue of abortion, placing a high value on personal freedom can lead to favoring a woman's right to choose. However, placing a high value on humanitarianism can lead to favoring the preservation of life at all costs. Each of us as an individual tries to find ways to resolve such value contradictions.

FIGURE 2-4 Thomas Edison was a strong proponent of the work ethic.

© Chris Hellier/Alamy

Emerging and Merging Values

Williams's work is now roughly 50 years old, and unfortunately there has not been a more recent study of broad cultural values. The closest is work by Geert Hofstede (1991), who studied workplace values surveys of more than 116,000 employees collected by IBM between 1967 and 1973 in more than 70 countries. He found four dimensions distinguishing different cultures, including individualism–collectivism, masculinity–femininity, power distance, and uncertainty avoidance. The individualism–collectivism dimension has received most attention and reflects a fundamental difference. Collectivist societies place high value on the group, including the family, clan, or organization, and emphasize the importance of conformity to the group, devotion, and loyalty. Individualist societies, in contrast, place high value on individual autonomy, individual achievement, and privacy. The United States scored higher than every other country on individualist orientation (an emphasis on autonomy and privacy). This high value placed on individualism affects many aspects of US culture and politics. The United States also scored in the lower third on power distance (more egalitarian and less hierarchical), in the top quarter in avoiding uncertainty (a desire for predictability and rules), and in the top third on femininity (a stronger emphasis on relationships than on achievement).

Beginning in 1981 and continuing through 2012, the World Values Survey Association has conducted several waves of surveys assessing values in 97 societies containing almost 90% of the world's population (worldvaluessurvey.org). They found that over time, as societies become more affluent, they change along two dimensions. First, societies de-emphasize traditional values such as religion and emphasize more secular-rational values such as technology and science. Second, increasingly affluent societies de-emphasize basic survival and place greater emphasis on self-expression values, such as physical fitness, youthfulness, and health. FIGURE 2-5 presents a diagram showing how different countries are grouped by values (Inglehart and Welzel 2010). In this diagram,

FIGURE 2-5 The World Value Survey Cultural Map: 2005–2008.
Source: Inglehart, Ronald and Welzel, Christian. 2010. "Changing Mass Priorities: The Link Between Modernization and Democracy" Perspectives on Politics 8(2): 554.

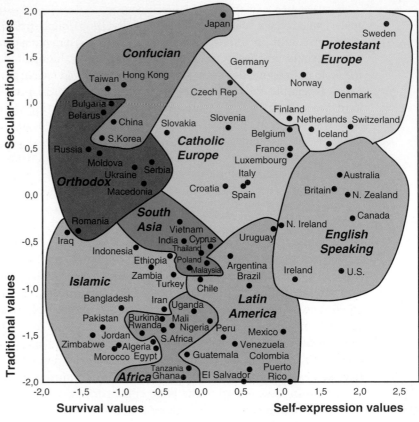

countries are placed not according to geographic position but based on their average position on the two dimensions. Notice that on this map, the United States tends to have values most like those of other English-speaking countries, and it is very high on self-expression and emphasizes traditional values like religion more than most English-speaking or European countries. In contrast, Islamic countries, for example, tend to place even greater emphasis on religion and much less emphasis on self-expression (Inglehart and Welzel 2010). It will be very interesting, in years to come, to see whether the trend toward greater secularism and less emphasis on traditional religious authority found in many Western countries continues to be reversed in Muslim countries like Iran.

Norms

Norms are expectations for behavior. Norms are part of the nonmaterial culture. Norms often apply to social roles that people are playing more than to the individuals themselves. For example, the expectation that a mother will care for her children is an expectation for the behavior of any person who is a mother, not just a particular person who happens to be a mother. Norms can proscribe (forbid) behavior or prescribe (require) behavior.

Folkways and Mores

An early sociologist, William Graham Sumner, distinguished two kinds of norms. **Folkways** are rules governing everyday conduct that are not considered to be morally important and are not strictly enforced. Conventions of dress such as wearing a tie to church, polite behavior such as men opening the door for women, saying *please* and *thank you*, and not staring at other people in an elevator are all examples of folkways. We give one another considerable discretion regarding folkways. If someone does not say *please* and *thank you* as a dinner guest at your house, you might raise an eyebrow, but you are unlikely to throw them out or call the police. Similarly, if someone does not wear a tie to church, older, more traditional churchgoers might give him dirty looks or his friends might tease him. On the other hand, if someone came to church wearing only a tie, he might be thrown

Norms Expectations for behavior.

Folkways Rules governing everyday conduct that are not considered to be morally important and are not strictly enforced.

out or even arrested, because he has violated a much more serious norm—what Sumner called *mores*. **Mores** (pronounced *mor-ays*) are serious norms for important activities that have a strong moral imperative and are strictly enforced. Someone who kills someone else, rapes someone, or steals is violating a more and will likely be sanctioned. The most serious of mores are taboos. A **taboo** is a norm considered so important that to violate it is seen as reprehensible and even to speak of violating a taboo is frowned upon. Incest, for example, is still considered inappropriate to discuss in polite company.

Laws and Social Control

Norms that are not regarded as terribly important such as folkways regarding polite behavior are **informal norms**—norms that are often expressed only informally and never written down. One example of this might be the norms for gift giving at Christmas, such as the norm that people closest to you should be given the best gifts. You will not find those norms written down anywhere, yet most people know and understand them (Caplow 1984). The most important social norms are typically the target of formal social control. **Formal norms** are written down and enforced. Colleges and universities, for example, typically have written regulations prohibiting students from cheating that define both what constitutes cheating and how it will be punished.

Sanctions are punishments or rewards designed to encourage behaviors conforming to norms and discourage behaviors that violate norms. Positive sanctions, such as congratulating someone who helped stop a crime, encourage and reward behavior consistent with cultural norms. Negative sanctions, such as glaring at a young boy skateboarding recklessly around a group of frail elderly, are designed to discourage behavior that violates a norm. Both glaring at someone and congratulating them are examples of informal sanctions. **Formal sanctions** are usually negative and are explicit punishments written into regulations or laws.

When a norm is regarded as of particular importance, it may become a law. A **law** is a formal norm that has been enacted by a legislature and is enforced by formal sanctions. For example, in the early 2000s, several states passed laws making it illegal to sell K2, a synthetic drug often marketed as not for human consumption but which, when consumed, mimics the effects of marijuana. The formal sanctions for violating this law often involve the possibility of several years in prison.

Ideal and Real Culture

Having norms for behavior and living up to them are two different things. There is often a bit of a disconnect between our ideal notions of what we should do and what people really do. The old parental standby "Do as I say, not as I do" recognizes that we often find ourselves unable to live up to standards of our "ideal" culture. For example, there is a norm in the United States of not having sex outside of marriage. Most people support this norm when asked on attitudinal surveys. However, surveys of sexual behavior, such as the highly regarded survey by Laumann and colleagues (1994), show that 10% of married women and 25% of married men do not follow this norm. In a survey of college students, Zimmerman and DeLamater (1983) found that many of them report having violated one or more norms at least once in their lives, including serious violations involving academic dishonesty as well as laws regarding the use of alcohol and drugs, as shown in FIGURE 2-6.

Mores Serious norms for important activities that have a strong moral imperative and are strictly enforced.

Taboo A norm considered so important that to violate it is seen as reprehensible and even to speak of violating a taboo is frowned upon.

Informal norms Norms that are often expressed only informally and never written down.

Formal norms Norms that are written down and enforced.

Sanctions Punishments or rewards designed to encourage behaviors conforming to norm and discourage behaviors that violate norms.

Formal sanctions Explicit punishments written into regulations or laws.

Law A formal norm that has been enacted by a legislature and is enforced by formal sanctions.

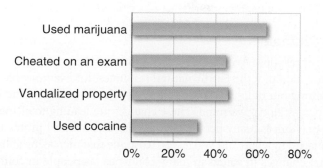

FIGURE 2-6 Percentage of students who reported violating different norms, 1983.
Source: Data from Zimmerman, R. and J. Delamater. 1983. "Threat of Topic, Social Desirability, Self-Awareness, and Accuracy of Self-Report." Unpublished manuscript cited in H. Andrew Michener and John D. DeLamater. 1994. Social Psychology. 3rd ed. Fort Worth, TX: Harcourt.

Moral holidays Times or places in which the usual norms are suspended and can be violated without punishment.

Differences between ideal culture and real culture are not just an individual matter. Many societies permit **moral holidays**—times or places in which the usual norms are suspended and can be violated without punishment. Gambling, for example, is illegal in most states except in specific places, such as riverboat casinos. Shooting off fireworks is against the law in most cities, but the law is routinely violated and only halfheartedly enforced on the Fourth of July. Underage drinking is against the law in all states, yet it would be quite unlikely that the police would enforce the law at someone's wedding celebration. In Missouri—the home state of one of the authors—"Party Cove" is an area at the Lake of the Ozarks where public nudity, public drinking, and even the occasional public sex occurs with regularity at what *The New York Times* called "the oldest established permanent floating bacchanal in the country." In a state that is usually socially conservative, laws against these behaviors are not rigorously enforced in that area. But if you were to try to do the same thing elsewhere, in the same lake or on some nonweekend day, you could expect strict enforcement and a heavy fine (Weber 2005). Similar moral holidays can be found in festivals like Burning Man, a week-long annual celebration of art, radical self-expression, and self-reliance (Saillant 2010); celebrations of Spring Break on Florida beaches; or—for some people—visits to Las Vegas.

CONCEPT LEARNING CHECK 2.2   Components of Culture

Match these concepts with examples of them.

_____ **1.** Law	**A.** It is impolite to eat with your hands.
_____ **2.** Informal sanction	**B.** A Mercedes hood ornament.
_____ **3.** More	**C.** Shushing someone who is talking in a theater.
_____ **4.** Folkway	**D.** An antilittering ordinance.
_____ **5.** Symbol	**E.** People should wear proper clothing in public.

2.3 Cultural Change

The world today is experiencing rapid cultural change, brought on in large part by changing technology and diffusion.

- Describe the basic processes of discovery, invention, and diffusion in cultural change.
- Examine the use of technology in sociocultural evolution.

Cultural change often occurs first in technology and then in the rest of culture as other cultural elements change to accommodate new technology. Technology, like the genie that cannot be put back in the bottle, often leads to fundamental changes in culture that then spread, through diffusion, to other societies and cultures. The impacts of technology on the rest of culture are so important that some sociologists use technology to explain the evolution of society and culture.

Causes of Cultural Change

Culture often changes in response to changing circumstances. The population explosion and extensive exploitation of the Earth's natural resources, for example, have led to concerns about running out of key natural resources such as fossil fuels and environmental damages such as global warming. These changes are leading to changes in values, norms, and behaviors as many people become more aware and protective of the environment. Similarly, Inglehart and Welzel (2010) argue that increasing affluence has led to fundamental changes in values in many countries, as people in countries enjoying great wealth are able to place less emphasis on the basics needed for survival and can "afford" to emphasize values related to self-fulfillment such as fitness, youthfulness, and health.

Cultural change often occurs as a result of one or more of three basic processes: discovery, invention, and diffusion. **Discovery** occurs when something that was unknown becomes known. In this sense, we can say that Christopher Columbus discovered America and Einstein discovered the famous relationship between energy, mass, and the speed of light represented by his formula, "$E = mc^2$." Notice that something (or some place) can be, and in fact often is, "discovered" independently by different people. Credit often goes to the person who first discovers something, so teams of scientists and teams of explorers often compete to be the first, such as the races to reach the North Pole and South Pole.

Knowledge, whether recently discovered or passed down for generations, can be used to create a new combination of cultural elements known as an **invention**. Inventions can be material artifacts, such as the cell phone, or nonmaterial combinations of cultural elements into a new form such as a new theory of how small groups work, a business model for an Internet startup, or the US Declaration of Independence. Since inventions require that some knowledge be available that can be used to direct the reorganization of cultural elements, discovery must precede invention. However, they do not necessarily happen in close succession. Knowledge can be widely available for decades or even centuries before someone gets the idea for a new invention based on that knowledge.

While much social change in a culture is the result of internal change, often the primary source of social change is diffusion from other cultures. **Cultural diffusion** is the spread of cultural elements including objects and ideas from one culture to another. This diffusion has always been common. With increased ease of travel, communication, and trade, cultural diffusion is becoming even more important (Carley 1994).

Discovery When something that was unknown becomes known.

Invention A new combination of cultural elements.

Cultural diffusion The spread of cultural elements, including objects and ideas, from one culture to another.

Contemporary examples of cultural diffusion.

(left to right) © Christian Kuber/
Getty Images; © dbimages/Alamy;
© Sunpix Travel/Alamy;
© imagebroker/Alamy

Sociologist Ralph Linton (1937) was among the first to point out how many items we use every day in our culture were invented elsewhere. For example, the umbrella originated in India, the train in Great Britain, glass in Egypt, coffee in Abyssinia, and rubber in Mexico. Today, more than 60 years after Linton's article, American culture is even more heavily influenced by other cultures. This paragraph was written using a computer with components measured by the metric system that we in the United States are still resisting. These words are represented in the computer with a computer language developed in the United States running on electronic computer chips designed in the United States but fabricated in several countries, including El Salvador. Some of the software was developed in India, some in the former Soviet Union, most in the United States. The computer may have been assembled in Korea. Beside the computer on the desk is a cup of hot tea imported from the UK but originally from China and a plate of hot Belgian waffles first invented in Scandinavia. A Japanese car sits in the driveway fueled by gasoline from Saudi Arabia.

Cultural lag theory A theory that argues technological change is the driving force for much change and that changes in other elements of culture often lag behind technology.

Cultural integration The coherence and consistency typically found among elements of a single culture.

Sociocultural evolution Development in human societies resulting from cumulative change in cultural information from inventions, diffusion, and discoveries.

Hunting and gathering societies The simplest societies, in which people rely on readily available vegetation and hunt game for subsistence.

Nomadic People who do not live in one place but move from place to place as conditions require for survival.

Horticultural societies Societies in which people plant crops in small gardens without the use of plows or more advanced technology for subsistence.

Cultural Lag

In 1964, sociologist William Ogburn proposed a theory of social change based on culture that he calls **cultural lag theory**. Ogburn argues that technological change is the driving force for much change and that changes in other elements of culture often lag behind technology. A cultural lag occurs when one part of culture changes while related parts do not change or change more slowly, leading to problems (Ogburn 1964). A classic example of cultural lag provided by Ogburn is the atomic bomb. "The atomic bomb was produced in two and one-half years . . . a decade later we have (not yet controlled) atomic energy (nor have we) banned the atomic bomb." (Ogburn 1964:132). His point was that the atomic bomb (a new technology) was so devastating that it made the ways countries were willing to pursue war, including all-out war (other aspects of culture that made sense before that new technology), a losing proposition for everyone. Those other aspects of culture needed to change to take into account the enormous damage that could be caused by this new technology. However, even today, more than 70 years later, the jury is still out on whether we will be able to escape further devastation from atomic bombs either in warfare or through an act of terrorism.

Cultural lag theory is based on **cultural integration**—the tendency for different elements of the same culture to be consistent. The theory argues that change occurs first in material culture. Rapid technological change causes maladjustment because old norms, roles, and in some cases, values no longer seem to apply to the situation created by the new technology. Eventually, the nonmaterial culture must change to adjust to the new technology. This tendency for changes in the nonmaterial culture to lag behind changes in the material culture is what Ogburn called cultural lag.

Technology can cause change by creating new possibilities, changing interaction patterns, or creating social problems needing action. For example, life-saving medical technology makes it possible to prolong life and permits people to remain healthy much later in life but raises important ethical and healthcare policy issues that must be addressed due to the high cost and low quality of life it provides. Similarly, genetic testing makes it possible to identify people with genes that cause specific diseases and raises the possibility of treatments tailored for a person's specific genetic makeup, while society still struggles with ways to regulate who should have access to that information and whether it should be permitted for insurance companies to cancel those people's insurance or employers to dismiss them based on that genetic information.

Technology and Cultural Change

Lenski and Lenski (1982) argue that the material culture of societies throughout the world can be understood by looking at the dominant technology used for production in that culture. Their framework describes a process of **sociocultural evolution**—development in human societies resulting from cumulative change in cultural information from discoveries, inventions, and diffusion. They distinguish four distinct levels of development: hunting and gathering, horticultural and pastoralism, agricultural, and industrial. These along with a fifth (postindustrial) society are illustrated in FIGURE 2-7.

Hunting and gathering societies are the simplest societies, in which people rely on readily available vegetation and hunt game for subsistence. Only a few people can be supported in any one area in subsistence societies; hence, they usually have no more than about 40 members and must be **nomadic**—people who do not live in one place but move from place to place as conditions require for survival. These societies usually have very little division of labor, with most people performing the same basic jobs, and since all their belongings must be carried from place to place by hand, there is little incentive to accumulate goods and, hence, very little inequality.

The domestication of plants and animals for food production permitted the development of horticultural and pastoral societies. These societies were the first in human history to have a dependable food supply, making possible larger societies, increased inequality due to the accumulation of wealth, trade, and a division of labor with some people freed to become merchants or artisans. **Horticultural societies** are societies in

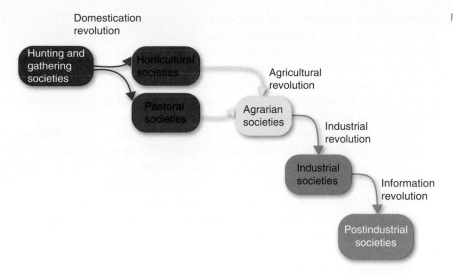

FIGURE 2-7 Sociocultural evolution.

which people plant crops in small gardens without the use of plows or more advanced technology for subsistence. Horticultural societies made it possible to establish permanent settlements. **Pastoral societies** are societies in which animals are domesticated and raised for food in pastures. Pastoral societies tend to develop in arid regions where there is insufficient rainfall to raise crops on the land. Pastoral societies are usually nomadic, moving on to a new area after the animals exhaust the food supply in each pasture.

Agricultural societies were made possible by the invention of the plow drawn by animals, making agricultural production vastly more efficient, leading to an even greater food surplus, permitting a much more complex division of labor. The agricultural revolution had such a profound impact on society that many people call this era the "dawn of civilization." During the same period that the plow was invented, the wheel, writing, and numbers were also invented. During this period, great wealth was accumulated by a few, and stratification became a major feature of social life. An elite gained control of surplus resources and defended its position with arms. This centralization of power and resources eventually led to the development of the institution of the state to further consolidate the gains of the rich and powerful.

Industrial societies are societies relying heavily on machines powered by fuels for the production of goods. These societies were made possible by the **industrial revolution**—a dramatic change in the nature of production in which machines replaced tools; steam and other energy sources replaced human or animal power; and mostly unskilled workers replaced skilled workers. Such societies have many large manufacturing plants such as steel mills, automobile factories, and machine shops. The increased efficiency of production of the industrial revolution produced an even greater surplus than before. Now the surplus was not just agricultural goods but also manufactured goods. This larger surplus caused all of the changes discussed earlier in the domestication revolution to become even more pronounced. Once again, population levels soared. Increased productivity made more goods available to everyone. However, inequality became even greater than before. The breakup of agriculture-based feudal societies caused many people to leave the land and seek employment in cities. This created a great surplus of labor and gave capitalists plenty of laborers who could be hired for extremely low wages.

A fifth type of society based on a distinct technology is **postindustrial society**—a society dominated by information, services, and high technology more than the production of goods. Postindustrial societies began during the last half of the 20th century in which service jobs—many high-technology jobs, including professions that produce and transfer knowledge, but other low-skill jobs like short-order cook—are becoming more common than jobs in manufacturing or agriculture. The product of skilled professionals is the information or knowledge they provide. The information revolution

Pastoral societies Societies in which animals are domesticated and raised for food in pastures.

Agricultural societies Societies made possible by the invention of the plow drawn by animals, making agricultural production vastly more efficient, leading to an even greater food surplus, permitting a much more complex division of labor.

Industrial societies Societies relying heavily on machines powered by fuels for the production of goods.

Industrial revolution A dramatic change in the nature of production in which machines replaced tools, steam and other energy sources replaced human or animal power, and mostly unskilled workers replaced skilled workers.

Postindustrial society A society dominated by information, services, and high technology more than the production of goods.

began with the invention of the integrated circuit or computer chip. Those chips have revolutionized our lives, running our appliances and providing calculators, computers, and other electronic devices to control our world. It is still early enough that no one knows precisely what all of the implications of the information revolution will be for social life. But clearly technological innovations, such as the Internet, smart phones, genetic mapping, and CT scans, are changing the nature of work, how families spend their time, our health, and virtually every aspect of our lives.

The different technologies available to these different societies mark important differences in cultures. Industrial societies, for example, are starkly different from hunting and gathering societies. However, within each of these categories, there is also great variation. Not every postindustrial culture is the same. China and the United States, for example, have fundamental differences even though both are now largely postindustrial societies. The individualistic culture of the United States contrasts with the collectivist culture of China, and their different views on human rights reflect just some of the differences.

Evolving technologies continue to transform our culture in many ways ranging from modern medicine, to threats to privacy, to the ways in which Internet social use is changing our lives. For example, the Pew Internet and American Life Project in 2012 (Brenner 2012) found that 66% of all Internet users use social networking sites, with most use by those between 18 and 29 (86%), but more than half of all users are younger than 65 and more than a third of users are 65 and over. About two-thirds use social media to stay in touch with current friends, and half say reconnecting with old friends is a major reason for their use. On a typical day, nearly half (48%) of online adults use social networking. Social networking site users have more friends and more close friends than nonusers (Brenner 2012).

CONCEPT LEARNING CHECK 2.3   Sociocultural Evolution

Match each of the following items with the related items among the answers.

_____ **1.** The primary technology that made agricultural societies possible.

_____ **2.** The primary technology that makes postindustrial societies possible.

_____ **3.** The first societies whose dominant economic activity was the production of goods.

_____ **4.** Societies in which most people must devote most of their time to basic survival needs like food.

_____ **5.** The type of society associated with "the dawn of civilization" as large surpluses made it possible for more people to perform activities other than the production of food.

A. Industrial societies

B. The plow

C. Hunting and gathering societies

D. Agricultural societies

E. Information technology

2.4 Cultural Diversity

Within societies, there is also cultural diversity reflecting social class differences, varying cultures brought by immigrants from other societies, and resistance to the dominant culture.

- Define high culture, popular culture, subcultures, and countercultures.
- Illustrate how each is related to social class and resistant to the dominant culture.
- Discuss the differences between multiculturalism and a global culture.

We have already seen that there is great cultural diversity around the globe. But what about *within* societies? Many societies, such as Japan and Sweden, are **homogeneous societies** in which members are generally from the same ethnic, racial, and religious backgrounds and share a common culture. Other societies, such as the United States, are **heterogeneous societies** with members from diverse ethnic, racial, and religious backgrounds. In the United States, as in other areas of the world, a major source of cultural diversity is differences in cultural heritage or ethnicity. Much of the diversity of the United States has resulted from immigration. Early immigration was primarily from Western Europe. More recently, the great majority of new immigrants are either from Latin America or Asia. In 2009, Latin Americans accounted for 53.1% of all the foreign-born population in the United States, Asians were 27.7%, Europeans were 12.7%, Africans were 3.9%, and other regions were 2.7%. See FIGURE 2-8 (Grieco and Trevelyan 2010).

The number of people more than five years old who spoke a language other than English in the home increased from 21.8 million in 1980 to 55.4 million in 2007 (19.7%, or almost one in five US residents). In FIGURE 2-9, we see the percentage of the population speaking a language other than English in the home by state for 2007 (Shin and Kominski 2010). This proportion varies dramatically from state to state, and—as a measure of cultural diversity—some regions of the country display much less cultural diversity than others. In three states—California, New Mexico, and Texas—this number has reached 30% or more of the population. Nine more states have 20 to 29%, 11 states have 10–19%, and 28 states have less than 10%.

Homogeneous societies Societies in which members are generally from the same ethnic, racial, and religious backgrounds and share a common culture.

Heterogeneous societies Societies with members from diverse ethnic, racial, and religious backgrounds.

High Culture and Popular Culture

Ethnic heritage and language are not the only important sources of cultural diversity in the United States, or any society for that matter. Social class (as measured by education,

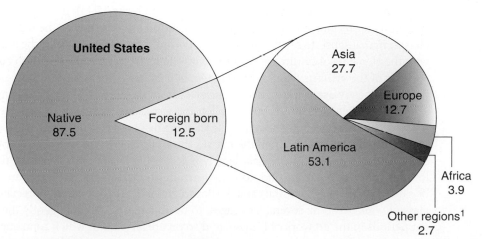

FIGURE 2-8 Percentage of foreign-born population in United States by region of birth (2009).
Source: Grieco, Elizabeth M. and Trevelyan, Edward N. 2010. "Place of birth of the foreign-born population: 2009." American Community Survey Briefs. U.S. Census Bureau.

[1]Other regions include Oceania and Northern America.

FIGURE 2-9 Percentage of the population who spoke a language other than English in the home by state (2007).
Source: Shin, Hyon B. and Kominski, Robert A. 2010. "Language Use in the United States: 2007." American Community Survey Reports. U.S. Census Bureau. Retrieved November 2011 (http://www.census.gov/prod/2010pubs/acs-12.pdf).

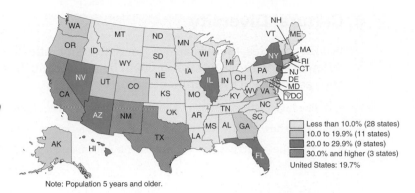

Less than 10.0% (28 states)
10.0 to 19.9% (11 states)
20.0 to 29.9% (9 states)
30.0% and higher (3 states)
United States: 19.7%

Note: Population 5 years and older.

Examples of high culture.

(left to right) © Anastasios71/Shutterstock, Inc.; © Photos.com; © iStock Photo

High culture The artifacts, values, knowledge, beliefs, and other cultural elements that elites in a society use to distinguish themselves from the masses.

Popular culture All of the artifacts, values, knowledge, beliefs, and other cultural elements that appeal to the masses.

income, and occupational status) is also related to culture, with some elements of culture reserved for only some members of society (Hall and Neitz 1993). In fact, in everyday usage, the term *culture* is often used to mean culture associated with the higher social classes. In that sense, to say that someone is "cultured" would mean he or she is familiar with the elements of culture we associate with the higher social classes. "**High culture**" consists of the artifacts, values, knowledge, beliefs, and other cultural elements that elites in a society use to distinguish themselves from the masses. High culture includes such things as classical music, opera, ballet, and works by "great authors." High culture represents a strategy of distinction—it is an effort by people in the upper social classes to differentiate themselves from the masses through the creation and consumption of cultural elements that may remain largely inaccessible or not understood by those in lower social classes. If someone grows up learning about elements of high culture it can be said that they have "cultural capital" (Bourdieu 1979). To be able to appreciate a fine glass of wine, to speak several languages, to be able to discuss intelligently the different periods in the art work of Picasso, and so on are all ways in which someone in the upper classes may be able to distinguish themselves from the rest of the masses. High culture is often distinguished from **popular culture**, which refers to all of the artifacts, values, knowledge, beliefs, and other cultural elements that appeal to the masses—for

example, rock music, popular television shows, toys, comic books, movie stars, and fast food. While most members of a society may view high culture as somehow superior to popular culture, when it comes to comparing cultures, it is a lot easier to say that they are different than it is to determine that on some objective measure of worth, one is better than the other.

Subcultures

Large industrial and postindustrial societies like the United States tend to have a number of additional important cultural differences within each society. In fact, most societies include within them not only a single dominant culture but also many different subcultures. The United States is particularly diverse due to the influence of immigrants from different countries, regional differences, and class differences; but many other societies also display a great deal of cultural diversity as well.

> **Dominant culture** The culture that takes precedence over other cultures in activities or events involving people from many categories of the population.
>
> **Subculture** A culture containing many elements of the dominant culture but having unique features that distinguish its members from the rest of the population.

The **dominant culture** in a society is the culture that takes precedence over other cultures in activities or events involving people from many categories of the population. The dominant culture often is so pervasive that it is not questioned by most societal members but is taken for granted. The dominant culture usually supports the interests of the ruling class. Typically, that dominant culture justifies elite domination and, through ideologies, values, and beliefs, helps perpetuate the status quo. Nazi Germany made extensive use of all aspects of culture to justify rule by the Third Reich. The Soviet Union under Stalin did the same. In the United States, the dominant culture, from the narrow-waisted "Gibson girl" of 1900 to today's fashion models, both male and female, is used as often to sell mouthwash as it is to promote public policy.

Within a single society, subcultures reflect differences among various categories of people. A **subculture** is a culture containing many elements of the dominant culture but having unique features that distinguish its members from the rest of the population. A wide range of categories of people can establish subcultures. People sharing a common

Examples of subcultures.

(left to right) © Kobby Dagan/Shutterstock,Inc.;
© ZUMA Wire Service/Alamy; © nobleIMAGES/
Alamy

ethnic heritage, such as Jewish immigrants from the Soviet Union, Irish Catholics, or Asian Americans may share a common subculture of beliefs, rituals, artifacts, music, and values that distinguish them from other categories of people. Subcultures can also be associated with a wide range of other categories of people based on life style choices, social class, regional differences, age, race, gender, or a myriad of other categories. Examples of categories of people sharing a subculture in the United States include Hasidic Jews, rural Southerners, young black males, computer programmers, cross country skiers, Star Trek enthusiasts, or college students.

Keep in mind that membership in a category does not necessarily mean an individual will share all aspects of the subculture with other members of that category. Not all Star Trek enthusiasts attend conventions and wear pointy ears. Not all politicians would do anything to get elected. Not all college graduates have high intellectual standards. However, being a member of a category predisposes individuals to adopt the subculture shared by other members of that category as a way of showing solidarity with other category members and as a strategy of distinction to set themselves apart from other categories to which they do not belong and do not wish to belong.

Countercultures

Counterculture A subculture that challenges important elements of the dominant culture such as beliefs, attitudes, or values and seeks to create an alternative life style.

When members of a subculture undertake deliberate measures to set themselves apart from the rest of society, theirs is called a counterculture. A **counterculture** is a subculture that challenges important elements of the dominant culture such as beliefs, attitudes, or values and seeks to create an alternative life style. Examples of countercultures in the United States include beatniks in the 1950s, hippies in the 1960s, and skinheads and militias in the 1990s. Many hippies in the 1960s, for example, rejected the materialism of corporate America and the violence of the Vietnam War, choosing to "drop out" of society and seek personal growth and expanded consciousness through communal living and psychedelic drugs. People who are members of minority categories, such as blacks or homosexuals, are likely to share a subculture but are not necessarily members of a counterculture. It is only when they adopt a culture that challenges the dominant culture, such as by becoming a member of the Civil Rights movement or the Gay Rights movement, that they share a counterculture. In some cases, members of countercultures become assimilated into the broader culture as the dominant culture shifts to accommodate some of their interests.

That the normative culture of a counterculture is at odds with the dominant culture in society is illustrated by sociologist Elijah Anderson's account of the street culture of poor inner-city black communities (Anderson 1994). This counterculture calls for behaviors that are dramatically different from the behaviors expected in more affluent, predominantly white suburbs. Anderson finds that among poor inner-city black communities, a street culture has arisen that is essentially an oppositional culture with norms for behavior that are often in direct opposition to those of the dominant culture.

Examples of counterculture.

(left to right) © Photodisc; © Photos.com;
© Cora Reed/Shutterstock, Inc.

Anderson describes this street culture as "the code of the streets"—a set of rules for interpersonal behavior in public settings prescribing the kind of image a person should try to project, how to respond if challenged, and when to employ violence. Knowledge of these expectations for behavior is virtually essential for someone to survive in public places in the inner city.

FIGURE 2-10 illustrates some of the key distinctions among types of culture. The dominant culture is the one that is typically invoked in important public events, and it tends to be imposed throughout the culture. Subcultures reflect many aspects of the dominant culture but also have some differences, such as those that we find with immigrants who bring elements of their original culture to the society and try to maintain at least some of those. Countercultures, on the other hand, actively oppose at least

Homogeneous societies have members who are generally of the same background and share a common culture.

Heterogeneous societies have members from diverse backgrounds with varying cultures.

Multiculturalism is like a big tent that embraces the contributions of many.

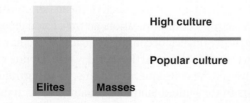

High culture

Popular culture

Elites   **Masses**

High culture consists of cultural elements that elites use to distinguish themselves from the masses.

Popular culture consists of cultural elements that appeal to the masses.

The dominant culture takes precedence over other cultures in shared events.

Subcultures contain many elements of the dominant culture plus distinguishing features.

Countercultures have elements that challenge important elements of the dominant culture.

FIGURE 2-10 Types of cultures.

some elements of the dominant culture while also perhaps being influenced by external factors such as immigration or adoption of ideas from other cultures. High culture is often used to add credibility to the dominant members of society and provides them with a way to set themselves off from the masses. This culture of distinction erects a barrier between the elites and the rest of society designed to remind those not among the elite that they do not deserve to be among them. In contrast, popular culture is more widely shared among members of society at different levels, and rejection of elements of popular culture may be used by elites, subcultures, or countercultures to further separate themselves from the masses.

Multiculturalism

Conventional wisdom has assumed that cultural diversity was handled swiftly, cleanly, and fairly in a "melting pot" in which diverse cultures became a single new, distinctly American culture. In reality, however, this was far from the case. Instead, the diverse cultures of different subpopulations remained more or less intact and a hierarchy of cultures was formed, changing as the mix of immigrants changed, often with the latest immigrant groups at the bottom of the hierarchy. At the top of the hierarchy, with the greatest influence on the dominant culture, were the cultures of Western Europe, particularly, the English, whose people had first settled the Northeastern seaboard. The resulting American culture was dominated by what might be called a Eurocentrism—a view of the world based on the perspective of early European immigrants. Other groups were often encouraged to shed their own cultural heritage and become Anglicized. This view typically ignored the contributions of others to United States culture, including downplaying the contributions of blacks and the long history of French and Spanish influences in much of the South and Southwest, as well as the contributions of other minorities.

Multiculturalism is a perspective that recognizes the contributions of diverse groups to our society and holds that no single culture is any better than all the rest. This perspective has sparked controversy with regard to a number of issues. There have been debates over how new history books for use in public schools should be written, with critics denouncing multicultural texts that recognize the contributions of blacks and Hispanics to American history and give less weight to the European settlement of the Eastern seaboard, which traditionally was the major focus of early American history texts. Perhaps even more controversial have been attempts by Congress to declare English the official language of the United States. This issue has not been decided in the US Congress, but 16 state legislatures have already made English the official language in their states. Multiculturalism appears destined to be at the heart of many controversies in the United States for years to come.

Multiculturalism A perspective that recognizes the contributions of diverse groups to our society and holds that no single culture is any better than all the rest.

A Global Culture?

Today, more than ever before, there are many effective means of cultural diffusion, including global migration, electronic communication, air travel, and global commerce. Together, they are reshaping the world. Is it becoming a single global culture? A half century ago, Marshall McLuhan (1964) first argued the world was becoming what he called "the global village." Today we see the consequences of this, as an earthquake in Japan affects the availability of cars in the United States and financial uncertainty in Greece causes turmoil in stock markets around the world. Civil unrest in a Latin American country disrupts the flow of electronic parts for computers in the United States. A bad harvest in Russia affects corn prices in Kansas. The Internet lets people around the world communicate, buy and sell to each other, and experience nearly simultaneously important political and social events.

This greater interdependence has made many elements of culture readily available around the world. You can travel to most major capitals in the world today and still eat your McDonald's hamburger or have wings at Kentucky Fried Chicken, listen to music on your smart phone, and, increasingly, drive an automobile.

If there is a global culture, it is not accessible to everyone. Rural areas of the world, including in the United States, and poor peoples in all countries often lack access to this global culture and the technology that makes it possible. Even in the United States, for example, there are many less populated areas that lack cell phone access and have slow dial-up Internet access. Similarly, in developing countries, large proportions of the population lack access to the global culture.

Another concern is that the uniformity encouraged by cultural diffusion may produce a drab cultural sameness. Cultural diffusion, while often having positive consequences, is not always a good thing. For example, one common consequence of cultural diffusion is **cultural leveling**—the reduction of differences (both good and bad) between cultures resulting in a loss of cultural uniqueness and the loss of cultural heritage. Left unchecked, cultural leveling might lead to cultural hegemony with a single dominant culture and a drastic reduction in cultural diversity.

Cultural leveling also takes place between subcultures within the same society. One notable example of cultural leveling is the disappearance of language dialects in different regions of the United States as television and radio lead to more uniform patterns of speech. A New England accent, a Southern accent, even the Minnesota accent popularized in the film *Fargo* are being replaced by speech that sounds more and more like that of the nightly news anchors. Cultural leveling often occurs when minority groups are assimilated into the larger culture. Sometimes members of a subculture who hope to preserve their own distinct cultural heritage resist such cultural leveling.

Societies often resist the diffusion of culture from other societies. At the start of the industrial revolution in England, the Luddites resisted new technologies that transformed work and caused many of them to lose their livelihoods (Thomis 1970). More recently, the United States has resisted moving to the metric system of measurement despite almost uniform acceptance by the rest of the world. Economic agreements between European countries and the United States almost failed when France insisted on taxing US movies and television shows. In the former Soviet Union, the Berlin Wall restricted travel and communication with the West, radio broadcasts for Radio Free Europe were jammed, and print and broadcast journalism were tightly controlled by the state.

> **Cultural leveling** The reduction of differences (both good and bad) between cultures, resulting in a loss of cultural uniqueness and the loss of cultural heritage.

THE SOCIOLOGICAL IMAGINATION   Protecting Your Own Subculture

Often, resistance to cultural change also comes from subcultures or countercultures from within a society. An example of resistance to cultural change is provided by Hawaiian sociologist Haunani-Kay Trask (1993) who argues that Hawaiian culture has been prostituted in the interests of promoting tourism.

Tourism in Hawaii, argues Trask (1993), treats Hawaiian culture as a commodity that can be exploited for profit. Multinational corporations, large landowners, and the state and local governments together collaborate to exploit the Hawaiian people for commercial gain. "High schools and hotels adopt each other and funnel teenagers through major resorts for guided tours of everything from kitchens to gardens to honeymoon suites in preparation for postsecondary jobs in the lowest-paid industry in the state (Trask 1993:84)." Land that was once sacred to islanders is now reserved for commercial use by large resorts. Hawaiians have little choice but to enter the military, work in the tourist industry, join unemployment lines, or leave the island. Slick commercial advertisements for the tourist industry paint an idyllic picture of island life, while the "awful exploitative truth" is that tourism is the primary cause of land dispossession, exploitative wages, environmental destruction, and the highest cost of living in the United States. Hawaiians are increasingly leaving the islands for the mainland not out of choice but out of economic necessity. Trask (1993:86) ends her article by saying, "If you are thinking of visiting my homeland, please don't. We don't want or need any more tourists, and we certainly don't like them."

EVALUATE

1. Do people in subcultures and countercultures have the right to resist the rest of society?

2. Does the rest of society or the dominant culture have the right to impose itself on people in subcultures?

3. Specifically, how far should someone like Trask be permitted to go to protect her culture?

4. Do you think more diverse complex societies such as the United States are more likely to be accepting of cultures and subcultures than would be more homogeneous societies?

CONCEPT LEARNING CHECK 2.4   Cultural Diversity

Match the following terms with statements that give the best examples of them.

_____ **1.** Multiculturalism

_____ **2.** Counterculture

_____ **3.** High culture

_____ **4.** Popular culture

_____ **5.** Dominant culture

A. During the first weekend since its release, sales of the iPhone 4S topped 4 million.

B. Protests begun by the Occupy Wall Street movement spread to additional cities in the United States and elsewhere in the world.

C. When Ronald Reagan died on June 5, 2004, a state funeral service with religious overtones and military tradition was conducted in the National Cathedral in Washington, D.C.

D. In this museum are displayed examples of art from diverse groups of people in the metropolitan area, including Navajo rugs, Japanese origami, and audio recordings of bluegrass songs recorded in Tennessee in the 1940s.

E. The Louvre Museum in Paris has one of the largest collections of fine art in the world.

2.5 Theoretical Perspectives on Culture

The three major theoretical perspectives each provide different insights into culture.

- Illustrate how the functional, conflict, and symbolic interaction theories provide different insights into culture.

Sociological theories can be used to help us observe and understand culture. As we pointed out previously, no single theory appears able to explain all that is interesting about social life. But together, these theories help us gain a deeper understanding of culture.

Functionalist Perspectives

Functional theory explains culture by identifying the positive functions performed by cultural elements. This theory is often used to explain cultural universals by arguing that such cultural elements appear in all or nearly all societies because they perform some important function necessary for societies to survive.

This perspective can be illustrated by something long regarded as puzzling by people in the United States—the Hindu religion's prohibition against the slaughter or eating of cattle. In the predominantly Hindu kingdom of Nepal, cow slaughter is severely punished. Even during a famine in India in the 1960s, starving people begged for food while cows roamed freely in the streets. To many Westerners, the sacred cow of India appears illogical and even tragic.

In a classic article, Marvin Harris (1974) argued that the veneration of cows in India serves a number of important and positive functions for Indian culture. Harris argues that cows, and the oxen they produce, pull plows and provide manure that is dried and used for fuel, fertilizer, and even housing blocks. After they die, cows are used for leather, and untouchable castes, in the privacy of their homes violate Hindu teachings by cooking and eating the meat, providing an important source of protein to the poorest members of the population who most need it. Harris argues the prohibition against slaughtering cows probably arose first as an unwritten taboo because farmers who slaughtered their cattle in times of hardship were unable to continue farming. Only later did the priesthood codify it.

Functional theory argues that cultural elements tend to persist across generations when they perform a useful function for society as a whole. Hence, functionalists look for and explain the presence of cultural elements by functions they appear to perform. Harris's explanation of India's sacred cows clearly relies on a functional argument, pointing out the many positive functions of cows in that society. In addition, this argument may be viewed as an example of "cultural ecology" because it emphasizes the relationship between culture and the natural environment. Functional theory is also sometimes linked to efforts by anthropologists to identify the cultural universals discussed earlier.

Conflict Perspectives

Conflict theory argues that cultural elements tend to persist when they support the interests of powerful members of society and tend to be resisted and even eliminated when they are in conflict with those interests. Elites are usually successful at imposing their own ideologies on the masses in a society, successfully justifying elite power and privilege. Often, when the elite dominate cultural industries in society, this control is exerted so effectively that there emerges within a society a unified, coherent view of the world that not only serves the interests of the elite over those of people in general but also may effectively prevent people from recognizing or considering alternatives. This control is often exerted through a process in which elites manage the interpretation of events in ways that mobilize support for their own agenda and thwart the agenda of others (Snow et al. 1986).

This view emphasizes ways in which the system of production within societies—for instance, capitalism in the United States—tends to appropriate popular culture and align it with the interests of the rich and powerful members of society (Cantor 1980). This can be seen in the themes found in many popular films and television shows. There are dozens of popular crime shows devoted to catching the "bad guys" who are stealing, murdering, or in other ways challenging the existing social order. Such shows reinforce the message that people who threaten the existing system should be punished. Films often show people who struggle to obtain financial success of some sort and in the end realize that "money isn't everything." This message provides a rationale for accepting inequality even when some financial success may be unfairly achieved. After all, why fight a large corporation that makes huge profits at the expense of workers when "money isn't everything"? Other sociologists point to ways in which popular culture such as films and television tend to perpetuate unfavorable stereotypes of women and minorities (Jewell 1993).

Other sociologists have argued that people in the upper social classes, finding that money and other material resources are not sufficient to differentiate themselves from people in the lower social classes, use culture as a way to distinguish themselves from members of other classes:

> At the bottom, people tend to believe that class is defined by the amount of money you have. In the middle, people grant that money has something to do with it, but think education and the kind of work you do almost equally important. Nearer the top, people perceive that taste, values, ideas, style, and behavior are indispensable criteria of class, regardless of money or occupation or education. (Fussell 1983)

This use of culture as a class barrier is illustrated for both art museums and music.

In a study of museum visitors in France, sociologist Pierre Bourdieu (1979) found that highly educated people came well prepared and knowledgeable about the museum and preferred to tour alone or with competent friends, while the middle-class visitors sought out tour guides and guidebooks. By making their desire to gain cultural knowledge visible, he argued, they broadcast their acceptance of the legitimacy of their "betters" and became accomplices in their own subordination. Similarly, surveys by the US Census Bureau find that art museums are more likely to be attended by professionals, managers, and students and less likely to be attended by laborers, machine operators, or service workers (Robinson 1987). In both France and the United States, Zolberg (1992) points out, the art educator (the person who serves as advocate for the public) has much lower status in museums than the art curator, who serves as advocate for the art. All of these findings suggest museums help perpetuate social class barriers. However, Zolberg (1992) points out that, even though there may be a correlation between social class and cultural "adeptness," until longitudinal studies are carried out, we have little idea how much cultural adeptness influences individual career paths.

The conflict perspective predicts that tastes in music are used as status markers to help mark the boundaries among occupational status groups. To determine whether this is true, Richard Peterson and Albert Simkus (1992) used the 1982 national Survey of Public Participation in the Arts (SPPA), collected for the National Endowment of the Arts by the US Census Bureau, to examine whether people in different occupational statuses have different musical tastes.

In the survey, respondents were asked to identify which of 13 categories of music they enjoyed and the single type of music they like best. They were also asked their occupational category. Results of the survey are summarized in FIGURE 2-11. Peterson and Simkus found that musical preference discriminated better at the upper end of the occupational prestige hierarchy, with classical music being a clear favorite for highest prestige. This provides support for the conflict perspective, with classical music being a marker used by those with higher occupational prestige to distinguish themselves from people with less prestige.

However, among moderate- to low-prestige forms of music, there were less clear divisions, producing a pyramid as displayed in the figure, with some categories having a number of forms of music with very similar prestige scores, such as rock, religious, soul, and country. The researchers conclude there is a clear consensus that classical music is the most elite form of music, but there is less consensus on rankings as one moves down the hierarchy. They also found that it is not the case, as it once might have been, that people in high-prestige occupations prefer classical music to the exclusion of all others. Rather, people in higher-prestige occupations demonstrate an appreciation for a wide range of music types—a pattern they call the "omnivore." In contrast, people in lower-prestige occupational categories are more likely to prefer a single form of music, and typically a form that distinguishes themselves from other people having similar occupational prestige but differing in race, gender, or age—the "univore" pattern. That is, people in the lower-prestige occupations appear to be using the univore preference for a single form of music to separate themselves from others in similarly low-prestige categories. So, for example, rural whites might prefer country music while urban blacks might prefer rap.

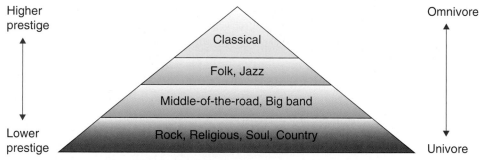

FIGURE 2-11 The American musical taste hierarchy.
Source: Adapted from Peterson, Richard A. and Simkus, Albert. 1993. "How Musical Tastes Mark Occupational Status Groups." Cultivating Differences: Symbolic Boundaries and the Making of Inequality, *edited by M. Lamont and M. Fournier. Chicago: University of Chicago Press. 152–186.*

Symbolic Interactionist Perspectives

Symbolic interactionist theories examine the ways in which culture is socially constructed, both in the ongoing reconstruction of existing cultures in everyday life and during periods of dramatic cultural change. Those efforts are guided by a desire to find meaning and consistency in culture.

A 16th-century proverb says, "Custom without reason is but ancient error." At first glance, this sounds like a very negative comment about customs and therefore about culture. It seems to be a criticism of custom and, perhaps, a call for change. However, it has another interpretation as well. This statement can be viewed not as a criticism of culture but as a standard to which we should hold elements of culture. In this view, we would expect societies to discard elements of culture that have no reason for existing. What are left are meaningful elements of culture that are reasonable by the standards of a culture and that have significance in that culture. In fact, this demand for consistency in culture produces one of the strongest patterns we find in social life—what we earlier identified as cultural integration. Cultural elements tend to be consistent with one another and to have shared meaning to members of the culture.

Sociologist Greg Matoesian (1993) describes in detail interactions in rape trials and shows how in the cross-examination of the victim, attorneys seek to impose a patriarchal interpretation of the act that redefines the female's individual experience of rape as an act of consensual sexual activity. The relationship between the victim and assailant, the context of their interaction, and the prior sexual history and overall moral character of the victim are all reinterpreted through courtroom interaction in an effort to persuade the judge or jury that the meaning of the event should be interpreted from the man's perspective rather than that of the woman. Matoesian argues that this "courtroom talk" is but one example of the way in which everyday interactions reproduce and perpetuate a normative culture based on existing inequalities in society.

THE SOCIOLOGICAL IMAGINATION Gaining Respect

Sociologist Elijah Anderson describes how the normative patterns of interaction among inner-city blacks serve to separate them into a distinct subculture in opposition to the dominant culture. According to Anderson (1994), the code of the streets provides "a framework for negotiating respect" among impoverished inner-city blacks who often have few other ways of obtaining status and respect. To be respected on the streets of the inner city is to not be "bothered" or "dissed" by others. Forms of "dissing" range from physical assault to maintaining eye contact too long. On the street, seemingly mild forms of dissing test the other person and may serve as warnings of potential violence. Consequently, people on the street become very sensitive to slights. Letting someone else "diss" you without responding causes a loss of respect or a loss of face among your friends and opens you up for further assault in the future. Thus, out of self-protection, people seek to project an aura of a willingness to engage in violent behavior to gain respect or "juice" on the streets. This image is conveyed through dress, physical appearance, facial expressions, gait, and verbal and nonverbal behavior—all intended to deter aggression. "Juice" (respect) can be claimed both by retaliating when someone else tries to "diss" you and by "dissing" someone else. "This code of the streets contributes to a vicious cycle further separating the subculture of the inner city from the dominant culture of the broader society" (Anderson 1994).

Bourgois (2002), decades later, found the desire for respect to be an important factor in the lives of Puerto Rican drug dealers in East Harlem. The oppositional street identity they project earns them respect in the streets that contrasts with the humble, obedient social interaction expected of those who had once worked as low-level office workers. The two cultures are incompatible. "Obedience to the norms of high-rise, office-corridor culture is interpreted as overwhelmingly humiliating by street culture standards—especially for males" (p. 27). Many of the dealers experienced deep humiliation in previous efforts to participate in the broader culture. For example, when one had worked as a messenger for a trade magazine, his boss would talk to other people in the office, saying, "He's illiterate," while he was standing there as if he was stupid enough to not understand what she was saying (p. 27). Another had been humiliated when working as a messenger; he had ridden the elevator with a white woman and coincidentally stepped off on the same floor after her. She was terrified and "fled from him shrieking down the hallway of a high-rise office building" (p. 28).

EVALUATE

Remember that the sociological imagination encourages us to see our individual biographies in the context of the broader social problems of the times in which we are living. We can only understand our individual lives if we consider the structural factors that influence individual opportunities. One example above illustrates how Puerto Rican men who tried to fit into the dominant culture found themselves in subordinate positions treated with little or no respect. Certainly this must have encouraged them to consider seeking alternative identities in the street.

1. Imagine you are an inner-city black or Puerto Rican man. Which life do you think you would prefer—being a disrespected subordinate in the broader culture or being a crack dealer? What could you do to go beyond those two options and how likely would you be to succeed?

2. Now imagine you are a suburban white woman. How different would be the "code" of behavior that applies to you? How different would be the opportunities you face? What similarities and dissimilarities are there? How could you claim greater respect in your life? How can you "diss" someone? How would you defend yourself if someone disrespected you?

CONCEPT LEARNING CHECK 2.5　　Theoretical Perspectives on Culture

Indicate whether each of these statements is true or false and briefly explain why.

_____ **1.** The argument that pornography is found in most societies because it fulfills a need in order for the society to survive is consistent with conflict theory.

_____ **2.** Examining the ways in which immigrants to the United States must negotiate with other people to find out what is expected of them and how to accomplish everyday tasks illustrates symbolic interactionist theory.

_____ **3.** People from lower occupational statuses are more likely to distinguish themselves from others with similar status but different race, gender, or other characteristics by their "univore" preference for a single form of music.

_____ **4.** The most popular type of music for people in the highest-status groups is big band music.

Visual Overview Theoretical Perspectives on Culture

Each of the major theoretical perspectives raises different issues regarding culture. Three such issues are illustrated below, including the consequences of sacred cows, the ways musical preferences distinguish different social classes, and the ways courtroom interactions seek to support competing views in rape trials.

Structural-Functional View

This view argues society adopts this cultural element (sacred cows) because it has social consequences which are good for society.

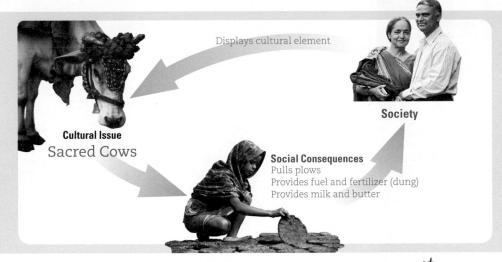

Displays cultural element

Society

Cultural Issue
Sacred Cows

Social Consequences
Pulls plows
Provides fuel and fertilizer (dung)
Provides milk and butter

Conflict View

This view argues that people with higher occupational prestige distinguish themselves from those with lower prestige by their liking of classical music even though they are "omnivores" who like most forms of music.

In contrast, people in lower prestige occupations distinguish themselves from other groups by liking a narrow "univore" preference for a single form of music.

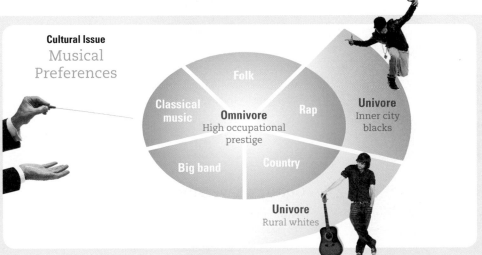

Cultural Issue
Musical Preferences

Folk

Classical music

Omnivore
High occupational prestige

Rap

Big band

Country

Univore
Inner city blacks

Univore
Rural whites

Symbolic Interactionist View

This view argues that men and their lawyers attempt to show consistency between their claim the relationship was consensual and other cultural elements such as the woman's prior sexual history and overall moral character.

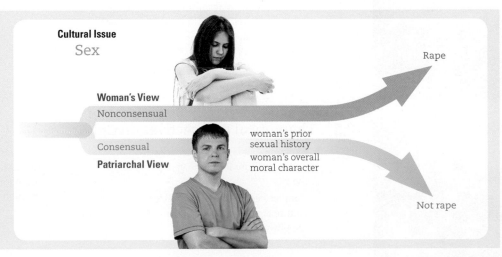

Cultural Issue
Sex

Rape

Woman's View
Nonconsensual

Consensual
Patriarchal View

woman's prior sexual history
woman's overall moral character

Not rape

Visual Summary Culture

2.1 Culture

- Culture is all around us and so pervasive we are often unaware of it.
- We depend on our culture so much we sometimes have difficulty reacting to other cultures.
- All societies share cultural universals but achieve those in diverse ways.

- Ethnocentrism and cultural relativism are competing responses to cultural diversity.
- Culture includes both material and nonmaterial components.

2.2 Components of Nonmaterial Culture

- Nonmaterial culture includes cognitive elements, which express our thoughts, beliefs, and preferences (symbols, language, values, and beliefs) and normative elements (folkways and mores), which express how we should behave.

- Values sometimes are contradictory and evolve over time.
- There is often a gap between ideal and real culture and between what people say they should do and what they actually do.

2.3 Cultural Change

- The world today is experiencing rapid cultural change.
- Cultural change is often brought on by changing technology and diffusion.

- Different components of culture change at different rates and may lag behind one another.

2.4 Cultural Diversity

- Within societies, there can be considerable cultural diversity.
- High culture is often used to separate elites from the rest of society.
- Subcultures display cultural variety, while countercultures go further and oppose the dominant culture.

- Globalization may tend toward cultural leveling and the rise of a shared global culture.

2.5 Theoretical Perspectives on Culture

- Functional perspectives emphasize passing culture from one generation to the next.
- Conflict perspectives emphasize ways that culture is determined by the interests of the powerful in society.

- Symbolic interactionist perspectives emphasize ways culture constrains behavior and ways culture is created through interaction.

2.1 Culture

1. Which of the following is *not* part of the material culture?
   A. Trash
   B. Skyscrapers
   C. Factories
   D. Rock music

2. Which of the following is not an example of a cultural universal as reported by Murdock?
   A. A high-rise apartment in New York City
   B. An igloo
   C. A house on stilts
   D. All of these are examples of the same cultural universal—housing

3. Which of the following is *not* an example of a technology?
   A. A digital recorder
   B. A typewriter
   C. Fertile agricultural soil
   D. A computer manual

2.2 Components of Nonmaterial Culture

4. At the football game for his college, Fred tailgated with friends and got a bit drunk even though he was not yet 21 and it was illegal for him to drink alcohol. There were many other younger college students doing the same thing that day, yet the campus police generally ignored them unless they got too rowdy, and even then did not check to see if they had been drinking. This is best described as a:
   A. more.
   B. moral holiday.
   C. counterculture.
   D. law.

5. Which of the following is not one of the common values of Americans found by Robinson?
   A. Science and technology
   B. Racism
   C. Freedom
   D. Preserving the environment

6. Fernando suddenly realized that today was his anniversary, and he had forgotten to get his wife a present. He has violated:
   A. a law.
   B. a taboo.
   C. an informal norm.
   D. a more.

2.3 Cultural Change

7. Cultural lag theory states that:
   A. some components of a culture change more slowly than others.
   B. cultural components tend to be passed down from one generation to the next.
   C. cultural components tend to be spread from one society to another.
   D. cultural diffusion always precedes other forms of social change.

8. What term best describes social change that results when a YouTube video "goes viral" and is played and talked about by hundreds of thousands of people?
   A. Cultural lag
   B. Technology
   C. Invention
   D. Diffusion

9. In the late 1970s, Steve Jobs and Steve Wozniak, working in a garage, put together the first computer designed for home use with a keyboard for input and a color television monitor to display the output. What term best describes this?
   A. Invention
   B. Discovery
   C. Diffusion
   D. Cultural integration

2.4 Cultural Diversity

10. When the US National Anthem, *The Star Spangled Banner*, is played before a football game, this is best described as an example of:
    A. subculture.
    B. dominant culture.
    C. counterculture.
    D. high culture.

11. Which of the following is more likely to be regarded as part of high culture?
    A. French fries
    B. The film *Titanic*
    C. A four-year old automobile
    D. Classical music

2.5 Theoretical Perspectives on Culture

13. Which theoretical perspective places great emphasis on cultural universals?
    A. Conflict theory
    B. Functional theory
    C. Interactionist theory
    D. Cultural lag theory

14. A culture of distinction is associated with:
    A. functional theory.
    B. high culture.
    C. countercultures.
    D. ethnocentrism.

12. What is the relationship between immigration and cultural diversity in the United States today?
    A. The two are unrelated.
    B. Immigration is reducing cultural diversity because most immigrants are from the same parts of the world as the majority of US citizens.
    C. Immigration increases cultural diversity because most immigrants are from the same parts of the world as the majority of US citizens.
    D. Immigration is increasing cultural diversity because most immigrants are members of racial or ethnic minorities in the United States.

15. The study by Peterson and Simkus found that musical tastes are associated with:
    A. ethnicity.
    B. race.
    C. gender.
    D. class.

CHAPTER ESSAY QUESTIONS

1. Briefly define each of the following three concepts and identify which of these three examples, A, B, or C best illustrates each concept:

   (1) Culture shock

   (2) Ethnocentrism

   (3) Cultural relativism

   A. I just cannot get over the fact that in some Asian countries people eat dogs. That is so sad.
   B. When I first arrived in Germany, I was a bit put off by the gruffness and unwillingness to engage in small talk I often saw. But by the time I left, I was amazed at how well Germans seemed to stay focused on their work and to run everything from their trains to meetings with precision and on time. I decided a little less socializing might not be such a bad thing. It certainly seems to work for them.
   C. My first night in Paris, I managed to get to the hotel all right, but then it seemed to take forever to check in as I struggled with language differences, did not know quite what to do or how to behave as I waited for a room to open, and felt a little overwhelmed doing even something as simple as ordering from the lunch menu.

2. Fill in the blanks with short answers for each of the following:
   A. The most common language spoken on the Internet is _____.

   B. The most common language spoken in the world is _____.

   C. Most of us are not auto mechanics, and if someone asked you to pass them the torque wrench, you might not be able to distinguish it from a crescent wrench or a monkey wrench. What cultural principle does this example illustrate? _____.

3. Read this hypothetical news article, then select three of the following concepts: cultural lag, invention, discovery, and cultural diffusion. Define those concepts and indicate a quote from the text that best illustrates each.

AP—Sep, 2036, Hong Kong. Today Geneticon Inc. reported sales of its home antiwrinkle genetic kit, NoplaStick®, reached the 1 billion mark. The meteoric rise of this company began 21 years ago when, in the spring of 2015, scientists at UCLA unexpectedly identified the gene that causes facial wrinkles while they were looking for a gene to cause a permanent tan. It took two years of development for Geneticon to perfect the process of preventing the appearance of wrinkles, followed by five more years of modifying the formula so that users have to redo the process annually, ensuring Geneticon of continued profits. This was followed by eight years of clinical trials before it was approved by the US Food and Drug Administration, as well as other drug and genetic safety agencies around the world. Now it is widely used in 23 countries around the world and is the attributed cause of the near-catastrophic decline in incomes of plastic surgeons.

CHAPTER DISCUSSION QUESTIONS

1. What are likely to be important trends in cultural change in the next 10 or 20 years? For example, should we expect continued increases in cultural diversity within and between countries? Is it likely that clashes over culture such as efforts to resist cultural diffusion will decrease or increase? Will cultural differences continue to be politicized in the United States, such as clashes over gay marriage, abortion, or the role of religion in the United States?

2. Multiculturalism and cultural relativism recognize the diverse contributions of different cultures and judge cultures by their own standards. Yet people often believe there are at least some things their own culture does particularly well. Let's try to take an objective look at it and see if you can identify two things you think US culture does better than other cultures and two things you think US culture does worse than at least some other cultures. Explain why you think those are better or worse.

3. Why do you think cultures have various "moral holidays"? Is it a bad thing? Is it a good thing? Do you think every culture has such moral holidays? Would a perfect culture have a moral holiday?

4. This chapter examined a lot of nonmaterial components of culture. What do you think are the three most important nonmaterial components of culture and what role do they play in your life?

5. Share with the class an example from your life when you experienced either culture shock or you were ethnocentric. Also discuss these experiences using cultural relativism.

6. Using the Sapir-Worf hypothesis, discuss how words in the English language are constructed to reflect both cultural meanings and change. For example, "cool," "epic," and "sick" or "tangelo" and "broccoflower".

7. Discuss cultural transmission. For example, how are American dominant values taught to children through the family, schools, media, and religion? What new values have you noticed emerge that are also changing norms?

8. Share with the class folkways you have broken and how others have responded. At what point do mores become taboos? Provide examples and discuss how society formally sanctions these behaviors.

9. Discuss current examples of cultural lag and make predictions about how society will resolve these issues. For example, how will laws related to genetics and robotics differ in the future?

10. How does cultural diffusion affect the emergence of new subcultures in the United States? Provide and discuss examples.

11. Share with the class symbols that are used to express meaning and understanding within a counterculture(s). Over time, have any of these symbols become socially accepted?

12. Discuss how holidays reflect aspects of both popular and dominant cultures. For example, how does the popular culture affect the expression of love on Valentine's Day while at the same time support the dominant values of a capitalist economy?

CHAPTER PROJECTS

INDIVIDUAL PROJECTS

1. Go online to learn about the differences between *individualist* and *collectivist cultures*. Write an analysis paper with a focus on relationships and interactions for example within the family, workplace, or business.

GROUP PROJECTS

1. Imagine you run a travel agency in a foreign country. Create a pamphlet for tourists planning to visit the United States. Include in your brochure key aspects of the material and nonmaterial culture, norms, symbols, gestures, gender roles, as well as food, clothing, and other important cultural facets of the American culture.

2. Search online for the *Urban Dictionary*. Browse and read through a sample of the slang terms. How many of these are you familiar with and use? As you browse through the definitions what patterns begin to emerge and how do these relate to what you read about in this chapter? Write a report summarizing your findings.

2. Should people always practice cultural relativism? Can ethnocentrism ever be good? Why or why not? Think about issues such as violence, conflict and war, and group solidarity. Write an analysis paper detailing your viewpoints. Include in your analysis US relations with foreign countries and how cultural relativism and ethnocentrism affects foreign affairs.

3. If you are living away from your home and going to college, then the next time you go home for a visit, try to notice some of the ways the culture at college and at home are different. If you live at home while going to college, you may find it harder since you see both every day. If that does not work for you, then the next time you visit a distant relative, try to notice cultural differences between that person's home and your own. Write down at least five such differences. Then, when you return to campus, compare your observations with those of two or three other students and decide together on a list of the five most important differences you found.

Agricultural societies
Counterculture
Cultural diffusion
Cultural integration
Cultural lag theory
Cultural leveling
Cultural relativism
Cultural transmission
Cultural universals
Culture
Culture shock
Discovery
Dominant culture
Ethnocentrism
Folkways
Formal norms

Formal sanctions
Heterogeneous societies
High culture
Homogeneous societies
Horticultural societies
Hunting and gathering societies
Industrial revolution
Industrial societies
Informal norms
Invention
Language
Law
Material culture
Moral holidays
Mores
Multiculturalism

Nomadic
Nonmaterial culture
Norms
Pastoral societies
Popular culture
Postindustrial society
Sanctions
Sapir-Whorf hypothesis
Society
Sociocultural evolution
Subculture
Symbols
Taboo
Technology
Values
Work ethic

2.1 Culture

1. Cultural transmission [D. The transfer of cultural components from one society to another]
2. Cultural universals [C. Cultural components that address common issues faced by all cultures and important for their survival, but the specific way they are addressed can vary considerably]
3. Cultural relativism [B. Judges cultures by the standards of that culture, not those of the observer]
4. Material culture [F. Buildings and roads]

2.2 Components of Culture

1. Law [D. An antilittering ordinance.]
2. Informal sanction [C. Shushing someone who is talking in a theater.]
3. More [E. People should wear proper clothing in public.]
4. Folkway [A. It is impolite to eat with your hands.]
5. Symbol [B. A Mercedes hood ornament.]

2.3 Sociocultural Evolution

1. The primary technology that made agricultural societies possible [B. The plow]
2. The primary technology that makes postindustrial societies possible [E. Information technology]
3. The first societies whose dominant economic activity was the production of goods [A. Industrial societies]
4. Societies in which most people must devote most of their time to basic survival needs like food [C. Hunting and gathering societies]
5. The type of society associated with "the dawn of civilization" as large surpluses made it possible for more people to perform activities other than the production of food [D. Agricultural societies]

2.4 Cultural Diversity

1. Multiculturalism [D. In this museum are displayed examples of art from diverse groups of people in the metropolitan area, including Navajo rugs, Japanese origami, and audio recordings of bluegrass songs recorded in Tennessee in the 1940s.]
2. Counterculture [B. Protests begun by the Occupy Wall Street movement spread to additional cities in the United States and elsewhere in the world.]
3. High culture [E. The Louvre Museum in Paris has one of the largest collections of fine art in the world.]
4. Popular culture [A. During the first weekend since its release, sales of the iPhone 4S topped 4 million.]
5. Dominant culture [C. When Ronald Reagan died on June 5, 2004, a state funeral service with religious overtones and military tradition was conducted in the National Cathedral in Washington, D.C.]

2.5 Theoretical Perspectives on Culture

1. [F] Meeting an important need is a key part of the functional argument.
2. [T] The interactionist perspective examines how interactions are affected by culture and lead to the development of cultural items.
3. [T] This is a finding of Peterson and Simkus.
4. [F] The most popular music for them is classical music.

ANSWERS TO CHAPTER REVIEW TEST

2.1 Culture

1. D. Rock music is not a tangible material product like the rest.
2. D. They are all examples of housing.
3. C. Soil is not a technology. It is neither a tool nor knowledge of how to use it.

2.2 Components of Nonmaterial Culture

4. B. A moral holiday occurs when people are free to violate norms they would normally be required to obey.
5. D. Robinson's work in the 1960s preceded Earth Day, and preserving the environment was less commonly shared as a value then.
6. C. This is an informal norm that is not written down anywhere but is widely recognized.

2.3 Cultural Change

7. A. Cultural lag theory gets its name from the lag between new technology and the rest of culture that must be changed to accommodate it.
8. D. This is an excellent example of diffusion when thousands of people consume a cultural element created elsewhere.
9. A. Inventions occur when people put together cultural elements in a new way to create a new product or service, such as the Apple II computer.

2.4 Cultural Diversity

10. B. A national anthem is part of the dominant culture and is often invoked at important public gatherings.
11. D. Classical music is part of high culture along with fine art.
12. D. Most immigrants today are members of racial or ethnic minorities, and increases in those groups increase cultural diversity.

2.5 Theoretical Perspectives on Culture

13. B. Functional theory emphasizes cultural components having important consequences (or functions) for society and, hence, those are likely to be found in all societies.
14. B. High culture is used to distinguish people of higher status from others less familiar with the culture.
15. D. They found musical tastes are associated with occupational prestige (a measure of social class).

ANSWERS TO CHAPTER ESSAY QUESTIONS

1. **(1)** Culture shock: Disorientation when first experiencing a new culture, Example C

   (2) Ethnocentrism: The view that your own culture is the standard against which other cultures can be judged right or wrong, Example A

   (3) Cultural relativism: A view that judges other cultures not by standards of the observer's culture but by the standards of the other culture itself, Example B

2. Answer: A—English
   Answer: B—Chinese
   Answer: C—The Sapir-Whorf hypothesis
   Rationale: Mechanics use many different words to distinguish different kinds of wrenches, while the rest of us may find it difficult to make distinctions, not having a specialized vocabulary to help.

3. Cultural lag: Definition—when components of culture that were once consistent become inconsistent as one changes faster than the other.

   Example text—either of the following:

   • followed by five more years of modifying the formula so that users have to redo the process annually, ensuring Geneticon of continued profits.

   • After that came eight years of testing before it gained approval by the US Food and Drug Administration, as well as other drug and genetic safety agencies around the world.

   Invention: Definition—create a new combination of cultural components.

   Example text—It took two years of development for Geneticon to perfect the process of permanently removing wrinkles.

   Discovery: Definition—when something that was unknown becomes known.

   Example text—was unexpectedly identified by scientists at UCLA.

   Cultural diffusion: Definition—the spread of cultural components including objects and ideas from one culture to another.

   Example text—Now it is widely used in 23 countries around the world.

REFERENCES

Aberle, David F., A. K. Cohen, A. K. David, M. J. Leng, Jr., and F. N. Sutton. 1950. "The Functional Prerequisites of a Society." *Ethics* 60(Jan):100–111.

Anderson, Elijah. 1994. "The Code of the Streets." *Atlantic Monthly* May. Accessed October 2012 at http://www.theatlantic.com/magazine/archive/1994/05/the-code-of-the-streets/306601/.

Basow, Susan A. 1992. *Gender Stereotypes and Roles.* 3rd ed. Pacific Grove, CA: Brooks/Cole.

Benedict, Ruth. 1938. In Franz Boas (ed.) *General Anthropology.* Boston: D. C. Heath and Company.

Bourdieu, P. 1979. *Distinction: A Social Critique of the Judgement of Taste.* Cambridge: Harvard University Press.

Bourgois, Phillipe. 2002. "Understanding Inner City Poverty: Resistance and Self-Destruction Under US Apartheid." Pp. 15–32 in *Exotic No More: Anthropology on the Front Lines,* edited by Jeremy MacClancy. Chicago: University of Chicago Press.

Brenner, J. 2012. Pew Internet: Social Networking (full detail). Pew Internet & American Life Project. Accessed July, 2012 at http://pewinternet.org/Commentary/2012/March/Pew-Internet-Social-Networking-full-detail.aspx.

Cantor, Muriel G. 1980. *Prime-Time Television: Content and Control.* Newbury Park, CA: Sage.

Caplow, Theodore. 1984. "Rule Enforcement without Visible Means: Christmas Gift-Giving in Middletown." *American Journal of Sociology* 89(6):1306–1323.

Carley, Kathleen M. 1994. "Communication Technologies and Their Effect on Cultural Homogeneity, Consensus, and the Diffusion of New Ideas." *Sociological Perspectives* 38(4):547–571.

Fussell, Paul. 1983. *Class: A Guide Through the American Status System.* New York: Simon & Schuster.

Grieco, Elizabeth M. and Edward N. Trevelyan. 2010. Place of birth of the foreign-born population: 2009. *Table 1, The Foreign-Born Population, Showing Percentage of the Population by Region of Birth: 2009.* US Census Bureau. Accessed November 2011 at http://www.census.gov/prod/2010pubs/acsbr09-15.pdf.

Hall, Edward T. and Mildred Reed Hall. 1990. *Understanding Cultural Differences.* Yarmouth, ME: Intercultural Press, Inc.

Hall, John R. and Mary Jo Neitz. 1993. *Culture.* Englewood Cliffs, NJ: Prentice-Hall.

Harris, Marvin. 1974. *Cows, Pigs, Wars and Witches: The Riddles of Culture.* New York: Vintage Books.

Hofstede, G. 1991. *Cultures and Organizations: Software of the Mind.* London: McGraw-Hill.

Inglehart, Ronald and Christian Welzel. 2010. "Changing Mass Priorities: The Link Between Modernization and Democracy." *Perspectives on Politics* 8(2):54.

Jewell, K. Sue. 1993. *From Mammy to Miss America and Beyond: Cultural Images and the Shaping of US Social Policy.* New York: Routledge.

Laumann, Edward O., John H. Gagnon, Robert T. Michael, and Stuart Michaels. 1994. *The Social Organization of Sexuality: Sexual Practices in the United States.* Chicago: University of Chicago Press.

Lenski, Gerhard and Jean Lenski. 1982. *Human Societies: An Introduction to Macrosociology.* 4th ed. New York: McGraw-Hill.

Lewis, M. Paul (ed.). 2009. *Ethnologue: Languages of the World.* 16th ed. Dallas, TX: SIL International. Online version: http://www.ethnologue.com/.

Linton, Ralph. 1937. "The One Hundred Percent American." *The American Mercury* 40:427–429.

Matoesian, Greg. 1993. *Reproducing Rape: Domination through Talk in the Courtroom.* Cambridge, UK: Polity Press.

McLuhan, Marshall. 1964. *Understanding Media: The Extensions of Man.* New York: Mentor.

McWhorter, John H. 2000. *Losing the Race: Self-Sabotage in Black America.* New York: The Free Press.

Miller, Casey and Kate Swift. 1991. *Words and Women: New Language in New Times.* Updated ed. New York: Harper Collins.

Miner, Horace. 1956. "Body Ritual among the Nacirema." *American Anthropologist* 58:3.

Modern Language Association. 2011. *Number of Speakers per Language in the United States.* Accessed November 2011 at http://arcgis.mla.org/mla/default.aspx.

Murdock, George Peter. 1945. "The Common Denominator of Culture." Pp. 123–142 in *The Science of Man in the World Crisis,* edited by Ralph Linton. New York: Columbia University Press.

Ogburn, William F. 1964. *On Culture and Social Change.* Chicago: University of Chicago Press.

Peterson, Richard A. and Albert Simkus. 1992. "How Musical Tastes Mark Occupational Status Groups." PP. 152–186 in *Cultivating Differences,* edited by Michele Lamont and Marcel Fournier. Chicago: University of Chicago Press.

Robinson, John P., Carol A. Keegan, and Timothy A. Triplett. 1987. Survey of Public Participation in the Arts: 1985, Volume I Project Report. University of Maryland and National Endowment for the Arts, Washington, D.C., 1987, (ERIC No. 289763).

Rosenberg, Jennifer. 2012. "History of the Swastika." About.com 20th Century History. Accessed February 2012 at http://history1900s.about.com/cs/swastika/a/swastikahistory.htm.

Saillant, Catherine. 2010. "Burning Man Becomes a Hot Academic Topic." *Los Angeles Times,* October 20. Accessed August 6, 2011 at http://articles.latimes.com/2010/oct/20/local/la-me-burning-man-20101020.

Sapir, Edward. 1929. "The Status of Linguistics as a Science." *Language* (5): 207–14.

Sapir, Edward. 1949. *Selected Writings of Edward Sapir in Language, Culture, and Personality.* Edited by David G. Mandelbaum. Berkeley: University of California Press.

Shin, Hyon B. and Robert A. Kominski. 2010. *Language Use in the United States: 2007.* US Census Bureau. Accessed November 2011 at http://www.census.gov/prod/2010pubs/acs-12.pdf.

Snow, David A., E. Burke Rochford, Jr., Steven K. Worden, and Robert D. Benford. 1986. "Frame Alignment Processes, Micromobilization, and Movement Participation." *American Sociological Review* 51:4(Aug):464–481.

Sumner, William Graham. 1906. *Folkways: A Study in the Social Importance of Usages, Manners, Customs, Mores, and Morals.* New York: Ginn.

Thomis, Malcolm I. 1970. *The Luddites: Machine-Breaking in Regency England.* Hamden, CT: Archon Books.

Trask, Haunani-Kay. 1993. *From a Native Daughter: Colonialism and Sovereignty in Hawaii.* New York: Common Courage Press.

Weber, Bruce. 2005. "Party Cove: Wild in the Ozarks." *The New York Times.* July 22. Accessed November 2011 at http://travel.nytimes.com/2005/07/22/travel/escapes/22cove.html?pagewanted=all.

Whorf, Benjamin Lee. [1941] 1956. *Language, Thought and Reality.* Cambridge, MA: The Technology Press of MIT/New York: Wiley.

Williams, Robin M., Jr. 1965. *American Society: A Sociological Interpretation.* 2nd ed. New York: Alfred A. Knopf.

Zimmerman, R. and J. Delamater. 1983. "Threat of Topic, Social Desirability, Self-Awareness, and Accuracy of Self-Report." Unpublished manuscript cited in H. Andrew Michener and John D. DeLamater. 1994. *Social Psychology.* 3rd ed. Fort Worth, TX: Harcourt.

Zolberg, Vera L. 1992. "Barrier or Leveler? The Case of the Art Museum." PP. 187–212 in *Cultivating Differences: Symbolic Boundaries and the Making of Inequality,* edited by Michele Lamont and Marcel Fournier. Chicago: University of Chicago Press.

© Photos.com/Thinkstock

Chapter Overview ▼

3 Socialization

Learning Objectives ▼

3.1 ▪ Discuss how societal experience impacts an individual's socialization.

3.2 ▪ Compare and contrast the key theories of the process of socialization.

3.3 ▪ Identify the major agents of socialization and describe their impact on an individual's understanding of culture.

3.4 ▪ Describe the five general stages of development and identify the major challenges and changes that occur in socialization at each stage.

© Monkey Business Images/Shutterstock, Inc.

My seven-year-old son and I developed a bedtime ritual that he lovingly called "thoughts." After our reading time, we reflected on all of the good things that happened that day and talked about why they were special and what we learned from the experiences.

"I have a thought," he would say. "We got to go on a picnic. It was fun because there was a playground and we got to play Frisbee!"

Then it was my turn. "I have a thought," I added. "You got to have cake for dessert!"

"That's a good thought," he said with a smile.

As my daughter approached her third birthday, we began to develop our own bedtime ritual. First, we would read her favorite story. Then each of her stuffed animal friends would give her a kiss and tell her goodnight in its own unique voice. She would giggle, then choose one stuffed animal to cuddle as she drifted into sleep.

One night, however, my daughter refused to choose an animal to cuddle. "I want to do thoughts," she said.

"It's time for bed," I told her. After all, "thoughts" were something that my son and I shared. My daughter and I had our own ritual, which she no doubt would have resisted sharing.

"No, Daddy. I want to do thoughts. My thought is that I have a very nice brother."

"That's a good thought," I said, relenting.

"I have another good thought," my daughter said, raising her hand.

And so the nightly ritual of thoughts spread. Now, I am expected to do thoughts with both my son and my daughter. To save time, we now do them together, with my daughter dutifully raising her hand to give her thoughts. Although at first she did not quite understand every aspect of the practice, she quickly learned the expectations. Now she participates fully and enjoys the last bit of family time before bed.

Reflecting on the development of our nighttime rituals, I guess that I should not have been so surprised that my daughter adopted the practice that my son began. After all, she was exposed to the ritual every night. She was, as sociologists would say, socialized into that particular bedtime observance. Within the boundary of her limited social experience, my daughter had observed and learned a ritual and sought to be a part of it. It also illustrated Merton's concept of anticipatory socialization. My daughter keenly observed her older brother and often tried to imitate his actions. She wanted to be like him, and this night-time ritual was another way that she could fulfill that desire. It was sociology in action.

Socialization is the way in which people learn the beliefs, values, and behaviors of their social groups. It is a lifelong process of learning. Sociologists see the process of socialization as vitally important to understanding the development of the sociological imagination. Although we are rarely conscious of this process, it operates all around us all of the time. My daughter provided me with a window into this interesting process. Now, as my daughter gets older and learns new skills and behavior, I think about how I can use my understanding of socialization to guide her development appropriately.

3.1 Socialization through Societal Experience

Socialization is the process by which a person learns the beliefs, values, and behavior of his or her society.

- Discuss how societal experience impacts an individual's socialization.

Socialization The process by which an individual learns the beliefs, values, and behaviors that are appropriate for his or her society.

What makes us who we are? Are we simply a product of our genetic heritage, or is who we are largely the result of the social structure that surrounds us? Sociologists are not the first to ask these questions, but while researching them, they have gained critical and unique insights into the development of the individual and what it is that makes us who we are. The process by which a person learns the beliefs, values, and behaviors that are appropriate for his or her society is called **socialization**. Throughout this lifelong process, a person develops his or her personality and sense of self. Socialization is also the way a person learns about his or her culture. Although most sociologists recognize that biological factors play a role in the development of the individual, sociologists believe that society plays a much larger role in who a person becomes.

Sociologist C. Wright Mills FIGURE 3-1 saw socialization as a process that allows us to see beyond the immediate causes of our beliefs and behaviors. Mills called this process the sociological imagination. According to Mills, the sociological imagination develops along two paths. First, the history and structure of the society that we live in shape our general values and the way we look at the world. These broad values are refined through personal experience as we interact in our social world. Thus, our socialization is achieved as the influence of society and the influence of our interactions work together to shape who we become. Mills suggested that when we understand how our beliefs, values, and behaviors are shaped, we are able to look at the world in new ways. Mills was not the first to attempt to understand how the world around us shapes who we become, however. Many others have paved the way in trying to understand how we become who we are.

Human Development: Nature and Nurture

Since Charles Darwin (1874) demonstrated that much of human behavior is rooted in our evolutionary history, human development has often approached behavior in terms of whether biology (nature) or society (nurture) is more important to who we become. However, recent research suggests that this approach is too simplistic. Charles Darwin's view of human behavior has often been misinterpreted as suggesting that humans are solely a product of instinctual drives. Yet, while Darwin did acknowledge that human behavior had its roots in biological processes, he also recognized that human beings possessed a unique trait—culture. Indeed, for Darwin, culture was an important part of understanding how human beings develop and grow. Early misinterpretations of Darwin's theory were instrumental in justifying prejudices and discrimination against certain groups of people whose behaviors were viewed as both primitive and instinctual. Differences in cultures were misattributed to differences in intelligence and understanding rather than to differences in the ways in which cultures can be constructed.

In contrast to the extreme biological view of human behavior, psychologist John B. Watson FIGURE 3-2 argued that all behavior is learned. Watson denied that human beings have any instincts at all but rather believed we exist as empty vessels to be filled by social learning. Watson believed that people vary only in their cultural patterns and learning. Following in the footsteps of Watson, a number of influential anthropologists noted that while cultures may differ in fundamental ways, all cultures are equally complex.

Neither of these extreme views is entirely correct. It is clear that nature does place limits on the ways in which humans can construct culture, as the existence of cultural universals reveals. **Cultural universals** are cultural patterns that are part of every known culture. Because these traits are a part of every known culture, it is difficult to make the argument that the traits are the result simply of social learning. Rather, as Darwin suggested, these universals are probably rooted in our evolutionary history. At the same time, the considerable diversity of cultures throughout the world attests to the strength and pervasiveness of human choice in the construction of culture. Other evidence for the influence of culture on the development of the individual can be seen in studies of social isolation.

FIGURE 3-1 C. Wright Mills developed the idea of the sociological imagination to describe how the process of socialization operates to make each person a unique product of society.

© 2003 Hulton Archive/Getty Images

FIGURE 3-2 Psychologist John B. Watson believed that all behavior is learned.

© Underwood & Underwood/Corbis

Social Isolation in Monkeys

Psychologists Harry and Margaret Harlow conducted early studies of social isolation using rhesus monkeys. In 1962, the Harlows placed infant monkeys in conditions of varying isolation. What they found was startling. The greater the degree of social isolation, the greater was the degree of developmental disturbance. Monkeys placed in total isolation for six months showed disturbing and irreversible developmental

Cultural universals
Cultural patterns that are part of every known society.

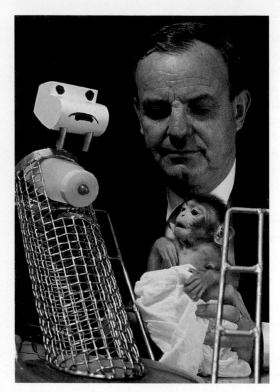

FIGURE 3-3 Psychologist Harry Harlow did experiments to test the effects of social isolation on monkeys.

© Nina Leen/Time Life Pictures/Getty Images

Feral children Children raised by wild animals or without appropriate socialization.

deficiencies, even when adequate nutrition was provided. When these monkeys were brought into a room with other rhesus monkeys, they exhibited extreme passivity in interaction, anxiousness, and fear of other monkeys.

The Harlows (1964) conducted another experiment in which infant rhesus monkeys were provided with an artificial mother. This artificial mother had a wire body, wooden head, and a feeding tube. Monkeys raised by this mother suffered similar developmental deprivations as monkeys raised in isolation FIGURE 3-3. Another group of infant monkeys was given an artificial mother made from soft terrycloth. Although these infants did suffer some developmental setbacks, they were able to interact to some degree when placed in a group. Furthermore, monkeys raised in social isolation who later become mothers themselves exhibited consistent inability to care for their infants. Most commonly, the new mothers were indifferent to their young, neglecting them to the point of death.

Based on these experiments, the Harlows concluded that social interaction is a key component to proper development. While short-term isolation appears to be reversible to some degree, isolation for longer than about three months appears to lead to permanent developmental damage FIGURE 3-4.

Social Isolation in Children

Of course, the kinds of experiments that the Harlows conducted on monkeys cannot be done on human infants for ethical reasons. However, documented cases of children growing up in isolation suggest that the results of the Harlows' experiments would apply to humans as well. Despite the tragic nature of these cases, they shed light on the importance of social interaction on the development of the human mind.

The notion of **feral children**—that is, children raised in the wild or by animals—is nearly as old as recorded history. For example, Romulus and Remus, legendary founders of the city of Rome, were allegedly raised by wolves. Indeed, through the years, many stories have been told about feral children. Often surrounded by fantastic tales and insufficient recordkeeping, it is difficult to disentangle the myth from the reality. Many cases, such as the case of Kaspar Hauser,

FIGURE 3-4 Monkeys were forced to choose from a soft monkey with no food, or a wire monkey with food. Harlow's experiments showed that monkeys prefer attachment to the soft monkeys to food.

© Inc - Photo/Photo Researchers/Getty Images

a German youth who claimed to have been raised in an isolated dungeon, have since been legitimately dismissed by historians. However, credible modern cases of feral children do exist, and they shed light on the effects of isolation on the human mind.

One such case is the story of Anna. Discovered in 1938 by social workers on the second story of a farmhouse in rural Pennsylvania, Anna lived a life of virtually total isolation from her mentally challenged mother and elderly grandfather. The two fed Anna only milk and kept her locked in a storage room until her discovery at age six. The emaciated Anna could not speak or walk, and she rejected human contact. After extensive socialization over the course of 10 days, Anna was able to interact with others. She began to walk. She found joy in the ability to feed herself and play with toys. However, it also became clear that her years of social isolation had caused permanent developmental damage. By age eight, Anna's development was below that of an average two-year-old. By age 10, Anna was using simple words. Unfortunately, Anna died at age 10 of a blood disease that may have been related to the years of neglect that she had suffered (Davis 1947).

In 1970, another feral child was found in California. Genie was 13 and had spent her life strapped to a potty chair in a dark room. She was rarely spoken to by her blind mother and mentally unstable father. Her only source of stimulation was a raincoat hung on a hook in front of the chair, which Genie could reach out and play with as she sat alone. When Genie was found, she had the mental capacity of an average one-year-old child. Scans of her brain revealed no obvious abnormality or retardation, so the deficiency is presumed to be the result of her years of isolation.

Although Genie's physical health improved dramatically, her cognitive improvements were not as spectacular. After nearly five years of intensive work, her language skills were still equivalent to a small child's. While Genie has learned to do many things for herself, 13 years of social isolation have meant that she must live in a group home for developmentally disabled adults (Rymer 1993) FIGURE 3-5.

The cases of Anna and Genie illustrate both the power and limitations of socialization. Individuals who lack appropriate early socialization tend to display developmental delays. Children who are not socialized properly do not develop properly. On the other hand, the failure of attempts at socialization to overcome years of isolation means that there are limits to the plasticity of the human brain.

These findings have led sociologists to develop two key hypotheses about socialization. The first hypothesis is that socialization occurs on three levels. The first of these levels is called **primary socialization** and refers to the basic and fundamental aspects of interacting that help an individual develop self-awareness. This level of socialization occurs most often through infancy and childhood and is influenced most strongly by the family. **Secondary socialization** occurs in later childhood through adolescence. As the social sphere widens, social influence moves beyond the family and extends to peer groups and other nonfamily forces. Finally, **adult socialization** occurs as the individual takes on adult roles such as spouse, employee, or parent, adapting to the complexity of changing roles that occurs throughout the adult years. The cases of Genie and Anna reveal the importance of primary socialization in opening the gates for the subsequent levels of socialization. Individuals who do not undergo adequate primary socialization within a given period of time will likely not proceed through secondary or adult socialization. Instead, as their biological potential is not met, the individuals will remain trapped at the level of a child. Thus, the second key hypothesis about socialization, the **critical period hypothesis**, suggests that there is a window of time for primary socialization to operate. Once this period has passed, primary socialization becomes increasingly difficult and less effective. This suggests that the effects of socialization are strongest and most important at the earlier stages in life.

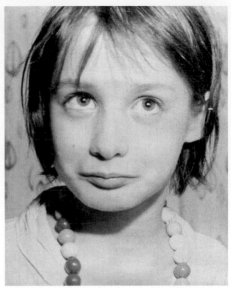

FIGURE 3-5 Found after nearly 13 years of social isolation, Genie now lives in a group home.

© Bettmann/CORBIS

Primary socialization The basic and fundamental aspects of interaction that help an individual develop self-awareness.

Secondary socialization Social influences that extend beyond the family.

Adult socialization Socialization that occurs as the individual takes on adult roles.

Critical period hypothesis Hypothesis that suggests there is a window of time for primary socialization to operate.

CONCEPT LEARNING CHECK 3.1   Socialization through Societal Experience

Choose the correct answer for the following questions.

1. The Harlows' research with rhesus monkeys showed that:

    A. monkeys will choose food over comfort.

    B. monkeys do not suffer ill effects from social isolation.

    C. monkeys suffer developmental effects as a result of prolonged social isolation.

    D. monkeys prefer a real mother over a surrogate mother.

2. Which of the following is untrue based on studies of feral children?

    A. Socialization has unlimited power to mold the human brain.

    B. There is a critical window in which certain skills are learned more easily.

    C. Socialization is essential for early attachment and learning.

    D. Lack of socialization has negative developmental and social consequences.

Match the life event with the appropriate level of socialization. Each question has more than one answer.

_____ **3.** Primary socialization	**A.** Learning to share	
_____ **4.** Secondary socialization	**B.** Dating	
_____ **5.** Adult socialization	**C.** Learning to talk	
	D. Transitioning into a new career	
	E. Having children	
	F. Getting a driver's license	

3.2 Understanding Socialization through Theorists and Their Research

Socialization is a lifelong process that may be understood in a variety of ways.

- Compare and contrast the key theories of the process of socialization.

Even though the effects of socialization are strongest during infancy and childhood, most people consider socialization to be a lifelong process. Often, the exact mechanisms and processes of socialization remain difficult to discover. Yet various theorists in both psychology and sociology have made lasting contributions to our understanding of the process of socialization.

Freud and the Psychoanalytic Perspective

Sigmund Freud FIGURE 3-6 was an Austrian physician whose interests led him to theorize about how the human mind develops and maintains personality. Eventually Freud developed the theory of psychoanalysis, which has maintained an influential role in psychology, psychiatry, and medicine. At the time of its development, the idea that human behavior was biologically determined was dominant. Freud's theory reflects the core of this belief, but with important caveats. Freud believed that humans have two basic general instincts that guide behavior toward the satisfaction of those instincts. The first instinct, which Freud called *eros*, is the instinct for life. According to Freud, this is often represented in the form of a sexual drive. In contrast, *thanatos* is the death instinct. This instinct is often represented by the need to destroy or act aggressively.

These two drives operate in a constant state of tension, vying for the primacy of satisfaction. Freud believed that the tension caused by these opposing instinctual forces formed the basis for the human personality (Slee 2002).

Freud's Model of the Human Mind

Freud represented the tension between *thanatos* and *eros* with a single concept—the id. The **id** represents the most basic part of the human personality, containing all of the basic impulses and drives that are necessary for human survival. The id is present at birth and is geared solely toward the satisfaction of the basic instincts. Freud noted that infants are constantly needy, demanding attention, contact, and food. However, as children grow, they realize that in many cases, their desires may not be satisfied or their needs may go unmet. This creates a level of frustration that is acted upon by the id in the form of crying or tantrums.

As the child learns to deal with the frustration that accompanies unmet needs, the second aspect of Freud's personality emerges. The **ego** represents the conscious part of the personality. As the conscious individual realizes that he or she cannot always satisfy his or her basic desires, the ego helps balance these desires with the demands of society.

As the demands of society are learned and reinforced through interaction, the norms and values of the society become part of the individual psyche. The **superego** is the expression of these internalized societal values, reinforcing the ego's conscious realizations and lessons learned from early childhood. Freud's model is frequently explained using the metaphor of an iceberg FIGURE 3-7.

Freud believed that personality development—and thus socialization—ended by the end of adolescence. His views reflected a radical departure from the prevailing views of his time. Freud's theory has subsequently become one of the most novel and influential approaches to understanding the human mind. The legacy of Freud was the challenge to rethink our views of children and the importance of socialization in the early years. At the same time, Freud's views have been widely criticized and challenged from many different professions. Indeed, Freud did no actual experiments, and the only corroboration we have of his theories come from his own reports of treatments he gave to his own patients. Subsequent investigations of these cases have shown his reports of successful treatments to likely be exaggerated (Kramer 2010). Empirical investigations into other aspects of his theory have revealed general but pervasive problems with the validity of the theory (Fisher and Greenberg 1996).

FIGURE 3-6 Sigmund Freud was an Austrian physician who developed a theory about how a person develops his or her personality.

Library of Congress, Prints & Photographs Division, [reproduction number LC-USZ62-1234]

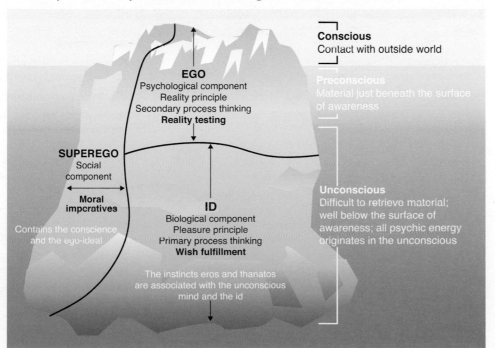

FIGURE 3-7 Freud hypothesized that there were three elements to the human mind.

© Jones & Bartlett Learning

EGO
Psychological component
Reality principle
Secondary process thinking
Reality testing

Conscious
Contact with outside world

Preconscious
Material just beneath the surface of awareness

SUPEREGO
Social component

Moral imperatives

Contains the conscience and the ego-ideal

ID
Biological component
Pleasure principle
Primary process thinking
Wish fulfillment

The instincts eros and thanatos are associated with the unconscious mind and the id

Unconscious
Difficult to retrieve material; well below the surface of awareness; all psychic energy originates in the unconscious

Id Freud's terms for the most basic part of the human personality, geared toward satisfaction of the basic instincts.

Ego Freud's term for the conscious part of the personality that seeks to balance instinctual desires with the demands of society.

Superego Freud's term for the expression of internalized cultural values that reinforces the conscious understanding of the ego.

Normative crisis The struggle people go through between what society expects them to do and what they actually accomplish.

FIGURE 3-8 Erik Erikson believed that personality spanned the life course.

© Ted Streshinsky/CORBIS

During Freud's oral stage, children explore the world by sticking objects in their mouths.

© iStockphoto/Thinkstock

Erikson's Psychosocial Theory

A student of Freud's, Erik Erikson, broke from traditional Freudian ideas as Erikson came to doubt that personality development stopped at adolescence. Instead, Erikson believed that every individual passes through eight stages of psychosocial growth that span the entire life course FIGURE 3-8. At each stage, the individual must navigate successfully through a normative crisis resulting from the tension between biological desires and societal expectations. A **normative crisis** is defined as the struggle that people go through between what society expects them to do and what they actually accomplish. How an individual accepts and resolves these crises depends upon the success of transitions through earlier stages. In contrast to Freud, who placed most of his emphasis on what is wrong with people, Erikson focused on how the biological, social, and individual dimensions of a person's personality converge to give a person a strong personal identity and make him or her psychologically healthy.

Most important for our understanding is that Erikson believed that socialization occurred throughout the life course TABLE 3-1. Adding three stages beyond adolescence, Erikson argued that people continue to be influenced by their social world in adulthood as well as in childhood.

Like Freud, Erikson has been very influential in developing our understanding of how personality is shaped through interaction. Also like Freud, Erikson's theory has been both widely defended and widely criticized. Erikson's theory is not easy to study empirically, and this makes it hard to make an accurate assessment of it (Cole 1970; Cole & Cole 1989). Some critics claim that Erikson's theory is more applicable to males than to females. Others suggest that Erikson's ideas about identity formation are too rigid and ignore cases of people who rediscover themselves or develop new understandings of their lives. Still others say that despite claims of being a theory of the lifespan, Erikson's theory puts more emphasis on the childhood years than on the adult years.

Piaget and Cognitive Development

Swiss psychologist Jean Piaget developed a theory of how children come to know about the world FIGURE 3-9. By observing his own children, Piaget hypothesized that children pass through a series of stages as they develop cognitively TABLE 3-2. It is important to note that Piaget was concerned only with the ability to understand the world through the

TABLE 3-1 Erikson's Stage Theory in its Final Version

Age	Conflict	Resolution or "virtue"	Culmination in old age
Infancy (0–18 months)	Basic trust vs. mistrust	Hope	Appreciation of interdependence and relatedness
Early childhood (18 months–3 years)	Autonomy vs. shame	Will	Acceptance of the cycle of life, from integration to disintegration
Play age (3–6 years)	Initiative vs. guilt	Purpose	Humor; empathy; resilience
School age (6–12 years)	Industry vs. inferiority	Competence	Humility; acceptance of the course of one's life and unfulfilled hopes
Adolescence (13–18 years)	Identity vs. confusion	Fidelity	Sense of complexity of life; merging of sensory, logical, and aesthetic perception
Early adulthood (19–24 years)	Intimacy vs. isolation	Love	Sense of the complexity of relationships; value of tenderness and loving freely
Adulthood (25–64 years)	Generativity vs. stagnation	Care	Caritas, caring for others, and agape, empathy and concern
Old age (65–death)	Integrity vs. despair	Wisdom	Existential identity; a sense of integrity strong enough to withstand physical disintegration

Source: Adapted from Slee, P.T. 2002. Child, Adolescent and Family Development. 2nd ed. Cambridge, UK: Cambridge.

FIGURE 3-9 Jean Piaget studied cognitive development by observing his own children.

© Bill Anderson/Getty Images

TABLE 3-2　Piaget's Stages of Development

Stage (age range)	Description
Sensorimotor (0–2 years)	Explores the world through sensory and motor contact
Preoperational (2–6 years)	Uses symbols (words and images) but not yet logic
Concrete operational (7–12 years)	Thinks logically about concrete objects
Formal operational (12 and on)	Reasons abstractly and thinks hypothetically

process of thinking rather than any emotional components of personality. This emphasis on cognition led Piaget to divide his theory into two parts. In the stage-independent component, Piaget addressed the issue of how cognitive development emerges. He identified four factors that are essential for the development of proper cognitive functioning. The first of these factors, maturation, emphasizes the role that biology plays in the development of the mind. At birth, the brain is not fully developed and thus acts as a limiting factor to cognition. As brain growth and development proceed, they provide both the upper and lower limit for cognitive development.

The second factor is experience. Piaget believed that within the limits set by maturation, the child experiences the world in two general ways. The first is through direct physical experience, such as playing with objects and exploring the world. As the child interacts with the world, he or she also gains experience with the way that various aspects of the world relate to one another.

Maturation and experience are child-centered processes. That is, the child is the center of the developmental process. However, in Piaget's third stage-independent component, the child moves from the center of the process to being a part of the process itself. Social transmission refers to the ways in which social interaction acts as a motivator of development. This occurs both through the transmission of social values as well as through conflict. Through the process of interaction, the child is forced to challenge the view of the child as the center of the process of development and gradually develops a multitude of conflicting ideas, which the child must learn to effectively choose from.

The final factor is equilibration. As the child struggles with the conflicts that arise in social transmission, he or she must find a balance between things that are understood and things that are not yet understood. The child attempts to relate the unknown to the known, to make the unfamiliar familiar. In other words, the child tries to make everything he or she encounters fit into his or her picture of the world. Equilibration is thus achieved through a process of accommodation, in which a child fits a novel object or idea into an existing cognitive category, or assimilation, in which the child creates a new category for the novel object or idea.

Piaget's contribution to understanding the development of cognition is properly recognized, but it is not without its critics. Maccoby (1980) and others have accused Piaget's theory of neglecting the role of emotions in cognitive development. Additionally, the stage theory may be too rigid. For example, some research suggests that there are various decision points in children's lives involving different aspects of the world that may lead different children to follow different paths of development (Slee 2002). For example, a child in adolescence may have to choose between pleasing friends or pleasing parents. The choice that the child makes can shape the availability of future choices, such as when the child chooses a delinquent behavior to impress friends at the expense of obeying parents. Russian psychologist Lev Vygotsky coined the term **scaffolding** to refer to a kind of socialization whereby a parent or other person helps a child bridge a gap between the child's current skill level or knowledge and a more advanced state of knowledge or skill. In the absence of scaffolding, children may make choices that are inappropriate for their developmental level. In other words, Piaget's theory is less a theory of socialization and more a theory of cognitive structuring. That is, Piaget explains the ways in which a person learns to respond to agents of socialization.

Scaffolding Socialization whereby a parent or other person helps a child bridge a gap between the child's current skill level or knowledge and a more advanced state of knowledge or skill.

Kohlberg's Six Stages of Moral Development

Support for Piaget's theory of moral development has been mixed (Slee 2002). A much more widely accepted theory of moral development comes from psychologist Lawrence Kohlberg FIGURE 3-10.

Building on Piaget's idea of a sequence of developmental stages, Kohlberg interviewed boys between the ages of 10 and 16, asking them to judge the morality of certain actions in a variety of stories. Unconcerned with whether the children thought the action right or wrong, Kohlberg focused his attention on the reasons why the child thought that the action was right or wrong. From this data, Kohlberg developed a three-level, six-stage theory of moral development TABLE 3-3.

Numerous criticisms of Kohlberg's theory of moral development have been offered. Despite Kohlberg's claim that the stages are universal, Simpson (1974) and others (e.g., Harkees, Edwards, and Super 1981) have credibly challenged this claim (Slee 2002). Similar to criticisms of Piaget, some researchers claim that Kohlberg's stages create artificial separations that assume that the process of moral development is unnaturally rigid, ignoring the considerable variation that occurs in how people develop their moral ideas. Also similar to criticisms of Piaget, Meadows (1986) has argued that Kohlberg neglects the role of emotions in the development of morality.

FIGURE 3-10 Lawrence Kohlberg studied the development of moral sentiment in children.

© Lee Lockwood/Getty Images

Carol Gilligan and Gender in Moral Development

Perhaps the most relevant criticism of Kohlberg's theory comes from Carol Gilligan, who noted that Kohlberg drew his data only from males FIGURE 3-11. In testing Kohlberg's theory on females, Gilligan (1977) noticed that females rarely moved beyond stage two, level three of Kohlberg's theory. In other words, females appear to judge moral rightness in terms of living up to what others expect of them (Slee 2002). Whereas Kohlberg saw this as a deficiency on the part of females, Gilligan argues that this reflects societal standards to see male patterns as the norm, as well as an inability or unwillingness to acknowledge different developmental trajectories for women and men. While Gilligan agrees with Kohlberg that women and men develop their moral sense through interaction, Gilligan believes that the interactions of women are fundamentally different from the interactions of men, which lead them to different developmental outcomes in terms of their moral sense.

TABLE 3-3 Kohlberg's Three-Level Theory of Moral Development

Premoral level	Stage 1: Punishment avoidance and obedience	Make moral decisions strictly on the basis of self-interests; disobey rules if can do so without getting caught.
	Stage 2: Exchange of favors	Recognize that others have needs, but make satisfaction of own needs a higher priority.
Conventional level	Stage 3: Good boy/girl	Make decisions on the basis of what will please others; concerned about maintaining interpersonal relations.
	Stage 4: Law and order	Look to society as a whole for guidelines about behavior; think of rules as inflexible, unchangeable.
Principled level	Stage 5: Social contract	Recognize that rules are social agreements that can be changed when necessary.
	Stage 6: Universal ethical principle	Adhere to a small number of abstract principles that transcend specific, concrete rules; answer to an inner conscience.

Source: Adapted from Slee, P.T. 2002. Child, Adolescent and Family Development. *2nd ed. Cambridge, UK: Cambridge.*

Charles Horton Cooley and the Looking-Glass Self

Charles Horton Cooley was an American sociologist who was interested in how people developed their sense of self. Cooley believed that individuals developed their sense of who they are through social interaction, and he set out to describe the process by which the self emerges. Like Erikson, Cooley saw the process of socialization as lifelong FIGURE 3-12.

Cooley argued that the most basic forms of interaction occur in **primary groups**. These are small groups, such as family, characterized by intimacy, face-to-face interaction, and strong commitments to one another. Socialization through primary groups is highly personal. Thus, in primary groups, the self is defined in relation to the group. According to Cooley, primary groups exert a lasting influence on us and serve as the foundation for the development of our social selves. In contrast to primary groups, with which we interact because it fulfills a basic need, **secondary groups** are larger, more impersonal groups that fulfill strictly instrumental needs. That is, we join secondary groups to achieve a specific goal or to accomplish a particular task. Examples of secondary groups include schools, clubs, governmental organizations, or work.

As we interact through primary and secondary groups, we notice that the people in these groups react to our behaviors. If these reactions are negative, we will change our behaviors to meet the expectations of the group. If the reactions are positive, those behaviors are reinforced. Thus, we judge our actions and ourselves by how think we appear to others. Cooley (1902) termed this the **looking-glass self** because this process resembles looking in a mirror.

> We see . . . our face, figure, and dress in the glass, and are interested in them because they are ours, and pleased or otherwise with them according as they do or do not answer to what we should like them to be; so in imagination we perceive in another's mind some thought of our appearance, manners, aim . . . and so on, and are variously affected by it. (Cooley 1902:182)

The concept of the looking-glass self implies that the self emerges through the process of interaction. The self is continuously constructed through judgments we make

FIGURE 3-11 Carol Gilligan criticized Kohlberg's theory as applicable only to males. Gilligan expanded Kohlberg's theory to females.

© 2005 Paul Hawthorne/Getty Images

Primary groups Cooley's term for small groups characterized by intimacy or strong commitments to one another.

Secondary groups Cooley's term for larger, impersonal groups that fulfill instrumental needs.

Looking-glass self Cooley's process of the development of the self, in which individuals interpret how they think others see them and adjust their behavior accordingly.

about how others see us. Thus, the self is a product of socialization. According to Cooley, without socialization a sense of self will not emerge.

George Herbert Mead and the Social Self

Building on the work of Cooley, George Herbert Mead argued that children begin to develop a social self as they imitate the world around them. Unlike Cooley, who failed to clearly identify a mechanism by which the self emerges, Mead outlined the actual process of the emergence of the self through social interaction. Play behavior, according to Mead, is essential to the process of developing a sense of self. Play behavior, and the sense of self that emerges from it, occurs in three stages FIGURE 3-13.

At first, infant play is limited to **imitation**. Children may see their parents talking on a phone. While the child may have no understanding of the significance of the action, she or he will nonetheless imitate the motions by placing an object to her or his ear. Children watching a parent cook will often imitate stirring motions even without understanding the significance of cooking.

As children move beyond the imitation stage, they progress into the **play stage**. At this stage of play, the child adopts a specific role and acts out that role as a form of play. For example, a child may wrap a towel around his shoulders and pretend to be a superhero. At this stage of play, however, the adoption of the role is limited to the individual. In other words, the role is not dependent upon other roles for its structure. The role is independent of any other person; it is egocentric.

By about age six, the child progresses into the **game stage**. At this stage, the child adopts roles that are dependent upon other roles for their structure. Mead used the game of baseball as an example of this interdependence. At any position, it is not sufficient for a player to understand only his role on the field. He or she also must understand the roles of others in the game and their relationships to every other position. It is during this stage of play, when the child learns to take the role of the other, that Mead says the self emerges. Children learn to see themselves as individual selves by seeing themselves as others see them.

FIGURE 3-12 Charles Horton Cooley hypothesized that the self emerges through the process of social interaction.

Courtesy of The American Sociological Association.

Cooley described the process of personality development as looking through a mirror and reacting to the image that we see.

© Alison Williams/Shutterstock, Inc.

Imitation Mead's first stage in the development of the self, in which the child imitates the behaviors of adults without understanding the actions.

Play stage Mead's second stage in the development of the self, in which the child adopts and acts out a specific role.

FIGURE 3-13 George Herbert Mead believed that personality development was reflected in play behavior.

© Photos.com

Mead argued that progressing through the stages of play, individuals learn to distinguish the *me* from the *I*. The *I* is the unsocialized, biologically driven child. Much like Freud's id, the *I* is a collection of spontaneous desires and wants. In contrast, the *me* is the socialized aspect of the individual. The *me* understands the role of the individual as it relates to others in society because the *me* is the social self, that part of the self that is able to take the role of the other.

Mead agreed with Cooley that socialization begins with the family and other groups with close emotional ties to the individual. Mead called these agents of socialization the **significant other**. Like Cooley, Mead also recognized the importance of the wider society in the process of socialization. Mead referred to these broader social groups and the values that they instill as the **generalized other**. For Mead, both significant others and the generalized others are important for the development of the distinction of the *I* and *me*. It is important to note, however, through the process of socialization, the *I* remains even as the *me* is discovered. Mead considered both the *I* and the *me* to be essential components of the individual self. Thus, the self is composed of a biological component as well as a socialized component.

It is important to note that although Mead saw the self as emerging in childhood, he still considered socialization a lifelong process. Mead argued that just as the sense of self emerges through socialization, so do our cognitive structure and moral sentiment. In other words, Mead was the first person to put all of the psychological pieces together to form a coherent theory of how socialization makes us who we are.

> **Game stage** Mead's third stage in the development of the self, in which the child adopts roles that are dependent upon other roles for their structure and meaning.
>
> **Significant other** Mead's term for family and other intimate or close agents of socialization.
>
> **Generalized other** Mead's term for broader social groups and the values they instill in the individual.

CONCEPT LEARNING CHECK 3.2	Understanding Social Theorists

Fill in the blank with the name of the appropriate theorist.

_____ **1.** Socialization leading to an understanding of the self proceeds through three stages: the imitation stage, play state, and game stage.

_____ **2.** Human personality develops throughout the life course as each person tries to resolve a central crisis associated with each of eight stages.

_____ **3.** The child develops a sense of self through play, progressing through three stages to the eventual emergence of the *me*.

_____ **4.** Boys and girls are socialized toward morality differently, with girls being socialized toward an other-oriented moral system and boys being socialized toward an individualist moral system.

_____ **5.** We watch the reaction that other people have to our behaviors and adjust our behavior accordingly so that we gain the approval first of primary groups and later of secondary groups.

3.3 Agents of Socialization

There are numerous agents of socialization that teach a person the beliefs, values, and behaviors that are appropriate in his or her society.

- Identify the major agents of socialization and describe their impact on an individual's understanding of culture.

As previously noted, sociologists see socialization as taking place in three general stages that span the life course: primary, secondary, and adult. At each stage, various agents of socialization affect the individual's cultural learning. **Agents of socialization** are groups, individuals, or circumstances in society that socialize an individual. Socialization is strongest in infancy and childhood, probably because there is simply so much cultural learning that needs to take place. Additionally, the brain is most susceptible to

> **Agents of socialization** Groups, individuals, or circumstances that socialize the individual.

Agents of socialization impact who we become in a variety of ways.

© Jones & Bartlett Learning; Photographed by Sarah Cebulski

learning at younger ages. At this stage, the family is by far the strongest agent of socialization. By adolescence, the agents of socialization change and the overall impact of socialization begins to weaken. Peer groups, school, and the media replace family as strong agents of socialization. By adulthood, although socialization continues to occur, the brain has matured and the individual core personality has stabilized. As a result, socialization is weakest at this stage.

The major theoretical perspectives in sociology offer significant insight into both the products and process of socialization. Using the various theoretical perspectives, we can better understand how socialization operates to make us who we are and develop our sociological imagination and how we think about the world. These perspectives also give us a backdrop to help us understand how socialization works in our lives.

Functionalist Perspectives on Socialization

The functionalist perspective analyzes the social world in terms of the functions that institutions have within the whole social system. What function does socialization have in society? Most obviously, socialization is the way in which each individual learns about his or her social world. Socialization functions as a process by which individuals learn the roles they will play in society, as well as the norms that are appropriate for those roles. Socialization functions as a means by which our status in society is constructed and maintained. Socialization also functions as a means of cultural transmission. That is, socialization is the process by which we teach others what are appropriate beliefs, values, and behaviors in our society. It is how we pass our culture on to our children.

Socialization through the Conflict Perspective

The conflict perspective tries to understand the world in terms of competition between groups and individuals for scarce resources. Although we will discuss this more in depth in a later chapter, the conflict perspective sees socialization as the process by which individuals and groups are taught to compete for resources in society. Prejudice and discrimination are taught to individuals as ways for them to justify their position as well as to legitimize differential access to resources. In other words, the conflict perspective seeks to understand socialization in terms of how individuals and groups are socialized to compete in society. Largely, the conflict perspective sees this competition as socially undesirable and uses this knowledge to develop ways to reduce social conflict and increase social justice.

Socialization and Symbolic Interactionism

As we have already learned, symbolic interactionism is a perspective that is interested in how social reality is constructed through the use of symbols. Since socialization is often transmitted and received through symbols such as language, symbolic interactionism seeks to understand how the process of socialization is transmitted. For example, many people see a doctor's white lab coat as a symbol of education, experience, and authority. Yet how is this message transmitted? Clearly, the white coat is a symbol of a doctor, but how do we learn this? Symbolic interactionism seeks to understand how individuals become socialized to understand the workings of our society and how they use this knowledge to be successful in society.

The Family

Ways of structuring a family and raising children vary from culture to culture. In some cultures, the family is broadly defined to include extended kin or even the entire community. In others, the family is more narrowly defined to include only parents and children. Nevertheless, wherever children are born, the family remains the most important agent of socialization in infancy and childhood. In modern societies, nuclear family units are most common, and most socialization of young children takes place in this context. However, even in modern society, there is variation in the structure of the family that may have an impact on the socialization of the child.

Infancy and Early Childhood

Some children grow up in single-parent homes; others grow up in blended families or in extended family units. In some families, the mother stays home to raise children; in others, the mother enters the paid labor force and places the child in day care. Regardless of the circumstances, the family socializes us to our basic sense of self as well as to the values, beliefs, and behaviors that we hold throughout childhood. The structure of the family has a strong impact on how the child is socialized.

The family is the strongest agent of socialization.
© Diana Lundin/Dreamstime.com

Socialization in infants and young children has been widely studied. According to McCartney and Galanopoulos (1988), these studies were conducted in two major waves. The first wave, conducted in the 1960s, focused on whether day care was harmful to the development of children. Generally, the research led to the conclusion that day care did not negatively impact attachment to parents. However, the body of research also concluded that children who spend even moderate amounts of time in day care tend to be more aggressive than children who are cared for at home. Despite this negative finding, the studies also concluded that spending time in day care may help accelerate the level of intellectual development of children from disadvantaged backgrounds.

Two decades later, more sophisticated studies focused on the effects of various qualities of day care (Belsky 1990). In large measure, these later studies confirmed the conclusions of the earlier studies, but only for high-quality day care centers. These studies also noted that child–staff ratios, staff supervision, staff resources, and quality of staff training were important factors in how day care affected the development of children over time. These studies have led some researchers, such as Richard Fiene, to call for national standards of high-quality day care.

Socialization and Social Class

One of the key findings about the ways in which families socialize children is that the social class of the family affects the way in which the child is socialized. Working-class and middle-class parents tend to raise their children in different ways. For example, Kohn (1977) found that working-class parents focus on raising their children to stay out of trouble. To that end, they tend to use physical punishment as a means of achieving compliance. In contrast, middle-class parents tend to be more concerned with developing creativity, self-expression, and self-control in their children. Rather than use physical punishment, middle-class parents tend to try to reason with their children or to use nonviolent forms of punishment.

Studies show that children who spend significant time in day care are more likely to solve problems aggressively.
© matka_Wariatka/Shutterstock, Inc.

Despite wide confirmation of these findings, sociologists at first did not understand why the differences occur. Now it is believed that parents are reflecting their work experiences in their parenting. For example, many working-class jobs are highly regimented, with bosses telling workers exactly what to do. Since parents generally expect their children's lives to be similar to their own, they stress obedience in their child rearing just as this value is expressed in their work. On the other hand, middle-class parents, who often work at white-collar jobs, often have greater opportunities to take the initiative and be creative at work. These parents may pass those values on to their children and socialize them toward those characteristics.

Kohn also found that basic understanding of child development varied in a similar way. Kohn discovered that middle-class parents tend to believe that children need guidance to master skills necessary in life, while working-class parents are more likely to believe that children develop naturally and thus need less guidance. These beliefs shape the expectations that parents have of their children with regard to behavior, school performance, and elsewhere.

Race and Socialization

Just as parental socialization differs with social class, different races and ethnic groups tend to socialize their children differently. African Americans tend to be either very permissive parents or very strict parents. Asian-American parents tend to strictly adhere to traditional values of their country of origin and expect children to show deference to those values. White parents tend toward parenting styles that offer both structure and flexibility and that give children the ability to make some choices in their behaviors.

There are other racial differences that impact socialization. One of the most notable is the attitude toward education that people of different racial or ethnic backgrounds take. For example, many families of Asian descent place a very high premium on education relative to other racial groups. Given that the number-one predictor of how well students do in school is how well they enjoy going to school (Duncan 2007), racial differences in attitudes toward education will no doubt have an impact on how a child is socialized through school.

Gender and Socialization

Parents socialize boys and girls differently because society expects different things from males and females. The transmission of these expectations begins at birth. For example, certain colors are associated with certain genders—blue for boys and pink for girls. Parents also socialize children through the toys that they buy for their children. Parents often buy dolls for girls but action figures for boys. Dress-up toys for girls are frequently pink with frills and fairy wings, while dress-up toys for boys includes shields, swords, and helmets.

Generally speaking, society expects boys to be less emotional and more aggressive than girls. Society also expects parents to be more protective of girls than of boys. For this reason, boys are typically given more freedom than girls. In a classic study of gender socialization, Goldberg and Lewis (1969) found that mothers subconsciously rewarded their daughters for being dependent and passive. On the other hand, mothers rewarded sons for being independent and active. Other studies have found that parents will allow their male preschool children to wander farther from them than their female children of the same age. Subsequent research has confirmed these results.

Although we know that socialization plays an important role in the development of gender roles, there is some evidence that biology may play a role as well. Do parents create dependency behaviors in girls and independence in boys, or are parents responding to innate behaviors that the children exhibit? Do parents buy gendered toys because they want to socialize children in a certain way, or do they buy these toys because those are the types of toys that children ask for? There is some evidence that biology may play a role in toy preference and play behavior.

Researchers have long known that girls are more likely to play caretaking games, often using dolls. In contrast, boys are more likely to play aggressive games. This coincides with additional research that shows that boys are interested in things, while girls tend to be more interested in people. These results seem to be true even when possible socialization effects are eliminated. Researchers explain these results with the suggestion that these play behaviors reflect biologically expected roles that the children will adopt in adulthood—parenting for women and competitive work for men.

Several recent studies have suggested that these biologically predisposed play behaviors may influence the kinds of toys that boys and girls prefer. A study in 2002 by Alexander and Hines showed that gendered toy preferences exist not only in humans but in monkeys as well. In this study, the researchers gave two stereotypically masculine toys, two stereotypically feminine toys, and two gender-neutral toys to 44 female and 44 male vervet monkeys. The result was that male vervets preferred the masculine toys, while the female vervets preferred the feminine toys. The two sexes did not differ in their preference for the gender-neutral toys.

There is also considerable evidence of brain differences between male and female children at birth (Moir & Jessel 1989). These differences are seen before the effects of socialization can affect the individual. These and other studies suggest that while socialization certainly plays a large role in the development of sex roles, biology also matters. A likely explanation is that while biology provides a foundation to our behavior, socialization reinforces and expands those predispositions.

Socialization and School

School is also an important agent of socialization. While parents provide basic values to children, the school imparts specific knowledge and skills that society has deemed important. School formalizes the process of acquiring these skills. Schools also teach broader social values, such as diversity and multiculturalism, both through curriculum as well as through the process of interacting with peers. As sociologists have begun to study school, they have identified these as separate trends. The first trend, the **hidden curriculum**, refers to values that are taught during the presentation of the standard curriculum but that are not an explicit part of that curriculum. For example, a question about history may impart a subtle message about patriotism or democracy, or reading a particular story in English class may teach a lesson about justice or fairness.

The second trend, called the **corridor curriculum**, refers to the lessons that children teach one another at school while not in class. Unlike the hidden curriculum, which may impart positive social values, the corridor curriculum often teaches schoolchildren undesirable social values, such as racism or sexism. Often, the corridor curriculum emphasizes popularity as a value to be strived for. The pursuit of popularity often creates peer pressure that may lead schoolchildren to engage in behaviors that are contrary to the positive social values taught by parents and schools.

School and Gender

Schools often reinforce gender socialization that occurs in the home. Studies show that at school, boys are more likely to engage in activities that are physical in nature, while girls are more likely to engage in behaviors that are social in nature. Boys are also more likely to engage in aggressive behaviors while at school and appear less able to sit still than girls.

In addition to behavioral differences, there are also learning differences between boys and girls. Studies have shown that boys tend toward hands-on learning and visual learning styles, while girls exhibit stronger verbal learning skills. For example, on tests in which words are read aloud and the child is asked to identify which words contained a particular letter, girls performed better than boys. However, when the test was administered as a visual task, boys outperformed girls (Moir & Jessel 1989). On average, girls learn to read more quickly than boys, too.

Schools often teach in a manner that favors the learning styles of girls, presenting the material in verbal form. Early research from Dianne McGuinness (1979) suggests that education is biased against the aptitudes of males, at least initially. McGuinness notes that in the early years, schools focus on reading and writing skills, which largely favors girls. She notes that young boys are more than four times more likely than girls to be identified as learning disabled; and more than 95% of children labeled as hyperactive are boys. Subsequent research on levels of ADD and ADHD largely confirm these early studies. However, boys often make up for this deficiency later in their school careers. As schools move into mathematical and science-oriented curriculums, boys begin to outpace girls. In fact, by the time they enter high school, the disadvantage has been reversed and now favors males.

Hidden curriculum Values that are taught through the presentation of standard curriculum that are not an explicit part of that curriculum.

Corridor curriculum Lessons that children teach one another at school while not in class.

Schools often have a hidden curriculum that socializes students to the values, beliefs, and behaviors of their society.
© Monkey Business Images/Dreamstime.com

Schools often have a corridor curriculum that socializes students toward being popular and well liked.
© Jupiterimages/Photos.com/Thinkstock

Race and Class in School

Because schools are funded largely by taxes on property values, schools in inner cities are often underfunded relative to schools in suburban areas. This means that urban schools typically have fewer resources to work with as they strive to educate children. Students in urban schools are more likely to have learning disabilities, including ADHD. The additional resources needed to effectively educate children with learning disabilities are often lacking in inner city schools. Inner cities are also populated disproportionately by racial and ethnic minorities. This means that there exists a structural bias in the educational system against minority groups.

Drop out rates for minorities are substantially higher than for whites. Hispanics have the highest high school dropout rate, approaching 18%. The dropout rate for Native Americans is around 13%, and it is more than 9% for African Americans. Whites and Asian Americans have the lowest dropout rates, with whites at just over 5% and Asian Americans at around 3½%. Dropout rates for all races and ethnic groups are higher in inner cities than in suburban school districts. We also know that minorities underperform on standardized tests relative to whites. We should not infer from these results, however, that dropout rates are solely a problem of race. Social class also plays a role. On average, minority families earn less than whites, which means that they are less likely to live in suburban school districts and more likely to attend poorly funded inner schools.

Socialization and Peer Group

Peer group A group of people, usually of similar age, background, and social status.

As a child ages, his or her social sphere gradually widens. The influence of the family gradually wanes, and the influence of peers increases. The process likely begins at school, as the child interacts more and more with peers. A **peer group** is defined as a group of people, usually of similar age, background, and social status.

Peer groups gradually come to exert a strong influence over the individual. Peer groups often separate themselves into discrete units (Adler & Adler 1998). In elementary school, peer groups separate themselves by sex. Males at this age tend to prefer the company of other males, and females prefer the company of other females. However, as the children transition into adolescence, peer groups gradually become mixed.

During early childhood, peer groups are usually segregated by gender.

© Jupiterimages/Comstock/Thinkstock

In addition to segregating by sex, peer groups also segregate in other ways. Each of these groups develops its own set of norms and socializes members of that group to accept those specific norms. These may be based on characteristics such as athletic ability or toughness in boys or physical appearance in girls. For males, academic success is tacitly discouraged because it diminishes their popularity. For females, however, academic success increases popularity.

According to researchers, by adolescence, peers replace the family as the most important agent of socialization. This effect tends to be short lived, however. As the adolescent transitions into adulthood, work and other obligations often take precedence over friendships and peer groups.

Socialization and the Workplace

Anticipatory socialization Learning to play a role before entering it.

By young adulthood, the influence of peer groups tends to diminish. Work becomes an increasingly important agent of socialization as an individual attempts to match his or her interests and skills to a job. Often, this means that a person tries many different jobs involving different skills. This in turn involves **anticipatory socialization**—that is, learning to play a role before entering it. This involves learning the expectations of the role prior to adopting it. Sociologists Robert Merton and Alice Kitt introduced the concept in 1950. Since then, it has become one of the most widely used sociological terms. Through the process of anticipatory socialization, a person gains a sense of identity and understanding with the role, which may help with the actual transition into that role. On the other hand, anticipatory socialization may help us avoid roles that we would find to be unrewarding.

Anticipatory socialization works in many ways. Merton and Kitt (1950) categorized the processes generally as occurring through either push or pull forces. *Push forces* refers to forces that push you away from a particular role, or behaviors associated with that role; *pull forces* refers to forces that pull you toward a particular role or forces associated with that role. For example, the threat of jail may push a person away from committing a crime. Programs like DARE and Scared Straight are designed to push people away from undesirable behaviors by offering a glimpse into the negative consequences of those behaviors. These programs serve as a means to dissuade people from adopting socially undesirable identities.

During adolescence, peer groups become mixed in terms of gender.
© Monkey Business Images/Dreamstime.com

Conversely, the promise of a high salary and good benefits may encourage a person to pursue a particular career. Employers often take great pride in the benefits they offer employees and even advertise those benefits in their job advertisements. Many jobs also have a measure of social prestige that attracts people to a particular profession. For example, most people see lawyers and doctors as important professions in society.

Anticipatory socialization is important for the development of social identity. As we will later learn, research suggests that people have a desire for a positive social identity. The push and pull forces in anticipatory socialization help us to develop a positive sense of social identity by pushing us away from negative beliefs, values, and behaviors and pulling us toward socially desirable ones. The roles that we play—and that we are socialized into—play an important part in the development of the sociological imagination. Anticipatory socialization helps us to narrow the focus of the constant bombardment of social stimulation. By focusing on a limited number of behaviors that we wish to mimic, we exclude aspects of socialization that we consider less important. We will learn more about these concepts in later chapters. Work as an agent of socialization is important for another reason. As a person stays at a job, the work becomes more and more important. Work becomes a part of the self-concept. Indeed, people often identify themselves by the work that they do. The roles and norms of the profession we are in can have either a negative or a positive impact on our self-image, depending on how the occupation is perceived in society. Generally, professions with high status rankings, such as lawyer or doctor, increase self-esteem, while professions with low status rankings, such as custodian or server, may reduce self-esteem.

Anticipatory socialization prepares people for roles they may adopt at a future time.
© Jaimie Duplass/Shutterstock, Inc.

Socialization and Religion

Religious institutions influence the core values and beliefs that people hold. For many people, religion defines the boundaries between right and wrong and offers a means of dealing with crisis and emotional trauma. More than 65% of Americans say that they belong to a religious congregation, and 40% say that they have attended services in a typical week. Religious beliefs, customs, and rituals have the effect of creating a sense of solidarity among a religion's members. Religion offers people a sense of social identity, a sense that they belong to something greater than themselves. In this way, religion has a stabilizing effect on society.

Growing up in a religious household has distinct advantages. On average, people who are religious live longer, tend to be happier, and have less stress. This is manifest in a variety of behavioral outcomes, including quicker recovery times from surgery. Studies have also revealed that regular attendance at religious services is linked to stable families, strong marriages, and lower delinquency rates among children. Men who regularly attend religious services are less likely to engage in acts of abuse against spouses and children. They are also much less likely to commit a crime or abuse drugs or alcohol. Interestingly, these findings hold regardless of the particular religious views that a person holds (Koenig 2008).

More than 65% of Americans belong to a religious congregation.
© Jupiterimages/Polka Dot/Thinkstock

However, just as religion can have a stabilizing effect on society, religion can also be a source of social conflict. Religions frequently socialize members to believe that their particular religious beliefs are true to the exclusion of other systems of beliefs. This can lead to tensions between religious views that sometimes erupt into violence, such as between Christians and Muslims or Sikhs and Hindus. Even people who do not identify as religious are affected indirectly by religion. For example, researchers from the University of Minnesota (Edgell, Gerteis, and Hartmann 2006) found that people who identify as agnostic or atheist are among the least trusted members of society. In this way, religion serves to divide as well as to join.

Socialization, Mass Media, and Social Media

Mass media Means of delivering impersonal communication to large audiences.

Every day, we are bombarded with advertisements and other messages from newspapers, magazines, television, radio, and the Internet. These messages have an effect on what we believe, what we buy, and what we value. **Mass media**, defined as a means of delivering impersonal communication to a large audience, thus act as agents of socialization. Usually, the socialization occurs in limited, short but intense bursts. However, the pervasiveness of these forms of socialization is due to the repetition of the message. More importantly, these messages are often radically different from or opposed to the messages of other agents of socialization. This makes them stand out and captures the attention of people in such a way as to make the message desirable.

Television

Television was invented in 1926, but did not make its way into American homes until the 1930s. The machine quickly became a sensation, becoming the dominant medium for news and information by the 1950s. Today, more than 98% of American households have at least one television. Even the poorest Americans have access to television services, with 97% of American households below the poverty line owning a television. Of those, 62% have cable or satellite services. This gives America the highest rate of television ownership in the world.

Americans have the highest rate of television ownership in the world.
© iStockphoto/Thinkstock

Today, television watching remains a popular pastime. On average, adults spend about 4.5 hours a day watching television, which is about half of an individual's daily free time. However, minorities and the elderly generally watch more television than the national average. The youth of America spend an average of 6.5 hours per day in front of video screens or television. When they are young, screen time is usually limited to television. However, as the child gets older, video games, the Internet, and social networking comprise an increasing amount of time in front of a screen. Many American children spend more time in front of a screen than they do in school or playing outside with friends. Studies have documented that too much television can lead to developmental problems in youth (Robinson et al. 2000). Studies such as Crespo and colleagues (2001) have demonstrated that children who watch television tend to be less physically active and are at greater risk for obesity.

Television has also received criticism for not portraying minorities equitably. For much of the history of television, minorities have either been invisible on television or portrayed in a very stereotypical manner. In recent years, minority groups have become more widely represented on television, both in the numbers presented as well as in the roles that they play. Other criticisms that have been offered are that television portrays a liberal bias in its reporting of the news and political issues. However, the increasing popularity of conservative talk shows suggests that television offers the political viewpoints of both sides of the political spectrum.

A much more poignant criticism suggests that the increasing amount of programming showing violent scenes on television may be negatively influencing America's youth. Bushman and Huesman (2001) found that the amount of violence on television exceeds the amount of violence that occurs in real life. By the time the average American child enters the first day of junior high school, he or she will have viewed more than 8,000 murders and 100,000 total acts of violence on television (Kirsch 2006). Critics contend that exposure to so much violent content has a direct link to increasing violence among American youth. However, crime statistics show, contrary to the assertion of critics, that violent crime in America has been declining, even among youth.

Studies of the impact of television violence on children show mixed results. Some studies show few if any negative effects, while other studies show pronounced and clear effects. Much of the discrepancy in the research may be the result of the way in which violence is measured and the group being studied. Results do converge, however, on two key points. First, the effects of television violence on aggression tend to differ based on the way in which the violence is presented. For example, violence that is punished or violence that shows the victim in severe pain tends to decreases the likelihood of the viewer acting aggressively. On the other hand, aggressive behavior that is presented as unpunished or that is trivialized tends to have the opposite effect (Kirsch 2006). Thus, the way in which violence is portrayed on television seems to make a difference in how that programming affects the viewer. Research shows that much of the violence portrayed on television is glamorized. Nearly 70% of heroes committing acts of violence went unpunished, and almost one third of them were rewarded. Even more disturbingly, nearly 80% of villains faced no immediate punishment for their violent actions.

The effects of television violence have been widely studied.

© Anita Patterson Peppers/Shutterstock, Inc.

Video Games

Children's first exposure to mass media is usually through television. However, as children get older, the screens they spend their time in front of shift from those of television to video games, computers, and cell phones. Like television, many of the images in video games often contain scenes of vivid violence. Even more than television, many researchers contend that violence in video games is damaging to children and increases the risk of childhood aggression (Kirsch 2006). This fear has led to hearings before Congress and attempts by some states to ban certain video games that are labeled as too violent. In Germany, video games that show human deaths are heavily restricted because they violate the nation's decency standards. Australia has banned many violent video games outright (Kirsch 2006). Much of this fear has been fueled by a handful of cases such as the Columbine shooting, in which students who had experience playing violent video games suddenly killed people in a violent rampage. Nevertheless, violence in video games has increased substantially in the last 30 years.

Some violent video games have been banned in Europe.

© Pixland/Thinkstock

While television is typically a passive activity, video games require the player to interact. That is, players are active participants in the fictionalized violence. This may make it more likely that children who play video games will have an increased risk of exhibiting violent behavior in other situations. However, research on the effects of violent video games is mixed. Some studies indicate that playing violent video games does indeed make children more violent, while other studies find only a small effect or no effect at all. The disparity in research results can have many causes. Some is doubtless due to the methods of study, as well as the particular video games that are used in the study. Studies also investigate different age groups, which may make a difference in the effect that particular media have on levels of aggression. Clearly, more research is necessary.

Movies

Violence has also increased in movies over the last decade. Unlike television and video games, which are usually viewed on a small screen, movies are often watched on a large screen. Recent research has found a heightened physiological response and heightened memory of violence when viewed on a large screen (Heo 2004). Additionally, while violence on television is often broken up by commercials, movie violence is usually shown continuously. Thus, the exposure to violence is often continuous rather than sporadic. Finally, movies are often watched in the presence of a larger group of people than is television. For all of these reasons, many researchers believe that the effects of movies may be greater than the effects of watching television (Kirsch 2006). However, very little research has actually been done to confirm these suspicions.

Social Media

Mass media are changing rapidly. Emerging technologies are changing the ways in which we communicate and connect with one another. The rate of technological change is increasing, especially in the area of communication. As emerging forms of mass media, social media such as Facebook or Twitter have not yet been widely studied. However, there is little question that these new ways of spreading information will have an effect in how individuals are socialized.

One such effect may be an increase in the ability to multitask. On average, 16- to 18-year-olds can effectively perform seven tasks simultaneously. People in their early 20s can perform only about six, and those in their 30s can perform fewer still (Koechlin et al. 1999; Wallis 2006). Another effect of the increase of technology is the change in the availability of personal information. Technologies like Twitter and Facebook have broken down many traditional boundaries of privacy and make users' intimate details and mundane activities public.

At the same time, many of these new technologies create an increasing sense of anonymity. For instance, how do you know that the people you are chatting online with are indeed who they claim to be? A man can pretend to be a woman; a woman can represent herself as a man. This allows criminals and predators new ways of finding and approaching targets.

Still another effect of this technology is the speed at which communication now occurs. What just a decade ago would take a few days can now be transmitted and received within moments. For example, prior to the advent of email, sending a letter across the country took several days. The same message sent as an email, however, reaches its destination in a matter of moments. This leads to increasing expectations of receipt of information as well an increased expectation of response to information. The speed and availability of information is greater than ever before. While this availability is often a good thing, it also means a proliferation of misinformation.

As technology continues to accelerate and change, it will no doubt continue to affect how people learn the values, beliefs, and behaviors of their society. While much of this technology offers new opportunities for learning and growth, it also offers opportunities for emerging criminal activity and the proliferation of misinformation. What the future of social media holds is uncertain. However, it is clear that social media is changing the way in which people interact with one another.

Because social media are a relatively recent cultural construct, sociologists have only begun to study their effects. Sociologists are unsure what the long-term effects of such rapid social media will be on the socialization of individuals. Some hypotheses include a change in the language and literacy of the culture. As an example, many people argue that texting has led to a decline in a grammar and spelling skills of American youth.

Cell phones are the number one interface among adolescents.

© Samuel Borges/Shutterstock, Inc.

THE SOCIOLOGICAL IMAGINATION   Social Media and Changing Communication

We said that C. Wright Mills defined the sociological imagination as the intersection between personal experience and history. A person's individual experiences within the framework of the broader culture go a long way toward shaping who we become. Changes in society will change how we experience the world.

The advent of social media such as Facebook and Twitter is fundamentally changing the way in which individuals communicate with one another. These changes will certainly have an impact on how individuals interact with the world around them. Twitter limits communication to 140 characters. For this and other reasons, text messaging has evolved into phonetic bursts that are often not grammatical. This new way of communicating has even been given its own name—textspeak. Emoticons—pictures made with keyboard characters—have also become popular as a way to express emotions in online interactions that often appear bereft of emotional content.

EVALUATE

1. How might the changing ways we communicate electronically affect the way in which we communicate in classrooms or workplaces?

2. Are there limitations to what can be communicated through text messaging and emoticons? Try experimenting with different messages to determine the limitations of communicating in textspeak.

CONCEPT LEARNING CHECK 3.3   Agents of Socialization

Answer the following questions.

1. Values that are taught through the presentation of standard school curriculum are called the:

   A. latent curriculum.

   B. corridor curriculum.

   C. secret curriculum.

   D. hidden curriculum.

2. Learning to play a role before entering that role is called:

   A. socialization.

   B. anticipatory socialization.

   C. resocialization.

   D. agency socialization.

3. Which of the following groups has the highest high school dropout rate?

   A. African Americans

   B. Native Americans

   C. Hispanic Americans

   D. Asian Americans

4. By adolescence, this replaces family as the strongest agent of socialization.

   A. Mass media

   B. Religion

   C. School

   D. Peers

5. This term refers to the lessons that children teach one another at school while not in class.

   A. Hidden curriculum

   B. Latent socialization

   C. Corridor curriculum

   D. Peer socialization

3.4 Socialization through the Life Course

Socialization is a lifelong process that has varying impact at different stages of life.

- Describe the five general stages of development and identify the major challenges and changes that occur in socialization at each stage.

We have learned that socialization is a lifelong process. However, the process of socialization and the effects it has on shaping beliefs, values, and behaviors differs at different stages of life. There are five general stages of development that are important for understanding socialization through the life course. These stages are infancy, childhood, adolescence, adulthood, and old age.

Infancy

The brain is most malleable at birth. The infant comes into the world with biological predispositions and reflexes. One of those predispositions is the ability to bond. Research shows that from birth, infants respond positively to faces. This is believed to facilitate the bonding process, as infants gradually learn to identify familiar faces. Infants also respond to smell. Within days of birth, an infant recognizes the unique smell of its mother and identifies that smell with safety, warmth, security, and food.

As the infant develops and grows, certain skills, such as sitting, rolling over, and crawling, come naturally. However, the child learns the significance of these actions only through the reinforcement that is given at each developmental milestone. The child's world expands through the process of development, but its understanding of that world develops through socialization.

Childhood

In early childhood, the child begins to speak. The development of speech signifies a milestone because it allows the child to communicate in increasingly complex ways with the adults who care for him or her. Speech also allows the adult to teach the child in new ways. Thus, socialization takes on a new dimension as the child begins to enter the symbolic world of the adult. The child gradually learns to use language not just to express needs and wants but to express ideas as well. But speech is important in other ways. By about age two or three, the child is able to form friendships with other children. The growing sphere of social interaction is gradually widening.

In many countries, children work in unsafe conditions for substandard wages.

© paul prescott/Shutterstock, Inc.

Secular trend The increasingly early onset of puberty seen in children.

For many children, however, childhood is also a time of stress. In many nations, childhood is seen as a time when the child can begin to contribute to the household. While in developed nations we may begin teaching children responsibility by giving them light chores, such as setting the table, in some countries, children are expected to work outside of the home. In fact, throughout the world, more than 160 million children work outside of the home. About half of these jobs are full-time positions. Often, the pay is low and the work environment poses significant physical or psychological danger to the child.

Of course, we do not allow children to work outside the home in the United States. In high-income nations, it is not necessary for children to earn an income. Instead, we see childhood as a time for children to explore, learn, and develop their skills and understanding of the world. We delay the responsibility of adulthood much longer than most cultures. Because childhood lasts so long in our culture, many children mature physically before they reach adolescence. In fact, the developed world is in the midst of a secular trend. The **secular trend** refers to the increasingly early onset of puberty seen in children. The trend has been particularly pronounced in girls. One in every seven girls will develop breasts and pubic hair by the age of eight. Among African Americans, the number is one in two.

Although no one is certain what is causing the secular trend, many researchers hypothesize that the increasing abundance of calories—particularly fatty foods—may be driving this effect. Other researchers claim that the increasing bombardment of sexual images in the mass media may be responsible for the secular trend. Although the mechanism is unknown at this time, many hypothesize that these messages somehow affect the brain and cause it to stimulate early onset of puberty.

Whatever the cause, the secular trend is changing not only the way in which children experience childhood but also the way society views childhood. For example, while boys who experience early sexual maturation typically experience an increase in self-esteem and popularity, girls who experience early sexual maturation typically see a reduction in their popularity among other girls and often experience an increase in sexual advances by males. The secular trend also leads to earlier sexual onset for both males and females. This is particularly problematic because while their bodies may have matured physically, their emotional and psychological development may not have kept pace. Reduction in parental supervision has also led many children to turn increasingly to peers and mass media to get information about adulthood. What they see is often inaccurate, however, as Hollywood portrays a world of violence, drugs, and sex. For these reasons, many youth are unprepared for the realities of adulthood in modern society.

Adolescence

Many cultures do not have a life stage known as adolescence. These cultures transition from childhood to adulthood through a rite of passage. The new adult is then entitled to all of the benefits that adulthood has to offer in that society. In the developed world, however, adolescence is a transition time between childhood and adulthood. When one is no longer a child but not yet an adult, adolescence can be a time of significant stress.

Research shows that most adolescents transition through this stage quite well. Still, a significant proportion faces an unusual mix of physiological and cultural change that makes this period of life challenging. Unlike other societies, in the developed world, there is no single ritual that marks the transition into adulthood. Adolescents are allowed to drive at 16. They can vote and join the military at 18. However, these same individuals are prevented from legally drinking alcohol until they are 21. While parents tell adolescents to delay sex, mass media seems to encourage sexual behaviors.

This cultural confusion can lead some adolescents to engage in rebellious behavior. They may dress in socially inappropriate ways or deliberately defy other cultural norms in an effort to express their independence. This rebellion is often an attempt at negotiating the cultural contradictions that manifest themselves most clearly during adolescence. During this time, the adolescent seeks to find his or her place in the world, deciding which values he or she wishes to adopt and which values to reject.

In some cultures, the idea of adolescence is unknown. Instead, children complete a right of passage into adulthood. In the Masai tradition, male children must kill a lion to progress into adulthood.

© Anup Shah/Photodisc/Thinkstock

Adulthood

By the time an individual enters adulthood, his or her sense of self is largely stabilized. The formation of a family and the pursuit of a career generally mean the end of adolescent rebellion. Individuals in adulthood tend to adopt the dominant cultural values and integrate fully into society.

However, the period of adulthood is also a time of challenge. Individuals struggle to balance the many roles they have now adopted—spouse, parent, worker. The expectations of society require increasing demands for time for all roles, which can cause stress.

The tensions that emerge as a person tries to successfully balance societal expectations for all of the roles of adulthood can lead to negative outcomes, such as divorce or depression. This is particularly true for women. Societal expectations have socialized women toward marriage, motherhood, and a career. Yet society has not provided the structure to help the women successfully navigate all of these competing roles. For this reason, many women find themselves overwhelmed, contributing to rates of depression that are higher than those of men. Societal expectations for men are somewhat less complex. Still, the expectation of financially caring for a family looms large in our society. As the American population ages, an additional burden of caring for elderly parents while simultaneously supporting young adult children threatens to overwhelm the American family.

Old Age and the End of Life

The later years of adulthood also offer unique opportunities for socialization. People are living longer than ever before, and the population of elderly is growing. Currently in America, about one person in eight is over the age of 65. That number is expected to double by the year 2030, when it will reach about 72 million Americans. This **graying of America**—the increasing proportion of the population over the age of 65—will doubtless have significant effects not only on the economics of the United States but also on the values and beliefs we hold as well. This has spurred an increase in the study of aging and the elderly, known as **gerontology** FIGURE 3-14.

Graying of America The increasing proportion of the population over the age of 65.

Gerontology Study of aging and the elderly.

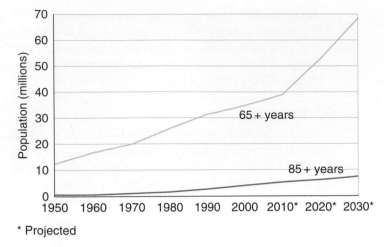

FIGURE 3-14 By the year 2030, the number of Americans over the age of 65 is projected to exceed 70 million.
Source: US Department of Health and Human Services. 1999. Health, United States, 1999 (www.cdc.gov/nchs/data/hus/hus99.pdf).

Increasing demands for health care, retirement, and other social benefits will likely be strained as the proportion of elderly Americans rises relative to the proportion of working adults. This will likely force a re-evaluation of these programs and services. Additionally, as seniors become more visible in society, there will likely be a change in the way in which they interact and integrate with the younger generation. Rather than be tucked away in a nursing home or retirement community, the growing number of elderly in America will be more likely to appear in mainstream society.

We are socialized to think of old age as a period of physical and mental decline. However, this is the reality only for a minority of seniors in our society. Although old age does increase the risk of injury, disease, and chronic illness, advances in modern medicine have allowed an increasing number of seniors to lead active lives through the retirement years. Only about 16% of seniors said that they could not walk a quarter mile unassisted, and fewer than 5% require assisted living. Nearly three fourths of seniors describe their health as good or excellent.

In developing nations, the elderly are often given more social power and more respect that in developed nations. This is because in developing nations, the elderly have had time to accumulate land and other scarce resources. They are also believed to have a considerable amount of wisdom and knowledge—a fact that makes them highly valued in that society. Societies in which the elderly have the most wealth, power, and prestige are called **gerontocracies**. In contrast, in the developed world, the elderly typically have less social power. It should be noted, however, that the demographic group with the most accumulated wealth is the elderly. However, the wealth is masked by the limitations of a fixed income, which often makes the elderly seem poorer than they really are. In other words, because the elderly often have a fixed monthly disposable income, it often appears that their economic resources are more limited than they actually are. Rather, the lack of social power probably comes from the view that the elderly in developed nations are out of touch with the rapidly changing technologies and the related social environment. Their knowledge and wisdom are seen as obsolete.

Of course, we all must face the fact of our mortality. However, in developed nations, death is coming later than ever before in human history. In America, only about 15% of people die before the age of 55. More than ever, people are living longer, happier lives. However, when death approaches, we can identify a process by which people come to grips with their own mortality.

Psychiatrist Elisabeth Kübler-Ross identified five distinct stages leading to acceptance of death. At first, a person is in *denial* about his or her impending death. He or she may claim that everything is fine, that he or she is healthy, or that there is some mistake. The second phase is *anger*. The person may see death as an injustice, as something unfair. The individual will eventually transition into *negotiation*, in which the person attempts to bargain with God in exchange for his or her life. The fourth

Gerontocracies Societies in which the elderly have the most wealth, power, and prestige.

stage, *depression*, is the knowledge that the person is actually going to die, but the knowledge is accepted only unwillingly. Sadness is common at this stage. Finally, the person comes to terms with his or her mortality during the *acceptance* stage. All of the anxiety about death fades, and the person seeks to make the most of the time that he or she has left FIGURE 3-15.

FIGURE 3-15 Elisabeth Kubler-Ross identified five distinct stages in the acceptance of death.

An aging population means a changing culture. As the population of the country ages, our culture is gradually becoming more comfortable with discussing death and planning for it. Discussing death has ceased to be taboo and is now an integral part of planning the life course. Many businesses have emerged to help people prepare for end of life, including estate planning and financial planning for the surviving spouse or children. This is particularly important for women, since they typically outlive men.

Although it remains widely used and accepted, Kübler-Ross's research has been criticized for a couple of reasons. First, critics such as Worden (1991) and Corr (1993) contend that Kübler-Ross's model is too linear and rigid. Rather, people do not necessarily pass through the stages of grief in the same order; and some people seem to experience more than one stage at the same time. Others, such as Bonanno (Bonanno et al. 2002) have attempted to replace Kübler-Ross's stage model with a model of resilience. Bonanno asserts that resilience, a personality characteristic that measures the ability to deal with change and stress, means that some people will grieve more than others, and some people may not grieve at all. Still others have criticized Kübler-Ross for ignoring cultural differences in grieving. For instance, while in American society, grieving is largely a personal matter, in other cultures, grieving for a loved one is a public matter.

Resocialization and Total Institutions

Sometimes, initial attempts at socialization are not sufficient to ensure that an individual will fully adopt the values, beliefs, and behaviors that a society expects. In those cases, people are often confined to a **total institution**, a place where a person is set apart from the rest of society and controlled by an authority within a structured environment. Examples of total institutions include psychiatric hospitals and prisons. In these facilities, the behavior of residents is strictly controlled. Everyone generally wears the same uniforms, eats the same food, sleeps at the same time, and has the same leisure activities to choose from.

The purpose of a total institution is **resocialization**, which is the process of changing a person's personality through careful control of that person's environment. Currently more than 2 million Americans are undergoing the process of resocialization in total institutions FIGURE 3-16. This process occurs in two stages. First, authority figures break down the person's existing sense of identity. This is often done through confiscating their personal possessions and replacing them with a standard uniform and/or a standard appearance, such as very short hair, that makes everyone in confinement look alike. After stripping away the individual's identity, the staff then strips away the person's sense of independence through frequent searches, examinations, and invasions of private space. The person may be referred to only as a number, thereby losing his or her name and the identity that goes with it.

Total institution A place where a person is set apart from the rest of society and controlled by an authority within a structured environment

Resocialization The process of changing a person's personality through careful control of that person's environment.

FIGURE 3-16 Prisons are an example of a total institution that attempts to resocialize inmates.

© Thinkstock/age fotostock

The second stage in the process is the construction of a new identity. This is often done through a system of rewards and punishments that seeks to make the identity of the person compliant. Correct behavior may be rewarded with a personal item or a luxury, such as watching television. Punishment for incorrect behavior might include solitary confinement or the removal of a personal item.

Not everyone responds positively to resocialization. While some people do indeed rehabilitate and adopt the values of the dominant culture, others become resentful of the control. People confined to total institutions for long periods of time may lose the skills necessary to successfully reintegrate into society and may therefore need to be institutionalized for the rest of their lives. In fact, some research (Bowers and Pierce 1980) has found that harsh punishments such as the death penalty may even increase crimes rates through a **brutalization effect**. The brutalization effect occurs because individuals see punishment by law enforcement as legitimizing violence, therefore making it appropriate to use violence against others as a means to solve problems. For most of us, however, socialization itself is effective. It does raise a question, though, of just how socialized we are. Does socialization restrict our behaviors, or does it help us to achieve our human potential within society?

Brutalization effect The idea that executions increase the rate of violence in society.

How Socialized Are We?

Socialization really is the process of creating the sociological imagination. Socialization is the intersection of our cultural history and our personal biography that shapes us into the person we become. It influences our values, beliefs, and behaviors. It influences how we think about the issues in our lifetime and how we behave toward those issues. Yet we must be careful not to see socialization as the only thing that makes us who we are. As already noted, our biological predispositions also play a role in the person we become. For example, biology can shape our personality in subtle and not-so-subtle ways, making some types of socialization more or less effective. Additionally, agents of socialization, for example, schools and mass media, often send contradictory messages. Even the same agents of socialization may send different messages at different times or in different social situations. What determines which of these messages are adopted and which are rejected? Just how much does socialization really influence our beliefs and behaviors?

Sociologists are not in agreement about how much socialization really influences a person's values, beliefs, and behaviors, Sociologists ask these kinds of questions when they study the extent to which individuals in a society think and act freely. This inquiry has led some sociologists to conclude that the influence of socialization on our behavior is pervasive and deterministic. In other words, our culture determines who we become, and our choices are limited to those that our culture offers us. Other sociologists argue that although society profoundly influences who we become, we are nevertheless free to choose which societal beliefs and values to accept and which to reject. It seems reasonable to suggest that some people are more influenced by the forces of socialization than others. Although far from settled, these and other forms of sociological inquiry offer unique insights into who we are in the context of the world in which we live.

CONCEPT LEARNING CHECK 3.4	Socialization through the Life Course

Match the life event to the most likely stage in the life course.

_____ **1.** Infancy

_____ **2.** Childhood

_____ **3.** Adolescence

_____ **4.** Adulthood

_____ **5.** Old age

A. Making friends for the first time

B. Mixed-sex peer groups

C. Resignation about death

D. Family recognition and bonding

E. Starting a family of your own

Visual Overview Stages of Development

Although all social theorists agree that development occurs in stages, they disagree about the number and nature of those stages. Socialization, though strongest during the early years of development, is a lifelong process and can occur cognitively, morally, and psychologically.

	Freud	Erikson	Piaget	Kohlberg	Mead
Infant 0–18 months	Oral-Stage	Oral-Sensory trust vs. mistrust	Sensori-motor	Preconventional	Imitation
Toddler 18 months– 3 years	Anal Stage	Muscular-Anal autonomy vs. self-doubt	Sensori-motor	Preconventional	Imitation
Early Childhood 3–6 years	Phallic Stage	Locomotor intiative vs. guilt	Pre-operational	Conventional	Play
Middle Childhood 6–12 years	Latency Stage	Latency industry vs. inferiority	Concrete- operational	Conventional	Game
Adolescence 13–18 years	Genital Stage	Adolescence identity vs. role confusion	Formal- operational	Post- conventional	
Young Adulthood 19–24 years		Young Adulthood intimacy vs. isolation			
Middle Adulthood 25–64 years		Middle Adulthood generativity vs. stagnation			
Old Age 65 years–death		Maturity ego integrity vs. depair			

Visual Summary Socialization

3.1 Socialization through Societal Experience

- Socialization is the lifelong process by which a person learns the beliefs, values, and behaviors of his or her society.
- Social contact is essential for socialization.
- Social isolation has significant and irreversible developmental effects.
- There are three basic levels to socialization: primary socialization, secondary socialization, and adult socialization.

3.2 Understanding Socialization through Theorists and Their Research

- Socialization can be understood in a variety of ways, but always as a process that occurs in stages.
- Freud believed that the development of personality required proper social attachment and development.
- Freud believed that personality stabilized during adolescence.
- In contrast to Freud, Erikson believed that development of the personality was a lifelong process.
- Erikson identified eight stages of development, each with a normative crisis that must be successfully dealt with for proper development.
- Piaget identified four stages to cognitive development.
- Kohlberg identified three levels and six stages of moral development in boys.
- Gilligan expanded Kohlberg's research to include girls and discovered that girls develop moral sentiment differently than boys.
- Charles Horton Cooley theorized that personality emerges through social interaction as individuals interpret how they think others see them and adjust their behaviors accordingly.
- George Herbert Mead believed that the self emerges through three stages of play that become increasingly social.

3.3 Agents of Socialization

- The family is the strongest agent of socialization.
- Other important agents of socialization include religion, work, school, and mass media.
- Peers replace family as the strongest agent of socialization during adolescence.
- Increasing violence in mass media may have a negative impact on youth, as it socializes them toward violent behaviors.
- Emerging social media will offer new forms of socialization.

3.4 Socialization through the Life Course

- Socialization is a lifelong process.
- In infancy, socialization is oriented toward attachment to caregivers and mastering early developmental milestones.
- In childhood, the social sphere widens as the child begins to develop friendships.
- School becomes an important influence in the socialization of the child.
- During adolescence, peers become the most important agent of socialization.
- During adulthood, socialization centers around beginning a family and work.
- During old age, a person is socialized toward acceptance of the end of life.

3.1 Socialization through Societal Experience

1. Carl turned 16 and went out with his friends to a club rather than spending time with his family. Carl is experiencing:
   A. primary socialization.
   B. secondary socialization.
   C. adult socialization.
   D. critical socialization.

2. The idea that learning a new language is more difficult as a person gets older is an example of the:
   A. critical period hypothesis.
   B. socialization hypothesis.
   C. language learning hypothesis.
   D. sociological imagination.

3. Every time that Aram and his brother Artashes fight, their mother punishes them and explains that violence is not an appropriate way to solve problems. Aram is experiencing:
   A. adult socialization.
   B. secondary socialization.
   C. primary socialization.
   D. peer socialization.

3.2 Understanding Socialization through Theorists and Their Research

4. As a teenager, Glenda finds it very difficult to learn to speak French. Her difficulties might be the result of what phenomenon?
   A. Secondary socialization
   B. Critical period hypothesis
   C. Primary socialization
   D. Adult socialization

5. Arthur is reflecting on his current career, wondering if his work has helped to make the world a better place for future generations. According to Erikson, Arthur is experiencing a:
   A. moral dilemma.
   B. crisis of self.
   C. ego crisis.
   D. normative crisis.

6. Jerome is in Erikson's adolescent stage. The normative crisis he will likely experience is:
   A. generativity versus stagnation.
   B. intimacy versus isolation.
   C. identity versus role confusion.
   D. trust versus mistrust.

7. Boris considered his football team a second family that helped shape his values of hard work and perseverance. Cooley would say that for Boris, the football team is a:
   A. normative crisis.
   B. primary group.
   C. generalized other.
   D. secondary group.

8. Gene has just signed up for little league baseball. As he learns how all of the positions work together on the team, he will master Mead's _____ stage.
   A. game
   B. play
   C. latency
   D. imitation

9. Tyra is beginning to read, but her mother still has to help her with difficult words. This is an example of:
   A. formal operations.
   B. secondary socialization.
   C. scaffolding.
   D. preconvention.

10. Ivan just got married. He is quickly learning about the responsibility that is involved with managing a household. What level of socialization is Ivan experiencing?
    A. Secondary socialization
    B. General socialization
    C. Primary socialization
    D. Adult socialization

11. Bart's coach has also served as a mentor, helping Bart through some very rough times in his life. According to Cooley, Bart's coach would be:
    A. a significant other.
    B. part of a primary group.
    C. a generalized other.
    D. part of a secondary group.

12. Jeannette is a teacher. Every time she lectures, she notices students falling asleep in class. Jeannette concludes that she is not a very good teacher. This is an example of:
    A. the looking-glass self.
    B. self-actualization.
    C. secondary socialization.
    D. primary socialization.

13. Belinda is playing dress-up while her mother gets ready to go out for the evening. Belinda is in which of Mead's stages of development of the self?
    A. Play
    B. Imitation
    C. Operational
    D. Game

3.3 Agents of Socialization

14. Amy has been in day care since she was six months old. Which of the following is not a likely outcome of Amy's experiences in day care?
- **A.** Amy will learn to read earlier than her peers who have not attended day care.
- **B.** Amy will be more aggressive than her peers who have not attended day care.
- **C.** Amy will have stronger bonds with her mother than her peers who have not attended day care.
- **D.** Amy will act out when challenged by an authority figure.

15. LaToya's parents both have working-class jobs. What would we predict about the way they parent LaToya?
- **A.** They are likely to spank LaToya when she is not compliant.
- **B.** They encourage LaToya to be creative in her approach to problems.
- **C.** They try to get LaToya to comply using reason.
- **D.** They encourage LaToya to express herself openly.

3.4 Socialization through the Life Course

19. Elmer is more interested in hanging out with his friends than with his family. He has also taken up smoking because his friends think it is cool. Elmer is likely in what life stage?
- **A.** Adolescence
- **B.** Adulthood
- **C.** Infancy
- **D.** Childhood

20. Vinny was so aggressive and disruptive that his parents sent him to a special boot camp to try to make him compliant. At the boot camp, they tell Vinny when to sleep and when to get up. They tell him when to eat and even when to go to the bathroom. Vinny is experiencing:
- **A.** anticipatory socialization.
- **B.** primary socialization.
- **C.** total institution.
- **D.** adult socialization.

16. Herman and Albert are standing by their school lockers talking about how lazy some of the minority students in their class are. This is an example of:
- **A.** primary socialization.
- **B.** hidden curriculum.
- **C.** anticipatory socialization.
- **D.** corridor curriculum.

17. Jose wants to own his own restaurant. He uses his current job as a line cook to practice skills he will need to achieve his goal. This is an example of:
- **A.** primary socialization.
- **B.** adult socialization.
- **C.** anticipatory socialization.
- **D.** secondary socialization.

18. Ted is in prison undergoing a rehabilitation program. Ted is experiencing:
- **A.** anticipatory socialization.
- **B.** resocialization.
- **C.** primary socialization.
- **D.** secondary socialization.

21. Dobu lives in a society in which the elders are highly respected, have most of the social power, and control most of the wealth. Dobu lives in a:
- **A.** matriarchy.
- **B.** gerontocracy.
- **C.** filiarchy.
- **D.** pastorality.

CHAPTER ESSAY QUESTIONS

1. Rates of attention deficit disorder are higher among boys than among girls, especially at younger ages. How might this be explained using concepts of socialization?

2. Discuss why rates of successful resocialization are low in total institutions.

CHAPTER DISCUSSION QUESTIONS

1. How do you think the media influence the way in which we perceive and understand other agents of socialization, such as school or the family?

2. What has a greater affect on humans: nature (biology/evolution) or nurture (socialization)? How do your viewpoints compare or differ to your beliefs about the differences between men and women? Share your thinking with the class.

3. How might anticipatory socialization be beneficial to an individual? How might it be detrimental?

4. Based on what you read about primary socialization and the critical period hypothesis, should social workers and the court system have more leniencies in removing toddlers from abusive homes? Should all parents have to undergo mandatory parenting courses? Why or why not? How does society balance the well-being of children versus the rights of biological parents?

5. In cultures that are more group centered, do you think children and adolescents experience Freud's id, ego and superego or Erickson's normative crises in the same way that children and adolescents do in western cultures that are more individual centered?

6. In what ways do interactions that occur in a classroom during a discussion reflect the main components of Cooley's looking glass self?

7. Using Mead's Development of the Self (imitation, play, and game stages) discuss why playing pee-wee sports or other organized group activities may be important agents of socialization for children in the U.S.

8. Share with the class your favorite cartoon characters from when you were a young child. Observe the nonverbal behaviors as your colleagues share their early childhood memories. Does the class appear more animated and lively? How does this reflect the influence of the mass media?

9. Does corridor curriculum exist in college? How does college facilitate anticipatory socialization?

10. In what ways is the military a total institution and how are soldiers resocialized into the values and norms of the military culture? How does this affect the reentry into society following active military duty for example soldiers coming home from the wars in Iraq and Afghanistan?

CHAPTER PROJECTS

INDIVIDUAL PROJECTS

1. Recall that at the elementary levels, schools tend to benefit females because they emphasize skills that are more consistent with the ways in which society socializes girls. Conversely, secondary schools tend to benefit boys because they emphasize skills that are consistent with the ways in which society socializes boys. Considering the ways in which society socializes gender roles in children, construct a plan to change elementary schools to be more amenable to the needs of boys. Construct a plan to change secondary schools to be more amenable to the needs of girls.

2. The essence of socialization is learning the beliefs, values, and behaviors that are considered acceptable to society. Through the process of socialization, individuals learn the moral boundaries of their culture. Design a test to determine where a child falls in Kohlberg's levels of moral judgment.

3. Interview an individual outside of your family who is at least 20 years older than yourself. Your questions should reflect *Erickson's Psychosocial Theory* and *Socialization through the Life Course*. Write a paper detailing your findings.

4. Write a self-reflection paper about your self-identity. Include in your paper *significant others* and *agents of socialization* that had the greatest impact on your personality development. How do you think your self-identity will evolve as you age and move through the life course?

GROUP PROJECTS

1. Find a public place such as a playground, restaurant, or mall with a play area where you can observe groups of children at play. Look for patterns in how children play and interact with each other and their significant others. Discuss how your observations are related to the material in this chapter. Write a summary of your findings.

2. Go online and search "Final Note on a Case of Extreme Isolation by Kingsley Davis." After you read the paper, discuss the two cases of Anna and Isabelle with your colleagues. How are the two case studies similar and how do they differ? What do these two examples teach us? Write a summary of your group discussion.

CHAPTER KEY TERMS

Adult socialization	Gerontocracies	Primary groups
Agents of socialization	Gerontology	Primary socialization
Anticipatory socialization	Graying of America	Resocialization
Brutalization effect	Hidden curriculum	Scaffolding
Corridor curriculum	Id	Secondary groups
Critical period hypothesis	Imitation	Secondary socialization
Cultural universals	Looking-glass self	Secular trend
Ego	Mass media	Significant other
Feral children	Normative crisis	Socialization
Game stage	Play stage	Superego
Generalized other	Peer group	Total institution

ANSWERS TO CONCEPT LEARNING CHECKS

3.1 Socialization through Societal Experience

1. [C] The Harlows' research with rhesus monkeys showed that monkeys suffer developmental effects as a result of prolonged social isolation.

2. [A] The following statement is untrue based on studies of feral children: Socialization has unlimited power to mold the human brain.

3. Primary socialization involves the development of skills learned in childhood. [A. Learning to share; C. Learning to talk].

4. Secondary socialization involves the development of skills in adolescence [B. Dating; F. Getting a driver's license].

5. Adult socialization involves socializing skills used in adulthood [D. Transitioning into a new career; E. Having children].

3.2 Understanding Socialization Through Theorists and Their Research

1. Socialization leading to an understanding of the self proceeds through three stages: the imitation stage, play state, and game stage. [George Herbert Mead]

2. Human personality develops throughout the life course as each person tries to resolve a central crisis associated with each of eight stages. [Erik Erikson]

3. The child develops a sense of self through play, progressing through three stages to the eventual emergence of the *me*. [George Herbert Mead]

4. Boys and girls are socialized toward morality differently, with girls being socialized toward an other-oriented moral system and boys being socialized toward an individualist moral system. [Carol Gilligan]

5. We watch the reaction that other people have to our behaviors and adjust our behavior accordingly so that we gain the approval first of primary groups and later of secondary groups. [Charles Horton Cooley]

ANSWERS TO CHAPTER REVIEW TEST

3.1 Socialization through Societal Experience

1. B. Secondary socialization occurs during adolescence as the individual's social sphere widens to include peers.

2. A. The critical period hypothesis states that there is an optimal period for learning certain skills, such as language.

3. C. Primary socialization is learned from the family in childhood and refers to basic values and behaviors acceptable to society.

3.2 Understanding Socialization through Theorists and Their Research

4. B. The critical window hypothesis suggests that it becomes harder to learn a foreign language as a person gets older.

5. D. Erikson identified eight normative crises that involve an individual reflecting on their individual lives and contributions.

6. C. In Erikson's theory, the normative crisis for the adolescent stage is identity versus role confusion.

7. B. Because his football team functioned as a second family, helping to shape his values of hard work and perseverance, the football team is a primary group.

8. A. Mead's game stage involves an understanding of how various roles interact with other roles.

9. C. Scaffolding refers to a kind of socialization whereby a parent or other person helps bridge the gap between a child's current skill level and a more advanced skill level.

10. D. At the conventional level, understandings of morality take a social focus. Morality becomes oriented toward rules that are applicable to the peer group.

3.3 Agents of Socialization

1. [D] Values that are taught through the presentation of standard school curriculum are called the hidden curriculum.

2. [B] Learning to play a role before entering that role is called anticipatory socialization.

3. [B, C] The following groups have the highest high school dropout rate: Native Americans, Hispanic Americans

4. [C, D] By adolescence, the following replace family as the strongest agent of socialization: School, peers.

5. [C] This term refers to the lessons that children teach one another at school while not in class: corridor curriculum

3.4 Socialization through the Life Course

1. Infancy [D. Family recognition and bonding]

2. Childhood [A. Making friends for the first time]

3. Adolescence [B. Mixed-sex peer groups]

4. Adulthood [E. Starting a family of your own]

5. Old age [C. Resignation about death]

11. B. Cooley defined primary groups as anyone with whom the individual has a close, personal relationship.

12. A. The looking-glass self is the process by which we adjust our behavior based upon our interpretations of how others see us.

13. B. During the imitation stage, children imitate the behavior of significant others even if they do not understand the action.

3.3 Agents of Socialization

14. C. Studies show that children who spend significant time in day care have weaker ties with their mothers than other children.

15. A. Studies suggest that working-class parents are more likely to use physical punishment as a means of achieving compliance in their children.

16. D. The corridor curriculum refers to lessons that children teach one another at school while not in class.

17. C. Anticipatory socialization refers to learning to play a role before your enter it.

18. B. Socialization such as rehabilitation, with the goal of promoting prosocial values, is called resocialization.

3.4 Socialization through the Life Course

19. A. During adolescence, peers replace family as the primary agent of socialization.

20. C. A total institution is a place that maintains total control over a person's action with the goal of resocialization.

21. B. A gerontocracy is a society in which the elderly maintain most of the wealth and social power.

1. Rates of attention deficit disorder are higher among boys than among girls, especially at younger ages. How might this be explained using concepts of socialization? Studies show that at young ages, boys are less capable of sitting still than girls. They are also more aggressive than girls and have shorter attention spans. However, society in general and schools in particular are structured so that the expectations of proper behavior favor girls. For example, boys are expected to sit still in class for long periods of time. They are also expected to solve problems in a nonaggressive way. Because these expectations are contrary to the natural behaviors of boys, they manifest themselves as behavioral problems such as attention deficit disorder or hyperactivity. However, as schools shift to male-oriented patterns in the later grades, many of these behaviors disappear as the child gets older.

2. There are several reasons why rates of successful resocialization are low in total institutions. First, research shows that the effects of socialization are weaker at later ages. This means that the attempts at resocialization are likely to have a reduced impact on the individual. Relatedly, attempts at resocialization may be unsuccessful because the original socialization toward negative values is extremely strong, and efforts at resocialization have not been applied for a long enough time to overturn the original values. Finally, efforts at resocialization frequently take place in total institutions. The total control of a person can have negative consequences, such as making the person experiencing it reject the dominant values even more strongly. For all of these reasons, resocialization in total institutions is often unsuccessful.

REFERENCES

Adler, P. A. and P. Adler. 1998. *Peer Power: Preadolescent Culture and Identity*. New Brunswick, NJ: Rutgers University Press.

Alexander, G. M. and M. Hines. 2002. "Sex Differences in Response to Children's Toys in Nonhuman Primates (*Cercopithecus aethiops sabaeus*)." *Evolution and Human Behavior* 23:467–479.

Belsky, J. 1990. "Infant Day-Care, Child Development and Family Policy." *Society* July/August:10–12.

Bonanno, G. A., C. B. Wortman, D. R. Lehman, R. G. Tweed, M. Haring, J. Sonnega, D. Carr, and R. M. Neese. 2002. "Resilience to Loss and Chronic Grief: A Prospective Study From Pre-loss to 18 Months Post-loss." *Journal of Personality and Social Psychology* 83:1150–1164.

Bowers, W. J. and G. L. Pierce. 1980. "Deterrence or Brutalization: What is the Effect of Executions?" *Crime and Delinquency* 26:353–383.

Bushman, B. J. and L. R. Huesmann. 2001. "Effects of Televised Violence on Aggression." Pp. 223–254 in *Handbook of Children and the Media*, edited by D. Singer and J. Singer. Thousand Oaks, CA: Sage.

Cole, M. and S. R. Cole. 1989. *The Development of Children*. New York: W. H. Freeman.

Cole, R. 1970. *Erik H. Erikson: The Growth of His Work*. London: Souvenir Press.

Cooley, C. H. 1902. *Human Nature and the Social Order*. New York: Scribner.

Corr, C. 1993. "Coping with Dying: Lessons That We Should and Should Not Learn from the Work of Elizabeth Kübler-Ross." *Death Studies* (17):69–83.

Crespo, C. J., E. Smit, R. P. Troiano, S. J. Bartlett, C. A. Macera, and R. E. Andersen. 2001. "Television Watching, Energy Intake, and Obesity in US Children." *Archives of Pediatric and Adolescent Medicine* 155:360–365.

Darwin, C. 1874. *The Descent of Man*. New York: Cromwell.

Davis, K. 1947. "Final Note on a Case of Extreme Isolation." *American Journal of Sociology* 52(5):432–37.

Duncan, G. J., C. J. Dowsett, A. Claessens, K. Magnuson, A. C. Huston, P. Klebanov, et al. (2007). "School Readiness and Later Achievement." *Developmental Psychology*, 43(6):1428–1446.

Edgell, P., J. Gerteis, and D. Hartmann. 2006. "Atheists as 'Other': Moral Boundaries and Cultural Membership in American Society." *American Sociological Review* 71(2):211–234.

Fisher, S. and C. R. Greenberg. 1996. *Freud Scientifically Reappraised: Testing the Theories and the Therapy*. New York: Wiley.

Gilligan, C. 1977. "In a Different Voice: Women's Conception of Self and Morality." *Harvard Educational Review* 47:481–517.

Goldberg, S. and M. Lewis. 1969. *Play Behavior in the Year-Old Infant*. New York: Bordwick.

Harkees, S., C. P. Edwards, and L. M. Super. 1981. "Social Roles and Moral Reasoning: A Study in a Rural African Community." *Developmental Psychology* 17:595–601.

Harlow, H. F. 1962. "Development of Affection in Primates." PP. 157–166 in *Roots of Behavior*, edited by E. L. Bliss. New York: Harper.

Harlow, H. F. 1964. "Early Social Deprivation and Later Behavior in the Monkey." Pp. 154–173 in *Unfinished Tasks in the Behavioral Sciences*, edited by A. Abrams, H. H. Gurner, and J. E. P. Tomal. Baltimore: Williams & Wilkins.

Heo, N. 2004. "The Effects of Screen Size and Content Type of Viewer's Attention, Arousal, Memory, and Content Evaluations." Dissertation Abstracts International, 64, 9-A. UMI No. AA3106253.

Kirsch, S. J. 2006. *Children, Adolescents, and Media Violence: A Critical Look at the Research*. Thousand Oaks, CA: Sage.

Koechlin, E., G. Basso, P. Pietrini, S. Panzer, and J. Graffman. 1999. "The Role of the Anterior Prefrontal Cortex in Human Cognition." *Nature* 399:148–151.

Koenig, H. G. 2008. *Medicine, Religion and Health: Where Science and Spirituality Meet*. West Conshohocken, PA: Templeton Foundation Press.

Kohn, M. 1977. *Class and Conformity: A Study in Values*. 2nd ed. Homewood, IL: Dorsey Press.

Kramer, P. 2010. *Freud: Inventor of the Modern Mind*. New York: Harper.

Maccoby, E. E. 1980. *Social Development, Psychological Growth and the Parent–Child Relationship*. New York: Harcourt.

McCartney, K. and G. Galanopolous. 1988. "Child Care and Attachment: A New Frontier the Second Time Around." *American Journal of Orthopsychiatry* 58:16–24.

McGuinness, D. 1979. "How Schools Discriminate Against Boys." *Human Nature* February:82–89.

Meadows, S. 1986. *Understanding Child Development*. London: Hutchinson.

Merton, R. and A. Kitt. 1950. "Contributions to the Theory of Reference Group Behavior." Glencoe, Illinois: Free Press. (Reprinted in part from *Studies in the Scope and Method of "The American soldier,"* edited by R. K. Merton and Paul Lazarfeld. Glencoe, IL: Free Press.)

Moir, A. and D. Jessel. 1989. *Brain Sex: The Real Difference Between Men & Women*. New York: Lyle Stuart.

Robinson, T. N., M. L. Wilde, L. C. Navacruz, K. F. Haydel, and A. Varady. 2000. "Effects of Reducing Children's Television and Video Game Use on Aggressive Behavior: A Randomised Controlled Trial." *Archives of Pediatrics and Adolescent Medicine* 155:17–31.

Rymer, R. 1993. *Genie: A Scientific Strategy*. New York: Harper.

Simpson, E. L. 1974. "Moral Development Research: A Case Study of Cultural Bias." *Human Development* 17:81–106.

Slee, P. T. 2002. *Child, Adolescent and Family Development*. 2nd ed. Cambridge, UK: Cambridge.

Wallis, C. 2006. The Multitasking Generation. *Time* (March 27):48–55.

Worden, W. 1991. *Grief Counseling and Grief Therapy: A Handbook for the Mental Health Practitioner*. 2nd ed. New York: Springer.

© Stockbyte/Thinkstock

Chapter Overview ▼

4

Society, Social Structure, and Social Interaction

Learning Objectives ▼

4.1 ■ Illustrate the three levels of sociological analysis.

4.2 ■ Identify the components of the social structure and their impact on the beliefs, behaviors, and values of individuals.
   ■ Define and discuss status characteristics.
   ■ Distinguish between primary and secondary groups.
   ■ Examine leadership styles.

4.3 ■ Identify the types of societies as identified by means of subsistence and the major characteristics of each.

4.4 ■ Compare and contrast the various macrosociological theories of social order and the theorists associated with each.

4.5 ■ Recognize the principles of microsociological analysis and its impact on the beliefs, values, and behaviors of individuals.

© AbleStock

Dramaturgy A microsociological approach that analyzes social life in terms of the stage.

My first day of teaching had finally arrived. After a year of shadowing a full professor, distributing, collecting, and grading his tests, getting his coffee, and making treks to the library in the cold northern winter to pick up loads of books for him, I had finally earned the right to teach my own class. I wanted desperately to make a good impression. I spent the previous evening carefully pressing my slacks, my shirt—and yes, even my socks. I spent half an hour choosing just the right tie to match my creaseless shirt. I shined my shoes.

My first class was simply a review of my carefully prepared syllabus, but I wanted it to be perfect. I rehearsed my lecture several times in front of a mirror, reviewed my notes, and made last-minute corrections in an effort to perfect my upcoming performance. I arrived at my classroom nearly a half hour early. As students began to filter in to the classroom, I handed each one a carefully prepared syllabus. When class began, I dutifully began my first lecture.

I went over classroom rules: Show up on time, turn off cell phones, bring your book every day. About halfway through the class, I noticed that several students had already begun peeking at their cell phones. Soon, several more had stopped taking notes and were playing on their laptops or cell phones. I mentioned to the students that they should put their cell phones away. It was not an easy sell. Cell phones should be off, I reminded them sternly, so that we can concentrate on the task at hand.

Just then, I heard loud music. A moment passed before I recognized the sound as a cell phone ringing. It took another several moments to track the sound—to my own bag! It was *my* cell phone that was ringing. Embarrassed, I fumbled through the pockets of my bag, nearly dropping my cell phone as it played music and vibrated in my hands. As I turned the sound off, I looked out over my bemused class. I fumbled for an explanation. When none was forthcoming, I desperately sought a way to save face.

I asked my students how it felt to be interrupted by the ringing phone. It was a distraction, they agreed. "Exactly," I exclaimed, "and that is why it is so important that you remember to turn your cell phones off." I went on to explain that distractions affect us all, and we need to minimize them to make sure we can concentrate on course material. The message was not lost on the class. I could tell that they truly understood.

As I reflected on that day's class, I realized that I had turned happenstance into a serious message. I realized that many of my students saw my ill-timed phone call as a deliberate exercise. I reflected on Goffman's concept of **dramaturgy**—analyzing social interaction in terms of the stage. I had turned a performance gone wrong into a demonstration about classroom etiquette. I had engaged in face-saving behavior and impression management, two of Goffman's most enduring contributions to sociology. Goffman would have seen my performance in the classroom as a microcosm of society—individuals bonding through the performance of social roles, complete with scripts that define the expectations for behavior. However, I did note that I missed the opportunity to link Goffman's concepts to the class. But that was a minor mistake, since we would cover that in class at a later time. At the time, I was glad simply to have survived my first day of teaching and glad to have impressed an important message to the class at the same time.

All social interactions are performances—some more authentic than others. We are socialized to play a variety of roles throughout our lives, and these roles shape our beliefs, values, and behaviors. The roles we play help shape our sociological imagination as well as help us navigate our increasingly complex social world.

4.1 Levels of Sociological Analysis

There are three levels of sociological analysis—microsociology, mesosociology, and macrosociology—each with its own perspective on how the social order affects the development of the sociological imagination.

- Illustrate the three levels of sociological analysis.

Just as social life can be understood through a variety of theoretical perspectives, we can also explore and understand social life using three levels of analysis FIGURE 4-1. These levels of analysis offer sociologists different views on the ways in which society affects the beliefs, values, and behaviors of individuals.

Macrosociology

Macrosociology refers to an analysis of social life that focuses on broad features of society, such as social institutions that influence us, such as education, the economy, and the media. By understanding how social institutions affect and influence the individual, we can infer, with reasonable accuracy, someone's beliefs and values as well as understand or anticipate his or her behaviors. Macrosociology helps us to understand how the broad social structure influences our beliefs, values, and behaviors. By understanding how large social institutions influence us, we gain insight into how society shapes who we become. These large social institutions set the context by which the lives of people are played out. Macrosociology is often used by sociologists using the conflict perspective or the functionalist perspective.

Microsociology

Microsociology analyzes social life by focusing on the specific aspects of social interactions. The microsociological perspective also examines small-scale social interaction, such as the interactions between small groups of people. This level of analysis is common to symbolic interactionists and social exchange theorists.

As an example, let us consider how each of these perspectives would analyze the effects of school on an individual. Macrosociologists might consider how the institution of schools socializes students toward the values that are appropriate for their society. The structure of the curriculum, the ways in which students are taught, and the expectations for learning might also be considered. Sociologists who adopt a microsociological perspective would be more interested in analyzing ways in which teachers interact with their students. For instance, do male and female teachers interact with students differently, and how might those interactions affect learning outcomes?

Mesosociology

A third level of analysis is **mesosociology**. As a level of analysis, mesosociology lies between the micro and macro levels. Mesosociology examines the middle layers of

Macrosociology Analysis of social life that focuses on broad features of society, such as social institutions.

Microsociology Analysis of social life that focuses on the specific aspects of interactions.

Mesosociology Analysis of social life that falls between the microsociological and macrosociological levels.

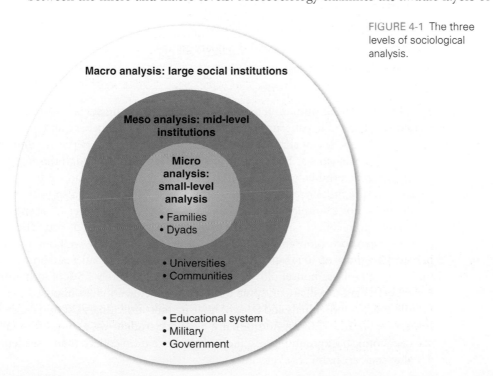

FIGURE 4-1 The three levels of sociological analysis.

Macro analysis: large social institutions

Meso analysis: mid-level institutions

Micro analysis: small-level analysis

- Families
- Dyads

- Universities
- Communities

- Educational system
- Military
- Government

society, such as communities or neighborhoods, that link personal interaction with the larger social institutions. To extend our example, a sociologist studying schools from a mesosociological perspective might look at how different classes within the same school differ in the ways in which they socialize students toward community values. Alternatively, mesosociology may seek an understanding of how different schools within the same geographic area increase or decrease social inequality.

While all three of these levels offer useful perspectives on social life, no one level is superior to the other two. All are essential to gain a full understanding of the ways in which society shapes the individual. All are necessary to gain insight into the sociological imagination.

CONCEPT LEARNING CHECK 4.1   Levels of Sociological Analysis

Identify which level of sociological analysis best fits each of the following elements of the social structure.

_____ **1.** The education system

_____ **2.** Interaction between a police officer and a citizen

_____ **3.** A neighborhood's block party

_____ **4.** A family

_____ **5.** A child in day care

_____ **6.** Christianity

A. Macrosociological

B. Mesosociological

C. Microsociological

4.2 Social Interaction at the Macrosociological Level

Sociologists view human behavior in relation to a broad framework of institutions that influence how people behave and interact with one another.

- Identify the components of the social structure and their impact on the beliefs, behaviors, and values of individuals.

- Define and discuss status characteristics.

- Distinguish between primary and secondary groups.

- Examine leadership styles.

Social structure Patterns or regularities in how people behave and interact with one another.

Sociologists believe human behavior is influenced by the social structure. **Social structure** refers to the patterns or regularities in how people behave and interact with one another. The social structure that surrounds a person is pervasive and frames that person's behaviors as he or she interacts in the world. Although the social structure is not a determinant of behavior, it certainly influences who we become. The social structure influences our values, beliefs, and behaviors. It also influences our life chances. For example, sociologists can estimate your chances of attending and graduating from college simply by knowing a few basic facts about you. The correlations between socioeconomic status and college attendance are well documented. A person who grows up in poverty is less likely to go to college than a person who grows up in a middle-class household. For example, approximately 55% of individuals in lower social classes will attend some form of higher education, as opposed to 67% of middle-income individuals and 84% of high-income individuals (National Center for Education Statistics 2012). Additionally, a college student who comes from a lower socioeconomic background is less likely to graduate from college than a student from a higher socioeconomic background.

The social structure is not just one thing. Instead, it is a complex mix of many aspects of the social world, all of which influence different people in different ways. This is largely because people are socialized in different ways. In terms of the sociological imagination, the social structure might be understood as that place where the individual's biography, or life history, intersects with social history. In order to begin to understand it and discuss it, sociologists generally break the social structure into six component parts: culture, social class, social status, roles, groups, and social institutions. Let us look at each one in more detail.

Culture

Culture and its effects on the individual are presented in depth in a different chapter. However, it is prudent to review some of the key points as they relate specifically to the social structure. Culture refers to the beliefs, values, behaviors, and objects that constitute a society's way of life. Culture is the broadest framework for the development of the beliefs, values, and behavior of an individual. As an example, think about how your life would be different if you had grown up in a different society. Aside from speaking a different language, your values and beliefs would also be very different. Your ambitions would also likely be different—perhaps you would have no desire to go to college. In fact, in some cultures, there are no universities at all. In other cultures, only certain people, such as males, are allowed to attend college. Thus, culture plays a role in who we become by framing the opportunities that a particular society offers and to whom it offers those opportunities.

Social Class

Social class is a broad measure of the place that a person occupies in the social structure. A person's social class is determined by his or her income, education, and occupational prestige. Thus, people who have similar education, work at jobs that are roughly equivalent, and earn roughly the same income are said to be members of the same social class.

These factors influence how a person views the world, what the person thinks, and how he or she acts. For example, because people of higher social class tend to have higher incomes than people in lower social classes, they may tend to view economics through the lens of conservatism. People of higher social class are more likely to vote Republican than people of lower social class, who see Democrats as closer to their values. Research shows that social class also affects the likelihood of going to college, likelihood of having strong religious values, and even the way in which a person parents children.

Social class A broad measure of the location that a person occupies in the social structure.

Status The position that a person holds in a group.

Prestige The esteem or reputation that accompanies a status.

Social Status

Sociologists use the term **status** to refer to the relative position that a person holds within a group. To distinguish status from social class, it may be helpful to think of the two concepts in the following way. Social class is a broad categorization, while status is the specific position that a person holds within a social class. In other words, while social class varies among large groups of people in society, people also vary in their specific positions within those particular social classes. Thus, status is somewhat more specific to individuals and a little less macrosociological than social class.

Status is perceived relative to the group to which a person belongs. A person's status will vary as he or she moves from group to group and situation to situation. For example, a person with a bachelor's degree will have high status among a group of high school dropouts. However, in a group of professors, the person with the bachelor's degree will have low status. In a room full of professors, everyone shares the same status. However, not all of the professors will be seen equally, because some may have more prestige than others. In contrast to status, which is a position that a person holds, **prestige** refers to the reputation or esteem that is attached to a particular status. Therefore, people may hold the same status but differ in prestige.

We all occupy multiple positions simultaneously. You might be a college student at the same time that you are a brother or sister and a member of an athletic team. All of

Ascribed status A status that a person takes on involuntarily, either through birth or through other circumstances.

Achieved status A status earned through some effort or activity within your control.

Status symbols Signs that identify a particular status.

Shaming Using status symbols to identify those who have violated societal expectations.

Salient characteristics Characteristics that distinguish between members of a group.

Diffuse characteristics Status characteristics that are presumed to always matter in determining a person's relative position in the group.

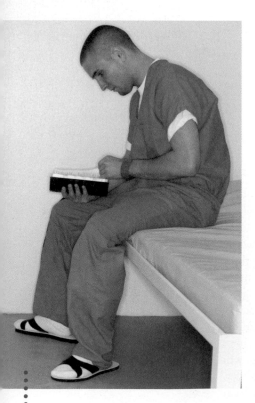

Prison uniforms function as a status symbol because they identify the individual's place in society.
© Thinkstock

these are statuses, and you hold all of these positions at the same time. Sociologists refer to this as a *status set*. Status sets will, of course, change as particular circumstances change. When you graduate from college, you drop one status and assume another. You acquire additional statuses if you get married or become a parent.

Each status is associated with a set of norms that guide behavior. To see how status affects your behavior in society, consider how your position as a student frames your actions. In the classroom, your behavior is likely very different from your behavior when you are not in class. Your status as a student means that you give deference to the instructor, who is of higher status by virtue of his or her higher educational attainment. The instructor sets the rules for the course, and your behavior is constrained by those rules. When you take on the status of student, you adopt the framework of behavior associated with that social position.

Status Characteristics

Some statuses, such as student, a person adopts voluntarily. Other statuses, such as that of son or daughter, a person receives involuntarily. An **ascribed status** refers to a status that a person takes on involuntarily, either through birth or through other circumstances beyond his or her control. In contrast, an **achieved status** is a position that is earned through some effort or activity within your control. In both cases, your status says something important about who you are. Both ascribed and achieved statuses provide a framework for beliefs, behaviors, and feelings.

Statuses may be positive or negative. Often, it is to our advantage to advertise our positive statuses and hide our negative ones. As a means of advertising our statuses, we use status symbols. **Status symbols** are signs that identify a particular status. This could be something as subtle as a wedding ring to show off your status as husband or wife, or it could be something more visible, such as a uniform that clearly identifies your status. Sometimes, society uses status symbols as a means of deterrence. For example, in some states, individuals convicted of driving while under the influence of alcohol must display a license plate that is noticeably different from the plates of everyone else. Another, more common example is the uniforms given to identify convicts in prison. These outfits stand in contrast to the uniforms worn by the guards. Using status symbols to identify those who have violated societal expectations is called **shaming**.

Often, status symbols serve not only to indicate individuals who are different from us but also indicate those individuals who are similar to us. For this to work, however, the status characteristic must be *salient*. In other words, it must be a characteristic of some but not all members of a group. For example, in a group of all females, sex is not a **salient characteristic** because it does not help us distinguish between and among members of the group. However, in a group with both men and women, sex is a salient characteristic because it can be used to distinguish members of a group from one another.

Thus, status symbols unite as well as divide. In fact, status characteristics are used in many social situations to make evaluations about a person's abilities and competencies. Sociologists Joseph Berger, Bernard Cohen, and Morris Zelditch (1972) identified six status characteristics that are used to evaluate people in every social situation (as long as they remain salient). Berger called these **diffuse characteristics**. The six diffuse status characteristics are sex, race, age, educational attainment, occupational prestige, and physical attractiveness. As long as they are salient, these six characteristics are used to determine a person's relative status in any group of people. Numerous studies have shown not only that these six characteristics are used to evaluate people in social situations but also that they are evaluated regardless of the situation. In every case, males are evaluated more positively than females, even by females (Hopcroft 2002). Whites are evaluated more positively than nonwhites. Older people are evaluated more positively than younger people, presumably because they are considered to have more knowledge and experience. Not surprisingly, individuals with more education are evaluated more positively than individuals with less educational attainment. Similarly, individuals who work in occupations with greater prestige are evaluated more positively than people who work in low-prestige jobs. Finally, research demonstrates that individuals who are considered more physically attractive are given higher status than individuals who are considered less attractive.

Of course, these are not the only status characteristics that matter. Sometimes an individual has skills or knowledge that are relevant to a particular task that the group is performing. Specific status characteristics are characteristics that are relevant for status distinctions only in particular situations. Often a person's status increases by virtue of her or his experience with the task.

To help distinguish between diffuse and **specific characteristics**, let us take an example. In a jury—a group formed to determine the innocence or guilt of an accused criminal—the amount of influence that a particular person wields on the jury can be predicted by assessing a person's relative status. We begin by comparing the relative status of the jury members by looking at their diffuse status characteristics. We compare the members on the basis of their sex, race, occupational attainment, age, educational attainment, and attractiveness. We then consider if any individuals have experience that is relevant to the purpose of the group. For instance, if one of the members has previous experience on a jury, then he or she would possess a specific status characteristic that increases his or her status relative to the other members of the group.

Some status characteristics are more important than others. Some status characteristics are so important to our identity and place in society that they overshadow all others. Sociologists call these **master status characteristics**. Master status characteristics may be achieved or ascribed. One commonly cited example of a master status characteristic is physical disability. Regardless of any other status characteristics that a person might possess, a person with a disability is usually evaluated solely on the basis of that disability. For example, if you encountered a person in a wheelchair, you might imagine his or her skills and abilities to be very limited. While the perception may indeed be correct, it may also be completely wrong, such as in the case of professor Stephen Hawking, a physicist with a disabling disease that confines him to a wheelchair. Whether the perception is correct or not, the point is that the individual is judged on the basis of perceived disability. Thus, physical disability acts as a master status characteristic.

As with the example of Stephen Hawking, on occasion our varying statuses may contradict or confuse. Such **status inconsistencies** are important reminders of the essential importance of status—its relation to expectations that other people have for us as we interact in the social world. Statuses guide the expectations that others have for us. When societal expectations are violated, as in the case of status inconsistencies, people often become uncomfortable because they are unsure how to react. The expectations that they rely on to guide them through the interaction are no longer valid.

Roles

As we now know, a status is a position that a person occupies in society. Each status comes with expectations for behavior, which is to say, each status comes with a role. Sociologists define a **role** as the behaviors that accompany a status. The expectations of these roles are created by society ahead of time and guide the behavior of the person playing that role. Like following a script in a play, a person learns and acts out the expected behaviors—plays the role—associated with each position.

Often, more than one role accompanies a single status. When more than one role is associated with a single status, these roles are called a **role set**. Of course, roles are only guidelines. Although we usually follow the script that is laid out for us, sometimes we deviate from it, and not always voluntarily. Sometimes, the expectations within a single status contradict themselves. This causes what sociologists call **role strain**. Role strain occurs when there is tension among the roles that are connected to a single position. Professors often occupy several roles: they teach, conduct research, write about the research they conduct, advise students, and usually serve on committees that help the university function smoothly. The demands of these

Specific characteristics Status characteristics that matter in determining a person's relative position in the group only if they are shown to be relevant to the circumstance of the group.

Master status characteristic A status characteristic that is so important that it overshadows all other status characteristics.

Status inconsistencies Statuses that contradict one another.

Role Expected behaviors that accompany a status.

Role set More than one role associated with a single status.

Role strain Tension between roles connected to a single status.

Dr. Stephen Hawking, a noted physicist, deals with Lou Gehrig's disease, a debilitating condition that confines him to a wheelchair and prevents him from speaking.

© Michael S. Yamashita/CORBIS

The demands of balancing a career with family create role conflict among many working women.

© zhu difeng/Shutterstock, Inc.

various roles compete for time and energy, of which there is often not enough. The resulting tension is known as role strain because all of these roles are connected to a single position—professor.

Additionally, roles connected to two or more positions may also contradict one another. This is called **role conflict**. Role conflict is more common than role strain because roles connected to a single status are usually consistent in their expectation, while roles connected to multiple statuses more commonly clash. In an increasingly fast-paced world, role conflict poses a significant challenge to people in modern society. As we try to adopt more and more roles, in trying to accomplish more and more, role conflict is an inevitable part of modern life. To continue with our example, many professors have families. Often, in trying to complete expected work on time, professors must choose whether to bring work home. Of course, bringing work home conflicts with the roles of spouse and parent. This is role conflict, since the tension involves two or more statuses—that of professor, parent, and spouse.

Sometimes, a role becomes so demanding that people find it impossible to continue occupying the status associated with that role. Role conflicts or role strains make the person doubt her or his ability to continue in a particular role. For instance, if the demands of being a university professor become so great that they threaten a professor's marriage, the professor may decide to leave the university and pursue a different career. The process by which a person disengages from a status and the social roles attached to it is called **role exit**. Often, this is a legitimate resolution for role strain and role conflict.

THE SOCIOLOGICAL IMAGINATION   Status and Role Inventory

We said earlier that sociologists believe human behavior is influenced by the social structure. We have just examined two critical elements of social structure: *status* and *role*.

Status can be thought of as a way for society to categorize individuals. We know that some of these categories, or statuses, can be altered and others cannot. Think about someone you know and list her or his *status set* in a notebook or journal. Try to think of each status this person holds, perhaps listing them in order of importance. Note which are *ascribed* and which are *achieved*. Underline any that could be considered a *master status*. List any *status symbols* that reflect a specific status. Can you think of an example of someone who belongs to only one group and has only one status?

Now consider roles, which we said are the behaviors that

accompany status. As you look at your list of statuses, note some of the roles, or behaviors, this person exhibits that seem to reflect each status. Can you think of a *role set* associated with one status? Have you witnessed or become aware of any *role strain* or *role conflict* associated with one or more statuses this person holds? Can you think of an example of *role exit* associated with a particular status? To what extent do you think these behaviors reflect this person's attitudes and beliefs about her or his status?

Now imagine that three or four of your family, friends, or acquaintances were to perform this same exercise using you as their subject. You might guess that, depending on their relation to you, their responses might vary considerably.

EVALUATE

1. Which responses about your status and roles do you think are most likely to be accurate?

2. Which are most likely to be inaccurate? Why?

3. What might this say about the influence of status and role in the social structure compared to its other components, such as social class and social institutions?

Groups

As already indicated, status is relative to the group that you are in. A **group** consists of individuals who share common beliefs and values and who regularly interact with one another. This is in contrast to an **aggregate**, which is people who occupy the same space and time but who have no common goals or purpose. Groups are an essential element of the social structure because they also influence behavior. A member of a group will usually conform to the expectations and norms of the group. In this way, groups also form an important part of a person's identity. We frequently define ourselves—at least in part—by the groups that we belong to. For example, think back to your high school yearbook. Underneath the pictures of various peers are lists of groups or clubs that the person was a part of. There are perhaps groups not listed that the person belonged to informally, such as being labeled a jock or a nerd. All of these groups, whether formal or informal, help to shape the person's beliefs, values, and behaviors.

However, some groups have more influence over your beliefs and behaviors than others. **Primary groups** are groups that have a strong influence over your socialization. Primary groups are typically small and characterized by lasting personal relationships. An example of a primary group is the family. **Secondary groups** are large and impersonal groups whose members share a specific goal or activity. Members adopt the roles expected of them within the group and act out the expected behaviors associated with each status. Often, the ties between members of a secondary group are weaker than those in a primary group. Thus, the influence of secondary groups on the beliefs, values, and behaviors of an individual is often weaker than in primary groups.

Leadership in Groups

In every group, leaders emerge. In formal groups that have a specific task or goal, leaders are often chosen through some formalized structure. In naturally forming groups, leaders often emerge through a natural process. In such cases, leadership is usually tied to status. That is, those individuals with the highest status typically emerge as group leaders.

In most groups beyond a group of two, two types of leaders will emerge. **Instrumental leadership**, also called task leadership, refers to group leadership that focuses on the completion of tasks. Instrumental leaders guide the group through the process of completing goals or tasks in a variety of ways, as we will explore below. But it is important to remember that the function of the instrumental leader is to make sure that the group functions appropriately to the task. In contrast, **expressive leadership** focuses on maintaining well-being and morale in the group. Expressive leaders are less concerned with completion of goals or tasks. Rather, they focus on minimizing tension between group members. They function to keep the group running smoothly by keeping morale high.

Instrumental leaders may govern the group in one of three ways. **Authoritarian leaders** take personal charge of the task, dictate the jobs of each of the group members, and expect them to follow orders. In other words, authoritarian leaders are dictatorial in their style. This leadership style works well in crisis situations when strong leadership is necessary. However, it often backfires in less demanding situations because it makes the leader unpopular. It also fails to allow other group members to give input into the process of accomplishing the goal.

Democratic leaders, on the other hand, seek input from group members. This type of leader attempts to include everyone in the process of accomplishing a task. For that reason, democratic leaders are usually popular. However, since democratic leadership requires a substantial investment of time as group members negotiate, democratic leadership is often not very effective in a crisis situation.

A person may also be a **laissez-faire leader**. This leader allows the group to function more or less on its own, offering guidance only when necessary. In most cases, laissez-faire leadership is not particularly effective in achieving group goals. One exception, however, is when the goal and the process to accomplish the goal are well known. In such cases, strong leadership is not necessary and the group can usually accomplish the goal without much guidance. **TABLE 4-1** compares three leadership styles and characteristics.

Role conflict Tension between roles connected to two or more statuses.

Role exit Disengaging from a status and the social roles attached to it.

Group Individuals who share common beliefs and values and who regularly interact with one another.

Aggregate People who occupy the same space and time but who have no common goals or purpose.

Primary groups Groups that are characterized by small, intimate relationships and that have a strong influence over your socialization.

Secondary groups Large and impersonal groups whose members share a specific goal or activity.

Instrumental leadership Leadership that focuses on the completion of tasks.

Expressive leadership Leadership that focuses on the well-being and morale of group members.

Authoritarian leaders Leaders who take personal charge of the task, dictate the jobs of other group members, and expect them to follow orders.

Democratic leaders Leaders who seek input from all members of the group before accomplishing a task.

Laissez-faire leader A leader who lets the group function more or less on its own, offering guidance only when necessary.

TABLE 4-1 Three Leadership Styles and Characteristics of Each

Leadership style	Characteristics	Appropriate use	Drawbacks
Authoritarian	Leader dictates tasks and expects obedience. Leader takes personal charge of the task.	Used most effectively when the task is time limited, and when strong leadership skills are necessary.	Morale of the group tends to be low. Often stifles creativity within group.
Democratic	Leader seeks input from members of the group.	Used appropriately when creative solutions are desirable and there is no time limit to completion of the task.	Often very hard to create consensus on the best way to complete the task.
Laissez-Faire	Group leader takes hands-off approach and lets the group function more or less on its own.	Used most effectively when the group is highly trained or experienced with completion of the task.	Often, group members do not perform to expectations unless they are monitored.

Social Institutions

Social institutions The ways in which a society meets it basic needs.

Social institutions are another important feature of the social structure. The term **social institution** refers to the ways in which a society meets its basic needs. Examples of institutions that meet the needs of society are family, religion, and school. While in tribal societies, social institutions are typically informal, technologically advanced societies usually develop formal ways of meeting societal needs. For example, while schooling in most hunter-gatherer societies is done informally through the family or extended kin, in developed societies schooling is usually done in a formal setting outside of the home.

Often, the effects of social institutions are taken for granted. Returning to our example of school, for instance, reveals how social institutions guide us in the organization of our lives. In developed societies, formal schooling is structured around a rigid schedule. School begins at the same time on the same days of the week and ends at the same time each day. Individuals in the school must organize their schedules around this school time. Other activities must also be organized in such a way as to accommodate the formal structure of the school. Yet the influence is not limited to the students. Parents and siblings must also adjust their schedules to the demands of formal education. Parents are responsible for making sure that their children get out of bed on time and get to school on time, as well as navigate the myriad of other activities that children participate in.

Schooling also affects how we see other aspects of the social structure. How we interact in groups, for instance, is at least partly learned in schools. Leadership and problem-solving skills are learned and developed within all of our educational institutions. Thus, social institutions have wide-reaching effects on the beliefs, values, and behaviors of the individual.

CONCEPT LEARNING CHECK 4.2   Social Interaction at the Macrosociological Level

For each scenario, identify the type of leadership style.

_____ **1.** Bill gives the group a task, then lets the group function without much direction.

_____ **2.** Bill assigns each member of the group a task and monitors their progress closely, often giving each of them direction.

_____ **3.** Bill seeks input from the members of the group on the best way to accomplish the task.

_____ **4.** Whenever a conflict arises in the group, Bill makes a joke and attempts to smooth over differences.

A. Democratic leader

B. Laissez-faire leader

C. Expressive leader

D. Authoritarian leader

4.3 Societies, Technology, and Change

Cultures can be defined by their general mode of subsistence, which develops and changes over time.

- Identify the types of societies as identified by means of subsistence and the major characteristics of each.

Culture is composed of two elements. **Nonmaterial culture** refers to the symbols and ideologies that define culture. Language and religion are examples of symbolic culture. **Material culture** refers to the physical items, also known as artifacts, that reflect the ideologies of the culture. Additionally, material culture reflects the level of technological development of a particular culture. A society's technological development determines how that society satisfies its basic needs. Societies are therefore classified by their means of subsistence. Six primary subsistence strategies have been identified and are used to classify almost every type of society, past and present: hunting and gathering, horticultural, pastoral, agricultural, industrial, and postindustrial FIGURE 4-2.

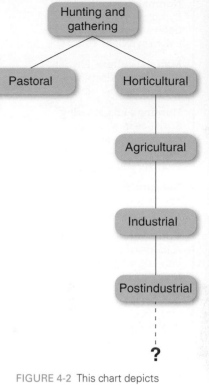

FIGURE 4-2 This chart depicts the ways in which societies have evolved their means of subsistence over time.

Hunting and Gathering Societies

For nearly all of human history, humans have subsisted by hunting wild animals and gathering food where they could find it. In fact, **hunting and gathering** was the dominant means of subsistence from the evolution of our proto-human ancestors six million years ago until horticulture was introduced 10,000 years ago. Now, however, only a few societies maintain a hunting and gathering life style. Most of the remaining hunting and gathering societies live in remote regions of the world, such as the Amazon jungle and central Africa.

Because hunting and gathering requires a large investment of time and because the carrying capacity of the land is limited, these societies usually number fewer than 50 people. Often, these small societies are simply extended kin **networks**, composed of one or two family groupings that are related. Hunter-gatherer societies are also transient. That is, because they deplete resources in an area, they are forced to relocate to new areas while the used land recovers. Hunter-gatherer societies follow an **optimum foraging strategy**—a pattern of foraging that leaves enough flora and fauna in a foraged area for the land to recover in a reasonable amount of time.

Both women and men, adults and children, young and old, contribute to foraging efforts. Thus, men and women are relatively equal in terms of social power. Men hunt almost exclusively, while women maintain the hearth, care for children, and forage near the camps. In many hunting and gathering societies, foraging by women and children accounts for more than half of the daily caloric intake for the group. Yet gender divisions are still evident. The reason is that the relative scarcity of meat compared to plant calories makes meat a highly desired commodity. Coupled with the fact that success rates for hunters are typically below 30%, successful hunting acts as an important status marker. Bringing home meat to the group would certainly increase the status of the hunter.

The transience of hunting and gathering societies means that individuals can own only what they carry as they move from place to place. For this reason, the rate of technological development is extremely slow and relatively limited. Most of the time, significant technological change in hunting and gathering societies is imposed from the outside. As more advanced societies encroach on hunting and gathering societies, some of the new technologies will doubtless find their way into the hunting and gathering societies.

Hunting and gathering was the dominant means of subsistence for most of human history.

© Uros Ravbar/Dreamstime.com

Nonmaterial culture
Symbols and ideologies that define a culture. Sometimes called symbolic culture.

Material culture Physical items that reflect the ideologies of a culture.

Hunting and gathering Societies in which the dominant means of subsistence is hunting animals and gathering food.

Network A small society of one or two family groupings that are related.

Optimum foraging strategy A pattern of foraging that leaves enough flora and fauna in a foraged area for the land to recover in a reasonable amount of time.

Horticulture Farming using simple hand tools to raise crops.

Pastoralism A means of subsistence that relies on the domestication of animals as the primary food supply.

Horticultural Societies

Domestication of plants first emerged around 10,000 years ago in an area of the Middle East known as the Fertile Crescent. By 6,000 years ago, the technique had spread as far as China and Western Europe. These early farmers used simple tools and human labor to raise crops. Known as **horticulture**, this represented a significant change in the way in which food was acquired.

Horticulture emerged as an alternative to hunting and gathering in areas where the soil was relatively fertile and easily cultivated. Einkorn wheat was likely the first domesticated plant, cultivated in the Fertile Crescent and hybridized over time. This offered groups a relatively stable supply of food, in contrast to the instability of hunting and gathering. However, due to the low technology used in horticulture, yields were often low and were at the mercy of the climate and weather of the region. Horticulture was thus often combined with other means of subsistence, such as hunting and gathering. So, while horticulture was often insufficient by itself as a means of subsistence, it nonetheless represents a significant leap in subsistence technology.

One change that horticulture established is a sedentary way of life. Farming requires that people remain near the farm in order to tend to the crops. The transition to a sedentary life is significant in that it allows for the accumulation of material possessions and technology. This means that some people can accumulate more possessions or wealth than others in the society. Horticulture represents the first real division of social classes, although this division remains minimal when compared to more technologically advanced societies.

Through farming, fewer people are needed to feed the entire group. Thus, some people are free to explore the development of new technologies and new ways of doing things. This means that technological development is accelerated relative to hunting and gathering societies. Indeed, in horticultural societies, we see the beginnings of economic specialization and the emergence of social classes based on ways of making a living.

Horticulture does have one significant drawback, however. As groups rely more and more on domesticated plants, their diet begins to vary less and less. This can lead to a reduction in vital nutrients needed for a healthy life style. Indeed, studies show that sedentary societies often have higher rates of nutrient-related diseases such as pellagra, rickets, and scurvy.

Pastoral Societies

In areas where the climate or the soil was not amenable to the domestication of plants, people learned to domesticate animals for food. This method of subsistence, known as **pastoralism**, is common in arid climates, such as the deserts of Africa, and in colder climates found in mountainous regions. Animals native to those climates, such as goats, sheep, and reindeer, were among the first animals domesticated for food. As with horticulture, pastoralism is often combined with gathering and hunting as a means of subsistence. Like horticultural societies, pastoral societies often must contend with nutrient-deficient diseases such as beri beri, rickets, or scurvy.

Unlike sedentary horticultural societies, pastoral societies must move from place to place. This is because herds of animals require large investments of grasses and other foods, which deplete environments rapidly. Herds must be migrated to where available food sources are located. For this reason, pastoralists can possess only that which they can carry, so possessions are few and the rate of technological change is low. Despite this limitation, however, many pastoral societies have developed significant social inequalities, with some members emerging as a ruling class. Interestingly, pastoral societies are an evolutionary dead end. Where hunting and gathering societies and horticultural societies have led to the emergence of new societal forms, pastoral societies have not evolved past their present state.

While there are several theories about why many pastoral societies have not evolved past their present state, perhaps the most widely accepted theory comes from Jared Diamond. Diamond (1999) hypothesizes that geographic conditions influence the

Horticultural societies farm using hand tools and human labor.

© iStockphoto/Thinkstock

development of cultures. For example, Asia is laid out along a horizontal axis on the globe, while Africa is laid out along a vertical axis. The orientation of continents affects many things, including the types of plants, animals, and other resources that are available for people to exploit. Additionally, because pastoral societies are not sedentary, they are limited in what items or technologies they can take with them when they move about. This means that the rate of culture change is likely to be slow.

Agrarian Societies

Agriculture developed from horticultural societies roughly 5,000 years ago. **Agriculture** differs from horticulture in the ways in which the farming is accomplished. In horticultural societies, farming is accomplished using human labor and simple hand tools. By contrast, agriculture relies on more complex farming implements as nonhuman labor. At first, animals were used to pull plows and sow seeds. Later, this developed into the use of powered machinery as a means of farming.

Pastoral societies rely on domesticated animals as their primary source of food.
© iStockphoto

Yields in agriculture are high compared to those in horticulture. In fact, agriculture usually results in significant food surpluses. This means that larger sedentary groups can be fed with less human labor. With fewer people needed to farm, more people can be free to develop new technologies and new ways of thinking. The development of new technologies, coupled with surplus food supplies, means that societies can trade with one another to a significant degree while advancing the pace of technological development and cultural diffusion. Communities grew and extended beyond the extended family. This began a trend of increasing individualism that continues to the present day.

It is perhaps not surprising that the first cities emerge in the same regions and at about the same time as the development of agriculture. The huge surplus that accumulates, coupled with the increasingly complex trade networks, means that these sedentary communities offer unique opportunities that do not occur in other means of subsistence. Opportunities for accumulating wealth and technologies are unprecedented, leading to people converging on these locations to take advantage of the opportunities offered. The opportunities afforded by agriculture are not guaranteed, however. Despite a general increase in quality of life, levels of social inequality rise dramatically in agricultural societies. While some people become very rich and powerful, others decline into serfdom or slavery.

Agricultural societies farm using machines powered by advanced energy sources.
© Jack Dagley/Shutterstock, Inc.

Additionally, because of the surplus, agricultural societies have much to protect. Warfare develops as a profession in order to protect the interests of the cities. The development of warfare parallels the development of strong political leadership in agrarian societies.

Industrial Societies

Just as agriculture gave rise to the emergence of cities, it also greatly increased the rate of technological development. By the middle 1700s, technological advances and capitalism ushered in the age of industry. **Industry** is defined as the production of goods using machinery driven by advanced sources of energy. Engines driven by steam or oil gradually replaced animal power as industry was born.

While in agrarian societies, people work close to home, in industrial societies, people's residences began to be separate from their places of work. People began to work in large factories under direct supervision of other people. This had a profound impact not only on the ways in which people made their living but also on the values and norms that had been dominant for centuries. Values surrounding the family changed significantly with the advent of industrialism. For the first time, the majority of people made their living away from the home, thus increasing the division of labor between men and women.

Agriculture Farming using machinery powered by engines.

Industry A means of subsistence that relies on the production of goods using machinery driven by advanced sources of energy.

Industrial societies produce goods in large factories powered by machines and augmented by human labor.

© Photodisc

Postindustrialism A means of subsistence that relies on the production of services and information.

Many aspects of life traditionally performed by the family became institutionalized. For example, formal schooling became significantly more popular, particularly among the emerging middle class. This trend occurred because the changing economic trends required greater knowledge and skills than had previously been necessary. The downside of this change, however, was that many roles that had previously been achieved through the family were now relegated to formal institutions run through the government.

Industry also made travel faster and less expensive. As railroads began to crisscross the country and steamships raced people across the oceans, trade continued to accelerate between cities and between nations. Increased trade brought unprecedented wealth, such that the lifespan and standards of living for most people rose dramatically. Travel also became more accessible to the average person in society, allowing more people to travel and explore more opportunities than had previously been offered.

Despite an increasing standard of living for most people, poverty became more visible as it migrated from the countryside to the city. This led to a misperception that poverty was increasing (Griffin 2010; Ridley 2010) and that steps were necessary to combat the problem. This misperception contributed significantly to the development of sociology as a discipline.

Postindustrial Societies

Many early theorists believed that industry was the culmination of society. However, many industrial societies have moved beyond the limitations of industry and into a new means of subsistence based on the creation and proliferation of information and information-related technologies. Termed **postindustrialism**, this is now the dominant way of life among Western cultures. As opposed to industrialism, which relies on the production of material things as a means of subsistence, postindustrial societies rely on the production of ideas and information. This shift to nonmaterial production has had a significant impact on the socialization of people living in postindustrial societies. Postindustrial societies come to rely heavily on the global marketplace, since most of the material goods that people rely on are now produced in other countries.

The first major change is the number and type of skills that are necessary to be successful in a postindustrial economy. As opposed to general skills that are often sufficient for industrial societies, highly specialized skills and knowledge are necessary to compete in an increasingly global information economy. For this reason, educational expectations are high, and education is highly formalized beginning in early childhood and extended through adulthood. Written and oral communication skills have become more important than building or other industrial skills.

In postindustrial economies, many of the traditional functions of the family have been relegated to formal organizations in an effort to control economic situations of the family such as child support and education, as well as control the use and dissemination of information. Social control, however, may be becoming more difficult. The advent of social media has increased the freedom and flow of information. However, social media have also lowered our standards for acceptable written communication and may be lessening our comfort and facility with face-to-face communication. In addition, social media have become increasingly important agents of socialization, as well as a means for creating identity and connecting in an increasingly individualistic world.

It is difficult to predict how society will evolve in the future. Regardless of the particular form it takes, it is clear that changes in society will lead to changes in the way that individuals are socialized and in the ways in which social life will be organized. It is likely that society will become increasingly individualistic and that identity formation and communication will become more reliant on technology. Already, technologies such as robotics, nanotechnology, and cloning are challenging us to think about what future society will be like. While these emerging technologies fascinate us, they also raise new

In postindustrial societies, the primary means of subsistence is the production of services and information.

© ImageSource/age fotostock

questions and concerns. As the pace of technological change accelerates, answers to the ethical, legal, and moral questions raised by such technologies have not kept pace. **Cultural lag**, the idea that some elements of culture change faster than others, presents its own set of challenges for navigating the society of the future.

> **Cultural lag** The idea that some elements of culture change faster than others.

| CONCEPT LEARNING CHECK 4.3 | Societies, Technology, and Change |

Match the kind of society with the means of subsistence.

_____ **1.** Hunting and gathering

_____ **2.** Pastoral

_____ **3.** Agricultural

_____ **4.** Horticultural

_____ **5.** Industrial

_____ **6.** Postindustrial

A. Produces goods using machinery driven by advanced sources of energy.

B. Animals are domesticated for food and serve as the primary source of calories.

C. Society primarily produces services and information.

D. Seeks food by gathering and hunting.

E. Farming using hand tools and human labor.

F. Farming using powered machinery.

4.4 What Holds Societies Together?

Macrosociological frameworks offer important insights into how societies are developed and maintained over time.

■ Compare and contrast the various macrosociological theories of social order and the theorists associated with each.

> **Capitalists** Marx's term for the owners of the means of production.

How does a society that is composed of thousands—or millions—of people pursuing their own objectives and interests manage to stay whole and intact? How does a society successfully maintain the interests of so many people for so long, even when those interests are radically different from and often contradictory to one another? How can a society survive the many changes that occur over time in its social structure? Sociologists have long struggled with these fundamental questions by asking the more basic question: What holds society together? Of course, this question is difficult to answer. Different sociologists have come up with a number of theories to explain the prevalence and pervasiveness of society over time. Early sociologists such as Karl Marx, Emile Durkheim, and others tried to answer these questions amid rapid and radical social change. Although their answers are different and even a little dated, these explanations laid the groundwork for much of our current macrosociological understanding.

Society and Conflict

Marx believed that the history of all societies could be interpreted as the struggle between people of two social classes. For Marx, a person's social class was determined by their relationship to the means of production.

Marx defined **capitalists** the highest social class. This class comprised the owners of the means of production. Capitalists are the people who own the factories and corporations that employ other people. Capitalists earn their living from the profits of their factories. Their wealth is accumulated, according to Marx, by using the labor of other people for their own benefit. Capitalists set the rules within their

FIGURE 4-3 Karl Marx explained how the struggle for scarce resources creates various forms of social order.

© Photos.com

Marx used the term capitalist *to refer to the highest social class. Capitalists own the means of production.*
© Photodisc

Proletariat Marx's term for the working class who provide labor for the capitalists.

Lumpenproletariat Marx's term for the dispossessed, criminals, mentally ill, and disabled in society.

Alienation Marx's term for the limitations in life choices that accompany low social status.

Marx used the term proletariat *to refer to the unskilled workers who labor in the factories.*
© Stockbyte

businesses and within society to advance the goals of their own social class and to keep members of the lower classes working for them.

Marx used the term **proletariat** refer to the working class. The proletariat provides the labor for the factories, as well as any other group that relies on selling their labor in order to make a living. Because they sell their labor to survive, they are at the mercy of the capitalists for their livelihood and are exploited when they are paid less than their labor is worth. The proletariat has very little social power. According to Marx, they rarely accumulate wealth because the capitalists structure society to keep the proletariat perpetually poor and dependent, through generations, in order to maintain a large, ongoing source of factory labor.

Marx did recognize other groups in society including farmers and peasants, a middle group of self-employed professionals, and the **lumpenproletariat**. Marx included in the lumpen-proletariat the unemployed, mentally ill, dispossessed, criminals, and other people who were unable generally to participate in the labor force. The lumpen-proletariat has the lowest amount of social and economic power and is unable to participate in the political process in order to further their position in life. However, Marx regarded these other groups as insignificant to the conflict between capitalists and the proletariat.

Marx argued that the capitalists, because they own the means of production, generally control the political process and therefore set the rules by which society operates. Of course, they will set the rules to benefit themselves to the disadvantage of other groups, whom the capitalists rely on for their continued economic success. In fact, Marx noted, the capitalists systematically prevent the proletariat from obtaining many of the material possessions that they produce in the factories! In this way, the proletariat is exploited for their labor. Through exploitation, the proletariat loses determination over their lives. Because they are relegated to manual labor, they are limited in their life choices. Marx called this **alienation**. Really, Marx's theory is a theory of social order through social conflict. Social order is established and maintained through competition for societal resources. Marx, however, did not believe that this was the best way to achieve social order. Marx felt that social problems such as crime and poverty were the inevitable result of a social order based on conflict. As an alternative, Marx advocated for the elimination of social classes through the abolition of private property. In that way, Marx believed, all people would have the same amount of social and political power. No one would need to resort to crime, and no one would suffer the ill effects of poverty. Social problems would be eliminated and society would progress further as everyone worked cooperatively for the good of the social order.

Marx's theory suffers from some serious flaws, however. First, Marx's analysis of history has been shown to be rather one-sided and selectively employed. Second, Marx neglected to consider the evolution of the capitalist system that he criticized. Marx believed that the capitalist system was inherently flawed and was destined to collapse upon itself, leaving only one social class. Marx failed to see the capitalist system as an evolving system that could raise the standard of living for even the lowest social classes. Marx also failed to anticipate the flexibility of the capitalist system. During times of crisis, capitalism has been able withstand the discontent of the proletariat by offering concessions. For example, during the Great Depression, many workers were given food, jobs, or retraining to help them weather the storm.

Despite these criticisms, Marx's perspective on the world offers us valuable insight into how conflicts are structured in society. Since Marx first explained society through social conflict, many other theorists have extended his analysis to include many more specific aspects of the social structure. For example, there are conflict analyses of the family, schools, gender relations, and sports. In all of these, the primary focus remains on how different individuals and groups compete in society for scarce resources. How this competition is structured and resolved remains a key component to understanding how society is maintained over time.

Society and Rationalization

German sociologist Max Weber FIGURE 4-4 believed Marx's analysis of modern life was too simplistic. Weber agreed with Marx that capitalism was alienating, but for different reasons. Weber argued that Marx understated the role of social structure in determining life chances. Additionally, whereas Marx related alienation to the means of production, Weber argued that it was the growing reliance on bureaucracy that was the cause of modern alienation.

Bureaucracy refers to an organizational model designed to perform tasks rationally and efficiently. Global capitalism that spurred the shift from agriculture to industry both influenced bureaucracy and helped develop and refine bureaucratic principles.

Although Weber was also critical of capitalism, he put more emphasis on the economic benefits of capitalism than Marx did. The efficiency provided through the creation of bureaucracy increased production and made it less expensive, thus making goods less expensive for everyone concerned and increasing the standards of living for all.

Weber identified six characteristics of bureaucracy that make it work efficiently and rationally. *First*, bureaucracies rely on specialization. Each person within a bureaucratic structure specializes in one or two tasks. Each person becomes an expert at accomplishing that specialized task and rarely shifts to another task. *Second*, bureaucracies are organized hierarchically, with a very few people at the top and many workers at the bottom. Each person is told who to report to—usually the person immediately above him or her. *Third*, bureaucracies guide their operations using numerous rules and regulations. Usually, these are codified and strictly enforced. Workers are expected to know and abide by the rules of the organization as a means of achieving consistent and efficient results. *Fourth*, officials in a bureaucracy have the technical competence to meet or exceed the expectations of the organization. Rather than hire workers indiscriminately, bureaucracies seek out the most competent workers, monitor them closely, and evaluate them using objective, impersonal, task-related measures.

This impersonality translates beyond evaluations, however. The *fifth* characteristic of bureaucracy is that it places more value on the rules of the organization than on the individual. This ensures that all people within the organization are given the same expectations and are evaluated and treated in the same way. Similarly, clients are also treated in accordance with a customary set of procedures that are designed to standardize interactions with clients. *Finally*, bureaucracy tracks all of its movements by a formal process of paperwork and recordkeeping. This is designed as an efficiency measure but also as a means of protecting the bureaucracy and improving performance in the long run.

All of these characteristics of bureaucracies are designed to lead to rational, efficient, and predictable outcomes. The proliferation of bureaucracies led Weber to argue that society was becoming increasingly rationalized. Weber identified the **rationalization of society** as the historical process by which rationality replaced tradition as the main mode of human thought. No longer are things done in a certain way because that is the way they have always been done. Instead, things are done in a manner that accomplishes the task with the least amount of effort and cost.

The bureaucratic process also helps the organization successfully navigate the **organizational environment**. This is defined as factors external to an organization that affect its operation and outcomes. Some examples include the society's political and economic systems, available workforce, level of technological development, other organizations, current events, and the basic values of that society. For example, how a company structures its bureaucratic operations is in part a response to the political and economic climate. Societies with greater regulation

The lumpenproletariat *was Marx's term for the dispossessed, disabled, and those unable to earn a living.*

© Xavier Marchant/Dreamstime.com

Bureaucracy An organizational model designed to perform tasks rationally and efficiently.

Rationalization of society The historical process by which rationality replaced tradition as the main mode of human thought.

Organizational environment Factors external to an organization that affect its operation.

FIGURE 4-4 Max Weber agreed with Marx that capitalism can be alienating but disagreed about why.

© Keystone Pictures USA/Alamy

How do cubicles function in a bureaucratic setting to dehumanize and alienate workers?

© Jupiterimages/Photos.com/Thinkstock

Emotion regulation The idea that businesses try to regulate the emotions of their workers.

Iron cage of bureaucracy Limitations on creativity and flexibility that are placed on workers by the bureaucratic process that causes alienation.

Bureaucratic ritualism Rigid focusing on rules and regulations that undermine an organization's goals.

Bureaucratic inertia The tendency of a bureaucracy to perpetuate itself over time.

of industry typically breed businesses with more bureaucracy because the business must embed additional layers of bureaucracy in order to effectively deal with the regulatory climate. Conversely, during an economic recession, the structure of the business may be streamlined to eliminate redundancy in the bureaucratic structure in order to reduce operating costs. Similarly, businesses can use new technologies to more effectively conduct business, as well as to more effectively manage their workforces. Technology improves the accuracy of doing business as well as provides new opportunities for cost cutting and growth.

For Weber, a perfect bureaucracy would regulate every activity. In fact, as Arlie Hochschild (1983) noted, businesses have even gone so far as to practice **emotion regulation**. That is, businesses try to regulate the emotions that their workers feel in order to improve the customers' perception of the business. An example of this can be seen among salesmen. They smile and act enthusiastic as they try to sell you their products. They do this even when they may be feeling down or depressed. Their happiness and enthusiasm are more than simply an act—they are an expectation of the employer, the employee, and the person who will be buying the product. Even more illustrative of this phenomenon are the workers at theme parks. As enclaves of fun, theme parks require employees to reflect the values of the theme park, regardless of personal circumstance. Employees dressed as popular characters must display a cheerful disposition even in the midst of personal crisis. Employees are often evaluated on their demeanor as part of their performance evaluation. In this way, employers attempt to regulate how their employees feel as well as how they act.

At the same time that Weber touted the efficiency of bureaucracy as a model of productivity and consistency, he also recognized that bureaucracy came with unique problems. One of the main problems that Weber identified is the tendency of a bureaucracy to dehumanize the people who work within its boundaries. Unlike Marx's alienation that is tied to the means of production, Weber's alienation is tied to the rigid rule orientation of bureaucratic structures. In bureaucracies, the rules become the defining feature of organization. These rules are interpreted consistently and rigidly. In many ways, the rules become more important than the person who is enforcing them. In fact, the unique talents of the individual become lost in the rigid enforcement of the rules. This inability to bring creativeness and flexibility to the workplace Weber termed the *iron cage of rationality*. It is this iron cage that causes alienation. The iron cage is not limited to the employees, of course. It applies to customers as well when rigid enforcement of the rules leads to the inability to meet the personal needs of the customer. Owners and managers are often limited by the **iron cage of bureaucracy** as well, making it more difficult to adapt to circumstances, thus constraining the ability of business to meet changing market demands.

Often, the rigidity that emerges in bureaucracies can hurt the organization. As society changes, businesses need to be able to adapt to changing technologies and changing social values. In many cases, situations change faster than formalized bureaucratic structures. When this happens, the bureaucracy that was designed to act efficiently often becomes highly inefficient and incapable of coping with a changing organizational environment. Sociologist Robert Merton built on Weber's early analysis of bureaucracies, coining the term **bureaucratic ritualism** to refer to the rigid adherence to rules and regulations that ultimately undermines an organization's goals. Rather than remaining a means to an end, the regulations of the bureaucracy become an end in themselves. This leads to **bureaucratic inertia**, which is the tendency of a bureaucracy to perpetuate itself over time. For example, according to the Government Accountability Office (2011), there are dozens of redundant programs in the United Stated federal government, including 82 programs to help improve teacher quality, 56 programs to help people understand finances, and 15 that oversee food safety. Another example is the Department of Agriculture, which maintains offices in every county in the United States to oversee agricultural production despite the fact that fewer than 15% of counties have working farms. Of course, the Department of Agriculture defends this action by noting that the original purpose of aiding farmers has grown to include environmental research and nutrition awareness. This **mission drift**, the tendency of formal organizations to shift their goals for their own survival, is another characteristic of bureaucracies.

Another disadvantage of bureaucracies was identified in 1915 by German sociologist Robert Michels. He noted that the hierarchy of leadership and responsibility that causes bureaucracies to operate efficiently can also weaken governmental democracy. Individuals at the top can and often do use their power to promote their own interests rather than the interests of the organization. Their position of dominance and influence tends to insulate them from public scrutiny and government investigation. Thus, Michels's **iron law of oligarchy** states that bureaucracy always means the rule of the many by the few.

More recently, sociologist George Ritzer has written an account of how deeply bureaucratic principles have become embedded in modern life. In his book *The McDonaldization of Society* (1996), Ritzer argues that the principles of bureaucracy outlined by Weber have led to a restriction of personal choice. The ideals of bureaucracy have been fulfilled, according to Ritzer, as society has become more efficient and rationalized and less concerned with quality. Ritzer shows how bureaucratic principles have infiltrated everything from food to education and the news.

Discussion of the drawbacks of bureaucracy shows that rationalization is perhaps easy to achieve but difficult to maintain. As bureaucratic systems formalize, they often lose creativity and flexibility needed to succeed in a changing organizational environment. This leads to a facelessness of bureaucracy and a rigid reliance on rules and regulations. In many ways, people come to work for the bureaucracies rather than the bureaucracies working for the people.

Weber wrote his analysis of bureaucracies largely as a response to Marx. However, the two views are not mutually exclusive. That is, both may be correct. At the core, they agree that modern life is alienating. They disagree, however, on what causes this alienation. As already noted, Weber's theories have been expanded over the years. His analysis of bureaucracies has proven invaluable in understanding modern life from both a microsociological and a macrosociological point of view. Through Weber's writings, we have a clearer picture of how institutions in society change and how those changes affect the behaviors of individuals in those societies.

Sociologist Arlie Hochschild discussed how employers attempt to regulate the emotions of workers.
© PhotoDisc

Society from a Functionalist Perspective

As the last remnants of feudalism collapsed, global capitalism, fueled by industry, brought about rapid and radical social change. Traditional assumptions about the nature of society were fundamentally altered or were no longer valid. People were moving from the countryside, where they had worked as peasant farmers, into the cities as they sought new economic opportunities brought about by the boom in industry and its accompanying need for labor.

In all, this industrial revolution improved the quality of life for most people. Even the urban poor were generally better off than those who remained in the countryside (Ridley 2010). However, at the same time that the quality of life improved, the gap between the very rich and the very poor widened considerably. In addition, poverty was now more visible because it was concentrated in cities. These social changes disconcerted many people, including early sociologists, who sought to explain the changes in an effort to improve conditions for the urban working poor.

Mission drift The tendency of formal organizations to shift their goals for their own survival.

Iron law of oligarchy An idea, developed by Robert Michels, that suggests that bureaucracy always means the rule of the many by the few.

Gemeinschaft Tönnies's term for societies based on a strong sense of community developed around strong traditions about how members of the village should interact.

Gesellschaft Tönnies's term for a society based on individual self-interest.

Mechanical solidarity Durkheim's term for societies based on strong moral values and a deep sense of community among members.

Tönnies used the term gemeinschaft to refer to close-knit societies with deeply rooted traditions.

© Sam DCruz/Shutterstock, Inc.

Organic solidarity Durkheim's term for societies based on individualism, specialization, and interdependence.

Ferdinand Tönnies

German sociologist Ferdinand Tönnies FIGURE 4-5 was one of the first to write about the radical social changes that were occurring in Europe during the 1800s. Tönnies wanted to understand how life in the newly expanding cities differed from life in rural villages. Through his insightful comparison, Tönnies developed two terms that capture the distinction between life in the city and life in rural areas.

Tönnies argued that rural villages were tightly knit communities. Each person in the village had to rely on every other person in the village for survival and success. This led to a strong sense of community developed around strong traditions about how members of the village should interact. For Tönnies, the entire village was a single primary group. Tönnies called these types of societies **gemeinschaft**.

As people moved to the cities, the sense of gemeinschaft was gradually lost. People became more individualized and dependent upon themselves for their livelihoods. Rather than seeking to improve the entire community, individuals in the cities seek to satisfy their own needs and interests. Tönnies called this type of society **gesellschaft**. The sense of community that permeates small villages is lost in the city. People associate with one another not because they desire the familiarity of interaction but rather because the other person has something that the individual sees as fulfilling a specific immediate need. Thus, Tönnies saw the city as weakening close, long-lasting primary ties in favor of impersonal secondary relationships.

Emile Durkheim

Durkheim FIGURE 4-6 was a French sociologist who was greatly influenced by the work of Tönnies. Durkheim agreed with Tönnies that city life differed in fundamental ways from life in the country. However, Durkheim disagreed with the assertion that people living in cities lack social bonds. Rather, Durkheim suggests that people in cities simply organize their social lives differently than people living in rural areas.

Durkheim believed that people in rural societies operated under a system of **mechanical solidarity**. In such societies, social bonds are based on shared moral values and a deep sense of community among members. Like a finely tuned machine, all of the parts must work together if society is to function as it should. However, in cities, mechanical solidarity gives way to another way of organizing social life. **Organic solidarity** occurs when people organize their social bonds around a sense of individualism,

FIGURE 4-5 Ferdinand Tönnies tried to understand the changes that were happening during the industrial revolution.

© Mary Evans Picture Library/Alamy

FIGURE 4-6 Emile Durkheim explored how the values of the city differ from the values held in rural communities.

© Bettmann/CORBIS

Tönnies contrasted his close-knit societies with societies based on self-interest, which he termed gesellschaft *communities.*

© Photos.com

specialization, and interdependence. While more traditional societies were based on similarities, the new urban life style is based on differences.

For Durkheim, this change had many negative consequences, such as a disconnect from the dominant norms of society—what Durkheim called **anomie**. This anomie is a result of increased role specialization and individualism that accompanies life in an industrial society. Yet organic solidarity has some positive effects as well. For example, urban societies are often more diverse and tolerant than traditional societies. Urban societies also offer more opportunities for personal choice and privacy than in traditional societies.

Anomie A feeling of normlessness caused by a disconnect from the dominant norms of society.

CONCEPT LEARNING CHECK 4.4   How Societies Function

Answer the following questions.

1. List the three classes identified by Marx in order from lowest to highest.

2. Tönnies's term for societies with tightly knit communities that have strong traditions about how members should interact is:

   A. gemeinschaft.

   B. organic solidarity.

   C. gesellschaft.

   D. mechanical solidarity.

3. Durkheim's term for societies with deep social bonds based on shared moral values and a deep sense of community is:

   A. gemeinschaft.

   B. organic solidarity.

   C. gesellschaft.

   D. mechanical solidarity.

4. Tönnies's term for societies based on individual self-interest is:

   A. gemeinschaft.

   B. organic solidarity.

   C. gesellschaft.

   D. mechanical solidarity.

5. Durkheim's term for societies with organizational bonds based around a sense of individualism, specialization, and interdependence is:

   A. gemeinschaft.

   B. organic solidarity.

   C. gesellschaft.

   D. mechanical solidarity.

4.5 Social Interaction from a Microsociological Perspective

Microsociological frameworks offer important insights into how societies are developed and maintained over time.

- Recognize the principles of microsociological analysis and its impact on the beliefs, values, and behaviors of individuals.

For most of this chapter, we have explored sociology through a macrosociological perspective. However, there are many valuable insights that can be gained from looking at face-to-face interaction among individuals and small groups. Microsociological analysis can span any one of three basic interactive frameworks: individual-to-individual interaction, individual-to-small group interaction, or interactions between small groups. While not the only way to approach microsociological interaction, by far the most common theoretical perspective to analyze microsociological interaction is the symbolic interactionist perspective.

Recall that the symbolic interactionist perspective is a theoretical approach that explores how people use symbols to interact with one another. The terms we give to the things around us and how we understand those terms influence our beliefs and behaviors. This aspect of the social structure is vital to gain a full understanding of how society works. Of course, there are too many specific aspects of interaction to cover here, so we will look at some of the more basic and prevalent aspects of microsociological interaction. We shall explore stereotyping, personal space, and facial expressions.

Stereotypes

Stereotype A general assumption that a person holds about a particular group of people.

Personal space Space surrounding a person that, when violated, causes discomfort.

A **stereotype** refers to general assumptions that someone holds about a particular group of people. Stereotypes may be true or false. They may also be negative or positive. More importantly, stereotypes shape the ways in which we interact with one another because they frame many of our first impressions of others. For example, we will no doubt interact differently with individuals who belong to groups that have made a positive impression on us than groups that have made a negative impression.

There are many characteristics that can form the basis of stereotypes. Often, these are noticeable physical features that inform us about the person. For example, race is often used to make evaluations about a person's competencies or beliefs. We may also form evaluations and stereotypes based on sex, age, and attractiveness. There are even stereotypes around hair color, often presented as jokes.

Although we like to think that we do not think in terms of stereotypes, the pervasiveness of stereotypes is embedded deeply in society and shapes our understandings of the world indirectly. Stereotypes have deep roots in our biological and cultural ancestry. Stereotypes often persist because they are functional or useful in terms of how we interact. Consider that if stereotypes did not exist, every individual would be required to make separate evaluations for every person he or she met. The investment in time and resources that this would require would make much of our interaction prohibitive. Stereotypes streamline the process of evaluation to make interaction predictable. Of course, stereotypes are sometimes inaccurate and even offensive. However, they help us streamline social interactions well enough that the benefits usually outweigh the costs. Thus, it is unlikely that we will ever eliminate stereotypes from the repertoire of human behavior.

Personal Space

Each of us has a space around us, defined by an invisible boundary. When this boundary is violated, we feel discomfort. For some people, this **personal space** is small. For others, this personal space is quite large. However big the personal space is, each person goes to great lengths to protect that space. As a simple experiment, see how close you can get to a friend without touching her or him. As you do so, notice how the person's body language changes. Usually, it will not take long for the subject of your experiment to become visibly uncomfortable with the invasion of personal space. As another example, observe the distance between people as they stand in line at the supermarket or at the post office.

Of course, we do allow some people into our personal space. For instance, when we hug, kiss, or touch people we are close to, they cross the boundaries of our personal space. Yet we often go through great pains to keep other people out of our personal space. In this way, our personal space acts as a way to categorize people into primary or secondary groups.

The amount of personal space that is typical for a person varies from culture to culture. Anthropologist Edward Hall (1959) studied personal space in a variety of cultures. His research showed great variation among cultures in the amount of personal space that their members maintained. For example, many hunter-gatherer tribes get very close to one another when they speak, often coming close to having their faces touch. To those in industrial societies, this would likely be extremely uncomfortable. In most Western societies, our personal space is much larger.

Hall noticed that in Western society, there are four levels of personal space—what Hall termed distance zones FIGURE 4-7. The zone closest to our bodies is called intimate distance. This usually extends about 18 inches beyond our bodies and is reserved for intimate contact. From about 18 inches to about 4 feet is the zone of personal distance. This distance is typically reserved for friends and acquaintances. It is also the distance used for normal conversations. Social distance encompasses from about 4 feet to 12 feet and is the appropriate distance for formal contacts, such as a job interview. Finally, the zone beyond 12 feet, called public distance, is used to separate people in highly formal and structured circumstances. For example, this distance is often used to separate a speaker from his or her audience. Not surprisingly, levels of discomfort increase as violations of space move toward the inner zones.

Facial Expressions and Body Language

There is considerable research to suggest that many facial expressions are innate. First studied scientifically by Charles Darwin (1872), the evidence suggests that many facial

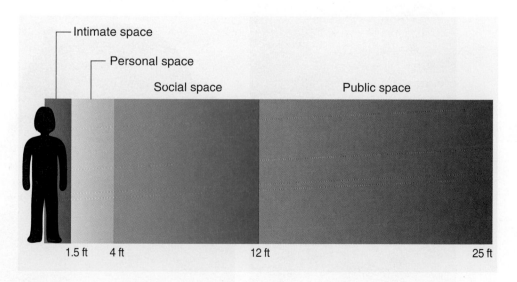

FIGURE 4-7 Hall identified four levels of personal space—called distance zones— to mark different aspects of social interaction.
Source: Data from Hall, Edward T. 1966. The Hidden Dimension. *Garden City, NY: Doubleday.*

Intimate space
Personal space
Social space
Public space

1.5 ft   4 ft   12 ft   25 ft

FIGURE 4-8 Many, though not all, facial expressions have the same meanings across cultures.
Reproduced with permission from John van Wyhe ed. The Complete Work of Charles Darwin Online. (http://darwin-online.org.uk/)

expressions are the same in similar circumstances, even across cultures. Even more compelling is the fact that people who are born blind and who have therefore never seen facial expressions exhibit socially appropriate facial expressions themselves. These facial expressions also tend to have similar meanings across cultures FIGURE 4-8. Body language also has an innate component. Numerous gestures and body postures have similar meanings regardless of the culture in which they appear. Indeed, some of the most common gestures and facial expressions can also be seen in our ape cousins, suggesting deep evolutionary roots FIGURE 4-9 (Corballis 2002; Darwin 1872).

However, this does not mean that all facial expressions or gestures are innate. There does appear to be some body language that is unique to particular cultures. In fact, the meanings of some gestures vary widely from culture to culture. This can lead to confusion, even frustration, when people from two different cultures attempt to communicate. This illustrates an important assumption of symbolic interactionism: in order to communicate effectively, individuals must have some degree of common understanding.

The importance of body language cannot be overstated. Gestures and body language communicate meaning in interactions. Studies show that between 60 and 90% of the meaning taken from a face-to-face interaction is communicated non-verbally (Burgoon, Buller, and Woodall 1989). Experimental situations in which a person's verbal statements contradict their body language show that people are more likely to believe the body language than the verbal statement (Burgoon, Buller, and Woodall 1989).

Body language and verbal language combine effectively to create and maintain communication between individuals. The benefit of language is that it allows shared meaning to become cumulative. This allows for the creation of complex culture. Language also allows for the maintenance of a shared and common past, as well as understandings of a shared future. Finally, language allows for the creation of common goals, as well as allowing for collaboration and planning toward the accomplishment of those goals. Thus, while nonverbal communication forms the basis of face-to-face interactions, language is vital to the construction of advanced culture.

Dramaturgy

Sociologist Erving Goffman FIGURE 4-10 was a great fan of the theater. He enjoyed watching the actors and actresses on stage bring a drama to life. However, as real as

FIGURE 4-9 We share many common facial expressions with our primate ancestors, suggesting deep evolutionary roots.

(right) © John Sartin/Shutterstock, Inc. (left) © iStockphoto

he may have wanted it to be, Goffman knew, of course, that he was witnessing an act. The actors and actresses were not who they appeared to be on stage—they were playing roles. The scenery and props were only there to make the production more believable. Still, it was all just an act.

Goffman saw the stage as a metaphor for understanding social life. He believed that our interactions—like a play without a defined script—was merely an act. When we interact with others, we play a role. Like the actors and actresses on the stage, however, the person we present is not who we really are. From this metaphor, Goffman developed **dramaturgy** (or dramaturgical analysis) as an approach to microsociological interaction that analyzes social life in terms of the stage.

As we are socialized into our society, we adopt various roles. The roles are accompanied by norms that guide the behavior that is acceptable for each role. Norms are like a script. While there is not necessarily a specific dialogue, the actions of the norm and sometimes even specific terms or jargon are specified for that norm. When we adopt the role, we adopt the script as well. When we encounter someone in the context of the norm, we play the role that has been assigned to us using the script that we have learned through socialization. We go through great lengths to make this performance convincing. For example, a professor may use specific language that is part of his or her role, known as **jargon**, as a part of his or her performance. The specialized nature of jargon is meant to confirm or certify this person in his or her role. The professor may also don a tie in an effort to differentiate himself from other roles at the university as part of his performance. Such "props" offer detail, context, and verisimilitude to the performance.

Yet what the students in the classroom see is just that—a performance. Like watching a play, the students see only the **front stage behaviors**. That is, they see only those behaviors that are part of the role being played. The professor likely has a life that the students never see, comprising many roles. These **back stage behaviors** may be very different from the tie-wearing, stuffy professor that students are used to. As a father or husband, the professor may act very differently. Of course, for his family, these roles constitute front stage behavior, while his backstage behavior may be his behavior in the classroom. Thus, the same setting may serve as a backdrop for both front stage and back stage behaviors, depending upon the audience.

When we play a role onstage, a script is usually provided. Social scripts are somewhat different, however. Although social scripts do provide us with a template for the role, they also permit a great deal of flexibility. **Role performance**, the way in which we play a particular role, is best thought of as the way in which we improvise a scene within a given framework. While the script sets the limits of an acceptable performance, we are free to improvise within those limits. Goffman noted that people often become the roles that they play. In other words, people adopt the roles they play often as part of their self-concept. Research suggests that when people exit roles that once played a key part in defining them, a period of confusion follows in which the individual struggles with maintaining a sense of identity (Ebaugh 1988).

Goffman noted that the way in which we interact with others loosely follows the process an actor goes through on stage. As the curtain goes up, you find yourself on stage. Around you are scenery and props that set the mood and give clues to the upcoming scene. You begin to deliver lines and use the scenery to enhance the performance. These three elements—social setting, scenery, and appearance—act as **sign-vehicles** that communicate the message of your performance effectively. Your body language and facial expressions coincide with your lines, making the performance seem more real. Of course, this is not a one-person play. There are usually other people involved in the performance as well. **Teamwork** refers to two or more people working together to make the performance more realistic and appropriate.

Usually, the performance is convincing and appropriate. However, on occasion, a performance lacks one or more elements. In such cases, the performance may draw a negative reaction from the audience. Actors will often engage in **face-saving behavior** in an attempt to salvage a performance that is going wrong. For example, when something does not go according to plan, a joke is often told to make light of the situation.

FIGURE 4-10 Erving Goffman developed dramaturgy, which analyzes interaction in terms of performance.

© Courtesy of The American Sociological Association

Dramaturgy A microsociological approach that analyzes social life in terms of the stage.

Jargon Specialized language that indicates the authenticity of the person in the role.

Front stage behavior Behaviors that are part of the role being played.

Back stage behavior Behaviors that are not part of the role being played.

Role performance The way in which a person plays a particular role within a given framework.

Sign-vehicles Elements that communicate the message of a performance, comprised of the social setting, scenery, and appearance.

Teamwork Two or more people working together to make a performance more realistic or appropriate.

Face-saving behavior Actions that seek to salvage a performance that is going wrong.

Sign-vehicles such as social setting, scenery, and appearance all contribute to the authenticity of the performance.

© AbleStock

This makes the audience feel better, as well as relieving stress the actor feels, having made an error in performance.

Goffman saw **impression management** as the core of dramaturgy. Just as an actor's goal is to convince the audience that the performance reflects reality, an individual playing a role in a social interaction will try to control the performance such that others are convinced by the performance. Using these techniques, individuals performing a particular role try to control the impressions that others form about them.

The Social Construction of Reality

The social construction of reality forms the cornerstone of the symbolic interaction approach. Through interaction, individuals in groups develop background assumptions that influence how they see the world around them. These background assumptions influence how the individuals interpret and understand the world around them. How people see and understand events depends in large part on the background assumptions that they hold. To put it another way, reality is socially constructed.

Sociologist W. I. Thomas took the concept of the social construction of reality even further. He argued that while our understandings of the world may be fluid, the effects of those understandings are very real. In other words, the Thomas theorem states that situations that are defined as real are real in their consequences.

One classic example of the Thomas theorem comes from the national oil shortages in 1973. One rumored effect of the oil shortage was that there would be a shortage of toilet paper. Because of the pervasiveness of this rumor, people began to stockpile toilet paper, thus helping to create the very shortage they feared.

Ethnomethodology

Another way of looking at the effects of the social construction of reality is through **ethnomethodology**. Usually considered a type of symbolic interactionism, this approach seeks to understand how individuals make sense of the everyday surroundings in their social world. **Background assumptions** are understandings of the way the world works that are deeply embedded in our social understanding. For example, imagine your reaction if you were to walk into your sociology class and your instructor began class by trying to sell you a blender. Some students would probably laugh, but most would not know how to respond. This is because the professor has violated the background assumptions for that social situation.

Harold Garfinkel FIGURE 4-11 founded the ethnomethodological approach by completing a series of experiments that show the importance of background assumptions on performance. Garfinkel asked his students to violate background assumptions and note the reactions. In one case, he asked students to pretend to be guests in their own homes. Students asked to go to the bathroom, called their parents "mister" and "missus," and spoke only when spoken to. In another experiment, students were instructed to violate a friend's personal space by getting as close to him or her as possible without touching and by staring directly at the person. In each of these cases, the reactions of the audience ranged from bewilderment to confusion and even anger. These reactions show how important background assumptions are in maintaining performance. Thus, there is more to performance than merely knowing lines. Body language is also important. But so are the assumptions and expectations of the audience watching the performance.

In sum, microsociological approaches reveal that the social structure operates not only through large-scale social institutions but also on the level of the individual. Microsociological interactions form an important part of the social structure, guiding and framing interactions.

FIGURE 4-11 Sociologist Harold Garfinkel developed the technique of ethnomethodology to understand how background assumptions contribute to social interaction.

Photo credit: Arlene Garfinkel

Ethnomethodology and the Development of the Sociological Imagination

Ethnomethodology provides some fascinating insights into the development of the sociological imagination. Much of our understanding of our social world is built upon the multiple background assumptions and ritual interactions that are the subject of ethnomethodological study. Our social experiences are often strongly influenced by these seemingly meaningless interactions. For example, when you shop at a grocery store, you may be welcomed by someone at the door. As you approach the checkout counter, you are asked by the cashier "How are you today?" or "Did you find everything all right?" These seemingly innocuous interactions do serve an important purpose, however.

Large grocery store chains are large, impersonal entities. They go out of their way to cultivate an image of caring for their customers in order to give the appearance of having a personal concern for their customers. Ritualistic interactions such as those described above provide social experiences that shape customer impressions of the business. Through repeated experiences, we begin to see the store and the people who work in it more personally—almost as friends. To put it another way, our social experience is shaped by the background interactions that are dictated by the store. Over time, this becomes part of our social history and shapes our understanding of the social world.

Impression management The ways in which an individual playing a role will try to control the performance such that others are convinced by the performance.

Ethnomethodology A type of symbolic interactionism that seeks to understand how individuals make sense of their everyday surroundings.

Background assumptions Understandings of the way the world works that are deeply embedded in our social understanding.

CONCEPT LEARNING CHECK 4.5   Social Interaction from a Microsociological Perspective

Identify the following components of dramaturgy.

1. Attempts to control the performance so that others are convinced by the performance are called _____.

2. The way in which a person plays a particular role within a given context is known as _____.

3. Elements such as social setting, scenery, and appearance that communicate the message of a performance effectively are called _____.

4. Garfinkel's approach that seeks to understand the social world through an understanding of background assumptions is _____.

5. The way in which people make sense of the everyday surroundings in their social world is called _____.

Visual Overview The Social Structure

Sociologists organize their thinking about social structure into six categories. Understanding the meaning and nature of each category gives you a solid grasp of the way sociologists think about society.

Culture
Culture refers to the beliefs, values, behaviors, and objects that constitute a society's way of life.

Social Class
Social class is a broad measure of the place that a person occupies in the social structure, determined primarily by income, education, and occupational prestige.

Social Institutions
Social institutions are permanent patterns of roles and rules through which major social functions are performed.

Social Structure
The social structure might be understood as a system organized by a pattern of relationships.

Social Status
Social status is the relative position that a person holds within a group or society.

Groups
Groups consist of individuals who share common beliefs and values and who regularly interact with one another and are working toward a common goal.

Role
Sociologists define a role as the behaviors that accompany a status; a person learns and acts out the expected behaviors associated with each position.

Visual Summary Society, Social Structure, and Social Interaction

4.1 Levels of Sociological Analysis

- There are three basic levels of sociological analysis.
- Macrosociology explores how large social institutions impact human beliefs, values, and behaviors.
- Microsociology analyzes the ways in which individual interaction influences the beliefs, values, and behaviors of individuals.

- Mesosociology approaches social analysis as a bridge between the macrosociological and microsociological levels of analysis.

4.2 Social Interaction at the Macrosociological Level

- *Social structure* refers to patterns or regularities in how people behave and interact with one another.
- *Social class* refers to a broad measure of the place that a person occupies in the social structure based on income and occupational prestige.
- *Status* refers to the position that a person holds in a group.
- There are various kinds of status characteristics that indicate where a person falls in the status hierarchy of a group.

- Roles are behaviors that accompany a status.
- There are several leadership styles in groups that affect how a group functions to complete a task.
- The ways that societies meet their basic needs are known as social institutions.

4.3 Societies, Technology, and Change

- Societies may be defined by their means of subsistence, which usually develop and change over time.
- Hunting and gathering was the dominant means of subsistence until horticulture was introduced 10,000 years ago.
- Horticultural societies subsist primarily from farming with hand tools.
- Pastoral societies subsist primarily through the domestication of animals.

- Agricultural societies farm using machinery driven by advanced forms of energy.
- Industrial societies focus on the production of material goods as a means of subsistence.
- Postindustrial societies subsist through the production of services and information.

4.4 What Holds Societies Together?

- There are a variety of theories to explain the prevalence and pervasiveness of society over time.
- Marx examined the social structure in terms of social conflict, focusing on how groups compete for scarce resources.
- Marx identified three social classes defined by their relationship to the means of production: capitalist, proletariat, and lumpenproletariat.
- Max Weber focused on the ways in which bureaucracy influences modern society.
- Weber identified six characteristics of bureaucracy: a formal hierarchical structure, management by rules, organization by functional specialty, a mission or goal, impersonality, and employment based on technical qualifications.
- Weber documented how bureaucracy influences the operation of society and individual behavior.
- Tönnies documented how societies change from community-based societies to individualistic societies as they urbanize, introducing the terms *gesellschaft* and *gemeinschaft* to describe this transition.
- Durkheim documented how societies change from community-oriented to individualistic as they develop and modernize.

4.5 Social Interaction from a Microsociological Perspective

- Most microsociological analysis is conducted through the symbolic interactionist perspective.
- *Stereotypes* refer to general assumptions that someone holds about a particular group of people.
- Edward Hall identified four levels of personal space that influence interactions.
- Much of human interaction is conducted nonverbally.
- Goffman developed dramaturgical analysis as an approach to microsociological interaction that analyzes social life in terms of performance.
- Ethnomethodology seeks to understand how individuals make sense of the everyday surroundings in their social world.

4.1 Levels of Sociological Analysis

1. Lydia is conducting a study that examines how the military influences the way in which people think about society. Which level of sociological analysis is Lydia is using?

- **A.** Microsociological
- **B.** Mesosociological
- **C.** Macrosociological
- **D.** Ethnomethodological

2. Aris wants to understand how a professor's gestures affect learning outcomes for students. Aris is conducting research at which level of analysis?

- **A.** Microsociology
- **B.** Mesosociology
- **C.** Macrosociology
- **D.** Ethnomethodology

4.2 Social Interaction at the Macrosociological Level

3. Oscar and Grover have similar education, similar incomes, and work at similar jobs. Oscar and Grover share a similar:

- **A.** status.
- **B.** culture.
- **C.** society.
- **D.** social class.

4. Mavis just received a degree in sociology. This is an example of:

- **A.** achieved status.
- **B.** master status.
- **C.** ascribed status.
- **D.** diffuse status.

5. Chloe has been asked to be the foreman of a jury in a criminal case because she has served on a jury twice before. This is an example of:

- **A.** ascribed status.
- **B.** specific status.
- **C.** master status.
- **D.** diffuse status.

6. Rachel has just gotten engaged to a dentist. She shows her friends the large engagement ring on her finger, indicating her new position in life. The ring is an example of:

- **A.** ascribed status.
- **B.** master status.
- **C.** status symbol.
- **D.** role strain.

7. Tyler is a star football player for his college. However, the demands of football practice do not leave him enough time to pursue his academic studies. This is an example of:

- **A.** master status.
- **B.** role strain.
- **C.** diffuse status.
- **D.** role conflict.

8. Aimee is responsible for making sure her group finishes the task on time. She takes personal charge of the group, dictates each group member's task, and monitors them closely. Aimee's leadership style would best be described as:

- **A.** expressive leadership.
- **B.** authoritarian leadership.
- **C.** democratic leadership.
- **D.** laissez-faire leadership.

4.3 Societies, Technology, and Change

9. Tony is an archaeologist who has discovered the site of a previously unknown civilization. Tony digs up pieces of pottery, tools, and clothing. He is attempting to understand the civilization through its:

- **A.** means of subsistence.
- **B.** leadership style.
- **C.** material culture.
- **D.** symbolic culture.

10. Akmu is a young girl learning how to choose ripe berries to eat while leaving the unripe berries alone. Akmu learns that this means there will always be berries in the future. Akmu is learning:

- **A.** gathering techniques.
- **B.** hunting strategies.
- **C.** pastoral techniques.
- **D.** optimal foraging strategy.

11. Akbar uses his hand tools to cultivate the field and harvest einkorn wheat. Akbar likely lives in what kind of society?

- **A.** Industrial
- **B.** Agricultural
- **C.** Horticultural
- **D.** Pastoral

12. Ernest works in a factory that produces engines for large trucks. Ernest makes his living through:

- **A.** pastoralism.
- **B.** hunting and gathering.
- **C.** industry.
- **D.** postindustrialism.

4.4 What Holds Societies Together?

13. Phillip owns a factory. According to Karl Marx, Phillip is a member of what social class?
    A. Lumpenproletariat
    B. Bourgeoisie
    C. Proletariat
    D. Capitalist

14. Orville works in a factory assembling parts. Marx would classify Orville in what social class?
    A. Lumpenproletariat
    B. Bourgeoisie
    C. Proletariat
    D. Capitalist

15. Wilbur is disabled and unable to work. Marx would classify Wilbur as what social class?
    A. Lumpenproletariat
    B. Bourgeoisie
    C. Proletariat
    D. Capitalist

16. Willie works as a server in a restaurant. His employer expects him to smile and be polite to customers, even when he is having a bad day. This is an example of:
    A. iron cage of bureaucracy.
    B. rationalization of society.
    C. emotion regulation.
    D. organizational environment.

17. Clarence lives in a small town. In this town, everyone knows everyone else, and there is a strong sense of community as people help each other out as needed. Durkheim would say that this community operates under a system of:
    A. gesellschaft.
    B. organic solidarity.
    C. gemeinschaft.
    D. mechanical solidarity.

4.5 Social Interaction from a Microsociological Perspective

18. Everyone in his class believes that Li Fau is good at math because he is of Asian descent. This belief is an example of a:
    A. prejudice.
    B. stereotype.
    C. front stage behavior.
    D. background assumption.

19. Edric was very surprised to see his teacher at the local grocery store wearing shorts, flip-flops, and a wrinkled t-shirt, talking on his cell phone. Edric got a rare glimpse into his teacher's:
    A. back stage behavior.
    B. impression management.
    C. face-saving behavior.
    D. front stage behavior.

CHAPTER ESSAY QUESTIONS

1. Discuss the ways in which the emergence of horticulture accelerated the pace of cultural change.

2. Discuss why leaders usually exhibit instrumental leadership qualities or expressive leadership qualities, but rarely both.

CHAPTER DISCUSSION QUESTIONS

1. Societies are always changing. What kind of society do you think will emerge after postindustrialism? Why do you think so?

2. Race and gender have traditionally been considered diffuse status characteristics. Yet with increasing equality among races and between genders, do you think that race and gender will always function as diffuse status characteristics? Why?

3. What are the macrosociological, mesosociological, and microsociological affects of Facebook on society?

4. Share with the class how your *life chances* are influenced by the social structure. Based on your and others' viewpoints, which of the six components of the social structure appear to be the most pervasive?

5. Imagine yourself winning the Mega Million Lotto. How would winning the lotto affect your master status? Share with the class how you would cope with status inconsistency or role conflict. Do any patterns emerge in your class discussion? How many people would attempt to isolate themselves from the public?

6. What evidence exists today that we are undergoing societal changes that push us into a new type of society? How do you think people will refer to this new society? What new social institutions might emerge?

7. What might be some functions of celebrity gossip in a gesellschaft or organic society? Make a list of 10 characterizations you make within the first few seconds of meeting a person for the first time. How these relate to diffuse characteristics, salient characteristics, status symbols, and stereotypes?

8. Discuss the main components of dramaturgy that can be used to analyze embarrassing situations such as an open pant zipper or smeared lipstick. Why is it difficult to approach some people while we openly make fun of others in awkward situations?

CHAPTER PROJECTS

INDIVIDUAL PROJECTS

1. Write an autobiography of your life with a focus on the six components of the social structure (culture, social class, social status, roles, groups, and social institutions). What patterns do you notice as you reflect on your life thus far?

2. Write a paper analyzing the types of leadership styles. Describe the different types of leadership styles you have experienced and the effectiveness of those leaders (examples may include employers, teachers, camp or club leaders, religious leaders, politicians, etc.). As you prepare yourself for your career, what kind of a leadership style do you think is important for you to practice?

GROUP PROJECTS

1. Design and implement an experiment in ethnomethodology. What background assumption are you exploring? What does your experiment say about these background assumptions?

2. Make a list of popular fast food corporate restaurants and look up their logos online. What two colors are prominent in the logos of nationwide chains? How does this relate to some of the problems of bureaucracies described by Max Weber and George Ritzer? How would Karl Marx analyze this pattern? Write a summary of your discussion.

3. All leadership styles are useful in specific situations. Develop a detailed outline or table of contents for a pamphlet or manual describing each leadership style and when that style is appropriate to use.

3. Choose a favorite food and make a list of the all the different occupations connected to the production, packaging, transportation, and marketing of each of the ingredients in your tasty nourishment. Were you able to complete your list? How many of these goods and services are global? Discuss how this activity is related to the types of societies that exist today, including organic and gesellschaft societies. Write an analysis paper of your group activity and discussion.

CHAPTER KEY TERMS

Achieved status	Horticulture	Prestige
Aggregate	Hunting and gathering	Primary group
Agriculture	Impression management	Proletariat
Alienation	Industry	Rationalization of society
Anomie	Instrumental leadership	Role
Ascribed status	Iron cage of bureaucracy	Role conflict
Authoritarian leaders	Iron law of oligarchy	Role exit
Back stage behavior	Jargon	Role performance
Background assumptions	Laissez-faire leader	Role set
Bureaucracy	Lumpenproletariat	Role strain
Bureaucratic inertia	Macrosociology	Salient characteristics
Bureaucratic ritualism	Master status characteristic	Secondary group
Capitalists	Material culture	Shaming
Cultural lag	Mechanical solidarity	Sign-vehicles
Democratic leaders	Mesosociology	Social class
Diffuse characteristics	Microsociology	Social institutions
Dramaturgy	Mission drift	Social structure
Emotion regulation	Network	Specific characteristics
Ethnomethodology	Nonmaterial culture	Status
Expressive leadership	Optimum foraging strategy	Status inconsistencies
Face-saving behavior	Organic solidarity	Status symbols
Front stage behavior	Organizational environment	Stereotype
Gemeinschaft	Pastoralism	Teamwork
Gesellschaft	Personal space	
Group	Postindustrialism	

ANSWERS TO CONCEPT LEARNING CHECKS

4.1 Levels of Sociological Analysis

1. The education system [A. Macrosociological]
2. Interaction between a police officer and a citizen [C. Microsociological]
3. A neighborhood's block party [B. Mesosociological]
4. A family [C. Microsociological]
5. A child in day care [C. Microsociological]
6. Christianity [A. Macrosociological]

4.2 Social Interaction at the Macrosocial Level

1. Bill gives the group a task, then lets the group function without much direction. [B. Laissez-faire leader]
2. Bill assigns each member of the group a task and monitors their progress closely, often giving each of them direction. [D. Authoritarian leader]
3. Bill seeks input from the members of the group on the best way to accomplish the task. [A. Democratic leader]
4. Whenever a conflict arises in the group, Bill makes a joke and attempts to smooth over differences. [C. Expressive leader]

4.3 Societies, Technology, and Change

1. Hunting and gathering [D. Seeks food by gathering and hunting].
2. Pastoral [B. Animals are domesticated for food and serve as the primary source of calories].
3. Agricultural [F. Farming using powered machinery].
4. Horticultural [E. Farming using hand tools and human labor].
5. Industrial [A. Produces goods using machinery driven by advanced sources of energy].
6. Postindustrial [C. Society primarily produces services and information].

4.4 What Holds Societies Together?

1. List the three classes identified by Marx in order from lowest to highest [Lumpenproletariat, proletariat, capitalists].
2. Tönnies's term for societies with tightly knit communities that have strong traditions about how members should interact is [A. gemeinschaft].
3. Durkheim's term for societies with deep social bonds based on shared moral values and a deep sense of community is [D. mechanical solidarity].
4. Tönnies's term for societies based on individual self-interest is [C. gesellschaft].
5. Durkheim's term for societies with organizational bonds based around a sense of individualism, specialization, and interdependence is [B. organic solidarity].

4.5 Social Interaction from a Microsociological Perspective

1. Attempts to control the performance so that others are convinced by the performance are called [impression management].
2. The way in which a person plays a particular role within a given context is known as [role performance].
3. Elements such as social setting, scenery, and appearance that communicate the message of a performance effectively are called [sign-vehicles].
4. Garfinkel's approach that seeks to understand the social world through an understanding of background assumptions is [ethnomethodology].
5. The way in which people make sense of the everyday surroundings in their social world is called [ethnomethodology].

ANSWERS TO CHAPTER REVIEW TEST

4.1 Levels of Sociological Analysis

1. C. Macrosociology involves the analysis of social life that focuses on how broad features of society, such as the military, impact human beliefs and behavior.
2. A. Microsociological analysis focuses on specific aspects of social interactions.

4.2 Social Interaction at the Macrosociological Level

3. D. Social class is a broad measure of the location that a person occupies in the social structure. It is typically measured by a combination of educational attainment, occupational prestige, and income.
4. A. An achieved status refers to a position earned through effort or activity, such as a college degree.
5. B. A specific status is a status that is particular to the task that the group is dedicated to perform.

6. C. Status symbols are physical objects that identify a particular status.
7. D. Role conflict refers to tension between two or more statuses, such as football player and student.
8. B. Authoritarian leadership is characterized by taking personal charge of the task and dictating the jobs of each of the group members.

4.3 Societies, Technology, and Change

9. C. Material culture refers to the physical items that distinguish a culture.
10. D. Optimal foraging strategy is a pattern of foraging that leaves enough flora and fauna for the land to recover in a reasonable amount of time.
11. C. Horticultural societies are characterized by farming using hand tools.
12. C. Industry refers to a means of subsistence characterized by the production of durable goods.

4.4 What Holds Societies Together?

13. D. According to Marx, individuals who own the means of production are considered capitalists.

14. C. Proletariat is defined as someone who labors in the factories or works other unskilled labor jobs.

15. A. The lumpenproletariat are defined as those who are unable to participate in the labor force.

16. C. Hochschild's emotion regulation states that employers will attempt to regulate the emotions of their employees.

17. D. Durkheim used the term *mechanical solidarity* to refer to communities based on a strong sense of moral values and a deep sense of community.

4.5 Social Interaction from a Microsociological Perspective

18. B. Stereotypes refer to general assumptions that someone holds about a particular group of people.

19. A. Back stage behavior refers to the role performance that is not part of the known role.

ANSWERS TO CHAPTER ESSAY QUESTIONS

1. The transition from hunting and gathering to horticulture changed the direction and pace of culture in several significant ways. First, in contrast to the transience of hunting and gathering cultures, horticultural societies are sedentary. This allows for the accumulation of goods over time, thus making cultural innovation more important. Since the innovation can be stored, it can be passed down more effectively and efficiently to future generations, thus making culture cumulative. In addition, horticultural societies allowed for the creation and storage of surplus food, which increased the opportunities for specialization, thus allowing even more accumulation of innovation over time. Thus, the surplus, coupled with the sedentary life style, allowed for the acceleration of material culture over time that led to the development of new cultural forms and new technologies.

2. Instrumental leaders are concerned with the completion of tasks. Expressive leaders are concerned with the morale of the group. Often, these two goals are in conflict. Successfully dealing with both of these aspects of the group also requires two different skill sets. For example, instrumental leaders must decide what is the best way to accomplish the goal. This may involve a leadership style that temporarily reduces the morale of the group. Decisions that drive forward the completion of the task often require individuals within the group to sacrifice their individual well-being or interest for the good of the group. Such decisions require an understanding of the nature of the task and the talents and abilities of each group member. Expressive leadership requires a different set of skills. Expressive leaders must understand the individual needs of members of the groups, as well as the dynamics of interaction between group members.

REFERENCES

Berger, J., B. P. Cohen, and M. Zelditch. 1972. "Status Characteristics and Social Interaction." *American Sociological Review* 37:241–255.

Burgoon, Judee K., David Buller, and W. Gill Woodall. 1989. *Nonverbal Communication*. New York: Harper and Row.

Corballis, M. 2002. *From Hand to Mouth: The Origins of Language*. Princeton, NJ: Princeton University Press.

Darwin, C. 1872(1965). *The Expression of Emotion in Man and Animals*. Chicago: University of Chicago Press.

Diamond, J. 1999. *Guns, Germs, and Steel: The Fates of Human Societies*. New York: Norton.

Ebaugh, Helen Rose Fuchs. 1988. *Becoming an EX: The Process of Role Exit*. Chicago: University of Chicago Press.

Gerald, D. E., and W. I. Hussar. 2012. Projections of Education Statistics to 2012. *National Center for Education Statistics Annual Report*. Washington,

D.C.: Institute for Education Sciences. Government Accountability Office. 2011. Retrieved October 2011 from http://online.wsj.com/article/SB10001424052748703749504576172942399165436.html.

Griffin, E. 2010. *A Short History of the British Industrial Revolution*. New York: Palgrave.

Hall, Edward. 1959. *The Silent Language*. New York: Doubleday.

Hochschild, A. 1983. *The Managed Heart: Commercialization of Human Feeling*. Berkeley: University of California Press.

Hopcroft, R. L. 2002. "Is Gender Still a Status Characteristic?" *Current Research in Social Psychology* 7(20):339–346.

Ridley, M. 2010. *The Rational Optimist: How Prosperity Evolves*. New York: Harper Collins.

Ritzer, G. 1996. *The McDonaldization of Society*. New York: Pine Forge Press.

Chapter Overview ▼

© Heather Renee Shutterstock, Inc.

5 Groups and Organizations

Learning Objectives ▼

5.1 ■ Define what a social group is and describe types of groups.

5.2 ■ Describe the ways in which individuals interact within a group.
■ Illustrate leadership styles in relation to the group structure.

5.3 ■ Explain how group dynamics influence social interaction.
■ Discuss concepts of group dynamics.

5.4 ■ Describe the role and function of a formal organization.
■ Illustrate types of formal organizations.

5.5 ■ Describe two important ways that organizations are adapting to contemporary environments.

A storm raged outside. Rain pelted the windows and high winds scattered branches through the streets. Thunder roared and lightning flashed. Through the storm, my wife and I decided to stream a movie on our computer. As I popped popcorn in preparation, my wife turned on the computer and attempted to log on to the Internet. It was not long before her disappointed sighs were noticed. The Internet was down due to the storm. There would be no movie. Instead, we read between handfuls of buttered popcorn.

The next day, I called our Internet provider to inform them that our service was out. As I tried to explain about the previous night's fierce storm, I was interrupted by the customer service representative.

"Well, it's probably your router," she said.

"No," I objected. "You see, we had a storm. Service is out. Can you send someone out to fix it?"

"I will have a new router sent to you," she said. When I again protested, she explained that she must follow the protocol for repairs. She could not, she said, send a repair technician until all other options had been exhausted. With my frustration mounting, I again tried to explain about the storm. It was to no avail. The customer service representative was unwilling to violate the company's procedural rules.

Three days without Internet service and the router arrived. I then began the laborious process of setting up the new router. With a new customer service representative on the phone, I was walked through the process step by step. Forty minutes later, the new router was up and running. However, there was still no Internet service.

"Perhaps the router we sent you is bad," suggested the faceless person on the other end of the phone.

"No," I told her. "We had a storm that knocked out service. Can you give me any idea of when service might be restored?" After a long pause, she promised to call me back and let me know.

Two more days passed without any word, and with no restoration of service. As my frustration mounted, my wife began making calls to find out when service would be restored. No one seemed able to give her an answer, although she had several more requests to replace our brand new router. Finally, my wife was contacted by a supervisor, who assured her repeatedly that service would be restored within 24 hours.

When we attempted to log on to the Internet the following day, we found that service still had not been restored. More phone calls, more promises, but no one agreed to have a technician come to our house. Another week passed with no results. Finally, my wife and I had had enough. With a threat to find a new service provider if we did not have Internet in two days, a supervisor finally agreed to send someone to our house to figure out what the problem was.

Late the next day, a friendly technician took just 15 minutes to restore the outside transfer box that had been blown apart in the storm.

I should not have been surprised at the events that transpired. Max Weber predicted that tendency of bureaucracy to focus on rules and regulations even when it threatened the ultimate goal of the organization—in this case, good customer service. The customer service representatives and even the supervisors were unwilling to vary their routine to help a single customer. The process proved more important than the people involved.

Ultimately, the delay in getting our Internet restored cost the company more than it would have had they simply sent a technician out on the first day. My wife and I negotiated a free month of service, plus credit for the days we were without service. We also had a brand new router for our troubles.

At work, I related the story to my colleagues. It seemed that everyone had a story to tell about negative experiences with large bureaucracies. Some told stories about their cell phone companies. Some told stories about their gym memberships. Others told tales of problems with their banks or retirement accounts. Throughout the day, we shared these stories. We had bonded over a common cause—shared a common goal. We had, in short, become a group.

5.1 Types of Social Groups

Sociologists investigate the role of groups in society, offering important insights into this essential component of daily life.

■ Define what a social group is and describe types of groups.

Previously, we have seen how the social structure impacts the development of the sociological imagination by affecting the beliefs, values, and behaviors of the people in a society in a variety of ways. We know that the social structure consists of various components, including social groups. In this chapter, we are going to delve more in depth into social groups in order to gain a more detailed understanding of how these social groups contribute to the development of the sociological imagination.

A **social group** may be defined as two or more people who have something in common and who interact with one another based on that commonality. In other words, groups are people who interact with one another because they share something in common that leads them to interact preferentially with each other. People may choose to interact with one another based on shared interests, such as stamp collecting or a love of science fiction movies. People may also choose to interact with one another because they share a common goal. For example, students may work together because they are assigned the same project or they are on the same sports team. People may also interact with one another because they share common values, such as political or religious affiliation.

Social group Two or more people who have something in common.

Emergent properties Properties of a group that emerge through the process of interaction.

Groups

Because there are many reasons for groups to exist, there are many different kinds of groups. Groups also come in a variety of forms and sizes. Still, while there are many different kinds of groups, there are also many things that groups have in common that exert influence over their members.

When analyzing groups, sociologists often note that the group itself, not the specific members of the group, exerts influence over individual members of the group. That is, the group has properties that emerge in the process of the interaction of its members. These **emergent properties** arise as members of the group continue to interact with one another. As people with common values or interests interact, they gradually come to consensus about the norms of the group. They come to consensus on how members of the group will act around each other and what will happen when those expectations are violated. Groups, therefore, develop their own set of roles and norms for members of the group. Group membership constrains the behaviors of the members of the group in accordance with the emerging rules and norms. These norms may become more important than the members of the group. This can be seen by realizing that the norms of the group will persist even as members of the group change. Many group norms may persist even after all of the original group members have been replaced, testifying to the importance and pervasiveness of emergent properties of groups. Emergent properties are the key defining characteristics of a group.

However, not all group norms emerge in the same way, and the values and expectations of groups may vary from group to group. Indeed, groups can be categorized in a variety of ways. It is important to remember that many of these categorizations are not discrete. That is, groups can be categorized in different ways depending on the criteria used to distinguish them. Different sociologists using different theoretical perspectives are likely to categorize and analyze groups in different ways.

A group is defined as people who interact with one another and who have something in common.

© Igor Karon/Shutterstock, Inc.

FIGURE 5-1 Gordon Allport denied the existence of emergent properties of groups.

© Bettmann/CORBIS

An aggregate is defined as people who occupy the same physical space, but who have nothing in common.

© Purestock/Thinkstock

Aggregate Individuals who temporarily share the same physical space but who do not share a sense of belonging.

Primary group Cooley's term for a group with which we feel a deep sense of belonging or intimacy.

Aggregates

While it might seem obvious that groups exert pressure on the beliefs and behaviors of members, some sociologists take the position that groups and the influence that they hold are more illusory than real. Indeed, some sociologists challenge the notion that groups have emergent properties. Social scientists such as Gordon Allport (1960) FIGURE 5-1 argued that groups—as defined above—do not actually exist. Rather, they insist, groups are merely an aggregate of people, each with their own individual interests that happen to coincide, thus giving the illusion of emergent properties. Because the interests of individuals change over time, emergent properties do not really exist. Instead, what guides interaction is not a constructed normative structure but, rather, a series of momentarily overlapping interests.

Still, most sociologists accept the idea of groups, although it is recognized that not every incidence of interaction constitutes a group. Consider the following example. You are sitting at a bus stop on a rainy day. Several other people have gathered under the canopy of the bus stop, some waiting for the bus, and others just to get out of the rain. By most accounts, this would not be considered a group. Rather, sociologists would classify this chance meeting of people as an aggregate. Sociologically, an **aggregate** is defined as individuals who temporarily share the same physical space but who do not share a sense of belonging. Unlike a group, which is based on mutual interests, goals, or values, members of an aggregate may have nothing more in common than being in the same place at the same time.

Unlike groups, which are seen as having a significant impact on the individual, aggregates often have little or no impact on the development of the sociological imagination. Aggregates may merge into groups, such as when a chance encounter at a bus stop leads to a long-term romantic relationship. But most of the time, aggregates are passing encounters that occur by virtue of chance rather than because of socially significant circumstances.

Primary and Secondary Groups

Sociologist Charles Horton Cooley (1909) FIGURE 5-2 coined the term **primary group** to refer to groups with which we feel a deep sense of belonging or intimacy. Groups such as the family give us our first sense of identity and provide us with our strongest and most enduring socialization. In fact, Cooley referred to primary groups as the "springs of life" because they are essential to our physical, psychological, emotional, and social well-being. Primary groups are essential for the development of our individual identities and form the core of how we understand our larger social world.

Our attachment to primary groups is rooted in our human biology. Humans have evolved as a unique social species. Unlike most primates that have a relatively short childhood and adolescent stage, humans are dependent upon caregivers for a much longer period of time. For most of us, these caregivers are in the form of our family, which provides us with nourishment, security, and protection, as well as teaches us how to care for ourselves. The human brain is wired toward early attachment as a necessary criterion of survival. As the experiments of Harry Harlow reveal, failure to attach to some primary caregiver has disastrous and often irreversible effects in later life.

Cooley contrasted the role of primary groups with secondary groups. **Secondary groups** are larger, more formal and impersonal groups that also affect our socialization. Whereas primary groups inculcate us with our basic values and behaviors, secondary groups expand our understanding of the social world by guiding our roles and norms beyond the limitations of the primary group. For many people in contemporary society, school represents the first exposure to secondary groups. Often, the rules in a classroom are more formal and more impersonal than at home. Thus, a child learns that expectations can differ from one circumstance to the next.

Secondary groups are a necessary part of modern life. However, they do not come without a cost. Secondary groups often put demands on people that can conflict with our attachment to primary groups. For example, when the demands of a career interfere with the demands of a family, the expectations of the secondary group clash with the expectations of our primary group. For an increasing number of people, this is a cause of role conflict, which is defined as tension between two roles. Often, though by no means always, our attachment to our primary group is stronger and offers a welcome respite from the increasing demands of secondary groups. However, the power of secondary groups in the shaping of our beliefs and behaviors should not be underestimated.

One way to think about the difference between primary and secondary groups is through the lens of the sociological imagination. Recall that the sociological imagination develops at the intersection between an individual's personal experiences and the history of her or his society. Our personal experience is shaped largely through our attachment to primary groups, while our historical experiences are shaped by our interactions with secondary groups. Through the process of socialization, influenced by both primary and secondary groups, our sociological imagination develops.

FIGURE 5-2 Charles Horton Cooley described primary group and secondary groups to categorize the way in which groups impact socialization.

Courtesy of The American Sociological Association

In-Groups and Out-Groups

Groups that we belong to or identify with are called **in-groups**. This is contrasted to **out-groups**, groups toward which we feel a sense of competition or antagonism. Because we identify with in-groups, we often feel a strong sense of loyalty to them. We also tend to develop the attitude that groups we have identified as in-groups are superior to other groups, which can then lead to discriminatory practices. Sociologist Robert Merton (1968) FIGURE 5-3 observed that many times traits that we identify as part of an in-group are seen as desirable, while the same trait seen in out-groups is considered undesirable. For example, within the framework of an in-group, tattoos may be seen as a sign of strength and identity, while tattoos observed in an out-group may be seen as showing off.

Thus, the in-group and out-group distinction can be a source of divisiveness. Too often, these distinctions, which are often presented as stereotypes, are used to justify discrimination against particular groups. For example, after the attacks of September 11, 2001, many Americans—from a wide variety of backgrounds—began to view Muslims as violent and sadistic. This caused a wave of prejudice and accompanying discriminatory behavior against Arabs across the United States despite the fact that most Arabs were equally appalled by the attacks. The in-group/out-group distinction that followed the terrorist attacks gained traction as many politicians advocated for violence—and even torture—against suspects who were viewed as the enemy. Mainstream journalism contributed to this attitude by reporting on this and related events around the clock, thus reinforcing the divisiveness.

Of course, the same in-group/out-group distinctions that can lead to divisiveness can also serve to unite. As already mentioned, after the September 11 attacks, Americans of all persuasions temporarily put their differences aside to unite behind a common cause. Groups that normally viewed themselves as adversaries or rivals suddenly became united under a larger cause—liberals and conservatives, Protestants, Jews, Catholics, and Muslims united in a show of solidarity against the attacks. These examples show that the way in which we construct in-group and out-group identification often reflects the circumstances we find ourselves in. That is, these distinctions depend on social factors.

This identification with and loyalty to in-groups means that they often exert a substantial influence over our socialization. We tend to adopt not only the norms and values of the group but also the language and shared understanding of in-groups. However, we should not dismiss the power of out-groups to shape our values, beliefs, and behaviors. As we decide how to divide our loyalties, we solidify our beliefs and values in favor of some views and in opposition to others. Thus, out-groups also serve an important role in the development of our sociological imagination, providing an orientation to our social and cultural history.

Primary groups are closely tied, intimate groups that are essential for the development of our identities.

© Monkey Business Images/Dreamstime.com

Secondary groups Cooley's term for formal, impersonal groups that impact socialization.

In-groups Groups to which we belong or identify with.

Out-groups Groups toward which we feel a sense of competition or antagonism.

Secondary groups are formal, impersonal groups that impact our socialization.

© kristian sekulic/Shutterstock, Inc.

FIGURE 5-3 Robert Merton discussed how our perceptions of groups are shaped by our membership in those groups.

Courtesy of The American Sociological Association

Reference groups Groups by which we gauge ourselves and that act as reference points for future behavior.

Social networks Links that connect people to one another in a web of connections.

Strong ties Ties that link people in a close fashion.

Clique A small group of people who are part of a larger group and who interact with one another as a group in and of themselves.

Reference Groups

Often, we use groups as a standard measure in an effort to evaluate ourselves. This can include family, friends, members of a church, or even a group that you do not belong to. **Reference groups** are an important part of our socialization, as they provide a means of anticipatory socialization. That is, since we often gauge ourselves relative to reference groups, we may begin to dress or act like members of the reference group in anticipation of later becoming a member of that group.

Reference groups are important because they tell us not only who we are but also who we are not. They act as a compass to point us to who we might want to become as we continue to navigate through our social world. In many cases, this has a positive effect, driving us toward the completion of social goals. However, sometimes reference groups can have a negative effect on an individual, as is the case when we are unable to meet the expectations of the reference group. For instance, a student decides that she wants to be a professor of sociology. As a result, she uses her current professors as a reference group, adopting their style of dress, their views of the world, even their language and jargon as a way or preparing herself for graduate school. However, the student soon realizes that her grades are probably not good enough to get into graduate school, and her writing skills are inadequate. In this case, the reference group can become a source of disappointment and even resentment. The student may even begin to project her own inadequacies onto members of the reference group, thus further distancing herself from the group she aspires to join. Reference groups are more likely drawn from in-groups than out-groups. This is because we both identify with and strive to be more like members of in-groups and seek to differentiate ourselves from out-groups.

Thus, reference groups can act as a means of social control, guiding behavior toward a particular end and constraining behavior to the norms and expectations of that particular group. Reference groups can be a source of accomplishment or dejection or a source of conformity or conflict. Reference groups are an important part of our socialization and of our development of the sociological imagination.

It is important to clarify the distinction between these many related terms. Reference groups are groups that we use to evaluate ourselves and often seek to imitate. By contrast, primary groups are groups that we have a strong, intimate connection to. Such a connection may not exist with reference groups. In-groups are a little different still. In-groups are simply groups that we belong to. These may be primary or secondary. We also may or may not belong to reference groups.

Social Networks

Social networks are not groups *per se*. Rather, **social networks** are the links that connect people to one another, like a web of ties that extends outward from a person that can be used to locate her or him in the social world. These ties can take the form of either weak ties or strong ties.

Strong Ties

Strong ties refer to ties that link people closely. Strong ties link an individual to primary groups or other people with whom they interact often. Indeed, strong ties are called strong ties precisely because they link us to people with whom we have a strong relationship. For example, we are usually connected to our primary groups through strong ties—our friends, family, and other people who are connected to us in significant ways. They are connected to us with strong ties—ties that are solid and very hard to break. Strong ties tend to cluster close to the individual. These clusters are called **cliques**. A clique is a small group of people that are part of a larger group and who interact with one another as a group in and of themselves.

Strong ties provide us with secure and definite links to individuals in our social world that we can rely on in most situations. Typically, we consider strong ties to be preferable to weak ties. However, recent research has called this assumption into question.

Often, in-group and out-group distinctions are sources for divisiveness and discrimination.

Weak Ties

Weak ties are links to people with whom we do not interact often or with whom we have weak social relationships. Weak ties may be people we know as acquaintances or friends of friends. Weak ties may be someone you met in passing with a similar interest and with whom you may have exchanged names and addresses. Sociologist Mark Granovetter (1973) FIGURE 5-4 has shown that weak ties can offer us distinct advantages over strong ties.

Although strong ties are more reliable than weak ties, there are usually fewer strong ties than weak ties. The greater number of weak ties means that there may be a greater likelihood of using weak ties to some advantage. Granovetter (1973) showed how weak ties can be more useful than strong ties in finding employment, because they provide a greater number of possible connections and options than strong ties do. The same logic may be used in applying to colleges. Having many weak ties at a variety of colleges may be more advantageous than maintaining only a few strong ties.

> **Weak ties** Links to people with whom we do not interact often, or with whom we have weak social relationships.

Social Networks and Online Groups

The advent of the Internet has led to the emergence of new ways of connecting with people. People connect online for many reasons. Some people connect to chat in real time with people about nearly every topic imaginable. Some people connect online to gather information, to get the news, or even to make new friends. Others use the Internet as a way to organize events. Whatever the reason, connecting online offers new ways of connecting to other people.

In many respects, online groups meet the definition of groups discussed above. People have common interests and come together to interact based on those common interests. However, rather than meeting face to face as in traditional groups, these meetings occur in virtual space.

For this reason, it is often difficult to verify the authenticity of the people you are connecting with. In fact, many parents and law enforcement officials have become increasingly concerned with growing deception on the Internet, particularly when it is aimed at minors. It is extremely easy to hide your real identity online. For example, when people construct profile pages, there is no way to ensure that the pictures they post are actually pictures of themselves. Nor is there any way to ensure that the information they present about themselves is true. A person online can represent him- or herself as just about anything. A woman can pass herself off as a man; a teenager can claim to be an adult. Currently, there are very few laws or regulations to ensure the veracity of information presented online. Such laws and regulations that do exist are nearly impossible to enforce.

At the same time, online groups provide unique opportunities to create or expand social networks. Online groups allow an individual to connect and communicate with people all over the world without ever meeting them face to face. Although many of these people will remain weak ties, united only in the virtual world, we have already

FIGURE 5-4 Mark Granovetter demonstrated how weak ties can be more useful than strong ties.

Photo by Ellen Granovetter.

Social media sites helped to usher in the Arab Spring that led to the overthrow of several dictatorial leaders.

© Nasser Nasser/AP Images

learned how weak ties can benefit an individual. One illustration of the strength of weak ties developed online can be seen in the rallies and protests that occurred across the Arab world in 2010 and 2011.

Called the Arab Spring, protests erupted in Egypt, Libya, Syria, and other Arab nations to protest the existing governments. Many of these protests were organized online, through social media sites. Most of the people involved were strangers, brought together through networks developed online. These networks linked people from many different parts of the nations and brought them together at prearranged times and places to protest perceived injustices. The power of these online networks to affect social change is evident in the fact that several of these protests led to significant political change, including the overthrow of several national governments.

For good or ill, online communication is changing the ways in which people interact with one another. Although some scholars are concerned with the inevitable dangers that online communication brings, others see significant opportunities to develop new avenues of social change. All scholars do agree, however, that online communication is changing the way in which sociologists think about groups in general and about how groups impact our beliefs, values, and behaviors.

CONCEPT LEARNING CHECK 5.1   Types of Social Groups

Based on what you have just read, answer the following questions.

1. Identify each of the following as either a primary group or secondary group.

   A. Mother

   B. Schoolteacher

   C. Media

   D. Best friend

   E. Sister

2. Identify each of the following as a group or an aggregate.

   A. People waiting for a bus

   B. Students in a sociology class

   C. Church congregation

   D. Students studying in a library

   E. Members of the chess club

5.2 Group Interaction and Leadership

Groups and their leaders function in a variety of well understood ways that offer insights into the individuals' behavior in group settings.

- Describe the ways in which individuals interact within a group.
- Illustrate leadership styles in relation to the group structure.

Now that we have reviewed the different kinds of groups, we can begin to explore the more sophisticated question of how people interact in groups. Of course, people do not all interact with one another in the same way. Additionally, the same two people may interact differently with one another as circumstances change. Gaining a clear understanding of the ways in which people interact with one another and why is an essential tool in understanding how groups operate to help us develop our sociological imaginations.

Fiske and the Four Elementary Forms of Social Action

Anthropologist Alan Page Fiske (1991) FIGURE 5-5 spent years studying the Moose (pronounced MOOS-say) tribe in the African nation of Burkina Faso. He noticed that in every society, there are four basic ways in which people interact. According to Fiske, all forms of social action are rooted in one or more of these four forms of interaction. Like building blocks, these forms can be used separately or combined to form a more complex structure of interaction.

Fiske sees these forms as equal in their validity and importance TABLE 5-1. Each of the elementary forms of social action is just as important as the next. The forms are merely descriptive of the ways in which interaction can take place. Furthermore, each form is rooted in one of four social structures.

FIGURE 5-5 Alan Page Fiske identified four elementary forms of social action.

Courtesy of Alan Fiske.

Communal Sharing

Earlier, we discussed *gemeinschaft* communities. In these types of communities, individuals are intimately connected, as each individual relies on all of the others to help him or her subsist from day to day. In gemeinschaft communities, there is a deep sense of tradition and rules that bond all of the individuals to one another in a strong sense of solidarity. Furthermore, all individuals interact on equal footing.

It is this structure that forms Fiske's first category of social action. Fiske calls this form of action **communal sharing**, because the interaction is based on the principles of a communal society in which the interests of society outweigh the interests of individuals. In communal sharing, the individuals who interact are presumed to be equal, and they work for a common interest.

Communal sharing One of Fiske's four elementary forms of social action, in which the group is more important than the individual and in which all members of the group work for a common interest.

Authority Ranking

Of course, in most interactions, one person usually possesses more resources or social power than another. Typically, the person who has more resources gets to dictate—at least to some degree—the terms of the interaction. A person who has more authority than another has more social power and therefore will likely receive more benefit from the interaction than someone with less authority and less social power. For example, when a supervisor and a worker interact with one another, it is recognized by both parties that the supervisor has more authority than the worker. Therefore, the supervisor will be able to use his or her authority to dictate the terms and outcome of the interaction in his or her own favor.

Fiske recognizes this structure as **authority ranking**. In this form of interaction, all members of the group recognize the existence of a social hierarchy and their place in it. Members will usually defer to individuals who have higher status and will expect deference from members who have lower status. All members seek to gain something from the interaction, but they realize that this gain may be limited by their place in the social hierarchy.

Authority ranking One of Fiske's four elementary forms of social action, in which one person has more status or authority than another and can thus dictate the terms of interaction.

Equality matching One of Fiske's four elementary forms of social action, in which individuals are presumed to be equal in status and authority but seek individual goals.

Equality Matching

In **equality matching** interactions, the individuals in the group are presumed to be equal in status and authority. However, unlike communal sharing, the individuals do not seek a communal goal. Rather, each individual is interested in his or her own distinct goal. Each individual interacts with others on a separate but equal status to benefit him- or herself. Usually, the benefit is also presumed to be of equal value, even though what is actually gained may differ from person to person. Let us take the example of two individuals interacting with one another. The first individual has a bag of candy, and the second individual has a bag of marbles. In an equality matching exchange, the individuals each seek their own benefit. Even though they are exchanging different items, they presumed the items to be of equal value to the other. The person who trades away the candy values marbles because he plays marbles competitively; the person who trades away his marbles for candy has a serious sweet tooth. Both engage in a presumed equal trade, although what they trade may be very different.

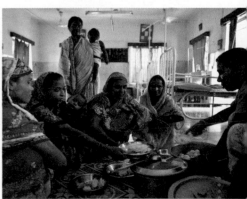

In communal sharing, the needs of the group are more important than the needs of the individual.

© Shannon Fagan/Corbis

TABLE 5-1 Fiske's Four Elementary Forms of Social Action

Relational Model	Description	Examples
Communal sharing	People treat each other as equivalent and undifferentiated in terms of contribution to community.	• Using a commons or shared resource • People intensely in love • Shared suffering for common well-being
Authority ranking	People have asymmetric positions in a linear hierarchy in which subordinates defer, respect, and obey while superiors take precedence and control.	• Military hierarchies • Ancestor worship • Monotheistic religions' moralities • Class or ethnic rankings • Sports team standings
Equality matching	Relationships keep track of the balance or difference among participants and know what is required to restore balance.	• Turn taking • One-person, one-vote elections • Equal share distribution • Eye for an eye vengeance
Market pricing	Relationships are oriented to socially meaningful ratios or rates such as prices, wages, interest, rents, tithes, or cost-benefit analysis.	• Property/stock values • Arranged marriage value • Standards of equity in judging entitlements

Source: Adapted from Fiske, A. P. 1991. Structures of Social Life: The Four Elementary Forms of Human Relations. *New York: Macmillan.*

In authority ranking, one person has more authority or status than another.

© Jonathan Ross/Dreamstime.com

Market pricing One of Fiske's four elementary forms of social action, in which the terms of exchange are dictated by market forces.

Leader A person who influences the beliefs, values, and behaviors of others.

Market Pricing

Often, when people interact to get something, they are willing to pay more than the item is typically considered to be worth. Many people, for instance, will pay higher prices for organic produce than for conventionally produced produce. This is because they consider the environmental benefits of organic produce to be worth the extra cost. People will likewise pay a very high price for tickets to a sports championship, even though the original price was considerably lower. These prices are dictated not by what the item is actually worth but by what people will actually pay. Many times, people who pay such high prices still believe that they got their money's worth because the value to them of watching the championship game is greater than the money expended. Of course, the person who sold the tickets at a high price also feels that he has benefited, since he has profited himself from the interaction.

In **market pricing** interactions, the cost of something is dictated not by its intrinsic value but rather by what people are willing to pay for it. Presumptions of equality or authority are no longer relevant, as the interaction is dictated solely by the value of the interaction. Nor should it be presumed that the value that each person gets from the interaction will be equal. However, all individuals who interacted will generally feel as though they benefited from the interaction.

Fiske's four models of elementary social action offer a foundation for understanding group interaction. Subsequent studies have shown Fiske's typology to be quite useful in categorizing interactions as well as in analyzing interactions.

Leadership Styles: Democratic, Authoritarian, and Laissez-Faire

As we examine the main types of leadership styles, it is important to remember that none of them is better or worse than others. Rather, all leadership styles are situational. To put it another way, in certain situations, some leadership styles work better than others. No leadership style is superior in every situation. It is also important to take note of the fact that leadership styles are limited to the completion of tasks and do not necessarily apply to groups that are not task oriented.

First, we should define what a leader is and why leaders are socially significant. A **leader** is defined as a person who influences the beliefs, values, or behaviors of others. Leaders emerge in nearly every task situation, and although the specific characteristics of leaders may vary, sociologists have identified some common characteristics that most leaders share. Experiments conducted by sociologist Robert Bales (1950) showed that leaders of groups tend to do more talking than other group members. They are also the individuals usually spoken to the most by others. Leaders also have their suggestions adopted most often by others. A leader is often the person who has the highest status in the group.

There are three basic leadership styles **TABLE 5-2**. Democratic leadership is desirable in situations in which the task to be completed is new. Democratic leadership also results in high morale among group members. This is because in novel situations, the input of many people offers a greater chance of coming up with an appropriate solution. Individuals tend to become highly invested in their own ideas; this narrow-mindedness is balanced by considering the ideas and opinions of other people.

Authoritarian leadership is often considered the least desirable, perhaps because it resembles a dictatorship. Certainly, very few people like to be told what to do or how to do it. However, authoritarian leadership does have distinct advantages that make it a necessary and even superior leadership style in certain situations. In cases in which the task requires the guidance of a clear leader, authoritarian leadership is best. For example, if a group is lost in the woods, a democratic or laissez-faire style of leadership is almost certainly not desirable. In such a situation, a knowledgeable, authoritarian leader making definitive decisions would offer the highest chance of successful rescue.

Laissez-faire literally means "let it alone." Laissez-faire leaders let the group function more or less on its own, offering guidance only when absolutely necessary. At first glance, this may seem like an inadequate leadership style, and many people consider laissez-faire leadership to be the least desirable. However, there are situations in which laissez-faire works quite well, such as when the members of the group are highly skilled at the task or very experienced. In such cases, little direct leadership is necessary. In fact, direct leadership may be considered a hindrance to the completion of the task. Direct leadership imposed on specialists often slows down their progress, reduces their morale and investment in the task, and may even breed resentment. Laissez-faire leadership allows individuals in the group to function in the best way they know how and at a pace that is suited to their particular life style. It demonstrates a sense of trust in group members and instills a sense of responsibility among all members of the group.

In equality matching, individuals have the same status or social power.
© Creatas Images/thinkstock

Leadership Functions: Instrumental versus Expressive Leadership

The leadership styles discussed above refer to leadership in task situations. However, the completion of a task is not the only time that leadership is necessary for a group. Often, group members disagree with one another, to the point of decreased morale for the entire group. Setbacks in accomplishing the task can also negatively impact the morale of the group. Often, the task leader is unaware of or unconcerned with issues that affect morale. Instead, her or his focus is on accomplishing the task. However, just as the task leader—also called the **instrumental leader**—is functional for the group to aid in the accomplishment of the task, **expressive leaders** are functional for the group to aid in the maintenance of the group's morale.

Expressive leaders improve morale in many ways. They may make jokes to help ease a stressful situation. They may offer sympathy when things go wrong. They may even organize events that help to reduce stress and improve the moods of group members. Because the role of the expressive leader is often in conflict with the role of the instrumental leader, they are usually not the same person. Usually, the expressive leader is someone further down the social hierarchy but who is widely liked and respected.

Most of the research on group leadership has been done on instrumental leadership. However, as sociologists begin to recognize and study expressive leadership, the

Market pricing models allow supply and demand to determine the terms of the interaction.
© Steven Collins/Shutterstock, Inc.

Instrumental leader Also known as a task leader, a person who is responsible for leading a group toward the completion of a task.

Expressive leader Also called a socioemotional leader; a person who is responsible for maintaining group morale and smoothing tensions in a group.

Visual Overview Four Ways a Group Can Be Formed

Fiske's four elementary forms of social action may be used to describe the fundamental interactions between individuals. These types of interactions can be combined in various ways to construct complex and enduring social groups.

Communal Sharing

Major Assumptions:
People are part of an integrated group.
The welfare of the group is more important than the welfare of the individual.

Contribution:
Everyone gives according to their ability. Everything belongs to the entire group; property is shared.

Group Decision Making:
The group seeks consensus and unity on major decisions.

Social Influence:
There is a desire to be similar to others in the group, and to maintain social harmony. This tends to lead to conformity.

Equality Matching

Major Assumptions:
People are individuals, but equal in status.
Equality may also occur when the value of the exchange is the same for all people.

Contribution:
Contributors match each other's contributions equally.

Group Decision Making:
The group usually makes decisions in a democratic way. All people have equal part in the decision-making process.

Social Influence:
There is a desire to keep social harmony by keeping contributions and rewards equal for all members. However, group members may differ in their beliefs and behaviors.

Fiske's four elementary forms of social action

Authority Ranking

Major Assumptions:
People are part of a hierarchical structure. Those with greater status are able to dictate the terms of the exchange.

Contribution:
Individuals at the top of the hierarchy demonstrate their power by giving generously. Subordinates are beholden to those who give gifts.

Group Decision Making:
Group decisions are made by individuals high in status.

Social Influence:
There is a desire to show obedience to authority and deference to group members of high status. Subordinates seek to display loyalty and strive to gain favor of individuals of high status.

Market Pricing

Major Assumptions:
People engage in exchanges dictated by market forces. The positions of individuals are irrelevant.

Contribution:
The value of contributions is assessed according to prevailing market forces.

Group Decision Making:
Group decisions are made based on the resolution of supply and demand.

Social Influence:
Influence is weighed through a cost/benefit analysis that accompanies the exchange. Individuals bargain with one another to improve their position in the exchange.

TABLE 5-2 Three Major Styles of Leadership

Authoritarian	Democratic	Laissez-Faire
Policies determined by leader	Policies determined by group discussion and decision, encouraged and assisted by the leader	Policies determined by group or individuals with minimal leader participation
The leader dictates work tasks and determines who works together	Group determines division of tasks and members work with whomever they chose, leader facilitates	Group determines division of tasks and members work with whomever they chose, leader does not participate

Source: © Jones & Bartlett Learning.

importance of maintaining happiness in the group has become increasingly appreciated. Individuals who are happy tend to work more efficiently and more effectively. They also tend to be more optimistic about accomplishing the task. For that reason, keeping the morale of the group high is an important consideration.

CONCEPT LEARNING CHECK 5.2   Group Interaction and Leadership

For each of the following situations, identify which leadership style is most appropriate.

1. You are leading a team of inexperienced workers to build a railroad bridge across a waterway. You have a strict deadline of three weeks to build the bridge.

2. You have been chosen to lead a team of scientists spread out across the United States on a project to construct a new space vessel that will travel to Neptune.

3. You are the new club president. Your task is to build membership in the club as well as to arrange meeting times and activities for the club.

5.3 Group Dynamics: Size, Diversity, and Conformity

Exploring group dynamics offers unique insights into the way groups influence and are influenced by individuals.

- Explain how group dynamics influences social interaction
- Discuss concepts of group dynamics

In addition to type of interaction and leadership style, there are other ways of thinking about and researching groups. When we do this, we are generally looking at **group dynamics**, or how groups influence the individual and how the individual influences groups. For example, by examining groups of different sizes, we gain a deeper understanding of how group size influences the beliefs, values, and behaviors that we hold. One of the first to understand this was Georg Simmel (1955), who studied how interaction in social groups differed depending on the size of the group.

Group dynamics How the individual influences the group and how the group influences the individual.

Group Size

As a way to begin thinking about how group size influences social interaction, think about the last time you were at a large gathering. As people begin to arrive, they form together in small groups of two or perhaps three people. As new guests arrive, they will sometimes form their own groups or join and therefore enlarge existing groups. When these groups reach about four or five people, they will often slowly divide into two smaller groups. Rarely will you see more than five people standing together in a discussion. To understand why this occurs, let us start with an understanding of the dyad and work our way toward an understanding of larger groups.

The Dyad

Dyad A group consisting of two people.

The **dyad**, a group of two people, is the most basic social group FIGURE 5-6. There is no group smaller than the dyad; there are just individuals. The group begins when two people interact. They may interact for any number of reasons, such as emotional connection. However, most sociologists believe that exchange is the basis for all interaction. That is, we interact with other people because we believe that it will benefit us. The other person interacts with us because he or she believes that it will benefit him or her in some way.

Why do we exchange with others? It depends on who you ask. Different theoretical perspectives offer different explanations for why exchange is so important. Conflict theorists believe that people exchange with one another as a way to accumulate resources that are valued in society. Functionalists argue that exchange is functional for society because no one person can gain all of the resources that society values by him- or herself. We exchange as a means to meet our needs and desires. Symbolic interactionists see exchange as a form of communication. Through exchange, we communicate to others what is valued and what we are willing to sacrifice to get that thing of value. An evolutionary approach to exchange argues that humans need to exchange to get resources that are vital to survival that we could not procure on our own. If we did not exchange, we could not survive. Whatever perspective we approach exchange from, it is clear that exchange forms a cornerstone of interaction. Of course, exchange does not necessarily have to take on material form. We can exchange emotional connections, friendship, or spiritual connections in addition to material or physical items.

The dyad, or group of two people, forms the basis of exchange and therefore the basis of the group. This basic social group forms the foundation of all other social groups. In fact, most of our conversations, exchanges, and interactions operate at the level of the dyad, even in a large social group. Think back to the example of the large social gathering. Even as more and more people flood into the room, the predominance of interaction occurs within small groups. You can see this for yourself with a very simple experiment. Invite a large group of friends to have lunch at the same time. Have everyone sit at the same table. Watch what happens. More than likely, the conversation will start big but will eventually break down into small groups—usually dyads.

Although the dyad is the most basic social group, it is inherently unstable. This is because if either of the members of the dyad stops interacting, the group no longer exists. To put it another way, there is a 1 in 2 chance that the dyad will dissolve. This makes exchange within the dyad ever more important, because if either person becomes unsatisfied with the exchange, the group will not exist for very long. Because the dyad is unstable, if both members of the dyad want the interaction to continue, they seek ways to develop the relationship over time. For this reason, the dyad is often the most intimate social group. Group dynamics change, however, as the group gets larger.

FIGURE 5-6 Because there is only one possible interaction, a dyad remains a highly unstable social group.

The Triad

The addition of a third person fundamentally changes the way in which the members of a group interact FIGURE 5-7. The old cliché "two is company, but three is a crowd" captures this sentiment well. A group of three people is called a **triad**, and Simmel (1955) noted that interaction in a triad is very different than it is in a dyad. Because the dyad has only two members, each member can interact only with the other. There are no choices about with whom a person will interact. However, in a triad, each person has a choice of who he or she would like to interact with. Usually, each person will develop a preference for which other member of the group he or she wishes to interact with. The addition of preference means that some member of the triad will often get excluded from interaction.

Triad A group consisting of three people.

Coalition The formation of preferential interaction in a group.

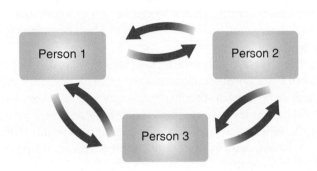

FIGURE 5-7 Because there are three possible interactions in a triad, it forms the basis for group stability.

As an example, consider a young married couple. When the couple first weds, they spend a considerable amount of time together. When the first child is born, it is so dependent that much of the new mother's attention turns from her husband to her newborn child. This can often leave the husband feeling excluded, leading to resentment or anger. Indeed, while many marriages are made stronger when children are born, the resentment that occurs when the first child is born often causes the marriage to deteriorate. This means that triads are also often unstable as two of the members interact differentially. The formation of preferential interaction in a group is called a **coalition**. As already noted, this can often make group members who are not part of the coalition feel excluded. However, these members may also act as arbitrators when conflict emerges in coalitions. Arbitration serves several functions in the group. First, arbitration serves the function of the expressive leader. That is, it helps to keep the morale of the group high by smoothing over differences of group members. It also functions to make the excluded member feel useful in the group. Although a hierarchy usually develops even in a dyad, in a triad, both the instrumental leader and expressive leader become evident.

Larger Groups

As groups become larger, the number of possible interactions grows as well. In a group of four, there are six possible relationships. In a group of five, there are 10 possible relationships. As the group expands to seven people, there are 21 possible relationships. Most of us cannot follow the conversations of more than two or three people at a time. This is why coalitions form. We break our interactions down into small, manageable pieces to make them easier to follow.

As group size increases, group stability also increases. However, as the group becomes larger, the intimacy of interaction declines. Because of this, as the size of the group increases, the group tends to become more formalized, with an identifiable status hierarchy. Leadership roles become more pronounced. Additionally, as the group becomes larger and larger, the ways in which the group influences an individual also change.

Intuitively, it might seem as though larger groups would influence an individual more than smaller groups. Most people think that conformity is bred through interactions with large groups. However, this is not the case. As we have already learned, smaller primary groups such as families generally provide more pervasive and lasting socialization than larger secondary groups. Remember that larger groups tend to be less intimate. Therefore, they tend to have less of an influence over the individual. There is another reason as well. In a small group, dissent from group consensus is easy to spot. However, as group size increases, it is easier to remain anonymous and therefore easier to dissent from consensus without rebuke. It is also much easier to justify leaving a large group than a small one, since the interactions are less intimate.

Group Diversity

Heterogeneity Diversity in groups.

Homogeneous A group in which all people are similar.

Diversity in groups—what sociologists call **heterogeneity**—can offer significant advantages in accomplishing a task. Group members bring unique experiences and histories to the group. The variety of experience that diversity brings to the group offers a wider range of possible solutions to the novel task, making successful completion of the task more likely and often more creative than it would be in a group of like individuals. Task leadership in a diverse group is often easier than in a **homogeneous** group—that is, a group in which all people are similar.

While diversity is typically an asset in a task situation, diversity can present challenges to the emotional connections of the group. Many times, differences in values, norms, or beliefs that accompany diversity lead to clashes that can range from the mild to the most severe. Often, these clashes can become emotionally charged as the views of two radically different cultures collide. Group morale can suffer as diverse views interact. Thus, expressive leadership is often made more difficult by diversity.

Heterogeneous groups are groups that are very diverse.

© Sandra Baker/Alamy

Group Conformity: The Asch Experiment

Imagine that you have volunteered to participate in a study. You are greeted at the door by one of the lab assistants and ushered into a room. In the room is a row of chairs. Five of the chairs are already occupied. You sit in the sixth. Soon, the final chair is taken up by another volunteer. All of the people are strangers to one another. Then, the director of the study, Dr. Solomon Asch, comes into the room to explain the study. He tells you that he will show you a card imprinted with a vertical line. Then, you will see another card with three other lines on it. Your task, explains the doctor, is to determine which of the three lines on the second card matches the length of the line on the first card FIGURE 5-8.

The instructions are simple, and so is the task. The answer is obvious to even the most untrained eye. One by one, the subjects sitting in the chairs answer the question—all of them answer correctly. The second series is just as easy as the first. Again, everyone gives the correct answer. On the third trial, however, the person sitting at the end of the row of chairs surprises you by giving what appears as an obviously incorrect answer. Then, almost miraculously, the next person in the row gives the same incorrect answer. One by one, each subject gives the same incorrect answer. Now, it is your turn. What do you do?

This time, you give the answer you believe to be correct. As the next cards are presented, the subject at the end again gives an incorrect answer. Again, one by one,

FIGURE 5-8 Typical question from Asch's experiment in which individuals were pressured to give incorrect answers to questions.

Source: © Jones & Bartlett Learning.

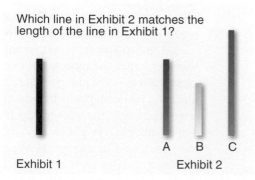

Which line in Exhibit 2 matches the length of the line in Exhibit 1?

A   B   C

Exhibit 1   Exhibit 2

each of the people sitting in the row gives the same incorrect answer. Again, you are forced to make a choice. Again, you decide to give the answer you know to be correct. Over and over, the row of people confidently gives incorrect answers. You begin to doubt yourself. Perhaps they are right, you think. Perhaps you are seeing things. After several trials, you begin to answer in accordance with the rest of the group. From that point on, your answers are the same as the other subjects, even though you often believe them to be wrong.

You might object at this point, saying that you would never give an answer that you knew was incorrect. Most people make that claim. While all of us would like to believe that we would not bow to conformity when we know that others are incorrect, the reality is that we cannot be certain what we would do. Even though nearly everyone states that they would stick to their guns, Asch's (1952) experiment tells a different story. One-third of the people tested gave answers they knew to be incorrect in at least half of the trials. Another 40% gave wrong answers, though less frequently. Only about one in four of the subjects tested stuck to their guns on every trial and always gave the correct answer.

Of course, the other people in the experiment were all people who worked for the experimenter. You were the only real subject in the experiment. The real experiment was not about lines but rather about whether you would conform to the pressure of a group. The test is a test of the power of groups to induce conformity on an individual.

It is certainly possible that this experiment—and the disturbing result—is an anomaly. However, the Asch experiment has been replicated numerous times, and the results are always the same. Despite our claims to a strong sense of individuality, many people in society appear willing to conform to the group such that they will say or believe things that they know are not true. The results of Asch's experiment are even more surprising when we remember that the experiment was completed with complete strangers. It is likely that groups of people we know well exert even more influence over our beliefs and behaviors. It is also important to understand how the authority structure of groups influences the way in which we behave.

Group Conformity: The Milgram Experiment

From 1939 to 1945, Adolph Hitler's Third Reich incarcerated and executed more than 10 million Jews, communists, Poles, Romani, homosexuals, and other members of perceived inferior and dangerous racial, ethnic, cultural, or political backgrounds. Only at the end of World War II did the full extent of the Nazi atrocities come to light. Many people wondered how the German citizens could allow these horrible events to unfold, essentially becoming complicit in the deaths of millions of people. One psychologist, a student of Solomon Asch, decided to find out.

Originally, Stanley Milgram FIGURE 5-9 intended his experiment to be done in the United States, and then in Germany, with the idea of comparing the results cross-culturally. Milgram hypothesized that there was a fundamental difference between German culture and American culture that allowed the Nazi atrocities to be tolerated—even sanctioned—by the German people. What Milgram found, however, shocked not only him but the rest of the world as well. Milgram's experiment never made it to Germany. He found his answer here in America, and the answer was both unexpected and disturbing.

Milgram designed an experiment to test how authority influences how people behave FIGURE 5-10. Like the Asch experiment, Milgram's experiment made use of a confederate—that is, actors who were in on the experiment. To begin, your participation was solicited through a local newspaper and offered payment for an experiment in learning. As you arrive, you are seated next to another subject in a waiting room. The other person strikes up a conversation. He tells the subject that he is looking forward to participating in the study, since he will be paid for it. He explains that he has been unable to work because he has a heart condition.

Before long, a researcher in a white lab coat emerges carrying a clipboard. He asks each of you a few basic questions, then assigns you the role of teacher and the other

FIGURE 5-9 Stanley Milgram conducted a controversial experiment on the influence of authority on individual behavior.

Source: © Jones & Bartlett Learning.

FIGURE 5-10 Milgram's experiment involved encouraging subjects to administer an electric shock to another person even to the point of injury.

Source: © Jones & Bartlett Learning.

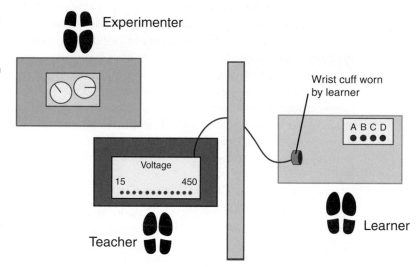

subject the role of learner. He leads the two of you to the back of the lab to prepare for the experiment. On the way, he explains that this is a test of learning. Specifically, the researcher wants to know how punishment affects learning. The other subject is led into a small room. You watch as he is hooked up to a series of wires. He appears a little nervous and asks if this is dangerous. "There will be some mild shocks," the researcher explains, but the experiment is not dangerous.

Next, you are led into a room filled with knobs, dials, and switches. The switches are labeled from 15 volts to 450 volts. A small sign by the 15-volt switch reads "Mild Shock," while a sign above the final switch warns "DANGER: SEVERE SHOCK." As you survey the room, the researcher explains that you will be the teacher. You will be given a pair of words. You will read the first word into a microphone. The other subject will respond. If he responds with the second word in the pair, you will move on to the next word pair. However, if the learner responds incorrectly, you will administer a shock. Each shock will be progressively more severe, working up to the maximum of 450 volts.

As you begin, the learner does not fare well. He misses more word pairs than he gets right. You dutifully administer progressively greater shocks. Before long, you can hear the learner begin to moan and scream with each shock. By the time you have reached 300 volts, the learner is screaming for you to stop. You hesitate to administer the next shock, but the researcher tells you to go on. Reluctantly, you continue. At the next level, the learner screams "my heart!" which is followed by silence.

Again, the researcher urges you to continue. Ever more reluctantly, you continue to increase the shock. There are no more responses from the learner. You fear that his bad heart has finally given out. You begin to sweat and shake. You plead with the researcher to stop. Your entreaties are meaningless to the researcher, who continues to insist that you proceed. What do you do?

Milgram (1963) was stunned by how many of the subjects complied with the researcher's demands to continue the experiment despite their obvious distress. Nearly two-thirds of the subjects eventually administered the maximum shock. Even when the subjects could see the person they were injuring, 40% of the subjects continued to administer shock all the way to the maximum level.

Milgram's experiment demonstrates the power of authority over human behavior. When interviewed after the experiments, subjects indicated that they felt pressured to continue by the authority figure. Recognition of the authority figure influenced the behavior of otherwise peaceful individuals such that they performed significant acts of violence. Our response to authority is essentially the same in the lab as it is in real life. Just as the subjects in Milgram's study responded to authority in the lab, so the citizens of Germany responded to the authority of their Nazi leaders.

Milgram expanded his experiments, including one scenario in which another actor was also made a learner alongside the subject. In these experiments, the actor was instructed to object to the continued administration of shock. In such cases, only about 5% of the actual subjects continued all the way to the highest level. This indicates that the influence of authority can be mitigated by the development of coalitions or other support by members of the group.

The Ethics of Milgram's Experiment

Milgram's experiment caused significant psychological distress to a number of subjects because they were led to believe that they had harmed another person. Even after they were told the truth about the nature of the experiment, many people still reported significant distress. Many sociologists and psychologists debated the ethics of conducting experiments that cause harm to the subjects. From these debates, review boards were formed at research institutions throughout the United States and Europe. The purpose of these review boards is to assess the ethics of experiments in an effort to reduce harm to subjects while preserving the integrity of the experiment. Today, nearly every experiment that a sociologist does must be approved by a review board before it can be conducted. Noncompliance with the review board process can result in the loss of money used in research, the loss of publication opportunities, and even the dismissal of the scientist.

Groupthink

As we have learned, working in a group can have significant advantages. When functioning well, groups can efficiently accomplish tasks and even develop and implement novel solutions to problems. However, sometimes groups can have the opposite effect. When some groups interact for long periods of time, they may begin to become rigid in their thinking. Psychologist Irving Janis (1972; 1982) studied groups that evolved such rigid thinking. Janis found that the tendency toward this rigid thinking is not as uncommon as one might expect, and that the process of developing this rigid mentality was common across groups. Janis identified eight characteristics FIGURE 5-11 of what he termed **groupthink**, the tendency for groups to develop a rigid way of thinking. It is important to recognize that the development of these characteristics does not necessarily appear all at once or in any particular order. However, they are often related to one another and thus tend to develop together.

The first characteristic is the *illusion of invulnerability*. Groups gradually come to believe that their views are absolutely correct. In fact, they often believe that there can be no other way of looking at a situation that is different from that of their group. For this reason, the group may take excessive risks in order to promote or defend its views.

Groupthink The tendency for groups to develop a rigid way of thinking.

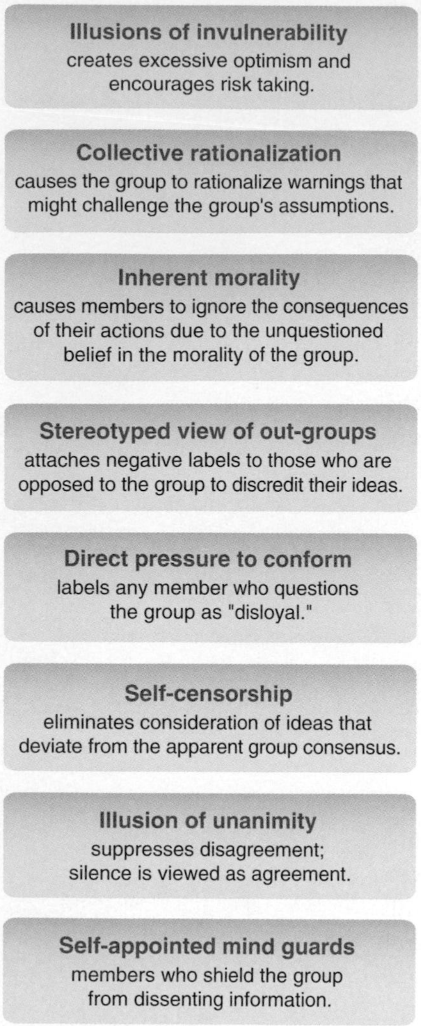

Illusions of invulnerability
creates excessive optimism and encourages risk taking.

Collective rationalization
causes the group to rationalize warnings that might challenge the group's assumptions.

Inherent morality
causes members to ignore the consequences of their actions due to the unquestioned belief in the morality of the group.

Stereotyped view of out-groups
attaches negative labels to those who are opposed to the group to discredit their ideas.

Direct pressure to conform
labels any member who questions the group as "disloyal."

Self-censorship
eliminates consideration of ideas that deviate from the apparent group consensus.

Illusion of unanimity
suppresses disagreement; silence is viewed as agreement.

Self-appointed mind guards
members who shield the group from dissenting information.

FIGURE 5-11 Irving Janis identified eight characteristics of groupthink.

As group thinking becomes rigid and the group becomes more confident of its own views, it often neglects warnings from outsiders and refuses to entertain alternative views and assumptions. Janis called this *collective rationalization* because the group as a whole uses a variety of techniques to avoid entertaining alternative ideas. The illusion of invulnerability and collective rationalization leads to the third characteristic of groupthink, which is a belief in the *inherent morality* of the group's position. That is, as the group moves toward groupthink, the group adopts the view that its beliefs are ordained and therefore inherently correct. All other views are inherently wrong or flawed. Because of the inherent morality of the group's view, groups often ignore the possible moral or ethical consequence of their decisions.

The fourth characteristic of groupthink is a *stereotyped view of out-groups*. Out-groups are portrayed as enemies. Thus, these stereotypes are most often negative and sometimes dehumanizing. This serves the purpose of making responsible responses to out-group demands or ideas unnecessary.

In addition to vilifying out-groups because they disagree with the views of the group, groupthink also leads to *direct pressures on group members to conform* unwaveringly to the rigid views of the group. Members of the group are discouraged from expressing any view that is inconsistent with the rigid views that have developed in the group. Because there is direct pressure for members to conform to the views of the group, doubts about the group or its ideas are often self-censored. This *self-censorship* means that alternative views, which might benefit the group, are suppressed and therefore lost, contributing to the development of further rigidity.

Because self-censorship is common in groupthink, the group maintains the *illusion of unanimity*. In other words, because no one speaks out against the views of the group, everyone in the group believes that everyone else in the group agrees with the views of everyone else in the group. With such a belief, any attempt to contradict the views of the group is suppressed for fear of reprisal.

Indeed, groupthink also leads to the *development of self-appointed mind guards*. These are members of the group who take it upon themselves to make sure that all opposition within the group is squashed. Mind guards also protect the leader of the group from any information that might pose a problem for the group or that might threaten the cohesiveness of the group.

Groupthink tends to occur when all eight of these traits occur. These traits are likely to occur when the group is highly cohesive and under significant pressure to make a quality decision. The pressure to balance continuing group cohesion with making a decision leads to irrational thinking and poor decision making. To illustrate groupthink, Janis analyzed the decision making that led to the tragedy of Pearl Harbor on December 7, 1941.

Although we are often taught that the Japanese attack on Pearl Harbor was a complete surprise, the fact is that there were many warnings of the impending attack. American Admiral H. E. Kimmel, who was tasked with monitoring the Japanese fleet, was told that contact with the Japanese aircraft carriers had been lost. Rather than explore the possibility of an attack, Kimmel joked about the situation, refusing to believe that the Japanese would launch a full-scale attack against the American naval base. Nevertheless, Kimmel reported the incident but convinced his superiors that the Japanese would not dare attack. Even though it was later reported that several officers felt an attack was imminent, they did not speak out because they feared reprisal.

People in all stages of the military hierarchy, from the sailors on the ships to the president, offered rationalizations to explain away the possibility of a Japanese attack. Most commonly, they posed the argument that the Japanese knew they could not win a protracted war with the United States and therefore would not dare to attack. Because no attack was coming, no one prepared to defend the island base. When the attack happened, the nation was stunned. The social and political ramifications of this incidence of groupthink would be felt for years as the nation was plunged into a war that cost more than 400,000 American lives.

Of course, groupthink is not limited to the military or to history. More recently, American unpreparedness for the collapse of the housing market and the financial sector can be seen as a result of groupthink. Morgenson and Rosner (2011) documented the events leading up to the recent crash of the financial and housing markets. Although there were many indications of an impending collapse, the warnings were ignored by bank executives and politicians who believed that the markets were sufficiently capitalized as to be impervious to a serious collapse. Morgenson and Rosner write:

> A handful of analysts and investors, for example, tried to warn of the rising tide of mortgage swindlers; they were met with a deafening silence. . . . Some brave souls in academia argued that renting a home was, for many, better than owning. They were refuted by government studies using manipulated figures or flawed analysis to conclude that homeownership was a desired goal for all. (p. 6)

The mentality that preceded the financial collapse serves as a classic example of Janis's idea of groupthink. Few people believed that a financial disaster of this magnitude could happen. Those who did were ignored or attacked by people who had a stake in maintaining the status quo. The result was a colossal downturn in the American economy that resulted in many Americans losing their jobs and their homes.

THE SOCIOLOGICAL IMAGINATION — A Different Outcome: Race, Culture, and Gender

While diversity is typically an asset in a task situation, diversity can present challenges to the emotional connections of the group. Many times, differences in values, norms, or beliefs that accompany diversity lead to clashes that can range from the mild to the most severe. Often, these clashes can become emotionally charged as the views of two different cultures collide. Group morale can suffer as diverse views interact. Thus, expressive leadership is often made more difficult by diversity.

EVALUATE

1. Think about a time you worked in a group. Was the group homogenous or heterogeneous? How did the composition of the group affect how the task was accomplished?

2. How did the experiences and world views of individuals in the group impact the expression of emotions in the group? How did these emotions impact the way in which the group functioned?

3. Which type of group do you prefer to work in? Why?

4. How might your preferences limit or enhance your performance at work with your coworkers, your manager, and your customers?

CONCEPT LEARNING CHECK 5.3 — Group Dynamics: Size, Diversity, and Conformity

Match the description with the characteristic of groupthink that it describes.

_____ 1. Groups believe that their beliefs are infallible and correct and thus the group will take excessive risks to defend its views.

_____ 2. Out-groups are portrayed as enemies and thus are portrayed in a generally negative way.

_____ 3. Members of the group take it upon themselves to make sure that opposition within the group is squashed.

_____ 4. Alternative views that might benefit the group are suppressed and therefore lost.

_____ 5. The group uses sanctions to encourage members to agree with the group's decision.

_____ 6. Groups believe that their position is ordained and therefore inherently correct.

_____ 7. The group believes that everyone in the group agrees with everyone else in the group.

_____ 8. The group as a whole uses a variety of techniques to avoid entertaining alternative ideas.

A. Illusion of invulnerability

B. Stereotyped view of out-groups

C. Self-appointed mind guards

D. Illusion of unanimity

E. Self-censorship

F. Direct pressure on group members to conform

G. Collective rationalization

H. Inherent morality

5.4 Formal Organizations

Formal organizations are characterized by a variety of clear, recognizable characteristics designed to achieve specific goals.

- Describe the role and function of a formal organization.
- Illustrate types of formal organizations.

Organization A group that is deliberately constructed to achieve a purpose common to its members.

Formal organization An organization that is rationally structured to efficiently achieve specific goals using rules and regulations.

People interact in groups to achieve goals that they would otherwise not be able to achieve alone. As groups evolve, they develop consistent goals and consistent means of achieving those goals. In other words, the group engages in deliberate action to achieve a purpose common to all of its members. Sociologists call this an **organization**. Although small, intimate groups can by definition be considered organizations, more often, organizations are large and less intimate. Examples of organizations include churches, universities, and businesses.

Organizations are a key part of all societies. However, in the Western world, organizations have become increasingly central to our way of life. This phenomenon was predicted by Max Weber (1925), who noticed a trend that organizations become more formal over time. Part of this trend is due to increasing regulation and requirements for legal standing. For example, a formal legal process is necessary for a business to become incorporated. This may involve, among other things, a statement of the goals of the organization and an outline of the structure of the organization. Another reason that organizations may formalize is that they find themselves competing with other organizations for the same rewards. Organizations that are more formalized are often more efficient, thereby gaining a competitive advantage over less efficient organizations.

A **formal organization** is defined as an organization or a group that is rationally structured to efficiently achieve specific goals using rules and regulations. Schools, hospitals, and even the government are formal organizations. Indeed, from the time we are born until the time we die, we are subjected to the rules and regulations of formal organizations. Parents are required to register the birth of their child in the form of a birth certificate. Babies are also issued a Social Security card—a form of identification. This information is used to track citizens through school, work, and old age. Indeed, even death is registered with the government. This information, of course, is used to assist citizens and government in efficiently navigating the complexities of society.

Even though formal organizations can be seen as an efficient way of conducting business, there are drawbacks to the pervasiveness of formal organizations in our lives. One of the most obvious drawbacks is that formal organizations take power and agency away from the individual and place it in the hands of the organization. To put it another way, the more rules and regulations we are expected to adhere to, the fewer choices we have about how to conduct our lives. Our own choices inevitably become subordinate to those of experts and officials who are bounded by the rules of the organization.

Types of Formal Organizations

Not all formal organizations are the same. For instance, they may be classified according to the reasons that people choose to participate in them. Three general classifications of formal organizations have been identified: utilitarian, normative, and coercive **TABLE 5-3**.

Utilitarian Organizations

Members of utilitarian organizations commit themselves to the organization voluntarily. The utilitarian organization rewards people for their efforts in the organization. This reward is material in nature. Working for a company is an example. A person takes a job to earn money, a very utilitarian goal. There is no coercion to join the organization; the person chooses to take the job or not take the job. The end goal, however, is the material reward associated with participating in the organization.

TABLE 5-3 Three Major Types of Organizations and Their Characteristics

Type of Organization	Characteristics of Membership	Example
Utilitarian	Members join for a practical reason, such as personal economic gain.	A job
Normative	Members join because they want to pursue a goal they see as morally worthwhile.	A charity
Coercive	Membership is involuntary. The goal of the coercive organization is to change the beliefs or behaviors of members.	A prison

Normative Organizations

Some people chose to join organizations even when they receive no material gain for their participation. Instead, they join the organization for a sense of belonging or to pursue a goal they believe is morally worthwhile. As with utilitarian organizations, participation in normative organizations is voluntary. Examples of normative organizations include political parties, Habitat for Humanity or other charity organizations, and religious organizations.

Coercive Organizations

Unlike normative organizations and utilitarian organizations in which participation is voluntary, membership in a coercive organization is involuntary. People participate in these organizations through no choice of their own. They may be forced into these organizations for a variety of reasons, such as being admitted into the hospital due to an illness or being sent to prison for committing a crime.

Many times, coercive organizations exist for the purpose of changing a person's beliefs, values, or behaviors. For that reason, coercive organizations often have special features, such as facilities to limit a person's movements, isolate a person from society, or provide some form of surveillance.

It should be noted that a formal organization may be classified in more than one category, depending upon the perspective. For example, a hospital may be classified as a utilitarian organization by a doctor, as a coercive organization for a patient in the hospital, and as a normative organization for a person who volunteers at the hospital.

> **Bureaucracy** An organizational model designed to achieve specific tasks in a very efficient way.

Bureaucracies

A **bureaucracy** is an organizational model designed to achieve specific tasks in a very efficient way. This model is prevalent in formal organizations, with officials in the organization often revising and rewriting policies to increase efficiency. What characteristics define efficiency in bureaucracies? Max Weber (1968/1925) FIGURE 5-12 studied bureaucracies and identified six traits that describe an ideal bureaucracy.

The first trait that Weber identified is *specialization*. In contrast to earlier societies, in which people often performed a variety of tasks to make a living, bureaucracies require individuals to engage in highly specialized and narrowly defined jobs. Bureaucracies also arrange these specific tasks in a *hierarchy of positions*. That is, workers are arranged in a vertical ranking, with each position supervised by a person of higher ranking. Usually, this hierarchical arrangement takes the shape of a pyramid, with fewer people at the top of the hierarchy and greater numbers of workers at the bottom of the pyramid.

Weber noted that bureaucracies maintain their efficiency through *rules and regulations*. These rules and regulations are clearly defined and make the operation of the bureaucratic organization predictable and consistent. Because of the proliferation of

FIGURE 5-12 Max Weber identified six characteristics of ideal bureaucracies.

© Keystone Pictures USA/Alamy

rules and regulations, workers in a bureaucracy develop a level of *technical competence*. This technical competence begins with the hiring process, which is typically formalized according to a set of standards specifically tailored to the job. Rules and regulations define the job, and the evaluation of performance is also formalized with a set of standards that allow technical competence to be evaluated in a rational and efficient way.

All of these rules led Weber to conclude that bureaucracies put rules ahead of the people who are obliged to abide by them. Weber called this *impersonality*. This ensures that all employees perform consistently and adequately the tasks that are prescribed them. Additionally, by placing rules before people, bureaucracies ensure that all clients are treated in the same way.

Finally, Weber noticed that all of the rules, regulations, and communications are done in a formal way and written down and recorded for reference. Bureaucracies rely on this *formal, written communication* to document the existence and effectiveness of the other bureaucratic characteristics. This also serves to provide a record to protect the integrity of the bureaucratic organization in a changing environment.

It should be stressed that Weber recognized that not all bureaucracies will exhibit all six of these characteristics. Some will exhibit them to greater or lesser degree. Weber described these characteristics as **ideal types**—that is, as a pure form of a concept usually used for the purpose of categorization.

Ideal types A pure form of a concept usually used for the purpose of categorization.

Organizational environment Outside forces that influence the structure and performance of an organization.

Organizational Environment

Organizations operate in the context of the broader society. The success of the organization depends not only on the structure and performance of the organization itself but also on forces outside of the organization itself. These outside forces, called the **organizational environment**, can include limits imposed by the government, political trends, the economy, current events, available technology, competition from other organizations, and the available workforce. Organizational environments are not characteristics of bureaucracies. Rather, they are the environments in which bureaucracies exist, and they affect the operations of bureaucracies in several ways.

Governmental regulations are limits that are imposed by the government that is in power in a society. Regulations are legislative rules that define responsibilities or constrain actions. In many cases, the regulations guide and shape elements of the organizations. Regulations, in turn, are frequently shaped by political trends and current events that influence the direction of politics. As an example, consider how increasing concerns about the environment have led to political regulation on certain organizations. This necessarily changes the way in which certain organizations must function.

Organizations are also affected by periods of economic recession and growth, as well as by competition with other organizations that have similar goals. For example, although people may want to join many organizations that are consistent with their values and beliefs, they are often able to participate in only one organization. Thus, organizations with similar goals often must compete for membership. Also, economic conditions affect the amount of time or money that people are willing to invest in participation in an organization. Economic factors also affect the operation of the organization in various ways. In good economic times, organizations seek to expand their operations, profits, and customer base. When the economy is in decline, organizations often find themselves restructuring their organization to remain efficient and competitive.

Technologies also help to shape the way in which organizations operate. One of the main impacts of advances in technology is that they give employees greater and faster access to information. Additionally, technology improves the ability of organizations to monitor their employees and customers over time.

Finally, the availability of workers or members also influences how organizations function. As bureaucracies rely more on technology, an educated workforce becomes increasingly important. This is why many jobs that did not require a college degree in the past now require workers with higher education credentials. Age may play an increasingly important role in the operation of organizations as the population continues to age. A decline in the birth rate means a shrinking workforce for organizations in the future. Doubtless, this will put pressure on the organizations that may change the way in which these organizations are forced to operate.

Informal Aspects of Bureaucracy

Although Weber's description of bureaucracy describes an ideal type in which the bureaucratic organization regulates every aspect of employee and client relations, it must be recognized that humans do possess agency, or free will, which allows them to resist the rigidity of bureaucratic rules and regulations. Most often, this resistance is not overt but rather takes the form of minor rejection of the rules and regulations in the form of cutting corners at work, showing up a little late to work, leaving a little early, or even minor incidents of stealing. These may seem like minor issues, but in the rigid world of a bureaucratic organization, these seemingly minor forms of rebellion are effective coping mechanisms to maintain a sense of individuality and creativity that is vital to the psychological and emotional health of the individual.

Informality may also be influenced by the leadership style of those at the top of the organizational hierarchy. Halberstam (1986) and Baron, Hannan, and Burton (1999) found that the structure and outcomes in bureaucratic settings are strongly influenced not only by the leadership styles of those in charge but also by their personality traits, such as their interpersonal skills, charisma, and approach to problem solving. People with more compulsive personalities tend to be less likely to condone informality in the bureaucratic structure than people with more laid-back personalities.

Lastly, the way in which the communication is structured may also contribute to the degree of informality in bureaucracies. For example, organizations that insist that communication strictly obey the chain of command tend to be more formal than organizations that allow employees a degree of latitude in communicating with the leadership of the organization. The pervasiveness of email has helped to level the communicative hierarchy and generally increase the level of informality within bureaucratic organizations.

Dysfunctions of Bureaucracy

Bureaucracies are generally successful at creating efficient organizations, and we rely on the myriad of bureaucracies to help us navigate an increasingly complex society. However, the effects of bureaucracy have not been all positive. Indeed, negative effects of bureaucracy have been noted and widely discussed among sociologists. Most notably, debate has centered around three problems in particular: the tendency of bureaucracies toward ritualism and rigidity, the tendency toward bureaucratic inertia, and the tendency of bureaucracies to alienate their members.

Bureaucratic Ritualism and Rigidity

As bureaucratic organizations grow in size, they also grow in complexity. Regulations and rules expand to encompass every aspect of behavior in the bureaucracy. As noted, it is not uncommon for the rules and regulations to become more important than people in bureaucracies. It is also possible for the rules and regulations to become more important than the goals the bureaucracy was designed to accomplish. In such cases, the bureaucracy may become highly ritualized to the point of inefficiency.

As an example, consider the tragedy wrought by Hurricane Katrina in 2005. After the storm struck, rescue workers and other first responders were dispatched from around the country to aid victims in New Orleans. As the rescue workers assembled and awaited their assignments, they were told by officials of the Federal Emergency Management Agency (FEMA) that prior to being dispatched to the disaster zone, they would be required to attend a series of lectures covering such topics as equal opportunity, customer service, and sexual harassment. When one of the rescue workers objected because the lectures did not have anything to do with saving lives, an angered FEMA official shouted "You are now employees of FEMA, and you will follow orders and do what you are told!" ("Places" 2005).

Rescue workers after Hurricane Katrina were often hampered by rigid rules and regulations.

Andrea Booher/FEMA

Bureaucratic ritualism A focus on rules and regulations to the point of undermining the goals of the organization.

Bureaucratic inertia The tendency of bureaucracies to perpetuate themselves over time.

This was not the only criticism of the government's handling of the situation in the aftermath of Hurricane Katrina. Nearly every criticism involved delays in reaching and helping victims of the storm due to the excess of regulations and rigid enforcement of those regulations. This delayed help to hundreds of people who were in desperate need of assistance and who relied on the promised efficiency of government bureaucracy. These criticisms extended from the federal government down to the state and even local level.

Another example involves a Boy Scout who became separated from his group on a hike deep in the woods. Lost, and with only a box of cookies to eat, the boy was quickly located by helicopter. The child waved his hands to signal to the aircraft, but the helicopter flew away, leaving the confused child in the woods for three days even though there was a clear landing place nearby. Bureaucratic ritual delayed the boy's rescue because federal regulations prohibited the landing of the helicopter in the national forest except in cases of emergency. Federal agents argued that since the boy was able to wave his arms, he was in no immediate danger, and thus there was no emergency.

Federal agents insisted that the boy be rescued by a party on foot, even though rescue workers argued that the terrain would prevent such a rescue. Indeed, as rescue workers attempted to cut a path through the hilly terrain, they were unable to reach the child. Eventually, three days after the boy was located, federal agents consented to bypass the regulations and allow the helicopter to land and rescue the boy (Gregory 2003).

These are just two examples of what sociologist Robert Merton (1968) termed **bureaucratic ritualism**. Merton defined this as a focus on rules and regulations to the point of undermining the goals of the organization. While not all bureaucracies will become ritualized, it does appear to be a frequent occurrence in large bureaucracies.

Bureaucratic Inertia

Bureaucratic inertia refers to the tendency of bureaucracies to perpetuate themselves over time. As bureaucracies expand over time, they often grow beyond their original purpose. In such cases, it is not uncommon for the bureaucracy to take on a life of its own, sometimes even switching goals in an effort to remain intact. For example, the March of Dimes was formed as a charity to fight polio. Once a vaccine for polio was discovered and the disease virtually eliminated, the March of Dimes was no longer needed. Rather than disband the complex bureaucracy, however, the organization expanded its mission to raise money to fight other diseases as well.

Alienation

Although Max Weber recognized that bureaucracies significantly increase the productivity of organizations, he also noted that bureaucracies tend to alienate the very people that they were designed to serve. This alienation affects not only customers but also those who work in the bureaucracy, both the managed and their managers. This is because, as we have already learned, bureaucracies become rule oriented, often to the point of impersonalization. Individualism becomes lost in the process. Individuals become cogs in the machine, subject to the whims of the organization. As Weber put it, the threat of bureaucracy is that although bureaucracies were designed to serve people, the alienation caused by bureaucracies may cause people to serve the bureaucracies instead.

CONCEPT LEARNING CHECK 5.4   Formal Organizations

Identify each of the following types of formal organizations as either normative, coercive, or utilitarian.

1. Being drafted into the military
2. A charity organization
3. Going to college
4. Working at a sub shop
5. Joining a church

5.5 **Future Opportunities for Organizations**

Organizations are leveraging their knowledge and technology to help them become more global and flexible in response to opportunity.

■ Describe two important ways that organizations are adapting to contemporary environments.

Like all social institutions, organizations change over time. When Weber first wrote about bureaucracies, he concentrated on the tendency of bureaucracies toward rigidity and hierarchical organization. Although this view remains largely valid to this day, bureaucratic organizations have begun to change in ways that Weber could not have predicted. These changes present new challenges to the bureaucratic structure. To respond to these changes and remain competitive, many bureaucratic structures have become more adaptive to their environment, changing their organization and operation.

Globalism

Communication and transportation technologies have dramatically increased the size and number of networks of the global marketplace. Corporations have responded by globalizing their operations, often having manufacturing based in one country, customer service in another, and packaging and distribution in still another, all while maintaining their corporate headquarters in still another nation. Although it is often hard to see how such an organization promotes efficiency, by dividing each task among different nations, large organizations can capitalize on opportunities that otherwise would not exist. Additionally, since not every task requires a high degree of education or skill, many jobs can be outsourced to other countries at less cost, thus increasing profits and allowing the bureaucracy to expand. Globalism also allows the opening of new potential markets for the organization. However, the idiosyncrasies of each culture mean that often, bureaucratic organizations must adapt to the beliefs, values, and expectations of a variety of ways of life.

Globalism has also brought opportunities to many developing nations that otherwise would not be possible. The expansion of bureaucratic organizations to other countries brings technologies, ideas, and, of course, jobs to nations that typically have high rates of poverty. These jobs provide opportunities for people in developing nations to improve their quality of life as well as contribute to the local and national economy.

Flexible Workplace

Increasing demands to balance work and family, coupled with advances in computer and communication technology, have led some organizations to provide a flexible workplace. The flexible workplace may take many forms. It may take the form of allowing workers to work from home, offer flexible work hours, and allow liberal leave time to attend to family matters. Flexible work environments may also take the form of flexible work hours, in which workers have some discretion to decide the hours they arrive at and leave work. Employees may also have the option to work four days a week for longer hours or five days a week with shorter hours each day.

The flexible workplace may also encourage workers to work and solve problems in a team setting. Work groups or teams carry distinct advantages that generally improve the outcomes of tasks. Interestingly, groups no longer need to meet face to face. Communication technologies allow for people to interact across geographic boundaries. Groups can work together in real time from home, from the office, or across the country.

Finally, the flexible workplace offers new forms of remuneration for employees. Benefits such as on-site child care, retirement benefits, and health care are highly sought after by modern workers. These types of job perquisites increase the competitiveness of the organizations because they attract workers who are trying to balance family, work, and other responsibilities of modern life.

CONCEPT LEARNING CHECK 5.5	Future Opportunities for Organizations

Provide a complete answer to the following question.

1. List five ways that modern bureaucratic organizations are adapting to social and economic changes.

Visual Summary   Groups and Organizations

5.1   Types of Social Groups

- A social group is defined as two or more people who have something in common.
- Groups are believed to have emergent properties, while aggregates are merely individuals who temporarily share the same physical space.
- Primary groups refer to groups with which we feel a deep sense of belonging.
- Secondary groups are larger, impersonal groups to which we belong
- In-groups are groups that we identify with and that form key parts of our identity.
- Out-groups are groups toward which we feel a sense of competition or antagonism.

- Reference groups provide a means of anticipatory socialization.
- Social networks are links that connect people to one another.
- Strong ties are connections within a network that link people in a close fashion.
- Weak ties are connections within a network that we interact with infrequently.
- Emerging technologies are changing the ways in which networks are created and maintained.

5.2   Group Interaction and Leadership

- Fiske identified four elementary forms of social action.
- Communal sharing is a form of interaction in which the group takes precedence over the individual.
- In authority ranking, one person in the interaction possesses more social power than the other.
- In equality ranking, the individuals are presumed to be equal in status and authority.
- In market pricing, the free market determines the circumstances of interaction.

- There are three basic leadership styles in groups.
- Democratic leaders give everyone a say in the operation of the group.
- Authoritarian leaders run the group in a dictatorial fashion.
- Laissez-faire leaders allow the group to function more or less on its own.
- Leadership can also be divided into task and expressive leadership.

5.3   Group Dynamics: Size, Diversity, and Conformity

- The dyad is the most basic social group.
- Group stability begins with the triad.
- As groups become larger, the number of possible interactions increases, making groups more stable.
- The Asch experiment demonstrated the effect of group pressure on individual decision making.

- The Milgram experiment demonstrated the effects of authority on individual decision making.
- Irving Janis developed the concept of groupthink to describe the tendency of groups to form rigid views.
- Janis identified eight characteristics of groupthink.

Andrea Booher/FEMA

5.4 Formal Organizations

- A formal organization is an organization that is rationally structured to efficiently achieve a specific goal.
- There are three kinds of formal organizations: utilitarian, normative, and coercive.
- Members of utilitarian organizations commit to the organization voluntarily and for personal gain.
- Members of normative organizations join to pursue a sense of belonging or to pursue a moral goal.

- Membership in coercive organizations is not voluntary, and the goal of such organizations is often to change the beliefs or behaviors of members.
- A bureaucracy is an organizational model that is designed to achieve specific tasks in a very efficient way.
- Max Weber identified six traits of bureaucratic organizations.
- Although bureaucracies have many benefits, they also have significant drawbacks.

© Daryl Lang/Shutterstock, Inc.

5.5 Future Opportunities for Organizations

- Organizations change over time.
- Organizations are becoming more global.

- Organizations are becoming more flexible.

5.1 Types of Social Groups

1. Tyrone and Phillip are waiting together at a bus stop with three other people. Sociologists would most likely describe this gathering as a(n):
   A. social group.
   B. aggregate.
   C. bureaucracy.
   D. formal organization.

2. Carlita grew up in a close-knit, loving family that gave her a strong sense of values. Cooley would call her family a:
   A. secondary group.
   B. generalized other.
   C. primary group.
   D. significant other.

3. As Carlita goes to school, her world view expands beyond the values of her family. Cooley would describe her school as a:
   A. secondary group.
   B. generalized other.
   C. primary group.
   D. significant other.

4. Pablo is a member of the Knights of Rest, a chess club at his school. Soon, they will play their arch rivals, the Kings of Heart High. Pablo sees the Kings as a(n):
   A. secondary group.
   B. in-group.
   C. primary group.
   D. out-group.

5. Pablo feels a deep sense of belonging with the Knights of Rest, and his position as team captain comprises a key part of his identity. The Knights of Rest would be considered a(n):
   A. secondary group.
   B. out-group.
   C. in-group.
   D. aggregate.

6. Ulla wants to be a college professor. She begins to dress and act like her course instructors, even reading many of the books that she sees them reading. For Ulla, college professors form a(n):
   A. aggregate.
   B. reference group.
   C. out-group.
   D. bureaucracy.

7. Bill has an acquaintance that he sees only once or twice a year at club meetings. His acquaintance might be considered a(n):
   A. strong tie.
   B. structural hole.
   C. weak tie.
   D. clique.

8. Reginald has kept in touch with his favorite professor, cultivating the connection in the hopes that the professor will write him a letter of recommendation. This connection would be described as a(n).
   A. in-group.
   B. weak tie.
   C. secondary group.
   D. strong tie.

5.2 Group Interaction and Leadership

9. Burma lives in a society that shares all resources. Fiske would describe their primary form of interaction as:
   A. communal sharing.
   B. market pricing.
   C. equality matching.
   D. authority ranking.

10. Bertha exchanged Christmas gifts with her best friend Rachel. Fiske would describe this exchange as:
    A. communal sharing.
    B. market pricing.
    C. equality matching.
    D. authority ranking.

11. Peter goes to the local farmer's market and pays four dollars for a pint of strawberries. Fiske would describe this exchange as:
    A. communal sharing.
    B. market pricing.
    C. equality matching.
    D. authority ranking.

12. Cathy allows her employees to work at their own pace and in their own way. She allows them to make many decisions for themselves and advises them only when asked. Cathy's leadership style would be described as:
    A. expressive leadership.
    B. laissez-faire leadership.
    C. authoritarian leadership.
    D. democratic leadership.

13. Samson solicits input from all group members and attempts to create consensus before making a decision. His leadership style would best be described as:
    A. expressive leadership.
    B. laissez-faire leadership.
    C. authoritarian leadership.
    D. democratic leadership.

5.3 Group Dynamics: Size, Diversity, and Conformity

14. Tracy is listening to a song and trying to learn the lyrics. Although she believes that the lyrics say one thing, all of her friends tell her that the lyrics say something else. Who would predict that Tracy will come to hear the lyrics as her friends suggest?
A. Milgram
B. Fiske
C. Asch
D. Lawler

15. Billy's club is comprised solely of males between the ages of 18 and 24. His club has a high degree of:
A. homogeneity.
B. groupthink.
C. heterogeneity.
D. expressive leadership.

5.4 Formal Organizations

16. Belinda starts a charity that is structured to achieve the goal of eliminating child illiteracy. Her charity might be considered a(n):
A. coercive organization.
B. formal organization.
C. homogeneous organization.
D. heterogeneous organization.

17. Ben joins Belinda's charity because he believes that every child should be able to read. For Ben, the charity represents a(n):
A. coercive organization.
B. expressive group.
C. utilitarian organization.
D. normative organization.

18. Jason is sentenced to jail for petty theft. From his perspective, prison represents a(n)
A. coercive organization.
B. expressive group.
C. utilitarian organization.
D. normative organization.

5.5 Future Opportunities for Organizations

19. Kelly is a customer service representative for a major company. She feels bad that a customer who requested help hung up in anger because she was unable to help her with her problem due to company regulations. Kelly and the customer are encountering what dysfunction of bureaucracy?
A. Alienation
B. Bureaucratic inertia
C. Bureaucratic ritualism
D. Groupthink

20. Because of Kelly's inability to help customers, she feels like she has become lost in the bureaucratic process. Weber would describe her feelings as:
A. globalism.
B. alienation.
C. bureaucratic inertia.
D. groupthink.

CHAPTER ESSAY QUESTIONS

1. Describe how online communication is changing the ways in which networks are constructed.

2. Discuss the role of task leaders and expressive leaders in avoiding groupthink.

CHAPTER DISCUSSION QUESTIONS

1. How do you think that bureaucracies will change in the next 20 years? What do you think will drive these changes?

2. What role do emotions play in Fiske's elementary forms of social action?

3. Have you ever been part of an aggregate that turned into a social group? What were the emergent properties that resulted in the transformation?

4. Share with the class some of your secondary groups. How do these groups contribute to your sense of belonging in society? How are your personal values shaped by your membership in these social groups?

5. How does the two party political system produce in-group and out-group attitudes and behaviors among Americans? What are the outcomes?

6. Share with the class how your reference groups affect your decisions about your occupational choices and consequently your behaviors. For example, are you mindful of how you interact online and face-to-face in formal and informal social environments?

7. Do you agree with Granovetter (1973) that weak ties may be more advantageous than strong ties in pursuing opportunities through our social networks? Why or why not?

8. Examining the findings of Bales (1950), discuss how definitions of status influence the emergence of leaders in groups. For example, does the sex, race, or social class of an individual affect authority ranking? Why or why not?

9. Discuss how groupthink and group dynamics may have contributed to the mortgage crisis and consequently the

Great Recession. Use the findings of Asch (1952) and Milgram (1963) to frame your discussion.

10. Discuss the formal organization structure of your college using Weber's (1925) six traits of an ideal bureaucracy. As a student have you experienced some of the bureaucratic dysfunctions such as bureaucratic ritualism?

CHAPTER PROJECTS

INDIVIDUAL PROJECTS

1. Go online to learn about the social network, LinkedIn. Write an analysis paper incorporating chapter information and key terms.

2. Write an analysis paper about groups such as juries, legislators, and/or boards of directors, among others

GROUP PROJECTS

1. Visit a public social environment in which you find an aggregate. Observe the interactions including any social groups and group dynamics. What patterns did you observe? Write a report of your findings incorporating chapter information and key terms.

2. Imagine you work for the human resources department at a large corporation. You have been tasked with developing a brochure helping employees cope with bureaucratic

that make group decisions. Consider group dynamics such as group conformity, obedience to authority, coalitions, cliques, factions, and leadership styles that influence decisions and consequently have broad societal implications such as judicial rulings, laws, jobs, etc.

dysfunction. What information, programs, and resources would you include in this brochure?

3. Design a pamphlet that explains what groupthink is and how to avoid it.

4. Draw a map of one of your social networks. Identify at least two strong ties and two weak ties. Discuss ways in which the network provides advantages for you and ways in which the network could be improved.

CHAPTER KEY TERMS

Aggregate	Formal organization	Organizational environment
Authority ranking	Group dynamics	Out-groups
Bureaucracy	Groupthink	Primary group
Bureaucratic inertia	Heterogeneity	Reference groups
Bureaucratic ritualism	Homogeneous	Secondary groups
Clique	Ideal types	Social group
Communal sharing	In-groups	Social networks
Dyad	Instrumental leader	Strong ties
Emergent properties	Leader	Triad
Equality matching	Market pricing	Weak ties
Expressive leader	Organization	

ANSWERS TO CONCEPT LEARNING CHECKS

5.1 Types of Social Groups

1. A. Mother [Primary Group]; B. Schoolteacher [Secondary Group]; C. Media [Secondary Group]; D. Best friend [Primary Group]; E. Sister [Primary Group]

2. A. People waiting for a bus [Aggregate]; B. Students in a sociology class [Aggregate]; C. Church congregation [Group]; D. Students studying in a library [Aggregate]; E. Members of the chess club [Group]

5.2 Group Interaction and Leadership

1. You are leading a team of inexperienced workers to build a railroad bridge across a waterway. You have a strict deadline of three weeks to build the bridge. [Authoritarian]

2. You have been chosen to lead a team of scientists spread out across the United States on a project to construct a new space vessel that will travel to Neptune. [Laissez-faire]

3. You are the new club president. Your task is to build membership in the club, as well as to arrange meeting times and activities for the club. [Democratic]

5.3 Group Dynamics: Size, Diversity, and Conformity

1. Groups believe that their beliefs are infallible and correct and thus the group will take excessive risks to defend its views. [A. Illusion of invulnerability]

2. Out-groups are portrayed as enemies and thus are portrayed in a generally negative way. [B. Stereotyped view of out-groups]

3. Members of the group take it upon themselves to make sure that opposition within the group is squashed. [C. Self-appointed mind guards]

4. Alternative views that might benefit the group are suppressed and therefore lost. [E. Self-censorship]

5. The group uses sanctions to encourage members to agree with the group's decision. [F. Direct pressure on group members to conform]

6. Groups believe that their position is ordained and therefore inherently correct. [H. Inherent morality]

7. The group believes that everyone in the group agrees with everyone else in the group. [D. Illusion of unanimity]

8. The group as a whole uses a variety of techniques to avoid entertaining alternative ideas. [G. Collective rationalization]

5.4 Formal Organizations

1. Being drafted into the military [coercive]

2. A charity organization [normative]

3. Going to college [utilitarian]

4. Working at a sub shop [utilitarian]

5. Joining a church [normative]

5.5 Future Opportunities for Organizations

1. Five ways that modern bureaucratic organizations are adapting to social and economic changes: allowing employees to work from home; providing on-site child care; allowing people to work across geographic boundaries; outsourcing and globalization; providing medical insurance.

ANSWERS TO CHAPTER REVIEW TEST

5.1 Types of Social Groups

1. B. An aggregate is defined as individuals who temporarily share the same physical space but who do not share a sense of belonging.

2. C. Primary groups refer to groups to which we feel a deep sense of belonging and that give us our sense of identity.

3. A. Secondary groups are larger, formal groups that expand our understanding of the social world.

4. D. An out-group is a group toward which we feel competition or antagonism.

5. C. In-groups are groups to which we feel a sense of belonging and that form a part of our identity.

6. B. Reference groups are groups that provide a guide for future roles.

7. C. People with whom we do not interact with often or with whom we have weak social relationships are called weak ties.

8. D. Strong ties refer to ties that link people in a close fashion.

5.2 Group Interaction and Leadership

9. A. In communal sharing interactions, the interests of society outweigh the interests of individuals.

10. C. In equality matching, individuals are presumed to be equal in status and authority.

11. B. In market pricing, the exchange is dictated by conditions of supply and demand.

12. B. Laissez-faire leaders allow the group to function more or less on its own.

13. D. Democratic leaders give everyone in the group input into the functioning of the group.

5.3 Group Dynamics: Size, Diversity, and Conformity

14. C. Asch's experiment demonstrates the ability of groups to influence the perceptions of individuals.

15. A. Groups in which all people are similar are called homogeneous groups.

5.4 Formal Organizations

16. B. A formal organization is an organization that is rationally structured to efficiently achieve a specific goal.

17. D. A person joins a normative organization because he or she believes that the goal of the organization is worthwhile.

18. A. Coercive organizations exist for the purpose of changing a person's beliefs, values, or behaviors.

5.5 Future Opportunities for Organizations

19. C. Bureaucratic ritualism is a focus on rules and regulations to the point of undermining the goals of the organization.

20. B. Weber described alienation as a feeling of impersonalization caused by excessive adherence to rules and regulations within a bureaucratic organization.

ANSWERS TO CHAPTER ESSAY QUESTIONS

1. Describe how online communication is changing the ways in which networks are constructed. Online communication is changing the ways in which networks are constructed because it eliminates many of the physical barriers that normally prevent the formation of networks. For example, one of the most salient barriers to network construction is proximity of individuals. In other words, the closer people are to one another, the greater the likelihood of interaction; the farther individuals are from one another, the less likelihood of interaction. Online communication is significant in that it renders proximity irrelevant to the formation of networks. Additionally, online communication allows groups to communicate efficiently across time. As opposed to traditional mail, which can take days, email, chat, or text is nearly instantaneous.

2. Discuss the role of task leaders and expressive leaders in avoiding groupthink. Groupthink can be a dangerous result of groups becoming rigid in their thinking. The two types of leaders—task and expressive—can engage in certain practices to avoid groupthink. Task leaders can be sure to allow all differences of opinion to surface and be entertained. The task leader can also take steps to deter stereotypes and the illusion of invulnerability. Similarly, the expressive leader can ensure that individuals who would evolve into self-appointed mind guards remain respectful of members in the group who may disagree with the group's decision. The expressive leader can also ensure that individual ideas are not censored and that the group does not place undue pressure on dissenting members to conform.

REFERENCES

Allport, G. 1960. *Personality & Social Encounter.* Boston: Beacon Press.

Asch, S. 1952. "Effects of Group Pressure upon the Modification and Distortion of Judgments." Pp. 202–256 in *Readings in Social Psychology*, edited by Guy Swanson, Theodore M. Newcomb, and Eugene L. Hartley. New York: Holt, Reinhart, and Winston.

Bales, R. F. 1950. *Interaction Process Analysis.* Reading, MA: Addison-Wesley.

Baron, J. N., M. T. Hannan, and M. D. Burton. 1999. "Building on the Iron Cage: Determinants of Managerial Intensity in the Early Years of Organizations." *American Sociological Review* (64)4:527–47.

Cooley, C. H. 1909. *Social Organization: A Study of the Larger Mind.* New York: Charles Scribner's Sons.

Fiske, A. P. 1991. *Structures of Social Life: The Four Elementary Forms of Human Relations.* New York: Macmillan.

Grannovetter, M. S. 1973. "The Strength of Weak Ties." *American Journal of Sociology* 78(6, May):1360–1380.

Gregory, L. 2003. *Hey Idiot!: Chronicles of Human Stupidity.* New York: Andrews McMeel.

Halberstam, D. 1986. *The Reckoning.* New York: Avon Books.

Janis, I. L. 1972. *Victims of Groupthink.* Boston: Houghton Mifflin.

Janis, I. L. 1982. *Groupthink: Psychological Studies of Policy Decisions and Fiascoes.* Boston: Houghton Mifflin.

Merton, R. K. 1938 (1968). "Social Structure and Anomie." *American Sociological Review* 3:672–682.

Milgram, S. 1963. "Behavioral Study of Obedience." *Journal of Abnormal and Social Psychology* (67)4:371–378.

Morgenson, G., and J. Rosner. 2011. *Reckless Endangerment: How Outside Ambition, Greed, and Corruption Led to Economic Armageddon.* New York: Times Books.

"Places Where the System Broke Down." 2005. *Time* (September 19):34–41.

Simmel, G. 1955. *Conflict and the Web of Group Affiliation.* Glencoe, IL: Free Press.

Weber, M. 1925 (1968). *Economy and Society: An Outline of Interpretive Sociology.* New York: Bedminster Press.

Chapter Overview ▼

6 Deviance and Crime

Learning Objectives ▾

6.1
- Explain the concept of deviance as a social construct.
- Analyze how societies exert control.
- Discuss the psychological views of deviance.

6.2
- Explain the structural-functional approach and the four positive functions of deviance.
- Compare and contrast opportunity theory and strain theory.

6.3
- Describe symbolic interactionism's perspective on deviance and the major theories associated with it.

6.4
- Discuss the social conflict perspective, distinguishing between different social constructs as they relate to deviance.

6.5
- Give examples of various categories of crime.
- Discuss and compare the attributes of at least two categories of crime.

6.6
- Discuss age, race, gender, and social class as they relate to crime statistics.

6.7
- Describe the criminal justice system in the United States and the roles played by the police, courts, and corrections.

© Andrew Buckin/Shutterstock, Inc.

It was 15 minutes before the deadline for submitting the homework online when Charlie, one of my students, began to panic. He had spent the past 30 minutes submitting his essay to be automatically graded only to be repeatedly disappointed as his score came back three times: 45% . . . 50% . . . 52%. He cursed himself for not starting on the essay sooner. He began to realize that he was unlikely to get a decent score before the deadline. In desperation he used his Internet browser to search for information on the topic, found an article in an online encyclopedia, and found a section that seemed to be about the topic of his assignment. He copied and pasted the text into his essay, which he then submitted online as his essay. In a few seconds he had his results back . . . 93%. "Whew!" he thought, "I dodged a bullet this time."

Unfortunately for Charlie, the program continued to process the submitted assignments. But now it was no longer grading student essays; it was looking for evidence of cheating or plagiarism. By 8:33 the next morning as I settled into my desk chair and pulled up the reports from yesterday's assignment, Charlie's essay was at the top of a list of essays that looked suspiciously similar to essays from other students and Internet sources. I had the computer generate a side-by-side comparison of Charlie's essay and the online article and could clearly see he had copied most of his essay directly from the article. By 9:15 AM, I had concluded that Charlie had plagiarized his essay. I changed his grade to a zero for the assignment and sent an email to both Charlie and the dean's office with the report attached. Charlie was eventually called in to speak with the dean and was placed on academic probation.

Cheating is not unique to Charlie but is found in many academic settings. For example, sociologist Peter Demerath, in his ethnographic study of the culture of an American high school, found cheating to be very common. One teacher said, "cheating is instrumental in getting what they want." Another said, "They cheat and they are open about it. They need the points. They need to get in. They need to get into college." (Demerath 2009).

6.1 Overview: Understanding Deviance and Crime

What a society considers to be deviant is relative and varies with time and place.

- Explain the concept of deviance as a social construct.
- Analyze how societies exert control.
- Discuss the psychological views of deviance.

Why do some people cheat and not others? Who decides what is cheating? Who decides how someone should be punished when caught? How do theories of deviance help us understand why deviance occurs and who will be deviant? How does society react to deviance and through what institutions? How does all of this change as so much of our lives are lived out over the Internet, where the information can be examined and judged by others—now, or even years from now? All these questions, and more, are questions that can be asked of deviance in general and are the focus of this chapter.

What is Deviance and Who Defines It?

Deviance The violation of norms of a group, society, or one's peers.

Deviance is the violation of norms of a group, society, or one's peers. Since norms are often different in different cultures, notions of what is deviance also differ. What is considered deviant in one culture, in a subculture, or at one time may be considered perfectly normal in another culture, subculture, or time. Consider different cultures. In most cultures, suicide is considered deviant. Yet in traditional Japanese culture, *hari-kiri*—in which someone commits suicide by ritual disembowelment—is expected of disgraced noblemen or leaders. In traditional Eskimo culture, when an older person is no longer able to contribute to society, his or her suicide is approved.

Notions of deviance also change over time. Cigarette smoking was banned as deviant in 14 states in the early 1900s, was regarded as socially approved behavior throughout much of the mid-20th century, and today is once again regarded as deviant behavior that should be banned in many public places. Nowhere are changing definitions of deviance over time more evident than when we review recent milestones in American gay rights, as summarized in FIGURE 6-1.

FIGURE 6-1 Milestones in American gay rights.

1969	Riots follow a police raid on the gay bar, Stonewall Inn, in Greenwich Village, New York City. Seen as the start of the gay rights movement in the United States and around the world.
1970	The first LGBT pride parade is held in Los Angeles and the first gay liberation day march is held in New York City.
1975	Homosexuality is legalized in California with passage of a bill in the state legislature.
1977	Openly gay politician, Harvey Milk, is elected to the San Francisco board of supervisors, only to be killed within a year by fellow city supervisor, Dan White.
1979	The first national homosexual rights march is held in Washington, DC.
1977	Heavily supported by former beauty queen Anita Bryant, a group called Save Our Children, Miami-Dade overturns a county ordinance prohibiting discrimination based on sexual orientation.
1993	"Don't ask, don't tell" becomes the policy for the US Armed Forces. The military could not ask military personnel if they were gay, and so long as someone did not make their sexual preference known they could serve.
1996	The US Defense of Marriage Act is signed into law, permitting the federal government and other states to choose not to recognize same sex marriages from other states.
1998	The torture and murder of a young gay man, Matthew Shepard in Laramie, Wyoming inspired demonstrations across the United States.
2004	The first same-sex marriage certificates in the United States are issued by San Francisco Mayor Gavin Newsom only to be later nullified by the California Supreme Court. Massachusetts recognizes same-sex marriages. Eleven states pass laws or constitutional amendments prohibiting same-sex marriage.
2007	New Hampshire, Oregon, and Washington take major strides by either legalizing civil unions (New Hampshire) or domestic partnerships. California's and Connecticut's supreme courts legalize same-sex marriage.
2008	Opponents of gay marriage win enough electoral support in California to roll back the state supreme court decision with Proposition 8, which is promptly challenged in court.
2009	Iowa, Vermont, Maine, and New Hampshire approve same-sex marriage.
2010	Judge Vaughn Walker of the US District Court for the Northern District of California declares Proposition 8 unconstitutional. The case is promptly appealed.
2011	The military policy of "don't ask, don't tell" is repealed making it possible for gays and lesbians to serve openly in the military. A year later a major study of the military finds no negative impacts of the repeal.

Within the same society, subcultures define deviance differently. Most of us would probably be embarrassed to be found naked in a public or semipublic place. Yet people who attend nudist camps routinely appear unclothed in front of unrelated people of both sexes and carry on otherwise normal daily activities such as having meals, playing games, or discussing the weather (Weinberg 1976). In the United States, some states ban gambling completely, other states permit gambling anywhere, and in still other states gambling is permitted in restricted locations such as riverboat casinos or Indian reservations.

What this means is that no one particular action, thought, or belief is deviant by nature. Deviance is not absolute but relative. To become deviant, an act must be defined as deviant by particular cultural norms. In short, deviance is socially constructed.

Crime A violation of criminal law.

Social control Efforts by society to regulate people's behavior and thoughts.

Negative sanctions Actions directed against a person or persons in response to an act of deviance.

Ostracism Excluding someone from the normal activities of a group.

Positive sanction An action aimed at a person that seeks to reward good behavior and encourage the person and others to continue such acts.

Galileo was labeled deviant because of his belief that Earth was not the center of the universe.

© Elena Korn/Shutterstock, Inc.

The most serious forms of deviance, viewed as deviant by the larger society, are crimes. A **crime** is a violation of criminal law. The laws that define something as a crime are socially constructed. People who commit crimes are subject to formal sanctions applied within the criminal justice system. We will return to discuss types of crime and the criminal justice system below.

Most of the discussion of deviance in this chapter will focus on deviance defined by the dominant culture within a society, the culture that most influences laws and the criminal justice system that enforces them. But we should not lose sight of the fact that societies today are complex and diverse, with subcultures and countercultures having their own sets of norms and their own views of what is deviance. Each of those subcultures seeks to define what is deviance, but some of them have more influence on the larger society than others.

Varieties of Deviance

Deviance occurs when someone's thoughts or behaviors are *different* from those of other people. They do not necessarily have to be *worse* or less desirable. The focus is usually on negative deviance, such as lying, theft, rape, or fraud. However, sociologists Alex and Druann Heckert (2004) point out that there are also many examples in which too much of a good thing can lead to criticism of people who "overdo" it. Examples include "rate busters" who work much harder than other workers, making the rest look bad, "fanatics" such as members of religious cults who display too much group loyalty, tactless people who are brutally honest, or "yes men" who never stand up to people.

Deviance doesn't always involve behavior. Since norms (expectations for behavior) can be expectations for beliefs or attitudes people hold, someone whose beliefs or attitudes are much different from those of others can also be regarded as a deviant and punished. During the Inquisition, for example, Galileo was forced to recant his view that the Earth was not the center of the universe. It was not sufficient that he change his behavior by no longer talking about it; he could not even believe it. *Political correctness* is a phrase sometimes used in American culture to describe social or political beliefs currently favored in a culture for which disagreement is regarded as deviant.

Social Control

Social control consists of efforts by society to regulate people's behavior and thoughts. Often social control takes the form of responses to deviance. **Negative sanctions** are actions directed against a person or persons in response to an act of deviance. Those actions are often intended to make it clear something is viewed as deviant, to punish the person or persons responsible, and to discourage them and others from repeating the deviant behavior. A mild slap on the wrist by a mother when a child reaches across her plate at the dinner table, an angry honking of your horn when someone cuts you off on the highway, or a "shh" from other moviegoers when you talk too loudly at the theater are all examples of relatively mild negative sanctions. Negative sanctions can also be much more severe. A particularly severe form of negative sanction is **ostracism**—excluding someone from the normal activities of a group. Some religious subcultures such as the Amish use ostracism as a form of social control by ignoring a person and forbidding them to talk, eat, or socialize with other members of the group. A **positive sanction** is an action aimed at a person that seeks to reward him or her for good behavior and encourage the person and others to continue such acts. Medals handed out to troops for bravery in battle, honor rolls at college, and blue ribbons at county fairs are all examples of positive sanctions designed to affirm the righteousness of individuals.

Competing Biological and Psychological Explanations of Deviance

Early attempts to understand deviance often focused on the individual and sought explanations for deviance in biological or psychological factors. Early biological views on deviance were relatively naive and are not generally respected today. Cesare Lombroso (1911) thought criminals were throwbacks in evolutionary development and were more likely to look apelike, with considerable body hair, deeply inset eyes, and a strong forehead and prominent cheek and jaw bones. American psychologist William Sheldon (1949) identified three body shapes—endomorphs (overweight), mesomorphs (muscular), and ectomorphs (lean) FIGURE 6-2. Sheldon argued that criminals were more likely to be muscular mesomorphs. But later research found criminals to include people of all body shapes, and those perspectives were abandoned. More recent biological approaches have attempted to isolate genetic factors related to particular personality traits that in turn predict deviance. Results of early studies were mixed (Kringlen 1967; Wilson and Herrnstein 1985) and were more often applied to street crime committed by people from lower social classes and less to white-collar crimes committed by people in higher social classes, suggesting a strong class bias (Empey 1982).

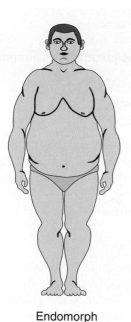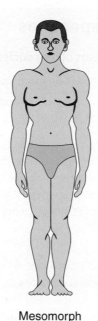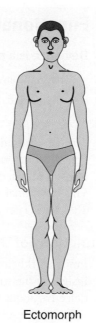

| Endomorph | Mesomorph | Ectomorph |

FIGURE 6-2 American psychologist William Sheldon identified three body shapes—endomorph, mesomorph, and ectomorph.

© Norbert Sobolewski/Shutterstock, Inc.

Psychological views of deviance also focus on the individual and his or her personality traits that might influence deviance. Personality theory argues that some personalities, such as the extrovert personality, are more impulsive and more likely to exceed the bounds of acceptable behavior (Eysenck 1977). Containment theory argues that some people are less able to constrain their impulses and behavior by deferring pleasure. Learning theory argues that deviance is socially learned from the observation of others. Children watching violence on television, even if they do not engage in the behavior, learn how to be violent (Bandura 1973). Finally, the frustration-aggression hypothesis argues that when people have unfulfilled or blocked needs, wishes, or biological urges, those can produce frustration, which in turn can lead to aggressive behavior (Berkowitz 1962).

It appears likely that genetic factors and psychological factors may contribute to our understanding of deviance. However, our knowledge of those factors is still limited, and it is clear that social factors, such as social class, which cannot be explained biologically or psychologically, play a strong role in deviance. Even more striking, biological and psychological explanations completely ignore key aspects of deviance, including how we decide what is deviant, the role of power in influencing those decisions, why some people are defined as deviant while others are not, and the positive consequences of deviance for society. For answers to these questions, we turn to sociological perspectives on deviance.

CONCEPT LEARNING CHECK 6.1   Understanding Deviance and Crime

Match the following concepts with phrases consistent with them.

CONCEPT	PHRASE
_____ 1. "Positive" deviance	**A.** Children watching violence on TV are more likely to be violent.
_____ 2. Positive sanction	**B.** Criminals are more likely to have certain body types.
_____ 3. Early biological view of deviance	**C.** Honor roll
_____ 4. Learning theory view of deviance	**D.** Is not limited to behaviors but can be about attitudes or beliefs.
_____ 5. Deviance	**E.** Rate busters

6.2 Functionalist Perspectives

Deviance is a necessary part of any society and has positive consequences.

- Explain the structural-functional approach and the four positive functions of deviance.
- Compare and contrast opportunity theory and strain theory.

The functionalist perspective emphasizes how societies are able to maintain **social order**—a level of social organization based on institutions, customs, and patterns of interaction capable of providing the conditions for their continuing survival. This functional perspective was first proposed by sociologist Emile Durkheim (1893, 1895) and later elaborated on in strain theory and opportunity theory.

Social order A level of social organization based on institutions, customs, and patterns of interaction capable of providing the conditions for their continuing survival.

Functions of Deviance

Emile Durkheim was the first to describe what is now recognized as the fundamental insight of the structural-functional approach: deviance is not something abnormal or defective about society but is an essential part of society. Deviance, argues Durkheim, reflects both society's highest goals and its darkest fears. Deviance has four important positive functions.

1. **Society's response to deviance clarifies moral boundaries.** Singling out deviants and treating them differently reminds others of the limits of acceptable behavior. White-collar criminals caught and sent to prison, students punished for cheating, and murderers executed each help map out what behaviors are not to be tolerated in society.

2. **Deviance promotes social unity.** People who may have little else in common become unified by their shared revulsion at acts of terrorism such as the World Trade Center bombing or the Oklahoma City federal building explosion.

3. **Deviance affirms cultural values and norms.** We cannot have good without bad, virtue without vice. Every society needs forms of deviance viewed as bad in order to generate and sustain a sense of morality, a sense of what is good. Even a nation of saints, Durkheim argued, would need to identify bad acts—actions so minor as to be largely ignored in less perfect societies—to reaffirm the difference between good and evil. This is precisely what (Erikson 1966) found in his classic study of the early Puritans in Massachusetts Bay. Even in that Puritan society composed of conscientious, religious people, every year a consistent proportion of people were convicted of what most of us would regard as trivial or insignificant crimes.

4. **Deviance can promote necessary social change.** Deviance, argued Durkheim, can be "an anticipation of future morality." Acts viewed as deviant at one time can challenge the status quo and eventually become viewed as morally acceptable,

The Puritans routinely convicted people of what seem today like insignificant crimes.

© North Wind/North Wind Picture Archives

even morally required behavior in the future. Acts of civil disobedience during the Civil Rights Movement, such as Rosa Parks' refusal to give up her seat on a bus to a white man, or efforts by blacks to enroll in segregated schools, illustrate this point. While they may have been illegal at one time, they are viewed as morally responsible acts to be commended rather than condemned.

Notice that structural-functional theory emphasizes social structures and explains why we have deviance. This is fundamentally different in approach to biological or psychological approaches that focused on internal factors within individuals that explain why that particular individual is deviant.

Strain Theory

While Durkheim's work considers why deviance occurs, Robert Merton's strain theory focuses on why a particular individual might be deviant. Merton (1968) argues that whether deviance occurs and the kind of deviance that occurs depends on whether society provides culturally acceptable means to achieve cultural goals. **Cultural goals** include widely shared objectives like financial success, while **institutionalized means** for achieving those goals include job opportunities and education. When an individual both subscribes to the cultural goals of society and has access to legitimate means for achieving them, then this is described as **conformity**. Rags-to-riches stories of people such as the late Steve Jobs, CEO of Apple, Inc., who achieve great financial success through hard work and education, are examples of conformity. However, when an individual lacks access to accepted means for achieving success or rejects those goals, he or she experiences strain and may resort to any of four possible forms of deviance.

Merton argues that people who accept the cultural goal of financial success but lack legitimate means to achieve it, such as the poor who lack access to education and employment opportunities, are likely to reject legitimate means in favor of other ways of reaching their objective, such as selling drugs or stealing. This response Merton calls **innovation**—accepting cultural goals (e.g., wealth) but rejecting accepted means in favor of unconventional ways of achieving those goals (e.g., crime). In this view, "Al Capone represents the triumph of amoral intelligence over morally prescribed 'failure,' when the channels of vertical mobility are closed or narrowed in a society which places a high premium on economic affluence and social ascent for all its members" (Merton 1968).

The second form of deviance, **ritualism**, occurs when someone rejects cultural goals while continuing to pursue legitimate means. People who have given up on achieving their goals but who cling to their jobs are ritualists. They include teachers who have given up on inspiring students but who still go through the motions in their classes, politicians who no longer expect to make the world better but continue to hold on to their elected offices, and public defenders who recognize they will never have the time needed to defend their clients properly but who continue plodding through their caseloads.

When an individual both rejects cultural goals and rejects legitimate means for achieving them, she may commit either of two types of deviance. If she essentially drops out of society, participating only minimally, like alcoholics or drug addicts, then it is described as **retreatism**. If, on the other hand, she rejects these goals and accepted means and actively offers an alternative, such as political revolutionaries or members of countercultures, including radical survivalists, then it is described as **rebellion**.

Merton's strain theory has been used to explain why poor people and minorities often have higher arrest rates because they lack access to legitimate means of achieving economic affluence. It fits into the structural-functional perspective because it emphasizes the effect of social structures on deviance rather than individual characteristics. However, it is better at explaining crimes such as theft by poor people than it is explaining white-collar crime by the relatively affluent; and it does not predict which kind of deviance people will choose.

Cultural goals Widely shared objectives like having financial success.

Institutionalized means Legitimate means, such as job opportunities and education, for achieving goals.

Conformity When an individual both subscribes to the cultural goals of society and has access to legitimate means for achieving them.

Innovation The idea of accepting cultural goals (e.g., wealth) but rejecting accepted means in favor of unconventional ways of achieving those goals (e.g.,crime).

Ritualism When someone rejects cultural goals while continuing to pursue legitimate means.

Retreatism When a person drops out of society, participating only minimally.

Rebellion When someone rejects these goals and accepted means and actively offers an alternative.

Famed criminal, Al Capone, accepted the cultural goal of economic success while rejecting accepted means for attaining it.

© Underwood & Underwood/Corbis

Opportunity Theory

Richard Cloward and Lloyd Ohlin (1966) extended Merton's theory by applying it to juvenile delinquency and, in the process, shed more light on the kind of deviance an individual might choose. They argue that the kind of deviance that occurs depends not only on a lack of access to legitimate opportunity but also on the availability of **illegitimate opportunity structures**—ready access to illegal means. When someone has little or no access to legitimate opportunities to get ahead and has easy access to illegitimate opportunities, then, Cloward and Ohlin predict, criminal subcultures, such as street gangs or even organized crime, will likely result. If neither legitimate nor illegitimate opportunities are available, Cloward and Ohlin predict deviance will be in the form of retreatist subcultures composed of people who disengage from social life and abuse drugs or alcohol or conflicting subcultures of people who lash out at others out of frustration but with little hope of achieving their goals. More recent research has provided some empirical support for opportunity theory. For example, some gangs specialize in one form of criminal behavior or another, depending on the available opportunities or resources (Sheley et al. 1995). However, all of the structural-functional theories of deviance have sometimes been criticized for focusing on structural conditions in society that lead to deviance without examining individual-level factors that influence whether any single individual becomes deviant.

> **Illegitimate opportunity structures** Having ready access to illegal means.

CONCEPT LEARNING CHECK 6.2   How Do Functional Theories Explain Deviance?

For each of the following examples, indicate the theory within the functionalist perspective that best explains the example. Then identify the particular concept or function that best applies.

Example	Theory	Concept
1. An adolescent sees her friend caught shoplifting and resolves to never shoplift herself.		
2. Monique is a freshman in college but doesn't know what she wants to do with her life. She stays in college because her parents want her to go and people respect her when she says she is a college student.		
3. Jerome learned from his friends how to download music and videos from the Internet without paying for them. He soon stopped paying for CDs and DVDs.		

THEORY

A. Strain theory

B. Opportunity theory

C. Functional theory

CONCEPT

A. Illegitimate opportunity structure

B. Society's response to deviance clarifies moral boundaries

C. Ritualism

6.3 Symbolic Interactionism

Individuals define deviance based on a variety of factors and interactions with others.

- Describe symbolic interactionism's perspective on deviance and the major theories associated with it.

Where the functionalist perspective focuses on social structures that constrain individual behavior, symbolic interactionism examines how individuals interpret events and make decisions about whether to commit deviant acts. Theories within the symbolic interactionism tradition include differential association theory, differential reinforcement theory, control theory, and labeling theory. They each emphasize different processes, but they all share a view of people whose actions are affected by their own interpretations of the situation and, in the case of labeling theory, by the interpretations of others.

Differential Association Theory

One of the earliest theories of crime was first proposed by sociologist Edwin Sutherland (1940) and later expanded by Sutherland and Donald Cressey (1978). This **differential association theory** argues people are more likely to be deviant to the extent they are exposed to deviants. **Differential association** refers to the tendency of someone to spend more time with some individuals and less with others. In this view, people are more likely to be deviant if significant others are deviant, if more of their associates are deviant, and if they are exposed to deviance early in their lives. Hence, primary groups, and in particular peer groups, are where criminal behavior is learned.

A survey of high school and junior high students by Hirschi (1969) provided data consistent with differential association theory. Students were much more likely to commit two or more deviant acts when three or more of their friends had been picked up by the police (45%) than when none of their friends had been picked up by the police (7%). These results are displayed in FIGURE 6-3.

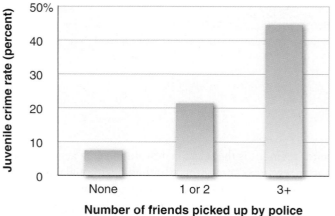

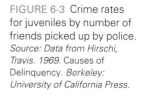

FIGURE 6-3 Crime rates for juveniles by number of friends picked up by police. *Source: Data from Hirschi, Travis. 1969.* Causes of Delinquency. *Berkeley: University of California Press.*

Differential Reinforcement Theory

Differential association theory was reformulated by Akers (1973) as **differential reinforcement theory**, which argues individuals learn criminal behavior through differential association, differential reinforcement, definitions of acceptable acts, and imitation. In this view, these four major concepts from learning theory are used to explain the occurrence of crime.

- Differential association again refers to the tendency of someone to spend more time with some individuals and less with others. People are exposed to illegal behavior through differential association. For example, they may learn from friends or family how to download music illegally.

- **Definitions of acceptable acts** are views of which acts are tolerable and which are unacceptable. Their view of the acts is based on definitions or ways of thinking about particular acts as acceptable, unacceptable, or tolerable. For example, they may view illegal music downloading as tolerable given the high price of music.

Differential association theory A theory which argues that people are more likely to be deviant to the extent they are exposed to deviants.

Differential association The tendency of someone to spend more time with some individuals and less with others.

Differential reinforcement theory A theory which argues that individuals learn criminal behavior through differential association, differential reinforcement, definitions of acceptable acts, and imitation.

Definitions of acceptable acts Views of which acts are tolerable and which are unacceptable.

Differential association theory argues that people adopt the behaviors of those with whom they associate.

Using differential association theory, sociologists (Martin and Hummer 1989) examined the social context of campus fraternities that appeared to encourage the sexual coercion of women. They conducted open-ended interviews with both Greek and non-Greek students, university administrators, and alumni advisers to Greek organizations.

They found that Greek fraternities compete with one another to convey an image of aggressive heterosexuality and masculinity to achieve status. They seek pledges who are athletic, sports oriented, can hold their liquor, and who "relate to girls." They avoid pledges who do not appear to be sufficiently masculine or appear to be "wimpy" and actively ostracize members suspected of being gay. Their culture emphasizes loyalty to their brothers (right or wrong), protection of one

another, and secrecy. There is considerable interfraternity rivalry and competition. As part of that rivalry, fraternities routinely commodify women, using them as bait for new members, servers, and sexual prey. Little Sisters programs, for example, recruit women to play a subordinate, supportive role for the fraternity, hosting parties and "taking care" of their "big brothers." Women are viewed as sexual conquests, and plying them with excessive alcohol to obtain sex is routine.

In short, Martin and Hummer conclude, fraternities provide a sociocultural context that encourages the sexual coercion of women (a felony) as a contest or game (Sato 1988). Fraternities, they argue, provide a social organization that effectively transmits a culture supporting abuse of women.

EVALUATE

1. This study took place more than 20 years ago. If you were to study fraternities today, how do you think the results might change?

2. Even if fraternities have a very different culture today and are more accepting of gays and more respectful of women, how, if at all, does differential association theory help explain how individual fraternity members might be influenced through their associations with other members?

Differential reinforcement
The selective reward of some acts and punishment of others.

Imitation When an individual copies the behavior of others.

Differential reinforcement theory may explain how people learn criminal behavior.

© eldeiv/Shutterstock, Inc.

- **Differential reinforcement** is the selective reward of some acts and punishment of others. The act is rewarded or punished through differential reinforcement. For example, they may often get away with downloading music.

- **Imitation** occurs when individuals copy the behavior of others. For example, they might first download music after watching a friend do it.

This perspective is illustrated in a study of computer crime among college students by Skinner and Fream (1997). They studied 581 students at a university, looking at various kinds of computer crime the students engaged in, including pirating software and gaining illegal access to sites. Their findings generally supported differential reinforcement theory. They found these forms of computer crime to be more common when peers also did it (differential association), and they learned about pirating by seeing family and teachers do it (imitation), and crime was much less common for students who firmly defined it as illegal (definitions), but there was little effect on their behavior of possible penalties (differential reinforcement).

In a classic work, Howard Becker (1953) used participant observation to study the process of learning to be a marijuana smoker in the 1950s. In the 1950s, smoking marijuana was much more hidden than it has become since. Becker described how a person must first overcome fears of negative effects and images. He found people usually learned by smoking with friends, that smoking could be fun, that they would not become slaves to the drug (as claimed by much of the public rhetoric of the time), that getting caught was unlikely, and how to hide being high if necessary. He pointed to the importance of learning, observation, and imitation for a person to learn the proper way to smoke and how to enjoy its effects. Additional studies find examples of deviance learned informally, through "hanging around" or in after-the-fact coaching, as occurs in learning to be a card hustler (Prus and Sharper 1977). Other studies have found relatively formal procedures for instructing newcomers, for deviance ranging from becoming a professional thief (Maurer 1964) to becoming a professional prostitute (Heyl 1979). Some forms of deviance, such as police corruption (Sherman 1974) even have a "career," a commonly followed sequence of actions leading to deeper and deeper involvement in the deviance.

Control Theory

Sociologist Walter Reckless (1967) proposed **social bond theory** in which he argued that everyone is tempted by opportunities for deviant behavior, but deviant acts are less likely when the individual's bonds to society are strong. The stronger the bond, the more likely the individual will resist temptation. The threat of losing a job or being condemned by family and friends is stronger for people who have a job and who have a strong link to family and friends. On the other hand, people who have few connections to society, who have no family or friends whose opinion they value, who have no job and no house they could lose, are less likely to be influenced by these concerns and, hence, are more likely to commit deviant acts.

Only two years later, Travis Hirschi (1969) expanded on social bond theory to better understand why, even though we all may be tempted to do something deviant at one time or another, most people are usually able to resist those temptations. His **control theory** argues that people have an inner control system supported by a conscience, internalized morality, a desire to be good, religious principles, fear of punishment, and a sense of integrity. People, he reasoned, would be more able to resist temptation if they are bonded to society through *commitments* (things such as a family, a job, and a home that we value and do not want to risk losing), *involvements* (an investment in legitimate activities, such as holding down a job, going to school, participating in family events), *shared beliefs* (such as a sense of morality or religious beliefs that discourage deviance), and *attachments* (the respect and affection we have for friends, teachers, and colleagues). Individuals are better able to resist temptation, he argues, if they have these things because they do not want to lose them.

To test this theory, Hirschi conducted a survey of 4,077 students in public high schools and junior high schools in a single metropolitan area. He asked questions about the bonds students had with their parents, specifically the extent of supervision by their mother and the extent to which they shared their thoughts and feelings with their father. When he compared student acts of deviance as measured by school and police records, he found that students who confided less in their fathers or were supervised less by their mothers were each far more likely to get in trouble for deviance. These results can be seen in FIGURE 6-4.

Howard Becker studied the process of learning to be a marijuana smoker in the 1950s.
© Sophie Bassouls/Sygma/Corbis

Social bond theory A theory which argues that everyone is tempted by opportunities for deviant behavior, but deviant acts are less likely when the individual's bonds to society are strong.

Control theory A theory which argues that people have an inner control system supported by a conscience, internalized morality, a desire to be good, religious principles, fear of punishment, and a sense of integrity.

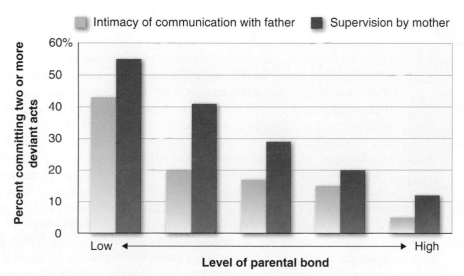

FIGURE 6-4 Deviance as a function of bonds with society.
Source: Data from Hirschi, Travis. 1969. Causes of Delinquency. *Berkeley: University of California Press.*

Labeling Theory

Labeling theory A theory which argues that an act becomes deviant only when it is labeled as deviant by others.

Primary deviance Occasional minor deviance that does not affect an individual's reputation or self-image.

Secondary deviance When an individual is labeled a deviant by others and comes to see himself as a deviant.

Stigma A distinctive, strongly negative label that marks the person as socially unacceptable or disgraced.

Sociologist Howard Becker (1963) proposed **labeling theory**, which argues that an act becomes deviant only when it is labeled as deviant by others. This means that deviance is relative because some people may define an act as deviant while others view it as acceptable behavior. In this view, then, it becomes important to understand the process by which people are labeled as deviant because the deviant label can have far-reaching consequences and can lead to great pain and embarrassment. How is it that, even though virtually everyone occasionally commits minor offenses—such as occasionally speeding, underage drinking, or engaging in sex outside of marriage—most of us neither see ourselves as deviants nor are seen as deviant by others. Instead, we are seen as generally good people who just happen to occasionally "sow our wild oats," "experiment," or "go through a phase." Sociologist Edwin Lemert (1951, 1972) called this **primary deviance**—occasional minor deviance that does not affect an individual's reputation or self-image.

But, if violations are too common or too severe, then the individual experiences **secondary deviance** in which he is labeled a deviant by others and comes to see himself as a deviant. This marks the beginning of what Goffman (1963) called a deviant career leading to **stigma**, a distinctive, strongly negative label that marks the person as socially unacceptable or disgraced. Powerful negative labels, such as *whore, nut, crook,* or *terrorist* draw a stark line between deviants and conforming members of society and can do irreparable damage to both one's social identity and self-image. Once so labeled, the person is likely to slip into what sociologist Merton (1968) called a "self-fulfilling prophecy," a cycle in which he is seen as a deviant, hence becomes more likely to do deviant things, and in turn is seen ever more clearly to be deviant.

A classic study by William Chambliss (1973) illustrates the power of labeling for two groups of high school males. He called them the Saints and the Roughnecks. The Saints were eight boys from middle-class families and the Roughnecks were six boys from lower-class families. In general, people in the community expected the middle-class boys to succeed in life, while the lower-class boys were widely regarded as troublemakers likely to fail. Chambliss reports how both groups engaged in surprisingly similar acts of deviance, such as vandalizing property, fighting, and skipping school. Yet the two were viewed very differently. The Saints were viewed as good boys overall who just made mistakes now and then, while the Roughnecks were viewed as inherently bad people and were punished or prosecuted more often for their acts of deviance.

Following up years later, Chambliss found lasting consequences for these two groups of boys. Seven of the eight Saints went on to graduate from college, with most having managerial or professional careers (including a physician, a lawyer, and a college professor). The Roughnecks suffered in comparison. The two most successful Roughnecks went to college on athletic scholarships and became high school coaches, two others never graduated high school, and two ended up in prison, one of whom was convicted for murder.

Chambliss found that the social class of the boys had a great deal to do with other people's initial perceptions of them and the way others responded to their actions. His results demonstrate how an initial label as a deviant can become a self-fulfilling prophecy. People expected little of the Roughnecks and much of the Saints, and the boys in each group eventually fulfilled those expectations. Stigmatized persons have what Goffman (1963) described as a "spoiled identity," making it difficult for them to manage the impressions others have of them. Sociologists have examined the effects of stigma in a wide range of cases, from people with eating disorders (Taub 1987) to AIDS (Weitz 1991) to airline passengers deemed risky (Cousineau 2010). To test whether deviant labels affect employment opportunities, sociologist Jerome Skolnick (1962) posed as a representative of an employment agency and contacted one hundred potential employers with four fictitious cases. Each case was the same in all respects but

People selected for more intensive screening in airport security lines experience a bit of what it is like to be stigmatized.

© iStockphoto.com/gchutka

one—a 32-year-old single male with a high school education and a record of a succession of short-term laborer jobs. There were four experimental conditions: (1) the person had no criminal record, (2) he was tried for assault but acquitted, (3) he was tried and acquitted with a supportive letter from the judge, and (4) he had been convicted and sentenced. The percentage of employers interested in hiring the "client" for each of the four conditions is displayed in FIGURE 6-5. Clearly, even being charged with a crime is sufficient to stigmatize a person, and the labeling process is powerful enough to result in significant loss of status and decreased job opportunities even when the person is acquitted. Similar stigmatizing effects have been found in other countries (Dijksterhuis 1971) and for other offenses including drunk driving (Johnson 1975) and marijuana possession (Goodstadt 1979).

Support for the legalization of marijuana is a form of tertiary deviance.

© Frontpage/Shutterstock, Inc.

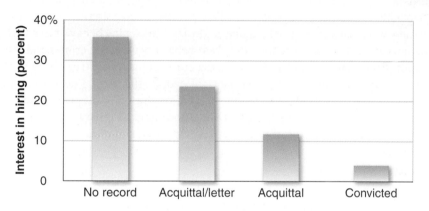

FIGURE 6-5 Percentage of employers indicating interest in hiring "client."
*Source: Data from Schwartz, R. D. and Skolnick, J. H. 1962. "Two studies of legal stigma."
Social Problems, 10:133-138.*

Sometimes a person's passage into a state of disgrace is marked by what Harold Garfinkel (1956) called a **degradation ceremony**, a public ritual in which the person's stigmatized status is made known. When a person is arrested and charged with a highly publicized crime, he or she is often subjected to such a degradation ceremony in the form of a "perp" (perpetrator) walk as he or she is paraded in handcuffs before an audience of news reporters to be humiliated and disgraced.

Given how powerful labels can be and how they can diminish life chances for someone so labeled, it should be no surprise that people have developed a wide array of strategies for resisting negative labels. Sykes and Matza (1957) and later Scott and Lyman (1968) identified a typology of what they call **techniques of neutralization**— strategies often used by individuals to excuse or justify actions that might otherwise be viewed negatively. These include strategies such as denying responsibility for the act, denying that anyone was seriously harmed, denying that one person is more a victim than another, condemning the condemners ("they are just as bad as us"), or appealing to higher loyalties ("my friend needed my help").

Resisting being labeled a deviant can also take place at a societal level. The gay rights movement is an example of **tertiary deviance** in which people attempt to redefine stigmatizing acts, characteristics, or identities as normal or even virtuous. While homosexuality was once condemned, this movement attempts to change public opinion and supports laws protecting the rights of homosexuals in the workplace, the family, and the military. Another interesting example of tertiary deviance is provided by criminology professors who are ex-convicts and who argue that they are better able to study and understand prison life based on their prison experience (St. John 2003). Other examples of tertiary deviance are efforts to legalize gambling, prostitution, or drugs.

Degradation ceremony A public ritual in which one's stigmatized status is made known.

Techniques of neutralization Strategies often used by individuals to excuse or justify actions that might otherwise be viewed negatively.

Tertiary deviance When people attempt to redefine stigmatizing acts, characteristics, or identities as normal or even virtuous.

THE SOCIOLOGICAL IMAGINATION   J.L.'s Story

Jared Loughner, the man accused of gunning down Representative Gabriele Giffords in Tucson, Arizona, at a Congress on Your Corner public appearance.

© AP Photo/Pima County Sheriff's Department via *The Arizona Republic*

Consider J.L. He is a college student who has come to believe that his instructors are trying to control him through grammar and their use of language. He has difficulty interacting with other people, and his behavior often worries or frightens his teachers and his fellow students. But his problem, if indeed he has a "problem," is not one that fits neatly into our established categories of crime. He has committed no crime, even though he sometimes behaves as if he is about to. Until he does, the criminal justice system is all but powerless to respond to his threatening behavior. The criminal justice system does not respond to all forms of deviance, only those that society has defined as criminal. Perhaps another powerful social institution, the mental health system, can provide some reasonable way to respond to such threats and exert control.

In case you did not recognize him, "J.L." is Jared Loughner, the gunman who attempted to assassinate Congresswoman Gabrielle Giffords in Tucson, Arizona, in January of 2011. He shot Giffords through the head and killed six other people. In the ensuing investigation, there were many reports of Loughner's odd and threatening behavior that frightened students and teachers at his school. But these behaviors were not crimes and therefore were not reported to the police. Although the criminal justice system was powerless to restrain Loughner before he acted, if the right people, the mental health system, had been informed, they might have been able to get him some help and prevent this tragedy. Ironically, after he was arrested, there was a question about whether he should stand trial for murder in the first degree or plead not guilty by reason of insanity.

EVALUATE

The sociological imagination helps us see both the intersection between biography and history and that between private troubles and public issues.

1. How does Jared Loughner's violent act reflect a broader set of social issues about the ways in which we recognize and treat the mentally ill?

2. How did his action highlight the intersection of history and biography for his victims?

3. How might this act of political violence be a reflection of the public issue of the breakdown of civil discourse in American politics?

4. What role did social labeling play in not being able to treat him before he committed this violent act?

5. Think of an incident in which someone you know or have met reacted badly to an event outside his or her control. Consider the circumstances and people involved. Then consider the role played by social forces according to social control and/or social labeling theory. How does thinking about social forces change your thinking about the incident, if at all?

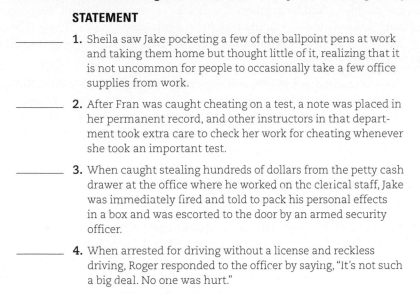

CONCEPT LEARNING CHECK 6.3   Distinguishing Concepts of Labeling Theory

Match each of the following statements to the concept from labeling theory that best describes it.

STATEMENT

_____ **1.** Sheila saw Jake pocketing a few of the ballpoint pens at work and taking them home but thought little of it, realizing that it is not uncommon for people to occasionally take a few office supplies from work.

_____ **2.** After Fran was caught cheating on a test, a note was placed in her permanent record, and other instructors in that department took extra care to check her work for cheating whenever she took an important test.

_____ **3.** When caught stealing hundreds of dollars from the petty cash drawer at the office where he worked on the clerical staff, Jake was immediately fired and told to pack his personal effects in a box and was escorted to the door by an armed security officer.

_____ **4.** When arrested for driving without a license and reckless driving, Roger responded to the officer by saying, "It's not such a big deal. No one was hurt."

CONCEPT

A. Degradation ceremony

B. Primary deviance

C. Secondary deviance

D. Techniques of neutralization

6.4 Conflict Perspectives

Three branches of conflict theory emphasize different factors that shape society's views of deviance: power, capitalism, and gender.

- Discuss the social conflict perspective, noting the importance of power, capitalism, and gender.

The **social conflict perspective** on deviance emphasizes factors influencing which behaviors are viewed as deviant or criminal. One branch of the social conflict perspective emphasizes how people having greater power use it to define deviance and crime in ways that protect their interests. Another branch focuses on the role capitalism plays in shaping what is considered to be deviant. A third branch, based on feminist theory, emphasizes effects of gender. Once again, this perspective—by examining issues such as who decides what is deviant and how laws are made that define deviance—is fundamentally different from biological and psychological approaches to deviance that focus solely on factors within the individual that might lead him or her to be deviant.

Social conflict perspective
A theory which emphasizes competing interests of groups of people having different amounts of power and how those having more power use it to exploit those with less power.

Deviance and Power

The conflict perspective argues social class and power influence what is considered deviant and how it is treated. Proponents of this view include Quinney (1977), Chambliss (1974), Chambliss and Seidman (1982), and Archer (1985). They argue that people who are rich and powerful generally shape our notions of what is deviant. We have already seen how they influence crime legislation that makes particular actions a crime. Behaviors that threaten the influence of the dominant social class are the ones more likely to become the targets of criminal legislation. It is the rich and powerful who determine *what is deviant* and *to what extent* deviants should be punished. Instead of laws reflecting consistent and balanced application of societal values, laws are the result of competing interests. This is why it is illegal to smoke marijuana, while cigarettes

Former Illinois governor, Rod Blagojevich, shortly before he entered prison.

© Frank Polich/Getty Images

and alcohol, both of which are well known to harm users, are sold legally with very few restrictions.

In those rare cases when the behavior of rich and powerful people is called into question, they are able to use their resources to resist being labeled and punished as deviants. For example, Rod Blagojevich, the former governor of Illinois, was found guilty of only one count of 24 in his trial for corruption. A news article (Harris 2010) in *The Guardian* details some of the ways he used his resources to resist the criminal label.

> While he was awaiting trial, Blagojevich appeared as a contestant on Donald Trump's *Celebrity Apprentice* reality TV show. A judge in the case also refused a Blagojevich request to go to Costa Rica to take part in the US version of *I'm a Celebrity . . . Get Me Out of Here!* His wife, Patti, went instead and used the show to talk about how she felt the couple was being unfairly persecuted. Blagojevich also took to the talk show circuit to protest his innocence and was a frequent Twitter user. He even made a cameo appearance in a Chicago musical about his life that was called *Rod Blagojevich Superstar* (Harris 2010).

Similarly, business executives in charge of companies that perform illegal acts of pollution, provide unsafe working environments, and pose health hazards to their employees and people living near their plants are rarely held personally accountable for any of those actions. At every stage in the criminal justice process, people from higher social classes are in a better position to influence the outcome in their favor. Affluent people are less likely to be perceived as criminals, can afford to make bail, can afford competent lawyers who can reduce their chances of coming to trial or being convicted, can often reduce their sentence, and are more likely to receive probation or alternative forms of punishment.

Deviance and Capitalism

Social conflict theorists maintain that law and culture support capitalist interests in many ways. For example, socialists are seen as deviants because they challenge capitalism. Those who threaten private property (especially the property of the rich) are seen as deviants. Those who will not work are seen as deviants because work is required for capitalism. Formal organizations require hierarchy, so those who challenge authority such as union agitators or nonviolent demonstrators are seen as deviant. Meanwhile, activities supportive of the economic system, such as sports, are encouraged because they promote competition (Spitzer 1980). It is often much easier for critics to see the inequities in the application of laws but to lose sight of the inherent unfairness of the laws themselves (Quinney 1977). People who do not contribute to the capitalist system are subject to control. The elderly and those with mental or physical disabilities pose a "costly yet relatively harmless burden" to society (Spitzer 1980) and are controlled by social welfare agencies, while those who pose a challenge to capitalism, including the "underclass" and revolutionaries, are controlled by the criminal justice system. Individuals, not the system, are seen as the problem. Labels asserting blame for those individuals are easily found, including *worthless freeloaders* for those in the welfare system, *radicals* or *communists* for those who dare to criticize the system, *criminals* for those who resort to illegal acts, or *rioters* for those who protest violently. As one proponent of the social conflict view put it, "Capitalist justice is by the capitalist class, for the capitalist class, and against the working class" (Quinney 1977).

Those who do not contribute to the capitalist economy, such as these aid recipients, are labeled as outcasts or freeloaders.

© Justin Sullivan/Getty Images

Feminist theory A theory which looks closely at ways in which men and women are treated regarding deviance and crime and how those differences are influenced by gender.

Feminist Theory

Feminist theory looks closely at the different ways in which men and women are treated regarding deviance and crime and how those differences are influenced by gender. Where traditional conflict theory emphasizes differences in social class, feminist theory focuses on gender differences. Feminist theorists argue that deviance and crime have often been approached with only the male perspective in mind, leading to notions of crime and deviance that favor men. For example, women who engage in frequent sex with many different sexual partners are viewed more negatively than men who do so.

Feminist theorists point out that women face a division of labor due to their sex, with women expected to perform more of the duties in the home—work that has traditionally been undervalued and undercompensated. This leaves women more dependent economically when men have greater earning power, making them less likely to report abuse for fear of losing financial support. Further differences result because men and women are socialized into stereotypical gender roles, with men expected to be more aggressive and women treated as sex objects. Together, gender differences in traditional roles in work and the family have led women to be more vulnerable.

Gender differences in the commission of crimes, they argue, can also be explained, at least in part, by traditional gender role differences. Men have traditionally had greater power in the workplace and hence greater opportunity to engage in some forms of crime such as embezzlement and fraud. But as more women work and have more powerful positions, those differences have diminished (Adler 1975; Adler, Mueller, and Laufer 2007). Nowhere is this clearer than when comparing powerful women such as Secretary of State Hilary Rodham Clinton with the traditional stereotype of the stay-at-home-mom of the 1950s.

Women are often victims of crimes, with the victimization, including rape and sex trafficking, varying in different countries. The crime of rape is often cited as an example of the way laws are constructed to favor men. In the United States, it wasn't until 1993 that husbands could be prosecuted for rape of their wives under most circumstances in all 50 states. Thirty states still prohibit prosecution under some circumstances, such as when force was not used because the wife was unconscious, mentally or physically impaired, or asleep. Bergen (2006) points out that such exceptions are based on a view that marriage entitles the husband to sex. The rates of assault and rape of women are much higher in some countries than others. Limited research suggests that 16% to 52% of married women in the Middle East are assaulted per year, while only 1.3% to 12% are assaulted in Europe and North America over the course of one year (Krug et al. 2002).

Traditional gender roles lead to different likelihoods of engaging in deviance or being a victim for women in the 1950s and today.

top: © iStockphoto.com/EdStock;
bottom: © CBS Photo Archive/Getty Images

CONCEPT LEARNING CHECK 6.4   Explaining Events with Conflict Theories

Match each of the following facts with the theory and key proposition that best explains it.

FACT

_____ **1.** Access to representation by a lawyer and the money to make bail are two of the reasons people from higher social classes are less likely to be convicted and imprisoned for crimes in the United States.

_____ **2.** In courtroom trials of rape cases, it sometimes seems as though the woman is on trial as much as the man she accuses of rape.

_____ **3.** Blacks and other minorities are more often prosecuted for smoking crack cocaine, while more affluent whites are more likely to use powdered cocaine. Average penalties are much harsher for crack cocaine than for similar amounts of powdered cocaine.

THEORY AND KEY PROPOSITION

A. Deviance and power—Social class and power influence what is considered deviant and how it is treated.

B. Feminist theory—Traditional perspectives of deviance favor men and overlook gender differences.

6.5 Crime

There are many types of crime differing in severity and in how they are punished.

- Give examples of various categories of crime.
- Discuss and compare the attributes of at least two categories of crime.

Criminology The scientific study of crime and its causes.

Crimes against persons Crimes involving the threat of injury or force against people.

Crimes against property Crimes involving stealing or damaging property.

White-collar crime Crime committed by relatively affluent white-collar workers, usually in the course of conducting their daily business activities.

Corporate crime Illegal acts conducted by or on behalf of a corporation.

Organized crime Crime committed by collections of criminals who coordinate activities much like a business.

Criminology is the scientific study of crime and its causes. This section examines the many types of crime, while the next section will examine crime statistics.

The Federal Bureau of Investigation (FBI) provides annual statistics on 29 categories of crimes and provides a well-publicized summary crime index consisting of only 8 types of crimes. Indexed crimes include **crimes against persons**—crimes involving the threat of injury or force against people, including aggravated assault, robbery, forcible rape, and murder; and **crimes against property**—crimes involving stealing or damaging property, including larceny/theft, burglary, motor vehicle theft, and arson.

In addition to the indexed crimes tracked by the FBI annually, there are several other important types of crime. We now turn to those.

White-Collar Crime

White-collar crime was first defined in 1940 by Edwin Sutherland as a crime committed by relatively affluent white-collar workers, usually in the course of conducting their daily business activities. In June of 2009, Bernie Madoff was convicted and sentenced to 150 years in prison for running the largest Ponzi scheme in history. Early investors with his firm received large profits, leading them to encourage others to invest, not knowing they were actually being paid from investments of other investors. The fraud continued undetected for more than 10 years and involved thousands of investors and billions of dollars (Frank et al. 2009). This is only one of tens of thousands of white-collar crimes committed every year, many of which go undetected. Common types of white-collar crime include embezzlement, business fraud, price fixing, bribery, and insider trading.

Corporate Crime

Corporate crime involves illegal acts conducted by or on behalf of a corporation. Corporate crimes include many possible actions, including knowingly polluting the environment, knowingly selling faulty or dangerous products, or violating accounting and business practices to mislead the public and stockholders regarding the real value of the company. Several well-known cases of the latter include Enron Corporation and Tyco International, where such practices were discovered and the company's stock price plummeted, leading to bankruptcy and losses of billions of dollars by stockholders and the loss of jobs and pensions of tens of thousands of employees. The collapse of Enron alone is estimated to have cost more than $50 billion.

The loss of money each year from corporate crime is generally several times greater than the loss of money from common theft, and deaths due to job-related hazards far exceed the number of deaths each year from violent crime (Herbert and Landrigan, 2000). For example, in 1992, approximately 65,000 workers died of work-related illnesses and injuries (Herbert and Landrigan, 2000), and in 2009, work-related injuries alone accounted for 4,340 deaths (Bureau of Labor Statistics 2010).

Organized Crime

Organized crime is crime committed by collections of criminals who coordinate activities, much like a business. Unlike corporate crime, where a legal corporation is involved, the business of organized crime is more secret, with members often even denying the existence of the business, just as criminals accused of being in the Italian Mafia in the 1960s denied it even existed. Organized crime has been a significant factor in US crime

THE SOCIOLOGICAL IMAGINATION | Technology and Cybercrime

On Thursday May 4, 2000, *BBC News* online reported that a computer virus spread by email messages with the subject line: "I LOVE YOU" had crippled government and business computers in Europe and Asia, and in the United States had affected the White House, the American State Department, the CIA, both houses of Congress, and the Pentagon, as well as major companies like Ford and Time-Warner. Within a day, it was estimated 1.27 million computers were infected worldwide, with nearly 1 million in the United States. Before it was over, the virus had spread to countless millions more computers, forcing users to disconnect their computer systems from the Internet and spend billions of dollars to remove the virus (*BBC News* 2000).

While rates of many other crimes are declining, newer technologies such as the Internet and cell phones have inspired an explosion of new forms of deviance and criminal activity. **Cybercrime** is crime executed with the use of a computer and usually over the Internet. Cybercrime is rapidly growing and is a significant portion of all crimes. Fifty-three percent of consumer-fraud complaints made to the US Federal Trade Commission (FTC) in 2004 were Internet-related (Bank and Richmond 2005). Cybercrime and cyberterrorism are currently the number-three priority for the FBI, behind only counterterrorism and counterintelligence (Kshetri 2006).

Some cybercrimes attack computers and networks themselves, such as denial-of-service attacks—attempts to make a computer site inaccessible to its intended users by overwhelming it with automated activity from multiple computers. Malware is software that has malicious functions, such as adware that repeatedly displays undesired pop-up advertisements, and spyware, which tracks what people do on their computers without their knowledge.

Malware spreads from one computer to another in any of several ways. Computer viruses are programs like the I Love You virus that attach themselves to existing programs, infect computers, copy themselves, and spread to other computers. Computer worms are computer programs that don't need to be attached to other programs to send copies of themselves to other computers on the network. Finally, a Trojan horse is a malware program that appears to be desirable before it is installed but actually performs malicious functions.

Cybercrime sometimes uses computers and networks to commit other crimes. Some of the most common examples are spam—sending unsolicited bulk email, usually for commercial purposes—and phishing—attempting to acquire sensitive personal information by posing as a trusted person or institution. A common phishing example is an email claiming to be from your bank asking you to provide passwords or other sensitive information, followed by using that information to pose as you online to withdraw funds. Computer fraud includes many acts such as altering or deleting data on someone else's computer. Copyright infringement occurs when copyrighted music or videos are downloaded without the owner's permission. Cyber bullying is the use of the Internet or cell phones to harass someone.

> **Cybercrime** Crime executed with the use of a computer and usually over the Internet.

EVALUATE

1. This author was one of the victims of the I Love You virus. I lost several days of work and spent over $100 getting my computer repaired. I kicked myself over and over for being such a fool to download the virus. That was my personal issue, but this problem reflects a broader social problem. How should we treat such problems differently when we know they transcend individuals?

2. The I Love You virus did its damage back in 2000. This intersection of my biography with history is a bit old now. How might this experience be different today or a few years from now as history marches on?

3. If the Internet has led to this variety of cybercrimes, what kinds of crimes might come from advances in other technologies such as genetic engineering?

4. A computer virus that appears aimed at destroying centrifuges used in Iran's nuclear program crosses yet another line and does actual physical damage to equipment. Can you imagine possible cybercrimes against people as opposed to crimes against property?

for well over a century, and the organizations that conduct it are often largely made up of people from a single immigrant ethnic group, as those groups experienced restricted opportunities. The Italian Mafia is perhaps best known, but other organized crime organizations involve Russians, Colombians, Haitians, Chinese, and other immigrant populations. Organized crime is often involved in gambling, prostitution, illegal drugs, credit card fraud, and human trafficking of immigrants (Valdez 1997). Today it increasingly involves transnational organized crime, including illegal drug and arms sales, cybercrime, and human trafficking of immigrants (Office of Justice Programs 2010).

Violent Crime

Violent crime Crime that attempts to harm a person.

Hate crime A crime against persons or property when the offender is motivated by bias.

Terrorism The use of violence and threats to intimidate or coerce a government or civilian population to further some political or social objective.

Violent crime is crime that attempts to harm a person. Crimes against persons, as defined by the FBI (termed *index crimes*) are often described as violent crimes. There are two additional types of crimes that sometimes involve horrific violence: hate crimes and terrorism.

Hate Crimes

In October 2010, in New York City, two 17-year-olds and a 30-year-old man were tortured and beaten by nine attackers because they were believed to be gay (Wilson and Baker 2010). New York City Mayor Michael Bloomberg said at a press conference,

> When you hear the details of what occurred, torture really is the only word that comes to mind. I was sickened by the brutal nature of these crimes and saddened at the anti-gay bias that contributed to them. Hate crimes such as these strike fear into all of us. (*Opposing Views* 2010)

A bomb disposal team inspects a vehicle connected with an attempted car bombing in New York City's Times Square.

© AP Photos/New York Daily News/Ken Goldfield

In August of 2010, a 21-year-old student in New York City asked the driver of his taxi if he was a Muslim, and after the driver said he was, the student slashed his throat with a utility knife (Zraick and Newman 2010). In June of 2010, an African man in South Carolina was murdered, and then his body dragged behind a truck for more than 10 miles. These are but three examples of hate crimes in the United States.

A **hate crime** is a crime against persons or property when the offender is motivated by bias. In 2008, 7,783 hate crime incidents were reported in the United States. Of those, 51% were racially motivated, 20% were motivated by religious bias, 17% were motivated by sexual-orientation bias, 12% were motivated by ethnic bias, and 1% were motivated by bias against someone with a physical disability (FBI Uniform Crime Report, 2009). Most states and the federal government have laws providing stronger penalties for hate crimes.

Terrorism

There are many different definitions of terrorism (Record 2003) and the term is politically charged, often being used to delegitimize opponents. **Terrorism** is the use of violence and threats to intimidate or coerce a government or civilian population to further some political or social objective. Terrorism often targets noncombatants and is carried out by nongovernment agencies, though it is sometimes sponsored by particular governments. Terrorism is sometimes said to involve unlawful violence and war because it does not follow the Geneva Conventions or international agreements, such as attempting to minimize the impact on noncombatants. There are all too many examples of terrorism, including the bomb attack on the Oklahoma City federal building in 1995, the September 11 attacks on New York and Washington, DC, in 2001, and the London Underground bombings of 2005.

Political Crime

While terrorism is usually a politically motivated act, it should be distinguished from other forms of political crime. **Political crimes** are crimes committed within or directed against a political system, such as terrorism. Political crimes also include crimes such as the Watergate scandal, voter fraud, and violations of campaign contribution laws. A more recent and technologically sophisticated political crime is tampering with the hardware or software of electronic voting machines. Feldman, Halderman, and Felten (2006) of the Center for Information Technology Policy at Princeton University conducted an analysis of a Diebold AccuVote-TS voting machine to assess its vulnerability to election fraud. They showed that an attacker with access to the machine for as little as one minute could install malicious code that could steal votes undetected, modifying all of the logs, counters, and records required to appear consistent. They also demonstrated that the malicious software could be a voting machine virus spreading invisibly from one voting machine to the next during normal voting activities.

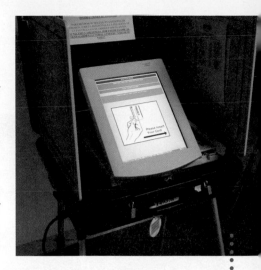

A common type of electronic voting machine.

© Frontpage/Shutterstock, Inc.

Juvenile Delinquency

Juvenile delinquency includes all of the usual crimes that might be committed by adults but are committed by minors, such as theft, arson, and murder. In addition, there are other nondelinquent and noncriminal acts that juveniles commit when the act is an offense for underage persons but not for adults. The latter are called status offenses because they are offenses only because of the person's status as an underage person. These include truancy, running away, underage drinking, and curfew violations. In 2008 juveniles accounted for 16% of all violent crime arrests and 26% of all property crime arrests. Between 2007 and 2008 there was a 3% decline in overall juvenile arrests and a 2% decrease in juvenile arrests for violent offenses (Office of Juvenile Justice and Delinquency Prevention 2010).

Victimless Crime

Victimless crimes are violations of the law that have no obvious victims. These include prostitution, illegal drug use, public drunkenness, and gambling. These crimes might result in violence or suffering, such as when accidents are caused by drunk driving, but those constitute different additional crimes, such as driving under the influence. In many cases, the people committing the victimless crime may be victims themselves, such as young women or men forced into prostitution. Sometimes it is controversial whether or to what extent a crime causes damage to someone. For example, while there is great concern that violations of intellectual property law, such as peer-to-peer downloading of music, seem likely to hurt music sales, economists (Oberholzer-Gee and Strumpf 2007) studied data for music sales and downloads for a large number of albums and found no statistically significant effect of downloads on sales.

> **Political crimes** Crimes committed within or directed against a political system.
>
> **Juvenile delinquency** All of the usual crimes that might be committed by adults but are committed by minors, such as theft, arson, and murder.
>
> **Victimless crimes** Violations of the law that have no obvious victims.

CONCEPT LEARNING CHECK 6.5   Categorizing Types of Crime

Sometimes real crimes can be more than one type of crime at the same time. Other times, one type of crime is enough to describe it. For each of the following crimes, name at least two categories of crime that describe it.

_____ **1.** A car bombing that injures 30 people but no one dies.

_____ **2.** Online gambling where it is illegal.

_____ **3.** A man is tied up and beaten by a group of other men because they think he is gay.

6.6 Crime Statistics

Crime statistics help identify important issues affecting public policy.

■ Discuss age, race, gender, and social class as they relate to crime statistics.

Crime rates have fallen steadily over the last 20 years.

© Richard Levine/Alamy Images

Street crime Crime that often occurs in public settings.

In the last section, we identified many types of crime. Now we turn to crime statistics, which play a crucial role in the study of crime. What sociologists look for in these statistics are trends over time, such as rapid increases or reductions in certain kinds of crime. Those help to measure progress or to spot trends that are leading to greater problems. The other most common use of crime statistics is to compare crime statistics for different categories of people. Knowing which people are more likely to be victims of crime and which people are more likely to commit crimes helps us understand the causes of crime and ways to reduce or prevent crime. They also help us assess the relative fairness of punishments.

Crime rates in the United States (as measured by the eight FBI index crimes) have declined significantly between 1991 and 2009, with the biggest declines between 1991 and 2000 and smaller declines from 2000 to 2009. Rates have declined in all crime categories, as shown in FIGURE 6-6 and FIGURE 6-7. In the last year for which data are available (2009), there were 10.6 million serious crimes according to the FBI annual crime report of index crimes.

Street Crime, the Criminal Profile

The crimes routinely reported by the Federal Bureau of Investigation and most often discussed in the media are **street crime**—crimes that often occur in public settings. Government statistics identify several categories of people more likely to be arrested for violent and property crimes.

Age

Arrest rates increase during adolescence, peak in the late teens, and then fall off at a high rate for older age groups (Bureau of Justice Statistics, 2009). Most arrests for crime, whether for property crime or violent crime, are of adolescents and young adults. FIGURE 6-8 shows the arrest rates for all offenses by age in 2009. Notice the arrest rate for 15- to 19-year-olds is more than twice the rate for 35- to 39-year-olds

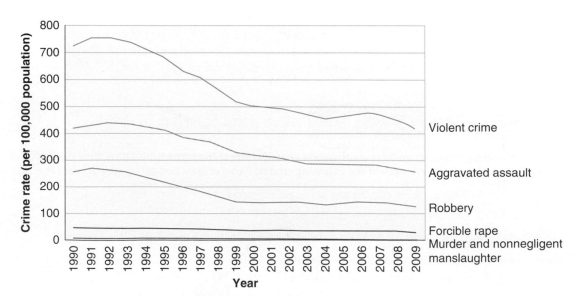

FIGURE 6-6 US crime rates (1990–2009): Crimes against persons.
Source: Data from the Federal Bureau of Investigation, Uniform Crime Reporting Statistics. Retrieved January 2012 (http://www.ucrdatatool.gov/index.cfm).

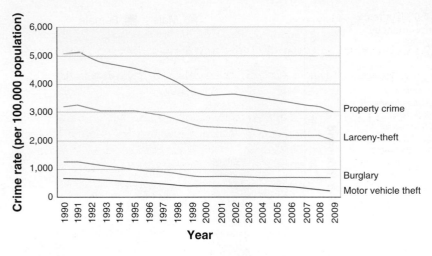

FIGURE 6-7 US crime rates (1990–2009): Crimes against property.
Source: Data from the Federal Bureau of Investigation, Uniform Crime Reporting Statistics. Retrieved January 2012 (http://www.ucrdatatool.gov/index.cfm).

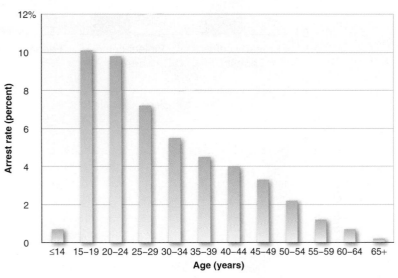

FIGURE 6-8 US arrest rate by age (2009).
Source: Maguire, Kathleen, ed. Sourcebook of Criminal Justice Statistics. University at Albany, Hindelang Criminal Justice Research Center. 2009. Table 4.4.2009. Retrieved January 2012 (http://www.albany.edu/sourcebook/csv/t442009.csv).

and nearly nine times the rate for 55- to 59-year-olds (Bureau of Justice Statistics 2009).

Gender

Men are more likely to be arrested than women and more likely to be federal prisoners. In FIGURE 6-9, we can see that the arrest rates in 2009 for males are nearly twice as high as those for females for property crimes and nearly five times higher than those for females for violent crimes. Men are 11 times as likely to be federal prisoners than are women. The difference in arrest rates between men and women is declining. Between 1998 and 2007, there was a 6.1% drop in overall arrests of men, while the overall arrests of women increased by 6.6% (Federal Bureau of Investigation 2007). This likely reflects increasing gender equality over time.

Race

Race is strongly related to arrests, imprisonment, and executions. FIGURE 6-10 shows rates for 2009 after adjusting for the different sizes of the black and white population (US Census Bureau 2011). Blacks were 2.7 times more likely to be arrested for a property crime than whites and more than 4 times as likely to be arrested for a violent crime (Bureau of Justice Statistics 2009). Similarly, blacks were more than 4 times as likely to be federal prisoners (Bureau of Justice Statistics 2003) or to be sentenced to execution when compared to whites (Bureau of Justice Statistics 2009).

There are several issues that should be considered in interpreting these statistics. Race in the United States relates to social opportunities. Blacks are more likely to grow up

Does the rule of law favor some while penalizing others?
© JustASC/Shutterstock, Inc.

FIGURE 6-9 US arrests and imprisonment by gender (2009). *Source: Maguire, Kathleen, ed. Sourcebook of Criminal Justice Statistics. University at Albany, Hindelang Criminal Justice Research Center. 2009. Table 4.9.2009, Sourcebook of Criminal Justice Statistics. 2003. p. 517. Retrieved January 2012 (http://www.albany.edu/sourcebook/pdf/t49.2009.pdf).*

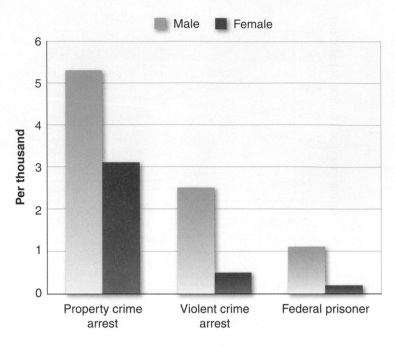

FIGURE 6-10 US arrests, imprisonment, and executions by race (2009). *Source: Maguire, Kathleen, ed. Sourcebook of Criminal Justice Statistics. University at Albany, Hindelang Criminal Justice Research Center. 2009. Table 4.10.2009, Table 6.28.2009, Sourcebook of Criminal Justice Statistics 2003. p. 517. Retrieved January 2012 (http://www.albany.edu/sourcebook/pdf/t4102009.pdf).*

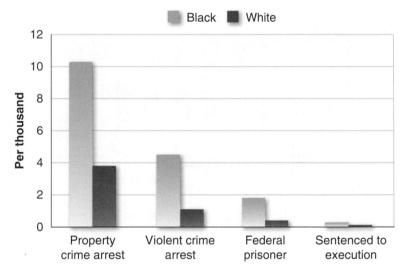

in single-parent homes and are more likely to be poor, and poor people are more likely to resort to crime (Anderson 1994; Martinez 1996). More blacks live in less-affluent inner cities, where they are more likely to participate in street crime and more likely to be victims of it. This is consistent with statistics indicating that blacks are more than six times more likely to be murder victims than whites (Federal Bureau of Investigation 2007). In addition, blacks who are victims of violent crime are much more likely to be victimized by other blacks (72.8%) than by whites (9.9%), while whites who are victims of violent crime are much more likely to be victimized by other whites (68.0%) than by blacks (13.3%) (Bureau of Justice Statistics 2007).

It is important as well to keep in mind limitations of these crime statistics. The FBI does not track ethnicity of offenders, so official statistics are limited to considerations of race. These FBI index crimes are street crimes and do not include white-collar crime or cybercrime, which is more likely to be committed by more affluent whites. If the full range of crimes were tracked equally well and included in crime statistics the proportion of white offenders would likely rise substantially.

Social Class

Just as data are not easily available for ethnicity, the FBI also does not track the social class of offenders. So our understanding of the relationship between social class and criminality has to rely on studies by social scientists rather than official statistics. For example, Thornberry and Farnsworth (1982) examined the correlation between arrest data and social class for a sample of men followed over time in Philadelphia. They found a strong relationship between social status and criminality among adults, with people of higher status less likely to be arrested. That is, poor people are more likely to be arrested for crimes. However, one reason poor people are more likely to be arrested may be because they are often regarded with less respect (Elias 1986) and hence more likely to be viewed as criminals. Again, it is important to keep in mind the limitations of the FBI crime statistics because they focus on street crime and do not include white-collar crime or other types of crime that may be more common among people of higher social classes.

Crime Victims

The chances of being a victim of either a property crime or violent crime have declined substantially since the early 1990s for all categories of people. However, your chances of being a victim of a violent crime or a property crime can be very different depending on your social characteristics.

Age

Teens and young adults are more likely to be victims of violent crime than middle-age and older adults, though that difference has declined dramatically since the early 1990s (Bureau of Justice Statistics 2007, Table 3.6.2007). Heads of household 65 and older were least likely to be victims of all property crimes. FIGURE 6-11 clearly shows the decline in personal victimization rates by age groups relative to the 16- to 19-year-old category.

Gender

Males continue to experience higher rates of victimization than females for all types of violent crime except rape/sexual assault. As the data in FIGURE 6-12 show, in 2009 males were 16% more likely to be victims of a violent crime than women (Bureau of Justice Statistics 2009: Table 3.4.2009). In 2005 (the last year for which data are available), males were more than twice as likely to be murder victims as women (Bureau of Justice Statistics 2005: Table 3.125.2005).

Race

In general, the data show that racial and ethnic minorities are more likely to be victims of all crimes for which there are statistics. Blacks are more likely to be victims of violent crimes than whites FIGURE 6-13. Blacks were just over 20% more likely than whites to be victims of property crimes, 70% more likely to be victims of violent crimes, and more than six times as likely to be murder victims than whites.

Hispanics were more than 30% more likely than non-Hispanics to be victims of property crime and slightly (less than 10%) more likely to be victims of violent crime FIGURE 6-14.

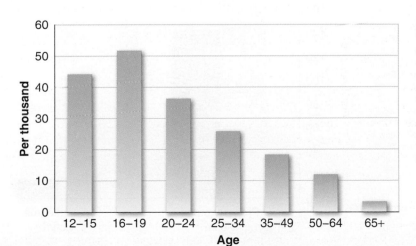

FIGURE 6-11 US personal victimization rate by victim age (2007).
Source: Maguire, Kathleen, ed. Sourcebook of Criminal Justice Statistics. University at Albany, Hindelang Criminal Justice Research Center. 2007. Table 3.6.2007. Retrieved January 2012 (http://www.albany.edu/sourcebook/pdf/t362007.pdf).

Social Class

In FIGURE 6-15, we see victimization rates as a function of annual household income in 2007. You may recall that, when asked why he robbed banks, bank robber Willie Sutton replied, "because that's where the money is." Apparently that message did not get

FIGURE 6-12 US crime victimization by gender of victim (2005, 2009). *Source: Maguire, Kathleen, ed. Sourcebook of Criminal Justice Statistics. University at Albany, Hindelang Criminal Justice Research Center. 2005. Table 3.125.2005 and Sourcebook of Criminal Justice Statistics 2009. Table 3.4.2009. Retrieved January 2012 (http://www.albany.edu/sourcebook/pdf/t342009.pdf, http://www.albany.edu/sourcebook/pdf/t31252005.pdf).*

FIGURE 6-13 US crime victimization by race of victim (2009). *Source: Maguire, Kathleen, ed. Sourcebook of Criminal Justice Statistics. University at Albany, Hindelang Criminal Justice Research Center. 2007. Table 3.22; 2009. Table 3.4; 2005. Table 3.125. Retrieved January 2012 (http://www.albany.edu/sourcebook/pdf/t3222007.pdf, http://www.albany.edu/sourcebook/pdf/t342009.pdf, http://www.albany.edu/sourcebook/pdf/t31252005.pdf).*

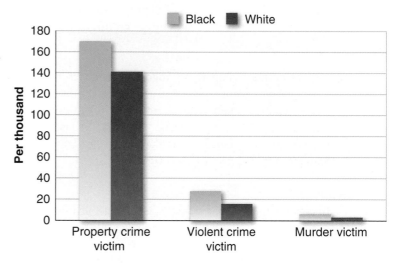

FIGURE 6-14 US crime victimization by ethnicity of victim (2009). *Source: Maguire, Kathleen, ed. Sourcebook of Criminal Justice Statistics. University at Albany, Hindelang Criminal Justice Research Center. 2007. Table 3.23.2007 and Sourcebook of Criminal Justice Statistics. 2009. Table 3.4.2009. Retrieved January 2012 (http://www.albany.edu/sourcebook/pdf/t342009.pdf, http://www.albany.edu/sourcebook/pdf/t3232007.pdf).*

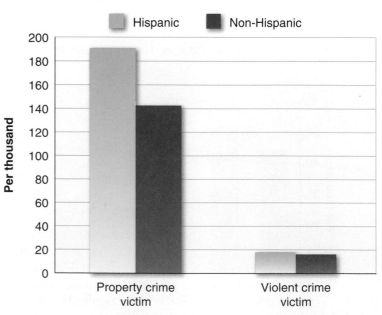

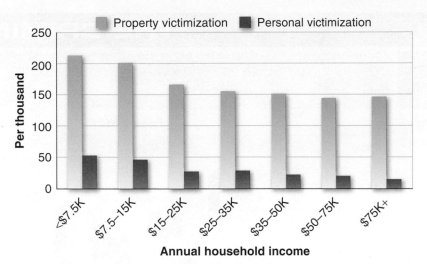

FIGURE 6-15 US victimization rates by annual household income of victim (2007). *Source: Maguire, Kathleen, ed. Sourcebook of Criminal Justice Statistics. University at Albany, Hindelang Criminal Justice Research Center. 2007. Table 3.12.2007 and 3.24.2007. Retrieved January 2012 (http://www.albany.edu/sourcebook/pdf/t3242007.pdf, http://www.albany.edu/sourcebook/pdf/t3122007.pdf).*

through to everyone, because for both property victimization and personal victimization, the lower your household income, the *more* likely you are to be a victim. People living in households with annual incomes less than $7,500 are nearly 50% more likely to be victims of property crime and well over three times as likely to be victims of violent crime than people whose annual household incomes are $75,000 or more (Bureau of Justice Statistics 2007, Tables 3.4.2007 and 3.12.2007).

CONCEPT LEARNING CHECK 6.6   Using Crime Statistics to Shape Social Policy

Which of the following is true and which is false?

_____ **1.** Racial and ethnic minorities are more likely to be victims of violent crimes than are whites.

_____ **2.** Women are more likely to be victims of violent crime than men.

_____ **3.** Over the past few years crime rates have risen at an alarming rate.

_____ **4.** Older adults are more likely to be victims of crime than younger adults or middle-age adults.

6.7 The Criminal Justice System

The criminal justice system includes all of the institutions that arrest, judge, and punish criminals.

■ Describe the criminal justice system in the United States and the roles played by the police, courts, and corrections.

The **criminal justice system** is the social institution whose primary purpose is to exert formal social control in a society. It is a *criminal* justice system because it attempts to control crime. It is a criminal *justice* system because it is based on the underlying principle of **due process**—that is, the criminal justice system must operate within the bounds of law. The US Constitution, including the Bill of Rights, guarantees important

Criminal justice system The social institution whose primary purpose is to exert formal social control in a society.

Due process The stipulation that the criminal justice system must operate within the bounds of law.

THE CRIMINAL J

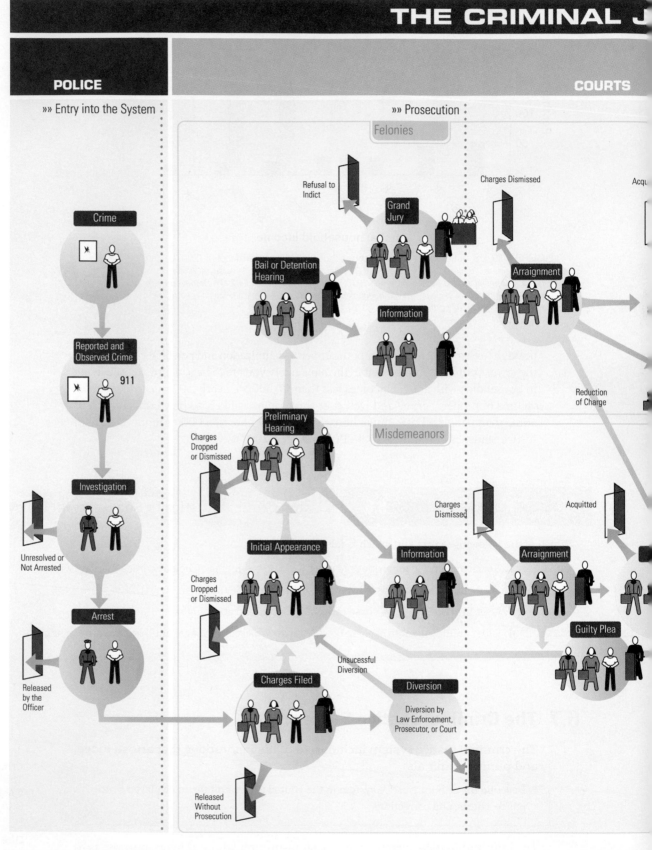

FIGURE 6-16 The criminal justice system.

JUSTICE SYSTEM

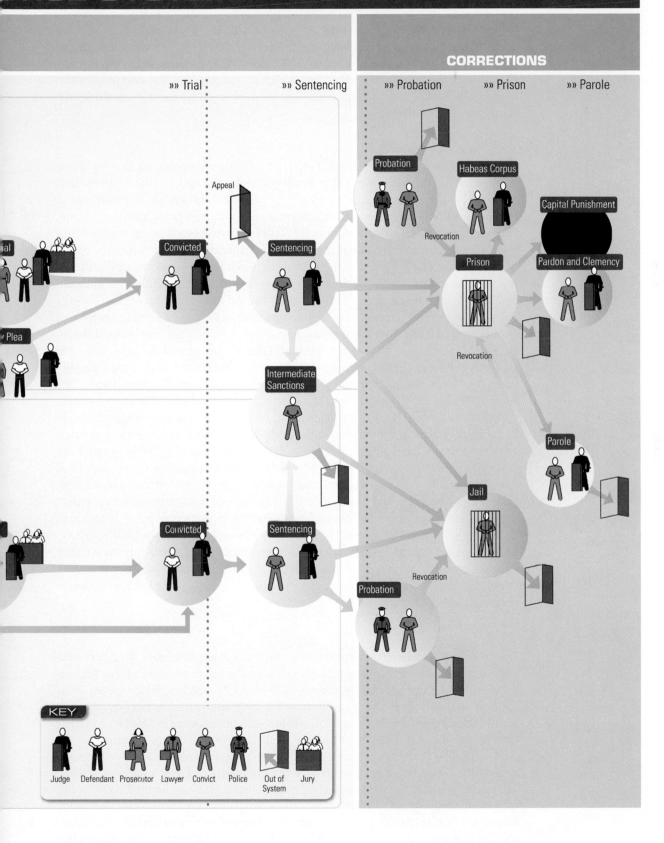

»» Trial   »» Sentencing

CORRECTIONS

»» Probation   »» Prison   »» Parole

Probation

Habeas Corpus

Capital Punishment

Appeal

Convicted

Sentencing

Revocation

Prison

Pardon and Clemency

Plea

Revocation

Intermediate
Sanctions

Parole

Jail

Convicted

Sentencing

Revocation

Probation

KEY

Judge | Defendant | Prosecutor | Lawyer | Convict | Police | Out of System | Jury

protections for someone accused of a crime, including the right to refuse to testify against oneself, the right to counsel, the right to a speedy and public trial, the right to a jury trial if desired, and freedom from being tried twice for the same crime, excessive bail, "cruel and unusual punishment," or being deprived of "life, liberty, or property without due process of law." Important components of the criminal justice system include the police, who enforce the laws, the courts, which determine whether a defendant is guilty or innocent, and the correctional system, which includes federal and state prisons and local jails in which convicted criminals and those charged with crimes awaiting trial are imprisoned FIGURE 6-16.

Police

It is the police who receive reports of crime, decide which crimes deserve more investigation, assess the criminality of alleged violators, and ultimately assert that someone has committed a crime by arresting that person and asking the prosecutor to file charges. Police organizations include municipal police, state highway patrols, the Federal Bureau of Investigation, and other federal agencies such as the Border Patrol and the Immigration and Naturalization Service. **Police discretion** refers to the power of police to exercise judgment in their interactions with suspects, deciding whether to arrest a husband or wife in the midst of a domestic dispute, deciding who to question about a crime, and selecting which motorists to stop on the highway (Silko 1994).

Stereotypes and perceptual biases have been shown to influence police. Sociologist Aaron Cicourel spent two years studying police and probation agencies in two different cities using participant observation. He found that young men whose behaviors were relatively harmless were more likely to be labeled criminals and treated more harshly when they were members of minorities or lower social classes (Cicourel 1969). In a study of people caught shoplifting, Mary Cameron (1964) found that among people apprehended, 58% of blacks were subsequently charged with larceny, compared to only 11% of non-blacks. Still other studies have shown that whether someone is arrested and charged depends a great deal on how cooperative a person is (Pilliavin and Brian 1964). They found that only 2 of 45 polite youths were arrested, compared with 14 of 21 uncooperative youths. Arrests are much more likely when a complainant requests that an arrest be made, and black citizens request arrests much more commonly than whites, producing distorted arrest statistics (Reiss 1971). A study of police behavior in five cities (Smith and Visher 1981) found added support for each of the findings above. In addition, the researchers found that police were more likely to make an arrest if they believed the situation was serious, the person had been arrested before, there were bystanders present, or if the suspect was a person of color such as a black or Hispanic person rather than a white person.

Courts

Once someone is arrested or charged with a crime, the courts determine the defendant's guilt or innocence. In theory, courts operate with the full protections of due process provided by the Constitution to protect individuals. In practice, however, the great majority of criminal cases never go to trial. Most criminal cases are resolved through **plea bargaining**—a formal negotiation in which defendants agree to plead guilty rather than appear in court. Usually, prosecutors reduce the initial charge in return for the guilty plea. Plea bargaining is extremely common in US courts. In 2009, in US district courts, 96.3% of all cases were resolved with a guilty plea and only 3.7% went to trial. The court system is so overburdened with cases that if plea bargaining did not occur, the system would grind to a halt. As it is, it often takes weeks, months, or even years before defendants have their day in court. Plea bargaining is most common for lesser offenses like immigration cases (99.3%) and less common for more serious offenses like murder (73.1%) or sexual abuse (87.4%) (US Sentencing Commission 2010). From the perspective of the criminal justice system, plea bargaining helps the system function and focuses overburdened courts on the most serious cases.

Police discretion The power of police to exercise judgment in their interactions with suspects.

Plea bargaining A formal negotiation in which defendants agree to plead guilty rather than appear in court.

However, plea bargaining is often criticized because it pressures defendants to plead guilty to a lesser crime or risk being convicted of the more serious crime they were charged with originally. For low-income defendants who have to rely on overworked and underpaid public defenders, the likelihood of a successful court hearing is less than that for affluent defendants who can hire their own counsel. Worse yet, plea bargaining further erodes the rights of defendants because public defenders often find it in their best interest—even if it is not in the best interest of the defendants—to encourage their clients to plea bargain.

Punishment and Corrections

When a crime is committed in the United States and the perpetrator is found and convicted, the next most likely consequence is some form of punishment for the criminal. In the United States, much more than in most other countries, the result is often imprisonment. The United States imprisons a larger proportion of its citizens than any other country in the world, with 2.3 million people in state and federal prisons and local jails currently (Bureau of Justice Statistics 2010). This is five times the number 30 years ago and reflects a strong increase in the number of people in state and federal prisons, as shown in FIGURE 6-17 (The Sentencing Project 2010). More than 5.6 million US adults have served time in federal or state prison (Bureau of Justice Statistics 2003). Black males are incarcerated at a rate more than six times higher than that of whites and 2.6 times higher than Hispanic males (Bureau of Justice Statistics 2010). "One of every three black males born today can expect to go to prison at some time in his life if current trends continue" (The Sentencing Project 2010).

Unfortunately, despite the heavy dependence on prisons in the United States, one of the most-often-cited measures of success, the **recidivism rate**—the rate at which former prisoners are rearrested, reconvicted, and re-imprisoned—suggests prisons are not very effective. In the latest data from the Bureau of Justice Statistics, of prisoners released in 1994, within three years, 67.5% had been rearrested, 46.9% had been reconvicted of some new crime, and 51.8% were back in prison either for a new crime or for violating parole (Bureau of Justice Statistics 2002). When those rates are compared with similar rates for prisoners released in 1983 the recidivism rate is increasing, as shown in FIGURE 6-18.

One explanation for why prisons are ineffective may be because reasons for putting someone in prison have changed over time, and there is not a strong consensus as to what we want to accomplish by imprisonment today. Four commonly cited reasons include retribution, deterrence, societal protection, and rehabilitation. The first three of these developed in different historical periods and represent evolving views of imprisonment.

Recidivism rate The rate at which former prisoners are rearrested, reconvicted, and re-imprisoned.

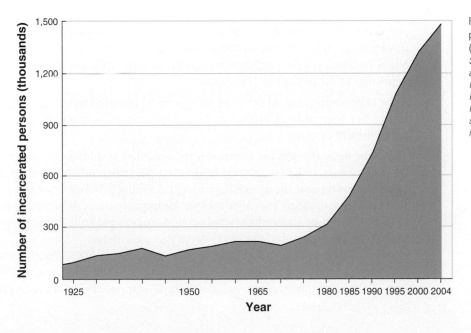

FIGURE 6-17 Incarcerated persons in US and federal prisons (1925–2004).
Source: King, Ryan S., Marc Mauer, and Malcolm C. Young. 2005. Incarceration and Crime: A Complex Relationship. The Sentencing Project. Retrieved January 2012 (http://www.sentencingproject.org/doc/publications/inc_iandc_complex.pdf).

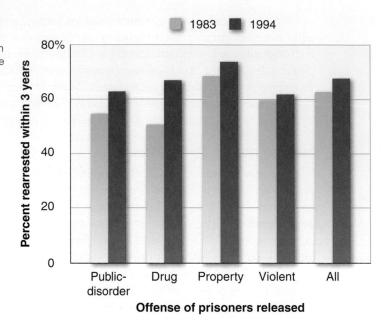

FIGURE 6-18 Percent of released prisoners in US rearrested within three years, by offense (1983 and 1994). *Data from the Bureau of Justice Statistics. 2002. Recidivism of Prisoners Released in 1994. Retrieved January 2012 (http://bjs.ojp.usdoj.gov/content/reentry/tables/recidivismtab.cfm).*

Retribution Punishment to seek vengeance.

Deterrence The attempt to discourage criminal behavior through punishment.

Rehabilitation The process of helping criminals become productive citizens.

Societal protection Seeking to remove offenders from society to make them incapable of further crimes.

- **Retribution**—punishment to seek vengeance—is the oldest justification for punishment and was common as long ago as the Middle Ages, when crime was viewed as a sin that must be punished. Retribution attempts to "set things right" by restoring a moral balance with punishment proportionate to the crime. The Biblical notion of an "eye for an eye" or the Muslim Sharia law that punishes theft by amputating one or both hands of the thief each reflect this notion of retribution.

- **Deterrence** attempts to discourage criminal behavior through punishment. Deterrence arose during the Enlightenment in the 18th century and assumes people are rational. Therefore, we should be able to prevent criminal behavior by making the punishment outweigh the benefits of the crime. Historically, deterrence arose in a reform movement in response to harsh punishments based on retribution and provided a rationale for milder punishments that might not be sufficient for retribution but still could be sufficient to deter criminal behavior by rational people.

- **Rehabilitation** seeks to help criminals become productive citizens. This view arose during the 19th century along with social sciences like sociology that point to ways the environment and social structures can lead individuals to become criminals. The logic of rehabilitation is that people can learn to be productive citizens able to survive in the economy outside of prison and become less likely to return to a life of crime once released. Where deterrence focuses on negative punishments to prevent crime, rehabilitation includes supportive steps to help reform the person. Where retribution seeks punishments that fit the crime, rehabilitation seeks treatments that fit the individual offender.

- **Societal protection** argues the offender should be removed from society to make him or her incapable of further crimes. This may be accomplished through imprisonment or execution.

Unfortunately, these reasons for imprisonment are often at odds with one another. Making prisons miserable may increase retribution but may not be needed for deterrence and may even harm efforts to rehabilitate. Educating prisoners may rehabilitate them but does little to satisfy the other reasons for imprisonment. Whether or not we believe offenders can be successfully rehabilitated leads to radically different notions of how long people need to be kept in prison to protect society.

Prisons are also very expensive, costing an average of $22,650 annually per state inmate. Prison expenditures increased 150% between 1986 and 2001 to $29.5 billion (Stephan 2004). For these reasons, alternatives to imprisonment are increasingly used. These all fall under the broad category of **community-based corrections**—correctional programs operating outside traditional prisons in the community at large. Community-based programs emphasize rehabilitation and are often offered only to offenders who have committed less serious crimes and pose less of a threat to the rest of society. Such programs cost less than prison, carry less of a stigma than imprisonment, reduce overcrowding in prisons, and permit offenders to avoid the greater hardship of imprisonment.

Community-based programs include probation and parole. **Probation** allows a convicted offender to be supervised in the community under conditions imposed by the court instead of going to prison, while **parole** releases prisoners to serve the remainder of their sentence in the community supervised by the court. Both probation and parole require the offender to meet the conditions of the court, typically including reporting to a probation or parole officer periodically and not associating with other convicted criminals. Conditions may also include getting a job, attending a drug rehabilitation program, or other requirements. Some sentences prohibit parole, and for those that do permit parole, prisoners become eligible after serving some portion of their sentence and must often go before a parole board, which decides whether they qualify.

The use of parole has increased proportionate to imprisonment between 1980 and 2008, while the use of probation has increased at a much higher rate, with more than 4 million people in the United States on probation at any one point in time FIGURE 6-19 (Bureau of Justice Statistics 2008). Unfortunately, these programs too often have high recidivism rates, and as a result, some states have discontinued parole programs entirely (Inciardi 2000).

The Death Penalty

Even more extreme than imprisonment is the death penalty. According to Amnesty International, in 2009 at least 2,390 people were executed in 25 countries and at least 8,864 were sentenced to death in 52 countries. The United States executed the fourth-largest number of convicted criminals, with 37 executions, behind China with at least 1,718. Iran executed at least 346, and Saudi Arabia executed at least 102 convicts (Amnesty International 2009).

There is disagreement in the United States over whether people should be executed, and fifteen states have no death penalty. One of the most common criticisms of the death penalty is that its application is often influenced by race. One study found that ". . . defendants with white victims face average odds of receiving a death sentence that are 4.3 times larger than those faced by similarly situated defendants with black victims"

Community-based corrections Correctional programs operating outside traditional prisons in the community at large.

Probation Allows a convicted offender to be supervised in the community under conditions imposed by the court instead of going to prison.

Parole Release of a prisoner to serve the remainder of his or her sentence in the community supervised by the court.

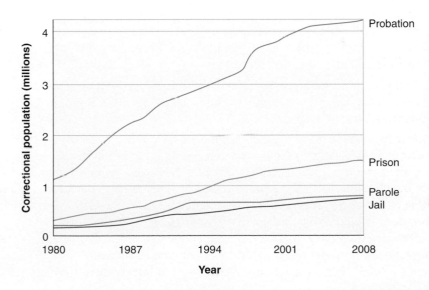

FIGURE 6-19 US adult correctional populations (1980–2008).
Data from the Bureau of Justice Statistics, Correctional Population Trends Chart 2008. *Retrieved January 2012 (http://bjs.ojp.usdoj.gov/content/glance/tables/corr2tab.cfm).*

(Baldus, Woodworth, and Pulaski 1990). Another common criticism points out that since 1973, there have been more than 130 people released from death row after convincing evidence, such as new DNA findings, surfaced and proved their innocence (House Judiciary Subcommittee on Civil and Constitutional Rights 1993; Death Penalty Information Center 2010).

| CONCEPT LEARNING CHECK 6.7 | What Are the Facts about the Criminal Justice System? |

Decide whether each of the following statements is true or false.

_____ **1.** Plea bargaining is rare in US courts.

_____ **2.** The United States is in the mid-range of developed countries when it comes to the per-capita rate of imprisonment.

_____ **3.** Your probability of being arrested is likely to increase if you are impolite to the police.

_____ **4.** Sentencing convicted offenders to probation has declined along with the drop in crime rates.

Visual Overview Deviance and Crime: Theoretical Perspectives

The major theoretical perspectives offer important, sometimes competing insights into the nature of deviance and crime. Use this graphic to begin to form a bigger picture of each perspective, examples, and how they relate to one another.

According to **Functionalist** perspectives, deviance and crime form a necessary part of society with some positive consequences.

Structural-Functional Approach

Society's response to deviance clarifies moral boundaries.

Deviance:
- promotes social unity
- affirms cultural values and norms
- promotes necessary social change

Strain Theory

Deviance occurs when society provides the means to achieve cultural goals.

- conformity
- innovation
- ritualism
- retreatism
- rebellion

Criminal Al Capone is an example of strain theory's innovation.

Opportunity Theory

The kind of deviance that occurs depends on a lack of access to legitimate opportunity and on access to illegal means.

According to **Symbolic** interactionism, deviance and crime are viewed according to a society's symbols, frameworks, behaviors, and attitudes. This view questions the possibility of an objective definition.

Differential Association

People are more likely to be deviant to the extent they are exposed to deviants.

Differential Reinforcement

Individuals learn criminal behavior through association, reinforcement, tolerance, and imitation.

Control Theory

People have an inner control system supported by conscience, morality, religion, fear of punishment, and integrity.

Labeling Theory

An act becomes deviant only when it is labeled as deviant by others.

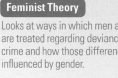

Howard Becker uses labeling theory to describe the process of becoming a marijuana smoker.

Deviance and Power

Social class and power influence what is considered deviant and how it is treated.

Deviance and Capitalism

Law and culture support capitalist interests and influence what is considered deviant.

Feminist Theory

Looks at ways in which men and women are treated regarding deviance and crime and how those differences are influenced by gender.

According to **Conflict** perspectives, deviance and crime reflect competing interests among different social classes, genders, and racial/ethnic groups.

Fraudulent practices that led to the collapse of the US housing market are an example of deviance and capitalism. Millions of people were victims, yet few were prosecuted.

Visual Summary Deviance and Crime

6.1 Overview: Understanding Deviance and Crime

- What is considered deviant is relative and varies with time and place.
- Deviance can refer to thoughts, not just behaviors.

- Deviance consists of thoughts or behaviors that are different from those of other people but not necessarily worse.
- Biological and psychological views of deviance focus on the individual.

6.2 Functionalist Perspectives

- Deviance is a necessary part of any society and has positive consequences.
- Strain theory argues that whether deviance occurs and the kind of deviance that occurs depends on whether society provides culturally acceptable means to achieve cultural goals.

- Opportunity theory argues that the kind of deviance that occurs depends not only on a lack of access to legitimate opportunity but also on the availability of illegitimate opportunity structures—ready access to illegal means.

6.3 Symbolic Interactionism

- This perspective focuses on how individuals define particular acts as deviant and how they respond to them through interactions with others.
- Differential association theory argues people are more likely to be deviant to the extent they are exposed to deviants.
- Differential reinforcement theory argues individuals learn criminal behavior through differential association, differential reinforcement, definitions of acceptable acts, and imitation.

- Control theory argues that people have an inner control system and are more able to resist temptation if they are bonded to society through commitments, involvements, shared beliefs, and attachments.
- Labeling theory argues that an act becomes deviant only when it is labeled as deviant by others and distinguishes primary, secondary, and tertiary deviance.

6.4 Conflict Perspectives

- The different social classes, genders, and racial and ethnic groups in society have competing interests, and some are more effective at shaping society's view of deviance than others.
- The social conflict perspective emphasizes competing interests of groups of people having different amounts of power, and those having more power use it to exploit those with less power.
- Social status and power influence what is considered deviant and how it is treated.

- Conflict theorists maintain that law and culture support capitalist interests in many ways.
- Race, social class, and gender interact, and people having particular combinations of characteristics are treated much differently than others.
- Feminist theorists argue deviance and crime have often been approached with only the male perspective in mind, leading to notions of crime and deviance that favor men.

6.5 Crime

- There are many types of crime, which differ in severity and in how they are punished.
- Crimes are often distinguished by who commits the crime and who is the target of the crime.

- Some "crimes" occur in areas where other social institutions such as the military or health care compete with the criminal justice system to regulate behavior.
- New kinds of crimes such as cybercrimes must be defined as social change makes possible new behaviors.

6.6 Crime Statistics

- Crime statistics—how often different types of crimes occur, who commits them, and who are the victims—help identify important issues affecting public policy.
- Crime rates in the United States (as measured by the eight FBI index crimes) have declined significantly between 1991 and 2009, with biggest declines between 1991 and 2000.

- Arrest rates are generally higher for teenagers and young adults, males, and blacks than other groups.
- Victimization rates are higher for minorities, generally for both crimes against property and crimes against persons.

6.7 The Criminal Justice System

- The criminal justice system includes the institutions that arrest, judge, and punish criminals.
- Important components of the criminal justice system include the police, who enforce the laws, the courts, which determine whether a defendant is guilty or innocent, and the correctional system, which includes federal and state prisons and local jails in which convicted criminals and those charged with crimes awaiting trials are imprisoned.
- The United States imprisons a larger proportion of its citizens than any other country in the world.

- Imprisonment is often criticized for being ineffective, at least in part because there is not a strong consensus as to what we want to accomplish by imprisonment today.
- Four commonly cited reasons for imprisonment include retribution, deterrence, societal protection, and rehabilitation.
- One of the most common criticisms of the death penalty is that its application is often influenced by race.

6.1 Understanding Deviance and Crime

1. Glaring at someone who is being impolite at the dinner table is an example of:
- **A.** a positive sanction.
- **B.** a negative sanction.
- **C.** ostracism.
- **D.** deviance.

2. Changing events in American gay rights provide evidence that deviance
- **A.** varies in different cultures.
- **B.** is something that is universally recognized in every subculture in a society.
- **C.** is sometimes viewed very differently at different times.
- **D.** should always be punished.

3. Which of the following, if true, would be *inconsistent* with the argument that deviance is relative?
- **A.** Killing someone is forbidden under any circumstances in every culture.
- **B.** At various times, smoking was illegal, then legal, and now often illegal again in particular settings.
- **C.** In some societies, men may have multiple wives, while in other societies, that is illegal.
- **D.** Gambling is legal in some places in many states but not legal in other locations.

6.2 Functionalist Perspectives

4. Which of the following is *not* an example of legitimate institutionalized means for achieving societal goals?
- **A.** A job
- **B.** Being accepted to college
- **C.** Joining the military
- **D.** Learning how to steal cars

5. What is the key difference between strain theory and opportunity theory?
- **A.** Opportunity theory emphasizes the importance of access to legitimate means of achieving societal goals.
- **B.** Strain theory emphasizes how a person's internal control system helps them resist deviance.
- **C.** Opportunity theory adds to strain theory the availability of illegitimate opportunity structures.
- **D.** Opportunity theory emphasizes social structures, while strain theory does not.

6. A college student telling her friend that she is just going to college because her parents insist would be an example of which kind of deviance according to strain theory?
- **A.** Rebellion
- **B.** Innovation
- **C.** Conformity
- **D.** Ritualism

6.3 Symbolic Interactionism

7. Michael had a tough childhood and, as a young adult, he was convicted of felony auto theft and spent a year in prison. When he later applied for a job at a factory, his application was rejected because they have a policy of not hiring convicted felons. In a sentence or two, indicate which theory best accounts for this example and what concept from that theory applies.

6.4 Conflict Perspectives

8. Which theory is most likely to make an argument that females are more disadvantaged than males?
- **A.** Functional theory
- **B.** Conflict theory
- **C.** Feminist theory
- **D.** Class theory

9. Who is more likely to be able to influence passage of legislation to legalize marijuana?
- **A.** A respected businessman in the community
- **B.** An immigrant farm laborer
- **C.** A housewife
- **D.** A college dropout

6.5 Crime

10. Which of the following crimes is *not* included in the annual FBI crime reports?
- **A.** Theft
- **B.** Computer crime
- **C.** Rape
- **D.** Assault

11. Subtypes of crime: Which of the following is *not* included among street crimes?
- **A.** Fraud
- **B.** Crimes against persons
- **C.** Crimes against property
- **D.** Corporate crime

6.6 Crime Statistics

12. Victims of violent crime are more likely to be victimized by:
- **A.** whites.
- **B.** blacks.
- **C.** someone of the same race.
- **D.** someone of a different race.

13. Which is not true of the people arrested for crimes against persons?
- **A.** They are more likely to be teenagers or young adults than older adults.
- **B.** They are more likely to be men than women.
- **C.** They are more likely to be illegal immigrants than American citizens.
- **D.** They are more likely to be black than white.

14. FBI crime statistics do not track all but one of the following. Which item *is* tracked by the FBI?
- **A.** Ethnicity of offenders
- **B.** Social class of offenders
- **C.** White-collar crime
- **D.** Race of offenders

6.7 The Criminal Justice System

15. Which of the following arguments against the death penalty is correct?
- **A.** DNA and other evidence that may later show a person innocent come too late if the person has already been executed.
- **B.** The death penalty is much more common when the victim was black and hence influenced by race.
- **C.** The majority of people put to death are women and hence it is gender biased.
- **D.** It is often used because it saves the state money.

16. True or False: Within three years of being released from prison, more than two-thirds of former prisoners in the US are likely to be rearrested and more than half end up back in prison.

17. Which of the following is *not* true of plea bargaining?
- **A.** It is very common in the United States.
- **B.** It makes the interests of the public defender in settling quickly conflict with the interest of the defendant in getting a fair trial.
- **C.** It slows the court process, making it almost impossible to get anything done.
- **D.** It often results in the defendant pleading guilty to a reduced charge.

ESSAY QUESTIONS

1. Your congressman is struggling to win reelection and wants to get tough on crime. He argues we do not put enough offenders in prison and that we should focus particularly on the worst offenses, such as violent interracial crimes and the victimization of children, women, and older adults. He also thinks we should put more emphasis on protecting more affluent households because they are more likely to be victimized than poorer households. In a few sentences, tell your congressman what you think he should emphasize and at least two things he should know about crime in America that influence your judgment.

2. Jorge is married with two small children. He and his family live in a modest house they just bought located within a mile of where Jorge works in a software firm. He works very hard at his job while trying to spend time with his children and be a good father. He is very active in his church and has many friends from both church and work. One friend in particular is a woman at work who is about 10 years older. She treats him like he was her son and he often turns to her for advice when things get rough. Write a brief one or two paragraph essay that addresses the following questions: Would control theory suggest that Jorge is likely or unlikely to be deviant? Identify at least three types of social bonds that Jorge has and indicate the word or phrase in the description that illustrates that type of bond.

CHAPTER DISCUSSION QUESTIONS

1. How does the sociological view of deviance reflect the sociological imagination? Consider any of the sociological theories of deviance and contrast it with psychological or biological views of deviance to show how the sociological imagination is reflected in the sociological theory but not the psychological or biological views.

2. How does smoking illustrate deviance as a social construct?

3. Was Durkheim right that every society needs deviance? How are his functions of deviance illustrated in the United States today?

4. Of the many types of crime, which do you think are the most serious crimes that should be punished most harshly? Why? What factors make some crimes more serious than others?

5. The criminal justice system has been compared to a big funnel in which the vast number of reported crimes is followed by a smaller number of arrests, followed by fewer criminal charges, followed by fewer court cases, followed by fewer convictions, followed by fewer prison sentences. Is this a good thing or a bad thing? Why? What does this imply about the old saying "crime doesn't pay"?

6. Make a list of behaviors and/or beliefs that used to be considered deviant in the past but today are a socially accepted. How do these examples reflect the relativity of deviance and cultural values? How do these examples reflect Emile Durkheim's functions of deviance?

7. Think about the norms related to college students. Provide examples to the class how students deviate from these norms. Discuss both positive sanctions and negative sanctions used to socially control college students.

How many of these sanctions involve informal versus formal means of social control? Do students also use sanctions amongst themselves to control behaviors and beliefs that might be defined as deviant?

8. Share with the class an example from your life when you experienced primary deviance by being labeled mildly deviant by someone. Did you attempt to use techniques of neutralization to justify yourself? You can use examples related to school, family, friends, work, etc.

9. Discuss how illegitimate opportunity structures that affect crimes against persons or crimes against property are related to social class status. Do you agree or disagree with the social conflict perspective on deviance which posits that groups of people with access to power are in positions to define and punish deviance?

10. Should minors who engage in bullying behaviors be labeled as juvenile delinquents and bullying defined as a status offense? What steps can schools take to lessen bullying and violence especially against GLBT students?

11. Discuss the pros (for) and cons (against) arguments regarding the decriminalization of certain illicit drugs or prostitution, keeping in mind the notion that these are defined as victimless crimes that may result in additional crimes against persons or property.

12. Examine the data related to *crime victims*. Discuss societal contributors that might affect the differences in victim rates related to age, gender, race, and social class.

13. Do you think that the US recidivism rate is acceptable or unacceptable? Discuss the effectiveness of various current deterrence and rehabilitation strategies including the death penalty.

CHAPTER PROJECTS

INDIVIDUAL PROJECTS

1. Go online to learn more about the "*medicalization of deviance*." Write an analysis paper based on your findings and consider issues such as *deviance and capitalism*, *social control*, and *stigma*.

2. Write a self-reflection paper about a time in which you were in a position to deviate but decided not to because you imagined yourself disappointing your family members, friends, or other people who you cared about or tried to impress. Incorporate key terms and theories throughout your reflection piece. Think about how the theories and key terms from the symbolic interaction perspective relate to your experience(s).

3. Over the course of a week, visit the social networking sites of a few people you know. Look for examples of social norms that are or have been violated. Describe what norm was violated and how people responded. Consider whether differences in people's responses depended on what role they played. What might this tell you about the role of social control in our lives?

4. Scan through a week's worth of news stories in the *New York Times* or your local newspaper and summarize what role deviance plays in the news. Do they report some kind of crime virtually every day even when nothing very serious seems to have happened? Do they focus on some types of crimes more than others? Do they discuss the crimes from a sociological perspective or more from a psychological perspective focusing on the individual criminal?

GROUP PROJECTS

1. Based on the sociological explanations of deviance how would each theory explain the recidivism rates in the United States?

2. Go online and search for the Uniform Crime Report (published by the FBI). Visit the Uniform Crime Report website and examine the statistics and information about the collection of crime data. Evaluate the statistics and collection methods and write a report documenting your group's findings.

KEY TERMS

Community-based corrections
Conformity
Control theory
Corporate crime
Crime
Crimes against persons
Crimes against property
Criminal justice system
Criminology
Cultural goals
Cybercrime
Definitions of acceptable acts
Degradation ceremony
Deterrence
Deviance
Differential association
Differential association theory
Differential reinforcement
Differential reinforcement theory
Due process

Feminist theory
Hate crime
Illegitimate opportunity structures
Imitation
Institutionalized means
Innovation
Juvenile delinquency
Labeling theory
Negative sanctions
Organized crime
Ostracism
Parole
Plea bargaining
Police discretion
Political crimes
Positive sanction
Primary deviance
Probation
Rebellion
Recidivism rate

Rehabilitation
Retreatism
Retribution
Ritualism
Secondary deviance
Social bond theory
Social conflict perspective
Social control
Social order
Societal protection
Stigma
Street crime
Techniques of neutralization
Terrorism
Tertiary deviance
Victimless crimes
Violent crime
White-collar crime

ANSWERS TO CONCEPT LEARNING CHECKS

6.1 Understanding Deviance and Crime

1. "Positive" deviance [E. Rate busters]

2. Positive sanction [C. Honor roll]

3. Early biological view of deviance [B. Criminals are more likely to have certain body types.]

4. Learning theory view of deviance [A. Children watching violence on TV are more likely to be violent.]

5. Deviance [D. Is not limited to behaviors but can be about attitudes or beliefs]

6.2 How Do Functional Theories Explain Deviance?

1. An adolescent sees her friend caught shoplifting and resolves to never shoplift herself. [C. Functional theory; B. Society's response to deviance clarifies moral boundaries.]

2. Monique is a freshman in college but doesn't know what she wants to do with her life. She stays in college because her parents want her to go and people respect her when she says she is a college student. [A. Strain theory; C. Ritualism]

3. Jerome learned from his friends how to download music and videos from the Internet without paying for them. He soon stopped paying for CDs and DVDs. [B. Opportunity theory; A. Illegitimate opportunity structure]

6.3 Distinguishing Concepts of Labeling Theory

1. Sheila saw Jake pocketing a few of the ballpoint pens at work and taking them home but thought little of it, realizing that it is not uncommon for people to occasionally take a few office supplies from work. [B. Primary deviance]

2. After Fran was caught cheating on a test, a note was placed in her permanent record, and other instructors in that department took extra care to check her work for cheating whenever she took an important test. [C. Secondary deviance]

3. When caught stealing hundreds of dollars from the petty cash drawer at the office where he worked on the clerical staff, Jake was immediately fired and told to pack his personal effects in a box and was escorted to the door by an armed security officer. [A. Degradation ceremony]

4. When arrested for driving without a license and reckless driving, Roger responded to the officer by saying, "It's not such a big deal. No one was hurt." [D. Techniques of neutralization]

6.4 Explaining Events with Conflict Theories

1. Incarceration rates among young, black, lower-class men are much higher than for most other categories of people in the United States. [A. Deviance and power]

2. In courtroom trials of rape cases, it sometimes seems as though the woman is on trial as much as the man she accuses of rape. [B. Feminist theory]

3. Blacks and other minorities are more often prosecuted for smoking crack cocaine, while more affluent whites are more likely to use powdered cocaine. Average penalties are much harsher for crack cocaine than for similar amounts of powdered cocaine. [A. Deviance and power]

6.5 Categorizing Types of Crime

1. A car bombing that injures 30 people but no one dies. [Assault or crime against persons or violent crime, terrorism]

2. Online gambling where it is illegal. [Victimless crime, cybercrime]

3. A man is tied up and beaten by a group of other men because they think he is gay. [Assault or violent crime or crime against persons, hate crime]

6.6 Using Crime Statistics to Shape Social Policy

1. Racial and ethnic minorities are more likely to be victims of violent crimes than are whites. [T]

2. Women are more likely to be victims of violent crime than men. [F]

3. Over the past few years crime rates have risen at an alarming rate. [F]

4. Older adults are more likely to be victims of crime than younger adults or middle-age adults. [F]

6.7 What Are the Facts about the Criminal Justice System?

1. Plea bargaining is rare in US courts. [F]

2. The United States is in the mid-range of developed countries when it comes to the per-capita rate of imprisonment. [F]

3. Your probability of being arrested is likely to increase if you are impolite to the police. [T]

4. Sentencing convicted offenders to probation has declined along with the drop in crime rates. [F]

ANSWERS TO ESSAY QUESTIONS

1. Well-written responses should be about one to two paragraphs long and cite statistics that support the writer's point of view, such as the following:
   - The United States has more people in prison per capita than all other countries.
   - Whites are more likely to be victimized by other whites, and blacks are more likely to be victimized by blacks.
   - Teens and young adults are more likely to be victims of crimes than children or older adults.
   - Men are more likely to be victims than women.
   - Victimization rates are higher for poorer households.

2. A good answer should indicate that control theory suggests that he is unlikely to be deviant because he has several social bonds. These include:
   - Commitments, illustrated by children, house, and job.
   - Involvements, illustrated by church,
   - Attachments, illustrated by affection for his friends and family
   - Shared beliefs, illustrated by religious beliefs.

   A good answer should mention at least three of the social bonds and provide at least one example of each.

ANSWERS TO CHAPTER REVIEW TEST

1. B. Glaring is a negative sanction intended to punish.

2. C. Our notions of deviance change over time.

3. A. Something forbidden in every culture is absolute, not relative.

4. D. Learning how to steal cars is an illegitimate means for achieving goals because it is illegal.

5. C. Opportunity theory suggests that some become criminals because they feel that the success goals shared by all can only be achieved through the illegitimate opportunity structures of criminal subcultures.

6. D. Her actions can be described as ritualism because her overt behavior conforms to family norms, yet she doesn't have the values that are the basis for those norms.

7. Michael is experiencing stigma and secondary deviance, either of which is a good answer. The theory that best accounts for this is labeling theory.

8. C. Feminist theory focuses on ways in which women are disadvantaged relative to men.

9. A. Since the rich and powerful play a big part in shaping our definitions of deviance, a respected businessman in the community is more likely to influence marijuana legalization laws.

10. B. Computer crime is not one of the index crimes included in the FBI's annual crime reports.

11. D. Corporate crime is not a street crime because it does not necessarily occur in public settings.

12. C. FBI statistics indicate that the race of offenders is likely to be the same as the race of their victims.

13. C. Data are not available regarding arrest rates for illegal immigrants versus American citizens for crimes against persons.

14. D. While the FBI does not keep track of white-collar crime, social class, and ethnicity, it does collect statistics on race.

15. A. DNA evidence exposing the innocence of defendants was explicit in the chapter. The other choices are incorrect. Death penalties are more likely when the victim is white, not black. There is nothing in the chapter about death row defenders by gender. Usually the death penalty costs more than life imprisonment because of all the legal appeals that must occur.

16. T. US Bureau of Justice Statistics (2002) show that among prisoners released in 1994, within three years 67.5% had been rearrested, 46.9% had been reconvicted of some new crime, and 51.8% were back in prison either for a new crime or for violating parole.

17. C. Plea bargaining does not slow down the court process. In fact, it has quite the opposite effect. It helps the courts process cases quickly by minimizing the cases seen in courts, which helps them decide some cases more quickly.

REFERENCES

Adler, Freda. 1975. *Sisters in Crime: The Rise of the New Female Criminal.* New York: McGraw-Hill.

Adler, Freda, Gerhard O. W. Mueller, and William S. Laufer. 2007. *Criminology and the Criminal Justice System.* 6th ed. New York: McGraw-Hill.

Akers, Ronald L. 1973. *Deviant Behavior: A Social Learning Approach.* Belmont, CA: Wadsworth.

Amnesty International. 2009. *Death Sentences and Executions in 2008—In Numbers 2009.* Available from http://www.amnesty.org/en/library/asset/ACT50/008/2009/en/3fc7fe75-97d0-425b-bf89-23df453e3009/act500082009en.html.

Anderson, Elijah. 1994. "The Code of the Streets." *Atlantic Monthly,* May, 81–94.

Archer, Dane. 1985. "Social Deviance." Vol. 2, 3rd ed., pp. 743–804 in *The Handbook of Social Psychology,* edited by G. Lindzey. and E. Aronson. New York: Random House.

Baldus, David C., George Woodworth, and Charles A. Pulaski Jr. 1990. *Equal Justice and the Death Penalty: A Legal and Empirical Study.* Boston: Northeastern University Press.

Bandura, Albert. 1973. "Social Learning Theory of Aggression." Pp. 201–250 in *The Control of Aggression,* edited by J. F. Knutson. Chicago: Aldine.

Bank, D. and R. Richmond. 2005. "Where the Dangers Are: The Threats to Information Security that Keep the Experts Up at Night—And What Businesses And Consumers Can Do To Protect Themselves." *Wall Street Journal,* July 18, p. R1.

BBC News. 2000. "'Love Virus Chaos Spreads." *BBC News,* May 4, 2000.

Becker, Howard S. 1953. "Becoming a Marihuana User." *American Journal of Sociology* 59(3):235–242.

———. 1963. *Outsiders: Studies in the Sociology of Deviance.* New York: Free Press.

Bergen, Raquel Kennedy. 2006. *Marital Rape: New Research and Directions.* Harrisburg, PA: VAW Net.

Berkowitz, L. 1962. *Aggression: A Social Psychological Analysis.* New York: McGraw-Hill.

Buikhuisen, W. and F. Dijksterhuis. 1971. "Delinquency and Stigmatization." *British Journal of Criminology* 11:185–88.

Bureau of Justice Statistics. 2002. *Recidivism of Prisoners Released in 1994.* US Department of Justice.

———. 2003. *Sourcebook of Criminal Justice Statistics.* US Department of Justice. Table p. 517.

———. 2007. *Sourcebook of Criminal Justice Statistics.* Table 3.22.2007.

———. 2009. *Sourcebook of Criminal Justice Statistics.* Table 4.4.2009, Table 4.10.2009, Table 6.28.2009, Table 3.4.2009, Table 4.92.2009. Available from http://www.albany.edu/sourcebook/pdf.

———. 2010. *Prevalence of Imprisonment in the US Population, 1974–2001.* 2003. Available from http://bjs.ojp.usdoj.gov/index.cfm?ty=pbdetail&iid=836.

———. *Correctional Population Trends Chart 2008.* 2008. Available from http://bjs.ojp.usdoj.gov/content/glance/corr2.cfm.

———. *Criminal Victimization in the United States, 2007.* 2007. Available from http://bjs.ojp.usdoj.gov/index.cfm?ty=pbdetail&iid=1743.

———. *Prison Inmates at Midyear 2009, June 23, 2010.* Available from http://bjs.ojp.usdoj.gov/content/pub/press/pim09stpy09acpr.cfm.

———. *Victim Age Trends 2010.* 2010. Available from http://bjs.ojp.usdoj.gov/content/glance/vage.cfm.

———. *Victim Characteristics 2010.* 2010. Available from http://bjs.ojp.usdoj.gov/index.cfm?ty=tp&tid=92.

Bureau of Labor Statistics. 2010. *Injuries, Illnesses, and Fatalities 2010.* Available from http://www.bls.gov/iif/.

Cameron, Mary O. 1964. *The Booster and the Snitch: Department Store Shoplifting.* New York: Free Press.

Chambliss, W. 1973. "The Saints and the Roughnecks." *Society,* Vol. 11, No. 1 (November/December 1973), pp. 24–31.

Chambliss, William J. 1974. "The State, The Law, and the Definition of Behavior as Criminal or Delinquent." Pp. 7–43 in *The Handbook of Criminology,* edited by D. Glaser. Chicago: Rand McNally.

Chambliss, William J. and Robert B. Seidman. 1982. *Law, Order, and Power.* Rev. ed. Reading, MA: Addison-Wesley.

Cicourel, Aaron. 1969. *The Social Organization of Juvenile Justice.* New York: Wiley.

Cloward, Richard A. and Lloyd E. Ohlin. 1966. *Delinquency and Opportunity: A Theory of Delinquent Gangs.* New York: Free Press.

Cousineau, Matthew J. 2010. *Passenger Identity Work in the Risk Society.* Northern Illinois University, DeKalb, IL.

Death Penalty Information Center. 2010. *Facts About the Death Penalty 2010.* Available from http://www.deathpenaltyinfo.org/documents/FactSheet.pdf.

Demerath, Peter. 2009. *Producing Success: The Culture of Personal Advancement in an American High School.* Chicago: University of Chicago Press.

Douglas, Mary and Aaron Wildavsky. 1982. *Risk and Culture.* Berkeley: University of California Press.

Durkheim, Emile. [1893] 1964. *The Division of Labour in Society.* New York: Free Press.

———. [1895] 1964. *The Rules of the Sociological Method.* Translated by S. A. Solovay. and J. A. Mueller. Edited by G. E. G. Catlin. New York: Free Press.

Elias, Robert. 1986. *The Politics of Victimization: Victims, Victimology and Human Rights.* New York: Oxford University Press.

Empey, LaMar T. 1982. *American Delinquency.* 2nd ed. Homewood, IL: Dorsey.

Erikson, Kai T. 1966. *Wayward Puritans: A Study in the Sociology of Deviance.* New York: Wiley.

Eysenck, Hans. 1977. *Crime and Personality.* London: Routledge and Kegan Paul.

Federal Bureau of Investigation. 2009. *Uniform Crime Reports 2009.* Available from http://www.fbi.gov/about-us/cjis/ucr/crime-in-the-u.s/2009/crime2009.

———. 2007. *Crime in the United States 2007.* Available from http://www.fbi.gov/ucr/cius2007/data/table_33.html.

Feldman, Ariel J., J. Alex Halderman, and Edward W. Felten. 2006. *Security Analysis of the Diebold AccuVote-TS Voting Machine 2006.* Available from http://dl.acm.org/citation.cfm?id=1323113

Frank, Robert, Amir Efrati, Aaron Lucchetti, and Chad Bray. 2009. "Madoff Jailed After Admitting Epic Scam." *The Wall Street Journal.* Mar 13, 2009. Available from http://online.wsj.com/article/SB123685693449906551.html.

Garfinkel, Harold. 1956. "Conditions of Successful Degradation Ceremonies." *American Journal of Sociology* 61(2):420–424.

Gay Rights Timeline. 2010. *Time.* Available from http://www.time.com/time/interactive/0,31813,1904681,00.html.

Glassner, Barry. 1999. *The Culture of Fear: Why Americans are Afraid of the Wrong Things.* New York: Basic Books.

Goffman, Erving. 1963. *Stigma: Notes on the Management of Spoiled Identity.* Englewood Cliffs, NJ: Prentice Hall.

Goodstadt, P. and M. Erickson. 1979. "Legal Stigma for Marijuana Possession." *Criminology* 17:208–216.

Harris, Paul. 2010. "Rod Blagojevich Guilty on Just One Count of 24 in Corruption Trial." *The Guardian.* Aug 17, 2010. Available from http://www.guardian.co.uk/world/2010/aug/18/rod-blagojevich-guilty-one-count-corruption-trial.

Heckert, Alex and Druann Maria Heckert. 2004. "An Integrated Typology of Deviance Applied to Ten Middle-Class Norms." *The Sociological Quarterly* 45(2):209–228.

Herbert, R. and P. Landrigan. 2000. "Work-Related Death: A Continuing Epidemic." *American Journal of Public Health.* 2000 April; 90(4): 541–545.

Heyl, Barbara Sherman. 1979. *The Madam as Teacher: The Training of House Prostitutes,* edited by D. H. Kelly. New York: St. Martin's.

Hirschi, Travis. 1969. *Causes of Delinquency.* Berkeley: University of California Press.

House Judiciary Subcommittee on Civil and Constitutional Rights. 1993. *Staff Report*. Feb 15. US House of Representatives.

Inciardi, James A. 2000. *Elements of Criminal Justice*. 2nd ed. New York: Oxford University Press.

Johnson, R. and D. Boshier. 1975. "Does Conviction Affect Employment Opportunities?" *British Journal of Criminology* 14:264–268.

Kane, Paul, Murray Shailagh, and Matt DeLong. 2010. "Times Square Bombing Arrest Allows GOP to Revive 'Miranda' Debate." *The Washington Post*, May 4. Available at http://voices.washingtonpost.com/44/2010/05/gop-seizes-on-times-square-arr.html.

Kringlen, Einar. 1967. *Heredity and Environment in the Functional Psychoses: An Epidemiological-Clinical Twin Study*. London: Heinemann Medical.

Krug, E. L., J. Dahlberg, Zwi A. Mercy, and R. Lozano. 2002. *World Report on Violence and Health*. Geneva, Switzerland: World Health Organization.

Kshetri, Nir. 2006. "The Simple Economics of Cybercrimes." *Security and Privacy* 4(1):33–39.

Lemert, Edwin M. 1951. *Social Pathology: Systematic Approaches to the Study of Sociopathic Behavior*. New York: McGraw-Hill.

———. 1972. *Human Deviance, Social Problems, and Social Control*. Englewood Cliffs, NJ: Prentice Hall.

Lombroso, Caesar. 1911. *Crime: Its Causes and Remedies*. Translated by H. P. Horton. Boston: Little, Brown.

Martin, Patricia Yancey and Robert A. Hummer. 1989. "Fraternities and Rape on Campus." *Gender and Society* 3(4):470–473.

Martinez, Ramiro Jr. 1996. "Latinos and Lethal Violence: The Impact of Poverty and Inequality." *Social Problems* 43(2):131–146.

Maurer, David W. 1964. *Whiz Mob: A Correlation of the Technical Argot of Pick-Pockets with Their Behavior*. New Haven, CT: College and University Press.

Merton, Robert K. 1968. *Social Theory and Social Structure*. New York: Free Press.

Oberholzer-Gee, Felix, and Koleman, Strumpf. 2007. "The Effect of File Sharing on Record Sales: An Empirical Analysis." *Journal of Political Economy* 115(1):1–42.

Office of Justice Programs. 2010. *Transnational Organized Crime 2010*. Available from http://www.ojp.usdoj.gov/nij/topics/crime/transnational-organized-crime/welcome.htm.

Office of Juvenile Justice and Delinquency Prevention. 2010. *Statistical Briefing Book 2010*. Available from http://www.ojjdp.gov/ojstatbb/

Opposing Views. "Rash of Brutal Anti-Gay Attacks in New York 2010." Available from http://www.opposingviews.com/i/rash-of-brutal-anti-gay-attacks-in-new-york-city.

Pilliavin, Irving and Scott Brian. 1964. "Police Encounters with Juveniles." *American Journal of Sociology* 70:206–214.

Prus, Robert C. and C. R. D. Sharper. 1977. *Road Hustler: The Career Contingencies of Professional Card and Dice Hustlers*. Lexington, MA: Lexington Books.

Quinney, Richard. 1977. *Class, State and Crime. On the Theory and Practice of Criminal Justice*. New York: David McKay.

Reckless, Walter C. 1967. *The Crime Problem*. 5th ed. New York: Appleton.

Record, Jeffrey. 2003. *Bounding the Global War on Terrorism 2003*. Available from http://www.strategicstudiesinstitute.army.mil/pdffiles/pub207.pdf.

Reiss, Albert. 1971. *The Police and the Public*. New Haven, CT: Yale University Press.

Rosenbaum, Ron. 1995. "The Great Ivy League Nude Posture Photo Scandal: How Scientists Coaxed America's Best and Brightest Out of Their Clothes." *The New York Times Magazine*. Jan. 15. Available at http://www.nytimes.com/1995/01/15/magazine/the-great-ivy-league-nude-posture-photo-scandal.html?pagewanted=all&src=pm.

Sato, Ikuya. 1988. "Play Theory of Delinquency: Toward a General Theory of the 'Action'." *Symbolic Interaction* 11:191–212.

Scott, Marvin B. and Stanford M. Lyman. 1968. Accounts. *American Sociological Review*. 33:46–62.

Sheldon, William. 1949. *Varieties of Delinquent Youth: An Introduction to Constitutional Psychiatry*. New York: Harper.

Sheley, James F., Joshua Zang, Charles J. Brody, and James D. Wright. 1995. "Gang Organization, Gang Criminal Activity, and Individual Gang Members' Criminal Behavior." *Social Science Quarterly* 76(1):53–56.

Sherman, Lawrence. 1974. *Police Corruption*. New York: Doubleday.

Silko, Leslie Marmon. 1994. "The Border Patrol State." *The Nation*, October 17, 412–416.

Skinner, William F. and Anne M. Fream. 1997. "A Social Learning Theory Analysis of Computer Crime among College Students." *Journal of Research in Crime and Delinquency* 34(4):495–518.

Skolnick, J. and R. Schwartz. 1962. "Two Studies of Legal Stigma." *Social Problems* 10:133–138.

Smith, Douglas and Christy Visher. 1981. "Street-Level Justice. Situational Determinants of Police Arrest Decisions." *Social Problems* 29(2):167–177.

Spitzer, Steven. 1980. "Toward a Marxian Theory of Deviance." Pp. 175–191 in *Criminal Behavior: Readings in Criminology*, edited by D. H. Kelly. New York: St. Martin's Press.

St. John, Warren. 2003. "Professors with a Past." *New York Times*, Aug 9.

Stephan, James J. 2004. *State Prison Expenditures*. Bureau of Justice Statistics 2004. Available from http://bjs.ojp.usdoj.gov/index.cfm?ty=pbdetail&iid=1174.

Sutherland, Edwin H. 1940. "White Collar Criminality." *American Sociological Review* 5(1):1–12.

Sutherland, Edwin H. and Donald R. Cressey. 1978. *Criminology*. 10th ed. Philadelphia: J. P. Lippincott.

Sykes, Gresham and David Matza. 1957. "Techniques of Neutralization: A Theory of Delinquency." *American Sociological Review*. 22(Dec.):664–670.

Taub, P. and D. McClorg. 1987. "Anorexia Nervosa and Bulimia: The Development of Deviant Identities." *Deviant Behavior* 8:298–304.

The Sentencing Project. 2010. Available from http://www.sentencingproject.org/template/page.cfm?id=107.

Thornberry, Terence P. and Margaret Farnsworth. 1982. "Social Correlates of Criminal Involvement: Further Evidence on the Relationship Between Social Status and Criminal Behavior." *American Sociological Review* 47(4):505–518.

US Census Bureau. 2011. *Statistical Abstract 2011*. Available from http://www.census.gov/compendia/statab/cats/population.html.

US Sentencing Commission. 2010. *Sourcebook of Federal Sentencing Statistics 2009*. Available from http://www.ussc.gov/Data_and_Statistics/Annual_Reports_and_Sourcebooks/2010/ar10toc.htm

Valdez, A. 1997. "In the Hood: Street Gangs Discover White-Collar Crime." *Police* 21(5):49–50, 56.

Weinberg, Martin S., ed. 1976. *The Nudist Management of Respectability, Sex Research: Studies from the Kinsey Institute*. Oxford, UK: Oxford University Press.

Weitz, Rose. 1991. *Life with AIDS*. New Brunswick, NJ: Rutgers University Press.

Wilson, James Q. and Richard J. Herrnstein. 1985. *Crime and Human Nature: The Definitive Study of the Causes of Crime*. New York: Simon and Schuster.

Wilson, Michael and Al Baker. 2010. "Lured into a Trap, then Tortured for Being Gay." *The New York Times*. Oct 8, 2010. Available at http://www.nytimes.com/2010/10/09/nyregion/09bias.html?pagewanted=all.

Zraick, K. and A. Newman. 2010. "Student Arraigned in Anti-Muslim Stabbing of Cabdriver." *The New York Times*. Aug 25, 2010. Accessed Sep 2012 at http://cityroom.blogs.nytimes.com/2010/08/25/cabbie-attacked/.

© Design Pics Inc./Alamy

Chapter Overview ▼

7 Class and Stratification in the United States

Learning Objectives ▼

7.1 ■ Compare and contrast the key principles of the four stratification systems.

7.2 ■ Describe how stratification systems have changed over time, highlighting differences between traditional and modern stratification systems.

7.3 ■ Contrast competing theories of social stratification.

7.4 ■ Illustrate the amount of inequality found in various measures of income and wealth in the United States.

7.5 ■ Define social mobility and identify the factors that affect it.

7.6 ■ Describe how the United States characterizes poverty.
■ Explain the culture of poverty.

7.7 ■ Explain the consequences of stratification for health, education, family, crime, and technology.

7.8 ■ Describe social stratification trends in the United States during the 20th and 21st centuries.

Courtesy of Jocelyn Augustino/FEMA

Hurricane Katrina. It was almost impossible to watch, yet I could not turn away. It was late August 2005 as I and millions of other people around the world watched the tragic story unfold in New Orleans. Pictures of people on their roofs looking for rescue, stories of still others tragically trapped in their attics as water levels rose faster and farther than they had anticipated, and scenes of hundreds of people in and around the New Orleans Super Dome, which was being used as a shelter, asking, sometimes angrily, always poignantly, for someone, anyone to help them. Hurricane Katrina grew to a Category 3 storm by the time it made landfall in southeast Louisiana. New Orleans's aging levee system failed, leading to massive flooding. Months and years later, after studies were completed of who died, it became clear that social class, along with race, age, and gender, affected the life chances of the victims. A legacy of economic and racial segregation left some neighborhoods particularly vulnerable to a disaster like Katrina in what Briggs (2006) calls a "geography of risk." Poor and black neighborhoods were more likely to experience flooding and structural damage (Logan 2006). Sharkey (2007) examined deaths and missing persons reports attributed to Katrina and found that the elderly were much more likely to die in the disaster and, after taking into account the effects of age, blacks were more likely to die than whites, and men were more likely to die than women. Elderly 65 and older had a death rate of 65.5 per 10,000—15 times higher than the death rate of 4.3 per 10,000 for nonelderly. For both elderly and nonelderly, blacks had significantly higher death rates than whites, and the most severe impact of the storm was in poor black neighborhoods, which were more often closer to the levees and at lower elevations than more affluent white neighborhoods.

7.1 Social Stratification Overview

Social stratification systems characterize all societies, persist from one generation to the next, and are justified by ideologies.

- Compare and contrast the key principles of the four stratification systems.

© Kurhan/Shutterstock, Inc.

Certain social statuses are viewed as somehow better than others and therefore deserving of greater privilege.

© Creatas/Thinkstock

This chapter is concerned with one of the fundamental issues of sociology: social inequality. As Hurricane Katrina illustrates, even natural disasters—events that at first glance we would expect would affect all people similarly—often extract far greater suffering from people in the lower social classes.

Every society has inequality, in which some people receive greater prestige, wealth, and power than others. In each society, social inequality displays a pattern with regularities that help us understand the nature and extent of inequality. This pattern of social inequality takes the form of a **social stratification system**, the structured ranking of people in a society based upon selected social statuses. A social status is a position in society, and individuals occupy many positions at once, such as someone who is married, black, a teacher, a father, and so on. In a social stratification system, people do not merely have different social statuses. Some social statuses are viewed as somehow better than others and therefore deserving of greater privilege. A physician and a janitor are not just different occupations; one is preferred over the other and generally thought to deserve greater deference, respect, opportunity, and privilege.

In this chapter, we examine inequality and the social stratification system in the United States. Sociologists seeking to better understand systems of social stratification have raised a number of important issues we will explore in this chapter. Why is there inequality? What are the important dimensions of inequality in our society? Is there a single dimension or several? What are the important groups or categories of people distinguished by the stratification system? How can inequality be measured? How much inequality exists in the United States? Is inequality increasing or decreasing? Given that there are different categories in a stratification system, can people move from one category to another to increase their standing, or must they always remain in their initial status? If social mobility is possible, how easy is it to change and how much change can one expect? Finally, why does inequality matter—that is, what are the important consequences of inequality?

Key Principles of Social Stratification Systems

There are several important principles of social stratification. Those principles are common to all theoretical perspectives FIGURE 7-1. First, social stratification is a universal characteristic of all societies, but societies differ widely in the criteria used to rank different social statuses and the amount of inequality found. Criteria often include factors such as wealth, prestige, and power. Historically, some societies have stressed some of these criteria more than others, and sociological theories explaining stratification sometimes emphasize some more than others.

Second, stratification is a characteristic of the entire society, not just single individuals. Hence, whether any one individual is wealthy or poor, powerful or powerless, honored or reviled is very much affected by the society itself and its system of stratification, not just by the characteristics of that individual. A general tendency for whites to be ranked more highly than blacks in the United States, for example, describes a structural characteristic of the US stratification system, not a characteristic of individuals. The fact that any one black person, such as LeBron James, may be able to achieve higher status than most whites through great personal effort and accomplishment does not erase the general trend for whites to experience greater privilege than blacks.

Third, social stratification is carried over from one generation to the next. Just as parents pass genetic traits to their children, they also pass their social position on to

Social stratification is a universal characteristic of all societies.

© North Wind/North Wind Picture Archives

Social stratification system
The structured ranking of people in a society based upon selected social statuses.

	Davis and Moore (1945)	Marx (1844)	Wright (1974)	Weber (1922)	Bourdieu
Dimensions		1. Social class	1. Social class	1. Class 2. Prestige 3. Power	1. Class 2. Prestige 3. Power 4. Cultural capital
Categories		• Bourgeoisie • Proletariat	• Bourgeoisie • Petty bourgeoisie • Manager • Worker	• Continuum, often measured by socio-economic status	• Elite • Masses
Concepts and insights	• Inequality universal • Inequality has positive functions for society	• Social class • Class consciousness • False consciousness • Worker revolt leading to a classless society	• Need more categories to reflect contemporary social life	• Prestige • Power • Social ranking based on 3 dimensions • Status consistency	• Cultural resources further distinguish elite from the masses

FIGURE 7-1 Key principles of social stratification.

The success of an individual such as LeBron James does not erase the general trend for whites to experience greater privilege than blacks.

© Domenic Gareri/Shutterstock, Inc.

Just-world hypothesis A tendency for people to want to believe the world is predictable, orderly, and fair.

their children. Wealthy parents, in fact, often go to great efforts to pass on their privileges to their children in the form of inherited wealth, education, values, and culture. As a consequence, people tend to achieve social positions similar in rank to those of their parents.

Fourth, social stratification systems include belief systems or ideologies justifying that inequality. Ideologies can be used to legitimize existing social order and justify existing inequalities. When ideologies are successful, the differences are viewed as just, legitimate, even necessary. Sometimes religion is the basis for a stratification system, while in other cases science is used to justify stratification, as when studies of IQ and inheritance take a social Darwinist perspective arguing that advantaged groups may be genetically superior. Darwin's theory of the survival-of-the-fittest is similar to the ideology most commonly invoked to justify stratification as a consequence of personal merit. This ideology justifies social inequality by emphasizing equality of opportunity. In this perspective, affluence is perceived as the just reward for personal worth and hard work. Similarly, the poor are seen not as the unfortunate victims of stratification, but as people who have earned their low position in society or at least failed to earn a higher position. This last point is illustrated by what social psychologists call the **just-world hypothesis** (Lerner 1980)—a tendency for people to want to believe the world is predictable, orderly, and fair. As a result, when we see people who contradict this belief, we tend to try to restore justice or to persuade ourselves that what we see is just because the victim "deserved" their fate. Such beliefs help account for why stratification systems can persist over many generations.

CONCEPT LEARNING CHECK **7.1**   Characteristics of Stratification Systems

Match the following principles of stratification systems with phrases consistent with them.

_____ **1.** Stratification is universal but varied.

_____ **2.** Stratification is supported by beliefs.

_____ **3.** Stratification is a characteristic of the entire society.

_____ **4.** Stratification is carried over from one generation to the next.

A. "No man suffers from poverty unless it be more than his fault—unless it be his sin." —preacher/Social Darwinist Henry Ward Beecher.

B. In the United States, most racial and ethnic minorities tend to have lower incomes than white non–Hispanics.

C. Some stratification systems are based primarily on inherited statuses, while others are based primarily on achieved statuses such as education and occupation.

D. The likelihood a child will grow up to be in the top 20% of the US population as measured by income is far greater if his or her parents are already in the top 20% today.

7.2 Social Stratification Systems

Social stratification systems have evolved from closed systems to more modern open systems.

- Describe how stratification systems have changed over time, highlighting differences between traditional and modern stratification systems.

In this section, we put social stratification in broad historical context. We begin by discussing work by Lenski and Lenski (1982), who argue that social inequality became much greater as societies developed, hence making stratification systems more important. Next, we discuss closed stratification systems that have dominated most of human history, providing little opportunity for changing one's social position; and finally, we consider more open systems that permit more social mobility (Tumin 1985).

Stratification and Technology: A Global Perspective

Lenski and Lenski (1982) argued that the amount of inequality in social stratification systems differs greatly depending on the stage of development of a society. In this view, societies with simple technologies, such as hunter-gatherer societies, barely produce enough to survive. In this instance, basic necessities needed for survival are distributed nearly equally, since the society's survival depends on the survival of most members. In contrast, when societies have surpluses, almost all surpluses are distributed unequally. The result is that societies with larger surpluses tend to have greater inequality. The size of the surplus for any society is a function of the society's technological development. Those who control the technology generating the surplus will tend to have more resources. Thus, hunting and gathering societies with low technology and little surplus would have little or no stratification and all members would be relatively equal. There would be little advantage in accumulating many goods since they must all be moved frequently. Advanced horticultural and agricultural societies should have larger surpluses and greater inequality. Because those societies are less mobile, goods can be accumulated and land itself can become the primary basis for wealth.

By this same reasoning, we might expect industrial societies to produce even greater inequality because they produce far larger surpluses. However, as the Nobel Prize–winning economist Simon Kuznets (1955, 1966) first pointed out with the "Kuznets curve," FIGURE 7-2 inequality begins to decline again in industrial societies. One reason for this decline in inequality may be because industrial economies produce so much surplus that the living standards of the majority are raised significantly. In addition, the specialized work in industrial societies requires technical training and schooling, with literacy rising for most. That, in turn, leads to greater participation in politics by the masses and eventually reduces inequality in the society.

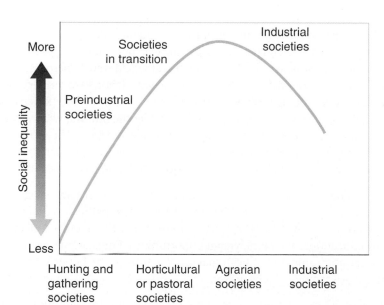

FIGURE 7-2 The Kuznets curve. *Source: Adapted from Kuznets, Simon. 1955. "Economic Growth and Income Inequality." The American Economic Review 45(1): 1–28.*

Today, as we will see below, the United States and most developed societies are in the postindustrial age as the information revolution transforms the nature of work and services dominate their economies. Social inequality has once again been increasing in the United States and other countries, suggesting that the postindustrial era may see a reverse in the Kuznets curve.

Traditional Stratification Systems

A **caste system** is a system of social stratification based on birth. Caste systems are rigid systems with almost no opportunity for changing one's caste. A person is born into a caste, and it is irrevocable. Moving from one caste to another is generally not permitted. The best-known example of a caste system is India's traditional system; however, caste

Caste system A system of social stratification based on birth.

systems are also found in other South Asian countries, including Nepal, Sri Lanka, and Pakistan; East Asian countries including Bali, China, Japan, and Korea; and some countries in Africa. According to tradition, people in caste systems are born into a caste, which determines the kind of work they will do in life. They must marry within their caste (a form of practice called endogamy). Their culture encourages them to accept their fate as a moral duty, and contact with members of other castes is strictly regulated to avoid members of higher castes becoming "polluted" from inappropriate contact with members of lower castes. Exogamy (primary and secondary relationships such as marriage that cross caste lines) is not permitted. India's caste system, which was outlawed in 1950, still influences people in rural agrarian villages but has less influence in large modern cities.

Clan systems and feudal estate systems are similar to caste systems but offer somewhat more social mobility. A **clan system** is a stratification system in which social standing is based on membership in an extended network of relatives. In a clan system, like a caste system, the basis for stratification is birthright, and a person's family ties are the primary determinant of his or her social standing. However, in a clan system, people can marry outside their own clan (exogamy), and this is often employed as a means to forge alliances among clans. The countries of Somalia and Iraq are dominated by clan systems. In feudal Europe and some Asian nations, stratification was based on an **estate system** in which there are three strata or estates—the nobility, the church, and peasants—and position is determined largely by inheritance. Since the eldest sons inherited all the wealth, other sons of noblemen had to enter the clergy or make a living in some other way. Thus, estate systems permit more social mobility than castes system.

Clan system A stratification system in which social standing is based on membership in an extended network of relatives.

Estate system A system with three strata or estates: the nobility, the church, and peasants; position is determined largely by inheritance.

THE SOCIOLOGICAL IMAGINATION   In His Own Words: Caste and a 21st-Century Nepali

FIGURE 7-3 Yangmali Rai.
Source: Courtesy of Yangmali Sahadev Rai.

"Years back, when Nepal was divided into several independent states, people were categorized into several castes based on their work. People who performed religious duties were named Brahmins, those who were pioneers in the battlefield were Kshetriyas, those who dealt with business were Vaishnavs, and those who were laborers or farmers were Shudra. Slowly, these were subdivided into several sub-castes. Many orthodox Nepalese viewed castes as divine identities. So-called low castes, like the Shudra, were viewed as untouchables and were excluded from all sorts of social gatherings. They were not allowed to enter temples or fetch water from local wells. They were beaten severely even if they unknowingly cast their shadows upon so-called high castes FIGURE 7-3.

"But things have changed. Education has instilled the view that people are recognized by their deeds and not their caste. Even the constitution of Nepal makes practicing untouchability a crime. Today, quotas are often used to ensure that members of every caste have many educational and employment opportunities. For example, each caste might receive a certain number of educational scholarships to the better schools as well as in different governmental jobs in Nepal.

"Socially, caste plays an even stronger role in my life. Born and brought up in a Rai community, I am required to live in accordance with my community's norms and traditions. From the day of one's birth to his/her death bed, Rais are guided by their own cultural beliefs. People in my caste celebrate our own festivals like Sakela (twice a year), and have our own religion (Kiranti) and religious book (Mundhum). I am expected and required to marry a girl from my own caste, else I will be excluded from my caste and family. If I marry a woman from another caste she would not be allowed to prepare food for members of my family or my caste and we would be excluded from much of the socializing and celebrating my family normally does. We have a large extended family of cousins, aunts, and uncles, and I communicate with them often and they are a big part of my life. To be excluded from the family would be a very big deal in my life.

"As a member of the Vaishya tribe in Nepal I have greater opportunity to enter certain jobs but not others. For example, members of my caste are often recruited into the armed forces. This is pretty ironic because members of my caste are supposed to be good at business. Yet many showed bravery in World War II fighting for the British government. As a result, people from my caste are recruited every year for their honesty and bravery by the British government." —Yangmali Sahadev Rai

EVALUATE

1. The sociological imagination helps us understand an individual's life experiences by relating them to the social context in which the person lives. How does growing up in a caste society make Yangmali's life different from your own?

2. Even though caste has been part of Nepali life for many years, it is changing. How different do you think it might be in another 10 or 20 years? Do you think Yangmali is less likely to follow caste rules than his parents or grandparents?

3. Are there any ways in which your own life is similar to that of a member of a caste, even in the United States?

Modern Class Systems

In each of the traditional stratification systems (caste, clan, and estate), the primary basis for social standing is **ascribed social statuses**, the categories into which one is born. In contrast, modern industrialized societies most commonly have a class system. In a **class system**, social standing is based primarily on individual achievement. **Achieved social statuses** are statuses earned through individual effort facilitated by opportunity. Social status in a class system is influenced greatly by one's education, income, and occupational prestige. All of those are achieved statuses. If everyone had equal opportunity for achieving those important social statuses, then the class system would be very efficient, permitting the most capable individuals to rise to the top of society and claim the most important positions, while less capable individuals found their own level of achievement at lower levels. Such a system would be a **meritocracy**, a system of social stratification based entirely on personal merit. To the extent that people do not have the same chance of achieving higher social statuses in a stratification system, then it will be less efficient and, by most standards, unfair, permitting some people to enjoy wealth and prestige beyond what they have rightfully earned, while others are not permitted their fair chance. Modern societies typically resemble meritocracies only partially and continue to have within them elements of caste systems in which some categories of people do not have the same opportunities for advancement through social mobility as others. We will return to this issue of equal opportunity later on.

Ascribed social statuses The categories into which one is born.

Class system A stratification system in which social standing is based primarily on individual achievement.

Achieved social statuses Statuses earned through individual effort facilitated by opportunity.

Meritocracy A system of social stratification based entirely on personal merit.

CONCEPT LEARNING CHECK 7.2   Common Social Stratification Systems

Match the following stratification systems with phrases consistent with them.

_____ **1.** Caste system

_____ **2.** Meritocracy

_____ **3.** Class system

_____ **4.** Clan system

A. Getting ahead in this society is solely based on how hard the individual is willing to work and their own innate ability.

B. Birthright is the sole basis for social position in this system.

C. This system is very high on consistency among a person's statuses.

D. This is the stratification system that characterizes most modern societies.

E. This is an ideal-typical stratification system that is unlikely to be found in practice.

F. Marrying outside one's own group (exogamy) can be a way to get ahead in this stratification system.

G. People are expected to marry within their own group in this stratification system.

H. A person's social status in this system is primarily affected by achieved statuses such as education, occupation, and income.

THE SOCIOLOGICAL IMAGINATION   Elements of Caste and Meritocracy in the United States

While the class system in the United States is based primarily on achieved statuses, the social standing of individuals is still influenced to a greater or lesser extent by ascribed social statuses such as race, ethnicity, gender, and family. On the one hand, there are examples of individuals who began with a modest background and who then went on to use education or other opportunities to achieve great fame or fortune. Examples include John Boehner, who rose from a working-class family to become Speaker of the United State House of Representatives, and Barack Obama, who rose from a single-parent household to become President of the United States FIGURE 7-4. On the other hand, there are also many examples of people who achieved fame or fortune whose parents were affluent and whose family name undoubtedly helped. Examples include Bill Gates, one of the founders of Microsoft, whose father was a very successful businessman as well; Michael Douglas, movie actor, who is the son of another famous movie actor, Kirk Douglas; and George W. Bush, the former US president who was preceded both at Yale and in the presidency by his father.

FIGURE 7-4 Barack Obama as a young man (left) and as president (right).

© Joe Wrinn/Harvard University/Handout/Corbis

© Anna Frajtova/Shutterstock, Inc.

EVALUATE

1. Overall, do you think the United States is more like a caste system or more like a meritocracy? To answer this, think about your own life and that of people you know personally. Can you identify instances in which your opportunities have been limited or enhanced because of ascribed social statuses? How did those statuses affect your wealth, the neighborhood in which you grew up, your education, who you marry, or job opportunities?

2. Which elements of US society resemble caste systems and which resemble class systems? You might want to consider, for example, inheritance laws that permit parents to pass on some or all of their wealth to their children, legacy admissions programs through which prestigious schools give some level of preference to children of alumni, the importance of higher education degrees in qualifying for many jobs, equal opportunity employment regulations, and so on.

7.3 Sociological Perspectives on Social Stratification

The functional, conflict, and interactionist perspectives make very different assumptions about stratification and focus on different issues.

■ Contrast competing theories of social stratification.

The Functional View of Social Stratification

In the 1940s and 1950s, Kingsley Davis and Wilbert Moore (1945) laid out the functional view of stratification FIGURES 7-5, 7-6. Functional theory argues that inequality is universal in all societies, and it persists because it has positive functions for society. Inequality, they argue, ensures that the most competent people fill the most important positions in society and that people perform important positions competently. Money and prestige provide rewards to persuade people to undergo the years of training and hard work required to perform important jobs.

Sociologist Herbert Gans (1971) illustrates this functional view when he argues that poverty persists in our society because it serves important social functions FIGURE 7-7.

- Poverty ensures that society's dirty, dangerous, dead-end jobs will be done.

- Because the poor are paid less, they subsidize economic activities that benefit the affluent by serving as underpaid domestics.

- Poverty creates jobs for people in professions that either serve the poor, such as social workers, or protect society from them, such as prison guards, police, and parole officers.

- The poor buy goods others no longer want, such as day-old bread, second-hand clothes, and used cars, thus prolonging the economic life of those goods.

- The poor can be punished as real or alleged deviants to uphold the legitimacy of conventional norms.

- The poor offer upward social mobility to those just above them who can exploit them with payday loans at exorbitant interest rates, slum housing, narcotics, gambling, and other goods and services sold at inflated prices to people who do not have the means to shop elsewhere.

- And the poor help ensure the status of those who are not poor by providing someone who is at the bottom of the social hierarchy with whom they can be compared.

In a well-known debate within sociology carried out during the 1940s and 1950s, the functional perspective described by Kingsley Davis and Wilbert Moore (1945) was criticized by sociologist Melvin Tumin (1953). Tumin argued four main points:

- First, Davis and Moore's view that the greatest rewards go to the most competent and deserving is contradicted by rules of inheritance. The wealth, power, and prestige of social class are often relatively stable across generations and are handed from one generation to the next through inheritance. If opportunity were based solely on competence, we should expect greater variation from generation to generation.

- Second, the extreme rewards accorded some individuals are often inconsistent with these individuals' influence, importance, and benefit to society. Why, for example, do many rock singers, film stars, and professional athletes make far more than the president of the United States?

- Third, there are many unfair barriers to competition restricting access to good jobs for the poor, minorities, the aged, and women, regardless of their competence.

- Finally, the functionalist perspective presumes that people compete for rewards in a society, and this may be less true in other societies than in capitalist economies like

FIGURE 7-5 Kingsley Davis.
Courtesy of The American Sociological Association

FIGURE 7-6 Wilbert Moore.
Courtesy of The American Sociological Association

the United States. In societies in which competition plays less of a role, inequality may not be as effective at motivating performance.

Karl Marx and Conflict Views of Stratification

In contrast, the conflict approach argues that stratification persists because it helps powerful people maintain the status quo, and functional arguments merely serve to justify this inequality. This perspective was first articulated by Karl Marx (1844) and was later revised and expanded to meet changing times by sociologist Erik Wright (1985) FIGURE 7-8.

The conflict view is based in large part on Karl Marx's critique of capitalism in which he argued the **proletariat** (workers who sell their productive labor for wages) were exploited by the **bourgeoisie** (the capitalist owners of the means of production). By **means of production**, he meant the technologies and resources required for producing goods or services in an economy, such as factories, raw materials, and machines.

Marx argued that workers tend to accept the dominant ideology of the existing stratification system as a form of false consciousness. However, he predicted that workers would eventually realize they were being exploited and overthrow the bourgeoisie, creating a socialist society. This socialist society would be a transitional one, leading eventually to a classless society, that is, a society having little or no inequality. Marx argued that economics is the basis of social stratification. To him, economics lay at the root of all the important processes in a society and everything else paled in comparison.

Marx has been criticized on many grounds, including what some critics see as an overemphasis on economics. He has also been criticized for separating performance from rewards. Marx believed communism (his theoretically possible society, not the social systems that actually developed later in Russia and elsewhere) would be a classless society based on the principle "from each according to ability; to each according to need." This meant that people who had to learn more, train harder, and work harder to perform the more important jobs in society would be paid no more than people who had jobs requiring little training or effort. Many critics objected that this would lead to a society in which the important jobs would not be performed well and the economy would suffer accordingly. Notice that this argument is based on the functional perspective.

Marx has also been criticized as less relevant in today's world because of dramatic changes in capitalism since his time—changes that may help explain why his workers' revolution never materialized. Those changes include the rise of white-collar workers in the form of professionals and managers and the changing nature of capitalism brought about by corporations owned by thousands of stockholders. Each of these clouds differences between the proletariat and the bourgeoisie. For example, white-collar and service workers constitute a much larger proportion of the labor force today, and blue-collar workers are much less a force than they once were. It is harder to see how Marx's theory of worker exploitation applies to new white-collar occupations, professionals, or managers. Braverman (1974) argued the key issue is buying and selling of labor and that the same issues apply for white-collar and service occupations, but the exploitation may not be so extreme as for blue-collar workers. In the corporate capitalism of today, most large corporations are now owned by thousands of stockholders, and many workers also own stock in corporations; hence, it is more difficult to separate workers from capitalists. And what about people who were once workers themselves but eventually bought their own business and now have a small business with a few workers? Are they more like capitalists who own huge businesses employing thousands of workers or more like workers?

Sociologist Erik Wright (1985) argued that these changing conditions made it necessary to modify Marx's analysis to include four classes:

1. **Capitalists**—people who own large businesses employing many workers, such as Microsoft owner Bill Gates or the family of Sam Walton, the founder of Wal-Mart

FIGURE 7-7 Herbert Gans.

Courtesy of The American Sociological Association

Proletariat Workers who sell their productive labor for wages.

Bourgeoisie The owners of the means of production (particularly large businesses employing many workers) in a capitalist economy.

Means of production The technologies and resources required for producing goods or services in an economy, such as factories, raw materials, and machines.

Capitalists People who own large businesses employing many workers.

2. **Petty bourgeoisie**—people who own small businesses, such as someone who owns a car repair shop, a small software company, a consulting business, or a small medical practice

3. **Managers**—people who sell their own labor but exercise authority over other employees, such as a dean in a college or a vice president in a corporation

4. **Workers**—people who sell their labor, such as someone who works on an assembly line, at a fast-food restaurant, or in an all-night gas station

Wright thus expands Marx's basic model, maintaining the basic distinction between worker and capitalist but recognizing the need for two additional categories: petty bourgeoisie and managers.

FIGURE 7-8 Erik Wright.

Courtesy of The American Sociological Association

Max Weber: Class, Status, and Power

Unlike Karl Marx, who believed only the economic dimension is important for stratification, Max Weber (1922) argued that there are three important dimensions: class, status, and power.

1. **Social class**, according to Weber, is a continuum instead of a dichotomy between proletariat and bourgeoisie. For Weber, social class could be measured by a combination of **wealth**—the property or economic resources owned by someone and not required for immediate consumption, such as buildings, factories, cars, stocks, bank accounts—and **income**—the money they receive as rents, royalties, wages, or profits.

2. **Prestige** is the respect and admiration accorded a social position or occupation and people in those positions by others. Prestige can result from respected acts (such as the prestige that comes from acts of bravery or great compassion). Prestige can sometimes be bought with money or claimed by power. Prestige can also be used to gain power or money.

3. **Power** is the capacity to influence or control the behavior of others. Power is the hardest of the three dimensions to measure, and there is some controversy over how power is distributed in the United States (we will return to this issue in the chapter on political life).

Where Marx saw power and prestige as minor factors largely determined by social class, Weber believed each of the dimensions was important, with their relative importance varying in different historical time periods. Agrarian societies, argued Weber, emphasized prestige, while industrialized societies emphasize social class based on economic position. As states become more bureaucratic, such as in welfare societies or in many of the formerly communist countries, power becomes more important. While Marx believed a revolution would end inequality, Weber believed it would only shift the base from one dimension, such as social class, to another, such as power.

Weber's multidimensional model of social stratification views inequality not in terms of black or white, worker or capitalist, but as a more complex continuum based on several different dimensions operating at the same time. This has led many contemporary sociologists to measure social inequality using **socioeconomic status (SES)**, a composite index based on occupational prestige, income, and educational attainment. This method relies heavily on **status consistency**, the tendency for people having high status in one area of their lives to also have high status in other areas. In general, rich people tend to be more highly educated and to occupy high-status occupations. However, there is not always consistency between different measures of status. For example, the highly prestigious political positions of president of the United States and Supreme Court justice are both paid far less than many corporate directors or physicians.

SES is widely used as the basis for measuring social class, particularly in the United States. SES has the advantage of placing people along a continuum with many different

Petty bourgeoisie People who own small businesses.

Managers People who sell their own labor but exercise authority over other employees.

Workers People who sell their labor.

Class (social class) Ranking in a stratification system based on either one's level of wealth and income (Max Weber) or one's relationship to the means of production (Karl Marx).

Wealth The property or economic resources owned by someone and not required for immediate consumption, such as buildings, factories, cars, stocks, and bank accounts.

Income The money people receive as rents, royalties, wages, or profits.

Prestige The respect and admiration accorded a social position or occupation and people in those positions by others.

Power The capacity to influence or control behavior of others.

Socioeconomic status (SES) A composite index of social status based on occupational prestige, income, and educational attainment.

Status consistency The tendency for people having high status in one area of their lives to also have high status in other areas.

Cultural capital The tastes, language, attitudes, and general ways of thinking that influence our interactions with one another.

Conspicuous consumption Blatant efforts to display status through the possession or consumption of status symbols such as expensive cars or clothes.

gradations and providing a measure of social class that reflects a person's income, occupational prestige, and education. However, it may be criticized for encouraging us to focus on small variations in income or occupational prestige when Marxist-oriented scholars argue the important distinctions lie with the class conflict between the proletariat and the bourgeoisie.

Interactionist Perspectives: The Social Construction of Inequality

Both the functional and conflict perspectives attempt to explain why social inequality exists. In contrast, the interactionist perspective shifts the focus to how inequality is perceived and socially constructed. Interactionist views look at how individuals perceive, report, and define their own social class.

Bourdieu and Cultural Capital

While Marx saw stratification as class conflict over material resources, and Weber saw stratification as based on the three factors of class, prestige, and power; Pierre Bourdieu (1984) pointed to the significance of multiple resources including what he calls cultural capital. **Cultural capital** includes the tastes, language, attitudes, and general ways of thinking and behaving that influence our interactions with one another. In this perspective, stratification systems distinguish people not solely based on material goods but also on other dimensions, including culture. This perspective accounts for the way in which "old money" distinguishes itself from "new money" based on cultural tastes such as the social graces that come from being brought up among the rich. Those cultural differences are socially constructed, and the elite are able to define their cultural preferences as somehow superior to those of the masses (Wilson 2007). In this perspective, movement from one social status to another requires a change not only in material goods but also in life style, as reflected in cultural differences in tastes, preferences, attitudes, and behaviors (Bourdieu 1984:374).

More recently, sociologists have argued that people in the upper social classes, finding that money and other material resources are not sufficient to differentiate themselves from people in the lower social classes, use culture as a way to distinguish themselves from members of other classes.

> At the bottom, people tend to believe that class is defined by the amount of money you have. In the middle, people grant that money has something to do with it, but think education and the kind of work you do almost equally important. Nearer the top, people perceive that taste, values, ideas, style, and behavior are indispensable criteria of class, regardless of money or occupation or education (Fussell 1983).

Claiming class: "Putting on airs." Individuals sometimes claim a higher status than they actually have. People use status symbols such as expensive jewelry, clothes, or cars to communicate our status to others. A blatant effort to display status through the possession or consumption of status symbols is called **conspicuous consumption** (Veblen 1899). Status symbols can be misleading when the person displaying the symbol does not actually have the status implied by it. C. Wright Mills (1956) argued there is a status panic in the United States because status symbols were so easily adopted by lower classes. In their panic to differentiate themselves from other classes, people go to extremes seeking symbols hard to fake. (Recall the earlier discussion about culture in which we described how culture is sometimes used as a barrier between the social classes.) Of course, not everyone deliberately displays the status symbols that many of us use to show off our social class, making it difficult or impossible to measure their social class by their life style. For example, Sam Walton, the founder of Walmart and, at the time, the richest man in the United States, would often drive around town in a pickup truck.

Conspicuous consumption is the blatant effort to display status through status symbols such as expensive jewelry, clothes, or cars.

© Maxim Blinkov/Shutterstock, Inc.

Subjective self-reports of social class. One method sometimes used to measure social class is the subjective self-report method, in which people are asked to identify their own social class. However, this method is often inaccurate. Decades of research have found people are often unable to correctly classify themselves within the US stratification system. For example, during the Depression, 8 out of 10 Americans claimed to be in the middle class (DeMott 1990). Self-reports are also affected by the categories used. When respondents are asked to place themselves in the upper, middle, or lower class, 75% or more place themselves in the middle class. However, when a fourth category, "working class," is available, about 40 to 45% place themselves in that category, and the "middle class" category drops to about 40 to 45% (DeMott 1990).

Underestimating inequality. Misperceptions of one's own social class may reflect a general tendency of people in the United States to underestimate the amount of inequality in our society. A survey by Norton and Arieley (2011) suggests people are often unaware of the differences in distribution of wealth in the United States. The data in FIGURE 7-9 illustrate this point. Individuals in a nationally representative online sample of 5,522 respondents were asked to estimate the distribution of wealth among quintiles in the United States and to indicate the distribution of wealth they thought each quintile *should* have. Respondent estimates of wealth were far less unequal than the actual distribution of wealth and much closer to the distribution respondents thought would be fair. The wealthiest quintile actually controlled about 84% of the wealth, while respondents estimated the wealthiest quintile to control about 59% of the wealth and thought that the wealthiest quintile *should* control only 32% of the wealth. These results are consistent with Marx's argument that the proletariat would display **false consciousness** (a lack of awareness of the severity of class differences by members of the proletariat)—that is, they would be unaware of how severe class differences were between themselves and the bourgeoisie.

One of the reasons there is relatively little class consciousness in the United States may be the way inequality is portrayed in the mass media. Sociologist Gregory Mantsios (1995) argues that the mass media in the United States are primarily owned by the upper class and serve the interests of that class. The media tend to hide class differences, providing little coverage of poverty and the poor and being misleading when they are covered. When it comes to the middle class and the wealthy, the media send mixed messages, either lionizing the wealthy or trying to create a sense of "we-ness" that implies the interests of the wealthy and the middle class are the same. The result, he claims, is that people in the middle and working classes learn from the media to fear and blame those below them in the class structure rather those above them. He argues we learn to resent the billions spent on welfare to help the needy but hear little about the billions the federal government spends on affluent people and corporations in the form of tax breaks, incentives, and loopholes in the US tax code (Mantsios 1995).

False consciousness A lack of awareness of the severity of class differences by members of the proletariat.

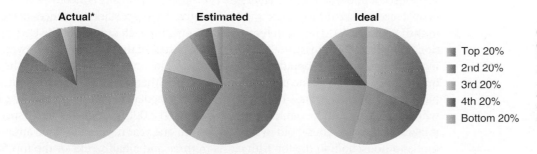

Actual*   Estimated   Ideal

■ Top 20%
■ 2nd 20%
■ 3rd 20%
■ 4th 20%
■ Bottom 20%

*Included but not visible are 4th 20% (0.2%) and bottom 20% (0.1%).

FIGURE 7-9 The actual, estimated, and ideal distribution of wealth in the United States.
Source: Data from Norton, M. I., & Ariely, D. 2010. Building a better America—one wealth quintile at a time. Perspectives on Psychological Science.

CONCEPT LEARNING CHECK 7.3   How Do Sociological Theories Explain Stratification?

As you read the case study below, consider what insights are offered by the theories of Marx, Weber, Wright, and Bourdieu into Fernando's situation. What sociological concepts are reflected in his story?

CASE STUDY

Fernando just graduated from college and was hired to be an entry-level manager at a startup webpage design firm in a large Midwestern city. He is proud of his recent MBA and his new position, but his salary is not as high as he had hoped given the difficult economy and the fact that he works for a new company struggling to make it big. He hopes that the company will succeed and grow rapidly, permitting him to increase his salary and receive stock options to eventually become rich.

One thing that worries him a bit is that it is a very small company and he spends social time with the owner/founders. He does not seem to fit in well with them, since they are from wealthy families and grew up going to private schools and then Ivy League universities. They are always talking about music he is not familiar with and plays and books that he has only read about in the paper. They do not seem interested in the sports events and movies he goes to see. He is trying to learn more about the arts so he can participate more in their lunchtime conversations. But he is convinced his MBA training at a state university is good preparation for the job.

RESPONSE

Write a paragraph about Fernando's situation in which you identify two or more sociological concepts associated with each theorist: Marx, Weber, Wright, and Bourdieu. Include examples and/or quotations from the case study that illustrate each concept.

7.4 Inequality in the United States: Income and Wealth

The two most common measures of inequality for social class are income and wealth, both of which are distributed very unevenly in the United States.

- Illustrate the amount of inequality found in various measures of income and wealth in the United States.

A key characteristic of any stratification system is just how much inequality there is. In this section, we begin by examining the distribution of income and wealth in the United States. As we saw in the previous section, most people in the United States are not aware of how much inequality there is. Here, we will report the latest numbers and try to make those numbers more understandable with some specific examples.

The Distribution of Income

The most commonly considered measure of economic inequality is income—the money people receive as rents, royalties, wages, or profits. There are stark differences in income in the United States. The mean household income for each quintile of the US population in 2009 is shown in FIGURE 7-10. A quintile is 20% of the people. So the lowest fifth includes the 20% of the population with the lowest income, the second fifth is the 20% making the next lowest income, and so on. Clearly there is an uneven distribution of income in the United States. The highest fifth has a median income of nearly $171,000, while the lowest fifth has an income of less than $12,000. To put this in perspective, it takes the average household in the lowest fifth one year to earn the same amount of money a household in the top fifth earns in three and a half weeks or the top 5% of households to earn in slightly more than two weeks!

If we look at the relative share of income for each quintile and then compare the shares in 2009 with the shares in 1979, there is a clear trend for the bottom 80% of the population (the first four-fifths) to lose share over time and only the top fifth and top

5% to increase share, as shown in FIGURE 7-11. This means there is greater inequality of income over that 30-year period. In 2009, the bottom 20% of people had only 3% of the total income. In contrast, the highest quintile (the top 20%) had 50% of the total income—a ratio of more than 16:1. The top 5% of people that same year received 22% of the total income. The share of total income for the top 5% of people that year was greater than the combined incomes of the lowest 50% of people.

Sociologist G. William Domhoff cites a wide range of data detailing inequality in America (2011). Inequalities in income become much more real if we consider specific examples. For example, in 2006, Lockheed Martin paid CEO Robert Stevens more than $24 million—787 times the annual pay of a typical US worker ($30,617), while in 2007, Wal-Mart CEO H. Lee Scott, Jr. made $29,682,000—1,314 times as much as the company's average full-time workers (Anderson et al. 2008:9). FIGURE 7-12 plots the ratio of the average CEO pay to average worker's pay based on several hundred large US corporations from 1960 to 2007. Notice that the ratio rose from 42:1 in 1960 to more than 500:1 in 2000 and, although it bounced around during recessions afterward, was still at 344:1 in 2007. In contrast, the same ratio in Europe is about 25:1.

The Distribution of Wealth

Wealth consists of the property or economic resources owned by someone and not required for immediate consumption, such as buildings, factories, cars, stocks,

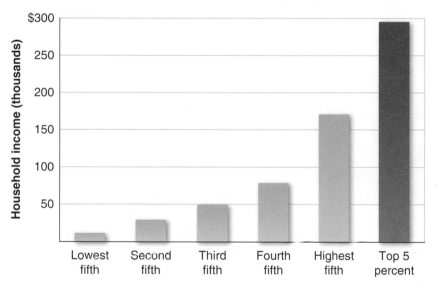

FIGURE 7-10 Mean US household income by quintile and top 5 percent (2009). *Source: Data from the U.S. Census Bureau, Current Population Survey, Table H-2. Retrieved October 2011 (http://www.census.gov/hhes/www/income/data/historical/inequality/H02AR_2009.xls).*

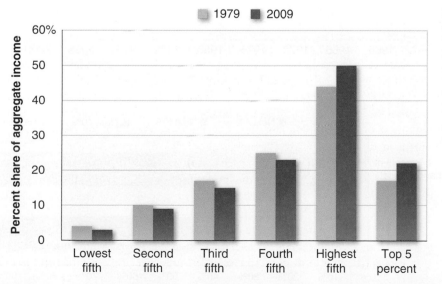

FIGURE 7-11 Share of aggregate income for each fifth and top 5 percent of households (1979, 2009). *Source: Data from the U.S. Census Bureau, Current Population Survey, Table H-3. Retrieved October 2011 (http://www.census.gov/hhes/www/income/data/historical/inequality/H03AR_2009.xls).*

Net worth Household wealth based on the difference between assets and liabilities.

Net financial assets Household wealth after equity in homes has been deducted.

bank accounts. The most common method of measuring wealth is **net worth**—household wealth based on the difference between assets and liabilities, or differences between what you own minus what you owe. Inequality is more pronounced in wealth than in income, with wealth much more concentrated in the upper extremes of the population. In FIGURE 7-13 are reported the distribution of net worth and net financial assets among US households in 2007. In 2007, the top 1% of households owned 35% of all privately held wealth in the United States, the next 19% owned 50% of all wealth. That is, the top 20% of the population owned 85% of all the privately held wealth. The remaining 80% of people owned only 15% of the wealth (Wolff 2010).

Much wealth in the United States is in the form of home ownership. **Net financial assets** (household wealth after equity in homes has been deducted) provide a more realistic estimate of the liquid assets of people (liquid assets are financial assets that can be easily and quickly converted to cash). Net financial assets are considerably lower than net worth. The overall household median net worth in 2007 was $120,300 (US Census Bureau 2011a), while median net financial assets are only $23,500 (Wolff 2010:43). Net financial assets are distributed even more unevenly than net worth. The top 1% own 43% of net financial assets and the top 20% own 93% of net financial assets, while the bottom 80% own the remaining 7% of net financial assets.

Some assets are distributed much more unevenly than others. The distribution of various assets is displayed in FIGURE 7-14. Home ownership (principal residence) is most evenly distributed, with 61.5% of wealth in principal residences owned by the bottom 90%. Next are life insurance, deposits, and pension accounts, with between 40.8 and 45.1% ownership among the bottom 90%. Much more unequal is the distribution of

FIGURE 7-12 CEO pay as a multiple of the average worker's pay (1960–2007). *Source: Data from Anderson, S., Cavanagh, J., Collins, C., Lapham, M., & Pizzigati, S. 2008. Executive Excess 2008: The 15th Annual CEO Compensation Survey. Washington, DC: Institute for Policy Studies/ United for a Fair Economy. Cited in Domhoff. 2011. Who Rules America? (http://www2.ucsc. edu/whorulesamerica/power/ wealth.html).*

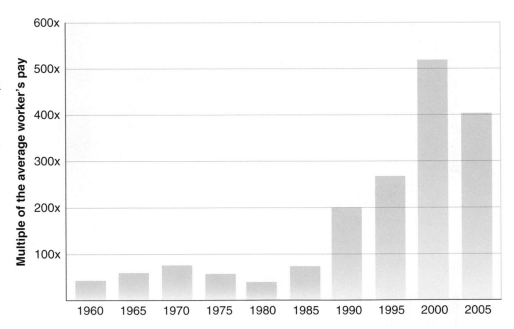

FIGURE 7-13 Distribution of net worth and financial wealth among US households (2007). *Source: Data from Wolff, E. N. (2010). "Recent trends in household wealth in the United States: Rising debt and the middle-class squeeze—an update to 2007." Working Paper No. 589. Annandale-on-Hudson, NY: The Levy Economics Institute of Bard College.*

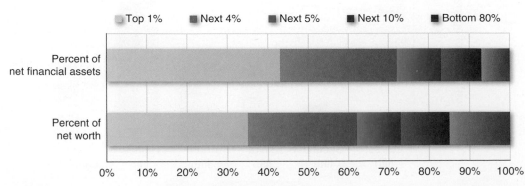

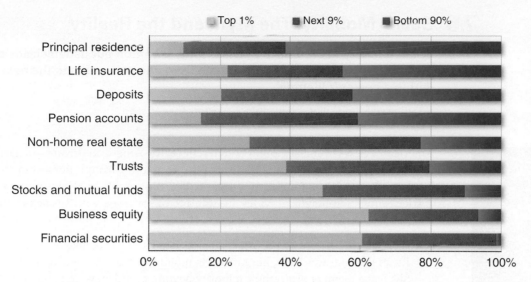

FIGURE 7-14 Distribution of various assets in the United States (2007).
Source: Data from Wolff (2010:51) Wolff, E. N. (2010). "Recent trends in household wealth in the United States: Rising debt and the middle-class squeeze—an update to 2007." Working Paper No. 589. Annandale-on-Hudson, NY: The Levy Economics Institute of Bard College.

nonhome real estate and trusts at 23.1% and 20.6%, respectively, owned by the bottom 90%. The greatest inequalities are found in stocks and mutual funds, business equity, and financial securities at 10.6%, 6.7%, and 1.5%, respectively. The top 1% of the US population owns 62.4% of business equity and 60.6% of financial securities (Wolff 2010:51).

These data provide some support for each of the perspectives on social stratification. Weber's view that social class is a continuum based on multiple dimensions is supported by the fact that the distribution of assets varies so widely depending on the asset. Huge discrepancies in distribution of ownership of the means of production as measured by real estate other than own home, stocks, and businesses clearly supports Marx's conflict view that a relatively small number of people own most of the means of production in the United States. Finally, these findings provide some support for the evolutionary view of Lenski and Lenski. That view suggests the basic needs for survival will be distributed based on function, but surpluses beyond basic needs will tend to be distributed based on power. This is consistent with the finding that basic assets, such as a home, that are important for survival and functioning in our society are distributed much more evenly than "surplus" wealth such as stocks and bonds.

CONCEPT LEARNING CHECK 7.4   Income and Wealth Inequality

Indicate whether each of the following statements is true or false.

_____ **1.** The top 5% of income earners account for 10% of total income.

_____ **2.** The top 5% of income earners saw a 5% increase in the percent of total income they received between 1979 and 2009.

_____ **3.** The share of total income for the top 5% of people in 2009 was greater than the combined incomes of the lowest 50% of people.

_____ **4.** Between 1979 and 2009, the only quintile that gained in their relative share of income was the bottom fifth.

_____ **5.** The average pay of CEOs as a multiple of the average worker's pay since 2003 has been lower in the United States than in Europe.

_____ **6.** The average pay of CEOs as a multiple of the average worker's pay since 2003 has been 300 or more.

_____ **7.** Wealth is distributed more unevenly than income in the United States.

_____ **8.** A large portion of the wealth possessed by most Americans is their home or principal place of residence.

_____ **9.** The bottom 80% of the US population collectively owns 7% of the net financial assets while the top 1% owns 43% of them.

7.5 Social Mobility: The Myth and the Reality

Social mobility in the United States is fairly common but usually leads to moderate net changes up or down both from one generation to the next and within a person's lifetime.

- Define social mobility and identify the factors that affect it.

Justice Sonia Sotomayor.
© Alex Wong/Getty Images/iStock

American's views of social mobility often reflect "the American dream"—a narrative in which a person can start with almost nothing and through perseverance and hard work, reach the heights of success. The biography of US Supreme Court Justice Sonya Sotomayor provides an example of someone who has achieved "the American dream."

> On June 25, 1954, when the first child of Juan and Celina Sotomayor, both of Puerto Rican descent, was born, her prospects might not have seemed very promising. She was a member of an ethnic minority, a woman, and grew up in the Bronx. Her father died when she was only nine years old and her mother had to work very hard to raise two children as a single parent. Yet Sonya Sotomayor was impressed with what she later labeled her mother's "almost fanatical emphasis" on education, graduating from high school in 1972 and entering Princeton University. She went on to study law at Yale and passed the bar in 1980. She worked first as an assistant district attorney in Manhattan, entered private practice in 1984, and was appointed US District Court Judge in 1992. On October 3, 1998, she was elevated to the US Second Court of Appeals. In August of 2009, she was confirmed by the US Senate as the first Latina Supreme Court justice in US history (biography.com).

How Much Social Mobility Is There?

There is a pervasive and romantic notion that the United States is "the land of opportunity," a place where the values of freedom, equality, and opportunity rule and where everyone can hope for and most can achieve "the American dream" of a life of material comfort and personal happiness. Often, our personal version of the dream is even greater. Many Americans are driven by the belief that they have a reasonable chance of achieving tremendous wealth and success. We retell in novels, television soap operas, and film countless variations of the Horatio Alger "rags to riches" story in which the hero experiences dramatic upward mobility. This formula that appears over and over in American popular culture was named after Horatio Alger (1834–1899), the author of juvenile novels that followed a formula: a brave but poor youth makes a daring rescue and thereby wins the gratitude and patronage of a wealthy benefactor. Alger's novels were immensely popular, and more than 20 million copies were sold during his lifetime. "Dream big" self-help books like *Think and Grow Rich*, by Napoleon Hill (1953), echo this theme. This book was first published in 1937 in the middle of the Great Depression and sold 20 million copies during his lifetime. The rags-to-riches myth is reflected in our beliefs about social mobility in the United States in several ways. We tend to believe the United States allows, even encourages, greater upward social mobility than other countries, with extreme upward social mobility a real possibility for us all. Attaining this prize, we believe, is the result of innate ability, hard work, and a little luck. How true is this belief? Before we can answer that, we must first clarify what we mean by social mobility.

Changes in the wealth and success of individuals reflect an important dimension of the broader social stratification system. **Social mobility** is changing one's social status and thereby changing one's social ranking in the stratification system. Social mobility is an important measure of a stratification system. Despite the huge differences in wealth, income, prestige, and power in the United States documented above, those differences are viewed as entirely acceptable and even a good thing by many people because this

Social mobility Changing one's social status and thereby changing one's social ranking in the stratification system.

country is perceived to be "the land of opportunity," in which each person can work hard and go from "rags to riches" and achieve the "American dream." Inequality, even dramatic inequality, is acceptable so long as each of us has "equal opportunity" to end up at the top.

Such opportunity is measured by social mobility—not "horizontal social mobility" in which sons are no better off than their fathers in terms of social prestige, wealth, or power, but "vertical social mobility" in which most sons and daughters can reasonably expect to do better than their mothers and fathers. **Vertical social mobility** occurs when there is a significant increase (upward mobility) or decrease (downward mobility) in social standing as measured by social status, class, or power. *Intergenerational social mobility* is the change in social standing of children in relation to their parents. Another important kind of mobility, *intragenerational social mobility*, refers to changes in social standing for one person over the course of his or her lifetime.

Most upward social mobility in the United States is due to **structural mobility**, that is, mobility resulting from changes in a society's occupational structure or stratification system rather than from individual achievement. This type of mobility was initially made possible by the industrialization of the economy and the expansion of new white-collar jobs. This expansion of well-paying jobs at the top, along with low birth rates among the upper classes, has made upward mobility possible, or what Olsen (1990) called the "prosperity escalator." The threat is that this upward mobility may be reduced when the economy experiences a downturn, as happened during the 1980s when Newman (1993) found that more than half her respondents reported falling incomes and nearly one-third had substantial reductions in income. Even more worrisome is how vertical social mobility may change as the economy evolves into a postindustrial economy with rapid increases in low-paying service jobs and the potential of a dwindling middle class.

To find out how much social mobility there is in our society, we need to consider both intergenerational mobility and intragenerational mobility. The focus here is primarily on income mobility (changes in income), but similar findings have been reported for occupational mobility (changes in occupational status).

Intergenerational social mobility. Social mobility in the United States is fairly common, but the extent of change is usually modest and less at the top and bottom of the occupational structure than in the middle. It usually occurs in steps between adjacent strata, for example, lower middle to middle, such as a father who is a merchant and a

Vertical social mobility A significant increase or decrease in social standing as measured by social status, class, or power.

Intergenerational social mobility An upward or downward change in social standing or social status of children relative to their parents.

Intragenerational social mobility An upward or downward change in social standing for an individual over the course of his or her lifetime.

Structural mobility Mobility resulting from changes in a society's occupational structure or stratification system rather than from individual achievement.

THE SOCIOLOGICAL IMAGINATION   Social Mobility

Below are descriptions of a few people and their jobs. Next to each description, in parentheses, is the social prestige score for that occupation according to the National Opinion Research Center (NORC 2011).

A. William had only a high school education and was first a carpenter (39), then a welder (42) for a few years before becoming a farmer (40).

B. William's daughter, Holly, went to college to get a degree in architecture and became an architect (73).

C. William's oldest son, Michael, did not go to college but worked on the farm with his dad and eventually inherited the farm and became a farmer (40).

D. William's youngest son, Adam, had no interest in farming and did not go to college, eventually becoming a truck driver (30).

E. Evan never went to college and first worked several years as a machinist (47). However, his company downsized, moving most of the jobs to Mexico, and he lost that job. To make ends meet, he became a janitor (22) and continued doing that until retirement.

F. Luis was a farm worker (23) on a large farm in central California when he was accepted into a local college, where he studied for a degree in education. While in college, he worked as a waiter (28) to pay his bills. Finally, after several years, he graduated from college and went on to join a startup software company as a computer programmer (61).

These occupational careers are presented in FIGURE 7-15. For each of the following questions, indicate which person (A–F) best answers that question.

(Continues)

THE SOCIOLOGICAL IMAGINATION *(Continued)*

FIGURE 7–15 Sample occupational careers illustrating different kinds of social mobility.

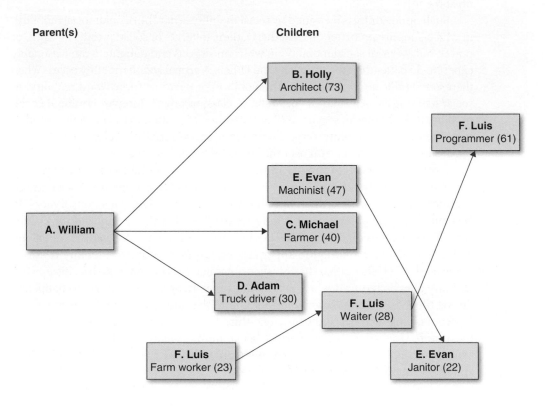

EVALUATE

1. Which person's story is the closest to a "rags to riches" story?

2. Who experiences intragenerational downward mobility?

3. Who experienced upward social mobility due to structural mobility?

4. Who experienced downward social mobility due to structural mobility?

5. Who experienced intergenerational downward social mobility?

6. Who experienced intergenerational upward social mobility?

Answers: 1. F, 2. E, 3. F, 4. E, 5. D, 6. B

son who becomes a lawyer. Large jumps, such as that of Supreme Court Justice Sonia Sotomayor, are rare (Kurz and Muller 1987). In a classic study of social mobility in the United States, sociologists Herbert Blau and Otis Dudley Duncan (1967) examined educational and occupational information from a representative sample of more than 20,000 American men. Only 1% of Blau and Duncan's sample had moved all the way from the bottom to the top of the class system.

Occupational inheritance is greatest at the top and bottom of the occupational structure. More intergenerational mobility occurs between extremes. For example, nearly two-thirds of CEOs in 243 major corporations were raised in upper-middle-class or upper-class families. (Boone et al. 1988; Kerbo 1983; Tumin 1985). Similarly, Blau and Duncan (1967) found that 72% of laborers' sons also had blue-collar jobs and 68% of salaried professionals' sons became white-collar workers. When compared to other countries, the overall rates of social mobility in the United States are much like those in other Western industrialized countries (Blau and Duncan 1967). Notice that many of the early studies of occupational mobility in the United States, such as the study by Blau and Duncan (1967), only studied men. Given that women participate much more in the workforce today, it is clear that contemporary studies need to consider both men and women.

A more recent report by economist Bashkar Mazumder (2008) provides detailed information on the income of parents and their children—both men and women—over a 25-year period. In FIGURE 7-16, we see the percentage of children reaching each income quintile according to their parents' income quintile. These data show the chances of each form of intergenerational income mobility.

If there were perfect mobility, the percentage in each income category for children would be the same regardless of parents' income. However, this is clearly not the case. The two largest percentages are people at the low and high extremes in income. Roughly 34% of people whose parents had low incomes in the bottom quintile were also in the bottom quintile themselves as adults; and roughly 38% of people whose parents had high incomes in the top quintile were also in the top quintile themselves as adults. Clearly the very rich tend to be able to pass on their high incomes to their children, while the children of parents from the bottom quintile find it difficult to escape the bottom quintile in their own adulthood. These findings show most income mobility is moderate and often ends in quintiles close to those of the parents. Only 7% of people displayed the "rags to riches" pattern in which parents in the bottom quintile had children who ended up in the top quintile. Similarly, only 11% of people displayed a "riches to rags" pattern in which parents in the top quintile had children who dropped to the bottom quintile in income.

An analysis of the same intergenerational income mobility broken down by race and ethnicity demonstrates that prospects for upward mobility for blacks are less than for whites. While 10.6% of whites display the "rags to riches" mobility, only 4.1% of blacks do. Looking at children "trapped" in the lowest income category, we find 24.9% of whites compared to 43.7% of blacks. So blacks raised in the lowest-income households are much more likely to end up in the lowest category themselves and far less likely to break out to achieve the American Dream (Mazumder 2008:17).

Intragenerational social mobility. It was intragenerational social mobility that Abraham Lincoln was referring to when he said, "There is no permanent class of hired laborers amongst us. Twenty-five years ago, I was a hired laborer. The hired laborer of yesterday labors on his own account today, and will hire the labor of others tomorrow." Lincoln was referring to the common tendency for individuals over the course of their lives to experience upward mobility. For most people, the low-paying jobs they have as inexperienced young people are replaced by dramatically better-paying jobs as they gain experience, training, and education. As FIGURE 7-17 shows, this upward trend is substantial, as reflected in household income, and begins to decline only at

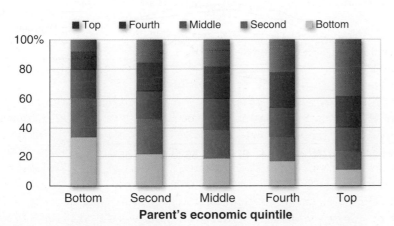

FIGURE 7-16 Percent of children reaching each income quintile by parent's quintile.
Source: © 2011 Pew Charitable Trusts. http://www.pew-states.org/uploadedFiles/PCS_Assets/2012/Pursuing_American_Dream.pdf.

retirement age. This commonly experienced trajectory of increased income over much of a person's working life produces a pattern of intragenerational mobility that gives people a sense of upward social mobility. As a result, many of us can live out, in at least some small way, our own Horatio Alger story of success at overcoming our meager beginnings. Unfortunately, severe or prolonged economic downturns, such as the Great Recession beginning in 2009, can upset this pattern as individuals confront temporary or permanent downturns in their own lives.

Social Mobility and Hard Work: Education Matters

Part of the romanticized "rags to riches" narrative is the belief that people can achieve the American dream through hard work. If upward social mobility within a person's lifetime is increased with hard work, then we should expect to see greater mobility for people who work hard, as measured by factors such as education. In FIGURE 7-18, we see the average income for men of various ages as a function of their education

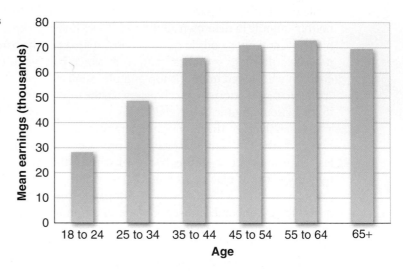

FIGURE 7-17   Mean earnings by age for males (2008). *Source: Data from the US Census Bureau. 2011. Statistical Abstract of the United States. Retrieved October 2011 (http:// www.census.gov/compendia/ statab/2011/tables/11s0702.pdf).*

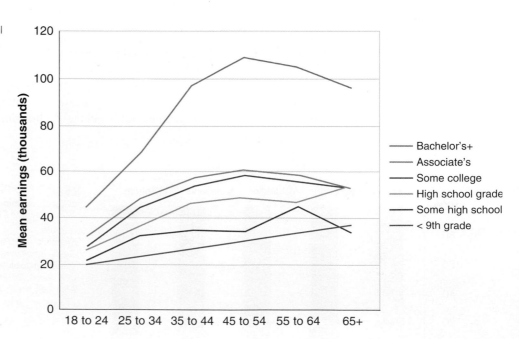

FIGURE 7-18   Intragenerational income mobility by education for men (2008). *Source: Data from the US Census Bureau. 2011. Statistical Abstract of the United States. Retrieved October 2011 (http:// www.census.gov/compendia/ statab/2011/tables/11s0702.pdf).*

(US Census Bureau, 2011b). Men having a bachelor's degree or more experience far greater upward social mobility during their lifetimes as measured by their average income at different ages than do men with less education. In this sense, at least, the notion of America as a land of opportunity is supported. However, we should keep in mind that some people have much greater access to higher education than others. While children of the affluent typically have access to some of the best private schools, those who are poor may be stuck in underfunded schools with few resources and high dropout rates. As a result, educational attainment is affected by other factors in addition to hard work. For the rich, education becomes a mechanism of achieving success, while for many of the poor, lack of access to education becomes a barrier to success.

Social Mobility and Opportunity

An essential element of the dominant view of stratification in America is the belief that ours is a land of equal opportunity where anyone can achieve success. How true is this? To answer this question, let us examine the measure of intragenerational social mobility considered above—mean income by age—and determine how the income trajectory varies for people of different sexes and educational levels FIGURE 7-19. Again we see the basic pattern of intragenerational upward mobility, with older people making more than younger people, though that trend reverses after middle age. But clearly, the upward mobility experienced by males is higher than that for females for both those with high school degrees and those with at least a bachelor's degree. These findings clearly show that opportunities for intragenerational income mobility for men and women are decidedly unequal.

The Dark Side of Social Mobility

Other evidence suggests that upward social mobility also has a down side. Sociologists Richard Sennett and Jonathan Cobb (1988) studied working-class parents in Boston who had sacrificed so that their children could go to college and experience upward social mobility. These parents limited their spending on themselves, while the fathers worked long hours and were often not home in order to earn enough to send their children to college. Ironically, instead of children who were grateful for their sacrifices, the children became estranged from the fathers because they spent so little time together, found that they had little in common with their parents as they went on to college and entered a higher social class, and the parents felt betrayed and bitter because their children seemed unappreciative. Thus, they found that upward social mobility carried with it a hidden cost for these families.

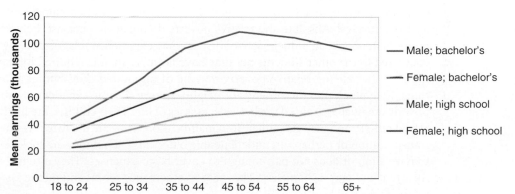

FIGURE 7-19 Mean earnings by age, sex, and education (2008).
Source: Data from the US Census Bureau. 2011. Statistical Abstract of the United States. Retrieved October 2011 (http://www.census.gov/compendia/statab/2011/tables/11s0702.pdf).

For each of the example cases below, identify two findings regarding social mobility that help answer the questions posed. Hint: The text identifies one factor affecting social mobility that the individual can influence and three factors that are largely beyond his or her control. Each of those factors can make it more or less likely that the individual will end up in a high income category.

1. Noah is just graduating from high school. He has been accepted into college and plans to major in business. Eventually he wants to get an MBA and start his own business. Noah is black, and his parents are in the lowest quintile in income. Noah's parents never graduated from high school and he relies on scholarships to attend college, yet he is still confident he has a bright future ahead of him. Does he? What factors make him more likely to succeed? What factors make it less likely he will succeed?

2. Shana is thinking of dropping out of high school. She is black and lives in the inner city of Chicago with three brothers and her mother in subsidized housing for the poor. Her mom has a part-time job and receives some welfare to help them get by. Shana's mother is in the lowest quintile for income. What are Shana's chances of ending up in the middle quintile? What factors make it less likely she will experience upward social mobility? What factors make it more likely she will experience upward social mobility?

3. Jonathan is just graduating from high school. Jonathan is white and lives in a popular upper-class community in a house next to the golf course. His parents are both white-collar professionals and his family is in the upper fifth of income. Jonathan hopes to be in the same upper-fifth bracket one day himself. What additional information about Jonathan do you need to assess his chances? What could Jonathan do to increase or decrease his chances of success? What factors about Jonathan that he cannot change make it more likely that Jonathan will succeed or more likely that he will fail?

7.6 Poverty in the United States

Those at the lowest end of the stratification system are most in need of a social safety net, which raises questions of the amount of poverty, who is poor, and how we account for poverty.

- Describe how the United States characterizes poverty.
- Explain the culture of poverty.

Relative poverty Deprivation experienced by some people in contrast to others who have more.

Absolute poverty A condition of deprivation in which people have too little money or other resources to obtain all they need for basic survival.

Poverty line or poverty threshold Roughly three times the amount of money required for a family to spend for food.

Since stratification systems produce "haves" and "have-nots," people in the latter category will at minimum experience **relative poverty**, deprivation experienced by some people in contrast to others who have more. More importantly, the United States, even though a wealthy society by many standards, includes large numbers of people experiencing absolute poverty. **Absolute poverty** is a condition of deprivation in which people have too little money or other resources to obtain all they need for basic survival. Absolute and relative poverty do not always coexist. For example, poorer students in an affluent school district may experience relative poverty when compared to the other students but may have far more than is required for survival. People experiencing relative poverty may be disappointed they cannot afford the same designer clothes their friends or neighbors wear. People experiencing absolute poverty are unable to afford the basic necessities of life. Their children are likely to go to bed hungry and may also suffer from malnutrition. They are likely to rely on public transportation or perhaps an undependable older car. Even if they are lucky enough to have a job, it does not pay enough to cover basic expenses. They struggle to pay their rent and may be homeless. They rely on emergency rooms and public assistance to obtain needed health care.

In order to track poverty in a consistent manner, the US government assumes poor families spend one-third of their income on food and defines the **poverty line or poverty threshold** as roughly three times the amount of money required for a family to spend for food. Since food costs vary by family size, this number varies. In 2009, for a family of four with two children under 18 years old, the poverty threshold was $21,756 (DeNavas-Walt, Carmen, and Smith 2009:55).

Obviously, the poverty threshold is a crude, somewhat arbitrary designation that does not take into account changes in food consumption, much less changes in costs of basic goods and services like housing (Katz 1989). Small changes in this definition of poverty can make it appear that hundreds of thousands of people either become or are no longer poor. Despite its obvious shortcomings, this definition of poverty is the basis for deciding who receives government help, and it is also the basis for most official statistics on poverty in the United States.

It is important to keep in mind that the poverty threshold is just that—a threshold—and many poor families have incomes much lower than that threshold. In 2009, 14.3% of the US population, 43.6 million people, lived in households earning less than the poverty threshold, and 6.3%, just over 19 million people, lived in households earning less than 50% of the poverty threshold (DeNavas-Walt et al. 2009:18).

US Poverty in Historical Context

In 2009, 43.6 million people or 14.3% of the population fell below the poverty line in the United States (DeNavas-Walt et al. 2009:14). Fifty years earlier, poverty rates in the United States were over 22%. As can be seen in FIGURE 7-20, between 1959 and 1974, poverty was cut almost in half, from 22.2% to 12.6%. But since 1975, the poverty rate has remained between 10% and 15%, actually increasing a little to its current rate of 14.3%. While public assistance programs associated with the War on Poverty in the 1960s and early 1970s made headway on reducing poverty in the United States, cutbacks in those programs during the 1980s and subsequent decades resulted in modest increases in poverty.

Who Are the Poor?

There are a number of misconceptions about poverty in the United States. People in the United States are more likely to be poor if they are children, women, or members of racial or ethnic minorities, if they are members of single-parent households with children or households in which only one adult works, or if they live in inner cities or rural areas. Changing rates of poverty for different age groups are displayed in FIGURE 7-21.

Absolute and relative poverty are related ideas but may describe people in very different circumstances.

(top) © James Woodson/Photodisc/Thinkstock; (bottom) © Joe Belanger/Shutterstock, Inc.

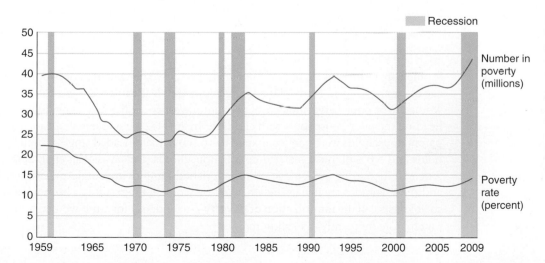

FIGURE 7-20 Number in poverty and poverty rate in the United States (1959–2009).
Source: DeNavas-Walt, Carmen, Bernadette D. Proctor, and Jessica C. Smith, U.S. Census Bureau, Current Population Reports, P60-238, Income, Poverty, and Health Insurance Coverage in the United States. 2009. US Government Printing Office, Washington, DC, 2010.

FIGURE 7-21 Percentage in poverty and poverty rate by age in the United States (1959–2009).
Source: DeNavas-Walt, Carmen, Bernadette D. Proctor, and Jessica C. Smith, U.S. Census Bureau, Current Population Reports, P60-238, Income, Poverty, and Health Insurance Coverage in the United States. 2009. U.S. Government Printing Office, Washington, DC, 2010.

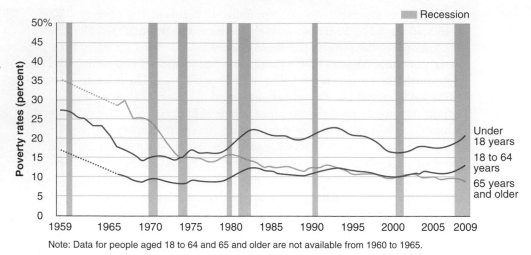

Note: Data for people aged 18 to 64 and 65 and older are not available from 1960 to 1965.

Children

In the 1950s through the mid-1970s, the elderly were more likely to be poor than were other adults or children. But today, children are far more likely to be poor than adults, and the elderly are actually less poor than the population as a whole. Social Security and private pension plans have dramatically transformed old age for many people from a time of poverty to a time of relative comfort in which they can continue to live much the same life style they experienced while working. While people 65 and older make up 12.7% of the US population, they are only 7.9% of people below the poverty line (DeNavas-Walt et al. 2009:19). For many of the elderly with incomes below the poverty line, their only significant source of income is Social Security, and they face increasing costs over future years while trying to make ends meet on a fixed income. A more recent concern is the loss of pension coverage or reductions in benefits for many private companies and even government workers along with threatened reductions in Social Security benefits. Many pension plans still have millions of dollars more in unfunded benefits promised to future retirees, and the rapid rise in retirement-age people as Baby Boomers approach retirement poses threats to the continued financing of Social Security benefits.

Infants and children are the age group most likely to be poor today. They constitute 35.5% of the poor in the United States. More than one of every five children under 18 (20.7%) is poor, compared to 12.9% of adults younger than 65 and 8.9% of people over 65 (DeNavas-Walt et al. 2009:15). Why are children more likely to be poor? Part of it has to do with the changing family structure in the United States. Forty years ago, most poor families still had both parents in the household and women were the single-parent heads of only 25% of all poor families. By 2009, this percentage had doubled to more than half (50.5%).

Women and Single Heads of Households

Women are more likely to be poor than men. Sixty-two percent of poor people over the age of 18 are women. Many of the same factors that lead children to be poor also lead women to be poor. Large numbers of poor adult women are the struggling single parents heading the poor households with children. In 2009, 29.9% of female-headed single-parent households were poor compared to 16.9% of male-headed single-parent households and 5.8% of intact married-couple households (DeNavas-Walt et al. 2009:15). Since an increasing percentage of impoverished families are single-parent families, and those families are increasingly headed by women, the result has been what many sociologists call the **feminization of poverty**—a tendency for adult women to be poor much more frequently than adult men.

Feminization of poverty A tendency for adult women to be poor much more frequently than adult men.

Racial or Ethnic Minorities

Both blacks and Hispanics are about three times as likely to be poor as are whites. Yet, because of the much larger number of whites in the United States, about two-thirds of the poor are whites. In 2009, the poverty rate for blacks was 25.8%, for Hispanics the rate was 25.3%, for Asians it was 12.5%, and for non–Hispanic whites the rate was 9.4% (DeNavas-Walt et al. 2009:16).

(Inequality as a function of race and ethnicity is also covered in Chapter 9. The issue of inequality by gender and age is also covered in Chapter 10.)

Inner-City Residents and Residents of Poor Rural Counties

Poverty is most common in central cities (18.7%) and outside metropolitan areas (16.6%). For people living inside metropolitan areas and not in central cities, poverty rates are 11% (DeNavas-Walt et al. 2009:17–18). Counties with higher levels of poverty are most likely to be in the South and least likely to be in the Midwest. In 2009, the lowest poverty rate occurred in the Northeast (12.2%), the second-lowest in the Midwest (13.3%), the second-highest in the West (14.8%), and the highest poverty rate was found in the South (15.7%) (DeNavas-Walt et al. 2009:17).

Workers

Critics of the poor argue that they should be forced to work—that is, "workfare" programs. And indeed, in 1996, the US welfare system was restructured under the Personal Responsibility and Work Opportunity Reconciliation Act, which requires welfare recipients to look for jobs and accept available jobs while placing a lifetime cap on welfare assistance for each individual. Yet others point out that many of the poor are children or over 65 and may be unable to work, other people in poverty are already working at jobs that pay too little to raise them above poverty, and for some, jobs simply are not available. Many of the people living below the poverty threshold in the United States are children under 18 (35.6% and 15.5 million people) or 65 and older (7.8% and 3.4 million people) and are unlikely to work. Of those in poverty 18 to 64 years old (56.7% and 24.7 million people), many are the **working poor**—working people whose incomes fall below the poverty line. In 2009, 32.4% (8 million) worked part time and 10.5% (2.6 million) worked full time but were paid so little that they were still poor. The poverty rate among all workers aged 16 and over was 6.9%. For people who worked less than full time, the rate was 14.5% (8 million people). For year-round, full-time workers, the rate was 2.7% (2.6 million workers) (DeNavas-Walt et al. 2009:15).

Making Sense of Poverty: How Does It Happen?

Sociologists have proposed a number of possible explanations of why poverty exists. These touch on important issues that shape public policy debates about poverty and the need for a social safety net in the form of the welfare system.

The Culture of Poverty

Some sociologists (Lewis 1961; Harrington 1962) argue that some of the poor are trapped in a **culture of poverty**—a subculture associated with people in lower social classes thought to encourage them to become resigned to their fate and to discourage personal achievement. These authors assume that the cultural values and norms of behavior for the poor are significantly different from those of others. They thus explain poverty by arguing that those who are poor have adopted a different culture than the rest of us. That culture creates a self-perpetuating cycle of poverty in which the poor lose hope of getting out of poverty, quit trying, and thus remain poor. Even worse, say these authors, this culture of poverty is passed on to the next generation, leading many of their children to remain poor throughout their lives as well.

Working poor Working people whose incomes fall below the poverty line.

Culture of poverty A subculture associated with people in lower social classes thought to encourage them to become resigned to their fate and to discourage personal achievement.

Blaming the Victim

William Ryan (1976) objects to the view that it is the culture of poverty that leads to poverty. Instead he argues that it is social-structural conditions within society as a whole, such as the availability of jobs and access to education, that lead to poverty. To support his argument, he points out that other countries, such as Sweden and Japan, display less overall inequality and also have less poverty. The culture of poverty, he argues, is a reasonable response to the difficulties of being poor. It is a *consequence* of poverty, not its *cause*. To argue otherwise, said Ryan (1976), is "blaming the victims" for their own suffering.

A Permanent Underclass

Underclass The most impoverished segment of American society, for whom poverty is relatively permanent.

Sociologist William J. Wilson (1987) further extends this debate by describing what he sees as a permanent underclass. The **underclass** is the most impoverished segment of American society, for whom poverty is relatively permanent (Wilson 1987). Like Oscar Lewis and Michael Harrington, he believes there is a relatively permanent class of people unlikely to escape poverty. However, he differs fundamentally from them by arguing that structural conditions in society, not the values and behaviors of members of that class, perpetuate the underclass. He goes on to characterize the members of the underclass. They are primarily residents of inner-city areas high in unemployment, out-of-wedlock births, female-headed families, welfare dependence, homelessness, and serious crime. They are also disproportionately black and Hispanic. Wilson argues the underclass is the result of major economic changes. Jobs once held by inner-city residents have largely moved out of inner cities to the suburbs, to the "Sun Belt" states in the South or Southwest, or overseas. Many inner-city residents are unqualified for the few jobs now available in their area and lack the means to travel to jobs in the suburbs. As their economic base crumbled, the stability of neighborhood social institutions like schools and churches was undermined.

The Permanence of Poverty

Both the culture-of-poverty view and the permanent-underclass view assume that poverty is a relatively permanent condition that people enter and only rarely escape. However, more than two decades of studies have repeatedly shown that, for most people, poverty is temporary, and far more people move in and out of poverty than are poor at any one time. As far back as 1989, economist Patricia Ruggles (1989) examined national statistics of people who are poor over time to assess whether there is a self-perpetuating culture causing people to be poor throughout their lives and to pass on poverty to the next generation. She found that many of the poor are "short-term poor," who move out of poverty in a period ranging from a few months to less than eight years. The others are "long-term poor" who remain poor for eight years or more, some even for most of their lives. However, even among the long-term poor, she found that most eventually overcome their poverty. Perhaps even more surprising, she found that passing poverty on from one generation to the next was uncommon. Only about 20% of people who are poor as children remain poor as adults (Ruggles 1989; Sawhill 1988). Gottschalk, McLanahan, and Sandefur (1994:89) found that 59% of people in poverty were poor for only one year or less, in large part because much poverty occurs as a result of dramatic life changes such as a divorce, loss of job, or medical bills (O'Hare 1996). Since the number of people who are poor each year remains relatively constant, this means that roughly as many people become poor as leave poverty.

More recent evidence also supports the view that poverty, for most, is a temporary condition. A US Census report (Anderson 2011) found that, of the 28.1 million people who were poor in 2004, 31.4% (8.8 million) were no longer poor in 2005 and 41.6% (11.7 million) were no longer poor in 2006. Of people who were not poor in 2004, 3.5% (8.4 million people) became poor in 2005 and 4.2% (10.1 million) became poor by 2006 (Anderson 2011). These results are displayed in FIGURE 7-22.

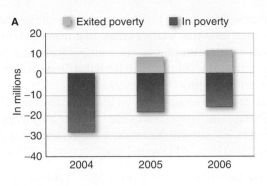

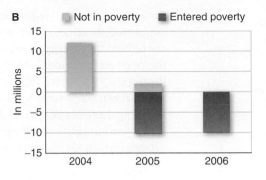

FIGURE 7-22 Numbers of people entering (A) and leaving (B) poverty in the United States (2004–2006). *Source: Data from the U.S. Census Bureau. 2011. "Dynamics of Economic Well-Being: Poverty, 2004–2006." Retrieved October 2011 (http://www.census.gov/hhes/www/poverty/publications/dynamics04/P70-123.pdf).*

Note: 0 represents the poverty line

That same census report found that from January 2004 to December 2006, 28.9% of the US population was in poverty for at least two months, while 2.8% were in poverty for the entire three-year period. Hence, poverty, for the great majority of poor people, is not chronic poverty—a long-term state they will experience most or all of their lives—but episodic poverty—a temporary condition, or episode, they must endure for a period of time while they try to marshal the resources required to break out of their poverty.

Even though the above studies show that people in poverty escape poverty fairly commonly, they may not go far. Studies of income mobility across generations such as those reported earlier in this chapter find what Mazumder (2008:11) describes as "stickiness" at the lowest income quintile, with 33.5% of people whose parents were in the bottom income quintile remaining in the bottom quintile as adults. Similarly, the census study by Anderson (2011:2) found that more than half of the people who exited poverty in that study continued to have incomes less than 150% of the poverty threshold.

Welfare Versus Wealthfare

We tend to focus on government expenditures for the poor and other entitlement programs, with many arguing that these programs can no longer be afforded because they unbalance the budget and increase the federal deficit. The amount budgeted for welfare in the US budget increased roughly 2% to 3% a year from 2007 to 2008, but increased rapidly from $301 billion in fiscal year 2009 (FY2009) to $496 billion in FY2012 as the United States and world economies attempted to deal with financial crisis. This is certainly a large expense and a significant chunk of the total spending for FY2012 budgeted at $3.819 trillion (Chantril 2011).

However, benefits to different groups in our society do not always come in the form of expenditures. Wealthy people and corporations benefit considerably more than do the poor from federal government generosity. Most benefits to these people come not as direct expenditures by the federal government but as revenue reductions based on tax breaks or tax subsidies. **Wealthfare**—government policies and programs that primarily benefit the wealthy and large corporations—provide billions of dollars in financial benefits to the wealthy and large corporations while remaining largely invisible in the government accounting procedures. A widely cited example is the "Bush tax cuts" passed under President George W. Bush that reduced the tax rates for middle- and upper-income taxpayers. Other examples are federal government tax breaks for oil companies, home mortgage interest deductions, and employer-sponsored health insurance; price supports for agricultural products; and tariffs on goods manufactured in other countries. Those benefits go disproportionately to wealthy people and rival and sometimes exceed the costs of welfare.

Some argue the Bush tax cuts appear to be replicating a situation that occurred under President Reagan during the 1980s in which major tax reductions for the rich

Wealthfare Government policies and programs that primarily benefit the wealthy and large corporations.

dramatically reduced federal revenues, producing huge deficits. The same people who supported those tax reductions then used the "budget crisis" manufactured by those tax reductions to support reduced expenditures for entitlement programs that benefit the poor and the elderly. In effect, this resulted in a massive redistribution of income during the 1980s from the poor to the wealthy (Braun 1997).

A particularly large form of corporate wealthfare was the TARP bailout of banks during the financial crisis of 2008 in which more than $700 billion of taxpayer money was used to help banks "too big to fail" survive the crisis. A subsequent audit by the Government Accountability Office (GAO 2011) found that

> the Federal Reserve provided more than $16 trillion in total financial assistance to some of the largest financial institutions and corporations in the United States and throughout the world. This is a clear case of socialism for the rich and rugged, you're-on-your-own individualism for everyone else. (Sanders 2011)

Even a US senator with strong conservative credentials, Tom Coburn (R–Okla.), in 2011 argued these tax subsidies should be eliminated to help reduce the deficit. He argued, "Tax expenditures are not tax cuts. Tax expenditures are socialism and corporate welfare. Tax expenditures are increases on anyone who does not receive the benefit or can't hire a lobbyist . . . to manipulate the code to their favor" (Gleckman 2011). The home mortgage interest deduction alone is estimated to reduce federal revenue by $600 billion between 2009 and 2013 (Pogol 2010). The reduced revenues due to the Bush tax cuts have been estimated at between $1.3 trillion and $2.8 trillion over 10 years. To put this in perspective, the cost of the Iraq and Afghanistan wars was $1.26 trillion through 2011 (Kessler 2011).

"IT GOES IN CYCLES, JUNIOR. SOMETIMES, THE RICH GET RICHER AND THE POOR GET POORER. SOMETIMES, THE RICH GET RICHER AND THE POOR STAY THE SAME."

The rich get richer.

Photo © Harley Schwadron/
CartoonStock.com

CONCEPT LEARNING CHECK 7.6   Poverty: Who Are the Poor?

For each of the following pairs of people, identify which one is more likely to be poor.

_____ **1.** A. 12-year-old child in a single-parent family   B. 70-year-old retired man

_____ **2.** A. 50-year-old man   B. 70-year-old retired man

_____ **3.** A. Hispanic man   B. White non–Hispanic man

_____ **4.** A. Someone who was poor last year   B. Someone who was not poor last year

_____ **5.** A. Someone living in a rural area   B. Someone living in a suburb

---

7.7 Why Class Matters

Social class has important consequences for people's lives, affecting everything from health to access to new technologies.

- Explain the consequences of stratification for health, education, family, crime, and technology.

Life styles Activities, behaviors, possessions, and other, often visible characteristics of how an individual spends her or his time and money.

Social stratification affects nearly every important dimension of our lives. People in different social classes differ markedly in both life styles and life chances. **Life styles** refer to the activities, behaviors, possessions, and other, often visible characteristics of how an individual spends her or his time and money. These things often reflect social class and may be used as ways for an individual to advertise his or her social class to others. Obviously, people from higher social classes are more likely to have nice homes, drive expensive cars, and be able to afford a broader range of leisure activities. If the only difference between people in different social classes was differences in life styles, then this might frustrate and annoy all but the wealthy, but it would have a generally inconsequential effect.

However, social class affects far more than how we spend our leisure time and what we wear while we are doing it. Social class also dramatically affects our life chances. **Life chances** refer to the likelihood of realizing a certain quality of life, or the probability of experiencing important positive outcomes in life such as material goods and favorable life experiences such as higher education, or important negative outcomes in life such as malnutrition, disease, or death. People born into higher social classes are more likely to go to college, get a good job, and be healthy than someone born into a poor family. In some cases, life chances can be interpreted literally because they reflect an individual's chances of living or dying. We do not have to look far to find situations in which people in lower social classes live shorter lives than people in higher classes.

> **Life chances** The likelihood of realizing a certain quality of life or the probability of experiencing certain positive or negative outcomes in life such as material goods and favorable life experiences.

Family Life

People in higher social classes tend to have families very different from those of people in lower social classes. People in lower social classes tend to marry earlier, have more children, and have children sooner. The 2000 Census found that the average age of first marriage for women with high school diplomas was 25, but for women with graduate degrees it was 30. The birthrate of women with high school diplomas was twice that of women with graduate degrees. Also, for women with less than a high school education, 64% were unmarried when they gave birth to their first child (US Census 2000). The net result is that the family places more demands for resources on people in lower classes and fewer resources are available to assist children in achieving higher social class or higher income.

Social class also influences child rearing. Sociologist Melvin Kohn (1977) found that lower-class parents have jobs in which they are strictly supervised. Therefore, they encourage children to respect authority in order to be successful in such jobs. In contrast, middle-class parents often have greater autonomy at work and hence encourage their children to be more creative. In a separate study, Lareau (2002) found that working-class parents are more likely to expect their children to develop naturally given basic support like food, shelter, and comfort. Hence, they tend to set basic limits but then let their children play on their own within those limits. In contrast, middle-class families are more likely to believe children need more guidance to develop and encourage play activities designed to strengthen their children's mental and social skills.

Education

Children in higher-social-class families are more likely to obtain more education than those in lower-social-class families and are also more likely to be enrolled in elite schools. A report provided by the US Department of Education (2005) examined the educational level 12th graders expect to earn in low-, medium-, and high-socioeconomic-status families. Only 22% of 12th graders in low-SES families expected to earn graduate or professional degrees, compared to 31% for middle-SES and 53% for high-SES—more than twice as many as for low-SES families.

Upper-middle-class parents, believing in the importance of education for helping their children succeed, often go to great lengths to enroll their children in prestigious preschools and private schools that feed into exclusive prep schools (Gross 2003), and parents in the upper class are routinely able to send their children to exclusive private schools that prepare them for prestigious universities (Cookson and Persell 2005). Working-class families and poor families are forced to rely on public schools. For the poor in particular, schools in their community are struggling schools where many students drop out. As a result, for the upper classes, schools provide a means for their children to achieve upward mobility or to maintain their privileged position, while for working-class and poor families, schools become a barrier that closes off opportunities for their children.

Crime and Criminal Justice

As was discussed previously, the effects of social class on being the victim of crime or entering the criminal justice system as an alleged offender are not tracked systematically in the United States. Nevertheless, studies looking at the effects of social class offer evidence that people in lower social classes are more likely to be regarded as criminals and, at every stage in the criminal justice process, they are more likely to be treated more harshly. Thornberry and Farnsworth (1982) in a study in Philadelphia found people of higher status were less likely to be arrested. White-collar criminals such as Bernie Madoff, who cheated clients out of billions of dollars (Frank et al. 2009), tend to be prosecuted less often and less vigorously than criminals from lower social classes. This may be due in part to the higher social status and influence of white-collar criminals.

Technology

The Internet and other relatively new digital technologies provide important opportunities to people with access to them. For example, computer literacy can help someone obtain or keep a job. The Internet can be used not just for entertainment but also for important tasks such as finding out about and applying for jobs, searching for information, and even working on an online course. The **digital divide** is a term often used to identify inequalities in access to these technologies. The poor, minorities, rural residents, inner-city residents, and people in developing countries often have far less access to these technologies than do affluent residents in cities and suburbs. In an information-based service economy, this digital divide increasingly limits opportunities for people who do not have the computer skills necessary for most good jobs, who may not have broadband access, and who may not have access to library resources on the Internet. The Pew Internet and American Life Project (2010) documented significant differences in access, with 93% of US college graduates using the Internet regularly, compared to only 77% of all US adults, 40% of people with less than a high school education, 63% of respondents with household incomes under $30,000, and 66% of Hispanic Americans. A similar disparity is found for broadband access, with 67% of whites and 56% of African Americans having broadband access at home (Smith 2010). When asked in a Pew Foundation survey what they saw as major disadvantages of not having broadband access, respondents mentioned job opportunities and career skills (43%), health information (34%), learning new things to improve and enrich life (31%), government services (29%), keeping up with news (23%), and keeping up with what is happening in their communities (19%) (Smith 2010).

Digital divide Inequalities in access to technologies such as the Internet and computers.

Health

When it comes to health, we find that social class is a strong predictor of both quality of life, as measured by many health indices, and life expectancy. Here, perhaps more than in any other area, the term *life chances* takes on a stark meaning, since social class influences a person's chance of living or dying. Income and education, two measures of socioeconomic status, are each related to health in many ways, with people having higher incomes and greater educational attainment being significantly healthier than those with low incomes or less education. More education and higher incomes are linked with living longer.

The relationship between education and health is presented in FIGURE 7-23. College graduates (both men and women) are expected to live at least five years longer than those who have not completed high school. Babies born to mothers with less than 12 years of education are twice as likely to die in their first year as those born to mothers with a college degree. Rates of poor or fair health for children are reported more than six times more frequently for parents with less than 12 years of education than for those with a college degree (Robert Wood Johnson Foundation 2008).

Income also is related to health, as shown in the following two charts. In FIGURE 7-24, we see that men and women with higher incomes can expect to live more than six years more than those with low incomes. In the next chart, FIGURE 7-25, we see that

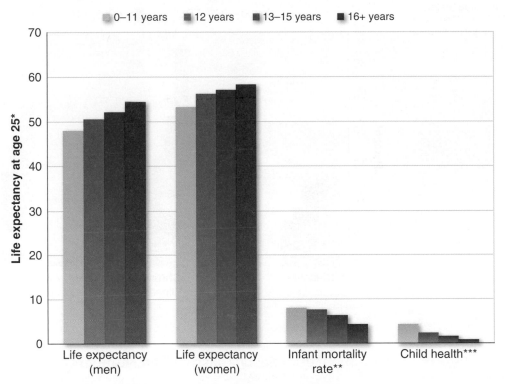

*This is the life expectancy at age 25, or the number of years they are expected to live beyond 25. For example, males with incomes less than the poverty level would be expected to live 45.5 more years for a total of 70.5 years.

FIGURE 7-23 Life expectancy, infant mortality, child health by number of years of education in the United States.
Source: © 2008 Robert Wood Johnson Foundation/Overcoming Obstacles to Health.

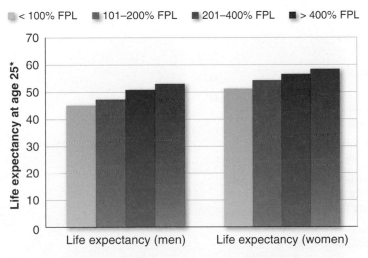

*The number of years they are expected to live beyond 25. For example, males with incomes less than the poverty level would be expected to live 45.5 more years for a total of 70.5 years.

FIGURE 7-24 Life expectancy by income in the United States.
Source: © 2008 Robert Wood Johnson Foundation/Overcoming Obstacles to Health.

people with low family incomes are twice as likely as those in affluent families to have diabetes—a major cause of disability and death. The poor are nearly 50% more likely to have coronary heart disease, five times as likely to report being in fair or poor health, three times as likely to report suffering from chronic illness, and seven times as likely to have children in fair or poor health.

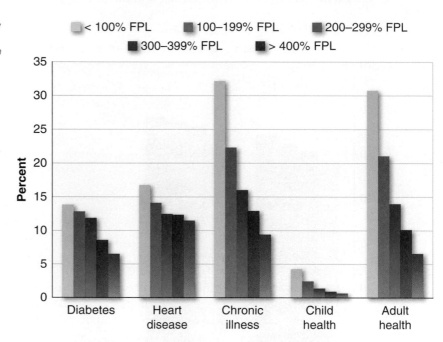

FIGURE 7-25 Health indicators by income in the United States.
Source: © 2008 Robert Wood Johnson Foundation/Overcoming Obstacles to Health.

| □ < 100% FPL | ■ 100–199% FPL | ■ 200–299% FPL |
| ■ 300–399% FPL | ■ > 400% FPL | |

CONCEPT LEARNING CHECK 7.7   Consequences of Social Class: By the Numbers

Connect the statements on the left with the appropriate letter for the statistic on the right.

_____ **1.** How many years longer a man is expected to live who obtains a bachelor's degree compared to a man who does not finish high school.

_____ **2.** Percentage of US college graduates who use the Internet regularly.

_____ **3.** Percentage of people with less than a high school education who use the Internet regularly.

_____ **4.** Percentage of 12th graders in low-SES families expecting to earn graduate or professional degrees.

_____ **5.** Percentage of 12th graders in high-SES families expecting to earn graduate or professional degrees.

_____ **6.** Percentage of women with less than a high school education who were unmarried when their first child was born.

_____ **7.** How many years longer a woman is expected to live whose income is greater than four times the poverty level, compared to a woman whose income is below the poverty level.

_____ **8.** How many times more likely is chronic illness for someone whose income is below the poverty level compared to someone making over four times the poverty level.

A. 22%

B. 40%

C. 53%

D. 64%

E. 93%

F. 3

G. 7

H. 7

7.8 Summing Up: Social Stratification in the United States Now and in the Future

Recent trends reverse a long-term tendency toward greater equality in the United States, with clearly negative consequences for all but the most wealthy, and—some argue—even negative impacts for the most wealthy as well.

- Describe social stratification trends in the United States during the 20th and 21st centuries.

The dominant trend in the United States throughout most of the 20th century was a modest reduction in inequality. As the United States industrialized, the proportion of wealth possessed by the richest 1% of the population peaked just before the Great Depression at about 36% and then dropped modestly through the late 1960s.

A far more noticeable trend has been the increasing economic prosperity of all— Olsen's (1990) "prosperity escalator." This trend was most noticeable in the postwar period from 1947 to 1967. This was a period of unprecedented prosperity and economic growth. During this period, family income increased substantially. Average weekly earnings rose by 50%. The real median family income nearly doubled from $15,423 in 1947 to $27,000 in 1967. This period also witnessed a modest trend toward a more equitable distribution of income. The gap between rich and poor diminished, and a prosperous middle class expanded. During this period, there developed the widespread belief among Americans that the quality of their lives would be better than that of their parents and the quality of their children's lives would exceed that of their own. Olsen (1990) argued that, even though the overall distribution of income remained very unequal and inequality did not change significantly during this period, no one was concerned by this fact as long as the majority of people were experiencing rising incomes and standards of living.

In contrast, the period from the late 1960s until today has been a time of slower economic growth, uneven progress, and increased inequality in our stratification system. The period of rapidly rising American prosperity has ended. During this period, the economic position of the American middle class has stagnated. This has also been a period of increasing income inequality. All but the highest 10% of American families experienced a decline in "real" income, after adjusting for inflation, since the 1970s. The highest 1% of families, on the other hand, experienced larger increases during that same period. During this period of economic stagnation and decline, the "prosperity escalator" faltered, the poor got poorer, and the rich got richer.

Former US Secretary of Labor Robert Reich argues that there has been a "significant reversal of the move toward income equality" that characterized the postwar period. Most of the wealth added to the US economy since 1980, he argues, has gone to the rich. By 2007, America's top 1% of earners increased their share of the nation's total income to 23%, or nearly three times the 8% share they had in 1980. A single family, the family of Walmart founder Sam Walton, has an estimated $90 billion in wealth, which is almost as much as the $95 billion in wealth owned by the bottom 40% of the US population in 2005—120 million people (Reich 2009).

A report from the Pew Research Center (Kochhar, Fry, and Taylor 2011) finds that the economic meltdown—often called the Great Recession—beginning with the bursting of the housing market bubble in 2006 and the recession that followed from late 2007 to mid-2009—impacted whites and racial minorities differently, dramatically increasing the wealth gap between whites and those minorities. Between 2005 and 2009, median wealth after adjusting for inflation fell by 66% among Hispanic households, 53% among black households, and only 16% among white households FIGURE 7-26.

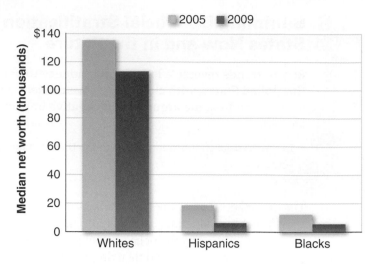

FIGURE 7-26 Median net worth of households by race and ethnicity in the United States. (2005 and 2009).
Source: © 2011 Pew Research Center, Social & Demographic Trends Project. Wealth Gaps Rise to Record Highs Between Whites, Blacks and Hispanics. (http://pewresearch.org/pubs/2069/housing-bubble-subprime-mortgages-hispanics-blacks-household-wealth-disparity)

By 2009, the median wealth of white households reached 20 times that of black households and 18 times that of Hispanic households, roughly twice the ratio of the gap that had prevailed for the 20 years before the Great Recession. The biggest cause of the drop in wealth were plummeting house values, and for blacks and Hispanics, the great majority of their wealth was in their house, while whites also had significant portions of their wealth in stocks and mutual funds and 401(k) or individual retirement accounts, all of which rebounded significantly since the recession, while house prices remained low. Recall that earlier in this chapter, we pointed out that people in lower-income quintiles tended to have most of their wealth in houses and less in stocks and other securities. So we can expect that an analysis of the impact of the Great Recession on people in different income quintiles would find the lower quintiles to suffer more from the erosion of wealth than those in higher quintiles. To assess this, the Pew Research Center also examined the share of wealth for the wealthiest 10% of households and found that it rose to 56% from 49% during this time. Controlling for the effects of racial or ethnic group, the share for the wealthiest 10% of households increased. For Hispanics, the share of the wealthiest rose from 56% to 72%; for blacks it rose from 59% to 67%.

Is Inequality Bad for All?

This chapter has focused on inequalities and the consequences for individuals. Clearly, inequality has far better consequences for the rich and powerful than it has for the poor. However, Kate Pickett and Richard Wilkinson (2009) make an intriguing argument that inequality is not just bad for the poor but bad for everyone. They examine a range of measures of social well-being as a function of the amount of inequality found in different states in the United States and in different countries around the world. They find that greater inequality is associated with lower life expectancy, lower women's status, lower trust, increased infant mortality, higher dropout rates, greater childhood obesity, higher teen pregnancy rates, higher imprisonment rates, and higher homicide rates. For example, FIGURE 7-27 shows a tendency for life expectancy to be lower in countries with greater income inequality. Their argument is that even the wealthy in a society benefit when living conditions improve for the poor and for society as a whole. Everyone becomes less likely to become victims of crime, and the taxes needed to address such social problems can be less. Critics have raised varying objections to the book, including its lack of sophisticated statistics (Kay 2009) and inconsistent support for the book's thesis from other studies (Sargent 2009).

Is inequality bad for all?
© 2007 Andy Singer/Politicalcartoons.com

Economic Growth

The focus of this chapter has been on inequality in stratification systems, or how the "pie" is divided. But another fair question related to stratification systems is

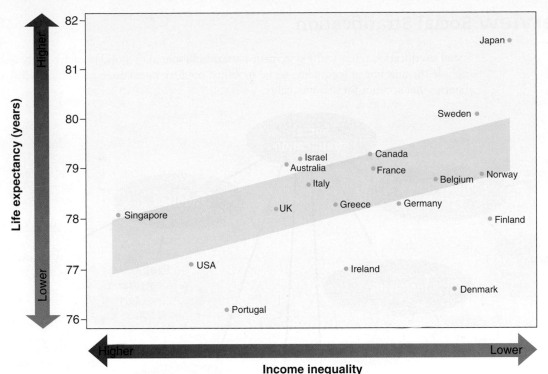

FIGURE 7-27 Life expectancy in years by income inequality in different countries.
Source: Adapted from Pickett, Kate and Wilkinson, Richard. 2009. The Spirit Level: Why Greater Equality Makes Societies Stronger. *New York: Bloomsbury Press.*

how big the pie should be. Many researchers and authors question whether the United States or any country can sustain the emphasis on consumerism and material wealth that dominates modern life. Their argument is that our race to achieve the American Dream of upward social mobility has led to an emphasis on consumption that leads people to work harder and faster while feeling less satisfied and more insecure than previous generations (DeGraaf, Waan, and Naylor 2002). For example, a study by Sayer and Mattingly (2006) found that Americans feel they are more rushed and have less free time than did similar respondents 30 years ago. This rush to have more and more not only leaves people unsatisfied but also endangers the environment. Our production system is designed to be linear, from raw materials to manufacturing to consumption, with products often designed to wear out or break and be thrown out, only to be replaced with others. Thus, the more we consume the more we use up natural resources and endanger our environment (The Story of Stuff Project 2009). We discuss this issue further in the chapter on Work and the Economy.

CONCEPT LEARNING CHECK 7.8 The Future of Stratification in the United States

During the past few years, which of the following changes in the US stratification system are true and which are false?

_____ 1. Inequality has continued to decrease gradually as the middle class catches up with the upper classes.

_____ 2. Overall wealth has increased relatively uniformly for all social classes, leading to few or no changes in inequality.

_____ 3. The share of the overall wealth increased from 8% to 23% for the top 1% of earners between 1980 and 2007.

_____ 4. Pickett and Wilkinson (2009) argue that greater equality leads to improvements in a broad range of social indicators of well-being for everyone in the society, not just those in the lower classes.

_____ 5. Robert Reich argues that increases in inequality in the past few years are slowing down and are likely to be reversed dramatically in the near-term future.

Visual Overview Social Stratification

Social stratification refers to the systematic patterns of inequality found in each society. Issues include the amount of inequality, social mobility, poverty, consequences of inequality, and theories that account for that inequality.

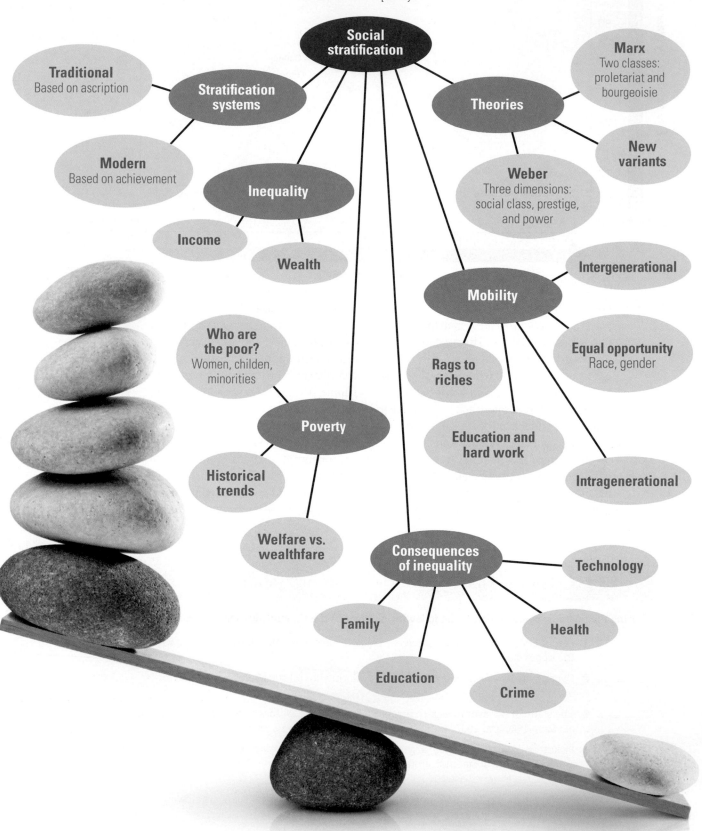

Social stratification

Stratification systems
- **Traditional** Based on ascription
- **Modern** Based on achievement

Inequality
- Income
- Wealth

Theories
- **Marx** Two classes: proletariat and bourgeoisie
- **New variants**
- **Weber** Three dimensions: social class, prestige, and power

Mobility
- Intergenerational
- Equal opportunity Race, gender
- Rags to riches
- Education and hard work
- Intragenerational

Poverty
- **Who are the poor?** Women, childen, minorities
- Historical trends
- Welfare vs. wealthfare

Consequences of inequality
- Family
- Education
- Crime
- Technology
- Health

Visual Summary Class and Stratification in the United States

7.1 Social Stratification Overview

- Social stratification systems characterize all societies.
- Stratification is a characteristic of the society, not single individuals.
- Stratification systems persist from one generation to the next.
- Stratification systems are justified by ideologies.

7.2 Social Stratification Systems

- Social stratification systems have evolved from closed systems to more modern open systems.
- Lenski and Lenski (1982) argue inequality increased as the complexity of societies increased.
- Traditional stratification systems, such as caste, clan, and estate systems, depend primarily on ascribed statuses.
- Modern stratification systems rely primarily on achieved statuses.

7.3 Sociological Perspectives on Social Stratification

- Functional theory argues stratification performs important functions needed for societies to survive.
- Conflict theory argues stratification persists because it helps powerful people maintain the status quo.
- Marx developed the conflict perspective, arguing that much of human history has been the result of class conflict between the bourgeoisie and the proletariat.
- Eric Wright updated and expanded conflict theory to also include two additional categories: the petty bourgeoisie and managers.
- Unlike Marx, who believed only the economic dimension is important for stratification, Max Weber (1922) argued there are three important dimensions: class, prestige, and power.
- The social interactionist perspective looks at how individuals perceive, report, and define their own social class; finding a tendency to claim higher status than people actually have, to overestimate middle class membership, and to underestimate the amount of inequality in the United States.

7.4 Inequality in the United States: Income and Wealth

- Income and wealth are the two most common measures of inequality and both are distributed very unevenly in the United States.
- Wealth is distributed much more unevenly than income.
- In recent years, inequality in both wealth and income have been increasing in the United States.

7.5 Social Mobility: The Myth and the Reality

- Social mobility in the United States is fairly common but usually leads to moderate net changes up or down both from one generation to the next and within a person's lifetime.
- The "rags to riches" American Dream happens only infrequently, but most people experience at least modest upward mobility during their lifetime.

- An important source of social mobility is structural mobility, in which the types of jobs available change.
- Upward mobility is harder for some categories of people such as minorities and women but is more possible for people who work hard to achieve an education.

7.6 Poverty in the United States

- Poverty is measured in the United States by the poverty line (three times the amount a family would be expected to spend for food).
- Poverty dropped dramatically in the United States during the 1960s but has remained relatively stable or increased somewhat since then.
- Children, minorities, women, and residents of inner cities or poor rural counties are more likely to be poor.

- Several myths persist about poverty, including the notion that poverty is always a permanent state from which people cannot escape.
- Consideration of whether welfare devotes too much of society's resources to the poor should be considered in light of ways in which those resources are also provided to the rich in the form of wealthfare.

7.7 Why Class Matters

- Social class affects life chances, not just life styles.

- Social class influences many important life chances including family, education, crime, health, and technology.

7.8 Summing Up: Social Stratification in the United States Now and in the Future

- Recent trends reverse a long-term tendency toward greater equality in the United States with clearly negative consequences for all but the most wealthy, and—some argue—even negative impacts for the most wealthy.

© Alex Wong/Getty Images/iStock

© Joe Belanger/Shutterstock, Inc.

Courtesy of Jocelyn Augustino/FEMA

© Kurhan/Shutterstock, Inc.

7.1 Social Stratification Overview

1. Which of these is *not* a principle of stratification systems?
   A. Stratification is universal but varied.
   B. Stratification is supported by beliefs.
   C. Stratification is a characteristic of individuals.
   D. Stratification is carried over from one generation to the next.

2. Which is *not* true of the relationship between ideologies and stratification?
   A. They are used to justify stratification.
   B. They may be based on personal merit.
   C. They legitimize the existing social order.
   D. They play no role in stratification.

7.2 Social Stratification Systems

3. Modern systems of stratification:
   A. include caste systems.
   B. are based on ascribed social positions.
   C. are only found in a few countries.
   D. are based on achieved social positions.

4. Which is *not* true of a caste system?
   A. A person is born into her or his social position.
   B. A person's social position is irrevocable.
   C. Exogamy (marriage outside one's caste) is often used to forge alliances.
   D. Members of castes are often expected to have particular occupations.

7.3 Sociological Perspectives on Social Stratification

5. Buying a huge house and driving an expensive car are examples of:
   A. cultural capital.
   B. conspicuous consumption.
   C. status consistency.
   D. social power.

6. Which of the following are concepts found in Marx's conflict theory?
   A. Petty bourgeoisie
   B. Prestige
   C. Proletariat
   D. Cultural capital

7. What group of people would be examples of petty bourgeoisie?
   A. A physician who is a part owner of a medical practice
   B. Bill Gates, one of the founders of Microsoft
   C. A professional football player
   D. A manager at McDonald's

7.4 Inequality in the United States: Income and Wealth

8. When the income distribution in the United States during 1979 is compared with 2009, we see that:
   A. all quintiles gained in relative share of total income between 1979 and 2009.
   B. the lower three income categories gained relative share.
   C. only the top quintile gained in relative share of income.
   D. the top three income categories increased moderately in their relative share.

9. Given that some assets are distributed more unevenly than others and that the largest drop in value during the Great Recession of 2006 to 2009 was in housing prices, this implies:
   A. all social classes were likely hurt the same amount by the recession.
   B. the more affluent were likely hurt more by the recession because they tend to have bigger houses.
   C. the less affluent were likely hurt more by the recession because their share of wealth in their homes is larger than their share of other assets.
   D. all people were hurt very little by the recession because homes are not a big part of their wealth.

7.5 Social Mobility: The Myth and the Reality

10. The probability of a child ending up in the same income quintile as her parents is greatest for which two quintiles?
    A. The lowest and second-lowest quintiles
    B. The highest and second-highest quintiles
    C. The middle quintile and the one just above it
    D. The lowest and highest quintiles

7.6 Poverty in the United States

11. In the three-year study of the permanence of poverty by Anderson (2011), the proportion of people who were poor only part of the three years was how big compared to the proportion who were poor the entire three years?

- **A.** 5x
- **B.** 10x
- **C.** 20x
- **D.** 30x

12. If the average cost to feed a family of four for a year is $8,000, then, according to the US government definition of the poverty threshold, a family of four would be living in poverty if they made less than how much each year?

- **A.** $8,000
- **B.** $16,000
- **C.** $24,000
- **D.** $32,000

7.7 Why Class Matters

13. Which of the following lists contains only measures of life chances, not life styles?

- **A.** A place to live, wearing designer clothes
- **B.** Favorite sports, access to a gym
- **C.** Internet access, expected highest education obtained
- **D.** Rate of coronary heart disease, membership in a country club

7.8 Summing Up: Social Stratification in the United States Now and in the Future

14. Which of the following best describes the impact of the Great Recession on different groups of people in the United States?

- **A.** It affected people in different income quintiles and blacks and whites about the same.
- **B.** It affected people in all categories much the same.
- **C.** It affected whites worse than blacks, closing the gap in wealth differences between the races considerably.
- **D.** It affected blacks worse than whites, further widening the wealth differences based on race.

15. Pickett and Wilkinson argue, in *The Spirit Level*, that greater inequality:

- **A.** raises the spirit of people as a whole.
- **B.** leads to greater economic productivity and innovation.
- **C.** is bad for society in general and hurts even those at the highest ends as well as the poor.
- **D.** is the inevitable result of high rates of alcoholism.

CHAPTER ESSAY QUESTIONS

1. Write a few sentences identifying the three dimensions in Weber's view of stratification and the measure most often used to assess social inequality from this perspective.

2. Takeshi graduated from college with an engineering degree and was hired by a large corporation. However, Takeshi's company closed its US headquarters and laid off all the members of Takeshi's design team. Takeshi has taken a temporary job as a substitute teacher at the local high school, hoping this will feed his family until the economy gets better. Identify three types of mobility illustrated by this example and justify your answer.

3. Imagine that you are in the lowest income quintile and your identical twin is in the highest income quintile. List at least three health-related measures for which your twin is likely to have much more desirable outcomes than you.

4. Michael is a black male 16-year-old living in a suburb with his divorced mom. Do you expect he will be living in poverty? What are two factors that increase his chances of being poor? What are two factors that decrease his chances of being poor?

5. Your friend is having an argument with you about the distribution of wealth in the United States. To support her argument that inequalities are relatively small, she mentions the distribution of income and houses. What other financial assets does she not talk about? Are those assets distributed as evenly as these two? Finally, is inequality as measured by income increasing or decreasing?

CHAPTER DISCUSSION QUESTIONS

1. Given the amount of inequality in the United States and the amount of social mobility, do you think the United States would be a better or a worse place if there was less inequality? Is some inequality a good thing (as functionalists argue)?

2. Many people are surprised at how many people experience occasional poverty (28.9% in a three-year period) and how few remain poor the entire time (2.8% during that three-year period). What does this imply for social policy regarding welfare? For example, does welfare as a strategy to help people get out of poverty make more sense given how few remain in poverty?

3. What do you think our stratification system will look like in the future? Do you think there will be greater inequality? Less? Why?

4. Given all the people who lost jobs in the Great Recession and who became poor as a result, does this change your attitude about welfare? For example, are people made poor in a recession less to blame for being poor and more deserving of help?

5. The consequences of social class for important life chances of individuals include big differences in health and mortality outcomes. Given those effects, does this make it even more important that people have equal opportunity to get ahead?

6. If failure was not an option what would you like to do and accomplish throughout your life? What is keeping you from doing these things today? How are your limitations related to your ascribed statuses? Compare your answers with your colleagues.

7. Share with the class your definition of the American Dream. How confident are you that you will be able to achieve the American Dream? How do your viewpoints differ or concur with your colleagues? Discuss how cultural capital, life chances, and structural mobility all affect social mobility.

8. Based on the measures of socioeconomic status (occupational prestige, income and education attainment) discuss occupations where individuals might not experience status consistency.

9. Provide examples of conspicuous consumption and then discuss how these actually benefit the bourgeoisie (capitalist owners of the means of production) and maintain false consciousness.

10. Discuss the advantages of home ownership for the middle class. With the spike in foreclosures during the Great Recession, how did this affect wealth, intragenerational and intergenerational mobility? Do you have a personal example(s) to share with the class?

11. What kind of social issues might income and wealth inequality create in the United States? What problems, consequences, or reactions have you already observed in the last few years?

12. Discuss benefits to the US government and politicians when the poverty line is primarily based on food expenditures rather than for example housing expenditures.

13. How would a functionalist sociologist view wealthfare as opposed to a conflict sociologist?

CHAPTER PROJECTS

INDIVIDUAL PROJECTS

1. Create a budget that includes typical monthly expenditures based on minimum wage earnings (go online to find the minimum wage for your state of residence). Did this exercise affirm your thinking about the working poor or are you surprised at the level of financial difficulty people face? Next, go online to learn about executive pay or executive compensation. What is your viewpoint about the income disparities that exist today among the middle and lower classes and top corporate executives? Write an analysis of your findings and also incorporate information from the chapter.

2. Write a self-reflection paper that includes your experiences related to your social class status when you were growing up. Reflecting back on your childhood how do you think your family, neighborhood, and schools compared to what you now know about social class and information from the section titled: "Why Class Matters." What values do you hold as an adult that are connected to your social class upbringing?

3. Volunteer at a food bank or homeless shelter in your community. Look around while you are there. Try to understand a little bit what it is like for some of the people who go there for help. Think about the kinds of people you see there and those you do *not* see there. Can you see any patterns, such as children, minorities, and women being more likely to need assistance? Do you see any problems with the way these services are delivered or have any ideas of how they could be improved?

GROUP PROJECTS

4. Brainstorm with your colleagues and write a list of examples how the mass media maintains cultural values related to meritocracy and the Horatio Alger myth. Next, write a list of examples how the mass media constructs stereotypes about the different social classes in the United States. What patterns emerged from your two lists? Report and explain your findings using one of the three perspectives on social inequality (functional, conflict, or interactionist perspectives).

5. Go online to learn more about the works of William Julius Wilson and Oscar Lewis. Discuss the opposing explanations of poverty and how these effect political policies and social programs. Include in your discussion how the general public views the causes of poverty and how these may affect voting patterns or trends. Write an analysis based on your group discussion.

CHAPTER KEY TERMS

Absolute poverty
Achieved social statuses
Ascribed social statuses
Bourgeoisie
Capitalists
Caste system
Clan system
Class (social class)
Class system
Conspicuous consumption
Cultural capital
Culture of poverty
Digital divide
Estate system
False consciousness

Feminization of poverty
Income
Intergenerational mobility
Intragenerational mobility
Just-world hypothesis
Life chances
Life styles
Managers
Means of production
Meritocracy
Net financial assets
Net worth
Petty bourgeoisie
Poverty line or poverty threshold
Power

Prestige
Proletariat
Relative poverty
Social mobility
Socioeconomic status (SES)
Social stratification system
Status consistency
Structural mobility
Underclass
Vertical social mobility
Wealth
Wealthfare
Workers
Working poor

7.1 Characteristics of Stratification Systems

1. Stratification is universal but varied. [C. Some stratification systems are based primarily on inherited statuses, while others are based primarily on achieved statuses such as education and occupation.]

2. Stratification is supported by beliefs. [A. "No man suffers from poverty unless it be more than his fault—unless it be his sin." —preacher/Social Darwinist Henry Ward Beecher]

3. Stratification is a characteristic of the entire society. [B. In the United States, most racial and ethnic minorities tend to have lower incomes than white non–Hispanics.]

4. Stratification is carried over from one generation to the next. [D. The likelihood a child will grow up to be in the top 20% of the US population as measured by income is far greater if his or her parents are in the top 20% today.]

7.2 Common Social Stratification Systems

1. Caste system [B. Birthright is the sole basis for social position in this system. C. This system is very high on consistency among a person's statuses. G. People are expected to marry within their own group in this stratification system.]

2. Meritocracy [A. Getting ahead in this society is solely based on how hard the individual is willing to work and their own innate ability. E. This is an ideal-typical stratification system that is unlikely to be found in practice. H. A person's social status in this system is primarily affected by achieved statuses such as education, occupation, and income.]

3. Class system [D. This is the stratification system that characterizes most modern societies. H. A person's social status in this system is primarily affected by achieved statuses such as education, occupation, and income.]

4. Clan system [B. Birthright is the sole basis for social position in this system. F. Marrying outside one's own group (exogamy) can be a way to get ahead in this stratification system.]

7.3 How Do Sociological Theories Explain Stratification?

Concepts and theorists illustrated by each of the following passages of text are as follows:

- Fernando just graduated from college and was hired to be an entry-level manager at a startup webpage design firm in a large Midwestern city: Marx—social class and proletariat; Wright—manager

- He is proud of his recent MBA and his new position, but his salary is not as high as he had hoped given the difficult economy: Weber—prestige, status inconsistency, social class

- He hopes to receive stock options to eventually become rich; Marx—bourgeoisie

- One thing that worries him a bit is that it is a very small company and he spends social time with the owner/founders: Wright—petty bourgeoisie; Bourdieu—elite

- He does not seem to fit in well with them, since they are from wealthy families and grew up going to private schools and then Ivy League universities. They are always talking about music he is not familiar with and plays and books that he has only read about in the paper: Bourdieu—cultural capital, elite
- He is trying to learn more about the arts so he can participate more in their lunchtime conversations: Bourdieu—cultural capital, elite
- They do not seem interested in the sports events and movies he attends: Bourdieu—masses

7.4 Income and Wealth Inequality

1. [F] The top 5% of income earners account for 22% of total income.
2. [T] The top 5% of income earners saw a 5% increase in the percent of total income they received between 1979 and 2009.
3. [T] The share of total income for the top 5% of people in 2009 was greater than the combined incomes of the lowest 50% of people.
4. [F] Between 1979 and 2009, the only quintile that gained in their relative share of income was the bottom fifth.
5. [F] The average pay of CEOs as a multiple of the average worker's pay since 2003 has been lower in the United States than in Europe.
6. [T] The average pay of CEOs as a multiple of the average worker's pay since 2003 has been 300 or more.
7. [T] Wealth is distributed more unevenly than income in the United States.
8. [T] A large portion of the wealth possessed by most Americans is their home or principal place of residence.
9. [T] The bottom 80% of the US population collectively owns 7% of the net financial assets while the top 1% owns 43% of them.

7.5 Social Mobility: Realistic Expectations

1. Factors helping Noah: He is getting a higher education, he is male. Factors hurting Noah: He is black, his parents are in the lowest income quintile.
2. Factors helping Shana: No factors are helping her. Factors hurting Shana: She is black, her parent is in the lowest income quintile, she is female, and she is dropping out.
3. Additional information needed about Jonathan: his race and whether he will get more education. Factors Jonathan could change that could help: he can get more education. Factors helping Jonathan that he cannot change: His parents are in the highest income quintile, he is a male, and he is white.

7.6 Poverty: Who Are the Poor?

1. [A. 12-year-old child in a single-parent family] Children are more likely to be poor than anyone over 18.

2. [A. 50-year-old man] Older adults are less likely to be poor than people 18 to 64, and with Social Security and Medicare, they have a stronger safety net to prevent poverty than people still working.
3. [B. white non–Hispanic man] Members of minorities are more likely to be poor.
4. [A. Someone who was poor last year] While many leave poverty, people who were recently poor or in low-income categories barely over the poverty line are more likely to be poor than others.
5. [A. Someone living in a rural area] People in inner cities and rural areas are more likely to be poor than people in the suburbs.

7.7 Consequences of Social Class: By the Numbers

1. How many years longer a man is expected to live who obtains a bachelor's degree compared to a man who does not finish high school [G. 7]
2. Percentage of US college graduates who use the Internet regularly [E. 93%]
3. Percentage of people with less than a high school education who use the Internet regularly [B. 40%]
4. Percentage of 12th graders in low-SES families expecting to earn graduate or professional degrees [A. 22%]
5. Percentage of 12th graders in high-SES families expecting to earn graduate or professional degrees [C. 53%]
6. Percentage of women with less than a high school education who were unmarried when their first child was born [D. 64%]
7. How many years longer a woman is expected to live whose income is greater than four times the poverty level, compared to a woman whose income is below the poverty level [H. 7]
8. How many times more likely is chronic illness for someone whose income is below the poverty level compared to someone making over four times the poverty level [F. 3]

7.8 The Future of Stratification in the United States

1. [F] Inequality has continued to decrease gradually as the middle class catches up with the upper classes.
2. [F] Overall wealth has increased relatively uniformly for all social classes, leading to few or no changes in inequality.
3. [T] The share of the overall wealth increased from 8% to 23% for the top 1% of earners between 1980 and 2007.
4. [T] Pickett and Wilkinson (2009) argue that greater equality leads to improvements in a broad range of social indicators of well-being for everyone in the society, not just those in the lower classes.
5. [F] Robert Reich argues that increases in inequality in the past few years are slowing down and are likely to be reversed dramatically in the near-term future.

ANSWERS TO CHAPTER REVIEW TEST

7.1 Social Stratification Overview

1. C. Stratification is a characteristic of societies, not individuals.
2. D. Ideologies help justify stratification systems and legitimize the existing social order and are often based on personal merit.

7.2 Social Stratification Systems

3. D. While traditional stratification systems are based on ascribed statuses, modern systems emphasize achievement.
4. C. Marriage outside one's caste is typically forbidden.

7.3 Sociological Perspectives on Social Stratification

5. B. Conspicuous consumption is the visible display of wealth.
6. C. Marx focused on class conflict between the proletariat and the bourgeoisie. The other three concepts are found in other theories of stratification.
7. A. Petty bourgeoisie typically own or partially own a business and also work there themselves.

7.4 Inequality in the United States: Income and Wealth

8. C. The four lower quintiles all lost relative share of income.
9. C. For the less affluent, their primary asset is usually their homes, which lost value during this period.

7.5 Social Mobility: The Myth and the Reality

10. D. Part of the reason may be that for these extreme quintiles, they cannot move to a more extreme quintile and can only move in one direction.

7.6 Poverty in the United States

11. B. Ten times as many people were temporarily poor as were poor the entire period.
12. C. The poverty threshold is three times the cost of feeding the household.

7.7 Why Class Matters

13. C. Life chances refer to important consequential issues such as health rather than discretionary activities such as a favorite sport.

7.8 Summing Up: Social Stratification in the United States Now and in the Future

14. D. The less affluent typically are affected more by recessions, and blacks are less affluent than whites in general.
15. C. Social problems for individuals such as the poor cost society as a whole, including those who are more affluent, who pay more in taxes, or who may be victimized by crime.

ANSWERS TO CHAPTER ESSAY QUESTIONS

1. The three dimensions Weber discusses are social class, prestige, and power. Socioeconomic status is the most common way to assess inequality consistent with Weber's perspective.
2. Intragenerational mobility, downward mobility, structural mobility. These changes occurred within a single generation. Losing his job and taking a less prestigious job marks downward mobility, and closing companies removes jobs, creating structural mobility.
3. Life expectancy; infant mortality; rates of diabetes; rate of coronary heart disease; self-reported fair or poor health; chronic illness; children in poor health. All of these conditions are related to income, with poorer outcomes found for the less affluent.
4. The answer can be either yes or no regarding whether he is expected to be poor. Factors reducing his chances of being poor are that he is male and lives in a suburb. Factors increasing his chances of being poor are that he is black, 16 years old, and lives with his divorced mom.
5. Assets not talked about include life insurance, deposits, and pension accounts, non-home real estate, trusts, stocks and mutual funds, business equity, and financial securities. Those other assets are distributed more unevenly than income and houses. Inequality as measured by income has been increasing in recent years.

REFERENCES

Anderson, Robin J. 2011. "Dynamics of Economic Well-Being: Poverty, 2004–2006." *Current Population Reports*, pp 70–123. Washington, DC: US Census Bureau. Available from: http://www.census.gov/hhes/www/poverty/publications/dynamics04/P70-123.pdf.

Anderson, S., J. Cavanagh, C. Collins, M. Lapham, and S. Pizzigati. 2008. *Executive Excess 2008: The 15th Annual CEO Compensation Survey*. Washington, DC: Institute for Policy Studies/United for a Fair Economy.

Biography.com. 2011. *Sonia Sotomayor Biography*. Available from: http://www.biography.com/articles/Sonia-Sotomayor-453906.

Blau, Peter M. and Otis Dudley Duncan. 1967. *The American Occupational Structure*. New York: Wiley.

Boone, Louis E., David L. Kurtz, and C. Patrick Fleenor. 1988. "CEOs: Early Signs of a Business Career. *Business Horizons*, 31(5):20–25.

Bourdieu, Pierre. 1984. *Distinction: A Social Critique of the Judgment of Taste*, Richard Nice (translator). Boston: Harvard University Press.

Braun, Denny. 1997. *The Rich Get Richer*. Chicago: Nelson-Hall.

Braverman, Harry. 1974. *Labor and Monopoly Capital: The Degradation of Labor in the Twentieth Century*. New York: Monthly Review.

Briggs, X. 2006. "After Katrina: Rebuilding Lives and Places." *City & Community* 5(2):119–128.

Chantril, Christopher. 2011. *Estimated vs. Actual Federal Spending for Fiscal Year 2011 from Federal Budgets*. Available from: usgovernmentspending.com. www.usgovernmentspending.com/budget_news.

Cookson, Peter W., Jr. and Caroline Hodges Persell. 2005. "Preparing for Power: Cultural Capital and Elite Boarding Schools." Pp. 175–185 in *Life in Society: Readings to Accompany Sociology: A Down-to-Earth Approach*. Seventh Edition, edited by James M. Henslin. Boston: Allyn and Bacon.

Davis, Kingsley and Wilbert E. Moore. 1945. "Some Principles of Stratification." *American Sociological Review* 10(April):242–249.

DeGraaf, John, David Waan, and Thomas Naylor. 2002. *Affluenza: The All-Consuming Epidemic*. San Francisco: Berrett-Koehler.

DeMott, Benjamin. 1990. "The Myth of Classlessness." The *New York Times*, Oct. 10.

DeNavas-Walt, Bernadette Proctor Carmen, and Jessica Smith. 2009. *Income, Poverty, and Health Insurance Coverage in the United States: 2009*. US Census Bureau. Available from: www.census.gov/prod/2010pubs/p60-238.pdf.

Domhoff, G. William. 2011. *Who Rules America?* Whorulesamerica.net. Available from: http://sociology.ucsc.edu/whorulesamerica/.

Frank, Robert, Amir Efrati, Aaron Lucchetti, and Chad Bray. 2009. "Madoff Jailed after Admitting Epic Scam." *The Wall Street Journal,* March 13, 2009. Available from: http://online.wsj.com/article/SB123685693449906551.html.

Fussell, Paul. 1983. *Class: A Guide Through the American Status System*. New York: Simon and Schuster.

Gans, Herbert. 1971. "The Uses of Poverty: The Poor Pay All." *Social Policy* 2(July–Aug):20–24.

Gleckman, Howard. 2011. "Tom Coburn: Tax Subsidies Are Socialism." *Forbes*. July 19, 2011. Available from: http://blogs.forbes.com/beltway/2011/07/19/tom-coburn-tax-subsidies-are-socialism/.

Gottschalk, Peter, Sara McLanahan, and Gary Sandefur. 1994. "The Dynamics and Intergenerational Transmission of Poverty and Welfare Participation. Pp. 85–108 in *Confronting Poverty: Prescriptions for Change*, edited by Sheldon H. Danziger, Gary D. Sandefur, and Daniel H. Weinberg. Cambridge, MA: Harvard University Press.

Government Accountability Office (GAO). 2011. *Federal Reserve System: Opportunities Exist to Strengthen Policies and Processes for Managing Emergency Assistance*. GAO-11-696 July 21, 2011. Available from: http://www.gao.gov/products/GAO-11-696.

Gross, Jane. 2003. "Right School for a 4-Year-Old? Find an Adviser." *The New York Times*, May 28. Available from: http://www.nytimes.com/2003/05/28/nyregion/right-school-for-4-year-old-find-an-adviser.html?pagewanted=all&src=pm.

Harrington, Michael. 1962. *The Other America: Poverty in the United States*. New York: Macmillan.

Hill, Napoleon. 1953. *Think and Grow Rich*. Cleveland, OH: Ralston Publishing Co.

Katz, Michael B. 1989. *The Undeserving Poor: From the War on Poverty to the War on Welfare*. New York: Pantheon Books.

Kay, John. 2009. "The Spirit Level (review)." *Financial Times*. March 23, 2009. Available from: http://www.ft.com/cms/s/2/77b1bd26-14db-11de-8cd1-0000779fd2ac.html.

Kerbo, Harold R. 1983. *Social Stratification and Inequality*. New York: McGraw-Hill.

Kessler, Glenn. 2011. "Revisiting the Cost of the Bush Tax Cuts." *The Washington Post*. Available from: http://www.washingtonpost.com/blogs/fact-checker/post/revisiting-the-cost-of-the-bush-tax-cuts/2011/05/09/AFxTFtbG_blog.html.

Kochhar, R., R. Fry, and P. Taylor. 2011. "Wealth Gaps Rise to Record Highs between Whites, Blacks, and Hispanics." *Pew Research Center Social & Demographic Trends*. July 26, 2011. Available from: http://www.pewsocialtrends.org/files/2011/07/SDT-Wealth-Report_7-26-11_FINAL.pdf.

Kohn, Melvin L. 1977. *Class and Conformity: A Study in Values*. Second edition. Homewood, IL: Dorsey Press.

Kurz, Karin and Walter Muller. 1987. "Class Mobility in the Industrial World." *Annual Review of Sociology* (August):18(14):203–225.

Kuznets, Simon. 1955. "Economic Growth and Income Inequality." *The American Economic Review* XLV(1, March):1–28.

—————.1966. *Modern Economic Growth: Rate, Structure, and Spread*. New Haven, CO: Yale University Press.

Lareau, Annette. 2002. "Invisible Inequality: Social Class and Childrearing in Black Families and White Families." *American Sociological Review* 67(October):747–776.

Lenski, Gerhard and Jean Lenski. 1982. *Human Societies: An Introduction to Macrosociology*. Fourth Edition. New York: McGraw-Hill.

Lerner, Melvin. 1980. *The Belief in a Just World: A Fundamental Delusion*. New York: Plenum Press.

Lewis, Oscar. 1961. *The Children of Sanchez*. New York: Random House.

Logan, J. R. 2006. *The Impact of Katrina: Race and Class in Storm-Damaged Neighborhoods (Hurricane Katrina Project, Initiative on Spatial Structures in the Social Sciences)*. Providence, RI: Brown University.

Mantsios, Gregory. 1995. "Class in America: Myths and Realities." Pp. 131–143 in *Race, Class, and Gender in the United States: An Integrated Study*, Third Edition, edited by Paula S. Rothenberg. New York: St. Martin's Press.

Marx, Karl. [1844] 1964. "Contribution to the Critique of Hegel's Philosophy of Right." Pp. 261–313 in *Karl Marx: Early Writings*, edited by T. B. Bottomore. New York: McGraw-Hill.

Mazumder, Bashkar. 2008. *Upward Intergenerational Economic Mobility in the United States*. Economic Mobility Project, May. Available from: http://www.economicmobility.org/assets/pdfs/Upward_Fig_1.pdf.

Mills, C. Wright. 1956. *The Power Elite*. Oxford, UK: Oxford University Press.

National Opinion Research Center (NORC). 2011. *General Social Survey Codebook*. Available from: http://publicdata.norc.org:41000/gss/documents//BOOK/GSS_Codebook.pdf.

Newman, Katherine. 1993. *Declining Fortunes: The Withering of the American Dream*. New York: Harper & Row.

Norton, M. I., and D. Ariely. 2011. "Building a Better America—One Wealth Quintile at a Time." *Perspectives on Psychological Science* 6(9):9–12.

O'Hare, William P. 1996. "A New Look at Poverty in America." *Population Bulletin* 51(2):1–47.

Olsen, Marvin E. 1990. "The Affluent Prosper While Everyone Else Struggles." *Sociological Focus* 23(2):73–87.

Pew Internet and American Life Project. 2010. *Demographics of Internet Users*. Available from: http://pewinternet.org/~/media/Files/Reports/2012/PIP_Digital_differences_041312.pdf

Pickett, Kate and Richard Wilkinson. 2009. *The Spirit Level: Why Greater Equality Makes Societies Stronger*. New York: Bloomsbury Press.

Pogol, Gina. 2010. "Will Congress Phase Out the Mortgage Interest Deduction?" HSH.COM. Aug 19, 2010. Available from: http://library.hsh.com/articles/government-programs/will-congress-phase-out-the-mortgage-interest-deduction.html.

Reich, Robert. 2009. "Foreward." Pp. iii-vi in *The Spirit Level: Why Greater Equality Makes Societies Stronger*, edited by Kate Pickett and Richard Wilkinson. New York: Bloomsbury Press.

Robert Wood Johnson Foundation. 2008. *Overcoming Obstacles to Health: Report from the Robert Wood Johnson Foundation to the Commission to Build a Healthier America*. Available from: http://www.rwjf.org/files/research/obstaclestohealth.pdf.

Ruggles, Patricia. 1989. *Short and Long Term Poverty in the United States: Measuring the American Underclass*. Washington, DC: Urban Institute.

Ryan, William. 1976. *Blaming the Victim*. New York: Vintage Books.

Sanders, Bernie. 2011. *The Fed Audit*. July 21, 2011. Available from: http://sanders.senate.gov/imo/media/doc/GAO%20Fed%20Investigation.pdf.

Sargent, Michael. 2009. "Why Inequality is Fatal." *Nature* 458(7242):1109–1110. doi:10.1038/4581109a.

Sawhill, Isabel V. 1988. "Poverty in the U.S.: Why Is It So Persistent?" *Journal of Economic Literature* 26(3):1073–1119.

Sayer, Liana C. and Maribeth Mattingly. 2006. "Under Pressure: Gender Differences in the Relationship Between Free Time and Feeling Rushed." *Journal of Marriage and Family* 68(1):205–221.

Sennett, Richard and Jonathan Cobb. 1988. "Some Hidden Injuries of Class." Pp. 278–288 in *Down to Earth Sociology*, Fifth Edition, edited by James M. Henslin. New York: Free Press.

Sharkey, P. 2007. "Survival and Death in New Orleans: An Empirical Look at the Human Impact of Katrina." *Journal of Black Studies* 37:482. Available from: http://jbs.sagepub.com/cgi/content/abstract/37/4/482.

Smith, Aaron. 2010. *Home Broadband 2010*. Pew Internet & American Life Project. Available from: http://pewinternet.org/Reports/2010/Home-Broadband-2010.aspx

The Story of Stuff Project. 2009. *The Story of Stuff*. April 22, 2009. Available from: http://www.youtube.com/storyofstuffproject#p/u/22/9GorqroigqM.

Thornberry, Terence P., and Margaret Farnsworth. 1982. "Social Correlates of Criminal Involvement: Further Evidence on the Relationship Between Social Status and Criminal Behavior." *American Sociological Review* 47(4):505–518.

Tumin, Melvin M. 1953. "Some Principles of Stratification. A Critical Analysis." *American Sociological Review* 18(Aug):387–394.

————. 1985. *Social Stratification*. Second Edition. Englewood Cliffs, NJ: Prentice-Hall.

US Census. 2000. *Marital Status of Women 15 to 44 Years Old at First Birth by Selected Characteristics: 1990–94*. Statistical Abstract of the United States 2000. Washington DC: US Government Printing Office.

US Census Bureau. 2009. *Tables H-2 and H-3. Share of Aggregate Income Received by Each Fifth and Top 5 Percent of Households, All Races: 1967 to 2009*. Available from: http://www.census.gov/hhes/www/income/data/historical/inequality/.

————. 2011a. *Statistical Abstract of the United States: 2011. Table 720*. Available from: http://www.census.gov/compendia/statab/2011/tables/11s0719.pdf.

————. 2011b. *Statistical Abstract of the United States 2011: Table 702*. Available from: http://www.census.gov/compendia/statab/2011/tables/11s0702.pdf.

US Department of Education. 2005. *Education Longitudinal Study of 2002 (ELS:02/04), First Follow-Up, Student Survey, 2004*, Washington, DC: USDOE. October.

Veblen, Thorstein. [1899] 1953. *The Theory of the Leisure Class*. New York: New American Library.

Weber, Max. [1922] 1978. *Economy and Society*. G. Rogh and C. Wittich (Eds.) Berkeley: University of California Press.

Wilson, Carl. 2007. *Let's Talk About Love: A Journey to the End of Taste*. New York: Continuum.

Wilson, William J. 1987. *The Truly Disadvantaged: the Inner City, the Underclass, and Public Policy*. Chicago: University of Chicago Press.

Wolff, E. N. 2010. "Recent Trends in Household Wealth in the United States: Rising Debt and the Middle-Class Squeeze—an Update to 2007." *Working Paper No. 589*. Annandale-on-Hudson, NY: Levy Economics Institute of Bard College. Available from: http://www.levyinstitute.org/files/download.php?file=wp_589.pdf&pubid=1235.

Wright, Erik Olin. 1985. *Classes*. London: Verso.

Chapter Overview ▼

8 Global Stratification

Learning Objectives ▼

8.1
- Identify world regions that account for the largest share of world GDP.
- Identify a region that is undergoing a dramatic decrease in its share of world GDP as well as one that is experiencing a rapid increase.

8.2
- Identify key differences between countries in different income categories and how this is reflected in migration.

8.3
- Identify four theories of global stratification and what distinguishes them.

8.4
- Identify some of the important trends likely to affect global stratification in the future.

© Israel Leal/AP/Corbis

Mexico City, Mexico. My first visit to another country occurred in the 1980s when I attended a research conference in Acapulco, Mexico. Even in the tourist sections of Acapulco, it was quickly apparent that this was a very different country. There was something about seeing soldiers in uniforms with their automatic rifles at the ready on the beaches and in public areas in the city that suggested a society in which social order was tenuous and might be threatened at any moment. The ramshackle wooden scaffolding and workers scrambling on it to build tall buildings that in the United States would have been built with modern cranes and machinery were more evidence. Of course, I had been reminded by countless friends to "don't drink the water" and so drank only bottled Coca-Cola or alcoholic drinks the entire trip. I could not walk anywhere among the downtown streets without children trying to gain attention to sell silver trinkets costing what seemed to be far less than they would cost back home. But the difference became most obvious when I tried to change my flight reservation. Mysteriously, every time I walked the several blocks to the travel agency to get my ticket changed (this was back in the 1980s before everything was done online), it was locked in the desk of another agent who had just stepped out of the office. The other agents were all smiles and wanted to help, but "no" they could not do anything until the other agent returned. After visiting the office several times over 2 days, it finally dawned on me that they might want a bribe. So in the next visit, once I was told the ticket was locked in yet another desk I politely mentioned that I would be grateful if they could get it done now as I handed over my documents accompanied by a few notes of the local currency. Needless to say that was the last time I had to visit that office.

It is now more than 30 years later, and most of the differences between the United States and Mexico persist. As we will see in this chapter, there are great inequalities between nations of the world. Huge differences in per-capita income are reflected in health, infrastructure, and opportunities. While some theories of global stratification place much of the blame on poor countries and a culture that may slow development, others argue that those inequalities exist in large part because of historical processes in which rich countries have taken advantage of poor countries and forced them into asymmetric relationships that continue to this day.

8.1 Global Stratification Overview

There are extreme inequalities in per-capita income among nations of the world, with per-capita incomes in high-income countries more than 50 times those of low-income countries.

- Identify world regions that account for the largest share of world gross domestic product (GDP).

- Identify a region that is undergoing a dramatic decrease in its share of world GDP as well as one that is experiencing a rapid increase.

Regional Inequalities and Trends

Just as there is a stratification system with dramatic inequality among individuals within nations, there is also a global stratification system with great inequalities among nations. The distribution of world GDP among different regions is both very uneven and undergoing dramatic change. FIGURE 8-1 displays both the current share of world gross domestic product and changes between 1969 and 2009 in shares for five regions: the 15 states in the European Union (EU 15), the United States, Asia/Oceania, Latin America, and the Middle East/Africa. Clearly there is great inequality among nations. In 2009, three regions dominated the world, each producing roughly 26% of world GDP (the EU 15, the United States, and Asia/Oceania), while two other regions (Latin America and the Middle East/Africa) accounted for only about 7% of world GDP each.

When we compare different regions over time, we find dramatic shifts. One region (the EU 15) has seen its share of world GDP drop precipitously from well over one-third

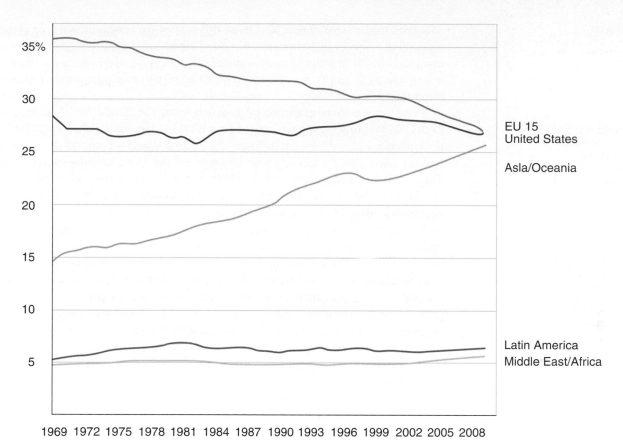

FIGURE 8-1 Share of world gross domestic product (1969–2009).
Source: Data from USDA. 2012. "International Macroeconomic Data Set." Retrieved January 2012 (http://www.ers .usda.gov/datafiles/International_Macroeconomic_Data/Historical_Data_Files/HistoricalRealGDPValues.xls).

of world GDP in 1969 to only slightly more than one-quarter of world GDP in 2009 (Schill, 2009). This drop reflects the economic crisis in the Euro Zone that continues to affect world markets today. A second region (Asia/Oceania) has grown dramatically in its relative share of world GDP, increasing from around 15% in 1969 to slightly more than 25% in 2009. This clearly reflects the ascendency of Asia as reflected in the dramatic expansion of Asian economies, including South Korea, Singapore, and China. During the same period between 1969 and 2009, the United States has held roughly steady with its share of about 27% of world GDP. While growth of the US economy has not slowed as much as that of the EU 15, it has clearly been outpaced by countries in Asia. This reflects the sense that the US economy has been stagnating for years and the concern (at least among those of us in the United States) that the dominance of the United States in the world economy is being challenged by rapidly expanding economies such as that of China. Meanwhile, during this same 40-year period, the Middle East/Africa and Latin America have remained mostly stable with about 7% of the world gross domestic product each.

When we consider this measurement for individual nations, we see how these broad trends lead to changes in their relative economic standing among other nations. The Centre for Economics and Business Research, for example, reports that Brazil has passed the United Kingdom as the world's sixth largest economy even while the UK is predicted to overtake France by 2016. These researchers also predict that by 2020, Russia, which was the world's ninth largest economy in 2011, will become the 4th largest economy, and India will move from 10th to 5th (*BBC News* 2011).

Income Distribution

Regional differences in nations, such as those described above, capture some of the important trends in global inequality. However, there are also large differences among countries in the same region, and those differences are masked if we only compare regional differences in economies. But there are too many nations to consider each one individually. In order to make sense of differences between nations of the world, it is necessary to group them into different categories that capture some of their most important differences.

This is not as trivial a task as it might at first seem. The "Three Worlds" classification from Cold War times distinguished the **First World**—industrialized nations allied with the United States and Western nations—the **Second World**—communist and socialist nations allied with the former Soviet Union—and the **Third World**—everything else. This political classification system has been out of date since the end of the Cold War era. More recent classifications pay less attention to politics and far more attention to economics. Another classification distinguishes three categories of development: the high category of "developed nations," the medium category of "developing nations," and the low category of "undeveloped nations." This classification has been criticized because it implies that undeveloped nations are necessarily inferior to developed nations. A similar classification is based on industrialization, distinguishing "most industrialized nations," "industrializing nations," and "least industrialized nations." The advantage of this classification is that industrialization may be more objectively measured than development, and the language does not imply that more industrialized nations are necessarily more or less desirable than less industrialized nations. However, many nations today are really postindustrial economies, and the most industrialized nations are actually becoming less industrial as their economies shift more and more into services and knowledge work. For these reasons, the rest of this chapter employs the World Bank's categorization of nations based on income. The World Bank classified 187 nations in 2011 along with 215 other economies with populations of greater than 30,000 (World Bank 2011a). This purely economic classification highlights inequalities among countries.

First World Industrialized nations allied with the United States and NATO, including many nations in Western Europe and North America, along with Japan, Australia, and New Zealand.

Second World Communist and socialist nations allied with the former Soviet Union, including many nations in Eastern Europe and Asia.

Third World Nations that did not fall into the Western or Eastern blocs.

The means of transportation for most people within a nation may reflect its economic realities.

(left to right) © iStockphoto/Thinkstock; © iStockphoto/Thinkstock; © iStockphoto/Thinkstock

Two statistical measures are often used to classify countries economically. Gross domestic product (GDP) is the monetary value of all finished goods and services produced within a country in a year. GNI (gross national income) is the GDP minus taxes on production plus the net income payable from abroad. In order to make meaningful comparisons across countries with very different-sized populations, the GNI or GDP statistics are often expressed on a per-capita basis. GDP per capita is a measure of the average economic productivity per person in a country during a year. GNI per capita is a measure of the average income a person in that country received in a year (OECD 2012). The World Bank (2011a) classifies nations into three categories based on GNI per capita.

Low-income nations have GNIs of $1,005 or less. **Middle-income nations** have GNIs between $1,006 and $12,275. **High-income nations** have GNIs of $12,276 or more. In FIGURE 8-2, these three categories of nations are identified.

High-income nations include most countries in Western Europe, the United States and Canada, Australia, Japan, South Korea, and a number of the oil-producing states, including Saudi Arabia, Oman, and the United Arab Emirates (UAE). Middle-income countries include the Russian Republic, China, and much of south and southeast Asia, most of South and Central America, and some countries in Africa. Low-income countries include several countries in Asia and many countries in Africa.

Low-income nations
Nations with a GNI of $1005 or less.

Middle-income nations
Nations with a GNI between $1006 and $12,275.

High-income nations
Nations with a GNI of $12,276 or more.

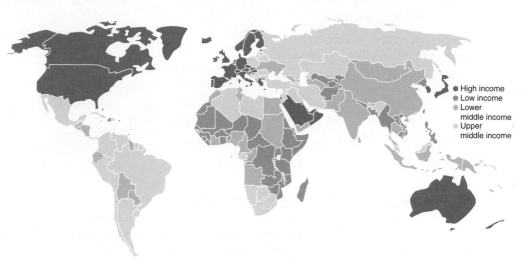

FIGURE 8-2 Nations according to income category.
Source: Data from The World Bank. Retrieved January 2012 (http://data.worldbank.org/indicator).

The distribution of the world's population and gross domestic product (GDP) among these three categories of countries is shown in FIGURE 8-3. High-income nations have 68% of the GDP but only 16% of the world's population (United Nations, 2008). On a per-capita basis, this is 4.25 times their expected share of 16% if GDP were distributed evenly. Middle-income nations have only 31% of the GDP but 72% of the population (less than half their expected share of 72% if GDP were distributed evenly), while low-income nations have only 1% of the world's GDP for 12% of the population (1/12 or .083 their expected per capita share). From these numbers, we can see that the ratio of the per-capita GDP of high-income countries to that of low-income countries is 4.25/.083 or more than 50:1. That is, the per-capita GDP of high-income countries is more than

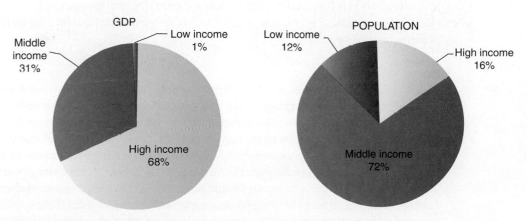

FIGURE 8-3 Worldwide distribution of GDP and income by national income categories.
Source: Data from The World Bank. Retrieved January 2012 (http://data.worldbank.org/country).

50 times the per capita GDP of people in the low-income countries (World Bank 2011a). This means that for every dollar earned by a person in a low-income country, someone in a high-income country would, on the average, earn more than $50!

| CONCEPT LEARNING CHECK 8.1 | Characteristics of the World Stratification System |

Match the following features with the appropriate classification of world countries.

_____ **1.** The primary basis for this classification is political.

_____ **2.** This classification is used by the World Bank.

_____ **3.** This classification distinguishes countries based on achieving a state many countries have now gone beyond.

_____ **4.** This classification implies that some nations are necessarily inferior to others.

A. Three worlds classification (First, Second, and Third World)

B. Development classification (developed, developing, undeveloped)

C. Industrialization classification (most industrialized, industrializing, least industrialized)

D. Income classification (high income, middle income, low income)

8.2 Wealth and Poverty: A Global View

Countries in different income categories differ dramatically on measures of poverty, inequality, health, and well-being.

■ Identify key differences between countries in different income categories and how this is reflected in migration.

The classification of countries into low-, medium-, and high-income categories by the World Bank provides a consistent way to look at important patterns of global stratification. Here we see how countries in each category differ in levels of poverty and income inequality, health, and several other measures of well-being. Finally, we consider how people in these countries react to these differences by examining differences in immigration rates.

Poverty and Income Inequality

The standard of living for people in a country—the level of material comfort they enjoy as a result of access to goods and services, both necessities and luxuries—is a direct reflection of their financial position. Here we consider two measures of standard of living: poverty rates and income inequality. We also examine how income inequality changes over time.

Poverty

Poverty rates vary dramatically for different countries. The map in FIGURE 8-4 shows the poverty rates (the percentage of the total population falling below the poverty line) based on a poverty line determined by that nation. We use each nation's own definition of poverty because exchange rates, varying costs of living, and other factors can cause a particular income figure expressed in US dollars to have very different meanings for the absolute poverty in each country. We are interested here in **absolute poverty**—a condition of deprivation in which people have too little money or other resources to obtain all they need for basic survival. It is important to acknowledge that people living in poverty in high-income nations may be living at a far higher standard of living than people living above the poverty line in some low-income countries.

Absolute poverty A condition of deprivation in which people have too little money or other resources to obtain all they need for basic survival.

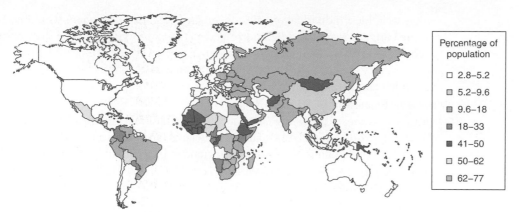

FIGURE 8-4 Poverty rate (percentage of population) according to each nation's own definition.
Source: IndexMundi. Global Poverty Working Group. Data are based on World Bank's country poverty assessments and country Poverty Reduction Strategies. Retrieved January 2012 (http://www.indexmundi.com/facts/indicators/SI.POV.NAHC).

Although each of these families falls below the poverty line for their nation, families living in poorer nations subsist on less than do families in richer nations.

(left) © David Butow/Corbis SABA (right) © Stockbyte/Thinkstock

Unfortunately, the World Bank map relies upon data provided by each country. Poverty rates for several countries, including the United States, are not shown. As a basis for comparison, in the United States, where the poverty line is defined as three times the amount required to feed a family, in 2009, 43.6 million people, or 14.3% of the population, fell below the poverty line (DeNavas-Walt et al. 2009:14). There are stark geographic differences in poverty rates among middle-income countries. In Asia, poverty rates are low for China (2.8%) and Malaysia (3.8%). In Eastern Europe, poverty rates are medium for the Russian Federation (11.1%) and the Ukraine (7.9%). In Africa and Latin America, poverty rates are high for Algeria (22.6%), Botswana (30.6%), Brazil (21.4%), and Mexico (47.4%). Low-income countries generally have even higher poverty rates, such as India (27.5%), Bangladesh (40%), Guinea (53%), and Bolivia (60.1%).

Income Inequality

Social scientists often use the **Gini coefficient** to measure inequality in wealth or income within countries. The Gini coefficient is named after Italian statistician and sociologist Corrado Gini, who first described this statistic in 1912. The Gini coefficient has a value between 0 and 100%. If all income were distributed equally among everyone in a nation (perfect equality), the Gini coefficient would be 0. If all income went to the

Gini coefficient The extent to which the distribution of income differs from an equal distribution.

single wealthiest individual (greatest inequality), the Gini coefficient would be 100%. So the Gini coefficient can be interpreted as the extent to which the distribution of income differs from an equal distribution. This coefficient can be compared for the same country over time to identify trends. It can also be compared across countries to see which countries have greater inequality.

Where is the Greatest Inequality within Nations?

FIGURE 8-5 is a map displaying Gini coefficients of national income distribution around the world (World Bank 2011a). These coefficients range from a low of 24.7 (Denmark) to a high of 74.3 (Namibia). Lowest values tend to be found in Scandinavian countries, next lowest in most of the rest of Western Europe, Canada (32.6), and Australia (35.2). The United States (40.8), Russia (42.3), and China (41.5) are in the high medium range. Highest values are found in some African countries, Bolivia (57.3), and many other South American countries.

FIGURE 8-5 Gini (income inequality) index for countries of the world, 2011.
Source: IndexMundi. World Bank, Development Research Group. Retrieved January 2012 (http://www.indexmundi.com/facts/indicators/SI.POV.GINI).

> **Human Development Index (HDI)** The composite measure of well-being first defined by the United Nations Development Program (UNDP 1990), including life expectancy, literacy rates, education, and other measures of standard of living.

Another way to measure income inequality that may be easier to understand is to measure the percentage of a country's total income held by the top 10% of the country's income earners. If income were distributed equally, this would be 10%. It is always more than 10%, however, with numbers as high as 65% for Namibia and as low as 20.8% for the Slovak Republic and 21.3% for Denmark. These numbers resemble the Gini coefficient, and a map of them would look nearly identical to the map for the Gini coefficient shown above (World Bank 2011a). Lowest values tend to be found in Scandinavian countries and the next lowest in most of the rest of Western Europe, Canada (24.8%), and Australia (25.4%). The United States (29.9%), India (31.1%), Russia (33.5%), and China (31.4%) are in the high medium range. Highest values are found in some African countries, Bolivia (45.4%), and many other South American and Central American countries such as Mexico (41.2%).

Increasing Inequality Over Time within Nations

The OECD (the Organization for Economic and Cooperative Development), in a 2011 report, provides data showing the gap between rich and poor in OECD countries. The OECD countries are 34 mostly high-income countries widely regarded as developed countries with "very high" **Human Development Index (HDI) scores**. The HDI is a composite measure of well-being first defined by the United Nations Development Program (UNDP 1990), including life expectancy, literacy rates, education, and other measures of standard of living. Even in OECD countries, the OECD reports, between 1985 and 2008, most of those countries saw the Gini coefficient (the commonly used measure of income inequality) rise dramatically to record high

Slums and other impoverished areas of large cities provide a stark and revealing contrast to signs of wealth and power.
© Dinodia Photos/Alamy

levels as shown in FIGURE 8-6. On release of the report in Paris, OECD Secretary-General Angel Gurría said,

> The social contract is starting to unravel in many countries. This study dispels the assumptions that the benefits of economic growth will automatically trickle down to the disadvantaged and that greater inequality fosters greater social mobility. Without a comprehensive strategy for inclusive growth, inequality will continue to rise. (OECD 2011)

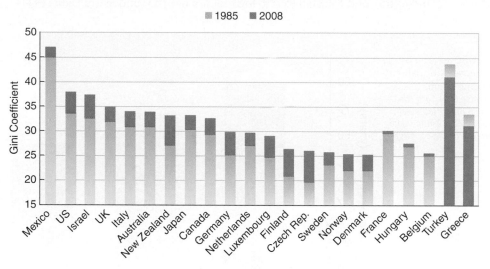

FIGURE 8-6 Income inequality has increased in most OECD countries in recent years.
Source: OECD. 2011. Divided We Stand: Why Inequality Keeps Rising. OECD Publishing. Accessed January 2012 (http://dx.doi.org/10.1787/9789264119536-en).

The report concludes that some of the main drivers behind rising income gaps have been greater wage gaps, as highly skilled workers benefit from technological progress and less skilled workers do not, along with changes in taxes that have cut top tax rates for high earners (OECD 2011). Increasing inequality within countries is one of the greatest concerns faced by nations in the 21st century. This is reflected in Occupy protests around the world highlighting the inequality between people who are economically in the top 1% versus the remaining 99% of the population (Berkowitz 2011). It is also reflected in US presidential election debates over the fairness of tax breaks for the wealthy and whether government should play a role in redistributing wealth to achieve greater equality (Klein 2012).

Health and Well-Being

The distribution of wealth and the gap between rich and poor in countries have consequences for many aspects of people's lives, including basic health and well-being. Two measures of health commonly used to compare countries are life expectancy at birth and infant mortality rates. Both of these vary considerably among countries and both tend to be highly correlated with many other measures of health. More importantly, what could be a more telling measure of the impact of inequality on people's lives than life expectancy? Inequalities between countries are so extreme that people in poor countries literally die on average more than two decades earlier than those in rich countries! Measures of well-being include educational opportunities, as measured by adult literacy rates and gender differences in education.

Life Expectancy at Birth

Inequalities among countries create markedly different life chances for people in those countries, both literally and figuratively. Nowhere is this more evident than in the stark differences in life expectancies at birth for these countries. In low-income countries, the life expectancy is 58, which is 11 years less than life expectancy for middle-income countries and 22 years—a whole generation—less than life expectancy in high-income countries FIGURE 8-7.

Individual countries display life expectancy differences as well. As we see in FIGURE 8-8, life expectancies at birth for high-income countries include: the United States (78), United Kingdom (80), Japan (83), and Australia (82). For middle-income countries, life expectancies are generally in the high 60s or low 70s, such as for the Ukraine (69), China (73), the Russian Federation (69), Brazil (73), and Mexico (76). Low-income countries have life expectancies ranging from highs like Bangladesh (68), India (65), and Pakistan (65) to lows for Guinea (53) and Sierra Leone (47).

FIGURE 8-7 Life expectancy by national income group.
Source: Data from The World Bank. Retrieved January 2012 (http://data.worldbank.org/country).

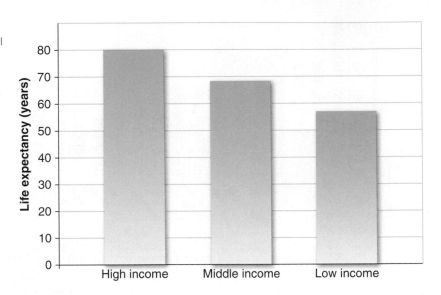

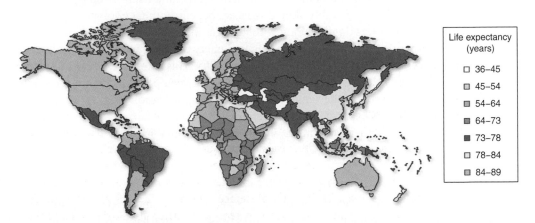

FIGURE 8-8 Life expectancy at birth by country.
Source: IndexMundi. Retrieved January 2012 (http://www.indexmundi.com/facts/indicators/SP.DYN.LE00.IN).

Infant Mortality Rates

Infant mortality The number of deaths per 1,000 infants born live in a year.

Infant mortality rates are often used as an index of overall health care in a country. **Infant mortality** is measured as the number of deaths per 1,000 infants born live in a year. Once again, as shown in FIGURE 8-9, high-income countries enjoy a great advantage, with an average infant mortality rate of 5 per 1,000 live births compared to 38 per 1,000 for middle-income countries and 70 per 1,000 for low-income countries.

In 2010, infant mortality rates range from a high of 113.7 deaths per 1,000 live births per year in Sierra Leone to a low of 1.6 for Iceland, as shown in FIGURE 8-10. It is a striking difference, with infants more than 70 times more likely to die in Sierra Leone than in Iceland. Lowest infant mortality rates tend to occur in Scandinavian countries, Western Europe, Canada (5.2), and Australia (4.1). The United States' rate of 6.5 places it 46th lowest in the world. Russia's is 9.1, China's is 15.8, Brazil's is 17.3, India's is 48.2, and Angola's is 97.9.

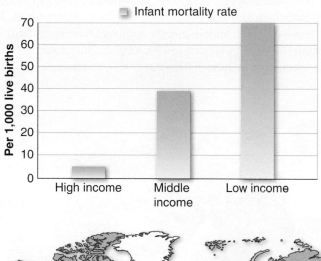

FIGURE 8-9 Infant mortality rate by national income group. *Source: Data from The World Bank. Retrieved January 2012 (http://data.worldbank.org/country).*

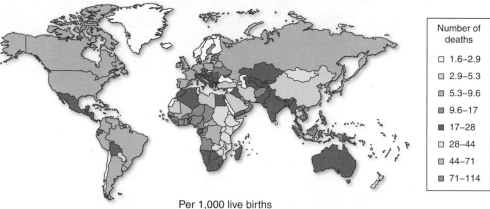

Per 1,000 live births

FIGURE 8-10 Map of infant mortality rates by country.
Source: IndexMundi. 2011. Level & Trends in Child Mortality. Estimates Developed by the UN Inter-agency Group for Child Mortality Estimation (UNICEF, WHO, World Bank, UN DESA, UNPD). Retrieved January 2012 (http://www.indexmundi.com/facts/indicators/SP.DYN.IMRT.IN).

Adult Literacy Rate

The literacy rate has important consequences for a society. If many people cannot read or write, it becomes much more difficult to have productive debates about public policies. Literacy enables people to participate more effectively as citizens, to function more effectively as workers, and to pursue leisure activities unavailable to the illiterate. The adult literacy rate (the percentage of people 15 and over who can read and write) also varies substantially by income category, as is shown in FIGURE 8-11. For high-income countries, literacy is almost universal (98%). It is substantially lower for middle-income

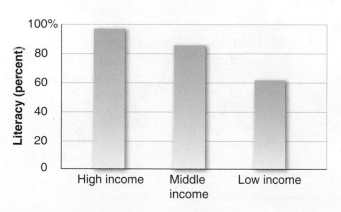

FIGURE 8-11 Literacy rate by national income group. *Source: Data from The World Bank. Retrieved January 2012 (http://data.worldbank.org/country).*

countries (83%) and only 61% for low-income countries. Clearly, the standard of living in these countries is very different.

Among high-income countries, the United States, the United Kingdom, Australia, Canada, and Japan all have literacy rates of 99%, as shown in the map FIGURE 8-12. Literacy rates are generally high for middle-income countries as well, with the Russian Federation at 100%. However, other middle-income countries have lower rates, including China (94%), Brazil (89%), and Mexico (86%). Low-income countries generally have very low literacy rates, such as those of Pakistan (49%), Bangladesh (48%), Bolivia (87%), and Haiti (53%).

FIGURE 8-12 Adult literacy rates by country.
Source: IndexMundi. CIA World Factbook. Retrieved January 2012 (http://www.indexmundi.com/ map/?t=0&v=39&r=xx&l=en).

Gender Differences in Education

A number of countries display disparities between men and women on key indicators. This is important for women, of course, since they are often disadvantaged. While equal treatment for women is consistent with Western values of gender equality, the issue also has pragmatic economic consequences for the countries as a whole. Within the United States, for example, dual-earner households tend to be much more affluent than single-earner households. If educational and occupational opportunities are fewer for women than for men, this disadvantages women and means that the country is underutilizing half of its population. This issue is reflected in gender access to secondary education. Countries in which roughly 50% of secondary education pupils are female are more likely to treat women fairly in other areas as well, as is shown in FIGURE 8-13.

Again, the income level of countries is related to this indicator. For high-income countries, most have roughly 50% female secondary students, including the United States (49.1%), the United Kingdom (49.1%), France (48.9%), and Japan (48.9%), with

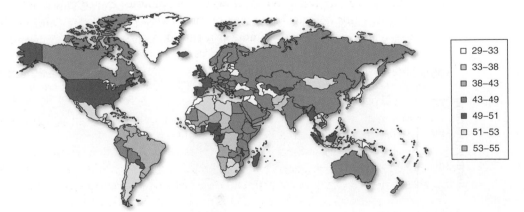

FIGURE 8-13 Percentage of secondary education pupils who are female by country.
Source: IndexMundi. United Nations Educational, Scientific, and Cultural Organization (UNESCO) Institute for Statistics. Retrieved January 2012 (http://www.indexmundi.com/facts/indicators/SE.SEC.ENRL.FE.ZS).

slightly lower numbers for Australia (47.6%) and South Korea (47.0%). Middle-income countries are also near 50% but show more variation, with Mexico (51.5%), Venezuela (51.3%), and Brazil (51.6%) all above 50%; and the Russian Federation (48.3%), China (48.0%), Iran (47.3%), Syria (48.7%), and Algeria (49.4%) slightly below 50%. Low-income countries tend to have a lower proportion of women in secondary school. Bolivia (48.6%) and Haiti (47.6%) are near 50%, but others are much lower, including India (44.6%), Pakistan (42.1%), and the Democratic Republic of the Congo (35.8%).

Infrastructure, Pollution, and Technology

Shared utilities, technologies, and consumption and their related pollution also vary greatly among countries. Infrastructure includes access to improved water supplies; technology includes phone and Internet use; and pollution can be measured by CO_2 emissions.

Water Quality

An infrastructure statistic that has implications for health and public welfare is access to improved water supplies. Access to a safe water supply is a public good that is essential for maintaining health. However, many low-income countries have not yet developed the infrastructure to provide safe water reliably in the amounts needed for their populations. The graph in FIGURE 8-14 shows the mean percentage of urban populations having access to an improved water supply in high-, medium-, and low-income countries. Specifically, it displays the percentage of urban populations that have access to at least 20 liters per person per day from an improved water source, such as a household connection, protected well, or public standpipe. This does not include water vendors, tanker trucks, or unprotected wells or springs.

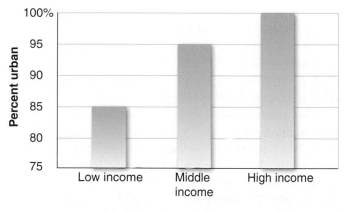

FIGURE 8-14 Access to improved water supply by national income group. *Source: Data from The World Bank. Retrieved January 2012 (http://data.worldbank.org/country).*

Such access is universal in high-income countries, somewhat lower (95%) in middle-income countries, and fairly low (85%) in low-income countries. Even 85% access means 15% of the population does not have access to improved water supplies and, hence, disease is likely to be more common, resulting in diminished health and lower productivity.

In all of our selected high-income countries, 100% of urban dwellers have access to improved water supplies, as seen in FIGURE 8-15. Many middle-income countries have access rates near 100%, such as China (98%) and Brazil (99%), but a few have less-than-complete access, such as Algeria (85%) and Syria (94%). The average access for low-income countries is only 85%, with low rates for the Democratic Republic of the Congo (80%), Bangladesh (85%), and Haiti (71%).

Why is it that some countries have never been able to develop an infrastructure of improved water supplies, good roads, and reliable power systems that can support demand even after decades of economic aid? Undoubtedly, in some cases, countries suffer from corrupt governments led by dictators who siphon off needed resources for themselves. In other cases, even countries that attempt to distribute resources more evenly may lack the funds required. The need for safe water in countries in which governments lack the resources to develop such water supplies opens an opportunity for private corporations

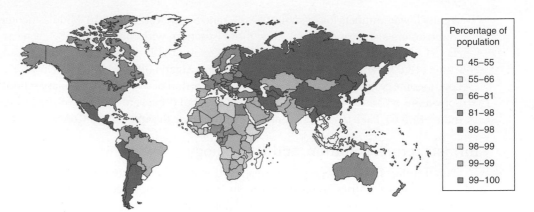

FIGURE 8-15 Percentage of urban population with access to improved water supply by country.
Source: IndexMundi. World Health Organization and United Nations Children's Fund, Joint Measurement Programme (JMP). Retrieved January 2012 (http://www.indexmundi.com/facts/indicators/SH.H2O.SAFE.UR.ZS).

to step in and develop private water supplies to meet the need. In some cases, this has worked successfully. However, critics often point to the failed privatization of water in Cochabamba, Bolivia. In that case, in order to obtain loans from the International Monetary Fund (IMF), Bolivia agreed to privatize major public enterprises, including national oil refineries and the Cochabamba local water agency. Bolivia leased the water agency to an international consortium, Aquas del Tunari, which included the major US corporation Bechtel. The consortium told the Bolivians that water prices would increase only 35% to cover upgrades, but in a matter of months, water bills doubled and then tripled. Peaceful protests began and quickly spread to other cities. By April of 2000, Bolivia's president declared a "stage of siege" similar to martial law and a 17-year-old boy protestor was shot during a demonstration. Widespread protests against the IMF and World Bank occurred in Washington, D.C., and the consortium's contract was revoked. Later Bechtel (whose 2000 revenues exceeded $14 billion) sued Bolivia (whose national budget is $2.7 billion) for $25 million in damages and for breach of contract (Sadiq 2002). Clearly, development of needed resources in poor countries is fraught with potential problems, and some of these countries are still struggling to find an approach that works for them.

Consumption and Pollution: CO_2 Emissions

Consumption and the resulting pollution in different countries are also highly related to the income categories, as is shown in FIGURE 8-16. Because there is far greater consumption in high-income countries than in low-income countries, the "carbon footprint" of people in high-income countries (the per-capita release of CO_2 emissions) is much higher. This is a reversal of the usual pattern in the sense that for CO_2 emissions, higher-income countries display the problem more than lower-income countries.

High-income countries clearly contribute much more to global pollution as measured by metric tons of CO_2 emissions (11.9 metric tons), compared to 3.5 metric tons for middle-income countries and 0.3 metric tons for low-income countries. This distribution is reflected among individual countries, too, FIGURE 8-16, with high values for the United States (17.9) and Australia (18.6) and lower, though still significant, values for the United Kingdom (8.5) and Japan (9.5). Middle-income countries generally have lower rates, such as China (5.3), Iran (7.4), and Mexico (4.3). However, the Russian Federation (a middle-income country), with a rate of 12, overlaps with some of the high-income countries. Low-income countries have the lowest rates as illustrated by India (1.5), Pakistan (1.0), Bolivia (1.3), and Haiti (0.2). The United States, due to its large population and large per-capita CO_2 emissions, contributes more than most countries to global emissions. However, both India and China, with their much larger populations, are increasing their per-capita carbon emissions rapidly. Both China and India illustrate an increasing emissions problem, as those countries with their huge populations undergo further development, leading to increased consumption with little

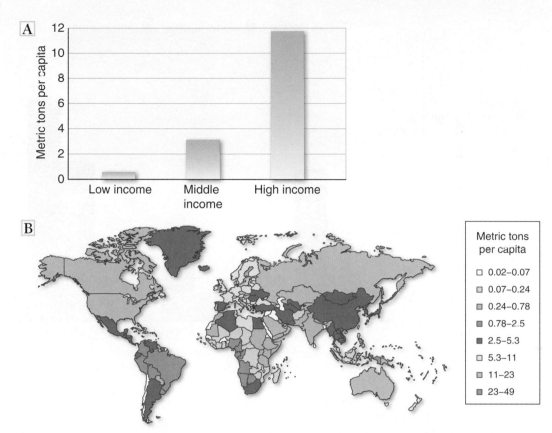

FIGURE 8-16 (**A**) CO_2 emissions by national income category. (**B**) CO_2 emissions per capita.
Source: (A) Data from The World Bank. Retrieved January 2012 (http://data.worldbank.org/country). (B) IndexMundi. Carbon Dioxide Information Analysis Center, Environmental Sciences Division, Oak Ridge National Laboratory, Tennessee, United States. Retrieved January 2012 (http://www.indexmundi.com/facts/indicators/EN.ATM.CO2E.PC).

regulation of emissions and heavy use of polluting energy sources such as coal. Any effort to reduce such emissions to slow or reverse global warming will need to include those countries as well.

Technology: Internet Users, Telephone Lines, and Cell Phones

New technologies also provide measures of opportunity and have interesting implications for the future. People living in countries with greater access to technologies such as the Internet, telephone lines, or cell phones have a better standard of living and greater opportunity afforded by those technologies for improving both their economic and social well-being. FIGURE 8-17 shows the number of Internet users, telephone lines, and cell phones per 100 people by income group. Of the three technologies, cell phones have been more widely adopted than either the Internet or telephone lines in all three income groups. One of the interesting implications of this is that the older technology of telephone lines, which require massive infrastructure investments and which have arrived very slowly in lower-income countries, are being leapfrogged by cell phones, whose infrastructure is much less expensive to establish. This illustrates how, at least occasionally, low-income countries, by being late to the game, can skip some of the initial investments that high- and middle-income countries made and catch up with wealthier countries.

All three technologies are used far more often in high-income countries, with much less use in middle-income countries and even less use in low-income countries. Because these technologies show similar distributions around the world, we only show distributions among Internet users here FIGURE 8-18.

High-income countries display the highest use of the Internet. This is illustrated by the high use in Scandinavian countries like Sweden (90.3%) and the United Kingdom (83.2%) and somewhat lower but still significant rates in the United States (78.1%),

Burning of fossil fuels accounts for more than 95% of CO_2 emissions.
© Photos.com/ Thinkstock

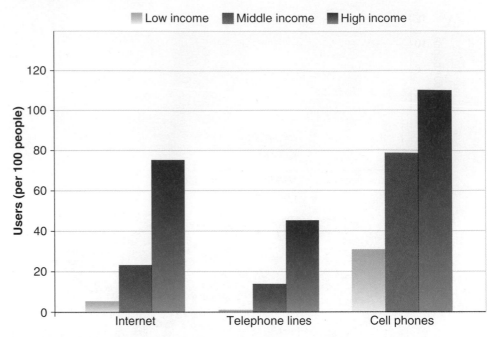

FIGURE 8-17 New technology adoption by national income group (2010).
Source: Data from The World Bank. Retrieved January 2012 (http://data.worldbank.org/income-level/LIC).

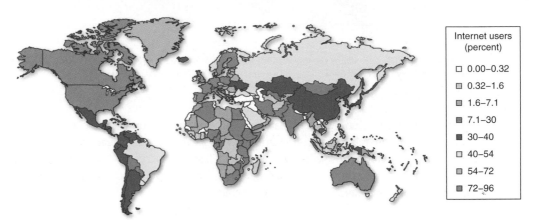

FIGURE 8-18 Percentage of Internet users in nations around the world.
Source: IndexMundi. International Telecommunication Union, World Telecommunication/ICT Development Report and database, and World Bank estimates. Retrieved January 2012 (http://www.indexmundi.com/facts/indicators/IT.NET.USER.P2).

Canada (77.7%), and Japan (77.7%). Middle-income countries have much lower rates, including Brazil (39.3%), Mexico (25.4%), and China (28.8%). Low-income countries have the lowest rates by far, including Pakistan (16.8%), India (7.8%), and Haiti (8.4%).

"Voting with Their Feet:" Migration Rates

Net migration rate The number of people moving into a country (immigration) minus the number of people moving out of the country (emigration).

Immigration The number of people moving into a country.

Emigration The number of people moving out of a country.

Another index of the overall standard of living in a country is the **net migration rate**—the number of people moving into a country (**immigration**) minus the number of people moving out of the country (**emigration**). In response to conditions within their own country and opportunities that may attract them to other countries, many people are "voting with their feet" and immigrating to countries with more favorable conditions, or at least the appearance of more favorable conditions. After all, the Berlin Wall and tightly controlled borders of communist states during the Cold War were in large part an effort to keep people in those countries from emigrating to the West. Today, more countries permit people to leave, and therefore immigration has become an even better indicator of standard of living.

We examine net migration rates for high-, medium-, and low-income countries in FIGURE 8-19. In 2010, only high-income countries showed a net in migration, or net gain, of about 14 people per 1,000. Middle-income countries lost about 3 people per

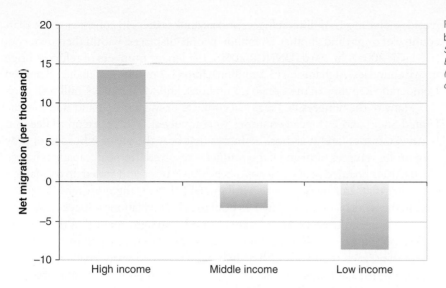

FIGURE 8-19 Net migration by national income group
Source: Data from The World Bank. Retrieved January 2012 (http://data.worldbank.org/country).

1,000, and low-income countries lost almost 9 people per 1,000 that year (World Bank 2011b). These results clearly support the notion that people tend to move out of countries with a lower standard of living and into countries with a higher standard of living.

We might expect that the United States had a net influx of people in recent years. Figures show that the United States had the highest net influx of any nation FIGURE 8-20 during the 5 years ending in 2010 (4.95 million). Other high-income countries also had net increases to their populations through migration. United Arab Emirates increased by 3.08 million, and Australia, Canada, and the United Kingdom each increased by more than a million. Some middle-income countries had net increases in population through migration, such as the Russian Federation (1.14 million), while other middle-income countries had net decreases, with more people leaving than migrating into the country, including China (–1.88 million), Mexico (–1.81 million), and Brazil (–.50 million). Almost all low-income countries showed net population decreases through migration, including Bangladesh (–2.91 million), Pakistan (–2.00 million), and Ethiopia (–.30 million). The country with the highest net loss of population through immigration during this period was India (–3.00 million).

Forced Migration: Refugees and Human Trafficking

Not all migration is by choice. There are millions of **refugees** around the world, people who were forced to leave their countries of origin to avoid violence and bloodshed in civil wars, regional conflicts, and other disputes. According to the United Nations High Commissioner for Refugees, in 2009, there were 42 million people uprooted around the

Refugee Someone who was forced to leave his or her country of origin to avoid violence and bloodshed in civil wars, regional conflicts, and other disputes.

FIGURE 8-20 Net migration by country (2005–2010).
Source: IndexMundi. United Nations Population Division, World Population Prospects. Retrieved January 2012 (http://www.indexmundi.com/facts/indicators/SM.POP.NETM)

world, including 16 million refugees and asylum seekers in countries other than their country of origin and another 26 million people displaced within their own countries (UNHCR 2009). In 2010 (UNHCR 2010), the largest numbers of refugees originated in five countries: Afghanistan (3.1 million), Iraq (1.7 million), Somalia (.8 million), the Democratic Republic of the Congo (.5 million), and Myanmar (.4 million).

Many of the refugees fled regional conflicts in Afghanistan and Iraq in which the United States and European countries were involved. Refugees tend to flee to neighboring countries, and it is those countries that bear the greatest burden of providing support for refugees until and if the conflict is resolved. Ironically, many refugees from North Africa boarded boats in hopes of reaching Europe and ended up on Malta, which is smaller than an American town, and in 2011, it had "the most refugees per square mile in the world according to figures from the United Nations refugee agency" (Alpert 2012). European Union countries are bound by an agreement that the first country to receive refugees is responsible for them. Some countries try to turn away refugees before they reach their soil, such as Italy, which turned away boats of refugees from Libya, and the United States, which has long turned away boats of Cuban refugees before they reach shore (Alpert 2012). Unfortunately, conflicts and the refugees they create sometimes go on for decades, as illustrated by the Palestinian refugee problem.

Even if migration is initially by choice, some people who chose to migrate end up the victims of human traffickers. **Human trafficking** is the modern equivalent of slavery. It may involve sexual exploitation or forced labor. Often it begins in the eyes of the victims as people smuggling, in which they voluntarily rely on someone else to help them enter a destination country illegally. However, victims are not allowed to leave once they reach their destination. In **forced labor**, they are physically coerced to work. Other times, they suffer a form **bonded labor** in which they become indebted to the smugglers under undefined or exploitative terms, making it impossible to pay off the debt. In **sex trafficking**, victims are forced to work against their will in the sex industry. Children are sometimes forced into slavery or required to participate in child pornography or forced labor or are even recruited as child soldiers in some conflicts. The United Nations Office on Drugs and Crime (2009) is engaged in a campaign to encourage countries to outlaw human trafficking and to combat it. In their study, the most common form of human trafficking (79%) is sexual exploitation, with victims predominantly women and girls. The next most common is forced labor. This is a worldwide problem, and a 2006 study (Kangaspunta 2006) identified 127 countries of origin and 137 destination countries for human trafficking. Victims were 54% women, 2% men, and 44% children (Kangaspunta 2006). Human trafficking victims are generally more likely to be from low-income countries and are taken advantage of by people in middle- or high-income countries.

Emigration of Highly Skilled People

There is an old riddle that asks how can it be that a person left his home in one country to live in another country and, in the process, raised the average IQ of both the country he left and the country he went to. I was told that riddle by a Scandinavian, so you might imagine Norway and Sweden being mentioned—I will not tell you which was which. In fact, you could substitute any two countries that compete and make the same riddle. The riddle illustrates an important point. It is not just how *many* people leave or take up residence in a country, but *which* people. If the "best and the brightest" people are leaving a country, then that country experiences what has been called **brain drain** or **bright flight**—emigration of highly skilled people. In this situation, highly skilled people leaving their home country lower the average level of education or skill in their country of origin and increase these averages in the country to which they immigrate.

The graph in FIGURE 8-21 shows the percentage of total tertiary, or service-sector, educated people who have emigrated from high-, medium-, and low-income countries. Three times the percentage of these highly trained individuals come from

---

Human trafficking The smuggling of humans, in which a victim relies on a smuggler to help him or her enter a country illegally.

Forced labor People who are physically coerced to work.

Bonded labor An exploitive arrangement in which the victim becomes indebted to undefined or exploitative terms, making it impossible to pay off the debt.

Sex trafficking Victims are forced to work against their will in the sex industry.

Brain drain/bright flight The emigration of highly skilled people from a country.

low-income countries as from high-income countries. This is a significant cost to low-income countries when they invest their limited resources in educating people, only to lose so many to emigration. For high-income countries, the relative loss is much less (4% compared to 12%), and there is often even a net gain because high-income countries are often the destination point of the "best and the brightest" from low-income countries.

We can also examine the emigration rates of highly skilled people by country, as seen in FIGURE 8-22. Emigration rates of highly skilled people vary considerably within each income category of countries. (These are expressed as percentages.) Among high-income countries, the United States has the lowest rate of less than one percent (.45). Japan is also low (1.2). Moderate rates are found for Australia (2.7), France (3.4), Sweden (4.5), Norway (6.2), and South Korea (7.5), but a surprisingly high amount for the United Kingdom (17.1). For middle-income countries, low emigration of highly skilled people is found for the Russian Federation (1.4), moderate amounts for China (3.8) and the Ukraine (4.4), and high amounts for Mexico (15.5). For low-income countries, moderate amounts are found for India (4.3) and Bangladesh (4.4) and a high amount for Pakistan (12.7). Emigration of highly skilled people is a huge problem for some of the smaller low-income countries, where more than 50% of their highly skilled people have left the country. This is true for Guyana (89.2), Haiti (83.4), Samoa (73.4), and Fiji (62.8).

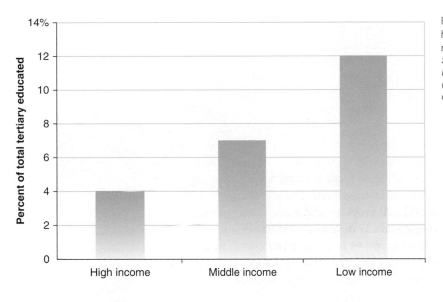

FIGURE 8-21 Emigration of highly educated people by national income group. *Source: Data from The World Bank. Retrieved January 2012 (http://data.worldbank.org/country).*

FIGURE 8-22 Emigration rate of highly educated people by country.
Source: IndexMundi. Frédéric Docquier, B. Lindsay Lowell, and Abdeslam Marfouk. 2009. "A Gendered Assessment of Highly Skilled Emigration." Retrieved January 2012 (http://www.indexmundi.com/facts/indicators/SM.EMI.TERT.ZS).

THE SOCIOLOGICAL IMAGINATION | Migration and Remittances

Migration sometimes benefits the country the migrant left. More than 215 million people live outside their countries of birth, and 700 million more migrate within their own countries. **Remittances** (money sent home to households by migrants) made up 2% of GDP for all developing countries in 2008 and 6% of GDP for low-income countries. For some small low-income countries, remittances make up more than 20% of GDP (World Bank 2011).

The importance of remittances to a country's economy is made clear when we look at Nepal. Sociologists Michael Kollmair and his colleagues (Kollmair et al. 2006) studied official figures for immigration and remittances in Nepal and also conducted a number of interviews with people to better estimate immigration and remittances. They estimate the total inflow of remittances to Nepal in 2003 was equivalent to $604 million USD—nearly double the total amount of all foreign aid to Nepal in that year. They estimate that 32% of all households in Nepal receive remittances and, among those households, remittances account for 35% of total household income. We can learn much from examining where Nepali workers have migrated and the amount of remittances these workers send back to families in Nepal during a typical year FIGURE 8-23. Clearly immigration and remittances have a big impact on the Nepali economy.

> **Remittance** Money sent home to households by migrants.

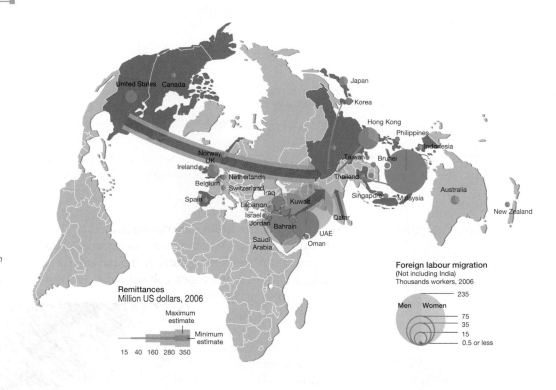

FIGURE 8-23 Labor migration from Nepal and annual remittances to Nepal.
Source: Data from Kollmair, M., et al., New figures for old stories: Migration and remittances in Nepal, Migration Letters, 2006; NHRC, Trafficking in Person Especially on Women and Children in Nepal, 2008. Cartographer: Riccardo Pravettoni, UNEP/ GRID-Arendal. Retrieved January 2012 (http://www .grida.no/graphicslib/detail/ labour-migration-from- nepal_8700).

EVALUATE

1. How might the situation in Nepal resemble the situations in Mexico or other Central American countries such as Guatemala and El Salvador?

2. How much do you think migrants from countries such as Mexico, Guatemala, or El Salvador send home in remittances every year? Try to find this information on the Internet, including estimates of what portion of each country's economy is based on remittances.

3. What effect are remittances likely to have on the country in which immigrants earn money and send it back to their country of origin?

4. To what extent does this make problems that originate in countries such as Mexico, Guatemala, or El Salvador the problems of the United States?

5. How, if at all, do problems that originate in the United States become the problems of Mexico, Guatemala, or El Salvador?

CONCEPT LEARNING CHECK 8.2 | Patterns of World Stratification

Match each statement with the number that makes it correct.

_____ **1.** The United States ranks below __ other countries in infant mortality rate.

_____ **2.** High-income countries have life expectancies that average __ years more than low-income countries.

_____ **3.** Infant mortality rates in low-income countries are on average __ times higher than those of high-income countries.

_____ **4.** In low-income countries, the percentage of the urban population with access to improved water supplies is __.

_____ **5.** Among low-income countries, the average percentage of highly skilled people who have emigrated to other countries is __%.

A. 14

B. 12

C. 85

D. 22

E. 45

8.3 Global Stratification: Theoretical Perspectives

Four theories of global stratification attempt to explain why and how global inequalities occur.

- Identify four theories of global stratification and what distinguishes them.

Several theories of global stratification try to explain inequality among the world's countries. The first, modernization theory, comes out of the functionalist tradition. The second, dependency theory, draws heavily on the history of colonialism and attempts to explain continuing patterns of inequality from a conflict perspective. The last two perspectives, world systems theory and the international division of labor theory, offer further revisions to attempt to account for the continuing evolution of global inequality.

Modernization Theory

A theory of social change that has roots both in structural-functionalism and in Weber's interactionist tradition is modernization theory. **Modernization theory** argues that progress could be made in poor countries through the greater economic and social development that comes from adopting modern technologies, cultural values, and economic institutions, such as those found in more highly developed economies (Rostow 1960). W. W. Rostow FIGURE 8-24 was an economic advisor to US president John F. Kennedy, and his conception of modernization theory dominated economic and social thinking about international development for more than 20 years.

Modernization theory provides a modern version of Weber's argument regarding the Protestant ethic—the view that the values and ideology of a culture can make it more or less able to use social change to its advantage. This theory argues that economic growth will occur first and most rapidly in countries having a cultural climate that can leverage technological innovation. From this perspective, the culture and social institutions of low-income countries conflict with the needs of rapid economic and technological development. The typically large families of low-income countries tend to encourage consumption rather than investment. Existing religious and spiritual values may be at odds with rapid technological development. Perhaps most important, argued Rostow, are fatalistic belief systems that view hardship as predetermined. Fatalism robs people of their initiative

Modernization theory A theory that argues that progress can be made in poor countries through the greater economic and social development that comes from adopting modern technologies, cultural values, and economic institutions.

FIGURE 8-24 W. W. Rostow (right) developed the modernization theory, which holds that poorer countries benefit from emulating richer countries.

© Bettmann/Corbis

by suggesting that there is no point in even trying to improve one's lot in life. Instead, as McClelland (1961) argues, countries that value individualism, self-reliance, deferred gratification, and achievement will benefit more from modernization than countries that do not have these values.

Rostow (1960) proposes that modernization occurs in four stages.

1. **Traditional stage**. This stage is characterized by fatalism, an emphasis on traditional values, little or no investment or saving for the future, little work ethic, and little or no change.

2. **Take-off stage**. This is a period of accelerating economic growth, a decline in the influence of tradition, the beginnings of a modern market economy, the growth of trade, increased individualism, risk taking, materialism, and saving for the future. Key to this is the development of a capitalist economy if a country is to move from a simple traditional society to a modern, complex society.

3. **Drive to technological maturity**. In this stage, the country adopts the cultural values that support a modern complex society, reinvests in industry, and begins to mature.

4. **High mass consumption**. In the final stage, the country's people enjoy a high standard of living based on the mass consumption of goods and services.

Modernization theory grew out of the 1950s and 1960s, when Western capitalist countries were in competition with Eastern communist bloc countries seeking to increase their influence with neutral (Third World) countries. This perspective provides a narrative for how less-developed Third World countries could benefit from partnership with the capitalist countries of the West. Another element of modernization theory identifies four ways affluent countries can help less developed countries by disseminating technologies that help control population growth, increase food production, and share industrial technologies, along with providing foreign aid. Many of the countries that have successfully made the transition from low income to middle income, including nations in East Asia, have become strongly involved in the capitalist world economy. This view began as a unilinear evolutionary theory of social change but has evolved into a more sophisticated multilinear view recognizing the importance of culture and not insisting that every country must evolve in precisely the same manner.

Dependency Theory

Modernization theory put the blame for lack of development squarely on the less developed nations and saw the role of rich nations as helping less developed nations earn their own place at the world economic table. In contrast, dependency theory reverses the argument, blaming rich countries for centuries of exploitation of the weaker countries. In this view, which builds on Marx's conflict theory, poorer nations are structurally dependent on richer nations for markets in which to sell their raw materials and the need for capital. It is not just that poor nations are underdeveloped but that they are "misdeveloped" (Amin 1974; Frank 1966). Richer countries exploit the poorer countries, extracting wealth from poorer countries and trapping them in a downward spiral of greater dependency and poverty.

We need look no further than at the history of colonialism to see the beginnings of this process. Under **colonialism**, powerful nations forced weaker nations to become colonies, thereby securing them as sources of raw materials and markets for goods produced by the stronger nations. This often involved European countries such as Britain, France, Spain, Belgium, Portugal, and Italy. In addition, Asian countries like Japan also established colonies, and even the United States—which began as 13 British colonies in North America—purchased the Louisiana territory from France and later Alaska from Russia and gained control of territories such as Guam, the Philippines, the Hawaiian Islands, Puerto Rico, and Haiti. Colonialism has nearly disappeared from the world today, with many countries gaining their independence since the end of World War II. But the legacy of colonialism persists as **neocolonialism**, in which former colonies

---

Traditional stage The first stage in development theory, characterized by fatalism, an emphasis on traditional values, little or no investment or saving for the future, little work ethic, and little or no change.

Take-off stage The second stage in development theory, a period of accelerating economic growth, a decline in the influence of tradition, the beginnings of a modern market economy, the growth of trade, increased individualism, risk taking, materialism, and saving for the future.

Drive to technological maturity The third stage of development theory, in which the country adopts the cultural values that support a modern complex society, reinvests in industry, and begins to mature.

High mass consumption The fourth and final stage of development theory, in which people in the country enjoy a high standard of living based on the mass consumption of goods and services.

Colonialism A world stratification system in which powerful nations forced weaker nations to become colonies, thereby securing them as sources of raw materials and markets for goods produced by the stronger nations.

Neocolonialism Former colonies often continue to be dominated by more powerful nations in the world economy.

often continue to be dominated by more powerful nations in the world economy. Today, that domination is not from the exercise of political force by colonizing countries but from the exercise of economic domination by multinational corporations that continue to exploit poorer countries, extracting their resources and their wealth while selling goods and services to them.

Dependency theory helps explain why many Latin American and African countries remain poor today but does not explain how India and a number of East Asian countries managed to overcome that dependency enough to graduate from low-income nations to middle-income nations and experience rapid economic growth.

European powers such as Belgium established and ruled foreign colonies, usually subjugating indigenous people to secure valuable natural resources.

(left) © Michael Nicholson/Corbis. (right) © UniversalImagesGroup/Contributor/Getty Images

World Systems Theory

Immanuel Wallerstein (1976, 1979, 1980)—building on Marx's conflict theory—proposed a theory of global stratification based on a global economic system. **World systems theory** argues that a process of globalization unites countries into a single worldwide political and economic system of interrelationships—a "capitalist world economy" (Wallerstein 1976). Thus, development or social change within any single country can only be understood in this global context. In this view, there is a division of power among three broad categories of countries: peripheral countries, core countries, and semiperipheral countries.

Peripheral countries are the most dependent countries in world systems theory, having low levels of industrialization. These countries have high levels of investment from other countries and are often unable to ward off interference in their internal politics by other countries. These countries are exploited by other countries for their raw materials and are a market for goods and services produced by more affluent countries. Peripheral countries are low-income countries, including Third World countries such as Bangladesh, Zimbabwe, and Sri Lanka. These countries have the fewest benefits from the current world order and are most likely to be supportive of revolution or to experience social disorder themselves. It is in these countries that most of the socialist revolutions of the 20th century have occurred.

Core countries are the high-income countries that dominate the world economic system. They have high levels of industrialization. Much of their economy is based on the provision of goods and services, and they have high levels of political autonomy to pursue their own interests. Core countries today include the United States, Germany, China, and Japan. Core countries dominate the world economy and are in positions from which they can influence the economies and political systems of peripheral and semiperipheral countries to serve their own interests. Core countries benefit most from the current world order and have the most at stake in seeing that it continues in its present form. These countries have been most resistant to revolutionary social change, whether in their own or other countries. Yet they sometimes create change in other countries to further their own interests. For example, in 1973, the US Central Intelligence Agency (CIA) sponsored a military coup in the South American country of Chile in which the freely elected socialist government of Salvadore Allende was overthrown and Allende himself was murdered. During the 1980s, the United States supported rebels attempting to overthrow the socialist government in Nicaragua.

World systems theory A theory that argues that globalization unites countries into a single worldwide political and economic system of interrelationships.

Peripheral countries The most dependent countries in world systems theory, having low levels of industrialization.

Core countries The high-income countries that dominate the world economic system.

Semiperipheral countries
The middle-income countries between the core countries and peripheral countries, having intermediate levels of industrialization, some manufacturing and services, and greater autonomy than peripheral countries.

International division of labor theory A theory that argues that multinational corporations split production into tasks that are then performed in whatever part of the world can provide the most profitable combination of labor and technology.

Global commodity chains Worldwide networks of production activities are required to produce the finished product for sale.

Semiperipheral countries are the middle-income countries between the core countries and peripheral countries, having intermediate levels of industrialization, some manufacturing and services, and greater autonomy than peripheral countries. Semiperipheral countries include countries like Brazil, Greece, and Spain. These countries are exploited by core countries, but they, in turn, exploit peripheral countries. So they both benefit and suffer from the world system. Because they, or at least their economic elites, enjoy some benefits from the world system, they have a vested interest in seeing the status quo continue.

In many respects, world systems theory is a modern revision of the theory of imperialism first developed by Lenin (1927). Imperialism argued that powerful countries used the resources of less powerful countries to favor their own interests without fair compensation for those resources. That is, powerful countries exploit weaker ones. Lenin argued that imperialism occurred because saturated markets and depleted natural resources in developed countries led to expansion through colonies to obtain new sources of raw materials and new markets for goods. For example, Baran (1957) describes how Great Britain systematically destroyed the textile industry in India when India was a British colony. While India continued to grow large amounts of cotton, instead of making cloth locally, the cotton was often shipped overseas to Great Britain, where it was made into cloth that was then sold back to consumers in India. This created a captive market for British textiles, provided a steady flow of income to Britain, and slowed the economic development of India.

Imperialism relied upon governments of powerful countries to conduct expansion through colonization, while in modern-day world systems theory, large multinational corporations are capable of conducting much of this expansion on their own. Today, much of the expansion is to obtain cheap labor. Unfortunately, primary-sector agricultural and mining production create only a few relatively low-paying, unskilled jobs while creating a class of elites dependent upon foreign investment. This kind of development thus increases the gap between rich and poor rather than reducing that gap as development did in core countries.

An example of this can be seen in *maquiladora* plants in Mexico built by multinational corporations. Components, often precision parts requiring skilled labor and technology, are manufactured in the United States. Then those components are shipped to Mexico to plants just across the border in which low-paid, unskilled Mexican workers assemble the components into products. The completed products are shipped back to the United States for sale. This illustrates a number of the consequences of the global economic system. Highly skilled high-technology jobs remain in the core country, the United States. Unskilled jobs that were once available in the United States are moved by the multinational corporation to peripheral or semiperipheral countries where workers are paid lower wages. Declining industries in the core countries become booming industries in peripheral and semiperipheral countries. There, workers move from the countryside to the cities, where housing is scarce, to work longer hours for lower wages in factories with fewer safety regulations.

The International Division of Labor Theory

The last global stratification theory to be discussed departs from earlier theories in that it emphasizes the role of multinational corporations and global economic production. **The international division of labor theory** argues that multinational corporations split production into tasks that are then performed in whatever part of the world can provide the most profitable combination of labor and technology to perform the task. This creates a division of labor among countries, with low-income countries providing low-cost, labor-intensive, assembly-oriented export production of commodities such as clothing and electronic products in plants with fewer regulations regarding workplace safety and environment (Waters 1995). This division of labor creates **global commodity chains** in which worldwide networks of production activities are required to produce the finished product for sale. This is illustrated by the iPhone. Apple is located in California, and the iPhone was entirely designed in the United States. However, it is assembled in China from parts made in other countries, including the touch screen and flash memory from Japan, the camera and GPS receiver from Germany, and the application processor from South Korea. Only 6% of the production costs are due to parts coming from the United States (Xing and Detert 2011). Global commodity chains reverse traditional trade patterns with developing countries, such as the People's Republic of China, exporting high-tech goods (like the iPhone) while industrialized countries such as the United States import the high-tech goods they themselves invented (Xing and Detert 2011). The dominant actor in this process is no longer a high-income country like the US but a multinational firm like Apple, making rational business decisions based on the interests of the firm and the profit motives of the stockholders. Those decisions may or may not benefit any of the countries in which product development and production occur.

Factory where iPhones are manufactured in China.
© Zou Haibin/Imaginechina/AP Images

CONCEPT LEARNING CHECK 8.3   Theoretical Perspectives on Global Stratification

Match the following characteristics with the correct theory.

_____ **1.** This theory explains how products such as high-tech electronics are manufactured in different countries.

_____ **2.** This theory is associated with W. W. Rostow.

_____ **3.** This theory assumes that high-income countries can help low-income countries through technology and foreign aid.

_____ **4.** This theory proposes that there are a few groups of nations in the world, with one group dominating the others.

A. Modernization theory

B. Dependency theory

C. World systems theory

D. International division of labor theory

8.4 Global Stratification Effects and the Future

Several trends and insights from theories of global stratification suggest issues we must face in the future.

■ Identify some of the important trends likely to affect global stratification in the future.

Today's global stratification system is based upon extreme inequalities among countries, and it has very real consequences for all of us. High-income countries, with 16% of the world's population, enjoy the benefits of 68% of the world GDP. That inequality has a pervasive effect on virtually all aspects of life in these countries.

The Consequences of Global Inequality

The greater consumption of high-income countries means they have far higher CO_2 emissions than other countries. Populations of high-income countries enjoy much better health, as illustrated by higher life expectancies at birth and much lower infant mortality rates. High-income countries score higher on measures of well-being than lower income countries as measured by higher literacy rates, lower poverty rates, and greater access to infrastructure such as access to improved water supplies and greater use of new technologies such as the Internet and cell phones.

Visual Overview Theories of Global Stratification

Stark inequalities exist among nations with high income nations enjoying huge advantages over medium and low income nations. Attempts to explain these inequalities have led to four competing theories of global stratification. The following map offers a closer look at the international division of labor theory and the role a hypothetical US auto company would play.

The International Division of Labor Theory

The dominant actors are no longer nation-states, but large multinational corporations that pick and choose the countries where their products are designed, manufactured, and assembled based on corporate interests.

Major automakers develop international infrastuctures that include:

● assembly   ● stamping   ○ engine   ● casting and forging   ● design

Classifiying Nations
■ High Income
■ Medium Income
□ Low Income

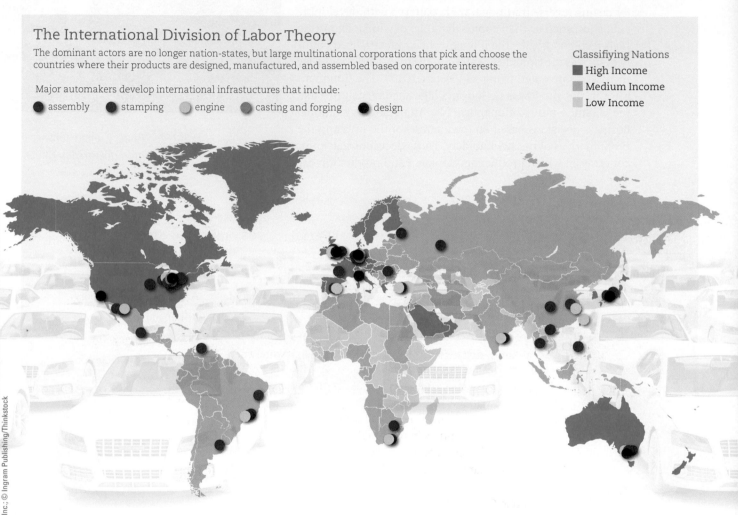

Other global stratification theories include:

Modernization Theory

Developed countries should help less developed countries overcome cultural barriers holding them back to modernize and become more like them

Dependency Theory

Powerful countries tend to dominate one or more dependent countries much like under colonialism

World Systems Theory

Nations can be divided based on power into core countries that dominate the semi-peripheral countries, and both of those dominate peripheral countries.

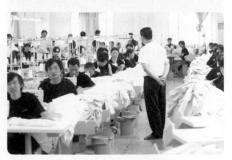

One indicator of the consequences of these inequalities among countries can be found in migration patterns. High-income countries have net population gains from immigration, while low- and middle-income countries have net losses to migration. Perhaps even more important, high-income countries generally have lower rates of emigration of highly skilled people (three times lower than low-income countries). For some small, low-income countries, emigration is a huge factor in their economies, as significant numbers of people emigrate to more affluent countries to find jobs and send back remittances to family members remaining behind.

Why Should We Care?

Selfishly, we might ask why this matters to people in high-income countries such as the United States. After all, high-income countries have benefited from global stratification for decades and, in some cases, for centuries. Is it not likely that these inequalities will continue for the foreseeable future? Of course, a moral argument could be made that wealthy countries should try to help low-income countries. But there are other reasons why people in high-income countries should not take their own continued prosperity for granted.

Increased Global Competition and Reshuffling at the Top

Global competition and the ability of multinational corporations to select which countries perform various parts of the design and production of products mean that workers in high-income countries now must compete with workers in low-income countries with far lower wages. The resulting exporting of jobs to low-wage countries has led to declining employment in these industries in higher-income countries. For Eurozone countries, this has resulted in a reduction of about 10% in their share of the world GDP between 1969 and 2009. The worldwide financial crisis of 2008 led to a sovereign debt crisis in many European countries when their bailouts of banks caused them to take on heavy debt loads. Ironically, several European countries were forced to take austerity measures and began looking to the World Bank and even to a middle-income country, China, for a bailout. That downturn left the United States and other high-income countries far more vulnerable to further economic downturns and competition as well. At the same time, the rise of many Asian countries economically is leading to a reshuffling of countries in the top tier of world economies, with Russia predicted to go from ninth largest economy in 2011 to fourth largest in 2020 and India moving from tenth to fifth largest by 2020 (*BBC News* 2011).

Increasing Inequality within Countries

Inequalities are found within nations as well as between them, and these inequalities seem to be growing. Historically, there has been greater inequality in low-income countries. However, inequality within countries is high and is increasing even among high-income countries. Instead of low-income countries developing and becoming more like high-income countries, in at least some respects, high-income countries are becoming more like low-income countries. Competition in the global economy leads to the exporting of jobs to countries with lower wages. As a result, even the high-income countries have to become more competitive to maintain their standard of living.

Problems for All: Migration and Political Instability

We have seen how the problems of poor countries may be shared somewhat by their rich neighbors as migrants seek a better future in richer countries. In addition, it is important to realize that countries themselves are not permanent unchanging entities. While some countries have persisted for centuries, others are relatively new, and all are more susceptible to fundamental

Arab Spring demonstration in Egypt.
© ASSOCIATED PRESS

change than we might imagine. The widespread civil uprisings among countries in the Middle East during the Arab Spring of 2011 in several cases led to changes in government. The Occupy Wall Street and other Occupy protests that occurred in many high-income countries during 2011 also reflect increased awareness and public protest of inequalities within countries. The global stratification system is very much a work in progress and will continue to evolve in the future.

Global Inequality: Theoretical Insights

Modernization theory helps explain some of the inequality among nations. Many low-income countries, for example, have high birth rates and rapidly growing populations along with crippling international debt. These factors have made it harder for these countries to develop successful economies. Policies of the World Bank and the International Monetary Fund are often based on the notion that, by encouraging low-income countries to live within their means to get their debt under control, those countries can then grow their economies. Some East Asian countries have undergone amazing economic development in the last few decades, moving from low-income to medium-income countries (such as China).

Dependency theory also helps account for the periodic dependent relationships between some countries. Certainly colonialism accounted for much of the inequality in the past, and the results are still evident. Some countries, while influenced by the entire global economic system, are heavily dependent on a single, more powerful neighbor. Examples of this are Mexico, which is heavily dependent on the United States, and Nepal, which is heavily dependent on India.

World systems theory looks beyond dependency relationships between nations and considers the entire global economy. In a global economy, each country typically has relationships with many other countries. Low-wage countries are often the site of manufacturing facilities for companies from several different other countries. High-income countries in general (the core countries) pursue markets for their goods and services in the middle-income (semiperipheral) and low-income (peripheral) countries.

Increased Worldwide Dependence

International division of labor theory highlights the increasing dependence of countries on one another in a world economy in which worldwide networks of production activities are required to produce a product for sale. As a result, something like an earthquake in Japan or floods in Thailand can mean that key components of automobiles or hard disks may be in short supply in the United States and Western Europe. That dependence is driven by technology when particular high-technology components may only be available from particular companies.

The Rise of the Corporation and the Decline of the Nation-State

The most striking insight of international division of labor is the importance of corporations. Where dependency theory sees one country dominating another and world systems theory sees core countries dominating the semiperipheral and peripheral countries, in the international division of labor theory, the dominant actor is not a country at all but a corporation. This is illustrated, as we saw earlier, by the failed effort to privatize the water supply in Bolivia by a consortium including a major US corporation, Bechtel (Sadiq 2002). The increasing influence of corporations on the world economy is not limited to low-income countries like Bolivia.

Multinational corporations play an increasingly important role in the world economy. Of the world's 50 largest economies in 2007, 6 are multinational corporations. The 26th largest economy is Walmart, with $408 billion, just below Norway's $414 billion and ahead of all but 25 countries. Other corporations among the top 50 economies are Royal Dutch Shell (35th at $285 billion), Exxon Mobil (36th at $284 billion), BP (British Petroleum), Toyota Motor, and Japan Post Holdings (*Fortune* 2010). It appears likely that the role of corporations in the world economy in the future will only become stronger, while the power of individual nation-states will decline. Even rich and powerful high income countries like the United States can become secondary to the very largest corporations. This was illustrated earlier by the Apple iPhone, which, though developed in the United States, is built from components made in several different countries and assembled in China. It is the Apple corporation that determines where the phone is built and which countries benefit most, not the United States.

Changes Driven by Technology

Many of the trends in the world stratification system are technology based. Communications technologies bring countries closer together and make it impossible not to be exposed to one another's cultures. However, as in all things, this is an asymmetric process. More powerful countries like the United States provide much of the content for the Internet, music, and the arts, and less powerful countries sometimes try to resist that influence. Transportation technologies coupled with advances in communications have made it possible to distribute the production of goods and services all over the world, making us all more interdependent. However, technology is a double-edged sword and can have its effects in many ways. Even though technology often supports the status quo, it can also be a powerful force to disrupt or challenge the world as we know it. It is technologies once again that have transformed political life and helped shape some of the recent events in the world. The Arab Spring demonstrations in many Arab countries in 2011 could have been very different without Facebook, cell phones, and Twitter helping demonstrators organize massive demonstrations and get the word out to the world about what was happening. "Leapfrog" technologies can help countries skip one or more stages of technological development, allowing them to adopt a newer, less expensive technology, as seen with cell phones becoming more widespread than telephone land lines in many low-income countries. Such technologies offer opportunities for low-income countries to skip some of the stages high-income countries went through and perhaps catch up to or surpass those countries faster. So technology supports existing trends as well as new ones. The only thing certain about the future of world stratification is that there will continue to be changes . . . and many of those changes will be brought about by new technologies

None of us knows what the future of technology will bring. But we all know it will lead to change.
© Nik Merkulov/ Shutterstock, Inc.

CONCEPT LEARNING CHECK 8.4   Future Trends

Which of the following trends are likely to affect global stratification in the future? Answer true or false.

_____ **1.** Increased competition

_____ **2.** Rising importance of multinational corporations

_____ **3.** The end of poverty

_____ **4.** Diminishing inequality within countries

Visual Summary Global Stratification

8.1 Global Stratification Overview

- The share of world gross domestic product has declined dramatically for Europe, increased dramatically for Asia/Oceania, and been relatively stable for the United States, Latin America, and the Middle East/Africa.
- Countries of the world have been classified by politics (First, Second, and Third World), levels of development, levels of industrialization, and income.

- The average per-capita income of individuals in high-income countries is more than 50 times larger than that of individuals in low-income countries.

8.2 Wealth and Poverty: A Global View

- Country income is inversely related to poverty rates.
- Income inequality within countries varies greatly, being lowest in Scandinavian countries and highest in Africa and South America.
- Income inequality is increasing in most countries, even high-income countries.
- Life expectancy at birth in low-income countries (58) is a full generation (22 years) behind that in high-income countries.
- Infant mortality rates are highest for low-income countries and lowest for high-income countries.
- Adult literacy is nearly universal for high-income countries, 83% for middle-income countries, and 61% for low-income countries.
- Equal access to education is highest for high-income countries and lowest for low-income countries.
- Access to a safe water supply for urban populations is highest in high-income countries and lowest in low-income countries.

- CO_2 emissions per capita are highest in high-income countries and lowest in low-income countries.
- Access to technologies such as the Internet, telephone lines, and cell phones is greatest for high-income countries and lowest for low-income countries.
- People tend to emigrate from lower-income countries and immigrate into higher-income countries.
- Forced migration includes refugees and human trafficking.
- Low-income countries are particularly hard hit by the emigration of highly skilled people.
- The economic loss to low-income countries from emigration is often reduced substantially when people living abroad send back funds (remittances) to family members still living in their country of origin.

Visual Summary Global Stratification, continued

8.3 Global Stratification: Theoretical Perspectives

- Modernization theory argues that the culture of low-income countries conflicts with development (the traditional stage), but with help from developed countries, this can change, leading the country to "take off," then drive to technological maturity, and eventually transform into a high-mass-consumption state.
- Dependency theory argues that rich countries exploit poorer countries that depend upon them, much like under colonialism.
- World systems theory argues the global economic system consists of peripheral countries exploited by other countries, semiperipheral countries that exploit peripheral countries but are themselves exploited by core countries, and core countries that have the highest income and dominate the world economic system.
- The international division of labor theory argues that large multinational corporations pick and choose which countries are used to manufacture various components of products to maximize their profit.

8.4 Global Stratification Effects and the Future

- Life in low-income countries is starkly different from that in middle and high-income countries and is reflected in efforts by people to migrate away from economic hardship.
- Increased global competition has left even high-income countries more vulnerable, and some, particularly in the Eurozone, are slipping in relative income.
- Inequality is increasing within most countries, even high-income countries.
- Problems of low-income countries impact all countries through migration issues and political instability.
- The global commodity chain for the production of many high-tech products makes countries more interdependent.
- Multinational corporations play an increased role in the world economy, and nation-states are more vulnerable.
- Much of the change in the global economy is driven by technology.

8.1 Global Stratification Overview

1. The income category of countries in the World Bank classification including the largest population is:
A. high income.
B. medium income.
C. low income.
D. OECD countries.

2. High-income countries (with 16% of the world's population) account for what proportion of the world GDP?
A. 68%
B. 30%
C. 16%
D. 90%

3. Low-income countries are most often found in which two continents?
A. North America and Africa
B. Africa and Asia
C. Asia and Europe
D. South America and North America

4. The ratio of income per capita for high-income nations compared to low-income nations is roughly:
A. 5:1.
B. 10:1.
C. 20:1.
D. 50:1.

8.2 Wealth and Poverty: A Global View

5. True or false: Poverty rates can vary considerably among even neighboring countries.

6. True or false: Income inequality is steadily diminishing in high-income countries.

7. True or false: Of the three technologies—Internet, telephone lines, and cell phones—low- and medium-income countries have greatest use of telephone lines because they have been around so much longer.

8. True or false: High-income countries contribute nearly 40 times as much CO_2 emissions per capita as low-income countries and more than 3 times as much as middle-income countries.

8.3 Global Stratification: Theoretical Perspectives

9. Which theory places greatest emphasis on the important role that multinational corporations play in global stratification?
A. Modernization theory
B. Dependency theory
C. World systems theory
D. International division of labor theory

10. Which theory assumes each vulnerable country is dominated by a single dominant country?
A. Modernization theory
B. Dependency theory
C. World systems theory
D. International division of labor theory

11. Which category of countries in world systems theory are most countries in Africa likely to fall into?
A. Third World countries
B. Core countries
C. Consumer countries
D. Peripheral countries

8.4 Global Stratification Effects and the Future

Consider how immigration looks to a high-income and a low-income country. For each characteristic below, indicate the type of country most likely to display it.

12. Higher rates of emigration of highly skilled people
A. High-income
B. Low-income

13. More likely to be a source of victims of human trafficking
A. High-income
B. Low-income

14. Less likely to receive remittances from people living abroad
A. High-income
B. Low-income

15. Net out-migration (emigration)
A. High-income
B. Low-income

CHAPTER ESSAY QUESTIONS

1. In 2009, this region of the world produced roughly between 25 and 28% of the world gross domestic product (GDP). Which three regions meet this description? Of those three, which one is undergoing a dramatic decline in its share since 1969? Which region increased dramatically in that same period?

2. Describe what you would expect regarding immigration and emigration for countries in the lowest income category.

3. List the three types of countries in world systems theory. Which category dominates the other two? Which type does Bolivia fall into? Which type describes Germany? Where do you think Brazil would fall?

CHAPTER DISCUSSION QUESTIONS

1. Do you know someone who has immigrated here from another country? Does his or her immigration fit the patterns discussed in this chapter? What factors led this person to immigrate?

2. As in many countries, inequality has increased in the United States. Can you think of examples or evidence in your own family or among your friends of ways in which increasing inequality has affected their lives? Use your sociological imagination to analyze and discuss how these people might explain these changes in their lives.

3. Discuss alternatives to the First, Second, and Third World classifications of countries. Are economic classifications independent of politics and political policies?

4. What are the best measures of poverty? Why is absolute poverty not used to define poverty in high- and middle-income countries? Should it be? Why or why not?

5. What policies should the United States adopt when it comes to refugees? Should there be a difference in immigration versus refugee policies? Why or why not?

6. Why do you think that women and children are significantly more likely than men to become victims of human trafficking, including forced and bonded labor?

7. Do you think the trends related to bright flight or brain drain should be global concerns, or is this more of an issue that should be dealt with at the local level by affected countries?

8. Which theory (modernization, dependency, world systems, or international division of labor) best explains global stratification? Why?

9. Will technological advances lessen the problems associated with global stratification? Why? How might modernization theory support your view?

CHAPTER PROJECTS

INDIVIDUAL PROJECTS

1. Go online and search the CIA World Factbook. Examine information about at least 12 different countries from at least three different continents. Write a report of your findings.

2. Go online and search the Better Life Index (OECD). Examine information including the categories that make up the index. How does the OECD's definition of a high quality of life compare with or differ from that of your own? Write an analysis of your findings.

GROUP PROJECTS

1. Many small towns in the United States are experiencing a net emigration, particularly of highly trained individuals, and are losing population. Consider how these communities might resemble a low-income country. What advantages do they have over low-income countries? Could any of the theories of global stratification be used to examine these communities by analogy? Prepare a brief report about a particular small US town or community in which you gather data and present your analysis of the ways this town resembles and differs from a low-income country.

2. Pick a country and find out its characteristics on all those dimensions described in section 8.2. You might review some of the websites cited for some of the statistics in that section. What income category does this country fall into? Does it meet all the expectations we have for that category? Are there ways it surprises you? Why do you think that country is different in those statistics on which it differs? Is there something special about its history or its culture that might account for those differences?

3. Go online and search for *world bank group*. Examine information of your choice, including the various topics and countries. Discuss with other students how the information and data relate to what you read about in this chapter. Write a summary of your findings and discussion.

4. Go online and search for *human rights watch*. Based on your examination of the topics, identify three of the most offensive violations of human rights and write a summary of your group discussion detailing why and how you reached your conclusions.

CHAPTER KEY TERMS

Absolute poverty
Bonded labor
Brain drain/bright flight
Colonialism
Core countries
Drive to technological maturity
Emigration
First World
Forced labor
Gini coefficient
Global commodity chains

High-income nations
High mass consumption
Human Development Index (HDI)
Human trafficking
Immigration
Infant mortality
International division of labor theory
Low-income nations
Middle-income nations
Modernization theory
Neocolonialism

Net migration rate
Peripheral countries
Refugee
Second World
Semiperipheral countries
Sex trafficking
Take-off stage
Third World
Traditional stage
World systems theory

ANSWERS TO CONCEPT LEARNING CHECKS

8.1 Characteristics of the World Stratification System

1. The primary basis for this classification is political.
   [A. Three worlds classification (First, Second, and Third World)]

2. This classification is used by the World Bank. [D. Income classification (high income, middle income, low income)]

3. This classification distinguishes countries based on achieving a state many countries have now gone beyond. [C. Industrialization classification (most industrialized, industrializing, least industrialized)]

4. This classification implies that some nations are necessarily inferior to others. [B. Development classification (developed, developing, undeveloped)]

8.2 Patterns of World Stratification

1. At 46th, the United States ranks below [E. 45] other countries in infant mortality rate.

2. High-income countries have life expectancies averaging [D. 22] years more than low-income countries.

3. Infant mortality rates in low-income countries are on average [A. 14] times higher than those of high-income countries.

4. In low-income countries, the percentage of the urban population with access to improved water supplies is [C. 85].

5. Among low-income countries, the average percentage of highly skilled people who have emigrated to other countries is [B. 12] %.

8.3 Theoretical Perspectives on Global Stratification

1. This theory explains how products such as high-tech electronics are manufactured in different countries. [D. International division of labor theory]

2. This theory is associated with W. W. Rostow. [A. Modernization theory]

3. This theory assumes that high-income countries can help low-income countries through technology and foreign aid. [A. Modernization theory]

4. This theory proposes that there are a few groups of nations in the world, with one group dominating the others. [C. World systems theory]

8.4 Future Trends

1. [T] Increased competition

2. [T] Rising importance of multinational corporations

3. [F] The end of poverty

4. [F] Diminishing inequality within countries

ANSWERS TO CHAPTER REVIEW TEST

8.1 Global Stratification Overview

1. B. Middle-income countries account for 72% of the world population.

2. A. High-income countries account for 68% of world GDP.

3. B. Africa and Asia together have most of the world's low-income countries.

4. D. 50:1. The per-capita income for high-income nations is roughly 50 times that of low-income nations.

8.2 Wealth and Poverty: A Global View

5. True. For example, Mexico's poverty rate is 47% while that of the United States is 14%.

6. False. It is increasing in most OECD countries, most of which are high-income countries.

7. False. Low- and medium-income countries have far less use of telephone lines than cell phones and, in large part, have been able to skip over that very expensive technology.

8. True. High-income countries contribute nearly 40 times as much CO_2 emissions per capita as low-income countries and more than 3 times as much as middle-income countries.

8.3 Global Stratification: Theoretical Perspectives

9. D. The international division of labor theory emphasizes the role of multinationals in deciding where different parts of a product are built.

10. B. Dependency theory emphasizes the dominance of one country over another as was common in colonialism.

11. D. Only B and D are world systems theory categories, and African countries are mostly peripheral countries.

8.4 Global Stratification Effects and the Future

12. B. Low-income. Higher rates of emigration of highly skilled people

13. B. Low-income. More likely to be a source of victims of human trafficking

14. A. High-income. Less likely to receive remittances from people living abroad

15. B. Low-income. Net out-migration (emigration)

ANSWERS TO CHAPTER ESSAY QUESTIONS

1. Three regions—the EU 15, Asia/Oceania, and the United States—each produced roughly 25 to 30% of the world GDP in 2009. The EU 15 is undergoing a dramatic decline, while Asia/Oceania increased dramatically.

2. Countries in the lowest income category tend to have high emigration with a net loss of population, high emigration of skilled workers, high remittances, high human trafficking, and high refugees.

3. World systems theory distinguishes core countries, semiperipheral countries, and peripheral countries. Bolivia is a peripheral country. Germany is a core country. Brazil is a semiperipheral country.

REFERENCES

Alpert, E. 2012. "Sharing refugees—a 'good idea' that's gone nowhere." *Los Angeles Times*, Sep. 20, 2012. Accessed October 2012 at http://latimesblogs .latimes.com/world_now/2012/09/sharing-refugees-united-nations-human-rights-humanitarian-relief.html.

Amin, Samir. 1974. *Accumulation on a World Scale: A Critique of the Theory of Underdevelopment.* New York: Monthly Review Press.

Baran, Paul A. 1957. *The Political Economy of Growth.* New York: Monthly Review Press.

BBC News. 2011. "Brazil Economy Overtakes UK, says CEBR." *BBC News* December 26, 2011. Accessed December 2011 at http://www.bbc.co.uk/news/business-16332115.

Berkowitz, B. 2011. "From a single hashtag, a protest circled the world." *Brisbane Times* October 19, 2011. Accessed January 2012 at http://www .brisbanetimes.com.au/technology/technology-news/from-a-single-hashtag-a-protest-circled-the-world-20111019-1m72j.html#content.

Centre for Economic and Business Research (CBR). 2011. "Brazil has overtaken the UK's GDP. CEBR News Release, Dec. 26, 2011. Accessed January 2012 at http://www.cebr.com/wp-content/uploads/Cebr-World-Economic-League-Table-press-release-26-December-2011.pdf.

CIA World Factbook. United Nations Educational, Scientific, and Cultural Organization (UNESCO), Institute for Statistics. Accessed January 2012 at http://www.indexmundi.com/map/?t=0&v=39&r=xx&l=en.

DeNavas-Walt, Carmen, Bernadette Proctor, and Jessica Smith. 2009. *Income, Poverty, and Health Insurance Coverage in the United States: 2009.* U.S. Census Bureau. Accessed January 2012 at http://www.census.gov/prod/2010pubs/p60-238.pdf.

Fortune. 2010. "Global 500." *Fortune.* Accessed October 2012 at http://money .cnn.com/magazines/fortune/global500/2012/full_list/.

Frank, Andre Gunder. 1966. *The Development of Underdevelopment.* New York: Monthly Review Press.

Kangaspunta, Kristina. 2006. *Trafficking in Persons: Global Patterns.* International Symposium on International Migration and Development. Turin, 28–30 June, 2006. Accessed January 2012 at http://www.un.org/esa/population/migration/turin/Turin_Statements/KANGASPUNTA.pdf.

Klein, E. 2012. "Would Obama or Romney Redistribute More?" *Washington Post.* Sep. 20, 2012. Accessed January 2012 at http://www.washingtonpost.com/blogs/ezra-klein/wp/2012/09/20/would-obama-or-romney-redistribute-more/.

Kollmair, Michael, Siddhi Manadhara, Bhim Subedı, and Susan Thieme. 2006. "New figures for old stories: Migration and remittances in Nepal." *Migration Letters*, 3(2):151–160. October 2006. (ISSN: *print:* 1741-8984 *&online:* 1741-8992) www.migrationletters.com. Accessed January 2012 at http:// www.google.com/url?sa=t&rct=j&q=&esrc=s&source=web&cd=1&sqi=2 &ved=0CDAQFjAA&url=http%3A%2F%2Fwww.icimod.org%2Fresource. php%3Fid%3D145&ei=AgcGT5r8NpKltwevj9XPBg&usg=AFQjCNGbqG ZL8TJmrpu50IGlRq3dxshrEQ.

Lenin, Vladimir Ilich. 1927. *Imperialism: The State and Revolution.* New York: Vanguard Press.

McClelland, D. 1961. *The Achieving Society.* New York, NY: Van Nostrand.

OECD. 2011. "Divided we stand: Why inequality keeps rising." Accessed December 2011 at http://www.oecd.org/social/socialpoliciesanddata/49170768.pdf.

OECD. 2012. Glossary of Statistical Terms. Accessed February 2012 at http:// stats.oecd.org/glossary/detail.asp?ID=1176.

Rostow, Walt W. 1960. *The Stages of Economic Growth: A Non-Communist Manifesto.* Cambridge, UK: Cambridge University Press.

Sadiq, Sheraz. 2002. "Timeline: Cochabamba water revolt." *PBS Frontline/World.* WGBH Educational Foundation. Accessed January 2012 at http://www.pbs .org/frontlineworld/stories/bolivia/timeline.html.

Schill, Mark. 2011. Share of world GDP by country, 1969–2009. New geography. Accessed January 2012 at http://www.newgeography.com/content/001562-share-world-gdp-country-1969-2010.

UNDP. 1990. *Defining and Measuring Human Development.* United Nations Development Program. Accessed February 2012 at http://hdr.undp.org/en/media/hdr_1990_en_chap1.pdf.

United Nations. 2008. United Nations Population Division, World Population Prospects 2008. Accessed January 2012 from http://www.indexmundi.com/facts/indicators/SM.POP.NETM.

United Nations High Commissioner for Refugees (UNHCR). 2009. *Annual Report.* Accessed January 2012 at http://www.unhcr.org/4a2fd52412d.html.

United Nations High Commissioner for Refugees (UNHCR). 2010. *Statistical Yearbook and Data Files 2010.* Accessed January 2012 at www.unhcr.org/statistics/populationdatabase.

United Nations Office on Drugs and Crime (UNODC). 2009. *Global Report on Trafficking in Persons.* United Nations. Accessed January 2012 at http://www.unodc.org/documents/human-trafficking/Executive_summary_english.pdf.

Wallerstein, I. 1976. *The Modern World System.* New York: Academic Press.

Wallerstein, I. 1979. *The Capitalist World-Economy.* Cambridge, UK: Cambridge University Press.

Wallerstein, I. 1980. *The Modern World System II: Mercantilism and the Consolidation of the European World Economy, 1600–1750.* New York: Academic Press.

Waters, Malcolm. 1995. *Globalization.* London and New York: Routledge.

World Bank. 2011a. *Data by Country.* The World Bank. Accessed January 2012 at http://data.worldbank.org/country.

World Bank. 2011b. *Migration and Remittances.* Accessed January 2012 at http:// go.worldbank.org/RR8SDPEHO0.

World Health Organization and United Nations Children's Fund, Joint Measurement Programme (JMP) (http://www.wssinfo.org/). Accessed January 2012 at http://www.indexmundi.com/facts/indicators/SH.H2O.SAFE.UR.ZS.

Xing, Yuqing and Neal Detert. 2011. *How the iPhone Widens the United States Trade Deficit with the People's Republic of China.* ABDI Working Paper 257. Tokyo: Asian Development Bank Institute. Revised May 2011. Accessed December 2011 at http://www.adbi.org/files/2010.12.14.wp257.iphone .widens.us.trade.deficit.prc.pdf.

© Ingram Publishing/Thinkstock

Chapter Overview ▼

9 Race and Ethnicity in Society

Learning Objectives ▼

9.1 ■ Describe the distinction between race and ethnicity.

9.2 ■ Explain the different concepts of race.
■ Identify the three major racial classifications.

9.3 ■ Compare and contrast race and ethnicity.
■ Discuss the three major ways in which new minority groups emerge in a culture.
■ Illustrate the four factors that influence the strength of a person's sense of ethnic or racial identity.

9.4 ■ Discuss the key perspectives on prejudice.
■ Describe the nature of stereotypes.

9.5 ■ Describe the difference between prejudice and discrimination.
■ Analyze the key theories of discrimination.

9.6 ■ Compare and contrast the ways in which the major theoretical perspectives interpret race and racial relations.

9.7 ■ Compare and contrast the major racial groups in the United States and how intersectionality theory dictates assumptions.

9.8 ■ Describe the key issues regarding race and ethnicity in the United States.

© luxorphoto/Shutterstock, Inc.

I opened our front door on a crisp morning and bent down to get the newspaper for my father. I could still detect the sour odor of the fresh paint on the door, and it took my eyes a moment to adjust to the bright red paint that dripped down to the stoop. Even though I was very young, I knew what it meant. I did not even have to read the words. A shiver of fright coursed through my body. Visibly upset, I called my father, who staggered out of the kitchen in his bathrobe, coffee in hand. He mouthed the words on the door "Go away Jews!" punctuated with a swastika. I started to cry.

My mother, hearing my sobs, came out of the bedroom and gasped when she saw the red lettering on the door. She hugged my father and me. "Why?" she whispered.

"How did anyone even know?" my father wondered aloud. We had only moved in a couple of weeks ago. We knew that in moving to a small, almost exclusively white town, we would be exposed to prejudicial attitudes that often viewed Jews as scapegoats. Many people blame Jews for a host of social problems, saying that they control the government through control of banking and media. These arguments are not new, of course, dating back even before Adolph Hitler used them to incarcerate and kill millions of Jews. Unfortunately, those attitudes did not die with the Third Reich.

We had tried to keep our Jewish heritage hidden. We did not tell anyone. I was told expressly to keep my heritage to myself, to be like everyone else. I was told to pray and eat and act like everyone else in the town. I did. Yet something felt dishonest about it. After all, I was a Jew. I was proud of my heritage, even though I did not understand all of it. I was proud of the contributions that the Jewish people had made to society. Torn between loyalty to my parents and loyalty to my ethnic heritage, I might have let my Judaism slip to one of my friends.

We never did solve the mystery of who painted those hateful words on our door, but it was the only such incident while we lived in that town. Today, I remain proud of my ethnic heritage and do not try to hide it. While some people still seem put off by ethnic heritage, I find most people to be accepting—and often supportive—of my Jewish heritage. I continue to work at my identity, seeking to establish a connection to my ancestry. In sociology, we call this ethnic work. We identify with our ethnic identity and incorporate it into our understanding of our self. Ethnic work helps us develop our sociological imagination because it merges history with experience. It helps us to understand how our understanding of self emerges from our social experiences.

9.1 Race and Ethnicity in Society

Sociological views of race center on how race is socially constructed and how race affects the social choices of people.

- Describe the distinction between race and ethnicity.

The importance of race in society is as old as civilization itself. However, the concept of race itself remains somewhat elusive and heavily debated among social scientists. Many social scientists argue that races exist only as a social construct. Other social scientists believe that races have a biological basis but that the meaning of race is determined by society. Still others remain ambivalent about the existence of races, focusing their attention instead on the ways in which the concept of race is used in society. Regardless of whether races exist as biological categories or merely as something socially constructed by society, it is clear that the concept of race is an important one in society for a variety of reasons. Race has an impact on status, education, income, and general quality of life. Race affects life chances.

A distinct but related concept is ethnicity. Ethnicity differs from race in significant ways. While the term *race* is generally used to refer to biological categories that distinguish groups of people, *ethnicity* refers to aspects of culture that distinguish one group from another. Ethnicities can be classified in a myriad of ways, such as through religion in the case of Judaism; language such as Hispanics; cuisine such as Thai; or nationality such as Chinese. There can even be multiple ethnicities within a single racial group. Indeed, within the white race, there exist a myriad of different ethnic groups ranging from English speakers to Spanish speakers, Christian to Buddhist, and everything in between. Because of the array of possible ethnic classifications, there are far more ethnicities than racial types. Like race, however, ethnicity affects life chances in a variety of ways. Ethnicity affects attitudes and behaviors toward education, income, socio-economic status, and quality of life. Ethnicity helps individuals form a sense of social identity and gives them a sense of connection to their heritage. In short, both ethnicity and race help people develop their sociological imagination.

CONCEPT LEARNING CHECK 9.1   Race and Ethnicity in Society

Based on what you have just read, answer the following questions.

1. List two ways in which race and ethnicity are different.

2. List two ways in which race and ethnicity are similar.

9.2 Race

Race refers to socially constructed categories based on biological traits that society considers important.

- Explain the different concepts of race.
- Identify the three major racial classifications.

> **Race** A socially constructed category of people who share some biologically transmitted traits that society considers important.

Although most social scientists believe that race is an artificial concept (Daynes and Lee 2008), scientists in many other disciplines do accept that races exist. For example, almost all forensic anthropologists—a branch of anthropology that works with law enforcement to identify skeletal remains—accept the fact that races have a biological origin (Gill 1990) FIGURE 9-1. Physical anthropologists also generally accept that races are real (Gill 1990). Similarly, most geneticists and evolutionary biologists also accept that the idea of races is biologically valid (Morning 2011). Practitioners in these disciplines argue that if a person can assess race with reasonable accuracy, then it must have some basis in biological reality (Gill 1990). Ordinary people are remarkably consistent in their assessment of racial origin. In addition, they are remarkably accurate in determining a person's racial ancestry. This gives some credence to the belief that races have some biological reality.

Racial diversity very likely had its origin deep in our evolutionary ancestry as human populations expanded from their African origins and began living in different geographic regions with different climates (Oppenheimer 2003). Over time, humans began to adapt to these different climates. For example, populations along the equator developed darker skins as protection from the intense sun, while populations living in more northern climates developed lighter skins in response to the more indirect sunlight found in those climates.

Social scientists, however, argue that these biological distinctions are unimportant. Rather, they take on importance only in social situations. They define **race** as a socially constructed category of people who share some

FIGURE 9-1 Anthropologist George Gill is one of the many scientists that accepts the validity of race as a scientific concept.

Courtesy of George W. Gill

biologically transmitted traits that society considers important. Social scientists note that all human beings, regardless of their place of origin, are of the same species. They point to the fact that definitions of race have changed over time. Early in our nation's history, individuals who could trace any of their ancestry to Africa were considered black. Today, however, these categorizations are no longer valid. Thus, the definitions of race have changed as social circumstances have changed. For example, in the years during and after slavery, having one drop of African-American blood was enough to have a person labeled African American. However, today, the definition of race has changed to allow an individual more choices about his or her racial identity. The United States census allows individuals to self-identify with one or even multiple racial categories.

Racial Types

Although racial categorization can be traced to the ancient world (Sarich and Meile 2004), the first scientist to offer a categorization of racial types was Swedish naturalist Carrolus Linneaus in 1735. Linneaus FIGURE 9-2 identified four identifiable races. This categorization was later expanded upon by various scholars and ballooned to as many as 34 categories (DeCamp 1995)!

As a society, Americans seem to view race as more important than citizens of other nations do. Generally speaking, American society recognizes three racial categories—black, Asian, and white. These categories are generally consistent with many modern scientific views on race (Gill 1990).

Generally, scientists who accept the biological reality of race divide mankind into three categories. *Caucasoid* is the general term applied to people with light skin and fine hair texture. *Mongoloid* peoples have yellow- or brown-toned skin and have folds in the eyelids that give a distinctive look. *Negroid* are people with darker skin and coarse, flat-shaped hair FIGURE 9-3. These categorizations are not universally accepted, of course, and social scientists point to the arbitrary nature of the categorizations as evidence of their claim against the reality of race. Sociologists further claim that distinctive categorization of people into racial categories is impossible. Rather than clear-cut racial distinctions, there exists only a range of physical variations among human beings. Sociologists also cite a study by biologist Richard Lewontin that there is more genetic variation within groups than between groups, even though this research and its conclusion have been strongly criticized.

Categorizations of race by nonscientists follow these basic categorizations quite closely and are remarkably reliable both throughout history and across cultures (Sarich and Meile 2004). As far back as the ancient Egyptians, reliable racial categories have been recognized and used. This process by which people are placed into racial categories is called **racialization**. In other words, people are placed into racial categories that are given social significance. Historically, racialization has been used as a means of oppressing certain groups and enriching others. For example, slavery in the American colonies was often justified through the process of racialization. Slavery advocates, often bolstered by the science of the time, argued that African races were inherently inferior to individuals of European descent. Nazi-run Germany also used racialization to justify horrific experiments on Jews and other groups. Even more recently, racialization has been used in Africa and Europe to fuel genocidal wars that have led to the death of thousands of people.

However, there is no necessary reason racialization must lead to discrimination. In fact, racialization can also be used for positive purposes. For example, forensic anthropologists use racial categorizations to help identify the remains of unknown individuals. In addition, modern medicine often relies on racial categorizations to accurately diagnose and treat many diseases. One example of how the medical profession has successfully used race in the treatment of disease is the creation of the drug BiDil. Doctors have long known that heart disease in African Americans

Karl von Linné.

FIGURE 9-2 Carrolus Linneaus was the first scientist to offer a categorization of racial types.

© Nicku/Shutterstock, Inc.

Racialization The process by which people are placed into racial categories.

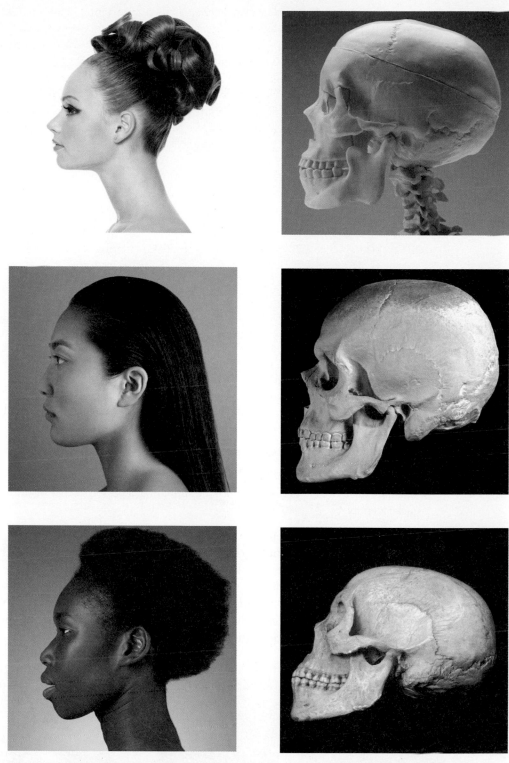

FIGURE 9-3 Most scientists identify three major racial groups: Caucasoid, Mongoloid, and Negroid.

(top row) © iStockphoto/Thinkstock; © StudioSource/Alamy; (middle row) © Thinkstock; © Patrick Landmann/Photo Researchers, Inc; (bottom row) © Hemera Technologies/Thinkstock; © E. R. Degginger/Photo Researchers, Inc.

is more aggressive and advances more rapidly, with greater chances of heart failure and other related problems than in other races. BiDil is a drug developed specifically for African Americans and does not work in other races. In the future, many such drugs will likely be targeted to the unique genetic and health profiles of different racial categories.

CONCEPT LEARNING CHECK 9.2　　Race

Answer the following multiple-choice questions.

1. The first scientist to offer a categorization of race was:

   A. Charles Darwin.

   B. Carrolus Linneaus.

   C. W. E. B. Du Bois.

   D. Richard Lewontin.

2. The process by which people are placed into racial categories is called:

   A. race aligning.

   B. race construction.

   C. racialization.

   D. race typing.

3. Most scientists recognize how many racial categories?

   A. 3

   B. 4

   C. 5

   D. 7

9.3 Ethnicity

Ethnicity refers to beliefs, values, and practices that characterize a particular group.

- Compare and contrast race and ethnicity.
- Discuss the three major ways in which new minority groups emerge in a culture.
- Illustrate the four factors that influence the strength of a person's sense of ethnic or racial identity.

Ethnicity Cultural practices that distinguish one group of people from another.

Often, the terms *race* and **ethnicity** are used interchangeably. They are, however, quite different conceptually. While *race* refers to distinctions based on physical characteristics, *ethnicity* refers to cultural practices that distinguish one group of people from another FIGURE 9-4. While there appear to be relatively few races, there are many ethnicities. Ethnic groups see themselves as distinct from other groups, and although there are many ways to make cultural distinctions between people, the most common distinctions

FIGURE 9-4 Ethnicity has significantly more variation than race.

(left to right) © Kobby Dagan/Shutterstock, Inc.; © Photodisc; © Uros Ravbar/Dreamstime.com

are based on language, religion, style of dress, history, or perceived ancestry. Some examples of ethnic groups in America are Jewish Americans, Dominican Americans, and Hispanics. It is important to know that while many people consider Hispanics a race, both the United States census and forensic anthropology consider Hispanics to be several ethnic groups, categorized under the Caucasian racial category.

As you can see, ethnicity is highly variable. It is also less strictly defined, and those definitions may change over time as cultures and cultural practices change. Because of their general denial of the reality of racial categories, sociologists are generally more concerned with ethnicity than race. Despite their denial of race, however, sociologists quite often continue to act as though races are real and include race as a variable in much social science research. College applications, applications for public assistance, and even census forms rely on a combination of ethnic and racial categorization. Sociologists often act as if races are real because the consequences of racial categorizations have real consequences in society.

Like race, ethnicity has often been used as justification for oppression of certain groups and the enrichment of others. American history is replete with examples of oppression of groups such as the Irish, Jews, and Chinese. This oppression has been the focus of considerable research in sociology and has shaped the development of the sociological imagination in significant ways.

Minority Groups

When most people think of a minority group, they think of a group in a society that is numerically inferior. However, this definition is vague and misleading. Almost everyone can be considered a minority in one way or another. Like race or ethnicity, the perceptions we take on minority groups depend a great deal on the way in which we choose to define the term. For instance, individuals with red hair are a numerical minority. Yet they are not a social minority. Sociologists define **minority groups** as groups that society sets apart in some away and disadvantages due to the traits that set them apart. So while people with red hair might be numerically inferior in a population, they are not subordinated or disadvantaged relative to other groups. Therefore, they are not a minority group. While there are more women than men in society, women are often subordinated and discriminated against. Therefore, women would be considered a minority group by sociologists.

Minority groups can thus be understood only in reference to dominant groups. A **dominant group** is a group that has greater power, privilege, or prestige than other groups. Usually, dominant groups can be recognized easily because they are the groups with the most social power. Dominant groups need not be numerical majorities. Rather, they simply wield a considerable amount of social power over other groups. For this reason, minority groups usually feel isolated or disconnected from the dominant social values. Sometimes they also become physically isolated, as in the case of **segregation**. Sometimes, the isolation is imposed by the dominant social groups FIGURE 9-5. Other times, the segregation is self-imposed. In either case, segregation often serves to increase tensions between the dominant and minority groups.

As noted, both race and ethnicity have been used as justification for oppression throughout history. There appears to be a natural tendency in humans to categorize people into in-groups and out-groups. Generally speaking, people tend to believe that the groups they belong to are superior to other groups. This leads to the development of prejudice and discrimination, which have historically created significant conflict between groups of people. Like the confusion between the concepts of race and ethnicity, prejudice and discrimination are often used interchangeably. Yet, although they are related, they have very different definitions with very different implications.

Minority groups Groups that society sets apart in some way and disadvantages due to the traits that set them apart.

Dominant group A group that has greater power, privilege, and prestige than other groups.

Segregation The physical or social isolation of a group of people from the rest of society.

The Emergence of Minority Groups

Dominant and minority groups appear in nearly every culture. There are a variety of ways that groups become dominant or minorities, with each minority group having its

FIGURE 9-5 After slavery was abolished in the United States, African Americans were forced to use separate schools, restaurants, and even drinking fountains.

(top to bottom) © Bettmann/CORBIS; © Bob Adelman/Corbis; © Bettmann/CORBIS

own story. Generally, however, sociologists recognize three major ways in which new minority groups emerge in a culture.

The first way a minority group may emerge in a culture is through the process of migration. For example, consider the thousands of Mexicans who cross the border into the United States every year. As they cross the border, they vacate their place in the dominant culture in Mexico and take their place among a minority group of Mexican immigrants in the United States. In this case, the migration is voluntary. However, it need not be so. Thousands of Africans, for example, were forcibly brought to the United States in chains during the peak years of slavery.

The second way in which minority groups emerge is through the process of expansion of political boundaries. This may take any of several forms, including colonialism, war, or economic dominance. For example, as the United States expanded its borders in the middle 1800s, it incorporated large areas that once belonged to Mexico. These territories became the states of New Mexico, Texas, and Arizona. The people who lived in those territories, once citizens of Mexico, became subject to the rule of the United States. However, because these people lacked a connection with the dominant culture under which they now found themselves, they were relegated to the status of a minority group.

The third process for the emergence of a minority group is somewhat less understood than the other two. In this process, minority groups are created within the society itself through social processes. Any group that is singled out within a society can be transformed into a minority group, though the process may differ for each group. For example, the phenomenon of women having less social power than men is not the product of overt forces of the kind already described. Rather, the process is internal to the society and evolves over time as society changes.

Constructing Racial and Ethnic Identity

If you are asked "who are you?" how would you answer the question? You might define yourself in a variety of ways. You might identify yourself as a student, as a son or daughter, or by what your job title is. Most likely, part of your identity is defined by your racial or ethnic identity as well. Although racial or ethnic identity is stronger for some people than others, nearly everyone identifies with it to some degree in defining who they are.

Why do some people feel a greater sense of ethnic or racial identity? Sociologists have identified four factors that influence the strength of a person's sense of ethnic or racial identity TABLE 9-1. The first is the relative size of the group. Generally speaking, the larger the size of the group, the less influence it has in shaping your identity. The second factor is the power that the group wields in society. Again, groups that wield significant social power seem to have less influence on identification of racial or ethnic identity.

The third factor that influences a person's sense of identity is the appearance of members of the group. If the group has a distinguishing mode of dress, for example, that makes it stand out from the dominant group, it is more likely to be used as a point of identity. In other words, if your group looks different or acts different from other groups, you are more likely to use this in constructing your racial or ethnic identity.

The final factor is discrimination. The more discriminated against a group is, the stronger the influence generally is on constructing racial or ethnic identity. This is because as a member of a discriminated-against group, you are likely to feel excluded or, more likely, to lack a sense of belonging with the dominant group. Thus, you are more likely to define yourself as a member of the minority group. In contrast, if you are a member of the dominant group, you will likely already feel a high sense of belonging and thus feel no need to identify as a member of the group.

Sociologists use the term **ethnic work** to refer to the process by which a person identifies with and constructs her or his ethnic identity. This includes how people with strong ethnic identity maintain or enhance their identity through distinctions from the dominant culture. For people with weaker ethnic identities, the term is often used to refer to the ways in which a person seeks to discover or recover her or his ethnic heritage. This may take a number of forms, such as tracing genealogical records or rekindling the celebration of a holiday unique to that ethnic group. For example, many Asians continue to celebrate Tet, a holiday celebration centered around the new year on the Asian calendar.

While ethnic work is important for the development and maintenance of identity, it does have latent consequences. One is that the development of strong ethnic identity does tend to inhibit assimilation into the dominant culture. That is why the claim of America being a **melting pot**—a blending of ethnic traditions—has not materialized in the way sociologists once predicted. Instead, ethnic work has allowed groups to maintain unique and valued elements of their specific ethnic or racial groups. Thus, America resembles less of a melting pot and more of a salad bowl!

Ethnic work The process by which a person identifies with and constructs their identity.

Melting pot A blending of ethnic traditions in a society.

TABLE 9-1 Four Main Influences in the Construction of Racial and Ethnic Identity

Factors in Discrimination	Social Influence
Size of group	The larger the social group, the less influence it has on identity.
Social power of the group	Groups that have more social power have less influence in identity formation.
Appearance of group members	Distinctive dress or other physical characteristics make a group more likely to be a point of identity.
Discrimination	The more discriminated against a group is, the stronger the influence in constructing racial or ethnic identity.

Match the definition to the correct term.

_____ **1.** Cultural practices that distinguish one group from another

_____ **2.** Groups that society sets apart and subordinates

_____ **3.** The physical isolation of groups of people

_____ **4.** The process by which a person identifies with and constructs her or his ethnic identity

A. Segregation

B. Minority group

C. Ethnic work

D. Ethnicity

9.4 Prejudice

Prejudice has many causes, but the sociological consequences of prejudice remain constant.

- Discuss the key perspectives on prejudice.
- Describe the nature of stereotypes.

Prejudice Beliefs or attitudes about a particular group.

Prejudice refers to beliefs or attitudes about a particular group. Everyone has prejudices. If you like corn but hate peas, you have a prejudice. That is, you prefer one type of vegetable to another. Of course, we can also be prejudiced against certain groups of people. These prejudices typically form very early in life and often become habitual. Many times, prejudices against groups of people are based on folklore and myth rather than on reality. Prejudicial attitudes are sometimes hard to change, and people often seek out selective evidence to justify their prejudices. For example, an individual with a prejudicial attitude toward a particular group may feel that members of that group are lazy. When he sees a member of that group napping on the job, he will tend to generalize this behavior to every member of the group, as well as to see it as evidence of his belief.

It is important to note that prejudice is natural in the human species. Generally speaking, prejudices are harmless because they are merely attitudes that we have toward a particular idea. However, sometimes prejudices can have negative consequences, such as when they translate into behaviors that seek to disadvantage certain groups. Such behaviors are called discrimination, which is discussed later in the chapter.

Defining and Measuring Prejudice

As noted, everyone has prejudices of one sort or another. In many cases, those prejudicial attitudes are relatively innocuous, as in the case of preferring one sport to another or preferring one type of food to another. However, when prejudices are directed at a specific group of people, they often threaten to develop into negative behaviors or attitudes that are harmful to other groups of people.

The extent of prejudice is hard to measure. Because prejudice is an attitude, it cannot be seen. Researchers must rely on the self-reporting of subjects for their information about prejudice. Often, prejudices are so ingrained in a person's mentality that the person is unaware he or she holds such deep-seated prejudices. Additionally, even when people are aware of their particular prejudices, they may be unwilling to admit them to other people. For this reason, research on prejudice is difficult to conduct accurately. Of course, researchers are typically interested in only one kind of prejudice, which may be confusing to the subjects if not clearly defined.

One additional problem is that people frequently confuse prejudice and discrimination. As we will come to see, they are distinctly different concepts. While most of the time discrimination constitutes evidence of prejudice, the same cannot be said in reverse. It is not necessary that prejudicial attitudes lead to discriminatory action. Yet people often assume that prejudice automatically leads to discrimination. This fallacy plagues not only ordinary people but sociologists as well. Because discrimination is a behavior rather than an attitude, it is much easier to get a reliable measure than prejudice.

Origins and Perspectives on Prejudice

There is considerable debate among social scientists about the origins of prejudicial behavior. Not surprisingly, the different theoretical perspectives approach the problem of prejudice formation differently. One thing that they all agree on, however, is that prejudice is universal in societies and among individuals.

Functionalism sees prejudice as functional for the maintenance of the individual or the social group. It may be functional for the maintenance of an individual's identity, because holding a prejudicial attitude against another group allows an individual to make positive comparisons with the out-group. Recall that we learned the process by which people create strong racial or ethnic identities. Functionalism seeks to understand *why* a person would want to have a strong ethnic or racial identity. After all, why would a person want to be associated with a group that is perceived as socially having less power or prestige than other groups? Functionalism provides a possible answer. People use their identity to compare with other people and to develop a sense of belonging with a particular social group. Generally, people tend to glorify groups they share a sense of belonging to and vilify groups they do not belong to. Thus, people gain a positive sense of identity even through association with oppressed groups. Similarly, prejudice can be functional for a group as well because it serves to unite members in a common bond against another group. By emphasizing differences between groups, boundaries for membership and identification with groups are clarified. In this way, groups create their own distinct identities in comparison with other groups.

The conflict perspective analyzes prejudice in terms of competition over scarce social resources. Prejudice is a means by which the dominant social group gains and secures access to scant resources. Prejudicial attitudes provide justifications for why minority groups are not entitled to the same resources as the dominant group. By perpetuating prejudice, the dominant group creates a means of social control by which not only members of its group but also other groups come to see unequal distribution of resources as normal or appropriate.

Through the symbolic interactionist perspective, the specific ways in which prejudice is constructed and understood in society can be studied. For example, symbolic interactionists might try to understand how certain characteristics come to be associated with particular groups, as well as how these terms come to be used in society. This perspective is valuable in understanding how stereotypes are constructed and used in society.

Stereotypes

Stereotypes are generalizations that are applied to a group of people. Stereotypes often arise from prejudices that people hold. In fact, stereotyping can be seen as the primary mechanism through which prejudice operates. Examples of stereotypes that you may be familiar with are that people of Asian descent are very good at math or that individuals of African descent are good at sports but bad at school. Of course, these stereotypes may be true for some members of those groups and untrue for many others. People who believe these stereotypes will act as if they apply to everyone. When faced with counterevidence, they are likely to admit that, of course, there are exceptions, but the stereotype is still generally true. In fact, the power of stereotypes is that they are nearly impossible to disprove by examining individual cases.

Stereotypes may be positive, such as the stereotype that all Asians do well at school.
© Bobby Deal/RealDealPhoto/Shutterstock, Inc.

Stereotypes may also be negative, such as the stereotype that all Hispanics are lazy.
© Jupiterimages/Thinkstock

Stereotypes Generalizations that are applied to a group of people.

Scapegoats Groups that are blamed for the problems of society that are not their fault.

Displacement The process of individual feelings of hostility, inadequacy, or anger are directed against groups that are not the origins of those feelings.

Projection The process whereby a person unconsciously projects their own characteristics on others.

It is worth noting that not all prejudices are negative, as the above examples demonstrate. People often have favorable prejudices toward in-groups and negative prejudices toward out-groups. Nor are prejudices necessarily a problem in society. When prejudices are kept private, they can sometimes serve the function of helping an individual navigate the social universe. It is only when prejudicial attitudes are translated into action that they cause social concern. When this happens, it often takes the form of scapegoating. **Scapegoats** are groups that are blamed for the problems in a society that are not their fault.

Almost always, scapegoating is directed at groups with little social power. As such, these groups are often unable to defend themselves against attacks.

Research by sociologists suggests that prejudice and the accompanying scapegoating is often the result of **displacement**, in which individual feelings of inadequacy, hostility, or anger are directed against objects or groups that are not the origins of those feelings. The process through which displacement typically occurs is called **projection**. This is the process whereby a person unconsciously projects his or her own characteristics onto others. This is why many people who direct attacks toward a group of people are often socially similar to them in some way.

CONCEPT LEARNING CHECK 9.4	Prejudice

Fill in the missing term.

1. _____ refers to beliefs or attitudes about a particular group.

2. Generalizations that are applied to a group of people are called _____.

3. _____ are groups that are blamed for the problems in a society that are not their fault.

4. _____ is a phenomena in which individual feelings of inadequacy, hostility, or anger are directed against objects or groups that are not the origins of those feelings.

5. The process whereby a person unconsciously projects his or her own characteristics onto others, it is called _____.

9.5 Discrimination

Discrimination is behaviors that deny rights, privileges, or opportunities to specific groups.

- Describe the difference between prejudice and discrimination.
- Analyze the key theories of discrimination.

Discrimination usually takes the form of denying a minority group access to the same rights and privileges as the majority.
© Karin Hildebrand Lau/Shutterstock, Inc.

As we have learned, prejudice is an attitude that is directed at a particular group. Although negative attitudes are generally not healthy, they are not generally socially harmful unless they translate into action. When prejudice leads to an action against a group, it is called **discrimination**. Usually, this takes the form of denying a particular group access to the same rights, privileges, or opportunities as the dominant group. For example, during the 1960s, American society was a segregated society. In certain parts of country, blacks were not permitted to attend the same schools, eat at the same restaurants, or even drink from the same water fountains as whites. In nearly every situation, the facilities reserved for blacks were inferior to those afforded to whites.

Discrimination is more socially troublesome than attitudes because behaviors are generally more harmful than beliefs. Because discrimination denies opportunities to particular classes of people, it tends to weaken society as a whole. Individuals who have particular skills, education, knowledge, or talents are systemically excluded from full participation in society. Thus, social progress is slowed, inevitably harming everyone.

Racism

Racism is discrimination that is directed at a particular race. It usually takes place in the context of a belief that one racial group—usually the dominant group—is superior to others. Racism may occur in a variety of forms. Racism may be individual, such as a bank officer denying a loan to an African-American based solely on his race. Racism may also occur in groups, such as the Ku Klux Klan (KKK), which advocates white supremacy.

Although most people think of racism as occurring through the actions of individuals or small groups, sociologists recognize that racism can also be embedded in the structure of society. Termed **institutional racism**, it is the belief that society is structured to favor the dominant group. Racism, in other words, is built into the very fabric of society. Such racism is often hard to measure, however. Often, accusations of institutional racism come from actions against specific individuals and may not be indicative of a pervasive social discrimination. Still, sociologists and others have uncovered evidence of institutional racism in society. One example comes from the analysis of racial redlining. The term *redlining* refers to red lines that were drawn on maps to indicate places that banks would not invest. Usually, these areas were predominantly minority. The effects of this institutional behavior were to keep predominantly minority areas poor and underdeveloped while facilitating the development of areas that are already developed and populated by dominant racial and ethnic groups.

Sociologists consider racism to be harmful not only to individuals and groups but also to society as a whole. Groups that are marginalized in society lack opportunities for education, employment, and social advancement that improve the conditions of the general society. For this reason, many sociologists have begun studying ways in which racism can be eliminated in society. In the 1960s, the term **antiracism** gained popularity. The term refers to ideologies or practices that seek to eliminate or ameliorate racism (Bonnett 2000). Certainly, great progress has been made in reducing racism in America. Political commitments, education, and social movements have all played a part in reducing discriminatory practices aimed at particular races. Much work still needs to be done, however.

> **Discrimination** Actions against a group that are designed to deny access to the same rights, privilege, and opportunities as the dominant group.
>
> **Racism** Discrimination that is directed at a particular race.
>
> **Institutional racism** The belief that racism is built into the structure of society, and that society is structured to favor the dominant group.
>
> **Antiracism** Ideologies or practices that seek to eliminate or ameliorate racism.

Racism can occur individually, or in groups, such as the Ku Klux Klan.

© JIM LO SCALZO/epa/Corbis

Theories of Discrimination and Racism

We have already learned a little about why people hold prejudicial attitudes. Understanding why people act on those prejudices to discriminate against other people requires a somewhat deeper understanding. It is important to note that no one theory is sufficient to explain all acts of discrimination. People may discriminate for different reasons. Therefore, we should see these theories as attempts to add to our understanding of why people engage in discriminatory behaviors rather than to explain every action of discrimination.

Theories of discrimination may be divided into several broad categories. Psychological theories seek to understand why people discriminate by looking at individual beliefs, values, and behaviors. Social-psychological theories emphasize the way in which a person's beliefs and values are embedded in the cultural practices of his or her society and how a person uses that understanding to find his or her place in society. Social-structural and elite theories focus on the ways in which groups interact with one another. These theories assume that groups are arranged hierarchically in society and that they compete for scarce resources. Finally, evolutionary theories argue that discrimination is an evolved response that helped some individuals or groups survive and thrive at the expense of other groups. Therefore, discrimination can be seen as an attempt to maximize reproductive fitness of individuals or groups.

Psychological Theories of Discrimination

Psychological theories of discrimination and racism focus primarily on the internal processes that take place within the individual (Sidanius and Pratto 1999). The emphasis is usually confined to the aspects of personality that an individual possesses, the basic values, beliefs, and stresses that a person maintains, or the ways in which individuals process information. While sociologists generally see such theories as incomplete, it is worth a cursory look at the major psychological theories of discrimination because they lay the foundation for other theories of discrimination.

The frustration-aggression hypothesis is perhaps the most basic and easy to understand of the psychological theories. According to the **frustration-aggression hypothesis**, discrimination against other groups is the result of displaced anger for an individual's ability to achieve highly desired goals. Because taking out anger on others is often dangerous, the anger frequently becomes directed at marginalized individuals or groups because they are less able to defend themselves or retaliate. For example, a student who fails to get accepted to the college of her choice may direct her anger toward groups who are the recipient of affirmative action programs, acting out against members of those groups.

Authoritarian personality theory was developed in the 1950s by sociologist Theodore Adorno FIGURE 9-6. This theory suggests that authoritarianism is a personality trait of individuals rather than a societal construct. Adorno argued that the characteristics of authoritarian personality are developed in childhood when the child is denigrated by his or her parents. Children that are repeatedly embarrassed, put down, or subjugated in childhood are more likely to develop a series of characteristics as a defense against these parenting practices. Later, these characteristics are projected onto groups that are perceived as powerless or marginalized in order to give the individual a sense of social power and individual worth that he or she lacked as a child.

Social-cognitive theory argues that stereotyping and discrimination are normal parts of each individual's information processing. In other words, the way in which humans process information to understand the world in which we live requires a degree of discrimination. People make connections between traits that seem unusual to them and certain racial or ethnic groups. This creates the foundation for stereotypes about those groups of people. Even if the stereotype is based on a false correlation, because of the way in which individuals organize the world, the stereotypes are acted upon as if they were true.

Social-Psychological Theories of Discrimination

Psychological theories of discrimination have been criticized because they exclude social forces in their explanation of discrimination. Social-psychological theories recognize the individual's role in constructing and engaging in discrimination while at the same time recognizing the importance of social forces in influencing those behaviors.

Social learning theories argue that people engage in prejudice and discrimination because they have been socialized to feel and behave in those ways. In other words, discrimination is taught through social interaction. Significant others teach beliefs and behaviors that are hostile toward other groups. When an individual mimics those beliefs or behaviors, the person is reinforced with praise from trusted individuals. Eventually, behaviors that are reinforced will be maintained and built upon, while behaviors that are not reinforced are removed from the behavioral repertoire.

Groups often compete with one another for societal resources. Although some resources are abundant, others are more limited. According to **realistic group conflict theory**, discrimination is the result of competition between groups for limited societal resources. For example, many people oppose illegal immigration because they argue that the immigrants are taking jobs—a limited resource—away from citizens. For that

---

Frustration-aggression hypothesis The idea that discrimination is the result of displaced anger for an individual's inability to achieve highly desired goals.

Authoritarian personality theory Authoritarianism is a personality trait of individuals that is the result of a poor upbringing.

Social learning theory People engage in prejudice and discrimination because they have been socialized to feel and behave in those ways.

Realistic group conflict theory Discrimination is the result of competition between groups for limited societal resources.

FIGURE 9-6 Sociologist Theodore Adorno suggested that discrimination has its roots in the personality of the individual.

© Getty Images

reason, they often act in discriminatory ways against members of the group they perceive as a threat to their livelihoods.

Another social-psychological theory of discrimination is **social identity theory**. This theory begins with the assumption that people have a desire to build and maintain a positive social identity. This is often accomplished by the construction of meaning of group membership and with the assumption of the in-group's superiority. When those boundaries are unclear, discrimination occurs as a means to re-clarify boundaries and return to a stable, positive social identity. This theory suggests, then, that discrimination is lowest when all groups know and accept their position in the social hierarchy. Conversely, discrimination is greatest when minority groups attempt to increase social power by confusing the boundaries between themselves and the dominant group.

Social-Structural and Elite Theories

Social-psychological theories are not fully sociological, however. They still maintain an element of individual agency in their understanding of the origins of discrimination. In contrast, social-structural and elite theories are fully sociological. They argue that the structural relationships between groups are the basis for discrimination. All of the theories in this category share the basic assumptions that social systems are arranged in a hierarchical fashion and are controlled by a small group of people who are dominant in that group.

Group position theory asserts that when groups interact, they are in a state of power imbalance. Inevitably, the dominant group will try to maintain its powerful position over the minority group by promoting social policies, attitudes, and beliefs that advantage the dominant group over others. Segregation provides an excellent example of this phenomenon. After slavery ended, the social position of blacks rose. However, segregation laws were implemented in many states as a means by which whites could continue to maintain power and privilege. Because the dominant group has more social power, it is able to manipulate policies to its advantage and continue to thrive at the expense of other groups.

Critical race theory seeks to understand how race, law, and social power operate to keep dominant groups in power. Critical race theory has its roots in Marxist theory. It assumes that institutional discrimination exists in many social institutions, including the legal and penal systems. Critical race theory notes, for example, that African Americans are arrested for crimes at a rate much higher than we should expect for their proportion of the population. Critical race theory also notes that African Americans have higher conviction rates and receive harsher punishments than whites for the same crimes. The theory suggests that the legal system is used by dominant groups as a means of controlling minority groups. By putting minorities in prisons, dominant groups can control the labor market by keeping incarcerated minorities from working. Additionally, in some states, individuals with felony convictions are ineligible to vote. Thus, by convicting minorities of felonies, whites use the legal system to control the democratic process and advantage themselves.

When an individual has a felony conviction, it often becomes more difficult for him or her to acquire a good-paying job. Thus, many African Americans who have been the victims of differential incarceration and sentencing continue to suffer the effects after they are released because their job opportunities are limited by their conviction. Critical race theory seeks to use its critical understanding to combat the institutional discrimination in the legal and political systems that proliferates the systematic disadvantages of minorities.

Evolutionary Theories of Discrimination

As we have already learned, evolutionary theory argues that prejudice has a strong innate component that served us well in our evolutionary ancestry. Consistent with that position, evolutionary theory offers insight into the nature of discrimination as well. According to evolutionary theory, discrimination is a behavioral adaptation to increase reproductive fitness.

Social identity theory People desire a positive social identity, and will discriminate to elevate their own identity.

Group position theory When groups interact, the dominant group will promote social policies and attitudes that advantage themselves over other groups.

Critical race theory A theory that examines the intersection of race, law, and power.

In our evolutionary ancestry, helping others to survive was a risky game. There was no guarantee that the individual you helped would return the favor. However, it is generally more likely that the individual would reciprocate if he or she were related to you in some way. The closer the relation, the greater the likelihood of reciprocation. Therefore, humans evolved a disposition to aid individuals who are most like themselves. But how do you know how closely related a person is to you? Generally speaking, individuals that physically appear most like us are most genetically similar to ourselves.

Research shows that individuals prefer to interact with people they perceive as more similar to themselves. Individuals are also more likely to aid individuals who are similar and distrust those who are less similar to themselves. The greater the degree of perceived dissimilarity, the greater the distrust. So prejudice and discrimination appear to have an evolutionary component as well.

None of this means that we are destined to discriminate. The social environment of the modern world is very different from the environment in which we evolved. This will undoubtedly change the way in which we structure relationships between people who are not related to us, and probably for the better. As thinking beings, we are able to make decisions about the ways in which we treat people that move beyond our evolutionary history and biology.

CONCEPT LEARNING CHECK 9.5   Discrimination

Organize the specific theories in the right-hand column under their correct general theoretical orientation on the left-hand column.

THEORETICAL ORIENTATIONS	THEORIES OF DISCRIMINATION
_____ **1.** Psychological	**A.** Social learning theories
_____ **2.** Social-psychological	**B.** Marxist theory
_____ **3.** Social-structural and elite	**C.** Frustration-aggression hypothesis
	D. Authoritarian personality theory
	E. Realistic group conflict theory
	F. Group position theory
	G. Social identity theory

9.6 Theoretical Perspectives on Race and Ethnic Relations

The major theoretical perspectives offer important insights into understanding prejudice and discrimination.

- Compare and contrast the ways in which the major theoretical perspectives interpret race and racial relations.

The major theoretical perspectives frame all of the theories of prejudice and discrimination we have discussed thus far. The ways in which we understand race and ethnicity are multifaceted and complex. Using the theoretical perspectives to organize and understand racial and ethnic relations helps to clarify many of these complex issues.

Functionalism

Functionalism sees prejudice as functional for the maintenance of the individual or the social group. It may be functional for the maintenance of an individual's identity, because holding a prejudicial attitude against another group allows an individual to make positive comparisons with the out-group. Recall that we learned the process by which people create strong racial or ethnic identities. Functionalism seeks to understand *why* a person would want to have a strong ethnic or racial identity. After all, why would a person want to be associated with a group that is perceived as socially having less power or prestige than other groups? Functionalism provides a possible answer. People use their identity to compare with other people and to develop a sense of belonging with a particular social group. Generally, people tend to glorify groups they share a sense of belonging to and vilify groups they do not belong to. Thus, people gain a positive sense of identity even through association with oppressed groups. Similarly, prejudice can be functional for a group as well because it serves to unite members in a common bond against another group. By emphasizing differences between groups, boundaries for membership and identification with groups are clarified. In this way, groups create their own distinct identities in comparison with other groups.

Social Conflict

The conflict perspective analyzes prejudice in terms of competition over scarce social resources. Prejudice is a means by which the dominant social group gains and secures access to scant resources. Prejudicial attitudes provide justifications for why minority groups are not entitled to the same resources as the dominant group. By perpetuating prejudice, the dominant group creates a means of social control by which not only members of their group but also other groups come to see unequal distribution of resources as normal or appropriate.

The conflict perspective has led to the development of many theories of prejudice and discrimination, such as group position theory and critical race theory, both discussed previously. All of these theories have their roots in the writings of Karl Marx and have been influential in developing an understanding of prejudice and discrimination.

Symbolic Interactionism

Through the symbolic interactionist perspective, the specific ways in which prejudice is constructed and understood in society can be studied. For example, symbolic interactionists might try to understand how certain characteristics come to be associated with particular groups, as well as how these terms come to be used in society. This perspective is valuable in understanding how stereotypes are constructed and used in society.

Many social-psychological theories of prejudice, such as social identity theory, have their roots in symbolic interactionism. Understanding how words used to describe races are connected to images of those races provides significant insight. For example, what kind of image is introduced when the word *kike* is used instead of the word *Jew*? How might the difference in terms affect perceptions of that group of people?

Biosocial Perspectives

Although most sociologists believe that prejudices are learned, the biosocial perspective suggests that prejudices may have an innate component as well. Other animals also display prejudice in the form of preferring members of their own group or pack to individuals from other groups. For example, chimpanzees often show remarkable compassion to members of their own social group; but will relentlessly attack chimpanzees from other groups who wander into their territory. As human beings were emerging on the planet, they undoubtedly encountered conflicts with other groups. Those groups that could most successfully navigate conflicts were more successful than other groups. Prejudice provided a means by which in-group and out-groups distinctions could be maintained, thus ensuring that scarce resources were given preferentially to members of the in-group. As human culture developed, these basic predispositions were elaborated upon over time and increased in complexity.

Biosociologists recognize that although prejudice may have an innate component, the specific target of preferential attitudes are in fact a learned behavior. In other words, while a person may have an inborn predisposition to maintain prejudicial attitudes, the specific groups that those attitudes are aimed at are learned through the process of socialization. Thus, prejudices can be both innate and learned.

CONCEPT LEARNING CHECK 9.6   Theoretical Perspectives on Race and Ethnic Relations

For each scenario, identify which theoretical perspective is being used.

1. Carlos is studying the ways in which prejudicial behaviors influence the roles people adopt in the family and how those roles help the family to bond.

2. Petunia seeks to understand how people use prejudice to justify defending their households from other people. She believes that the justifications stem from an innate need to protect a person's family.

3. Steven believes that people of lower socioeconomic status have more prejudices than people of higher socioeconomic status because they are jealous of the successes of the wealthy.

4. Nita is researching how terms used to refer to different groups affects the way in which school children perceive the quality of their teacher.

9.7 Racial and Ethnic Relations in the United States

The history of races and ethnicities in the United States is entwined in the history of the nation.

- Compare and contrast the major racial groups in the United States and how intersectionality theory dictates assumptions.

Despite much progress in the area of racial and ethnic relations in the United States, tension between racial and ethnic groups still exists. Prejudice and discrimination continue to manifest themselves in the actions of individuals, as well as in American society as a whole. While often the controversies are largely academic—such as what terms are appropriate to describe a particular group—many times the issues have broader social consequences. For example, recent discussions about immigration have erupted in the public debate, polarizing people and influencing government policy that will no doubt have significant long-term consequences for the direction of our nation.

Long-term study of racial and ethnic relations reveals several interesting points. First, it is difficult to say that discrimination has decreased. Rather, it seems as though the emphasis of discriminatory behavior moves from one group to another. As debates over immigration from Mexico have heated up, for example, the focus of discrimination shifts from African Americans to Hispanics. Other groups that have become recent targets for discrimination include homosexuals and the obese.

Another important long-term trend is that minority groups have become more organized in their response to discrimination. Sometimes, organized groups from different minority statuses form coalitions to promote the common interests of both groups. For example, during the civil rights era, feminists frequently joined with African-American advocacy groups to fight for equal rights.

The way in which debate over racial and ethnic issues is framed and discussed strongly influences how the situation is resolved. Often, minority groups cluster into regions FIGURE 9-7, which makes the debate more real in some areas than in others. The visibility of minority groups influences the perceptions that people have about those groups. As the percentage of different racial and ethnic groups changes relative to the dominant group, views about those groups and their place in society will necessarily

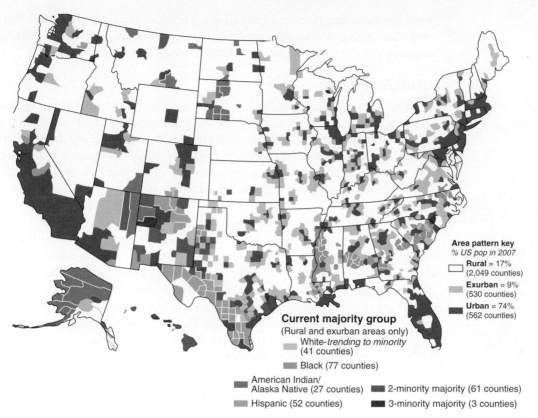

FIGURE 9-7 Some minority groups tend to cluster into regions.

Source: Courtesy of The Daily Yonder (*http://www.dailyyonder .com/counties-minorities-majority-grow-rural-america*) *and Timothy Murphy.*

Area pattern key
% US pop in 2007

Rural = 17% (2,049 counties)

Exurban = 9% (530 counties)

Urban = 74% (562 counties)

Current majority group
(Rural and exurban areas only)

White-*trending to minority* (41 counties)

Black (77 counties)

American Indian/ Alaska Native (27 counties)

Hispanic (52 counties)

2-minority majority (61 counties)

3-minority majority (3 counties)

change as well. All of these factors, as well as others, influence the state of racial and ethnic relations in America today.

European Americans

In large part, this country was settled by immigrants from Europe seeking greater religious and political liberty. Because the country was founded largely by white European, this group became the dominant group and established the cultural foundations for the entire country. Initially, European immigrants were the minority, since the land was occupied by Native Americans. However, Native Americans were fragmented into more than 560 tribes, all with complex cultures but relatively low technological sophistication when compared to the Europeans who occupied their shores.

The immigrants who settled the lands from Europe were also of more than one cultural background. However, exposure and familiarity to the traditions of other European nations, similar technology, and a common goal of survival in a new world unified the settlers with a common goal. For this reason, it was comparatively easy to overcome any resistance by the natives. Thus, whites became the dominant group in settled areas rather rapidly and constructed cultural values and norms that became the cornerstone of American culture.

Early racial policy made the attitude of the new nation clear. In 1790, political leaders passed the Naturalization Act, which decreed that only white immigrants could apply to become US citizens. Even among white immigrants, a hierarchy quickly emerged, with immigrants from England seen as superior to immigrants from other European nations. Those who emigrated from Europe to America were expected to **assimilate**. That is, they were expected to adopt the values, beliefs, and practices of the dominant culture. Often, this meant abandoning the unique customs, practices, and language of their native nationalities.

Generally, children of immigrants assimilated rather quickly and helped to reinforce the dominant cultural norms. Each subsequent generation became more and

Assimilation The adopting of the values, beliefs, and practices of the dominant culture.

more uniquely American and less and less a product of its native culture. The more American these individuals became, the more they shaped policy that influenced the way in which others would be viewed and treated in American culture.

African Americans

The first African immigrants came to America not as slaves but rather as indentured servants. This arrangement involved finding an individual or family of means to sponsor passage to the colonies. In exchange, the individual would agree to work for the family for a set number of years—usually five or seven years. The individual would live with the family and serve them until the period of indenture ended, at which time the person would be free to form his or her own family and establish a home.

Slavery came later as the benefits of free labor and the ease of capturing slaves became evident. Slavery already existed in Europe and other areas of the world, so the infrastructure to bring slaves to the new colonies was easily expanded. By the time of the first American census in 1790, nearly 750,000 individuals of African descent populated America—most of them as slaves. From the beginning, slavery was the subject of controversy. Advocates of slavery attempted to justify the practice by claiming that Africans were somehow less human than other races and therefore less intelligent and less civilized. They ultimately argued that slavery was a benefit to the black race because it offered them opportunities to become more civilized.

Brown v. Board of Education *ended school segregation in America.*
© Bettmann/CORBIS

After slavery was abolished, Southern states passed a series of statutes to segregate blacks and whites. These statutes were upheld by the Supreme Court in the case of *Plessy v. Ferguson*. In this case, the Supreme Court established the doctrine of separate but equal. In other words, segregation was legal as long as blacks were afforded equal accommodations. Blacks were segregated with separate neighborhoods, schools, restaurants, and even drinking fountains. Of course, these accommodations were rarely equal. Black schools were woefully underfunded, poorly equipped, and poorly managed. While drinking fountains for whites ran with cool, clean water, fountains "for coloreds only" were often filthy and produced only warm water.

More importantly, the dominant culture declared that the political process was white. Therefore, blacks were systematically excluded from voting in the primary elections until 1944, when the Supreme Court ruled that political primaries must be open to all voters. In response, many states passed laws that permitted only literate people to vote. Most blacks were, not surprisingly given the state of their schools, deemed illiterate and therefore not eligible to vote.

In 1954, after much controversy and struggle, the Supreme Court overturned *Plessy v. Ferguson* and ruled that blacks were legally entitled to attend the same schools as whites. Other aspects of segregation, however, persisted until well into the 1960s. In 1964, the Civil Rights Act became law, making it illegal to discriminate on the basis of race. A year later, literacy tests as a condition for voting were outlawed by an act of Congress. These gains were not universally accepted and were often accompanied by violent reactions. Over time, however, blacks were afforded the same legal status as whites in society. Despite the progress that has been made, blacks still lag behind whites in many areas.

Barack Obama was sworn in as America's first minority president in 2009.
© Medford Taylor/National Geographic Society/ Corbis

African Americans currently make up about 13% of the population of the United States. Yet African Americans comprise only about 10% of the House of Representatives, and there have been only six individuals of African descent to serve in the US Senate since it was first convened. One of those six senators, Barack Obama, was sworn in in January 2009 as the first minority president. On the whole, African Americans continue to lag behind whites in political representation, although it is equally clear that gains are being made.

African Americans are also expanding into the middle class. As African Americans become more educated, their incomes have risen. **Affirmative action**, a set of policies that encourages or mandates preferential hiring or admissions for previously oppressed

Affirmative action Policies that mandates preferential hiring, promotion, and college admission of historically disadvantaged groups.

minorities, has also helped many African Americans to improve their quality of life. Affirmative action is controversial, however, and is often portrayed by critics as a form of reverse discrimination. Recent court cases have been mixed in how they interpret and defend affirmative action in work and education. Nevertheless, the programs remain popular among minorities, and do appear to have helped somewhat to improve the standard of living for African Americans and help them emerge into the middle class. Nearly two-thirds of African-American families today earn more than $50,000 a year, and 10% earn more than $100,000 a year. Still, on average, African Americans earn only about 58% of what whites earn FIGURE 9-8. African Americans also continue to be more vulnerable to job loss during recessions and remain more likely to be unemployed than whites. As a percentage of the population, African Americans are still more likely than whites to live in poverty.

There are also differences between African Americans and whites with regard to crime. Although they make up only about 13% of the population, African Americans make up 28% of all arrests. Blacks are also more likely to be convicted of crimes and tend to get harsher sentences than whites. Additionally, blacks are more likely to be the victims of crime. In fact, African Americans are six times as likely to be murdered as whites. Most of these murders occur at the hands of other African Americans.

It is important to understand, however, that unequal outcomes are not necessarily evidence of unequal opportunities. For example, it is possible for two people to have the same opportunity to participate—say on an exam—but have radically different outcomes. It is dangerous to argue that unequal outcomes must be due to unequal opportunity. Having said that, there is some truth to the claim that many of the negative outcomes of blacks in society have their roots in the discrimination of the past. Discriminatory acts such as segregation and slavery have led to a systematic disadvantage of blacks in America. Although much progress has been made, there is much work to be done.

Hispanic Americans

Hispanics are the largest and fastest-growing minority group in the United States. Census counts estimate around 44 million Hispanics in America, with an estimated 9 million living in the United States illegally. Most of these immigrants come from Mexico and Puerto Rico, and many more come from Central America. Most immigrants come to America seeking economic and social opportunities that do not exist elsewhere. The influx of illegal immigration has become an area of political and social concern. Many people believe that illegal immigration harms the US economy because immigrants

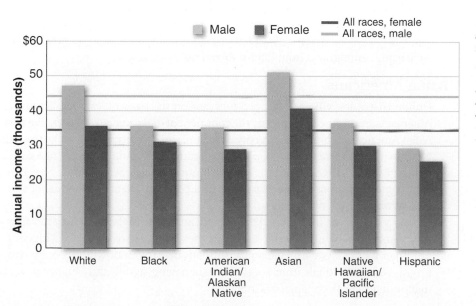

FIGURE 9-8 Race and ethnicity affect life chances in the United States, as shown by this chart.

Source: Data from U.S. Census Bureau. 2008. "Income, Earnings, and Poverty Data From the 2007 American Community Survey." Accessed January 2012 (http://www.census.gov/prod/2008pubs/acs-09.pdf).

typically avail themselves of public resources such as schools and medical care, which drives up the cost of maintaining those services. If immigrants fail to pay taxes but use those services, the cost must be picked up by citizens. Critics also contend that immigrants take jobs from citizens who may be looking for work, because the immigrants will typically work for less money and fewer benefits.

On the other hand, some people point out that immigrants take jobs that American citizens do not want to do. Many manual labor jobs are very demanding and receive little pay and few benefits. Immigrants fill this labor void with cheap labor that helps keep prices low and products readily available. Although we do pay a social cost to educate the children of immigrants, this is a small price to pay for their continued participation in the American labor market.

These opposing views have fueled the debate about the social benefits and costs of illegal immigration. Most people agree that the United States needs to reform its immigration policy, but there is little agreement on what that reform should look like. Recently, the US government began building a 670-mile fence on the US side of the Mexican border in an attempt to curb illegal immigration from Mexico. Illegal immigration is on the decline. However, the decline is probably not due very much to the efforts noted above. Rather, the decline in immigration can be traced to a sagging American economy and increased freedoms and opportunities in immigrants' native countries.

Although they are often lumped together as a single group, connected by a single language, Hispanics are a diverse ethnic group that encompasses many traditions and cultures. In fact, country of origin is very important for most Hispanics because it defines their cultural traditions and beliefs. Many Hispanics, indeed, identify themselves by their nationality first, such as Cuban or Peruvian. The country of nationality—rather than the language or ethnic identification—defines most Hispanics.

When compared to white Americans, Hispanics are underrepresented in media and politics. Currently, Hispanics make up just under 15% of the population of America but have only three seats in the Senate and 5% of the seats in the House of Representatives. However, as Hispanics increase in number, and as issues such as immigration move to the forefront of political debate, it is likely that the role of Hispanics in shaping US policy will increase.

In other areas, Hispanics fare similarly poorly. When compared with white Americans, Hispanics are generally of lower social class, make less money, and have lower educational attainment and higher unemployment and poverty. Hispanics are also less likely to own their own homes. Hispanics are the group with the highest high school dropout rate and the group that is least likely to attend college. Additionally, Hispanics have the highest rate of teen pregnancy of any racial or ethnic group. However, it needs to be stated that these figures aggregate all Hispanics. There are certainly differences in social class, income, and education among Hispanics with different countries of origin. For example, while people of Cuban origin typically score high on measures of social well-being, immigrants from Puerto Rico tend to score low.

Asian Americans

Unlike Hispanics, who are grouped together on the basis of a shared language, Asian Americans are grouped together by the continent of their origin. However, like Hispanics, Asian Americans represent a diversity of cultures and traditions that make them difficult to lump into one general category. There are roughly 13 million people of Asian descent living in the United States, representing more than a dozen nations. Nevertheless, it is possible to approach them as a group and compare them to other racial and ethnic groups on a variety of measures.

As a whole, the income of Asian Americans is the highest of every racial or ethnic group, including whites. At the same time, however, Asians also have a higher poverty rate than whites. As with Hispanics, this can be broken down largely by country of origin, with individuals from Southeast Asia having significantly higher poverty rates than individuals from Japan or China.

Asian Americans also have high graduation rates from high schools and college. They rank lowest in teen pregnancy and tend to delay marriage longer than other racial or ethnic groups. Asian Americans remain underrepresented in American politics and media. However, this seems to have limited impact on their successes.

Asian Americans are no stranger to discrimination and prejudice. In the mid 1800s, many immigrants were lured from Asian with promises of good wages to build railroad lines across the United States. Indeed, although the wages were good by Chinese standards—about a dollar a day—the conditions were often brutal, and many workers perished from heat and exhaustion. Railroads also charged workers for living in railroad housing and purchasing food at the railroad store, which was mandatory. At its peak, 90% of the railroad workers for the Central Pacific Railroad were from China. Still, when the railroad was complete, only the white workers were included in the historic photograph documenting the completion of the rail line.

The railroads were not the only institution to discriminate against people of Asian descent. The California Supreme Court ruled that Chinese could not testify against whites because they were considered untrustworthy witnesses. California also passed a law charging Chinese and other immigrants a $20-a-month fee to work in the state, cutting deeply into the wages of already exploited workers. After the Japanese attack on Pearl Harbor that initiated America's military involvement in World War II, Japanese immigrants as well as citizens of Japanese descent were systematically rounded up and forced to live in large camps. The American government justified the forced internment of Japanese Americans through fears of sabotage or spying against America. It is important to note that individuals who were interned in these camps were never charged with a crime, nor were there any opportunities for a trial or for appeals.

Given the history of discrimination against individuals of Asian descent, what accounts for the relative success of Asian Americans? There are several factors that sociologists have identified. The first factor is family life. Compared to other racial and ethnic groups, Asian American children are more likely to live in two-parent families. These families, as already noted, have incomes above the median income for American families. Additionally, Asian Americans are least likely to be born to teenage mothers or in single-parent households. Asian American families are typically rooted in traditional values that stress self-discipline, hard work, and thrift. Asian American children are strongly socialized toward valuing education and achievement.

Because of the strong socialization toward education and achievement, Asian Americans have very high rates of high school and college graduation. Indeed, nearly half of all Asian Americans graduate from college. This high rate of college graduation creates opportunities for economic success that place Asian American families high on the socioeconomic ladder.

Finally, a strong trend of assimilation has also contributed to the success of Asian Americans in modern society. Of all the racial and ethnic groups discussed in this chapter, Asian Americans have the highest rate of intermarriage. Among Asian Americans with college degrees, nearly half marry someone outside of their racial or ethnic group. More than half of children being born among Americans of Asian descent have a parent who is not of Asian descent (Alba and Nee 2005).

Despite the success of Asian Americans, they remain underrepresented in American politics. Only three states—Hawaii, Washington,

Asian immigrants were used to build American railroads, often working in horrendous conditions for little pay.

© Josef Scaylea/CORBIS

During World War II Japanese were interned in camps in the United States for fear of sabotage.

Library of Congress Prints and Photographs Division LC-DIG-ppprs-00368

and Louisiana—have elected governors of Asian descent. Eight members of the current House of Representatives claim Asian American descent, along with two Senators— both from Hawaii. It is unclear at this time if this trend will change in the near future.

Native Americans

When the first European settlers landed in America, they found it inhabited by more than 560 tribes of native people totaling approximately 10 million people. As the set- tlers expanded, they encroached upon the lands of the native people, setting the stage for significant conflict that would decimate the native populations. Native Americans did not have resistance to many of the diseases that European settlers exposed them to. Smallpox and other diseases that Europeans had developed an immunity to caused the populations of natives to plummet. In 1890, the United States census counted only 250,000 Native Americans.

At first, relations between the Native Americans and European settlers were gen- erally amiable. However, as European settlers encroached on Native American lands and began raiding Native American villages, relations quickly began to break down (Horn 2006). Gradually, the federal government adopted policies of systemic deception and trickery to maintain dominance over the Native Americans and annex their land. This deception often took the form of making a treaty with tribes, only to violate the treaty later, often with the use of force.

As European settlements expanded westward, discrimination against Native Americans intensified. In 1838, the US Army was ordered to relocate 15,000 Cherokee. The relocation involved a 1,000-mile march from the Carolinas to Oklahoma during the fall and winter months. More than 4,000 Native Americans perished on this forced march. In 1890, more than 300 Native American men, women, and children were slaughtered at Wounded Knee, South Dakota, by the US cavalry. These are only two examples of the persistent discrimination faced by Native Americans as America grew.

Today, Native Americans exist largely on the margins of society. A sizable percentage of Native Americans are isolated in reservations scattered throughout the nation. Half of the Native American populations live in rural areas. For these reasons, many people are unaware of the presence of Native Americans in their own state or region. Years of attempted genocide, violent discrimination, and attempts to destroy Native American culture have fueled systemic disadvantages among Native American populations. For example, Native Americans have the lowest life expectancy of any racial or ethnic group. They are also the group most likely to live in poverty. Only about 14% of Native Americans graduate from college. Rates of suicide are also the highest among racial and ethnic groups.

Gradually, Native Americans appear to be slowly reversing those trends. A string of legal victories in the 1960s and 1970s have created opportunities for Native Americans to open businesses such as casinos and other tourist attractions that have netted con- siderable sums of money. This has helped many Native American families rise out of poverty and has allowed for the creation of many services to help Native Americans overcome years of systemic discrimination.

Despite the fact that Native Americans are an extremely diverse group, comprising more than 560 distinct tribes, the common fate shared by all of them at the hands of the United States government has led to pan-Indianism. **Pan-Indianism** is the idea that all Native Americans share a common identity that is rooted in the experiences of past prejudice and discrimination. Proponents of this view believe that only by recognizing a common past can the various tribes recognize a common future of progress and prosperity.

In 1838, the US government forcibly relocated over 15,000 Cherokee, resulting in thousands of deaths.
© CORBIS

Pan-Indianism The idea that all Native Americans share a common identity that is rooted in the experiences of past prejudice and discrimination.

Intersectionality Theory

Intersectionality theory was largely developed by sociologist Patricia Hill Collins (2008). The core assumption of intersectionality theory is that variables that influence life chances do not operate alone. Instead, variables intersect and work in groups to create what Collins describes as interlocking systems of oppression FIGURE 9-9. That is,

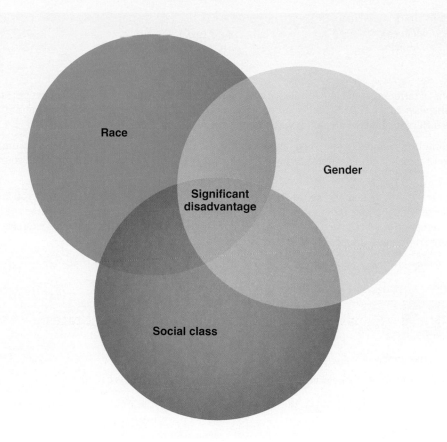

FIGURE 9-9 Intersectionality theory discusses how race, sex, and social class work together to influence life chances.

intersectionality theory explores the ways in which race, social class, gender, and other variables interact with one another to create advantages or disadvantages in life. For example, research shows that African Americans, on average, earn less than whites, and that women, on average, earn less than men. Intersectionality theory takes this knowledge a step further and asks how the earnings of an African-American woman would compare with either alternative. Intersectionality theory predicts that African-American women would earn less than either an African-American male or a white woman because race and gender intersect to create multiple layers of social disadvantage. Social class becomes relevant because it influences the opportunities for employment and the types of the jobs that are available. An African-American woman living in the inner city would likely have a significantly lower income than an African-American woman living in a suburban neighborhood.

THE SOCIOLOGICAL IMAGINATION   Race as a Public and Private Issue

The sociological imagination is shaped by social experience in the context of social history. In terms of race, the social history of the United States is filled with examples of white privilege exercised at the expense of other races. Past and present voting laws are a reflection of the social inequalities that exist between dominant and minority groups. For example, in 1787, only white male landowners could vote in most states, while Native Americans were not allowed to vote until 1924. The Voting Rights Act of 1965 made literacy tests and other restrictions illegal. Yet during the 2012 elections, recent new voter identification laws were challenged as disproportionately affecting minorities. The legacy of slavery and segregation remains, affecting many areas of life including education, health, poverty, and employment despite significant progress in creating racial and ethnic equality. History continues to shape individual social experiences and racial and ethnic relations.

(Continues)

EVALUATE

1. Think about how the assumptions of different racial and ethnic groups might be shaped by their awareness of events of the past. How might this affect the ways in which individuals interact with others in society? For example, how might the assumptions of a black driver be different than a white driver when pulled over by a police officer?

2. List at least five background assumptions related to your own racial identity and then attempt to examine these assumptions from the point of view of a different racial or ethnic identity. How does this change the ways in which you interpret your social world?

3. Think of a dominant group (e.g., race, ethnicity, sex, age, social class, sexual orientation, ability, religion, etc.) that you identify with and make a list of the privileges that you take for granted that are often denied to the minority group. Reverse the list by writing down privileges that are denied to you because of your membership in a minority group. How does this exercise reflect the view that privilege is invisible to dominant groups yet visible to minority groups?

CONCEPT LEARNING CHECK 9.7   Racial and Ethnic Relations in the United States

Answer the following multiple-choice questions.

1. The expectation of immigrants to adopt the values, beliefs, and practices of the dominant culture is called:

    A. emigration.

    B. assimilation.

    C. immigration.

    D. affirmative action.

2. A set of policies to promote hiring, promotion, and college admission to historically disadvantaged groups is called:

    A. emigration.

    B. assimilation.

    C. immigration.

    D. affirmative action.

3. The racial or ethnic group most likely to assimilate after immigration is:

    A. Hispanics from Mexico.

    B. Africans.

    C. Asians.

    D. Hispanics from Cuba.

4. The idea that all Native Americans share a common identity rooted in discrimination and prejudice is called:

    A. Pan-Indianism.

    B. intersectionality theory.

    C. Native American unity theory.

    D. affirmative action.

5. The idea that race, sex, and social class all work together to help create cultural advantage or disadvantage is called:

    A. affirmative action.

    B. intersectionality theory.

    C. triangulation theory.

    D. racialization.

9.8 Key Issues in the Future of Race and Ethnicity

Although there has been much progress, racial and ethnic relations in the United States remain strained.

- Describe the key issues regarding race and ethnicity in the United States.

Most of America's social problems involve dimensions of race or ethnicity. For example, poverty can be discussed both as an independent issue but also in terms of race or ethnicity. Poverty rates differ for different racial and ethnic groups, and for different reasons. Issues surrounding public education also cross over into discussions of race and ethnicity. Indeed, it is difficult to think of a social issue in America that does not have a racial or ethnic dimension.

The pervasiveness of discussions of race and ethnicity in America has opened up many opportunities for minority groups, however. Acknowledgement of past indiscretions and a willingness to discuss issues of race and ethnicity in political and educational venues has led to significant improvements in American attitudes toward minority groups. Clearly, however, substantial work still remains. As American society changes, so will attitudes toward race and ethnicity.

Immigration and Emigration

The issue of **immigration** is as old as the nation itself. Immigration refers to people moving into a country. America, founded by immigrants from other nations, has often welcomed those who wish to reap the benefits of coming to America. At the same time, immigration has often led to feelings of paranoia and mistrust. Today, immigration remains one of the most contested issues in American politics. More than one million immigrants come to America each year, most of them through legal channels. More than 38 million immigrants live in the United States—more than at any time in our nation's history.

> **Immigration** The movement of people into a given country.
>
> **Emigration** The movement of people out of a given country.

Many people fear that unchecked immigration is harmful to America. Critics of immigration argue that immigrants take jobs away from citizens and absorb resources such as health care and education that should be given preferentially to citizens. Additionally, many people fear that unchecked immigration will change the politics and culture of the United States, thus threatening what many perceive as the "American way of life." The American way of life, as we have already learned, however, is more of a myth than a reality. America is composed of many ethnic, racial, and religious groups that have distinctly different beliefs, values, and norms. There are many American ways of life, a product of our long history of immigration.

The face of immigration has changed over time. Early in American history, immigrants most commonly came from Western Europe or from Africa as slaves. Today, immigrants are much more diverse in terms of their country of origin. Because of the close proximity to the United States, immigrants from Mexico and Central America are common. As previously noted, Hispanics are the fastest growing minority group in American, in part due to immigration from Latin American nations.

Immigrants come to America for a variety of reasons. The most common are improved economic opportunities and to escape political persecution. As political and economic circumstances change throughout the world, the influx of immigration from various regions of the world will ebb and flow. For example, improving economic circumstances in Mexico and Central America are already leading to slowing rates of immigration to America from that region of the world.

Less common in America is **emigration**—movement out of a given nation. Rates of emigration from America are far less than rates of immigration. In other words, more people are coming into America from other nations than are leaving America to live elsewhere. Still, rates of emigration from America are increasing slowly. Lower costs of living and an increasingly positive attitude toward American expatriates have made emigration an attractive option for middle-class retirees seeking a high quality of life.

Affirmative Action

As we have learned, America is an ethnically and racially diverse nation with a long history of racial and ethnic tension. The degree to which America should embrace a multicultural society is the subject of considerable debate. However, one thing is quite clear: American treatment of minorities has been historically discriminatory, which has resulted in the denial of equal opportunities to minority groups.

In an effort to increase opportunities for minorities, President John F. Kennedy initiated policies of affirmative action, which promoted differential hiring, promotion, and college admission for minority groups (including women). Research conducted on the effects of affirmative action has shown the impact of these programs to be quite modest (Reskin 1998). Part of the reason for this is that affirmative action is often inadequately enforced. Additionally, affirmative action is about ensuring opportunity rather than ensuring a particular outcome. For example, while the policies may help African-American students to get admitted to college, the policies do nothing to ensure success once the students are admitted.

From their adoption, affirmative action policies have been the subject of significant controversy. Critics of affirmative action policies argue that such policies are nothing more than reverse discrimination because they give preferential treatment to minority groups over the dominant groups. They argue that this is fundamentally no different than the discrimination against minority groups. Through the implementation of affirmative action policies, individuals who have never discriminated against others are themselves discriminated against. They also argue that affirmative action can stigmatize people who benefit from it, since others might believe that they got their job because of their race or sex rather than through personal merit.

Proponents of affirmative action argue that the program is warranted restitution for past discrimination and that affirmative action is the most efficient way to achieve equality of opportunity. They see it as fundamentally fair that some whites will lose out on positions they deserve in order to make up for past wrongdoings. They also argue that the promotion of women and minorities strengthens society because it makes social institutions more diverse.

This debate has been fueled by a series of court rulings. In 1996, voters in California voted on Proposition 209, which added an amendment to the state constitution that made it illegal to give preference in promotion, college admission, and hiring to women and minorities. Despite vigorous opposition, voters passed the amendment by a considerable margin. Civil rights groups immediately appealed the decision all the way to the United State Supreme Court, but the court upheld the amendment.

In 2003, a more ambiguous ruling also seemed to cast some doubt on the constitutionality of affirmative action laws. White students who had been denied entrance to a Michigan law school sued the school when they discovered that less qualified minorities had been admitted. In a complicated decision, the court ruled that schools can use race as a criterion of college admission, but that mechanical formulas that give extra points for minority status are unconstitutional.

In response to the controversy of affirmative action, several states have attempted to address the issue through amendments to state constitutions. Michigan and Nebraska passed amendments that prohibit public institutions from using race or sex as criteria for hiring, promotions, or college admissions. However, in several other states, attempts at changing the law have failed. There is little doubt that the debate on affirmative action will continue for some time to come.

Race: Looking Back and Looking Ahead

More than 100 years ago, sociologist W. E. B. Du Bois (1903) FIGURE 9-10 wrote that one of the most pressing problems of the 20th century is the problem of the color line. In other words, this is the problem of how the darker and lighter races relate to one another in society. In 2008, America elected its first African-American president. Although many people interpreted this as a sign of improvement in race relations, many others

FIGURE 9-10 W. E. B. Du Bois believed that the problem of race relations would remain for many years.

© Bettmann/CORBIS

believed that this will merely exacerbate racial tensions. In some ways, both of these predictions have been shown to be correct. Clearly, the election of President Obama demonstrates that significant progress has been made in our acceptance of race. At the same time, however, there is every appearance that what remains of racial disparities is becoming increasingly polarized.

If Du Bois were alive today, what might he make of the interesting dynamic that has evolved around race in America? He might not be surprised that race still plays a significant role in American society. He would probably not be at all surprised that race still influences a person's life chances—education, employment, income, and family. At the same time, Du Bois would probably be flabbergasted at the progress that has been made. He would no doubt be surprised to see the end of racial segregation—to see people of all colors living, working, and going to school together. He would be encouraged by the increasing numbers of minorities in higher education and politics.

Du Bois would also concur that there was much work left to do. Even though segregation has ended legally, Du Bois would point out that economically imposed segregation still relegates many racial minorities to the inner cities and therefore to segregated schools. Although legally integrated, many key aspects of society remain socially segregated. Du Bois would argue that there is still much work to do to improve race relations in America—but he would also nod, smile, and say that we are on the right track to a future of greater racial and ethnic equality.

CONCEPT LEARNING CHECK 9.8	Key Issues in the Future of Race and Ethnicity

Answer the following multiple-choice questions.

1. Margo moves from Montreal, Canada, to Los Angeles, California. Her move out of Canada would be:

   A. emigration.

   B. immigration.

   C. affirmative action.

   D. triangulation.

2. Margo's move into Los Angeles would be considered:

   A. emigration.

   B. immigration.

   C. affirmative action.

   D. triangulation.

3. Carson is an African American who was promoted ahead of his white colleagues. Carson was the recipient of what policies?

   A. Proposition 209

   B. Affirmative action

   C. Emigration

   D. Intersectionality theory

Visual Overview Race and Ethnicity in Society

Sociologists study the effects of both race and ethnicity on life chances. While race refers to biological characteristics that society recognizes, ethnicity refers to cultural divisions that include religion, place of origin, or cultural heritage.

race

Scientists who accept the biological reality of race generally divide mankind into three categories: Caucasoid, Mongoloid, and Negroid.

These racial categories are also known as white, Asian, and black.

In the 2010 census

32%

of US respondents self-identified as multi-racial (www.census.gov).

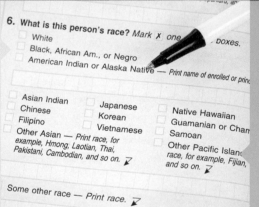

6. What is this person's race? Mark X one ... boxes.
☐ White
☐ Black, African Am., or Negro
☐ American Indian or Alaska Native — Print name of enrolled or prin...

☐ Asian Indian
☐ Chinese
☐ Filipino
☐ Japanese
☐ Korean
☐ Vietnamese
☐ Other Asian — Print race, for example, Hmong, Laotian, Thai, Pakistani, Cambodian, and so on. ↗

☐ Native Hawaiian
☐ Guamanian or Cham...
☐ Samoan
☐ Other Pacific Island race, for example, Fijian, and so on. ↗

☐ Some other race — Print race. ↗

Ethnicity, on the other hand, is based on cultural characteristics, such as differences in religion or national origin.

ethnicity

I am Jewish-American.

I am Bengali.

We are a family.

My mom is Mexican.

My dad is Greek.

My abuelo still lives in Guanajuato.

Visual Summary Race and Ethnicity in Society

9.1 Race and Ethnicity in Society

- Race is a very important concept for understanding how people relate to one another.

- Whether race has roots in biology or culture is debated among social scientists.

9.2 Race

- Race is a socially constructed category of people who share biologically transmitted traits that society considers important.
- Most social scientists believe that race is an artificial concept.

- The way that individuals and society place people into racial categories is called racialization.

9.3 Ethnicity

- Ethnicity refers to cultural practices that distinguish one group from another.
- Ethnic work refers to the process by which a person constructs their ethnic identity.

- Dominant groups hold greater power, privilege, or prestige than other groups.
- Minority groups are groups that society sets apart and disadvantages in some way.

9.4 Prejudice

- Prejudice refers to the beliefs or attitudes a person holds about a particular group.
- Prejudice is a universal behavior among human beings.
- While prejudice has its roots in biology, the specific groups a person is prejudiced against are learned through social interaction.

- Stereotypes are generalizations that are applied to a group of people.
- Scapegoats are groups that are blamed for the problems in society.

9.5 Discrimination

- Discrimination is an action against a particular group that seeks to deny the group the same power, privilege, or opportunities as other groups.
- Racism is discrimination that is directed against a particular race.
- Institutional racism is racism that is embedded in the structure of society.
- Psychological theories of discrimination seek to understand discrimination as individual personality characteristics.
- Social-psychological theories of discrimination recognize an individual's role in engaging in discrimination while at the same time recognizing the importance of social forces in influencing individual behaviors.

- Social-structural and elite theories of discrimination argue that discrimination is caused by the structural relationship between groups.
- Evolutionary theories of discrimination believe that the roots of discrimination are located in our evolutionary ancestry and once were functional for survival.

9.6 Theoretical Perspectives on Race and Ethnic Relations

- The ways in which we understand race and ethnicity are multifaceted and complex.
- Functionalism sees prejudice as functional for the maintenance of the individual or the social group.
- The social conflict perspective analyzes prejudice in terms of competition over scarce resources.
- Symbolic interactionism analyzes the ways in which prejudice is constructed and understood in society.
- Biosocial perspectives suggest that prejudice may have an innate component.

9.7 Racial and Ethnic Relations in the United States

- Although much progress has been made in ethnic and racial relations, tension between groups still exists.
- Early immigrants from Europe quickly became the dominant group and established the cultural foundation for the entire nation.
- Immigrants who came to America were expected to assimilate—that is, to adopt the ways of life of the dominant culture.
- Many African Americans were transported to America as slaves to provide free labor for the dominant group.
- Slavery was followed by segregation that forced African Americans into separate schools, neighborhoods, restaurants, and other social institutions.
- Today, African Americans make up about 13% of the population but remain underrepresented in many aspects of American culture.
- Affirmative action policies were set in place to give preferential hiring, promotion, and college admission to groups who have been historically disadvantaged.
- Hispanic Americans comprise roughly 15% of the population yet remain underrepresented in American politics, media, and education.
- Asian Americans have the highest average income of any racial or ethnic group.
- Among racial and ethnic groups, Asian Americans are the most likely to assimilate.
- Native Americans continue to exist on the margins of American society.
- Pan-Indianism is the idea that all Native Americans share a common identity based on past discrimination.
- Intersectionality theory explores how race, sex, and social class interact with one another to create or limit privilege, power, and opportunity.

9.8 Key Issues in the Future of Race and Ethnicity

- Immigration is a key issue in modern American politics.
- Immigration refers to people moving into one country from another country.
- People moving out of a given country is called emigration.
- Affirmative action has also been the cause for significant political and social debate.
- Although much progress has been made in improving relations between different racial and ethnic groups, much work still needs to be done.

9.1 Race and Ethnicity in Society

1. Kyria is a sociologist. She most likely believes that:
   A. races are socially constructed categories of people based on biological traits.
   B. races do not exist.
   C. races exist as biological categories of people rooted in human evolution.
   D. races have no impact on a person's life chances.

9.2 Race

2. Hardeep is a forensic anthropologist. He most likely believes that:
   A. races are socially constructed categories of people based on biological traits.
   B. races do not exist.
   C. races exist as biological categories of people rooted in human evolution.
   D. races have no impact on a person's life chances.

3. Nya believes that anyone with one drop of Pudumu blood is automatically a Pudumu. Nya is engaging in the process of:
   A. ethnic work.
   B. racialization.
   C. ethnic cleansing.
   D. segregation.

4. Carl is from the United States, while Bill is from Brazil. Which is probably true?
   A. Bill will probably see race as more important than Carl.
   B. Carl and Bill will identify different racial categories.
   C. Carl will probably see race as more important than Bill.
   D. Carl and Bill will have identical views about race.

9.3 Ethnicity

5. Elvira belongs to a group that is not allowed to vote. Elvira's group would be considered a(n):
   A. race.
   B. dominant group.
   C. ethnicity.
   D. minority group.

6. Oskar is forced to live with his culture away from the rest of society, including going to a separate school. Oskar is experiencing:
   A. prejudice.
   B. segregation.
   C. ethnic work.
   D. racialization.

7. Takeya is exploring her heritage in an effort to understand herself better. She finds, for example, that she is the descendant of slaves. She decides, however, to keep that information secret from her friends. Takeya is engaged in:
   A. ethnic work.
   B. racialization.
   C. segregation.
   D. identity exploration.

9.4 Prejudice

8. Harvey gets disgusted every time he sees a Hispanic person taking a nap, because he thinks that Hispanics are lazy. Harvey is displaying:
   A. discrimination.
   B. ethnic work.
   C. racialization.
   D. prejudice.

9. Edny believes that all African Americans want to overthrow the government and take money from rich people to keep for themselves. In which theoretical perspective is Edny's prejudice rooted?
   A. Biosocial
   B. Functionalism
   C. Conflict
   D. Symbolic interactionism

10. Kendra believes that all Asian Americans are geniuses. She is engaging in the creation of a:
    A. projection.
    B. stereotype.
    C. prejudice.
    D. scapegoat.

11. Ichabod believes that immigrants from other countries are taking jobs away from Americans, ruining our public schools, and eroding our family values. Ichabod is engaging in:
    A. scapegoating.
    B. racism.
    C. ethnic work.
    D. racialization.

12. Ichabod believes that immigrants from other countries are taking away jobs from Americans because he is insecure about getting a good-paying job. Ichabod's insecurity forms the basis for his:
    A. discrimination.
    B. racialization.
    C. displacement.
    D. ethnic work.

9.5 Discrimination

13. As a banker, Galen denies loans to Native Americans because he thinks they are rude and unclean. His behavior is an example of:
    A. prejudice.
    B. ethnic work.
    C. discrimination.
    D. projection.

14. The bank that Galen works for routinely denies large loans to African Americans because they have higher default rates than other groups. The bank's policy might be an example of:
    A. institutional discrimination.
    B. scapegoating.
    C. projection.
    D. prejudice.

15. A doctor believes that Murtha's prejudice is the result of Murtha's childhood, in which he was consistently put down by his parents and punished often. The doctor is operating under what theory of prejudice?
    A. Realistic group conflict theory
    B. Social identity theory
    C. Frustration-aggression hypothesis
    D. Authoritarian personality theory

16. Niklaus puts down other groups of people because it makes him feel good about himself and helps him strengthen his own identity. Niklaus's prejudice might best be understood through which theory?
    A. Social learning theory
    B. Social identity theory
    C. Frustration-aggression hypothesis
    D. Group position theory

17. Cuthbert was taught by his parents from a young age that he should fear other races, since they desire to take over the country and enslave his. His prejudice might best be understood using which theory?
    A. Authoritarian personality theory
    B. Social learning theory
    C. Social identity theory
    D. Realistic group conflict theory

9.6 Theoretical Perspectives on Race and Ethnic Relations

18. Raynald is studying how prejudice emerges in neighborhoods because of inequalities in the number of public parks. What theoretical perspective is Raynald using?
    A. Biosocial perspective
    B. Symbolic interactionism
    C. Functionalism
    D. Conflict perspective

19. Aphrodite is studying how nicknames affect perceptions of racial identity in schools. Her work would best be understood through which theoretical approach?
    A. Biosocial perspective
    B. Symbolic interactionism
    C. Functionalism
    D. Conflict perspective

20. Pele believes that prejudice is inherent in social relations, because all animals show some in-group and out-group distinctions. Pele's beliefs are best exemplified by which theoretical perspective?
    A. Biosocial perspective
    B. Symbolic interactionism
    C. Functionalism
    D. Conflict perspective

9.7 Racial and Ethnic Relations in the United States

21. Toby was one of the first people of African descent to come to America. He most likely came as a(n):
- **A.** indentured servant.
- **B.** slave.
- **C.** free man.
- **D.** ship's captain.

22. Gretchen was promoted over her friend Alice because Gretchen is a member of a minority group. Gretchen is the recipient of:
- **A.** reverse discrimination.
- **B.** racial atonement.
- **C.** affirmative action.
- **D.** assimilation.

23. Kurtwood believes that all Native Americans should band together to advocate for group rights because, despite their cultural differences, all Native Americans are bound by a common identity rooted in their past experiences of discrimination. Kurtwood is advocating for:
- **A.** antiracism.
- **B.** social identity theory.
- **C.** realistic group conflict theory.
- **D.** pan-Indianism.

9.8 Key Issues in the Future of Race and Ethnicity

24. Mark is a recent immigrant to America. He is most likely from what nation?
- **A.** Sweden
- **B.** Mexico
- **C.** South Africa
- **D.** Laos

25. Tony is an immigrant to America coming from another country in the early 1900s. He most likely came from what region of the world.
- **A.** Greenland
- **B.** Asia
- **C.** South America
- **D.** Europe

CHAPTER ESSAY QUESTIONS

1. Discuss why the melting pot has not developed the way in which sociologists predicted.

2. List and describe what factors may influence whether or not an immigrant is likely to assimilate.

CHAPTER DISCUSSION QUESTIONS

1. How do the ways in which politicians and the media discuss race influence the ways in which people understand race in America?

2. Which theory of discrimination provides the best explanation of modern racism? Why?

3. People who identify with a minority group typically identify with the values, beliefs, and behaviors of that group. Why do some people who belong to dominant groups have difficulties seeing themselves as part of the dominant group? How is the denial of power and social position in society an example of privilege?

4. The US Census defines people who identify as Hispanic or Latino as an ethnicity and then prompts them to choose their race as either white, black, Native American, or other. There are current efforts to redefine Hispanic and Latino as a standalone category. What do you think of this racialization? How might definitions affect research findings and consequently public policies?

5. While ethnic work is an individual process, what issues might people who identify as biracial and multiracial experience, including how others might stereotype and interact with them?

6. About how old were you when you became aware of race? Which socialization agents—family, schools, or media—have the greatest impact on children's prejudices and stereotypes? Why?

7. Which is more problematic in the United States today, institutional or individual racism? Why?

8. How might assimilation create intergenerational conflicts within one's own family? How does this affect feelings of belonging for first-generation immigrant children?

9. Why should Americans be concerned with emigration patterns? What latent problems exist for the United States as global economic conditions continue to improve? Consider how immigration patterns historically have shaped the United States's economic power.

10. How might affirmative action policies be restructured to ensure both constitutionality and equal opportunities?

INDIVIDUAL PROJECTS

1. Create a chart that compares how different scientific disciplines view the concept of race. Include their understanding of the origins of race, the process of racialization, and the social nature and consequences of understanding race in that way.

2. Interview someone—whose racial or ethnic identity differs from your own—about his or her viewpoints on the state of current racial and ethnic relations in the United States. Write an analysis paper including similarities and difference in your own thinking about the topic.

GROUP PROJECTS

1. Although significant progress has been made in eliminating racism in America, significant work still remains. Using at least two of the theories that have been discussed in this chapter, design a plan to help young children avoid racism as either perpetrators or victims.

2. Your group has been charged with creating a workshop for college students that teaches racial and ethnic tolerance. Which of the theories on prejudice and discrimination are useful in how you structure your workshop and the information you present? Write an outline of your workshop.

3. Go online and research the immigration history of your ethnic group(s) to the United States. Write an analysis paper incorporating your findings and chapter information.

3. Go online to find the latest FBI hate crime statistics. How do the statistics reflect the information you read in this chapter? Write a summary of your discussion.

CHAPTER KEY TERMS

Affirmative action	Ethnic work	Race
Antiracism	Frustration-aggression hypothesis	Racialization
Assimilation	Group position theory	Racism
Authoritarian personality theory	Immigration	Realistic group conflict theory
Critical race theory	Institutional racism	Scapegoats
Discrimination	Melting pot	Segregation
Displacement	Minority groups	Social identity theory
Dominant group	Pan-Indianism	Social learning theory
Emigration	Prejudice	Stereotypes
Ethnicity	Projection	

ANSWERS TO CONCEPT LEARNING CHECKS

9.1   Race and Ethnicity in Society

1. Race refers to biological categories, while ethnicity refers to cultural traits; there are relatively few racial categories, while there are many ethnic categories.

2. Both race and ethnicity impact life chances; both race and ethnicity help a person develop an identity and a sociological imagination.

9.2   Race

1. The first scientist to offer a categorization of race was [B. Carrolus Linneaus].

2. The process by which people are placed into racial categories is called [C. Racialization].

3. Most scientists recognize how many racial categories? [A. 3]

9.3   Ethnicity

1. Cultural practices that distinguish one group from another [D. Ethnicity]

2. Groups that society sets apart and subordinates [B. Minority group]

3. The physical isolation of groups of people [A. Segregation]

4. The process by which a person identifies with and constructs her or his ethnic identity [C. Ethnic work]

9.4   Prejudice

1. [Prejudice] refers to beliefs or attitudes about a particular group.

2. Generalizations that are applied to a group of people are called [stereotypes].

3. [Scapegoats] are groups that are blamed for the problems in a society that are not their fault.

4. [Displacement] is a phenomena in which individual feelings of inadequacy, hostility, or anger are directed against objects or groups that are not the origins of those feelings.

5. The process whereby a person unconsciously projects his or her own characteristics onto others, it is called [projection].

9.5 Discrimination

1. Psychological [D. Authoritarian personality theory; C. Frustration-aggression hypothesis]

2. Social-psychological [A. Social learning theories; G. Social identity theory; E. Realistic group conflict theory]

3. Social-structural and elite [Group position theory; B. Marxist theory]

9.6 Theoretical Perspectives on Race and Ethnic Relations

1. Carlos is studying the ways in which prejudicial behaviors influence the roles people adopt in the family and how those roles help the family to bond. [Functionalism]

2. Petunia seeks to understand how people use prejudice to justify defending their households from other people. She believes that the justifications stem from an innate need to protect a person's family. [Biosocial]

3. Steven believes that people of lower socioeconomic status have more prejudices than people of higher socioeconomic status because they are jealous of the successes of the wealthy. [Conflict]

4. Nita is researching how terms used to refer to different groups affects the way in which school children perceive the quality of their teacher. [Symbolic interactionism]

9.7 Racial and Ethnic Relations in the United States

1. The expectation of immigrants to adopt the values, beliefs, and practices of the dominant culture is called [B. Assimilation].

2. A set of policies to promote hiring, promotion, and college admission to historically disadvantaged groups is called [D. Affirmative action].

3. The racial or ethnic group most likely to assimilate after immigration is [C. Asians].

4. The idea that all Native Americans share a common identity rooted in discrimination and prejudice is called [A. Pan-Indianism].

5. The idea that race, sex, and social class all work together to help create cultural advantage or disadvantage is called [B. Intersectionality theory].

9.8 Key Issues in the Future of Race and Ethnicity

1. Margo moves from Montreal, Canada, to Los Angeles, California. Her move out of Canada would be [A. Emigration].

2. Margo's move into Los Angeles would be considered [B. Immigration].

3. Carson in an African American who was promoted ahead of his white colleagues. Carson was the recipient of what policies? [B. Affirmative action]

ANSWERS TO CHAPTER REVIEW TEST

9.1 Race and Ethnicity in Society

1. A. Most sociologists believe that races are social constructs based on biological traits that society considers important.

9.2 Race

2. C. Most forensic anthropologists accept that races are biological categories rooted in human evolution.

3. B. The process by which people are placed into racial categories that are given social significance is called racialization.

4. C. Americans generally see race as more important than citizens of other nations do.

9.3 Ethnicity

5. D. A minority group is a group that society sets apart in some way and disadvantages.

6. B. Segregation occurs when the dominant group physically or socially isolates a minority group.

7. A. The process by which a person identifies with and constructs her or his ethnic identity is called ethnic work.

9.4 Prejudice

8. D. Prejudice is a belief or attitude about a particular group.

9. C. The conflict perspective sees prejudice as emerging from competition over scarce resources.

10. B. A stereotype is a generalization that is applied to a group of people.

11. A. Scapegoating is the process of blaming the ills of society on particular groups of people.

12. C. Displacement occurs when individual feelings of inadequacy or anger are directed against objects or groups that are not the origins of those feelings.

9.5 Discrimination

13. C. Discrimination is an action taken against a particular group, usually with the goal of denying them the same rights or opportunities as others.

14. A. When discrimination is embedded into some aspect of the social system, it is called institutional discrimination.

15. D. Authoritarian personality theory suggests that prejudicial attitudes develop in childhood when a child is denigrated and put down by parents.

16. B. Social identity theory states that people exhibit prejudicial attitudes against others to build their own positive social identity.

17. B. Social learning theory argues that prejudice is learned through agents of socialization.

9.6 Theoretical Perspectives on Race and Ethnic Relations

18. D. Conflict perspective analyzes the way in which prejudice results from scarce resources.

19. B. Symbolic interactionism seeks to understand how prejudice and discrimination are constructed in society.

20. A. The biosocial perspective believes that prejudice and discrimination are innate in human social relations

9.7 Racial and Ethnic Relations in the United States

21. A. The first African immigrants came to America as indentured servants.

22. C. Affirmative action refers to policies that give preferential hiring, promotion, or college admissions to historically disadvantaged groups.

23. D. Pan-Indianism is the idea that all Native Americans share a common identity that is rooted in common experiences of past prejudice and discrimination.

9.8 Key Issues in the Future of Race and Ethnicity

24. B. Most immigrants to the United States today come from Hispanic nations.

25. D. In early American history, most immigrants came from Europe.

ANSWERS TO CHAPTER ESSAY QUESTIONS

1. There are several reasons the melting pot has not developed the way in which sociologists predicted. The melting pot idea relies on the assumption that immigrants will willingly assimilate to the values of the dominant culture while still maintaining elements of their own culture. However, many immigrants may desire to keep significant elements of their culture that are functional for them, such as traditional family values. Additionally, many values of the dominant culture may clash with the traditional cultural values that have been strongly socialized in the immigrant. For these reasons, many immigrants choose to preserve key elements of their own culture rather than assimilate to major aspects of the dominant culture.

2. There are many factors that influence whether an immigrant is likely to assimilate. Age is important, because immigrants who immigrate at a younger age are more likely to be influenced by and therefore to adopt key elements of the dominant culture. The older a person is, the less likely he or she is to assimilate. It may also matter where the immigrant is originally from. For example, immigrants from Asia may be more inclined to cling to their traditional values and cultural practices than immigrants from Europe. Finally, the reason for immigration may also play a role in whether an immigrant is likely to assimilate to the dominant culture. Individuals who immigrate to escape political or economic persecution are more likely to assimilate than individuals who immigrate for other reasons.

REFERENCES

Adorno, T. 1950. *The Authoritarian Personality*. New York: Norton.

Alba, R. and V. Nee. 2003. *Remaking the American Mainstream: Assimilation and Contemporary Immigration*. Cambridge, MA: Harvard University Press.

Bonnett, A. 2000. *Anti-Racism*. New York: Taylor and Francis.

Collins, P. H. 2008. *Black Feminist Thought: Knowledge, Consciousness, and the Politics of Empowerment*. New York: Routledge.

Daynes, S., and O. Lee. 2008. *Desire for Race*. Cambridge, UK: Cambridge University Press.

DeCamp, L. S. 1995. *The Ape-Man Within*. New York: Prometheus.

Du Bois, W. E. B. 1903. *The Souls of Black Folk: Essays and Sketches*. Chicago: McClurg.

Gill, G. W., and S. Rhine, eds. 1990. *Skeletal Attributions of Race: Methods for Forensic Anthropology*. Albuquerque, NM: Maxwell Museum of Anthropology.

Horn, J. P. 2006. *Land as God Made It: Jamestown and the Birth of America*. New York: Basic Books.

Mills, C. W. 1957. *The Power Elite*. London: Oxford University Press.

Morning, A. 2011. *The Nature of Race: How Scientists Think and Teach about Human Difference*. Riverside: University of California Press.

Oppenheimer, S. 2003. *The Real Eve: Modern Man's Journey Out of Africa*. New York: Carroll & Graf.

Reskin, B. F. 1998. *The Realities of Affirmative Action in Employment*. Washington, DC: American Sociological Association.

Sarich, V., and F. Meile. 2005. *Race: The Reality of Human Difference*. New York: Westview Press.

Sidanius, J., and F. Pratto. 1999. *Social Dominance*. Cambridge, UK: Cambridge University Press.

(right and left) © iStockphoto/Thinkstock

Chapter Overview ▼

10 Sex and Gender

Learning Objectives ▼

10.1 ▪ Distinguish the concepts of sex, gender, and sexuality from the perspectives of biology, behavior, and inequality.

10.2 ▪ Illustrate biological and cultural aspects of sexual behavior.

10.3 ▪ Compare and contrast the three main theoretical perspectives on sexuality.

10.4 ▪ Identify common agents of socialization and show how they operate in gender socialization.

10.5 ▪ Describe the role of patriarchy in gender inequality.

10.6 ▪ Illustrate aspects of gender stratification and inequality in the United States

10.7 ▪ Compare and contrast different theoretical perspectives on gender inequality.

© Rob Marmion/Shutterstock, Inc.

When I first met Shawna she was 25, had just moved back in with her mother, and was working as a house cleaner. Her husband had walked out on her and their four-year-old son some months earlier. At first she was not sure how she could ever survive taking care of her son by herself. The combined incomes of herself from house cleaning and her husband from his job as a night janitor had only barely made ends meet. On the other hand, she admitted to me one day, she was secretly relieved. Marriage had not been at all what Shawna had expected. Shortly into her first year of college she fell in love and within months was pregnant. Over the objections of her mother, they had a hasty courthouse marriage. She dropped out of school to work so that he could continue college. But he too dropped out two years later because she could not earn enough as a house cleaner to support the family. By their second year of marriage, they were struggling. Her job paid poorly and, despite working hard, the few men employees of the house cleaning company were paid better and got the few promotions. After working a full shift cleaning houses, she would come home exhausted, yet her husband expected her to do all of the housework and child care. He would get drunk and "treat her rough," expecting her to wait on him hand and foot. He did not like her friends or spending time with her family, and she felt more and more isolated and helpless.

Shawna's problems, unfortunately, are not all that different from the problems faced by many women who, even in this the second decade of the 21st century, all too frequently find themselves in jobs in which they are paid less than men doing similar work, are often passed over for promotions, are subjected to abuse or even violence by an intimate partner, and do most of the housework and child care in the home while working outside the home as well. This chapter will examine these and other problems faced by women, many of which have faced women throughout history and can be found in both this and other societies. There are plenty of issues to fill the complete chapter focusing exclusively on women and gender issues. However, the problems women face have been in large part because of men and men's treatment of women as sexual objects. To fully understand the impact of gender, we must also consider issues of sexuality.

10.1 Defining Sex, Gender, and Sexuality

The concepts of sex, sexuality, and gender bring together issues of biology, behavior, and inequality.

- Distinguish the concepts of sex, sexuality, and gender from the perspectives of biology, behavior, and inequality.

In this chapter, we examine issues related to three distinct but interrelated concepts: sex, sexuality, and gender. These concepts span issues of biology, inequality, and behavior. We begin with sex.

Sex

Sex The biological distinction between males and females.

Primary sex characteristics A person's genitalia and a woman's ability to bear children and nurse.

Secondary sex characteristics Physical characteristics not directly related to reproduction, such as general body shape, the amount and distribution of body fat, height, weight, muscular strength, the amount of body hair, and the tone of one's voice.

Sex is the biological distinction between males and females. Males and females are distinguished by characteristics of their bodies. These include both primary sex characteristics and secondary sex characteristics. **Primary sex characteristics** are the sexual organs used for reproduction—the male and female genitals—and the ability of females to bear children and nurse. As males and females pass through puberty to reach sexual maturity, they take on additional **secondary sex characteristics**—physical characteristics not directly related to reproduction, such as general body shape, the amount and distribution of body fat, height, weight, muscular strength, the amount of body hair, and the tone of their voices. Mature males tend to have lower voices, more body hair, and greater muscular strength than females. Mature females tend to have wider hips needed to permit childbirth, milk-producing breasts for nursing, and more fatty tissue, providing reserve stores of nutrition useful during pregnancy and nursing. There is, of course, a great deal of variation within both males and females, and physically there is overlap. So, for example, while most men are taller than most women, some women are taller than some men.

Gender

Gender is the social status associated with a person's sex and all of the expectations for behaviors, beliefs, and attitudes that are associated with that status. Where sex is biological, gender is social. Where sex refers to being a male or female, gender refers to masculinity or femininity, social standards of what it means to be a male or female. Because gender is a social status, unlike sex, gender is socially constructed. That is, cultural beliefs about femininity and masculinity evolve as part of the larger culture. Those values, norms, and ideologies about gender justify and reproduce gender inequalities. Thus, gender varies from one society to another, and the expectations for how a man or woman should behave can be very different in those different societies. Whereas sex is biologically determined, gender is learned through a process of socialization. As sociologists Candace West and Don Zimmerman (1987) argued, gender is not an innate quality of human beings but is a performance that is judged by others in terms of how well it meets societal expectations. Thus people are "doing gender" while others evaluate the appropriateness of their behavior. Gender has social significance because it is used by most societies to sort people into different categories and treat them differently. A person's gender is one of the more important social statuses he or she occupies and has consequences for the individual throughout his or her lifetime.

In everyday discourse, people often confuse sex and gender because they do not recognize the distinction. There is a tendency to think that differences between men and women are due to the biological differences of sex. Attributing these differences to biology leads people to perceive these differences as "natural" and not easily changed. However, many differences between men and women are arbitrary differences of gender and are neither "natural" nor unavoidable but lead to persistent inequalities that disadvantage one gender over another.

Gender is an important status that people carry with them throughout their lives, influencing the way people are perceived and treated in the workplace, in the home, in the healthcare system, in education, across cultures, and over time. Over the last 100 years, there have been dramatic changes in some areas and persistent gaps in others. Women now participate in the labor force at almost the same rate as men and go to college in higher proportions than men. However, women are often shunted into less prestigious jobs and are usually paid less than men for the same job, while in the home, women still bear the greater burden of housework, cooking, and child care. We will discuss gender inequalities at length in the section on gender stratification.

Sexuality

Sexuality refers to a person's sexual behavior and attitudes about sexual behavior. Whereas sex is based on biological differences and gender is based on different cultural expectations and inequalities, sexuality is based on sexual behaviors. There is a wide range of sexual behaviors found in our own and other cultures. In the next section, we will examine some of the varieties of sexual behavior found in various cultures and attitudes regarding those behaviors. These include issues of sexual orientation, prostitution, pornography, abortion, sexual violence, premarital sex, and forms of sexual behavior made possible by new technologies.

> **Gender** The social status associated with a person's sex.
>
> **Sexuality** A person's sexual orientation, sexual behavior, and attitudes about sexual behavior.

CONCEPT LEARNING CHECK 10.1   Basic Concepts of Sex, Gender, and Sexuality

Match the following characteristics with the correct term.

_____ **1.** Gender   **A.** Biological

_____ **2.** Sexuality   **B.** A social status

_____ **3.** Sex   **C.** Attitudes and behaviors

Miss Canada, 2012, Jenna Talackova.

© AP Photo/*The Canadian Press*, Chris Young

Intersexual people People whose bodies have the characteristics of both sexes.

Transsexuals People who have the biological characteristics of one sex but identify with the other sex.

Transgendered People of one sex who live as a members of the opposite sex, with which they identify.

Gender reassignment Usually surgery and hormone treatment to make a person's body conform to his or her self-identity.

Sexual orientation A person's preference for sexual partners of a particular sex.

Heterosexual Someone attracted to members of the opposite sex.

Homosexual Someone attracted to members of the same sex.

Bisexual Person is attracted to members of either sex.

Asexual A person who has no sexual attraction to other people regardless of their sex.

10.2 Sexuality and Varieties of Sexual Behavior

There are many varieties of sexual behaviors, and people's attitudes toward those are changing dramatically.

- Illustrate biological and cultural aspects of sexual behavior.

Biological Perspectives

Biology, of course, plays a role in sexual behaviors and attitudes. The biological characteristics associated with a person's sex are the beginning points for their sexual behavior and attitudes. For the great majority of people, their sex is a given. Sex is determined at conception based on the chromosomes carried by the male sperm. However, in rare cases, individuals are sometimes born with some combination of the internal and external sex organs of both sexes. Such people are called **intersexual people**—people whose bodies have the characteristics of both sexes. Another notable exception to the usual pattern is provided by **transsexuals**—people who have the biological characteristics of one sex but identify with the other sex. Often they become **transgendered**—that is, they ignore conventional rules of how people should behave based on sex and live as members of the sex with which they identify. In some cases, they may undergo **gender reassignment**—usually surgery and hormone treatment to make their bodies conform to their self-identities. In India and other South Asian countries, intersexual people are widely recognized in society as hijras and are thought of as a "third sex" (Nanda 1998). In 2012, after some controversy, the Miss Universe Organization decided to permit contestants who were not born as women to compete for the title, clearing the way for Miss Canada, 23-year-old Jenna Talackova, to compete.

Apart from their role in reproduction, the biological differences between men and women are relatively inconsequential in today's world. Men tend to weigh about 25 pounds more than women on average. Men have greater upper-body strength, yet women tend to have greater long-term endurance. The overall intelligence of men and women is about the same, although adolescent males tend to do better on tests of mathematical ability, while adolescent females tend to perform better at tests of verbal ability, and those differences appear to be as much due to socialization as to any biological differences (Lengermann and Wallace 1985).

Cultural Perspectives

Sexuality, like gender, is socially constructed. Different societies have very different norms regarding sexual behavior, and behaviors regarded as quite normal in some societies may be severely punished in others. Lorber (1994) identifies a wide range of possible sexual practices, including sex with men, women, or both; with one partner at a time or two or more partners; with no one (celibacy); with oneself (masturbation); with transsexuals or cross-dressers; or even sex with animals. He also mentions the use of pornography or sexual devices and the use of bondage and/or pain for sexual arousal.

Sexual orientation refers to a person's preference for sexual partners of a particular sex (Lips 1993). Sexual orientation of people is influenced by the prevailing norms in their society as well as by their own socialization experiences. The prevailing norm in modern industrial and postindustrial societies is for heterosexual behavior. A **heterosexual** person is attracted to members of the other sex. Other sexual orientations, though less common, are found in all societies. A **homosexual** person is attracted to members of the same sex. Male homosexuals are often described as "gay," while homosexual women are often referred to as "lesbians." A **bisexual** person is attracted to members of either sex. An **asexual** person has no sexual attraction to other people regardless of their sex (Plummer 1984).

Societal norms in virtually all societies endorse heterosexuality. Indeed, since heterosexuality is required for reproduction, we cannot expect societies to survive if they do not at least permit heterosexual behavior. Norms regarding homosexuality more often forbid it or at most tolerate it. However, in some rare cases, there have been societies in which homosexuality is looked upon with more favor. In ancient Greece, for example, elite men practiced homosexuality, and heterosexuality was regarded as little more than a necessity for reproduction. Thus, their favorable disposition toward homosexuality grew out of **sexism**—a belief that one sex is superior to the other (Greenberg 1988; Kluckhohn 1948). Among the Azande people in Southern Sudan in Africa, sexual relations among men and boys are accepted (Evans-Prichard 1970).

> **Sexism** A belief that one sex is superior to the other.

Societal norms regarding sexual behaviors are not limited to passing judgments on the rightness or wrongness of heterosexuality and homosexuality. Societies often have strong norms regarding with whom a person can engage in sexual activities, the kind of sexual activities, and the number of partners. The study of sexual norms, beliefs, and behaviors has been a topic of investigation by social scientists for decades. Anthropologists studying various cultures by visiting and living with indigenous peoples have often included an examination of those peoples' sexuality. Typically, anthropological studies of sexuality in other cultures have been based upon direct observation and interviews. In contrast, studies of sexual behaviors and beliefs in our own culture have usually been based upon face-to-face interviews or mailed questionnaires. Direct observations have been uncommon, have typically been in laboratory settings rather than natural settings, and have usually focused upon the physiological aspects of sexuality rather than the social and cultural elements (Masters, Johnson, and Kolodny 1988).

The Kinsey Studies. The first widely read and cited study of human sexuality in the United States was produced by a biologist, Alfred Kinsey (Kinsey et al. 1948). The Kinsey study was based on surveys in which he asked both men and women to describe their sexual histories, including the types of behaviors in which they had engaged and the frequency. Kinsey's work produced quite a response in the public at the time of its publication because his results showed major discrepancies between the rather restrictive norms of sexual behavior of US society during the 1940s and 1950s and the actual behaviors reported by his respondents. His data reported a much higher incidence of sexual behaviors such as masturbation, homosexuality, and premarital sex than expected. Kinsey's work has been criticized for using a convenience sample—people sampled because they were easy to find and persuade to respond. As Kinsey traveled and talked about his research, he would interview groups of people at his talks, a PTA here, a group of homosexual men there, or a college class at yet another site. But those groups were not necessarily representative of the US population. His audience members were mostly white, educated, and Midwesterners. Since many were volunteers who sought him out, it was possible his interviewees responded differently to his survey than the general population would. Despite the study's limitations, Kinsey's data both shocked and fascinated the nation for decades.

The National Health and Social Life Survey. It was not until years later that a national survey of human sexual behavior was able to gather data using methods that were more valid than Kinsey's. The National Health and Social Life Survey was conceived in 1987 as a way to gather useful data about sexual practices in the United States that could be used to help control AIDS. By identifying groups at risk due to their sexual behaviors, this study could help medical scientists target subpopulations for medical education to help reduce the spread of AIDS. The study conducted 90-minute face-to-face interviews with a national probability sample of 3,432 adults. A probability sample was selected to give people of all types a chance of being included and to result in a sample that represented the broader population. Nearly 80% of people contacted agreed to participate in the study. The resulting sample of people was compared to the US population on various characteristics and found to be quite similar. Thus, the sample is likely to be representative of the US population in general (Michael et al. 1994:26–29).

This National Health and Social Life Survey found a number of results that might be expected, while other results challenge conventional wisdom about sexuality. In FIGURE 10-1, for example, are the number of sexual partners people have had since

FIGURE 10-1 Number of sexual partners since age 18 as reported by adults ages 18 to 59 (1994). *Source: Data from Laumann, Robert Michael, Stuart Michaels, and John Gagnon. 1994. The Social Organization of Sexuality. Chicago: University of Chicago Press.*

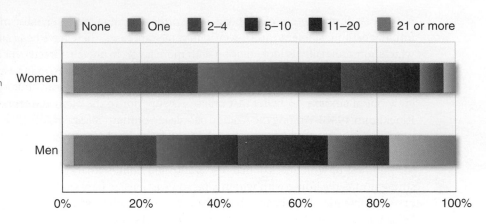

Double standard Different standards of sexual behavior for men and women.

the age of 18 for men and women, college graduates, and high school graduates. As might be expected, men report more partners than women. The pattern for college graduates more nearly resembles the pattern for men (more partners) and the pattern for high school graduates resembles the pattern for women (fewer partners). The findings regarding men and women are consistent with the **double standard**—different standards for men and women when it comes to sexual behavior. This double standard shows up in both behaviors and attitudes. For example, both male and female college students displayed more negative evaluations of women who had experienced a casual first sexual relationship at the age of 16 than men (Blumstein and Schwartz 1983). Another study of preadolescent boys found that they tended to view women who were sexually active as "sluts" and "prosties" while sexually active boys were viewed more favorably (Fine 1987:107).

Some of the more surprising findings from the National Health and Social Life Survey contradict traditional stereotypes of sexual behavior. Despite popular myths of love being the primary basis for selecting sexual partners and the notion that anyone can marry anyone, as when Cinderella marries the prince, the reality is more like *Romeo and Juliet,* in which the animosity between their respective families first kept the lovers apart and eventually led to their deaths. That is, people are far more likely to choose sex partners similar to them in race, ethnicity, religion, age, and social class. Finally, both marital infidelity and the number of homosexuals in the population were less common than many had thought. However, both of those may have been underreported, particularly during the middle of the AIDS epidemic.

Sexual Orientation

Earlier, we defined sexual orientation as a person's preference for sexual partners of a particular sex. An important question is to what extent sexual orientation is influenced by biological factors versus environmental factors. Most social scientists agree that both nature and nurture play a role in whether someone becomes a homosexual. However, it is difficult to create a study that can isolate the effects of biological factors such as genetics or hormones and social factors such as early childhood socialization.

The role of genetics. Studies of genetically identical twins offer some intriguing evidence. For example, Bailey and Pillard (1991) and Bailey et al. (1993) studied 167 pairs of brothers and 143 pairs of sisters, at least one of whom identified him- or herself as homosexual. By comparing identical twins (who share all genes) with fraternal twins (who share some genes) with adopted siblings (who share no genes), we can assess the impact of genetics on homosexual orientation. On the one hand, if genetics completely determined homosexuality, then all of the identical twins should be homosexual, somewhat fewer of the fraternal twins, and even fewer of the adopted siblings. On the other hand, if socialization completely determined homosexuality, then the rates of homosexuality among all pairs should be quite similar (assuming the pairs spent their entire childhood together in the same household and exposed to the same socialization).

As usual with such studies, the results provided some partial support for the influence of both biology and socialization. Roughly one-half of the identical twins were both homosexual when one of them was homosexual, while only about 1 in 5 fraternal twins were homosexual and about 1 in 10 adopted siblings were homosexual. This suggests genetics plays some role in homosexuality. However, since about half of the identical twins were not homosexual even though their twins were, obviously something in addition to genetics must be at work here.

The effect of hormones. Other studies of homosexuality relative to birth order suggest that men with older brothers are more likely to be homosexual, with each additional older brother increasing the odds of homosexuality by roughly 33% (Blanchard and Klassen 1997). Those authors argue that mothers who have previously given birth to males develop antibodies to male hormones that may interfere with the hormonal development of later boys, leading them to be more likely to be homosexual. Hormones thus provide another mechanism by which biology influences homosexuality.

The effects of socialization. Sociologist Peter Bearman (2002) examined some of the ways socialization experiences may interact with genetics and hormones to influence homosexuality. He found that males with an opposite-sex (OS) twin were twice as likely to be homosexual as other males. This finding could be due to either hormones (sharing the uterus with a female twin could lead to greater feminization of the male due to hormone transfers between the fetuses) or to socialization (norms of equality could encourage parents to treat twins more alike, thus reducing socialization supporting gender-stereotypical behaviors). Next, Bearman examined the rate of homosexuality for men having OS twins when an older brother was present in the household. The hormonal hypothesis based on Blanchard and Klassen (1997) would predict an older brother would lead to increased homosexuality, while the socialization hypothesis, argued Bearman (2002), would predict decreased homosexuality because gender-socializing mechanisms may be locked in from earlier socialization of the older brother. Bearman's results supported the socialization hypothesis rather than the hormonal hypothesis, with reduced homosexual attraction for male OS twins having an older brother.

These results are consistent with the American Academy of Pediatrics (2004), which stated that "sexual orientation probably is not determined by any one factor but by a combination of genetic, hormonal, and environmental influences." Clearly biology has a lot to do with sexual orientation through both genetics and hormones, and the effects of socialization are also beyond the control of the individual. Together, studies such as these support the widespread view that sexual orientation is not something someone chooses. By 1994, the General Social Survey found that 54% of respondents believed being homosexual is something an individual cannot change (NORC 2011).

Homosexuality in the United States. Kinsey (Kinsey et al. 1948; Kinsey 1953) conceptualized homosexuality not as a discrete "yes" or "no" issue but as a continuum, with some people exclusively heterosexual at one extreme, others exclusively homosexual at the other extreme, but with many people displaying more or less homosexuality and heterosexuality in between. He estimated that about 4% of men and 2% of women were exclusively homosexual, while one-third of men and one-eighth of women had had at least one homosexual experience in which they reached an orgasm. In contrast, the much more precise survey conducted by Laumann and colleagues (1994) measured homosexuality somewhat differently. They distinguished between men and women who define themselves as entirely or partly homosexual (2.8% of men and 1.4% of women), those reporting homosexual activity prior to puberty only (7.1% of men and 3.8% of women), and those who had ever engaged in any homosexual activity at any time in their lives (9.1% of men and 4.3% of women). The results of the Laumann and colleagues (1994) survey are displayed in FIGURE 10-2. More recently, the National Survey of Sexual Health and Behavior (Herenick et al. 2010) reported 4% of adult men self-identified as gay and 7% as either gay or bisexual, while 13.8% of men 40 to 49 years old and 14.9% ages 40 to 59 years old reported engaging in one or more forms of same-sex behavior during their lifetime (Herbenick et al. 2010).

FIGURE 10-2 The heterosexual–homosexual continuum in the United States.
Source: Data from Laumann, Robert Michael, Stuart Michaels, and John Gagnon. 1994. The Social Organization of Sexuality. Chicago: University of Chicago Press.

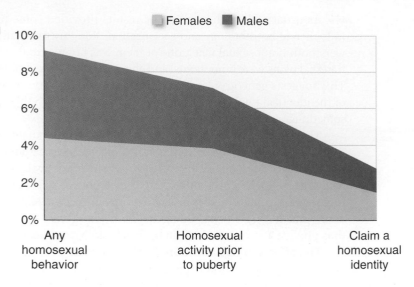

Social movements for homosexual rights. While homosexuals have existed throughout history and in all societies, for most of history, they hid their sexual orientation. It is only within the last 50 years that many homosexuals in the United States have been willing to "come out of the closet" and openly acknowledge their homosexuality. Today many large cities, such as New York and San Francisco, have substantial openly gay and lesbian populations and a distinct gay and lesbian subculture.

A turning point in the movement for homosexual rights was the Stonewall Riots of June 28, 1969. Before Stonewall, the great majority of gays wished to keep their sexual orientation a secret to avoid the stigma of being gay. This left them vulnerable to harassment by police. In the Stonewall riots, gays who had grown tired of repeated police harassment openly fought New York City police for two days (D'Emilio 1983; Weeks 1977). Stonewall became a symbol of gay pride and led to the recognition by many gays that they had to speak out if they were ever to expect to gain equal treatment under the law.

Following Stonewall, during the 1970s, openly gay people and openly gay-run businesses such as publishing houses, bath houses, discos, and counseling services became much more common, and gay communities in large urban areas began to become much more visible and politically active. Another victory for homosexual rights occurred in 1973 when, after considerable pressure and lobbying from homosexual rights groups, the medical community finally removed homosexuality from the list of mental illnesses. By 1992, there were 1,600 gay and lesbian social and political organizations in the United States (Cohn 1992), and in April of 1993, between 300,000 and a million people attended a march on Washington for gay rights (Houston 1993). Today, marches for gay rights are held annually in many large cities, including Los Angeles, San Francisco, Boston, New York, and Chicago. Such marches would have been unthinkable 50 years ago.

Homosexuals and civil rights. There is considerable evidence that attitudes toward homosexuals are becoming less negative. In FIGURE 10-3 are reported attitudes toward homosexuals and their civil rights from 1973 to 2010 based on the General Social Survey (NORC 2011). When asked whether homosexual sex is wrong, only 6% responded in 1973 that it is "not wrong at all." Beginning around 1994, this has steadily increased until by 2010, 35% of all respondents agreed homosexual sex is not wrong at all. Over that same period, attitudes regarding the civil rights of homosexuals have also improved dramatically. When asked whether homosexuals should be permitted to give a speech in their community, only 47% were in favor of allowing it in 1973. By 2010, 82% were in favor. Regarding homosexuals teaching in college, approval more than doubled from 33% in 1973 to 80% in 2010. Similarly, when asked if they approved of excluding or removing a book by a homosexual from the library, numbers went from 38% who

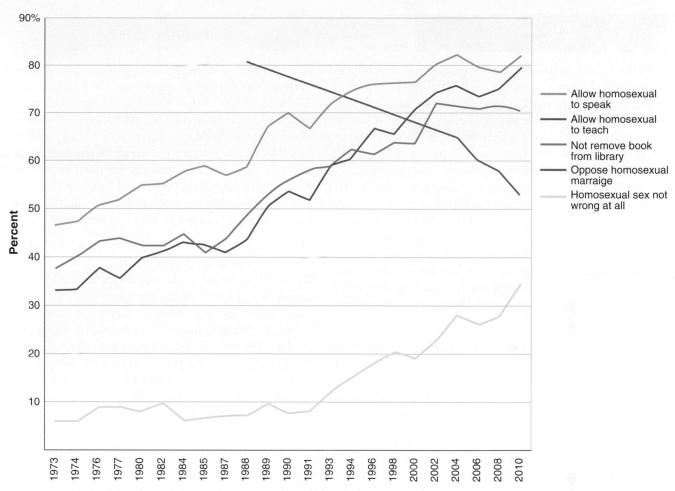

FIGURE 10-3 US attitudes about homosexuals and their civil rights (1973–2010).
Source: Data from National Opinion Research Center (NORC). 2011. General Social Surveys, 1972–2010 Cumulative Codebook.
Accessed November 2012 (http://www.ropercenter.uconn.edu/data_access/data/datasets/general_social_survey.html).

would not remove the book in 1973 to 71% in 2010. The data are not available for every year during this time period. However, in 1981, 81% of respondents opposed homosexuals marrying each other, and by 2010, that had dropped to only slightly more than half (53%).

Despite these more favorable attitudes toward homosexuality, homosexuals still find themselves victims of discrimination and acts of violence. **Homophobia** is prejudice and discrimination against homosexuals driven by an aversion to or even hatred of homosexuals and their life styles. Well-known terms in our language such as *fag*, *homo*, or *dyke* provide ample evidence of the long history of verbal abuse. Physical abuse and harassment of gay, lesbian, bisexual, and transsexual people is also not difficult to find. Many gays find themselves the victims of bullying, such as Tyler Clementi, the 18-year-old Rutgers University student who committed suicide after his roommate streamed live video of Clementi and another man in his dorm room (*The New York Times* 2012). The suicide rate among gay youths, while hard to estimate (Best 2001), is widely reported to be significantly higher than the suicide rate among heterosexual youths (Suicide Prevention Resource Center 2008). It was not until 2009 that President Obama signed into law legislation expanding hate crime classifications to include crimes based on sexual orientation and gender identity.

Homophobia Prejudice and discrimination against homosexuals driven by an aversion to or even hatred of homosexuals and their life styles.

Sexual Issues

There are many additional issues of sexuality and sexual behavior in the United States today, including prostitution, pornography, pregnancy and abortion, sexual violence, and the circumstances of sex, including when, with whom, and the role of technology.

THE SOCIOLOGICAL IMAGINATION   Gay Suicide and the "It Gets Better" Project

In the Fall of 2010, there was a rash of highly publicized suicides by young gay men, including the death of Tyler Clementi, that raised public consciousness about gay bullying and suicide. In response to this, Dan Savage, a gay sex advice columnist, started the "It Gets Better" project. Savage and eventually more than 40,000 others posted online videos, which usually took the form of a talking head looking straight into the camera and speaking to young gays who feel they are being bullied. Some videos were posted by famous actors or politicians, including President Barack Obama. However, in most of the videos, adults who experienced bullying as teenagers or young adults would describe some of their own bad experiences then explain how their lives are better now. The message, reflected in the name of the campaign, is that things will get better: just hang in there, do not despair, your life will get better.

Sociologist Jeffrey McCully (2012) conducted a detailed analysis of 400 videos from this project to look at the themes that occur. While he recognized that the intent of the project was to help prevent suicides, McCully criticized the project on sociological grounds, arguing that the project reproduces some of the very ideologies and practices that contribute to homophobia and gender oppression that it seeks to combat. One basis for his criticism is the way the project lacks a sociological imagination. Remember, the sociological imagination argues that we should not confuse public issues with private troubles. Yet this project seeks to reduce gay suicides by asking bullied youth to wait until it gets better. Doesn't this send a message to the bullied youth, said McCully, that it is their problem rather than the problem of the bullies? If they could just be stronger, wait longer, they can get through it.

McCully argues the "It Gets Better" project tackles the problem on the individual level, ignoring the structural conditions that make it a broad social issue. A sociological analysis, he argues, would lead us to also recognize that the cause of the problem is bullying by others. Instead of asking the victim to wait for things to improve (a proposed solution focusing on the individual), why do they not argue for trying to make things better today for people in general? Why do we not address the social issue at a societal or community level? For example, why do more high schools not have antibullying policies that are actually enforced?

EVALUATE

1. What do you think? Was this Tyler Clementi's problem, or is it a broader social issue? Have you or someone you know experienced bullying? Was that bullying an individual problem or a social issue? If one victim of bullying is able to overcome the problem, does that do anything to help other victims or to stop the bully? Would it be wise to try to address the problem at a social level rather than at the individual level?

2. Finally, consider how people might respond to an "It Gets Better" project for blacks or women or other oppressed minorities. Would not women or blacks be outraged (and rightly so) if a woman suffering sexual harassment at work or a black man experiencing job discrimination was told to just wait and it will get better?

Prostitution Paid sex.

Pornography The portrayal of sexual subject matter for the purpose of sexual arousal.

Prostitution

Prostitution, or paid sex, has been part of social life for centuries in societies throughout the world. There is a long tradition of hypocrisy regarding prostitution in the United States. In the United States, for example, prostitution is illegal everywhere in the country except for a few places in Nevada, yet when asked whether they had ever paid for sex or been paid for having sex, roughly one out of five men (20%) responded yes (NORC 2011). Prostitution is a gendered activity in the sense that men and women participate in it very differently. Most prostitutes are women and most customers are men. Fewer than 2% of women report having ever paid for sex or having been paid for sex in that same national survey (NORC 2011). While prostitution is sometimes called a "victimless crime" because the victim is not so obvious, in fact, prostitutes (or sex workers, as they prefer to be called) are often victims of violence from their pimps or clients (Estes and Weiner 2001), and gay prostitutes are often the victims of rejection or violence by family and friends (Kruks 1991).

Pornography

Pornography is the portrayal of sexual subject matter for the purpose of sexual arousal. That is easy enough to say, but it turns out it has been very difficult for US courts to specify clearly what constitutes pornography and what constitutes reasonable expression permitted under the First Amendment. Because of this difficulty, courts have permitted local communities to decide for themselves. The broad standards address whether the material violates "community standards" and lacks "redeeming social value." Most countries, including the United States, attempt to restrict access to pornography by minors, but this has become very difficult to enforce given the easy access to pornography over the Internet. Some types of pornography, such as child pornography involving one or more minors, are illegal and are more tightly enforced in many countries, including the United States.

Critics of pornography argue that it demeans women (Mackinnon 1984) and may encourage violence against women (Malamuth 1986). Pornography, they argue, leads to sexual objectification and dehumanization in which women are viewed merely as sex objects for another's sexual gratification, with little or no regard for their individuality or humanity (Bartky 1990). This view of women as objects of sexual pleasure encourages body modifications designed to increase their perceived beauty and sexuality, such as genital circumcision (the surgical removal of the clitoris). However, it is difficult to establish a clear causal link between pornography and these possible effects. Part of the problem is typified by a University of Montreal study that attempted to compare views of men who had never been exposed to pornography with regular users. They could not find any men who had not been exposed to pornography (Liew 2009).

Over the past 40 years, attitudes toward pornography, as measured by the General Social Survey between 1973 and 2010, displayed in FIGURE 10-4, have changed dramatically. Between 1973 and 2010, there has been an increasing tendency for people to believe pornography should be illegal for people under 18, increasing from 32% who agreed in 1973 to 49%, while those feeling pornography should be illegal for everyone dropped from 61% in 1973 to 41% in 2010. Over this same period of time, the percentage of respondents reporting they had seen an X-rated movie last year ranged from 5 to 15% and averaged slightly more than 10% (NORC 2011). When asked between 2000 and 2004 whether they had used a pornographic website in the past 30 days, 11% of males and only 1.6% of females responded yes (NORC 2011).

Pregnancy and Abortion

Teen pregnancy is a long-standing concern because most teens, though biologically capable of having children, are often not ready to handle the burdens of parenthood and are less likely to complete their education once they are responsible for a child. In 2008, there were 733,000 pregnancies among teenagers (women aged 15 to 19) and a pregnancy rate among teenagers of 7%. This was the lowest pregnancy rate among teens in more than 30 years, down 42% from its peak in 1990 when the rate was 12%. The teenage abortion rate was 17.8%, 35% lower than the peak rate of 61.8% in 1991 (Kost and Henshaw 2012). Issues of teen pregnancies and abortions are greatest for minorities. Both birth and abortion rates are higher for blacks and Hispanic teenagers than for non–Hispanic white teenagers. The birth rate for both blacks and Hispanics is twice that of non–Hispanic white teenagers. When compared to non–Hispanic teenagers, the abortion rate for black teens is four times higher and the abortion rate for Hispanic teenagers is two times higher.

Prostitution has been part of social life for centuries.
© Corbis

A growing number of people believe pornography should be illegal for people under 18 years of age.
© Martyn Vickery/Alamy

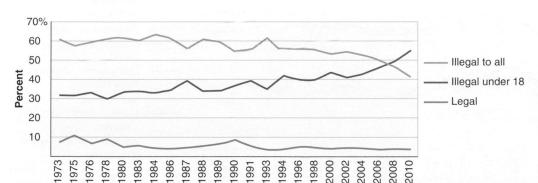

FIGURE 10-4 US attitudes about pornography (1973–2010). *Source: Data from National Opinion Research Center (NORC). 2011.* General Social Surveys, 1972–2010 Cumulative Codebook. *Accessed November 2012 (http://www .ropercenter.uconn.edu/data_access/ data/datasets/general_social_survey .html).*

The General Social Survey, throughout its history from 1972 to 2010, has found relatively consistent support for abortion when the woman's health is seriously endangered (near 90%) and somewhat less support for abortion when she is pregnant as a result of rape or there is a strong chance of a serious defect (around 75% or 76% most recently). This is shown in FIGURE 10-5. Other reasons for abortions (married and wanting no more children, low income and cannot afford more children, not married, or for any reason) receive mixed support (between 30 and 50% earlier and generally in the low 40% range in recent years). Generally, these rates have been mostly stable over time but have dropped somewhat since the 1970s.

Sexual Violence

Women are often subjected to violent acts both in the United States and throughout the world. In the United States, violence against women often takes the form of rape. **Rape** is forced, nonconsensual vaginal, oral, or anal intercourse. Rape is often thought to be one of the most underreported crimes. One study in England estimates that between 75% and 95% of rapes are never reported to police (Her Majesty's Inspectorate of Constabulary 2007). The US Department of Justice estimates there were 255,630 rapes/sexual assaults reported in 2006, with 99,910 involving strangers and 155,720 involving nonstrangers (USDOJ 2008, Table 37). While the great majority of rapes involve women victims of men, men also rape other men in all-male environments such as prison. The National Inmate Survey in 2007 reported an estimated 60,500 inmates (4.5% of all state and federal inmates) experienced one or more incidents of sexual victimization in 2007 (BJS 2007).

In addition to violent rape, "date rape" or "acquaintance rape" is rape occurring between nonstrangers. As the data above suggest, this is the most common form of rape. One of the difficulties regarding rape is that between rape and consensual sex is "a continuum of pressure, threat, coercion, and force" (Kelly 1987). Men accused of rape often argue that the incident was actually consensual sex, and in the process they call into question the motives and responsibility of the woman. Establishing the lack of consent by one married partner in the case of marital rape can be even more difficult (Frieze 1983). Women who are subjected to physical rape then sometimes experience a kind of emotional assault on their own character in the courtroom.

Intimate partner abuse is not limited to rape. The National Center on Domestic and Sexual Violence distinguishes a range of ways in which one partner can abuse another. These include physical coercion and threats, intimidation, emotional abuse, isolation, and additional strategies to assert power and control summarized in FIGURE 10-6 (NCDSV 2012).

Sex: When and with Whom?

Premarital sex. Attitudes about premarital sex among adults have changed dramatically between 1972 and 2010 as measured by the General Social Survey (NORC 2011).

Rape Forced, nonconsensual vaginal, oral, or anal intercourse.

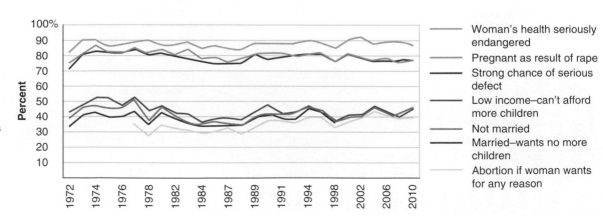

FIGURE 10-5
Approval of abortion depending on circumstance: Support for abortion is much higher in the case of serious birth defects, rape, or if the woman's health is endangered.
Source: Data from General Social Survey. 2010.

— Woman's health seriously endangered
— Pregnant as result of rape
— Strong chance of serious defect
— Low income–can't afford more children
— Not married
— Married–wants no more children
— Abortion if woman wants for any reason

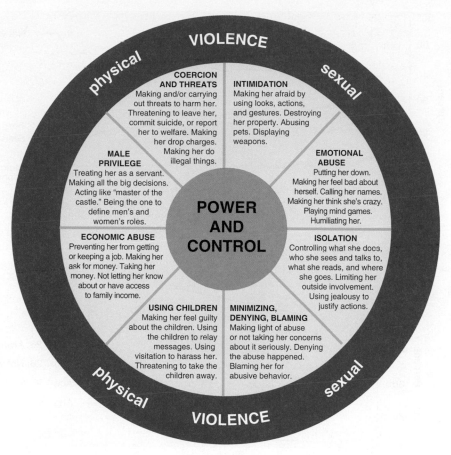

FIGURE 10-6 Abuse often occurs in more than one form, which is, in part, why it is so powerful.
Source: Courtesy of The Duluth Model, Domestic Abuse Intervention Programs (http://www.theduluthmodel.org).

These attitudes are plotted in FIGURE 10-7. In 1972, only 27% of respondents indicated it is not wrong at all for a man and woman to have sex relations before marriage, while 37% indicated it was always wrong. By 2010, 53% of respondents indicated it was never wrong and only 22% indicated it was always wrong.

When we break down attitudes by age, we find that the majority of young adults (between 18 and 25) viewed sex before marriage as not wrong at all in 1972 (51%) and an even stronger majority did so in 2010 (60%). In contrast, in 1972, a majority of adults 50 and older (51%) believed sex before marriage was always wrong, but by 2010, that had dropped to only 27%, while the percentage of adults 50 and older who viewed sex before marriage as not wrong at all rose from 16% in 1972 to nearly half (47%) in 2010. This is displayed in FIGURE 10-8.

A hookup culture. Given the favorable view of premarital sex for young people, it is not surprising that on college campuses, sex before marriage is relatively common. Sociologist Paula England (England, Fitzgibbons, and Fogarty 2008) surveyed students at a Midwestern university and found evidence that many students are putting off serious relationships longer and are not expecting or trying to begin their families yet. As a result, many students engage in "**hookups**"—casual, usually one-time encounters with others that may lead to sexual activity but often stop short of intercourse. Hookups do not necessarily mean that either person is interested in a relationship, but they might be. In her survey, she found that half of student respondents reported their last sexual partner was someone with whom they had slept only once.

Not all sex is right. We might be tempted, given the increasing acceptance of sex before marriage, to think that attitudes toward all forms of sexuality are becoming more accepting in the United States. But this is not true. Some forms of sex are no

Hookups Casual, usually one-time encounters with others that may lead to sexual activity but often stop short of intercourse.

FIGURE 10-7 US attitudes about premarital sex.
Source: Data from National Opinion Research Center (NORC). 2011. General Social Surveys, 1972–2010 Cumulative Codebook. Accessed November 2012 (http://www .ropercenter.uconn.edu/data_access/ data/datasets/general_social_survey .html).

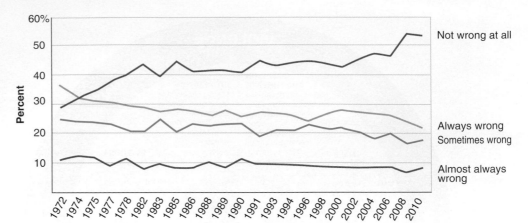

FIGURE 10-8 US attitudes about premarital sex, by age (1972 and 2010).
Source: Data from National Opinion Research Center (NORC). 2011. General Social Surveys, 1972–2010 Cumulative Codebook. Accessed November 2012 (http://www .ropercenter.uconn.edu/data_access/ data/datasets/general_social_survey .html).

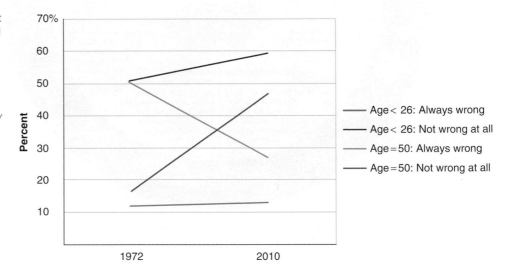

more acceptable today than they were decades ago, and some are even less acceptable today. Two examples of this are attitudes toward sex among teenagers aged 14 to 16 and extramarital sex. When asked their attitudes toward premarital sex among teenagers age 14 to 16, roughly 70% (between 67% and 72%) of respondents indicated it was always wrong in every survey between 1986 and 2010. Similarly, when asked about extramarital sex, respondents were even less accepting, with 79% indicating it was always wrong in 1991 and 81% in 2008 (NORC 2011). Despite that, the percentage of respondents who report having had sex with someone other than their spouse while married rose from 11% in 1991 to 21% in 2010. This is displayed in FIGURE 10-9.

Technology and Sexuality

A hookup culture based on casual sexual encounters can be facilitated by new technologies such as the Internet, social networking, and cell phones. **Virtual sex** occurs when two or more people use some form of communications technology to arouse each other sexually by transmitting sexually explicit messages such as text, photos, or videos. **Sexting** is the transmission of sexually explicit photographs, videos, or messages by cell phone. **Cyber sex** is virtual sex using computers over the Internet. If an underage person is involved, it has sometimes been regarded as child pornography (Irvine 2009). When former US Congressman Anthony Weiner sent a link to a sexually explicit photograph of himself to women both before and during his marriage, he was forced to resign from his seat in Congress (MSNBC 2011).

The explosion in use of the Internet and social networking programs such as Facebook and Twitter helps people find others with similar interests. Variants of social network applications include networking sites whose primary use is to permit people

Virtual sex When two or more people use some form of communications technology such as text, photos, or videos to arouse each other sexually by transmitting sexually explicit messages.

Sexting The transmission of sexually explicit photographs, videos, or messages by cell phone.

Cyber sex Virtual sex using computers over the Internet.

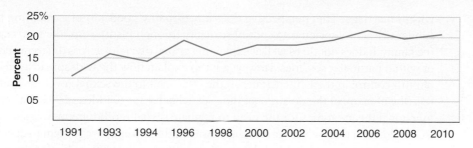

FIGURE 10-9 Percentage of adults who report having had extramarital sex (1991–2010). *Source: Data from National Opinion Research Center (NORC). 2011.* General Social Surveys, 1972–2010 Cumulative Codebook. *Accessed November 2012 (http://www. ropercenter.uconn.edu/data_access/ data/datasets/general_social_survey .html).*

to find sexual partners with whom they can meet and engage in sexual activity. Online classifieds sites, such as Craigslist, also often have personals sections such as "women seeking men." The latest, and by some accounts the creepiest, of smart phone apps include geospatial social networking programs that, when installed on your smart phone, can access all of your Facebook and other networking connections, letting you know when you are near someone who shares similar interests. Some of these are explicitly focused on helping users hook up with sexual partners (Bartz and Ehrlich, 2012).

CONCEPT LEARNING CHECK 10.2 | Recent Trends in Sexual Behavior

Match the following attitudes regarding sexuality with trends in recent years according to the data presented in this chapter.

_____ **1.** Premarital sex

_____ **2.** Abortion

_____ **3.** Pornography (for adults)

_____ **4.** Sex outside marriage

_____ **5.** Homosexuality

A. Attitudes toward this issue are becoming *more favorable* over time.

B. Attitudes toward this issue are *about the same* as they have been for decades.

C. Attitudes toward this issue are becoming *less favorable* over time.

10.3 Theoretical Perspectives on Sexuality

Human sexuality has been examined by the dominant theoretical perspectives of sociology, and one of them, conflict theory, has extended to feminism and queer theory.

- Compare and contrast the three main theoretical perspectives on sexuality.

The three broad theoretical perspectives that sociologists use to examine other aspects of social life also can be used to interpret sexuality. In addition to these three (structural-functional theory, symbolic interaction theory, and social conflict theory), conflict theory has been extended to feminism and queer theory.

Structural-Functional Theory

Structural-functional theory attempts to understand sexuality in terms of the positive functions for society of various forms of sexuality. In this view, the importance of legitimate procreation (from sex within marriage) as opposed to illegitimate procreation (illegitimate births from sex taking place outside marriage) reflects the desire to regulate sexuality (in what circumstances and with whom one can have sex) in order to preserve family, inheritance, and the provision of support needed to raise children. In the functional view, the argument is that we forbid some forms of sexuality, such as incest, extramarital sex, or even homosexuality because we wish to restrict sexual expression to forms that support the continued survival of society—that is, heterosexual relationships within marriage. This perspective does a reasonably good job of explaining broad similarities across societies to control sexuality through institutions like marriage and the family. It does not do as well at explaining sexual diversity across different societies or within particular societies. However, it can explain how the widespread availability of birth control in the United States in the 1960s led to the sexual revolution and the relaxing of many of the norms regarding sexual behavior (Giddens 1992). Structural-functional theory argues for the need to regulate sexual reproduction to assure males that children of their wives are also their own children to encourage them to devote the resources needed to raise the children. Birth control makes it possible for the woman to have sex with other men without having their children by use of birth control with other men, but not with their spouse. Of course, this relaxation of norms of sexual exclusivity also challenged the family.

Symbolic Interactionism

Symbolic interaction theory emphasizes the social construction of reality through interaction. For this reason, it is better able than structural-functional theory to account for diversity in sexual behavior throughout the world and over time. This perspective can help explain differences across societies in sexual practices like circumcision. Male circumcision (the surgical removal of all or most of the foreskin of the penis) of infant males, for example, is quite common in the United States but quite rare in European countries. In contrast, female circumcision is very rare in the United States but common in some parts of Africa and the Middle East (WHO 2012). Interestingly, in the United States, we sometimes refer to the practice that is rare in our society as *female genital mutilation*, while a similar phrase, *male genital mutilation*, is not used to refer to the practice that is common in our society.

Symbolic interaction theory can account for changes in sexual behavior and attitudes over time, since in this view, the meaning of particular sexual practices or behaviors arises from interaction among people in that time and place. One often-cited example of changing sexual norms is the importance of virginity. In this view, virginity was once regarded as very important before marriage in the United States, when it was the best assurance to the man that his would-be-bride was not carrying another man's baby. However, with the widespread availability of birth control, the importance of virginity has declined to the point where, for people born between 1963 and 1975, only 16.3% of men and 20.1% of women reported being virgins when first married (Laumann et al. 1994:503).

While symbolic interaction theory can account for varieties of sexuality around the world, the presence of a widespread persistent trend across societies and times is more likely to be the result of some broader structural factor that might be better explained by functional theory or conflict theory.

Social Conflict, Feminist, and Queer Theories

Social conflict theory argues that class conflict accounts for much of social life. This perspective has been used to explain differential enforcement of laws against prostitution. Being arrested is much more likely for the less-powerful female prostitute than the more-powerful male client. Similarly, among women prostitutes, those with less income and more likely to be members of minorities (streetwalkers) are more likely to be arrested than more-affluent and more-likely-to-be-white call girls.

Feminist theory and queer theory, in many ways, begin from a conflict perspective and extend it to gender and sexuality. Feminist theory takes the conflict perspective and focuses on the domination of women by men. In this view, sexuality may be at the heart of inequality between men and women, with women defined in sexual terms and thereby devalued by men. As support for this perspective, they point out that pornography is consumed primarily by men and usually portrays men as having power over women.

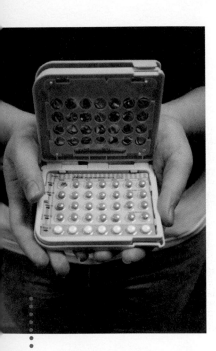

Birth control led to the relaxing of many of the norms regarding sexual behavior.

© Jones & Bartlett Learning. Photographed by Jessica Elias.

Queer theory expands the argument from feminist theory—based on conflict between men and women—to argue there is a heterosexual bias in contemporary American culture. It expands the notion of men dominating women to recognize a **heterosexism** in the United States—a view that labels anyone who is not heterosexual (including homosexuals, lesbians, bisexuals, and transsexuals) as "queer." Queer theorists point out that bias against nonheterosexuals is tolerated in American society far more than bias against women or racial and ethnic minorities. In many states, for example, there are laws against racial or gender bias in housing and jobs, while the Defense of Marriage Act explicitly prohibits gays from enjoying the benefits of marriage enjoyed by every other member of our society.

Often, people in the majority are not aware of how biased they are in their treatment of minorities. In the case of heterosexism, this seems particularly true because many heterosexuals take the view that nonheterosexual life styles are inherently immoral. One effort to sensitize people to this taken-for-granted moral judgment is the Heterosexual Questionnaire, attributed to Martin Rochlin, PhD, 1977, reproduced here in FIGURE 10-10.

If you are heterosexual and take the questionnaire seriously, you may be a bit offended at the negative assumptions it makes about heterosexuality. The point of the

> **Heterosexism** A view that labels anyone who is not heterosexual (including homosexuals, lesbians, bisexuals, and transsexuals) as "queer."

The Heterosexual Questionnaire
attributed to Martin Rochlin, PhD 1977

1. What do you think caused your heterosexuality?
2. When and how did you first decide you were a heterosexual?
3. Is it possible your heterosexuality is just a phase you may grow out of?
4. Is it possible your heterosexuality stems from a neurotic fear of others of the same sex?
5. Isn't it possible that all you need is a good Gay lover?
6. Heterosexuals have histories of failures in Gay relationships. Do you think you may have turned to heterosexuality out of fear of rejection?
7. If you've never slept with a person of the same sex, how do you know you wouldn't prefer that?
8. If heterosexuality is normal, why are a disproportionate number of mental patients heterosexual?
9. To whom have you disclosed your heterosexual tendencies? How did they react?
10. Your heterosexuality doesn't offend me as long as you don't try to force it on me. Why do you people feel compelled to seduce others into your sexual orientation?
11. If you choose to nurture children, would you want them to be heterosexual, knowing the problems they would face?
12. The great majority of child molesters are heterosexuals. Do you really consider it safe to expose your children to heterosexual teachers?
13. Why do you insist on being so obvious, and making a public spectacle of your heterosexuality? Can't you just be what you are and keep it quiet?
14. How can you ever hope to become a whole person if you limit yourself to a compulsive exclusive heterosexual object choice and remain unwilling to explore and develop your normal, natural, healthy, God-given homosexual potential?
15. Heterosexuals are noted for assigning themselves and each other to narrowly restricted stereotyped sex-roles. Why do you cling to such unhealthy role-playing?
16. Why do heterosexuals place so much emphasis on sex?
17. With all the societal support marriage receives, the divorce rate is spiraling. Why are there so few stable relationships among heterosexuals?
18. How could the human race survive if everyone were heterosexual, considering the menace of overpopulation?
19. There seem to be very few happy heterosexuals. Techniques have been developed with which you might be able to change if you really want to. Have you considered aversion therapy?
20. Do heterosexuals hate and/or distrust others of their own sex? Is that what makes them heterosexual?

FIGURE 10-10 The heterosexual questionnaire.
Source: Martin Rochlin, Ph.D., 1977. Unpublished and uncopyrighted.

questionnaire is that these are the kinds of questions often asked of homosexuals in real life by well-meaning heterosexuals. The questionnaire asks you to question your own feelings of sexuality and to defend this whole class of people with whom you share only one thing, most of whom you have never met. This predicament is something often experienced by homosexuals as questions like this are asked of them by their family, friends, teachers, and others.

CONCEPT LEARNING CHECK 10.3   Theoretical Perspectives on Sexuality

Match the following arguments with the theory most closely associated with them.

_____ **1.** This theory argues against the bias against anyone who is not a heterosexual.

_____ **2.** This theory argues the importance of legitimate births helps regulate sexual behavior to ensure that children will receive the support they need to grow up.

_____ **3.** This theory argues that notions of what is right or wrong in terms of sexual behavior are formed through interactions among people and can vary from one society to the next or one time to the next.

_____ **4.** This theory argues that women are viewed sexually as part of the domination of women by men.

A. Feminist theory

B. Queer theory

C. Symbolic interactionism

D. Structural-functional theory

10.4 Gender Socialization

Gender is socially constructed and is influenced by a person's interactions with parents, peers, teachers, mass media, and sports.

- Identify common agents of socialization and show how they operate in gender socialization.

Nature versus nurture. How much of the differences between males and females is due to biological differences and how much is due to socialization? Or, to state the question another way, which is more important: sex or gender? To answer this question, sociologists and anthropologists have examined different societies around the world. On the one hand, if the primary differences are biological, then we should find *cultural universals* with all societies displaying the same basic relationships between men and women. On the other hand, if societies display very different patterns, then this cultural diversity suggests that biological factors play less of a role in male/female differences.

Margaret Mead (1935) studied three societies in New Guinea: the Arapesh, the Mundugumor, and the Tchambuli. She found that among the Arapesh, men and women behaved very much alike and in a manner we usually attribute to women. That is, they displayed sensitivity and were cooperative with one another. In contrast, among the Mundugumor, males and females also behaved much like one another. However, the Mundugumor engaged in headhunting and cannibalism, and both the men and women were selfish and aggressive—traits we usually attribute to men. Finally, in the third society, the Tchambuli, she found that men and women were different, but their roles reversed our traditional notions of male/female differences. There, the males were emotional, submissive, and nurturing, while the females were more dominant and rational. Mead argued that these diverse societies demonstrate that these differences are due more to culture than to biology, more to gender than to sex. Additional support for the importance of culture over biology comes from a broad study of more than 200 preindustrial societies conducted by anthropologist George Murdock (1937). Murdock found that only a few activities tended to be regarded by virtually all societies as masculine or feminine. Warfare and hunting tended to be viewed as male activities, while cooking and child care tended to be viewed as female activities. Most other areas, such as building shelters and engaging in agriculture, are about as likely to be performed by women as by men.

These findings provide some early support for the view that gender is socially constructed, and what it means to be masculine or feminine can be expected to vary from one society to the next.

Parents

Gender roles are expected behaviors associated with males or females. Traditional gender roles have stereotyped personality traits of males and females. Men are supposed to be masculine, women are supposed to be feminine. Those stereotypes view women as submissive, unintelligent, emotional, dependent, receptive, weak, sensitive, and timid, while men are viewed as dominant, intelligent, rational, assertive, strong, brave, competitive, insensitive, and independent (Bernard 1980). These stereotyped roles are most clear in the traditional family, in which women are expected to perform supportive tasks, be subordinate to men, and assume primary responsibility for home and children. The male role in families includes expectations they will provide for and defend families. Men are more likely to believe in gender stereotypes than women; however, husbands and wives tend to influence each other's views regarding gender roles. Traditional gender roles have many negative consequences for women. They place women in subordinate and less-valued positions than men, they call upon women to make more sacrifices than men, and in general, traditional gender roles work to the disadvantage of women in most spheres of life, particularly in the "public world" beyond the family.

However, other social scientists, including Warren Farrell, argue that gender roles also have a number of negative consequences for men relative to women. It is men who were for much of modern history expected to bear most of the burdens of war, as evidenced by the male-only military draft in the United States. In addition, men make up the great majority of workplace deaths, are less likely to gain custody of children in a divorce, have lower life expectancy than women, and have higher suicide rates (Farrell 2000).

Children are socialized for gender roles very early. By the time they are six years old, children of both sexes can give good descriptions of appropriate gender-role behavior for each sex. Kohlberg (1966) offered a theory of gender-role learning. He argued people acquire gender roles as a result of organization of the ideas and experiences encountered in early life. As people organize their behaviors and attitudes to make their worlds simpler to manage, gender provides a very helpful category for predicting behavior. Recognition of one's gender and acceptance of characteristics associated with that gender is gender identity. This socialization of children for gender roles comes from several sources, including the family, peers, schools, and the mass media.

Parents respond to infants and children differently depending on their gender. They expect and reward different behaviors by boys and girls. Several studies have found that people respond differently to the same infant depending on whether the child is dressed as a boy or a girl. For example, when the child is dressed as a boy, people treat the male child less carefully, bouncing "him" on the knee or lifting "him" high in the air; and when the child is dressed as a girl, "she" is handled more carefully and given more hugs and caresses (Travis and Wade 2001). Even the same behaviors are interpreted differently depending on whether the baby is thought to be a girl or a boy. When college students were shown a videotape of a baby crying after being startled by a jack-in-the-box, the "girl" infant was thought to be frightened while the "boy" was described as angry (Condry and Condry 1976).

Gender roles Expected behaviors associated with males or females.

Parents often buy toys for children consistent with stereotypical sex roles.

© George Doyle/Stockbyte/Thinkstock

Gender socialization in the family occurs in many ways. We described some ways in which parents respond to children differently depending on their gender. The way in which significant others respond to behaviors by children can reinforce or punish gender-role-consistent behaviors. Children also learn gender roles through modeling, by observing significant others of the same sex and behaving as they do.

Family socialization often occurs through play behaviors and the toys associated with them. Parents often buy toys for kids consistent with stereotypical gender roles. In one study, researchers visited homes of 120 infants and children, finding boys to be given sports equipment, tools, and vehicles, while girls were given dolls, children's furniture, and kitchen appliances (Pomerleau et al. 1990).

Peers

Peers influence us throughout our lives. Barrie Thorne (1986) observed boys and girls interacting on playgrounds. For both boys and girls, peer interactions provided models for how they were expected to behave and reinforced behaviors supporting "gender-appropriate" behaviors and punished "gender-inappropriate" behaviors. Martin (1989) reports that children who conform to gender stereotypes find greater social acceptance among their peers.

Teachers and Schools

Children spend much of their lives in school. Thus, teachers (like parents) have many opportunities to influence gender socialization. Teachers, through their own behaviors, model appropriate gender roles for students. Eisenhart and Holland (1983) studied fifth- and sixth-grade classrooms and found that teacher behaviors often unconsciously perpetuated gender-role differences. The male teachers tended to perform outside tasks such as loading busses and supervising sports, while female teachers were more likely to stay inside and work on bulletin boards. Women teachers also would ask male teachers to move furniture, stand on chairs to change light bulbs, and other activities.

Teachers tend to treat boys and girls differently, too. Many studies have found that boys are more likely to receive attention from teachers than girls. Boys are more likely to be given second chances to solve the problem, while girls are more likely to be told the solution. Girls are interrupted more in class than boys, and boys tend to dominate class discussion (Sadker and Sadker 1985). Boys are often expected to excel at math and science, while girls are expected to do well in English and literature (AAUW 1992; Sadker and Sadker 1985). School textbooks tend to devote little space to problems of girls, ignore them, and stereotype them (AAUW 1992). Perhaps as a result of these factors, self-confidence of girls declines twice as much as that of boys during the early adolescent years (AAUW 1992).

Mass Media and Technology

According to one study, the average American child watches television 27 hours per week (Tracy 1990). Thus, mass media, including television, film, magazines, and radio, have abundant opportunity to influence gender roles. Men and women tend to read different magazines, with women's magazines focusing on diet, health, physical appearance, and relationships, while men's magazines tend to focus on athletics and women as sex objects. Most of the announcers, news anchors, even the voiceover announcers in television and radio are men (Courtney and Whipple 1983). Mass media provide many examples of role models for women. Women are portrayed as preoccupied by laundry, cleaning, and household chores or portrayed as sex objects to help sell products. Women are usually depicted in television shows as young, with traditional roles, and occupying low-level occupations (Signorielli 1989).

Gender socialization is also influenced by technology. A content analysis of video game characters by Dill and Thill (2007) found that male characters were more likely than female characters (83% vs. 62%) to be portrayed as aggressive, while female characters were more likely to be sexualized (60% vs. 1%) and scantily clad (39% vs. 8%). In a study of 340 Greek elementary school boys and girls, sociologists Ioanna Vekiri and Anna Chronaki (2008) found evidence that boys and girls are socialized differently regarding computer use and computer self-efficacy. Boys reported greater perceived support for their use of computers from both parents and peers. Boys also reported greater self-efficacy than girls—that is, boys saw themselves as more competent in their use of computers than girls. Sociologists William Dutton and Grant Blank (2011), in the Oxford Internet Survey, examined Internet use and attitudes of men and women in Britain. They found that, while there is no gender gap in use, there is a gender gap in attitudes, with 31% of women indicating they are likely to "get nervous using technologies, because I might break something," compared to only 16% of men, and 25% of women feel that "technologies fail when you need them most" compared to only 19% of men.

Sports

Much of the time children are not in structured learning activities in school, they are playing games or sports. However, girls and boys in the United States typically engage in different types of games. Boys learn to participate in highly competitive, rule-based games with lots of participants (such as soccer, basketball, and football), while girls more often engage in games with small groups of girls their same age, such as jump rope or hopscotch (Ignico and Mead 1990).

For men and boys, playing sports often becomes a defining activity, helping them and others to see themselves as masculine. Michael Messner (1990) interviewed 30 male former athletes, most of whom had played the "major sports" in the United States. He talked with them about what sports meant to them as young boys, experiences, and successes and failures. Sports in the United States, Messner points out, are both a "gendered institution"—one organized by gender relations, with men segregated from women in most of the activities—and a "gendering institution"—one that helps reconstruct the gender order in society by socializing men and women into gender roles. For many of these men, Messner found that their sports activities helped to shape their self-concept and their own conception of their masculinity. For many of these men, when they were boys, sports was "just what you did . . . and if you didn't, there was something wrong with you." When asked what it meant to be a man at that age, one respondent replied, "I didn't want to be a so-called scaredy-cat. You want to hit a guy even though he's bigger than you to show that, you know, you've got this macho image . . . and I began to notice a change, even in my parents—especially in my father—he was proud of that, and that was very important to me" (Messner 1990). For the boys in Messner's study, it became natural to equate masculinity with competition, physical strength, and skills—all of which were measured in sports that only boys could play. Girls simply could not participate.

CONCEPT LEARNING CHECK 10.4   Gender Socialization

Indicate whether each of these statements is true or false.

_____ **1.** Michael Messner's study found that for the men in his study, it became natural to equate masculinity with sports.

_____ **2.** Boys are interrupted more in elementary classrooms than girls and girls tend to dominate classroom discussions.

_____ **3.** During adolescence, self-confidence of girls declines twice as much as that of boys.

_____ **4.** Traditional gender roles have both negative and positive consequences for both males and females.

_____ **5.** Video games portray males and females differently, with males more likely to be scantily clad.

10.5 Gender Inequality around the World

Women are often a repressed minority, subject to violence and disadvantage justified by systems of patriarchy.

- Describe the role of patriarchy in gender inequality.

Females: A Minority?

Even though women outnumber men in the world, women have been discriminated against historically. In this sense, women are a sociological minority—a group of people who are discriminated against based on physical or cultural characteristics. It is not just that this occurs sometimes in a few societies. Every society distinguishes between men and women, giving them different access to power and resources. Women have been discriminated against in virtually every society (Lerner 1986).

The Concept of the Patriarch

When we consider the possible arrangements among the sexes within societies, there are three logical possibilities: **patriarchy**—a system of social relationships in which men dominate women—**matriarchy**—a system of social relationships in which women dominate men—and an **egalitarian system** in which both sexes have equal authority. The great majority of contemporary societies are patriarchal. In fact, there is debate as to whether *any* society was ever truly matriarchal (Lengermann and Wallace 1985). While some researchers claim there is evidence of nonpatriarchal societies, particularly egalitarian ones (Eisler 1988), most researchers believe all societies have been patriarchal to some degree (Brown 1991; Harris 1977). Even though patriarchy is present in all societies, different sectors of the same society and different societies vary markedly in the amount of inequality between men and women. For example, in the United States, patriarchy is more evident among working-class families, while egalitarian families are more common among middle-class families. Of course, among families with a female single head of household, matriarchy is the rule. Scandinavian societies, like Norway and Sweden, for example, approach egalitarian societies in most matters, while many Muslim societies like Saudi Arabia, Afghanistan, and Iraq display enormous inequality between men and women.

Patriarchy is often justified by sexism—a belief that one sex is superior to the other (Greenberg 1988; Kluckhohn 1948). Since societies are patriarchal, sexism tends to favor males over females the great majority of the time. In FIGURE 10-11 are displayed

Patriarchy Any social relationships in which men dominate women.

Matriarchy A system of social relationships in which women dominate men.

Egalitarian system A system in which both sexes have equal authority.

THE SOCIOLOGICAL IMAGINATION   Female US Soldiers in Muslim Countries

Imagine for a minute how difficult it might be for a woman from the United States to be treated the same way Muslim women are treated in Saudi Arabia. When female American soldiers were stationed in Saudi Arabia before and during the Gulf War, they found themselves in precisely that situation, forced to experience being women in a culture quite unlike their own. These women troops had trained side by side with men in the United States, had slept in the same tents with men during military exercises in the United States and other countries, and performed jobs ranging from truck driver to communications technician to intelligence specialist.

Yet, in Saudi Arabia, these same women troops suddenly found themselves in a society in which women were treated very differently. Women were not allowed to drive in Saudi Arabia,

and the United States had to get special permission from the Saudi government to permit the many women drivers to operate trucks and forklifts. Women were not permitted to shop on their own. So, when a woman soldier wanted to take her clothes to the laundry or even purchase a bar of soap, she had to be accompanied by a male who paid for her purchases while she stood by meekly with eyes focused on the floor to avoid offending the Saudi shopkeepers. Women were not permitted to share quarters with men soldiers but were housed in a separate barracks. And if a woman soldier wanted to swim in the gymnasium pool, she had to wait for the few hours a week when the gym was closed to men, and then she had to swim wearing a loose-fitting blouse and knee-length shorts (Moore 1990).

Martha McSally, a retired US Air Force colonel, sued then Defense Secretary Donald Rumsfeld over a directive requiring female soldiers in Saudi Arabia to wear the abaya—traditional Muslim dress for women. As late as 2011, some women soldiers continued to object to the practice, which, by then, was made optional. As McSally wrote, "American servicewomen will continue to be viewed as second-class warriors if leaders push them to take up the customs of countries where women are second-class citizens" (Marcelo 2011). Meanwhile, in 2012, Saudi Arabia announced plans to build a new city exclusively for women (Davies 2012). While women are permitted to work, only 15% are in the workforce because they are expected to take care of all essential homemaking duties and to limit interactions with unrelated men in accordance with Sharia law. Saudi Arabian women were still not permitted to drive, but they were allowed to compete in the Olympic Games for the first time ever.

EVALUATE

1. Would you also expect large differences in the treatment of American men in Saudi Arabia when compared to their treatment in the United States? Why or why not?

2. Would you expect a woman from Saudi Arabia living in the United States to prefer the way women are treated in the United States? Why or why not?

3. Have you or someone you know been to Saudi Arabia or another Muslim country and experienced this first hand? Or have you interacted with people from Saudi Arabia elsewhere and experienced the same things?

the percentages of respondents agreeing with the statement "It is much better for all if the man is the achiever outside the home and the woman takes care of the home and family." These results are provided from the General Social Survey (NORC 2011) for both 1977 and 2010 (the earliest and the most recent years available). In that 33-year span, there was a huge decrease in people agreeing with this statement, from 66% agreeing in 1977 to 36% agreeing in 2010. This suggests sexism and patriarchy in the United States have diminished considerably during that time.

Violence Against Women

Violence against women takes many forms internationally. **Dowry deaths** is a term used to describe the murder of Indian brides in which they were tortured, murdered, or driven to suicide by continuous harassment by husbands and in-laws attempting to extort more resources from the women's families (NCRB 2008). In 2010, the National Crime Records Bureau of India reports 8,391 dowry deaths were reported across India

Dowry deaths The murder of brides for failing to provide adequate dowry payments.

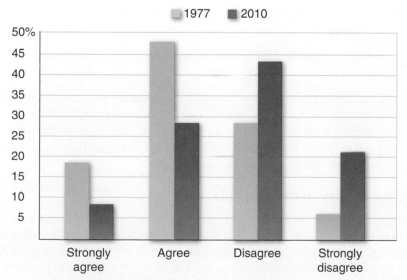

Is it better for all if the man is the achiever outside the home and the woman takes care of home and family?

FIGURE 10-11 Patriarchal attitudes in the United States (1977 and 2010).
Source: Data from National Opinion Research Center (NORC). 2011. General Social Surveys, 1972–2010 Cumulative Codebook. *Accessed November 2012 (http://www .ropercenter.uconn.edu/data_access/ data/datasets/general_social_survey .html).*

(Bedi 2012). Many brides, even after bringing a dowry at the time of marriage, are subject to continuing demands for more money and goods long after the wedding is past. If their families refuse or are unable to pay, the brides are sometimes set afire by the grooms or the grooms' family members (Bedi 2012).

In no small part due to the expensive dowries expected of brides, Indian families often much prefer a male child to a female one. Families often undergo ultrasound scans or other procedures to determine the sex of a fetus, often aborting the child if it is female. As a result, since 1991, the sex ratio (the ratio of females to males) in India has dropped in 80% of districts, with statistics overall dropping from 947 girls to 1,000 boys in 1991 to 927 girls for 1,000 boys in 2001 (Gupta 2012).

Yet another form of violence often directed at women internationally is human trafficking. By one estimate, 2.5 million people are in forced labor, including sexual exploitation, at any one time (UN.GIFT 2007). A study by the United Nations Office on Drugs and Crime (2009) found that the most common form of human trafficking (79%) is sexual exploitation. By UN estimates, 43% of victims, 98% of whom are women and girls, are used for forced commercial sexual exploitation (ILO 2007).

CONCEPT LEARNING CHECK 10.5   Gender Inequality around the World

Match the following items with the correct item in the other list.

_____ **1.** Dowry death

_____ **2.** Sexism

_____ **3.** Patriarchy

A. The murder of the husband who criticizes the dowry the bride's family brought to the wedding

B. The murder of the bride whose dowry is viewed as inadequate by the husband and his family

C. A system of social relationships in which men dominate women

D. The belief that one sex is superior to the other

E. The belief that heterosexual sex is the only acceptable form of sexual behavior

---

10.6 Gender Stratification/Inequality in the United States

Women are disadvantaged relative to men in most key aspects of American society.

- Illustrate aspects of gender stratification and inequality in the United States.

Gender stratification
The distribution of wealth, power, and social prestige among men and women.

Patriarchy and sexism ensure that gender as a social status has a great deal to do with social stratification. In this section, we will examine **gender stratification**—the distribution of wealth, power, and social prestige among men and women. We will see that there are dramatic differences based on gender in the workplace, the family, education, politics, and health care. We begin with the workplace.

Gender Inequality in the Workplace

More women work today than ever before, and women make up an increasing proportion of the labor force. The demographics of women have shifted to include married women with children as well as single women or women without children. As can be seen in FIGURE 10-12, the percentage of women participating in the labor force increased from 34% in 1950 to 59% in 2010 (BLS 2007, 2012). The demographics of women in the labor force have also shifted. Before 1940, most working women were single. Now, married women predominate. Seventy-five percent of married women with

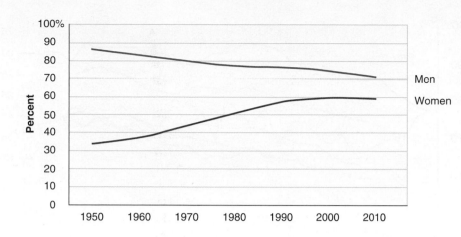

FIGURE 10-12 US labor force participation by men and women (1950–2010).
Source: Data from US Bureau of Labor Statistics (BLS). 2007. Changes in Men's and Women's Labor Force Participation Rates. *Accessed May 2012 (http://www.bls.gov/opub/ted/2007/jan/wk2/art03.txt); US Bureau of Labor Statistics (BLS). 2012. Civilian Labor Force Participation Rates by Age, Sex, Race, and Ethnicity. January 2012 Monthly Labor Review. Table 3.3. Accessed May 2012 (http://www.bls.gov/emp/ep_table_303.htm).*

school-age children work, while 59% of those with preschool children work. More than 80% of widowed, divorced, or separated women with school-age children work; more than 70% of those with preschool children work (*Statistical Abstract of the United States, 2006*:Table 586). In 60% of married couples, both work outside the home.

There are several likely reasons for this rise in female participation in the workforce. Changing attitudes and the rise of feminism have surely encouraged more women to think of working outside the home. Reductions in sexual discrimination in the workplace and the opening up of many of the better-paying professional jobs to women provide increased incentives for women to work. In the home, decreased family sizes, urbanization, and opportunities to "out-source" child care and food preparation in the form of day care and fast food restaurants permit at least some of the household tasks that traditionally fell to women to be accomplished even if the woman works outside the home. A higher divorce rate and a sometimes stagnant economy, in which the adjusted take-home pay for the male worker has not increased and sometimes actually declined, increase the need for women to work. Whatever the reasons for individual women to work outside the home, it appears likely that high participation in the workforce by women is here to stay.

The Gender Pay Gap and Comparable Worth

Although women now participate in the workforce nearly as much as men, women tend to be paid less for their work. In 2009, the mean earnings of full-time workers for women were $657 per week, roughly 80% of the $819 median for men. In other words, this means that women are paid on the average about 80 cents for each dollar a man is paid (BLS 2010). This is called the **gender pay gap**—the difference in average wages for men and women. In fact, in the past, the gap was even larger. In 1979, women earned about 62 cents per dollar a man was paid. It peaked at 81% in 2005 and 2006 (BLS 2010).

The gender pay gap is greater for older workers than younger ones FIGURE 10-13. Women under 35 who work full time earn roughly 90 cents for each dollar a man earns. But for women over 35, the average is only about 75 cents per dollar (Rampell 2010b). In a surprising reversal in recent years, in some large metropolitan areas young women earn more than young men because women are more likely to complete college (Hagrey, 2007; Roberts, 2007).

A gender pay gap is found in other countries as well FIGURE 10-14. In 2006 (or the latest year data were available), the average income of men in Organisation for Economic Co-operation and Development (OECD) countries was 17.6% higher than the average for women, with a high of around 37% greater in Korea, around 33% in Japan, around 19% for Switzerland and the United States, around 11% in France, and less than 10% in Belgium (Rampell 2010a).

Why is there a gender wage gap? Perhaps the strongest factor is the fact that women tend to have different kinds of jobs than men. A number of occupations and professions

Gender pay gap The difference between average pay for men and women.

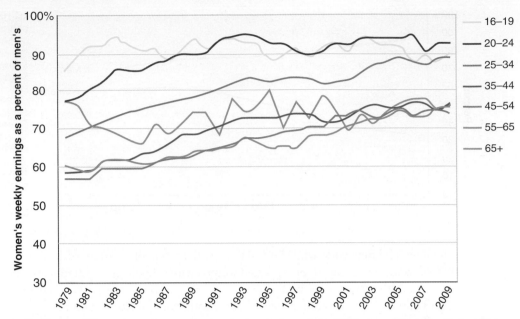

FIGURE 10-13 Women's median earnings as a percent of men's for full-time workers in the United States (1979–2009).
Source: US Bureau of Labor Statistics (BLS). 2010. Highlights of Women's Earnings in 2009. Report 1025. *Accessed May 2012 (http://www.bls.gov/cps/cpswom2009.pdf).*

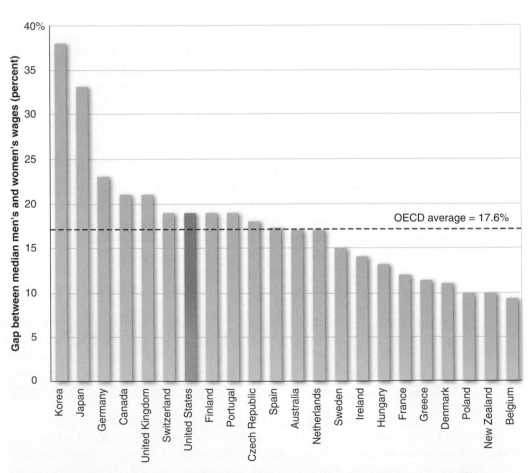

FIGURE 10-14 Wage gap between median men's and women's wages for full-time workers in different countries.
Source: OECD. 2010. Gender Brief Prepared by the OECD Social Policy Division. Accessed May 2012 (www.oecd.org/els/ social http://www.oecd.org/social/familiesandchildren/44720649.pdf).

have traditionally been dominated by either women or men, and the occupations most dominated by women are often regarded as "women's work" and are sometimes perceived to have less importance (Blum 1991). Sociologists often refer to women-dominated occupations as **pink-collar jobs**. For example, in **TABLE 10-1**, we see several occupations that, historically, have been held primarily by males and others that were historically female, along with the percentage of females in those occupations in 2004 and 2010. While for most of these occupations, the imbalance between males or females is now less, clearly these occupations are still most common to members of one sex, and the predominantly male occupations, such as engineers, dentists, and physicians, are paid more than predominantly female occupations such as receptionists, teachers, and restaurant servers.

A second factor leading to lower pay for women is a tendency for women to choose jobs that give them more time to handle family responsibilities such as taking care of a sick child or taking time off from work while they care for children, particularly newborns (Chaker and Stout 2004). However, it may be argued that women may not have chosen such jobs but may be less able to obtain better jobs.

However, both of these factors—the different kinds of jobs and choosing jobs that permit meeting family responsibilities—only account for between one-half and two-thirds of the pay gap (Fuller and Schoenberg 1991; Kemp 1990). The remainder of the pay gap is due to one or more forms of gender discrimination (Roth 2003). In response to the gender wage gap, some people have argued in favor of a policy based on "**comparable worth**" in which jobs requiring similar levels of education and training should be paid at comparable levels regardless of whether they are predominately female or predominately male occupations. Nations such as Great Britain have adopted such policies. However, efforts to pass similar legislation in several states in the United States have generally met with failure. An effort to pay women back pay based on a comparable-worth study in Washington State was ultimately defeated in a decision by the United States Court of Appeals for the Ninth Circuit, which overturned this decision, stating that "the state did not create the market disparity" and going on to argue that the free-market system was a legitimate way to set wages (*AFSCME et al. v. State of Washington et al.* 1985).

Pink-collar jobs Female-dominated occupations.

Comparable worth The principle that jobs requiring similar levels of education and training should be paid at similar levels regardless of whether they are predominately female or predominately male occupations.

TABLE 10-1 Male- and Female-Dominated Occupations

	Percent Female	
Predominantly Male Occupations	**2004**	**2010**
Engineers	13.8%	12.9%
Dentists	22.0	25.5
Physicians	29.4	32.3
Lawyers and judges—2010 just lawyers	29.4	31.5
Firefighters	5.1	3.6
Predominantly Female Occupations		
Elementary and middle school teachers	81.3	81.8
Librarians	83.2	82.8
Registered nurses	92.2	91.1
Receptionists	92.4	92.7
Secretaries	96.9	96.1
Restaurant servers	73.1	71.1

Source: U.S. Census Bureau. 2006. Statistical Abstract. Accessed May 2012 (http://www.census.gov/compendia/statab/2006/labor_force_employment_earnings/labor.pdf); U.S. Census Bureau. 2012. Statistical Abstract. Accessed May 2012 (http://www.census.gov/prod/2011pubs/12statab/labor.pdf).

Glass ceiling A barrier that, while not obvious or easily visible, blocks women's movement into the top ranks of management.

Institutional sexism Discrimination against one sex that results from the day-to-day operations, rules, and policies of organizations and institutions.

Sexual harassment Unwanted attention based on someone's sex or sexuality that interferes with job performance or causes discomfort.

Executive Positions (Glass Ceiling)

A common form of gender discrimination in the workplace is called the **glass ceiling**—a barrier that, while not obvious or easily visible, blocks women's movement into the top ranks of management. While corporations have hired more women in recent years, women are often relegated to lower-level management positions and passed over for promotion to higher levels. A study of CEOs of the largest US corporations in 2012 found that only 18 women led Fortune 500 companies—a record high (Hoare 2012).

Women are often victims of discrimination in the workplace in a variety of ways, with the gender pay gap being only one of the consequences of that discrimination. As we know, sexism is the view that one sex is inherently superior to the other. **Institutional sexism** occurs when the day-to-day operations, rules, and policies of organizations and institutions discriminate against one sex. Examples of institutional sexism include: female jobs leading only to other female jobs, preference for jobs granted to military veterans, machines and tools designed for average men not women, employer policies limiting child care that have more negative impact on women than men, and organizations that limit activities of women. For example, some armed forces prohibit combat by women even though that is crucial for promotion. Some religious organizations have sex-linked roles such as rabbi, priest, and minister.

A report by the US Equal Employment Opportunity Commission (2004) uses data from the 2002 Survey of Firms in Private Industry to examine the status of women in management. They found that between 1990 and 2002, the percentage of women officials and managers in the private sector increased from 29% to 36%, yet the percentage of employees who are women is 48%. So women continue to be underrepresented in management positions relative to men.

Harassment

Sexual harassment consists of unwanted attention based on someone's sex or sexuality that interferes with job performance or causes discomfort. An extreme and obvious example would include a supervisor making threats or offering benefits in return for sexual favors from an employee. Sexual harassment can also be much more subtle, such as in a work environment in which sexual teasing, jokes, or other behaviors make the person feel singled out and create the effect of a hostile environment even if that was not the intent (Cohen 1991). In 1982, the US Court of Appeals ruled that sexual harassment violates the Civil Rights Act because it discriminates against an individual based on his or her sex.

Most victims of sexual harassment are women. This is because sexual harassment usually occurs when one person takes advantage of his or her power in the workplace, on campus, or in other settings. Historically, men have often had greater power in such settings and often oversee the work of women. This is particularly true in the military. A survey of women graduates of the Air Force Academy found that 12% of them reported being the victims of rape or attempted rape (Schemo 2003). Sexual harassment is not limited to females, but females are much more often the victims than males. In a nationally representative survey, 27% of women respondents reported they had been the object of sexual advances or propositions from supervisors (NORC 2011). That same survey found that 19% of males reported being the object of sexual advances or propositions from supervisors (NORC 2011). Sexual harassment does not have to be based on a desire to have sex with the victim. This was made clear in a later Supreme Court decision ruling that it also applies to homosexuals harassed on the job by heterosexuals (Felsenthal 1998).

Sexual harassment usually occurs when one person takes advantage of his or her power in the workplace.

© Ron Chapple Studios/Thinkstock

Gender Inequality in Family Roles

Increased participation of women in the workforce has led to dramatic changes in family life. Yet gender roles have not changed fast enough to cope with those differences. Traditional gender roles in which women perform most of the household work have persisted even in families in which wives are employed outside the home. In a 1990 study, researchers found that women in the US did about three times as much domestic work as men. Husbands did "less than one-quarter of the total work done by all household members" (Nock and Kingston 1990:136). When both outside work and household work are considered, women often end up working many more hours per day than their husbands do. The result often is women who must bear all of the responsibilities of the workplace during the day, then return home to a "**second shift**" in which they spend many more additional hours performing child care duties, cooking, and cleaning (Hochschild and Machung 1989).

> **Second shift** The extra hours women often spend performing child care duties, cooking, and cleaning after a full shift of work outside the home.

The gap between the number of hours men work each week and the number women work is not limited to the United States, either, if we are to believe a survey by the International Labor Organization (*Associated Press* 1992). They report that African women work 15 hours more per week than men; Asian women, 14 hours more; Latin American women, 6 hours more; and European women, 5 hours more.

Two more recent studies suggest women continue to work more around the house than men. In a study of the leisure-time activities of men and women in two-career families with at least one child, an observer visited their home and recorded the activity of men and women in 10-minute intervals. Women spent about 30% of their time engaged in housework, while men spent 20% of their time doing housework (Saxbe et al. 2011). Another study (ICPSR 2009) found that women spend an average of 28 to 29 hours per week on all household duties, while men contribute 16 to 20 hours per week (depending on whether the result is reported by the man or the woman).

Gender Inequality in Health Care

Women and men are treated differently in health care, both for diseases and conditions that we all may face regardless of sex (such as heart disease) and for those that are specific to their sex, such as hysterectomies (removal of the uterus and ovaries in women) and cancer of the prostate in men. When enterprising medical researchers noticed that women were twice as likely to die as men from coronary bypass surgery, they at first thought such surgery might be harder to perform on women. However, that would likely mean the surgery took longer for women than men, and it was found that the operations were actually faster for women. Eventually, researchers found that the problem was unintended sexual discrimination. Doctors were less likely to take seriously women's complaints of chest pains. Physicians were more than 10 times as likely to subject men to tests to diagnose heart disease as women, and by the time women got to the operating table, they were generally much sicker than men on the average and, hence, died more often (Bishop 1990). This tendency to overlook heart disease in women is part of a long history of medical research that gave greater emphasis to men. It was only in 1993 that the National Institutes of Health were directed to develop guidelines to ensure the inclusion of women and minorities in clinical research (NIH 2001).

Sexual discrimination is even more obvious when it comes to health issues related to distinct male and female anatomy. When a medical examination discovers that a woman has fibroids in her uterus, physicians are sometimes quick to perform a hysterectomy even though many women have fibroids, and they usually do not turn into cancer. Seventy-six percent of these operations were found to be inappropriate—that is, they did not meet criteria established by the American College of Obstetricians and Gynecologists (Broder et al. 2000).

In contrast to women whose ovaries are often removed even without getting cancer, men experiencing prostate enlargement or even prostate cancer are often not operated on at all. In fairness, it should be pointed out that most prostate cancer is often slow growing and usually occurs among older men, who are more likely to die of something else before prostate cancer can kill them.

Gender Inequality in Education

Historically, in the United States—as in many other countries—the education of women was seen as less important than the education of men. However, this has changed dramatically over the last few decades. In the United States, college enrollments for women have exceeded those for men since the late 1970s. In 1980, women made up 52% of college enrollments. By 2009, women constituted 56% of all college enrollments (Statistical Abstract for the United States 2012:Table 281). In 2009, women received 62.1% of all associate's degrees, 57.2% of all bachelor's degrees, 60.4% of all master's degrees, 49.0% of all first professional degrees, and 52.3% of all doctoral degrees (NCES 2011:Table A-26-2).

The proportion of women earning professional degrees has increased dramatically for degrees like medicine, dentistry, law, and theology, increasing from single digits in 1970 to 49% for medicine, 46% for law and dentistry, and 33% for theological degrees by 2009, as can be seen in FIGURE 10-15.

However, there are still discrepancies. Even when women achieve the same levels of education as men, women tend to paid less. In FIGURE 10-16 are displayed the mean annual incomes of males and females having different levels of educational attainment. At every level of education, women are consistently paid lower, on average, than men.

Gender Inequality in Politics

Women play less of a role in politics than men in most countries. Many of the world's oldest democracies gave women the right to vote only as recently as the last century. The first to do so was New Zealand in 1893. Following New Zealand were: Australia in 1902, Denmark in 1915, the former Soviet Union in 1917, England in 1918, the United States in 1920, Japan in 1945, and Switzerland in 1971. Internationally, women held 3% of parliamentary positions in 1945, which grew to 20% by December 2011 (Inter-Parliamentary Union 2012). In FIGURE 10-17 is displayed the percentage of women in parliament worldwide, by region, and for the United States (Inter-Parliamentary Union 2012).

FIGURE 10-15 Percent of professional degrees earned by women (1970–2009).
Source: Data from Statistical Abstract for the United States. 2012. Table 304. (http://www.census.gov/prod/2011pubs/12statab/educ.pdf).

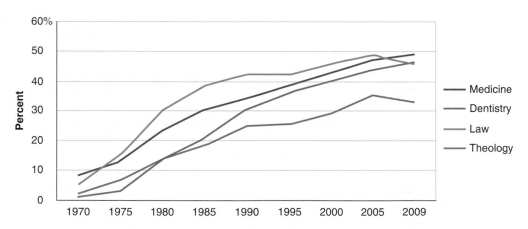

FIGURE 10-16 Annual income by education level and sex (2009).
Source: Data from Statistical Abstract for the United States. 2012. Table 703. (http://www.census.gov/prod/2011pubs/12statab/income.pdf).

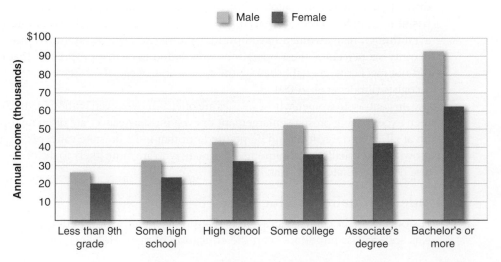

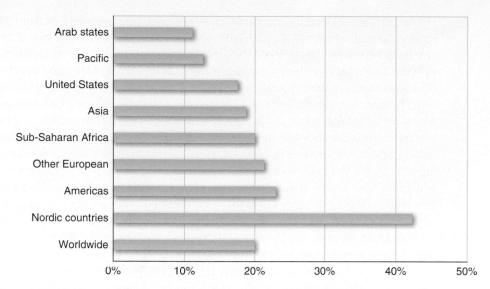

FIGURE 10-17 Percentage of women in parliament or national legislatures (2011).
Source: Data from UNDP. 2011. Human Development Report. *Accessed May 2012 (http://hdr.undp.org/en/media/HDR_2011_EN_Table4.pdf).*

In the United States, the first female senator was elected in 1932 (US Senate 2012). There were only 2 out of 100 members until 1993, when there were 7. In 2012, 17 members were women (Statistical Abstract of the United States 2012). The US House had 22 women members out of 434 in 1985 and 75 out of 435 in 2012 (17.2%) (Congressional Research Service 2012).

The United Nations computes a Gender Inequality Index for countries based on several measures, including seats in national parliament, labor force participation rate, and other factors. By this index, the United States ranks 47th in the world, well behind Canada (20th), Norway (6th), and Japan (14th; UNDP 2011:142, Table 4). By that standard, it could not be said that the US leads the world in gender equality.

Gender Inequality in the Military

An increasing number of women serve in the military, though still in much fewer numbers than do men. In 1994, a new policy was enacted by the US Department of Defense expanding the range of positions in which women could serve to include fighter pilots and ship commanders. Fully 10% of soldiers serving in Iraq were women (Corbett 2007). Yet women are still precluded from serving in ground combat units such as the infantry, giving them less access to opportunities to earn medals and promotions. Ironically, in the wars in Iraq and Afghanistan, much of the violence occurs behind the front lines in the form of sniper attacks or IED (improvised explosive device) explosions. So while women bear much of the risk of war, they enjoy fewer of the opportunities for career advancement. PTSD (post-traumatic stress disorder) is a debilitating condition that often results after exposure to extreme trauma and stress. Women combat veterans (10% of the force in Iraq) make up about 11% of the victims of PTSD, suggesting that women bear much the same risk as men in combat.

Violence, Gender, and Sexuality

Women, both in the United States and throughout the world, are most likely to be victimized by men, while men are far less likely to be victims of violence by women. Domestic violence is a leading cause of death for women ages 15 to 44, according to the Centers for Disease Control and Prevention. It is a leading cause of death of pregnant women, mortality research shows. And African-American and Native-American women are at the highest risk of intimate partner homicide (Tessier 2008). In 2009, violent crimes by intimate partners (current or former spouse, boyfriend or girlfriend) accounted for 26% of nonfatal violent crimes against females and 5% against males (BJS 2010). Of female murder victims in 2009, 35% were killed by an intimate partner (FBI 2010).

In 2009 in the United States, victims ages 12 or older experienced a total of 125,910 rapes or sexual assaults (BJS 2010:Table 1). Eighty percent of rape or sexual assault victims in 2009 were female (BJS 2010:Table 1). Of female rape or sexual assault victims in 2009, 21% were assaulted by a stranger. Thirty-nine percent of offenders were friends or acquaintances of their victims, and 41% were intimate partners.

The story is much the same on US campuses and in the military. College students who were victims of rape or sexual assault were about four times more likely to be victimized by someone they knew than by a stranger (Krebs 2007:4). Fourteen percent of undergraduate women were victims of at least one completed sexual assault since entering college; 5% were victims of forced sexual assault, and 8% were sexually assaulted while they were incapacitated due to voluntary use of alcohol or drugs (Krebs 2007). One study of female veterans found that 79% reported being sexually harassed during military service and 30% reported an attempted or completed rape (Sadler et al. 2003).

For LGBT (lesbian, gay, bisexual, or transgendered) youth, the threat of violence is also real and greater than that for non–LGBT youth (Human Rights Campaign 2012). The Human Rights Campaign surveyed 10,000 LGBT youth between the ages of 13 and 17 years old around the country. LGBT youths' biggest problems relate to family acceptance (26%), school bullying (21%), and fear of being out or open (18%). In contrast, the focus of non–LGBT youth is on schooling and careers, with their biggest problems being classes/exams/grades (25%), college/career (14%), or financial pressures related to college or job (11%).

CONCEPT LEARNING CHECK 10.6   Gender Inequality in the United States

Match the following concepts with the statements most closely related to them.

1. Comparable worth

2. Glass ceiling

3. Second shift

A. A term used to refer to the transparency that exists in the corporate world regarding the actions of upper management

B. The relative worth of men and women as measured by physicians' likelihood of diagnosing heart attacks

C. A tendency for women to be relegated to the second shift in factories because men are given preference

D. The tendency for women to do most of the household work even though they work outside the home as well

E. The relative worth of different traditionally male and female jobs based on education and training required

F. The tendency for women to not be promoted past a certain point in companies

---

10.7 Theoretical Perspectives on Gender

Four theoretical perspectives, including feminism, offer insights into gender inequality.

- Compare and contrast different theoretical perspectives on gender inequality.

Each of the three major theoretical perspectives addresses the issue of gender, with structural-functional and conflict views emphasizing the origins of gender inequality and the interactionist perspective emphasizing the mechanisms that continually reproduce gender inequality in everyday life. In addition, feminism, a perspective born out of a social movement for greater gender equality, offers insight into gender inequality as well.

Structural-Functional

The structural-functional view of gender differences explains the dominance of males as a consequence of biological differences between men and women related to reproduction (Wood and Eagly 2002). In early human history, life expectancies were short, and many children died in childbirth or early infancy, while methods of birth control were limited or nonexistent. Hence, much of their adult lives, women were often either pregnant, nursing an infant, or caring for a young child. This, of course, limits their ability to move about, engage in combat, or carry out strenuous physical activities. For this reason, in most (but not all) early societies, men became the ones responsible for engaging in warfare, hunting, and gathering food, while women became responsible for child care and managing the home (Huber 1990). Because the tasks performed by the male often resulted in life or death for the males and their families and produced valued goods in the form of food or valuables traded with other people, men's work was often seen as more valuable than the routine, mundane, but essential tasks of women. Thus, men became dominant in most cultures and, over many generations, that dominance became taken for granted and an institutionalized part of the culture.

Consistent with this functional view, Parsons and Bales (1955) argued there are positive consequences in the traditional division of labor in which women were "better suited" to perform *expressive* roles providing for supportive emotional relationships in the family unit, while men were better for *instrumental* roles performing goal-directed behavior. They argued, using the functionalist perspective, that these two roles were different and complementary, best performed by different individuals. Men and women learn their different roles in gender-differentiated socialization experiences, as growing boys learn that they should "be a man" while growing girls learn what it means to be female. When members of either sex step outside the realm of accepted behaviors for their gender, they are quickly reminded of the inappropriateness of boys who are "sissies" or girls who are "tomboys."

This view has become less influential as women have gained control of reproduction and as many of today's jobs can be performed equally well by males or females (Collins 1988; Layng 1990). Biological differences between men and women are generally less important today and have little or no bearing on the performance of most jobs. It is a great waste of talent and resources when women who might be superb members of traditionally male occupations are prevented from achieving their potential.

Conflict

Conflict theory views traditional gender roles as instruments of oppression by society, preserving advantages of males over females (Basow 1986; Collins 1971, 1975). It argues that cultural ideologies evolved to support male dominance over females, stressing the "natural" physical and intellectual superiority of males and nurturing instincts of females. Although Karl Marx was generally silent on issues of gender, his colleague, Frederich Engels (1942, orig. 1884) was among the first conflict theorists to address issues of gender. Engels argued that, while men and women performed different activities in early hunting and gathering societies, it was only when surplus production became available that men began to truly dominate women. He argued that men wished to control property through inheritance, and that required knowledge of paternity, hence requiring the faithfulness of wives to their husbands and the monogamous marriage. In Engels's view, capitalism exacerbated male dominance by creating more wealth, giving men greater power as the primary producers, heirs, and owners of wealth. The role of women was to take care of the home so that men could work in factories and to become consumers to purchase the products produced by men. The tragedy of capitalism, in Engels's view, was the exploitation of males through *low* wages for their labor and the exploitation of women through *no* wages for "female" work (Eisenstein 1979).

Critics of this view argue that it overemphasizes conflict, suggesting women and men rarely or never do anything cooperatively (Barry 1979). Marxist versions of conflict theory argue gender oppression is a product of capitalism, yet gender oppression is also found in noncapitalist societies (Crompton and Mann 1986). This view is also criticized because it paints families as exploitative relationships when most people believe families are good.

Symbolic Interactionism

While the functional and conflict views focus on the macro-level structures and origins of gender inequality, the interactionist view focuses at the micro level on the everyday interactions that continually reproduce gender inequalities (Henley 1977; Matoesian 1993). Symbolic interactionists examine ways gender differences are reflected in male/female interactions.

Gender differences pervade social interaction, including even patterns of nonverbal interaction in which the dominance of men over women is subtly reinforced. More powerful people tend to touch less powerful people more than vice versa. Men tend to touch women more, conveying their claim to power. Males also tend to take up more space in the way they stand and sit, indicating greater freedom and control over space (Henley 1977). Interruptions may reflect power differences between males and females. Males are more likely to interrupt females than vice versa. In one study of male–female couples, 74% of the males interrupted, while only 26% of the females interrupted. In same-sex couples, interruptions were about even. In other studies, parents were found to be more likely to interrupt daughters than sons. Females are more tentative in speech, qualifying with "I think," "I suppose," and so on. Women also tend to speak more softly and use softer words (West and Zimmerman 1983).

These patterns of interaction between men and women have a lasting impact on the opportunities of women by reproducing patriarchy throughout social life. For example, in classroom interaction, teachers in elementary and junior high schools treat males and females differently. Boys dominate communication in schools. In part, this is because boys are more assertive, but teachers respond differently, too, encouraging boys to speak more. Matoesian (1993) examined detailed court transcripts of rape trials and showed how the interactions between attorneys, judges, and female accusers are influenced by patriarchy and reproduce the hierarchical relationships between men and women.

The interactionist perspective on gender inequality does provide useful insights into some of the mechanisms through which that inequality is expressed and reproduced in everyday life. However, it offers little insight into the origins of gender inequality. Nor is it clear that changes in those micro-level patterns of interaction could reduce inequality without accompanying structural changes at the macro level. Men interrupting women less, for example, will do little to achieve equality so long as women continue to be paid less than men for comparable work.

Feminism

Feminism A perspective that argues men and women are essentially equal and should be treated equally in social life.

Feminism is a perspective that argues men and women are essentially equal and should be treated equally in social life. In this sense, feminism is a direct contradiction of patriarchy. While most sociological theories have been developed by academics, feminism developed initially as a social movement and its associated ideology. There have been three distinct periods or "waves" of feminist advocacy in the United States. The first feminist wave began to take shape during the 1830s when women supporting the abolitionists and antislavery groups began to draw parallels to their own plight. It was formally launched in 1848 when Elizabeth Cady Stanton and Lucretia Mott held a convention in Seneca Falls, New York, to mobilize support to address women's issues. Once this first wave achieved its primary objective of securing for women the right to vote in 1920, the movement lost its momentum and fell apart.

The "second wave" of feminism as a social movement began in the 1960s in response to continuing inequalities of treatment relative to men, stimulated by events such as the publication of Betty Friedan's *The Feminine Mystique* in 1963. Once again, the feminist movement was inspired at least in part through women's participation in the other social movements of the time, particularly the Civil Rights and anti–Vietnam War social movements (Bernard 1981; Friedan 1963). This wave has not had a single driving issue like obtaining the right to vote, but it has attempted to achieve greater equality for women in the workplace and to reduce violence against women.

The "third wave" of feminism, dating roughly from the 1990s to the present, grew out of both the victories of and the criticisms and backlash against the second wave. This perspective places greater emphasis on the diversity of women of different racial, ethnic, religious, and cultural backgrounds (Tong 2009). It emphasizes contemporary problems facing women, including infanticide, rape warfare, human trafficking, and child brides. This perspective argues that young men are negatively impacted by social constructions of masculinity (Pollock and Shuster 2000) just as are women (Pipher 1994).

After women won the right to vote in 1920, the movement lost its momentum and fell apart.

© Bettmann/CORBIS

There are many varieties of feminism. In addition, there are many people who oppose gender inequality but who do not regard themselves as feminists. While the differences among these people are many and sometimes subtle, it is possible to distinguish several broad perspectives within feminism (Freedman 2002; Tong 2009; Vogel 1983).

Liberal feminism seeks to improve the lot of women through reform of existing social institutions. Liberal feminists argue that traditional values regarding femininity prevent women from achieving their full potential and instead are in many ways oppressive (Friedan 1963). Liberal feminists supported the Equal Rights Amendment—a failed attempt in the 1970s and 1980s to amend the US Constitution to explicitly declare equal rights for men and women. They favor a woman's right to reproductive freedom and seek to elect women and supporters of women's rights to political positions.

Socialist (Marxist) feminism evolved from conflict theory and the work of Frederich Engels (1942, orig. 1884). Socialist feminists see the reforms advocated by liberal feminists as inadequate for achieving gender equity. Capitalism itself, they believe, is at the heart of the exploitation of women. They argue the form of family fostered by capitalism imposes a kind of "domestic slavery" on women. To achieve gender equity, they believe it is necessary to have a more socialist society, including in particular socialized means of child care. They believe this requires a socialist revolution creating a socialist state.

Radical feminism agrees with socialist feminism that reform of exiting social institutions is inadequate to eliminate gender inequality. It goes even further to argue that a socialist revolution will also be inadequate to achieve inequality (Tong 2009). Proponents of this view point out that socialist economies have not achieved gender equality any more than have capitalist ones. This view, in part, was born from the frustration experienced by women participating in the Civil Rights movement and anti–Vietnam War movements of the 1960s. While the men were giving the dramatic speeches about equality and justice, women in the movements were often relegated to stereotypical "behind-the-scenes" activities. Proponents of this view argue that equality requires the elimination of patriarchy and, some argue, the creation of new kinds of alternate institutions, as typified by communities of women working around specific issues like rape crisis intervention or shelters for battered women.

Postmodern feminism rejects the notion that all women share a single perspective and experience that could be explained by a single grand theory. Instead, they argue, there are many different standpoints, and the experience of being a woman can be quite different for black women, lesbians, heterosexuals, blue-collar workers, and so on. Postmodernists reject all the other feminist perspectives and, instead of seeking a single theory to account for "women's experience," they value diversity and the "otherness" of different individuals and groups. As Tong (2009) puts it, there are many truths and many constructions of reality characterizing "womenness."

Opposition to feminism has come both in society and in academia. Much of the criticism of feminism is a reaction to the socialist and radical forms of feminism. Some men, undoubtedly, oppose feminism because they enjoy their current privileges as men. Much of the opposition to feminism takes the form of a defense of traditional notions of masculinity (Doyle 1983), femininity (Marshall 1985), or the family (Baydar and Brooks-Gunn 1991), and argues that feminism ignores considerable empirical evidence of differences in the ways men and women think and act.

CONCEPT LEARNING CHECK 10.7   Theoretical Perspectives on Gender

Match the following statements to the theoretical perspectives most closely related to them.

_____ **1.** This theoretical perspective on gender is a sociological theory and is also related to a social movement that has been prominent in one form or another in the United States over a span of decades.

_____ **2.** This theory explains inequalities between men and women as deriving from biological differences such as women having to carry children to birth and nurse them, thus limiting their mobility and their ability to carry out certain necessary tasks.

_____ **3.** This theory emphasizes the ways in which patterns of interaction between men and women reproduce inequalities.

_____ **4.** This theory argues the role of women is to take care of the home so men can work in factories and to become consumers of new wealth produced by men.

A. Conflict theory

B. Feminist theory

C. Structural-functional theory

D. Symbolic interactionism

Visual Overview Sex, Gender, and Sexuality

Gender and sexuality represent the two largest classes of issues related to sex. Notions of how men and women should behave, and the different opportunities they have, vary dramatically in the the United States and throughout the world, along with the varieties of sexual behavior.

sex

Sex is biological. Sex refers to being male (♂) or female (♀).

gender

Gender is a social construct. Gender refers to perceptions of masculinity or femininity.

sexuality

Sexuality is a behavior or attitude. Sexuality refers to person's sexual orientation or preference.

Gender socialization is influenced by:
Parents
Peers
Education
Mass media

Gender inequality in the United States
Family roles
Health care and life expectancy
Education
Violence and victimization
Economics
Workplace issues

Sexuality is influenced by:
Cultural perspectives
Biological perspectives
Sexual orientation

Gender inequality around the world
Females a minority?
The concept of the patriarch
Violence against women

Sexual Issues
Prostitution and pornography
Sexual violence
Pregnancy and abortion
Sex: when and with whom?
Sexually transmitted infections
Sexual trafficking

Visual Summary Sex and Gender

10.1 Defining Sex, Gender, and Sexuality

- Sex is the biological distinction between males and females, gender is the social status associated with sex, and sexuality refers to sexual behavior and attitudes.

10.2 Sexuality and Varieties of Sexual Behaviour

- There are a great many varieties of sexual behaviors, and people's attitudes toward those are changing dramatically.
- Intersexual people have the characteristics of both sexes; transsexuals have the biological characteristics of one sex but identify with the other and may become transgendered by living as a member of the sex with which they identify.
- In some cases, people undergo gender reassignment to make their bodies conform with their self-identities.
- People's sexual orientation (their preference for sexual partners of a particular sex) can be heterosexual (they are attracted to members of the opposite sex), homosexual (they are attracted to members of the same sex), bisexual (they are attracted to both), or asexual (they are not sexually attracted to others).
- Studies of human sexuality include the Kinsey studies (Kinsey et al. 1948), the National Health and Social Life Survey (1994), and the National Survey of Sexual Health and Behavior (Herbenick et al., 2010).
- Studies of sexuality often find a double standard—different standards for men and women regarding sexual behavior.
- Several studies suggest that whether someone is a homosexual is influenced by both genetics and socialization.
- Studies of sexual behavior in the United States find varying proportions of men and women who consider themselves exclusively homosexual, with more who see themselves as either homosexual or bisexual and still more who have at least once in their lives had a homosexual experience.
- The social movement for homosexual rights in the United States is widely regarded as having begun in earnest in the Stonewall Riots of June 1969, when gays grew tired of repeated police harassment and openly fought New York police for 2 days.
- Attitudes toward homosexuals have generally become much less negative over the past few decades, one example of which is increasing support for gay marriage.
- Prostitution (sex for pay) displays a strong double standard, with women more likely to be prostitutes or sex workers and men are more likely to be the clients.
- Pornography (the portrayal of sexual subject matter for the purpose of sexual arousal) is difficult to prohibit while protecting free speech, is quite common in the United States, and, over the last few decades, has become more acceptable for adults while still generally unacceptable for anyone under 18.
- Teen pregnancy rates are higher for blacks and Hispanics than for whites, but rates for all have diminished from their peak in 1990.
- Over the last 40 years, surveys have found relatively consistent support for abortions when the woman's health is seriously endangered or for rape or a strong chance of serious defect but overall disapproval of abortions for other reasons.
- Women around the world are often victims of violence, from dowry deaths in India to human trafficking to rape.
- Rape is one of the most underreported crimes, with most victims being women and most rapes and sexual assaults involving acquaintances or "date rape" in which men accused of rape often challenge the woman's account, claiming the sex was consensual.
- Attitudes toward premarital sex are much more accepting today than 40 years ago, with greatest acceptance among younger respondents.

- A "hookup culture" can be found on some college campuses, in which students engage in casual, usually one-time encounters that may involve some form of sexual activity.
- Two areas of sexual behavior that remain unacceptable today much as they were decades ago involve sex among teenagers aged 14 to 16 and extramarital sex.
- The Internet, smartphones, and social networking sites make possible (and even common) new forms of technology-mediated sexual behaviors.

10.3 Theoretical Perspectives on Sexuality

- Human sexuality has been viewed from the three dominant theoretical perspectives of sociology (structural-functional theory, symbolic interaction theory, and social conflict theory), and conflict theory has been extended to feminism and queer theory.
- Structural-functional theory attempts to understand sexuality in terms of its positive functions such as raising children or preserving the family.
- Symbolic interactionism emphasizes how sexuality is socially constructed and can vary dramatically from one culture to the next, as illustrated by male and female circumcision.
- Social conflict theory points to the inequalities of social class that account for things such as the differential enforcement of laws against prostitution for males and females.
- Feminist theory focuses on the domination of women by men, as is illustrated by pornography, which is most often consumed by men and portrays men having power over women.
- Queer theory argues that there is a heterosexual bias throughout society against nonheterosexuals, as illustrated by the Defense of Marriage Act (prohibiting gays from enjoying the benefits of marriage), which is tolerated much more than biases against women or racial and ethnic minorities.

10.4 Gender Socialization

- Gender is socially constructed and is influenced by a person's interactions with parents, peers, teachers, mass media, and sports.
- If nature is the most important factor in gender socialization, we would expect to find cultural universals (e.g., differences between men and women found in every society), yet research by Margaret Mead and George Murdock found considerable diversity in male and female activities in different cultures.
- Parents influence gender roles (expected behaviors associated with males or females) in gender-stereotypical behaviors by parents that children see, rewarding behaviors differently depending on whether the child is a boy or girl, and, of course, the toys they provide to kids, which tend to be gendered (e.g., dolls for girls, sports equipment and tools for boys).
- Peers influence gender roles by the types of behavior that are rewarded on the playground, where boys are punished for acting too girlish and girls are punished for being tomboys.
- Teachers often provide role models reinforcing gender-appropriate behaviors, as reflected in the tasks male and female teachers perform in the school. Teachers also tend to expect boys to excel at math and science and pay more attention to boys and give them more second chances in classroom interaction.
- Television programs, movies, magazines, and radio shows often reinforce gender differences, as some are aimed mainly at women while others are aimed at men.
- Technology also influences gender roles, with women characters in video games more likely to be sexualized and women less likely to see themselves as competent with computers.
- For boys, organized sports and athletic programs in school help shape their identity as men.
- The various games boys and girls play in grade school are very gender specific, such as jump rope for girls and touch football for boys.

10.5 Gender Inequality around the World

- Around the world, women are often a repressed minority subject to violence and other disadvantages justified by systems of patriarchy in which men dominate women.

- Women, though outnumbering men in the world, have been discriminated against historically and hence are a sociological minority.

- Most researchers believe all societies have been patriarchal to some degree.

- Sexism is a belief that one sex is superior to the other and supports patriarchy.

- Internationally, women are exposed to many forms of violence, including dowry deaths in which brides are murdered by the groom or his family members, abortions of female fetuses when male children are preferred, and human sex trafficking.

10.6 Gender Stratification/Inequality in the United States

- Women are disadvantaged relative to men in most aspects of American society, including in the workplace, family roles, health care, education, and politics.

- From 1950 to 2010, women participating in the labor force increased from 34% to 59%, and women working outside the home appears likely to continue indefinitely.

- Women historically, in both the United States and other countries, have been paid significantly less than men. However, that pay gap is declining slowly over time.

- One factor influencing the pay gap is the fact that women have traditionally dominated low-paying occupations, known as pink-collar jobs.

- Comparable worth is the concept that people should be paid similar wages if their jobs require similar levels of education and training, regardless of whether the jobs are held mainly by men or by women.

- Glass ceilings refer to invisible barriers that prevent women from occupying top management or executive leadership jobs.

- Institutional sexism occurs when the day-to-day operations, rules, and policies of organizations discriminate against one sex (usually women).

- Sexual harassment is unwanted attention based on one's sex or sexuality that interferes with job performance or causes discomfort. It is most commonly directed against women but can also be directed against homosexuals harassed on the job by heterosexuals.

- Although women work in the workforce at rates nearly equal to men, women still are often tasked with traditionally women's work in the home such as child care, cooking, and housework. This has been called the "second shift."

- Men and women are treated differently in health care, as illustrated by the greater tendency of physicians to check men for heart disease than they do women and a tendency for women to be subjected to inappropriate hysterectomies.

- Historically, women lagged behind men in education in the United States, but since the 1970s, college enrollments for women have exceeded those of men, and women now earn the majority of college degrees.

- Women play lesser roles in politics than men, having gained the right to vote long after men in most countries and having fewer seats in legislatures globally.

- LGBT (lesbian, gay, bisexual, or transgendered) youth are more likely to be victims of bullying than their straight counterparts and find themselves most worried about violence and acceptance, while their straight friends are focusing on school, careers, and college.

10.7   Theoretical Perspectives on Gender

- Structural-functional theory explains gender differences as something that grew out of biological differences related to reproduction.
- Conflict theory explains gender roles as instruments of oppression that preserve male advantages over females.
- Symbolic interactionism explains gender inequality based on mechanisms of everyday interaction that reproduce inequality.
- Feminism is a perspective that argues men and women are essentially equal and should be treated equally.

- Liberal feminism seeks greater gender equality through reform of existing social institutions. Socialist feminism believes capitalism is at the heart of exploitation of women and a more socialist society is required to achieve equality. Radical feminism argues that even a socialist revolution will not result in gender equality and only the elimination of patriarchy will do that. Finally, postmodern feminism argues that women experience life differently depending on their own standpoints based on social class, race, sexuality, and so on; hence, a single theory cannot account for women's experience.

10.1 Defining Sex, Gender, and Sexuality

1. Which of the following is likely to be the same regardless of country and even century?
   A. Sex
   B. Sexuality
   C. Gender
   D. Societal attitudes toward abortion

2. Which of the following best describes gender?
   A. The differences between men and women
   B. Behavior and attitudes related to sex
   C. The differences between masculinity and femininity
   D. Both a and c

10.2 Sexuality and Varieties of Sexual Behaviour

3. Which of the following statements about pornography is *not* true?
   A. Pornography has been defined by US courts as material that violates community standards and lacks redeeming social value.
   B. Over the past 40 years, there has been a decrease in the percentage of people feeling pornography should be illegal for everyone.
   C. While men are more likely to engage in extramarital sex, women are more likely to access pornography.
   D. Most countries attempt to restrict access to pornography by minors.

4. Which of the following is a "hookup" according to sociologist Paula England?
   A. A first date
   B. A monogamous relationship between two unmarried people
   C. A drug deal
   D. A casual, often one-time encounter that might lead to sexual activity

5. Which of the following is a true statement about attitudes toward sex before marriage?
   A. A majority of respondents over 50 believed it is always wrong in both 1972 and 2010.
   B. A majority of respondents over 50 believed it was always wrong in 1972, but nearly that many believed it was not wrong at all by 2010.
   C. A majority of respondents under 26 believed it was wrong in 1972 but not in 2010.
   D. Respondents of all ages believed it is always wrong in both 1972 and 2010.

6. The studies of twins by Bailey and Pillard (1991) and Bailey et al (1993) found that:
   A. All identical twins are either both homosexuals or both not homosexuals.
   B. One's chances of being a twin are higher if one's brother is a homosexual.
   C. Twins are less likely to be homosexual than nontwins.
   D. One is more likely to be a homosexual if one's identical twin is homosexual than if one's fraternal twin is homosexual.

10.3 Theoretical Perspectives on Sexuality

7. The importance of virginity before marriage in the United States has declined significantly over the decades. Which theory accounts for the changing importance of virginity over time?
   A. Feminist theory
   B. Queer theory
   C. Symbolic interactionism
   D. Structural-functional theory

8. The Heterosexual Questionnaire in this chapter is:
   A. a serious questionnaire intended to help heterosexuals guard against becoming homosexuals.
   B. a tongue-in-cheek questionnaire intended to help heterosexuals recognize some of the taken-for-granted assumptions about homosexuality reflected in questions often faced by homosexuals.
   C. a questionnaire designed to help assess whether you are heterosexual.
   D. a questionnaire intended to assess your knowledge of heterosexuality.

10.4 Gender Socialization

9. Which of the following is least likely to help socialize someone for gender roles?
   A. His or her father
   B. A friend he or she spends hours with each day
   C. Television shows
   D. A neighbor down the street

10. Which of the following is most likely to be among the expected behaviors for a traditional female role?
    A. Provide for the family
    B. Defend the family
    C. Be brave
    D. Assume primary responsibility for child care

11. Which of the following statements is true?
    A. Boys reported less perceived support for their use of computers from both parents and friends.
    B. Male video game characters are more likely to be sexualized.
    C. Male video game characters are more likely to be portrayed as aggressive.
    D. Male video game characters are more likely to "get nervous using technologies."

10.5 Gender Inequality around the World

12. Studies of societies around the world both now and in the past have consistently found that:

A. women are most often placed in revered positions of favor compared to men.

B. women are most often treated as inferior to men, with less access to power and resources.

C. roughly half of societies favor women and half favor men.

D. relations between men and women in different societies tend to change quickly, and one may be favored in one decade and the other in some other decade.

13. Which of the following best describes women in Saudi Arabia based on information in this chapter?

A. Women are not allowed to exercise.

B. Women must always travel in pairs.

C. Women are not permitted to drive.

D. Women do all the household shopping.

10.6 Gender Stratification/Inequality in the United States

Indicate whether each of the following statements is true or false.

14. The percentage of women participating in the labor force has increased dramatically between 1950 and 2010, increasing from around one-third to nearly 60%.

15. The gender pay gap is greater for older workers than for younger workers.

16. In Scandinavian countries such as Norway and Denmark, there is a "reverse gender pay gap" with women on the average being paid more than men.

17. Which of the following is not among reasons often given for why women participate more in the labor force?

A. The number of men working has decreased, dramatically causing the need for more women to work.

B. Higher divorce rates.

C. Women are more often the heads of single-parent households.

D. Some traditional household "women's work" such as cooking, cleaning, and child care is now more often "outsourced," making it possible for women to work outside the home.

10.7 Theoretical Perspectives on Gender

18. Which theoretical perspective argues that there is no one perspective that characterizes women, but there are many standpoints, and being a woman can be quite different for blue-collar workers, black women, lesbians, and so on?

A. Radical feminism

B. The conflict perspective

C. Postmodern feminism

D. Liberal feminism

CHAPTER ESSAY QUESTIONS

1. Molly is a 16-year-old girl. Unlike most of her friends, Molly does not watch television very often. Her parents bought her lots of sports equipment, along with dolls, while she was growing up. Today she is a cheerleader and does not play sports herself.

In school, she sometimes gets frustrated when she raises her hand in the classroom and the teacher seems to call on boys first. This is particularly frustrating because boys usually do not know the material any better than she does. What she likes most about school is learning about computers. She sees herself as more competent at computers than most of her friends, both girls and boys.

What is it about Molly and sports that you would expect given what we know about gender role socialization, and which thing is unexpected?

Similarly, what about her school experience is consistent with the literature on gender socialization and which thing is a surprise given what we know from the literature?

2. Although prostitution is illegal, a surprising number of men have paid (or been paid) for having sex. What proportion of men report they have done this? Sociologists sometimes say that prostitution is "gendered." What does this mean? How is this supported by the proportion of women who report they have paid (or been paid) for having sex?

3. Aaron is talking to Monica, and he says that he does not believe women are discriminated against any more. "After all," says Aaron, "more women go to college than men." He points out that there are nearly as many women graduates in professional programs in medicine (49%), dentistry (46%), and law (46%) as men. Is Aaron right that men and women are treated nearly the same? What evidence is there to support your answer? What terms identify three additional ways in which women are discriminated against in the workplace?

CHAPTER DISCUSSION QUESTIONS

1. In what area of life do you think gender inequality is most serious for women? Education? In the home? At work?

2. How does gender socialization reflect our patriarchal society in general? Do you see patterns of sexism?

3. At work, which do you think is worse for women: the pay gap, glass ceilings, sexual harassment, or institutional sexism?

4. The great majority of inequalities between genders favor men. However, there are some cases in which women are favored. What are some of those? Do those benefits for women "even out" the benefits for men?

5. Are gender roles more rigid for girls or for boys, or are they about the same? Would you allow your male child to dress up in princess outfits? Why or why not?

6. In what ways does society still blame the victim when it comes to sexual violence such as rape, stalking, and other forms of intimate partner abuse? Is there a double standard when it comes to men and women? What messages regarding sex and violence do men and women receive from the pornography industry and the mass media in general?

7. Which of the theoretical perspectives on gender reflect your own beliefs? Do you consider yourself a feminist? Why or why not?

CHAPTER PROJECTS

INDIVIDUAL PROJECTS

1. Think back to your high school experiences. Can you remember at least one example of gender socialization involving your parents? Peers of the same sex? Peers of the opposite sex? The school itself? Mass media?

2. Go to a social networking site that you are a member of, such as Facebook, LinkedIn, or Twitter. Look at the entries and look for examples of gender stratification that you see there. For example, does someone's tweet about an activity reflect an opportunity that is more available to men than women or vice versa? When you look at postings on your wall or profiles of friends on Facebook, do you see gender differences in work, family household responsibilities, or other areas?

3. Go online and search for the term *third gender*. Write an analysis paper of your findings using chapter information. Include in your analysis an example of a contemporary culture that uses this classification and the status of this group. Are they respected or do they face sexism?

GROUP PROJECTS

1. Interview someone you know who is of the opposite sex about what it means to be a male or female in society today (depending on their sex). Write a self-analysis paper comparing your interview findings to your own experiences and viewpoints.

2. Go online to find the following information: how many women hold CEO positions in Fortune 500 companies, the number of female governors and congresswomen, and what percentage of college presidents are female. Discuss your findings with your colleagues and write a summary of your data analysis.

CHAPTER KEY TERMS

Asexual	Glass ceilings	Prostitution
Bisexual	Heterosexism	Rape
Comparable worth	Heterosexual	Second shift
Cyber sex	Homophobia	Secondary sex characteristics
Double standard	Homosexual	Sex
Dowry deaths	Hookups	Sexism
Egalitarian system	Institutional sexism	Sexting
Feminism	Intersexual people	Sexual harassment
Gender	Matriarchy	Sexual orientation
Gender pay gap	Patriarchy	Sexuality
Gender reassignment	Pink-collar jobs	Transgendered
Gender roles	Pornography	Transsexuals
Gender stratification	Primary sex characteristics	Virtual sex

ANSWERS TO CONCEPT LEARNING CHECKS

10.1 Basic Concepts of Sex, Gender, and Sexuality

1. Gender [B. A social status]
2. Sexuality [C. Attitudes and behaviors]
3. Sex [A. Biological]

10.2 Recent Trends in Sexual Behavior

1. Premarital sex [A. More favorable]
2. Abortion [B. About the same]
3. Pornography (for adults) [A. More favorable]
4. Sex outside marriage [B. About the same]
5. Homosexuality [A. More favorable]

10.3 Theoretical Perspectives on Sexuality

1. This theory argues against the bias against anyone who is not a heterosexual. [B. Queer theory]
2. This theory argues the importance of legitimate births helps regulate sexual behavior to ensure that children will receive the support they need to grow up. [D. Structural-functional theory]
3. This theory argues that notions of what is right or wrong in terms of sexual behavior are formed through interactions among people and can vary from one society to the next or one time to the next. [C. Symbolic interactionism]
4. This theory argues that women are viewed sexually as part of the domination of women by men. [A. Feminist theory]

10.4 Gender Socialization

1. [T] Michael Messner's study found that for the men in his study, it became natural to equate masculinity with sports.
2. [F] Boys are interrupted more in classrooms than girls and girls tend to dominate classroom discussions.
3. [T] During adolescence, self-confidence of girls declines twice as much as that of boys.
4. [T] Traditional gender roles have both negative and positive consequences for both males and females.
5. [F] Video games portray males and females differently, with males more likely to be scantily clad.

10.5 Gender Inequality around the World

1. Dowry death [B. The murder of the bride whose dowry is viewed as inadequate by the husband and his family]
2. Sexism [D. The belief that one sex is superior to the other]
3. Patriarchy [C. A system of social relationships in which men dominate women]

10.6 Gender Inequality in the United States

1. Comparable worth [E. The relative worth of different traditionally male and female jobs based on education and training required]
2. Glass ceilings [F. The tendency for women to not be promoted past a certain point in companies]
3. Second shift [D. The tendency for women to do most of the household work even though they work outside the home as well]

10.7 Theoretical Perspectives on Gender

1. This theoretical perspective on gender is a sociological theory and is also related to a social movement that has been prominent in one form or another in the United States over a span of decades. [B. Feminist theory]
2. This theory explains inequalities between men and women as deriving from biological differences such as women having to carry children to birth and nurse them, thus limiting their mobility and their ability to carry out certain necessary tasks. [C. Structural-functional theory]
3. This theory emphasizes the ways in which patterns of interaction between men and women reproduce inequalities. [D. Symbolic interactionism]
4. This theory argues the role of women is to take care of the home so men can work in factories and to become consumers of new wealth produced by men. [A. Conflict theory]

ANSWERS TO CHAPTER REVIEW TEST

10.1 Defining Sex, Gender, and Sexuality

1. A. Sex is a biological attribute that does not change with culture or over time.
2. C. Gender is a social status and describes differences between what it means to be masculine or feminine.

10.2 Sexuality and Varieties of Sexual Behaviour

3. C. Men are more likely to access pornography than women (NORC 2011).
4. D. A hookup is a casual usually one-time encounter that may lead to sexual activity but often stops short of intercourse.
5. B. In 1972, 51% of respondents over 50 believed it was always wrong, but by 2010, 57% of respondents over 50 believed it is not wrong at all (NORC 2011).

6. D. They found that roughly one half of the identical twins were both homosexual when one of them was homosexual, while only about 1 in 5 fraternal twins were homosexual and about 1 in 10 adopted siblings were homosexual.

10.3 Theoretical Perspectives on Sexuality

7. C. Symbolic interactionism can account for changes in cultural practices over time, since the meaning of particular sexual practices or behaviors arises from interaction among people in that time and place.
8. B. It is a questionnaire designed to help heterosexuals recognize some of the taken-for-granted assumptions about homosexuality reflected in questions often faced by homosexuals.

10.4 Gender Socialization

9. D. While an interfering neighbor might try to influence sex role behavior, family, peers, and social media are widely regarded as stronger influences.

10. D. Traditional women's roles include an expectation that the woman will assume primary responsibility for household cooking, cleaning, and child care.

11. C. Male video game characters are more likely than female characters (83% vs. 62%) to be portrayed as aggressive.

10.5 Gender Inequality around the World

12. B. Women are treated as inferiors to men in most societies today and in virtually all societies historically.

13. C. Women are not permitted to drive.

10.6 Gender Stratification/Inequality in the United States

14. True. Bureau of Labor Statistics (2007, 2012)

15. True. Women under 35 are paid roughly 90 cents for each dollar a man earns, while for women over 35, the average is only about 75 cents per dollar.

16. False. Women are paid less than men in every country for which data are available.

17. A. The number of men working has decreased only slightly over the past few decades and is nowhere near as large as the increase in women working.

10.7 Theoretical Perspectives on Gender

18. C. Postmodern feminism argues there are many constructions of reality characterizing what it means to be a woman (Tong 2009).

ANSWERS TO CHAPTER ESSAY QUESTIONS

1. Regarding sports, it is unusual and unexpected that she would grow up with lots of sports equipment. It is expected and usual that she would have dolls and would be a cheerleader and not play sports herself.
   Regarding school, it is expected that teachers might call on boys first. It is unexpected that she views herself as more competent at computers than boys.

2. Twenty percent of (about one in five) men have engaged in prostitution.
   About 2% of women have engaged in prostitution.
   It is gendered because men and women participate in it very differently. Men participate more. Men are more likely to be customers and women participate less often but are more like to be the sex workers or prostitutes.

3. There is a lot of evidence that men are treated better than women and women are discriminated against. So in most respects Aaron is wrong.
   The percentage of females in those same professions is low (less than men).
   Terms identifying other ways women are discriminated against in the workplace include the gender pay gap, institutional sexism, sexual harassment, and glass ceilings.

REFERENCES

American Academy of Pediatrics. 2004. "Sexual Orientation and Adolescents." *Pediatrics* 113(6):1827–1832.

American Association of University Women (AAUW). 1992. *The AAUW Report: How Schools Shortchange Girls*. Washington, DC. American Association of University Women Education Foundation.

American Federation of State, County and Municipal Employees, AFL-CIO (AFSCME), et al. v. State of Washington et al. 770 F.2d 1401 (9th Cir), 1985.

Associated Press. 1992. "Women Worldwide Work Harder for Less, Study Says." (September 7):A-3.

Bailey, J. Michael, and Richard C. Pillard. 1991. "A Genetic Study of Male Sexual Orientation." *Archives of General Psychiatry* 48(12):1089–1096.

Bailey, J. Michael, Richard C. Pillard, Michael C. Neale, and Yvonne Agyei. 1993. "Heritable Factors Influence Sexual Orientation in Women." *Archives of General Psychiatry* 50:217–223.

Barry, Kathleen. 1979. *Female Sexual Slavery*. Englewood Cliffs, NJ: Prentice-Hall.

Bartky, Sandra Lee. 1990. *Femininity and Domination: Studies in the Phenomenology of Oppression*. Oxford, UK: Routledge.

Bartz, A., and B. Ehrlich. 2012, March 22. "The Year's Hottest, and Creepiest, Apps." *CNNTech*. Accessed March 2012 at http://www.cnn.com/2012/03/22/tech/mobile/creepy-social-apps-netiquette/index.html?iref=allsearch.

Basow, S. A. 1986. *Gender Stereotypes*. Pacific Grove, CA: Brooks/Cole.

Baydar, Nazli, and Jeanne Brooks-Gunn. 1991. "Effect of Maternal Employment and Child-Care Arrangements on Preschoolers' Cognitive and Behavioral Outcomes: Evidence from Children From the National Longitudinal Survey of Youth." *Developmental Psychology* 27:932–935.

Bearman, P. 2002. "Opposite-Sex Twins and Adolescent Same-Sex Attraction." *American Journal of Sociology* 107:1179–1205.

Bedi, Rahul. 2012, February 27. "Indian Dowry Deaths on the Rise." *The Telegraph*. Accessed May 2012 at http://www.telegraph.co.uk/news/worldnews/asia/india/9108642/Indian-dowry-deaths-on-the-rise.html.

Best, Joel. 2001. *Damned Lies and Statistics: Untangling Numbers from the Media, Politicians, and Activists*. Berkeley: University of California Press.

Bernard, J. 1981. *The Female World*. New York: Free Press.

Bernard, Larry C. 1980. "Multivariate Analysis of New Sex Role Formulations and Personality." *Journal of Personality and Social Psychology* 38 (2):323–336.

Bishop, J. E. 1990. "Study Finds Doctors Tend to Postpone Heart Surgery for Women, Raising Risk." *Wall Street Journal*, April 16:B4.

Blanchard R, and P. Klassen. 1997. "Review H-Y antigen and homosexuality in men." *Journal of Theoretical Biology* 185(3):373–378.

Blum, Linda M. 1991. *Between Feminism and Labor: The Significance of the Comparable Worth Movement*. Berkeley: University of California Press.

Blumstein, Phillip, and Pepper Schwartz. 1983. *American Couples*. New York: Morrow.

Broder, M. S., D. E. Kanouse, B. S. Mittman, and S. J. Bernstein. 2000. "The Appropriateness of Recommendations for Hysterectomy." *Obstetrics and Gynecology* 95(2):199–205.

Brown, Dee. 1991. *Wondrous Times on the Frontier*. Little Rock, AR: August House.

Chaker, Ann Marie, and Stout, Hilary. 2004, May 6. "After Years Off, Women Struggle to Revive Careers." *Wall Street Journal*. Accessed December 2012 at http://online.wsj.com/article/0,,SB108379813440903335,00.html.

Cohen, Lloyd R. 1991. "Sexual Harassment and the Law." *Society* 28(4):8–13.

Cohn, Bob. 1992. "Discrimination: The Limits of the Law." *Newsweek* September 14:38–39.

Collins, Randall. 1971. "A Conflict Theory of Sexual Stratification." *Social Problems* 19:3–21.

Collins, Randall. 1975. *Conflict Sociology: Toward an Explanatory Science*. New York: Academic Press.

Collins, Randall. 1988. *Sociology of Marriage and the Family: Gender, Home, and Property*. Second edition. Chicago: Nelson-Hall.

Condry, J. C., and S. Condry. 1976. "Sex Differences: A Study of the Eye of the Beholder." *Child Development* 47:812–819.

Congressional Research Service. 2012. *Women in the United States Congress: 1917–2002*. Accessed March 2012 at http://www.fas.org/sgp/crs/misc/RL30261.pdf.

Corbett, S. 2007, March 18. "The Women's War." *The New York Times*. Accessed April 2012 at www.nytimes.com/2007/03/18/magazine/18cover.html?scp=1&rcsq=&rcst=cse.

Courtney, Alice E., and Thomas W. Whipple. 1983. *Sex Stereotyping in Advertising*. Lexington, MA: D. C. Heath.

Crompton, R., and M. Mann, Eds. 1986. *Gender and Stratification*. Cambridge, UK: Polity Press.

Davies, C. 2012. "Saudi Arabia Plans New City for Women Workers Only." *The Guardian*. Accessed August 2012 at http://www.guardian.co.uk/world/2012/aug/12/saudi-arabia-city-women-workers.

D'Emilio, John. 1983. *Sexual Politics, Sexual Communities: The Making of a Homosexual Minority in the United States 1940–1970*. Chicago: University of Chicago Press.

Dill, Karen E., and Kathryn P. Thill. 2007. "Video Game Characters and the Socialization of Gender Roles: Young People's Perceptions Mirror Sexist Media Depictions." *Sex Roles* 57:851–864.

Doyle, James A. 1983. *The Male Experience*. Dubuque, IA: Wm. C. Brown.

Dutton, William H., and Grant Blank. 2011. "Next Generation Users: The Internet in Britain." *Oxford Internet Survey 2011 Report*. Table IIB. Oxford, UK: Oxford University.

Eisenhart, M. A., and D. C. Holland. 1983. "Learning Gender from Peers: The Role of Peer Group in the Cultural Transmission of Gender." *Human Organization* 42:321–332.

Eisenstein, Zillah R., Ed. 1979. *Capitalist Patriarchy and the Case for Socialist Feminism*. New York: Monthly Review Press.

Eisler, Riane. 1988. *The Chalice and the Blade*. San Francisco: Harper.

Engels, Frederich. 1942 (1884). *The Origins of Family, Private Property, and the State*. New York: International.

England, Paula, Emily Fitzgibbons Shafer, and Alison C. K. Fogarty. 2008. "Hooking Up and Forming Romantic Relationships on Today's College Campuses." PP. 531–546 in *The Gendered Society Reader*. Third edition, edited by Michael Kimmel and Amy Aronson. New York: Oxford University Press.

Estes, Richard and Weiner, Neil. 2001. *The Commercial Sexual Exploitation of Children in the U.S., Canada, and Mexico*. University of Pennsylvania School of Social Work. Accessed March 2012 at http://www.sp2.upenn.edu/restes/CSEC_Files/Exec_Sum_020220.pdf.

Evans-Prichard, E. E. 1970. "Sexual Inversion Among the Azande." *American Anthropologist* 72(6):1428–1434.

Farrell, Warren. 2000. *The Myth of Male Power: Why Men are the Disposable Sex*. Berkeley, CA: Simon and Schuster.

Federal Bureau of Investigation (FBI). 2010. "Crime in the United States, 2009: Expanded Homicide Data." Calculated from Tables 2 and 10. Washington, DC: GPO. Accessed October 2010 at http://www.fbi.gov/about-us/cjis/ucr/crime-in-the-u.s/2009.

Felsenthal, Edward. 1998. "Justices' Ruling Further Defines Sex Harassment." *Wall Street Journal* (Mar 5):B1–B2.

Fine, Gary. 1987. *With the Boys: Little League Baseball and Preadolescent Culture*. Chicago: University of Chicago Press.

Freedman, Estelle B. 2002. *No Turning Back: The History of Feminism and the Future of Women*. New York: Ballantine Books.

Friedan, Betty. 1963. *The Feminine Mystique*. New York: Boston.

Frieze, I. 1983. "Investigating the Causes and Consequences of Marital Rape." *Signs* 8(3):532–553. Accessed October 2012 at http://www.jstor.org/stable/3173950.

Fuller, R. and Schoenberger, R. 1991. "The Gender Salary Gap: Do Academic Achievement, Intern Experience, and College Major Make a Difference?" *Social Science Quarterly* 72(4):715–26.

Giddens, Anthony. 1992. *The Transformation of Intimacy*. Cambridge, UK: Polity Press.

Greenberg, David F. 1988. *The Construction of Homosexuality*. Chicago: University of Chicago Press.

Gupta, Alka. 2012. *Female Foeticide in India*. UNICEF. Accessed May 2012 at http://www.unicef.org/india/media_3285.htm.

Hagrey, Keach. 2007, August 3. "Big-City Gals Earn More Than Guys." *CBS News*. Accessed June 2012 at http://www.cbsnews.com/2100-501203_162-3130645.html.

Harris, Marvin. 1977. "Why Men Dominate Women." *The New York Times Magazine* (November 13):46, 115–123.

Henley, Nancy M. 1977. *Body Politics: Power, Sex and Non-verbal Communication*. Englewood Cliffs, NJ: Prentice-Hall.

Her Majesty's Inspectorate of Constabulary. 2007. *Without Consent: A Report on the Joint Review of the Investigation and Prosecution of Rape Offences*. Accessed April 2012 at http://www.hmic.gov.uk/media/without-consent-20061231.pdf.

Herbenick, D., M. Reece, V. Schick, S. Sanders, B. Dodge, and J. Fortenberry. 2010. "Sexual Behavior in the United States: Results from a National Probability Sample of Men and Women Ages 14–94." *Journal of Sexual Medicine* 7(suppl 5):255–265.

Hoare, Rose. 2012, May 9. "Meet Fortune 500's Female Powerbrokers." *CNN*. Accessed May 2012 at http://edition.cnn.com/2012/05/08/business/f500-leading-women/index.html.

Hochschild, Arlie, and Anne Machung. 1989. *The Second Shift: Working Parents and the Revolution at Home*. New York: Viking Penguin.

Houston, Paul. 1993. "Huge March Seeks Gay Rights." *Los Angeles Times* (April 26):A-1.

Huber, J. 1990. "Macro–micro Links in Gender Stratification: 1989 Presidential Address." *American Sociological Review* 55:1–10.

Human Rights Campaign. 2012. *Growing up LGBT in America: HRC Youth Survey Report*. Accessed June 2012 at http://www.hrc.org/files/assets/resources/Growing-Up-LGBT-in-America_Report.pdf.

ICPSR (Inter-university Consortium for Political and Social Research). 2009. *Exploring the Second Shift: A Data-Driven Learning Guide*. Ann Arbor, MI: Inter-university Consortium for Political and Social Research [distributor], 2009-04-16. Doi:10.3886/secondshift.

Ignico, Arlene A., and Barbara J. Mead. 1990. "Children's Perceptions of the Gender-Appropriateness of Physical Activities." *Perceptual and Motor Skills* 71:1275–81.

International Labour Organization (ILO). 2007. *Forced Labour Statistics Factsheet*. Accessed December 2012 at http://www.ilo.org/sapfl/Informationresources/Factsheetsandbrochures/WCMS_181921/lang--en/index.htm.

Inter-Parliamentary Union. 2012. *Women in National Parliaments*. Accessed March 2012 at http://www.ipu.org/wmn-e/world.htm.

Irvine, M. 2009. "Porn Charges for 'Sexting' Stir Debate." *Associated Press* (Feb. 4, 2009). Accessed December 2012 at http://www.msnbc.msn.com/id/29017808/ns/technology_and_science-tech_and_gadgets/t/porn-charges-sexting-stir-debate/.

Kelly, L. 1987. "The Continuum of Sexual Violence." Pp. 46–60 in *Women, Violence, and Social Control*. Edited by J. Hammer and M. Maynard. Atlantic Highlands, NJ: Humanities Press.

Kemp, A. 1990. "Estimating Sex Discrimination in Professional Occupations with the *Dictionary of Occupational Titles*." *Sociological Spectrum* 10(3):387–411.

Kinsey, Alfred C. 1953. *Sexual Behavior in the Human Female*. Bloomington: Indiana University Press.

Kinsey, Alfred C., Wardell B. Pomeroy, and Clyde E. Martin. 1948. *Sexual Behavior in the Human Male*. Philadelphia: W. B. Saunders.

Kluckhohn, Clyde. 1948. "As an Anthropologist Views It." Pp. 88–104 in *Sex Habits of American Men*. Edited by Albert Deutsch. New York: Grosset and Dunlap.

Kohlberg, Lawrence. 1966. "A Cognitive-Development Analysis of Children's Sex-Role Concepts and Attitudes." Pp. 82–166 in *The Development of Sex Differences*. Edited by Eleanor Macoby. Stanford, CA: Stanford University Press.

Kost, K., and S. Henshaw. 2012. *U.S. Teenage Pregnancies, Births and Abortions, 2008*. Guttmacher Institute. Accessed April 2012 at http://www.guttmacher.org/pubs/USTPtrends08.pdf.

Krebs, Christopher P. 2007. "The Campus Sexual Assault Study." Washington, DC: National Institute of Justice. Accessed September 2010 at http://www.ncjrs.gov/pdffiles1/nij/grants/221153.pdf.

Kruks, G. N. 1991. "Gay and Lesbian Homeless/Street Youth: Special Issues and Concerns." *Journal of Adolescent Health*. (Special Issue 12):515–18.

Laumann, Robert Michael, Stuart Michaels, and John Gagnon. 1994. *The Social Organization of Sexuality*. Chicago: University of Chicago Press.

Layng, A. 1990. "What Keeps Women 'in Their Place.'" Pp. 148–151 in *Anthropology 90/91*. Edited by E. Angeloni. Guilford, CT: Dushkin Publishing Group.

Lengermann, Patricia Madoo, and Ruth A. Wallace. 1985. *Gender in America: Social Control and Social Change*. Englewood Cliffs, NJ: Prentice Hall.

Lerner, Gerda. 1986. *The Creation of Patriarchy*. New York: Oxford.

Liew, J. 2009. "All Men Watch Porn, Scientists Find." *The Telegraph*. Accessed March 2012 at http://www.telegraph.co.uk/relationships/6709646/All-men-watch-porn-scientists-find.html?science.

Lips, Hilary. 1993. *Sex and Gender: An Introduction*. Second edition. Mountain View, CA: Mayfield Publishing Co.

Lorber, J. 1994. *Paradoxes of Gender*. New Haven, CT: Yale University Press.

Mackinnon, Catherine A. 1984. "Not a Moral Issue." *Yale Law and Policy Review* 2:321–345.

Malamuth, Neil M. 1986. Do Sexually Violent Media Indirectly Contribute to Antisocial Behavior? *Report of the Surgeon General's Workshop on Pornography and Public Health (Aug 4, 1986)*. United States Public Health Service. Office of the Surgeon General.

Marcelo, Philip. 2011, April 10. "Muslim Dress Optional for Female U.S. Soldiers." *Providence Journal*. Accessed May 2012 at http://news.providence-journal.com/politics/2011/04/muslim-dress-op.html.

Marshall, Susan E. 1985. "Ladies against Women: Mobilization Dilemmas of Antifeminist Movements." *Social Problems* 32(4, April):348–362.

Martin, Carol L. 1989. "Children's Use of Gender-Related Information in Making Social Judgments." *Developmental Psychology* 25:80–88.

Masters, William H., Virginia E. Johnson, and Robert C. Kolodny. 1988. *Human Sexuality*. Third edition. Glenview, IL: Scott, Foresman/Little, Brown.

Matoesian, Greg. 1993. *Reproducing Rape*. Cambridge, UK: Polity Press.

McCully, Jeffrey. 2012. *It Gets Better? Gay Teen Bullying and Suicide*. Doctoral dissertation, University of Missouri, Columbia.

Mead, Margaret. 1935. *Sex and Temperament in Three Primitive Societies*. New York: William and Morrow.

Messner, Michael. 1990. "Boyhood, Organized Sports, and the Construction of Masculinities." *Journal of Contemporary Ethnology* 18 (4, January):416–44.

Michael, Robert T., John H. Gagnon, Edward O. Laumann, and Gina Kolata. 1994. *Sex in America: A Definitive Survey*. Boston: Little, Brown & Company.

Molly Moore. 1990. "Crossing the Culture Gulf; For Female Soldiers, Different Rules." *The Washington Post. HighBeam Research*. Accessed December 2012 at http://www.highbeam.com/doc/1P2-1143845.html.

MSNBC. 2011, June 16. "New York Rep. Anthony Weiner Resigns." Accessed March 2012 at http://www.nytimes.com/2011/06/17/nyregion/anthony-d-weiner-tells-friends-he-will-resign.html?pagewanted=all&_r=0.

Murdock, George Peter. 1937. "Comparative Data on the Division of Labor by Sex." *Social Forces* 15(4, May):551–553.

Nanda, Serena. 1998. *Neither Man Nor Woman: The Hijras of India*. Belmont, CA: Wadsworth Publishing.

National Center on Domestic and Sexual Violence (NCDSV). 2012. *Power and Control Wheel*. Accessed October 2012 at http://www.ncdsv.org/images/PowerControlwheelNOSHADING.pdf.

National Center for Education Statistics (NCES). 2011. *The Condition of Education 2011* (NCES 2011-033), Table A-26-2. U.S. Department of Education. Accessed March 2012 at http://nces.ed.gov/fastfacts/display.asp?id=72.

National Crime Records Bureau (NCRB). 2008. *India*. Accessed May 2012 at http://ncrb.nic.in/cii2008/cii-2008/Chapter%205.pdf.

National Institutes of Health (NIH). 2001. *NIH Policy and Guidelines on the Inclusion of Women and Minorities as Subjects in Clinical Research*. Accessed October 2012 at http://grants.nih.gov/grants/funding/women_min/guidelines_amended_10_2001.htm.

National Opinion Research Center (NORC). 2011. *General Social Surveys, 1972–2010 Cumulative Codebook*. Accessed November 2012 at http://www.ropercenter.uconn.edu/data_access/data/datasets/general_social_survey.html#codebook.

The New York Times. 2012, March 16. "Tyler Clementi." *New York Times*. Accessed March 2012 at http://topics.nytimes.com/top/reference/timestopics/people/c/tyler_clementi/index.html?offset=0&rs=newest.

Nock, Stephen L. and Paul W. Kingston. 1990. *The Sociology of Public Issues*. Belmont, CA: Wadsworth.

Parsons, T., and R. F. Bales. 1955. *Family, Socialization and Interaction Process*. Glencoe, IL: Free Press.

Pipher, M. 1994. *Reviving Ophelia: Saving the Selves of Adolescent Girls*. New York: Random House.

Plummer, Kenneth. 1984. "Sexual Diversity: A Sociological Perspective." Pp. 219–253 in *The Psychology of Social Diversity*. Edited by Kevin Howells. New York: Basil Blackwell.

Pollock, W., and T. Shuster. 2000. *Real Boys' Voices*. New York: Random House.

Pomerleau, Andree, Daniel Bolduc, Gerard Malcuit, and Louise Cossette. 1990. "Pink or Blue: Environmental Gender Stereotypes in the First Two Years of Life." *Behavioral Science* 22(5–6):359–367.

Rampell, Catherine. 2010a, March 9. "The Gender Wage Gap, Around the World." *The New York Times*. Accessed May 2012 at http://economix.blogs.nytimes.com/2010/03/09/the-gender-wage-gap-around-the-world/.

Rampell, Catherine. 2010b, May 9. "For Younger Women, a Smaller Wage Gap." *The New York Times*. Accessed May 2012 at http://economix.blogs.nytimes.com/2010/07/08/for-younger-women-a-smaller-wage-gap/.

Roberts, Sam. 2007, August 3. "For Young Earners in Big City, a Gap in Women's Favor." *The New York Times*. Accessed June 2012 at http://www.nytimes.com/2007/08/03/nyregion/03women.html?pagewanted=all.

Roth, Louise Marie. 2003. "Selling Women Short: A Research Note on Gender Differences in Compensation on Wall Street." *Social Forces* 82(2, Dec.): 783–802.

Sadker, Myra, and David Sadker. 1985. "Sexism in the Schoolroom of the 80s." *Psychology Today* 19(3):54–57.

Sadler, A. G., B. M. Booth, B. L. Cook, and B. N. Doebeling. 2003. "Factors Associated with Women's Risk of Rape in the Military Environment." *American Journal of Industrial Medicine* 43(3): 262–273.

Saxbe, D. E., R. L. Repetti, and A. P. Graesch. 2011. "Time Spent in Housework and Leisure: Links with Parents' Physiological Recovery from Work." *Journal of Family Psychology* 25(2):271–281.

Schemo, Diana J. 2003, August 29. "Rate of Rape at Academy is Put at 12% in Survey." *The New York Times*. Accessed December 2012 at http://www.nytimes.com/2003/08/29/us/rate-of-rape-at-academy-is-put-at-12-in-survey.html.

Signorielli, Nancy. 1989. "Television and Conceptions about Sex Roles: Maintaining Conventionality and the Status Quo." *Sex Roles* 21(5/6):341–360.

Statistical Abstract of the United States. 2006. Table 586. Accessed May 2012 at http://www.census.gov/compendia/statab/.

Statistical Abstract of the United States. 2012. Accessed May 2012 at http://www.census.gov/compendia/statab/.

Suicide Prevention Resource Center. 2008. *Suicide Risk and Prevention for Lesbian, Gay, Bisexual, and Transgender Youth*. Newton, MA: Education Development Center. Accessed April 2012 at http://www.sprc.org/sites/sprc.org/files/library/SPRC_LGBT_Youth.pdf.

Tessier, Marie. 2008, July 25. *Intimate Violence Remains a Big Killer of Women*. Womensenews.org. Accessed April 2012 at http://womensenews.org/story/crime-policy-and-legislation/080725/intimate-violence-remains-big-killer-women.

Thorne, Barrie, and Luria, Zella. 1986. "Sexuality and Gender in Children's Daily Worlds." *Social Problems* 33(3, February):176–190.

Tong, R. 2009. *Feminist Thought: A More Comprehensive Introduction*. Philadelphia: Westview Press.

Tracy, L. 1990. "The Television Image in Children's Lives." *The New York Times*. May 13:M-1, M-5.

Travis, Carol, and Carol Wade. 2001. *Psychology in Perspective*. Third edition. Upper Saddle River, NJ: Prentice Hall.

UN.GIFT (Global Initiative to Fight Human Trafficking). 2007. *Human Trafficking: The Facts*. Accessed May 2012 at http://www.unglobalcompact.org/docs/issues_doc/labour/Forced_labour/HUMAN_TRAFFICKING_-_THE_FACTS_-_final.pdf.

United Nations Development Program (UNDP). 2011. *Human Development Report*, p. 142, Table 4. Accessed March 2012 at http://hdr.undp.org/en/media/HDR_2011_EN_Table4.pdf.

UNODC (United Nations Office on Drugs and Crime). 2009. *Global Report on Trafficking in Persons*. United Nations. Accessed January 2012 at http://www.unodc.org/documents/human-trafficking/Executive_summary_english.pdf.

US Bureau of Justice Statistics (BJS). 2007. *Sexual Victimization in State and Federal Prisons Reported by Inmates, 2007*. Accessed April 2012 at http://bjs.ojp.usdoj.gov/index.cfm?ty=pbdetail&iid=1149.

US Bureau of Justice Statistics (BJS). 2010. *Criminal Victimization, 2009*. Table 1. Accessed October 2010 at http://bjs.ojp.usdoj.gov/content/pub/pdf/cv09.pdf.

US Bureau of Labor Statistics (BLS). 2007. *Changes in Men's and Women's Labor Force Participation Rates*. Accessed May 2012 at http://www.bls.gov/opub/ted/2007/jan/wk2/art03.htm.

US Bureau of Labor Statistics (BLS). 2010. *Highlights of Women's Earnings in 2009*. Report 1025. Accessed May 2012 at http://www.bls.gov/cps/cpswom2009.pdf.

US Bureau of Labor Statistics (BLS). 2012. "Civilian Labor Force Participation Rates by Age, Sex, Race, and Ethnicity." *January 2012 Monthly Labor Review*. Table 3.3. Accessed May 2012 at http://www.bls.gov/emp/ep_table_303.htm.

US Department of Justice (USDOJ). 2008. *Criminal Victimization in the United States, 2006 Statistical Tables*. Table 37. Accessed April 2012 at http://bjs.ojp.usdoj.gov/content/pub/pdf/cvus0602.pdf.

US Equal Employment Opportunity Commission. 2004. *Glass Ceilings: The Status of Women as Officials and Managers in the Private Sector*. Accessed April 2012 at http://www.eeoc.gov/eeoc/statistics/reports/glassceiling/index.html.

US Senate. 2012. *Women in the Senate*. Accessed October 2012 at http://www.senate.gov/artandhistory/history/common/briefing/women_senators.htm.

Vekiri, Ioanna, and Anna Chronaki. 2008. "Gender Issues in Technology Use: Perceived Social Support, Computer Self-efficacy and Value Beliefs, and Computer Use Beyond School." *Computers & Education* 51:1392–1404.

Vogel, Lise. 1983. *Marxism and the Oppression of Women: Toward a Unitary Theory*. New Brunswick, NJ: Rutgers University Press.

Weeks, Jeffrey. 1977. *Coming Out: Homosexual Politics in Britain, from the Nineteenth Century to the Present*. New York: Quartet.

West, Candace, and Don H. Zimmerman. 1983. "Small Insults: A Study of Interruptions in Cross Sex Conversations between Unacquainted Persons." Pp. 86–111 in *Language, Gender and Society*. Edited by Barrie Thorne, Cheris Kramarae, and Nancy Henley. Rowley, MA: Newbury House.

West, Candace and Don H. Zimmerman. 1987. "Doing Gender." *Gender and Society* 1(2 Jun):125–151.

Wood, Wendy, and Alice Eagly. 2002. "A Cross-cultural Analysis of the Behavior of Women and Men: Implications for the Origins of Sex Differences." *Psychological Bulletin* 128(5, Sep):699–727.

World Health Organization (WHO). 2012. *Female Genital Mutilation*. Accessed April 2012 at http://www.who.int/mediacentre/factsheets/fs241/en/.

Chapter Overview ▼

11 Aging and the Elderly

Learning Objectives ▼

11.1
- Illustrate the biological and psychological changes that occur as we age.
- Describe the social constructs of aging.
- Analyze the impact of the aging population from a global perspective.

11.2
- Examine the demographic factors related to the graying of America.
- Discuss the consequences of aging for different genders and minorities.

11.3
- Analyze the different theoretical views of aging and recognize when they are illustrated by specific examples.

11.4
- Illustrate different examples of how people respond to the prospect of death and the implications for quality of life and closure for both the dying and their families.

11.5
- Discuss some of the common misconceptions of the elderly and their impact on the aging demographic.

© iStockphoto/Thinkstock

The restaurant had the same massive oak door that I remembered from when my high school classmates waited tables there 40 years ago. As I reached for the handle, the door was opened by an older couple coming out. She had gray hair and wrinkles but seemed basically in good health. He seemed older. He carried with him the extra weight that so often comes with advanced years. I was about to excuse myself and go looking for the people there for our class reunion when he suddenly recognized me, grabbed me in a bear hug, and started talking about high school as though it had been only yesterday.

Later, inside, I visited with old friends and acquaintances, most of whom I hadn't seen except for occasional reunions once a decade. By this time, we were all so much easier to recognize, wearing buttons with our high school graduation photos on them. Some had done quite well for themselves: the lawyer known for his multimillion-dollar settlements, the military officer working in the Pentagon, and my old friend, John, who teaches at a small college one state over. Many were nearing the end of their working careers and talking about retirement dreams financed with pensions, investments, and savings. Most of this group had aged gracefully, continued to exercise and eat well, and looked surprisingly healthy.

But for others, life had not been so kind. Some had already been forcibly retired as they lost jobs and could not get rehired or faced medical crises that left them with no savings and unable to work. I couldn't help but notice the ravages of age on some who had battled cancer or alcohol or divorce or unemployment. Jack, the older-looking fellow coming out the door earlier, was in the midst of radiation treatments for cancer and looked both grim and determined. Then, of course, there were those who were not there, honored with their high school graduation photos and names posted on a rickety easel near the entrance—Roger, who died in a car accident a few years after high school; Sandy, who died in her 30s of ovarian cancer; and a few others, but surprisingly few given we were now all approaching 60 years of age.

Baby Boomers—that's what they called us in the 1950s and 1960s when we filled public schools and stimulated a commercial boom that followed us as we aged, from diapers to schools to cars to houses and now, it seems, to health care. My 40-year high school reunion provides a microcosm for understanding aging. While I looked in the mirror at myself every day, I didn't notice (or continued to deny) the changes that come with aging. It was only when confronted with others my age and seeing how they looked at me that I remembered just how old I was getting. It is still the same "me" inside here, just like I was 40 years ago, but now I could see how the wrapping on the package had been changing all these years. It is common for people to deny aging, and most of us have negative stereotypes of "old folks." This chapter exposes some of the myths about what it is like to be old, looks at the implications for societies as populations age, and explores how different old age is depending on social class, gender, race, and ethnicity.

11.1 Aging and Becoming Elderly

We can look at aging as a series of questions, such as "What is aging and what does it mean to be old? How is aging shaping societies, and how is aging different in different societies?"

- Illustrate the biological and psychological changes that occur as we age.
- Describe the social constructs of aging.
- Analyze the impact of the aging population from a global perspective.

Biological and Psychological Changes

There are several biological markers of aging that occur gradually in everyone as they age, though the sequence in which they occur and at what age they become evident varies from person to person. These include visible changes such as gray hair, wrinkles, and a general loss of skin tone. There is a general decline in senses including vision, hearing, taste, touch, and smell. Overall strength and fitness decline through reduced cardiovascular efficiency, a loss of muscle mass, and increased body fat. Bones become more brittle after 50, making them more likely to break and to take longer to heal. The older one gets, the more likely one is to suffer from chronic illnesses such as diabetes or arthritis and life-threatening illnesses such as heart disease or cancer. While this sounds like a death sentence, and eventually it leads to death, the process can be slowed measurably by a healthy life style, including good nutrition and exercise (Butler 2010), as well as new medical and assistive technologies. Assistive devices include canes, walkers, hearing aids, eyeglasses, magnifying glasses, and "grabbers" to help elders reach and grip items on high shelves. Gerontologists also often recommend homes with fewer stairs, grab rails, no loose rugs and other hazards that might lead to falls, improved lighting, and other design modifications to make the home environment safer and more accessible for the elderly. Together, assistive devices and universal design changes can help the elderly remain independent, improve their quality of life dramatically, and help them stay in their own homes longer, rather than moving into expensive assisted-living environments or nursing homes. Taking advantage of these options should make it possible for more and more people to spend the majority of their years relatively healthy, with only a brief period of sickness just before death (Fries 1980; Vaupel et al. 1998).

Psychological changes accompanying aging are less obvious and appear to occur later than many biological changes. Cognitive functions such as reasoning, intelligence, and memory do not appear to decline significantly until the late 80s (Atchley 2000; Cohen 2005); however, the speed of recall and analysis slows somewhat. That slowing sometimes may appear to be mental impairment, but usually it is not. The most common form of dementia is **Alzheimer's disease**—an incurable degeneration of the brain leading to a progressive loss of mental capacity. Alzheimer's is relatively rare among people younger than 75 years old, but it may affect up to half of all people over 85 (Kukull and Ganguli 2000).

The US Administration on Aging (Greenberg 2012) reports that in a 2010 survey, more than one-third (37%) of older persons reported some type of disability, such as problems in hearing, seeing, cognition, ambulation, self-care, or independent living. For people over 80, this increased to 56% having a severe disability and 29% needing assistance. In 2000 to 2009, 40% of noninstitutionalized older persons (those not in hospitals or nursing homes) report their health is excellent or very good, compared to 64.7% for people 18 to 64 years old. Most older persons have at least one chronic condition and many have more than one. The most frequently occurring conditions in 2007 to 2009 were diagnosed arthritis (50%), uncontrolled hypertension (34%), all types of heart disease (32%), any cancer (23%), and diabetes (19%; Greenberg 2012).

Assistive devices and universal design can help the elderly remain independent, improve their quality of life, and help them stay in their own homes longer.

© iStockphoto/Thinkstock

Alzheimer's disease
An incurable degeneration of the brain leading to a progressive loss of mental capacity.

The Social Construction of Aging

However, it turns out that biological and psychological changes do not account for what we mean by *aging*. Aging is socially constructed, and several factors affect our definition of what is "old."

To say that aging is socially constructed means that its meaning derives from social processes within each society as people interact and form opinions about when old age starts, how people should be expected to behave when they are old, and the relative value of older versus younger people. If it is socially constructed, we should expect different meanings of old age in different societies and different views depending on one's own age. The latter is not hard to imagine. Probably most of us can remember when we were children thinking someone in his or her early 20s was "old." In the 1960s, a common phrase was "Don't trust anyone over 30," reflecting a generational divide in which people 30 and over were considered not only "old" but also opponents.

Individuals often participate actively in the social construction of their own status in an effort to resist being viewed as "old."

© Noel Hendrickson/Photodisc/Thinkstock

Chronological age The number of years since birth.

Biological age Changes in physical characteristics such as graying hair, wrinkles, declining health, reduced strength, and greater susceptibility to injuries.

Social age Changes in the social and/or economic roles the person can competently perform.

Young old People between 65 and 74 years of age.

Old old People between 75 and 84.

Oldest old People 85 and older.

Old age is socially constructed. Being "old" in the United States can be quite different than being "old" in other societies or other times or other circumstances. Different societies employ different markers of old age, and the age at which one becomes "old" can vary dramatically in different societies. The application of the "old" label to individuals varies for people in the same society having different characteristics or living in different times or circumstances. Individuals often participate actively in the social construction of their own status in an effort to resist being viewed as "old."

Evidence of the social significance of age is found in the nearly universal conception of being "old" (Sokolovsky 2004:218). How that label is constructed varies substantially from one society to the next (Ikels and Beall 2000). Anthropologists Anthony Glascock and Susan Feinman (1981) examined a sample of 60 societies and found three common means of identifying whether someone is "old":

1. **Chronological age**—the number of years since birth

2. **Biological age**—changes in physical characteristics such as graying hair, wrinkles, declining health, reduced strength, and greater susceptibility to injuries

3. **Social age**—changes in the social and/or economic roles the person can competently perform

They found that the most common marker for being designated "old" was social age. This includes changes in roles brought on by changes in their ability to perform economically productive activities, having grandchildren, or beginning to receive more goods and services than they give. Ironically, biological age was the least common marker of being designated "old." They reason that this is because most societies tend to create a category of "old" that occurs before most people undergo strong signs of physical decline. They found that most societies use two or more of these to define "old" and often included graduated phases of oldness marking the loss of normal functioning and approaching death (Glascock and Feinman 1981).

In the United States, the increasing diversity among the elderly leads to a common distinction between three categories of old people. Sociologists often distinguish between the **young old** (people between 65 and 74 years of age), the **old old** (people between 75 and 84) and the **oldest old** (people 85 and older). The young old are most likely to be financially independent, healthy, and active, while the oldest old are most likely to be in poor health, financially stressed, and lonely. These differences are at least in part due to biological and psychological consequences of aging. But they also reflect cohort differences, as the young old and oldest old are 20 years or an entire generation apart. They experienced different economic booms and busts, different healthcare technologies, and different wars, each of which has further differentiated life for people in these different cohorts **TABLE 11-1** (Treas 1995). Many of today's oldest old lived through World War II, for example, when people placed great faith in their government; the young old include the first of the Baby Boom generation of children born just after World War II and who came of age during the Vietnam War and the sexual revolution of the 1960s, when young people were much more liberal socially and less trusting of government politically.

From the perspective of the aging person—at least in the United States and probably in most modern postindustrial societies—being "old" is a part of their identity that they often resist. Sociologist Rebecca Jones (2006) reports a study in which she examined the talk of older people and identified various strategies they use to distance themselves from being old. One commonly cited strategy (Featherstone and Hepworth 1989) is "the mask of ageing." In this example, people often describe the experience of growing older as one in which they continue to see themselves as the same young person they always were, but a mask of an older person appears on their face (Jones 2006:Section 8). The phrase "age is just a number" is another expression often used to convey the notion that age is what you make of it and we should not let age define us but should create our own identities.

TABLE 11-1 Generations in the United States: 1927 to Present

Years of Birth*	Title	Characteristics
1927–1945	Silent Generation or Traditionalists	Children of the Great Depression and World War II; affected by anti-communism, Cold War, Korean War, Vietnam War, 50s conformity; marriage is for life
1946–1964	Baby Boomers	Children of post-World War II era, demographic bulge so big they reshaped society as they aged, giving them a sense of being a special generation; rejected values of earlier generations; influenced by anti-war and civil rights protests, hippies, rock and roll, AIDS; first acceptance of gays
1965–1983	Gen X, Baby Busters	Children of boomers; decline in birth rates, so fewer born; influenced by Reagan, first Gulf War, end of Cold War, personal computers; young adults on 9/11 terrorist attacks; late to marry, quick to divorce, many single parents
1984–2002	Gen Y, Millennials	More racially and ethnically diverse; social networking, texting, smart phones; peer oriented, seeking instant gratification; influenced by Great Recession, rising higher education costs, student loans, parents facing housing crisis; few serve in military; children/teens during 9/11 (Pew Research Center, 2010)
2003+	Gen Z, Digital Natives	Digital technology was always part of their lives, smart phones, social networking; rise of China; post-9/11 childhood, ???

*Precise years vary by different authors.

Source: Adapted from Pew Research Center. 2010. "The Millennials: Confident. Connected. Open to Change." Pew Research Center Publications. Accessed November 2012 (http://pewresearch.org/pubs/1501/millennials-new-survey-generationalpersonality-upbeat-open-new-ideas-technology-bound).

Aging in a Global Perspective

At what age does "old age" begin? A 2011 report by the Nielsen Company reports results of a global survey that provides additional evidence of the social construction of aging. The researchers found that the perception of when old age begins, as measured by chronological age, is older in countries with older median ages and younger in countries with younger median ages.

In the 14 oldest countries surveyed (median age of 42), 70% think old is over the age of 70, with nearly one in three thinking old is over age 80. In the 14 youngest countries surveyed (median age of 27), 27% say being in your 60s is old and an equal percentage believe that 70s is old. Less than 1% in the youngest countries surveyed say you are not old until your 80s (Nielsen Company 2011:3).

The Nielsen survey also found that as an individual's age rises, his perception of when old age begins also rises. Of respondents over 60, nearly half thought old age begins over the age of 80, while for those less than 60, roughly a third say old age begins at 60, a third say it begins at 70, and a third say it begins at 80 (Nielsen Company 2011:3). FIGURE 11-1 shows the percentage of respondents indicating different ages at which old age begins by region of the globe. Notice that in North America, we are more likely to say older ages such as 80 (43%) or 70 (25%), while in the Asia/Pacific countries, only 7% say 80 and 24% say 70. In the Middle East/Africa region, 35% say old age begins before 60 (Nielsen Company 2011:3). Generally, the longer the life expectancy in a country, the later someone is viewed as old.

A Social Contract between Generations

Just as notions of when someone is "old" vary dramatically around the globe, the meaning of being old and the consequences for the old person also vary dramatically across different societies and over time. All societies differentiate people by age—that is, they have an age stratification system. This is natural given different capabilities of children, adults, and the elderly. However, the nature of age stratification varies dramatically from one culture to the next, with extremes ranging from **geronticide**—the killing of the aged—to **gerontocracy**—rule by the aged.

Geronticide The killing of the aged.

Gerontocracy Rule by the aged.

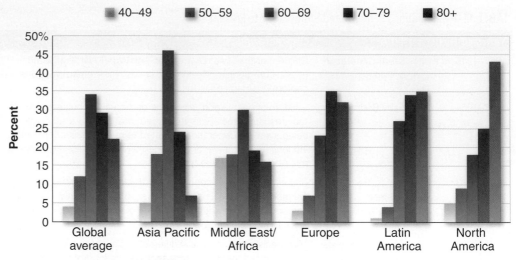

FIGURE 11-1 How old is old in different regions of the world?
Source: Data from The Nielsen Company. 2011. The Global Impact of an Aging World, February 2011. Accessed November 2012 (at.nielsen.com/site/documents/GlobalReportonAging.pdf).

In some societies, elders are revered. In China, for example, the age period after 55 is the one most comfortable and secure. Sweden, a welfare state, also treats the elderly with great respect. In 1987, Sweden had 1,500 home helpers per 100,000 older people in need. In contrast, the United States during that same time had only 66 helpers per 100,000 elderly in need (Szulc 1988:7).

In other societies, the elderly are sometimes seen as unproductive members who drain society's resources when they become frail and require much assistance. Barker (1997) found geronticide or death-hastening acts against the frail aged on Niue Island—an island country in the South Pacific Ocean 1,500 miles northeast of New Zealand. Among the Fulani of Africa, older men and women move to the edge of the homestead and the elderly sleep over their own graves. They are already socially dead long before they actually die. Among the Mardudjara (a hunting and gathering culture in Australia), older members are given food, but they may be left behind to perish when they can no longer keep up (Tonkinson 1978). Traditionally, Eskimos encouraged elders to leave the family home and go off into the cold to die alone.

Vincentnathan and Vincentnathan (1994) studied untouchable communities (untouchables are one of the lowest castes in the Indian caste system) in the South Tamil Nadu area of India. They found that, in the poorest communities, increased education of the young through modernization programs led many children and young adults to feel superior to parents, over time leading to strained generational relations "sometimes involving high levels of abuse and killing of the aged" (Sokolovsky 2004:221). Separate worldwide statistical studies of aging found killing of the aged in one-fifth of societies studied (Glascock 1997) and harsh treatment including death-hastening behavior in 62% of cases (Silverman and Maxwell 1987). Both of those studies found that such "death-hastening" behaviors are generally directed not at intact, fully functioning aged, but at "*decrepit* individuals who find it difficult to carry out even the most basic tasks" (Sokolovsky 2004).

Ethnographic studies by anthropologists suggest that whether the elderly are able to bring more resources and services to society than they take from society is a critical factor—a kind of "social contract" across generations that becomes the standard by which the elderly are treated (Bengtson and Achenbaum 1993). Pamela Amoss and Steven Harrell argue that, in any particular society, the elderly are accorded greater respect and dignity when the contributions they make to the society are greater, and they receive less respect and dignity when the costs they impose on society are great (Amoss and Harrell 1981:6). Several studies examining the Human Relations Area Files (ethnographic reports of studies of hundreds of world cultures) provide evidence that the impact of this net balance of contributions and costs is moderated by the extent to which old people control resources important to the society (Amoss and Harrell 1981:6). When older adults control administration and consultation, they tend to receive beneficent treatment. However, cultures in which the elderly were thought to possess supernatural power such as witchcraft viewed them as a threat and put them to death, as occurred frequently in Europe during the Middle Ages (Bever 1982) and in parts of East Africa in the mid-1990s (Kibuga and Dianga 2000).

Aging in Historical Perspective: Modernization Theory of Aging

Sociologist Donald Cowgill (Cowgill 1986; Cowgill and Holmes 1972) studied aging in different cultures and found dramatic differences in the way the elderly are treated in modern industrial societies and in developing societies. Developing countries generally have rapidly growing young populations with a relatively small percentage of the population that is elderly. Yet there are problems for elderly in those countries. Modernization in the form of urbanization, industrialization, and other long-term trends often undercuts the traditional status and role of the elderly in developing countries. Younger people are able to learn more quickly and hence are better able to adapt to rapid changes those countries are experiencing. This calls into question the traditional leadership role held by the elderly (Cowgill 1986). Urban housing in developing countries is typically too small for extended families. Yet more young family caregivers are moving to cities to find work, while elderly may be left behind in the rural areas without help from their children. This gap in care for the elderly is unlikely to be made up by government social programs such as Social Security, because those programs are rare and typically small in developing countries. Such programs are more frequent in South America but almost nonexistent in Africa, where economies are often weaker.

In industrialized nations, families play a decreasing role in taking care of the elderly.

© Stockbyte/Thinkstock

In industrialized nations, families play a decreasing role in taking care of the elderly, and government programs such as Social Security have taken over some of that role. The role of the family in taking care of the elderly, the role of elderly in society, and relationships among age groups are changing as societies become industrialized. Government social programs such as Social Security are often the primary source of income for older citizens.

From these differences, Cowgill and other sociologists developed a modernization theory of aging. Modernization theory argues the status of the elderly declines in more modern societies because modern industrial societies stress youth and highly skilled occupations requiring ever-increasing amounts of training beyond that given the elderly when they were educated. Industrial, urbanized societies also tend to discourage the extended family that provides support for the elderly in more traditional societies. The transition from agricultural to industrial economies is not always good for the elderly. The traditionally valued role of the elderly tends to change. The lowered status of older people is reflected in prejudice and discrimination against them, age segregation, and unfair job practices.

However, as Sokolovsky (2004) points out, critics have argued that this modernization theory of aging is not historically accurate and idealizes the past (Kertzer and Laslett 1994; Laslett 1976). This creates a "world we lost" syndrome that overlooks the harsh realities of growing old. For much of human history, people's lives were plagued by "continual fear and danger of violent death" and lives were "nasty, brutish, and short" (Hobbes, 1651 [Revised 2010], XIII. 9). In many cultures, "the treatment of the old was harsh and decidedly pragmatic: dislike and suspicion, it is said, characterized the attitudes of both sides" (Plakans 1989). So, while this theory may work well describing some cultures where the elderly are highly respected, it should not be assumed to describe every culture.

The Increased Global Significance of Aging

While the modernization theory claim that the status of the elderly is declining with modernization may be suspect, the demographics of modernization are clear. Around the world, country after country is undergoing rapid development, with corresponding increases in population and improvements in life expectancy. As a result, the populations in most countries are becoming older on average. This effect can be seen by comparing more developed regions (e.g., North America, Europe, Japan, Australia, and New Zealand), least developed regions (sub-Saharan Africa), and less developed regions (all other countries; *National Atlas of the United States* 2011). While this effect has been stronger in developed regions, the percentage of populations 60 and older is increasing dramatically throughout the world. This is illustrated in FIGURE 11-2, in which in even the less developed regions of the world, by 2050, projections are that 12% of the total population will be 60 years or older. In the more developed regions, this number shoots up to 33%. The consequences of these changes in age distribution become clearer from the last column in that same table, where we can see that the support ratio (the number of persons aged 15–64 years old per person aged 65 years or older) decreases from 5 to 2 in more developed regions and from 18 to 8 in least developed regions between 1999 and 2050. This highlights the increased burden on economies that will come from the aging of populations. By 2050, in more developed regions, there will be two people working for each retiree; in less developed regions, it will be four working per retiree; and in least developed regions, it will be eight workers per retiree. This will tax the economic resources of many of these economies and may exacerbate intergenerational conflicts over resources. As these populations age around the globe, the issue of how societies cope with the burdens of aging populations becomes increasingly important.

In FIGURE 11-3, the percentage of the population of each country 65 and older is mapped. Countries with the highest percentage of elderly are darker blue. This is one of the unusual cases in which more developed countries face a bigger problem than developing countries. It is the more developed regions of the world, such as North America, Europe, Australia, and Russia, that have the oldest populations and in which the increased economic burden of supporting the elderly will be most severe.

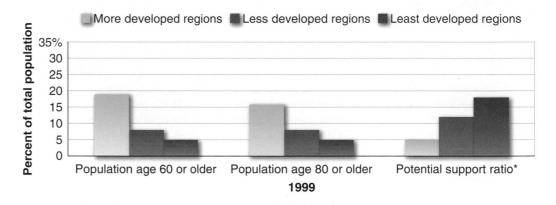

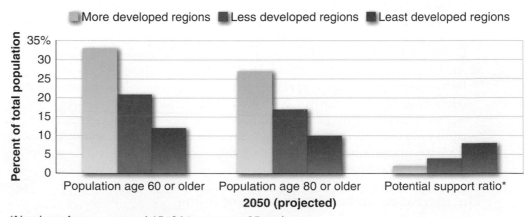

*Number of persons aged 15–64 to persons 65 and over.

FIGURE 11-2 Elderly as percentage of population and support ratio (1999–2050 global regions).
Source: Data from United Nations. 1999. Population Aging, 1999. United Nations, Population Division, Sales No. E.99.XIII.11.

FIGURE 11-3 Elderly percentage of population by country.
Source: IndexMundi. 2012. Population ages 65 and above (% of total). Data from the United Nations Population Division's World Population Prospects, Accessed January 2012 (http://www.indexmundi.com/facts/indicators/SP.POP.65UP.TO.ZS).

CONCEPT LEARNING CHECK 11.1   Aging and Becoming Elderly

Which of the following statements is true and which is false?

_____ **1.** The elderly are treated more favorably by their society if they are seen as controlling magical or supernatural powers.

_____ **2.** The social contract between generations implies there should be some generational equity in the distribution of resources.

_____ **3.** People over 65 are remarkably similar to one another, and age tends to reduce any remaining differences based on race, gender, or social class.

_____ **4.** The problem of aging populations, like most other problems globally, occurred first and is greater for developing nations with low average incomes.

_____ **5.** In many cases, someone viewed as chronologically old in developing countries such as in Asia or Africa may still be viewed as young or middle aged chronologically in the United States.

11.2 The Graying of America

The US population is growing older, and people in old age are living longer, both of which have different consequences for men, women, and minorities.

- Examine the demographic factors related to the graying of America.

- Discuss the consequences of aging for different genders and minorities.

Since 1900, the average age of the population of the United States has been increasing. The percentage of people age 65 and older is plotted in FIGURE 11-4, beginning in 1900 and projected through 2050. In 1900, people 65 and older made up 4% of our population. By 1970, they constituted 10%. That percentage continued to increase until around 1990, when it leveled off until near 2010. This period reflected the low birth rates during the Great Depression and World War II. Then, beginning in 2010, the Baby Boomers born in the period after World War II begin to turn 65, raising the percentage dramatically to 20% by 2040, then leveling off at that level. This is clearly going to have dramatic repercussions as more elderly retire, changing their life styles and consumption patterns, including the use of greater medical care.

The Increased Average Age of the Population

The dramatic increase in the proportion of the population 65 and over in the United States is impressive enough. But it is only part of the story. To understand the complete picture, we must also examine the changing mix of the elderly and the demographic factors that are driving this change. It turns out the aged are aging. "Old folks" are getting even older!

To understand how the elderly are themselves becoming older, in FIGURE 11-5 is plotted the number of elderly broken down by whether they are the young old (65–74), the old old (75–84), or the oldest old (85+). It is the latter category of people that is likely to have the greatest disabilities and the greatest need for special care and medical services. It is clear from this graph that the proportion of the elderly who are in the oldest two categories increases dramatically as Baby Boomers move out of the old category into the old old and the oldest old categories. By 2040, people 75 and older will be more than half of the elderly. To put this in perspective, in 1950, there were well over twice as many people between 65 and 75 as those 75 and older. By roughly 2035, there will be as many people 75 and older as there are 65 to 75. This is why the US government is struggling to finance programs like Social Security and Medicare.

Why is the proportion of old people in the population increasing, and why are they older than in the past? These two questions can be answered by examining the effects of two demographic factors: increased life expectancy and changes in birth rates.

Life Expectancy

The first demographic factor leading to the increased average age of the population is the obvious cause: increased life expectancies. Throughout the 20th century and first part of the 21st century, there have been dramatic increases in **life expectancy**—the average number of years people are expected to live. Those increases have been greatest

Life expectancy The average number of years people are expected to live.

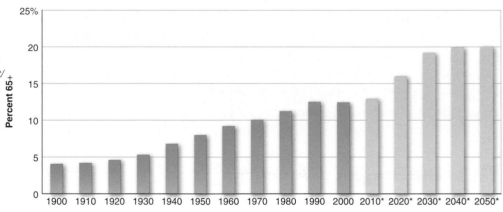

FIGURE 11-4 Percentage of US population 65 and older (1900–2050). *Source: Data from US Administration on Aging (AOA). 2012. Projected Future Growth of the Older Population. Accessed October 2012 (http://www.aoa.gov/aoaroot/aging_statistics/future_growth/future_growth.aspx#age).*

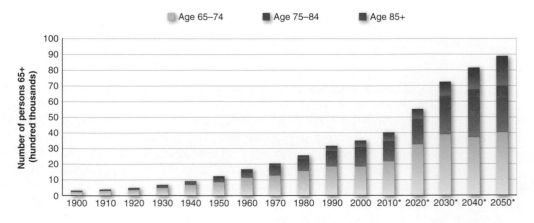

FIGURE 11-5 Number of US elderly in young old, old old, and oldest old categories (1900–2050). *Source: Data from Hobbs, Frank and Nicole Stoops. 2002. U.S. Census Bureau, Census 2000 Special Reports, Series CENSR-4, Demographic Trends in the 20th Century. Washington, DC: U.S. Government Printing Office. Accessed November 2012 (www.census.gov/prod/2002pubs/censr-4.pdf); Vincent, Grayson K. and Victoria A. Velkoff. 2010. U.S. Census Bureau: The Next Four Decades The Older Population in the United States: 2010 to 2050. Washington, DC: U.S. Department of Commerce Economics and Statistics.Administration. Accessed November 2012 (http://www.census.gov/prod/2010pubs/p25-1138.pdf).*

in industrialized countries like the United States, where the life expectancy rose from 40 years in 1900 to 78.1 years by 2008. Of course, there are still differences in life expectancy by gender, race, and ethnicity, with higher expectancies for females (75.6 for males, 80.6 for females), lower life expectancies for blacks (74.0 for blacks compared to 78.5 for whites), but higher life expectancies for Hispanics (81.0 for Hispanics and 78.4 for non–Hispanic whites and 73.7 for non–Hispanic blacks; Arias 2012:1). Even when someone lives to be 65, his life expectancy at that point is still 18.8 years (17.3 for males and 20.0 for females). That means that nearly half of the people who are 65 today will live to be in the 85-and-older category of the oldest old in the next 20 years.

Birth Rates

The second demographic factor leading to increased average age of the population is less obvious: variable birth rates. It was birth rates 65 years ago that led to people turning 65 this year. The same is true for each year of age. Since birth rates increased dramatically during the Baby Boom years, this has led to a bulge of people working its way through the system as they age. Those Baby Boomers are just starting to turn 65 now, and the increased numbers of people 65 years old will continue for the next decade or two. This means that there are disproportionately more people turning 65 during this time. At the same time, birth rates after the Baby Boom dropped significantly, so the relative size of those younger cohorts of people is smaller. Together, these changing birth rates lead to this increased proportion of the population becoming elderly.

Baby Boomers are just starting to turn 65 now, and increased numbers of people 65 and older will continue for the next decade or two.
© Comstock/Thinkstock

Who Are the Aged? Race, Ethnicity, Class, and Gender

In 2010, there were 23 million women and 17.5 million men 65 and older in the United States. This is a sex ratio of 132 women for every 100 men. Because women have a longer life expectancy, the sex ratio of women to men increases with age, as men die sooner than women. For 65- to 69-year-olds, the sex ratio is 112. But for people 85 and older, the sex ratio is 206 (Greenberg 2012:2; see FIGURE 11-6). Women are much more likely to outlive their husbands and to live alone than are men (see FIGURE 11-7). Most men 65 and older are married (72%), with 13% widowed, 12% divorced or separated, and 4% never married. Women 65 and over are almost as likely to be widowed (40%) as married (42%), with 13% divorced or separated and 5% never married (Greenberg 2012:4).

Minority populations tend to be younger (i.e., more children and fewer older adults) than non–Hispanic whites, with only 7.2% of minorities 65 and over in 2010, compared to 16.5% of non–Hispanic whites. Only one in five people 65 and over were minorities FIGURE 11-8, with 8.4% African-Americans, 6.9% Hispanics, 3.5% Asian or Pacific Islanders, and less than 1% American Indian or Native Alaskan (Greenberg 2012:6).

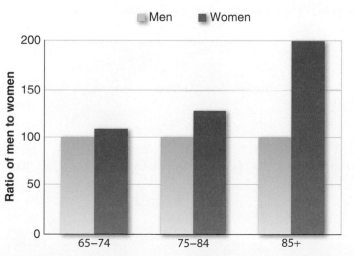

FIGURE 11-6 US sex ratio by age group among the elderly.
Source: Data from U.S. Department of Health and Human Services. 2011. A Profile of Older Americans: 2011. Accessed January 2012 (http://www.aoa.gov/aoaroot/aging_statistics/Profile/2011/docs/2011profile.pdf).

FIGURE 11-7 Marital status by gender for people 65 and older in the United States.
Source: U.S. Department of Health and Human Services. 2011. A Profile of Older Americans: 2011. Accessed January 2012 (http://www.aoa.gov/ aoaroot/aging_statistics/Profile/2011/ docs/2011profile.pdf).

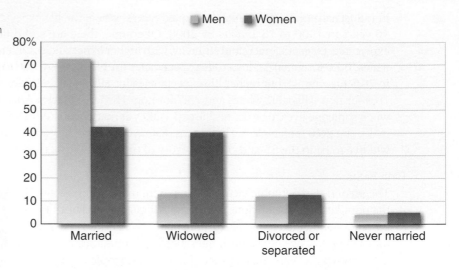

FIGURE 11-8 Elderly minorities in the United States.
Source: Data from U.S. Department of Health and Human Services. 2011. A Profile of Older Americans: 2011. Accessed January 2012 (http://www. aoa.gov/aoaroot/aging_statistics/ Profile/2011/docs/2011profile.pdf).

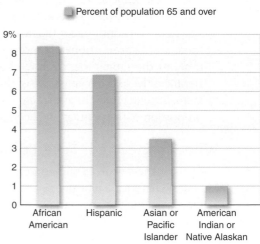

Only 4.1% of people over 65 in 2009 lived in institutional settings such as nursing homes—a percentage that increases to 13.2% for people 85 and older. Of noninstitutionalized elderly, 55.1% lived with their spouse in 2010 (69.9% of men and 41.3% of women), while about 29.3% (37.3% of older women and 19.1% of older men) lived alone (Greenberg 2012:5).

CONCEPT LEARNING CHECK 11.2   The Graying of America

1. You just heard that the apartment next to you has been rented by someone 65 or older. Is this person more likely or less likely to be:

   A. male?

   B. a minority?

2. How would this change if you knew the new renter was 85 or older? Compared to people between 65 and 85, is this person more likely or less likely to be:

   A. male?

   B. healthy and able to live on his or her own?

3. If you find out that this person is a woman, then, when compared to males of that age, does that make it more or less likely that she is:

   A. living with her spouse?

   B. living alone?

11.3 Sociological Perspectives in Aging

There are several theoretical views of aging within sociology. These include theories within the tradition of structural-functionalism, symbolic interactionism, and conflict theory, as well as a life course perspective.

■ Analyze the different theoretical views of aging and recognize when they are illustrated by specific examples.

Structural-Functional Theory

Structural-functional theory, which was popular in sociology during the 1950s and 1960s in the United States, looks at aging in terms of its consequences for society. It generally assumes that as people age, they will have declining health and declining ability to perform the roles they had played throughout their life and will require changes to accommodate those changed abilities (Hendricks 1992). In this perspective, Talcott Parsons (1960), one of the most respected proponents of structural-functional theory, argued US society places too much emphasis on youth and needs to find new roles for the elderly as they age to take advantage of their wisdom and maturity. This theory pays some attention to the consequences for the aging individual. Both society and the aging individual would be better served by understanding how to accommodate changing roles to reflect changing capabilities. However, structural-functional theory emphasizes the consequences for society as a whole. The structural-functional approach applied to aging emphasizes how the roles of individuals may change as they age to accommodate their changing needs and abilities in disengagement theory.

Talcott Parsons argued that US society needs to find new roles for the elderly to take advantage of their wisdom and maturity.

© iStockphoto/Thinkstock

Disengagement Theory

Disengagement theory takes the view that society benefits when, as people age, they are eased out of positions of responsibility (Cumming and Henry 1961). This has positive functions both for society and for the aging individual. Society benefits because positions of responsibility continue to be performed competently and there is a smooth transition as the elderly pass on their job skills and knowledge to younger workers. There is no disruption such as would occur if people continued in important positions right up until they died, and then the important job was performed badly until someone new was trained. Younger workers benefit from the positions made available as the elderly retire. The retiring individuals benefit because they no longer experience the pressure of performing an increasingly difficult job and are free to pursue leisurely activities of their own choosing (Palmore 1979). In this perspective, the aging individual withdraws as his or her capacities diminish. Society withdraws, too, by segregating the elderly residentially (into retirement homes and communities), educationally (through programs for senior citizens), and recreationally (by establishing senior centers). This theory is consistent with a functional interpretation in which the stability of society is ensured when the aged pass their social roles from one generation to another in preparation for their own deaths. This theory has implications for social policy, suggesting we should help the elderly withdraw gracefully.

Many sociologists object to the notion that older people want to be ignored and "put away" and should be encouraged to withdraw. Critics of this view argue this is painful to the elder and often involuntary. Empirical studies fail to support disengagement theory. Instead, results suggest elders are as likely to increase some activities as to decrease them. In addition, there are considerable differences in how fast and how much elders withdraw. For example, sociologist Don Cowgill, who was internationally respected for his comparison of aging in developing and developed societies, only retired when he was 70, still kept active in his sociology department office, and was active in the discipline until he died unexpectedly from a heart attack after jogging. Some people are unable to disengage even if they wished to do so because they need to keep working due to financial pressures. For these reasons, most sociologists do not regard disengagement theory as a valid explanation of aging (Riley 1987).

Symbolic Interactionism

Unlike the structural-functional theory that emphasizes the consequences for society, symbolic interactionism focuses on the individual and encourages viewing the benefits for individuals that they can derive from remaining active.

Activity Theory

Activity theory argues the elderly person who remains active will be best adjusted. This perspective argues that people construct their social identities from the statuses and roles they occupy and find meaning and satisfaction from those. This view argues that elderly people may not have the same capabilities but may have the same need for social interaction as middle-aged people. Hence, they tend to replace earlier activities with new pursuits. Instead of withdrawing, elderly should maintain activities of middle age and "full membership in the social world" (Havighurst 1961). Where disengagement theory stresses the benefits to society from an orderly transition as the elderly are replaced with younger, more competent workers, activity theory emphasizes the aging individual and what benefits him or her.

Empirical research generally supports activity theory and fails to confirm disengagement theory. This research has suggested greater involvement and social support helps reduce mortality rates among the elderly. For example, sociologist Richard Hessler and his colleagues (1990) report results of a 25-year prospective study of elderly in small towns. They found that the biggest factor affecting mortality was social supports and that the elderly tended to deteriorate more rapidly when they withdrew from activities and supports.

The arguments of activity theorists have been further strengthened by significant improvement in the overall health of the elderly. Generally, someone who is 60 today is healthier than someone who was 60 years old 10 years ago. As elderly maintain good health later in life, they are better able to remain active. Many proponents of activity theory believe the elderly would find more value in their activities when they are valued by society—that is, if society valued them enough to pay for their labor (Dowd 1980:6–7; Quadagno 1987). However, US society does little to encourage continued involvement and activity by the elderly. Forced retirements and a reluctance to hire older workers have led many elderly to seek unpaid volunteer work in order to stay active, while others continue to participate in the paid workforce because they have to financially (Pew Research Center 2006).

While much research supports activity theory as described above, this is not always the case. In one study of retired people in France, some respondents were found to be more happy when they were very active, while others were more happy when they were less involved (Keith 1982). Nor is it always clear what kinds of activities are best for the elderly. In a study by Beck and Page (1988) of 2,000 retired American men, solitary activities such as performing home repairs had about the same impact on life satisfaction as more intimate activities.

Continuity Theory

Continuity theory is a modification of activity theory that incorporates the normal life course. Activity theory in its most extreme form implies there are no changes and a person remains active throughout life. In contrast, continuity theory recognizes aging can be a time of great change but points to continuity as well (Atchley 1989, 1999; House et al. 2005). According to continuity theory, individuals do not change so much when they age as they adapt in ways that preserve continuity over their lifetimes (Atchley 1999). Even when subjected to considerable changes in health or social circumstances as they age, continuity theory points out there tend to be consistent patterns of thought, habits, and activities for the individual. They are still who they are, and that sameness is

Proponents of activity theory believe the elderly would find more value in their activities when they are valued by society—that is, if they are paid for their labor.

© iStockphoto/Thinkstock

the basis for their continuity. This theory does not argue that continuity is essential for successful aging, and it recognizes that some changes will occur along with elements of continuity (Atchley 1999). For example, someone who loves baseball as a child may continue to love baseball throughout his life, even when he can no longer play baseball in middle age, and even when he can no longer even go to the games when he becomes old and frail. That individual may experience changes in physical health and social relationships but still maintain that continuity. While they may abandon roles they can no longer fulfill, the elderly continue with roles that benefit society, including their roles as parents and grandparents, as well as volunteers helping provide social services.

Critics of continuity theory sometimes argue that it leaves out older adults who may not experience normal aging due, for example, to chronic illness, and that it has developed a notion of normal aging based on males (Quadagno 2007).

Conflict Theory

Conflict theorists criticize both disengagement theory and activity theory, asking why social interaction must change with age and arguing both disengagement and activity theory fail to consider the impact of social structure on patterns of aging. Conflict theory focuses on the disadvantaged elderly and political and social structures that foster their dependence. It asks what role social class, gender, race, ethnicity, and other inequalities have in lives of the elderly. Aging can be much more difficult for working-class people and minorities than it is for the affluent or whites. Working-class people and minorities are exposed to more health risks, hazards, and job-related injuries. These disadvantaged people also have greater dependence on Social Security and private pensions. Among the elderly, it is the women, racial and ethnic minorities, and low-income people who are more economically distressed (Atchley 2000; Hendricks 1992). Fixed incomes of the elderly often do not keep up with inflation. None of these issues are satisfactorily addressed by either disengagement or activity theory.

Conflict theorists argue old age is socially constructed to support the needs of the economy at the expense of the elderly (Estes 1979). They argue that "older people came to be viewed as a burden on western economies, with demographic change . . . seen as creating intolerable pressures on public expenditure" (Phillipson 1998:17). In both the UK (Phillipson 1982) and the United States (Estes, Swan, and Gerard 1982), the state decides who is allocated resources and who is not. The elderly retirement experience is affected by macro-level economic changes that can force withdrawal from work while also threatening reductions in retirement benefits (Powell 2001). In the United States, for example, the retirement age for Social Security has increased to 66 and is scheduled to increase again.

Generational Equity?

Conflict theory encourages us to examine sources of conflict. One of those sources is intergenerational conflict. **Generational equity** is the concept of a balance in costs and benefits going to each generation (Quadagno 1989). If the elderly seek too large a portion of society's resources, they can be seen as "greedy geezers," while if they are denied too much of those resources, they can be viewed as "forsaken elders." Somewhere between those two extremes lies generational equity. This revisits the same issue discussed earlier as the social contract between generations. In the United States, this takes form as conflicts over entitlement programs.

The most obvious potential sources of inequity today are entitlement programs that benefit the elderly, including Social Security and Medicare. The Social Security Act, providing monthly benefits for retirees who had paid into the system during their working years, was passed in 1935. Medicare legislation, guaranteeing access to health insurance for Americans 65 and older and young people with disabilities, became law in 1965. While these programs reduce poverty among the elderly, an argument can be made that those resources might be needed more elsewhere and people paying to support Social Security are sometimes poorer than those receiving retirement benefits

Generational equity The concept of a balance in costs and benefits going to each generation.

(DeNavas-Walt et al. 2010). For example, there are nearly four times as many children under 18 in poverty as there are people over 65 in poverty. Since 1959, poverty rates for the elderly have dropped from over 30% to less than 9%. During the same period, poverty rates for children have generally been around 7 to 8% higher than those for the elderly and were over 20% in 2009 (DeNavas-Walt et al. 2010).

The most pressing problem with these programs is their continued financing in the face of a number of factors that lead to increased costs, including an increased percentage of the population eligible for benefits, rising healthcare costs, and increased life expectancies (Social Security and Medicare Boards of Trustees 2012). Beginning in 2011, the oldest members of the Baby Boom generation began retiring and, for every day over the next 19 years, 10,000 baby boomers will reach 65 (Pew Research Center 2012). In the 1940s, shortly after Social Security became available, only 54% of males and 61% of females survived from age 21 to age 65. By 1990, that increased to 72% of males and 84% of females surviving to age 65, while life expectancies increased about 3 years for men and almost 5 years for women. So the burden of benefit payments for Social Security is much greater today (Social Security Online 2012). Already in 2011, Social Security accounted for 20% of the federal budget, while Medicare accounted for roughly 14% (Center on Budget and Policy Priorities 2012). Each year, benefits paid out by Social Security and Medicare are paid from revenues in withholding and interest, with deficits reducing the trust fund reserves. By 2033, the Social Security trust fund is projected to be exhausted, requiring either additional funding or reduced benefits or both (Social Security and Medicare Boards of Trustees 2012).

Age dependency ratio for the elderly The ratio of people 65 and older to the working-age population.

A commonly used measure of the relative costs of the elderly is the **age dependency ratio for the elderly**—the ratio of people 65 and older to the working-age population. The financial base for Social Security in the United States is threatened by the increasing proportion of our population that is elderly. In 1937, there were 12 workers for each retiree. In 2011, it was less than five workers per retiree. By 2030, it is projected there will be fewer than three workers for each retiree (Shrestha 2006). This has already led Social Security taxes for working men and women to be raised substantially and is likely to require additional raises or reduced benefits for retirees.

Younger Americans are concerned about paying Social Security taxes, fearing they will not receive full benefits themselves. However, there is some evidence that inter-generational conflict over scarce resources may not be the best explanation of public opinion regarding Social Security. Street and Cossman (2006) report poll data in which younger Americans support increased spending on Social Security more than older adults, while older adults have higher support for education. Those results suggest each generation is concerned with the needs of the other generations and society as a whole, not just its own self-interests.

We do not want to overreact to these statistics. The money spent providing Social Security benefits to the elderly was not directly taken out of the pockets of children any more than was money spent on defense or other federal expenditures. The fact that the United States has not done much to address the increasing poverty among children is due to many factors, not just our expenditures to help the elderly. We also need to keep in mind that there are other intergenerational transfers of wealth, and many of those benefit younger age groups more than they do the elderly. Yes, the elderly are the beneficiaries of most federal spending for social entitlement pro-grams, primarily Social Security. However, the elderly are also the *sources* of many other intergenerational transfers of wealth, including inheritances and gifting to younger generations. In the middle and upper classes, elderly primarily give to their children. In working classes, children primarily give to their parents (Atchley 1985). Middle-aged people are often descried as the "sandwich generation," caught between generations, sometimes simultaneously providing support to an older generation of aging parents and a younger generation of children with college expenses and in need of assistance to help purchase their first homes and meet the expenses of having grandchildren.

Life Course Perspectives

Another view of aging views people as actors or agents who shape their lives through their own actions and the objects of broader-level structural factors in society that provide them with both opportunities and challenges. An individual, for example, may make a decision to go to college that transforms her life. Yet an economic recession while she is in college might force her to drop out. This view recognizes that as people age throughout their lives, advantages or disadvantages they began life with tend to accumulate. This leads to increasing diversity among the elderly as they age, with some elderly relatively well off and able to have fulfilling retirements, while others struggle to survive from day to day. In effect, social structures (as discussed in Chapters 1 and 4) evolve that constrain their lives.

The argument made by life course perspectives can be understood by examining age cohorts. An **age cohort** consists of people born within the same time frame who experience different ages as they age together. Age cohorts help us understand social life because they call attention to the intersection of biography and history that is a key element of the sociological imagination. For example, people born in 1950 would be an age cohort. They grew to adulthood with the Vietnam War raging through their teen and early adult years. They were 30 when Ronald Reagan was elected President, 42 when the Berlin Wall was torn down, 51 when the 9/11 terrorist attacks occurred, and 58 in 2008 when the Great Recession began. In contrast, people born in 1990 never experienced the Berlin Wall, much less the Vietnam War, were only 11 years old when the 9/11 terrorist attacks occurred, were just entering college as the Great Recession of 2008 began, are much more likely to incur large college loans before graduation than their parents, and were first able to vote for Barak Obama or John McCain in the 2008 election. For example, a male born in the 1950 cohort of parents who were not affluent was likely to have been drafted and served in the Vietnam War, perhaps leading to injury and a lifetime of near poverty; someone in the same cohort born of affluent parents might have gone to college and been deferred from the draft, eventually having a life of affluence. In contrast to both of these, someone born in 1990 would not have been exposed to the military draft at all, since it was inactivated years earlier.

This view makes it clear that quality of life for the elderly is influenced by all the things that happen to those people throughout their lives. If they began life as the son or daughter of well-off parents, they have an initial advantage that tends to persist over time. The challenges and opportunities they face in life can be better understood by understanding the times in which they were living as reflected in their age cohort. In general, initial advantages or disadvantages tend to accumulate over time so that inequalities early in life lead to greater inequalities later on and can lead to enormous inequalities by old age (O'Rand 1996).

Some elderly are relatively well off and able to have fulfilling retirements, while others struggle to survive from day to day.

© iStockphoto/Thinkstock

> **Age cohort** People born within the same time frame who experience different ages as they age together.

THE SOCIOLOGICAL IMAGINATION   Forcibly Retired During the Great Recession

In the summer of 2007, Maria's future life looked promising. Although widowed at an early age, she had been working at an auto parts supplier for a nearby auto plant producing Saturn cars as a machinist for the past 20 years and had built up what, for her, would be an adequate pension to help in her retirement. She never thought she would be able to afford to buy a house given her low income and marginal credit rating. But five years earlier, she had received a loan to purchase a modest house with payments small enough that she could continue to afford them once retired. At 60, she was looking forward to retiring as soon as she could. However, the Social Security retirement age had been raised to 66 so she would have to work one more year than she had hoped.

But by the summer of 2009, Maria's dream had been crushed. During the fall of 2008, the mortgage crisis hit, and "for sale" signs were sprouting from every third yard on her street. When financial markets began to fall apart, the Saturn plant closed and her employer went out of business. She lost both her job and any hope of ever getting the pension they had promised. Because she was already over 60, no one seemed to want to hire her, and her unemployment benefits were about to run out. To add insult to injury, people she worked with who had already retired and were already drawing their company pension as well as Social Security benefits were unaffected. Unable to pay her house payments, she tried unsuccessfully to sell her house for 25% less than she had paid for it.

(Continues)

THE SOCIOLOGICAL IMAGINATION *(Continued)*

EVALUATE

The sociological imagination helps us understand the intersection between history and biography and the link between private troubles (or successes) and public issues (Mills 1959). The life course perspective helps highlight the intersection of history and biography in Maria's life.

1. We tend to look at how individuals like Maria are affected by broad public issues and historical events. But individuals, through their own actions added to those of millions of other people making similar decisions, also contribute to those public issues and historical events. For decades, buying a house was a safe investment. What made the housing market collapse and to what extent did Maria contribute to that collapse?

2. Clearly Maria was hurt by the financial crisis, and that historical downturn came at a time in her life when she was vulnerable to its effects. How would it have affected her differently if she had been 67 when it happened? How do you think it affected her grandson, who was 18 in 2007 and just entering college?

3. Maria's private troubles (her loss of job and pension and the loss of value of her house) clearly reflect public issues. What could Maria have done at earlier stages in her life to set herself on a different path that might have helped her avoid those impacts? Is there anything she could have done?

CONCEPT LEARNING CHECK 11.3   Sociological Perspectives in Aging

Match each of these statements with one of the four theoretical perspectives most consistent with the statement.

_____ **1.** Well over two-thirds of men over 65 live with their spouse, while only 42% of women over 65 do so, and women who live alone are much more likely to live below the poverty line.

_____ **2.** Many people, when they retire, devote more time to travel or hobbies or grandkids to help fill their time.

_____ **3.** David never liked school, so immediately upon graduating from high school, he enlisted in the Army, where he served two tours of duty in Afghanistan. Unfortunately, on his second tour, he was wounded and lost his left leg below his knee. He was fitted with a prosthetic and recovered well, but now he faces a lifetime in which he has to work around this disability.

_____ **4.** Most people retire at or shortly after 65.

A. Disengagement theory

B. Activity theory

C. Conflict theory

D. Life course perspectives

11.4 Death and Dying

Reactions to death range from fierce rejection to preparation and acceptance.

- Illustrate different examples of how people respond to the prospect of death and the implications for quality of life and closure for both the dying and their families.

"I prefer old age to the alternative."

—Maurice Chevalier, 1962, at the age of 74

One of the constants that all people must face at some point in their life is death. Responses to death range the full gamut. At one extreme is acceptance of the inevitability of death as reflected in the lines from the Book of Ecclesiastes in the Bible:

To every thing there is a season,
And a time for every matter under heaven:
A time to be born and a time to die. . .

At the other extreme is a fierce resistance to death, as reflected in the poem "Do Not Go Gentle into that Good Night" by Dylan Thomas:

> Do not go gentle into that good night,
> Old age should burn and rave at close of day;
> Rage, rage against the dying of the light. . . .

These extremes can be seen in how people face death. At one extreme there are people such as Michigan Dr. Jack Kevorkian, who, until his own death in 2011, became controversial for championing a patient's right to die by physician-assisted suicide and who claimed to have assisted in the deaths of more than 100 patients himself (Schneider 2011). At the other extreme are people like computer scientist Ray Kurzweil, who argues that by 2045, the world will experience the **singularity**—the point in time at which computer intelligence will equal human intelligence. Eventually, humans will be able to become immortal, extending their lives forever by scanning our consciousness into computers and living on inside them as software forever (Grossman 2011). No less intriguing are those who advocate using cryonics—the use of very low temperatures to preserve humans considered dead by current legal definitions who might eventually be resuscitated with more advanced technologies (Perlin 2007).

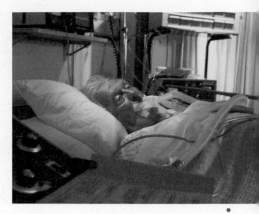

Most deaths in developed societies today take place in the hospital, and most of those deaths are among the elderly.

© Ken Tannenbaum/Shutterstock, Inc.

Less extreme versions of these two approaches to death can be found in common medical practice. But first, let us put this in context. Most deaths in developed societies today take place in the hospital, and most of those deaths are among the elderly. In fact, for most people alive today in the United States, there is a good likelihood that they will live most of their lives relatively healthy, able to function much as they could when they were younger adults, and independent—except for a few months at the end of their lives, when their health deteriorates rapidly and they die. One consequence of this is that, as the author of one study of healthcare costs at the end of life reports, "We end up spending about a third of our overall healthcare resources in the last year of life" (Bergman, cited in Harding 2010). So a large portion of our healthcare costs is spent with little long-term benefit to the patient, often prolonging death at the cost of considerable agony and discomfort rather than extending a high quality life.

The problem is, of course, that often we do not know when someone is in the last stage of life or when he or she is merely experiencing an acute health crisis which, if resolved, may leave the person with years of happy productive life. Even worse, when the patient is severely ill, the patient is often unable to make such important life-or-death decisions. What most often happens, even with patients who are gravely ill and expected to die soon, is a resisting-death strategy. When the patient's heart stops or he stops breathing, a **code blue**—a hospital emergency code indicating a patient is in need of resuscitation—is initiated and medical staff rush to the patient and attempt to revive him. If a patient is in pain and near death anyway, he may prefer that such heroic measures not be taken so he can die with dignity.

To help ensure that patients have greater control over their own health care when they are near death, in 1991, the US Congress passed the Patient Self-Determination Act (PSDA), requiring most healthcare facilities to inform adult patients about their rights to execute an advanced directive (Jones et al. 2011). An **advance directive (AD)** is a statement by an individual communicating preferences for his or her own health care under possible future circumstances that might make it impossible for the patient to make those decisions. The objective is to ensure that the patient's wishes about her end-of-life care are honored. This represents the accepting-death approach. The most common advance directives are living wills and do-not-resuscitate orders. A **living will** is a written document in which a patient expresses his or her wishes regarding starting or discontinuing use of life support procedures in the event of a life-threatening illness or injury. A **no-code order**, also called a **do not resuscitate (DNR) order**, is a written order from a doctor directing that resuscitation not be attempted if the patient goes into cardiac or respiratory arrest. These orders provide a mechanism for patients to exert

Singularity The point in time at which computer intelligence will equal human intelligence.

Code blue A hospital emergency code indicating a patient is in need of resuscitation.

Advance directive (AD) A statement by an individual communicating preferences for his or her own health care under possible future circumstances that might make it impossible for the patient to make those decisions.

Living will A written document in which a patient expresses his or her wishes regarding use of life support measures in the event of a life-threatening illness or injury.

No code order; do not resuscitate (DNR) order A written order from a doctor directing that resuscitation not be attempted if the patient goes into cardiac or respiratory arrest.

An advance directive allows a patient's wishes about her or his end-of-life care to be recorded.

© iStockphoto/Thinkstock

some control over their health care and give healthcare providers the opportunity to find a balance between raging against death and acceptance that suits the individual patient. Such orders are normally initiated only for patients who are gravely ill and expected to die soon based on the living will of the patient. The latest study of nursing homes (2004) and home and hospice care (2007) found that 28% of home healthcare patients, 65% of nursing home residents, and 88% of discharged hospice care patients had one or more advanced directives on record. Older patients were more likely to have an AD than younger patients, and blacks were less likely than whites to have an AD (Jones et al. 2011). The authors do not explain why these differences occur. However, we might expect older patients who are more likely to be nearer death and more accepting of death to have an AD. Perhaps blacks have greater distrust of healthcare institutions and are less willing to trust such important decisions to others as a result.

The Dying Process: Coping, Bereavement, and a "Good Death"

Sociologists who have studied the death and dying processes see evidence of both resisting and accepting death. Elizabeth Kubler-Ross (1969) interviewed and observed dozens of people who were dying. She wanted to understand what went through their minds as they coped with their impending deaths. She identified five stages of grieving people typically experience.

1. **Denial**—they simply cannot believe it is happening to them.

2. **Anger**—at that point, they begin to realize it is actually happening to them, but they see it as a gross injustice.

3. **Bargaining**—they seek to postpone their death by changing their behavior, looking for new treatments, and even making promises to God.

4. **Resignation**—this stage is often accompanied by severe depression.

5. **Acceptance**—they come to terms with their death and attempt to make the most of the remaining time available to them to take care of business with relatives and friends before they die.

Not all people experience all of these stages, and they do not necessarily occur in this specific sequence (Lund 1989). Family and friends also go through bereavement along with the dying person, and how they cope with the death affects the person who is dying. More recent work argues there is a dual process of coping with bereavement for the surviving spouse or relative. These five stages all fall within the loss-orientation (LO) process, focusing on stress related to the loss itself, while a second process, restoration orientation (RO), refers to processes related to secondary stresses accompanying new roles such as learning to make important decisions on one's own and take greater initiative with one's own health care. Both of these processes must be addressed by the grieving relative (Lund et al. 2010). To help people through the dying process, a relatively new social institution has evolved—hospice care. **Hospice care** is care designed to help people have a "good" death experience by relieving pain and discomfort for the patient and providing emotional and spiritual support to both the patient and the patient's family. Unlike hospitals, in which the goal is to cure the patient, hospices recognize the person cannot be cured, and they strive to minimize pain and suffering and encourage the family to remain close throughout (Forman et al. 2003). The hope is, and research supports the conclusion that, when families are able to accept the death of a loved one and reach some level of closure, their grieving is less intense and they are better able to support one another after the death (Sanders 1979). Hospices were initially buildings, but today often hospice care is provided in the patient's home.

Hospice care Care designed to help people have a "good" death experience by relieving pain and discomfort for the patient and providing emotional and spiritual support to both the patient and the patient's family.

CONCEPT LEARNING CHECK 11.4 Death and Dying

Match each of the following with the strategy for approaching death that best describes it.

_____ 1. Code blue

_____ 2. Resignation

_____ 3. Trying alternative medicine therapies when conventional medical procedures fail

_____ 4. Denial

_____ 5. Hospice care

_____ 6. Advance directive

_____ 7. The singularity

A. Rage against death and resist it as long as possible

B. Accept death and come to terms with it

11.5 Aging and the Elderly: Revisiting Cultural Expectations

Common stereotypes about the elderly—that they are poorer, unhealthier, and less able to cope than younger people are—are often wrong.

- Discuss some of the common stereotypes of the elderly and their impact on the aging demographic.

There are many stereotypes of the elderly, more often negative than positive, that do not hold up when we look at the data describing the elderly. Part of the reason for this disconnect between conceptions of what it means to be old and reality is that the reality has changed dramatically over the past few decades. In this section, we consider many of the cultural expectations we have regarding the elderly, then see what the data actually show. In most cases, these data paint a picture of old age as more positive than the stereotypes would suggest.

Health among the Aged: 50 is the new 40!

Today's elderly are "younger" than yesterday's in the sense that they have experienced improved health, exercise, and nutrition throughout their lives when compared to people of the same age in earlier age cohorts. This improvement in the health of the elderly has been noticeable for several decades. As long ago as 1987, Sylvia Mertz was quoted as saying activities of a contemporary 70-year-old "are equivalent to those of a 50-year old a decade or two ago" (quoted in Horn and Meer 1987:76). This change over time is consistent with the differences among countries found earlier in the Nielson global survey (Nielsen Company 2011). As the proportion of elderly in the United States increases and as more old people are able to continue functioning at high levels for longer, our threshold for when we think of someone as "old" becomes older.

Recent statistical data regarding the health of the elderly bear out this notion of their general good health. In 2000 to 2009, 40.0% of noninstitutionalized older persons reported their health was excellent or very good (compared to 64.7% for all persons aged 18–64 years). Older men and women reported essentially the same results; however, lower rates were reported by African-Americans (26.0%), American Indians/Alaska Natives (24.3%), and Hispanics (28.2%); higher rates were reported by whites (42.8%) and Asians (35.3%). These differences in self-reported measures of health are consistent with other, more objective measures, which usually show minorities to suffer from more health problems than whites. While their general health is often good, most elderly live

When someone is viewed as "old," he or she gets pushed to an older age, although many elderly function at high levels later in life.

© Goodshoot/Thinkstock

with at least one chronic condition, and many have multiple conditions. From 2007 to 2009, the most frequently occurring conditions among older persons were uncontrolled hypertension (34%), diagnosed arthritis (50%), all types of heart disease (32%), any cancer (23%), diabetes (19%), and sinusitis (14%; Greenberg 2012:5).

Perceptions, Stereotypes, and Ageism

Being old is often a "master status" (the status that dominates a person's self-perception and the perception of others) in the United States and is generally viewed in negative terms. In one study, the same person was made up to look different ages, and responses of people to the person were studied. College students were significantly more negative in job evaluations for the older applicant. The "older" applicant was viewed as less competent, less intelligent, less reliable, and less attractive (Levin 1988). Thus, being labeled "old" carries with it a stigma that can have a major negative impact on perceptions of a person by others as well as on one's own self-perceptions. This "labeling" view of aging is reflected in negative stereotypes of the elderly and ageism. Because of such negative stereotypes, federal law (the Age Discrimination in Employment Act of 1967) makes it illegal to discriminate on the basis of age in hiring, firing, promotion, and pay decisions for anyone 40 years of age and older. That makes discrimination illegal, yet such discrimination still occurs.

Ageism Prejudice and discrimination against the elderly, usually based on negative stereotypes.

Ageism is prejudice and discrimination against the elderly, usually based on negative stereotypes. Ageism includes values, beliefs, and norms that justify prejudice against people based on their age. The targets of ageism are usually older people and the aging process. But it can also target younger people, such as adolescents, who are sometimes not taken seriously by adults or young adults who are denied jobs or other opportunities due to their age. When directed at the old, ageism reflects a deep uneasiness among young and middle-aged people about growing old. In this view, age symbolizes death, disease, and disability. Ageism among physicians, for example, influences the type of health care received. Physicians treat elderly women with breast cancer differently than younger women, significantly shortening their lives (Greenfield et al. 1987). Other examples of ageism are readily found in our society, including negative stereotypes of the elderly, age segregation of older people into retirement communities and special housing projects, competition among different generations in the labor force, and abuse of the elderly within family relationships.

There are a number of common stereotypes of the elderly. Those stereotypes are generally negative and patronizing. The elderly are often viewed as stubborn, touchy, quarrelsome, bossy, meddlesome, and sometimes depressed. Over the years, television has often presented unrealistic stereotypes of the elderly. In the 1970s, TV provided many negative stereotypes of the elderly as incompetent or unproductive workers. Yet older workers are as productive as younger workers, less accident prone, and more reliable (Barth 1997). Further study of late-life depression found that "aging per se is not necessarily associated with increases in depression" but that some age cohorts experience more depression than others due to stresses they faced such as wars or economic recessions (Yang 2007). Well into the 21st century, media continue to portray the elderly in stereotypical fashion as helpless victims faced with inevitable deterioration and decline or as sweet, pathetic figures (Walker 2010).

To better understand stereotypes of the aged, sociologists Mary Kite and her colleagues reviewed more than 200 published studies comparing attitudes toward older and younger adults and found consistent negative stereotypes for older adults. As expected, they found that people do seem to hold clear stereotypical beliefs that view older adults as less attractive and, to a lesser extent, less competent than younger adults. Their results also supported findings from earlier studies (e.g., Hummert 1999) that these stereotypes are complex and multidimensional (Kite et al. 2005:255). They found that younger adult respondents saw greater differences than older respondents between young and old for every dimension except evaluative judgment, where younger adults perceived smaller differences (Kite et al. 2005:256).

Kite and her colleagues looked for evidence to determine whether there is a double standard for men and women in stereotypes of the aged. They found that there are differences in stereotypes, but that some of them favor men and some favor women. For example, competence is a key theme in male stereotypes (Deaux and LaFrance 1998; Eagly 1987). Kite and colleagues (2005) found that aging males were viewed more negatively in terms of competence, while age differences in competence for females were much smaller. Men are seen as losing agency as they age (Kite 1996), meaning that they lose competence and are less in control of tasks requiring competence as they age (Kite et al. 2005:257). In contrast, for the dimension of behaviors and behavioral intentions, the double standard favors men (Kite et al. 2005:257).

Many of the negative stereotypes of the elderly fly in the face of actual behaviors of older people. Rock stars from the 1960s, who are now in their 60s, such as Paul McCartney, Bruce Springsteen, and the Rolling Stones, certainly challenge many preconceptions we have of how people over 60 are expected to behave. Older adults also use the Internet more often than many of us would expect. One-third of people 65 and older use the Internet in the UK (Dutton and Blank 2011), and 58% of Americans over 65 do so (Pew Internet and American Life Project survey (Pew Internet 2009). Older adults are often active in sports as well, as evinced by senior games held in many states for people over 50 that attract thousands of participants each year (Missouri State Senior Games 2012).

Loneliness and Social Isolation

It is a myth that most of the elderly are lonely. Seventy percent of older men and 41% of older women are living with a spouse. Only 19% of older men and 37% of older women live alone (Greenberg 2012:5). They have very low divorce rates and often have active sex lives into their 70s and 80s. However, there are four times more widows than widowers, so one might expect elderly women to experience loneliness more than elderly men (Greenberg 2012:4).

It is a myth that most of the elderly are lonely.
© LiquidLibrary

Sociologists Sharon Shiovitz-Ezra and Sara A. Leitsch (2010) used data from the National Social Life, Health, and Aging Project to study a nationally representative sample of individuals ages 57 to 85 in the United States. Respondents' mean level of loneliness was 3.99 on a scale from 3 to 9 (with 9 being more lonely), indicating a relatively low level of experienced loneliness. Women, nonmarried individuals, black and Hispanic people, people with poor perceived health, people with low income, and people with low education reported greater loneliness.

Shiovitz-Ezra and Leitsch (2010) also found that both objective and subjective social network characteristics were related to loneliness for people in later life. Respondents who reported higher frequency of contact with social network members (an objective indicator) were less lonely. They also found that subjective measures of the quality of the marital relationship for married or cohabiting people or the quality of family ties for the nonmarried respondents also affected loneliness. In short, people with higher frequency of contact and positive relationships with their spouses or families reported being less lonely (Shiovitz-Ezra and Leitsch 2010:157).

Age segregation is an important feature of age stratification in the United States. Elderly people tend to live in neighborhoods, apartment complexes, or condominiums with other elderly. Since only 4.1% of people over 65 in 2009 lived in institutional settings such as nursing homes (Greenberg 2012:5), and most enter in their late 70s or early 80s, residential segregation by age has little to do with the physical health of the elderly. Sometimes this segregation is a result of a preference by the elderly. As often as not, it is a result of efforts by the nonelderly to exclude elderly residents from their neighborhoods and apartment complexes. Some neighborhoods oppose elderly housing as well as apartments for students or fraternity or sorority houses. Affluent elderly often live in elderly communities, condominiums, hotels for the aged, or senior

Individuals in nursing homes often have high needs for care and assistance with activities of daily living.

© Alexander Raths/Shutterstock, Inc.

housing projects. Other elderly are often trapped in older, decaying neighborhoods in inner cities. Increased age segregation in retirement communities, inner-city concentrations of the elderly, and aging populations in small rural communities have led to a subculture of the aged (Hendricks and Hendricks 1986; Rose 1965). Development of this subculture of the aged is further encouraged by political differences between the aged and other age groups over social issues regarding retirement, pensions, and Social Security.

Nursing Homes

Given the relatively good health and longer life span of today's elderly, being elderly is not a sentence to a nursing home. On the contrary, the great majority of people over 65 live independently, either alone or with their families. In 2009, 1.5 million people 65 and older (4.1%) lived in institutional settings (1.3 million of those lived in nursing homes). The percentage institutionalized increases with age. In 2009, 1.1% of people 65 to 74 old years lived in nursing homes, 3.5% for those 75 to 84 years old, and 13.2% for people 85 and older. An additional 2.4% of the elderly lived in senior housing with at least one supportive service available to residents (Greenberg 2012:7). Older adults make up roughly 90% of all nursing home residents. About half of them were 85 and older. Individuals in nursing homes often have high needs for care with the activities of daily living (ADL), such as eating, dressing themselves, walking, and so on. Many nursing home residents have severe cognitive impairment due to Alzheimer's disease or other forms of dementia (Greenberg 2012:6).

For the elderly who are in nursing homes, quality varies widely, with homes serving the poor of far lower quality than those serving the more affluent elderly. It is not difficult to find news accounts of abuse or even deaths of elderly nursing home residents. However, it is difficult to accurately assess the incidence of abuse. One measure of care that is much easier to measure is the prevalence of pressure ulcers among nursing home residents. In 2004, about 11% of US nursing home residents (159,000) had pressure ulcers, also known as bed sores, that are caused from unrelieved pressure on the skin. Pressure ulcers are serious and common medical conditions that should be treated, yet only 35% of residents with a pressure ulcer of stage 2 or higher received wound care in accordance with clinical practice guidelines. While most elderly are not in nursing homes during most of their years since turning 65, as many as 20% of the elderly are expected to spend some time in a nursing home before they die (Rosenwaike and Logue 1985).

Elder Abuse

Elder abuse is defined by the National Research Council (NRC) report *Elder Mistreatment: Abuse, Neglect, and Exploitation* (Bonnie and Wallace 2003) as intentional actions by a caregiver or someone trusted by the vulnerable elder that (a) cause harm or risk of harm (even if unintended) to the elder or (b) a failure to protect the elder from harm or to meet basic needs. Abuse can be any of many types, including financial, physical, emotional, sexual, neglect, or abandonment (National Center on Elder Abuse 1998).

Elder abuse is difficult to measure because most elderly victims are embarrassed or fear retaliation. Hood (2002) estimates abuse occurs to between 4 and 6% of the elderly in the home. Some particular forms of abuse such as financial abuse are estimated to be reported only about 4% of the time (National Center on Elder Abuse 1998).

It is widely thought that elder abuse occurs when family members such as children are frustrated by the demands of caring for an elderly parent or spouse (e.g., Yates 1986). However, the first nationally representative study asking older adults about their experience of mistreatment—the National Social Life, Health and Aging Project (NSHAP) study—found most mistreatment came from someone other than a member of the elder's immediate family (Laumann et al. 2008). Nine percent of older adults reported verbal mistreatment, 3.5% financial mistreatment, and 0.2% physical mistreatment by a family member (Laumann et al. 2008).

Aging, Labor Force Participation, and Retirement

Younger workers often view the elderly as job stealers and display biases against elder workers similar to biases against immigrants. Yet in the United States during the 20th century, there was a marked decline in participation of older workers in the labor force as retirement made it possible for many people 65 and over to retire. In 1900, two-thirds of men 65 and older worked at least part time. By 1990 11.8% of older men worked. Ironically, since 1990 that percentage has increased to 17.4% in 2010 and is projected to reach 22.6% by 2020 (Toossi 2012).

Retirement is a relatively recent phenomenon in history. Historically, people tended to continue working so long as they were physically able. In 1935, the passage of the Social Security Act established the concept of retirement in the United States. In 1900, 65% of men over 65 were still active in the workplace. One hundred years later, by the year 2010, only 17.4% of people 65 and over were still in the workplace (Toossi 2012). Retirement has been encouraged in the United States by "mandatory retirement" rules in many companies, fewer workers on farms and more in large corporations with retirement plans, the addition of Medicare to cover health benefits in 1966, and the tying of Social Security benefits to the cost of living. Retirement usually brings with it a substantial drop in income. For the average retired couple, retirement income from Social Security and pensions is about half of their preretirement incomes (Foner and Schwab 1981). The major sources of income as reported by older persons in 2009 were Social Security (reported by 87% of older persons), income from assets (reported by 53%), private pensions (reported by 28%), government employee pensions (reported by 14%), and earnings (reported by 26%; Greenberg 2012:13).

Poverty

Social Security transformed the United States from a society in which the elderly were poorer than the rest of society into one in which the poverty rate of the elderly roughly matches that of working age adults in general. In 2011 (the latest year available), 8.7% of elderly lived below the poverty line (DeNavas-Walt et al. 2012). FIGURE 11-9 shows how this number declined from more than 30% in 1959 to roughly the same rate as working adults and much less than the 15 to 20% poverty rate for children under 18 years old. In fact, during the Great Recession beginning in 2008, poverty rates among the elderly remained relatively constant, while poverty rates among working adults increased by approximately 3%. The elderly were protected by the social safety net of Social Security, while working adults had much less protection (Morin and Taylor 2009).

It is often said that without Social Security, one-half of the elderly would live below the poverty line (Greenberg 2012:1). Social Security is small compared to similar programs in other nations, yet it accounts for 38% of all income received by the elderly.

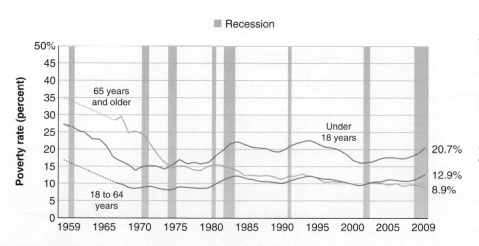

FIGURE 11-9 US poverty rates by age (1959–2009).
Source: DeNavas-Walt, Carmen, Bernadette D. Proctor, and Jessica C. Smith, U.S. Census Bureau. 2010. Current Population Reports, P60-238, Income, Poverty, and Health Insurance Coverage in the United States: 2009, U.S. Government Printing Office, Washington, DC. Accessed October 2012 (http://www.census.gov/prod/2010pubs/p60-238.pdf).

Notes: Data for people aged 18 to 64 and 65 and older are not available from 1960 to 1965.

"Social Security constituted 90% or more of the income received by 35% of beneficiaries (22% of married couples and 43% of nonmarried beneficiaries)" (Greenberg 2012:11). The income of elderly often declines relative to their income at a younger age, and income by age displays an inverted U-shaped distribution, with highest income by middle-aged people and lower incomes for the young and the old. The elderly often have greater accumulated wealth than people of other ages. The elderly do not have many of the costs younger people have for tuition, home payments, and so on, but they have far higher medical costs. Average out-of-pocket health costs for people over 65 were $4,843 in 2010, up 49% from 2000, and nearly $2,000 more than the average of $3,157 for the total population. Older Americans spent more than twice the proportion of their total expenditures on health care (13.2%) compared to the 6.6% spent by all consumers (Greenberg 2012:13).

Since most elderly are not poor, the question becomes "Who are the elderly poor?" Like other age groups, there is significant variation in wealth and power among the elderly. The poorest elderly were usually also among the poorest before they became old (e.g., female-headed households and racial and ethnic minorities). Older women experience the double burden of being female and being old. In 2011, as can be seen in FIGURE 11-10, 10.7% of elderly women lived below the poverty line, compared to 8.7% of all elderly and 6.2% of elderly men. Similar patterns are found for ethnic and racial minorities. In 2011, among the elderly 65 and over, 17.3% of blacks, 18.7% of Hispanics, and 11.7% of Asians fell below the poverty line, compared to only 7.7% of whites and 6.7% of white non–Hispanics (DeNavas-Walt et al. 2012).

Elderly living alone are three times more likely to be poor (16.0%) than those living in families (5.3%). The poverty rate for widows is 18.6%, for divorced women it is 22%, and for never-married women it is 20%. Older women of color are poorest, with 32.5% of single African-American women and 43.7% of single Hispanic women poor. Without Social Security, things would be much worse, with more than half of elderly women of all races and ethnicities living in poverty (Greenberg 2012:1).

The Future of Old Age and Political Participation

The elderly have both benefited and suffered over the past 50 to 100 years. Social Security and other entitlement programs have boosted most elderly out of poverty and dramatically improved their quality of life. The increased health, functionality, and life expectancy of the elderly make a much more appealing picture of the future most of us will face than the much bleaker negative stereotypes of the elderly as in poor health,

FIGURE 11-10 US poverty rates among elderly by race, ethnicity, and gender (2011).
Source: Data from DeNavas-Walt, Carmen, Bernadette D. Proctor, and Jessica C. Smith, U.S. Census Bureau. 2012. Current Population Reports, P60-243, Income, Poverty, and Health Insurance Coverage in the United States: 2011, U.S. Government Printing Office, Washington, DC. Accessed October 2012 (http://www.census.gov/prod/2012pubs/p60-243.pdf).

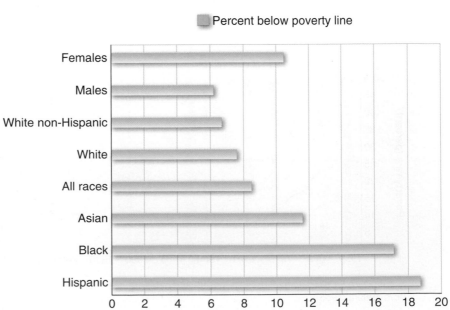

dependent on others for support, perhaps even greedy geezers taking much more from society than they give. However, economic downturns and political debates over the fate of entitlement programs put some of those benefits in jeopardy. It seems clear that the future state of the elderly in this country and others will rest heavily on political decisions made by our governments and others.

The elderly are very much aware of this. They tend to be more active in politics than other age groups. In 2008, more than 70% of people 60 and older voted, compared to only 51% of people aged 18 to 29 (US Election Project 2010). During the 1970s, elderly people organized in a collective movement similar in some ways to the student movements of the 1960s. The Gray Panthers were founded to work for rights of the elderly. The largest elderly organization is AARP (formerly the American Association of Retired Persons). This organization provides elders with many benefits ranging from discount insurance to political lobbying. AARP is the second-largest voluntary association in the world (just behind the Roman Catholic Church; Birnbaum 2005). AARP's political activities include voter registration campaigns and advocacy for Medicare and Social Security, as well as nursing home and pension reform. When it comes to political participation, the elderly appear to be much better described by their activity than by their disengagement.

Clearly, there are many stereotypes and misconceptions about the aged that are not true today even if they might have been true once. As our population continues to age, both in the United States and around the globe, it is becoming ever more important to understand how aging and the elderly will shape our future.

CONCEPT LEARNING CHECK 11.5   Aging and the Elderly: Revisiting Cultural Expectations

Match the items in the first list with the corresponding numbers in the second list.

_____	**1.** The percentage of US elderly women who live alone	**A.** 4%
_____	**2.** The percentage of US elderly men who live alone	**B.** 5–10%
_____	**3.** The percentage of US elderly living in nursing homes at any one time	**C.** 15–20%
_____	**4.** The percentage of US elderly receiving 90% or more of their income from Social Security	**D.** 35–40%
_____	**5.** The percentage of US men 65 and over in the labor force in 2010	**E.** 70%
_____	**6.** The percentage of US elderly living in poverty in 2009	

Visual Overview Aging and the Elderly

Aging populations around the world and in America strain the capacity of societies to provide needed services such as health care. Yet the overall health and well-being of the elderly today is generally much better than it was decades ago and even our notions of when someone is "old" are changing.

Elderly

- World populations are getting older
- Number of workers contributing to benefits per elderly beneficiary:

Retirees   Workers

1937

2011

projected 2050

- Individuals resist being labeled old
- **Young old** Age 65–74; **Old old** Age 75–84; **Oldest old** Age 85+
- Major health problems most likely in oldest old

Graying of America

- Proportion of elderly is increasing, and projected to approach 20% by 2040

1900   2010   2040

- Elderly are less likely to be minorities
- Among the elderly, the oldest old segment is increasing.
- Baby Boomers are perceived as placing increased demands on society.
- More women then men are old and the difference increases with age.
- Most elderly men live with a spouse. Elderly women are about as likely to be widowed as married.

Characteristics and Stereotypes

- 50 is the new 40—most elderly are healthy.
- Only about 4% of elderly live in nursing homes

  - Social Security
    - major source of income
    - reduced poverty
    - the future of entitlements under political debate
    - permitted retirement

  - Negative stereotypes:
    - less attractive
    - less competent
    - less productive

Aging

often measured first by social aging

- Biological wrinkles, gray hair, loss of strength
- Psychological diminished cognitive functioning
- Social changing roles

Perception by Region

- Decade in which 50% or more people view someone as old by world region

Country	Age by Decade			
Asia Pacific	50	60	70	80
Europe	50	60	70	80
Middle East/Africa	50	60	70	80
Latin America	50	60	70	80
North America	50	60	70	80

Sociological Perspectives

- Activity theory (symbolic interactionism): elderly benefit by remaining active
- Conflict theory: highlights generational equity and aging more difficult for minorities, women, and lower classes
- Life course perspective: cohorts face different challenges and opportunities reflecting historic events
- Disengagement theory (structural-functional): elderly should withdraw gracefully
- Modernization theory: diminished role of the family

Visual Summary Aging and the Elderly

11.1 Aging and Becoming Elderly

- Aging leads to biological changes such as gray hair and wrinkles, loss of skin tone, decline in senses, reduced strength, diminished cardiovascular efficiency, and often increased body fat, along with greater prevalence of chronic diseases.

- Psychological changes from age include diminished cognitive functioning and tend to occur late in the aging process.

- Aging is socially constructed, and being "old" tends to be marked by social aging as reflected in changing roles the individual can perform competently more than by chronological age, as measured in years, or even biological aging measured by decreasing strength, decline in senses, and so on.

- Old age spans more than 30 years between turning 65 and the death of the great majority of people by their 90s. The old between 65 and 75 are more likely to be financially independent, healthy, and active, while the oldest old are most likely to be in poor health, financially stressed, and lonely.

- Negative stereotypes of the elderly tend to view all elderly as typified by the oldest old, while the great majority of those chronologically 65 and over are in much better shape.

- Individuals tend to resist being labeled old, talking as though they are not old and seeing age as a mask hiding the still-young person inside.

- There are large differences globally in the chronological age at which people are thought to be old.

- How elderly are viewed and treated is based on how their contributions and costs are viewed—that is, how well they fulfill the social contract between generations.

- Modernization theory points to a diminishing role of families in caring for the elderly as younger people move to cities in search of jobs, leaving elderly family members behind. Its critics, however, remind us that much of human history was plagued by continual fear and danger of violent death.

- Graying populations the world over burden societies with a larger proportion of elderly that must be supported and raise questions of the relative contributions and costs of elderly for each society.

- Ironically, more developed and affluent societies saw the earliest and largest increases in life expectancy, meaning the problem of aging populations is greater for those countries than for poorer, less developed countries.

11.2 The Graying of America

- Since 1900, the population of the United States has been growing older on average, from 4% age 65 and older in 1900 to 10% in 1970, then increasing dramatically beginning in 2010 as Baby Boomers turned 65, rising to 20% by 2040.

- Among those 65 and older, the proportion of old old (75–85) and oldest old (85+) is increasing dramatically (the increased average age of the population), further increasing dependency demands on society.

- The aging of society has been due to increasing life expectancy and irregularity in birth rates, as higher rates produced larger numbers of Baby Boomers who are now turning old, while lower birth rates have diminished the ranks of those still young enough to work and help support them.

- There are nearly a third more women than men aged 65 and over (132 per 100 men), and the disparity increases with age since women have longer life expectancies.

- Most men over 65 live with their spouse (72%), while most women over 65 are as likely to be widowed (40%) as married (42%).

- Minorities are younger on average than whites because of their lower life expectancies and higher birth and immigration rates.

11.3 Sociological Perspectives in Aging

- Structural-functional theory applied to the elderly leads to disengagement theory arguing that as people age, society benefits if there is a smooth transition as they are moved out of positions of responsibility, suggesting we should encourage the elderly to withdraw gracefully.

- Symbolic interactionism focuses on the individual and encourages viewing the benefits for the individual that they can derive from remaining active, leading to activity theory.

- Activity theory makes more sense today than years ago, as the elderly today are in better health and live longer than they would have decades ago, leaving today's elderly more capable of interaction and with more time to continue contributing actively to society.

- Conflict theory emphasizes the disadvantaged elderly and political structures that foster their dependence, pointing out that aging is much more difficult for minorities, women, and those in lower social classes. It also points to the issue of generational equity that influences debates over entitlement programs such as Social Security and Medicare that benefit the elderly.

- Life course perspectives emphasize the way structural factors occurring throughout a person's life provide opportunities and challenges, and advantages or disadvantages with which they began life tend to accumulate to produce greater diversity among the elderly.

- Different age cohorts are exposed to different opportunities and challenges that reflect the historic times and the influence of historic events on individuals in those cohorts.

11.4 Death and Dying

- While death is inevitable, people's approaches to death and dying range from raging against death (illustrated by "code blue" attempts to resuscitate a patient near death) to accepting its inevitability (illustrated by advance directives such as living wills or do-not-resuscitate orders designed to ensure patient's wishes are fulfilled even when he or she can no longer voice them).

- Our confrontation with death can be denied and postponed for most of our lives because death has been removed from the home, is hidden in the hospital, and for roughly 75% of people does not come until after the age of 65. Even then, most of our lives, we are likely to be relatively healthy and able to function except for a few months at the end.

- Both the dying patient and his or her family usually go through a grieving process involving noticeable stages, including denial, anger, bargaining, resignation, and acceptance. Hospice care is designed to help people through this process while minimizing pain and suffering.

11.5 Aging and the Elderly: Revisiting Cultural Expectations

- Today's elderly are "younger" than yesterday's in the sense that they have experienced improved health, exercise, and nutrition throughout their lives, and more old people are able to continue functioning at high levels for longer.

- Stereotypes of the elderly are generally negative and patronizing. The elderly are often viewed as less attractive, less competent, and less productive, with younger people perceiving the differences as greater.

- The elderly appear less lonely than common expectations would predict. In the United States, only 19% of older men and 37% of older women live alone. Greater loneliness was found for women, nonmarried individuals, black and Hispanic people, people with poor perceived health, people with low income, and people with low education.

- Only about 4% of the elderly live in nursing homes at any one time, but they make up 90% of all nursing home residents. Quality of care in nursing homes varies dramatically, and 11% of US nursing home residents in a recent study had pressure ulcers—one measure of poor quality of care.

- Elder abuse can be financial, physical, emotional, sexual, neglect, or abandonment and is estimated to occur for between 4 to 6% of elderly.

- Social Security is a major source of income for the elderly, making it possible for many elderly to retire in the United States, leading labor force participation of men 65 and older to drop from 65% in 1900 to only 17.4% by 2010.

- As a result of Social Security, poverty among the elderly dropped from over 30% in 1959 to roughly the same rate as working adults (around 9%) and less than the 15 to 20% poverty rate for children under 18 by 2008.

- Social Security accounts for 38% of all income received by the elderly and constituted 90% or more of the income received by 35% of beneficiaries.

- Poverty rates among the elderly are higher for women, ethnic and racial minorities, and those living alone. Poverty is highest for elderly single women of color.

- The future of entitlement programs such as Social Security and Medicare will rest on political decisions about the allocation of resources tempered by views of the relative contributions and costs of the elderly. Many of the elderly are well aware of this and are actively engaged to lobby for their interests through organizations such as the AARP.

11.1 Aging and Becoming Elderly

1. Which of the following is *not* one of the ways people resist their own aging discussed in this chapter?

A. Speaking as though they are not among the old

B. Viewing their old external appearance as a mask that hides the young person they remain inside

C. Immigrating to a country where someone their chronological age is regarded as younger

D. Using assistive devices such as canes to maintain functionality

2. Which is a measure of social aging?

A. Age in years

B. Having grandchildren

C. Having trouble remembering dates

D. Diminished vision

11.2 The Graying of America

5. Which of these statements about aging in the United States is true?

A. The increased proportion of people 65 and over in the United States is due entirely to increased life expectancies.

B. Women 65 and over are more likely to live alone than men that age.

C. Men over 65 outnumber women over 65, but by 85 women outnumber men.

D. The proportion of people among those 65 and older who are 85 and older is decreasing.

6. By 2040, the percentage of people aged 65 and over in the United States is projected to be

A. 10%.

B. 15%.

C. 20%.

D. 25%.

11.3 Sociological Perspectives in Aging

8. How is disengagement theory consistent with structural-functional theory?

A. They both emphasize the importance of individual agency or choice.

B. They both emphasize the consequences of individual actions on society.

C. Actually, disengagement theory is more consistent with symbolic interactionism.

D. They both emphasize the cumulative effects of individual action over time.

11.4 Death and Dying

10. Which of the following is the last stage in Elizabeth Kubler-Ross's five stages of grieving?

A. Resignation

B. Acceptance

C. Bargaining

D. Anger

3. What are the three types of aging and which is most often used to decide when someone is old?

A. Chronological age is most important, followed by biological age and psychological age.

B. Social age is most important, followed by psychological age and financial age.

C. Biological age is most important, followed by chronological age and social age.

D. Social age is most important, followed by biological age and chronological age.

4. True or false? A person's age is the same regardless of what society he or she lives in, so whether someone is viewed as "old" is generally the same for all societies.

7. Most men over 65 live with their spouse (72%), while most women over 65 are as likely to be widowed (40%) as married (42%). How can these numbers add up? If 72% of men over 65 are married, why are not 72% of women over 65 married? Which statement below best explains this?

A. There are about 30% more women than men who are over 65.

B. The numbers do not make sense. Something must be wrong.

C. Today's elderly are more healthy than the elderly were years ago.

D. The proportion of women increases with age due to their longer life expectancy.

9. Which of the following statements is most consistent with activity theory?

A. People who retire sometimes seem to lose interest in life.

B. People who spend more time with friends and family tend to live longer and be happier than those who do not.

C. Most people retire relatively soon once they are able to do so.

D. Women over 65 are much more likely to live alone than men over 65.

11. Who is it who believes there will be a time in 2045 when computer intelligence equals human intelligence, making it possible to upload our consciousness onto computers and live forever?

A. Elizabeth Kubler-Ross

B. Dylan Thomas

C. Jack Kevorkian

D. Ray Kurzweil

11.5 Aging and the Elderly: Revisiting Cultural Expectations

12. Poverty rates among the elderly are higher for all but one of the following when compared to elderly not in that category. Which one does not belong?
   A. Men
   B. Ethnic and racial minorities
   C. Those living alone
   D. Single women of color

13. Which of the following is a common stereotype of the elderly discussed in this chapter?
   A. Less competent
   B. Less productive
   C. Less attractive
   D. All of the above

14. Fill in the blanks in this sentence with one item in each blank. Today's elderly, when compared to the elderly 50 or 100 years ago are less likely to be _____ and more likely to be _____.
   A. poor, lonely
   B. healthy, retired
   C. lonely, poor
   D. poor, healthy

15. Which is not true of elder abuse?
   A. Elder abuse is particularly frequent for elderly women and is estimated to occur to roughly one in five of elderly women.
   B. Elder abuse can be financial.
   C. Elder abuse occurs to an estimated 4 to 6% of the elderly.
   D. Elder abuse can be sexual.

CHAPTER ESSAY QUESTIONS

Use the following description of Winston for questions 1 and 2:

Winston is 65. He no longer plays tennis regularly with friends as he once did. He admits *he has* gained a bit of a bulge around his waist and buys bigger pants than when he was younger. His hair is about half gray—he says it makes him look distinguished. He has a little more trouble seeing than he once did and has a little trouble hearing well enough to understand when children, with their high-pitched voices, talk to him. He also admits it is a little harder to remember things now and it takes him longer to balance his checkbook. He always feels busy and rushed nowadays. He continues his volunteer work with his church. He always enjoys the time spent there. However, he no longer coaches Little League baseball every summer. He lives with his wife, and together they manage to keep up with household chores and enjoy living on their own. The last thing he would want to do now or ever, he says, is go into a nursing home. He still works and does not plan on retiring until he is at least 70 years old.

He is a professional who is paid well and does not live beyond his means. Most of his life, he did well financially. However, he lost a lot of money in the dotcom bubble around 2000 and again in 2008 when stocks tanked after the housing crisis. Truth be told, that is part of why he does not plan to retire until 70, by which time he hopes to catch up to where he wanted his wealth to be. He is optimistic and expects to be able to travel and enjoy life when he finally retires.

1. Write a brief essay identifying one sign of chronological aging in Winston, at least two signs of biological aging, and at least two signs of social aging.

2. Do you think Winston's description provides more support for activity theory or for disengagement theory? Briefly define each of those theories and then identify at least two characteristics of Winston that are consistent with one of those theories and two characteristics consistent with the other theory.

3. A community in a Midwestern state has just heard that a large firm is planning to build a new subdivision with more than 1,000 new housing units aimed at attracting people over 65. It will be a mix of less expensive, multifamily rental units along with single-family dwellings. However, the area in which the subdivision is planned is currently zoned for agricultural use and has to be rezoned for residential use. One of the speakers is strongly opposed and makes the following statements.

I'm opposed to this new subdivision because I don't think the community can afford the drain it will place on our resources. I don't want to live next door to a bunch of lonely old men living alone in poverty. Most of them are totally supported by Social Security and other government handouts. If they need more money to live on, they aren't going to be able to hold down a real job. Even if they wanted to work part-time, they are likely to be slower, less productive, and less reliable at coming to work on time than someone younger. Plus, they will overwhelm our nursing homes here in town. Already, 90% of our nursing home residents are elderly, and we can't afford to build new ones.

Write a brief paragraph identifying one thing this person got right. He got several of his facts wrong. For at least two things he got wrong, tell the zoning commission what the data actually says about those issues.

CHAPTER DISCUSSION QUESTIONS

1. Several strategies for denying aging were discussed. Think about people you know. Do any of them do any of those things? If you have not seen them do them, do you expect they do? Is it wrong for them to try to deny aging or becoming old? What is good about denying your own aging? What is wrong with it?

2. With life expectancy rates increasing, what public issues can you predict may occur in terms of society caring for those diagnosed with Alzheimer's disease?

3. Which do you think makes more sense—disengagement theory or activity theory? Can you support your argument with examples from people you know? What general trends support your view? When you retire, do you expect to continue being active or slow down a lot?

4. How do current societal trends related to the economy, health, family, and technology impact the social construction of chronological, biological, and social age?

5. What disputes might arise in the workplace between different age cohorts, for example, Baby Boomers, GenXers, and Millennials?

6. Do you think the five stages of grieving identified by Elizabeth Kubler-Ross explain how people respond to their own death or that of a loved one? Should everyone end up at the acceptance stage? Is it so bad if they do not? Do you think the stages would usually occur in that sequence? Did she miss any stages? Do you know any people who died who were close to you? Did they go through those stages? Did you go through those stages while grieving for them?

7. How can hospice care as a social institution contribute to societal and cultural perceptions of death and dying?

8. By law, it is illegal to discriminate on the basis of age when hiring, promoting, or firing workers. You are one of the 10 people, all under 30, currently employed in a startup company and you are charged with hiring the next three employees. One of the applicants has experience in the same type of business and good references, but that applicant is over 50. Do you honestly think you would hire them? Why or why not? What do you expect him/her to be like? Do you really believe it when the book says elders are as productive, more reliable, and less accident prone than younger workers? Do you think you would enjoy working with an older person? Would they fit in? Is it fair to consider that when hiring? To put this in perspective, would a black, a Latino, or an Asian person fit in? A gay or lesbian?

CHAPTER PROJECTS

INDIVIDUAL PROJECTS

1. In many respects, the problem an older population raises for societies is one of dependence, with large numbers of elderly unable to contribute much to the economy but needing assistance. But another group that increases dependence is children too young to work and contribute economically in a society. Developed societies generally have a larger percentage of elderly than developing societies, but developing societies usually have a larger percentage of children too young to work. So overall, the proportion of the population that depends on others for economic support may already be greater in developing societies. Does this argument make sense? Each person in your project group should pick three developing societies and three developed societies of interest to them, then go on the Internet and find reliable data describing the percentage of people under 18 and the percentage 65 and over for each of those countries. Add both for each country and compare them. Do developing societies have a larger proportion of their population that is dependent?

2. Numerous studies have been conducted over the past few decades of how television and film portray the elderly in ways that perpetuate unfair stereotypes. It is reasonable to expect that YouTube might have videos that also portray the elderly unfairly. Search for videos involving older people on YouTube and look for the kinds of stereotypes those videos portray. If there are several people in the project group, then each person should identify and analyze at least three videos. Combine the results from all of the group members and make a case for whether you think these videos unfairly portray the elderly.

3. Go online to learn more about the Baby Boom generation. Write a paper detailing your views and predictions on how this generation might reshape retirement norms, keeping in mind the theories presented throughout the chapter.

4. Go online and educate yourself about Social Security and Medicare. Write an analysis paper of your findings including the future of these two entitlement programs.

GROUP PROJECTS

1. Go online to learn more about geronticide and gerontocracies. Write a report and be prepared to share with the class your group's findings.

2. Imagine you are part of a hospital team tasked with developing a pamphlet aimed at informing seniors about elder abuse. Create a document that includes statistics, definitions, and resources.

CHAPTER KEY TERMS

Advance directive (AD)	Code blue	No code order; do not resuscitate (DNR) order
Age cohort	Generational equity	Old old
Age dependency ratio for the elderly	Geronticide	Oldest old
Ageism	Gerontocracy	Singularity
Alzheimer's disease	Hospice care	Social age
Biological age	Life expectancy	Young old
Chronological age	Living will	

ANSWERS TO CONCEPT LEARNING CHECKS

11.1 Aging and Becoming Elderly

1. [F] They are treated more poorly, such as being burned at the stake.

2. [T] The elderly tend to be viewed based on their contributions to society minus their costs.

3. [F] Differences of race, gender, and social class remain and may even be stronger among the elderly as initial differences are magnified over time by the opportunities or challenges they present for individuals.

4. [F] The problem of aging populations occurred first in more developed societies, and the proportion of the population that is elderly is likely to be much higher there.

5. [T] The Nielson Company survey suggests that someone in the United States in her 60s would be seen as old by only 32% of the population, but someone that old in Africa would be seen as old by 65% of the population.

11.2 The Graying of America

1. [A, less] Women outnumber men among those 65 and older because of their longer life expectancy.

   [B, less] Minorities are less common among the elderly because most minorities have shorter life spans and their higher birth rates increase their proportions among those under 65.

2. [A, less] The proportion of women increases with age due to their longer life expectancy.

   [B, less] People 85 and older are more likely to be in poor health and need assistance than those between 65 and 75.

3. [A, less] Women are more likely to be widowed than men among the elderly.

   [B, more] Most women over 65 are as likely to be widowed (40%) as married (42%), while 72% of men over 65 live with their spouse.

11.3 Sociological Perspectives in Aging

1. Well over two-thirds of men over 65 live with their spouse, while only 42% of women over 65 do so, and women who live alone are much more likely to live below the poverty line. [C. Conflict theory]

2. Many people, when they retire, devote more time to travel or hobbies or grandkids to help fill their time. [B. Activity theory]

3. David never liked school, so immediately upon graduating from high school, he enlisted in the Army, where he served two tours of duty in Afghanistan. Unfortunately, on his second tour, he was wounded and lost his left leg below his knee. He was fitted with a prosthetic and recovered well, but now he faces a lifetime in which he has to work around this disability. [D. Life course perspectives]

4. Most people retire at or shortly after 65. [A. Disengagement theory]

11.4 Death and Dying

1. [A, A code blue calls for an all-out effort to revive a dying patient.]

2. [B, Resignation does not fight death.]

3. [A, Alternative therapies are a way to not give up.]

4. [A, Denial certainly does not accept death and is more likely to fight it.]

5. [B, Hospice care helps people accept death and minimize pain and suffering.]

6. [B, Advance directives typically instruct when to withhold further treatment when it becomes evident someone is likely to die soon.]

7. [A, The singularity hopes that someone can escape death by uploading their consciousness onto a computer (yes, it really believes that!).]

11.5 Aging and the Elderly: Revisiting Cultural Expectations

1. [D, 37% of elderly women live alone.]

2. [C, 19% of elderly men live alone.]

3. [A, 4% of elderly live in nursing homes at any one time.]

4. [D, 35% of elderly receive 90% or more of their income from Social Security.]

5. [C, 17.4% of elderly men were in the labor force in 2010.]

6. [B, 9% of the elderly were living in poverty in 2009.]

ANSWERS TO CHAPTER REVIEW TEST

11.1 Aging and Becoming Elderly

1. C. All of the other ways were discussed in the chapter.

2. B. Anything that changes social roles in a manner correlated with aging contributes to social aging.

3. D. Social aging is usually the first criterion of deciding someone is old, and the other broad types of aging are biological and chronological.

4. False. Age is socially constructed and can be viewed very differently in different societies.

11.2 The Graying of America

5. B. Women over 65 are more likely to be widowed and hence more likely to live alone than men.

6. C. 20%

7. A. Many of the 30% more women than men who are over 65 are likely to be widows or unmarried since there are so many fewer men that age.

11.3 Sociological Perspectives in Aging

8. B. They both emphasize the consequences of individual actions for society.

9. B. People who spend more time with friends and family tend to live longer and be happier than those who do not.

11.4 Death and Dying

10. B. She believes people are better off if they eventually come to accept death.

11. D. Ray Kurzweil calls this time the singularity.

11.5 Aging and the Elderly: Revisiting Cultural Expectations

12. A. Elderly women are more likely to be poor than elderly men.

13. D. All of these are common stereotypes of the elderly.

14. D. Today's elderly are less likely to be poor and more likely to be healthy.

15. A. No statistics were given for elder abuse rates broken down by gender.

ANSWERS TO CHAPTER ESSAY QUESTIONS

1. A good answer should include 65 as a chronological sign of aging. Signs of biological aging include bulging waist and bigger pants, gray hair, trouble seeing, trouble hearing, harder to remember, and longer to balance checkbook. Signs of social aging include changes in roles such as no longer coaching, while hanging onto other roles suggests he is not aging socially much yet, such as still living with his wife, managing household chores, not retiring, and continuing to volunteer with his church.

2. A good answer should note that activity theory argues he should continue with activities or at least replace them with new ones. It is supported by new activities like traveling, not retiring right away, continuing to volunteer with his church and still working. Disengagement theory suggests he is likely to drop activities and is supported by no longer coaching and no longer playing tennis regularly.

3. A good answer should indicate he was right, that about 90% of nursing home residents are the elderly. It should also provide at least two of the following correct statistics. Most elderly do not live alone. Only about 4% of elderly live in nursing homes at any one time. Most elderly are not supported primarily by Social Security. Social Security only accounts for about 38% of all income received by the elderly. The elderly are generally more reliable, as productive, and less accident prone than younger workers. People 65 and older are no more likely to be in poverty than working adults. Most elderly are women, not men.

REFERENCES

Amoss, P., and S. Harrell (Eds.). 1981. *Other Ways of Growing Old: Anthropological Perspectives.* Stanford, CA: Stanford University Press.

Arias, E. 2012. United States Life Tables, 2008. *National Vital Statistics Reports* 61(3). Accessed October 2012 at http://www.cdc.gov/nchs/data/nvsr/nvsr61/nvsr61_03.pdf.

Atchley, R. C. 1985. *Social Forces and Aging: An Introduction to Social Gerontology.* Belmont, CA: Wadsworth.

Atchley, R. C. 1989. "A continuity theory of normal aging." *The Gerontologist,* 29:183–190.

Atchley, R. C. 1999. "Continuity theory, self, and social structure." Pp 94–121 in *The Self and Society in Aging Processes,* edited by C. D. Ryff and V. W. Marshall. New York: Springer.

Atchley, R. C. 2000. *Social Forces and Aging: An Introduction to Social Gerontology,* Ninth Edition. Belmont, CA: Wadsworth.

Barker, J. 1997. "Between Humans and Ghosts: The Decrepit Elderly in a Polynesian Society." Pp. 407–425 in *The Cultural Context of Aging: World-wide Perspectives,* Second edition, edited by J. Sokolovsky. Westport, CT: Bergin & Garvey.

Barth, M. C. 1997. "Older Workers: Perception and Reality." *U.S. Senate Special Committee on Aging Forum: Preparing for the baby boomers' retirement: The role of employment.* July 25, 1997.

Beck, S. H., and J. W. Page. 1988. "Involvement in Activities and the Psychological Well-being of Retired Men." *Activ. Adapt. Aging* 11(1):31–47.

Bengtson, V. L., and W. A. Achenbaum (Eds.). 1993. *The Changing Contract across Generations.* New York: Aldine de Gruyter.

Bever, E. 1982. "Old Age and Witchcraft in Early Modern Europe." Pp. 150–190 in *Old Age in Preindustrial Society,* edited by P. Sterns. New York: Holmes & Meier.

Birnbaum, J. H. 2005. "AARP Leads with Wallet in Fight over Social Security." *Washington Post.* March 30, 2005. Accessed November 2012 at http://www.washingtonpost.com/wp-dyn/content/article/2005/03/30/AR2005033000267.html.

Bonnie, R. J. and Wallace, R. B. (Eds.) 2003. *Elder Mistreatment: Abuse, Neglect, and Exploitation.* National Research Council (NRC) report. Accessed November 2012 at http://www.nap.edu/openbook.php?isbn=0309084342.

Butler, R. 2010. *The Longevity Prescription: The 8 Proven Keys to a Long, Healthy Life.* New York: Avery.

Center on Budget and Policy Priorities. 2012, August 13. *Policy Basics: Where Do Our Federal Tax Dollars Go?* Accessed November 2012 at http://www.cbpp.org/cms/index.cfm?fa=view&id=1258.

Cohen, G. D. 2005. *The Mature Mind: The Positive Power of the Aging Brain.* New York: Basic Books.

Cowgill, D. 1986. *Aging Around the World.* Belmont, CA: Wadsworth.

Cowgill, D., and L. D. Holmes (Eds.). 1972. *Aging and Modernization.* New York: Appleton–Century-Crofts.

Cumming, E., and W. E. Henry. 1961. *Growing Old.* New York: Basic.

Deaux, K., and M. LaFrance. 1998. "Gender." Pp. 788–827 in *The Handbook of Social Psychology,* Fourth edition, Volume 1, edited by D. T. Gilbert, S. T. Fiske, and G. Lindzey. New York: McGraw Hill.

DeNavas-Walt, C., B. D. Proctor, and J. C. Smith. 2010. *Income, Poverty, and Health Insurance Coverage in the United States: 2009.* US Census Bureau, Current Population Reports, P60–238. Washington, DC: U.S. Government Printing Office. Accessed October 2012 at http://www.census.gov/hhes/www/poverty/data/incpovhlth/2009/pov09fig05.pdf.

DeNavas-Walt, C., B. D. Proctor, and J. C. Smith. 2012, September. *Income, Poverty, and Health Insurance Coverage in the United States: 2011.* Current Population Reports. P60–243. Accessed October 2012 at http://www.census.gov/prod/2012pubs/p60-243.pdf.

Dowd, J. J. 1980. *Stratification Among the Aged.* Belmont, CA: Brooks/Cole.

Dutton, W. H., and G. Blank. 2011. *Next Generation Users: The Internet in Britain.* Oxford Internet Institute. Oxford, UK: University of Oxford.

Eagly, A. H. 1987. *Sex Differences in Social Behavior: A Social-Role Interpretation.* Hillsdale, NJ: Lawrence Eribaum Associates, Inc.

Estes, C. 1979. *The Aging Enterprise.* San Francisco: Jossey-Bass.

Estes, C., J. Swan, and L. Gerard. 1982. "Dominant and Competing Paradigms in Gerontology: Towards a Political Economy of Ageing." *Ageing and Society* 12:151–64.

Featherstone, M., and M. Hepworth. 1989. "Ageing and Old Age: Reflections on the Postmodern Life Course." Pp. 143–147 in *Becoming and Being Old,* edited by B. Byetheway, et al. London: Sage.

Foner, A., and K. Schwab. 1981. *Aging and Retirement.* Monterrey, CA: Brooks/Cole.

Forman, W. B., D. Kopchak Sheehan, and J. A. Kitzes. 2003. *Hospice and Palliative Care: Concepts and Practice,* Second edition. Sudbury, MA: Jones & Bartlett Publishers.

Fries, J. F. 1980. "Aging, Natural Death, and the Compression of Morbidity." *New England Journal of Medicine* 303:130–35.

Glascock, A. 1997. "When Killing is Acceptable: The Moral Dilemma Surrounding Assisted Suicide in America and Other Societies." Pp. 56–70 in *The Cultural Context of Aging: World-wide Perspectives,* Second edition, edited by J. Sokolovsky. Westport, CT: Bergin & Garvey.

Glascock, A., and S. Feinman. 1981. "Social Asset or Social Burden: Treatment of the Aged in Non-industrial Societies." Pp. 13–32 in *Dimensions: Aging, Culture, and Health,* edited by C. Fry. Hadley, MA: Bergin & Garvey.

Greenberg, Saadia. 2012. *A Profile of Older Americans: 2011.* US Administration on Aging. Accessed October 2012 at http://www.aoa.gov/aoaroot/aging_statistics/Profile/2011/docs/2011profile.pdf.

Greenfield, S., D. M. Blanco, R. M. Elashoff, and P. A. Ganz. 1987. "Patterns of Care Related to Age of Breast Cancer Patients." *Journal of the American Medical Association* 257(20):2766–2770.

Grossman, L. 2011, February 10. "2045: The Year Man Becomes Immortal." *Time Magazine.* Accessed October 2012 at http://www.time.com/time/magazine/article/0,9171,2048299,00.html.

Harding, A. 2010. "End-of-Life Care Costs Continue to Climb Upward." Reuters. Accessed October 2012 at http://www.reuters.com/article/2010/10/14/us-care-costs-idUSTRE69C3KY20101014.

Havighurst, R. J. 1961. "Successful Aging." *The Gerontologist* 1(1):8–13.

Hendricks, J. 1992. "Generation and the Generation of Theory in Social Gerontology." *Aging and Human Development* 35:31–47.

Hendricks, J., and C. D. Hendricks. 1986. *Aging in Mass Society: Myths and Realities.* Boston: Little, Brown.

Hessler, R. M., S. H. Pazaki, R. W. Madsen, and R. L. Blake. 1990. "Predicting Mortality among Independently Living Rural Elderly: A 20-year Longitudinal Study." *Sociological Quarterly* 31:253–67.

Hobbes, T. 1651(2010). *Leviathan.* Revised Edition, edited by A. P. Martinich and Brian Battiste. Peterborough, ON: Broadview Press.

Hobbs, Frank, and Nicole Stoops. 2002. "Table 5. Population by Age and Sex for the United States: 1900 to 2000." *Census 2000 Special Reports, Series CENSR-4, Demographic Trends in the 20th Century.* Washington, DC: U.S. Census Bureau.

Hood, J. R. 2002. "More Abuse Seen as Elder Population Grows." *Caregiver USA News.* Accessed October 2012 at www.andthoushalthonor.org/news/abuse.html.

Horn, J. C., and J. Meer. 1987. "The Vintage Years: The Growing Number of Healthy, Vigorous Older People Has Helped Overcome Some Stereotypes about Aging. For Many, the Best Is Yet to Come." *Psychology Today* 18:76–90.

House, J. S., P. M. Lantz, and P. Herd. 2005. "Continuity and Change in the Social Stratification of Aging and Health over the Life Course: Evidence from a Nationally Representative Longitudinal Study from 2986 to 2001/2 (Americans' Changing Lives Study)." *Journal of Gerontology* SS 60B (Special Issue II):15–26.

Hummert, M. L. 1999. "A Social Cognitive Perspective on Age Stereotypes." Pp. 175–196 in *Social Cognition and Aging,* edited by T. M. Hess and F. Blanchard-Fields. San Diego, CA: Academic Press, Inc.

Ikels, C., and C. Beall. 2000. "Age, Aging and Anthropology." Pp. 125–139 in *The Handbook of Aging and the Social Sciences,* Fifth edition, edited by R. Binstock and L. George. San Diego, CA: Academic Press.

Jones, A. L., A. J. Moss, and L. D. Harris-Kojetin. 2011. "Use of Advance Directives in Long-Term Care Populations." *NCHS data brief, no 54.* Hyattsville, MD: National Center for Health Statistics. Accessed November 2012 at http://www.cdc.gov/nchs/data/databriefs/db54.pdf.

Jones, R. L. 2006. "'Older People' Talking as if They Are Not Older People: Positioning Theory as an Explanation." *Journal of Aging Studies* 20(1):79–91.

Keith, J. 1982. *Old People, New Lives: Community Creation in a Retirement Residence,* Second edition. Chicago: University of Chicago Press.

Kertzer, D., and P. Laslett (Eds.). 1994. *Demography, Society and Old Age.* Berkeley: University of California Press.

Kibuga, K. F., and A. Dianga. 2000. "Victimisation and Killing of Older Women: Witchcraft in Magu District, Tanzania." *South African Journal of Gerontology* 9(2):29–32.

Kite, M. E. 1996. "Age, Gender, and Occupational Label: A Test of Social Role Theory." *Psychology of Women Quarterly* 20:361–74.

Kite, M. E., G. D. Stockdale, B. E. Whitley, and B. T. Johnson. 2005. "Attitudes Toward Younger and Older Adults: An Updated Meta-analytic Review." *Journal of Social Issues* 61(2):241–66.

Kubler-Ross, E. 1969. *On Death and Dying.* New York: Routledge.

Kukull, W., and M. Ganguli. 2000. "Epidemiology of Dementia: Concepts and Overview." *Neurologic Clinics,* 18:923–50.

Laslett, P. 1976. "Societal Development and Aging." Pp. 3–34 in *Handbook of Aging and the Social Sciences,* edited by R. Binstock and E. Shanas. New York: Van Nostrand Reinhold.

Laumann, E. O., S. A. Leitsch, and L. J. Waite. 2008. "Elder Mistreatment in the United States: Prevalence Estimates from a Nationally Representative Study." *Journal of Gerontology: Social Sciences* 63:248–254.

Levin, W. C. 1988. "Age Stereotyping." *Research on Aging* 10:134–148.

Lund, D. A. 1989. *Older Bereaved Spouses: Research with Practical Applications.* Washington, DC: Taylor-Francis/Hemisphere Press.

Lund, D., M. Caserta, R. Utz, and B. deVries. 2010. "Experiences and Early Coping of Bereaved Spouses/Partners in an Intervention Based on the Dual Process Model (DPM)." *Omega (Westport)* 61(4):291–313.

Marshall (Eds.). *The Self and Society in Aging Processes.* New York: Springer.

Mills, C. Wright. 1959. *The Sociological Imagination.* Oxford, UK: Oxford University Press.

Missouri State Senior Games. 2012. Accessed October 2012 at http://www.smsg.org/senior_games/.

Morin, R., and P. Taylor. 2009. "Different Age Groups, Different Recessions: Oldest Are Most Sheltered." Pew Research Center. Accessed October 2012 at http://www.pewsocialtrends.org/2009/05/14/different-age-groups-different-recessions/1/.

National Atlas of the United States. 2011. *The United States Population in International Context: 2000.* NationalAtlas.com. Accessed November 2012 at http://www.google.com/url?sa=t&rct=j&q=&esrc=s&source=web&cd=1&cad=rja&ved=0CDEQFjAA&url=http%3A%2F%2Fwww.nationalatlas.gov%2Farticles%2Fpeople%2Fa_international.html&ei=yZKyUPnNK8ebqwH0p4DADg&usg=AFQjCNH8H5UAKn_j2xgIldsfsxdt0XcejQ.

National Center on Elder Abuse (NCEA). 1998. *The National Elder Abuse Incidence Study.* Accessed October 2012 at http://www.aoa.gov/AoARoot/AoA_Programs/Elder_Rights/Elder_Abuse/docs/ABuseReport_Full.pdf.

Nielsen Company. 2011. "The Global Impact of an Aging World." *Global Online Survey.* Accessed November 2012 at http://www.nielsen.com/us/en/insights/reports-downloads/2011/global-impact-aging-world.html.

O'Rand, A. M. 1996. "The Precious and the Precocious: Understanding Cumulative Disadvantage and Cumulative Advantage over the Life Course." *Gerontologist* 36:230–238.

Palmore, E. B. 1979. "Predictors of Successful Aging." *Gerontologist* 19:427–431.

Park-Lee, E., and C. Caffrey. 2009. "Pressure Ulcers among Nursing Home Residents: United States, 2004." *NCHS data brief, no 14.* Hyattsville, MD: National Center for Health Statistics. Accessed November 2012 at http://www.cdc.gov/nchs/data/databriefs/db14.htm.

Parsons, T. 1960. *Structure and Process in Modern Societies.* New York: Free Press.

Perlin, A. A. 2007. "'To Die in Order to Live': The Need for Legislation Governing Post-Mortem Cryonic Suspension 2007." *Southwestern University Law Review* 36(1):33. Accessed November 2012 at SSRN: http://ssrn.com/abstract=1608140.

Pew Internet. 2009. "Demographics of Internet Users." *Pew Internet and American Life Survey.* Accessed October 2012 at http://www.pewinternet.org/Static-Pages/Trend-Data-%28Adults%29/Whos-Online.aspx.

Pew Research Center. 2006. "Working after Retirement: The Gap between Expectations and Reality." *A Social Trends Report.* Accessed November 2012 at http://pewresearch.org/assets/social/pdf/Retirement.pdf.

Pew Research Center. 2010. "The Millennials: Confident. Connected. Open to Change." *Pew Research Center Publications.* Accessed November 2012 at http://pewresearch.org/pubs/1501/millennials-new-survey-generational-personality-upbeat-open-new-ideas-technology-bound.

Pew Research Center. 2012. "10,000—Baby Boomers Retire." *The Databank.* Accessed November 2012 at http://pewresearch.org/databank/dailynumber/?NumberID=1150.

Plakans, A. 1989. "Stepping Down in Former Times: A Comparative Assessment of Retirement in Traditional Europe." Pp. 75–97 in *Age Structuring in Comparative Perspective,* edited by D. Kertzer and K. W. Schaie. Hillsdale, NJ: Lawrence Erlbaum.

Phillipson, C. 1982. *Capitalism and the Construction of Old Age.* London: Macmillan.

Phillipson, C. 1998. *Reconstructing Old Age.* London: Sage.

Powell, J. L. 2001. *Aging & Social Theory: A Sociological Review.* SSPP.net—Social Science Paper Publisher. Accessed October 2012 at http://homepages.uwp.edu/takata/dearhabermas/powell01bk.html.

Quadagno, J. 1987. "Theories of the Welfare State." *Annual Review of Sociology* 13:109–128. Accessed November 2012 at http://links.jstor.org/sici?sici=0360-0572%281987%2913%3C109%3ATOTWS%3E2.0.CO%3B2-M.

Quadagno, J. 1989. "Generational Equity and the Politics of the Welfare State." *Politics & Society* 17:353–76.

Quadagno, J. 2007. *Aging and the Life Course: An Introduction to Social Gerontology,* Fourth edition. Hightstown, NJ: McGraw-Hill Humanities/Social Sciences/Languages.

Riley, M. W. 1987. "On the Significance of Age in Sociology." *American Sociological Review* 52:1–14.

Rose, A. M. 1965. "The Subculture of the Aging: A Framework for Research in Social Gerontology." Pp. 3–16 in *Older People and Their Social Worlds,* edited by A. M. Rose and W. Peterson. Philadelphia: F. A. Davis.

Rosenwaike, I., and B. Logue. 1985. *The Extreme Aged in America: A Portrait of an Expanding Population.* Westport, CT: Greenwood Press.

Sanders, C. M. 1979. "A Comparison of Adult Bereavement in the Death of a Spouse, Child, and Parent." *OMEGA—Journal of Death and Dying* 10(4):303–22.

Schneider, Keith. 2011. "Dr. Jack Kevorkian Dies at 83: A Doctor Who Helped End Lives." *New York Times.* Accessed November 2012 at http://www.nytimes.com/2011/06/04/us/04kevorkian.html?pagewanted=all&_r=0.

Shiovitz-Ezra, S., and S. Leitsch. 2010. "The Role of Social Relationships in Predicting Loneliness: The National Social Life, Health, and Aging Project." *Social Work Research* 34(3):57–167. Accessed October 2012 at http://swr.oxfordjournals.org.proxy.mul.missouri.edu/content/34/3/157.full.pdf.

Shrestha, L. B. 2006. *Age Dependency Ratios and Social Security Solvency.* CRS Report for Congress. Washington, DC: Congressional Research Service, Library of Congress. Accessed October 2012 at http://aging.senate.gov/crs/ss4.pdf.

Silverman, P., and R. J. Maxwell 1987. "The Significance of Information and Power in the Comparative Study of the Aged." Pp. 43–55 in *Growing Old in Different Societies: Cross-Cultural Perspectives,* edited by J. Sokolovsky. Acton, MA: Copley.

Social Security and Medicare Boards of Trustees. 2012. *Status of the Social Security and Medicare Programs.* Accessed November 2012 at http://www.ssa.gov/OACT/TRSUM/index.html.

Social Security Online. 2012. *Life Expectancy for Social Security.* Accessed November 2012 at http://www.ssa.gov/history/lifeexpect.html.

Sokolovsky, J. 2004. "Aging." Pp. 217–223 in *Encyclopedia of Medical Anthropology: Health and Illness in the World's Cultures,* edited by Carol R. Ember and Melvin Ember. New York: Kluwer Academic Publishers.

Street, D., and J. S. Cossman. 2006. "Greatest Generation or Greedy Geezers? A Life Course Approach to Social Spending Preferences." *Social Problems* 53(1):75–96.

Szulc, T. 1988, May 29. "How We Can Help Ourselves Age with Dignity." *Parade* 4–7.

Tonkinson, R. 1978. *The Mardudjara Aborigines.* New York: Holt, Rinehart, and Winston.

Toossi, M. 2012. "Labor Force Projections to 2020: A More Slowly Growing Workforce." *Monthly Labor Review.* Accessed November 2012 at http://www.bls.gov/opub/mlr/2012/01/art3full.pdf.

Treas, J. 1995. "Older Americans in the 1990s and Beyond." *Population Bulletin* 50:1–48.

United Nations Population Division. 2012. *World Population Prospects. 2012.* Accessed October 2012 at http://www.indexmundi.com/facts/indicators/SP.POP.65UP.TO.ZS.

US Administration on Aging (AOA). 2012. *Projected Future Growth of the Older Population.* Accessed October 2012 at http://www.aoa.gov/aoaroot/aging_statistics/future_growth/future_growth.aspx#age.

US Census Bureau. 2008. *Table 12. Projections of the Population by Age and Sex for the United States: 2010 to 2050* (NP2008-T12). Washington, DC: Population Division, U.S. Census Bureau.

US Census Bureau. 2012. *Current Population Survey, 1960 to 2010 Annual Social and Economic Supplements.* Accessed Oct 2012 at http://www.census.gov/hhes/www/poverty/data/incpovhlth/2009/pov09fig05.pdf.

US Election Project 2010. 2010. *2010 Early Voting.* Accessed November 2012 at http://elections.gmu.edu/early_vote_2010.html.

Vaupel, J. W., et al. 1998. "Biodemographic Trajectories of Longevity." *Science.* 280(5365):855–60.

Vincentnathan, S. G., and L. Vincentnathan. 1994. "Equality and Hierarchy in Untouchable Intergenerational Relations and Conflict Resolutions." *Journal of Cross-Cultural Gerontology* 9:1–19.

Walker, J. 2010. "Elder Stereotypes in Media and Popular Culture." *Aging Watch Protection, Promotion, Participation.* Accessed Nov 2012 at http://www.agingwatch.com/?p=439.

Yang Y. 2007. "Is Old Age Depressing? Growth Trajectories and Cohort Variations in Late Life Depression." *Journal of Health and Social Behavior* 48:16–32.

Yates, R. E. 1986, August 14. "Growing Old in Japan: They Ask Gods for a Way Out." *Philadelphia Inquirer,* 3A.

© iStockphoto/Thinkstock

Chapter Overview ▼

12 Family and Intimate Relationships

Learning Objectives ▼

12.1
- Describe the four family forms and three marriage patterns.
- Explain the various residential patterns of families.
- Define and identify the various patterns of descent.

12.2
- Discuss different theoretical perspectives as they apply to the family unit.

12.3
- Illustrate the different stages in family construction.

12.4
- Illustrate the various forms that family violence takes and assess its impact on later social development.

12.5
- Identify the major transitional stages in the American family.

12.6
- Discuss the different alternatives to the classic family forms.

12.7
- Discuss how race, class, and gender affect our understanding and perceptions of the family.

© iStockphoto/Thinkstock

When my first marriage ended in divorce, the hardest part was explaining it to my five-year-old daughter. She was too young to understand, really. All that she knew was that daddy was moving out. My wife and I sat her on the couch and offered her a bowl of vanilla ice cream bought just for this occasion. As she devoured the frozen treat, we tried to explain to her exactly what was happening.

My daughter stared up at me with a ring of melted ice cream around her mouth. "Why do you have to go, Daddy?" she asked. "Did you do something wrong? Did I do something wrong?"

"No," I told her. "I just have to go. When you are older you will understand."

At first, I stayed close and visited regularly. Then, a distant job offer was too good to refuse in a struggling economy, so I moved far away.

"Don't worry," I exclaimed, "I will still come to visit." And I did, though with much less frequency. Visitations declined to once a year as the demands of work, distance, and beginning a new family all took their toll. I missed her learning to ride a bike. I missed her school plays.

By the time I moved close again, my daughter was 12, struggling in school and defiant. Visitation increased, but I could sense emotional distance between us. Several times, she asked me to explain why her mother and I split. I evaded the questions. Perhaps I was too embarrassed to answer, or perhaps I did not really understand myself.

As I studied the family in graduate school, I learned that my behavior was typical for many fathers, and I learned that my behavior had consequences for my child. I learned that many of my daughter's struggles in school may have been due to my inconsistent contact, feelings of abandonment, or a distrust of significant others. Her personality was shaped in part by her surroundings, which included a father who came sporadically and offered little in the way of explanation. She was, as sociologist C. Wright Mills predicted, a product both of her personal experiences with divorce and a changing society that has normalized divorce and absent parenting. I learned how the sociological imagination played a very real part in her behavior.

I came to see how the choices I made about career and family had affected others. I began to understand the perceptions of normlessness that underscore the modern family. And I wondered if it was too late to set the record straight.

12.1 Introduction to the Concept of Family

Although it takes a variety of forms, the family is a pervasive social institution that helps to shape who we are and who we become.

- Describe the four family forms and three marriage patterns.
- Explain the various residential patterns of families.
- Define and identify the various patterns of descent.

The family is the strongest agent of socialization.

© Monkey Business Images/Dreamstime.com

Think back to your earliest memory. It might include memories of playing catch with your father. It might include sitting at the dinner table with your mother and brother and sister. It might be a happy memory or a sad one. Whatever the memory, chances are that it involves not just you but members of your family as well. From the time we are born, we are part of a larger interactive world that may take a variety of forms and sizes. Yet despite an incredible variety of organization, the idea of family as a social institution has been a mainstay of human existence. Through our childhood and into adulthood, the family remains a cornerstone of our social life. In this chapter, we shall explore the many forms that families can take. We shall discuss how families affect us developmentally and socially and how changing family structures affect society.

Defining Family and Kinship

We spend a substantial part of our lives within a family. While most of us can easily identify individuals who are part of our family, it is another thing entirely to define what a family is. In fact, given the vast diversity of family forms, can we define what a family is at all?

Generally speaking, a **family** is a social institution that unites people in groups in order to cooperate and care for one another, including any children. Most families are based on ideas of **kinship**, bonds based on specific cultural relationships such as common ancestry or social conventions such as marriage or adoption. Notions of kinship and family are cultural universals. That is, they exist in every culture. However, the specific ways in which the institution of family is structured from culture to culture are highly varied.

Family Structures and Characteristics

While all families do have some things in common, there is also considerable variation in the ways in which families are structured across cultures and across time. The ways in which families are structured may vary with cultural mores, economic conditions, social convention, or other factors. Structurally, four family forms are possible FIGURE 12-1.

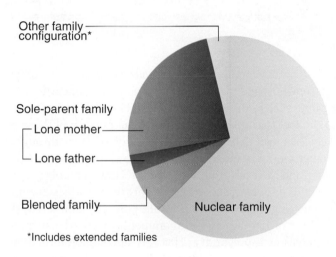

Other family configuration* (includes extended families)
Sole-parent family
Lone mother
Lone father
Blended family
Nuclear family

*Includes extended families

FIGURE 12-1 Modern society is comprised of a variety of family forms.
Source: Data from Kreider, Rose M. and Renee Ellis. 2011. "Living Arrangements of Children: 2009," Current Population Reports, P70–126. U.S. Census Bureau. Accessed January 22, 2013 (http://www.census.gov/prod/2011pubs/p70-126.pdf).

Family A group of individuals related to one another by blood, marriage, adoption, or social convention.

Kinship The linking of people through blood, marriage, adoption, or social convention.

Nuclear family A family consisting of two parents and children.

Sole-parent family A family composed of one parent and children.

Extended family A family consisting of more than two generations or relatives living within the same household.

Blended family A family created when people with children from previous relationships remarry. Also known as a stepfamily.

Marriage A socially approved union between individuals.

In the Western world, the most common family form is the **nuclear family**. This is typically defined as a husband, wife, and any mutual children. Yet many families lack one parent. Although such **sole-parent families** often have significant challenges, they can also be remarkably stable and developmentally appropriate. Some families include not only parents but additional kin as well. Grandparents, aunts, uncles, or other kin may reside with the nuclear family to create an **extended family**. Finally, a **blended family** consists of individuals that come together from previous relationships, with one or both of the parents bringing children from those previous relationships. Blended families may also have mutual children.

Marriage Patterns

Marriage may be defined as a group's socially approved means of uniting people in a mating arrangement. Often, this involves some degree of ritual or formality that is used to express commitment to forming a family. While these rituals vary greatly, the end result is universally a socially recognized and approved structure that forms the basis for the creation of a family. Understanding marriage patterns is sociologically relevant because family forms the basis of our social units. The great variety of marriage patterns lays the foundation for the vast ways in which families can be formed. Because families are the most important agent of socialization, understanding family forms helps us develop our sociological imagination.

Many American families are sole-parent families. Most sole-parent families are headed by females.
© LiquidLibrary

Extended families consist of parents, children, and other kin.

© digitalskillet/Shutterstock, Inc.

The Brady Bunch featured the challenges associated with the creation of a blended family.

© ZUMA Press, Inc./Alamy

Monogamy Marriage to only one partner at a time.

Polygamy Marriage that unites more than two partners.

Polygyny A form of marriage in which a man may have more than one wife.

Polyandry A form of marriage in which a woman has more than one husband.

Endogamous Marriage within one's own social group.

Exogamous Marriage outside of one's own social group.

Residential patterns Culturally determined patterns that dictate where new families will live.

Matrilocal A family system in which the new family lives near the wife's parents.

Patrilocal A family system in which the new family lives near the husband's parents.

Like families, marriages may take a variety of forms. While most people in the Western world believe in **monogamy**, a marital form that unites one man and one woman, this is certainly not the only way that marriage can be structured. Indeed, many cultures around the world practice **polygamy**, a marriage that unites a person with more than one spouse. Polygamy may take two forms FIGURE 12-2.

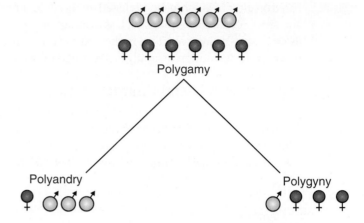

FIGURE 12-2 Polygamy is a broad term that refers to any marital structure in which there is more than one spouse. Polyandry refers to a marriage in which one woman has multiple husbands. Polygyny refers to polygamy in which a man has multiple wives.

Across the world, the most commonly sanctioned marital form is **polygyny**. In polygynous marriages, one husband may be united to more than one wife at the same time. Many African tribes, such as those in Botswana and Lesotho, sanction polygyny. This may be due to the fact that because of the extreme poverty of those regions, women are more likely than men to be unmarried or widowed. Also, throughout history, males have a higher mortality rate than females. Thus, polygyny functions as a means to ensure women and their offspring are cared for. However, polygyny requires considerable investment of resources, and generally only the wealthiest members of a society are capable of engaging in the practice. So while polygyny is culturally the most commonly sanctioned form of marriage, it is less commonly practiced than monogamy.

Another form of polygamy is **polyandry**. This very uncommon form of marriage unites one woman with more than one husband. Polyandry is uncommon largely because of the relative lack of social power and resources that women possess in society. However, in Tibet, polyandry is a traditional marriage form that emerged because farming the difficult terrain to support a family requires considerable physical strength and cooperation. Women take multiple husbands, often brothers to one another, to help tend the land.

Marriages may also be **endogamous** or **exogamous**. Endogamous marriages unite individuals of the same social category, such as village, social class, or caste. Conversely, exogamy unites individuals of different social categories. Endogamy provides continuity in the social hierarchy and allows parents to pass down their social standing to their children. Exogamy serves to link people of different social categories so as to ensure the spread of culture and to increase social ties with neighboring communities.

Residential Patterns

When new families are formed through marriage or other means, the question of where and with whom the new family should reside emerges as a consideration. **Residential patterns** of families are culturally determined patterns that dictate where new families will live. There are three general residential patterns.

Societies such as the Tlingit of the Pacific Northwest coast are **matrilocal**. In matrilocal societies, new families reside with or very near the wife's parents, forming an extended family clan based through the maternal line. Conversely, **patrilocal** societies are those in which the new family lives with or very near the husband's family.

Although historically many families have been shown to be patrilocal, the practice appears to be in decline worldwide.

Much of the Western world practices neolocality. **Neolocal** societies are ones in which the new family lives apart from both sets of parents. Neolocality is on the rise but tends to be limited to areas with sufficient resources for the new family to set up independent residence. In many societies in which resources are scarce, neolocality remains unrealistic as a residential pattern.

Patterns of Descent

As we shall explore in more depth later, one of the traditional functions of the family is to provide identity of children through descent. **Descent** refers to the way in which a society traces kinship through generations. Descent can be used not only to identify current family and ancestry but also to provide information about social class or status.

In **matrilineal** societies, kinship and sometimes property is passed from mothers to their children. Most hunter/gather and horticultural societies follow a matrilineal pattern of descent. This is because in such societies, women tend to be the main food producers. In societies in which food is scarce, it is important for the survival of society that the supply of food remains attached to the family line. Conversely, in agrarian and pastoral societies, men are the primary food producers and property holders. As such, these societies have adopted a **patrilineal** line of descent. In patrilineal societies, kinship is traced through the father. Industrial societies, in which a substantially greater degree of gender equality exists, practice **bilateral descent**. In bilateral descent, kinship is traced through both parents, and relatives of both the mother and father are counted among an individual's extended family.

Patterns of Authority and Power

Historically, despite considerable variation in the structure and composition of families, one cultural universal is patriarchy. **Patriarchy** is defined as a society or group in which men hold all or the majority of social power. **Matriarchy**, a system in which women hold more social power than men, has never been conclusively demonstrated to exist (Brown 1991). No current matriarchies exist, and all alleged historical accounts of matriarchies have either been discounted or have yet to be confirmed (Bamberger 1974; Goldberg 1973).

Despite the fact that gender norms in the Western world are gradually becoming more equal, many patriarchal family customs remain. One example of this is the custom of a new bride taking the surname of her husband. Similarly, children usually take the last name of their father. Another example of the persistence of patriarchy is the custom in which the parents of the bride pay for the wedding. This custom is a remnant of the dowry system, still practiced in many societies, in which fathers pay to marry off their daughters.

Polyandry is a rare form of marriage that unites one woman with multiple men.
© Chris Curtis/Shutterstock, Inc.

Neolocal A society in which the new family lives apart from both sets of parents.

Descent A system by which members of society trace kinship through generations.

Matrilineal A type of society in which kinship and sometimes property is passed from mothers to their children.

Patrilineal Describes a system of descent that considers only the father's side.

Bilateral descent A system by which members of society trace kinship from both the mother's and father's side.

Patriarchy A society in which males maintain the majority of social power.

Matriarchy A society in which women maintain the majority of social power.

CONCEPT LEARNING CHECK 12.1   Introduction to the Concept of Family

Please match the definition to the family form that it describes.

_____ **1.** A family consisting of one parent and children.

_____ **2.** A family created when people with children from previous relationships remarry; also known as a step-family.

_____ **3.** A family that consists of a mother, father, children, and other kin.

_____ **4.** A family consisting of two parents and children.

A. Extended family

B. Sole-parent family

C. Nuclear family

D. Blended family

12.2 Theoretical Perspectives on Families

Different theoretical perspectives can lead to very different conclusions about the family and its place in society.

- Discuss different theoretical perspectives as they apply to the family unit.

Families are remarkable in their variability of structure and characteristics. This variety is the result of cultural constructs rooted in the environmental and economic circumstances such that each society believes its own family form to be the most natural and most logical. We should not assume, however, that any particular means of descent, residential pattern, or marital pattern is necessarily better than another. Rather, these patterns are based on factors unique to the particular society. To appreciate this fact more fully, let us look at how each of the major theoretical perspectives views the family.

Functionalist Perspective

The functionalist perspective argues that each institution in society fulfills basic functions that contribute to the operation of society as a whole. Functionalists believe that families not only contribute to society, they also contribute many essential tasks in society, forming the very backbone of society.

Sociologist Talcott Parsons argued that the family performed two main functions. **Primary socialization** refers to a process by which children learn the values and norms of their society. Relatedly, the family plays a fundamental role in the development and maintenance of an individual's personality. **Personality stabilization** refers to the role that the family plays in the cognitive and emotional development of the individual. Indeed, considerable research shows that the family is the strongest agent of socialization and that the family plays a strong role in the emotional well-being of individuals.

For Parsons, marriage is an institution that developed as a means by which men and women may engage in mutual support of their physical and psychological well-being. For example, men who are married tend to live longer and have fewer health problems. Married women also tend to have better physical health and are less likely to engage in unsafe behaviors. However, research also shows that women, on average, benefit less from marriage than men (Wilson and Oswald 2005).

Parsons believed that the nuclear family provided the best family structure to handle the unique challenges of industrial society. Recent research confirms that from a developmental perspective, the nuclear family does offer significant advantages over other family forms. One such advantage is monetary. In industrial societies, it is common for both parents to work to contribute to a generally higher standard of living than sole-parent families. In situations in which one parent does not work, Parsons argued that the specialization of family roles resulting from one parent working and one parent staying home contributes to the emotional well-being of children and the stability of the family unit.

Building on his early work, other functionalists have suggested that the family performs functions beyond those specified by Parsons. For example, in addition to socialization and material and emotional security, families also provide a means by which society can regulate sexual activity and pass on social identity in terms of religion, ethnicity, and social class. Regardless of the society or the form that families take within those societies, functionalists consider these functions to be universal.

Yet despite some evidence in support of his views, Parsons's view of the family is generally considered dated and obsolete. Functionalist understandings of the family have often been interpreted as justifying rigid and conservative family roles and failing to acknowledge changing social norms and changing family values. Indeed, historically, families in the Western world have changed considerably over the last

Primary socialization The main process by which children learn the values and norms of their society.

Personality stabilization The role that family plays in the cognitive and emotional development of the individual.

200 years. Historical and economic forces have shifted family structures away from the dominant form of the nuclear family to a greater variety of family forms, which we will explore in more detail later in the chapter. Implicit in these changes is a shift in the functions of the family. For example, the advent of social welfare programs has had the latent consequence of eroding many of the traditional roles of the father. Inevitably, this spurs a redefinition of the roles within the family and of the family as a social institution.

Conflict Perspective

The central premise of the conflict perspective is the struggle over power and resources. In terms of the family, the conflict perspective explores the ways in which family creates and maintains social inequality.

As we have already learned, family structures the world over are based in patriarchy. Conflict theorists argue that patriarchy is a means by which males control the sexuality of women and gain control of social power and resources in society. Friedrich Engels (1884) FIGURE 12-3 argued that patriarchy arose as a means for males to keep track of inheritance. In this way, men are able to concentrate their wealth over time and pass their wealth along through bloodlines to renew the dominant class structure in subsequent generations.

Many feminists have approached marriage and family from a conflict perspective. Some feminists argue that marriage always implies a power imbalance because men and women in the family often adopt different roles that have socially defined boundaries that are patriarchal in nature. Feminism seeks to change the nature of relationships between men and women to equalize the power in the relationship.

Conflict is inevitable in all families. When two or more people work to function together as a unit, sharing resources, space, and stress, conflict is bound to occur. It is safe to say that conflict in families will never be completely eliminated. However, the feminist approach has had an impact on power relations in American families. Morin and Cohen (2008) examined decision making in American households. Surprisingly, they found that in nearly half of all American households surveyed, the wife makes more decisions about money, entertainment, and purchases. In another 30% of the sample, men and women made decisions jointly. Only in one quarter of the families surveyed did the husband make more decisions. These findings suggest that the power imbalance in families may be changing.

FIGURE 12-3 Freidrich Engels believed that the family is a means by which males maintain dominance over females.

© johnrochaphoto/China/Alamy

Domestic Violence through a Conflict Approach

Domestic violence in its various forms may be seen through the conflict perspective as a means of achieving and maintaining unequal power relationships between men and women. In this case, men use violence to control not only economic resources and social power that women have access to but also their specific behaviors within the family.

However, in the Western world, the power of wives has been increasing. More women are working for income, and they are making more money than ever before. Additionally, women are gaining more power in key family decisions (Rogers and Amato 2000). Still, despite significant strides in this area, research shows the **symmetrical family**—a family that is egalitarian in the distribution of responsibilities—remains elusive.

Criticisms of the conflict perspective include objections from scholars such as Yalom (2001) and Kompter (1989). They argue that while indeed men maintain a considerable advantage in overt social and political power, women maintain power covertly through their dominance in domestic spheres. Kompter points out that women, through the process of child rearing, have the power to socialize and shape the values, beliefs, and behaviors of future generations. She argues that this covert power is largely undetected by the dominant patriarchies, yet it remains an important dimension of social control and power.

Symmetrical family A family that is equal in the distribution of responsibilities.

Symbolic Interactionist Perspective

The functionalist and social conflict perspectives approach the family as a structural institution. That is, they study the family as if it were an entity in and of itself, as a whole that is greater than the sum of its component parts. In contrast, the symbolic interactionist perspective analyzes the family by looking at the parts of whole. Symbolic interactionism tries to understand how the roles and concepts of the family are constructed through the interactions that take place within the family. These interactions are influenced, in part, by the social institutions that shape families in society. At the same time, the unique experiences of each individual in the family also shape the interactions between family members. Symbolic interactionism places more emphasis on the latter. Symbolic interactionism argues that family roles are constructed as individuals within each family negotiate the roles through repeated interactions with one another.

For example, what comes to mind when you think of the word *mother*? You might think of a nurturing, loving person who cooks for the family, dresses children, and packs their lunch for school. Alternatively, you might think of someone who wears a suit, drops her child off at day care, and rushes to the office. In either case, symbolic interactionism argues that your understanding of the term *mother* is shaped by your experiences and interactions within your family. As evidence, symbolic interactionists present evidence that people tend to parent as they were parented. That is, people tend to replicate the behaviors of their parents through generations.

Constructing a Family

Constructing a family is one of the most important events in a person's life. Because it represents a radical change, we often rely on social scripts to help us transition into the new position. How we understand the new roles can be understood through a symbolic interactionist perspective.

Ask yourself what it means to be a husband or a wife. Different people will likely answer this question in different ways. Indeed, whatever preconceived notions of the role of wife or husband a person enters into a marriage with, they will likely be redefined several times as the relationship progresses. As circumstances change, roles are negotiated and redefined on an individual level. Thus, according to the symbolic interactionist perspective, the family is constructed through interaction rather than through the imposition of social structures.

Social Exchange Approach

Cost/benefit analysis The comparison of the costs and benefits of remaining in a relationship.

Relatedly, the social exchange approach is also a microsociological approach. The social exchange approach also sees marriage and the family as a form of negotiation. However, in this perspective, negotiations are framed in terms of **cost/benefit analysis**. In other words, people compare the costs and benefits of being in a relationship. If the benefits of remaining in the relationship are greater than the costs incurred, the individuals will remain in the relationship. However, if the costs of the relationship exceed the benefits, the relationship will likely end. Individuals continuously evaluate the relationship and make judgments about the desirability of the relationship in relation to alternatives.

These individual cost/benefit analyses can be framed in a variety of ways. Often, men and women seek different things from relationships. For example, cross-cultural studies of relational expectations indicate that men from all cultures seek the same characteristics in women, while women in all cultures seek the same general characteristics in men. These studies have repeatedly shown that women seek men who have potential to accumulate significant access to fundamental resources or other wealth. Men, on the other hand, prefer women who demonstrate reproductive potential (Bereczkei, Voros, Gal, and Bernath 1997).

Certainly, though, there is more to mate selection than these studies conclude. Women and men also seek as mates individuals with whom they have something in common. Most often, people pair with individuals that are similar to themselves on a number of characteristics. Recall that in most cultures, endogamy—marriage within one's own social category—is most common.

Evolutionary Perspectives

Decisions about who to start a family with are cost/benefit decisions. But unlike the social exchange perspective, which frames cost/benefit decisions in terms of an ongoing interaction between family members, the evolutionary perspective delves deep into our human heritage in an attempt to understand why we engage in the kinds of decisions that we do. Rooted in the work of Charles Darwin, who outlined the theory of evolution by natural selection in 1859, evolutionary perspectives on the family seek to understand how the family is both a cause and consequence of our evolved nature. In fact, the evolutionary approach to families is the oldest approach in sociology, dating back to the works of Finnish sociologist Edward Westermarck (1891). Contrary to popular beliefs of the time, Westermarck believed that the original form of human familial attachment was monogamy, with a strong tendency toward the nuclear family, which he considered to be the fundamental and universal unit of society.

Understanding the ancestry of humans offers us insight into how families are formed and how and why they change over time. However, this does not mean that sociological perspectives on the family are irrelevant. In fact, sociological perspectives on the family, as we have already seen, offer significant insight into how families are formed. Moreover, unlike evolutionary theories of the family, sociological perspectives offer significant insight into how families operate from day to day, how they are influenced by the social structure, and how families change over time.

CONCEPT LEARNING CHECK 12.2   Theoretical Perspectives on Families

Choose the best answer to the questions below.

_____ **1.** The process by which children learn the values and norms of their society is called:

    A. personality stabilization.

    B. secondary socialization.

    C. primary socialization.

    D. cost/benefit analysis.

_____ **2.** A family that is egalitarian in the distribution of responsibilities is called a(n):

    A. symmetrical family.

    B. egalitarian family.

    C. equal power relationship.

    D. progressive family.

EXPLAIN

3. Explain how the social exchange perspective and the evolutionary perspective are `similar. Explain how they are different.

12.3 Stages of Intimate Relationships

Families are constructed in stages that vary in their rate but are generally similar in their sequences within cultures.

- Illustrate the different stages in family construction.

Although they vary from culture to culture, all societies recognize distinct stages in the development of a family. In some societies, future spouses are chosen by the parents, often when their children are still very young. In such cases, romance and love are not considered essential elements of the marital bond, though they often develop

Dating scripts Culturally guided rules and expectations about dating practices.

Romantic love People being sexually attractive to one another and often idealizing one another.

Dating scripts are culturally guided rules and expectations about dating practices.

© Jupiterimages/Thinkstock

Although practiced in many different ways, marriage is a culturally universal way of forming a new family.

© PhotoCreate/Shutterstock, Inc.

after the marriage has already taken place. In other societies, marriage is left up to the individuals. In such cases, the development of romantic feelings and love usually precede the marital bond.

Love and Intimacy

Although dating usually begins in adolescence, children begin to form bonds with the opposite sex late in middle childhood. These relationships, though rarely progressing past the friendship stage, are fundamentally different than same-sex friendships. Children use these early relationships to practice dating scripts. **Dating scripts** are culturally guided rules and expectations about dating practices. For example, which sex should ask the other on the date? Who should pay? The scripts may, of course, change over time. While several generations ago, it was seen as generally inappropriate for a woman to ask out a man, it is now a much more socially acceptable practice. Because these expectations change, they need to be explored and practiced. As true dating develops, it becomes a means by which the individual learns not only societal expectations for courtship but also about her or his specific dating partner. In fact, dating becomes a way to determine the level of attraction to the dating partner.

Attraction is the foundation for romantic love. **Romantic love** is defined as people being sexually attracted to one another and often idealizing one another. Originally, social scientists believed that romantic love was a solely Western phenomenon. We now know that this is not the case. A study involving 166 cultures around the globe found that romantic love was present in 88% of the cultures surveyed (Jankowiak and Fischer 1992). However, as already pointed out, the process of forming a family varies from culture to culture. While in some societies the act of marriage precedes romantic love, in Western society, romantic love is seen as a precursor to marriage.

Although the norms of Western society allow us to choose our marital partner freely, such choices are seen by sociologists as constrained by the social structure. Most often, we marry people who have many similar characteristics as ourselves. This **homogamy** is usually due to the spatial proximity of individuals. For example, people in poverty tend to cluster in specific urban areas, with little access to suburban areas. Thus, it is likely that a person living in poverty will meet and marry someone who lives a similar life style. Similarly, people who live in the same area tend to work, go to school, and attend church in the same area, thus increasing the chances that they will marry someone who shares these commonalities. Therefore, both preference and proximity are key sociological variables that influence family formation (Kalmijn 1998). It is difficult to measure rates of homogamy, however, since there are many variables that influence mate choice, and researchers often focus on one or two at a time.

Marriage

The term *wedding* derives from a Greek word meaning *pledge*. The cultural universal called marriage is in fact nothing short of a pledge to form a family. Although practiced in many different ways, marriage is seen as the primary way in which a new family is formed, bonding two individuals together through a ceremony in which the couple pledges to uphold certain societal rules about how the family should function. The pledge may be witnessed only by family, by family and friends, or by the whole community.

In the United States, nearly every adult will marry at least once in her or his life. However, social scientists have noticed a trend toward later age at first marriage. In the 1960s, the average age at first marriage was 22.8 for men and 20.3 for women. However, in 2000, the average ages at first marriage had increased to 26.8 for men and 25.1 for women. Several explanations have been offered to explain this phenomenon.

One explanation is that an increase in rates of cohabitation among young adults is a primary cause of the delay in marriage. Another explanation is the increasing number of Americans—especially women—attending colleges. Most college students wait until after graduation to get married. While a study by Waite and Spitze (1981) found that premarital employment can actually hasten marriage, most research suggests that increased participation of women in the labor force may delay marriage as women work to establish careers before marrying (Cherlin 1981). As college graduation and increasing participation in the workforce have improved the economic position of women in society, women are less likely to see the need for a male breadwinner. As the economic position of men declines relative to that of women, males may be seen as less attractive mates and as less able to adequately take care of a family. Indeed, this explanation has been used to explain the low rates of marriage among blacks. As black men continue to suffer poor economic conditions, they may be viewed as poor prospects for marriage.

A final explanation may be that as society changes, people are becoming more individualized, thus making marriage less important than it has historically been. It is likely that no one of these explanations is sufficient to completely explain the trend. Rather, a combination of causes is probably the best way to view this phenomenon.

Homogamy The tendency of people with similar characteristics to marry one another.

Cohabitation Two people living together in a sexual relationship without being married.

Cohabitation

As the average age for first marriage has increased in America, so has the trend toward cohabitation. **Cohabitation** is defined as an unmarried couple sharing the same household. This practice is a relatively new development in the family, and although it seems to have emerged among poorly educated groups with low socioeconomic statuses, today it is primarily practiced by young adults. In 1970, rates of cohabitation hovered around 11%. By the 1980s, the rates had risen to nearly 45%. Today, the rate of cohabitation is slightly over 50% FIGURE 12-4.

As the trend emerged, society considered cohabitation to be a deviant practice. Social scientists, on the other hand, argued that cohabitation was a largely positive

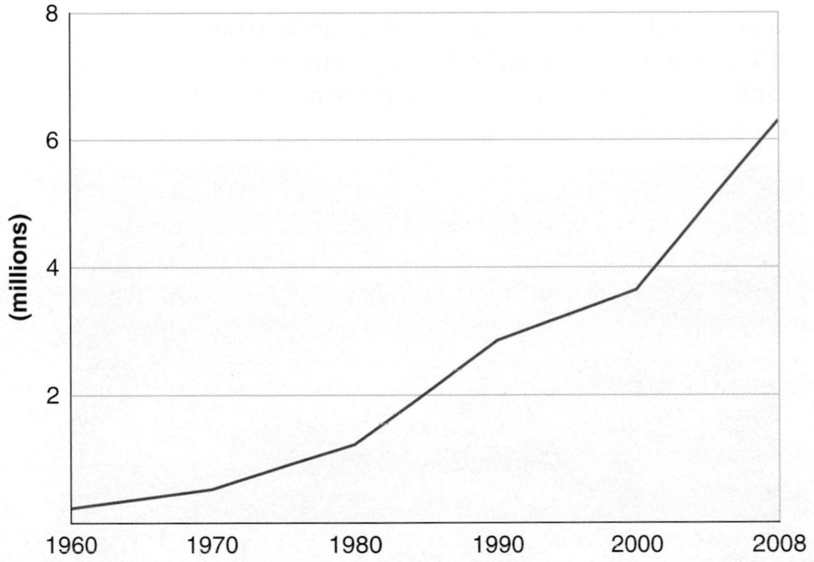

FIGURE 12-4 Cohabitation in America has been increasing over time. *Source: © 2009 The National Marriage Project and the Institute for American Values. "The State of Our Unions: Marriage in America 2009." Retrieved January 2012 (http://stateofourunions. org/2009/SOOU2009.pdf).*

development in the formation of the family. Initially, it was argued that cohabitation prior to marriage would strengthen marriages by acting as a practice for marred life. Couples could live together in order to work out any problems that might occur before they got married, thus making the transition to married life more smooth.

We now know that this assessment was in error. In fact, research on the transition from cohabitation to marriage met with two unexpected results. First, not all cohabiting couples who remain together get married. Among cohabiting couples who do marry, however, research has shown that the likelihood of divorce is significantly higher than for couples who do not cohabit prior to marriage (Axin and Thornton 1992). Andrew Cherlin (1992) has described cohabitation as part of phase of life for young adults who want to leave their options open. Thus, marriage and cohabitation are often unconnected. Rather than revealing itself to be a way to practice forming a marital bond, cohabitation has emerged instead as an alternative to marriage that is becoming increasingly popular in the Western world.

Children

Most people see children as an integral part of the family structure. Indeed, in most cultures, marriages are expected to produce children. In preindustrial societies, the expectation of children is culturally driven by the need for increased labor. The more children that are produced, the more work can be accomplished and the more food and goods the family can produce. Thus, children increase the wealth and social standing of the family. In industrialized nations, however, children are often prohibited from working until they are teenagers, and modern technology has rendered children largely unnecessary for household labor.

Therefore, children have shifted from being an asset to the family to being an economic liability. The average cost of raising one child in America from birth through college now exceeds $250,000!

Perhaps this helps to explain the decline in the average number of children in the United States. Two hundred years ago, the average number of children in America was eight per household. Today, the average is just over one child per household. There are other reasons for this trend. One is that the Western world has extended the length of childhood. Where many societies consider adulthood to begin at puberty, in the Western world, we delay adulthood until the end of adolescence. Another reason is that the death rate for children is considerably lower in industrial nations than in preindustrial countries.

Still, most Americans identify child rearing as one of the primary functions of the family and one of the great joys of life. In fact, parenting maintains a place as a central role in the identity of most Americans. However, that role is markedly different than in other societies. In less developed societies, children are often seen as little adults. Gendered work is often required for the welfare of the entire family, and children are expected to contribute. By contrast, America's substantial wealth has shifted our view of children to one of dependents who are in need of considerable

People in every society see children as an integral part of the family.

© ClickPop/Shutterstock, Inc.

In many societies child labor is necessary for the survival of the family; in America children are prohibited from working until they are teenagers.

(left) © iStock Photo; (right) iStock Photo

nurturing and care. This view creates a paradox, however. On one hand, parents want to provide for their children's needs. On the other hand, this often requires that both parents work outside the home, thus taking time away from parenting. This balance between the material and social needs of the children presents a dilemma for many American parents.

Visual Overview The Formation of the Family

Although the specific paths of family formation are varied across cultures and individuals, people generally form families in the same broad ways; and the family remains the most important social institution for the formation of the sociological imagination.

Dating usually begins in adolescence with dating scripts, culturally guided rules and expectations about dating practices.

Romantic love is defined as people being sexually attracted to one another and often idealizing one another.

Although practiced in many different ways, the pledge of **marriage** is the primary way in which a new family is formed.

Increasing numbers of couples are **cohabiting**—that is, living together as a couple without being married.

Even though the average number of children has declined in industrial nations, most Americans still identify **child rearing** as one of the primary functions of the family.

Separation or **divorce** is more common today than in the mid 20th century. Many divorced people choose to remarry and form blended or step families.

Despite social perceptions to the contrary, most couples find **renewed marital satisfaction** after the last child has left the home due to increased privacy, freedom, and disposable income.

THE SOCIOLOGICAL IMAGINATION   Changing Values and the Generation Gap

As we have learned, the family is the strongest and most pervasive agent of socialization. Parents are instrumental in developing a child's beliefs, values, and behaviors. Parents, of course, had to be socialized into their beliefs and values by previous generations. Societies change, however. Historical events often shape changes in the values that a society holds in a given generation. This means that the values of the older generations are sometimes inconsistent with the values of the younger generations. For example, while premarital sexual relations seem normative today, just two generations ago, this was not the case.

The generation gap raises an interesting question about the sociological imagination. How can older generations with unique historical experiences and values successfully pass on their experiences to generations with different historical circumstances? How can the continuity of culture be maintained in the midst of historical change?

EVALUATE

1. What values do you hold that are different from those of your parents and grandparents?

2. Where did you learn these different values? Think about how the values you hold may change over time.

3. How might the values of your children differ from the values you now hold?

Quality day cares may increase peer socialization among children, and may improve later school performance.

© Masterfile

Filiarchy Emphasis on the power of children in the family.

Permissive parenting A style of parenting in which parents make few demands on their children, imposing few rules and offering little guidance.

Authoritarian parenting A dictatorial style of parenting in which unquestioning obedience is expected from children.

Day Care

Between 20 and 25% of children spend some time in day care. While there do exist quality day care centers that offer warm, loving, and safe environments, most day cares fall short of this ideal. Since many parents do not know what to look for, they may choose a day care that is inappropriate for their needs. Furthermore, parents rarely get to see what goes on while the parents are not present. Although some researchers such as Richard Fiene have called for national standards for day care providers, such regulations have yet to materialize.

Research on the effects of day care on children has met with mixed results. While some research on day care has concluded that day care weakens the child's maternal bonds, other studies have argued that day care increases peer socialization and may even improve later school performance. The discrepancies in research are probably due to the quality of the day cares studied, the methods used in the studies, and the children used in the studies. It is likely that negative effects are most pronounced in poor day care settings and mitigated in more enriching environments where the positive effects are also found. As day cares increase in popularity, more research is clearly needed.

Ways of Parenting

Never the less, parents today are spending more time with their children than they did at any other time in history. This trend is largely due to decreases in time spent on housework driven by new technologies and an increased reliance on prepared foods and restaurants. Another reason for this trend is the new ways in which society perceives children. As already noted, views of children are distinctly different in industrial societies and preindustrial ones. As children have become more dependent upon parents, they have increasingly come to occupy a central role in the family. This trend toward **filiarchy** will likely continue as new technologies drive continued changes in the American family.

Developmental psychologist Diana Baumrind identified four general types of parenting styles TABLE 12-1. Building on her work, sociologists have discovered differences in child-rearing practices that vary with social class and race. While working-class parents tend to see children as developing naturally and with little guidance, middle-class parents tend to see children as needing more guidance. Working-class parents are also more likely to use physical discipline than middle-class parents. African-American parents tend to have either a **permissive parenting** style in which the child is given very little guidance and few rules or an **authoritarian parenting** style in which the parents are very strict and expect unquestioning obedience to the parents.

TABLE 12-1   Parenting Styles and their Developmental Consequences

Parenting Style	Description	Example	Developemental or Behavioral Outcomes
Authoritarian	Parents who are authoritarian set rigid rules for their children. These rules cannot be questioned and must be obeyed in order to avoid punishment. Their communication style is typically one-sided in favor of the parent without consideration of the child's feelings.	The parents choose the clothes that the child wears to school.	Children raised by authoritarian parents are generally obedient and proficient, but rank low in social competence, creativity, self-esteem, and happiness.
Authoritative	Authoritative parents give children choices within defined parameters or guidelines. The communication style is generally two-way, with the parents considering the child's point of view in a democratic fashion.	The parents let the child choose school clothes from three outfits.	Children raised by authoritative parents tend to be happy, well adjusted, successful, and socially competent.
Permissive	Permissive parents make few, if any, rules for their children. The children set their own boundaries. Communication is generally in favor of the child, perhaps informing the parents what the child will be doing.	The child chooses which outfit to wear for school without parental consultation.	Parents who are permissive often raise children who distrust or resent authority, perform poorly in school, and rank low on happiness and self-regulation.
Neglectful	Although the basic needs of the child are often fulfilled, neglectful parents are detached from their child's life. They communicate with their child only when absolutely necessary.	The child chooses which outfit to wear, and the parent is unaware of the choice.	Children of neglectful parents score the lowest across all domains. They are often lack self-control and self-esteem, and tend to rank very low on happiness and social competence.

Source: Adapted from Baumrind, D. 1967. "Child care practices anteceding three patterns of preschool behavior." Genetic Psychology Monographs, 75(1): 43–88. and Maccoby, E.E. 1992. "The role of parents in the socialization of children: An historical overview." Developmental Psychology 28:1006–1017.

By contrast, white parents tend to be more **authoritative** in their parenting, giving the child choices and responsibilities within a defined framework. Baumrind contrasts these three parenting styles with **neglectful** parenting, which occurs when parents systemically abuse their children, or do not attend to their basic needs.

Sociological analysis of the social structure provides some insight into why these patterns emerge. African-American families are more likely to be sole-parent, female-headed households. The demands of working and raising a family often lead to role conflict as the mother is forced to choose between time spent working and time spent parenting. Thus, permissive parenting becomes more common. Alternatively, the various demands placed upon a working mother may require considerable control over the environment in order to ensure that everything gets done. This may lead to authoritarian parenting.

Housework

While in many societies, gender roles remain clearly defined, in the Western world the boundaries between typical male and female roles have become increasingly blurred. The increasing number of women in the workforce and in colleges has driven a shift in perceptions about the roles of males and females in the family. As already noted, these trends have had an impact on the structure and operation of the family.

One area that has not seen a significant change in gender roles, however, is the division of housework. While industrialization has made housework generally easier and less time consuming, and while women have taken an increasingly large role in activities outside of the family, they still tend to do more housework than men FIGURE 12-5.

Authoritative parenting
A democratic style of parenting in which parents give guidance and encouragement with limited freedom.

Neglectful parenting
Parenting in which the parents neglect the child, or act as though the child does not exist.

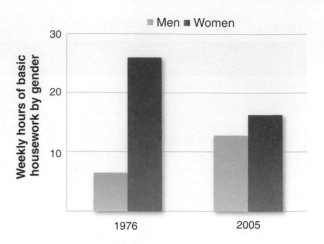

FIGURE 12-5 Although women still do more housework than men, men have increased the total amount of housework over time.
Source: Data from Panel Study of Income Dynamics, public use dataset. 1976, 2005. Produced and distributed by the Institute for Social Research. University of Michigan, Ann Arbor, Michigan.

In Western society, women who work outside of the home engage in what sociologist Arlie Hochschild (1989) has called a "second shift," as they then spend an average of 16.5 hours per week on housework, compared to just over 10 hours of housework per week for men. While men typically indicate that they favor women working outside of the home, men often fail to increase their participation in household work. At the same time, research does indicate that over time, men have increased the total number of hours they spend doing housework, while women have decreased the total hours they spend doing housework.

Interestingly, while both men and women recognize that women do more housework than men, both men and women indicate that they believe this arrangement to be equitable. These results demonstrate the pervasive nature of cultural influence on shaping the American family. However, these results should be interpreted with caution. While it is true that women do more housework than men, on average, men work eight hours a week more than women outside of the home—roughly the difference in hours per week spent on household labor. This fact means that men and women average about the same number of total hours worked in all spheres.

CONCEPT LEARNING CHECK 12.3   Stages of Intimate Relationships

1. List three examples of a dating script. Briefly identify how each one of these examples might contribute to the long-term development of the family.

2. Using Baumrind's styles of parenting, think about what style of parenting your parents or guardian fall into. How did their parenting style help shape who you are now? How might you be different if your parents had used different parenting techniques?

12.4 Problems in the Family

While the family is a safe and secure institution for most people, family violence is a legitimate and too-common social problem.

■ Illustrate the various forms that family violence takes and assess its impact on later social development.

For most people, the family is a safe and nurturing social environment. However, for too many, the family is an intimidating and even violent place. Family violence can come in a myriad of forms, yet all can leave lasting impressions on those who are victims of violence or who witness violence within the family.

Violence and Abuse

Intimate partner violence is a term that refers to any violent act committed against a sexual partner. This violence may be sexual, physical, emotional, or psychological in nature. Rates of intimate partner abuse vary by race, socioeconomic class, and age. Studies have consistently shown that lower socioeconomic status is associated with a higher level of partner abuse. Rates of domestic violence against African Americans are roughly 35% higher than those for whites, largely because African Americans are three times more likely than whites to live in poverty. Additionally, younger women are more likely than older women to be the victims of intimate partner violence. Domestic violence is most common among women between the ages of 16 and 24.

Although data show that rates of intimate partner violence in America are declining, it is important to note that not all abuse is reported to authorities. African Americans and Hispanics report approximately 65% of abuse cases, while whites report only around 50% of cases. Scholars typically credit the decline in intimate partner violence to increased awareness and education, better social support of victims, and tougher criminal justice response to reported incidences.

Intimate partners are not the only victims of abuse in families. Each year, more than 3 million child abuse cases are reported to authorities in the United States. Around 30% of those cases are substantiated. Most confirmed abuse happens at the hands of parents.

Unlike rates of intimate partner violence, rates of child abuse do not appear to be declining. In fact, the number of fatalities due to child abuse and neglect is increasing, despite efforts to increase awareness and strengthen laws protecting children FIGURE 12-6.

Children who are abused often suffer from a variety of negative outcomes, such as depression, delinquency, and other behavioral problems. Additionally, children who are

> **Intimate partner violence**
> Physical, emotional, or psychological abuse toward an intimate partner.

Witnessing abuse as a child doubles the risk that the child will become an abuser later in life.

© Gladskikh Tatiana/Shutterstock, Inc.

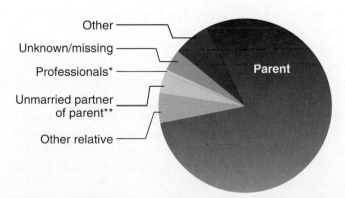

*Includes residential facility staff, child day care providers, and other professionals.

**Defined as someone who has a relationship with the parent and lives in the household with the parent and maltreated child.

FIGURE 12-6 The relationship to the victim to the perpetrator of child abuse (2011).
Source: Data from U.S. Department of Health and Human Services, Administration for Children and Families, Administration on Children, Youth and Families, Children's Bureau. 2012. Child Maltreatment 2011. Accessed January 18, 2013 (http://www.acf.hhs.gov/programs/cb/research-data-technology/statistics-research/child-maltreatment)

Intergenerational transmission of violence The tendency for people who are victims of abuse or who witness abuse to be perpetrators of violence at a later stage of the life course.

Resilience The degree to which a person can endure changes in his or her environment.

victims of abuse are more likely to themselves become abusers. This **intergenerational transmission of violence** is not limited to children who are victims of abuse. Simply witnessing abuse of another family member effectively doubles the chance that a child will become an abuser or a victim of abuse later in life.

Divorce and Dissolution

Although it is often claimed that the rate of divorce in America is around 50%, this figure is misleading. The figure actually refers to the fact that there are about half as many divorces each year as there are marriages. A better way to determine the rate of divorce is to look at the percentage of married people that gets divorced in any given year. Using these figures, fewer than 2% of couples get divorced each year. These effects, of course, are cumulative, though some of these will remarry. Effectively, then, the percentage of Americans who are currently divorced at any given moment is somewhere around 9%. This rate is higher for African Americans (13%) and whites (12.5%) and lower for Hispanics (8%) and Asian Americans (4.6%) FIGURE 12-7. These rates also vary by region of the country, with higher rates of divorce in the southern and western regions of the United States and lower rates in states in the far north FIGURE 12-8.

FIGURE 12-7 Divorce rates vary not only by socioeconomic status, but by race as well. *Source: Elliott, Diana B. and Tavia Simmons. 2011. Marital Events of Americans: 2009, American Community Survey Reports, ACS-13. U.S. Census Bureau, Washington, DC.*

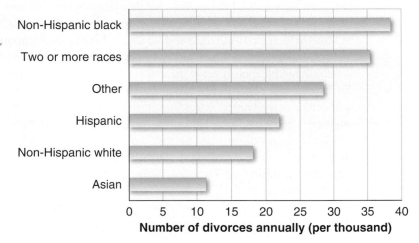

Divorce rates, of course, refer only to couples who were legally married at the time the relationship fractured. Not included in these figures are the high rates of dissolution of cohabiting couples. When these numbers are included, the impression is one of families in a state of flux. The familial changes caused by relational dissolution manifest themselves in developmental and behavioral changes in the individuals involved—particularly children.

The Effects of Divorce on Children

Children who experience divorce at any point along the life course have a greater chance of engaging in delinquent behavior.

Most children of divorced parents do fine, however. Hetherington and Kelly (2002) note that fewer than 15% of children of divorced parents suffer pervasive, long-term negative effects. Whether a child suffers long-term effects from parental dissolution is dependent upon a number of social and psychological ones. Psychologically speaking, a child's resilience is a key factor. **Resilience** refers to the degree to which a person can endure changes in his or her environment. Children with greater resilience are less likely to suffer serious negative consequences from their parents' divorce. Socioeconomic status seems to play a role in the child's adjustment to divorce, with children in the lower income brackets having a higher rate of long-term negative effects than children in middle and upper income brackets. Perhaps this is because children of low-income families are less resilient than other children because of the pervasive problems associated with living in poverty.

Indeed, divorce may actually be seen as a contributing factor to poverty! Social scientists have identified a trend called the **feminization of poverty**. This refers to the fact that a growing number of people in poverty are women, most with children FIGURE 12-9. These are often women who have been through the dissolution of a relationship and who have retained custody of their children. Since men earn more, on average, than women, this dissolution results in a substantial loss of income for the woman. Even with child support and other help, the standard of living for a divorced woman drops about one third.

Feminization of poverty The trend of an increasing number of women—usually with children—living below the poverty line.

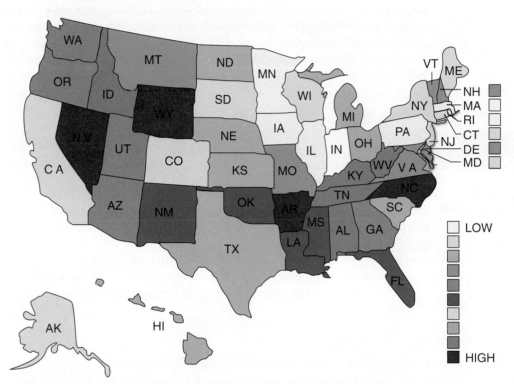

Note: In several cases where 2004 data is unavailable, data from earlier years has been used.

FIGURE 12-8 As this map shows, states in the north generally have lower divorce rates than states in the south and west.
Source: Courtesy of Bruce Wilson, Talk2Action.org. Retrieved January 2012 (http://www.talk2action.org/story/2006/7/13/14120/4811).

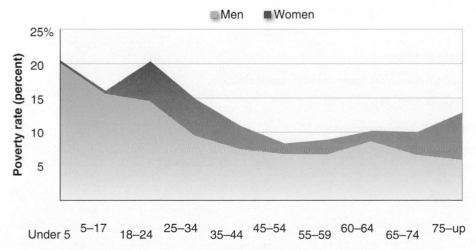

FIGURE 12-9 At all age ranges, more females in the United States live in poverty than males.
Source: Data from US Census Bureau. 2008. Current Population Survey, 2008 Annual Social and Economic Supplement.

Furstenberg and Cherlin (1994) have noted that men typically see marriage and fatherhood as a package deal. This means that if the marriage ends, the father will often gradually disconnect from the children of that marriage as well. Fewer than 20% of children who live apart from their fathers see them at least once a week. Just over half of children who live separate from their fathers have no contact with their fathers at all. Two-fifths of absent fathers pay no child support to their children, and most fathers who do pay do not pay the full amount of court-ordered support.

Despite the increasing risk of poverty due to divorce or relational dissolution, the poverty is often of short duration. Many women who are divorced will eventually remarry, thus adding the new spouse's income to the family and lifting the children out of poverty (Emery 1999). There are identified racial differences in rates of remarriage. While 58% of whites will eventually remarry, the numbers are somewhat lower for Latinas and African Americans—44% and 32%, respectively. Most divorced people marry other divorced people, and since we know that one divorce increases the likelihood for subsequent divorce, these new families are often at high risk for dissolution.

THE SOCIOLOGICAL IMAGINATION   A Matter of Recall

Overwhelmingly, women report more abuse in domestic situations than men, even when both the male and the female in a couple are questioned. This has led to a perception that men either deny many charges of abuse, have different definitions of abuse, or are simply less accurate at reporting abuse than women. A study by DeMaris, Pugh, and Harman (1992) found that these perceptions are inaccurate. Instead, they found that men are more accurate at reporting violent events than women, while women were more accurate at reporting nonviolent relational events.

Although crime rate statistics indicate that rates of domestic violence are declining, this trend may be explained in part by the reluctance of victims to report that they have been abused.

EVALUATE

1. What factors might explain the reluctance to report domestic violence?

2. Discuss how these factors are connected to an individual's development of the sociological imagination.

3. Discuss how the intersection of history (traditional views about the roles of men and women in families) and biography (the experiences of individuals who commit or are victims of domestic abuse) contribute to our understanding of the family.

CONCEPT LEARNING CHECK 12.4   Problems in the Family

Please fill in the blank with the appropriate answer.

1. The degree to which a person can endure changes in his or her environment is called _____.

2. The fact that a growing number of people living in poverty are women is called _____.

Please choose the correct answer for the following questions.

3. Approximately what percentage of the 3 million reported child abuse cases are substantiated?

   A. 10%

   B. 20%

   C. 30%

   D. 50%

4. Approximately what percentage of absent fathers pays no child support?

   A. 40%

   B. 25%

   C. 65%

   D. 10%

12.5 Transitions

The family is a constantly changing social institution that reflects changes in society.

- Identify the major transitional stages in the American family.

As has already been demonstrated, the family as a social institution is neither stable nor fixed. In fact, family forms evolve and change with changing social, economic, and political circumstances. Divorce, remarriage, cohabitation, and other behaviors have all contributed to changes in family forms. Although in society, the nuclear family is still the most widely accepted standard, it is increasingly obvious that alternative family forms are increasing in popularity and have now become a permanent part of our culture.

The considerable number of divorces has resulted in the proliferation of several family forms. While none of these forms are unique to Western culture, they are relatively new forms in Western society. As couples divorce, the parent with custody of the children takes on the role of sole-parent family. As already noted, with only one parent in the home—usually the mother—sole-parent families have a higher than average rate of poverty, with all of the challenges that go along with it. As sole parents transition into new relationships, they may cohabit with new partners and eventually remarry. This forms a blended family in which there is at least one stepparent. Still other families of divorce return to live with parents or other relatives to form an extended family.

Blended Families

Like sole-parent families, blended families face a unique set of challenges. Research from Vischer and Vischer (1979) has shown that blended families are structurally dissimilar to nuclear families. Stepparents often have unclear roles and responsibilities that often cause conflict within the family. For example, to what degree should a stepfather be allowed to discipline his stepchildren? This is no mere academic question. Research shows that stepparents are more likely to abuse their stepchildren than their biological children. Relatedly, evidence suggests that stepparents treat their biological children better than they treat stepchildren.

Structurally, blended families are most similar to adopted or foster families. In such cases, the roles of each family member are not the result of naturally occurring biological relationships but rather through socially and legally constructed means. As a result, the roles of each member must be negotiated, which often results in disagreement and conflict.

Launching Children

Marital happiness is greatest at two points during the lifespan of the marriage. In the first year, couples are in the honeymoon phase of marriage, which is generally characterized by a high level of marital satisfaction for both men and women FIGURE 12-10. When children are born, marital satisfaction declines for several reasons. First, expenses associated with raising children mean that couples often have to sacrifice some activities that they would otherwise have done as a couple. Of course, there is also the fact that children are highly dependent upon their parents, which further restricts the activities that parents—particularly mothers—can engage in. Finally, couples who have children find that they must now compete for time with the children. Where once all of the spouse's attention was focused on the other spouse, now much of that attention is focused on the children. This can cause marital stress in couples who are not prepared for the changes that children bring. This effect is particularly pronounced among men, who report higher drops in marital satisfaction after the birth of children than do women.

FIGURE 12-10 Marital happiness is highest at two points in the life course: during the honeymoon phase and after the last child leaves the home.
Source: Data from Gilbert, Daniel. 2005. Stumbling on Happiness. New York: Vintage Books.

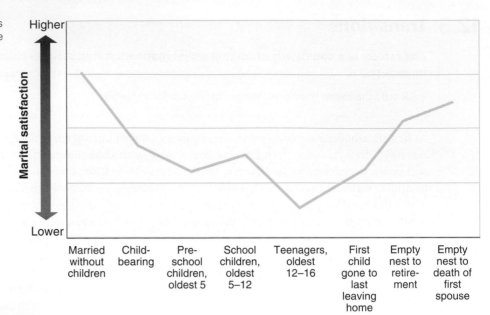

Empty nest syndrome
A myth that parents mourn after the last child leaves the home.

Marital happiness tends to increase after the last child leaves the house.

© Comstock Images/Thinkstock

The Empty Nest Syndrome

Although social scientists used to believe that parents become distraught after the last child leaves the house, research shows that the **empty nest syndrome** is largely a myth. In fact, marital happiness tends to increase substantially after the last child takes flight and leaves the house. In contrast to couples with children, couples who have launched their last child have, on average, more money and more privacy, with more attention given to each other than to children.

Many mothers with children decide to return to the home of their parents out of financial necessity. As divorced women with children move into the home of the mother's parents, the increasing financial burden may cause a delay in retirement for the parents. This return to the nest is also seen among a growing number of young college graduates, especially in times of economic downturn. This recent phenomenon has not been widely or comprehensively studied, so it is hard to assess the impact of this change on the family. However, it is clearly further evidence of the dynamic nature of the family in response to a changing economic and social climate.

CONCEPT LEARNING CHECK 12.5   Transitions

Please fill in the blank with the appropriate answer.

1. Blended families are structurally most similar to _____.

2. Blended families are structurally most dissimilar to _____.

Please answer the following question.

3. Using the concept of the sociological imagination, discuss why blended families may face unique challenges.

12.6 Family Alternatives

Understanding the diversity of the family includes recognizing the emergence of new family forms, which emerge as social norms change.

■ Discuss the different alternatives to the classic family forms.

As we have already learned, the family is a diverse institution. Part of understanding this diversity is the realization that simple definitions of the family are often not appropriate to describe all of the ways in which individuals can coexist. For example, most Americans, when asked, will define a family as a married couple with children. However, sociologists recognize that while this definition represents one kind of family, the definition is not exhaustive of all of the possible ways in which a family might be formed. Behavioral flexibility is often greater than institutional flexibility. Indeed, the emergence and perpetuation of new family forms has created considerable debate within American society about how a family ought to be defined and how society should respond to changes in family structure.

Gay and Lesbian Couples

One of the most controversial family forms is lesbian and gay couples. While many nations, beginning with Denmark in 1989, have legalized gay unions, in America, homosexual unions continue to meet with resistance. Although gay civil unions have been legalized in Hawaii, Vermont, Connecticut, and most recently New York, giving limited legal status to homosexual partnership, 13 states have passed voter-approved Constitutional amendments defining marriage as between one man and one woman. Despite this, trends show a slowly growing acceptance of homosexual relationships. More than one-third of Americans support marriage equality for homosexuals, and just under half support civil unions for homosexual couples that would grant them many legal benefits currently enjoyed by married couples.

Homosexual coupling remains a controversial family form.
© Fleyeing/Dreamstime.com

Gay and Lesbian Couples as Parents

Many gay and lesbian couples are expanding their families by raising children. Most of these children are the result of previous heterosexual relationships, but an increasing number of children raised by homosexual parents are adopted. This, too, has caused controversy. Fewer Americans support the rights of homosexuals to raise children than support their right to marry. Eleven states refuse to recognize the legality of adoptions by homosexual couples, even if the adoption occurred in another state. In some cases, courts have removed children from the custody of homosexual parents. Much of this opposition stems from the unsubstantiated belief that children raised by homosexual parents will be more likely to become homosexual themselves. However, no evidence of this has even been produced. In fact, evidence suggests that children raised by homosexual parents are typically as well adjusted and successful as children raised by heterosexual parents.

Sole-Parent Families

Society has come to legitimate sole-parent families somewhat more than gay and lesbian families. This has occurred perhaps because of the increasing prevalence of this family form in America as a result of the increasing number of divorces. However, somewhat less accepted is the conscious decision to be a sole parent. Women who have children outside of marriage have a much lower degree of support in society. This

While many gay couples choose to raise children, support for gay parenting remains low.
© Stuart Pearce/age fotostock

Racially mixed couples account for about 14.6% of all marriages in the United States.

© Jupiterimages/Thinkstock

has created a social stigma that may create additional challenges for the family. It has already been established that children raised in sole-parent households are more likely to live in poverty and are more likely to have behavioral and academic problems. The idea of intentionally exposing a child to increased risk factors may go a long way toward explaining the social disapproval of this common family form.

Staying Single

While some people never marry because they simply have not met the right person, other people consciously decide to remain single. This decision may be very difficult in a society in which marriage and family formation are part of the social expectation and form the cornerstone of our social fabric. Often, the choice to remain single is met with questions regarding the person's sexual preference or other derision. However, this choice may be rooted more in economic preferences or in the desire to maintain independence. For some, the choice not to marry may evolve from earlier decisions to delay marriage until educational or career goals have been met.

More and more women are choosing to raise children while bypassing the institution of marriage. Patterns of women who raise children outside of marriage tend to take one of two forms. On one hand, some women have children very young, even as early as their teens. In such cases, the prospects for the women and their children are generally poor. Often, these women fail to complete school or stop their education with a high school diploma. This lack of education limits the economic prospects of the family and increases the likelihood that the family will live at or below the poverty line. Increasing social supports for women with children have attempted to combat the struggles these women face. However, the rules for obtaining public assistance are often tedious and difficult to navigate, especially for a mother with limited education. Additionally, when benefits are obtained, they are often insufficient for the circumstances.

On the other side of staying single are women who delay having a child until they have achieved their education or career goals. These women are considerably less likely to live in poverty. They are also more likely to be emotionally and psychologically ready for the challenges of parenthood. Thus, on average, their children are likely to have fewer developmental and social difficulties than children of younger mothers with limited education. What both groups have in common, however, is the significant amount of time that they remain single. Although their feelings and circumstances may eventually change, the choice not to marry is becoming slowly more accepted in society.

Racially Mixed Marriages

Although it is still quite rare in American society, the number of racially mixed marriages is slowly increasing FIGURE 12-11, Currently, the number of racially mixed marriages is about 14.6%. The most common combination of racially mixed marriages is a white husband and an Asian wife. The western United States has the highest concentration of racially mixed marriages. Rates of mixed race marriage also vary by gender. For example, nearly 22% of black male newlyweds marry outside of their race, compared to just 9% of black female newlyweds. Conversely, women of Asian descent marry outside of their race nearly 44% of the time, compared with just 20% of their male counterparts.

There is little doubt that as society continues to change, the family will continue to change as well. New family forms will continue to emerge and flourish, and societal acceptance of those forms will likely follow the same pattern of disapproval followed by gradual acceptance of the new family form.

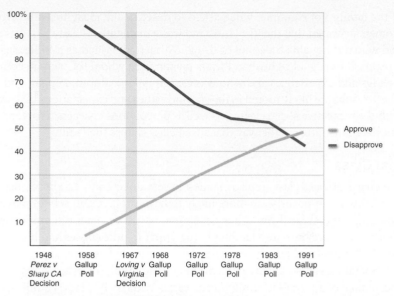

FIGURE 12-11 Support for interracial marriage continues to increase with changing social values.
Source: Data from Marriage Equality USA. 2010. "Polling Data and the Marriage Equality Movement." Retrieved January 2012 (http://www.marriageequality.org/polls-and-studies).

CONCEPT LEARNING CHECK 12.6   Family Alternatives

Please choose the best answer to the questions below.

1. The first nation to legalize gay unions was:

   A. Denmark.

   B. Sweden.

   C. United States.

   D. Canada.

2. How many states have passed Constitutional amendments banning gay marriage?

   A. 6

   B. 8

   C. 13

   D. 22

3. The number of mixed marriages as a percentage of the of the population is about:

   A. 15%.

   B. 4%.

   C. 2%.

   D. 11%.

Please indicate if each statement is true or false.

4. Children raised by homosexual parents are more likely to be gay as adults.

5. The highest concentration of racially mixed marriages in the United States occurs in the western states.

12.7 Families: Class, Race, and Gender

Race, class, and gender intersect to create multiple layers of inequality that manifest in the operation, definition, and understanding of the family.

■ Discuss how race, class, and gender affect our understanding and perceptions of the family.

Race, class, and gender are three dimensions of inequality that affect family structure, finances, and opportunities. They may also affect our understandings and perceptions of the family. For example, when asked to describe the ideal husband, working-class women answered that the ideal husband was a man with a steady job, was nonviolent, and who did not abuse alcohol or drugs. Women identified as middle class, however, answered that the ideal husband was a person with whom the woman could share her feelings and experiences and who was easy to talk to (Rubin, Peplau, and Hill 1981). These results are likely rooted in the specific values and expectations that are associated with the respective social classes, as well as perceptions of access to potential partners. They are illustrative of the way that social class shapes the family.

Social Class

The effects of social class are also manifest in very direct ways. As already noted, children who grow up in poverty are more likely to have problems in school, have behavioral problems, and suffer from other developmental and social difficulties. By contrast, children who are born into families in the upper middle classes and higher have better physical and mental health outcomes, have higher self-esteem, and are happier.

Social class also affects perceptions of the family in other ways. For example, acceptance of alternative family forms varies with social class. Families identified as lower social class tend to be less supportive of alternative family forms such as homosexual pairing than families of higher social class. At the same time, the acceptance of sole parenting as a legitimate family form is higher as social class declines.

Ethnicity and Race

Although we should be careful to avoid stereotyping, it is important to understand how race also helps to shape the family. Because race and ethnicity have real consequences in society that include access to jobs, education, and social power, differences emerge in both beliefs and behaviors associated with the family. While some ethnic and racial minorities attempt to retain their traditional views of the family in the face of rapid cultural change and pressures to assimilate, some views of the family are shaped by the way in which society institutionalizes minority status.

African Americans

African-American families have been widely studied. As a group, African-American families earn only 63% of the national average income. This means that African-American families are more than three times as likely to be poor as white families FIGURE 12-12.

FIGURE 12-12 Child poverty rates by race.
Source: Data from National Center for Children in Poverty. 2007. "Who are America's Poor Children? The Official Story." Retrieved January 2012 (http:\\www.nccp.org/publications/pdf/text_787.pdf).

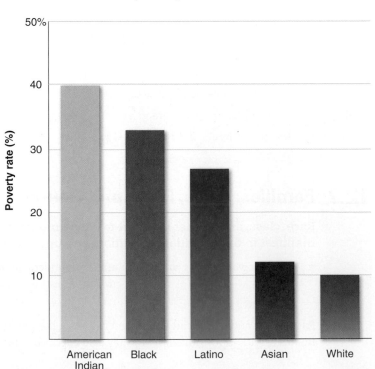

This poverty is often pervasive and may affect the health and well-being of members of the family. This poverty is coupled with the fact that African-American children are less likely to live in two-parent homes. In fact, 45% of African-American households are female headed. Nearly 30% of middle-aged African-American women with children have never been married, compared to about 8% of white mothers in the same age range. Nearly 70% of African-American children are born to single mothers. This means that the poverty of African-American families is likely to be more pervasive than for other racial groups, creating a sustained disadvantage that becomes intergenerational as it perpetuates stereotypes, which leads to further disadvantages.

Jennifer Hamer (2001) FIGURE 12-13 studied absent fathers in African-American cities. She found that contrary to social perceptions that African-American fathers were uninvolved fathers who contributed little to their children's upbringing, African-American fathers had constructed a model of fatherhood that was different than the model of dominant white society yet viable given their social and economic circumstances.

FIGURE 12-13 Jennifer Hamer studied absent black fathers.
Courtesy of Jennifer Hamer

Hispanics

Studying Hispanic families has proven challenging because of the variations in origin and immigration history. Nevertheless, some generalizations can be made about the state of Hispanic families in the United States. Research shows that in some ways, Hispanic families have kept the traditions and values of their native cultures. This includes high levels of family ties and strong family support. However, these ties seem to be weakening as Hispanic families assimilate into American culture. Hispanics generally also exhibit a higher fertility rate than other racial or ethnic groups. This has led to an increase in out-of-wedlock births and increasing sole-parent families among Hispanics, regardless of national origin or immigration history. Despite general declines in teen pregnancy, teenage Hispanic girls are more likely to be teen mothers than other groups. A latent effect of these trends is that currently, nearly 40% of Hispanic women live in poverty.

Native Americans

Another difficult group to study is Native American families. With nearly 240 separate tribes, Native Americans exhibit a wide variety of family structures that make generalization difficult. Again, however, patterns do emerge that allow some general comparisons with other racial and ethnic groups. These patterns are especially prevalent among Native Americans who live in cities.

The first noticeable pattern is the formation of **fictive kin**. These are unrelated people who are regarded as family. This may include members of the same tribe who are unrelated or members of another tribe who share some cultural traits. The formation of fictive kin often helps Native Americans become established in the cities. This often leads to an improvement of quality of life, since jobs on the reservation are scarce. Improved quality of life in the cities means more stable marriages and families.

Research on Native American families living on reservations or on Native ground shows that, generally speaking, family structures have become a mix between traditional family structures that maintain deference to the community and to societal elders and the norms of the dominant society that tend to promote individuality. The high level of poverty on many Native American reservations has exacerbated many problems, such as abuse, addiction, and absent parenthood.

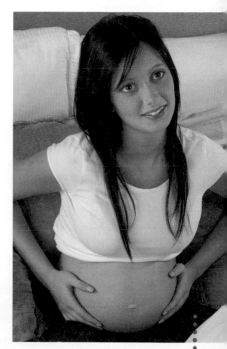

Hispanics have the highest rate of teen pregnancy in the United States.
© iStockphoto/Thinkstock

Asian Americans

Families of Asian descent make up almost 5% of the population of the United States. Most of these families are from China, Japan, or the Philippines, although populations of western Asia are on the rise. On average, Asian families are high-wage-earning families that strongly maintain the culture of their country of origin. They are the least likely ethnic or racial group to assimilate to the dominant American cultural norms.

Fictive kin Unrelated people who are regarded as family.

Asian Americans are the racial group most likely to live in an extended family.

© Monkey Business Images/ Shutterstock, Inc.

Asian Americans are also more likely than other racial or ethnic groups to live in extended families.

Asian American families tend to value education as a path to improvement. They maintain conservative family values that usually include a taboo on premarital sexual relations and strong marital ties. Asian American families have low rates of divorce and the latest onset of first sexual intercourse of all racial and ethnic groups. For example, while the average age of first sexual onset for African Americans is 15.7 years, the average age of first sexual onset for Asian Americans is just under 19 years of age. The result is a low rate of poverty and single motherhood for Asian Americans.

Gender

Gender also plays a role in the family. Bernard (1972) has argued that men and women see marriage in fundamentally different ways. Men, she argues, benefit more from marriage than do women. For men, marriage builds status and is viewed as a sign of the man's ability to care for a family. Women, on the other hand, become trapped by the identity of their husbands. She went on to document that men benefit from marriage in other ways as well. For example, men who are married tend to have better mental and physical health, make more money, have a longer life span, and report being happier than single men. By contrast, women who are married report higher rates of depression, make less money than single women, and report lower levels of happiness than single women. Bernard attributed these differences to the patriarchal structure of society. She argued that male domination of women is the reason that women do not reap the same benefits of marriage that men do.

At the same time, married women do report a generally high level of marital satisfaction. This pattern follows closely the pattern for couple happiness in general, in which marital happiness is high in the early years of the marriage, declines after the introduction of children, then rises again after the last child leaves the home. Over all, marriages in the United States bring a considerable degree of satisfaction to both male and female partners.

These three dimensions of inequality—race, gender, and socioeconomic status—do not operate independently but rather intersect with one another. If marriage is detrimental to women and poverty is detrimental, then a poor woman would be expected to have even greater total disadvantage. When race is factored into the equation, the multiple layers of disadvantage that can occur make family life extremely challenging for the most marginalized groups in society.

CONCEPT LEARNING CHECK 12.7   Families: Class, Race, and Gender

1. Using your understanding of how race, gender, and social class intersect, rank the following examples in order from highest status to lowest status within US Society.

_____ A middle-class African-American woman

_____ A poor white male

_____ A rich Asian American male

_____ A poor Hispanic female

_____ A middle-class white female

Visual Summary Family and Intimate Relationships

12.1 Introduction to the Concept of the Family

- The family is a social institution that takes a variety of forms to unite people in order to cooperate and care for one another.
- Families may take one of four forms: nuclear families, sole-parent families, blended families, or extended families.
- Marriage may take one of three basic forms: monogamy, polygyny, or polyandry.

- While polygyny is the most commonly sanctioned form of marriage worldwide, monogamy is the most commonly practiced marital form.
- Families may be divided by residential pattern.
- Families may be divided by patterns of descent.
- Patriarchy is a cultural universal.

12.2 Theoretical Perspectives on Families

- Families may be understood through several different theoretical paradigms.
- The functionalist perspective analyzes the family in terms of how the family fulfills functions that contribute to the operation of society as a whole.
- The conflict perspective seeks to understand how the family creates and maintains social inequality.
- The symbolic interactionist perspective tries to understand how the roles and concepts of the family are constructed through experience in the family.

- The social exchange perspective analyzes the family in terms of a cost/benefit analysis.
- The evolutionary perspective seeks to understand how families are formed and how they change by understanding how the family aids in human survival.

12.3 Stages of Intimate Relationships

- Although they vary from culture to culture, all societies recognize distinct stages in the development of the family.
- Culture provides guided rules and expectations about dating practices.
- Though practiced in many different ways, marriage is a cultural universal.
- In America, age at first marriage is increasing.
- Cohabitation is a growing trend in America.
- Cohabitation prior to marriage increases the risk of divorce.

- Child rearing is seen as a primary function of the family despite a decrease in fertility.
- Baumrind identified four parenting styles: permissive, authoritarian, authoritative, and neglectful.
- Parenting style varies with race and social class.
- While the division of housework has become more equal, women still do a majority of the housework.

Visual Summary Family and Intimate Relationships, continued

12.4 Problems in the Family

- Rates of intimate partner violence are declining.
- Rates of intimate partner violence vary by race and socioeconomic status.
- Children who are abused suffer from a variety of negative outcomes, such as depression and delinquency.
- Individuals who are victims of abuse or who witness abuse as children are more likely to become abusers later in life.

- The number of Americans who are currently divorced at any given moment is about 9%.
- Rates of divorce and relationship dissolution vary by race and social class.
- Witnessing divorce as a child increases the risk for delinquency or other social problems.
- Increasing divorce rates are a contributing factor to increases in poverty among women and children.

12.5 Transitions

- Family forms change as societal institutions and values change.
- Blended families face unique challenges, as the roles of all family members must be negotiated.

- Marital happiness is greatest early in the marriage and after the last child leaves the home.

12.6 Family Alternatives

- Simple definitions are often not appropriate to describe all of the ways in which people can coexist in a family.
- Denmark was the first nation to legalize gay unions.
- There is no evidence that children raised by gay parents are more likely to be gay.
- Society has increasingly legitimated sole-parent families as a legitimate family form.

- Although there is a social expectation toward marriage, some people choose not to marry.
- Approximately 15% of all marriages in the United States are racially mixed.
- Rates of racially mixed marriages vary with geographic location, race, and sex.

12.7 Families: Class, Race, and Gender

- Race, social class, and gender intersect to create multiple layers of family dynamics.
- Children who grow up in poverty are more likely to have problems in school, have behavioral problems, and suffer from developmental difficulties.
- Children who grow up in higher social classes tend to be healthier, have better self-esteem, become more successful, and be happier.
- African-American children are more likely to grow up in poverty and more likely to suffer sustained disadvantage.

- Hispanic women have the highest rate of teen pregnancy of all racial and ethnic groups.
- Native Americans often rely on fictive kin as a means to overcome systemic disadvantage.
- Asian Americans have the highest average wages and are the least likely ethnic or racial group to assimilate to the dominant cultural norms.
- Men tend to benefit from marriage more than women.

12.1 Introduction to the Concept of Family

1. Tietia lives with her mother, brother, and grandmother. Tietia lives in a(n):
  A. sole-parent family.
  B. blended family.
  C. nuclear family.
  D. extended family.

2. Dobu has just married his fourth wife. He is practicing:
  A. bilaterality.
  B. monogamy.
  C. polyandry.
  D. polygyny.

3. Rex and Judy are newlyweds. After the wedding, they move to a town away from both Rex and Judy's parents. This is an example of:
  A. neolocality.
  B. patrilocality.
  C. matrilocality.
  D. bilaterality.

12.2 Theoretical Perspectives on Families

4. Which theoretical perspective sees the family as an institution that helps men and women engage in mutual support of their physical and psychological well-being?
  A. Conflict perspective
  B. Functionalist perspective
  C. Evolutionary perspective
  D. Symbolic interactionist perspective

5. Sally is upset because her husband Bill does not give her access to the family checkbook. She argues that this a way for Bill to maintain power and control in the relationship. Which theoretical perspective is Sally operating from?
  A. Functionalist
  B. Social exchange
  C. Conflict
  D. Symbolic interactionism

12.3 Stages of Intimate Relationships

6. On their date, Arlo pulls out a chair for Alice at the restaurant. At the end of the meal, he takes the check and pays for dinner. Arlo is following a:
  A. cultural universal.
  B. romantic interlude.
  C. practice routine.
  D. dating script.

7. Ken and Tina live together for two years prior to their decision to get married. According to the research, what would sociologists of the family predict about Ken and Tina's marriage?
  A. They are more likely to get a divorce.
  B. They are less likely to get a divorce.
  C. They are less likely to have children.
  D. They will be happier than other couples.

8. Regina chooses her daughter's clothes, dictates who her friends are, and punishes her severely if her daughter disobeys. Regina is practicing what kind of parenting?
  A. Neglectful
  B. Authoritative
  C. Authoritarian
  D. Permissive

9. Suzy and Ed are a middle-class white couple. Based on these demographic factors, we would predict that their parenting style would generally be described as:
  A. neglectful.
  B. authoritarian.
  C. authoritative.
  D. permissive.

12.4 Problems in the Family

10. Jared witnessed abuse as a child. Which of the following is not a likely outcome in adulthood?
  A. Jared is more likely to suffer from depression.
  B. Jared is more likely to go to college.
  C. Jared is more likely to be arrested.
  D. Jared is more likely to become an abuser.

11. Tia's parents hardly ever speak to her. They keep her locked in her room most of the day. Their parenting style might best be described as:
  A. neglectful.
  B. authoritative.
  C. permissive.
  D. authoritarian.

12.5 Transitions

12. Becky and Samuel have just sent their last child off to college. According to most research, what would we predict about Becky and Samuel's marital happiness?
- **A.** Their marital happiness will remain the same.
- **B.** Their marital happiness will decline.
- **C.** Their marital happiness will increase.
- **D.** Becky's marital happiness will decline, but Samuel's marital happiness will increase.

12.6 Family Alternatives

13. Sue and Leah are a lesbian couple trying to adopt a child. Sue's family objects to the adoption. Sue and Leah should point out that:
- **A.** research shows that children raised by gay parents are no more likely to be gay than children raised by heterosexual parents.
- **B.** eleven states have passed laws preventing gay couples from adopting children.
- **C.** Denmark legalized gay unions in 1989.
- **D.** fewer Americans support the rights of gay couples to adopt children than support gay marriage.

14. Deborah had her first child at age 15. Statistically, we can predict that:
- **A.** Deborah will go on to complete college.
- **B.** Deborah will not have another child.
- **C.** Deborah will be likely to live in poverty.
- **D.** Deborah lives in the northern United States.

12.7 US Families: Class, Race, and Gender

15. Abe is a member of the Iroquois tribe. His family unit includes both family members as well as nonrelated members of his tribe. Abe has created a network of:
- **A.** extended family.
- **B.** fictive kin.
- **C.** tribal affiliation.
- **D.** urban acquaintances.

16. Elena is 17. Her parents emigrated to America from Japan. Statistically, we can predict that:
- **A.** Elena will not attend college.
- **B.** Elena's family is a blended family.
- **C.** Elena's family is living in poverty.
- **D.** Elena will not have premarital sexual relations.

CHAPTER ESSAY QUESTIONS

1. Discuss how economic conditions in a society might influence the development of the various marital forms.

2. Using conflict theory, explain differences in parenting styles between blacks and whites.

CHAPTER DISCUSSION QUESTIONS

1. Families change in response to changing economic and social circumstances. What changes do you think are in store for the family of the future? What will the family look like in 50 years? Discuss how you arrived at your prediction.

2. Over 1.5 million American families rely on cash assistance and food stamps to help make ends meet. Discuss how such social welfare programs might strengthen the American family. How might these programs weaken the family? Discuss your answer in terms of the various theoretical perspectives discussed in the chapter.

3. The family is the strongest agent of socialization. In what ways has your family shaped your beliefs, values, and behaviors? How might you be different if you had grown up in a different culture with a different family?

4. Share with the class your definition of the family. What social trends have changed societal definitions of the family (such as sole-parent, extended, and blended), including membership, size, parenting responsibilities, and legal rights?

5. What is it about US culture that supports specific norms related to marriage? Think about cultural values regarding monogamy, residential patterns, descent, endogamous and exogamous patterns, and the cultural values that support these norms. Are any of these ideologies consequences of a patriarchal society? Why or why not?

6. Discuss current dating scripts. What gender roles still exist today and how are dating scripts changing? Has the social acceptance of cohabitation changed the way people think about dating and marriage?

7. Share with the class the parenting style in which you were raised as a child (permissive, authoritarian, or authoritative). What patterns emerge? Expand your discussion to explain these patterns.

8. What political policies might lessen the feminization of poverty related to divorce? What might be some unintended consequences of these policies?

9. If the empty nest syndrome tends to be a myth, how might the economic realities of young adults contribute to conflicts within the family?

CHAPTER PROJECTS

INDIVIDUAL PROJECTS

1. Go online and search for "interracial marriage statistics." Write an analysis paper detailing your findings and include some of the conflicts that may occur within the interracial family. How might these conflicts be affected by societal policies of the past, extended family, and other societal factors? How are the experiences of an interracial couple similar to those of interfaith and same-sex couples?

GROUP PROJECTS

1. Go online and search for the "Power and Control Wheel" and statistics related to *intimate partner violence*. How do these behaviors affect the victim's inability to leave the relationship? Why might it be dangerous to encourage a victim to leave an abusive relationship? In what ways does US culture contribute to the social acceptance of violence? Write a summary of your discussion.

2. Imagine that you run an after school program for middle school children. Make a list of behavioral problems you might encounter. Think about how parenting styles might contribute to the behavioral problems. Develop suggestions for your employees for how to handle these issues and address them with parents. Go online and read about "types of child abuse" and "mandatory reporters." Include in your write-up information about mandatory reporting.

2. Imagine you are a family and marriage therapist. Which of the *theoretical perspectives on families* do you think would influence your work with clients that are considering *divorce*? Write an analysis paper of the theories to defend your thinking.

3. Analyze the use of day care centers using at least three theoretical perspectives covered in this chapter.

3. As an alternative project, you might create a plan to increase resiliency in children. Use at least three concepts from this chapter.

Authoritarian parenting
Authoritative parenting
Bilateral descent
Blended family
Cohabitation
Cost/benefit analysis
Dating scripts
Descent
Empty nest syndrome
Endogamous
Exogamous
Extended family
Family
Feminization of poverty
Fictive kin

Filiarchy
Homogamy
Intergenerational transmission of violence
Intimate partner violence
Kinship
Marriage
Matriarchy
Matrilineality
Matrilocality
Monogamy
Neglectful parenting
Neolocality
Nuclear family
Patriarchy

Patrilineality
Patrilocality
Permissive parenting
Personality stabilization
Polyandry
Polygamy
Polygyny
Primary socialization
Residential patterns
Resilience
Romantic love
Sole-parent family
Symmetrical family

12.1 Introduction to the Concept of Family

1. [B] Sole-parent families are defined as families with one parent in the home.

2. [D] When a sole parent remarries or cohabits with someone who is not his or her children's parents, a blended family is formed. This is also known as a stepfamily.

3. [A] Extended families include kin beyond parents and siblings.

4. [C] The nuclear family consists of two parents and mutual children.

12.2 Theoretical Perspectives on Families

1. [C] Primary socialization is the most influential and important way that a society imparts culture to the individual.

2. [A] In this case, symmetry refers to the way in which power relations are structured. A symmetrical family is one in which the power structure is divided equally between partners.

3. Both the social exchange perspective and the evolutionary perspective see the family as operating through cost/benefit calculations. Social exchange perspective argues that these cost/benefit calculations are multidimensional and ongoing through the process of interaction between various family members. By contrast, the evolutionary perspective sees the cost/benefit calculations as rooted in human evolutionary history as both men and women seek to maximize the fitness of their offspring.

12.3 Stages of Intimate Relationships

1. A man asking out a woman; a man paying for dinner; a man pulling out a chair for a woman to sit down. There are many possible connections. Students may choose to connect these dating scripts to the evolutionary perspective, for example, insofar as the scripts assess the male's ability and willingness to commit resources to the relationship. Alternatively, students could interpret the man paying for dinner as a reflection of patriarchal values.

2. There is not necessarily a right answer here. Students are to reflect on how the way in which they were parented reflects historical cultural norms as well as how it shaped their experiences. Instructors should use this opportunity to reinforce the links between the family and the sociological imagination.

12.4 Problems in the Family

1. The degree to which a person can endure changes in his or her environment is called [resilience].

2. The fact that a growing number of people living in poverty are women is called [feminization of poverty].

3. Approximately what percentage of the 3 million reported child abuse cases are substantiated? [C. 65%]

4. Approximately what percentage of absent fathers pays no child support? [A. 40%]

12.5 Transitions

1. Blended families are structurally most similar to [adopted families].

2. Blended families are structurally most dissimilar to [nuclear families].

3. The sociological imagination considers how the intersection of history and biography influences the beliefs, values, and behaviors of an individual. In forming a blended family, the cultural history of the various members may differ considerably. Similarly, the individual biographies of the various family members will differ. For this reason, blended families often have to renegotiate roles in the family in an effort to create common experiences.

12.6 Family Alternatives

1. [A] Denmark was the first nation to legalize homosexual unions in 1989.

2. [C] Thirteen states have voter-approved constitutional amendments defining marriage as between one man and one woman.

3. [B] Roughly 15% of marriages in the United States are racially mixed.

4. [F] No evidence exists that children raised in homosexual households are more likely to be homosexual.

5. [T] The highest concentration of racially mixed marriages in the United States occurs in the western United States, largely because of the greater racial and ethnic diversity in those states.

12.7 Families: Class, Race, and Gender

[3] A middle-class African-American woman
[4] A poor white male
[1] A rich Asian American male
[5] A poor Hispanic female
[2] A middle-class white female

ANSWERS TO CHAPTER REVIEW TEST

12.1 Introduction to the Concept of Family

1. D. An extended family consists of parents, children, and other kin.
2. D. Polygyny is the marriage of one man to multiple wives.
3. A. Societies in which a new family lives apart from both sets of parents are known as neolocal societies.

12.2 Theoretical Perspectives on Families

4. B. The functionalist perspective of Talcott Parsons sees the family as the social institution primarily responsible for developing and maintaining the physical and psychological well-being of its members.
5. C. The conflict perspective sees society in terms of a struggle over scarce resources. This includes the ways in which family relationships create and maintain social inequality.

12.3 Stages of Intimate Relationships

6. D. Dating scripts are culturally guided rules and expectations about dating practices.
7. A. Research on cohabitation shows that couples who cohabit prior to marriage have an increased risk of divorce.
8. C. Authoritarian parenting is characterized by the expectation of strict adherence to the rules, low freedom, and swift and severe punishment.
9. C. White and middle-class parents are more likely to exhibit an authoritative parenting style than other socioeconomic groups.

12.4 Problems in the Family

10. B. People who witness abuse as a child are more likely to suffer from a variety of negative outcomes, including problems in school.
11. A. Neglectful parents are defined as parents who systematically neglect their children, or who do not attend to their basic needs.

12.5 Transitions

12. C. Research shows that after the last child leaves the household, marital happiness tends to increase for both partners.

12.6 Family Alternatives

13. A. In defense of the objection to homosexual adoption, it should be pointed out that research shows that children raised by gay parents are no more likely to be gay than children raised by heterosexual parents.
14. C. Having a child as a teenager significantly increases the chances that the mother and child will live below the poverty line.

12.7 US Families: Class, Race, and Gender

15. B. Unrelated people who are regarded as family are called fictive kin.
16. D. Asian American families tend to maintain strong cultural ties that include taboos against premarital sexual intercourse.

ANSWERS TO CHAPTER ESSAY QUESTIONS

1. There are three basic marital forms. These are monogamy, polygyny, and polyandry. Monogamy is defined as a marriage between one man and one woman. Polyandry is defined as one woman with multiple husbands. Polygyny is defined as a marriage consisting of one man with multiple wives. The development of each of these marital forms can be explained by economic conditions. In societies in which resources are relatively abundant, polygyny is often normative. However, the resources are usually not distributed evenly among the males in society. Thus, although polygyny is sanctioned, many males do not possess enough resources to maintain multiple wives. Thus, monogamy is the most commonly practiced marital form. Conversely, in societies in which resources are scarce, multiple husbands are often necessary to secure adequate resources for the survival of the family unit.

2. Research into parenting styles identifies racial differences in parenting style. Specifically, the research shows that while whites tend to parent in an authoritative style, African Americans are more likely to parent in either a highly permissive style or in an authoritarian style. Conflict theory may be used to explain this phenomenon. Conflict theory approaches social phenomena as struggles by individuals or groups for scarce resources. African Americans, on average, earn less than whites and have less total wealth than whites. African Americans are also more likely to be single parents than whites are. As single African American parents struggle to maintain a livelihood, they often work long hours at menial jobs. In this struggle for resources, they have less time to invest in parenting. Therefore, they tend to adopt either a very permissive style of parenting, which requires very little investment in time, or they overcompensate by maintaining a very strict household to give them a sense of control over one aspect of their life.

REFERENCES

Axin, W. G. and A. Thornton. 1992. "The Relationship between Cohabitation and Divorce: Selectivity or Causal Influence?" *Demography* 29(3): 357–374.

Bamberger, J. 1974. "The Myth of Matriarchy: Why Men Rule in Primitive Society." Pp. 263–280 in *Women, Culture and Society*, edited by M. Rosaldo and L. Lamphere. Stanford, CA: Stanford University Press.

Bereczkei, T., S. Voros, A. Gal, and L. Bernath. 1997. "Resources, Attractiveness, Family Commitment; Reproductive Decisions in Human Mate Choice." *Ethology* 1(3):681–699.

Bernard, J. 1972. *The Future of Marriage*. New York Bantam Books.

Brown, D. 1991. *Human Universals*. Philadelphia: Temple University Press.

Cherlin, A. 1981. "American Marriage in the Early Twenty-First Century." *Marriage and Child Wellbeing* 15(2):33–55.

Cherlin, A. J. 1992. *Marriage, Divorce, Remarriage*, Second edition. Cambridge, MA: Harvard University Press.

DeMaris, Alfred, Meredith D. Pugh, and Erica Harman. 1992. "Gender Differences in the Accuracy of Recall of Witnesses of Portrayed Dyadic Violence." *Journal of Marriage and the Family* 54:335–345.

Emery, R. E. 1999. *Marriage, Divorce, and Children's Readjustment*, Second edition. Thousand Oaks, CA: Sage Press.

Engels, Freidrich. 1884. *The Origin of Family, Private Property and State*. Zurich: Hottingen.

Furstenberg, F. and A. Cherlin. 1994. *Divided Families: What Happens to Children When Parents Part*. Cambridge, MA: Harvard University Press.

Goldberg, S. 1973. *The Inevitability of Patriarchy*. New York: William and Morrow.

Hamer, J. 2001. *What it Means to be Daddy: Fatherhood for Black Men Living Away from Their Children*. New York: Columbia University Press.

Hetherington, M. and J. Kelly. 2002. *For Better or Worse: Divorce Reconsidered*. New York: Norton.

Hochschild, A. and A. Machung. 1989. *The Second Shift: Working Families and the Revolution at Home*. New York: Penguin.

Jankowiak, W. R. and E. F. Fischer. 1992. "A Cross-cultural Perspective on Romantic Love." *Ethology* 31(2):149–155.

Kalmijn, M. 1998. "Intermarriage and Homogamy: Causes, Patterns, Trends." *Annual Review of Sociology* 24:395–421.

Kompter, A. 1989. "Hidden Power in Marriage." *Gender in Society* 3:187–216.

Morin, R. and D. Cohn. 2008. *Women Call the Shots at Home; Public Mixed on Gender Roles In Jobs*. Pew Research Center Publications, September 28, 2008.

Rogers, S. J. and P. Amato. 2000. "Have Changes in Gender Relations Affected Marital Quality?" *Social Forces* 79(2):731–753.

Rubin, Z., L. A. Peplau, and C. T. Hill. 1981. "Loving and Leaving: Sex Differences in Romantic Attachments." *Sex Roles* 7(8):821–835.

Vischer, E. and J. Vischer. 1979. *Stepfamilies: A Guide to Working with Stepparents and Stepchildren*. New York: Routledge.

Waite, L. J. and G. Spitze. 1981. "Young Women's Transition to Marriage." *Demography* 18(4):681–694.

Westermarck, E. 1891. *The History of Human Marriage*. London: Macmillan.

Wilson, C. M. and A. J. Oswald. 2005. *How Does Marriage Affect Physical and Psychological Health? A Survey of the Longitudinal Evidence*. Bonn, Germany: Institute for the Study of Labor.

Yalom, M. 2002. *A History of the Wife*. New York: Harper Perennial.

© Ron Nickel*/Design Pics-Corbis

Chapter Overview ▼

13 Education and Religion

Learning Objectives ▼

13.1
- Discuss key contemporary issues in public education.
- Analyze the education choices available in the United States.

13.2
- Illustrate education systems in postindustrial, developing, and underdeveloped nations.

13.3
- Describe the sociological perspectives on education.

13.4
- Compare and contrast how sociologists view the role of religion in social life.

13.5
- Describe the sociological perspectives on religion.

13.6
- Compare and contrast the main religions of the world.

13.7
- Illustrate the continuum of religious organizations.

13.8
- Discuss the functions that religion plays in the lives of Americans.

© George Doyle/Stockbyte/Thinkstock

My five-year-old son bounded out of bed, rushed downstairs, and grabbed his backpack. "Ready to go!" he announced proudly, without losing a beat. It was his first day of school. Never mind that it was more than an hour before school started—he was excited. My wife and I gently encouraged him to relax and have some breakfast first. My wife reminded him about the importance of eating a good breakfast before school. Both my wife and I took some pictures to remember the day. The time could not go fast enough for my son, though. He fidgeted through his morning meal and paced the dining room until it was time to go.

My son had been talking about school for quite a while. As a sociologist, I knew that the number-one predictor of school success is how well a child likes school. I also knew that the number-one predictor of how well a child likes school is parental attitudes toward schooling. To that end, my wife and I had discussed school regularly with my son since his fourth birthday. We explained what school was, why it was important, and what was going to happen. We told him he would meet lots of new friends and get to do lots of fun and interesting things. We toured the school and met his teacher. As a naturally curious boy, he could not wait to start.

We did not send our child to just any school, however. We also knew that our local public schools had issues. Since we lived in the city, our son would be attending an underfunded urban school that had a disappointing educational record. That is why, despite the expense, my wife and I decided to send our child to a private school. There were several to choose from in our area. Some were extremely rigid and required uniforms. Some had no rules at all and did not even issue grades. We hunted around, looking at all of the options. We also let my son weigh in and give his opinions, even if he was not sure what he should be looking for.

"I like the windows in this one," he said. We laughed, but he was right. It was a religious school, and the stained-glass windows of the cathedral were impressive. As a sociologist, I understood the importance of religion for a healthy society, as well as the important place that religion has for individuals. Adding religion to the curriculum would help reinforce many of the values that my wife and I held about family, society, and charity. Ultimately, it was not the stained-glass windows that won us over, but we chose a private religious school for our son. Combining the benefits of a private education with the power of religious instruction, the school we chose was the right choice for us. We knew that both religion and school are important institutions to shape who our son will become. The beliefs, values, and behaviors that make him who he is will be strongly influenced by the education he receives, as well as by the influence that religion has on his development. The school we chose combined both of these powerful social institutions into one.

We are fortunate to be able to send our children to private school. Many families are not so fortunate and remain trapped in underfunded and underperforming schools with children whose families face multiple layers of disadvantage that push education down on the list of importance. As education in America struggles to keep pace globally, many American students are being left further and further behind. Sociology offers us unique insight into the problems of education, as well as into the way in which religion shapes our beliefs, values, and behaviors. Sociology helps us understand why my son loves school and how the school he attends shapes his sociological imagination. Sociology also helps us gain insight into what needs to be done to ensure that all children have access to quality schooling.

13.1 Education in the United States

Schooling in the United States has changed dramatically over the last 200 years.

- Discuss key contemporary issues in public education.
- Analyze the education choices available in the United States.

Schooling in the United States has changed dramatically since the nation began. For about half of the nation's history, formal education was piecemeal. Children went to school only when schooling did not interfere with work that they were required to do to help their families survive. This is why schools even today are typically on break during the summer. It is a social convention that dates back to a time when most people farmed for a living. Children were needed at home during the spring and summer months to tend to crops and livestock that were essential for a family's survival. Sending a child to school during those critical times meant less labor on the farm and potential disaster for a preindustrial family.

Schools in America have changed dramatically since the nation began.
© Monkey Business Images/Shutterstock, Inc.

Most schools were a small, single-room buildings in which children of different ages were taught together. Rather than placed in grades, children were placed by age, and the older children often helped to teach the younger ones. Schools were typically built and run by individual communities, and there was no formal curriculum. Teachers were scarce and poorly paid, often having their meager salaries supplemented by living for short periods with families of the children they taught before moving on to another family. These teachers lived with the family, ate their food, worshipped with them, and often tutored the children as well.

By 1850, only about half of school-aged children were actually enrolled. The rest received little to no formal education. In response, the federal government set a goal of mass education. Individual states were charged with the task of designing and implementing formal curricula and creating a structure of free, public education. By 1918, all states had passed compulsory education laws, requiring all children between the ages of 5 and 16 to attend school. States also began to standardize curricula so that all children in the state would learn essentially the same thing. Eventually, a formal structure evolved that divided students into grades, and students were placed with peers at the same skill level rather than by age. American education stressed key competencies such as literacy and practical skills that were considered relevant to the life style of Americans. As the economy changed from agricultural to industrial, our educational values also changed. Much of our education more recently has been with the goal of preparing people for future employment rather than simply imparting knowledge for the sake of knowledge.

The first schools were one room, with students of all ages placed together.
© iStockphoto/Thinkstock

By the end of the 1960s, more than half of the American population had a high school diploma. These numbers have continued to rise, and today nearly 70% of Americans complete high school (Alliance for Excellent Education 2012). National surveys conclude that Americans overwhelmingly believe that education is important to personal success and that our society offers an equal opportunity for everyone to get an education consistent with their talents and abilities. It should be noted, however, that these beliefs reflect an ideal more than a reality. Schools are far from equal in how they are funded and the education they provide. For example, inner-city schools deal with significant financial and social challenges that are fundamentally absent from suburban schools. Indeed, even today, the majority of men and women who attend college come from families with above-average incomes and attended suburban schools.

Schools and Segregation

Although the stated goal of compulsory education was to prepare students for future employment, schools clearly did not prepare everyone equally. During the years of segregation, African Americans were segregated in many ways. Blacks ate in separate restaurants, drank from separate water fountains, and attended separate churches. In the 1896 case *Plessy v. Ferguson*, the Supreme Court of the United States ruled that segregation was legal as long as the facilities were "separate but equal." Under this ruling, African-American children were segregated into separate schools. Despite the legal requirement, schools for blacks were rarely equal. These schools, often located in the inner cities, were housed in dilapidated buildings, were grossly underfunded relative to schools for whites, and often employed well-meaning but underqualified teachers.

By the end of the 1960s, more than half of the US population had a high school diploma.
© Christopher Futcher/Shutterstock, Inc.

During segregation, separate facilities were supposed to be equal.

© Bettmann/CORBIS

The Supreme Court case Plessy v. Ferguson *established segregated schools in America.*

© Bettmann/CORBIS

De jure segregation
Segregation that is allowed by law.

De facto segregation
Segregation that is part of social practice.

All of these factors converged to make education for blacks far inferior to the education received by whites at that time.

Over time, African-American leaders like Charles Hamilton Houston led legal charges against educational segregation. Houston primarily attacked segregation laws on the grounds that facilities were not, in fact, equal, and won numerous legal victories that forced states to provide increasing funding and other resources for segregated schools. These victories led to a reassessment of the separate-but-equal doctrine that had framed educational law in America.

Although Houston did not live to see the victory, in 1954, the Supreme Court revisited school segregation and ruled in *Brown v. Board of Education* that "racially segregated schools are inherently unequal." The ruling effectively desegregated schools—at least in law. The reaction among proponents of segregation was intense. In fact, even though desegregation became law, school integration happened only sporadically and slowly. Some school districts, such as Prince Edward, Virginia, actually closed schools rather than integrate. Instead, county officials issued vouchers for private school tuition, knowing full well that the only private school in the area had a white-only admission policy. It took another Supreme Court Case, nearly a decade later, to force Prince Edward, Virginia, schools to provide integrated public schooling.

Today, even though **de jure segregation**—that is, segregation allowed by law—has been overturned, **de facto segregation**—segregation in practice—still remains. In large part, this is more the result of social circumstances than overt discrimination. As minority groups have become increasingly concentrated in the inner cities, they have made up a growing percentage of inner-city public schools. As whites simultaneously vacated the inner cities, city revenue to fund public schools declined, leaving largely segregated, poorly funded schools in many urban communities in the nation.

Contemporary Issues in Public Education

Through the middle of the 1970s, America's public education system was the envy of the world. Other nations modeled their educational goals and methods after the American system. Yet while these nations continued to innovate and adjust their schools to meet changes in society, American education remained relatively rigid. Curriculums changed little, even as America began transitioning into a postindustrial society. School funding also failed to keep up with the times, and schools could not afford to keep pace with rapidly changing technological innovations and advancements. School buildings and equipment began to age, and many schools—particularly those in urban areas—could not afford to upgrade or repair equipment. Thus, American schools, and America's urban schools in particular, began to fall behind.

These problems were exacerbated by problems with the ways in which schools were funded. Typically, schools have been funded through the collection of property taxes. As the values of properties were assessed and taxes paid, inequities became evident. Homes in the inner cities are worth disproportionately less than suburban homes. Thus, urban schools received less funding than suburban schools. This left urban schools even further behind than suburban schools. Additionally, urban schools have less money to pay teachers, so they often are left with less skilled teachers. In several states, such as Ohio, this method of funding schools has been ruled unconstitutional. However, most states have failed to correct these funding inequities.

Changes in the family structure also played a role in school decline. Technologies such as television meant a change in the way in which children were socialized and a change in the way in which they interacted with one another. They began to read less. They received less teaching at home. As both parents now were engaged in the workforce, there was less emphasis on manners and behaviors in certain social situations. All of these cultural changes doubtless contributed to the decline of American public education.

In 1979, President Jimmy Carter made the Department of Education a cabinet-level department, effectively taking control of schools from states and nationalizing the educational process. Over time, this led to discussions of standardizing curriculum across all states. Not long after, public perception of public education began to decline. Critics asserted that public education was not adequately preparing students for the changing world. Relative to the rest of the world, America's public schools declined. However, it is unclear whether this was due to a deterioration of American schools or an improvement of schools in other nations. Some people suggest that federal control of public education led to a reduction in local control of resources needed to ensure functionally adequate schools. The expansion of bureaucracy that accompanied the change did not translate into more efficient governance of schools, nor did it translate into cost savings. Instead, resources that could have been used on education were absorbed by the increasingly complex bureaucracy.

President Jimmy Carter established the Department of Education as a cabinet-level department in 1979.

Karl Schumacher Official White House photograph
Library of Congress LC-USZC4-599

Liberalism and Public Education

Liberals blamed the deterioration of public education on a lack of funding. While they argued that funding inequities between urban and suburban schools should be addressed, they also broadened their arguments to suggest that all schools should see an increase in funding. After all, the argument went, no amount of money is too much to spend to educate our children.

Indeed, spending on education did increase relative to other government expenditures. In fact, only military spending increased faster than educational spending (USgovermentspending.com 2012). Yet school quality continued its general decline. By the end of the 1980s, America was spending more per pupil than nearly every other nation even as American schools fell further behind on the world stage. By 2008, expenditure per pupil averaged $10,694 (US Department of Education 2012). This figure includes only instructional-related expenses and excludes money spent on structural costs such as building repair.

Currently among nations of the world, America ranks third in spending per pupil, and school performance ranks 14th in reading, 25th in mathematics, and 17th in science FIGURE 13-1 (OECD Pisa rankings 2009). These rankings indicate that there is little correlation between expenditure per student and academic rankings. As public expenditure on students has increased, performance has, on the whole, decreased. Additionally, studies of private schools, which will be discussed in more detail later, have shown that while private schools spend significantly less per student than public schools, their academic outcomes are significantly higher (US Department of Education 2006). This has led an increasing number of scholars to question the wisdom of continued high expenditures in America's schools. Similarly, public support for additional education spending has waned somewhat, though it remains generally high.

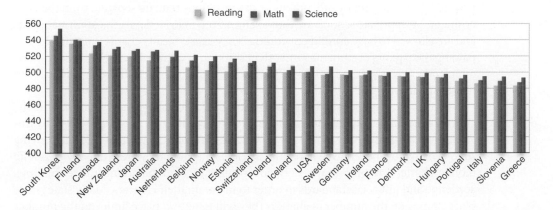

FIGURE 13-1 Rankings of schools throughout the world.

Source: Data from OECD. 2009. OECD Programme for International Student Assessment (PISA). Accessed October 2012 (http://www.oecd.org/pisa/46643496.pdf).

In 2001, President George W. Bush passed the No Child Left Behind Act to help reform American education.

© spirit of america/Shutterstock, Inc.

Compulsory education The legal requirement that all children attend school.

Charter school A school that is run by private individuals or corporations but funded with public tax dollars.

Conservativism and Public Education

Conservative approaches to public school are even more controversial than their liberal counterparts. Generally speaking, conservative criticisms of the American educational system argue that school reform begins with accountability. First, school administrators should be accountable for proper allocation of educational resources. Second, teachers should be held accountable for the learning outcomes of their students. Students, of course, should also be held accountable for their performance in the classroom. Parents also have a role, many critics argue, to make sure that children are adequately prepared for school academically, attitudinally, and nutritionally.

Conservatives generally favor strong government control in an effort to enforce accountability. In 2001, Under President George W. Bush, the No Child Left Behind Act was passed in an attempt to reform public education. The law established standards that schools had to meet and tied federal funding to school performance. Schools that fail to consistently meet standards and schools that fail to improve performance over time, can face sanctions, loss of funding, or even a ceding of control of the school to federal authorities.

Almost immediately, the No Child Left Behind Act met with derision among many school officials, teachers, academics, and even other conservatives. Critics complained that the law punished schools in urban areas because they were already so far behind academically that it would be nearly impossible to meet the goals outlined in the legislation. Additionally, the punitive measures outlined, such as financial sanctions against underperforming schools, would disproportionately harm already underfunded urban schools by taking away much-needed resources.

Although there is some evidence that the No Child Left Behind legislation has led to marginal improvements in education in America (Whittle 2005), it has certainly not been the panacea that some conservatives had hoped. Indeed, many urban and some suburban schools have been harmed by punitive reductions in funding. On the whole, schools continue to decline in world rankings; student standardized test scores remain low even as teachers spend increasing amounts of time teaching strictly to the test material; schools continue to struggle to keep pace with changing social and economic expectations; and students continue to lack many of the skills required of them.

Charter Education, Private Education, and Vouchers

Although the notion of **compulsory education**—that is, the legal requirement that all children attend school—remains a cornerstone of American educational ideals, there is no requirement that children attend public schools. A survey done in 1999 and repeated in 2009 showed that by a margin of nine to one, Americans believe that parents should have the right to choose their child's school (Council for American Private Education 1999). Private schools and charter schools offer a choice different from public education. In fact, private schools account for about 25% of all active schools and enroll nearly 10% of all school-aged children in America (Council for American Private Education 2012). Nearly 87% of private schools in America are religiously based. Private schools are run by individuals or organizations that are separate from the government. Most private schools are thus exempt from many federal education standards and are allowed to have enrollment criteria. They also typically charge tuition, which is paid by the parents of students rather than through tax dollars. Because these tuitions often come directly from families, private schools are criticized for being exclusive to higher-income families.

Charter schools offer another type of school choice. Unlike privately funded schools, **charter schools** are funded with public tax dollars, but they are run by private individuals or agencies. The agency must apply for and be granted a contract, or charter, from the state, which must be renewed at regular intervals. Because they are funded with public money, charter schools are subject to government regulation and must meet rigorous academic and financial standards in order to maintain their charters. Many states have placed limits on the number of charters they will issue and place limits on the number of students that the schools can admit FIGURE 13-2. For these reasons, charter schools are uncommon and there are often waiting lists to get children into them. Critics contend that using public money for private education is inappropriate and that charter schools create exclusivity that disadvantages minorities and the poor.

In response to criticisms of the cost of private education leading to exclusivity, some states have implemented a program of vouchers to help people pay for school choice. Vouchers are given by states to individuals who meet income eligibility requirements. Low-income families may use the vouchers to pay part or all of the tuition to private schools. Critics of voucher systems argue that vouchers take the best students from inner-city public schools and place them in private schools, thus reducing the quality of public schools. Additionally, critics vehemently argue that when vouchers are used to purchase tuition to private schools, it is a violation of the Constitutional separation between church and state. It should be noted, however, that in numerous court cases at all levels and in many states, voucher systems have been ruled constitutional. Indeed, states continue to expand voucher programs to help the poor achieve school choice. With an average tuition price of $8,549, private schools remain unaffordable for many families, even with the use of vouchers.

Recently, a new option for school choice has also emerged. **Magnet schools** are publicly funded schools that concentrate their curricula on a particular subject area, such as arts or science. Students typically compete for admission to magnet schools, which seek to prepare students for careers in their particular areas of concentration. Highly competitive admission standards and limited space make magnet schools an attractive option for some while seeming to systematically exclude others. There are simply not enough magnet schools to satisfy demand.

Magnet school A publicly funded school that concentrates its curriculum on a particular subject area.

Home Schooling

Currently, slightly more than 3% of all school-aged children are home schooled. That translates to more than 1.5 million children in the United States. Home schooling was

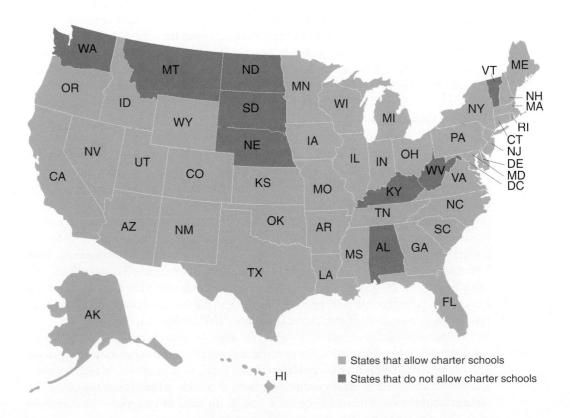

FIGURE 13-2 Nine states still do not permit charter schools as an avenue of school choice.
Source: Data from Alison Consoletti, ed. 2012. Charter School Laws Across the States 2012. Pg. 86. Washington: The Center for Education Reform. Accessed October 2012 (http://www.edreform.com/2012/11/charter-school-laws-across-the-states-2012).

Home schooling is gaining popularity across the country.

© Katrina Wittkamp/Digital Vision/Thinkstock

not always legal. Many states, such as Pennsylvania, had laws prohibiting parents from schooling their children at home. A series of lawsuits, spurred by home-schooling advocacy groups, opened the door for the legalization of home schooling. Now home schooling is legal in every state, giving parents yet another type of school choice. Home schooling is gaining popularity across the country.

There are racial differences in the rates of home schooling. More whites are home schooled than blacks or Hispanics (US Department of Education, National Center for Education Statistics 2012). Nearly 78% of home-schooled students are white. Fewer than 2% are Hispanic, and fewer than 1% are African American. Additionally, there are socioeconomic differences in home-schooling rates. Students in two-parent households made up 89% of the home-schooled population, and those in two-parent households with one parent in the labor force made up 54% of the home-schooled population (US Department of Education, National Center for Education Statistics 2012).

Home schooling represents a significant investment in time and money, so why would parents choose to home school their children? For some families, home schooling is an attempt to offer a strong religious education and upbringing. Parents want the values of their particular religion included in the curriculum, and home schooling offers one way of doing just that. More and more, however, parents are deciding to home school their children simply because they feel as though public schools are not adequately educating their children. In order to give their children the best possible chance at life, parents are investing time and money, rearranging their schedules, and even relearning material in order to be able to home school their children.

Advocates of home schooling point to studies that show students who learn at home outperform public school students in every subject. They point to the right of parents to choose their children's educational trajectory. Critics point out, however, that when students are home schooled, it removes good students from public schools. For schools that have a history of underperformance, this can exacerbate those problems. For those schools that receive funding based on the number of students enrolled, home-schooled students cost public schools money. Some critics have contended, too, that home-schooled students may excel academically, but they face a deficit in terms of being socialized because they are not being schooled with peers. Research has shown, however, that this fear is unfounded. There is no evidence that home schooled students face any social deficit.

Does School Choice Work?

School choice has many adherents but also many opponents. Critics of school choice, as we have seen, center their arguments on the ways in which school choice excludes students in marginal groups. They argue that private school students are more likely to come from certain advantaged groups while leaving students from disadvantaged groups behind. There is some truth to this criticism. As noted, private school tuition is often unaffordable for many families. Even with vouchers and tuition assistance, the cost of private schools remains prohibitive. Critics of private schools also point out that only about half of the teachers in private schools are certified to teach, and while more than half of public school teachers have advanced degrees, fewer than half in private schools complete a graduate degree. Teachers in public school also tend to be more experienced than private school teachers in the same subject, and the turnover rate for private school teachers is substantially higher than in public schools (*Public Purpose* 1998).

Proponents of school choice, however, point to an array of statistics that highlight the successes of private schools. For one, the average per-pupil expenditure for private schools was 30% lower than for public schools (*Public Purpose* 1998). In fact, if public schools could reduce student expenditure to meet private school costs, the estimated savings would be more than $115 billion a year. At the same time, a government analysis of public versus private and charter schools concluded that students in private schools outperform students in public schools in every subject (US Department of Education 2006) and demonstrate greater understanding and retention of material.

Perhaps not surprisingly, a greater percentage of private and charter school students go to college than public school students. The percentages are even higher for graduate education. Proponents also point out that, contrary to the claims of critics, more than 85% of upper-income families choose public schools for their children. In fact, some studies have shown that lower-income families are just as likely or even more likely to support school choice than upper-income families (Council for American Private Education 2012).

Teachers also report fewer security problems and behavior problems in private schools. For example, in a 2005 survey of teachers, more than 25% of public school teachers reported gang activity in or near the school, compared to 4% of private school teachers. A 2006 study done by the National Center for Education Statistics reported that more than 20% of teachers in public schools report student apathy to be a serious problem, while only 4% of private school teachers cited apathy as a serious problem.

Finally, private schools are far from the homogeneous enclaves that many critics claim. According to the US Department of Education, National Center for Education Statistics (2009), whites are slightly overrepresented in private schools, while other races are slightly underrepresented. In fact, studies of the racial, ethnic, and religious makeup of schools reveal that while private schools are slightly less diverse than many public schools, private schools are becoming increasingly diverse (Council for American Private Education 2012).

How would a sociologist respond to these debates? A sociologist might point out that the debate itself is sociologically interesting because it raises questions about the degree to which people should be expected to participate in public institutions. For example, as more public money is funneled into voucher programs, charter schools, and magnet schools, there is less money for the operation of public education systems. Some might see this as damaging to society because it removes many of the best students from the public education system. Sociologists might also be interested in how different schools socialize people differently. Do private schools, for instance, socialize children against full participation in other public social institutions?

There is little doubt that the debate about schooling in America will continue. As American schools continue to struggle on the world stage, perhaps lessons from other nations will help to guide American schools in new directions and provide creative solutions to many of the challenges facing American public education.

Deviance in Schools

Not that long ago, deviance in school consisted mainly of smoking, chewing gum, or tardiness. Today's schools, however, are dealing with much more serious issues such as drug addiction, gangs, teen pregnancy, and violence. These forms of deviance threaten the learning environment as well as require significant investment of resources to combat.

It should be noted that there is no evidence that schools are causing these deviant behaviors. In most cases, the violence and other deviant acts begin in the surrounding society and spill over into schools. To combat these problems, many schools have adopted zero-tolerance policies that require immediate and predetermined responses to serious deviance.

Zero-tolerance policies have been heavily criticized. Despite strong legislative support, studies of zero-tolerance policies have not been shown to be effective at combating deviance in schools (Casella 2003; Skiba 2004). There are two interrelated reasons for this. First, zero-tolerance policies are inflexible and thus cannot respond effectively to unique situations that might arise. Blogger George Clowes (2003) has collected numerous accounts of zero-tolerance policies that have resulted in harm to students rather than providing safer schools. For example, Clowes documents the case of a fifth-grade student with a spotless disciplinary record who had won several citizenship awards. The student dutifully turned in a pocketknife that he and a friend had found in the school cafeteria. He was promptly suspended for five days. School officials explained that the student had waited two hours to turn in the knife, and during that two hours he had broken school policy because his teacher might have thought the knife belonged to him.

Such cases are interesting sociologically. Although there is no evidence that schools as an institution are becoming less safe, school officials have implemented policies that in many ways resemble the rigid rules of a total institution such as prison. Perhaps school officials are responding to pressures from parents and politicians, who rely on media accounts of school violence rather than on empirical data. Sociologists note that, often, perceptions are more important for influencing behavior than reality is. If people believe that schools are fraught with violence, they will act accordingly, regardless of the veracity of the belief. Sociologist W. I. Thomas believed that if a situation is defined as real by a person, it will become real in its consequences. Known as the **Thomas theorem**, this may explain, in part, why schools enact zero-tolerance policies.

Despite the reality, many people believe that schools facilitate deviant behavior. Schools indeed do carry a **corridor curriculum**, things that students learn informally outside of the classroom. Often, such socialization is done by other students. Ways in which students interact with each other and attitudes toward school or toward a particular teacher are all part of the hidden curriculum. So is bullying. Bullying is considered a pervasive problem in public schools across the country. While **bullying** may have varying definitions, the government defines it as: unwanted, aggressive behavior among school-aged children that involves a real or perceived power imbalance. The behavior is repeated, or has the potential to be repeated, over time (stopbullying.gov 2012). Bullying includes actions such as making threats, spreading rumors, attacking someone physically or verbally, and excluding someone from a group on purpose. Statistics suggest that one in three children in public schools are either bullies or is a victim of bullying. Nearly every school now has a policy to prevent bullying, as well as plans to help reduce incidences of bullying in school. However, since these policies are relatively new, there are few data to suggest whether such programs actually reduce bullying.

Student Passivity

As already noted, public school teachers cite student apathy as a major problem. Some of this may be attributed to the proliferation of electronic devices, which consume increasing amounts of students' time and lead to boredom with traditional methods of instruction. Coleman, Hoffer, and Kilgore (1981) argue that schools encourage student passivity because they combine compulsory education with a one-size-fits-all curriculum and a passive system of learning. Part of the problem, too, is doubtless the increasing bureaucratization that can lead to rigidity and facelessness. The small, single-room schools of the past and close relationships with teachers have been replaced by large bureaucracies that have effectively structured education like a factory. Students enter the production line, are given an approved set of lessons, and then are pushed through the system as if all the students are fundamentally the same. In fact, the bureaucratization of schools has led to a series of issues that undermine education.

First, bureaucratic schools increasingly rely on numerical assessments to determine success or failure. Numbers such as dropout rates or achievement test scores are useful tools, but they are insufficient to measure dimensions of education such as motivation, creativity, and innovation. Schools have set rigid expectations that may not be appropriate for every student. Relatedly, the rigid uniformity that quantification and bureaucracy have bred in schools neglects the culture of individual communities, families, and individuals. It essentially treats all students as the same and neglects to attend to their special needs.

Rigid expectations set by the bureaucratization of schools lead to the assumption that all children should know the same material and learn it in the same way and at the same pace. They neglect the vast diversity in learning styles and speeds. Most schools discourage gifted students from advancing more quickly than their peers or graduating

Thomas theorem If something is perceived as real, it becomes real in its consequences.

Corridor curriculum Lessons that children teach one another at school while not in class.

Bullying Repeatedly being mean to another child.

early, and poor performers are pushed through the grades despite being deficient at key academic skills needed for success in higher grades.

Like most bureaucracies, schools have also adopted specialization. Student education is divided into specialized periods in which students learn math from one teacher, language arts from another, and science from still another. Often, no connection is made between the various subjects, so the knowledge gain is encapsulated and fragmented. Additionally, such specialization often keeps teachers from getting to know their students well.

Finally, bureaucratic schools tend to disempower both teachers and students. A rigid adherence to numerical ratings means that teachers must teach to the tests, giving them less power to determine what they teach. Students are rarely empowered to learn on their own, increasingly relying on teachers to tell them what is important to know, how to solve the problem, and what the correct answer should look like. Creativity that accompanies personal interest in a subject is discouraged, leading to increasing impersonalization and more student apathy.

Dropping Out

Although passivity is a major problem in America's public schools, dropping out may be an even bigger problem. **Dropping out** refers to leaving school prior to graduation. In many states, students may legally drop out at age 16, regardless of their academic performance. Despite the problems with public schools, dropping out leaves students even more unprepared for work in a postindustrial economy. Students who drop out are at significantly higher risk for poverty than people who complete high school. In fact, dropouts account for more than half of all people receiving welfare and more than 80% of the prison population (Christle, Jolivette, and Nelson 2004). Additionally, students who drop out of school are more likely to be unemployed or underemployed. They also earn less income, on average, over the course of a lifetime than people who complete high school.

Roughly 9% of Americans between the ages of 16 and 24 have dropped out of school. Racial and ethnic disparities in dropout rates are even more disturbing. The dropout rate for whites is roughly 5.3%. For African Americans, the rate is 8.4%. Most disturbingly, the rate for Hispanics is 21.4% (US Department of Education, National Center for Education Statistics 2009)! It should be noted that these numbers include only people that are known to have left school. However, it is likely that these numbers are higher than official statistics indicate. In fact, some researchers have estimated the numbers to be twice as high as officially reported (Thornburgh 2006).

Students drop out for a variety of reasons. Some students live in poverty and must work to help support their families. Time at school means time away from earning a wage that is necessary for family survival. In fact, students living in poverty are more than five times more likely to drop out of school than children living in high-income families (US Department of Education, National Center for Education Statistics 2009). Other students drop out because they become pregnant and must leave school to care for their children. Still others struggle with the English language and find school tedious or difficult to navigate. Whatever the reason, school dropouts constitute a serious issue because of the social costs involved with failing to complete high school.

One thing that may contribute to dropout rates is the self-fulfilling prophecy. First used sociologically by Robert Merton (1968), the **self-fulfilling prophecy** refers to actions or attitudes that make a preconceived belief come true. For example, if a person believes that he will not do well in school, he will likely not apply himself to his schoolwork and thus will do poorly in school. Given that the number-one predictor of how well a child does in school is how well she likes school, an attitude of dislike toward school may easily become a self-fulfilling prophesy. The concept works for teachers, too. If a teacher believes that a student or a class will

Dropping out Leaving school prior to graduation.

Self-fulfilling prophecy Actions or attitudes that make a preconceived belief come true.

Research shows that students who drop out make considerably less money over the course of a lifetime.

© Photodisc/Thinkstock

not perform well, he or she will be more likely to teach in a way that prevents good performance in school.

Grade Inflation

School bureaucratization has led to an increasing trend toward quantifying academic success and an increasing reliance on the use of grades to measure individual academic success. Because grades are quantifiable and clear, they are presumed to be an objective measure of a student's mastery of subject matter. However, in recent years, schools have seen a trend toward **grade inflation**, the trend to give everyone higher grades for mediocre work. The trend toward grade inflation is evident both in public schools and in colleges and universities throughout the country.

Grade inflation occurs for a couple of reasons. First, recent trends in educational philosophy have made teachers increasingly concerned with the self-esteem and morale of students. Although some people may see average grades as a means to motivate students, many people see average grades as deflating for a student. As American culture becomes more grade obsessed, average grades are seen as failures. The perceived competitiveness of getting into college and graduate school means that students and parents put more emphasis on grades than in previous generations. Teachers who do issue average grades for average work are often chastised by parents, students, and administrators and are often pressured to increase student grades to fend off such criticisms. Indeed, much of this trend may involve **credentialism**, the tendency to overemphasize the receipt of a diploma or academic degree rather than a particular skill or experience (Collins 1979). Grade inflation is particularly interesting sociologically when it is linked to credentialism because at the same time that the average grades of students have increased, scores on standardized test scores have not. This suggests that grade inflation is a real phenomenon with real consequences. Students certainly gain some self-esteem from receiving a good grade. Yet they are certainly exposed to mixed messages when they fail to master a subject as measured by standardized tests. This trend suggests a rising emphasis on grades rather than on knowledge and skill.

Academic Standards

Perhaps the most talked-about school issue is declining academic standards. A 1983 study by the National Commission on Excellence in Education issued a scathing report that demonstrated serious shortcomings in American public educational institutions. Among its findings is that fewer than 20% of public school students can write a persuasive essay, and only about one-third of students can correctly solve a math problem requiring several steps. More than one-third of students nationwide fail to achieve basic reading, science, and math skills. These percentages are considerably higher in urban schools. In fact, nearly 25% of America's students are **functionally illiterate**. This means that they do not possess basic reading and writing skills necessary for everyday living.

This sobering study called for radical reform, including stricter requirements for language and math, as well as the abolition of social promotion. **Social promotion** occurs when a student is passed through a grade level due to age, regardless of academic ability. Although social promotion is thought to promote self-esteem in students, it has the latent effect of reducing a student's motivation to work, as well as placing students in higher grades without proper foundational skills, thus disadvantaging them even more.

A follow-up study in 2008 showed only marginal progress in improving school academics. School dropout rates declined slightly, and a trend was noted of schools offering some more challenging content. The report also noted that more high school graduates are going to college. However, this may, in part, be caused by decreasing admission standards in colleges and universities rather than by improvements in public education. At the same time, the report noted that more and more elementary school students are failing to meet standards in reading and math.

Grade inflation The trend of giving everyone higher grades for mediocre work.

Credentialism The tendency to emphasize a diploma or academic degree rather than experience, skill, or subject knowledge.

Functionally illiterate The absence of basic reading and writing skills necessary for everyday living.

Social promotion Passing a student through grades as a result of age rather than academic ability.

CONCEPT LEARNING CHECK 13.1   Education in the United States

Identify the kind of school that each person goes to.

_____ **1.** Although Ryan's school teaches all of the subjects, its emphasis on music and dance will be key to helping Ryan become a Broadway actor.

_____ **2.** June was put on a waiting list because the state she lives in allows only 120 students to attend her private school.

_____ **3.** Chi'Lan's parents received money from the state to help them cover the cost of her private school.

_____ **4.** Tyson goes to a school that is open to anyone regardless of income, abilities, or interests.

_____ **5.** Nina attends a school run by the Episcopalian church.

13.2 Education around the World

By comparing American education to that of other countries, we can gain insight into how to improve our own schools.

■ Illustrate education systems in postindustrial, developing, and underdeveloped nations.

Part of what drives the differences in school performance around the world is the cultural values that a society holds about education. For example, students in the Unites States are, on average, less motivated to do homework than students in many Asian nations. Japanese culture places a premium on education, and Japanese students spend 60 more days in school each year than American students. Teachers in other countries are also given considerably more flexibility than in the United States, and their profession is generally more widely respected. Although it is impossible to survey schools from every nation, let us look at some nations with radically different educational views and outcomes from America to get a sense of the diversity of schooling methods and approaches. The countries discussed here were chosen because of their various levels of socioeconomic development and approaches to schooling.

Schooling and Economic Development

First, it should be noted that the way in which a culture views education and the methods that it uses to educate its children are strongly tied to the economic development of the nation. Low-income nations often have limited formal schooling, with families and communities expected to teach children essential skills and knowledge—much like it was in America's early days. In some of these nations, formal schools are exclusive to particular groups, such as boys or families who can pay to send their children to school. Wealthy people whose children do not need to work are thus at a significant advantage in such nations, as their children will likely get a much more comprehensive education than children of poor families. Some countries, such as Iran, tie their schooling to their religion, which reflects their national culture.

Higher-income nations generally have more inclusive, more comprehensive, and more formal schooling for students. Nations with postindustrial economies need more educated and more skilled workers, so education becomes even more important to preparing students for the demands of a rapidly changing workplace.

Schooling in Japan

Japanese schools consistently score above American schools in all subjects, and Japanese schools are well known on the world stage for producing some of the highest academic achievers. Japanese schools are structured so that the earlier grades are dedicated to teaching the roots of Japanese culture, such as dedication to family and country.

Japanese schools produce some of the world's highest academic achievers.
© Ingram Publishing/Thinkstock

Beginning in their early teens, Japanese students take a series of highly competitive standardized tests that help to determine their life trajectory. The top half of performers on these tests will enter college. The bottom half will generally not be admitted. Not surprisingly, Japanese families take these exams very seriously. Many families pay substantial amounts of money for "cram schools" to help prepare students for these tests. Many students study long into the night, sacrificing sleep to prepare for the exams. Sometimes, students even fall asleep in class—looked upon by teachers as an indication of a serious student.

For the Japanese, academic success is a family affair. Students who excel in school are seen as contributing to the success of their families, while academic failure is also shared among the family members. Thus, school success is an attitude that is deeply ingrained in the family and thus in the culture of Japan. This differs from American ideas of education, in which success or failure is usually attributed to the individual student rather than to the whole family.

Japanese schools teach very differently than US schools. For example, in a study of teaching methods in mathematics (Stigler and Hiebert 2009), researchers videotaped Japanese lessons in math. Then they did the same in US schools. The patterns they saw revealed significant differences in the ways in which the two nations approach teaching. While American teachers tended to dictate the process of solving the problem to students, teachers in Japan let students experiment in small groups with different ways of solving the problem for themselves. Thus, Japanese students learn to embrace struggle with novel concepts, while American students learn to follow directions and to believe that there is one way to solve a problem and one correct answer to a problem.

Schooling in India

Because India is a developing nation, Indian schools are still in the process of evolving. Indian schools also face significant challenges. India's population is the fastest growing in the world. Demographers estimate that if current trends continue, India will be the most populous nation on Earth by 2050. Class sizes in India already average nearly 60 students in a crowded classroom with few resources. While 90% manage to complete primary school, fewer than half continue through secondary school. Only one-third attend college. Thus, Indian schools will require an enormous investment in infrastructure, teachers, supplies, and hardware if India is going to keep up with population trends. Those investments will need to be even higher if Indian schools wish to compete on the world stage.

Indian schools are often overcrowded and underfunded.
© Andrew Aitchison/In Pictures/Corbis

Indian culture also shapes education. Despite significant economic gains in recent decades, the average Indian family earns only about 6% of the average American income. In India, boys are more valued than girls, particularly in poor families, because both the boy and his future wife will contribute income to the family. However, there are significant costs to raising a girl, such as the payment of a dowry. Additionally, the contributions of a daughter benefit her husband and his family. For these reasons, many Indian households shy away from significant investment in educating daughters. Instead, they put daughters to work in factories or other jobs to generate income for the family. More boys than girls complete primary grades and go on to secondary schools. Even boys in poor families are forced to work, often as many as 60 hours per week, which significantly limits the time they can spend in school.

How Indian schools respond to the demographic trends they are facing remains to be seen. While government officials often announce a commitment to improving schools, they face corrupt administrators, significant poverty, and a culture that is not committed to compulsory education.

Schooling in Liberia

The African nation of Liberia is among the poorest in the world. It has also been devastated by years of civil war that damaged the nation's infrastructure and destroyed families. The war also destroyed nearly all of the nation's schools. At the conclusion of the war, the new government began to work with agencies such as UNICEF to reconstruct their educational system from the ground up. Temporary structures were constructed and books provided so that classes could resume. Classes remain large due to a shortage of classrooms and teachers—many of whom were killed in the war.

Liberian education is mostly rote memorization in math, reading, and science. Schools generally lack technologies and supplies necessary for more advanced studies. Despite a lack of significant monetary investment, a dearth of qualified teachers, and a lack of classroom space, nearly 70% of males and 60% of females complete primary school. Liberia maintains a youth literacy rate of nearly 75%!

These numbers can be explained by two trends. First, Liberia has attempted to ingrain a desire for education into the national culture. Seeing education as a way to lift families and the nation out of poverty, it is easy to convince people to commit to compulsory education laws and take education seriously. Second, Liberia has reached out for foreign help. By pairing up with groups from around the world, Liberia has been able to bring supplies, teachers, and other educational infrastructure to the children. The government has continued to work with these organizations to establish both short- and long-term solutions to their educational crisis.

Wracked by years of civil war, the nation of Liberia is rebuilding schools with the help of the international community.

© Olivier Polet/Corbis

What Can Other Countries Teach Us about Education?

Obviously, discussion of schools in all of the more than 200 nations of the world is prohibitive. The three nations discussed here—one postindustrial nation, one developing nation, and one underdeveloped nation—can offer some important lessons about the way that social forces shape education as a social institution.

First, it is clear that while money is an important factor, it is not a panacea to educational problems. Nations that spend far less per student than the United States are able to compete effectively on the world stage. Second, education is more than simply teaching facts and figures. Cultural transmission remains an important foundation of education, shaping both how students approach education as well as what facts and figures are important for students in that society to learn. Finally, establishing a culture of education is important for a nation. Research in developmental psychology has established that the number-one predictor of how well a child does in school is how well the child likes his or her school (Slee 2002), and the number-one predictor of how much a child likes school is parental attitudes toward education (Slee 2002). Thus, a nation that fosters a positive attitude toward education will produce students who perform better than a nation that does not take education seriously.

THE SOCIOLOGICAL IMAGINATION Education and the Sociological Imagination

The sociological imagination is about learning how to view personal troubles as public issues. It comes from the way in which our personal experiences are shaped by social history. In 1957 during the Cold War, the Soviet Union successfully launched Sputnik, a Russian satellite, into orbit. Americans feared that the satellite would be used to spy on the United States and consequently this event spearheaded a revolution in mathematics and science curriculum. One year later Congress passed the National Defense Education Act (NDEA)

authorizing one additional billion federal dollars to be spent on college financial aid, and revised science, mathematics, and foreign language courses at all levels of the public school system designed to train and motivate students into careers that would allow the country to compete against the Soviet Union. Education as a social institution is integral to the development of the sociological imagination. After all, education is shaped by history, and education shapes individual experiences.

(Continues)

THE SOCIOLOGICAL IMAGINATION *(Continued)*

EVALUATE

1. What current national or global issues exist today that influence education policies and individual education goals?

2. Is the United States ready for another science-based education revolution? Why or why not?

3. How did your school reflect societal values? How did your school teach those values to you?

4. How did your experiences in school shape how you view education in America?

CONCEPT LEARNING CHECK 13.2   Education around the World

Choose the correct answer.

_____ 1. Bartholomew goes to school in a dilapidated building, with extremely overcrowded classrooms that are mostly male. Bartholomew likely attends school in what country?

    A. India

    B. The United States

    C. Liberia

    D. Japan

_____ 2. Eva goes to school underneath a tent, with no books or pencils. Her lessons consist mostly of memorizing. She likely goes to school in what nation?

    A. India

    B. The United States

    C. Liberia

    D. Japan

_____ 3. Carlita goes to school in a class with brand new computers. She works in groups to find novel ways to get the correct answers. She is pushed very hard to perform well on her tests. She likely goes to school in what nation?

    A. India

    B. The United States

    C. Liberia

    D. Japan

_____ 4. Peter attends school in the inner city in a run-down building. Although there are computers, they are old. His classroom is somewhat overcrowded, but his teacher is certified to teach. Peter likely goes to school in what nation?

    A. India

    B. The United States

    C. Liberia

    D. Japan

13.3 Sociological Perspectives on Education

Sociologists use the three major theoretical perspectives to understand how education shapes individuals in society.

- Describe the sociological perspectives on education.

Sociologists have analyzed schools in a variety of ways. Sociologists have used the major theoretical perspectives to look at the ways in which schools function as social institutions and the ways in which schools shape individuals. While each of the perspectives offers interesting and valuable insight into American schools, each also identifies some key differences in the way in which schools can be understood in American culture.

Functionalism in Schools

Functional analysis identifies at least five ways in which formal education functions in society. First, schools play a key role in socialization of students. For many children, school represents the first agent of socialization beyond the family. Primary schools teach language, mathematics, and basic science. But they also teach adherence to cultural norms such as turn taking, conflict resolution, and fair play. Civics classes teach the basics of political history and culture that help to develop students as patriotic citizens. Sports and other competitive activities function to teach teamwork, individualism, and good sportsmanship.

Second, schools function as a means of cultural innovation and change. Teachers not only reflect existing cultures, they also create culture. Many professors and teachers tend to have liberal social and economic philosophies, and these beliefs are often injected into their teaching. Additionally, certain subjects, such as social sciences, humanities, and arts, often lead to new ways of thinking about the world that have the potential to radically change a person's world view. For example, research in social sciences has led to understandings of the social world that have improved the quality of life for many people.

Third, schools function as a means of stratifying people. Through the use of testing and grades, students are separated into categories that have real social consequences. Consider how placement tests divide students into high achieving and low achieving. At a more macro level, schools reinforce meritocracy by rewarding talented students and punishing less talented students. These divisions often influence the opportunities that people have later in life. For example, students who are identified as high achievers are often placed in advanced-placement courses or talented and gifted courses, making it easier for them to get into college. Conversely, students who are identified as needing remedial classes are often tracked into vocational programs.

Fourth, schools function as a means of social integration. As American society becomes more diverse, so too are schools becoming more ethnically and racially diverse. Schools function as an institution that shapes a diverse population into a group that shares a common set of norms, values, and behaviors. Compulsory education, combined with a mandated curriculum and standardized testing, assimilates people of all walks of life into a single cultural view.

Finally, schools perform several latent functions that help the economy. Aside from providing jobs for people who work in the educational field, schools provide child care for parents. This is advantageous for both sole-parent families and dual-income families because they do not have to pay for child care. As students get older, high schools and colleges keep many students from working full time, which prevents the job market from being flooded with cheap labor. During this time, students often develop networks of professors, professionals, students, and other people that will help them get jobs in the future. Schools and colleges also function as a kind of marriage market, bringing together men and women of marriageable age.

Schooling and the Conflict Perspective

The conflict perspective analyzes schools in terms of how schools cause and perpetuate social inequality. The conflict perspective also analyzes schools in terms of how the creation of social inequality influences life chances by separating students into winners and losers. Unlike the functionalist approach, however, the conflict approach challenges the notion that such stratification is functional for society.

Schools can be used to divide students into high and low achievers.

© Hero/Corbis

Schools enforce rules that create an obedient workforce.

© Digital Vision/Thinkstock

Hidden curriculam Values that are taught through the presentation of standard curriculum that are not an explicit part of that curriculum.

Tracking Assigning students into different types of educational programs based on their perceived aptitude.

Schools can be seen as a way of controlling people, forcing them to accept the dominant cultural norms and values. As public education evolved over time, it became focused on teaching skills needed for industrial jobs, such as obedience, following directions, and discipline—skills that are part of what is called **hidden curriculum**. In school, children learn to raise their hands before speaking, defer to authority, and attend to tasks that others set out for them. Such skills inevitably benefit those who own the means of production, because they have a workforce that is trained in the values that make good, obedient workers.

Standardized tests, as already noted, are tools used by the educational system to divide students into high and low achievers. Most American schools practice **tracking**—assigning students into different types of educational programs based on their perceived aptitude. The conflict perspective, however, notes that the tests may not be accurate assessments of students' aptitudes. For example, consider the following question from California's standardized language arts exam:

A person who frequents the hallways of the legislature in order to influence public officials is called a:
A. congressman.
B. liaison.
C. lobbyist.
D. petitioner.

Although the answer to the question may seem obvious to us, consider the difficulty of the question for a recent immigrant. A student who has recently come to America from a nation with a strong totalitarian government will likely not have cultural knowledge of American politics. The lack of cultural knowledge alone may be enough to place the student in a low-achieving category, thereby disadvantaging the student and limiting his or her social mobility.

Tracking also tends to advantage children from higher-income families. These families are more likely to have parents who are college graduates and who can afford tutoring or other services that will help students perform well on standardized exams. On the other hand, students from low-income families often have parents who are less involved in their children's education and who do not have the resources to help their children succeed academically. Tracking, therefore, has become controversial. Although many schools do give students the ability to move from one track to another, the extent to which this actually happens has not been widely studied.

Just as students are divided into high and low achievers, so too are schools. As we have already learned, urban schools are often poorly funded relative to suburban schools, and the educational outcomes of these differences in funding lead to noticeable differences in educational outcomes. In nearly every case, the better-funded suburban schools outperform urban schools. Of course, this advantages students in suburban schools, whose families have generally higher incomes than families from the inner city. Thus, the poor remain poorly educated with limited opportunities for college or careers, while the middle class and upper class receive better educations and thus better opportunities.

Differences in public school affect access to higher education. Urban schools may prepare students less effectively for college. In addition, college is expensive. Some of the least costly state schools still charge more than $6,000 a year, excluding the cost of books and supplies. Private colleges charge considerably more—up to $45,000 per year! Family income influences not only which college a student might attend, but also whether the student attends college at all! While nearly 67% of children from families with incomes above $75,000 attend college, only 25% of children from families with incomes under $20,000 will go on to college. Even when they do, they usually must take out substantial student loans, to be paid back upon graduation. Thus, students from poor families that attend college start out with the added disadvantage of substantial debt.

The growth and expansion of community colleges has mitigated this problem somewhat. Offering two-year degrees, community colleges now enroll more than one-third of all college undergraduates. Tuitions at community colleges are substantially lower than at four-year institutions. This means that higher education is less expensive and within reach of more families than ever before. Community colleges benefit minorities in particular. Currently, almost half of all African-American and Hispanic undergraduates in the United States are enrolled in community colleges. Many students who receive two-year degrees from community colleges go on to complete four-year degrees at traditional colleges. Such students, having some college experience, tend to do better in their classes than students coming straight from high school.

In short, the conflict perspective sees school as a way to transform privilege into personal merit. The credentials that schooling provides are seen as a sign of accomplishment and expertise. These credentials provide considerable opportunity for economic and social advancement that are essential for social mobility.

Symbolic Interactionism and Education

As we have already learned, the symbolic interactionist approach suggests people actively create the social world that they live in through the use of symbols in their day-to-day interaction. The symbolic interactionist approach analyzes schools in terms of the way in which the language we use shapes our perceptions of education and how stereotypes can shape what goes on in a classroom.

Researchers (Rosenthal & Jacobson 1968) wanted to know how the labels we put on students affect their education. To test this, they performed an interesting experiment. First, they took students and randomly assigned them to one of two classes with the same teacher. Although the students were randomly assigned, students and the teacher were both told that the first class was filled with students identified as high achievers, while the other class was labeled as low achievers. What happened?

First, the students formed expectations about their performance. Students who were placed in the low-achieving class began to believe they would do poorly in class. Conversely, the students who had been placed in the high-achieving class began to show improved performance. Some of this effect can be attributed to the teacher, whose expectations of the low achievers made her teach more slowly and expect less from those students, while at the same time, her expectations for the high-achieving class rose. Other studies have confirmed these results. In addition, when students labeled high achieving interacted with students labeled low achieving, they often adopted an arrogant, domineering, and superior attitude toward the low-achieving students (Rist 1970).

Studies such as these show the power of a label to influence student performance and teacher expectations. Perhaps, then, tracking students into high and low tiers creates advantage and disadvantage simply due to the fact that students will begin to behave in accordance with their expectations for themselves, as well as according to the expectations of others.

CONCEPT LEARNING CHECK 13.3   Sociological Perspectives on Education

Answer the following questions.

1. List two functions of schooling in America.

2. List two ways that schools cause or exacerbate social inequality.

3. List two ways that labeling people can affect school performance.

13.4 Sociology of Religion

Religion is one of the most important institutions in any society.

■ Compare and contrast how sociologists view the role of religion in social life.

Profane Part of the realm of ordinary experience.

Sacred Things that are set apart as inspiring awe or reverence.

Religion A social institution involving beliefs, values, and behaviors based on the sacred.

Faith Belief based on conviction rather than on empirical evidence.

As an agent of socialization, religion stands as one of the most important in American culture. More than a third of Americans say that they attend religious services at least once a week. Many more belong to a church but attend infrequently. Still more claim to believe in a particular religion, even though they may rarely or never participate in religious ceremonies. Any way you look at the numbers, religion emerges as an important part of the fabric of American life.

Sociologists and Views on Religion

Early sociologists also recognized the importance of religion in social life. Emile Durkheim (1915) wrote an entire book dedicated to the subject, stating that the purview of religion is things that surpass the limits of human knowledge. Durkheim said that people separate objects, events, and experiences that are **profane**—that is, part of the realm of ordinary experience—from those things that are **sacred**—things that are set apart as inspiring awe or reverence. Religions, Durkheim argued, rely on the separation of the sacred from the profane. He thus defined **religion** as a social institution involving beliefs, values, and behaviors based on the sacred.

Karl Marx recognized the importance of religion for maintaining the status quo. Marx criticized religion as a tool by which those in power oppress the poor. For example, Marx pointed out that Biblical phrases like "it is easier for a camel to pass through the eye of the needle than for a rich man to enter into heaven" can be interpreted as justifying poverty in this life in exchange for redemption after death. Marx saw this as merely a method by which the owners of the means of production keep the poor in their place by promising them future rewards. In that way, the current hierarchical structure is kept intact.

Max Weber believed that religion can act as a strong force of social change. As an example, Weber discussed how Protestantism differed from Catholicism. While Catholicism, argued Weber, advocated for a strong social hierarchy, traditional values, and ritualism, Protestantism advocated innovation, meritocracy, and good works. Protestant values, argued Weber, helped to usher in the Industrial Revolution. So religion can be not just a source of social stagnation but a force for social change as well.

So sociologists have studied religion almost from the beginning. Sociological approaches to religion, however, are not concerned with whether a particular religion is true. Rather, sociologists are concerned with how religions and issues of **faith**—belief based on conviction rather than on empirical evidence—are developed, maintained, and used in society.

Durkheim divided the symbolic world into the profane and the sacred.

© Bettmann/CORBIS

CONCEPT LEARNING CHECK 13.4   Sociology of Religion

Match the idea with the sociologist.

_____ 1. Religion is a way to keep people from challenging the social hierarchy.

_____ 2. Religion is the way that societies separate what is common from what is awe inspiring.

_____ 3. Religion is a social institution that can lead to significant social change.

A. Max Weber

B. Karl Marx

C. Emile Durkheim

13.5 Sociological Perspectives on Religion

The major theoretical approaches offer unique sociological insight into the ways in which religion shapes social life and influences individuals.

- Describe the sociological perspectives on religion.

As we have seen, different sociologists have offered very different analyses of the role of religion in social life. At least some of those differences can be explained by the theoretical approach that these sociologists take in their analysis of religion. While there exists some overlap in their approaches, the major theoretical perspectives also offer some very unique insight into the ways in which religion shapes social life and influences individuals.

Functionalism and Religion

Emile Durkheim recognized that religion played an important part in the social lives of people in every society. Each society adopts certain items as symbols of its social life. In preindustrial societies, these objects are usually totems. A **totem** is defined as an object in the material world that a society collectively defines as sacred. The totem, according to Durkheim, functions as the cornerstone of rituals that symbolize the power of the sacred world and the power of society over the individual.

In industrial and postindustrial societies, the function of totems sometimes evolves from the material to the symbolic. For instance, the phrase "In God We Trust" that appears on every coin and currency represent values that bind Americans together. On a more micro level, consider how the logos of various sports teams bind fans together with a common sense of purpose. Of course, not all of our modern totems are symbolic. The American flag is a physical symbol of American values that is held sacred by society. Rules of etiquette for the American flag include not desecrating it, not allowing it to touch the ground when retiring the colors, and proper disposal of the flag. These totems, both physical and symbolic, bind people together with a common core of values, beliefs, and practices.

From this analysis, Durkheim identified three main functions of religion in society. The first, as already noted, is social cohesion. Religion serves to unite people through the creation and maintenance of a common sense of values and behaviors. Religion establishes a common set of practices, such as fair play, turn taking, and concern for others, that help us to organize our social lives successfully.

Second, religion functions as a means of social control. Like Marx, Durkheim recognized that religion can be used to promote conformity to desired social values. By defining what behaviors are consistent with religious practice and which ones are contrary to religious practice, religion encourages people to behave in a certain way. Additionally, by defining a higher power as a judge with the ability to reward and punish people for their behavior, religion ensures conformity. The power of religion to induce conformity in people has long been recognized and has formed the basis of many monarchical claims of divine right. Obedience to the king or queen was seen as obedience to God.

Finally, Durkheim argued that religion functions to give people a sense of meaning or purpose. In preindustrial societies, many aspects of nature are not well understood. This can make people feel isolated or frightened. Religion serves to orient people in nature and provides them with a way to fit the world to their understanding. In industrial and postindustrial societies, religion serves as a way to decrease anomie and gain direction in an increasingly individualistic society. Religion also gives a sense of direction during times of tragedy. Many people take comfort in trying times by putting the issue in a religious context. To help understand this idea, consider that many of our most important life events—birth, marriage, death—are marked with religious rituals.

Unlike Marx, Max Weber argued that religion can act as a strong force for social change.
© Keystone Pictures USA/Alamy

Totem An object in the material world that a society collectively defines as sacred.

As noted, Max Weber saw one of the functions of religion as promoting social change. As an example, Weber showed how the rise of global capitalism was encouraged by the emergence of Calvinism, a religious movement within the Protestant Reformation. John Calvin was a Protestant leader who believed that God had predetermined the fates of people by picking some for salvation while condemning everyone else. People who were chosen for salvation by God were destined to ascend to Heaven, while the rest of humanity was fated to a life in Hell.

Of course, individuals did not know whether they were predestined or Heaven or Hell. The anxiety of not knowing drove followers of Calvin to seek signs that they had been favored by God. Gradually, they came to see prosperity as a sign of that favor. People who were more prosperous were favored by God. This caused Calvinists to work hard and adopt a thrifty life style to amass wealth. The wealth was used not for spending on oneself and not for donating to charities to help the poor—after all, the poor were not favored by God. Rather, wealth was to be reinvested and used to make more wealth! To gain wealth, Calvinists advocated thrift and adopted new technologies. All of this laid the groundwork for industrial capitalism. As Calvinism waned, the values that it ushered in became more common and ingrained themselves in the broader culture, driving global capitalism and changing society forever.

Conflict Perspectives on Religion

As already noted, the conflict perspective emphasizes how religion is used to support social inequality. Marx argued that religion supports the ruling class by legitimizing its position in society. Weber's analysis of Calvinism provides an example of this. As Calvinists sought a sign that they were chosen, they used personal wealth as a measure of God's favor. Everyone who was wealthy was favored. Poor people were condemned to Hell. Calvinist wealth can therefore be justified as God's will, and it is dreadfully hard to argue with the will of God.

Again, consider how many leaders have justified their rule by claiming that they are descendants of deities. This claim alone is enough to establish social inequality between rulers and the rest of the population. Religion can also be used to maintain those divisions through the justification of servitude in this world with the promise of freedom in the next. In addition to creating and maintaining class division, religion also serves to create and maintain gender divisions. Nearly all of the world's major religions are patriarchal. In traditional Judaism, for example, women are forbidden to become rabbis. In Islam, women are required to wear clothes that cover nearly their entire body. In Christianity, passages in the Bible reflect and reinforce patriarchal values, such as the oft-repeated marital vow for a woman to "honor and obey" her husband.

Marx zeroed in on the ways in which religion not only created social class divisions but also prevented revolutionary social change. Religion, Marx argued, "is the opium of the people," (2012:27, orig. 1848) meaning it lulls them into a sense of complacency so that they ignore or accept the poor conditions around them.

Symbolic Interactionism and Religion

Symbolic interactionism believes that religion, like all societal institutions, is socially constructed. Religious beliefs and ritual behaviors create a common understanding that gives people a sense of collective meaning and identity. Through the rituals developed through religious practice, distinctions are made between the sacred and profane. More importantly, through the use of symbols used in these rituals, people identify themselves with a particular group. Because this group has a connection to the sacred, religion places our lives within a framework that extends beyond this life. Facing inevitable mortality, people find comfort in religion. The symbols of faith that are used by religions give people the feeling of security and permanence.

As an example, consider how religion acts symbolically to strengthen marriage. If two people see marriage merely as a contract, they can guiltlessly decide to end the marriage at any time. However, it is much harder to justify leaving a marriage when it is seen

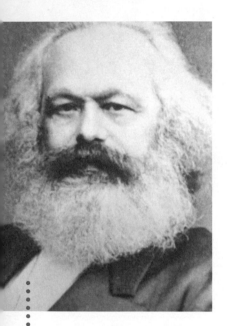

Marx argued that religion supports the ruling class by legitimizing its position in society.

© Photos.com/Thinkstock

Religion can symbolically strengthen marriage when it is seen as a covenant from God.

© Buccina Studios/PhotoDisc

as a covenant with God. The rings that are exchanged between spouses act as symbols of that covenant and bind the spouses through the use of that sacred symbol. This may be one reason why divorce rates are lower among people with strong religious beliefs.

In short, sacred symbols help people to overcome anomie and uncertainty as they navigate the social world. Religion serves as a symbol that binds people to others and as a symbol of what lies beyond the struggles of this world. Religion creates stability and order through the use of symbols and rituals. It gives people meaning and reminds them of that meaning through the use of religious symbols.

CONCEPT LEARNING CHECK 13.5   Sociological Perspectives on Religion

1. Tomie carries around a small icon that is symbolic of her religious views. Durkheim would call her symbol a _____.
2. Tomie also carries around her college textbook. Durkheim would suggest that this item represents the _____.
3. Marco believes that religions are just a way to keep people happy while the world is in crisis. His views most represent the view of what early sociologist?
4. Gina believes, as did _____, that religion functions to give people a sense of meaning in their lives.

13.6 Religions of the World

Like many social institutions, religion exhibits considerable diversity around the world.

- Compare and contrast the main religions of the world.

Like many social institutions, religion exhibits considerable diversity around the world. In fact, there are more than 730 established and recognized religions throughout the world. Many of them number only a few thousand or a few hundred followers. Still others have millions of followers around the globe. Six of the world's major religions include more than two-thirds of the human population. Each of them is briefly examined, along with atheism and agnosticism—the denial or doubt about the existence of a deity.

Christianity

Christianity is the most widespread religion in the world, with more than 2 billion professed followers. The bulk of these 2 billion Christians live in the North America, South America, and Europe. In fact, more than 85% of the North American population identifies as Christian. Christianity's dominance in the Western world is evident in several ways, most notably in the structure of the modern calendar, which begins on the alleged year of the birth of Jesus.

Like most religions, Christianity began as a small, cult-like religion that drew elements from the much older Judaism. Christianity was built on the personal character and charisma of Jesus bar Joseph, a Jew born in the town of Bethlehem in the land of Judah, who preached personal salvation. Rather than challenge the political authority of the conquering Romans, Jesus preached personal accountability to faith and love, which he saw as conquering sin and death.

Jesus preached **monotheism**, the belief in one god. Although he was not the first monotheist in history, the teachings of Jesus arose among the polytheism of Roman rule. In direct contrast to monotheism, **polytheism** recognizes many gods. Gradually, the monotheism of Christianity evolved into the belief in a single God in three forms—the holy trinity. God was seen as the father of creation and of Jesus. Jesus became of the symbol of God's presence on Earth, while the Holy Spirit represented the presence of God in the individual.

Monotheism The belief in one god.

Polytheism The belief in more than one god.

During Jesus' life, his followers were limited to a few hundred (Sanders 1993). Claims of his divinity emerged only after his persecution and death. Jesus was brought to trial by regional officials as a threat to the political establishment and sentenced to death by crucifixion, a slow and agonizing death that was common at the time. This explains why the cross has become a universal symbol of Christianity. According to Christian beliefs, Jesus was buried in a tomb and rose from the dead after three days, proving in the process that he was the son of God.

The followers of Jesus spread his teachings throughout the Middle East. For many years, Christianity remained a small and rogue religious group, often persecuted by the Roman authorities. However, by the 4th century, the Roman Empire under the rule of Constantine adopted Christianity as the official religion of Rome. Over time, as Christianity spread to other lands, it integrated practices from other cultures in order to make Christianity more palatable. For example, the Christmas tree was adopted as a symbol of Christmas—the alleged day of Jesus' birth—in order to integrate rituals from Druidic cultures that celebrated the winter solstice.

Today, Christianity takes many forms. Broadly divided into Catholic and Protestant views, each of these can be further subdivided into literally hundreds of denominations, each with slightly different views and rituals. Despite these differences, Christians everywhere are united in their belief in the divinity of Jesus.

Islam

The second-largest religion in the world is Islam, which comprises nearly one-fifth of the world's population. Followers of the Islamic religion are called Muslims. Although the majority of people in the Middle East identify as Muslim, followers of Islam are spread throughout the world, and the majority do not live in the Middle East. Muslims also have the highest birth rate of any major religion, and some demographers predict that Islam will become the world's dominant religion by 2100.

There are no solid figures about how many Muslims live in the United States. Estimates range from 2–8 million. Regardless, it is clear that Muslims compose an important part of the fabric of American life. American Muslims are diverse, coming from all over the world—Africa, Asia, and the Middle East. Some Muslims are born in the United State to Muslim parents and others are converts from other religions.

Islam is the word of God as revealed to the prophet Muhammad. Muhammad was born in the city of Mecca, Saudi Arabia, around the year 570. Unlike Christianity, which sees its prophet Jesus as a divine being, Islam considers Muhammad only as a prophet to whom the word of God is revealed. Islam is a religion based on the word of God as revealed in the Qur'an, the sacred book of the Islamic faith. The book urges the total submission to Allah (Arabic for God) as the path to inner peace. To show their devotion to Allah, Muslims engage in ritual prayers five times a day.

Islam spread rapidly after the death of Muhammad. Like Christianity, divisions arose within Islam over interpretations of the words of Muhammad. Despite these divisions, all Muslims are guided by the five tenets or pillars of the faith. The first pillar is the recognition that Allah is the one true God and that Muhammad is the true messenger of God's word. The second pillar is ritual prayer five times a day. The third pillar is the practice of charity by giving alms to the poor. The fourth pillar of Islam is fasting during the month of Ramadan. The fifth pillar is that all Muslims must make a pilgrimage to the city of Mecca at least once in their lifetime.

Although there are significant differences between the two religions, Christians and Muslims do have beliefs in common. For example, both religions are monotheistic. Additionally, although they use different names, they both believe in the same God. Like Christianity, Islam holds people accountable for their actions while on Earth. Individuals who do good deeds while on Earth will be rewarded in the afterlife, while those who do evil will be punished after death.

Muslims are also required to defend their faith, which in some cases has led to holy wars against unbelievers. Rising anti-Western sentiment has fueled some Muslims to

The city of Mecca is the birthplace of the Islamic prophet Muhammad, and is a holy city.

© iStockphoto/Thinkstock

vigorously defend their beliefs. Many Westerners hold stereotypical views of Muslims based on isolated but devastating terrorist attacks by a few radical Muslims. These misunderstandings have also helped increase the animosity between Muslims and Christians.

Some people in the United States are critical of Islam because they view Muslim women to be oppressed. Many Muslim women are not permitted to go to school, hold political office, drive a car, or work. In some Islamic societies, women must keep themselves covered in public. However, these limitations are more political and cultural than religious. The rights and limitations of Muslim women vary from nation to nation. Still, it is true that Muslim women do have relatively less social power than men. However, it should be noted that while it is tempting to be critical of Islam's treatment of women, we should avoid being ethnocentric. **Ethnocentrism** refers to the judgment of other systems of beliefs by the standards of our own beliefs. Sociologists generally believe that all cultural values are analyzable only on their own terms and thus cannot be compared. Indeed, some people suggest that Islam actually improved the conditions of women in society because the Qur'an requires a man to treat his wives justly. For example, the Qur'an allows a man to have up to four wives. However, it instructs him to have only one wife if having additional wives would cause him to act unjustly to any woman (Haddad and Stowasser 2004).

> **Ethnocentrism** The judgment of other systems of belief by the standards of our own beliefs.

Judaism

Judaism has deep historical roots that extend more than 4,000 years into the past. Although practiced by only around 15 million people around the world, the teachings of Judaism have provided the foundation for both Islam and Christianity. Together, these three religions form the Semitic (or Abrahamic) religions—that is, monotheistic faiths that trace their common origins through the ancestry of Abraham. Jews rely strongly on the lessons of the past to inform their present and future values, beliefs, and behaviors.

The first record of Judaism occurs among the ancient societies of the Mesopotamian valley. These early Jews were polytheistic wanderers and probably mercenary warriors. Their views were shaped through this history of wandering as their leader Jacob—the grandson of the Biblical hero Abraham—led the Jews into Egypt. For more than two centuries, the Jews languished in Egypt as servants at the bottom of the social hierarchy. According to Jewish history, Moses, an adopted son of an Egyptian princess, was called by God to lead the Jews out of Egypt and into lands that were promised to the Jews by God. When the Egyptians refused to allow the Jews passage out of Egypt, God sent a series of plagues on the people to convince the Pharaoh to allow the Jews to leave. Eventually, the Pharaoh permitted the Jews to depart for their own lands. Today, Jews remember this exodus as Passover, a major Jewish holiday.

After the Exodus, the Jews became monotheistic, and Moses revealed the Ten Commandments given to him by God that formed the foundations of Jewish law. The commandments accompanied another key tenet of the Jewish faith—the idea that the Jews are the chosen people of God. The covenant is a special relationship with God, which both defines the place of Jews as the chosen people and confers special responsibility to observe the laws of God. These laws are written as the history of the Jewish people, contained in the Old Testament in the Bible. Specifically, the first five books of the Bible, called by Jews the Torah, are the essence of Jewish law.

Jews have been one of the most persecuted groups in history. They have met resistance throughout history as they attempted to settle land that was promised to them by God. Recognized now as the nation of Israel, Jews have been subject to attacks by surrounding nations. Jews were also persecuted in Tsarist Russia, the Roman Empire, and Medieval Europe, and in modern times as they were rounded up and interred in Nazi concentration camps. In many ways, these experiences reflected the history of the Jewish people, became a part of that history, and have shaped much of modern Jewish thinking.

Like most other religions, Judaism has evolved many factions. There are three main denominations of Judaism. Orthodox Judaism, which represents nearly 600,000 people

Passover is a major Jewish holiday that celebrates the exodus of the Jewish people from Egypt.

© iStockphoto/Thinkstock

Orthodox Judaism is a sect of Judaism that largely sets itself apart from mainstream society.

© mikhail/Shutterstock, Inc.

Hinduism is probably the oldest extant religion.

© Matthew Wakem/Digital Vision/Thinkstock

in the United States, strictly observes Jewish law and cultural and dietary practices. Orthodox Jews also strictly enforce the segregation of women and men at religious services. Their strict adherence to traditional Jewish rules despite pressures to assimilate to more mainstream values has led Orthodox Jews to largely set themselves apart from the larger society. This means that in practice, Orthodox Judaism functions as a sect, which will be described later in this chapter.

Jews who assimilated into the larger society evolved into Reform Judaism. Reform Judaism is much more liberal in its thinking about Jewish law and tradition. It views Judaism as an evolving process rather than a static vision of religious life. For example, while in Orthodox Judaism men are dominant, Reform Judaism give substantially more social and religious power to women, even to the point of ordaining female rabbis. In short, Reform Jews tend to pick and choose among the laws and traditions that work for them as they navigate mainstream society.

Between the two poles of Reform Judaism and Orthodox Judaism is Conservative Judaism. Conservative Jews have strictly adopted some tenets of traditional Jewish law but rejected others. For example, traditional Jewish dietary laws are usually upheld, while laws prohibiting marriage between a Jew and a gentile (non-Jew) are often not followed.

Despite a legacy of enslavement, oppression, and attempted genocide, Jews have managed to survive. In fact, the social standing and socioeconomic standing of Jews are well above the world average. At the same time, many Jewish leaders remain concerned about the long-term fate of Judaism as a religion. Of the Jews that get married, more than half marry gentiles. Additionally, many children are not being brought up with the traditions, rituals, and history that has made the Jewish people strong and shaped their religion.

Hinduism

Hinduism is probably the oldest extant religion, dating back more than 4,500 years. Originating with the emergence of Indus River valley civilizations, Hindus live in what is now India and Pakistan, but some substantial populations can be found in Indonesia and some southern African nations.

Like Judaism, Hinduism has interwoven religious belief and practice with day-to-day life. Many social rules are prescribed by Hinduism that guide daily living. In fact, Hinduism is known as an "ethical religion," meaning that the core of the religion rests on an expectation of specific ethical responsibilities, or Dharma. For example, one of the principles of Dharma is the expectation that Hindus will observe the traditional caste system. Another is the giving of alms to the poor.

Although Hinduism has a concept of God, it is somewhat different than the physical God envisioned by Judaism, Islam, and Christianity. Rather, Hindus view God more as a moral force that permeates the universe than as a physical force that guides the direction of the universe. Hindus believe that each action has a moral consequence that affects the spirit. Positive actions result in moral development. Through positive action, karma—the belief in the spiritual progression of the soul—is cultivated. Karma works through reincarnation, a cycle of death and rebirth by which a person is born into a spiritual state that corresponds to the moral quality of his or her previous life. In contrast to the Semitic religions that view death as the ascent of the soul to ultimate judgment by God, Hindus believe that there is no ultimate judgment at the hands of a higher power. Rather, justice is achieved through reincarnation into a higher or lower form. When a person reaches Moksha, a state of spiritual perfection, the soul has no further need to be reborn, and reincarnation ceases.

Although the idea of Hinduism may seem strange to Westerners, the fact that Hinduism has thrived through the ages attests to the power of its ideas to shape human behavior. It is also illustrative of the fact that not all visions of God are the same. Semitic religions generally see God as transcendent—that is, a God that exists apart from nature and is beyond the realm of normal perception or understanding. In contrast, Hinduism sees God as immanent—within all things that exist. God, according to the Hindus, exists in all things, including the actions that we engage in.

Buddhism

Buddhism emerged nearly 2,500 years ago from Hinduism. Based upon the revelations of one person, Siddhartha Gautama, Buddhism now claims around 380 million followers. Gautama was born to a high-caste family in Nepal. A highly spiritual youth, Gautama left home at age 29 after a spiritual awakening. He travelled across the lands, meditating and preaching the path to enlightenment. Shaped by the extreme poverty that he witnessed on his travels, the Buddha believed that life involved suffering. The solution to the problem of suffering, according to the Buddha, is not wealth or power. On the contrary, the solution to suffering lies in the development of spiritual harmony. Through meditation, we develop the spirit to move beyond material desires and selfish acts. Only by focusing and quieting the mind can people achieve a connection with the universe.

Gautama founded the Buddhist religion, which now has around 380 million followers.
© Jim Esposito Photography LLC/Digital Vision/ Thinkstock

Based on the strength of his charisma, the Buddha quickly gained followers, who spread his message throughout Asia. When India's ruler converted to Buddhism in the 3rd century BCE, he spread the faith even further. Buddhism differs from Hinduism primarily in the way in which spiritual enlightenment is achieved. While Hinduism relies to a degree on rituals to achieve enlightenment, Buddhism relies on personal meditation and personal withdrawal.

Confucianism

K'ung Fu-tzu, more commonly known as Confucius, was born in China around 551 BCE. Like the Buddha, Confucius was heavily influenced by the suffering that he saw around him. While Buddhism relied on a withdrawal from the world as a way to mitigate worldly suffering, Confucius took a somewhat more formalized approach to the problem. Confucius instructed his followers to follow a code of conduct designed to alleviate suffering. This practice, called jen (humaneness), asserts that we should always place moral rightness above personal self-interest. For Confucianism, family forms the cornerstone of right living, because it teaches generosity, sacrifice, and consideration for others. Families also have a moral duty to the larger society. In this way, moral living is layered in such a way as to unite all people with a similar value system.

K'ung Fu-tzu, also known as Confucius, began one of the very few religions that lacks a concept of the sacred.
© iStockphoto/Thinkstock

Confucianism was the official religion of China from around 200 BCE until the beginning of the 20th century. After the people's revolution in 1949 that introduced communism to China, all religious expression was suppressed. Still, Confucianism remained. Today, hundreds of millions of people remain influenced by this religion. Indeed, the religion has spread out of China, with nearly 100,000 followers of Confucianism living in the United States.

Confucianism differs from other religions in its absence of a sense of the sacred. There are few ritual practices, no symbols, and no specific vision of a deity. Indeed, Confucianism seems more like a guide for disciplined living than an actual religion. At the same time, the goals of Confucianism are quite similar to the goals of other major religions—correct living, peace, and social harmony.

Agnosticism and Atheism

Of course, atheism and agnosticism are not religions. Indeed, in many ways, they represent the antithesis of religion. **Atheism** is the more extreme view, the complete denial of a higher power. **Agnosticism** refers to a personal doubt about the existence of God. Although these views represent only about 10% of people in the United States (Gervais, Shariff, and Norenzayan 2011), the number of people who identify with one of these two views is slowly rising. Estimates place the number of atheists worldwide at around half a billion people. When agnostics are included, the number is even higher.

Atheism The absence of a belief in God or the denial of belief in God.

Agnosticism Doubt or skepticism about the existence of God.

Minority group Any group that a society sets apart and treats differently.

More importantly, atheism and agnosticism are socially significant because of the way in which they are viewed in society.

Atheists and agnostics truly fit the sociological definition of a minority group. Sociologists define a **minority group** as any group that society sets apart in some way and treats differently. Indeed, some research shows that atheists and agnostics are among the least trusted members in society (Gervais, Shariff, and Norenzayan 2011). Nearly half of people surveyed indicated that they would not approve of their child marrying an atheist.

What is the cause of this distrust of atheists? At least part of the reason comes from the belief that religion is the only path to moral rightness. The argument suggests that religion offers the only moral guide. However, various authors, such as biologist Richard Dawkins (2006), have argued that a higher power is not necessary for the construction of morality. Dawkins marvels at the pervasiveness of distrust of atheists, since he notes that unlike other minority groups, atheists are not a coherent, visible, or even socially powerful group.

Some atheists have exhibited equally troubling behavior by being openly hostile to religion. For example, some atheists have sued to prevent any representations of religion in public places, such as nativities at Christmas. It should be noted, however, that most atheists do not condone such practices, and the rates of discrimination and hostility are markedly higher by religious people than by atheists. Still, atheists contributing to the vitriol simply feed into the social distaste for their views.

CONCEPT LEARNING CHECK 13.6	Religions of the World

Match the beliefs to the religion.

_____ **1.** This religion has no sense of the sacred.

_____ **2.** Probably the oldest extant religion.

_____ **3.** This religion was the foundation for Islam and Christianity.

_____ **4.** This is the largest religion in the world.

_____ **5.** Spiritual harmony is the way to eliminate suffering.

_____ **6.** The state religion for most of the Middle East.

A. Islam

B. Judaism

C. Christianity

D. Confucianism

E. Hinduism

F. Buddhism

13.7 Types of Religious Organizations

Religion as a social institution can be classified according to its acceptance of mainstream social values.

■ Illustrate the continuum of religious organizations.

As we have already learned, there are hundreds of different recognized religions and religious organizations. These organizations can be categorized along a continuum, with churches at one end and sects at the other. This categorization allows sociologists to describe any actual religion by comparing it to the ideal types and locating it on this continuum.

Church

Church A type of religious organization that is formally recognized and is well integrated into society.

A **church** is defined sociologically as a type of religious organization that is formally recognized and is well integrated into society. Churches usually exist in society for a long period of time and include members of the same families over generations of time. Churches are generally highly formalized, having well-established rules and regulations. Additionally, churches expect their leaders to be formally trained and ordained.

Churches focus their teachings on what is sacred. Yet churches also accept the ways of the profane in day-to-day living. Churches tend to separate discussions of God and morality from daily living. This allows churches to avoid social controversy. For example, churches may preach that all people are part of one worldly family and that we should celebrate human diversity as a work of God, while at the same time ignoring the homogeneity of their own congregations or ignoring their official stances on homosexuality. This type of strategy allows churches to preach their views while still maintaining a level of cooperation with the larger society.

Churches may exist independently in society, or they may operate under the official sanction of the state. A **state church** is a church that is formally allied with the state. State churches have existed for most of human history. The Roman Empire went through a number of state churches, from their early polytheism to Roman Catholicism. Confucianism, as we have already learned, was the official religion of China for several centuries. In modern times, examples can still be found. Islam is the official religion of many Middle Eastern nations. In England, the Anglican church—what we know as Episcopalianism—remains the official church of England. State churches consider everyone in that society a member of the church. This often has the effect of limiting tolerance of other religions.

The term **denomination** refers to a church, independent of the state, that recognizes religious pluralism. In other words, denominations recognize different beliefs, values, or behaviors within the same religion. For example, within the religion of Christianity, there are dozens of denominations, such as Catholics, Baptists, Presbyterians, Methodists, and Lutherans. While all of them share the basic tenets of Christianity, they also contain significant differences in their values, governance, and daily practice.

Sect

Next on the continuum is a sect. A **sect** is a type of religious organization that stands apart from the larger society. Members of sects are typically more rigid in their beliefs and deny the validity of the beliefs of others. While churches make an effort to appeal to as many people as possible, a sect forms an exclusive group, generally believed to be chosen by God. Members of sects view their religious beliefs not just as one aspect of life but as the cornerstone of life itself. In some cases, these views clash so much with the prevailing social norms that their practitioners withdraw from mainstream society. In America, the Amish present an excellent example of a sect. Although they exist within the boundaries of the broader society, the Amish isolate themselves in many ways, including not using electricity and refusing to drive automobiles.

Sects are often less formal than churches. Some members of sects are spontaneous and very emotional in their worship, breaking down in tears or spontaneously dancing. Leaders of sects often denounce the more formal intellectualism of churches, preferring instead the more inward, emotional, and personal aspects of religious experience. For this reason, many sects approach God as a personal experience rather than as a distant entity. Sects often have different leadership structure and style than churches. While the leadership of churches is often formally trained and ordained, leaders of sects often claim their leadership through their **charisma**—personal qualities that make people want to follow them.

Sects often form as groups that break away from mainstream religions, usually through a charismatic leader who is dissatisfied with the church. Because of the charismatic leadership and the highly emotional nature of sects, they are most often relatively short lived. Interestingly, the pattern of sects mimics the rise and fall of social movements. Those sects that do exist for long periods of time tend to evolve greater structure, more formality, and less emotional content until they come to resemble churches. To maintain membership, sects resort to **proselytizing**. This involves actively recruiting membership. Because sects value the process of conversion, they often feel compelled to share their own conversion stories with others. This gives the religious experience a personal aspect that many people may feel is lacking in more traditional churches.

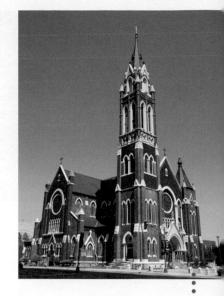

Churches are the most formal religious organization.

© Allan Baxter/Lifesize/Thinkstock

State church A church that is sanctioned by or allied with the government.

Denomination A church, independent of the state, that recognizes religious pluralism.

Sect A religious organization that sets itself apart from mainstream religious beliefs.

Charisma Personal qualities that make people want to follow you.

Proselytizing Actively attempting to recruit members to a particular religious view.

Cults usually remain small and isolated from the rest of society.

© Richard Baker/In Pictures/Corbis

Cult A religious organization that is completely outside a society's cultural traditions.

Sects and churches also differ in the composition of their members. Because churches are more tied to the world, they attract individuals of high social status. Conversely, because sects are often in conflict with the values of the larger society, they tend to attract a higher number of disadvantaged people. A deep personal experience that is shared by other people, combined with fulfillment in life and the promise of salvation, appeals to people that are social outcasts.

Cult

On the opposite end of the continuum from churches lie cults. A **cult** is a religious organization outside a society's cultural traditions. While most sects emerge from mainstream churches guided by a charismatic leader, cults typically form around a charismatic leader but lack a connection to mainstream religious views. The leader presents a radically different way of life. Marquand and Wood (1997) suggest that there may be as many as 5,000 existing cults in America at any one time. Cults usually remain small and isolated from society.

Because most cults have values, beliefs, and behaviors that differ radically from those of mainstream society, many people believe that cults are evil. The Heaven's Gate cult, a California cult that believed that death opened the doorway to a higher plane of existence with the help of an alien spaceship hiding in the tail of the Hale-Bopp comet, committed suicide 1997 as the comet passed close to earth. Such events feed the negative stereotypes that people hold about cults.

As sociologists, we should be very careful about passing such judgments. It is worth noting that many mainstream religions, such as Christianity and Islam, began as cults. Most cults, however, are short lived. Additionally, many beliefs about cults have not been confirmed by research. For instance, although many people accuse cults of brainwashing members, Williams (2002) found that most people who join cults experience no psychological harm.

| **CONCEPT LEARNING CHECK 13.7** | Types of Religious Organizations |

Fill in the blanks.

1. Barry belongs to a religion because the government officially sanctions the religion. Barry is a member of a _____.

2. Tyree is a member of the Methodist church, a _____ of Christianity.

3. Patsy belongs to a group that does not let her interact with the rest of society. She is likely a member of a _____.

4. Thomasina's religious organization broke away from her church to form a new group because they disagreed with the church's ideas about sins. Thomasina is a member of a _____.

13.8 Religions in the United States

There are many factors that influence how religious a person is.

- Discuss the functions that religion plays in the lives of Americans.

The United States is one of the most religious high-income nations in the world (Crabtree 2010). Nearly 80% of Americans say that they find some comfort and strength from belonging to a religion. However, there is a distinct difference between religious belief and religious practice, and there is considerable debate about how religious Americans really are. Few people doubt that religion forms a cornerstone of the American way of life, but perceptions about the decline of the American family and a growing acceptance of the tenets of science have led to concerns that religious faith is being weakened.

More than 85% of Americans claim to belong to some religion. More than half of adults in the United States identify with Protestantism, nearly 25% profess to be Catholic, and just under 2% are Jewish. At the same time, there are large numbers of Muslims, Buddhists, Jaynes, and even Sikhs that make America the most religiously diverse nation in the world. This is due in large part to the Constitutional ban on government-sanctioned religion as well as legal protections on religious practice. In addition, immigrants from all over the world come to America, bringing their religious beliefs and traditions with them.

Sociologists seek to understand the functions that religion play in the lives of Americans, as well as patterns that emerge in the distribution of religious views. For example, New England is predominantly Catholic, while the South is mostly Baptist. In Utah, most people are members of the Church of Jesus Christ of Latter-Day Saints—more commonly known as the Mormons. In the northern Plains, most of the residents are Lutheran.

Religious Affiliation and Religiosity

Sociologists use the term **religiosity** to refer to the importance that religion plays in a person's life. This can be conceived of in a variety of ways, including how many times a person participates in a religious ceremony, how many times a person goes to church, how many times the person prays, or a combination of factors. For example, while nearly 95% of Americans claim that they believe in a higher power, only about 60% claim that they have no doubts about God. While 60% of American adults say they pray at least once a day, fewer than one-third report attending a religious service on a weekly basis FIGURE 13-3.

These numbers vary among religions and among denominations. Members of sects tend to report the highest degree of religiosity. Among mainstream religious views, Catholics report the highest religiosity, with Protestants such as Presbyterians, Methodists, and Episcopalians being somewhat less religious. Not surprisingly, older Americans report higher degrees of religiosity than younger Americans, while women tend to be more religious than men.

Why does religiosity matter? Sociologists who study religion have made a number of connections between levels of religiosity and other social patterns. For example, studies show that individuals who are highly religious show lower rates of delinquency, lower rates of adult incarceration, and lower rates of divorce (Muller and Ellison 2001).

Religiosity The importance that religion plays in a person's life.

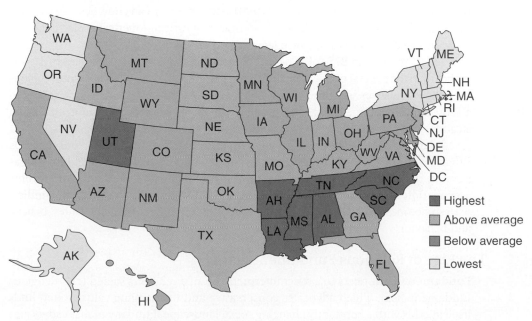

FIGURE 13-3 Levels of religiosity vary by region.
Source: Data from Newport, Frank. 2012. State of the States: Mississippi Is Most Religious U.S. State. Gallup. Accessed October 2012 (http://www.gallup.com/poll/153479/Mississippi-Religious-State.aspx#2).

African-American churches often contain a degree of emotional spontaneity.

© Digital Vision/Thinkstock

Gender, Race, Ethnicity, Class, and Religion

Anyone who attends a church in America will probably notice that congregations are composed of more women than men. Why? This interesting sociological question has no easy answer. Perhaps it is because as a minority group, women find strength and comfort in religion. At the same time, however, religions have been known to place women lower in the social hierarchy than men. One interesting theory about why women attend church in greater numbers than men was proposed by David Murrow (2004). Murrow hypothesizes that Christianity—and perhaps other religions as well—have become more feminized over the years, thus alienating men from the teachings and practices of the religion. For example, Murrow notes that in the time of their exodus from Egypt, the Jews were a warrior clan. They excelled at warfare and hunting. Modern religion, however, has reinterpreted the exodus story in a more peaceful way. Phrases such as "turn the other cheek" have become more important than other passages that may be interpreted as more aggressive or violent. Murrow suggests that church practices have also changed consistent with these feminized interpretations so that male-typical activities are generally excluded from the church.

Although Presbyterians, Episcopalians, and Church of Christ members collectively account for less than 10% of the population, they account for a reported 33% of the most economically and socially successful Americans. Jews, who make up only about 1.7% of the population, account for an astonishing 12% of the most successful Americans. Catholics and Methodists, on average, maintain moderate social standing, while Baptists, Lutherans, and members of sects generally fall among the lowest social standings (Keister 2000).

Ethnicity also plays a significant role, since it is often intimately connected to religion. For example, Judaism represents not only a religion but a way of life as well. The Middle Eastern world is predominately Muslim. Chinese culture is deeply rooted in Confucianism. We can also identify Irish Catholics, Greek Orthodox, and Anglo-Saxon Protestants, which adds to the religious diversity of the United States.

Since the first Africans were brought to America, religion has formed a significant part of African-American life. Many of those brought here as slaves converted to Christianity but blended Christian beliefs with elements of their traditional tribal religions. Much of this blending involved a degree of emotional spontaneity that is not typically seen among predominantly white congregations (Patillo-McCoy 1998). The church played a significant role in dealing with slavery and family separation and, later, extreme poverty and prejudice (Patillo-McCoy 1998). African-American churches also played a role in guiding youth and developing leaders among African Americans. Martin Luther King, Jr. was a minister, as are Jesse Jackson and Al Sharpton.

Today, more than 87% of African Americans claim a religious affiliation. This is higher than the general population, indicating that African Americans are more religious than the population as a whole. Most African Americans indicate that they belong to a Protestant denomination. However, the number of converts to Islam is increasing steadily among the African-American population, particularly in urban areas.

Asian Americans often retain many of their traditional ways of life and religious rituals, even after being in America for several generations. Religion functions both as a connection to personal heritage and as a guide for living that often slows or prevents assimilation to the dominant culture. Religion thus binds Asian American families, who sometimes struggle against the strength of the dominant culture's values, beliefs, and behavior.

The Rise of Religious Fundamentalism

Fundamentalism The literal and rigid interpretation of a sacred text.

Fundamentalism refers to a strict interpretation of a religion's sacred text. Religious fundamentalism, which advocates conservative and unchanging values, often finds itself at odds with a constantly changing social landscape. Fundamentalism advocates social stagnation and strict adherence to religious doctrine. It takes the position that its values, beliefs, and behaviors are applicable to everyone in society. The values are generally not seen as malleable or flexible in any way. Fundamentalism also believes that because the religious text is the direct word of God, it is not open to challenge or criticism.

Fundamentalism should not be confused with evangelicalism. Although the terms have overlapping historical origins, they have come to mean very different things in modern society. All evangelicals are fundamentalist, but not all fundamentalists are evangelicals. Broadly speaking, although they share a literal interpretation of the Bible, fundamentalists as a group tend to separate themselves from mainstream society far more than evangelicals. Evangelicals believe that a person needs to be transformed through a "born-again" experience. Social change for evangelicals is often through ministry or teachings rather than through overt political activism. In contrast, fundamentalists tend to be socially and politically active.

Although a small minority of the American population, religious fundamentalists have considerable social power. Much of this comes from their ability to transfer the zealotry of their beliefs with significant social organization. Fundamentalists were integral to the election of President George H. W. Bush, as well as several members of Congress. Christian fundamentalism has also helped to shape social policy in areas such as abortion and marriage. More than a decade ago, Christian fundamentalism helped to shape the wording of the Defense of Marriage Act, a federal law passed in 1996 that would define marriage as between one man and one woman and allowing states to disavow marriages that do not conform to those standards. Christian fundamentalists, forming a key voting base in some areas, used their influence to help push the legislation through Congress and onto the desk of President Bill Clinton, where it was signed into law.

In recent years, the influence of Christian fundamentalism has waned somewhat. Although fundamentalism, which in many ways resembles a social movement, remains strong in some areas of the United States, its political clout has diminished among mainstream Americans.

Secularization

Secularization refers to the historical decline in the importance of religion. Accompanying the decline in religious fundamentalism, the rise of secularization accompanies changes in society that put more emphasis on science and technology and deemphasize the sacred. In contrast to a century ago, when people spent most of their lives in the shadow of religion, people of today are more likely to spend the bulk of their significant life events in secularized institutions. For instance, most people are born in a hospital rather than at home. Death often occurs in a hospital rather than at home in the presence of a minister. This suggests that the importance of religion may be diminishing.

Secularization The declining importance of religion in society.

Can we infer from this that religion will someday disappear? Probably not. More people say that they believe in God than vote in national elections. In fact, despite the fact that some areas of society seem to be getting more secularized, other areas of society, such as politics, may be getting more religious. While younger people have reported a decline in religiosity, older people report increasing levels of religiosity. While some people are leaning more toward fundamentalism, others are becoming atheists.

Patterns of religion are changing. The nature of these changes, however, is not clear. Conservatives tend to emphasize the decline in religious values and interpret it as evidence of declining morality. On the other hand, progressives see the decline in religiosity as a positive sign that society is breaking free of traditional values and the limitations that religion places on human behavior.

Religion and the Sociological Imagination

Religion plays a significant role in the development of the socio-logical imagination. Religion offers us a sense of our own history as well as shapes our social experiences. Some religious views help us make sense of the world. One example is the end-of-the-world predictions that periodically recur. A poll conducted by Ipsos Global Public Affairs (2012) found that worldwide, nearly 15% or one in seven people believe that the world will end during their lifetime and 10% of respondents believed the end-of-the-world interpretations of the Mayan calendar in 2012. In the United States, end-of-the-world believers were 22% of the population compared with 6% in France. Lower education, lower household income, and age groups under 35 were demographic groups that were more likely to believe that the world is going to end or experience anxiety as a result of this contemplation. Reasons for the end of the world varied and included the world ending due to an act of God, natural, or political events.

EVALUATE

1. Why do you think that end-of-the-world predictions gain so many followers, even when previous predictions have not come true?

2. How do our social experiences shape our beliefs about the end of the world?

3. What do end-of-the-world predictions say about the state of society?

CONCEPT LEARNING CHECK 13.8 Religions in the United States

_____ 1. Which racial or ethnic group has the highest religiosity?

   A. Whites

   B. African Americans

   C. Asian Americans

   D. Hispanics

_____ 2. The historical decline in the importance of religion is called:

   A. fundamentalism.

   B. scientism.

   C. secularization.

   D. totemism.

_____ 3. A literal interpretation of a sacred text is called:

   A. fundamentalism.

   B. scientism.

   C. secularization.

   D. totemism.

Visual Overview Education and Religion

As American society has changed, education has changed to reflect emerging societal values and norms. The timeline below provides an overview of some major landmarks in American education.

Education Highlights, 1850–present

1850 Only about half of school-aged children were actually enrolled. Schools were controlled at the local or state level only. **Education was not compulsory**.

1896

Plessy v. Ferguson, the Supreme Court of the United States ruled that **segregation** was legal as long as the facilities were "separate but equal." Under this ruling, African-American children were segregated into separate schools. Despite the legal requirement, schools for blacks were rarely equal.

1918, all states had passed **compulsory education** laws, requiring all children between the ages of 5 and 16 to attend school.

'54

Brown v. Board of Education

The Supreme Court revisited school segregation and ruled in *Brown v. Board of Education* that "racially segregated schools are inherently unequal." The ruling effectively desegregated schools

1969 (By the end of the 1960s), more than half of the American population had a high school diploma.

1979 President Jimmy Carter made the **Department of Education** a cabinet-level department, effectively taking control of schools from states and nationalizing the educational process.

'01

Under President George W. Bush, the No Child Left Behind Act was passed in an attempt to reform public education.

2006 Government analysis of public versus private and charter schools concluded that **students in private schools outperform students in public schools** in every subject.

'09

Expenditure per pupil averaged $10,694. Compared to the rest of the world, America ranks:

country	rank	category
🇺🇸	**3rd**	spending per pupil
	14th	reading
	25th	mathematics
	17th	science

2012 nearly 70% of Americans complete high school. (Alliance for Excellent Education 2012).

There are more than 730 established religions throughout the world. The following are six of the world's major religions, encompassing more than two-thirds of the world's population.

Symbols of the World's Religions

Christianity	Buddhism	Islam	Hinduism	Judaism	Confucianism

Visual Summary Education and Religion

13.1 Education in the United States

- Schooling in America has undergone significant historical changes.
- School segregation sets the foundation for the systematic disadvantaging of African Americans in society.
- In the last few decades, public education in America has declined on the world stage.
- Liberal and conservative approaches to public education have failed to correct shortcomings in the public education system.
- Charter schools, magnet schools, private schools, home schooling, and vouchers offer alternatives to public education.
- Research on school choice shows that it provides a satisfactory alternative to public education.

13.2 Education around the World

- The way in which a culture views education is tied to the economic development of the nation.
- Japanese schools consistently score above American schools in all subjects.
- Schools in India are still in the process of evolving to teach many low-income students.
- Schools in Liberia face numerous challenges as they recuperate from civil unrest.
- Studying schools in other countries can help make American schools better.

13.3 Sociological Perspectives on Education

- Functionalism identifies at least five ways in which formal education functions in society.
- The conflict perspective analyzes schools in terms of how schools cause and perpetuate social inequality.
- Symbolic interactionism seeks to understand how the labels we place on students affect their education.

13.4 Sociology of Religion

- Early sociologists recognized the importance that religion plays in social life.
- Emile Durkheim understood religion as providing a division between the sacred and the profane.
- Karl Marx believed that religion was used by the capitalists to maintain social divisions between the rich and poor.
- Max Weber believed that religion can act as a strong force for social change.

13.5 Sociological Perspectives on Religion

- Functionalism analyzes how religion functions in our social life.
- Durkheim identified three main functions of religion in social life.
- The conflict perspective emphasizes how religion is used to support social inequality.
- Symbolic interactionism analyzes how the symbols and rituals in religion help us to construct meaning in our lives.

Visual Summary Education and Religion, continued

13.6 Religions of the World

- Christianity is the most widespread religion in the world.
- Islam, the preaching of the prophet Muhammad, is the second largest religion in the world.
- Judaism is the foundation of both Islam and Christianity. Followers of Judaism have been one of the most persecuted groups in history.

- Hinduism is probably the oldest extant religion and views God more as a moral force than as an actual physical force.
- Having its roots in Hinduism, Buddhism is based on the charismatic teaching of Siddhartha Gautama, the Buddha.
- Confucianism is unique among religions in its conspicuous lack of a concept of the sacred.
- Atheists and agnostics are the least trusted groups in American society.

13.7 Types of Religious Organizations

- A church is a religious organization that is formally recognized and is well integrated into society.
- A state church is a church that is formally allied with the state.
- A denomination refers to the various manifestations a church may take.

- A sect is a type of religious organization that stands apart from the larger society.
- A cult is a religious organization outside of a society's cultural traditions.

13.8 Religions in the United States

- The United States is one of the most religious high-income nations in the world.
- More than 85% of Americans claim to belong to some religion.
- The term *religiosity* refers to the importance that religion plays in a person's life.
- Race, ethnicity, and gender all play a role in the degree of religiosity.

- Religious fundamentalism refers to a rigid and strict interpretation of a religion's sacred text.
- In America, religious fundamentalism has demonstrated significant social and political power.
- Secularization refers to the historical decline in the importance of religion, usually accompanied by a rise in reliance on science and technology.

13.1 Education in the United States

1. Benjamin lives in Oklahoma in 1850. He most likely goes to school:
   A. in a school that has classrooms for each grade.
   B. with just boys.
   C. throughout the year.
   D. only sporadically.

2. Tyree goes to a school for students who want to pursue careers in science. He likely goes to a:
   A. magnet school.
   B. charter school.
   C. public school.
   D. voucher school.

3. Tracie goes to a school that is privately run but publicly funded. She likely goes to a:
   A. magnet school.
   B. charter school
   C. public school.
   D. religious school.

13.2 Education around the World

7. Paul was so tired from studying that he fell asleep during class. Rather than scold him, his teacher admired his dedication. Paul likely goes to school in what country?
   A. India
   B. United States
   C. Liberia
   D. Japan

8. Pitta goes to school under a tent. She uses a slate board and chalk to learn her letters and numbers. She likely goes to school in what country?
   A. India
   B. United States
   C. Liberia
   D. Japan

13.3 Sociological Perspectives on Education

10. Arturo notices how people in his school are divided into cliques such as jocks and nerds. He notices that these social divisions carry over from the classroom to society in general. Which theoretical perspective explains Arturo's observations?
    A. Functionalism
    B. Conflict
    C. Biosocial
    D. Symbolic interactionism

11. Toby studies the ways in which schools socialize students to raise their hands before speaking and to defer to authority. What theoretical perspective is Arturo working from?
    A. Functionalism
    B. Conflict
    C. Biosocial
    D. Symbolic interactionism

4. Of the following, who is most likely to attend college?
   A. Bill, a high school dropout
   B. Maureen, a public school graduate
   C. Peter, a charter school graduate
   D. Martin, who goes to a poor, inner-city public school

5. Of the following, who is most likely to drop out of high school?
   A. Lilivet, a Hispanic female
   B. Ho Jung, an Asian-American male
   C. Esther, an African-American female
   D. Doug, a white male

6. To keep students and parents from complaining, Tara gives all of her students an A, regardless of their performance in her class. Tara is practicing:
   A. social promotion.
   B. functional literacy.
   C. grade inflation.
   D. school choice.

9. Parakheet goes to a school that is mostly male, with nearly 60 students in his classroom, and few resources. Parakheet likely goes to school in what country?
   A. India
   B. United States
   C. Liberia
   D. Japan

12. Reynald has been told that his standardized test scores mean that he will be placed in a class for lower-performing students. His father is concerned because he fears that Reynald will now be disadvantaged in life. What theoretical perspective best fits these concerns?
    A. Functionalism
    B. Conflict
    C. Biosocial
    D. Symbolic interactionism

13. Barbara wants to understand how labels such as "jocks" and "Goths" influence academic performance in public schools. What theoretical perspective should Barbara use to frame her research?
    A. Biosocial
    B. Conflict
    C. Functionalism
    D. Symbolic interactionism

13.4 Sociology of Religion

14. Tanya wears a symbol of her religion on a chain around her neck. Whenever she feels scared or threatened, she grabs the symbol in her fist and begins to pray. Durkheim would say that the symbol functions as something:

A. magical.

B. profane.

C. sacred.

D. ridiculous.

15. Even though science has yet to demonstrate it, Yorba is convinced that everyone has a unique soul that leaves the body upon death. For Yorba, belief in the soul is a matter of:

A. faith.

B. positivism.

C. profane.

D. sacred.

13.5 Sociological Perspectives on Religion

16. Marissa lives in a society that worships at the statue of the ancestral gods. This statue is used for prayer and for spiritual and social guidance, as well as a way to bind members of the society together. Durkheim would consider this statue a:

A. profane item.

B. faith-based item.

C. totem.

D. symbol of the ridiculous.

17. The high priest in the tribe preaches to Alfonse that God has decreed that the congregation members should give all of their money to the church in order to ensure their salvation. Alfonse begins to suspect that the priests are using religion to make themselves rich at the expense of others. Alfonse is beginning to think like what early sociologist?

A. Karl Marx

B. Emile Durkheim

C. Max Weber

D. George Herbert Mead

13.6 Religions of the World

18. Katina is a member of the largest religion in the world. She is:

A. Islamic.

B. Hindu.

C. Christian.

D. Jewish.

19. Parker just completed a pilgrimage to the city where the founder of his religion was born, as required by the tenets of his religion. Parker is most likely:

A. Islamic.

B. Hindu.

C. Christian.

D. Jewish.

20. Reginald is a member of what is probably the oldest extant religion. He is:

A. Muslim.

B. Christian.

C. Jewish.

D. Hindu.

21. Tovah is a member of the religion that formed the basis for Christianity and Islam. Tovah is:

A. Hindu.

B. Confucian.

C. Jewish.

D. atheist.

22. Marco is a member of the most distrusted group in American society. Marco is:

A. African American.

B. atheist.

C. Hispanic.

D. Jewish.

23. Stan belongs to the only religion that does not contain a sense of the sacred. Stan is:

A. atheist.

B. Hindu.

C. Confucian.

D. Muslim.

13.7 Types of Religious Organizations

24. Yasmine belongs to a formal religious organization that has an ordained minister. She belongs to a:

A. church.

B. sect.

C. cult.

D. denomination.

25. Trevor joined a religious organization because of dissatisfaction with mainstream religion. In this new group, Trevor has curtailed some contact with the rest of society because his new beliefs conflict with some aspects of mainstream religion. Trevor believes his views are totally correct and that anyone who rejects his views will not attain salvation. Trevor most likely is a member of a:

A. church.

B. sect.

C. cult.

D. state church.

26. Wayne is a member of a religious organization that has no contact with the outside world. His total life and work are given over to the perpetuation of the religion. Wayne is a member of a:

A. sect.

B. church.

C. state church.

D. cult.

27. Elvira's church encourages members to shout out in the middle of sermons, to dance during songs, and to be expressive during the service. Elvira likely belongs to what racial or ethnic group?
- **A.** Hispanic
- **B.** White
- **C.** African American
- **D.** Asian American

28. Despite her church's belief in the healing power of prayer, Zia got an antibiotic from her doctor when she became ill. This is an example of:
- **A.** religiosity.
- **B.** secularization.
- **C.** denominationalism.
- **D.** agnosticism.

CHAPTER ESSAY QUESTIONS

1. Secretary of Education Arne Duncan once said that the proliferation of private schools had failed to lead to improvements in public education. Critics contend that the comparison of private with public schools is unfounded. Using at least one theoretical perspective in your analysis, do you believe that Secretary Duncan's comparison is valid?

2. Although religion performs several functions in society, it may also create social dysfunction. Identify and explain at least two social dysfunctions that religion may have in society.

CHAPTER DISCUSSION QUESTIONS

1. Using principles and concepts from sociology, discuss how American public schools might be improved. How might sociology help to fix identified problems in American education?

2. Discuss why adherence to religious fundamentalism might increase in society. Discuss what social factors might make it decrease. How can the degree of religious fundamentalism be used as a barometer for social change or stability?

3. What societal factors exist today that push large numbers of students into college? How do these compare or contrast to societal issues that existed 50 and 100 years ago?

4. Liberalism and conservatism both have differing viewpoints on public education. Share with the class the viewpoint you agree with the most. What pattern emerged in the class?

5. What kind of societal problems may result from grade inflation and social promotion? Given these factors, would you be willing to support school policies that restrict extra

credit and attendance points awarded just for showing up in class? Why or why not?

6. Discuss different ways that US schools teach students to accept capitalism.

7. Share with the class the type of labels that your teachers put on you as a child. How did these labels affect you? In what ways can cultural stereotypes related to ethnicity, gender, and social class affect teacher–student interactions?

8. Share with the class examples of how religious beliefs and teachings have been incorporated into societal laws and policies.

9. Why do you think that religious affiliation tends to cluster with demographic characteristics such as social class, ethnicity, and geographic location?

10. Given that the United States has become a more secularized society, why do you think there is such disdain for atheists?

CHAPTER PROJECTS

INDIVIDUAL PROJECTS

1. Choosing one sociological concept, come up with a creative and fun way to teach it to the class! How does your method of teaching draw on information you have learned about the sociology of education? What concepts discussed in this chapter influence the way in which you teach the material?

2. Choose a country other than the United States and go online to learn about its educational system. Prepare a class presentation based on your findings.

GROUP PROJECTS

1. Examine alternatives to traditional schools such as vouchers, homeschooling, and charter schools. Gather information online and prepare a slide presentation incorporating chapter information.

3. Choose a religion and write a report of the religious beliefs, totems, rituals, and demographic characteristics.

4. Go online to learn about interfaith marriage including statistics, issues, and parenting. Write an analysis of your findings.

2. Despite the extreme variety of religious tradition in the world, religions also have many things in common. Create a chart that outlines both the similarities and differences between major religions. What patterns do you see in the similarities? What patterns do you see in the differences?

KEY TERMS

Agnosticism
Atheism
Bullying
Charisma
Charter school
Church
Compulsory education
Corridor curriculum
Credentialism
Cult
De facto segregation
De jure segregation

Denomination
Dropping out
Ethnocentrism
Faith
Fundamentalism
Grade inflation
Hidden curriculum
Magnet school
Minority group
Monotheism
Polytheism
Profane

Proselytizing
Religion
Religiosity
Sacred
Sect
Secularization
Self-fulfilling prophecy
Social promotion
State church
Thomas theorem
Totem
Tracking

ANSWERS TO CONCEPT LEARNING CHECKS

13.1 Education in the United States

1. Although Ryan's school teaches all of the subjects, its emphasis on music and dance will be key to helping Ryan become a Broadway actor. [Magnet school]

2. June was put on a waiting list because the state she lives in allows only 120 students to attend her private school. [Charter school]

3. Chi'Lan's parents received money from the state to help them cover the cost of her private school. [Voucher]

4. Tyson goes to a school that is open to anyone regardless of income, abilities, or interests. [Public school]

5. Nina attends a school run by the Episcopalian church. [Private school]

13.2 Education around the World

1. Bartholomew goes to school in a dilapidated building with extremely overcrowded classrooms that are mostly male. Bartholomew likely attends school in what country? [A. India]

2. Eva goes to school underneath a tent, with no books or pencils. Her lessons consist mostly of memorizing. She likely goes to school in what nation? [C. Liberia]

3. Carlita goes to school in a class with brand new computers. She works in groups to find novel ways to get the correct answers. She is pushed very hard to perform well on her tests. She likely does to school in what nation? [D. Japan]

4. Peter attends school in the inner city in a run-down building. Although there are computers, they are old. His classroom is somewhat overcrowded, but his teacher is certified to teach. Peter likely goes to school in what nation? [B. The United States]

13.3 Sociological Perspectives on Education

1. Schools can function to socialize students. Schools can facilitate cultural innovation and change. Schools function to stratify people. Schools function as a means of social integration. Schools provide job training.

2. Schools can be seen as a way of controlling people, forcing them to accept dominant cultural norms. Schools can also be used as a means of tracking students into high and low achievers. Schools can advantage people if the schools are good and disadvantage them if the schools are bad.

3. Students who are labeled high achievers tend to do better than students who are labeled low achievers. Students tend to adopt the characteristics of stereotypes that are given to them at school.

13.4 Sociology of Religion

1. Religion is a way to keep people from challenging the social hierarchy. [B. Karl Marx]

2. Religion is the way that societies separate what is common from what is awe inspiring. [C. Emile Durkheim]

3. Religion is a social institution that can lead to significant social change. [A. Max Weber]

13.5 Sociological Perspectives on Religion

1. Tomie carries around a small icon that is symbolic of her religious views. Durkheim would call her symbol a [totem].

2. Tomie also carries around her college textbook. Durkheim would suggest that this item represents the [profane].

3. Marco believes that religions are just a way to keep people happy while the world is in crisis. His views most represent the view of what early sociologist? [Karl Marx]

4. Gina believes, as did [Emile Durkheim], that religion functions to give people a sense of meaning in their lives.

13.6 Religions of the World

1. This religion has no sense of the sacred. [Confucianism]

2. Probably the oldest extant religion. [Hinduism]

3. This religion was the foundation for Islam and Christianity. [Judaism]

4. This is the largest religion in the world. [Christianity]

5. Spiritual harmony is the way to eliminate suffering. [Buddhism]

6. The state religion for most of the Middle East. [Islam]

13.7 Types of Religious Organizations

1. Barry belongs to a religion because the government officially sanctions the religion. Barry is a member of a [state church].

2. Tyree is a member of the Methodist church, a [denomination] of Christianity.

3. Patsy belongs to a group that does not let her interact with the rest of society. She is likely a member of a [cult].

4. Thomasina's religious organization broke away from her church to form a new group because they disagreed with the church's ideas about sins. Thomasina is a member of a [sect].

13.8 Religion in the United States

1. Which racial or ethnic group has the highest religiosity? [B. African Americans]

2. The historical decline in the importance of religion is called [C. Secularization.]

3. A literal interpretation of a sacred text is called [A. Fundamentalism.]

ANSWERS TO CHAPTER REVIEW TEST

13.1 Education in the United States

1. D. Early American education was sporadic because children were often needed to tend the farm.

2. A. Magnet schools are designed to attract students interested in specific subject matter.

3. B. Charter schools are privately run but are funded with public tax dollars.

4. C. Students who graduate from charter schools are more likely to attend college than individuals who attend public schools or who drop out of school.

5. A. Hispanics have the highest dropout rate of any racial or ethnic group.

6. C. Grade inflation is the tendency for teachers to give everyone higher grades for mediocre work.

13.2 Education around the World

7. D. Falling asleep in class in Japan is seen as a sign of a dedicated student.

8. C. Schools in Liberia are often under tents, because most the infrastructure was destroyed during the civil war.

9. A. Schools in India are overcrowded and contain mostly boys, since educating girls in India is less culturally desirable than educating boys.

13.3 Sociological Perspectives on Education

10. B. Conflict perspective analyzes schools in terms of how they create and maintain social inequality.

11. A. Functionalism analyzes schools by seeking to understand how schools function to socialize students into the values, beliefs, and behaviors of society.

12. B. The conflict perspective seeks to understand how schools divide people into high and low achievers.

13. D. The symbolic interactionist perspective is concerned with how the labels we attach to people influence their values, beliefs, and behaviors.

13.4 Sociology of Religion

14. C. Durkheim referred to things that inspire awe or reverence as sacred.

15. A. Faith refers to a belief based on conviction rather than on empirical evidence.

13.5 Sociological Perspectives on Religion

16. C. Durkheim defined a totem as an object in the material world that a society collectively defines as sacred.

17. A. Marx believed that religion was a tool used by the wealthy to keep the poor in their place.

13.6 Religions of the World

18. C. Christianity is the largest religion in the world.

19. A. Islam requires its members to make a pilgrimage to Mecca—the city where Muhammad was born—at least once during their lifetime.

20. D. Hinduism is probably the oldest religion still in existence.

21. C. Judaism formed the cornerstone for both Christianity and Islam.

22. B. Research shows that atheists are the most distrusted group in American society.

23. C. Confucianism is unique among religions because it does not contain an idea of the sacred.

13.7 Types of Religious Organizations

24. A. A church is a formal religious organization that has an ordained clergy.

25. B. Sects are defined as religious organizations that are set apart from mainstream society and often have rigid and uncompromising values and beliefs.

26. D. Cults are religious organizations that are outside of a society's cultural traditions.

13.8 Religions in the United States

27. C. Because of their historical roots, African-American churches are often quite expressive, encouraging dancing and shouting during services.

28. B. Secularization refers to a rise in the beliefs of science and technology over religion.

ANSWERS TO CHAPTER ESSAY QUESTIONS

1. It is not necessarily valid to compare public and private education in America. The conflict perspective analyzes how social institutions cause and maintain social inequality in a society. Since private schools charge tuition, they will usually attract children who come from families with greater resources than public schools. Because private schools are also largely exempt from the rigid rules and bureaucracy of public schools, they can operate more freely than can public schools. For this reason, the functions of private schools may differ from those of public schools. Finally, because of the social expectations and standards associated with private education, the meaning of attending private schools may differ from the meaning attending a compulsory public school.

2. One of the key dysfunctions of religion was pointed out by Karl Marx. Marx noticed that religion can be used as a tool by the wealthy and powerful to keep the poor and weak in their place and keep them from seeking more social power. Relatedly, religion can function as a means of stifling social change. Another possible dysfunction of religion in modern society is the rejection of positivism that might prevent individuals from pursuing medical treatments or technologies that could help them. For example, if a person's religion teaches that all ailments can be healed through prayer, it may result in the person refusing to seek medical treatment, thus making her or him even more ill. Thus, religion can function to harm people as well as help them.

REFERENCES

Alliance for Excellent Education. 2012. "Graduation Rates." Accessed December 2012 at http://www.all4ed.org/about_the_crisis/students/grad_rates.

Casella, R. 2003. "Zero Tolerance Policy in Schools: Rationale, Consequences, and Alternatives." *Teachers College Record* 105:872–892.

Christle, C., C. M. Nelson, and K. Jolivette. 2004. "School Characteristics Related to the Use of Suspension." *Education & Treatment of Children* 27:509–526.

Clowes, G. 2003. "Zero Tolerance Horror Stories." Accessed December 2012 at http://heartland.org/editorial/2003/06/12/13-zero-tolerance-horror-stories.

Coleman, James, Thomas Hoffer, and Sally Kilgore. 1981. *Public and Private Schools.* Report to National Center for Education Statistics. Chicago: National Opinion Research Center.

Collins, R. 1979. *The Credential Society: An Historical Sociology of Education and Stratification.* New York: Academic Press.

Council for American Public Education. 1999. "Survey Finds Public Likes Private Schools." Accessed December 2012 at http://www.capenet.org/facts.html.

Crabtree, S. 2010. "Religiosity Highest in World's Poorest Nations: United States is among the Rich Countries that Buck the Trend." Accessed December 2012 at http://www.gallup.com/poll/142727/religiosity-highest-world-poorest-nations.aspx

Dawkins, Richard. 2006. *The God Delusion.* Boston: Houghton Mifflin.

Durkheim, Emile. 1915. *The Elementary Forms of Religious Life.* New York: MacMillan.

Gervais, W. M., A. F. Shariff, and A. Norenzayan. 2011. "Do You Believe in Atheists? Distrust Is Central to Anti-Atheist Prejudice." *Journal of Personality and Social Psychology* 101(6):1189–1206.

Haddad, Y. Y., and B. F. Stowasser. 2004. *Islamic Law and the Challenges of Modernity.* New York: Altamira Press.

Ipsos Global Public Affairs. 2012. "One in Seven (14%) Global Citizens Believe End of the World is Coming in Their Lifetime." Accessed December 2012 at http://www.ipsos-na.com/news-polls/pressrelease.aspx?id=5610.

Keister, L. A. 2000. "The Role of Religious Affiliation and Participation in Early Adult Asset Accumulation." *Social Forces* 82(1):175–207.

Marquand, R. and D. B. Wood. 1997. "Rise in Cults as Millenium Approaches." *Christian Science Monitor* (March 28, 1997):1,18.

Marx, Karl, and F. Engels. 1848 (2012). *The Communist Manifesto.* New York: Create Space.

Merton, Robert K. 1968. *Social Theory and Social Structure.* New York: Free Press.

Muller, C., and C. G. Ellison. 2001. "Religious Involvement, Social Capital, and Adolescents' Academic Progress: Evidence from the National Education Longitudinal Study 1988." *Sociological Focus* 34(2):155–183.

Murrow, D. 2004. *Why Men Hate Going to Church.* New York: Thomas Nelson.

OECD Pisa rankings (2009). Accessed December 2012 at http://www.guardian.co.uk/news/datablog/2010/dec/07/world-education-rankings-maths-science-reading.

Pattillo-McCoy, M. 1998. "Church Culture as a Strategy of Action in the Black Community." *American Sociological Review* 63(6):767–784.

The Public Purpose. 1998, January. "US Public Schools and Private Schools: Performance and Spending Compared." Accessed December 2012 at http://www.publicpurpose.com/pp-edpp.htm.

Rist, R. C. 1970. "Student Social Class and Teacher Expectations: The Self-Fulfilling Prophecy in Ghetto Education." *Harvard Educational Review* 40(3):411–451.

Rosenthal, R. and L. Jacobson. 1970. *Pygmalion in the Classroom: Teacher Expectations and Pupil's Intellectual Development.* New York: Holt, Reinhart, and Winston.

Sanders, E. P. 1993. *The Historical Figure of Jesus.* New York: Penguin.

Skiba, R. 2004. "Zero Tolerance: The Assumptions and the Facts." *Education Policy Briefs* 2(1):1–8.

Slee, P. 2002. *Child, Adolescent and Family Development.* Sidney, Australia: Cambridge University Press.

Stigler, J. W., and J. Hiebert. 2009. *The Teaching Gap: Best Ideas from the World's Teachers for Improving Education in the Classroom.* New York: Free Press.

Stopbullying.gov. 2012. *Bullying definition.* Accessed December 2012 at http://www.stopbullying.gov/what-is-bullying/definition/index.html.

Thornburgh, N. 2006, April 2006. "Dropout Nation." *Time Magazine.* Accessed December 2012 at http://www.time.com/time/magazine/article/0,9171,1181646,00.html.

US Department of Education. 2006. *Comparing Private Schools and Public Schools Using Hierarchical Linear Modeling.* Washington DC: National Assessment of Education Progress.

US Department of Education, National Center for Education Statistics. 2012. *Digest of Education Statistics, 2011* (NCES 2012-001), Table 191. Accessed December 2012 at http://nces.ed.gov/programs/digest/d11/tables/dt11_191.asp.

USgovernmentspending.com. 2012. "US Education Spending History from 1900." Accessed December 2012 at http://www.usgovernmentspending.com/education_spending.

Whittle, C. 2005. *Crash Course: A Radical Plan for Improving Public Education.* New York: Riverhead.

Williams, P. D. 2002. *America's Religions: From their Origins to the Twenty-First Century.* Urbana, IL: University of Illinois Press.

Chapter Overview ▼

14 Politics and Economy in Global Perspective

Learning Objectives ▼

14.1
- Distinguish political sociology from political science.
- Describe the major types of authority.

14.2
- Identify the four basic types of government and characteristics of each.
- Discuss some of the ways in which political authority is transferred.

14.3
- Compare and contrast the US political system with other democracies.

14.4
- Illustrate the functionalist and conflict perspectives on political power.

14.5
- Explain the causes, types, and cost of wars, as well as the ways warfare is evolving.
- Discuss the changing demographic composition of US armed forces.
- Discuss ways the United States has tried to deter attack as well as seek diplomatic resolutions.

14.6
- Identify and describe historically different economies and the nature of work within each.

14.7
- Compare and contrast the key characteristics, common differences, and historical trends of capitalism and socialism.

14.8
- Illustrate the functional, conflict, and symbolic interactionist perspectives as they apply to the economy and work.

14.9
- Describe the changes in economics and work demographics in the postindustrial era in the United States.

© Library of Congress Prints & Photographs Division LC-USE6-D-004076

What's in a Name?

"Floy?"

"Yes," my mother responded, and the man looked startled, then said, "Well, I guess you'll do."

And that was how I was able to go to college.

It was the 1950s, and most married women, particularly women with children, were stay-at-home moms. Those who braved the workforce most often found themselves relegated to what at that time was widely regarded as "women's work"—jobs like secretary, nurse, maid; jobs that paid much less than "men's work." But Floy would have none of that. She applied for a good-paying union job working in a factory at a defense plant in Kansas City—the job that later boosted our family income and made it possible for me to go to college. Once there, she completed the paperwork for the application and sat in a large room with other job applicants waiting as, one after another, men were called out of the room to be told they were hired. She and her friend, Helen, were among the few women there that day. Finally, after all the men had been hired, the recruiter came into the room, looked around puzzled, then left. Minutes later he returned and called her name, and—as they say—the rest was history. Floy was the only woman hired that day. The recruiter had come into the room expecting to find another male job applicant, "Floy." Luckily for her, she had a name that was often given to men. How does she know this? Well, of course, no one ever admitted it. But after she was hired, she met two of the other very few women working there. Their names? Van and Jo.

Of course, much has changed since this true story took place. More women participate in the labor market today, and they are more likely to have access to good jobs. However, many of those good jobs have been moved overseas or disappeared forever, and a much smaller proportion of workers belongs to unions. In this chapter, we will see that political and economic institutions have become increasingly interdependent, with political policies and governmental regulations influencing the growth and regulation of businesses, while corporations play increasingly important roles through unlimited donations to independent interest groups that influence political campaigns. We will examine changes in both the economy and politics that are transforming both the United States and the world.

14.1 Political Systems, Power, and Authority

Political sociology examines how politics takes place within the context of other social institutions and studies the distribution of power and authority.

- Distinguish political sociology from political science.
- Describe the major types of authority.

Politics is the social institution that sets policies and goals for society and a means through which power is both exercised and acquired. Politics takes place within a **state**—the political entity having a monopoly over the use of force in a specific geographic territory. **Government** is the formal organization that acts on behalf of the state to regulate interactions with other states and among citizens of the state. For example, the United States is a state whose government is the constitutionally established system of institutions that carry out the directives of the three branches of government: the legislative, executive, and judicial branches. US politics includes activities such as election campaigns and campaign fundraising. Politics involves the exercise of power within a political system, or, as Lasswell (1936) said, politics is "who gets what, when, and how."

Political sociology is different from political science in important ways. Political science often focuses on comparisons of political systems in different countries, relationships between governments and other countries or international bodies such as the United Nations, and the operations of the branches of government, including election laws and campaigns, public opinion, and efforts to pass legislation. In contrast, political sociology focuses on how politics is influenced by other social institutions such as the media, the economy, religion, and education.

Power is the ability to realize one's goals and interests, even in the face of resistance. There are three basic sources of power in any political system: force, influence, and authority. Force is the actual or threatened use of coercion to impose one's will on others. Examples of the exercise of force in political systems include imprisoning or executing someone and engaging in a war against another state. **Coercion** occurs when one person or group forces its will on another based on the threat of physical force or violence. Filling prisons with political prisoners from the opposition party to stifle dissent would be an example of coercion. **Influence** is the exercise of power through the process of persuasion. Examples of influence include newspaper editorials, expert testimony, and the opinions of friends or respected people.

Authority is power that has been institutionalized and is recognized as legitimate by the people over whom it is exercised. Democracies are based on authority. As Abraham Lincoln said in a speech in 1854, "No man is good enough to govern another man without that other's consent." Authority is typically limited by the constraints of a particular social status. For example, in the United States, judges—members of the judiciary—can supervise trials and make decisions about guilt or innocence, but they cannot make new laws or collect taxes.

Types of Authority

Max Weber identified three types of authority: traditional, legal-rational, and charismatic (Weber 1913).

Traditional Authority

Traditional authority is power conferred by custom and accepted practice. Traditional authority is usually institutionalized and accepted without question. The authority of a king or queen in a monarchy is based on tradition, as is the authority of the Pope in the Catholic Church. Traditional authority rests on custom. Traditional authority does *not* rest on personal characteristics, technical competence, or even written laws or regulations. If monarchs violate tradition, they do so at the risk of losing their position

State The political entity having a monopoly over the use of force in a specific geographic territory.

Government The formal organization that acts on behalf of the state to regulate interactions with other states and among citizens of the state.

Power The ability to realize one's goals and interests, even in the face of resistance.

Our political system invests judges with a great deal of authority.

© Jupiterimages/liquidlibrary/Thinkstock

The Pope is an example of traditional authority.

© MIMMO FERRARO/Shutterstock, Inc.

Coercion Occurs when one person or group forces its will on another, based on the threat of physical force or violence.

Influence The exercise of power through the process of persuasion.

Authority Power that has been institutionalized and is recognized as legitimate by the people over whom it is exercised.

Martin Luther King possessed charismatic authority.

© Hulton-Deutsch Collection/CORBIS

Traditional authority Power conferred by custom and accepted practice.

Legal-rational authority Derived from written rules and regulations of political systems.

Charismatic authority Power made legitimate by a leader's exceptional personal characteristics and emotional appeal to his or her followers.

of authority, as happened when King Edward VIII of England was forced to abdicate the throne in 1936 in order to marry a divorced American "commoner," Wallis Simpson. Many of the remaining monarchs around the world, such as Queen Elizabeth II of England, now defer to elected leaders, such as the prime minister, who have legal-rational authority.

Legal-Rational Authority

Legal-rational authority is derived from written rules and regulations of political systems. Examples include the authority of the President of the United States or the US Congress, both of which are based on the US Constitution. In legal-rational authority, specific areas of competence and authority are clearly delineated and limited by role. Violation of those explicit laws and constitutional provisions, if serious enough, can lead to loss of position. Richard Nixon resigned from the presidency in 1974 as Congress threatened him with impeachment proceedings.

Charismatic Authority

Charismatic authority is power made legitimate by a leader's exceptional personal characteristics and emotional appeal to his or her followers. Examples include the authority wielded by Martin Luther King, Mahatma Gandhi, or Jesus Christ. Charismatic authority tends to be unstable. Since it is based on personal characteristics of individuals rather than on law, there are no protections for various interests, and charismatic leaders like Adolf Hitler can cause great harm. Charismatic authority is not easily transferred to successors unless the charismatic leader helps create and legitimize a traditional or legal-rational system. For example, some of the emotional fervor with which people supported George Washington was successfully channeled into support for the new US Constitution.

CONCEPT LEARNING CHECK 14.1   Types of Authority

Match each example below with the most likely type of authority it represents.

_____ **1.** A judge in state court

_____ **2.** The founder of a new, fast-growing religion

_____ **3.** A revolutionary figure battling against the existing government in her country

_____ **4.** A priest in the Lutheran Church

A. Charismatic authority

B. Traditional authority

C. Legal-rational authority

14.2 Governments around the Globe

There are four primary types of government around the world, each of which must find some means to transfer authority from one set of leaders to the next.

- Identify the four basic types of government and characteristics of each.
- Discuss some of the ways in which political authority is transferred.

Examining the range of governments that have existed throughout history and those present today leads us to identify four broad types of government with very different consequences for those they govern: monarchy, democracy, authoritarianism, and totalitarianism.

Monarchy

A **monarchy** is a government ruled by a family, and the right to rule is passed from one generation to the next by inheritance. Monarchies are one of the oldest forms of government and were very common in agrarian societies. Monarchies can be traced back to **city-states**, small centers of power restricted to cities in which a monarch ruled the city surrounding a castle. As these city-states fought with one another, some extended their power to broader regions, conquering and absorbing other city-states, eventually resulting in larger **nation-states**—political entities covering a relatively large geographic region. An extreme example of this is the English Commonwealth, consisting of the United Kingdom and other nations, each of which recognizes Queen Elizabeth II as its reigning constitutional monarch.

Monarchies were the most common form of government in Europe well into the 19th century but are much less common today. **Absolute monarchs**, such as the royal families in Saudi Arabia and Kuwait, claim a monopoly on power in a country based on divine right. Most monarchies today have become **constitutional monarchies**, such as Great Britain, Norway, and Sweden, in which members of royalty serve as symbolic rulers while elected officials actually govern those countries. Because constitutional monarchies are ruled by elected officials, they are also a form of democracy.

Democracy

A **democracy** is a form of government in which the people governed have the opportunity to select those who govern and, in some cases, to participate directly in governance themselves. That is, a democracy is governed by all people or by their elected representatives, not by an elite. Democracies have traditional or constitutional limits to power, require leaders to periodically be re-elected, and recognize human rights, which usually include freedom of speech, freedom of the press, and freedom of religion. Political trends that led to changing many governments from monarchies to democracies, with added emphasis on personal liberties, often took place alongside economic transformation from rural agrarian societies to modern industrial societies. The United States is the oldest surviving democracy.

Small communities can exercise **direct democracy**, in which all members come together to make decisions, such as in a town hall meeting. However, democratic governments in all but the very smallest of societies practice **representative democracy**—a democracy in which representatives of the people are elected to govern on their behalf. These representatives make most routine decisions but sometimes resolve issues by popular vote. Representative democracies include constitutional monarchies, parliamentary systems, and democratic republics.

Parliamentary systems are representative democracies in which candidates for the national legislature (parliament) represent political parties. The prime minister is elected from among members of the party holding the majority of seats in parliament. When no party has a majority, coalitions are often formed. Parliamentary systems typically require the ruling party to call elections every few years and also have elections when a coalition breaks up or the ruling party loses a major vote. Most European parliamentary system elections are based on proportional representation, with a party winning 40% of the vote, for example, being awarded 40% of the seats in the legislature. This system encourages multiple parties because even a small party having only 5% or 10% of the vote can have elected representatives. Examples include France and Germany, along with many countries that are also constitutional monarchies, such as Great Britain, Sweden, and the Netherlands.

Monarchy A government in which the right to rule is passed from one generation to the next by inheritance.

City-states Small centers of power restricted to cities in which a monarch ruled the city surrounding a castle.

Nation-states Political entities extending throughout a relatively large geographic region.

Absolute monarchs Claim a monopoly on power based on divine right.

Constitutional monarchies Members of royalty serve as symbolic rulers while elected officials actually govern those countries.

Democracy The people governed elect those who govern and, in some cases, participate directly in governance.

A town hall meeting is a form of direct democracy.

© Toby Talbot/Associated Press

The origins of English parliamentary rule date back almost a 1,000 years.

© EMPPL PA Wire/Associated Press

Direct democracy A democracy in which all members come together to make decisions.

Representative democracy A democracy in which representatives of the people are elected to govern on their behalf.

Parliamentary systems Representative democracies in which candidates for the national legislature (parliament) represent political parties.

Democratic republics, such as the United States, are examples of representative democracy and are much like parliamentary systems except that democratic republics have popularly elected chief executives. Unlike most European parliamentary systems, US elections are winner-take-all affairs, with the party winning a majority of votes in a specific district being awarded the seat and other parties—even one gaining 49% of the vote—receiving nothing. Winner-take-all voting encourages a two-party system and discourages third parties since they are unlikely to win a majority, unlike European parliamentary systems, which encourage multiple parties. For example, in the United States, any attempt by a party other than Democrats or Republicans to seek elective offices is generally unsuccessful because most voters believe only Democrats or Republicans have a realistic chance of winning.

Authoritarianism

Authoritarian governments concentrate power in the hands of a strong leader who often rules for life and may exercise absolute power. Such governments often do not recognize human rights or freedoms and attempt to restrict the flow of information and to control the media in order to repress dissent. There are many kinds of authoritarian governments, including monarchies, dictatorships, oligarchies, totalitarian governments, and military juntas. A **dictatorship** is rule by a single person. It is an example of an authoritarian government. Examples include Iraq under Saddam Hussein and Libya under Muammar Gaddafi. **Oligarchies** are governments ruled by a select few. Leaders are subject to the whim of the ruling group and can be quickly replaced if they lose support of that group. Oligarchies are often authoritarian governments. Examples include the Soviet Union during the Khrushchev era and the People's Republic of China under Deng Xiaoping. However, not all oligarchies are authoritarian governments. Even a democracy may be an oligarchy if power is effectively in the hands of a few people. Military juntas are authoritarian governments and are usually either oligarchies or dictatorships. A **military junta** is a group of military leaders who have seized power from the prior government, such as the Panamanian government under Manuel Noriega.

Iraq under Saddam Hussein was an authoritarian government.
© Reuters/CORBIS

Totalitarianism

A **totalitarian government** is an extreme form of authoritarian government having complete control over all aspects of people's lives—even aspects having little or nothing to do with politics. Where authoritarian governments may have independent social and economic institutions not under control of the state, totalitarian governments rigidly control all major institutions, including families, the economy, and religion. Totalitarian governments typically have a single political party, have an elaborate ideology used to explain and justify the government, utilize terror in the form of secret police, torture, and punishment without trials, and rigidly control weapons, the media, and the economy (Friedrich and Brzezinski 1965). Examples include Nazi Germany, the Soviet Union under Joseph Stalin, and Cuba under Fidel Castro. For example, in both Nazi Germany and the Soviet Union during the Cold War, the government rigidly controlled art in an attempt to use it to glorify those in power and to stifle any attempt to use art as a means of dissent. Not all authoritarian governments become totalitarian governments, but there is a tendency for them to do so in order to consolidate and preserve their power.

Revolutions, Coups d'Etat, and Transfers of Authority

One of the first tasks of any political system is to provide for the orderly succession of power from one set of leaders to the next. Historically, in totalitarian countries ruled by a dictator, the succession plan is often for power to be inherited by a son or daughter, much like occurs in monarchies, such as in North Korea where President Kim Il-Sung successfully passed the role of head of state on to his son, Kim Jong-Il. In other cases, the autocratic ruler holds on to power stubbornly and a disorderly transition occurs through a coup d'état, a political revolution, or nonviolent protests.

The Soviet Union often used art for propaganda purposes.
© Prisma Bildagentur AG/Alamy

A **coup d'état** is the abrupt replacement of one government with another illegally, often relying upon coercive force or the use of violence. For example, Chile's government under General Augusto Pinochet, which came to power in a coup supported by the US government and Muammar Gaddafi, who seized power in Libya in 1969 in a bloodless coup d'état against the previous hereditary monarchy and ruled for 42 years before finally being killed in a revolution in 2011.

Usually more violent and long lasting than a coup d'état is a **political revolution**—the replacement of one political system with another through violent means. Political revolutions may be thought of as extreme examples of social change brought about through social movements. The downfall of Muammar Gaddafi in a political revolution in 2011 is a recent example. What factors lead some countries to experience a political revolution while others do not? A number of sociologists have studied revolutions that have occurred throughout the world during the last few hundred years (Paige 1975; Skocpol 1979). Many of the factors leading to revolutions are the same factors that lead to reformist social movements, including rising expectations, an unresponsive government, leadership by intellectuals, and legitimization of the movement. A wide range of social movements influences politics, and most of these are reform movements rather than revolutionary movements, leading not to violent political overthrows but to modification of existing laws or policies. For example, politics in the United States has been influenced by a number of broad-scale social movements, including the civil rights movement, the women's movement, the Tea Party movement, and the Occupy Wall Street movement.

In many cases, social and political movements pursue a deliberate course of **nonviolent resistance**—political actions relying on nonviolent acts to protest particular policies or regimes. Mahatma Gandhi in India and later Martin Luther King, Jr. in the United States are well-known examples of leaders who advocated nonviolent resistance. The Arab Spring uprisings in many North African and Middle Eastern countries in 2011 included many mostly nonviolent demonstrations throughout the region and led to changes in governments in Tunisia and Egypt, while resulting in violent repression in Syria and full-scale civil war in Libya.

Democracies usually have been more successful at providing for an orderly succession of power through **elections**—a formal decision process in which individuals are permitted to vote for their favorite option. However, even in the United States, orderly transition has sometimes been difficult and the credibility of the government has at times been strained when elections are extremely close, such as the election of George W. Bush in 2000, which was settled only after a 5–4 decision by the Supreme Court in which each justice voted in favor of the candidate belonging to the same party as that of the president who appointed him or her.

Democratic republics
A form of representative democracy in which chief executives are chosen by popular election.

Authoritarian governments
Concentrated power in the hands of a strong leader who often rules for life and may exercise absolute power.

Dictatorship Rule by a single person.

Oligarchies Authoritarian governments ruled by a select few.

Military junta A group of military leaders who have seized power.

Totalitarian government An authoritarian government having complete control over all aspects of people's lives— even aspects having little or nothing to do with politics.

Coup d'état The abrupt replacement of government leaders illegally, often relying upon coercive force or the use of violence.

Political revolution The replacement of one political system with another through violent means.

Nonviolent resistance Political actions relying on nonviolent acts to protest particular policies or regimes.

Elections Formal decision processes in which citizens vote for their favorite option.

CONCEPT LEARNING CHECK **14.2**	Types of Government

Match each of the following characteristics of government with the type of government most likely to display it.

_____ 1. A government having complete control over all aspects of people's lives

_____ 2. A democratic government with a popularly elected chief executive

_____ 3. A democratic government in which some people are elected to govern on behalf of the people

_____ 4. A government in which the leader claims a monopoly on power based on divine right

_____ 5. A democratic government with elected leaders and a figurehead whose position was inherited

_____ 6. A government ruled by a single individual who seized power from the prior government

A. Monarchy

B. Absolute monarchy

C. Constitutional monarchy

D. Democracy

E. Totalitarian government

F. Direct democracy

G. Representative democracy

H. Parliamentary system

I. Democratic republic

J. Dictatorship

14.3 The US Political System

> The US government is based on fundamental democratic principles recognizing human rights, and the political process is dominated by the exercise of power through the right to vote.
>
> - Compare and contrast the US political system with other democracies.

Government Structure and Driving Democratic Principles

The US Constitution created the first modern democracy and advanced the notion that there are basic human rights of people that should be honored by the government. Many of these are incorporated into the Bill of Rights and include key principles of freedom of speech, free association, the right to privacy, and the right of habeas corpus or protection from unlawful detention. To prevent any power from becoming too centralized, the Constitution sets up a number of checks and balances, including independent legislative, executive, and judicial branches.

A key principle underlying the structure of the US government is giving power to the people in the form of voting rights. While women and blacks were initially excluded from voting, over time, those voting rights were extended to people of any race and both men and women. Because voting is so central to democracies, much of the political process can be understood as an effort to gain votes in order to win elections. This can be seen in major aspects of the political system such as political parties.

Political parties
Organizations whose major purpose is to gain legitimate control of the government.

Political Parties and Elections

The US two-party system, winner-take-all elections, wedge issues, and efforts to get voters to the polls are just some of the many key factors influencing the outcome of elections.

The Two-Party System

In the United States, two major **political parties**—organizations whose major purpose is to gain legitimate control of the government—have accounted for 90% of the vote in most elections since the 1800s (Schmidt 1996). There have been more than 1,000 third parties during the same period, but most of those have received very few votes. Some of the best third-party showings included Ross Perot's winning 19% of the vote in 1992 and Theodore Roosevelt's Progressive (Bull Moose) party's 27% in 1912. Earlier, we discussed how a winner-take-all election system discourages third parties. In addition, the media heavily favors the two established parties, making it difficult for third-party candidates to appear in debates or to be given equal time.

In the United States, two major political parties have accounted for 90% of the vote in most elections since the 1800s.

© KamiGami/Shutterstock, Inc.

In the United States, each party has to appeal to the middle to get its candidate elected. This can be seen in the data on political party affiliation from the Gallup Poll (2011a). Strong Republicans are only 26% of the population, strong Democrats only 31%, and Independents are 41%. Hence, parties tend to take similar political positions and display fewer ideological differences (Granberg and Holmberg 1988). In contrast, candidates and parties in parliamentary systems often take clear and distinct positions representing class interests (e.g., the Labor Party in Great Britain) or special issues (the Green Party representing environmental issues in different European countries) and still expect to win enough votes to be represented in Parliament.

While American political parties are not as extreme in their differences as those in European parliaments, the Republican and Democratic parties take different stands regarding major social and economic issues. Republicans generally believe government should play a limited role, raising and spending as little as possible and relying on individual initiative and competition to drive the economy. Democrats typically believe that an unregulated economy leads to greater inequality and believe government should be bigger, raising more money in taxes to support social programs that attempt to provide a safety net for everyone and keep big business in check. Democrats tend to be more liberal on social issues, believing that government should play an active role in protecting the rights of minority groups. Republicans tend to be more conservative, supporting arguments based on religious views that limit individual rights on issues such as abortion or gay marriage, and prefer social policies that reward people based on merit rather than on minority status.

Elections

In the United States, elections are **winner-take-all elections** in which the party receiving the most votes in each district wins the whole district. In contrast, most parliamentary systems, such as that of Sweden, employ a **proportional representation** system in which seats in a legislature are divided among parties in proportion to the number of popular votes received by each party. The proportional representation system encourages the formation of minority parties representing special or extreme interests. Minority parties can sometimes play a crucial role in forming a coalition government, exacting political concessions from larger parties to create a majority coalition. The US winner-take-all system discourages third parties that have little chance of winning the majority in any district. Even people preferring those parties may still not vote for them for fear of throwing away their vote. Many states have complex petition processes before a third party can be placed on the ballot. Mass media often ignore third-party candidates, focusing instead on the two major parties they believe will have the most chance of winning.

Voter Participation

Voting rates in the United States are also lower now than they have been during many other periods in history. For example, during the period between 1874 and 1892, an average of 79% of all eligible citizens voted in US presidential elections, with voting rates averaging 93% in Indiana and 92% in New Jersey and Ohio during that period (Burnham 1980). This does not mean that the poor were better represented in the 19th century, however, because many groups denied voting rights at that time were impoverished (i.e., blacks and immigrants). The voting rate dropped dramatically after 1900 (Burnham 1980), reaching a rate of 43% in 1920 (about half the rate in 1876). Between 1945 and 2010, voting rates in the United States have ranged between about 50% and 65% (US Census Bureau 2012:Table 397).

Beeghley (1986) argues that voting participation rates are lower now than they were in the 19th century due to structural barriers excluding certain segments of the population such as the poor. In the United States, election day is on Tuesday, making voting difficult for those who lack access to child care or are unable to take time off from work. Voters are required to register well in advance of elections, are dropped from rolls if they do not vote within a specified time, and must reregister when they move. Almost half the US population moves every 5 years, and polls indicate recent movers are less likely to vote (Toner 1990a). In the 1988 election, 37% of nonvoters did not vote because they were not registered. Two-thirds of those reported they would have voted if they could do so without having to register (Dionne 1989).

The strongest structural factor leading to reduced voting in the United States is probably the "winner-take-all" elections. This system discourages voting in elections that are not close because in such elections, an individual vote has little likelihood of making a difference. Many legislative seats in the United States are "safe seats," making it less important to vote (93% of incumbents retained their seats in 1992, 96% in 1990, and 98% in 1988) (Mann 1987; Toner 1990b). The middle-of the road positions taken by the two centrist US parties further reduce voting by making it seem less important who wins (Downs 1957).

Voting rates are dramatically influenced by social characteristics. As can be seen in **TABLE 14-1**, voting rates are higher for older, more educated, employed, white non–Hispanics (US Census Bureau 2011b:Table 399). Political participation appears to be enhanced when people have more at stake, such as the affluent and well-educated, and when they have a sense of political efficacy—they feel they have the ability to make a difference through their participation.

Winner-take-all elections
Those in which the party receiving the most votes in each district wins the whole district.

Proportional representation
A system in which seats in a legislature are divided among parties in proportion to the number of popular votes received by each party.

TABLE 14-1 Percentage Reporting They Voted by Selected Characteristics, 2008 Presidential Election

Total	58.2
18–20 yrs	41
21–24 yrs	46.6
25–34 yrs	48.5
35–44 yrs	55.2
45–64 yrs	65
65+	68.1
Gender	
Male	55.7
Female	60.4
Race	
White	59.6
Black	60.8
Asian	32.1
Hispanic	31.6
Region	
Northeast	57.4
Midwest	63.4
South	57.7
West	54.6
Education	
< = 8	23.4
< High school	33.7
High school or GED	50.9
Some college	65
Bachelor's +	73.3
Employment status	
Employed	60.1
Unemployed	48.8
Not in labor force	55.5

Source: US Census Bureau. 2012. "Table 399 Voting-Age Population—Reported Registration and Voting by Selected Characteristics: 1996 to 2010." Statistical Abstract of the United States 2012. Retrieved October 2011 (http://www. census.gov/compendia/statab/2012/tables/12s0399.pdf).

Candidate Preference

Exit polls from elections are often used to examine the preference for candidates as a function of important demographic characteristics like race, ethnicity, and so on. In **TABLE 14-2**, we see the percentage of voters who indicated they voted for Barack Obama or John McCain. Obama received 95% of the vote among blacks and 66% among Hispanics, but he lost decisively among white voters with only 43% in his favor. The younger the age category of voters, the more they favored Obama, with 66% of those 18 to 29 voting for Obama compared to 52% of those 30 to 44, 49% of those 45 to 64, and 45% of those 65 and over. Similarly, voters from lower income categories were more likely to vote for Obama. There was also a rural–urban split, with urban voters most likely to vote for Obama (63%), while 50% of suburban voters and only 45% of rural voters indicating they voted for Obama (Kohut 2008). Many of these divisions reflect long-standing tendencies for the young, minorities, urbanites, and those with low income to favor Democrats.

In the 1980s, election polls for the first time in recent memory began to display a significant **gender gap**—a tendency for women and men to have different political

Gender gap A tendency for women and men to have different political preferences on many issues.

TABLE 14-2 Voter Preferences for Presidential Candidates by Selected Characteristics

	Obama	McCain	04–08 Dem Gain
Total	52	46	+4
White	43	55	+2
Black	95	4	+7
Hispanic	66	32	+13
18–29	66	32	+12
30–44	52	46	+6
45–64	49	49	+2
65+	45	53	–2
Under $50K	60	38	+5
$50–99K	49	49	+5
$100+K	49	50	+8
Republican	9	89	+3
Democrat	89	10	0
Independent	52	44	+3
Conservative	20	78	+5
Moderate	60	39	+6
Liberal	88	10	+3
Urban	63	35	+9
Suburban	50	48	+3
Rural	45	53	+3

Source: © 2008 Pew Research Center Publications. Post-Election Perspectives. http://pewresearch.org/pubs/1039/postelection-perspective.

preferences on many issues. In the 1980s, women were more likely to register as Democrats than as Republicans and were more critical of policies of the Reagan administration. In 1990, women voted 54% for Democratic candidates while men split their votes 50:50. Women are more in favor of abortion rights and less in favor of large defense budgets and military intervention overseas. This gender gap persisted through the 2012 presidential election in which women were, in general, more likely to vote for the Democratic candidate Barack Obama (56%), than were men (46%) (Gallup, 2012)

Getting Out the Vote

Today's political campaigns use a wide range of strategies to target voters who tend to favor their candidate. By knowing which groups favor their candidate, campaigns can target efforts to get out the vote. For example, candidate preference data, such as those seen in the table on voter preferences above, are taken from surveys leading up to the election. Such data provide a wealth of information that campaigns can use to target voters they want to encourage to get to the polls. Obama was clearly favored by blacks, Hispanics, younger voters, lower-income voters, urban voters, and women; McCain was favored by whites, older voters, and rural voters. So on election day, each campaign tried to make sure voters likely to favor its candidate were able to get to the polls and vote.

Opinion Polls, Wedge Issues, and Campaign Strategy

Contemporary political campaigns rely heavily on opinion polls to identify issues to emphasize and even which positions to take on controversial issues. The graph in **TABLE 14-3** shows results of Gallup polls during 2011 (Gallup Poll 2011b). When respondents were asked to identify the most important problem facing this country today, respondents were clearly most concerned about the economy, with 73% concerned about economic problems, including unemployment/jobs (32%) and the economy

TABLE 14-3   The Most Important Problem Facing the Country Today (2011)

What do you think is the most important problem facing the country today?

Trend	Oct 6–9, 2011	Sep 8–11, 2011	Aug 11–14, 2011	Jul 7–10, 2011	Jun 9–12, 2011	May 5–8, 2011	Apr 7 6–10, 2011

Economic problems
- Unemployment/jobs
- Economy in general

Noneconomic problems
- Dissatisfaction with government
- Poor health care/high cost of health care

Source: Data from Gallup Poll. 2011. "U.S. Satisfaction." Gallup Poll. Retrieved January 2013 (http://www.gallup.com/file/poll/150080/Satisfaction_MIP_111012.pdf).

in general (31%), and only 41% concerned with noneconomic problems, including dissatisfaction with government (13%) and health care (5%).

Each party tries to emphasize **wedge issues**—issues about which people have strong opinions and the position of their party receives greater public support than the other party. For example, throughout the 1992 presidential campaign, taped to the wall of the Clinton campaign headquarters was a sign with the simple message, "It's the economy, stupid." During the 1992 campaign, the economy was widely perceived as being in a recession, and many voters blamed the Bush administration for the sour economic times. Similarly, in the 2004 election, Republicans benefited when gay marriage bans were placed on the ballot in many states, encouraging more conservatives to participate in the election and re-elect George W. Bush. Many wedge issues in recent years have been based on religious beliefs regarding issues such as abortion, same-sex marriage, funding of contraceptives, or prayer in schools. The 2012 US presidential election, for example, saw much discussion of whether and how contraceptives should be funded, particularly for religiously affiliated employers such as the Catholic Church and Catholic hospitals. As former Senator Bob Kerry of Nebraska said, campaigns are not about changing the minds of voters but about convincing them the candidate's values align with theirs. "What you do is pretend to lead while basically you're trying to follow their opinions" (Bob Kerry cited in Miller 2012).

Lobbyists and Special-Interest Groups

> We have the best congress that money can buy.
> —Will Rogers

Interest groups are voluntary associations of citizens who attempt to influence public policy. Such groups are often concerned with regulatory legislation, but some also try to influence federal criminal code. Single-interest groups focus on specific issues such as gun legislation. An example is the National Rifle Association (NRA). Broader interest groups often represent large segments of the population and focus on issues of interest to that group. For example, the American Association of Retired Persons (AARP) focuses on issues of interest to older adults and the elderly. Public-interest groups claim to represent issues of interest to the broad public. Examples include Common Cause and consumer-oriented groups, such as Ralph Nader's Public Citizen group. Interest groups often attempt to influence the political process through lobbyists and political action committees. A **lobbyist** is someone who represents an interest group and meets with public officials to try to influence their decisions by providing information supporting the interest group's goals. The term *lobbyist* derives from the common practice of catching officials in public lobbies and trying to persuade them there. By an estimate from the Center for Responsive Politics, based on data from the Senate Office of Public Records, in 2010, there were 13,000 active registered lobbyists in Washington, DC, who collectively spent more than $3.51 billion on lobbying expenses, including lobbyists' salaries (OpenSecrets.org 2011).

> **Lobbyist** Someone who represents an interest group and meets with public officials to try to influence their decisions by providing information supporting the interest group's goals.
>
> **Political action committees (PACs)** Interest groups formed to campaign for or against political candidates, legislation, and ballot initiatives.

   Political action committees (PACs) are interest groups formed to campaign for or against political candidates, legislation, and ballot initiatives. The first PAC was founded by organized labor in 1943. By 1976, there were 922 PACs. By 2009, there were 4,611 PACs (Federal Election Commission 2009). PACs provide hundreds of millions of dollars to political candidates for media campaigns. PACs have become a significant way for groups and corporations to exert influence on issues important to them. PACs benefited from the Campaign Reform Act of 1974, which restricted individual contributions to political candidates to $1,000 and group contributions to $5,000, thus limiting the ability of individuals or political parties to act directly on behalf of the interests of the candidate. In contrast, the *Citizens United v. Federal Election Commission* decision by the Supreme Court in 2010 lifted funding limits for PACs, further strengthening the role of PACs in fundraising.

   While PACs try to influence decisions on high-visibility and controversial issues, they devote much more of their efforts to influencing low-visibility issues where it is less likely to be detected. Rather than focusing their energies on the final vote, PACs try to influence the way in which bills are worded, securing exemptions from government regulations. This is illustrated by the Clean Air Act Amendments of 1990. Members of Congress were able to vote almost unanimously for the act in the final vote and look good for their constituents on this environmental issue. However, before that final vote, dozens of loopholes were added in private meetings or subcommittee hearings, outside the attention of the public and the press. The public got a clean air act. The corporate interests got a bill that was severely weakened long before the final vote. Privately, members of Congress were able to assure their PAC contributors that the bill had been weakened while publicly assuring their constituents they voted for the bill in the end (Clawson et al. 1992).

   The impact of PACs on US politics is driven by an almost insatiable need for campaign funds. The US presidential election campaign in which Barak Obama defeated John McCain generated $1.7 billion in spending by candidates (Salant 2008). Campaigns for US senator or the governorship in most states cost millions of dollars. By 2000, the campaign cost for the average winning candidate was $847,000 for a House seat and $7.2 million in a Senate race (Cantor 2002). Because political campaigns are so expensive, most successful candidates must be rich. About 50% of US senators are millionaires (Barnes 1990). Many winning US senators spent more than $4 million on their campaigns. Even affluent candidates must raise money for their campaigns and hence are vulnerable to influence by contributors. For just one bill, the Affordable Care Act of 2010 that overhauled the US healthcare system, 4,500 lobbyists were hired by nearly 1,800 firms and spent millions of dollars to influence the legislation. This amounts to roughly eight lobbyists for every member of Congress (Eaton and Pell 2010).

Global Comparisons with Other Democratic Systems

When comparing the US political system with European systems, one of the most striking differences is the very low rate of voter turnout in the United States. In TABLE 14-4, we can see that the voting rate in presidential elections in the United States in 2008 was 57.47% and the turnout for congressional elections was 38.46%. In contrast, the turnout in Canada for parliamentary elections was 61.41% and for the United Kingdom it was 65.77%, while the turnout rate for Denmark was 86.59%. It is hard to even imagine 86% of American voters going to the polls to vote on any issue.

TABLE 14-4 Voter Turnout in Selected Democracies

Country	Election Type	Year	Voter Turnout (%)
Australia	Parliamentary	2010	93.22
	Presidential	—	
Canada	Parliamentary	2011	61.41
	Presidential	—	
Denmark	Parliamentary	2007	86.59
	Presidential	—	
France	Parliamentary	2007	59.98
	Presidential	2007	83.97
Germany	Parliamentary	2009	70.78
	Presidential	—	
United Kingdom	Parliamentary	2010	65.77
	Presidential	—	
United States	Parliamentary	2010	41.59
	Presidential	2008	70.33

Source: Data from International Institute for Democracy and Electoral Assistance. Voter Turnout. Retrieved October 2011 (http://www.idea.int/vt/).

Politics in the United States differs substantially from politics in most Western European democracies. Granberg and Holmberg (1988) conducted an exhaustive analysis of voting behavior and attitudes in dozens of national elections in both Sweden and the United States. They concluded several important differences were due to differences in the Swedish parliamentary system and the US democratic republic. While the United States is dominated by two political parties, Sweden has more political parties, and those parties take clearer, more easily perceived stands on political issues than the two US parties. Voting rates are considerably higher in Sweden than in the United States. Ideology is more closely linked to voting behavior in Sweden, where issues dominate voting decisions, while in the United States, voters are sometimes more influenced by candidate personalities than by the issues. Once again, it was structural differences in the two governments they believed led to those differences.

The United States also has a history of voting barriers sometimes directed at particular groups that reduce voter participation. The 1965 Voting Rights Act was designed to prevent barriers such as literacy tests that once limited voting by blacks. During the 2012 election, new concerns were raised about laws passed in several states by Republican-controlled state governments, including those requiring state-issued ID cards, efforts to purge the rolls of dead or no-longer-eligible voters, limitations on absentee balloting, and reductions in early voting. Proponents of those measures argue that they are efforts to prevent voter fraud (Truethevote 2012), while opponents argue voter fraud is very rare and such measures are more likely to prevent far more legitimate voters from exercising their right to vote (Brennan Center for Justice 2012). In parliamentary systems, the head of government is selected from among the majority party. In contrast, for most of the years in the period 1954 to 1992, the President of the United States was a Republican and the Democrats had a majority in Congress. This is possible because the president is elected by popular vote rather than appointed by the majority party in Congress, as in parliamentary systems. This is one factor contributing to what some call "**governmental gridlock**"—an inability to resolve important issues when neither party has sufficient votes to determine government policy. For example, in 2011, despite widely publicized hearings and vocal support for increasing the debt limit, Congress debated up until the last minute, nearly shutting down the government, with the result that the credit rating firm Standard & Poor's downgraded the United States' AAA credit rating for the first time in history (Brandimarte and Bases 2011).

Governmental gridlock An inability to resolve important issues when neither party has sufficient votes to determine government policy.

In fairness, it is true that the checks and balances in the US Constitution are designed to make it difficult for any one group to pass laws without broad consent. But when government threatens to grind to a halt from its inability to even agree on a budget, *gridlock* seems a fair description of the situation.

CONCEPT LEARNING CHECK 14.3 Demographics and Voting

Elections for US senator are occurring in three states. Match each of the following statements with the state it best describes.

_____ 1. The state most likely to elect the Republican candidate.

_____ 2. The state most likely to elect the Democratic candidate.

_____ 3. The state most likely to have the smallest voter turnout.

_____ 4. The state likely to have the highest voter turnout.

A. Western mountain state that is primarily rural with a large proportion of people 65 and older, relatively few 18- to 29-year-olds, and 75% whites.

B. Eastern state that is primarily urban with a large proportion of younger people, particularly 18- to 29-year-olds, and large minority populations of Hispanics and blacks.

C. Midwestern State that is evenly split among urban and rural voters, small minority populations, and a large proportion of younger people.

14.4 Theoretical Perspectives on Power and Political Systems

Two contrasting views of power in the US political system stress either government by the people or government by the few.

- Illustrate the functionalist and conflict perspectives on political power.

There are two contrasting models of the power structure in the United States that describe very different views of the distribution of power: the functionalist view and the conflict view.

Functionalist Perspectives: Pluralist (Government by the People) Model

The structural-functional perspective sees political systems as relatively stable, well-functioning systems. In this view, **pluralist models** are used to explain that many groups within a community or country have access to government officials and compete with one another in an effort to influence policy decisions (Cummings and Wise 1989:235). These **interest groups** consist of a voluntary association of citizens who attempt to influence public policy. Interest groups attempt to exert power by influencing people in positions of authority and supporting candidates whose positions are sympathetic to their cause. An interest group that is highly influential on one issue is often not the same group that has the greatest influence on another issue. In this case, power and influence are widely dispersed among many different interest groups, each having strong effects on a narrow range of issues.

Within the pluralist perspective, David Riesman (1961) argues that many interest groups are **veto groups** having the capacity to prevent the exercise of power by others. Riesman notes that to be re-elected, political leaders must be able to placate veto groups such as the farm lobby or the gun control lobby. This ensures that their interests have to be considered even when they are not the majority. Two studies of the power structure in New Haven, Connecticut, support the pluralist model. Those studies found that different groups controlled different issues (Polsby 1959) and power had become more dispersed over time (Dahl 1961). It could be argued that the division of power in the

Pluralist models Argue that many groups within a community or country have access to government officials and compete with one another in an effort to influence policy decisions.

Interest groups Groups that consist of a voluntary association of citizens who attempt to influence public policy.

Veto groups Interest groups that have the capacity to prevent the exercise of power by others.

US Constitution among the executive, legislative, and judicial branches was a deliberate attempt to encourage greater pluralism by giving different groups opportunities to influence the political process.

Conflict Perspectives: Elite (Government by the Few) Model

Inspired by Marx's conflict perspective, sociologist C. Wright Mills (1956) argued that a small ruling elite of military, corporate, and governmental leaders controls the fate of the United States. From this perspective, power rests in the hands of the few, both inside and outside government. According to Mills, these leaders come to constitute a "power elite" because they coordinate their decisions to their mutual benefit. The military, corporate, and governmental institutions form a power triangle that allows the powerful to realize their wills, even if others resist them. This is not quite a conspiracy theory, but Mills argues there is a community of interest and sentiment among a few influential Americans.

The elite belong to interlocking boards of directors (where individuals may sit on a number of boards and in that way come to know other elites), have memberships in elite clubs, attend elite schools, and in other ways associate with one another. In many cases, these elites often take turns in key positions on boards or as officers of corporations, moving from one institution to another. While Mills argues that power rests in the hands of the few both inside and outside government, he believed no one could be truly powerful unless s/he has access to the major institutions, because it is only through these institutions that power can be maintained and enhanced. As he says, "churches, schools, and families adapt to modern life; governments, armies, and corporations shape it. As they do so, they turn the lesser institutions into means for their ends" (Mills 1956). Power resides not in the individual members of the elite but in the institutional positions they occupy.

G. William Domhoff (1967, 1983), in a series of books beginning with *The Ruling Class*, agrees with Mills that America is run by a small elite. Unlike Mills, however, Domhoff argues that the nation is controlled by a social upper class that effectively is a ruling class due to its dominant role in the economy and government. Like Marx, Domhoff believes the upper class dominates the military and political elite. Unlike Marx, he believes it is a *social* elite, not just an *economic* elite that dominates. This ruling class, argues Domhoff, is socially cohesive and owns 20 to 25% of all privately held wealth and 45 to 50% of all privately held common stock. Members are recognized in *The Social Register*—a directory of the social elite available in many American cities. Members of the elite tend to hold public positions of authority, including important appointive government posts. For example, George H. W. Bush, before becoming president, held a number of important posts, including that of Director of the Central Intelligence Agency. Members of this ruling social class dominate powerful corporations, foundations, universities, and the executive branch of government.

A number of studies have provided support for elite models of community power structures. The Lynds (1937) studied Muncie, Indiana ("Middletown"), and found that a single family dominated the community, where their name was attached to the university, bank, a hospital, and a department store, in addition to their major business, a factory making glass canning jars. Similarly, in a study of Atlanta, Floyd Hunter (1963) found that as few as 40 people held all the top positions in the city's businesses and controlled community politics.

Visual Overview Pluralist versus Elite Models—Significant Differences

Pluralist models argue that because there are many competing interest groups attempting to influence policy on different issues, it is unlikely any one group will extert too much influence on its own. In contrast, elite models argue there is a relatively small number of elites that has the greatest influence on the full range of issues.

Pluralist Model

> Many groups have access to government officials and compete to influence policy.

> Because interest groups compete with one another and have divergent views, this makes the abuse of power by any one group unlikely.

> Power is widely dispersed among many different veto groups, each having strong effects on a narrow range of issues, hence people can influence policy by voting and participating in such interest groups.

> Public policy is the result of the competing goals of different interest groups, each of which wins only on some issues.

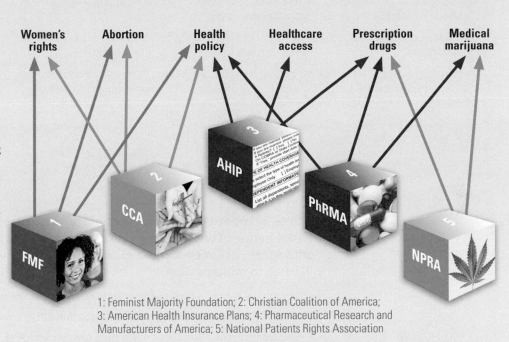

Women's rights   Abortion   Health policy   Healthcare access   Prescription drugs   Medical marijuana

FMF CCA AHIP PhRMA NPRA

1: Feminist Majority Foundation; 2: Christian Coalition of America; 3: American Health Insurance Plans; 4: Pharmaceutical Research and Manufacturers of America; 5: National Patients Rights Association

Elite Model

> A small group of elites make important policy decisions for the entire society.

> The elites recognize shared interests and values and generally work in concert to achieve their goals and overrule non-elites.

> Power is highly centralized in people at the top of a pyramid-shaped social hierarchy and efforts to influence policy by the non-elites will be ineffectual.

> Most or all public policy decisions reflect the interests of the elites.

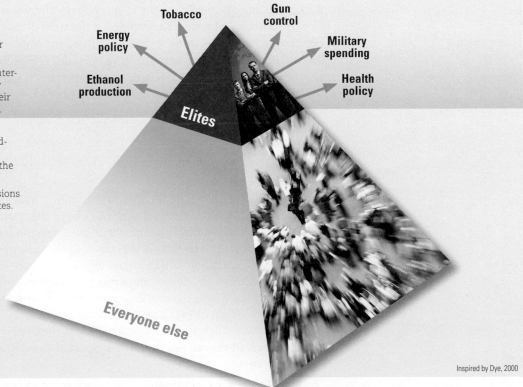

Tobacco   Gun control   Energy policy   Military spending   Ethanol production   Health policy

Elites

Everyone else

Inspired by Dye, 2000

CONCEPT LEARNING CHECK 14.4   Pluralist versus Elite Models of the US Political System

For each of the following hypothetical statements, indicate the model with which it is most consistent.

_____ 1. Government support for ethanol production was heavily favored by the corn growers' lobby but was opposed by many environmental groups because they believe it does not reduce carbon emissions.

_____ 2. A particular person serves on the boards of six large corporations and has held several important appointed posts in government.

_____ 3. I do not see much point in voting since I cannot really influence policy much as an individual.

_____ 4. Virtually no legislation regarding transportation can get past Congress without support from the Teamsters' Union, but the union's opposition to the government bailout of Wall Street banks was of no avail.

A. Pluralist model

B. Elite model

14.5 War and Peace

Efforts by countries to defend their citizens all too often lead to war, even as the nature of warfare evolves. Efforts to maintain the peace are divided, with some resources devoted to diplomacy and a far greater amount devoted to militarization.

■ Explain the causes, types, and cost of wars, as well as the ways warfare is evolving.

■ Discuss the changing demographic composition of US armed forces.

■ Discuss ways the United States has tried to deter attack as well as seek diplomatic resolutions.

War Organized conflict between nations.

A fundamental claim of any state is sovereignty and a state monopoly on violence. Governments are obligated to provide for the right of its citizens to engage in their everyday activities free from interference from any source other than the state. Historically, to protect their citizens, states sometimes engage in **war**—organized conflict between nations. The United States, for example, has engaged in 12 major wars since the Revolutionary War, including the wars in Iraq and Afghanistan, with a total loss of more than 1.3 million US men and women and several times as many injured.

Causes of War

Why do wars occur? There are as many theories about why wars occur as there are people who write about it.

A few of these illustrate the diversity of views. In _Why Nations Go to War_, John Stoessinger (1974/2005) argues that all sides argue that their position is morally right, and wars are often justified based on overly optimistic projections of the outcome and misperceptions of the intentions of the enemy. Evolutionary psychologist Steven Pinker, in _The Blank Slate_ (Pinker 2002), argues alliances and pre-emptive wars are attempts to provide deterrence by developing a reputation for retaliation, and war itself is often beneficial for the victors because they gain control over scarce resources. Political scientist Quincy Wright (1987) argues that there are five circumstances that increase the likelihood of war. These can be illustrated by how the United States went to war in Iraq.

1. **A perceived threat**—such as the suspected development of weapons of mass destruction.

2. **Moral objectives**—Operation Iraqi Freedom was presented as an effort to liberate the Iraqi people from an oppressive dictator.

3. **Political objectives**—The United States wanted to "stand up" to Saddam Hussein and show the world that we are a force to be reckoned with.

4. **Social problems**—The war helped divert attention from economic troubles at home.

5. **Absence of alternatives**—Diplomacy and UN monitoring of Iraq's military capabilities had failed.

It is interesting to consider how these same factors might apply to other nations such as North Korea or Iran, both of which are widely regarded as rogue states that frequently threaten to ignite a regional or even global conflict.

Types of War

People often speak of war as though it were a single homogeneous activity. But there are many different types of war, each of which poses different threats to the nation-state and requires different responses to prevent or to win such a war.

Conventional warfare such as occurred in World War II and the Korean War is largely symmetrical, with two or more nation-states battling each other to gain control of territory. Success in such a war could be measured by territory gained and losses inflicted upon the enemy. But the United States is unlikely to be engaged in symmetrical warfare in the near future because the United States has pumped trillions of dollars into its military budget over decades. According to the Stockholm International Peace Research Institute (2010), in 2010, the US military budget of $698 billion dwarfed the next highest budget (China at $114 billion). As a result, warfare today is often **asymmetric warfare**—war between opponents with significantly different military power and, consequently, significantly different tactics. The wars in Iraq and Afghanistan illustrate asymmetric warfare in which the United States and its allies rely on high-technology equipment and massive resources while their opponents wage a guerilla war with car bombs and roadside improvised explosive devices (IEDs) to inflict casualties and destroy property.

Terrorism—the systematic threat or use of violence to achieve a political end—is one form of asymmetric warfare. Unfortunately, we have no shortage of examples of terrorism, including the attacks of September 11, 2001, the bombing in Oklahoma City, suicide bombers who blow themselves up in crowded public areas, and the bombing of the Pan Am flight over Lockerbie, Scotland. Not every act of asymmetric warfare is terrorism. Most definitions of terrorism reserve the term for violent acts intended to create fear and that disregard the safety of civilians and noncombatants or explicitly target them. Terrorism is often carried out by extremist political groups whose members are unknown or in hiding, who deny accountability, and who are not affiliated with a sponsoring nation-state, making it extremely difficult for governments to effectively respond to acts of terrorism.

Sometimes acts of terrorism are carried out by totalitarian governments that use terror against their own citizens to suppress opposition or sponsor acts of terrorism against other countries. Both Iraqi leader Saddam Hussein and Muammar Gaddafi were accused of terrorist acts of violence against their own people. Gaddafi and his government in Libya were also accused by the United States and England of terrorism for supporting and protecting the people who blew up the Pan Am airliner over Lockerbie, Scotland. It hardly needs to be said that *terrorism* is a highly charged term and what one side calls an act of terrorism may be regarded as "resistance" by the other side. To discourage terrorism by not rewarding those who practice it, many countries, including the United States, have policies of refusing to negotiate with terrorists.

Often nations will wage war on the grounds that their cause is morally just.

© Bettmann/Corbis/AP Images

The bombing of the Alfred P. Murrah Federal Building in Oklahoma City in 1995.

© Ralf-Finn Hestoft/CORBIS

Asymmetric warfare War between opponents with significantly different military power and, consequently, significantly different tactics.

Terrorism The systematic threat or use of violence to achieve a political end; one form of asymmetric warfare.

Drone warfare is expanding as more nations add drones to their military arsenals.

© dvande/Shutterstock, Inc.

Cyberwarfare A form of information warfare using digital software and hardware to conduct sabotage and espionage.

Drone warfare The use of remotely controlled airplanes to conduct surveillance and to kill suspected militants with laser-guided rockets and other armaments.

Military-industrial complex The conjunction of interests of the combination of the federal government, the military, and the defense industry.

Technology is also transforming warfare. **Cyberwarfare** is a form of information warfare using digital software and hardware to conduct sabotage and espionage. The United States, for example, considered using cyberwarfare in the initial attack on Libya in 2011 (Schmitt and Shanker 2011) but ultimately chose not to do so, partly to avoid setting a precedent by using the technology visibly and to avoid revealing cyberwarfare tactics, which in turn could help other potential opponents develop ways to counter them. **Drone warfare**—the use of remotely controlled pilotless airplanes to conduct surveillance and to kill suspected militants with laser-guided rockets and other armaments—has been used extensively by the United States in Afghanistan and Iraq, as well as in Yemen and other countries.

Drone warfare has been so successful that much of the US military budget is being redirected from manned aircraft to drones, and in 2010, the US Air Force trained more pilots to "fly" drones than traditional fighter planes. Drone warfare is expected to expand in future wars because dozens of other countries around the world, including China and Russia, are developing their own drones. However, a number of legal and ethical questions have been raised by critics about the use of drones to perform targeted killing even in countries with which the United States is not at war and when there has been substantial loss of life for innocent civilians (Billitteri 2010).

Costs of War

War and the military exact a high price on countries. Worldwide, well more than one trillion dollars is spent each year on military budgets (Stockholm International Peace Research Institute 2010). In the United States in 2005, military expenditures accounted for 4.06% of gross domestic production (GDP). Lives lost and people wounded in military conflicts make up an even greater cost. The more than 1.3 million lost lives in the United States alone mentioned earlier is one measure. Wars throughout history have taken an enormous toll, with World War II alone estimated to have resulted in 60 million deaths worldwide. If we add in refugees, productivity loss, and physical damages, the losses are staggering.

Why do countries continue to accept the high costs of war? In the United States, one factor must certainly be what President Eisenhower called the **military-industrial complex**—the conjunction of interests of the combination of the federal government, the military, and the defense industry. Defense industries spend millions of dollars on lobbying to help ensure continued funding for their projects, and many of those lobbyists and key people in the industry are former military themselves, while other former military members take positions in the federal government. Members of Congress feel tremendous pressure from their constituents to support continued spending in their own districts. It is little wonder, then, that Lockheed Martin assigned production of the F-22 Raptor to subcontractors in 46 states in order to increase Congressional support for the program (Lobe 2009).

Gender, Race, and Class in the Military

Historically, the military has been made up primarily of men. In 2008, the percentages of women in the various military forces were 6% in the Marine Corps, 14% in the Army, 15% in the Navy, and 20% in the Air Force (DoD Statistical Information Analysis Division 2009). Women are excluded from a third of all Army jobs in occupational fields such as infantry, armor, and special forces (Manning 2005) and continue to experience harassment in the military, leading to higher turnover rates for women than men (Sims, Drasgow, and Fitzgerald 2005). Gays were banned from military service between 1950 and 1993, when President Clinton signed the "Don't ask, don't tell" (DADT) policy. In 2011, that policy was repealed, permitting gay men and women to serve openly in the armed forces.

One concern when the all-volunteer force was created was that the burden of warfare would be shifted more heavily onto the shoulders of disadvantaged minorities and the lower social classes. To some extent, this has happened. During the all-volunteer force era, African Americans have consistently been overrepresented in the military, hovering around 20%, while the civilian labor force participation of blacks has stayed between 11 and 13% (Marmion 1971). However, the percentage of Hispanics in the military (13% in 2006) has more nearly mirrored the percentage of Hispanics in the civilian workforce (Segal, Thanner, and Segal 2007). The bottom quartile of the socioeconomic status distribution is underrepresented in large part because of failing to meet educational, physical, mental aptitude, and moral requirements (such as no drug use or arrests), while the upper quartile is under-represented primarily because they chose other careers (Bachman et al. 2000). High school students with C grade averages were roughly two times as likely to enter military service as students with A grade averages (Bachman et al. 2000).

Maintaining the Peace

Given the high costs of war for countries, they pursue a number of strategies to achieve a lasting and just peace.

Deterrence and Defense

Much of the effort to preserve the peace since World War II has been essentially a peace-through-strength strategy. After World War II, with the proliferation of atomic weapons and the vastly more horrific possible consequences of all-out nuclear war between nations, much of the effort concentrated on **deterrence**—preventing war from occurring. During the Cold War, the dominant strategy was based on a premise of mutually assured destruction (MAD). The United States and the Soviet blocs of countries attempted to develop sufficient nuclear weapons shielded from destruction so that if one country were to launch a pre-emptive nuclear strike, it could expect the other nation would have enough weapons survive to launch a devastating counterattack. In other words, no one could win such a war. This policy, as mad as it sounds, has actually worked for more than 60 years to prevent nuclear war. However, it has not prevented all wars. Instead, other types of warfare have occurred, including the rise of terrorism and attacks by stronger nations on weaker nations. This also led to a massive arms race that eventually bankrupted the Soviet Union and diverted substantial US economic resources from the civilian economy into the military.

Another element of US efforts to prevent war has been increased reliance on high-technology weapons. Those weapons seek not only to deter attacks from others but also to dominate any conflicts that do occur. It may be argued that since World War II, the willingness of the American public to endure massive loss of lives in wars has decreased. By developing new weapons, we have sought the ability to execute wars with much less loss of life. These new weapons have included the drone aircraft and cyberwarfare mentioned above. With drone aircraft, "pilots" can fly planes in combat from thousands of miles away, no longer placing our military pilots at risk.

Diplomacy and Resolution

In contrast to building up military strength, many argue that the most effective way to maintain the peace is through diplomacy, disarmament, and the resolution of differences. The idea here is that diplomats can work together to negotiate reductions in weapons stockpiles, thereby reducing the chance of war and the amount of death and destruction that might result. This includes efforts to negotiate nuclear weapons reductions such as have taken place between the United States and Russia over decades. It also includes efforts to have the United Nations take an active role in reducing tensions, such as providing troops to monitor the peace or to apply sanctions against countries that persist in activities that violate human rights in their own country or threaten the peace with other countries. It also includes nation-building efforts in which richer countries help poorer nations to improve their infrastructure to provide better housing, education, and health care for their people.

Although the number of women in the military is increasing, they are excluded from a third of all Army jobs.
© DoD/Corbis

Deterrence Preventing war from occurring.

Diplomats from the US Department of State meet with their foreign counterparts to try to negotiate agreements between their respective nations.
© Asianet-Pakistan/Shutterstock, Inc.

CONCEPT LEARNING CHECK 14.5   The Demographics of the Military

Which of the following statements about military service by people with various demographic characteristics are true and which are false?

_____ 1. In 2011, a "Don't ask, don't tell" policy was put into place in the military, requiring that gay men and women not disclose their sexual preference.

_____ 2. The armed forces include a larger proportion of people from the bottom quartile of the socioeconomic distribution because they have fewer alternative opportunities to get ahead.

_____ 3. High school students with C averages are twice as likely to enter military service as students with A averages.

_____ 4. The proportion of African Americans in the military is nearly twice as high as their proportion in the civilian labor force.

_____ 5. The proportion of Hispanic Americans in the military is nearly twice as high as their proportion in the civilian workforce.

14.6 Economy and Economic Systems in Transition

Economies have transformed dramatically, with dramatic consequences for how people work.

- Identify and describe historically different economies and the nature of work within each.

Economy Consists of the organizations and processes that produce and distribute goods and services.

Agricultural economies Economies in which agricultural production is efficient, leading to a food surplus, permitting a more complex division of labor and making it possible to settle permanently in one place.

An **economy** consists of the organizations and processes that produce and distribute goods and services. Over thousands of years, societies have undergone transitions from agricultural economies to industrial economies and finally to information economies (Lenski and Lenski 1982).

Hunting and Gathering Economies

The earliest economies were hunting and gathering economies in which people hunted game and relied on readily available vegetation and water for subsistence. These were bare subsistence economies limited by the available food supply that could support no more than a few dozen members, all of whom performed the same task of acquiring food for survival. All societies began as hunting and gathering economies. These were still common until a few hundred years ago. Today only a few such societies remain, in remote areas, with most of the rest having had their territory overrun by other forms of economy.

Agricultural Economies

The agricultural revolution occurred with the invention of the plow drawn by animals, followed by other agricultural technologies. This made **agricultural economies** possible in which agricultural production was efficient, leading to a food surplus, permitting a much more complex division of labor and making it possible to settle permanently in one place. With people free to pursue other occupations, the wheel, writing, and numbers were also invented, leading to what many refer to as the "dawn of civilization." Permanent settlements became possible, and during this period, great wealth was accumulated by a few, with stratification becoming a major feature of social life. An elite gained control of surplus resources and defended its position with arms. This centralization of power and resources eventually led to the development of the institution of the state to further consolidate the gains of the rich and powerful. Agricultural economies dramatically changed economic life. The key technology is human and animal labor and the key resource is raw materials including land.

Industrial Economies

The Industrial Revolution dramatically changed the nature of production: Manufacturing became a central economic activity. The Industrial Revolution began in approximately 1750 in England, then spread throughout Europe and the United States, and eventually engulfed the entire world. By 1800, more British workers were employed in manufacturing than in agriculture, and the first industrial society was born. The United States did not reach this stage until 70 years later. Today the great majority of societies are industrialized.

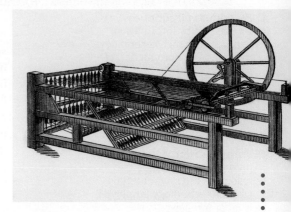

The spinning Jenny replaced the traditional spinning wheel, dramatically increasing productivity.
© Associated Press

Industrial societies have six important characteristics.

1. **Manufacturing and mass production**—People freed from agricultural labor were able to work in manufacturing jobs assembling raw materials into finished goods made up of standardized components.

2. **New machines increased productivity**—Beginning with inventions in the textile industry that increased the productivity of workers, new machines dramatically increased productivity and a surplus of inexpensive manufactured goods replaced handcrafted ones.

3. **New forms of energy replaced human muscle power**—New machines quickly became too big to be powered by humans or animals. In 1765, the steam engine, invented by James Watt, provided a solution that was hundreds of times more powerful than humans.

4. **Work became centralized in factories**—The size of these new machines and need for power meant that workers had to be centralized in factories rather than working individually in their homes.

5. **Independent craftsmen were replaced with wage laborers**—Craftsmen who worked independently and sold their products to buyers could not compete with the new factories and became factory workers who were paid wages in exchange for their labor. The breakup of agricultural-based feudal societies caused many people to leave the land and seek employment in cities. This created a great surplus of labor and gave capitalists plenty of laborers who could be hired for extremely low wages.

6. **Narrow specialization**—With mass production, skilled craftsmen capable of producing complete products were replaced with highly specialized workers, each performing a repetitive task that contributed to one small step in the production process.

In industrial economies, the key technology is capital intensive because of the wealth required to build and purchase machines, and the key resource is energy to power those machines.

Information Economies and Postindustrial Societies

The **information revolution** is a change that began during the last half of the 20th century in which service jobs are becoming more common than jobs in manufacturing or agriculture. Service jobs are high- and low-skilled jobs that produce and transfer knowledge. The information revolution overlaps the more recent phases of the Industrial Revolution, and both "revolutions" are occurring simultaneously in most parts of the world. The information revolution has lead to what is known as the **information economy**—an economy based on the product of skilled professionals, which is the information or knowledge they provide. The information revolution began with the invention of the integrated circuit or computer chip. These chips have revolutionized our lives, running our appliances and allowing us to produce calculators, computers, and other electronic devices to control our world. It is still too early to know precisely what

Industrial revolution A dramatic change in the nature of production in which manufacturing became a central economic activity.

Industrial societies These societies emphasize manufacturing and mass production in which machines replace much human labor and craftsmen are replaced by less skilled laborers.

Information revolution A change that began during the last half of the 20th century in which service jobs become more common than jobs in manufacturing or agriculture.

Information economy An economy based on the product of skilled professionals, which is the information or knowledge they provide.

the implications of the information revolution are for social life. Clearly, innovations such as the Internet, permitting people to communicate using computers all around the globe, satellite dishes, and cellular phones have changed how families spend their time, the kind of work we do, and many other aspects of our lives.

Postindustrial societies are dominated by information, services, and high technology more than by the production of goods. The key technology in postindustrial societies is knowledge as represented by copyrighted works, patents, and knowledge-intensive information-processing technologies. The key resource is information that can be used to generate additional information and knowledge. The United States was the first country to have more than half of the workforce employed in service industries. Service industries include government, research, education, health, sales, law, banking, and so on. As you can see in FIGURE 14-1, by 2010, several countries were well into the postindustrial age, with a low among these nations of 68.5% for Italy and 69.7% for Germany and highs of 81.2% for the United States and 80.7% for both the United Kingdom and the Netherlands (US Census Bureau 2011d:Table 1370).

Economic Sectors

Modern economies contain elements of each of the three most common types of economies. These elements, or categories, are known as **economic sectors**—large segments of the economy representing fundamentally different kinds of production. These three sectors of the economy parallel the development of societies over time as they evolved from hunting and gathering societies to postindustrial societies.

The Primary Sector

The **primary sector** is agricultural production, the major resources are raw materials, and the technology employed is labor intensive. The primary sector dominates preindustrial economies but plays a much more limited role in industrial or postindustrial economies.

The Secondary Sector

The **secondary sector** is manufacturing, its activity is goods producing, the key resource is energy, and the technology employed is capital-intensive machine production. The secondary sector dominates industrial economies.

The Tertiary Sector

The **tertiary sector** is the service sector, including entertainment, the food industry, professions, and so on. The tertiary sector dominates postindustrial societies.

Postindustrial societies Dominated by information, services, and high technology more than the production of goods.

Economic sectors Large segments of the economy representing fundamentally different kinds of production.

Primary sector Agricultural production; the major resources are raw materials and the technology employed is labor intensive.

Secondary sector Manufacturing; its activity is goods producing, the key resource is energy, and the technology employed is capital-intensive machine production.

Tertiary sector Dominated by services ranging from high-wage professional advice based on knowledge to low-wage menial services.

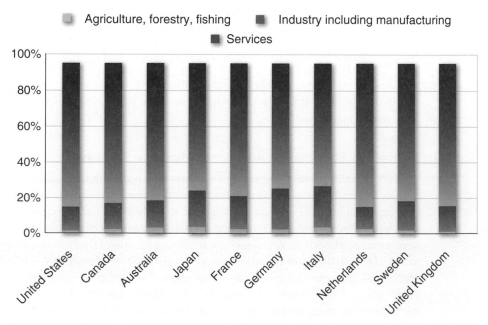

FIGURE 14-1 Civilian employment by industry and country.
Source: US Census Bureau. 2012. The 2012 Statistical Abstract The National Data Book, International Statistics. Retrieved October 2011 (http://www.census.gov/compendia/statab/cats/international_statistics.html).

CONCEPT LEARNING CHECK 14.6   Types of Economic Systems

Match these types of economies with their characteristics.

_____ **1.** Hunting and gathering economies   **A.** Little or no food surplus

_____ **2.** Agricultural economies   **B.** Requires massive amounts of energy

_____ **3.** Industrial economies   **C.** For the first time, food surpluses permit additional specialization and a renaissance in the sciences, the arts, and new forms of business.

_____ **4.** Postindustrial economies

D. The key resource is information.

14.7 Global Economic Systems

Both capitalism and socialism, while competing with one another, have their own variants and have evolved over time.

- Compare and contrast the key characteristics, common differences, and historical trends of capitalism and socialism.

Modern economies face several important issues, including what is to be produced, how much is to be produced, who decides what and how much to produce, and why people should work. Two competing economic systems—socialism and capitalism—offer very different answers to these questions. Both of these economic systems are ideal types that cannot be found in pure form in any society. All modern economies can be understood as a combination of elements of these two systems.

Four general dimensions of economies provide answers to the questions described above and distinguish socialism from capitalism. These are summarized in **TABLE 14-5**.

Capitalism

Capitalism is an economy based on private ownership of wealth, competition, profit, and noninterference by the government. Capitalism tends to be decentralized, with no single organization or government that makes most economic decisions. Individual companies decide how much they will produce each year and what they will charge. Capitalism is based on a **market economy** in which consumers are the key decision makers, the market drives the economy, and transactions are based on the profit motive and competition. The key assumption of capitalism is that people are permitted to engage in economic exchange out of their own self-interest, and through market forces, those individual self-interests lead to the common good. "It is not from the benevolence of the butcher, the brewer, or the baker that we expect our dinner, but from their regard to their own interest" (Smith 1776). Even though we are all motivated by our own personal gain, we all benefit from the increased productivity and greater efficiency that result from people trying to maximize their own profits.

Capitalism An economy based on private ownership of wealth, competition, profit, and noninterference by the government.

Market economy An economy in which consumers are the key decision makers, the market drives the economy, and transactions are based on the profit motive and competition.

TABLE 14-5 Key Characteristics of Capitalism and Socialism

Capitalism	Socialism
Decentralized economy	Centralized economy
Market economy	Planned economy
Private ownership of means of production	Public ownership of means of production
Profit motive	Collective goals

Competitive capitalism The capitalism of Marx's day in which no single capitalist or small group of capitalists could dominate a market.

Monopoly capitalism Occurs when one or only a few capitalists control a sector of the economy.

State capitalism Capitalism in which capitalistic enterprises exist side by side with state-owned production enterprises and the state regulates and manages the economy.

Corporate capitalism Capitalism dominated by public corporations owned by many stockholders.

Managerial capitalism Occurs where managers, through both their day-to-day involvement in the corporation and their ownership of large blocks of stock as part of their compensation, often dominate the corporation.

Institutional capitalism Capitalism in which large shares of corporations are owned by institutional investors such as pension, insurance, or trust funds.

Socialist economies Economic systems in which the means of production are collectively owned and the economy is government regulated.

Communism As envisioned by Karl Marx, an extreme form of socialist economic and political system in which all members of the society are equal.

Historically, there have been several variants of capitalism: **Competitive capitalism** is the capitalism of Marx's day in which no single capitalist or small group of capitalists could dominate a market. Baran and Sweezy (1966) argue modern capitalism should be called "monopoly capitalism." **Monopoly capitalism** occurs when one or only a few capitalists control a particular industry or segment of the economy. For example, in 1900, Standard Oil Corporation controlled 90% of the oil production in the United States. **State capitalism** is exemplified by the United Kingdom, where major businesses or organizations in key industries are owned by the state, while private corporations operate in other industries and the state regulates and manages the economy.

Today, capitalism in the United States and many other countries can best be described as **corporate capitalism**—capitalism dominated by public corporations owned by many stockholders. Corporate capitalism has evolved over time and there are four common variants, all of which can be found in the world today. Most larger corporations today have become public corporations owned by many stockholders. These many owners of stock depend heavily on worker-managers to control the corporation. The result is **managerial capitalism**, in which managers, through both their day-to-day involvement in the corporation and their ownership of large blocks of stock as part of their compensation, often dominate the corporation.

Another, more recent variation is **institutional capitalism**, in which large shares of corporations are owned by institutional investors such as pension, insurance, or trust funds. This latter form has arisen because of the shift of much individual investing from buying shares in a business to investing in such managed funds controlled by large financial institutions.

Socialism

Socialist economies are economic systems in which the means of production are collectively owned and the economy is government regulated. Socialist economies place primary emphasis on collective goals, ensuring that everyone has sufficient resources to meet their needs and minimizing inequalities. Basic resources such as health care, food, and housing are regarded as entitlements of all people, not something available only if you can afford it. Socialist economies tend to be centralized, planned economies, with state ownership of most resources and private trade occurring only in an illegal black market. State socialism occurs when the government determines what will be produced, how it will be produced, and the means of distribution of goods and services through centralized economic planning.

Communism, as envisioned by Karl Marx, is an extreme form of a socialist economic and political system in which all members of the society are equal and workers control decision making over production and issues affecting their lives. Communist economies would be guided by the principle "From each according to his abilities, to each according to his needs" (Marx 1875). Marx saw socialism as an intermediate step on the road to pure communism. Although some governments today call themselves communist societies, none has achieved the classless society Marx envisioned as communism. Despite efforts to reduce inequality, communist countries during the Cold War era generally displayed considerably less material wealth than capitalist countries and still had both economic and political inequalities, with political elites having much greater access to material wealth and large, cumbersome, bureaucratic governments required to manage such tightly regulated economies.

Capitalism and Socialism in Mixed Economies

Marx argued that capitalism was a flawed economic system that would inevitably lead to its own destruction and its replacement by communism. Ironically, in the late 1980s and early 1990s, it was communist governments around the world that were toppling like dominoes, leading in most cases to more democratic governments and the introduction of capitalism into countries in Eastern Europe and the former Soviet Union, most of which had been almost exclusively socialist. For example, as early as 1991 when the former Soviet Union formally dissolved, many of the former Soviet countries adopted various market reforms. Within 10 years, 75% of businesses were either partially or completely privately owned, and economic inequality in Russia was greater than in the United States (World Bank 2002). Even staunch communist countries like Cuba and the People's Republic of China are moving toward more capitalist economies.

But no economy is purely either capitalist or socialist. This point is illustrated by the United States. Clearly the United States is much closer to the capitalist end of the continuum than to the socialist end. But it also has socialist elements, including government-sponsored entitlement programs, publicly owned institutions for education and health care, and government policies and tax incentives to support business. Entitlement programs in the United States include aid programs such as food stamps, unemployment compensation, and Social Security. In a purely capitalist society, all schools and hospitals would be private, yet most schools and colleges are publicly owned, and the state provides subsidies to private colleges through scholarships and loans to their students. While many hospitals and insurance companies are private, some hospitals, such as the extensive Veteran's Administration hospitals, are publicly owned, and the government provides extensive subsidies for health care through Medicare and Medicaid that are slated to become even more involved as a result of the Affordable Care Act passed in 2010. Even for-profit corporations benefit from a wide range of government subsidies, including tax incentives and special grants and contracts. One such program is the Small Business Innovative Research program that awards millions of dollars each year to encourage the creation of new jobs and the development of new technology. Perhaps the most extreme recent example of such "corporate welfare" was the Emergency Economic Stabilization Act of 2008 that bailed out very large banks and insurance companies with more than $700 billion in government loans.

While capitalism and socialism offer almost diametrically opposed world views, most countries have generally chosen to develop economies that reflect a balance of socialism and capitalism appropriate for their own culture and history.

Even staunch communist countries such as China are moving toward more capitalist economies.

© Jake Wyman/Corbis

CONCEPT LEARNING CHECK 14.7 Types of Capitalism

Indicate which of the following sentences are true or false.

_____ **1.** In state capitalism, all corporations are owned by the state.

_____ **2.** In institutional capitalism, all important social institutions, such as education, are owned by corporations.

_____ **3.** In managerial capitalism, managers exercise the greatest influence over the corporation.

_____ **4.** In state capitalism, the state itself is a corporation.

_____ **5.** In monopoly capitalism, one or a very few capitalists control a segment of the economy.

14.8 Theoretical Perspectives on Economy and Work

The three major theoretical perspectives in sociology can be applied to the economy and work and emphasize different issues.

■ Illustrate the functional, conflict, and symbolic interactionist perspectives as they apply to the economy and work.

Functionalists, conflict theorists, and symbolic interactionists view the economy with very different assumptions and emphasize different issues. The differences between conflict and functionalist perspectives are illustrated by their divergent views of, for example, multinational corporations in the global economy. Examining this same topic, the symbolic interactionist perspective explores other issues, including work and identity, alienation and job satisfaction, and renegotiating the work contract.

Functionalist Perspective

Functionalists view the economy as a key social institution performing the important function of providing for the production and distribution of needed goods and services. The needs of society are met when the various components of the economic system work smoothly to fulfill their functions. When the system does not work smoothly, the economy and the society suffer and efforts must be made to cure the economy much like one might try to cure a sick patient.

Today we truly have a global economy in the sense that large portions of the products we use are manufactured in other countries, and large percentages of the products and services we produce and provide are sold to people in other countries. Advances in communications and transportation technologies have made it possible for products to be designed in one country, built in another with raw materials and components from still other countries, and the resulting product is sold in many countries around the world. This globalization of the economy is one of the most significant changes of the late 20th century and has transformed economies both in the United States and throughout the world, literally changing the way everyone lives and works.

Functionalists emphasize the positive benefits of globalization and "free trade" policies that encourage globalization, such as the North American Free Trade Agreement (NAFTA), believing it leads to benefits for all with greater efficiency, lower prices, increased productivity, and higher employment. In this view, the global division of labor builds what Durkheim called organic solidarity in which (like organs in a body) we all depend on workers around the globe. We may drive a car built in Japan whose gas tank is filled with Saudi Arabian oil, use an iPhone built in China, and wear clothes manufactured in Thailand. We are all linked in a global economic web of mutual dependencies.

The effects of the global economy are best understood by considering the commercial organizations that do business throughout the world: multinationals. **Multinational corporations (transnational corporations)** are commercial organizations whose operations span international boundaries, typically both producing and selling goods and services in multiple countries. Multinationals include very large corporations that play major roles in the economies within countries and, increasingly, even in the world economy, companies like IBM, Ford, Toyota, and Microsoft. Of the world's 50 largest economies in 2007, six are multinational corporations. The 26th largest economy is Walmart with $408 billion, just below Norway's $414 billion and ahead of all but 25 countries. Other corporations among the top 50 economies are Royal Dutch Shell (35th at $285 billion), Exxon Mobil (36th at $284 billion), BP (British Petroleum), Toyota Motor Corporation, and Japan Post Holdings (*Fortune* 2010).

The functional perspective emphasizes the positive benefits of multinationals for both the developing countries and developed ones. Multinationals can be good for developing countries by bringing in jobs. They also facilitate the exchange of ideas and technology around the world, perhaps even moderating national disputes. It may be in the economic interests of large multinational corporations to encourage countries in which they operate to settle their political disputes peacefully.

Conflict Perspective

The conflict perspective emphasizes inherent conflicts between workers and management. This perspective argues that globalization benefits large corporations at the expense of workers. Today's multinationals are not just buying and trading all over the world, they are also producing all over the world. This permits multinationals to **export jobs to low-wage countries**—moving production from high-wage countries to low-wage countries, resulting in a net loss of jobs in high-wage countries and a net increase of jobs in low-wage countries. Sometimes the company sets up its own plants in low-wage countries. In other cases, it may **outsource** work—discontinue production and

---

Multinational corporations (transnational corporations) Commercial organizations whose operations span international boundaries, typically both producing and selling goods and services in multiple countries.

Export jobs to low-wage countries To move production from high-wage countries to low-wage countries, resulting in a net loss of jobs in high-wage countries and a net increase of jobs in low-wage countries.

Outsource To discontinue production and contract with another company to supply those goods or services.

contract with another company to supply those goods or services. This can reduce the corporation's accountability for the working conditions and wages paid for that work. With new information technologies, many corporations have found it cheaper to export jobs to Third World countries where labor is cheaper, sending data and information back and forth for processing. For example, insurance claims and other kinds of transaction processing are often handled in this manner (Burgess 1989). Many workers in other countries are paid only a fraction of what similar labor would cost in the United States. For example, before October of 2010, average wages at Foxconn Technology, the company in China that produces the iPad and iPhone, were about $180 a month (Finch 2010). A job that was paying $7.91 per hour in Paterson, New Jersey, in 1989 was moved to Mexico, where workers received $1.45 per hour for the same work (Bartlett and Steele 1992). In FIGURE 14-2, we see huge differences in hourly compensation costs between the United States and other countries in 2009.

In their rush to profit from cheap foreign labor, multinationals often contribute to conditions that lead to human rights abuses and exploitation of workers. Multinationals can use their economic clout to extract benefits from countries. If labor makes demands they do not like, the multinationals may threaten to move to another country. Countries trying to create a "favorable climate for investment" may develop repressive antilabor laws. As far back as 1993, Walmart was found to be selling clothes produced by workers as young as nine years old in Bangladesh sweatshops (US Department of Labor 2011). More recently, Foxconn Technology (the factory in China at which iPhones are made) was widely reported to have 12-hour shifts, suicide nets on buildings to cut down on suicides, employees injured in worksite accidents, and many workers as young as 16 (the legal age for working in China). Another study examined the impact of foreign investment on infant mortality rates in 63 developing nations. Countries with fewer foreign companies operating in them had better health care by this index. The study concludes that foreign investment leads to low-wage labor and poverty (Wimberley

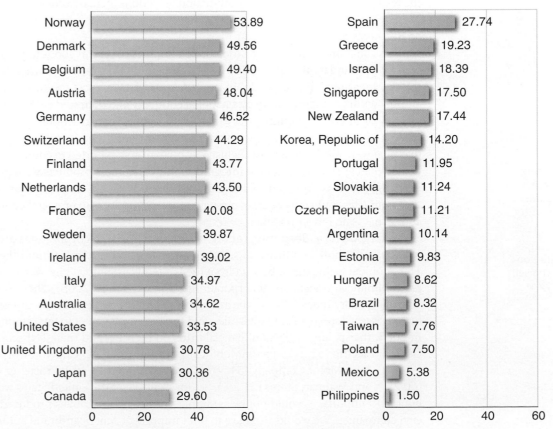

FIGURE 14-2 Hourly compensation costs by country in US dollars (2009).
Source: Bureau of Labor Statistics. 2011. International comparisons of hourly compensation costs in Manufacturing, 2009. News Release. Mar 8, 2011. Retrieved October 2011 (www.bls.gov/news.release/archives/ichcc_03082011.pdf).

1990). Conflict perspective theorists suggest that, on the whole, multinationals have a negative impact on workers in both industrialized and developing nations (Bluestone and Harrison 1982; Harrison and Bluestone 1988).

Multinationals, and the people running them, often play a role in the world economy that is largely independent of the country in which they are headquartered. In fact, the conflict perspective argues that these companies feel little loyalty to their nation of origin, preferring instead to focus on their own economic interests. This is reflected in remarks made by the chairman of Dow Chemical Company at a gathering hosted by President Richard Nixon at the White House:

> I have long dreamed of buying an island owned by no nation and of establishing the world headquarters of Dow Chemical Company on the truly neutral ground of such an island, beholden to no nation or society . . . rather than being governed by the laws of the United States. (Carl A. Gerstacker, Chairman, Dow Chemical Co. 1972)

According to the conflict perspective, multinationals can even threaten national sovereignty in both developing and developed countries. For example, in Canada, foreign corporations (most based in the United States) have controlled 60% of Canada's manufacturing, 75% of its petroleum and natural gas industry, and 60% of its mining and smelting for more than 30 years (Coleman and Cressey 1980). Perhaps the most extreme example occurred in Chile in 1970 when ITT (International Telephone and Telegraph) and the CIA conspired to overthrow the Marxist government of Salvador Allende in which President Allende was killed in a military coup.

The argument has been made that multinationals tend to increase economic inequality in developing countries. Studies of the impact of multinationals on developing countries suggest that initially, they increase the host country's wealth, but they also tend to increase economic inequality. Upper and middle classes benefit most by managing the local facilities and selling products and services to the multinationals. However, lower classes benefit much less. By opposing increases in minimum wage levels and favoring the restriction of union activities, multinationals' actions increase economic inequality.

Trade Restraints and Deep Integration

Nations sometimes attempt to restrict foreign imports of certain goods to protect their own workers and industries from low-wage competition from other countries. However, this is increasingly difficult to do. In the 1960s and 1970s, most products were made entirely within a single country by a national company and then sold either in the same country or in another country. For example, Caterpillar construction equipment was made in the United States and was sold all over the world. Similarly, Japanese cars at that time were produced almost exclusively in Japan and exported to countries like the United States. That was **shallow integration**, in which most products were produced in a single country and then sold in that country and abroad. Under shallow integration, countries could impose taxes on such imported products to protect their interests. Today that is no longer possible.

Today, we have **deep integration**, in which most large corporations are multinationals that both produce and sell their products and services around the world. This problem is illustrated by data from the United Nations 2008 list of the 100 largest nonfinancial transnational corporations (United Nations 2008). They compute a Transnationality Index (TNI) as the average of the following three ratios: foreign assets to total assets, foreign sales to total sales, and foreign employment to total employment. In 2008, the six largest US nonfinancial firms on their list and their TNI scores were General Electric (52.2%), ExxonMobil Corporation (67.9%), Chevron Corporation (58.1%), Ford Motor Company (54.3%), ConocoPhillips (43.4%), Procter & Gamble (60.2%), and Walmart Stores (31.2%). So, for example, if the United States wanted to limit auto imports, it would not be as simple as taxing automobiles produced by foreign companies. We would also have to limit imports of American-brand automobiles produced in other countries.

Shallow integration Occurs when most products were produced in a single country and then sold in that country and abroad.

Deep integration Most large corporations are multinationals that both produce and sell their products and services around the world.

Symbolic Interactionist Perspective

Symbolic interactionism emphasizes the ways in which people find or create meaning from their work and the social significance of work. As a result, this perspective emphasizes micro-level relationships between individuals and work. This approach is illustrated here by considering the social significance of work for a person's identity, why workers become satisfied or alienated by their work, and how workers use social interaction to construct meaning through renegotiating the work contract.

Work and Identity

Work is often the defining element of a person's life in modern industrial societies, heavily influencing both one's own self-esteem and one's status in the community. The importance of work is reflected in the fact that occupation is one of the three major indices of socioeconomic status (SES). In addition, occupation is often the master status for a person, the status that most clearly defines her or his identity. Work means more than just a steady income to people. Approximately 70% of US workers say they would continue working even if they did not have to do so (Kohut and Stefano 1989). More than 60% of million-dollar-plus lottery winners continued to work a year after winning the lottery (Kaplan 1985). Modern workers appear increasingly interested in achieving some form of self-fulfillment in work (Erikson and Vallas 1990).

Nowhere is the meaning of work more evident than among people unable to find work. Sociologist Thomas Cottle (1992) spent 15 years meeting with and interviewing men who experienced long-term unemployment, most of whom were in their late 40s and 50s and many of whom, during that time, came to realize that they would never work again. Initially, they vented their anger at the government and their former bosses. But somewhere around the first anniversary of losing their jobs, the men began to turn their anger inward, blaming themselves for their problems and seeing themselves as failed men, no longer worthy of a place in their own homes and looking forward only to death. As one man said it, "There's only two worlds: Either you work every day in a normal nine-to-five job with a couple weeks vacation, or you're dead! There's no in-between . . . Working is breathing . . . When you stop you die." Within a year, that former manager of a small tool company killed himself with a shotgun (Cottle 1992).

As an aside, some sociologists, such as George Ritzer (2005) argue that the significance of work for an individual's identity might be declining in societies like the United States, where people increasingly see themselves in terms of what they consume as well as what they produce.

Mass production has been criticized because it is boring, repetitive work that often leads to alienation from work.

© Photodisc/Thinkstock

Alienation and Job Satisfaction

Mass production has been criticized by many, including Karl Marx, because it is boring, repetitive work requiring little or no thought and often leads to alienation from work. **Alienation from work** is the breakdown of the natural connections people have with their work and with other people through their work. Alienation is typified by assembly-line work in which a worker performs a simple, repetitive task over and over for years at a time, having little control over the process and rigidly controlled by the pace of the line. To relieve the boredom, workers often find ways to vary activities to provide some meaning and "work the system" to avoid being given still more work and losing what freedom of activity they have (Roy 1954).

Alienation from work The breakdown of the natural connections people have with their work and with other people through their work.

Despite such evidence of alienation from work, surveys often find moderate to high levels of satisfaction with work. One national survey of job satisfaction found that 79% of US workers are generally satisfied with their jobs, while 28% are completely satisfied (Kohut and Stefano 1989). A classic and often-cited study (Work in America, Department of Health, Education and Welfare 1973) found the following factors to be associated with job satisfaction, ordered with the most important first:

1. High status, control, personal satisfaction, and prestige

2. Challenging jobs with autonomy and variety

3. Thoughtful, considerate, and consultative supervision

4. Peer interaction on the job

5. High wages

6. Clearly defined opportunities for advancement

7. Good work conditions

8. Employment security

Freeman and Rogers (1999) conducted a national telephone survey of 2,400 workers in the private sector in companies with 25 or more employees and followed up with in-depth interviews of 801 workers. The dominant finding of this study was that workers want to exert more influence in their work. Workers believe that if they had more influence, they would not only enjoy the job more but the company would be more productive and competitive. Workers see a need for cooperation between themselves and management, and, interestingly, 63% of workers prefer working in an organization run jointly by workers and management rather than one run by workers alone. Ultimately, job dissatisfaction can lead to low self-esteem for workers, low morale, sabotage in the workplace, high absenteeism, and high turnover, all of which reduce productivity.

Renegotiating the Work Contract

Many occupational groups are trying to renegotiate and redefine their occupational activities to make their work less demeaning and, as much as possible, more autonomous. Mary Romero, in her extensive study of Chicana domestic workers, describes how these workers attempt to renegotiate the work relation away from the preindustrial mistress–servant relation, even away from the industrial capitalist relation of worker–employer, toward a relation of customer–vendor. Romero identified several strategies these workers used, including negotiating which tasks they would perform, charging a flat rate rather than an hourly rate, and minimizing contact with employers. Charging a flat rate for cleaning a house rather than an hourly rate gives the domestic the opportunity to increase her profits if she is more efficient. But a flat rate requires clearly identifying which tasks will be performed to avoid being exploited. "I don't do windows," "that will cost you extra," and rotating different tasks on different days are all strategies used to handle employer requests for extra work for the same pay. To gain further control over their work and to avoid the stigma of servitude, domestics often prefer working for a family in which both spouses work outside the home and they can perform their chores unsupervised (Romero 1992).

CONCEPT LEARNING CHECK 14.8   Insights from Three Theoretical Perspectives

For each of the statements below, indicate whether it is true or false and, if true, which theoretical perspective led to that insight or finding.

_____ **1.** Multinationals bring jobs to developing countries.

_____ **2.** When asked, most workers would prefer to work in companies run by workers alone without management.

_____ **3.** Multinationals often export jobs from high-wage countries to low-wage countries.

_____ **4.** Workers often indicate they would like to exert more influence in their work.

_____ **5.** Work is often a defining element in a person's life.

_____ **6.** Hourly compensation costs in the United States in 2009 were the highest in the world.

14.9 Postindustrial US Economy and Work

Many key elements of the US economy and the nature of work have changed over the last 50 to 100 years as the United States has transformed into a postindustrial economy.

■ Describe the changes in economics and work demographics in the postindustrial era in the United States.

Transition from Agricultural Work to Factory Work to Service Work

The **occupational structure** in the United States—the number and types of jobs available—experienced major shifts during the 20th century (US Census Bureau 2011e). This is displayed in FIGURE 14-3. In 1900, the US economy was nearly equally distributed among the three economic sectors, with 38% of jobs in agriculture, 36% in manufacturing, and 26% in services. Today, the US economy is dominated by the services sector, with more than 90% of jobs in the services sector, only 5.5% in manufacturing, and less than 1% in agriculture. Most of the reduction in jobs in the agricultural sector occurred before 1950. In contrast, blue-collar manufacturing jobs remained nearly level until the mid-1970s but then began dropping precipitously. **Blue-collar jobs** are manual-labor occupations often having relatively low status, such as machinist, assembly-line worker, truck driver, or auto mechanic.

This transition in the nature of work reflected several important trends. The first half of the 20th century was dominated by the drop in agricultural employment as people left the farm and moved into the cities and take jobs in manufacturing. This was a period that saw rapid growth of **labor unions**—groups of workers who unite to negotiate as a group with corporations regarding issues such as wages, benefits, and working conditions. Labor unions are based on the recognition that, while both labor and management desire to keep the company competitive and to survive, there is an inherent conflict between them. Labor unions are found in all Western societies and are protected in the United States under the First Amendment right of freedom of association. Through collective organization, unions seek to reduce the power companies have over individual workers. Historically, labor unions have sought increased benefits for workers, such as higher wages, better working hours, increased job security, and improved safety.

Occupational structure In the United States, refers to the number and types of jobs available—experienced major shifts during the 20th century.

Blue-collar jobs Manual-labor occupations often having relatively low status, such as machinist, assembly-line worker, truck driver, or auto mechanic.

Labor unions Groups of workers who unite to engage in collective bargaining with corporations.

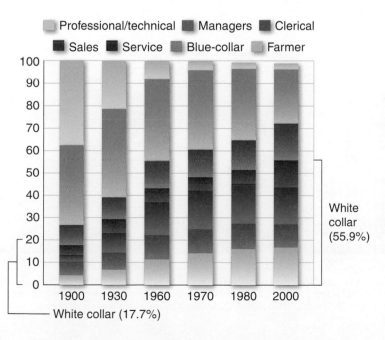

FIGURE 14-3 Changes in US occupational structure from 1900 to 2000.
Source: 1900 and 1930 data from Philip Hauser, "Labor Force" in Robert E. Faris (Ed.). 1964. HANDBOOK OF MODERN SOCIOLOGY. Chicago: Rand-McNally, p.183. 1960, 1970, and 1980 data from US Department of Commerce, Bureau of the Census. 1981. Projected data for 2000; Kutscher (1987). From The Social Organization of Work by Randy Hodson and Teresa Sullivan. Belmont, CA: Wadsworth.

Strikes Temporary work stoppages by a group of workers to seek changes in working conditions.

Work to rule The slowdown of work by meticulously following all regulations and doing only the minimum work legally required.

Lockout An action in which the company is locked up and workers are not permitted to work or draw pay until the conflict is resolved.

Unions and management often negotiate over specific conditions, and when they cannot resolve their conflicts, either unions or management may resort to some form of work stoppage or slowdown until their demands are met. Workers may resort to **strikes**—temporary work stoppages by a group of workers to seek changes in working conditions. When strikes are illegal or forbidden in existing contracts, workers may **work to rule**—slow down their work by meticulously following all regulations and doing only the minimum work legally required. Similarly, management may stop work by enforcing a **lockout** in which the company is locked up and workers are not permitted to work or draw pay until the conflict is resolved. Strikes were common in the United States up until the 1970s but dropped dramatically in the 1980s after President Ronald Reagan fired striking air traffic controllers, replacing them with new, nonunion workers. The number of strikes each year remains low today, as seen in FIGURE 14-4 (US Bureau of Labor Statistics 2011a).

Labor unions increased membership in the United States from 3% of the non-farm labor force in 1900 to 23% by 1945, peaking in the 1950s, with more than 33% of the nonfarm labor force (Chang and Sorrentino 1991). Since then, union membership has declined to 12.3% in 2009 (US Bureau of Labor Statistics 2010a; Unionstats 2011). Labor unions are not only losing members but have been forced to accept less favorable terms at the negotiation table in recent years—often including wage reductions and loss of benefits—to retain jobs. In contrast to the United States, 80% of workers in Scandinavian countries belong to unions, 50% in Europe, and 33% in Canada (Western 1993). The only areas in which union participation held steady or increased slightly in recent years in the United States were among state employees and service workers (US Bureau of Labor Statistics 2011b), as is shown in FIGURE 14-5. However, after the 2010 elections, many state governments attempted to handle ongoing budget crises by scaling back wages and benefits of unionized state workers. In some states, such as Wisconsin, controversial laws were passed limiting collective bargaining rights.

There are many reasons for the decline of labor unions in the United States. There was always strong management opposition to labor unions. In the 1930s, management sometimes hired people to beat up or kill labor organizers. In the 1980s, many union plants closed, laying off union workers, only to start up again with a new name as a nonunion shop, or the jobs were shipped overseas to countries with cheaper labor. The composition of the workforce has changed away from blue-collar workers and men (workers most receptive to unions) and toward women and faster-growing, white-collar and service occupations that are more resistant to unionization.

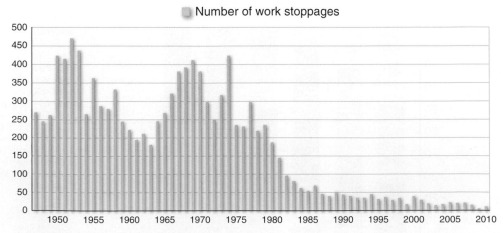

FIGURE 14-4 US work stoppages involving 1,000 or more workers (1947–2010).
Source: Data from Bureau of Labor Statistics. 2011. Work stoppages involving 1,000 or more workers, 1947–2010. Last revised Feb 8, 2011. Retrieved October 2011 (http://www.bls.gov/news.release/wkstp.t01.htm).

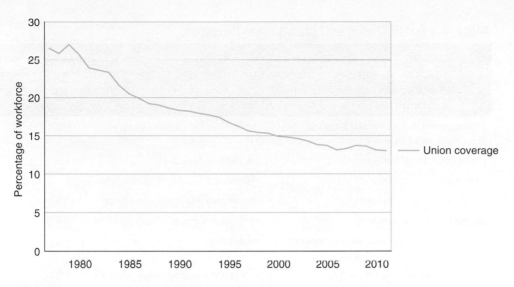

FIGURE 14-5 Labor union density (1973–2010).
Source: Data from Union Membership and Coverage Database from the CPS (Unionstats.com). 2011. Union density 1973–2010. Retrieved October 2011 (http://www.unionstats.com).

Technological change has often hurt the bargaining position of union workers or eliminated their jobs altogether. For example, skilled typesetters who were unionized have been replaced by computer operators who typically are not unionized.

The second half of the 20th century through the present is a period of rapid drop in manufacturing and blue-collar jobs and the rise of a services economy. **Deindustrialization** is the systematic withdrawal of private investment from manufacturing and the decline of industry through plant shutdowns, layoffs, and downsizing (Bluestone and Harrison 1982). **Downsizing** is reducing the size of companies to cut costs by laying off workers or even selling parts of the company. The US economy experienced a rapid and dramatic drop in "smokestack" industries such as steel. In the 10 years between 1979 and 1989, for example, the number of employees in steel mills declined from 570,500 to 274,300 (less than half). Many workers lost jobs or benefits as large companies like USX "downsized" from 100,000 employees in 1980 to fewer than 20,000 in 1987 (Ignatius 1988).

The number of professionals and technical workers almost quadrupled between 1900 and 2000 but is now more stable. This change is often attributed to increased technology, the greater role of new knowledge in our economy, and sufficient wealth that people can afford a wide array of professional services. Both clerical and managerial jobs increased during most of the century but were beginning to drop slowly by its end. Their early increases may have reflected the dawn of the information age and the increased need for people to manage and process information. Their more recent decrease may reflect the impact of the information age and early stages of employing computers to replace low-level clerical and managerial workers.

The changing occupational structure is reflected in the fastest-growing occupations, shown in **TABLE 14-6** (US Bureau of Labor Statistics 2010b:Table 2.3). The fastest-growing occupations are all in the services, including the health professions and computing. In contrast, the fastest-declining occupations are all in manufacturing.

Because many of these postindustrial jobs are based around information, they can often be performed from a distance through **telecommuting**, in which workers work from their homes and communicate with their workplace through communications technologies like Skype, including interactive voice, video, and data conferencing. More than 26 million American workers reported telecommuting at least part time in a 2006 survey (American Interactive Consumer Survey 2006).

Deindustrialization The systematic withdrawal of private investment from manufacturing and the decline of industry through plant shutdowns, layoffs, and downsizing.

Downsizing Reducing the size of companies to cut costs by laying off workers or even selling parts of the company.

Telecommuting Occurs when workers work from their homes and communicate with their workplace through communications technologies like Skype, including interactive voice, video, and data conferencing.

TABLE 14-6 Fastest Growing and Fastest Declining Occupations

Industry Description	Sector	Average Annual Rate of Change 2008–18
Fastest Growing		
Management, scientific, and technical consulting services	Professional and business services	6.2
Other educational services	Educational services	4.5
Individual and family services	Health care and social assistance	4
Home healthcare services	Health care and social assistance	3.9
Specialized design services	Professional and business services	3.8
Data processing, hosting, related services, and other information services	Information	3.8
Computer systems design and related services	Professional and business services	3.8
Lessors of nonfinancial intangible assets (except copyrighted works)	Financial activities	3
Offices of health practitioners	Health care and social assistance	3
Fastest Declining		
Cut and sew apparel manufacturing	Manufacturing	–8.1
Apparel knitting mills	Manufacturing	–7.1
Textile and fabric finishing and fabric coating mills	Manufacturing	–7.0
Fabric mills	Manufacturing	–6.1
Audio and video equipment manufacturing	Manufacturing	–6.0
Apparel accessories and other apparel manufacturing	Manufacturing	–6.0
Fiber, yarn, and thread mills	Manufacturing	–5.7
Textile furnishings mills	Manufacturing	–5.7
Railroad rolling stock manufacturing	Manufacturing	–4.7
Footwear manufacturing	Manufacturing	–4.5

Source: US Bureau of Labor Statistics. 2010. "Table 2.3, Industries with the fastest growing and most rapidly declining wage and salary employment." Retrieved October 2011 (http://www.bls.gov/emp/ep_table_203.htm).

THE SOCIOLOGICAL IMAGINATION | Globalization from Different Perspectives

The service sector spans a wide range of jobs, from high-salary professions to very low-wage fast-food clerks, maids, cab drivers, and so on. Robert Reich (1989) distinguishes two important categories of service workers. The top fifth of American workers with the highest incomes, says Reich, are **symbolic analysts**—people who manipulate information: data, words, and oral and visual symbols—including lawyers, management consultants, investment bankers, scientists, academics, and so on. Another large group of American workers are **routine personal service workers**—workers who perform repetitive tasks for providing a service. These workers, including fast-food clerks, cabdrivers, and so on, are paid low wages and compete with illegal aliens and displaced routine production workers from the declining manufacturing sector. Reich argues that the global economy contributes to inequality in the United States by boosting the income of symbolic analysts and reducing the incomes of the other four-fifths of American workers through global competition.

Remember that the sociological imagination encourages us to see our individual biographies in the context of the broader social problems of the times in which we are living. Use your sociological imagination to consider how the lives of individuals reflect these broad social divisions.

EVALUATE

1. Imagine that you are a routine personal service worker—say a clerk at a fast-food restaurant. How do you think your own life would be affected by globalization? How do you think you would feel about immigration? How optimistic would you be about things getting better for you and your children in the future?

2. Now imagine you are a symbolic analyst—a professional in a high-technology company with extensive sales all around the globe. How would you feel about restricting international trade? How would you feel about immigration? How optimistic would you be about things getting better for you and your children in the future?

Dual Labor Market and Workforce Diversity

The United States and most other industrial capitalist economies have a **dual labor market** in which there is a relatively advantaged primary form of employment and a relatively disadvantaged secondary form of employment. Workers in the **primary labor market** enjoy relatively good working conditions, reasonably high pay, opportunity for advancement, and—most important—job security. Primary labor market workers include physicians, lawyers, accountants, teachers, civil service workers, and unionized blue-collar jobs. Workers in the **secondary labor market** have none of these things. They routinely experience high turnover, low job security, few or no benefits, low wages, and little opportunity for advancement. The secondary labor market includes cashiers at fast-food restaurants, migrant workers, many construction workers, and "temps"—temporary workers hired only for short periods of time.

Workers in the secondary labor market are often women or members of minority populations who are less likely to be organized for collective bargaining (Jenkins 1986). One consequence of women and minorities being more likely to be in the secondary labor market is that their average incomes tend to be lower than those of white males. This can be seen in TABLE 14-7, in which the average incomes are displayed for men and women, whites, blacks, and Asians.

In addition to more often finding themselves in the secondary labor market, women for many years participated in the labor market much less than men. As late as 1950, only 34% of women aged 16 and older participated in the labor market, compared to 86% of men. But by 2015, those numbers are projected to rise to 62% for women and drop to 72% for men (Fullerton 1999). These labor force participation rates for men and women are found in FIGURE 14-6.

Many corporations in the United States rely on the secondary labor market much more than they once did. This represents a significant change in the labor contract, as many companies no longer offer the benefits and job security of permanent jobs. Highly skilled technical and managerial employees who were victims of downsizing are sometimes hired back by their same companies as temporary workers at a lower wage and with few or no benefits. Others become self-employed consultants, hiring themselves out temporarily at a range of jobs or even starting their own small businesses. Mayor Michael Bloomberg of New York, for example, started his very successful business because he was fired and could not get anyone else to hire him.

Symbolic analysts People who manipulate information: data, words, and oral and visual symbols.

Routine personal service workers Workers who perform repetitive tasks for providing a service.

Dual labor market One in which there is a relatively advantaged primary form of employment and a relatively disadvantaged secondary form of employment.

Primary labor market Enjoys relatively good working conditions, reasonably high pay, opportunity for advancement, and—most important—job security.

Secondary labor market Employees routinely experience high turnover, low job security, few or no benefits, low wages, and little opportunity for advancement.

TABLE 14-7 Median Usual Weekly Earnings of Full-Time Wage and Salary Workers in the United States, by Sex, Race, and Ethnicity (2007)

	Women	Men
Total	$614	$766
White	$626	$788
Black or African American	$533	$600
Asian	$731	$936
Hispanic or Latino	$473	$520

Source: Bureau of Labor Statistics. 2008. Earnings of women and men by race and ethnicity, 2007. Retrieved October 2011 (http://www.bls.gov/opub/ted/2008/oct/wk4/art04.htm).

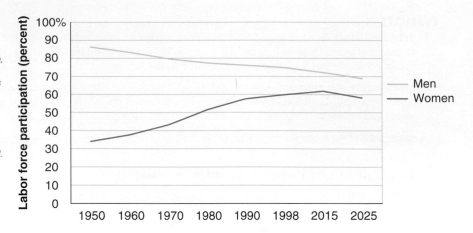

FIGURE 14-6 US labor force participation by gender, 75 years. *Source: Data from Fullerton, Howard N. 1999. Labor force participation: 75 years of change, 1950–98 and 1998–2025. Monthly Labor Review. Table 1. Bureau of Labor Statistics. Retrieved October 2011 (http://www.bls.gov/mlr/1999/12/art1full.pdf).*

Profession A high-status occupation based on abstract knowledge, enjoying considerable autonomy and authority and, in turn, serving the public good and regulating its members.

Professionalization A process of defining a type of work as a profession.

Professions

A **profession** is a high-status occupation based on abstract knowledge, enjoying considerable autonomy and authority and, in turn, serving the public good and regulating its members (Friedson 1970). Key features of professions include the following:

1. **Abstract knowledge**—Work is based on abstract, theoretical knowledge rather than just training, and members learn through education by other members of the profession.

2. **Autonomy**—Members enjoy considerable autonomy because their knowledge makes them more qualified to exercise judgment in their field than others.

3. **Self-regulation**—They regulate themselves with a code of ethics, and other members of the profession determine whether someone should be permitted to practice in the profession.

4. **Authority**—They have authority that is recognized by other subordinate occupations.

5. **Altruism**—They are expected to use their position of favor for the public good.

Because of the advantages of professions, many occupational groups attempt to renegotiate and redefine their occupational activities through **professionalization**—the process of defining a type of work as a profession (Goode 1960; Parsons 1954). Established professions include engineers, doctors, nurses, lawyers, accountants, and scientists. Many additional occupational groups have sought to become professions over the years, with varying degrees of success. Robert Habenstein (1954), for example, examined the process of professionalization for funeral parlor operators.

George Bernard Shaw famously said "A profession is a conspiracy against the layman." Like all good humor, there is an element of truth to Shaw's tongue-in-cheek characterization of professions. They are indeed a conspiracy against the layman in the sense that by becoming defined as professionals, members of professions gain more autonomy and control over their work and experience greater power over their clients. On the other hand, professions can also serve the interests of their clients because professionalism imposes a set of standards and discipline on the occupation designed to upgrade services and "weed out" incompetent practitioners. As we move further into the information age and as increasingly specialized bodies of knowledge play ever greater roles in our everyday lives, we should expect the number and scope of professions to continue to increase. For example, the website of Healthcare Providers Service Association (2011) lists more than 120 health professions for which it provides professional liability insurance.

The Rationalization of Work for Both Management and the Managed

One of the most important distinctions among occupations is that between managers and workers who are managed. According to the US Bureau of Labor Statistics (2011c:Table 9), in 2010, 11% of all US workers were classified as managers (15 million people). Historically, men have been more likely to be managers than women. In 2010, 62% of managers were men aged 20 and over, and 38% were women aged 20 and over. Only 9% of all women aged 20 and over were managers, compared to 13% of all men aged 20 and over.

The nature of work for both managers and workers who are managed has changed dramatically since 1900 as a result of pervasive rationalization of work. **Rationalization** is a process in which traditional methods and standards of social organization based on tradition, belief, and even magic are replaced with new methods and standards of social organization based on objectively calculable scientific criteria. In the area of work and the economy, rationalization includes the processes of scientific management, bureaucratization, and mechanization.

At the beginning of the 20th century, Frederick Taylor, an industrial engineer, created a process of scientific management to make work more efficient and economical. **Scientific management (Taylorism)** applies scientific and engineering principles to human labor by breaking a complex task into simple components and using time-and-motion studies to specify every detail of the job to maximize efficiency. Scientific management reduced extra steps to perform a task and made assembly lines more efficient. Incentive payment systems to workers (e.g., "piece-rates" or paying a fixed amount for each piece produced) were often used to further increase worker efficiency and effort (Watson 1995:44).

Classic examples of scientific management are mass production and the assembly line. **Mass production** is a process of production in which products are standardized, parts are interchangeable, precision tools fit parts together precisely, and the production is mechanized to produce a continuous high volume. An **assembly line** is a mode of production in which a complex task is broken into individual tasks, with each worker performing only one or a few of the tasks repeatedly. In one of the first examples of mass production, Henry Ford revolutionized the production of automobiles by (1) redesigning the car to be built from standardized parts, (2) developing an extensive division of labor in which the task of building an automobile was broken into simple steps, such as attaching a bumper or screwing in spark plugs, with each step performed by a different worker, and (3) putting the car together on an assembly line. This revolutionized the production of automobiles, resulting in a five-fold increase in productivity (Chandler 1964), creating thousands of jobs, and lowering costs enough to make cars affordable for large numbers of people. This assembly method of production today dominates many industries, including fast-food restaurants, in which automation and frequently conveyor belts produce food in standard fashion (Ritzer 1994, 1995).

Henry Ford made one additional innovation that was so important that his approach is sometimes called "Fordism" to distinguish it from other examples of scientific management. Ford recognized that if he was to have a good market for his automobiles, enough people had to earn enough money to make it possible to afford them. So he paid his assembly-line workers $5 a day, which was an incredibly good wage in those days, raising the standard of living for his workers to the point at which they could afford to purchase the automobiles they were producing.

The assembly line is but one example of the way technology is transforming work, changing the skills required of workers, the nature of work, and even how workers are controlled. **Technology** consists of the knowledge, tools, and machines used to produce artifacts or manipulate the environment. In industrial economies, technology often replaced the muscle power of people through the creation of more powerful machines such as steam engines. It also replaced the skilled craftsman with someone much less skilled. In today's information economy, the effects of technology are somewhat different.

Rationalization A process in which traditional methods and standards of social organization based on tradition, belief, and even magic are replaced with new methods and standards of social organization based on objectively calculable scientific criteria.

Scientific management (Taylorism) Applies scientific and engineering principles to human labor by breaking a complex task into simple components and using time-and-motion studies to specify every detail of the job to maximize efficiency.

Mass production A process of production in which products are standardized, parts are interchangeable, precision tools fit parts together precisely, and the production is mechanized to produce a continuous high volume.

Assembly line A mode of production in which a complex task is broken into individual tasks, with each worker performing only one or a few of the tasks repeatedly.

Technology Consists of the knowledge, tools, and machines used to produce artifacts or manipulate the environment.

Deskilling A reduction in expertise, training, and experience required to perform a job.

Bureaucracy The primary design principle of modern formal organizations, based on a hierarchical structure of authority, codified rules and regulations, and principles of fairness and efficiency.

Entrepreneur Someone who takes an innovative idea and, through financing and business savvy, turns it into a viable business.

Private equity Investors contribute funds in exchange for a share of ownership or equity in a company.

Zuboff (1982) identifies several ways in which computers are transforming work, including **deskilling**, a reduction in expertise, training, and experience required to perform a job. Computers make it possible for the same tasks to be performed by people having fewer skills because they can rely upon the computer to provide the necessary expertise. For example, American Express has an expert system computer program that makes decisions about whether to approve credit card transactions—a task once performed by many white-collar employees and requiring many managers.

In 19th-century capitalism, capitalists exerted extensive personal control over workers, hiring and firing them on the spot, exhorting, bullying, threatening, and rewarding them. Abuse and even violence were not uncommon in many work situations. In the 20th century, more impersonal and bureaucratic controls became common. These more subtle controls may make the conflict between workers and management less obvious and less personal, and may be one reason capitalism has not led to the workers' revolution Marx predicted (Edwards 1979).

Bureaucratization has affected the role of managers in much the same way that scientific management affected the role of workers (Hage and Powers 1992; Watson 1995). A **bureaucracy** is the primary design principle of modern formal organizations, based on a hierarchical structure of authority, codified rules and regulations, and principles of fairness and efficiency. The same principles that ensure decisions will be made objectively and fairly, according to recognized rules and procedures to the extent they are followed, tie the hands of managers, regulating their behavior in a manner similar to the detailed work plan created by time-and-motion experts for assembly-line workers. The more explicit the regulations and the more rigidly they are followed, the less the discretion of the manager and the fewer skills required.

While scientific management and mass production often produced gains in productivity and profitability, they also increased alienation from work and led to unemployment and deskilling. Deskilled workers are more easily replaced and hence have less power relative to management and are likely to have lower wages (Braverman 1974). As Nobel Prize–winning economist Wassily Leontief explains, we are not making a single individual more productive with machines any more than we are making horses that used to pull wagons more productive by the development of the automobile. They have simply been replaced (Leontief 1982). In short, all too often, another phrase for "gains in productivity" is "job loss."

Entrepreneurship, Self-Employment, and Venture Capitalism

An **entrepreneur** is someone who takes an innovative idea and, through financing and business savvy, turns it into a viable business. The term is often used in conjunction with starting a new business (startup companies) but can also be encouraged within existing organizations (intrapreneurship). Entrepreneurial activities range from modest to grand. Many entrepreneurs begin with self-employment and may have started only because they became unemployed. Others start even smaller, perhaps working at the entrepreneurial enterprise only part time while they keep their "day job." Steve Jobs and Steve Wozniak began Apple Computer in their spare time while continuing to work at Hewlett Packard. Their spectacular—and unusual—success led to the creation of a company employing thousands and whose products and services have changed our culture.

Participating in some type of entrepreneurial activity is fairly common. According to Paul Reynolds, creator of the Global Entrepreneurship Monitor, a project that tracks entrepreneurial activity, half of all working men in the United States have had a period of self-employment for one or more years by the time they retire (Reynolds 2007).

Financing is usually crucial for startup companies because they are often high risk and not well established enough to secure a bank loan or sell stock to the public. Entrepreneurial activity is often financed by some form of **private equity** in which investors contribute funds in exchange for a share of ownership or equity in a company. For smaller startups involving one or two individuals, initial funding may come in the form

Steve Jobs and Steve Wozniak began Apple Computer in their spare time while continuing their day jobs at Hewlett Packard.

© Featureflash/Shutterstock, Inc.

of "financial bootstrapping" or "sweat equity" in which the company's initial activities are used to generate funds to cover expenses or to reinvest profits in the new business to finance growth. For projects with a high estimated value, the funds needed are usually much larger, so initial funding may be sought from "**angel investors**"—affluent individuals who provide initial capital for a business startups, usually in return for a share of ownership. Later, a promising startup may seek additional funding from **venture capital** funds—companies in business to loan money to high-risk, high-potential, early-stage startup companies. However, here—as elsewhere—women are often at a disadvantage. According to Astia, a nonprofit organization dedicated to helping women form startup companies, women create only 8% of the venture-backed tech startups (Miller 2010).

One alternative source of funding that women might find more hospitable is **crowdfunding**—a process in which entrepreneurs post their idea and proposal on a website asking for people to contribute small amounts either to purchase a product in advance or to gain equity in the business (Cunningham 2012).

It is often claimed that new startups and small businesses account for a large proportion of new jobs in our economy. This is supported by data from the fourth quarter of 2010 that indicate that small firms with from 1 to 4 employees created 937,000 new jobs that quarter and accounted for 16.4% of gross job gains—more than the 15% of gross job gains produced by firms of 100 employees or more. Unfortunately, many small firms go out of business each year as well. That same quarter, small firms lost 893,000 jobs, accounting for 17% of gross job losses (US Bureau of Labor Statistics 2010c:Tables A and B). So, while startups and small businesses create jobs, those jobs may be less secure than positions at large corporations.

Unemployment and Underemployment

The **unemployment rate** in the United States is measured by the percentage of unemployed workers in the labor force who are actively seeking jobs based on a monthly survey of 60,000 households carried out by the US Bureau of Labor Statistics (2012). The unemployment rate in the United States has often been around 4 or 5%, but in 2010, it was 9.6% as the country struggled out of the Great Recession (US Census Bureau 2011c). Official statistics, though, are not perfect. They do not include "discouraged" workers who would like to work but have given up trying to get a job, those who have never worked, or those who are unable to work. Nor do these statistics include people who are **underemployed**—people working full time at a much lower salary than they used to make or people working part-time jobs or self-employed and working less than desired because they cannot get a full-time job.

Social scientists distinguish three kinds of unemployment: seasonal, cyclical, and structural. **Seasonal unemployment** is unemployment due to seasonal variations such as school teachers on summer vacation or jobs hampered by bad weather. **Cyclical unemployment** is unemployment resulting from lower production rates during recessions. **Structural unemployment** is unemployment that results when the skill set of unemployed workers does not match the skills required for available jobs or when the unemployed are in a different location than available jobs (McEachern 2000). Structural unemployment often arises from structural changes in the economy in which some jobs are replaced by automation or are moved overseas to low-wage countries. The rapid deindustrialization experienced in the last few decades in the United States has resulted in millions of workers losing jobs and having to either be retrained or, more likely, settle for lower-paying, less-skilled jobs than the ones they lost.

Underground and Informal Economies

Every society, whether capitalist or socialist, permits some forms of economic exchange and prohibits others. In some former communist countries, many forms of economic exchange between individuals were illegal, such as the buying and selling of foreign currency. In those countries, when such exchange occurred, it did so on what is called the "black market." In capitalist countries like the United States, a wider range of economic

Angel investors Affluent individuals who provide initial capital for a business startup, usually in return for a share of ownership.

Venture capital Companies in business to loan money to high-risk, high-potential, early-stage growth startup companies.

Crowdfunding A process in which entrepreneurs post their idea and proposal on a website asking for people to contribute small amounts either to purchase a product in advance or to gain equity in the business.

Unemployment rate In the United States, it is measured by the percentage of unemployed workers in the labor force actively seeking jobs.

Underemployed People working at part-time jobs or self-employed and working less than desired because they cannot get a full-time job.

Seasonal unemployment Unemployment due to seasonal variations, such as school teachers on summer vacation, or variations in weather, which often affect agriculture, construction, and tourism jobs.

Cyclical unemployment Unemployment resulting from lower production rates during recessions.

Structural unemployment Unemployment that results when the skill set of unemployed workers does not match the skills required for available jobs or when the unemployed are in a different location than available jobs

transactions are usually permitted, but there are strict laws requiring reports of those economic activities for purposes of computing taxes. In addition, some transactions, such as extortion, money laundering, the sale of illegal drugs, prostitution, illegal gambling, theft, and other criminal activities, are illegal. We often use the term the **underground economy** to indicate *all* economic transactions involving income that is not reported to the government as required by law. While most people do not engage in illegal activities, most do participate in the underground economy fairly regularly in a small (or not so small) way. For example, waiters, waitresses, hotel clerks, and other service workers routinely understate their income from tips. Self-employed people, such as carpenters, lawn workers, plumbers, and even physicians, who provide services or products to individuals, may not report all of their income when it was received in cash. By one estimate, there is as much as $170 billion in taxes lost each year on unreported income in the United States (Speer 1995). Individuals and households often engage in the "**informal economy**"—unpaid labor such as doing housework, repairing one's own car, or performing voluntary charity work. Friends sometimes trade or barter to exchange services with one another without exchanging money, such as a neighbor who helps you repair your brick patio after you helped him paint his house.

Corporations and the Economy

Modern capitalism has been increasingly influenced by corporations. In 2007, there were more than 6 million business firms in the United States employing one or more workers (US Census Bureau 2011f). A few large corporations account for the majority of corporate assets, with the largest 200 corporations controlling more than half of all manufacturing assets. Corporations thus tend to concentrate wealth.

In the United States, a **corporation** is a company that is incorporated, that is, a legal entity separate from its owners. For most intents and purposes, a corporation is treated as a person, with many of the same individual rights. A corporation can enter into contracts, buy and sell property, and sue and be sued. A corporation shields its owners from certain risks and liabilities. For example, even though a corporation might go broke and lose all of its assets, the people who own stock in the corporation would only lose the value of that stock. Any other assets of those individuals would remain untouched. In the United States, the political power of corporations increased enormously when, in 2010, the US Supreme Court ruled in *Citizens United v. Federal Election Commission* that, because corporations are "persons," the government could not restrict political expenditures by corporations so long as they do not contribute directly to a political candidate or party and they identify sponsors of advertisements.

There is one important way in which corporations are different from individuals, however. While individuals usually balance their own self-interest with some sense of social responsibility, corporations, by law, are required to maximize profits for their shareholders. As Milton Friedman put it (Friedman 1970), "There is one and only one social responsibility of business—to use its resources and engage in activities designed to increase its profits so long as it stays within the rules of the game . . ." This desire to maximize profits can lead to corporations bending or breaking rules to achieve competitive advantage. For example, Microsoft has maintained its dominant market share in computer operating systems over decades by continually changing its standards in software upgrades, forcing most computer users to continually upgrade their computers' software (Markoff 2007). Other companies, such as BP, cut corners on environmental regulations to maximize their profits, sometimes resulting in major environmental catastrophes such as the BP Deepwater Horizon drilling rig explosion (National Commission on the BP Deepwater Horizon Oil Spill and Offshore Drilling 2011).

Capitalism is based on free competition. That competition is limited when a single firm dominates an industry—a **monopoly**—or when a few firms dominate an industry—an **oligopoly**. To preserve competition and to make sure that capitalism leads to efficient and fair production, US law prohibits any one firm obtaining a monopoly. However, many industries are dominated by an oligopoly of only a few firms. When oligopolies are present, those few firms often cooperate in setting prices—known as

---

Underground economy All economic transactions involving income that is not reported to the government as required by law.

Informal economy Unpaid labor such as doing housework, repairing one's own car, or performing voluntary charity work.

Corporation A legal entity separate from its owners.

Monopoly Occurs when a single firm dominates an industry.

Oligopoly Occurs when a few firms dominate an industry.

price fixing—rather than competing. This is why most service stations in a given area tend to charge the same price for gasoline. Corporations often enhance their dominance over an industry through mergers and acquisitions, such as when German automaker Daimler-Benz purchased Chrysler for $38 billion. Independent competition is further reduced when there are extensive linkages among corporations through stock ownership or seats on boards of directors. For example, more than 30% of the stock in the largest 200 US corporations is owned by the largest 200 US financial firms. Corporations also often have interlocking boards of directors, permitting a few individuals to exercise influence over many different corporations.

Taken together, the wealth concentrated in corporations, their legal protections, and their ability to influence the governments that regulate them mean that corporations play a very powerful role in modern capitalist economies.

CONCEPT LEARNING CHECK 14.9   Issues in the Postindustrial Economy

For each of the following statements, identify the concept that best characterizes it.

_____ **1.** Imagine how much more expensive and time consuming it would be to make an automobile if every screw, every bolt, indeed every part of the car had to be individually crafted for that specific car. This was once the case, but this process changed all that.

_____ **2.** Alexi is a hotel maid.

_____ **3.** Kara is a software developer who works four days a week from her home and drives the 120 miles to work one day a week for meetings. The software she develops is on a server several thousand miles away and is accessed daily by people from all over the world.

_____ **4.** The retail industry routinely hires tens of thousands of additional sales workers during the holiday season; then, most of them are laid off once the season is over.

A. Routine personal service worker

B. Telecommuting

C. Mass production

D. Seasonal unemployment

Visual Summary Politics and Economy in Global Perspective

14.1 Political Systems, Power, and Authority

- Political sociology focuses on how politics is influenced by other social institutions, such as the media, economy, religion, and education.

- Types of authority include traditional authority (based on custom), rational-legal authority (based on written rules and regulations), and charismatic authority (based on the exceptional appeal of an individual.

14.2 Governments around the Globe

- Common types of government include monarchy (rule by a family), democracy (government by the people), authoritarianism (rule by a strong leader), and totalitarianism (government that completely controls all aspects of people's lives).

- Transfer of political power can occur by individuals voting in elections, through nonviolent resistance leading to regime change, through an abrupt and often violent coup d'état, or through the longer-lasting and more violent overthrow of a political revolution.

14.3 The US Political System

- The US political system is based on fundamental democratic principles recognizing human rights, and political decisions are made through voting.

- Voting dominates the US two-party system, in which winner-take-all elections determine who has power.

- The US political process focuses on elections, with campaigns using opinion polls to identify wedge issues favoring their candidates and getting out the vote by voters more likely to support them.

- US politics is also heavily influenced by lobbyists supporting special-interest groups and campaign donations directly to candidates or to "independent" political action committees able to spend unlimited funds exercising their free speech about issues in ways that favor their preferred candidate.

- In contrast to the United States, most other democracies are parliamentary systems, with representation based on the proportion of votes won by a party, permitting multiple parties and coalitions to gain power.

14.4 Theoretical Perspectives on Power and Political Systems

- The pluralist perspective argues that many interest groups compete to influence policy.

- The elite perspectives argue that a relatively few people form a ruling elite to dominate political life.

Visual Summary Politics and Economy in Global Perspective, continued

14.5 War and Peace

- Efforts by countries to protect their citizens through warfare have become more complex as conventional warfare gives way to asymmetric warfare, terrorism, and new technology-based forms of warfare.

- While men still make up most of US military personnel, women make up a larger proportion than before, blacks are over-represented relative to civilian populations, and Hispanics mirror civilian populations. Gay and lesbian people are now allowed to serve openly, and people at the very high or very low levels of socioeconomic status are less likely to serve than those in the middle.

- Efforts to maintain peace are divided between deterrence, which seeks to prevent war through strength, and diplomacy and the resolution of differences.

14.6 Economy and Economic Systems in Transition

- Economies produce goods and distribute services. Over hundreds of years, economies have evolved from early hunting and gathering economies in which everyone struggled to obtain food to agricultural economies in which the production of food became efficient to industrial economies in which much economic activity focused on producing things to postindustrial information economies focused on producing and sharing information.

- Today's economies mirror the evolution of societies in the three major economic sectors of agriculture, manufacturing, and services.

14.7 Global Economic Systems

- Major types of economies include socialism, in which the means of production are collectively owned and the economy is government regulated, and capitalism, in which there is private ownership of wealth, competition, people are driven by the profit motive, and there is noninterference by the government. Most economies are a mixture of both.

- Capitalism has evolved and includes variants such as competitive capitalism, in which no individual or small group dominates a market; monopoly capitalism, in which one or a few capitalists control an industry; and state capitalism, in which key industries are owned by the state while others are private. Other variants include corporate capitalism dominated by public corporations; managerial capitalism, in which managers control corporations and own much of the stock; and institutional capitalism, in which most stock in corporations is owned by investment funds.

14.8 Theoretical Perspectives on Economy and Work

- Multinational corporations, which produce and sell goods and services in multiple countries, illustrate the difference between the functional perspective, which emphasizes the positive benefits of multinationals, such as bringing jobs to developing countries, and the conflict perspective, which emphasizes negative consequences of multinationals, such as the loss of jobs from high-wage countries, poor working conditions, and worker exploitation.

- Resisting globalization through import restrictions becomes more difficult as products have evolved from shallow integration, in which products were mostly made in a single country, to deep integration, in which each product may be produced from components manufactured in several different countries.

- The symbolic interactionist perspective emphasizes how people find or create meaning from their work, including the importance of work for a person's identity and alienation from or satisfaction with work.

- Domestic workers sometimes try to negotiate expectations for their work to achieve higher occupational status to make their work less demeaning and more autonomous through strategies such as charging a flat rate, minimizing direct contact with employers, and negotiating which tasks they will perform.

14.9 Postindustrial US Economy and Work

- The occupational structure in the United States has changed dramatically, with deindustrialization as investment is withdrawn from manufacturing, often followed by downsizing to reduce the workforce.

- There have been large reductions in blue-collar, manual-labor jobs along with a decline in labor unions and tactics used by unions in negotiations with management such as strikes and work to rule.

- A dual labor market characterizes the US economy, with a primary labor market of good jobs with high wages and job security and a secondary labor market of low-paying, insecure jobs, with minorities and women more often found in the secondary labor market.

- Professions are high-status occupations based on abstract knowledge, enjoying considerable autonomy over their work, self-regulation, and authority over subordinate occupations; and they are expected to earn those benefits by being altruistic in their practice of their profession to serve the public.

- New businesses are often created by entrepreneurs who take an innovative idea and obtain financing through private equity investments in which investors contribute money in exchange for partial ownership of the company.

- Unemployment is measured in the United States by the percentage of unemployed workers in the labor force who are actively seeking jobs and includes seasonal unemployment, cyclical unemployment, and structural unemployment.

- In addition to the unemployed, there are those workers who have given up and are no longer actively seeking a job, as well as underemployed people who are working at jobs with less pay and/or fewer hours than they would like.

- In addition to the formal economy, there is also an underground economy in which income is not reported as required by law (such as waitresses who do not report their tips) and an informal economy in which people exchange labor without payment, such as a neighbor who helps you paint your house and you help her build a patio.

- In the United States, people can form corporations that are legal entities separate from their owners. Such corporations are legally required to maximize profits for their shareholders and are sometimes accused of acting in ways that harm the public good.

- Corporations sometimes dominate an industry individually (a monopoly) or with a few other firms (an oligopoly).

14.1 Political Systems, Power, and Authority

1. What is the most likely and most important source of authority for a US congressman from California?
  A. Historical precedent
  B. The US Constitution
  C. Charisma
  D. Coercion

14.2 Governments around the Globe

2. What form of government may be either democratic or authoritarian?
  A. Parliamentary system
  B. Military junta
  C. Monarchy
  D. A republic

3. Which type of government is more likely to determine succession from one leader to the next through elections?
  A. Parliamentary system
  B. Military junta
  C. Absolute monarchy
  D. Nation-state

14.3 The US Political System

4. Which of the following is an example of a PAC?
  A. A Little League baseball team
  B. The Association of Swine Producers
  C. The Democratic Party
  D. Apple Inc.

5. Which of the following percentages is closest to the percentage of registered voters who voted for members of Congress in the 2010 US election?
  A. 93%
  B. 85%
  C. 65%
  D. 40%

14.4 Theoretical Perspectives on Power and Political Systems

6. Which of these people is most associated with the power elite view?
  A. Robert Dahl
  B. David Riesman
  C. C. Wright Mills
  D. Nelson Polsby

14.5 War and Peace

7. Which category of people was the last to be permitted to serve in the military?
  A. Hispanics
  B. Women
  C. Blacks
  D. Homosexuals

8. An armed conflict in which one side relies mostly on snipers and roadside bombs to inflict damage on the enemy while the other side calls in drone strikes and bomb-resistant vehicles is best described as:
  A. an asymmetric war.
  B. terrorism.
  C. cyberwarfare.
  D. the Industrial Revolution.

9. Which strategy or strategies has the United States *not* pursued to preserve the peace?
  A. MAD (mutually assured destruction)
  B. The Nuclear Nonproliferation Pact
  C. Development of high-technology weapons
  D. A policy of paying ransom for kidnap victims of terrorists

14.6 Economy and Economic Systems in Transition

10. Currently, the US economy can best be described as a(n):
    A. agricultural economy.
    B. underground economy.
    C. industrial economy.
    D. service economy.

14.7 Global Economic Systems

11. Which of the following is a way in which the US economy is partially socialist?
    A. Any US citizen can start a small business and engage in activities designed to make profits as long as the specific activities do not violate laws.
    B. Individual companies make their own decisions about products and services to offer.
    C. The federal government, through agencies such as the Federal Reserve, sometimes rescues private financial institutions at risk of failing.
    D. The Congressional Office for Central Planning assigns yearly production quotas to companies engaged in interstate commerce, telling them what and how much they should produce.

12. Which of the following is *not* a characteristic of socialist economies?
    A. Planned economy
    B. Decentralized economy
    C. Public ownership of means of production
    D. Collective goals

14.8 Theoretical Perspectives on Economy and Work

13. Which of the following correctly describes shallow or deep integration?
    A. Shallow integration occurs when products are produced by different manufacturers and then combined into a more complex product.
    B. Deep integration occurs when workers are highly trained and experienced in producing the product.
    C. Shallow integration occurs in inefficient companies, particularly small startups that quickly fail.
    D. Deep integration occurs when products are produced in multiple countries, making it difficult to restrict trade in order to preserve jobs at home.

14.9 Postindustrial US Economy and Work

14. Strikes and union activity in the United States:
    A. have increased dramatically over the last 30 years.
    B. have decreased steadily over the last 20 years.
    C. have surpassed those of many European countries over the last 15 years.
    D. occur most often in the private sector.

15. Anadoxalists are developing a professional association of anadoxalists and are trying to get others to recognize them as a profession. Which of the following is *not* a requirement to be seen as a profession according to Friedson (1970)?
    A. Unique technologies or tools developed to perform anadoxia
    B. One or more theories to explain why anadoxia helps their clients
    C. Statewide Anadoxalist Review Boards staffed by licensed anadoxalists who review any complaints about practitioners of anadoxia
    D. Anadoxia assistants trained by and working under the supervision of licensed anadoxialists

CHAPTER ESSAY QUESTIONS

1. **Candidate Preferences and Campaign Strategies.** Consider the following poll results for three different issues in a hypothetical state. Given what you know about where Republicans and Democrats stand, write a few sentences indicating what a wedge issue is. Then identify which of these issues are wedge issues that could be emphasized by each party to increase its votes.
   A. 70% of people polled are worried about the high budget deficit and believe it should be reduced.
   B. 60% of people polled believe same-sex marriage should be legalized.
   C. Polls are just about tied, with 51% favoring legalized abortion and 49% opposing it.

2. Read the description below of a hypothetical economy. Then write a few sentences identifying at least one feature of that economy matching each of the characteristics of capitalism and each of the characteristics of socialism.

   This economy has a central bank that regulates interest rates. Major industries such as the automobile industry and the entertainment industry are largely unregulated, with private companies competing with one another for market share. One automobile manufacturer is investing heavily in all electric cars to reduce pollution, while another is still emphasizing production of large SUVs because of their high markup. The government has a strong commitment to having a healthy and educated population, however, and other areas of the economy, like education and health care, are dominated by nonprofit charitable agencies or government-run institutions. The government just completed a 10-year initiative to reduce carbon emissions by replacing 15% of their coal-burning plants with new nuclear reactors.

3. Mary Romero mentioned three strategies domestic workers use to attempt to renegotiate their role to make it less demeaning and more autonomous. Write a few sentences identifying these three strategies and why they use them.

4. **A case study of work in the postindustrial economy.** Joanna is a female African American who is currently working in a union job in a high-technology firm providing software services over the Internet. She lost her previous job in a multinational manufacturing company when the plant closed and the jobs were moved to India. So she went back to college and got a degree in computer science before landing this job. The company is a new startup just one year old. The two founders pooled their savings and took out a bank loan to get the company going. Write a few sentences indicating whether Joanna's experience is what you would predict given what we know about (1) multinational companies and manufacturing jobs in the United States, (2) women and minorities in the primary and secondary labor market, (3) unions in the private sector, (4) structural unemployment in manufacturing, and (5) financing and job creation and job loss in entrepreneurial startup companies.

5. Write a few sentences describing the difference between three strategies available during worker–management conflicts with unions. Identify the three strategies and briefly define each of them.

CHAPTER DISCUSSION QUESTIONS

1. What are some of the most important ways in which the economy and political life influence one another?

2. What proportion of our economy is capitalist and what proportion is socialist? If you could, how would you change these proportions, if at all? Why?

3. Think about your career plans. Are you planning to work in an occupation or profession that is growing or declining? What can you do to improve your chances of success in that occupation or profession? What policies could we, as a society, adopt to help more people end up in better jobs?

4. Think back to the most recent political election. Can you see how campaign advertisements and other strategies of the competing candidates reflect some of the issues discussed in this chapter, such as wedge issues or campaign financing regulations?

5. How have the political revolutions that have been part of the Arab Spring attempted to use power to gain authority?

6. Which of the two political system models influences the US economy more: pluralism or elite models?

7. What will cause future wars? How they will be fought? Consider concepts such as asymmetric warfare, terrorism, cyberwarfare, and deterrence.

8. Can small businesses and entrepreneurs compete with multinational corporations? What aspects of capitalism, working in the global economy, support your position?

9. Does our economy need more or less government regulation? Why?

CHAPTER PROJECTS

INDIVIDUAL PROJECTS

1. Go online and search for the website "Occupational Outlook Handbook" published by the US Bureau of Labor Statistics. Examine the predictions related to employment and industries of your choice. Write an analysis paper of your findings and relate it to chapter information.

2. Go online to learn more about the European Union, including its history, organization, and membership. Write an analysis paper of your findings and relate it to chapter information.

GROUP PROJECTS

4. Go online and search for the website Open Secrets or the Federal Elections Commission. Examine data related to the financing of campaigns. What patterns do you find related to corporate, labor union, and individual funding of campaigns? Prepare and present a report using chapter information to analyze your findings.

5. Search online and social media sites for references to the Occupy Wall Street movement and its variants for different cities (e.g., Occupy Washington, Occupy Oakland, etc.). What are some of the key issues the movement addresses, and how do they relate to both the political and economic issues discussed in this chapter?

3. Go to a local big-box store and pick any section that sells things that interest you. Look at 10 different products and find out the country in which they were manufactured. How many were made in the United States? Do you think it is important to "buy American"? Why or why not?

6. Go online and search for the latest federal budget expenditures, revenues, and the overall federal deficit. Create a balanced budget using the information from your search. Consider societal and economic consequences of making cuts and raising taxes, keeping in mind the size of the deficit.

CHAPTER KEY TERMS

Absolute monarchs
Agricultural economies
Alienation from work
Angel investors
Assembly line
Asymmetric warfare
Authoritarian governments
Authority
Blue-collar jobs
Bureaucracy
Capitalism
Charismatic authority
City-states
Coercion
Communism
Competitive capitalism
Constitutional monarchies
Corporate capitalism
Corporation
Coup d'état
Crowdfunding
Cyberwarfare
Cyclical unemployment
Deep integration
Deindustrialization
Democracy
Democratic republics
Deskilling

Deterrence
Dictatorship
Direct democracy
Downsizing
Drone warfare
Dual labor market
Economic sectors
Economy
Elections
Entrepreneur
Export jobs to low-wage countries
Gender gap
Government
Governmental gridlock
Industrial revolution
Industrial societies
Influence
Informal economy
Information economy
Information revolution
Institutional capitalism
Interest groups
Labor unions
Legal-rational authority
Lobbyist
Lockout
Managerial capitalism
Market economy

Mass production
Military-industrial complex
Military junta
Monarchy
Monopoly
Monopoly capitalism
Multinational corporations (or transnational corporations)
Nation-states
Nonviolent resistance
Occupational structure
Oligarchies
Oligopoly
Outsource
Parliamentary systems
Pluralist models
Political action committees (PACs)
Political parties
Political revolution
Postindustrial societies
Power
Primary labor market
Primary sector
Private equity
Profession
Professionalization
Proportional representation
Rationalization

Representative democracy
Routine personal service workers
Scientific management
  (or Taylorism)
Seasonal unemployment
Secondary labor market
Secondary sector
Shallow integration
Socialist economies
State

State capitalism
Strikes
Structural unemployment
Symbolic analysts
Technology
Telecommuting
Terrorism
Tertiary sector
Totalitarian government
Traditional authority

Underemployed
Underground economy
Unemployment rate
Venture capital
Veto groups
War
Wedge issues
Winner-take-all elections
Work to rule

ANSWERS TO CONCEPT LEARNING CHECKS

14.1 Types of Authority

1. A judge in state court [C. Legal-rational authority]

2. The founder of a new, fast-growing religion [A. Charismatic authority]

3. A revolutionary figure battling against the existing government in her country [A. Charismatic authority]

4. A priest in the Lutheran church [B. Traditional authority]

14.2 Types of Government

1. A government having complete control over all aspects of people's lives [E. Totalitarian government]

2. A democratic government with a popularly elected chief executive [I. Democratic republic]

3. A democratic government in which some people are elected to govern on behalf of the people [G. Representative democracy]

4. A government in which the leader claims a monopoly on power based on divine right [B. Absolute monarchy]

5. A democratic government with elected leaders and a figurehead whose position was inherited [C. Constitutional monarchy]

6. A government ruled by a single individual who seized power from the prior government [J. Dictatorship]

14.3 Demographics and Voting

1. The state most likely to elect the Republican candidate [A. Republicans are favored by rural, older whites]

2. The state most likely to elect the Democratic candidate [B. Democrats are favored by urban, younger minorities]

3. The state most likely to have the smallest voter turnout [3. Voter turnout is lower for younger minorities]

4. The state likely to have the highest voter turnout [A. Voter turnout is higher for older whites]

14.4 Pluralist versus Elite Models of the US Political System

1. Government support for ethanol production was heavily favored by the corn growers lobby, but was opposed by many environmental groups because they believe it does not reduce carbon emissions. [A. Pluralist model]

2. A particular person serves on the boards of six large corporations and has held several important appointed posts in government. [B. Elite model]

3. I do not see much point in voting since I cannot really influence policy much as an individual. [B. Elite model]

4. Virtually no legislation regarding transportation can get past Congress without support from the Teamsters' Union, but the union's opposition to the government bailout of Wall Street banks was of no avail. [A. Pluralist model]

14.5 The Demographics of the Military

1. [F] Don't ask, don't tell was repealed in 2011.

2. [F] People from the bottom quartile of the socioeconomic distribution are less likely to meet requirements to be accepted in the military and hence are underrepresented in the military.

3. [T] High school students with C averages are twice as likely to enter military service as students with A averages.

4. [T] The proportion of African Americans in the military is nearly twice as high as their proportion in the civilian labor force.

5. [F] Hispanic Americans serve in the military roughly in the same proportion as they appear in the civilian workforce.

14.6 Types of Economic Systems

1. Hunting and gathering economies [A. Little or no food surplus]

2. Agricultural economies [C. For the first time, food surpluses permit additional specialization and a renaissance in the sciences, the arts, and new forms of business].

3. Industrial economies [B. Requires massive amounts of energy]

4. Postindustrial economies [D. The key resource is information.]

14.7 Types of Capitalism

1. [F] In state capitalism, some corporations are owned by the state.

2. [F] In institutional capitalism, all important social institutions, such as education, are owned by corporations.

3. [T] In managerial capitalism managers exercise the greatest influence over the corporation.

4. [F] In state capitalism, the state itself is a corporation.

5. [T] In monopoly capitalism, one or a very few capitalists control a segment of the economy.

14.8 Insights from Three Theoretical Perspectives

1. [T, Functional perspective] Multinationals bring jobs to developing countries.

2. [F, Interactionist perspective] When asked, most workers would prefer to work in companies run by workers alone without management.

3. [T, Conflict perspective] Multinationals often export jobs from high-wage countries to low-wage countries.

4. [T, Interactionist perspective] Workers often indicate they would like to exert more influence in their work.

5. [T, Interactionist perspective] Work is often a defining element in a person's life.

6. [F, Conflict perspective] Hourly compensation costs in the United States in 2009 were the highest in the world.

14.9 Issues in the Postindustrial Economy

1. [C] Mass production is a process of production in which products are standardized, parts are interchangeable, precision tools fit parts together precisely, and the production is mechanized to produce a continuous high volume.

2. [A] Routine personal service workers perform repetitive tasks that provide a service.

3. [B] In telecommuting, workers work from their homes and communicate with their workplace through communications technologies like Skype, including interactive voice, video, and data conferencing.

4. [D] Seasonal unemployment is unemployment due to seasonal variations including variations in demand over holiday seasons.

ANSWERS TO CHAPTER REVIEW TEST

14.1 Political Systems, Power, and Authority

1. B. Legal-rational authority is relevant and, in this case, it rests with the US Constitution.

14.2 Governments around the Globe

2. C. An absolute monarchy is often authoritarian, while a constitutional monarchy is a democracy.

3. A. Most parliamentary systems determine leaders in elections based on proportional representation.

14.3 US Political System

4. B. This is likely to be an interest group that, among its other activities, lobbies Congress.

5. D. The voting rate was 38.46%.

14.4 Theoretical Perspectives on Power and Political Systems

6. C. C. Wright Mills wrote *The Power Elite*.

14.5 War and Peace

7. D. The Don't Ask, Don't Tell policy requiring gay men and women to not disclose their sexual preference while serving in the military was rescinded in 2011.

8. A. An asymmetric war occurs between two sides having very different capabilities and tactics.

9. D. Many nations refuse to negotiate with terrorists out of fear it encourages further terrorism.

14.6 Economy and Economic Systems in Transition

10. D. The service industry is much larger than either manufacturing or agriculture.

14.7 Global Economic Systems

11. C. In a true capitalist marketplace, companies would be allowed to fail to clear the system of inefficient companies and make way for more successful ones.

12. B. Socialist economies tend to be centralized.

14.8 Theoretical Perspectives on Economy and Work

13. D. Shallow integration is the opposite situation, in which products are produced primarily in a single country, making it easier to restrict trade such as with "buy American" campaigns.

14.9 Postindustrial US Economy and Work

14. B. Union activity and strikes have both decreased dramatically since the 1980s.

15. A. Special or unique tools are not mentioned as a requirement by Friedson.

ANSWERS TO CHAPTER ESSAY QUESTIONS

1. A wedge issue is one that members of a political party have strong opinions about. Their party's position on the issue receives greater public support than does the position of the other party on the same issue. Same-sex marriage is a wedge issue that favors Democrats. The budget deficit is a wedge issue that favors Republicans.

2. The economy demonstrates several characteristics of capitalism. A decentralized economy is suggested because one automobile manufacturer is investing heavily in all electric cars, while another is still emphasizing production of large SUVs. It is a market economy in the sense that the automobile industry and the entertainment industry are

largely unregulated, with private companies competing with one another for market share. Private ownership of the means of production is found in both the automobile and entertainment industry. It is the profit motive that motivates car companies to produce SUVs because of their high markup.

However, the economy also displays characteristics of socialism. The economy is centralized in that there is a single bank that regulates interest rates. The 10-year initiative to reduce carbon emissions reflects a planned economy. Public ownership of the means of production is found in both education and health care. Collective goals include reducing pollution and having a healthy and educated population.

3. Domestic workers often charge a flat rate or fixed rate instead of an hourly rate to increase profits. They specify which tasks they will perform to avoid being exploited with extra work. They prefer to perform the chores unsupervised to reduce stigma, maintain dignity, and avoid the need for being deferential.

4. Several characteristics of Joanna are surprising. It is unexpected that she is black and a female working in the primary labor market because blacks and minorities are more likely to have jobs in the secondary labor market. It is unexpected that an entrepreneurial startup was financed with a bank loan, since most startups are unable to obtain bank loans and have to seek investment financing. It is unexpected that she has a union job, since unions have declined in the private sector in the United States.

Other characteristics of Joanna are as we might expect. Her manufacturing job was exported to a low-wage country, as multinationals often do. Her new job is in a high-tech startup company is predictable, since small businesses tend to create lots of jobs. Finally, her returning to college and getting a very different job is consistent with high structural unemployment in which old jobs disappear.

5. Three strategies sometimes used include strikes (a temporary work stoppage by workers seeking changes); work to rule, in which workers meticulously follow regulations, slowing down work; and lockouts in which management does not permit workers to work or draw pay until the problem is resolved.

REFERENCES

American Interactive Consumer Survey. 2006. Retrieved October 2011 from www.workingfromanywhere.org/news/Trendlines_2006.pdf.

Bachman, Jerald et al. 2000. "Who Chooses Military Service? Correlates of Propensity and Enlistment in the U.S. Armed Forces." *Military Psychology* 12:1–30.

Baran, Paul A. and Paul M. Sweezy. 1966. *Monopoly Capital: An Essay on the American Economic and Social Order*. New York: Modern Reader Paperbacks.

Bartlett, Donald L. and James B. Steele. 1992. *America: What Went Wrong?* Kansas City, MO: Andrews and McMeel.

Beeghley, Leonard. 1986. "Social Class and Political Participation." *Sociological Forum* 1(3):496–513 (in Carter 1994).

Billitteri, Thomas J. 2010. "Drone Warfare: Are Strikes by Unmanned Aircraft Ethical?" *CQ Researcher* Aug 6, 2010, 20(28). Retrieved October 2011 from http://library.cqpress.com.proxy.mul.missouri.edu/cqresearcher/document.php?id=cqresrre2010080600

Blauner, Robert. 1964. *Alienation and Freedom: The Factory Worker and His Industry*. Chicago: University of Chicago Press.

Bluestone, Barry and Bennett Harrison. 1982. *The Deindustrialization of America: Plant Closings, Community Abandonment, and the Dismantling of Basic Industry*. New York: Basic Books.

Brandimarte, W. and D. Bases. 2011, August 6. "United States loses prized AAA credit rating from S&P." *Reuters*. Retrieved October 2011 from http://www.reuters.com/article/2011/08/06/us-usa-debt-downgrade-idUSTRE7746VF20110806.

Braverman, Harry. 1974. *Labor and Monopoly Capital: The Degradation of Work in the Twentieth Century*. New York: Monthly Review Press.

Brennan Center for Justice. 2012. "Policy Brief on the Truth about 'Voter Fraud.'" Brennan Center for Justice, New York University School of Law. Retrieved October 2011 from http://www.brennancenter.org/content/resource/policy_brief_on_the_truth_about_voter_fraud/.

Burgess, John. 1989. "Exporting Our Office Work." *Washington Post National Weekly Edition* 6(May 1):22.

Burnham, Walter Dean. 1980. "The Appearance and Disappearance of the American Voter." Pp. 35–73 in *Electoral Participation*. Edited by Richard Rose. Beverly Hills, CA: Sage.

Cantor, Joseph E. 2002. "Government and Finance Division, Congressional Research." *Campaign Finance*. Retrieved October 2011 from http://www.policyalmanac.org/government/archive/crs_campaign_finance.shtml.

Chandler, Alfred Dupont. 1964. *Giant Enterprise: Ford, General Motors, and the Automobile Industry; Sources and Readings*. New York: Harcourt Brace & World.

Chang, Clara and Constance Sorrentino. 1991. "Union Membership Statistics in 12 Countries." *Monthly Labor Review* December:46–53.

Clawson, Dan, Alan Neustadt, and Denise Scott. 1992. *Money Talks: Corporate PACs and Political Influence*. New York: Basic Books.

Coleman, James W. and Donald R. Cressey. 1980. *Social Problems*. New York: Prentice Hall.

Cottle, Thomas J. 1992. "When You Stop, You Die: The Human Toll of Unemployment." *Commonweal*, June 19.

Cummings, Milton C., Jr. and David Wise. 1989. *Democracy Under Pressure: An Introduction to the American Political System*. 6th edition. San Diego: Harcourt Brace Jovanovich.

Cunningham, W. 2012. "Commentary: Crowdfunding can provide new financing option for minority firms." *Washington Post*. June 3, 2012. Retrieved October 2011 from http://www.washingtonpost.com/business/capitalbusiness/commentary-crowdfunding-can-provide-new-financing-option-for-minority-firms/2012/06/01/gJQAThq7BV_story.html.

Dahl, Robert A. 1961. *Who Governs?* New Haven, CT: Yale University Press.

Department of Defense, Statistical Information Analysis Division. 2009. "Military Personnel Statistics." Retrieved October 2011 from http://siadapp.dmdc.osd.mil/personnel/MMIDHOME.HTM

Department of Health, Education, and Welfare (DHEW). 1973. *Work in America: Report of a Special Task Force to the U.S. Department of Health, Education, and Welfare*. Boston, MA: The MIT Press.

Dionne, Jr., E. J. 1989. "Voter-signup bill gains in Congress." *The New York Times*. May 7.

Domhoff, G. William. 1967. *Who Rules America?* Englewood Cliffs, NJ: Prentice Hall.

Domhoff, G. William. 1974. *The Bohemian Grove and Other Retreats: A Study in Ruling-Class Cohesiveness*. New York, Harper & Row, Publishers, Inc. (in Henslin 1995).

Domhoff, G. William. 1983. *Who Rules America Now? A View of the '80s.* Englewood Cliffs, NJ: Prentice Hall.

Downs, A. 1957. *An Economic Theory of Democracy.* New York: Harper and Row.

Eaton, J. and M. B. Pell. 2010, February 24. "Lobbyists Swarm Capital to Influence Health Care Reform." Center for Public Integrity. Retrieved October 2011 from www.publicintegrity.org/articles/entry/1953/.

Edwards, Richard. 1979. *Contested Terrain: The Transformation of the Workplace in the Twentieth Century.* New York: Basic Books.

Ehrenreich, Barbara and Annette Fuentes. 1981, January. "Life on the Global Assembly Line." *Ms Magazine* 9(7):52–59.

Erikson, Kai and Steven Peter Vallas (Eds.) 1990. *The Nature of Work.* New Haven, CT: Yale University Press.

Federal Election Commission. 2009, March. "Number of Federal PACs Increases." Retrieved October 2011 from http://www.fec.gov/press/press2009/20090309PACcount.shtml.

Finch, J. 2010. "Foxconn pay rises help life wages in China—and that can only be good." *The Guardian.* October 2, 2010. Retrieved February 2012 from http://www.guardian.co.uk/business/2010/oct/03/foxconn-pay-rises.

Fortune 2010. Global 500 2010. Retrieved December 2012 from http://money.cnn.com/magazines/fortune/global500/2010/index.htmlhttp://money.cnn.com/magazines/.

Freeman, Richard B. and Joel Rogers. 1999. *What Workers Want.* Ithaca, NY: ILR Press and Russell Sage Foundation.

Friedman, Milton. 1970. "The responsibility of business is to increase its profits." *The New York Times Magazine.* September 13, 1970, 32–33.

Friedrich, Karl and Zbigniew Brzezinski. 1965. *Totalitarian Dictatorship and Autocracy.* Cambridge, MA: Harvard University Press.

Friedson, Eliot. 1970. *Profession of Medicine: A Study of the Sociology of Applied Knowledge.* New York: Dodd, Mead.

Fullerton, Howard N. 1999. "Labor force participation: 75 years of change, 1950–98 and 1998–2025." *Monthly Labor Review.* Table 1. Retrieved October 2011 from http://www.bls.gov/mlr/1999/12/art1full.pdf.

Gallup Poll. 2011a. "Selected Trend on Party Affiliation: 2004–2011." Retrieved October 2011 from http://www.gallup.com/poll/15370/party-affiliation.aspx.

Gallup Poll. 2011b. "Most Important Problem." Retrieved October 2011 from http://www.gallup.com/poll/1675/most-important-problem.aspx.

Gallup Poll. 2012. Gender Gap in 2012 Vote Is Largest in Gallup's History. Gallup.org. Nov. 9, 2012. Retrieved December 2012 from http://www.gallup.com/poll/158588/gender-gap-2012-vote-largest-gallup-history.aspx.

Goode, William J. 1960. "Encroachment, Charlatanism, and the Emerging Profession: Psychology, Sociology and Medicine." *American Sociological Review.* 25:902–914.

Granberg, Donald and Soren Holmberg. 1988. *The Political System Matters: Social Psychology and Voting Behavior in Sweden and the United States.* Cambridge, UK: Cambridge University Press.

Habenstein, Robert W. 1954. *The American Funeral Director.* PhD Dissertation, University of Chicago, Department of Sociology.

Hage, Jerald and Charles H. Powers. 1992. *Post-Industrial Lives: Roles and Relationships in the 21st Century.* Newbury Park, CA: Sage.

Harrison, Bennett and Barry Bluestone. 1988. *The Great U-Turn.* New York: Basic Books.

Healthcare Providers Service Association. 2011. "Professions Covered." Retrieved October 2011 from http://www.hpso.com/professional-liability-insurance/professions-covered.jsp.

Hunter, Floyd. 1963 (1953). *Community Power Structure.* Garden City, NY: Doubleday.

Ignatius, David. 1988. "What's Left of Big Steel?" *Washington Post Outlook.* March 20, C-1.

Jenkins, R. 1986. *Racism and Recruitment: Managers, Organizations and Equality in the Labour Market.* Cambridge, UK: Cambridge University Press.

Kaplan, H. Roy. 1985. "Lottery Winners and Work Commitment." *Journal of the Institute for Socioeconomic Studies.* 82–94.

Kohut, A. 2008. "Post-election perspectives." Pew Research Center for the People and the Press. Retrieved Fall 2011 from http://pewresearch.org/pubs/1039/post-election-perspective.

Kohut, Andres and Linda Stefano. 1989. "Modern Employees Expect More from Their Careers." *The Gallup Report.* 288(Sep.):22–30.

Lasswell, Harold D. 1936. *Politics: Who Gets What, When, How.* New York: McGraw-Hill.

Leontief, Wassily. 1982. "The Distribution of Work and Income." *Scientific American* 247(September):188–90.

Lenski, Gerhard and Jean, Lenski. 1982. *Human Societies: An Introduction to Macrosociology.* New York: McGraw-Hill.

Lobe, Jim. 2009. "New, Old Weapons Systems Never Die" Inter Press Service, 17 July 2009. Retrieved December 2012 from http://www.ipsnews.net/2009/07/us-new-old-weapons-systems-never-die/.

Lynd, Robert S. and Helen M. Lynd. 1937. *Middletown in Transition.* New York: Harcourt, Brace and World.

Mann, Thomas. 1987. "Is the House of Representatives unresponsive to political change?" PP. 277 in *Elections American Style.* Edited by A. James Reichley. Washington, DC: Brookings Institute.

Manning, Lori. 2005. *Women in the Military: Where They Stand.* 5th edition. Washington, DC: Women's Research and Education Institute.

Markoff, John. 2007, January 7. "Tips for Protecting the Home Computer." *New York Times.* Retrieved October 2011 from http://www.nytimes.com/2007/01/07/technology/07tips.html.

Marmion, Harry A. 1971. *The Case against an All-Volunteer Army.* Chicago: Quadrangle Books.

Marx, Karl. 1875. *Critique of the Gotha Program.* Retrieved November 2012 from http://en.wikipedia.org/wiki/Critique_of_the_Gotha_Program.

McEachern, W. A. 2000. *Macroeconomics.* Fifth edition. New York: McGraw-Hill Irwin.

Miller, C. 2010, April 17. "Out of the Loop in Silicon Valley." *The New York Times.* Retrieved February 2012 from http://www.nytimes.com/2010/04/18/technology/18women.html?pagewanted=all.

Miller, M. 2012, February 29. "The Republican Crack-Up." *The Washington Post.* Retrieved February 2012 from http://www.washingtonpost.com/opinions/an-election-ripe-for-an-independent-candidate/2012/02/29/gIQAG6M0hR_story.html?hpid=z3.

Mills, C. Wright. 1956. *The Power Elite.* New York: Oxford University Press.

National Commission on the BP Deepwater Horizon Oil Spill and Offshore Drilling. 2011. *Deep Water: The Gulf Oil Disaster and the Future of Offshore Drilling.* Retrieved February 2012 from http://www.oilspillcommission.gov/sites/default/files/documents/DEEPWATER_ReporttothePresident_FINAL.pdf.

Organization for Economic Cooperation and Development (OECD). 2011. *Trade Union Density by Country and Year.* Retrieved October 2011 from http://stats.oecd.org/Index.aspx?DataSetCode=UN_DEN.

OpenSecrets.org. 2011. "Lobbying Database." Retrieved October 2011 from http://www.opensecrets.org/lobby/.

Parsons, Talcott. 1954. *Essays in Sociological Theory.* New York: Free Press.

Paige, Jeffery M. 1975. *Agrarian Revolution: Social Movements and Export Agriculture in the Underdeveloped World.* New York: Free Press.

Pinker, Steven. 2002. *The Blank Slate: The Modern Denial of Human Nature.* New York: Viking.

Pogue, David. 2012, February 29. "What Cameras inside Foxconn Found." *New York Times.* Retrieved February 2012 from http://pogue.blogs.nytimes.com/2012/02/23/what-cameras-inside-foxconn-found/.

Polsby, Nelson W. 1959. "Three Problems in the Analysis of Community Power." *American Sociological Review.* 24(6):796–803.

Reich, Robert B. 1989. "As the World Turns." *The New Republic.* 200(18, May 1): 23, 26–28.

Reynolds, Paul D. 2007. *Entrepreneurship in the United States: The Future Is Now.* New York: Springer Science + Business Media.

Riesman, David. 1961. *The Lonely Crowd.* New Haven, CT: Yale University Press.

Ritzer, G. 2005. *Enchanting a Disenchanted World: Revolutionizing the Means of Consumption*. Thousand Oaks, CA: Pine Forge Press.

Ritzer, George. 1994. *The McDonaldization of America*. Thousand Oaks, CA: Pine Forge Press.

Ritzer, George. 1995. *Expressing America*. Thousand Oaks, CA: Pine Forge Press.

Romero, Mary. 1992. *Maid in the U.S.A.* New York: Routledge.

Roy, Donald. 1954. "Efficiency and the 'Fix': Informal Intergroup Relations in a Piecework Machine Shop." *American Journal of Sociology*. 60.

Salant, Jonathan D. 2008, December 26. "Spending Doubled as Obama Led First Billion-Dollar Race in 2008." *Bloomberg*. Retrieved October 2011 from http://www.bloomberg.com/apps/news?pid=newsarchive&sid=aerix76GvmRM.

Schmidt, Manfred G. 1996. "When Parties Matter: A Review of the Possibilities and Limits of Partisan Influence on Public Policy." *European Journal of Political Research*. 30(2):155–183.

Schmitt, Eric and Thom Shanker. 2011, October 17. "U.S. Debated Cyberwarfare in Attack Plan on Libya." *The New York Times*. Retrieved October 2011 from http://www.nytimes.com/2011/10/18/world/africa/cyber-warfare-against-libya-was-debated-by-us.html.

Segal, Mady W., Meredith H. Thanner, and David R. Segal. 2007. "Hispanic and African American Men and Women in the U.S. Military: Trends in Representation." *Race, Gender & Class* 14(3–4):48–64.

Skocpol, Theda. 1979. *States and Social Revolutions: A Comparative Analysis of France, Russia, and China*. Cambridge, UK: Cambridge University Press.

Sims, Carra S., Fritz Drasgow, and Louise F. Fitzgerald. 2005. "The Effects of Sexual Harassment on Turnover in the Military: Time-Dependent Modeling." *Journal of Applied Psychology*. 90(6):1141–1152.

Smith, Adam. 1776. *An Inquiry into the Nature and Causes of the Wealth of Nations*. New York: The Modern Library. Republished 1937.

Speer, Tibbett L. 1995. "Digging into the Underground Economy." *American Demographics*. 17(2, Feb.):15–16.

Stockholm International Peace Research Institute. 2010. "SIPRI Military Expenditure Database." Retrieved October 2011 from http://www.sipri.org/research/armaments/milex/milex_database.

Stoessinger, John. 2005 (1974). *Why Nations Go to War*. Ninth edition. Belmont, CA: Thomson/Wadsworth.

Toner, Robin. 1990a, November 7. "The 1990 Election: Nonvoters; Turned Off by Campaigns, or Just Too Busy to Vote." *The New York Times*. Retrieved October 2011 from http://www.nytimes.com/1990/11/07/us/the-1990-election-nonvoters-turned-off-by-campaigns-or-just-too-busy-to-vote.html?pagewanted=all&src=pm.

Toner, Robin. 1990b, November 7. "The 1990 Elections: Congress; Helms and Other Incumbents Manage to Hold On." *The New York Times*. Retrieved October 2011 from http://www.nytimes.com/1990/11/07/us/the-1990-elections-congress-helms-and-other-incumbents-manage-to-hold-on.html?pagewanted=all&src=pm.

Truethevote. 2012. Retrieved October 2011 from www.truethevote.org.

Unionstats.com. 2011. "Union density 1973–2010." Union Membership and Coverage Database from the CPS. Retrieved October 2011 from http://www.unionstats.com/.

United Nations Conference on Trade and Development. 2008. "Largest Transnational Corporations." Retrieved October 2011 from http://www.unctad.org/templates/page.asp?intItemID=2443&lang=1.

US Bureau of Labor Statistics. 2008. "Earnings of women and men by race and ethnicity, 2007." Retrieved October 2011 from http://www.bls.gov/opub/ted/2008/oct/wk4/art04.htm.

US Bureau of Labor Statistics. 2010a. "Union members summary 2010." Retrieved October 2011 from www.bls.gov/news.release/union2.nr0.htm.

US Bureau of Labor Statistics. 2010b. "Table 2.3. Industries with the fastest growing and most rapidly declining wage and salary employment." Retrieved October 2011 from http://www.bls.gov/emp/ep_table_203.htm.

US Bureau of Labor Statistics. 2010c. "Table B. Firm size percentage share(1) of gross job gains and losses, fourth quarter 2010, seasonally adjusted." Retrieved October 2011 from http://www.bls.gov/web/cewbd/table_b.txt.

US Bureau of Labor Statistics. 2011a. "Work stoppages involving 1,000 or more workers, 1947–2010." Last revised February 8, 2011. Retrieved October 2011 from http://www.bls.gov/news.release/wkstp.t01.htm.

US Bureau of Labor Statistics. 2011b. "Union affiliation of employed wage and salary workers by occupation and industry, 2010." Retrieved October 2011 from http://www.bls.gov/cps/cpsaat42.pdf.

US Bureau of Labor Statistics. 2011c. "Table 9. Employed persons by occupation, sex, and age. Employment and Earnings, January, 2011." Retrieved October 2011 from http://www.bls.gov/cps/cpsa2010.pdf.

US Bureau of Labor Statistics. 2011d, March 8. *International comparisons of hourly compensation costs in Manufacturing, 2009*. News Release.

US Bureau of Labor Statistics. 2012. *Labor force statistics from the current population survey*. Retrieved October 2011 from http://www.bls.gov/cps/cps_htgm.htm#unemployed.

US Census Bureau. 2011a. "Table 397. Participation in Elections for President and US Representatives: 1932 to 2010." *Statistical Abstract of the United States 2012*. Retrieved October 2011 from http://www.census.gov/compendia/statab/2012/tables/12s0397.pdf.

US Census Bureau. 2011b. "Table 399. Voting-Age Population—Reported Registration and Voting by Selected Characteristics: 1996 to 2010." *Statistical Abstract of the United States 2012*. Retrieved October 2011 from http://www.census.gov/compendia/statab/2012/tables/12s0399.pdf.

US Census Bureau. 2011c. "Table 622 Unemployed Workers—Summary: 1990–2010." *Statistical Abstract of the United States 2012*. Retrieved October 2011 from http://www.census.gov/compendia/statab/2012/tables/12s0622.pdf.

US Census Bureau. 2011d. "Statistical Abstract of the United States: 2012, Table 1370." Retrieved October 2011 from Retrieved October 2011 from http://www.census.gov/compendia/statab/cats/international_statistics.html.

US Census Bureau, 2011e. "Statistical Abstract of the United States: 2012." Retrieved October 2011 from http://www.census.gov/compendia/statab/2012/tables/12s0620.pdf.

US Census Bureau. 2011f. "Statistics about Business Size (including Small Business) from the US Census Bureau." Retrieved October 17, 2011, from http://www.census.gov/econ/smallbus.html.

US Census Bureau, 2012. Statistical Abstract of the United States: 2012. Table 397. Participation in Elections for President and U.S. Representatives: 1932 to 2010. Retrieved January 2013 from http://www.census.gov/compendia/statab/cats/elections/voting-age_population_and_voter_participation.html.

US Department of Labor. 2011. "The apparel industry and codes of conduct: A solution to the international child labor problem?" Retrieved October 2011 from http://actrav.itcilo.org/actrav-english/telearn/global/ilo/code/apparel.htm#EXECUTIVE.

US News. 2008. "Data Points: Gender Gap in the 2008 Election." Retrieved October 2011 from http://www.usnews.com/opinion/articles/2008/11/06/data-points-gender-gap-in-the-2008-election.

Watson, Tony J. 1995. *Sociology, Work and Industry*. London: Routledge.

Weber, Max. 1913. *The Theory of Social and Economic Organization*. Translated by A. M. Henderson and Talcott Parsons. Edited by Talcott Parsons. Glencoe, IL: Free Press. Republished 1947.

Western, Bruce. 1993. "Postwar Unionization in Eighteen Advanced Capitalist Countries." *American Sociological Review*. 58(2):266–82.

Wimberley, Dale W. 1990. "Investment Dependence and Alternative Explanations of Third World Mortality: A Cross-National Study." *American Sociological Review*. 55(Feb):75–91.

World Bank. 2002. *Transition: The First Ten Years. Analysis and Lessons for Eastern Europe and the Former Soviet Union*. Washington, DC: World Bank.

Wright, Quincy. 1987. "Causes of War in the Atomic Age." Pp. 7–10 in *The Arms Race and Nuclear War*. Edited by William M. Evan and Stephen Hilgartner. Englewood Cliffs, NJ: Prentice Hall.

Zuboff, Shoshana. 1982. "New Worlds of Computer-Mediated Work." *Harvard Business Review*. 60(5):142–152.

© Wavebreak Media/Thistock

Chapter Overview ▼

15 Health and Health Care

Learning Objectives ▼

15.1 ■ Illustrate how culture-bound syndromes impact health in different cultures.

15.2 ■ Compare and contrast life expectancy and cause of death in high-, middle-, and low-income countries.

15.3 ■ Describe changes in life expectancy in the United States over the last century.
■ Identify demographic factors related to health and longevity.

15.4 ■ Illustrate how life style choices affect health and life expectancy.
■ Describe important life style trends and their impact on morbidity and mortality.

15.5 ■ Distinguish scientific medicine from alternative medicine.
■ Analyze trends in healthcare costs.
■ Describe healthcare delivery systems in the United States.
■ Discuss factors affecting both cost and quality of health care in the United States.

15.6 ■ Contrast spending on health care in the United States with other countries and identify some of the key differences in healthcare systems of different nations.

15.7 ■ Illustrate key differences in theoretical perspectives of health and medicine.

15.8 ■ Identify likely trends in the future of health care.

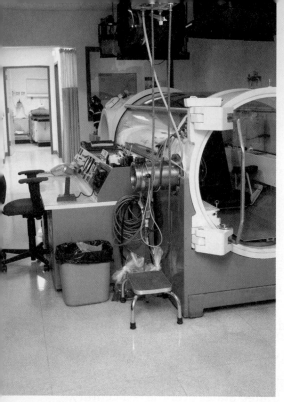

© Jupiterimages/Photos.com/Thinkstock

Health Defined by the World Health Organization (1946) as a state of complete mental, physical, and social well-being.

Culture-bound syndrome A conception of disease or ill health that is limited to a small number of cultures and is shaped by culture.

Death in the hospital. The call came early in the morning. My mother said simply, "Your father died this morning." And so it ended, much as it had begun years earlier when my parents called and first told me my father had inoperable lung cancer. As a construction worker, my father had always been healthy and fit. But on his last visit, he had been uncharacteristically quiet and seemed to cough a lot. He was a man of few words, but there was something about the way he carried himself and perhaps a hint of fear in my mother's eyes when he told us he was going to see the doctor to "get his cough checked out" the next week.

He survived the first rounds of radiation therapy. After several months, the tumor had shrunk and therapy stopped. For a few years, it seemed he had beaten cancer, but then the "cough" returned and he was once again in the hospital. The cancer was back. This time he was not so lucky. The tumor had grown and doctors decided to do exploratory surgery. While on the operating table, his heart stopped and he had to be resuscitated twice. Doctors were unable to remove the tumor. Nothing could be done, but he was so weak he had to stay in the hospital with a tube in his chest cavity to help drain his lungs. What followed was weeks of agony for him and anguish for his family. He had trouble breathing, was clearly in constant pain, and was given enough pain medication that he often did not know where he was. His physician and the family had to discuss the difficult decision of whether to issue a "no code" order so that if his heart stopped again, they would not aggressively try to save him. Mom stayed with him constantly while his children and grandchildren flew in from other states and we all had last visits with him. Forty-two days later, after several hundred thousand dollars of medical and nursing care, he died at the age of 69.

My father's story is not his alone. He died of cancer, one of the three leading causes of death in the United States. He died in a hospital, where most deaths occur, and after a period of intense medical care administered at great expense to his family and even greater expense to the third-party payer (his insurance). More money was spent on his health care during those last few weeks than had been spent on his health during the entire rest of his life. The length of his life was affected by life chances—he grew up during the Depression and never finished high school, worked in mines briefly after serving in WWII, and was a construction worker (all negatives), but had good health insurance that gave him access to care (a positive)—and by life style—he smoked much of his life (negative) but was fit from his work in construction (positive). He and his family had to face difficult ethical issues of what to do once it became clear he would not recover. This chapter will explore how these and other issues affect the health and healthcare experiences of all of us.

Health care provides an opportunity for us to look ahead and glimpse what work and society may be like in a 21st century dominated by knowledge workers whose expertise is based on science and whose influence can be measured at least in part by technological advances. We in the United States pay more per capita for health care than people in any other country in the world. Yet more than 50 million Americans are not insured and hence have only limited access to that care (Waananen 2012). This chapter examines the health-care system in the United States and contrasts it with those of other countries. We examine the rates of morbidity (sickness) and mortality (death) and the changing causes of death and increased life expectancy during the last hundred years, finding these to be closely related to gender, race, social class, and life style choices, such as smoking, unprotected sex, and alcohol consumption. We examine the institution of medicine and its functions, the social construction of health and illness, inequities of access to health care by race, gender, and class, and the rising dominance of physicians throughout most of the 20th century followed by the rationalization of health care in the first part of the 21st century.

15.1 Defining Health

People the world over value health, though their conception of what is meant by "health" varies in some respects from one culture to the next.

- Illustrate how culture-bound syndromes impact health in different cultures.

Many people think of health as the absence of disease. This is understandable when someone is suffering from a particular condition and looks forward to overcoming it and once again being healthy. However, health is not just the absence of disease. **Health** is defined by the World Health Organization (1946) as *a state of complete mental, physical, and social well-being.* Conceptions of whether a person is healthy are thus, at least in part, social. As a result, what is thought to be healthy varies in different cultural contexts.

Some medical and social scientists speak of **culture-bound syndromes**—conceptions of disease or ill health that are limited to a small number of cultures and are shaped by culture (Prince 1985; Ritenbaugh 1982). For example, eating disorders like anorexia nervosa (starving oneself out of a fear of becoming fat) and bulimia nervosa (binge-eating followed by self-induced vomiting) (Keel and Klump 2003), or even obesity (Ritenbaugh 1982) are more often found in the United States and some other high-income countries. Here, a culture of thinness is glorified by Barbie dolls and fashion models, while historically, and in many low-income countries today, thinness was a sign of poverty. Other examples of culture-bound syndromes include brain fog and fan death. Brain fog—depression and difficulty concentrating found predominantly among male students—was initially found almost exclusively in West Africa (Kataona and Robertson 2005). Many South Koreans believe in "fan death," the belief that leaving an electric fan running overnight in a closed room can kill the occupants (Korea Consumer Protection Board 2006).

Conceptions of health also change over time as we come to understand some of the causes of disease and recognize previous misconceptions. For example, 18th-century physicians would administer a type of medicine (a derivative of mercury) until the patient's hair began to fall out and his or her gums were bleeding. We now recognize those to be the symptoms of mercury poisoning (Remini 1984).

Despite these variations in how health is viewed in different cultures, it is safe to say that, regardless of culture and despite variations in precisely what is meant by being healthy, people the world over place great value on health. This is reflected in a well-known quotation from Ben Johnson's *Volpone.*

> O, health! health! The blessing of the rich! The riches of the poor! Who can buy thee at too dear a rate, since there is no enjoying the world without thee? (Ben Johnson, *Volpone* 1b, Act 2, Scene 1)

This chapter examines the issues that are the focus of medical sociology. **Medical sociology** is a special area within sociology focusing on "the phenomena of health and illness, the social organization of healthcare delivery, and differential access to medical resources" (ASA 2012). Chief among the concerns of medical sociology are the **social determinants of health**—"the circumstances in which people are born, grow up, live, work, and age, and the systems put in place to deal with illness. These circumstances are in turn shaped by a wider set of forces: economics, social policies, and politics" (WHO 2008).

With new medical advances, conceptions of health change as we recognize previous misconceptions.

© Everett Collection/Shutterstock, Inc.

Medical sociology The special area within sociology focusing on "the phenomena of health and illness, the social organization of health-care delivery, and differential access to medical resources."

Social determinants of health The circumstances in which people are born, grow up, live, work, an age, and the systems put in place to deal with illness. These circumstances are in turn shaped by a wider set of forces: economics, social policies, and politics."

CONCEPT LEARNING CHECK 15.1   Defining Health

Match each of the following four terms with the best definition.

_____ **1.** Fan death

_____ **2.** Bulimia nervosa

_____ **3.** An example of a culture-bound syndrome

_____ **4.** Health

A. Anorexia nervosa

B. A rock star's fear of being crushed to death by her fans

C. Cancer

D. The absence of disease

E. Starving oneself out of a fear of becoming overweight

F. The fear of dying from being in a closed room where a fan is left running

G. Repeated binge-eating followed by self-induced vomiting

H. A state of complete mental, physical, and social well-being

15.2 Global Health

Health and life expectancies vary dramatically from one nation to the next, and extreme differences are found depending on the income of each nation.

- Compare and contrast life expectancy and cause of death in high-, middle-, and low-income countries.

The Impact of Income on Health

When it comes to health, the world looks very different for high-, middle-, and low-income countries. These differences can be seen in three widely used measures of health differences: life expectancies, infant mortality rates, and causes of death. **Life expectancy** is the average number of years people are expected to live. **Infant mortality rate** is the number of deaths of infants under 1 years of age per 1,000 live births in a given year. **Causes of death** are categories of reasons attributed for deaths on birth certificates. In fact sheets available online from the World Health Organization (WHO 2011a), stark contrasts can be seen in all three of these measures of health. In high-income countries, more than two-thirds of the population lives beyond the age of 70; in middle-income countries, nearly half live to be 70; and in low-income countries, fewer than 20% live to be 70 and more than a third of all deaths occur among children under 15. FIGURE 15-1 highlights the stark differences in the age at which people die in high-, middle-, and low-income countries. Forty percent of deaths in low-income countries are among children under age 15, while in high-income countries, those children account for only 1% of deaths.

Major Health Problems in Different Countries

Causes of death vary dramatically by income. In high-income countries, only one infectious disease—lung infection—is among the leading causes of death. The most common causes are chronic diseases such as cardiovascular disease, cancers, diabetes, and dementia. In middle-income countries, like high-income countries, chronic diseases are the major killers. But middle-income countries also have additional leading causes of death in the form of tuberculosis (2.4%), HIV/AIDS (2.7%), and road traffic accidents (2.4%). In low-income countries, most people do not live long enough to be victims of chronic diseases. Instead, most die from infectious diseases including lung infections (11.3%), diarrheal diseases (8.2%), HIV/AIDS (7.8%), malaria (5.2%), and tuberculosis (4.3%). In low-income countries, leading causes of death also include complications of pregnancy and childbirth (8.7%; WHO 2011a).

Life expectancy The average number of years people are expected to live.

Infant mortality rate An age-specific death rate, the number of deaths of infants under 1 year of age per 1,000 live births in a given year.

Causes of death are categories of reasons attributed for deaths on birth certificates.

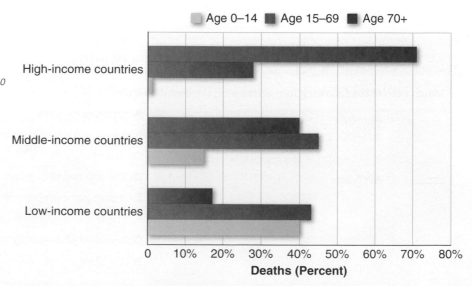

FIGURE 15-1 The age at which people die varies dramatically in high-, middle-, and low-income countries.
Source: Data from World Health Organization (WHO). 2011. The top 10 causes of death. WHO Fact Sheets. Retrieved August 2012 (http://www.who.int/mediacentre/factsheets/fs310/en/index1.html).

To put this in perspective, in low-income countries, the leading cause of death is infectious diseases, which account for 36.8% of deaths, while 8.7% of deaths are due to complications of pregnancy and childbirth. In middle-income countries, 14.9% of deaths are due to infectious diseases. In high-income countries, only 3.8% of deaths are due to the single infectious disease among the top 10 causes of death (lower respiratory infections). In both middle- and high-income countries, complications of pregnancy and childbirth are not among the top 10 causes of death.

Consider how different life is for someone born in a low-income or high-income country. An infant born in a low-income country has a greater chance of dying from birth complications (5 out of 1,000) or prematurity and low birth weight (5 out of 1,000) than dying at a much older age of heart disease (10/1,000). Forty percent of the people born in a low-income country will die before the age of 15, compared to only 1% of people born in a high-income country, and only 17% in a low-income country can look forward to living to be 70, compared to 71% of people in a high-income country.

In low-income countries, people are still dying from the health problems that plagued the United States back in 1900. In some of those countries, life expectancy today is even less than it was in the United States in 1900. How can those countries, with such poverty, improve health significantly? The major problems faced by low-income countries are problems that were solved decades ago in high- and middle-income countries through improved water supply, better sanitation, disease control, and inoculations. Therefore, many of the major efforts to improve health in low-income countries focus on delivering the resources and know-how to make these solutions available to those populations. One example is the World Health Organization's program to eradicate malaria (WHO 2011b).

Efforts to improve health in low-income countries focus on delivering resources, such as mosquito nets, in order to prevent the transmission of infectious disease.

© Liba Taylor/Alamy

CONCEPT LEARNING CHECK 15.2   Health Characteristics by Income Category

Match each of the following numbered items with the income category (low, middle, or high) for countries it best describes.

_____ 1. Most people will live to be 70 or more before dying.

_____ 2. The leading cause of death is infectious diseases.

_____ 3. Forty percent of people die before the age of 15.

_____ 4. Road traffic accidents are among the top 10 causes of death.

_____ 5. Nearly 8% of deaths are due to HIV/AIDS.

_____ 6. Fifteen percent of deaths occur among children younger than 15.

_____ 7. Only one infectious disease (lower respiratory infections) is among the top 10 causes of death, and it only accounts for 3.8% of deaths.

A. Low-income countries

B. Middle-income countries

C. High-income countries

15.3 Health in the United States: Demographic Factors

Health has improved dramatically in the United States over the last century or more, but substantial health differences remain for various demographic groups.

- Describe changes in life expectancy in the United States over the last century.
- Identify demographic factors related to health and longevity.

As a rich, developed country, the United States enjoys access to some of the best and most expensive health care available anywhere in the world. But how is our health? Which categories of people are more likely to be ill or to die? What life style behaviors

Demographics The study of populations.

Demographic characteristics Characteristics of populations such as age, sex, race, and ethnicity.

are associated with death and illness? **Demographics** is the study of populations, and **demographic characteristics** are characteristics of populations such as age, sex, race, and ethnicity. In this section, we will examine how demographic characteristics are related to health in the United States. Let us begin by putting this discussion into historical context.

Throughout the 20th century, death rates dropped substantially in most countries around the world. While these declines have been greatest in high-income nations, there have also been significant drops in death rates in most countries. As a result of decreased death rates, the life expectancy has increased substantially. As FIGURE 15-2 shows, in the United States, the average life expectancy increased from 47.3 years in 1900 to 78.7 years in 2010 (CDC 2011a). However, life expectancy varies by sex and race, with females living longer (81.1 years) than males (76.2 years) and whites living longer (79 years) than blacks (75.1 years).

The health and life expectancy of American Indians and Alaska natives also lag significantly behind that of the entire US population. The life expectancy of American Indians and Alaska Natives is 5.2 years lower than the population as a whole (Indian Health Service 2011). They have a 20% higher overall death rate, are six times more likely to die from alcohol-induced disease or tuberculosis, 2.8 times more likely to die from diabetes, 2.4 times more likely to die from unintentional injuries, 1.9 times more likely to die from homicide, and 1.8 times more likely to die from suicide when compared to the US population as a whole (Indian Health Service 2011).

There is a tendency to assume that the increased life expectancy we enjoy today is the result of the technological wonders of modern medicine. However, most of the increase in life expectancy occurred early in the 20th century as we made dramatic progress in simple public health and sanitation measures to clean up water supplies and halt the spread of infectious disease (McKeown 1976). Death rates from most infectious diseases began to decline long before the most effective medical treatment was discovered (McKinlay and McKinlay 1977). In many cases, medical treatments not only did not help but also hurt patients, who were sometimes bled to death or, as in

FIGURE 15-2 Life expectancy at birth in years by race and sex in the United States (1900–2010).
Source: Data from Centers for Disease Control (CDC). 2011. Life expectancy by age, race, and sex, 1900–2007. National Vital Statistics Reports. 59 (9), Sep 28, 2011. Retrieved August 2012 (ftp://ftp.cdc.gov/pub/Health_Statistics/NCHS/Publications/NVSR/59_09/Table21.xls).

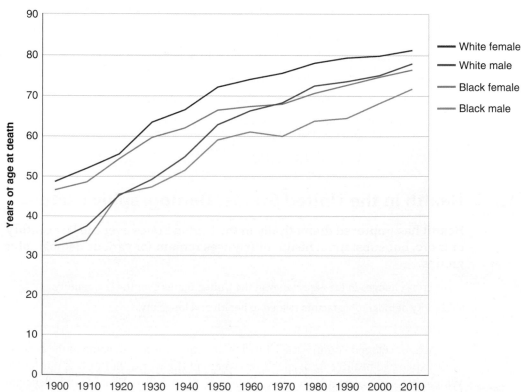

the case of President Andrew Jackson's wife, who was advised to take up smoking as a cure for tuberculosis, were given bad advice (Remini 1984).

As a result of improvements in sanitation and advances in health care, infectious diseases, which were once the top causes of death, have been largely eliminated. Today, people are much more likely to die from chronic, or persistent, illnesses such as heart disease and cancer, as can be seen in **TABLE 15-1**. In this table, the changes between 1900 and 1994 reflect long-term trends, while changes between 1994 and 2010 reflect more recent short-term trends. Four of the most common causes of death in 1900 (tuberculosis, diarrhea, bronchitis, and diphtheria)—all infectious diseases—are no longer among the top 10 causes of death in the United States. Note that the top four diseases in 1994 (and 2010) are all chronic diseases.

Comparing leading causes of death in 1994 to 2010 highlights recent trends in mortality. Both AIDS and homicides have dropped out of the top 10 causes of death. This reflects reductions in the homicide rate over the last decade and the reduced mortality rate due to AIDS after the introduction of drugs that permit many AIDS patients and HIV-infected patients to manage the disease. It is important to keep in mind that AIDS remains a major problem. Having AIDS is no longer a death sentence, but patients are not cured of AIDS and must deal with its dangers as well as the side effects and expense of drugs for the rest of their lives.

Another change between 1994 and 2010 is the increasing mortality due to kidney disease. Renal (kidney) disease can present (show up) in several ways, including nephritis (inflammation of the kidneys), nephrotic syndrome (a nonspecific form of kidney disease), or nephrosis (renal disease without inflammation). Why the increase in kidney disease? Diabetes is becoming more prevalent among the US population and often leads to kidney problems. Another factor is the dramatic increase in the abuse of both over-the-counter and prescription drugs, either of which can cause kidney failure. A second cause of death first appearing in the top 10 causes in 2010 is Alzheimer's disease. This is widely attributed to the aging of the population, since this disease occurs primarily among the elderly.

Social Epidemiology

Social epidemiology is the study of the distribution of mortality (death) and morbidity (disease) in a population. **Epidemiology** is related to the term *epidemic*, which refers

> **Social epidemiology** The study of the distribution of mortality (death) and morbidity (disease) in a population.
>
> **Epidemiology** is related to the term *epidemic*, which refers to an outbreak of a disease within a population.

TABLE 15-1 Top 10 Causes of Death in the United States (1900, 1994, and 2010)

1900	1994	2010
1. Tuberculosis*	1. Heart disease	1. Heart disease
2. Pneumonia	2. Cancer	2. Cancer
3. Diarrhea*	3. Blood vessel disease (stroke)	3. Lung diseases (not cancer)
4. Heart disease	4. Lung diseases (not cancer)	4. Blood vessel disease (stroke)
5. Nephritis	5. Accidents	5. Accidents
6. Accidents	6. Pneumonia and flu	6. Alzheimer's disease
7. Blood vessel disease (stroke)	7. Diabetes	7. Diabetes
8. Cancer	8. AIDS**	8. Nephritis, nephrotic syndrome, and nephrosis
9. Bronchitis*	9. Suicide	9. Pneumonia and flu
10. Diphtheria*	10. Homicide**	10. Suicide

* These four diseases are no longer among the top 10 causes of death in the United States.
** These two are no longer in the top 10.
Note: Some of the terms were standardized across the different tables.

Source: Murphy, S., J. Xu, and K. Kochanek. 2012. "Deaths: Preliminary Data for 2010." National Vital Statistics Reports 60(4): Table 2. Retrieved July 2012 from http://www.cdc.gov/nchs/data/nvsr/nvsr60/nvsr60_04.pdf; National Center for Health Statistics. 1997. Statistical Abstract 1997, Tables 129, 130.

to an outbreak of a disease within a population. John Snow is often credited with creating social epidemiology as a scientific discipline. Snow lived in London in the 1800s and became interested in stopping an outbreak of cholera in that city in 1854. At the time, the causes of cholera and how the disease was spread were not well understood. However, by plotting addresses of cholera victims on a street map, Snow found that most victims lived in a particular area of London. The next step was to determine what might be the cause of people in that area but not those in other areas contracting cholera. Eventually, Snow narrowed his suspicions to one source, a public water pump on Broad Street. Unable to convince authorities he was right, Snow secretly removed the Broad Street pump handle one night. People were no longer able to use the pump for water, and the spread of cholera stopped. Snow had not only helped us learn that contaminated drinking water was the source of cholera but also gave birth to the new science of epidemiology (Rockett 1994).

Today, epidemiologists working in universities and health centers often use extensive health statistics collected by national agencies such as the Centers for Disease Control and Prevention (CDC) to identify correlates and causes of disease and death. That information is then often used to guide social policies aimed at improving health. The top 10 causes of death discussed earlier are one example of how this information helps focus efforts on those factors that most affect health outcomes. Epidemiologists have also identified a number of characteristics of populations that are correlated with health: age, sex, race/ethnicity, social class, disability, and mental illness.

Age

In the United States, chronic disease and death are primarily issues for the elderly. Death is rare for the young, and when it occurs, it is primarily due to accidents or suicides. The CDC summarizes many of the relevant statistics for health of the elderly. Chronic problems increase with age. Among noninstitutionalized elderly, two-thirds or more of men and women aged 65 or older have hypertension, about 40% of men and women 65 to 74 are obese, along with between 25 and 30% of those 75 and over. Roughly a quarter (24.4%) of those 65 and over are in fair or poor health. Annual mortality rates increase with age, increasing from roughly 2% mortality for people aged 65 to 74 to nearly 5% for those 75 to 84 and 13% for those 85 and over. The leading causes of death for persons age 65 and over are heart disease, cancer, and chronic lower respiratory disease (CDC 2012b).

Sex

Women live longer than men in the United States and other countries. Ironically, the gap between men and women increased during the 20th century, and the effect of sex on life expectancy is greater than that of race (both white and black women live longer than either white or black men). A number of factors contribute to the difference between life expectancies for men and women. Kalben (2000) examined various causes of death and found the ratio of death rates for men compared to women to be greater than 1 for all causes and ranged from 1.2 for diabetes mellitus to 4.3 for suicide, with highest differences for suicide (4.3), homicides (3.5), and accidents (2.4). While some of the higher death rates for men appear due to biological factors, there are clear social risk factors that disadvantage men as well. Generally, men engage in more risky behaviors and suffer higher mortality rates as a consequence. For example, 93% of job-related deaths occur among men even though men constitute only 55% of the workforce (*The New York Times*, Oct. 3 1993c:13). Men also smoke more than women and hence suffer more smoking-related mortality and morbidity.

Race/Ethnicity

Whites live longer and experience less disease than blacks. Blacks experience higher rates of infant mortality and maternal deaths and have a life expectancy 4.3 years less than that of whites (CDC 2010a). The infant mortality rate is the number of deaths of infants under 1 year of age per 1,000 live births in a given year. Why these differences? Undoubtedly, some diseases (such as sickle-cell anemia among blacks) have a genetic or biological basis. However, social factors such as poverty or occupational health risks are the major cause of differences in health status among racial and ethnic groups. One reason blacks have a lower life expectancy is that race and education together lead to even greater differences than race alone. Blacks have lower life expectancies than whites, and people with less education have lower life expectancies than people with more education. When race and education differences are combined, the effects are even greater. Olshansky and colleagues (2012) report that in 2008, US adults with fewer than 12 years of education had life expectancies nearly as low as those of all adults in the 1950s and 1960s. Blacks tend to have lower educational attainment than whites in the United States, and when blacks with less than 12 years of education are compared to whites with 16 or more years of education, the difference in life expectancies is 14.2 years for men and 10.3 years for women.

Hispanics display higher incidence rates for some diseases and often lack access to health care when compared to whites. However, Hispanics have a longer life expectancy than whites by 2.4 years (CDC 2010a). When compared to the population as a whole, Hispanics have similar rates of strokes as the overall population; lower rates of heart disease and heart attack, cancer, and arthritis; and higher rates of diabetes. Hispanics are least likely to have health insurance among ethnic groups. In 2010, 30.7% of the Hispanic population lacked health insurance, compared to 11.7% of the non–Hispanic white population (DHHS 2012). Hispanics have higher rates of obesity than non–Hispanic whites and, largely due to lack of insurance, are more likely to lack access to preventive care. Leading causes of death and illness among Hispanics include "heart disease, cancer, unintentional injuries (accidents), stroke, and diabetes. Some other health conditions and risk factors that significantly affect Hispanics are: asthma, chronic obstructive pulmonary disease, HIV/AIDS, obesity, suicide, and liver disease" (DHHS 2012).

Social Class

There are many reasons to suspect that social class has important consequences for health. Those in higher social classes tend to work in safer jobs and live in safer neighborhoods. They have greater access to health care, better nutrition, and safe places to exercise. Social class influences life style choices that impact health, too. In a national study of physical inactivity and social class, Crespo and colleagues (1999) found that greater physical inactivity was found for people who are less educated, living below the poverty line, or retired. Studies of the impact of social class on health use measures of social class based on occupational status, income, wealth, education, and combinations of two or more; and numerous studies "show socioeconomic inequalities in health and mortality to be pervasive throughout the world" (Elo 2009:557). In the United States, life expectancy at age 25 in 2000 was seven years higher for individuals having attended at least some college when compared for those with a high school education or less (Meara et al. 2008).

Low-income Americans have lower life expectancies than middle- and higher-income Americans. In one study of factors predicting longevity, Muennig, Fiscella, Tancredi, and Franks (2010) found that people living at less than 200% of the federal poverty level had average life expectancies 8.2 years lower than those living at or above that amount. That factor was stronger than any other single factor in predicting mortality, including smoking, which was second at 6.6 years reduction in life expectancy. The gap in life expectancy due to income is in fact getting larger. One Social Security Administration study by Waldron (2007) found that since 1977, the life expectancy of male workers retiring at age 65 increased by 6 years for workers in the top half of the income distribution, but by only 1.3 years in the bottom half (Waldron 2007:Table 4). The United States National Health Interview Survey 1999–2010 (CDC, 2011b) found that, when asked, the poor are much more likely to report a number of chronic conditions when compared to the nonpoor. The poor are 135% more likely to have a stroke, 81% more likely to have had a heart attack, 63% more likely to suffer from coronary heart disease, 75% more likely to have cancer, 57% more likely to have diabetes, and 22% more likely to suffer from arthritis (CDC 2011b).

Disability

Disability A reduced ability to perform tasks expected of a normal person at that stage in life.

Stigma A distinctive social characteristic or attribute identifying its owner as socially unacceptable or disgraced.

A **disability** is a reduced ability to perform tasks commonly expected of a person at that stage in life. Not all disabilities are apparent to other people. One of the authors, for example, has very bad eyesight in one eye but is able to read, drive, and do most or all things people normally expect. He would make a bad sniper or astronomer, perhaps, but for the most part, this is not what we think of as a disability. On the other hand, he has a relative who suffers from a psychological disorder. This has made it difficult for her to hold a job for long and eventually led her to go through a legal process of qualifying for disability benefits through Social Security. Not everyone who is disabled applies for, needs, or receives those benefits, however.

People with chronic illness or disabilities can have enormous burdens in their lives, taxing both them and loved ones emotionally, physically, and financially. As Corbin and Strauss (1985) express it, there are three types of "work" they face: First, they face the "everyday work" of daily living such as maintaining relationships, a career, and a household. Second, they have "illness work"—visiting the physician, getting treated, managing pain, dealing with insurance claims, and all the things they have to do to manage their illness. Finally, they have "biographical work," as they have to both incorporate the illness into their own lives and explain it to others. These extra burdens are faced by the disabled or chronically ill so long as their condition remains. For example, a friend with diabetes must constantly not only manage his work and family life but also continue to medicate himself, monitor his health, deal with periodic bouts of hospitalization, and explain to friends like myself about his illness and how he copes with it.

All of this is made far more difficult when such people are victims of a stigmatized condition such as AIDS, psychological disorders, cancer, or alcoholism. **Stigma** was first defined by sociologist Erving Goffman (1963) as a distinctive, strongly negative label that marks the person as socially unacceptable or disgraced. Goffman distinguished between stigmas that were "abominations of the body" such as disfigurement and obesity and "character blemishes" such as laziness, untrustworthiness, and sexual promiscuity. Stigmatized people are generally treated poorly by others, as people try to separate themselves from the disease. Treatment by others can be particularly harsh if the person is viewed as in part to blame due to a character flaw, such as sexual promiscuity in the case of AIDS or lack of self-control when it comes to being overweight. For example, DeJong (1993) found in one study that adolescents were much less critical of someone who was overweight when they believed it was due to biological factors rather than a lack of self-control. People infected with HIV/AIDS have been stigmatized and subjected to extreme discrimination, including being refused admission to public places, denied treatment by health professionals, barred from entering countries, and losing promotions, wages, and even jobs as a result (USDOJ Disability Rights Division 2012).

Disability is socially constructed. It is not just a characteristic of the individual but also of the society in which the person finds him- or herself. The reduced ability to perform tasks expected of a normal person in one society may be different from those in another society or in a different time and place. Perhaps even more important, the extent to which a disability affects a person's life is affected by the larger society. This is the premise behind the Americans with Disabilities Act (USDOJ Disability Rights Division 2009). This act prohibits discrimination on the basis of disability in employment, state and local government, public accommodations, commercial facilities, transportation, and telecommunications. The idea is that, where possible, reasonable accommodations should be made to permit people with disabilities to accomplish the tasks of everyday life on their own. Wheelchair ramps, computer readers for the blind, sign language interpreters, and other accommodations can help many disabled people function at a higher level.

Stigmatized people are generally treated poorly by others as people try to separate themselves from the disease.

© Arman Zhenikeyev/Shutterstock, Inc.

Mental Illness and Psychological Disorders

The terms **mental illness** and *mental* or *psychological disorder* are often used interchangeably. Strictly speaking, however, mental health professionals use the term **psychological disorder** to describe what most of us think of when we hear the term *mental illness*: a psychological condition that is deviant, may cause harm to oneself or others, and may cause psychological distress. About one in every four adults is estimated to suffer from a diagnosable psychological disorder in the United States (Kessler et al. 2005). Psychological disorders are the leading cause of disability in the United States and Canada for people ages 15 to 44 (WHO 2004).

Kessler and colleagues (2005) and, indeed, the great majority of the psychiatric and psychological professions, regard mental illness and psychological disorders as very real and study them as the result of a combination of chemical, biological, environmental, psychological, and social factors. In contrast, some sociologists such as Thomas Szasz (1984) argue that mental illness is a myth. In his view, "mental illnesses" are merely behaviors or traits deemed unacceptable, deviant, or immoral by the larger society. Labeling people mentally ill does nothing to help them, he goes on, and in fact harms them because they come to see themselves as mentally ill and are treated as ill by others. The mental health movement, he argued elsewhere (Szasz 1970) is analogous to the Inquisition, leading to the same moral implications and political consequences as the belief in witchcraft.

Serious psychological disorders are highly stigmatizing, and people diagnosed with them often find themselves following a lifelong roller-coaster pattern of hospitalization, recovery, and ongoing medication, making it difficult or impossible to keep a job.

> **Mental illness** See *psychological disorder*.
>
> **Psychological disorder** A psychological condition that is deviant, may cause harm to oneself or others, and may cause psychological distress.

CONCEPT LEARNING CHECK 15.3 Life Expectancy and Disability in the United States

Which of the following statements about life expectancy in the United States are true and which are false?

_____ **1.** Life expectancy increased dramatically for everyone between 1900 and 2010.

_____ **2.** Women have longer life expectancies than men of the same race, and the gap increased between 1900 and 2010.

_____ **3.** Blacks have lower life expectancies than whites of the same sex, and the gap increased between 1900 and 2010.

_____ **4.** In 1900, blacks, regardless of sex, had lower life expectancies than whites, suggesting race was a bigger factor than sex.

_____ **5.** In 2010, women, regardless of race, had higher life expectancies than men, suggesting sex is a bigger factor affecting life expectancy than race.

Disabilities are:

_____ **6.** Always apparent to others.

_____ **7.** Characterized by an inability to perform tasks as well as others doing the same job.

_____ **8.** Socially constructed.

_____ **9.** Sometimes associated with stigmas.

15.4 Health in the United States: Life Style Factors

Life style choices by individuals can alter their health and change their life expectancy by years.

- Illustrate how life style choices affect health and life expectancy.
- Describe important life style trends and their impact on morbidity and mortality.

Life style behaviors contribute greatly to health. By life style behavior, we mean the things that people do that express who they are. These include eating habits, smoking, the use of alcohol, unprotected sexual activity, drug abuse, and other factors. Diseases related to life styles kill more people than communicable diseases, and the costs are staggering (Bittman 2011). More than 1/7th of our gross domestic product (GDP) is spent attempting to cure diseases most of which could be prevented by changes in life style. Costs of cardiovascular disease alone are projected to triple to more than $800 billion annually in the United States, with $276 billion in indirect costs like productivity losses. Type 2 diabetes (a disease that is nearly entirely preventable) is projected to affect half of all Americans and cost $500 billion a year by 2020 (Bittman 2011).

Life style-related activities cause more than 1 million deaths per year. As shown in FIGURE 15-3, smoking causes far more deaths than other behaviors. Surprisingly, some of the life style issues most often focused on by the media, such as unprotected sex and drug abuse—significant though they are—cause many fewer deaths than the top three life style issues: smoking, diet/exercise (referring, of course, to a poor diet and little or no exercise), and alcohol. That was true as far back as 1993 (*The New York Times*, 1993b:B7) and remains true today (Danaei et al. 2009; Murphy et al. 2012). TABLE 15-2 provides additional detail, including both estimated costs and estimated deaths.

The impact of life style factors is measured in this table by both numbers of deaths and estimated costs annually. However, some life style factors have their major impact on costs, while others have greater impact on deaths. Smoking ranks at the top of our list of life style hazards in deaths, but the estimated costs of alcohol are number one even while less than a fifth as many people die from alcohol-related hazards than from smoking-related hazards. HIV/AIDS-related deaths are much less common (8,352), having dropped considerably as medications have helped many with HIV to live much longer and have reduced the spread of the disease. In some cases, estimated costs are not available, and in all cases, it is difficult to encompass all costs and all deaths. For example, drug abuse costs would need to include not only medical treatment and prevention but also criminal justice system costs and deaths due to drug-related violence. But it is very difficult to know where to draw the line on such consequences. These statistics, for example, do not include the estimated 50,000 deaths in the last five years in Mexico since former president Felipe Calderon made the war on drugs a cornerstone of his policies (Archibald and Cave 2012). Clearly, those consequences are too distant to be counted here. Nevertheless, we should be aware that there are broader consequences.

Smoking

Smoking is the top preventable cause of death in the United States, causing about one out of every five deaths in the United States each year (CDC 2008). Smoking far exceeds other preventable causes of death. More deaths are caused each year by

FIGURE 15-3 Annual deaths in the United States related to different life style factors.
Source: Data from Centers for Disease Control (CDC). 2008. Smoking—Attributable Mortality, Years of Potential Life Lost, and Productivity Losses—United States, 2000–2004. Accessed March 2011 (http://www.cdc.gov/mmwr/preview/mmwrhtml/mm5745a3.htm). Murphy, S., Xu, J., and Kochanek, K. 2012. Deaths: Preliminary data for 2010. National Vital Statistics Reports. 60(4), Jan. 11, Table 2. Accessed July 2012 (http://www.cdc.gov/nchs/data/nvsr/nvsr60/nvsr60_04.pdf). Naumann R.B., Dellinger A.M., Zaloshnja E., Lawrence B.A., Miller T.R. 2010. Incidence and total lifetime costs of motor vehicle-related fatal and nonfatal injury by road user type, United States, 2005. Traffic Injury Prevention. 11:353–360. Centers for Disease Control. 2012. HIV in the United States: At a Glance. March, 2012. Accessed September 2012 (http://www.cdc.gov/hiv/resources/factsheets/PDF/HIV_at_a_glance.pdf). Danaei, G., Ding, E., Mozaffarian, D., Taylor, B., Rehm, J., Murray, C., and Ezzati, M. 2009. The preventable causes of death in the United States: Comparative risk assessment of dietary, lifestyle, and metabolic risk factors. Public Library of Science Medicine 6(4), April. Accessed July 2012 (http://www.ncbi.nlm.nih.gov/pmc/articles/PMC2667673/?tool=pubmed).

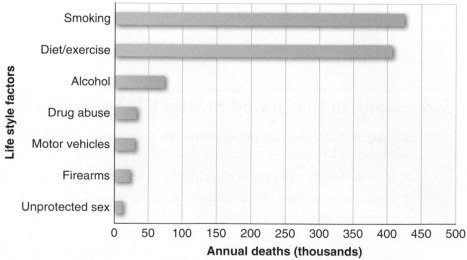

TABLE 15-2 Effects of life style on health: estimated annual costs and deaths

	Year	Estimated Costs	Rounded Death Estimates	Rounded Death Estimates[1]
Smoking	2004	$193 billion	433,000 (CDC 2008)	467,000
Diet/exercise	2008	$147 billion (obesity)	407,000[1] Obesity 216,000 Inactivity 191,000	
Alcohol	2011	$223.5 billion[4]	79,000 25,440 (alcohol-induced deaths)	64,000
Drug abuse			37,792	
Motor vehicles		$70 billion[3]	35,080	
Firearms Accidental Suicide Assault	2010 Unavailable		30,923 600 19,308 11,015	
Unprotected sex	2009		17,774[2]	
Total			1,031,147	

Sources: Data from Murphy, S., Xu, J., and Kochanek, K. 2012. Deaths: Preliminary Data for 2010. National Vital Statistics Reports. 60(4), Jan. 11, Table 2. Accessed July 2012 (http://www.cdc.gov/nchs/data/nvsr/nvsr60/nvsr60_04.pdf). [1]Danaei, G., Ding, E., Mozaffarian, D., Taylor, B., Rehm, J., Murray, C., and Ezzati, M. 2009. The preventable causes of death in the United States: Comparative risk assessment of dietary, lifestyle, and metabolic risk factors. Public Library of Science Medicine 6(4), April. Accessed July 2012 (http://www.ncbi.nlm.nih.gov/pmc/articles/PMC2667673/?tool=pubmed). [2]CDC. 2012. HIV in the United States: At a Glance. March 2012. Accessed September 2012 (http://www.cdc.gov/hiv/resources/factsheets/PDF/HIV_at_a_glance.pdf). [3]Naumann, R.B., Dellinger, A.M., Zaloshnja, E., Lawrence, B.A., Miller, T.R. 2010. Incidence and total lifetime costs of motor vehicle-related fatal and nonfatal injury by road user type, United States, 2005. Traffic Injury Prevention. 11:353–360. [4]Excessive Drinking Costs U.S. $223.5 Billion. CDC 24/7: Saving Lives. Protecting People. Retrieved July 2012 from http://www.cdc.gov/Features/AlcoholConsumption/.

tobacco than all the deaths from alcohol use, motor vehicle injuries, illegal drug use, HIV, suicides, and murders combined (CDC 2008). Roughly 433,000 people die each year from smoking-related diseases such as cancer, heart and blood-vessel diseases, and respiratory disorders. This includes 49,400 deaths per year from secondhand smoke exposure (CDC 2008). This is roughly 50 people every hour (Moseley and Cowley 1991). "Smoking accounts for more than one-quarter of all deaths among Americans 35 to 64 years old. . . . A third of all cancer deaths are smoking-related. . . . The North Carolina Assist project put it this way: 'The loss of life from smoking in North Carolina equals the death toll if two fully loaded Boeing 737 passenger planes crashed each week in our state, with no survivors'" (Brody 1993). On average, adults who smoke cigarettes die 14 years sooner than nonsmokers (CDC 2002), and cigarette smoking results in 5.1 million years of potential life lost in the United States annually (CDC 2008).

Efforts to reduce the death toll due to smoking encounter pushback from the tobacco industry. Tobacco is a big business in the United States. In 2010, more than 303 billion cigarettes were purchased in the United States (Maxwell 2011a), 13.3 billion cigars (Maxwell 2011b), and more than 122 million pounds of smokeless tobacco—including snuff, chewing tobacco, and other forms of tobacco that are placed in the mouth but not smoked (Maxwell 2011c). In 2008, the tobacco industry spent $10.5 billion on advertising and promotional expenses in the United States, or nearly $29 million each day (FTC 2011).

Despite industry resistance, progress has been made in reducing smoking. In 1965, when the US Surgeon General's Report first suggested a link between smoking and lung cancer, 52% of US adult men and 32% of adult women smoked. But the rising concerns over the health risks of smoking have cut this rate dramatically to 21.5% for men and 17.3% for women (45 million people). FIGURE 15-4 summarizes smoking rates for different groups. Roughly 20 to 22% of adults under 65 smoke compared to 9.5%

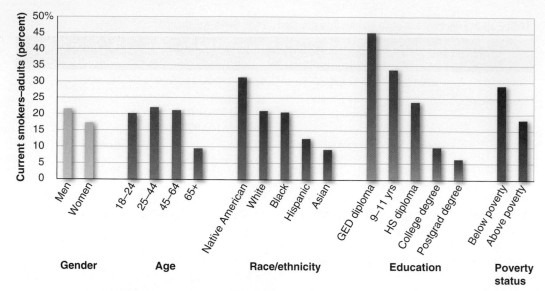

FIGURE 15-4 Smoking rates in the United States vary dramatically by gender, age, race/ethnicity, education, and poverty status.
Source: Centers for Disease Control and Prevention. 2011. Vital Signs: Current Cigarette Smoking Among Adults Aged ≥ 18 Years—United States, 2005–2010. Morbidity and Mortality Weekly Report 2011;60(33):1207–12.

of adults 65 and older. Asians and Hispanics are much less likely to smoke than are whites, blacks, and particularly American Indians (CDC 2010b).

Another measure of the changing views of smoking can be had by examining who smokes. Smoking was once considered stylish back when movie stars like Humphrey Bogart and Lauren Bacall routinely lit up on the silver screen. But today, smoking is much more common among the less well educated and people living below the poverty line. Smoking declines markedly with education, with 45% of adults with a GED degree smoking compared with fewer than 10% of college graduates. Roughly one third of people living below the poverty line (28.9%) smoke, compared to only 18.3% of those living above the poverty line (CDC 2010b).

The Body: Diet, Exercise, and Nutrition

Sociologists only fairly recently began to realize the importance of the body and ways in which our bodies are shaped by our social experiences, values, and culture, as well as ways in which our body affects those experiences. This field of research is called the **sociology of the body**. Here we consider several life style issues related to the body. These include the obesity epidemic with its negative consequences for our health, eating disorders, and bodybuilding.

Sociology of the body The study of how our bodies are shaped by our social experiences, values, and culture, as well as ways in which our bodies affect those experiences.

The Obesity Epidemic

The United States is in the middle of an obesity epidemic. Roughly 60% of US adults are overweight. More than one-third (37.5%) of US adults and nearly 17% of children and adolescents are obese (Ogden et al. 2012). In **TABLE 15-3**, we see the standards for common weight categories.

Obesity increases risks for a range of serious diseases, including coronary heart disease, Type 2 diabetes, some forms of cancer, hypertension, high cholesterol, and stroke (NIH 1998). In 2008, medical costs associated with obesity were estimated at $147 billion, and the medical costs paid by third-party payers (such as insurance companies) were $1,429 higher for people who were obese than for those with normal weight (CDC 2012c). By one estimate, obesity leads to roughly 216,000 deaths a year and physical inactivity leads to 191,000 (Danaei et al. 2009). Obesity has significant social consequences as well, often leading to employment discrimination, teasing, and insults (Carr and Friedman 2005).

Obesity is related to race and ethnicity, with non–Hispanic blacks having the highest rates of obesity (44.1%), then Mexican Americans (39.3%) and all Hispanics (37.9%), and lowest rates for non–Hispanic whites (32.6%; CDC 2012c). Obesity tends to be lower for women with more education and/or higher incomes. For non–Hispanic black

TABLE 15-3 Weight Categories Based on Body Mass Index (BMI)

Weight Category	Body Mass Index
Underweight	< 18.5
Normal	18.5 to 24.9
Overweight	25 to 29.9
Obese	30 to 34.9
Clinically obese	35 to 39.9
Morbidly obese	> 40

BMI = 703 × weight (lb)/height^2 (inches). For example, someone who is 5'4" weighing 174 pounds or more, or someone 5'9" weighing 203 pounds or more has a BMI of 30 or more and would be considered obese (Ogden et al. 2012).

Source: National Heart, Lung, and Blood Institute (NHLBI). 1998. Clinical Guidelines on the Identification, Evaluation, and Treatment of Overweight and Obesity in Adults. NIH Publication 98-4083. National Institutes of Health. Retrieved July 2012 (http://www.nhlbi.nih.gov/guidelines/obesity/ob_gdlns.pdf).

and Mexican-American men, obesity is lower for those with higher incomes, but not for those with higher education.

It may be tempting to place all of the blame for obesity on the individuals who become obese. However, there are many factors that contribute to obesity. Many people work at more sedentary tasks. There is less cooking in the home and greater reliance on fast food. Video games and the Internet have supplanted much of the time children once played outside. And reduced funding for education sometimes leads to fewer physical education classes. In addition, there is considerable evidence that structural characteristics of the food industry beyond the control of individuals play a role in the rise in obesity and make it particularly hard for some groups of people to avoid becoming obese. Former Food and Drug Administration (FDA) commissioner David Kessler argues that when we consume foods containing salt, sugar, and fat, this changes our brain biochemistry. By manipulating these three ingredients, food manufacturers can take advantage of this biochemistry to make and sell foods that stimulate our appetites, leading to a spiral of desire and consumption and a nation full of overweight overeaters. The food industry uses this to increase demand and profits for popular brand manufacturers, chain restaurants, and fast food franchises. Other factors also serve to increase obesity in the United States, particularly for the poor. Higher prices are often charged for less fattening food because people are willing to pay more for healthy food. The poor also face the unavailability of free places to exercise safely in many communities (Brownell and Horgen 2004), and the lack of grocery stores where healthy food can be obtained in many poor neighborhoods (Morland et al. 2002).

Exercise

The health benefits of physical activity have been documented in numerous studies. Some of the most important benefits are summarized by the CDC (2011f). Physical activity has more impact on health than does almost any other life style factor. People who are physically active for 7 hours a week have a 40% lower risk of dying early than people with less than 30 minutes of activity a week (CDC 2011f). Regular physical activity helps people control their weight, helps build and maintain muscle mass and strength, reduces the risk of cardiovascular diseases, lowers blood pressure, improves cholesterol levels, reduces the risk of Type 2 diabetes, reduces the risk of some cancers, strengthens bones and muscles reducing the loss of bone density that comes with age, reduces the chance of falls, improves mental health, and helps maintain the ability to perform the activities of daily living (CDC 2011f).

Eating Disorders

Eating disorders are extreme efforts to control weight through unhealthy means. These include **anorexia nervosa**—an intense fear of becoming fat and a distorted image of

Eating disorder An extreme effort to control weight through unhealthy means.

Anorexia nervosa An intense fear of becoming fat and a distorted image of one's own body, leading someone to drastically reduce body weight through starving.

Bulimia nervosa Binge-eating followed by self-induced vomiting.

Binge eating disorder Occurs when the person engages in recurrent binge eating (eating too much at a sitting).

Muscle dysmorphia A condition in which males see themselves as smaller than they are and work very hard to gain muscle mass.

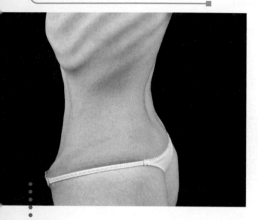

Eating disorders, such as anorexia nervosa, are related to a cultural norm that equates thinness with attractiveness.
© Baloncici/Shutterstock, Inc.

Muscle dysmorphia is a disorder related to a cultural norm that equates male muscle mass with attractiveness.
© Istvan Csak/Shutterstock, Inc.

one's own body, leading someone to drastically reduce body weight through starving—and **bulimia nervosa**—the practice of binge-eating followed by self-induced vomiting. A third eating disorder is **binge eating disorder**, in which the person engages in recurrent binge eating. Unlike bulimia, a person with binge eating disorder does not purge and, hence, is often overweight and feels a loss of control over eating. Such people often experience guilt and shame about their binge eating, sometimes leading to even more binge eating.

Much of the research on eating disorders argues they are related to a cultural norm of thinness. This "cult of thinness" encourages women to believe that men are only attracted to thin women, that thinness is essential to being attractive, and that they are not as thin as they should be (Hesse-Biber 1996). These eating disorders are seen by many sociologists as the product of a patriarchal culture that inculcates the importance of thinness to women on a daily basis through the media, through family, and through colleagues (Hesse-Biber 1996; Levine 1987).

This research recognizes that eating disorders are often "gendered," having greatest impact on women. However, other research suggests they are also raced and classed. White, middle-class women experience eating disorders in very different ways than African-American women or Latina women. Sociologist Becky Thompson (1992) argues that "by focusing on the emphasis on slenderness, the eating problems literature falls into the same trap of assuming that the problems reflect women's 'obsession' with appearance" (Thompson 1992:558). Instead, she found that many of the black and Latina women in her research—even those less influenced by the dominant standards of beauty and those one step from hunger and hence unlikely to be susceptible to eating problems—also display eating disorders. Those disorders, she argued, are not limited to middle-class white women but are strategies used to cope with a wide range of trauma and stress, including poverty, physical violence, and sexual abuse.

Anorexia nervosa occurs 10 times as often in females as in males (Woodside 2001). Men are less likely than women to be diagnosed with eating disorders (Anderson 1992). Some men's distorted body image is similar to that for females, and they work very hard to become thin. Other males have **muscle dysmorphia**, in which males see themselves as smaller than they are and work very hard to gain muscle mass. This becomes particularly unhealthy when, in their eagerness to bulk up, males sometimes resort to use of steroids or other dangerous drugs to increase muscle mass (Pope et al. 1997). A more "rational" but equally dangerous case occurs when males engaged in competitive sports use steroids or other dangerous drugs as performance enhancers (New York State Health Department 2012).

The National Institute of Mental Health (NIMH 2012) estimates that for at least some time in their life, 2.8% of US adults (3.5% of females and 2.0% of males) will suffer from binge eating disorder, 0.6% of adults will suffer from anorexia nervosa (.9% of females and .3% of males), and 0.6% of adults will suffer from bulimia nervosa (1.5% of females and 0.5% of males).

Sometimes one addiction combines with another. For example, some students on college campuses use the term *anorexiaholic* or *drunkorexia* (Treatment4addiction 2011) to describe a combination of anorexia and binge drinking. This refers to a tendency for some college students to "swap" food calories for alcohol calories, limiting food consumption during the day in order to be able to drink in excess at night while maintaining a trim figure.

Alcohol

Alcohol is widely understood to cause great loss of life and considerable expense to society. However, systematic studies of those effects have been few and far between. For the first time since 1998, an extensive study published in 2011 examined data from 2006 regarding the costs of excessive alcohol consumption in the United States. That study, by Boucherey and colleagues (2011), concluded that excessive alcohol consumption leads to an average of 79,000 premature deaths each year, increased disease, property damage, motor vehicle accidents, alcohol-related crime, and lost productivity. Their economic analysis concluded the economic costs of excessive drinking were $223.5 billion in 2006. Nearly half the cost was borne by the government. They estimate the economic impact of excessive alcohol consumption amounts to approximately $746 per person or $1.90 per drink FIGURE 15-5. Almost three-quarters of the costs were due to **binge drinking**—consuming four or more alcoholic drinks per occasion for women or five or more for men. The great majority of total costs (72%) were losses in workplace productivity, 11% due to health care required as a result of excessive drinking, 9% to criminal justice expenses, and 6% to motor vehicle accidents resulting from driving impaired.

Alcohol is a prevalent problem on college campuses, where nearly two-thirds of college students report using alcohol in the last 30 days and more than a third (37%) report binge drinking during the last two weeks. Since 1980, however, drinking by college students has dropped from 81.8% to 65%. Nevertheless, the percentage of college students reporting engaging in binge drinking in the last two weeks only dropped from 43.9% to 37%. These trends, along with trends in cigarette smoking and drug abuse on college campuses, are displayed in FIGURE 15-6.

Binge drinking Widely recognized as consuming four or more alcoholic drinks per occasion for women or five or more for men.

Drugs

As can be seen in Figure 15-6, reported use of marijuana and cocaine by college students have both dropped significantly between 1980 and 2010. Cocaine use dropped from 6.8% in 1980 to 1% in 2010, while marijuana use dropped from 34% to 17.5% during

1 Drink = $1.90 in economic costs or $746 per person annually

FIGURE 15-5 Economic costs of alcohol.
Source: CDC. 2012. Excessive Drinking Costs U.S. $223.5 Billion. CDC 24/7: Saving Lives. Protecting People. Retrieved July, 2012 (http://www.cdc.gov/Features/Alcohol Consumption/).

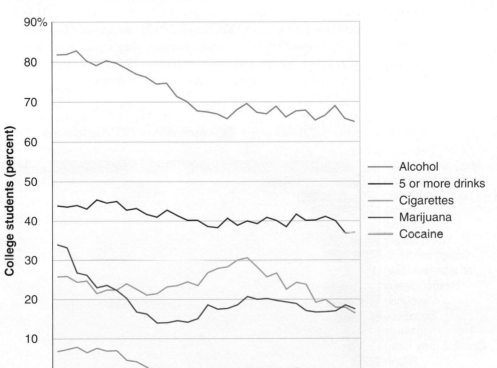

FIGURE 15-6 Reported drug use, alcohol use, and cigarette use in last 30 days among US college students (1980–2010).
Source: Johnston, L., O'Malley, P., Bachman, J., and Schulenberg, J. 2011. Monitoring the Future: National survey results on drug use, 1975–2010. Vol. II. College students & adults ages 19–50. U. of Michigan Institute for Social Research. Retrieved July 2012 (http://www.monitoringthefuture.org/pubs/monographs/mtf-vol2_2010.pdf).

Designer drugs Lab-made versions of drugs similar to designated controlled substances under US law

the same time period. Today's drug scene sometimes includes a wide range of **designer drugs**—lab-made versions of drugs similar to designated controlled substances under US law (Turney 2011). One variant of designer drugs that mimic the effects of cocaine or amphetamines is often sold as "bath salts" marked "not for human consumption" in an effort to get around drug laws (DEA 2012). In 2010, college students were about as likely to smoke marijuana as they were to smoke cigarettes, and they were less likely to smoke either one than their parents were 30 years earlier. However, the rate of use of marijuana reported by high school seniors in 2010 was more than twice that for college students at 36.4% (NIDA 2010).

Prescription and Over-the-Counter Drugs

Roughly one in nine youth abused prescription drugs in the past year. As can be seen in FIGURE 15-7, after marijuana, prescription and over-the-counter medications account for most of the commonly abused drugs among high school seniors (NIDA 2010). In 2007, prescription drugs caused more deaths than illicit drugs (CDC 2011d).

Drug abuse is a global problem. Drug use places a heavy financial burden on societies in terms of treatment, productivity loss, and drug-related crime. The United Nations Office on Drugs and Crime (UNODC) estimates that between $200–$250 billion US (.3 to .4% of global GDP) would be required to cover all drug treatment costs worldwide. Actual expenditures are much less, and fewer than one in five people needing drug treatment receive it. The impact on productivity is even greater, with productivity losses in the United States estimated at 0.9% of GDP and in other countries between 0.3 and 0.4% of GDP. Costs associated with drug-related crime are higher yet and are estimated to be around 1.6% of GDP based on studies in England and Wales (UNODC 2012).

Worldwide consumption of illegal drugs is well below levels of tobacco and alcohol. While 25% of the population aged 15 and above worldwide used tobacco, only 2.5% used illicit drugs. Annually, 42% of adults worldwide use alcohol, eight times more than the annual use of illicit drugs (5%).

Firearms

In 2010, there were 30,923 deaths from firearms reported in the United States. Most firearms-related deaths were due to suicides (19,308) or assault (11,015), while 600 were from accidents (Murphy and Kochanek 2012). We include firearms in our discussion of life style issues related to health because they are nearly as much of a risk as drug abuse (37,792 deaths) and motor vehicles (35,080). It might seem unfair to classify firearms as a life style issue, since—as with motor vehicles—you may be at

FIGURE 15-7 Drug use among high school seniors.

Source: National Institute on Drug Abuse (NIDA). 2010. National survey on drug use and health, 2010. Retrieved July 2012 (http://www.drugabuse.gov/related-topics/trends-statistics/infographics/prescription-drug-abuse-young-people-risk).

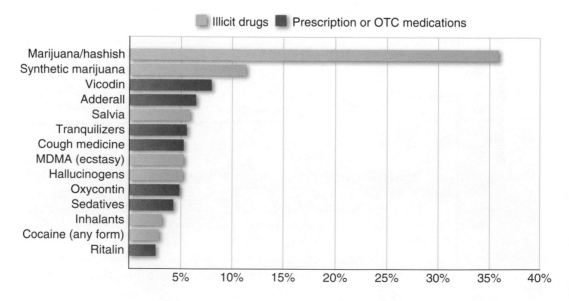

risk of dying from firearms due to the actions of other people (the 11,015 deaths due to assaults). However, an individual's chances of dying from an accident or assault involving a firearm can be influenced by whether the person spends time in situations where firearms are more likely to be present, and the most likely death by firearms comes from suicide (19,308). It should be pointed out that suicide rates in the United States are 16.6 per 100,000 persons for men and 4.0 per 100,000 for women. This is slightly lower than average suicide rates in Organization for Economic Cooperation and Development (OECD) countries of 17.6 for men and 5.2 for women (Rampell 2009) even though there is generally much greater access to guns in the United States. Thus, evidence suggests that suicide may not be more common in the United States, but when it occurs, it is more likely to involve use of a firearm.

Unsafe Sex and Sexually Transmitted Diseases

Sexually transmitted diseases (STDs) are infectious diseases transmitted through sexual activity. These include gonorrhea, syphilis, chlamydia, genital herpes, human papillomavirus (HPV), and, most notably, AIDS. About 1,308,000 cases of chlamydia, 309,000 cases of gonorrhea, and 13,000 cases of syphilis were reported in the United States in 2010 (CDC 2010c). Chlamydia cases increased by 5.1% from 2009 to 2010 and represent the largest number of cases ever reported to CDC for any STD (CDC 2010d). Chlamydia is caused by a bacterium and, though symptoms are usually mild or absent, can cause irreversible damage or infertility in women. Gonorrhea, if untreated, can result in sterility, and syphilis, untreated, can result in blindness, psychological disorders, and death. Most cases of these two diseases can be cured with antibiotics such as penicillin, but some strains of the microorganisms that are resistant to antibiotics are becoming increasingly common. Genital herpes is caused by a virus that infects one in seven US adults (about 20 to 30 million people) and is incurable. In 2010, there were 232,000 new cases of genital herpes reported in initial visits to physicians' offices in the United States (CDC 2010d). Genital herpes is not fatal to adults and may be symptomless but often produces periodic painful blisters on the genitals. If transmitted to infants during vaginal delivery, herpes may be fatal.

The most likely death by firearms is suicide.
© LiquidLibrary

HPV (human papillomavirus) is the most common sexually transmitted infection, including more than 40 types. A study between 2003 and 2005 found that nearly a quarter of the population in the United States has some form of HPV infection (Datta et al. 2008). Most people infected with HPV have no noticeable symptoms and do not realize they have it. There are more than 40 types of HPV. Some of those can lead to genital warts, while others can lead to anogenital cancers, including cervical cancer. In 2010, 376,000 cases of genital warts were reported in initial visits to physicians' offices in the United States (CDC 2010d).

AIDS (acquired immune deficiency syndrome), the final stage of HIV infection in which people have badly weakened immune systems, was first recognized in 1981 and is by far the most serious of STDs. Currently, AIDS is still incurable. However, there are medications that make it possible to live with the disease, dramatically prolonging the lives of those infected, and that reduce the transmission of the virus. AIDS is caused by a **human immunodeficiency virus (HIV)** that attacks the white blood cells, causing the victim's immune system to be ineffective against a wide range of infectious diseases. Untreated AIDS victims die of one of those infectious diseases in a matter of a few years. With treatment, people can live much longer—even decades—with HIV before they develop AIDS.

It would be a mistake to become complacent about HIV and AIDS. Current treatments are not a cure and do not work for some patients. Patients will have to continue taking the drugs the rest of their lives, and there are often significant side effects. The HIV virus remains in those patients in minute amounts and sometimes comes back in force. HIV also tends to mutate and to adapt to drugs, so over time, those drugs lose

HPV (human papillomavirus) The most commonly sexually transmitted infection, including more than 40 types.

AIDS (acquired immune deficiency syndrome) The final stage of HIV infection in which people have badly weakened immune systems.

HIV (human immunodeficiency virus) A lentivirus that weakens the immune system, leading to acquired immunodeficiency syndrome (AIDS).

their effectiveness. Finally, those drugs are also very expensive, with patients often needing several drugs and with a single drug, Atripla, costing as much as $25,000 per year for a single patient (Vastag 2012).

AIDS is not spread through casual contact such as touching, sharing food, or even coughing. The HIV virus is transmitted through sharing body fluids such as blood, breast milk, or semen. While the HIV virus is found in saliva, the risk of contracting AIDS through kissing is very low. Thus, people at risk of AIDS are people who engage in behaviors that involve the sharing of these body fluids. Homosexuals, intravenous drug users, and people who have multiple sex partners are most at risk of contracting AIDS. Anal sex is a high risk factor for both homosexuals and heterosexuals because it may result in rectal bleeding, permitting the easy transmission of the HIV virus. Sharing needles used to inject drugs is a common practice among intravenous drug users and has accounted for much of the spread of AIDS in this group (CDC 2012e).

Since the AIDS epidemic began, an estimated 1,129,127 people have been diagnosed with AIDS in the United States and 619,400 people have died, 17,774 of those in 2009. In 2010, 47,129 people were diagnosed with HIV and 33,015 were diagnosed with AIDS. FIGURE 15-8 shows how the epidemic has spread, beginning with rapid increases in new diagnoses, deaths, and prevalence, with new AIDS diagnoses first leveling off in 1993 at nearly 80,000 annually, then dropping to roughly 33,000 annually today. In 1996, the first effective drug treatments became available and annual deaths from AIDS dropped from a high of more than 50,000 annually to less than 20,000 annually today. However, the prevalence (the number of people living with a condition) continues to increase to nearly 500,000 people with AIDS and 1.2 million with HIV infection today (CDC 2012g).

Some categories of people are more at risk for HIV than others. The distribution of risk mirrors cultural norms related to gender and sexuality that are more accepting of multiple sexual partners for men than women and for homosexuals than heterosexuals. Highest are men who have sex with men (MSM), including gay and bisexual men. MSM make up approximately 2% of the US population, yet in 2009, they accounted for 61% of all new HIV infections overall and 69% of new HIV infections among persons aged 13 to 29. By the end of 2009, there were 441,669 MSM living with an HIV diagnosis in the United States (CDC 2012f). Among MSM, black MSM are more likely to have

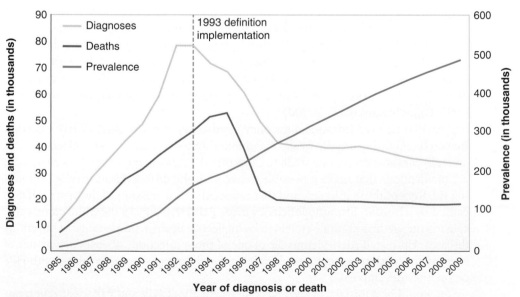

Note: All displayed data have been statistically adjusted to account for reporting delays, but not for incomplete reporting. Death may be due to any cause.

FIGURE 15-8 AIDS diagnoses, deaths, and persons living with AIDS (1985–2009) in the United States and six US-dependent areas.

Source: CDC, 2012. AIDS Surveillance—Trends (1985–2010). Retrieved July 2012 (http://www.cdc.gov/hiv/topics/surveillance/resources/slides/trends/index.htm).

new infections than other men, and young black MSM infections increased from 2006 to 2009 by 48% FIGURE 15-9. Among gay men in the United States, infection rates have been increasing by 8% each year since 2001, with 15% of MSM having HIV even while broader population rates are declining (Park 2012).

Among racial/ethnic groups, African Americans are the racial/ethnic group most affected by HIV, and in 2009, African Americans comprised 44% of all new HIV infections, while they are only 14% of the US population (CDC 2012d). After black MSM, HIV/AIDS is an emerging issue for black heterosexual women. This appears to be a consequence of the disproportionate numbers of black men who are incarcerated at least once during their lifetime, the lack of AIDS testing or condom distribution in prisons, and a tendency for many men who have sex with men in prison to self-identify as heterosexual and not consider the possibility of AIDS transmission to female sex partners in the community after their release from jail.

Several strategies can reduce the spread of HIV. Abstaining from sexual activities or having sex only in a long-term mutually monogamous relationship with an uninfected partner are most effective. Limiting the number of sexual partners and choosing only responsible HIV-negative partners reduces your risk. Practicing safe sex (using latex condoms) reduces risk. It is also important that people who might be at risk for HIV receive testing. If they know their HIV status, they can avoid exposing others. Also, early treatment of people infected with HIV even before they display symptoms both slows the deterioration of their immune system and reduces the amount of the virus in their bloodstream, making them less likely to spread the disease. Avoiding injecting drugs and not sharing needles also reduces risk (CDC 2012e).

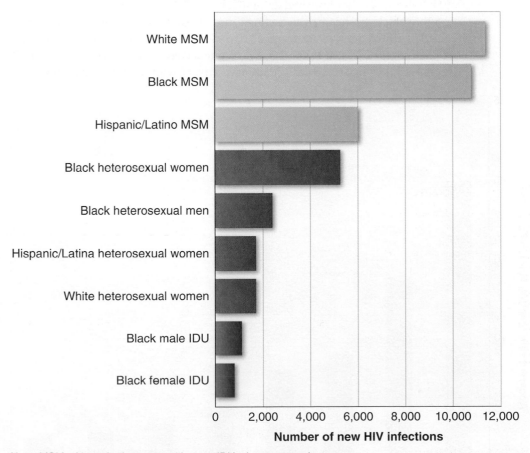

Note: MSM—Men who have sex with men; IDU—Intravenous drug users

FIGURE 15-9 Number of new HIV infections by risk category (2010).
Source: CDC. 2012. HIV among gay and bisexual men. Retrieved July 2012 (http://www.cdc.gov/hiv/topics/msm/index.htm).

In some parts of the world, HIV/AIDS is far more of a problem than in others. It is particularly acute in Sub-Saharan Africa, where an entire generation has been affected. There, the United Nations estimates there are 22.5 million people (5% of the entire population) living with HIV, 1.8 million new HIV infections per year, and 1.3 million AIDS-related deaths per year. South and South-East Asia are next, with 4.1 million people (0.3%) living with HIV, 270,000 new HIV infections a year, and 260,000 AIDS-related deaths per year. In total, there are estimated to be 33.3 million people around the globe living with HIV, 2.6 million new infections in 2009, and 1.8 million AIDS-related deaths in 2009 (UNAIDS 2012).

Motor Vehicle Accidents

In 2009, there were 35,080 deaths in the US due to motor vehicle accidents, while more than 2.3 million adult drivers and passengers were treated in emergency rooms as a result of being injured in motor vehicle accidents (CDC 2011e). One study estimated the cost of crash-related deaths and injuries to be $70 billion in 2005 (Naumann et al. 2005).

Accidents are more likely when there is distracted driving, impaired driving, or very young or very old drivers. Distracted driving leading to fatal crashes increased from 7% in 2005 to 11% in 2009 (NTSA 2009). Distracted driving involves taking your eyes off the road, your hands off the wheel, or your mind off driving. Common distractions include cell phones (25% of US drivers "regularly or fairly often" talk on their cell phones while driving) and texting or emailing (9% of US drivers do this "regularly or often" while driving; Novelli 2010). In 2009, more than 5,400 people died and 448,000 people were injured in accidents involving a distracted driver; more than 1,000 deaths involved cell phones (NTSA 2009). Nearly one-third of car crash deaths (10,839 in 2009) involve an alcohol-impaired driver (CDC 2012i).

Motor vehicle crashes are the leading cause of death for US teens, accounting for one-third of deaths. In 2009, teens ages 16 to 19 were four times more likely to crash than older drivers (CDC 2011e). In FIGURE 15-10 are accident rates by age group. In 2009, the overall accident rate was 8 per 100 licensed drivers, while for teen drivers it was 20.

FIGURE 15-10 US accident rates by age group (2009).
Source: Data from U.S. Census. 2012. The 2012 Statistical Abstract, Table 1114. Retrieved July 2012 (http://www.census.gov/compendia/statab/2012/tables/12s1114.xls).

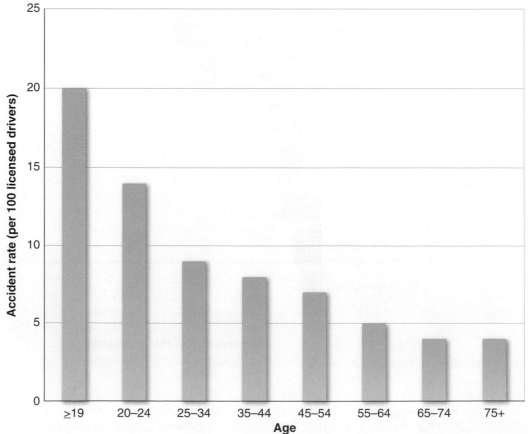

Crashes occur most often for males (CDC 2011e), teens driving with teen passengers (Chen et al. 2000), and newly licensed teens (IIHS 2009). Motor vehicle accidents are far higher in countries such as South Africa, India, and Egypt, for example, than in the United States. Poor roads, lack of vehicle maintenance, less driver education, and lax enforcement of traffic laws contribute to the higher death and accident rates in lower-income countries.

CONCEPT LEARNING CHECK 15.4   Life Style and Deaths

As measured by the annual number of deaths, indicate which of the following pairs of life style factors leads to more deaths.

_____ 1.   **A.** Smoking   **B.** Alcohol

_____ 2.   **A.** Alcohol   **B.** Drug abuse

_____ 3.   **A.** Unprotected sex   **B.** Diet/exercise

_____ 4.   **A.** Diet/exercise   **B.** Smoking

_____ 5.   **A.** Firearms   **B.** Unprotected sex

15.5 Health Care in the United States

The domination of the healthcare system in the United States by scientific medicine has led to increased use of technology, rising costs, and limited access to types of health care that have been the focus of healthcare reforms.

- Distinguish scientific medicine from alternative medicine.

- Analyze trends in healthcare costs.

- Describe healthcare delivery systems in the United States.

- Discuss factors affecting both cost and quality of health care in the United States.

Scientific Medicine

Medicine is the social institution that focuses on maintaining health and preventing or treating disease. Early in the 20th century, there were 160 medical schools in the United States. However, when the American Medical Association examined those schools in 1906, they found only 82 to be acceptable (Starr 1982). Training was often short, with no clinical training, and you could become a physician without even graduating from high school. Medical schools had very different philosophies of medicine, not all of which were based on science. Even Harvard University's medical school was only a two-year school. In response, the Carnegie Foundation funded Abraham Flexner to visit every medical school and recommend ways to improve the quality of medical education. Flexner found some schools had no books and many had totally inadequate laboratories. In his report in 1910, Flexner recommended raising the admissions standards of medical schools and encouraged philanthropies to fund only the most scientific ones. The Flexner Report was a watershed for medicine, leading to the professionalization of medicine and the accreditation of medical schools. Based on this report, some of the schools were funded very well and were then able to attract faculty and students, while many other schools were forced to close their doors.

Control of medical schools through accreditation was followed by efforts to make medicine a monopoly. Laws were passed making it illegal for anyone to practice medicine who was not a graduate of an approved medical school. Competing modes

Medicine The social institution that focuses on maintaining health and preventing or treating disease.

of health care became illegal, and medicine consolidated its hold over health care. Physicians tried to exclude other professions from the practice of health care of any sort—including chiropractors, osteopaths, and midwives. Physicians worked to prevent these others from being reimbursed by third-party payers. Physicians also succeeded in making the practice of some of these other health professions illegal in many states. Medicine became something practiced only by white Anglo-Saxon Protestant males, and for most of the rest of the century, medical schools rarely admitted women or minorities. This monopoly on health care by medicine led to the situation in which by law, only this small group of white men was permitted to diagnose and treat medical problems. The result, said anthropologist Horace Miner with tongue in cheek, could be viewed as a scientific priesthood (Miner 1956) complete with its own secret language (Latin), sacred pieces of parchment (prescription forms), and even translators (pharmacists). Only these men had the sacred knowledge of what was needed for people's health.

Holistic/Eastern Medicine

The rise of scientific medicine in the United States corresponded to the rejection of alternative forms of medicine, including holistic medicine from indigenous American Indians and Eastern medicine. Holistic medicine and Eastern medicine are examples of the kinds of health care that in the United States have often been relegated to a marginal role due to the dominance of the Western technologically oriented medicine commonly practiced by the American medical profession. The dominant position of scientific medicine in the United States led to many forms of **alternative medicine** (approaches to medicine that fall outside scientific medicine) being denied coverage in health insurance plans and established institutions within scientific medicine, such as the American Cancer Society, cautioning against their use and recommending that if they are used, it only be in conjunction with mainstream medical care (American Cancer Society 2012).

Holistic medicine emphasizes the whole person, including physical, environmental, emotional, social, and spiritual elements (American Holistic Medical Association 2012). Practitioners of holistic medicine often have little or no separation between medicine and the spiritual and religious belief systems that underlie health and healing. Holistic treatments often are based on the view that ill health is the result of an imbalance that needs to be corrected. Treatments include acupuncture, nutritional supplements, natural diet and herbal remedies, and homeopathic remedies. Homeopathy, for example, assumes that whatever causes the disease in healthy people, in small quantities, can cure the disease in sick people (Hahnemann, 1833). Many of these notions and treatments were widely regarded as quackery by the medical community, though some elements of holistic medicine, including acupuncture, are sometimes practiced along with scientific medicine.

Traditional Chinese medicine is another form of alternative medicine often criticized by scientific medical proponents. One current in Chinese medicine views disease symptoms as possible reflections of an imbalance of yin and yang, with some symptoms (such as heat sensations, night sweats, dry mouth, and rapid pulse) suggesting too little yin (Kaptchuck 2000:230), and other symptoms (such as aversion to cold, cold limbs, slow pulse) suggesting too little yang (Wiseman and Ellis 1996:142).

The Role of Technology in Medicine

There is a vast array of medical technologies available today that have transformed medicine. Just a few of these include vaccinations for polio, smallpox, and HPV; antibiotics, including penicillin and tetracycline; diagnostic tests and testing equipment, including CT scans, MRI scans, ultrasound, X-rays, HIV tests, and endoscopies; procedures, including laser cataract surgery, *in vitro* fertilization, and open-heart surgery; organ transplants, including heart, kidney, and liver; and insulin pumps, defibrillators, artificial hearts, pacemakers, stem cell therapies, and telesurgery. These technologies

Alternative medicine Several approaches to medicine that fall outside scientific medicine.

Holistic medicine Medicine that considers the whole person, including physical, mental, and spiritual needs, and is an alternative to scientific medicine.

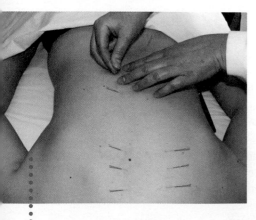

Some elements of holistic medicine, including acupuncture, are sometimes practiced along with scientific medicine.

© Cora Reed/Shutterstock, Inc.

have all been widely adopted and have transformed medicine. But have they produced improvements in health proportionate to their increased costs?

The use of high-tech medical tests and surgeries in the United States has risen steadily as new technologies become available, according to a report by the National Center for Health Statistics (1997). Between 1996 and 2006, the use of MRIs and CT scans tripled. Between 1994 and 2006, surgeries increased 70% for knee replacements, 31% for kidney transplants, and 43% for liver transplants. The use of prescription drugs also increased. In 1994, 38% of the population was taking at least one prescription. By 2006, that had risen to 47%. During the same period, the number of Americans taking three or more prescriptions nearly doubled to 20%, and the use of statin drugs increased by a factor of 10 (Alfonsi and Hutchison 2010)! The National Health Interview Survey of adults in 2011 found that 46.5% of them had used the Internet to look up health information (Cohen and Adams 2012).

However, it is not clear whether all this technology is actually improving health. CT scans, for example, expose patients to 500 times the radiation of a conventional X-ray, which many health experts believe raises the risk of cancer. Yet at least some improvement in health as a result of technology seems clear. CT scans, for example, replace risky and painful exploratory surgeries that would have occurred in the 1960s for conditions like unexplained abdominal pain. However, observers have noted a tendency to overuse technologies, at least in part, as defensive medicine, in which doctors use available technologies to avoid getting sued if they were to miss a diagnosis.

The Economics of Health Care

The United States has been tremendously successful at discovering new treatments and inventing new technologies for improving health care. It is often argued that the United States leads the world in innovations in health care, and certainly it is true that many of the new technologies, medicines, and vaccinations came from the United States. However, there is more to health care than invention. There must also be healthcare delivery. This requires having the resources and a system capable of delivering healthcare treatments to those who need it. Here we consider the economics of health care, including the rising costs of health care over time, who pays for health care, who has access to health care, and finally, efforts to reform health care in the United States.

Rising Healthcare Costs in the United States

People the world over value life and health so much we would sacrifice almost anything to get and keep it . . . and that is part of the basic problem. We value health so much that it is difficult to say no to a new technology or a new treatment that promises to improve health. To draw a line and say that something is too expensive and those people having that condition should be allowed to die is an explicit form of rationing of health care that is widely rejected in the United States.

As a result of our unwillingness to ration health care, healthcare costs in the United States are rising faster than any other sector of the economy. This is causing concern that medical care costs may outpace our ability to afford them. FIGURE 15-11 displays national health expenditures per capita in the United States, from 1960 to 2010. In 1970, total healthcare spending in the United States was $75 billion, or $356 per capita and 7.2% of the gross domestic product (GDP). By 2010, the United States spent $2.6 trillion on health care, or $8,402 per person, and 17.9% of the GDP (Kaiser Family Foundation 2012d). In the decade between 2000 and 2010 alone, per-capita healthcare expenditures increased by roughly 70% from $4,878 to $8,402, and the share of GDP rose from 13.8% to 17.9%. (Kaiser Family Foundation 2012d).

Technology and rising healthcare costs. Why are healthcare costs increasing so much faster than other sectors of the economy? Several factors have been cited as contributing to healthcare costs, including the aging of the US population and the higher costs of health care for the elderly, rising obesity, and increases in the prevalence of some diseases (Kaiser Family Foundation 2012d:25). Another oft-cited reason for

FIGURE 15-11 US health expenditures per capita (1960–2010).

Source: Data from Center for Medicare and Medicaid Services, 2012. National Health Expenditure Data. Office of the Actuary, National Health Statistics Group. Retrieved August 2012 (http://www.cms .gov/Research-Statistics-Data-and-Systems/Statistics-Trends-and-Reports/NationalHealthExpendData/ Downloads/NHEGDP10.zip).

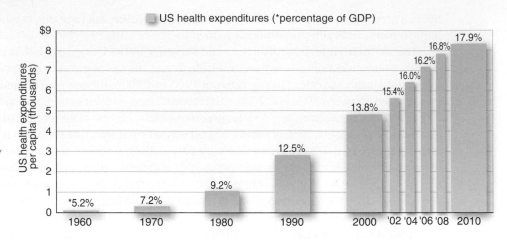

increasing costs is the high cost of new healthcare technologies such as transplants, CT scans, and open-heart surgery. Certainly the long list of new technologies mentioned above appears to be a likely source of at least some of the rise in costs of health care.

One effort to assess the impact of technology on healthcare costs is an analysis of the contribution of different factors to the costs of health care conducted by the US Congressional Budget Office (CBO) in January 2008. That report identified several factors that influence rising healthcare costs. For example, in 2001, spending per capita for a morbidly obese person averaged 70% more than for someone of normal weight.

Based on their review of the literature, the CBO concluded that roughly half of the increase in healthcare costs during the past several decades was associated with new technological advances that expanded the capabilities of medicine (CBO 2008:12). New technologies can sometimes reduce costs. The polio vaccine, for example, cost very little per person and dramatically reduced costly long-term treatments for the few people who contracted polio.

However, many advances involve ongoing treatment for chronic conditions that can require considerable costs where there once were none. Drugs to manage AIDS, for example, cost thousands of dollars a year, and their use can continue for decades. The CBO cites several technological advances that have led to increased costs even when at first blush the technology seemed likely to reduce costs. For example, coronary angioplasty—a procedure in which a tube is inserted into the artery and a balloon is used to expand the artery at a blockage to restore blood flow—appeared likely to reduce costs. It cost less than open-heart surgery and involved far less trauma. However, since it was less traumatic, it could be used on more frail patients, and many patients who would have foregone the trauma and risk of open-heart surgery chose to undergo angioplasty. As a result, spending for heart disease patients increased after angioplasty was introduced (Cutler and Huckman 2003). Other new medical technologies that have led to increased healthcare costs include renal dialysis and transplants, bone marrow transplants, neonatal intensive care, joint replacement, and diagnostic imaging (CBO 2008).

Preventive care: A way to reduce healthcare costs? While we repeatedly spend hundreds of thousands of dollars trying to save patients through high technology, we often overlook less dramatic but much more cost-effective preventive measures. For example, decades ago, it was pointed out that only 40 to 60% of preschool children in the United States in 1993 received recommended vaccinations and "in some inner-city neighborhoods the number is just 10 percent. . . . Studies show that for every dollar spent on childhood immunization, $10 is saved in later medical costs." The entire country could be inoculated for between $475–$600 million per year. This could save between $4–$6 billion per year in later medical costs (*The New York Times* 1993a).

Can preventive care help reduce healthcare costs? The basic logic of this argument is that it costs less to educate people and encourage them to live healthy life styles, thus avoiding expensive health problems. Persuading an adult to take a low-dose aspirin every day to help prevent heart attack, for example, should cost less than the very expensive procedures of cardiac catheterization or open-heart surgery after the person experiences a heart attack. However, the Robert Wood Johnson Foundation summarized three nationwide studies of preventive medicine and found that only two preventive measures—childhood immunizations and health education on the use of low-dose aspirin—were found by all three studies to be cost-saving measures that actually reduce eventual expenditures. In addition, alcohol screening and counseling was found to be cost saving in the two studies that included it, and tobacco screening and prevention and motor vehicle safety counseling were found to be cost saving in one study. Nevertheless, most other preventive measures cost more than the savings they produce. Hence, the report suggests that additional preventive care is unlikely to significantly reduce healthcare costs (Cohen and Neumann 2009).

Many other preventive healthcare measures do not actually save money but are cost-*effective* measures. That is, they lead to increased benefits in the form of additional **quality-adjusted life years (QALY)**. A QALY would be 1 for one additional year of life at optimal health, but between 0 and 1 for an additional year of life with an adverse condition causing pain or reducing participation in activities. Several screening interventions were found to be cost effective, including screening for hypertension, cholesterol, colorectal cancer, breast cancer, and HIV (Goodell, Cohen, and Neumann 2009).

Cost effectiveness of treatments, as measured by QALYs, is sometimes used to ration health services in order to keep costs down and maximize the improvement in quality of life per dollar spent. For example, in Britain, "the National Institute for Health and Clinical Excellence determines what therapies will be covered by the National Health Service. It generally recommends against paying for a therapy that costs more than $31,000 to $47,000 for each year of life gained, adjusted for quality." For example, the Institute has denied or limited coverage of expensive drugs for conditions including pancreatic cancer, macular degeneration, and Alzheimer's (Porter 2012). This, incidentally, is an example of the rationing of health care that we tend to resist strongly in the United States.

Who Pays and Who Has Access?

Most health care in the United States is paid for by **third-party payers**—someone other than the patient or the healthcare provider—such as the government or private insurance companies. In 2010, only 11.6% of national health expenditures in the United States were paid by the patient directly. Approximately one-third of expenditures (32.7%) were paid by private health insurers, another third (35.7%) were paid by federal and state government funding of Medicare and Medicaid, and the final 20% was paid by other third-party payers, public insurance programs, and investments (Kaiser Family Foundation 2012a:12).

Insurance coverage affects the amount of care received and the health outcomes. Doyle (2005) studied victims of auto accidents with and without health insurance who were admitted to emergency rooms in Wisconsin. He found that those without health insurance received 20% less care. Those without insurance were hospitalized an average of 6.4 days, while those who had insurance were hospitalized 9.2 days, and $3,300 more was spent on insured patients. The uninsured were 40% more likely to die from their injuries. Yet in 2012, before the Affordable Care Act was ruled constitutional by the US Supreme Court, there were well over 50 million uninsured Americans (Waananen 2012). Most people who have private health insurance in the United States get insurance through their employer, where group insurance rates make it more affordable. Most of the people who lack health insurance are those who do not have jobs that offer health insurance or who are unemployed. Differential access to health care based on the ability to afford health insurance turns out to be a form of de facto rationing of health care that we in the United States have long permitted.

Quality-adjusted life year (QALY) Would be 1 for one additional year of life at optimal health, but between 0 and 1 for an additional year of life with an adverse condition causing pain or reducing participation in activities.

Third-party payer Someone other than the healthcare provider or the patient who pays for the service.

Healthcare Reform

Historically, there have been many attempts to reform the delivery of health care to manage costs and improve quality. Some of the most significant efforts have come from private-sector innovations in health care. These include health maintenance organizations and managed care.

Traditionally, most health care in the United States has been paid for in a **fee-for-service** plan in which providers are paid for each visit, each operation, and so on. Critics have long argued that a fee-for-service plan encourages rising healthcare costs and unnecessary services by rewarding providers who perform more operations, see more patients, and so on. To combat rising healthcare costs and to provide better care, an alternative method of payment was first developed shortly after World War II. This is a **health maintenance organization (HMO)**—a prepaid healthcare plan delivering comprehensive care to members through designated providers. In an HMO, clients are charged a fixed fee each year. That money is then used to pay for all services provided, equipment costs, and other expenses of the providers each year plus the providers' salaries. If the providers have lower expenses from performing fewer operations, diagnostic tests, and other services, then some of those savings are passed on to the providers as a bonus. The HMO thus gives providers an incentive to reduce costs and to keep patients healthy through preventive care to keep costs down in the future. By 1995, 46.2 million people (about 18% of the population of the United States) were enrolled in one of 550 health maintenance organizations (NCHS 1997:Table 173).

Another effort to reduce healthcare costs is **managed care**—programs in which physicians no longer have complete freedom to decide what services are provided to patients but must first approve those services for payment with the insurance provider. Unfortunately, both HMOs and managed-care plans raise the possibility that providers will refuse to provide or pay for treatments that patients (and even physicians) feel are necessary. And, despite the rapid rise of both HMOs and managed-care plans, healthcare costs continue to rise at an alarming rate in the United States.

There have also been several attempts by the federal government to implement federally funded health care in the United States. While some form of universal health coverage was often the goal of such reform, the reform efforts have been met with significant resistance and the resulting systems have been limited to only some segments of the population.

The Veterans Health Administration (VHA) is the oldest government effort to provide health care to a class of American citizens—military veterans and their dependents. The Continental Congress of 1776 provided pensions for disabled soldiers in order to encourage enlistments during the Revolutionary War. Over the years, services were expanded. In 1811, medical services for veterans were authorized. In the 19th century, benefits were expanded to include veterans, their widows, and their dependents. After the Civil War, state veterans' homes were established. When the United States entered World War I in 1917, Congress established a new system of benefits. In 1930, services were consolidated into the Veterans Administration (VA) with 54 hospitals. Today, it includes 152 hospitals, 126 nursing home care units, as well as other facilities (US Department of Veterans Affairs 2012a).

However, efforts to improve benefits for veterans did not always progress smoothly. In 1924, Congress passed the World War Adjustment Compensation Act authorizing bonuses to veterans; however, those were not to be paid until 20 years later. The Great Depression left many veterans destitute, and in 1930, veterans marched to Washington, DC, to demand payment. Between 15,000 and 40,000 bonus marchers set up camp in the capital city and only left after a riot broke out and the Army was called in to remove protesters forcibly. It was not until 1936 that Congress authorized early payment of the bonuses, and it was not until late in World War II in 1944 that Congress passed the GI Bill of Rights, providing benefits including educational benefits and housing loans for veterans (US Department of Veterans Affairs 2012b).

Fee-for-service A method of payment in which providers are paid for each visit, each operation, and so on.

Health maintenance organization (HMO) A prepaid healthcare plan delivering comprehensive care to members through designated providers.

Managed care A program in which physicians no longer have complete freedom to decide what services are provided to patients but must first approve those services for payment with a third-party payer.

In the United States, efforts to provide universal health care began as early as Theodore Roosevelt's support for the concept in the 1912 election in which he was defeated (Corning 1969; Palmer 1999). Franklin Roosevelt included healthcare provisions in Social Security legislation but removed them in the face of resistance by the American Medical Association (AMA). Harry Truman championed universal health care in his Fair Deal and also removed them due to strong opposition. It was not until 1965 that President Lyndon Johnson was able to pass Medicare and Medicaid into law despite opposition from the AMA and insurance companies. However, Medicare applied only to the elderly and Medicaid applied only to those poor enough to pass a means test required to qualify. In the 1960s and 1970s, the nation came closer to passing universal healthcare coverage when President Richard Nixon introduced the Comprehensive Health Insurance Act. However, that act was defeated when Democrats, including Senator Ted Kennedy, opposed the bill for not going far enough.

In 1994, the Clinton administration proposed a sweeping reform of health care in the United States. In this proposal, the government would regulate a process in which employees would use collective bargaining to contract with any of several healthcare provider organizations for care. The hope was to create "managed competition" with the cost savings of collective bargaining but with the freedom to select from a wide range of provider organizations rather than being forced to use a single government program. That proposal was successfully defeated after an intensive lobbying campaign against it was waged by a number of healthcare provider organizations. Ironically, since the defeat of that program, many employment healthcare plans have sought to reduce their costs by negotiating for the delivery of health care by preferred provider organizations and conversion to health maintenance organizations or some form of managed care.

The Patient Protection and Affordable Care Act was passed by Congress and signed into law by President Obama on March 23, 2010. Like earlier efforts to reform health care, this law was the object of intense lobbying by many groups, including healthcare providers and insurers, along with partisan division. On June 28, 2012, the Supreme Court upheld the healthcare law, though Republicans in Congress continued attempts to repeal it. This law made comprehensive changes in healthcare. Some of the most important provisions include changes designed to increase the number of Americans who are covered by health insurance. Insurance companies are not permitted to cancel policies or deny benefits due to pre-existing health conditions. The act permits people under 26 to continue to receive health coverage under a parent's plan. The law also requires everyone to purchase health insurance or pay a penalty tax every year. It establishes health insurance exchanges in states to help individuals who do not have insurance provided through their work find affordable health insurance. The law also provides tax credits to small businesses to help reduce healthcare costs for their employees (www.healthcare.gov).

THE SOCIOLOGICAL IMAGINATION   A Healthcare Case Study

The US Department of Health and Human Services has a website on which it posts information to help people understand their rights under the Affordable Care Act. On that site is a blog containing case study descriptions of individuals including Jill.

Jill: Jill from North Carolina is a writer and a tutor, but she is also a runner. A few years ago, she was training for the Olympic trials in the marathon. One day, she suddenly passed out in a parking lot. She was diagnosed with a heart condition, atrioventricular nodal reentrant tachycardia (AVNRT). The good news was that the condition could be remedied with a surgical procedure. The bad news was that Jill could not afford the surgery.

For years following her diagnosis, she lived within reach of a cell phone just in case she had to call 911. Her condition worsened. "I did stop running; I stopped exercising completely because any kind of exertion would trigger an episode. So I went from running marathons competitively to doing nothing," Jill says.

(Continues)

THE SOCIOLOGICAL IMAGINATION *(Continued)*

She applied for insurance that might cover her surgery, but was turned down due to her pre-existing condition. Her appeal was denied. There did not seem to be a place in the healthcare system for her situation. *Source:* Salcido (2012).

The blog then goes on to talk about how Jill's needs are met by the Affordable Care Act.

This case illustrates how the sociological imagination can be used to help relate personal experiences to broad social policies. Jill's personal trouble of being unable to obtain health insurance is an example of a public problem the new law was designed to address: people who were unable to obtain health

insurance because of a pre-existing condition. Her biography reflects the fact that during the years when she was unable to afford the surgery she needed, she was living in a time when it was common for people to be denied health insurance because of pre-existing conditions.

In these examples, the sociological imagination seems to support the need for the Affordable Care Act. But the sociological imagination is nonpartisan. It can lead to insights that support or challenge any particular social policy. For example, individuals and companies are also likely to experience individual troubles that reflect public problems as a result of the Affordable Care Act.

EVALUATE

1. Have you or someone you know been turned down for health insurance, for example, due to a pre-existing condition, affordability, or denied coverage under parents' insurance before age 26? What were the circumstances, outcomes, and coping strategies?

2. What issues might companies and individuals experience that reflect public problems resulting from the Affordable Care Act, which imposes tax penalties on those who do not purchase health insurance?

3. What issues might healthcare providers and patients experience as the law is implemented and more and more people begin to carry health insurance?

CONCEPT LEARNING CHECK 15.5   Health Care in the United States

Match each of the following concepts with the phrase that defines it or illustrates it.

_____ **1.** Third-party payer

_____ **2.** Health maintenance organization

_____ **3.** Managed care

_____ **4.** Fee for service

A. Before this family physician can refer a patient to a surgeon, she must first have the decision approved by the patient's insurer.

B. I pay a fixed monthly fee for health care regardless of whether I need and receive no care or expensive procedures such as an operation.

C. This patient only pays his physician when he goes to see the physician for a checkup or a procedure.

D. This physician's office has to process claims for payments for several dozen different insurance companies.

15.6 Global Health Care

The United States spends far more on health care than any other nation, yet does not outperform other nations on measures of healthcare quality, a result of differences in how nations deliver health care.

■ Contrast spending on health care in the United States with other countries and identify some of the key differences in healthcare systems of different nations.

Healthcare Costs around the World

The United States spends considerably more per capita on health care than other Western industrialized countries. FIGURE 15-12 displays both per capita healthcare expenditures and percentage of GDP for selected countries in 2010. In 2010, the United States spent 17.6% of GDP and $8,233 per capita for health. This was roughly 60% higher than the next-highest per-capita expenditures of Norway ($5,400) and Switzerland ($5,300) (OECD 2012).

This graph makes it very clear that the United States spends far more on health care than other nations, whether measured as percentage of GDP or dollars per capita. The real surprise, however, comes when we examine how well the US healthcare system performs when compared to those of other nations. In two widely used measures of health care, the United States lags behind many other countries. In 2011, the United States ranked 41st in the world in infant mortality rates (Kaiser Family Foundation 2012c), and in 2012 the United States ranked 50th in the world in life expectancy (CIA 2012).

These figures prompted Matt Miller (2012) to argue, in a *Washington Post* column titled "The Real Medicare Villain," that both Republican criticism of the $176 billion in "cuts" Obama made reducing payments to providers but not affecting benefits, and criticism by Democrats of expected reductions in Medicare funding as a result of the Ryan proposal to offer vouchers are missing the point. The real Medicare villain is America's medical-industrial complex, which receives far higher payments than its counterparts abroad while producing lower-quality health care. He argues that instead of protecting funding for Medicare, we should be figuring out how to reduce costs to levels comparable to those in other countries while preserving or even improving healthcare quality.

A study funded by the Commonwealth Fund (Squires 2011) compared the US healthcare system to those of 12 other industrialized nations, examining more than

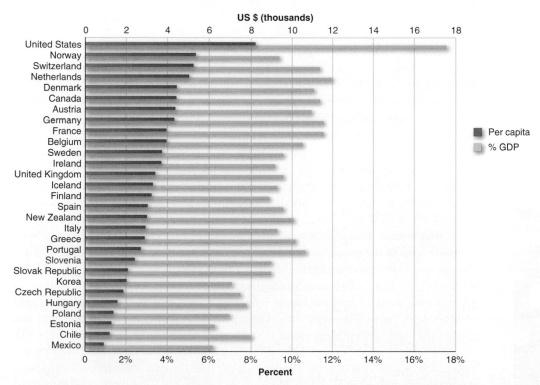

FIGURE 15-12 Annual per capital healthcare expenditures and percentage of GDP for selected countries (2010).

Source: Data from Organization for Economic Cooperation and Development. 2010. OECD.StatExtracts. Retrieved August 2012 (http://stats.oecd.org/Index.aspx?DataSetCode=SHA).

1,200 health system measures. That study found that even though healthcare spending in the United States is much higher than in other countries, the United States has fewer hospital beds, physicians, and hospital and patient visits than the other countries. The United States is particularly high compared to the other countries on utilization and spending for prescription drugs and diagnostic imaging. A comparison of drug prices in the United States compared to eight other industrialized countries found Canada and Germany closest to US prices (77% and 76% of US prices, respectively), while five other countries (the UK, Australia, the Netherlands, France, and New Zealand) had prices ranging from 51% of those in the United States to 34% (IMS Health, analysis by Gerard Anderson, cited in Squires 2011). Similarly, the United States had more than three times the median number of MRI scanners per capita, more than twice the number of scans per capita, and fees 70% higher than the median for the studied countries (Squires 2011). Regarding outcome measures, the researchers found that the United States compared favorably on five-year cancer survival, in the middle on in-hospital, case-specific mortality, and lower than other countries on hospital admissions for chronic conditions, including diabetes.

Different Healthcare Systems

The rise of scientific medicine that occurred in the United States was mirrored by similar developments the world over as medicine matured as a profession. However, there are important differences between the American healthcare system and that of other countries, differences that help explain some of the problems that are unique or exacerbated for the United States. Many other countries have some form of **universal health care**, in which health care is regarded as a right of citizens and available to all. In many cases, other countries have some form of **socialized medicine**—a healthcare system in which the government owns most of the medical facilities and employs most of the physicians. However, those healthcare systems take many forms, "from single-payer (Canada, England) to mandated private insurance (Switzerland, Holland) to creative public/private hybrids (Singapore)" (Miller 2012). Here we examine a few of those healthcare systems that illustrate this diversity.

Canada. Canada has a publicly funded healthcare system with universal coverage, and patients pick their doctor. Because Canada has a **single-payer system** in which the government pays all bills (instead of insurers, individuals, and the government), Canada's administrative costs are lower. They have about the same number of physicians per capita and more hospital beds per capita than the United States (Health Canada 2012). Drug prices are negotiated by the federal government with providers and tend to be much lower than prices for those same drugs in the United States. Patients can, however, be required to join waiting lists before receiving some advanced medical procedures. Canada emphasizes prevention and early detection and tends to have fewer high-cost surgeries than the United States. Canada also has lower infant mortality, and their medical costs were 11.4% of GDP in 2010 versus 17.6% for the United States (OECD 2012).

Great Britain. Everyone is guaranteed medical treatment in Great Britain. Physicians are paid by the government to serve in the National Health Service. England has a single-payer system of socialized medicine in which the government pays the bills, with relatively few cost-sharing fees at the point of use. Patients in this system complain of long waits for hospitalization. Some physicians provide private practices paid for directly by more affluent patients. Thus, Britain has a two-tier medical system like the United States, except that, unlike the United States, everyone is guaranteed health care. Private insurance covers 12% of the population, accounting for 1% of health expenditures, and 90% of private expenditures on health care are direct out-of-pocket payments (Vrangbaek et al. 2008). Medical costs in the UK were 9.6% of GDP in 2010 (OECD 2012).

The Netherlands. In the Netherlands, since 2006, all residents have been required to purchase health insurance from private insurers regulated by private law. It is estimated only 1.5% are not covered by insurance (Vrangbaek et al. 2008). Medical costs in the Netherlands were 9.2% of GDP in 2010 (OECD 2012).

Universal health care
Health care is regarded as a right of citizens and available to all.

Socialized medicine
A healthcare system in which the government owns most of the medical facilities and employs most of the physicians.

Single-payer system
A healthcare system in which the government pays all bills.

England has a single-payer system of socialized medicine.

© Jones and Bartlett Publishers.
Photographed by Kimberly Potvin.

Singapore. Singapore's healthcare system has among the lowest expenditures (3.1% of GDP and $1,148 per capita in 2007). This is roughly one-seventh the amount per capita spent on health care by the United States. Yet Singapore's infant mortality rate was 2 per 1,000 births compared to 7 per 1,000 births for the United States in 2010 (WHO 2010). The Singapore system emphasizes personal responsibility by requiring medical savings accounts for individuals (Medisave accounts). Most individuals also enroll in a voluntary catastrophic insurance plan (Medishield). Their system also emphasizes health promotion and preventive health care. Patients can choose providers, and the government subsidizes treatment with greater subsidies for less expensive care such as open wards rather than private rooms (Kaiser Family Foundation 2012b). The average waiting time for elective surgical operations is eight days (Liu and Yue 1999).

For a closer look at how healthcare systems around the world appear in practice, the 2008 PBS documentary *Sick Around the World* (Palfreman and Reid 2008) provides video of healthcare systems in five countries: Britain, Japan, Germany, Taiwan, and Switzerland.

CONCEPT LEARNING CHECK 15.6	Global Health Care

Match each of the following numbered items with lettered items that best correspond.

_____ **1.** The Netherlands

_____ **2.** Great Britain

_____ **3.** United States

_____ **4.** In this country, all citizens are entitled to free medical care when they need it regardless of ability to pay.

A. Socialized medicine

B. This country has more MRI scanners per capita, uses them more often, and charges more for their use.

C. Universal health care

D. A privatized healthcare system in which each resident is required to purchase health insurance from private insurers.

15.7 Theoretical Perspectives on Health and Health Care

The three dominant theoretical perspectives in sociology each highlight different issues when applied to health and medicine.

- Illustrate key differences in theoretical perspectives of health and medicine.

Functionalist Perspective: The Sick Role

In the structural-functional view, medicine is seen as an institution having positive functions for society by helping people to fulfill their normal daily obligations. From that perspective, sociologist Talcott Parsons (1951) argued illness is a form of deviance that is dysfunctional to society because it disrupts normal functions. Illness presents a problem for social control because it provides people with a free pass to ignore their usual obligations. As a result, Parsons argues, it was necessary to come up with a careful mix of expectations for how people behave when they are sick that can take into account when people really cannot function normally without giving them license to stop working altogether. This is the sick role.

The **sick role** is a set of expectations for how someone who is ill should behave. For people unable to carry out their normal roles due to illness, the sick role has the positive functions of temporarily relieving them of their usual obligations while encouraging them to seek treatment and become well. Parsons identified four basic components of the sick role: two freedoms and two obligations. Sick people are granted greater freedoms than other people because they are (1) exempted from normal day-to-day responsibilities and (2) not blamed for their condition. This is a good deal. Those freedoms give sick people flexibility to tend to their illness and get well. It is tempting, however, for people

Sick role A set of societal expectations for the behavior and attitudes of someone who is ill.

Illness presents a problem for social control because it provides people with a free pass to ignore their usual obligations.

© Jan Danel/Shutterstock, Inc.

to take advantage of the sick role even when they are not sick. To prevent people from abusing the sick role, there are also two additional obligations: (3) The sick person is obligated to try to get well and (4) the sick person should seek competent help. A person is allowed to take advantage of the freedoms of the sick role only so long as he or she is also fulfilling the responsibilities of trying to get well and seeking competent help.

Eliot Freidson (1970) elaborated on Parsons' concept of the sick role to identify three variations. First is the conditional sick role, which only applies temporarily when a person suffers from a condition that is likely to be cured. That person enjoys the benefits of the sick role only if he or she fulfills the obligations. If the illness is more severe or likely to last longer, the person may be treated more favorably, but ultimately, he or she must seek to get well and is expected to be in the sick role only temporarily. Second is the case of an incurable disease or terminal illness. In that case, there is no reasonable expectation that the person will get well; hence, they cannot be expected to do more than seek to minimize their pain and suffering and perform whatever partial functions they can. Someone with a permanent disability, for example, should work within his or her capabilities to perform his or her duties but is not expected to do more than that. The third case Freidson describes is an illegitimate role in which the illness is stigmatized or the person is viewed as largely responsible for it. AIDS patients who used intravenous drugs or engaged in unprotected sex or long-term smokers with chronic respiratory distress may not receive the same sympathy as a child victim of a drunken driver.

Critique of the Sick Role

As Freidson's work suggests, the sick role as conceptualized by Talcott Parsons (1951) does not work equally well for all people and all types of illness. In addition, people differ greatly in their tendency to adopt the sick role. Some people deny being sick both to themselves and others. Others are extremely reluctant to seek help from a doctor. Still others may not cooperate with the physician to help become well. This is particularly common when behavioral changes are required as part of the intervention—for example, dieting, exercise, stopping smoking, or refraining from use of alcohol. Finally, not everyone is able to take on the sick role even when they are ill. Uninsured workers may not be able to afford being sick, lacking resources to pay the physician fees or even to afford the loss of pay from missed work.

Conflict Perspective: Social Inequality

Researchers who take the conflict theory view of health and medicine argue that, as one of the few countries in the world without universal health care, health care in the United States is very unequal. They argue that (1) the quality of health care in the United States, as measured by infant mortality rates, is not as good as that in many other countries despite costing considerably more, (2) there is glaring inequality of access to health care in the United States, and (3) the US medical profession and the system of insurers, hospitals, and pharmaceutical companies has achieved a position of power in our capitalist economy permitting them to control medical work and the prices charged for that work to maximize profits at the expense of the rest of society.

Quality of Care

Variations in infant mortality rates are often used as an index of quality of health care around the world. The infant mortality rate is an age-specific death rate, the number of deaths of infants under 1 year of age per 1,000 live births in a given year. This rate is often taken as a measure of the quality of health care provided in countries and is a major factor in the reduction of mortality and the population explosion. In **TABLE 15-4** are the infant mortality rates for 2011 for selected countries around the world. Notice that relative to most other Western industrialized countries, the US rate of 6.06 is high (it is, however, nowhere near as high as India's). Hence, as measured by this standard, we receive a lower quality of care than most Western industrialized nations. In fact,

TABLE 15-4 Infant Mortality Rates for Selected Countries (2011)

Country	Infant Deaths (per 1,000 live births)
Sweden	2.74
Japan	2.78
Australia	4.61
Canada	4.92
United States	6.06
Russian Federation	10.08
China	16.06
India	47.57

Source: CIA World Factbook. 2011. Country Comparisons. Accessed August 2012 (https://www.cia.gov/library/publications/the-world-factbook/rankorder/2091rank.html).

when ranked by infant mortality rates, the United States ranks 41st in the world. Yet the United States spends more per capita on health care than these other countries. Why is our healthcare quality lower than that of countries paying much less for health care? Conflict theorists argue it is due to glaring inequities in access to health care.

Within the United States, there are also large differences in infant mortality for different racial and ethnic groups. In 2007 (the latest date with comparable data for these groups), the infant mortality rate overall was 6.75, while for non–Hispanic whites it was 5.63, for Puerto Ricans it was 7.71, for American Indian or Alaska Natives it was 9.22, and for non–Hispanic blacks it was highest of all at 13.31—well over twice the rate for non–Hispanic whites (MacDorman and Mathews 2011).

Access to Health Care

The United States is one of the few Western industrialized countries that does not view health care as a right of all its citizens and does not have some form of national health insurance. In 2012, before the Affordable Care Act was ruled constitutional by the US Supreme Court, there were well over 50 million uninsured Americans, and that number was projected to increase to 60 million by 2022 without the law. With the law, the Congressional Budget Office projected the number of uninsured would decrease to 27 million by about 2016. An estimated 17 million were projected to expand the Medicaid rolls and 22 million were expected to purchase insurance through state or federal exchanges, with modest decreases projected for the number of people receiving insurance at work or individually (Waananen 2012).

Even if the law took force completely, there were still projected to be 27 million uninsured people by 2022. However, since the Supreme Court decision gave states the option of not participating in the expansion of Medicare, the actual number of uninsured is likely to be millions more. Thus we can expect to see continued inequity in access to medical care in the United States for the foreseeable future. Medicaid is a means-tested program. It only covers people who meet a **means test**—a qualification procedure to determine whether someone's wealth and income are sufficiently low to qualify them for some form of federal support. For the more than 50 million people in the United States in 2012 who were uninsured, and for the 27 million or more who would remain uninsured by 2022 even with the Affordable Care Act in place, if they are ever faced with a catastrophic health problem, they would have to first use up all of their own financial resources before they qualified for assistance through Medicaid.

Minorities are more likely to be uninsured than whites. In 2010, nearly one-third of Hispanics and nearly one-quarter of black Americans were uninsured, while only 14% of non–Hispanic whites were uninsured (Kaiser Family Foundation 2012a). Lack of insurance has strong negative effects on a person's health. Uninsured adults are more than twice as likely to report being in fair or poor health than those with private insurance,

Means test A qualification procedure to determine whether someone's wealth and income are sufficiently low to qualify them for some form of federal support.

and almost half of uninsured nonelderly adults have a chronic condition (Davidoff and Kenney 2005). Uninsured nonelderly adults are far less likely than insured adults to have preventive care and screenings (*NewsHour with Jim Lehrer* 2003) and hence are more often diagnosed in later stages of diseases such as cancer and die earlier than those with insurance (Ayanian et al. 2000; Roetzheim et al. 2000). Because of these stark differences in access to health care, many argue that the United States has a **two-tier medical system** providing one level of care for the rich and a lesser level of care for the poor.

Two-tier medical system
Provides one level of care for the rich and a lesser level of care for the poor.

Critique of Conflict Perspective

The conflict view highlights inequalities in health care, particularly those related to race and social class. However, the conflict perspective does not help us understand the importance of health care for the society as a whole (as addressed in the structural-functional theory) or the ways in which people interpret illness and interact to provide treatment. The latter issues are addressed by symbolic interactionism.

Symbolic Interactionism: Social Construction of Illness and Treatment

As addressed by symbolic interactionism, physical and mental health are not predetermined social statuses but are statuses that must be achieved through negotiation and collaboration with others. This is illustrated by the sick role, which sometimes must be established through letters from a parent to a child's teacher or a letter from a physician to an employee's supervisor. Symbolic interactionism identifies ways in which both illness and its treatment are socially constructed.

The doctor–patient relationship and communication is an area in which numerous studies have examined differences based on age, gender, social class, race, and ethnicity (Roter and Hall 2006). They cite evidence that doctor–patient interaction is affected by patient gender and social class, physical attractiveness, and difficult versus easy patients (Roter and Hall 2006:51). For example, Cooper-Patrick and colleagues (1999) found that African-American patients perceived their visits with physicians as less participatory than white patients did, patients of the same race as the physician perceived their visits as more participatory than those of different races, and all patients generally wanted more participatory interactions.

Constructing Illness

Earlier we noted that some sociologists such as Thomas Szasz (1984) argue that mental illness is a myth. For example, he argues that ADHD (attention-deficit hyperactivity disorder) was "invented" rather than discovered (Szasz 2001), while others argue ADHD is a socially constructed explanation of behaviors that do not meet prescribed social norms but are not of themselves necessarily pathological (Parens and Johnston 2009). As evidence of the arbitrariness of the diagnosis, its critics often point out that ADHD is diagnosed roughly three to four times as often in the United States based on the DSM IV criteria as compared to the ICD 10 diagnostic criteria advocated by the World Health Organization (Singh 2008).

AIDS is another example of the social construction of illness. As noted above, there was initially a great deal of stigma, since AIDS was at first associated with people already considered to be deviant due to their life styles as homosexuals or intravenous drug users (Hassin 1994). Because of this stigma, taking on the sick role was far more problematic for someone with AIDS than for someone with other diseases. Contracting AIDS was often seen as the victim's own fault for engaging in illicit behavior, and people with the disease suffered discrimination in the workplace, in schools, and even at home. It was only after the disease spread into the heterosexual community and included growing numbers of children that the stigma began to lessen. AIDS victims began to be treated according to the sick role and granted the same legal protection and health care given people suffering from other contagious diseases (Fee and Fox 1992).

Constructing Treatment: The Gynecological Examination

In a now-classic study, sociologist Joan Emerson (1970) observed 75 different gynecological examinations of women by a male doctor. While women are familiar with the gynecological examination, men may be surprised to know that these examinations involve the woman exposing her genitals for inspection by the physician, a situation women typically find at least a little embarrassing. Needless to say, such intimate viewing and touching of the woman by a male physician could easily be misinterpreted as either a sexual act or even assault. Emerson found that the physician and healthcare professionals devote considerable attention to creating a setting that leaves little room for ambiguity. All healthcare personnel wear uniforms and only medical equipment is present in the examination room. Their behaviors, too, are designed to convey the impression that this is a routine professional activity. The physician tries to act in a manner that suggests he sees this as no different from examining other parts of the body. His actions are studiously nonchalant and his language carefully employs dictionary terms rather than everyday words to keep the interaction formal. Much of the woman's body is draped to minimize her exposure, and a female staff member (usually a nurse) is typically present in the room along with the male physician at all times so that the woman patient is never alone in the room with a man.

Critique of Interactionist Perspective

The interactionist view helps us see how health, illness, and treatments of illness must be socially constructed. This opens the door to understanding how nonmedical factors that influence the process of negotiation and defining the situation can influence a person's health and illness behavior. However, it would be a mistake to think that there is no objective component to this process. The more severe the symptoms of a disease are, the less flexibility there is for social construction of the situation.

CONCEPT LEARNING CHECK 15.7   Theoretical Perspectives on Health Care

Match each of these statements with the theoretical perspective that best encompasses it.

_____ **1.** The uninsured poor can receive health care in emergency rooms, but they often endure long waits, and the more expensive services that are not deemed essential for saving their lives may not be provided.

_____ **2.** When Sarah caught strep throat, she got a written excuse from the student health center that she gave to her professor so that she would be allowed to make up her missed work.

_____ **3.** Being drunk in public was once treated as a crime, but today it is usually treated as a disease, and the person is viewed as an alcoholic who needs treatment more than punishment.

A. Structural-functional theory

B. Conflict theory

C. Symbolic interactionism

15.8 Health Care: Future Possibilities

Key trends in health care likely to continue in the future include continuing increases in the use of technology, rising costs, and the domination of the healthcare system by physicians.

- Identify likely trends in the future of health care.

So, what should be expected for health care in the future? On one hand, it seems likely that both in the United States and throughout the world there will be continued increases in the costs of health care. As health improves and people live longer, populations age

In the United States it seems likely there will be continued controversy over how health care is provided and paid for and continued inequalities of access.

© Jose Gil/Shutterstock, Inc.

and the larger proportion of elderly have higher healthcare costs than the young. As poor countries become more affluent, more of their resources will likely be devoted to health care. Most countries—particularly the United States—have shown little ability to rein in healthcare costs to grow no faster than the rest of the economy. Business as usual seems unlikely to change that in the future.

On the other hand, business as usual, in which healthcare costs continue to outpace the rest of the economy, may lead to a crisis in which countries lack the economic resources or the political will to continue. The global economic downturn beginning in 2008 has stressed countries to the point where increasing costs that once would have been endured become unendurable. Exponential increases in the costs of health care cannot be sustained indefinitely, so we should expect continuing discussions and efforts to control costs. Here in the United States, it seems likely there will be continued controversy over how health care is provided and paid for and continued inequalities of access.

In an ever more rationalized society like that of the United States, scientific medicine's near-monopoly over health care is likely to continue over the long term. In the short term, the Affordable Care Act will make health care accessible to millions of people who lacked health insurance before. That will lead to a dramatic increase in the need for primary healthcare providers. If those continue to be predominantly physicians, then this will further increase the power of physicians in the healthcare system. If the Affordable Care Act leads to increased use of other health professionals such as nurse practitioners or physician assistants instead of physicians, then it might reduce the monopoly power that physicians have over health care.

Continuing improvements in technology seem likely to produce new advances in medicine. But it is not clear whether most new technologies will reduce costs or generate revenues for the companies that produce them. Pharmaceutical companies are eager to produce new and costly drugs for chronic diseases that patients are likely to use regularly for the rest of their lives, but few firms are willing to invest resources into developing new antibiotics to fight drug-resistant infections—antibiotics that are typically taken for a short period of time, then not needed by the patient and hence are much less profitable. Physicians often charge for their own services proportionate to the costs of treatments or drugs they provide. Hence, they may be more inclined to adopt expensive brand-name drugs and technologies rather than less expensive generics. As an article in the prestigious *New England Journal of Medicine* put it regarding two equivalent drugs, "Why use paclitaxel (and receive 6% of $312) when you can use Abraxane (for 6% of $5,824)?" (Gatesman and Smith 2011). Substantial reductions in the costs of health care seem unlikely so long as there are so many inducements for health system participants to maximize their own profits.

CONCEPT LEARNING CHECK 15.8   Future Possibilities in Health Care

Answer the following question.

1. Identify three key trends in health care mentioned in this section that are likely to continue in the future.

Visual Overview Life Style and Health

Life style choices play a role in more than one million deaths every year. Changes in life style provide opportunities for individuals to affect their own health.

LIFE STYLE CHOICES	👤 = 10,000 PEOPLE

Smoking
433,000 deaths annually

Adults who smoke cigarettes die 14 years sooner than nonsmokers (CDC, 2002).

Diet/Exercise
407,000 deaths annually

By manipulating salt, sugar, and fat, food manufacturers encourage greater consumption (Kessler, 2009).

Alcohol
79,000 deaths annually

The economic costs to society of alcohol are roughly $746 per person. 2/3 of college students used alcohol in the last 30 days. More than 1/3 report binge drinking in the last 2 weeks.

Drug Abuse
38,000 deaths annually

In 2007, prescription drugs caused more deaths than illicit drugs (CDC, 2011d).

Motor Vehicles
35,000 deaths annually

Motor vehicle accidents are more likely when there is distracted driving impaired driving, or very young or very old drivers (NTSA, 2009).

Firearms
31,000 deaths annually

Most firearms deaths are due to suicides (19k) or assaults (11k) and accidents (.6k; Murphy and Kochanek, 2012).

Unprotected Sex
18,000 deaths annually

Roughly 1.2 million people in the US are HIV positive and nearly 500,000 have AIDS (CDC, 2012g). Nearly 1/4 of the US population is infected by HPV, the most common STI.

Visual Summary Health and Health Care

15.1 Defining Health

- Health is more than just the absence of disease.
- Culture-bound syndromes include eating disorders and obesity, brain fog, and fan death.

- We place great value on being healthy.

15.2 Global Health

- Whether a country is a high-, medium-, or low-income country affects the age at which people die and the most common causes of death.
- In high-income countries, more than two-thirds of the population lives beyond 70. In middle-income countries, nearly half live to be 70. In low-income

countries, less than 20% live be 70 and more than a third of all deaths are among children under 15.
- In low-income countries, the leading cause of death is infectious diseases. In middle-income and high-income countries, the leading causes of death are chronic diseases.

15.3 Health in the United States: Demographic Factors

- In the United States, the life expectancy increased from 47.3 years in 1900 to 78.7 years in 2010.
- Women continue to live longer than men, and the gap has increased to exceed the gap between whites and blacks. White and black women live longer than men of either race.
- In the United States, the top 10 causes of death changed from infectious diseases in 1900 to chronic diseases in 2010. From 1994 to 2010, there have been short-term reductions in deaths from AIDS and homicide and increased roles of kidney disease and Alzheimer's.
- In the United States, chronic disease and death are primarily issues for the elderly.

- The gap in life expectancy for men and women has increased during the 20th century.
- Whites live longer and experience less disease than blacks in the United States. Hispanics have higher incidence rates of some diseases and less access, but a longer life expectancy than whites. Low-income Americans are more likely to report health problems and to have a lower life expectancy than middle- and higher-income Americans.
- People with chronic illness or disabilities face three kinds of work: everyday work, illness work, and biographical work.
- Psychological disorders are psychological conditions that are deviant, may cause harm to oneself or others, and may cause one psychological distress.

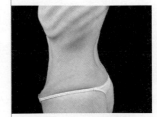

15.4 Health in the United States: Life Style Factors

- Life style factors account for more than one million deaths per year.
- The life style factors having greatest impact on deaths are smoking, diet/exercise, and alcohol use.
- Smoking causes about one out of every five deaths in the United States each year. Smoking rates have declined over time from 52% of men and 32% of women in 1965 to 21.5% for men and 17.3% for women in 2010. Smoking is more common among the poor and less educated.

- Roughly 60% of US adults are overweight and more than one-third are obese. Obesity increases risks for many serious diseases and increases healthcare costs. Structural factors contributing to obesity include higher prices for less fattening food and a lack of free places to exercise safely and healthy food stores in many poor neighborhoods.
- Eating disorders include anorexia nervosa, bulimia nervosa, and binge eating.

- Alcohol consumption in the United States leads to an average of 79,000 premature deaths each year and cost $223.5 billion in 2006. Most of the cost of alcohol consumption is due to binge drinking.

- Alcohol use is prevalent on US college campuses but drinking rates are dropping. Drug use on college campuses is also dropping.

- Roughly one in nine youths abused prescription drugs in the past year, and in 2007, prescription drugs caused more deaths than illicit drugs. Worldwide consumption of illegal drugs is well below levels of tobacco and alcohol consumption.

- There were 30,923 deaths from firearms in the United States in 2010, with most due to suicides or assaults.

- HIV/AIDS remains incurable but can be managed with drugs that are both expensive and have negative side effects. Deaths from AIDS have dropped from a high of nearly 80,000 in 1993 to roughly 33,000 annually today. There are nearly half a million people with AIDS and 1.2 million with HIV in the United States today.

- Motor vehicle accidents led to 35,080 deaths in 2009 and are the leading cause of death for US teens. Motor vehicle accidents are more likely for distracted, impaired, or very old or very young drivers.

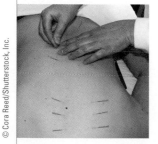

© Cora Reed/Shutterstock, Inc.

15.5 Health Care in the United States

- Medicine in the United States has become dominated by science since the early 1900s and discourages alternative forms of medicine. Technology has transformed modern medicine through vaccinations, antibiotics, diagnostic tests, and procedures.

- Healthcare costs in the United States are rising faster than any other sector of the economy and accounted for 17.9% of the GDP in 2010 and costs of $8,402 per person. Roughly half the increase in healthcare costs can be attributed to new technological advances.

- Some forms of preventive care, such as childhood immunizations and health education on the use of low-dose aspirin, both improve health and reduce costs.

Most preventive care improves health but adds to costs and may be cost effective but is not necessarily cost saving.

- Much of the healthcare cost in the United States is covered by third-party payers such as insurance companies, but millions of people lack insurance coverage.

- Efforts to reform health care in the United States have included health maintenance organizations and managed care.

- The latest effort to improve health care in the United States through legislation is the Affordable Care Act of 2010, which follows earlier legislation that established the VA system and the passage of Medicare and Medicaid in 1965.

© Jones and Bartlett Publishers. Photographed by Kimberly Potvin

15.6 Global Health Care

- The United States spends considerably more per capita on health care than any other country.

- In 2011, the United States ranked 41st in the world in infant mortality rates, and in 2012, it ranked 50th in the world in life

expectancy—two measures often used to assess overall healthcare quality.

- Many other countries have some form of universal health care and some form of socialized medicine.

Visual Summary Health and Health Care, continued

© Jan Danel/Shutterstock, Inc.

15.7 Theoretical Perspectives on Health and Health Care

- The structural functional view sees medicine as an institution having positive functions for society.

- The sick role expects people to be exempted from day-to-day responsibilities and not be blamed for being sick but also expects them to seek competent help and to try to get well.

- The conflict perspective argues that (1) quality of health care in the United States is less than in many other countries, (2) this is due to inequality in the United States limiting access to health care for the uninsured poor, and (3) the domination of health care by the medical profession allows them to maximize profits at the expense of the rest of society.

- Symbolic interactionism views physical and mental health as statuses that must be achieved through negotiation and collaboration with others. This is illustrated with the stigma associated with AIDS and the ways in which gynecological examinations are managed to convey an air of professionalism.

© Jose Gil/Shutterstock, Inc.

15.8 Health Care: Future Possibilities

- Three trends in health care likely to continue in the future are: increases in the use of technology, rising costs, and the domination of the healthcare system by physicians.

15.1 Defining Health

1. Brain fog is:
   A. a contagious disease thought to have been spread to humans from monkeys in Africa.
   B. a culture-bound syndrome first found among blond movie starlets.
   C. a neural condition often found among people receiving dialysis treatments.
   D. a culture-bound syndrome first found among men in West Africa.

15.2 Global Health

2. Fill in the blanks with the most likely broad category of disease. Most people in high-income countries will die from _____ diseases, while most people in low-income countries will die from _____ diseases.

3. Complications of pregnancy and childbirth are among the top 10 causes of death in which income category of countries?
   A. Middle-income
   B. Low-income
   C. High-income
   D. Both middle- and low-income

15.3 Health in the United States: Demographic Factors

4. Which of the following groups of people is likely to have the longest life expectancy?
   A. Hispanic males
   B. Hispanic females
   C. White males
   D. White females

5. The study by Muennig, Fiscella, Tancredi, and Franks in 2010 examined many factors affecting life expectancies, and they found a single factor that had the strongest effect on life expectancy. What was this factor and by how many years did it reduce life expectancy?

   A. Income—people living at less than twice the federal poverty level had average life expectancies of 8.2 years lower than those living at or above that line.
   B. Education—lacking a high school education reduced life expectancy by 5.3 years on average.
   C. Alcohol—people who regularly drink alcohol even at moderate levels had average life expectancies of 4.1 years lower than those who do not drink.
   D. Diet and nutrition—people who eat less than 1,500 calories a day had a reduced life expectancy of 6.1 years on average.

15.4 Health in the United States: Life Style Factors

6. The text mentioned several factors beyond the control of individuals that may particularly affect the poor, encouraging them to become overweight or obese. Which of the following is one of those factors mentioned in the chapter?
   A. The high price of food
   B. Higher prices for healthy, less fattening food
   C. The time it takes to exercise
   D. The availability of fast-food restaurants in the neighborhood

7. Which of the following statements is true about the use of drugs and alcohol on college campuses?
   A. Use of alcohol, cigarettes, and drugs since 1980 has increased steadily, with today's college students more likely to use marijuana than their parents were to use cigarettes.
   B. College students are about as likely to smoke marijuana as they are to smoke cigarettes, and they are less likely to smoke either than their parents were 30 years before them.
   C. College students in 2010 are more likely to smoke than they are to drink alcohol.
   D. The use of marijuana by college students has steadily increased over the last 30 years.

8. In the United States before 1992, the number of new diagnoses of AIDS was increasing exponentially, and by 1992, roughly 80,000 new diagnoses occurred annually. Since 1992, which of the following statements about AIDS is correct?
   A. Most new infections of HIV in the United States occur among men who have sex with women.
   B. The number of new diagnoses of AIDS has continued to rise exponentially.
   C. The number of people living with AIDS (the prevalence of AIDS) has continued to rise and now is roughly 500,000.
   D. Most new infections of HIV in the United States occur among intravenous drug users.

15.5 Health Care in the United States

9. Which statement about healthcare costs in the United States is closest to the facts?
   A. Healthcare costs are rising at roughly the rate of inflation.
   B. Healthcare costs were rising rapidly but have slowed since the recession.
   C. Healthcare costs have risen faster than the rate of inflation for decades.
   D. Healthcare costs sometimes rise and sometimes fall, depending on how the stock market does.

10. Coronary angioplasty is a procedure in which a tube is inserted into the artery and a balloon is used to expand the artery at a blockage to restore blood flow. This is much less intrusive than surgery and much less risky for the patient. It also costs much less than surgery. It was expected to reduce healthcare costs, but costs actually increased. Why?
    A. It actually costs more than surgery.
    B. It led to more court cases in which patients sued their physicians, driving up costs.
    C. It had to be repeated multiple times and hence cost more.
    D. It could be used for more frail patients; hence, more patients were willing to undergo the procedure, and it lead to increased costs.

11. What government-run system or systems of health care have been available in the United States since the 1950s?
    A. The VA system
    B. Medicare
    C. Medicaid
    D. All the above

15.6 Global Health Care

12. The United States' rankings (where 1 is the most or best) compared to other countries on healthcare expenditures, life expectancy, and infant mortality, are:
    A. First in expenditures, 4th in life expectancy, and 5th in infant mortality.
    B. First in infant mortality, 4th in life expectancy, and 50th in expenditures.
    C. First in life expectancy, 41st in expenditures, and 50th in infant mortality.
    D. First in expenditures, 41st in infant mortality, and 50th in life expectancy.

13. One difference between the United States and Canada is that:
    A. The United States has a third-party payer system, while Canada has a single-payer system.
    B. Canada spends more per capita for healthcare costs than the United States.
    C. The United States has universal healthcare and Canada does not.
    D. The United State's system is socialized medicine, while Canada's is not.

15.7 Theoretical Perspectives on Health and Health Care

14. When the surgeons meet with their patient's family after the operation to tell them how the operation went, they usually take on a serious demeanor consistent with the importance of the occasion in which a person's life was on the line. This is consistent with which theoretical perspective?
    A. Conflict theory
    B. Structural-functional theory
    C. Symbolic interactionism
    D. Exchange theory

15. What point did the text make about the use of expensive name-brand drugs versus generic drugs?
    A. Physicians are more likely to use expensive drugs because they are paid a salary proportionate to the drugs they prescribe.
    B. Physicians are encouraged to prescribe generic drugs because they reduce costs to patients.
    C. Physicians avoid the use of generic drugs because they are usually inferior to name-brand drugs.
    D. Physicians rarely prescribe generic drugs because they do not keep up with new innovations and often are unaware of them.

15.8 Health Care: Future Possibilities

16. One key trend in health care mentioned in this section that is likely to continue in the future is:
    A. further reductions in cost.
    B. less use of technology.
    C. domination of the healthcare system by physicians.
    D. dramatic reductions in costs due to technology.

CHAPTER ESSAY QUESTIONS

1. Between 1994 and 2010 in the United States, two new causes of death joined the top 10. What are those causes of death, and for each, name one factor that was cited in the text that may account for its increased occurrence.

2. Kaitlin smokes. She started in high school. But now she is a graduate student, 22 years old, earning a respectable wage as a teaching assistant. Her American Indian family has always been against her smoking and she hopes to stop. . . someday. Name at least two characteristics of Kaitlin that are associated with smoking *less* and two other characteristics of her that are associated with smoking *more*.

3. What is the difference between a cost-saving treatment and a cost-effective treatment? Which (cost-saving treatments or cost-effective treatments) need to be justified using a QALY (a quality-adjusted life year)? Finally, was education on the use of low-dose aspirin found to be cost-saving or cost-effective?

4. Drew worked at a small machine plant that manufactures ear buds. One weekend he went out drinking with his buddies at the local bar, and they got a bit too drunk. Drew's friend was driving them both but went off the road and hit a tree. Drew was thrown from the car (he did not have on his seat belt) and broke his leg. He could not drive with a cast on his leg, so he asked his boss for sick leave while he healed. His boss, Tom, was furious and said, no, explaining it was Drew's own fault for getting drunk and he should come in to work or lose his job. So Drew took a taxi to work every day. Even though Drew saw a doctor several times and worked hard to recuperate, he was not able to drive until several weeks later.

Which two expectations of the sick role were met for Drew in this example? Which two expectations were not met? Which, if any, of the three sick role variations identified by Freidson (1970) describes what happened here?

CHAPTER DISCUSSION QUESTIONS

1. Thinking back over this chapter, what are some of the most important factors that influence life expectancy? How many of those are life style characteristics individuals can change and how many are basic demographic categories over which they have no control?

2. The United States spends far more per capita on health care than any other country. Some people argue that the United States could dramatically improve health care while reducing healthcare costs by going after inefficiencies. But the United States is even more extreme in its defense funding, far outstripping other countries. Is there something unique about the United States that leads us to devote so many resources to things we value? Should we be proud that we spend more on health care even if it is less efficient?

3. It has been said that every dollar of potential healthcare savings is a dollar subtracted from somebody's income. If, as many suggest, we can reduce billions of dollars in inefficient health care, how are we going to do that when the people currently receiving those billions want to hang onto them? Who, by the way, are those people? Where are our healthcare dollars going?

4. Have you ever taken advantage of the sick role even when you were not really all that sick? How often do you suspect people do this? What do we do in our society to help limit taking unfair advantage of the sick role?

5. Share with the class your personal definition of health. What patterns emerged among your classmates' answers? How is one's definition of health affected by societal factors such as cultural norms and life styles, individual income and education, and the income classification of a country?

6. Which of the demographic characteristics identified by epidemiologists do you think has the greatest impact on life expectancy? How do these health differences support the conflict perspective that health care in the United States is a two-tier medical system?

7. Compare medicine as a social institution to the criminal justice institution. How do these institutions control and sanction human behavior? In what ways does the healthcare industry gain power when behaviors that were traditionally defined as deviant or ignored are now medicalized?

8. What are some of the problems with third-party payer systems that have failed to control healthcare costs? Do you think that the Affordable Care Act can lower healthcare costs? What American cultural values might need to change before healthcare costs can be lowered?

9. Why do Americans support universal access to education through tax-funded public schools but, for the most part, oppose universal health care, although exemptions are made for the poor and elderly?

10. Provide examples of medical conditions that do not fit the characteristics of the sick role and in which people are more likely to experience social stigma instead.

11. How do culture-bound syndromes support the symbolic interaction perspective that health and illness are social constructions?

CHAPTER PROJECTS

INDIVIDUAL PROJECTS

1. Go online to find the Centers for Disease Control and Prevention (CDC) website. Choose a topic or a specific group and population and write an analysis paper incorporating your findings and chapter information.

2. Go online to learn about the specifics of the Patient Protection and Affordable Care Act. Write an analysis paper incorporating both benefits and some of the problems that the new legislation might create. Include in your analysis your personal viewpoints about the high cost of health care, access to health care, and the role of the government in health care.

3. Look online at some of the many sites intended to help individuals find out more about specific diseases or seek help diagnosing or treating diseases (e.g., WebMD.com). What can you find out from searching the Internet about the kinds of help these provide and how many people use them? What potential problems do you see for such sites? What benefits do they offer? How do these sites reflect some of the sociological perspectives and findings discussed in this chapter?

4. Think about the last time you were sick and analyze the experience using concepts and perspectives from this chapter. You should discuss the sick role. You should also identify any technology used in your treatment. What is known about how common this health problem is? Is it more likely for people fitting your demographic characteristics? Is it something you may have influenced by your own life style choices?

GROUP PROJECTS

1. Go online to find the World Health Organization (WHO) website and examine various countries, health topics, and statistics. Discuss some of the patterns that emerge from your examination and write a report on your group's findings.

2. Go online and search for Healthy People 2020 website. Examine the various topics, including the program's objectives and leading health indicators. Discuss how the Healthy People program aims to resolve some of the issues presented in this chapter. Write an analysis paper of your group's findings and discussion.

3. Identify a particular medical technology and, using library resources and the Internet, develop a summary of the technology, how it was developed, how it has changed medical practice, how often it is used, and what it has done to affect healthcare costs.

CHAPTER KEY TERMS

AIDS (acquired immune deficiency syndrome)
Alternative medicine
Anorexia nervosa
Binge drinking
Binge eating disorder
Bulimia nervosa
Culture-bound syndrome
Demographic characteristics
Demographics
Designer drugs
Disability
Eating disorder
Fee-for-service

Health
Health maintenance organization (HMO)
HIV (human immunodeficiency virus)
Holistic medicine
HPV (human papillomavirus)
Infant mortality rate
Life expectancy
Managed care
Means test
Medical sociology
Medicine
Mental illness

Muscle dysmorphia
Psychological disorder
Quality-adjusted life year (QALY)
Sick role
Single-payer system
Social epidemiology
Social determinants of health
Socialized medicine
Sociology of the body
Stigma
Third-party payer
Two-tier medical system
Universal health care

ANSWERS TO CONCEPT LEARNING CHECKS

15.1 Defining Health

1. Fan death [F. The fear of dying from being in a closed room where a fan is left running]

2. Bulimia nervosa [G. Repeated binge-eating followed by self-induced vomiting]

3. An example of a culture-bound syndrome [A. Anorexia nervosa]

4. Health [H. A state of complete mental, physical, and social well-being]

15.2 Health Characteristics by Income Category

1. Most people will live to be 70 or more before dying. [C. High-income countries]

2. The leading cause of death is infectious diseases. [A. Low-income countries]

3. Forty percent of people die before the age of 15. [A. Low-income countries]

4. Road traffic accidents are among the top 10 causes of death. [B. Middle-income countries]

5. Nearly 8% of deaths are due to HIV/AIDS. [A. Low-income countries]

6. Fifteen percent of deaths occur among children younger than 15. [B. Middle-income countries]

7. Only one infectious disease (lower respiratory infections) is among the top 10 causes of death and it only accounts for 3.8% of deaths. [C. High-income countries]

15.3 Life Expectancy and Disability in the United States

1. [T] Life expectancy increased dramatically for everyone between 1900 and 2010.

2. [T] Women have longer life expectancies than men of the same race, and the gap increased between 1900 and 2010.

3. [F] Blacks have lower life expectancies than whites of the same sex, and the gap increased between 1900 and 2010.

4. [T] In 1900, blacks, regardless of sex, had lower life expectancies than whites, suggesting race was a bigger factor than sex.

5. [T] In 2010, women, regardless of race, had higher life expectancies than men, suggesting sex is a bigger factor affecting life expectancy than race.
Disabilities are:

6. [F] Always apparent to others.

7. [F] Characterized by an inability to perform tasks as well as others doing the same job.

8. [T] Socially constructed.

9. [T] Sometimes associated with stigmas.

15.4 Life Style and Deaths

1. [A. Smoking]

2. [A. Alcohol]

3. [B. Diet/exercise]

4. [B. Smoking]

5. [A. Firearms]

15.5 Health Care in the United States

1. Third-party payer [D. This physician's office has to process claims for payments for several dozen different insurance companies.]

2. Health maintenance organization [B. I pay a fixed monthly fee for health care regardless of whether I need and receive no care or expensive procedures such as an operation.]

3. Managed care [A. Before this family physician can refer a patient to a surgeon, she must first have the decision approved by the patient's insurer.]

4. Fee for service [C. This patient only pays his physician when he goes to see the physician for a checkup or a procedure.]

15.6 Global Health Care

1. The Netherlands [D. A privatized healthcare system in which each resident is required to purchase health insurance from private insurers.]

2. Great Britain [A. Socialized medicine]

3. United States [B. This country has more MRI scanners per capita, uses them more often, and charges more for their use.]

4. In this country, all citizens are entitled to free medical care when they need it regardless of ability to pay. [C. Universal health care]

15.7 Theoretical Perspectives on Health Care

1. [B. Conflict theory]

2. [A. Structural-functional theory]

3. [C. Symbolic interactionism]

15.8 Future Possibilities in Health Care

1. A good answer should include: continued cost increases or a crisis due to costs, continued physician dominance of health care in the United States, and continued use of new technology.

ANSWERS TO CHAPTER REVIEW TEST

15.1 Defining Health

1. D. It is a culture-bound syndrome and was first attributed to males in West Africa.

15.2 Global Health

2. Chronic, infectious

3. D. Complications of pregnancy and childbirth are among the top 10 causes of death in both middle- and low-income countries.

15.3 Health in the United States: Demographic Factors

4. B. Hispanics have longer life expectancy than whites, and females have longer life expectancy than males.

5. A. People living at less than twice the federal poverty level had average life expectancies of 8.2 years lower than those living at or above that line.

15.4 Health in the United States: Life Style Factors

6. B. Access to healthy, less fattening food is often difficult in inner-city neighborhoods where many poor people live.

7. B. College student use of drugs, alcohol, and cigarettes has generally decreased over the last years to the point where roughly 18% of them smoke or use marijuana.

8. C. Today, there are roughly 500,000 people in the United States who have been diagnosed with AIDS

15.5 Health Care in the United States

9. C. Healthcare costs have risen much faster than inflation for decades and take up an increasingly large percentage of GDP.

10. D. More patients had the procedure, so even though it cost less, the increased volume led to increased costs.

11. A. Only the VA system, because Medicare and Medicaid were not passed until 1965.

15.6 Global Health Care

12. D. Despite being first by far in expenditures, the United States lags behind many other countries in many indices of health care.

13. A. The United States uses third-party payers (insurance companies), while Canada has a single payer (the government).

15.7 Theoretical Perspectives on Health and Health Care

14. C. This is consistent with constructing a shared definition of the situation, as described in symbolic interactionism.

15. A. Physicians are often paid a salary proportionate to the cost of drugs they prescribe, so more expensive drug prescriptions can dramatically increase their fees.

15.8 Health Care: Future Possibilities

16. C. Physicians have dominated health care for decades and are likely to continue to do so in the future.

ANSWERS TO CHAPTER ESSAY QUESTIONS

1. The causes and their likely explanations are nephritis or kidney disease, which is likely due to drug abuse and diabetes, and Alzheimer's, which is likely due to an aging population.

2. A good answer should mention at least two of the following features that make smoking *less* likely: sex (female), education (college degree), above poverty line (income). Features that make her *more* likely to smoke are her age (less than 65) and her race/ethnicity (American Indian).

3. A good answer should include the following points: A cost-saving treatment must cost less than the money it saves. That is, it must reduce costs. A cost-effective measure does not actually save money, but it may increase the length and quality of life at small expense. A QALY is a quality-adjusted life year. Education on the use of low-dose aspirin is a cost-saving measure that reduces costs.

4. A good answer should say that he was *not* exempted from everyday responsibilities, he *was* blamed for the condition. So both of those expectations were not met. However, he tried to get well and sought help, so both of those expectations were met. This corresponds to Freidson's example in which the sick person is blamed for his or her own illness.

REFERENCES

Alfonsi, S., and C. Hutchison. 2010. "More Americans Using High-Tech Medicine, CDC Finds." *ABC World News*. Feb 17, 2010. Retrieved August 2012 from http://abcnews.go.com/Health/Wellness/technology-medicine/story?id=9864930#.UDVcl6MkKSo.

American Cancer Society. 2012. *Guidelines for Using Complementary and Alternative Methods*. Retrieved August 2012 from http://www.cancer.org/Treatment/TreatmentsandSideEffects/ComplementaryandAlternativeMedicine/guidelines-for-using-complementary-and-alternative-methods.

American Holistic Medical Association. 2012. *American Holistic Medical Association Website*. Retrieved August 2012 from http://www.holisticmedicine.org/index.asp.

American Sociological Association (ASA). 2012. "Mission Statement: Section on Medical Sociology." Retrieved Oct. 2012 from http://www.asanet.org/sections/medical.cfm.

Anderson, A. E. 1992. "Eating Disorders in Males: Critical Questions." pp. 20–28 in *Controlling Eating Disorders with Facts, Advice and Resources*, edited by R. Lemberg. Phoenix, AZ: Oryx Press.

Archibald, R., and D. Cave. 2012. "Candidates in Mexico Signal a New Tack in the Drug War." *The New York Times*. June 10. Retrieved July 2012 from http://www.nytimes.com/2012/06/11/world/americas/us-braces-for-mexican-shift-in-drug-war-focus.html?pagewanted=all.

Ayanian, J., et al., 2000. "Unmet Health Needs of Uninsured Adults in the United States." *Journal of the American Medical Association* 284(16):2061–2069.

Bittman, M. 2011. "How to Save a Trillion Dollars." *The New York Times*. April 12. Retrieved July 2012 from http://opinionator.blogs.nytimes.com/2011/04/12/how-to-save-a-trillion-dollars/.

Bouchery, E., H. Harwood, J. Sacks, C. Simon, and R. Brewer. 2011. "Economic Costs of Excessive Alcohol Consumption in the U.S., 2006." *American Journal of Preventive Medicine* 41(5):516–524. Retrieved July 2012 from http://www.ajpmonline.org/article/S0749-3797%2811%2900538-1/abstract.

Brody, Jane E. 1993. "17 States in the Vanguard of War on Smoking." *The New York Times*. Nov 10. Retrieved Nov. 2012 from http://www.nytimes.com/1993/11/10/health/17-states-in-vanguard-of-war-on-smoking.html?pagewanted=all&src=pm.

Brownell, K., and K. Horgen. 2004. *Food Fight: The Inside Story of the Food Industry, America's Obesity Crisis, and What We Can Do About It*. New York: McGraw-Hill.

Carr, D., and M. Friedman. 2005. "Is Obesity Stigmatizing? Body Weight, Perceived Discrimination and Psychological Well-Being in the United States." *Journal of Health and Social Behavior* 46:244–259.

Center for Medicare and Medicaid Services. 2012. *National Health Expenditure Data*. Office of the Actuary, National Health Statistics Group. Retrieved August 2012 from http://www.cms.gov/Research-Statistics-Data-and-Systems/Statistics-Trends-and-Reports/NationalHealthExpendData/Downloads/NHEGDP10.zip.

Centers for Disease Control and Prevention (CDC). 2002. *Annual Smoking-Attributable Mortality, Years of Potential Life Lost, and Economic Costs—United States, 1995–1999*. Retrieved March 11, 2011, from http://www.cdc.gov/mmwr/pdf/wk/mm5114.pdf.

Centers for Disease Control and Prevention (CDC). 2008. *Smoking-Attributable Mortality, Years of Potential Life Lost, and Productivity Losses—United States, 2000–2004*. Retrieved March 11, 2011, from http://www.cdc.gov/mmwr/preview/mmwrhtml/mm5745a3.htm.

Centers for Disease Control (CDC). 2010a. *CDC Health Data Interactive: Life Expectancy from Birth*. National Center for Health Statistics. Retrieved September 2012 from http://205.207.175.93/HDI/TableViewer/tableView.aspx?ReportId=169.

Centers for Disease Control (CDC). 2010b. *Adult Cigarette Smoking in the United States: Current Estimate*. Retrieved July 2012 from http://www.cdc.gov/tobacco/data_statistics/fact_sheets/adult_data/cig_smoking/.

Centers for Disease Control (CDC). 2010c. *Sexually Transmitted Disease Surveillance 2010*. Retrieved July 2012 from http://www.cdc.gov/std/stats10/surv2010.pdf.

Centers for Disease Control (CDC). 2010d. *Sexually Transmitted Diseases Surveillance Tables*. Retrieved July 2012 from http://www.cdc.gov/std/stats10/tables/44.htm.

Centers for Disease Control (CDC). 2010e. *Web-Based Injury Statistics Query and Reporting System (WISQARS)*. National Center for Injury Prevention and Control, Centers for Disease Control and Prevention (producer). Retrieved August 2012 from http://www.cdc.gov/injury/wisqars/.

Centers for Disease Control (CDC). 2011a. *Life Expectancy by Age, Race, and Sex, 1900–2007*. National Vital Statistics Reports. Spreadsheet version available from ftp://ftp.cdc.gov/pub/Health_Statistics/NCHS/Publications/NVSR/59_09/Table21.xls. Retrieved August 2012 from http://www.cdc.gov/nchs/fastats/lifexpec.htm.

Centers for Disease Control (CDC). 2011b. *CDC Health Data Interactive: Chronic Conditions, Ages 18+: US, 1999–2010*. National Center for Health Statistics. Retrieved Sept. 2012 from http://205.207.175.93/HDI/TableViewer/tableView.aspx?ReportId=101.

Centers for Disease Control (CDC). 2011c. *Vital Signs: Current Cigarette Smoking Among Adults Aged ≥ 18 Years—United States, 2005–2010*. Retrieved Jan. 2012 from http://www.cdc.gov/mmwr/preview/mmwrhtml/mm6035a5.htm?s_cid=%20mm6035a5.htm_w.

Centers for Disease Control (CDC). 2011d. *Fact sheet—CDC Health Disparities and Inequalities Report—U.S., 2011*. Retrieved July 2012 from http://www.cdc.gov/minorityhealth/reports/CHDIR11/FactSheet.pdf.

Centers for Disease Control (CDC). 2011e. *Vital Signs: Nonfatal, Motor Vehicle-occupant Injuries (2009).* Retrieved August 2012 from http://www.cdc.gov/mmwr/preview/mmwrhtml/mm5951a3.htm.

Centers for Disease Control (CDC). 2011f. *Physical Activity and Health: The Benefits of Physical Activity.* CDC 24/7: Saving Lives. Protecting People. Retrieved July 2012 from http://www.cdc.gov/physicalactivity/everyone/health/index.html.

Centers for Disease Control (CDC). 2012a. *Excessive Drinking Costs U.S. $223.5 Billion.* CDC 24/7: Saving Lives. Protecting People. Retrieved July 2012 from http://www.cdc.gov/Features/AlcoholConsumption/.

Centers for Disease Control (CDC). 2012b. *Older Persons' Health.* CDC 24/7: Saving Lives. Protecting People. Retrieved August 2012 from http://www.cdc.gov/nchs/fastats/older_americans.htm.

Centers for Disease Control (CDC). 2012c. *Overweight and Obesity.* CDC 24/7: Saving Lives. Protecting People. Retrieved July 2012 from http://www.cdc.gov/obesity/data/adult.html.

Centers for Disease Control (CDC). 2012d. *HIV among African Americans.* Retrieved Oct. 2012 from http://www.cdc.gov/hiv/topics/aa/index.htm.

Centers for Disease Control (CDC). 2012e. *Basic Information about HIV and AIDS.* Centers for Disease Control and Prevention. Retrieved August 2012 from http://www.cdc.gov/hiv/topics/basic/index.htm.

Centers for Disease Control (CDC). 2012f. *HIV among Gay and Bisexual Men.* Retrieved July 2012 from http://www.cdc.gov/hiv/topics/msm/index.htm.

Centers for Disease Control (CDC). 2012g. *AIDS Surveillance—Trends (1985–2010).* Retrieved July 2012 from http://www.cdc.gov/hiv/topics/surveillance/resources/slides/trends/index.htm.

Centers for Disease Control (CDC). 2012h. *HIV in the United States: At a Glance.* Retrieved Sept. 2012 from http://www.cdc.gov/hiv/resources/factsheets/PDF/HIV_at_a_glance.pdf.

Centers for Disease Control (CDC). 2012i. *Impaired Driving.* CDC 24/7: Saving Lives. Protecting People. Retrieved July 2012 from http://www.cdc.gov/Motorvehiclesafety/Distracted_Driving/index.html.

Central Intelligence Agency (CIA). 2012. *The World Factbook.* Retrieved Sept. 2012 from https://www.cia.gov/library/publications/the-world-factbook/rankorder/2102rank.html.

Chen, L., S. P. Baker, E. R. Braver, and G. Li. 2000. "Carrying Passengers as a Risk Factor for Crashes Fatal to 16- and 17-Year-Old Drivers." *Journal of the American Medical Association* 283(12):1578–82.

Cohen, J., and P. Neumann. 2009. "Cost Savings and Cost-Effectiveness of Clinical Preventive Care." *The Synthesis Project, Issue 18.* Robert Wood Johnson Foundation. Retrieved August 2012 from http://www.rwjf.org/pr/product.jsp?id=48508.

Cohen, R., and P. Adams. 2012. *QuickStats: Use of Health Information Technology among Adults aged >=18 Years—National Health Interview Survey (NHIS), US, 2009 and 2011.* Retrieved August 2012 from http://www.cdc.gov/mmwr/preview/mmwrhtml/mm6132a9.htm?s_cid=mm6132a9_w.

Congressional Budget Office (CBO). 2008. *Technological Change and the Growth of Health Care Spending. A CBO Paper.* Congress of the United States. Retrieved August 2012 from http://www.cbo.gov/sites/default/files/cbofiles/ftpdocs/89xx/doc8947/01-31-techhealth.pdf.

Cooper-Patrick, L., J. Gallo, J. Gonzales, H. Vu, N. Powe, C. Nelson, and D. Ford. 1999. "Race, Gender, and Partnership in the Patient–Physician Relationship." *Journal of the American Medical Association* 282(6):583–589. doi:10.1001/jama.282.6.583.

Corbin, J., and A. Strauss. 1985. "Managing Chronic Illness at Home: Three Lines of Work." *Qualitative Sociology* 8(3):224.

Corning, P. 1969. *The Evolution of Medicare…from Idea to Law.* Social Security Administration. Retrieved August 2012 from http://www.ssa.gov/history/corning.html.

Crespo, C., B. Ainsworth, S. Keteyian, G. Heath, and E. Smit. 1999. *Prevalence of Physical Inactivity and Its Relation to Social Class in U.S. Adults: Results from the Third National Health and Nutrition Examination Survey, 1988–1994.* Retrieved October 2012 from http://ukpmc.ac.uk/abstract/MED/10613434/reload=0;jsessionid=xuwVEKhxpKWZ0EzRYf7R.0.

Cutler, D., and R. Huckman. 2003. "Technological Development and Medical Productivity: The Diffusion of Angioplasty in New York State." *Journal of Health Economics* 22(2):187–217.

Danaei, G., E. Ding, D. Mozaffarian, B. Taylor, J. Rehm, C. Murray, and M. Ezzati. 2009. "The Preventable Causes of Death in the United States: Comparative Risk Assessment of Dietary, Lifestyle, and Metabolic Risk Factors." *Public Library of Science Medicine* 6(4):April. Retrieved July 2012 from http://www.ncbi.nlm.nih.gov/pmc/articles/PMC2667673/?tool=pubmed.

Datta, S. D., L. Koutsky, S. Ratelle, E. R. Unger, J. Shlay, T. McClain, et al. 2008. "Human Papillomavirus Infection and Cervical Cytology in Women Screened for Cervical Cancer in the United States, 2003–2005." *Annals of Internal Medicine.* 148(7):493–500.

Davidoff, A., and G. Kenney. 2005. *Uninsured Americans with Chronic Health Conditions: Key Findings from the National Health Interview Survey.* The Urban Institute and the University of Maryland. Retrieved Sept 2012 from http://www.urban.org/publications/411161.html.

DeJong, P. F. 1993. The relationship between students' behaviour at home and attention and achievement in elementary school. *British Journal of Educational Psychology,* 63 (1993):201–213.

Doyle Jr., Joseph J. 2005. "Health Insurance, Treatment, and Outcomes: Using Auto Accidents as Health Shocks." *Review of Economics and Statistics* 87(2, May 2005):256–270.

Drug Enforcement Agency (DEA). 2012. *Drug Fact Sheet: Bath Salts or Designer Cathinonones (synthetic stimulants).* Retrieved October, 2012 from http://www.justice.gov/dea/druginfo/drug_data_sheets/Bath_Salts.pdf.

Elo, I. 2009. "Social Class Differentials in Health and Mortality Patterns and Explanations in Comparative Perspective." *Annual Review of Sociology* 35:553–72.

Emerson, Joan P. 1970. "Behavior in Private Places: Sustaining Definitions of Reality in Gynecological Examinations," Pp. 74–97 in *Recent Sociology No. 2,* edited by P. Dreitsel. New York: Macmillan.

Federal Trade Commission (FTC). 2011. *Federal Trade Commission Cigarette Report for 2007 and 2008.* Washington, DC: Federal Trade Commission. Retrieved September 2012 from http://www.ftc.gov/os/2011/07/110729cigarettereport.pdf.

Fee, Elizabeth, and Daniel M. Fox (Eds.). 1992. *AIDS: The Making of a Chronic Disease.* Berkeley: University of California Press.

Freidson, Eliot. 1970. *Professional Dominance: The Social Structure of Medical Care.* New York: Atherton Press.

Gatesman, M., and T. Smith. 2011. "The Shortage of Essential Chemotherapy Drugs in the United States." *New England Journal of Medicine* 365:1653–1655.

Goffman, Erving. 1963. *Stigma: Notes on the Management of Spoiled Identity.* Englewood Cliffs, NJ: Prentice Hall.

Goodell, S., J. Cohen, and P. Neumann. 2009. *Cost Savings and Cost-Effectiveness of Clinical Preventive Care. Policy Brief No. 18, Sep, 2009.* Robert Wood Johnson Foundation. Retrieved August 2012 from http://www.google.com/url?sa=t&rct=j&q=&esrc=s&source=web&cd=3&ved=0CEkQFjAC&url=http%3A%2F%2Fwww.statereforum.org%2Fsystem%2Ffiles%2Freport_final.pdf&ei=suifUOXUKY_uqAHFl4DYDA&usg=AFQjCNElLrl39rygzRDl_M_9W9xDis2GnA.

Hahnemann, S. 1833. *The Homeopathic Medical Doctrine, or "Organon of the Healing Art."* Dublin: W. F. Wakeman, pp. iii.

Hassin, J. (1994). "Living a Responsible Life: The Impact of *AIDS* on the Social Identity of Intravenous Drug Users." *Social Science & Medicine,* 39(3):391.

Health Canada. 2012. Retrieved August 2012 from http://www.hc-sc.gc.ca/ahc-asc/index-eng.php.

Hesse-Biber, Sharlene. 1996. *Am I Thin Enough Yet?: The Cult of Thinness and the Commercialization of Identity.* Oxford, UK: Oxford University Press.

Indian Health Service. 2011. *The Indian Health Service Fact Sheets.* Retrieved October 2012 from http://www.ihs.gov/PublicAffairs/IHSBrochure/Disparities.asp.

Insurance Institute for Highway Safety (IIHS). 2009. *Fatality Facts: Teenagers 2008.* Arlington, VA: The Institute.

Johnson, Ben. 1606. *Volpone 1b,* Act 2, Scene 1. Retrieved November, 2012 from http://www.gutenberg.org/ebooks/4039.

Johnston, L., P. O'Malley, J. Bachman, and J. Schulenberg. 2010. *Monitoring the Future: National Survey Results on Drug Use, 1975–2010. Vol. II. College Students & Adults Ages 19–50*. U. of Michigan Institute for Social Research. Retrieved July 2012 from http://www.monitoringthefuture.org/pubs/monographs/mtf-vol2_2010.pdf.

Kaiser Family Foundation. 2012a. *The Uninsured: A Primer*. Retrieved July 2012 from http://www.kff.org/uninsured/upload/7451-07.pdf.

Kaiser Family Foundation. 2012b. *International Health Systems/Singapore*. Retrieved August 2012 from http://www.kaiseredu.org/Issue-Modules/International-Health-Systems/Singapore.aspx.

Kaiser Family Foundation. 2012c. *U.S. Global Health Policy. Infant Mortality Rate 2011*. Retrieved July 2012 from http://www.globalhealthfacts.org/data/topic/map.aspx?ind=91.

Kaiser Family Foundation. 2012d. *Health Care Costs: A Primer*. Retrieved July 2012 from http://www.kff.org/insurance/upload/7670-03.pdf.

Kalben, B. B. 2000. "Why Men Die Younger: Causes of Mortality Differences by Sex." *North American Actuarial Journal* 4:83–111.

Kaptchuck, T. 2000. *The Web That Has No Weaver*. 2nd edition. Chicago: Contemporary Books.

Katona, C., and M. Robertson. 2005. *Psychiatry from a Glance*. 3rd edition. Oxford, UK: Blackwell Publishing.

Keel, P., and K. I. Klump. 2003. "Are Eating Disorders Culture-Bound Syndromes? Implications for Conceptualizing their Etiology." *Psychological Bulletin*. 129(5):747–769.

Kessler, D. 2009. *The End of Overeating*. New York: Rodale.

Kessler, R. C., W. T. Chiu, O. Demler, and E. E. Walters. 2005. "Prevalence, Severity, and Comorbidity of Twelve-Month DSM-IV Disorders in the National Comorbidity Survey Replication (NCS-R)." *Archives of General Psychiatry* 62(6):617–27.

Korea Consumer Protection Board. 2006. Press Release. Retrieved August 30, 2012 from http://web.archive.org/web/20070927051420/http://english.cpb.or.kr/user/bbs/code02_detail.php?av_jbno=2006071800002.

Levine, Michael P. 1987. *Student Eating Disorders: Anorexia Nervosa and Bulimia*. Washington, DC: National Educational Association.

Liu, E., and S. Y. Yue. 1999. *Health Care Expenditure and Financing in Singapore*. Hong Kong: Legislative Council Secretariat. Retrieved August 2012 from http://www.legco.gov.hk/yr98-99/english/sec/library/989rp12.pdf.

MacDorman, M., and T. Mathews. 2011. *Understanding Racial and Ethnic Disparities in U.S. Infant Mortality Rates*. NCSH Data Brief No. 74, Sep. Retrieved July 2012 from http://www.cdc.gov/nchs/data/databriefs/db74.pdf.

Maxwell, J. C. 2011a. *The Maxwell Report: Year End & Fourth Quarter 2010 Sales Estimates for the Cigarette Industry*. Richmond, VA: John C. Maxwell, Jr.

Maxwell, J. C. 2011b. *The Maxwell Report: Cigar Industry in 2010*. Richmond, VA: John C. Maxwell, Jr.

Maxwell, J. C. 2011c. *The Maxwell Report: The Smokeless Tobacco Industry in 2010*. Richmond, VA: John C. Maxwell, Jr.

McKeown, Thomas. 1976. *The Modern Rise in Population*. London: Edward Arnold.

McKinlay, John, and Sonia McKinlay. 1977. "The Questionable Contribution of Medical Measures to the Decline of Mortality in the United States in the Twentieth Century." *Milbank Memorial Quarterly/Health and Society* 55.

Meara, E. R., S. Richards, and D. M. Cutler. 2008. "The Gap Gets Bigger: Changes in Mortality and Life Expectancy, by Education 1981–2000." *Health Affairs* 27:350–60.

Miller, M. 2012. "The Real Medicare Villain." *Washington Post*. August, 2012. Retrieved September 2012 from http://www.washingtonpost.com/blogs/she-the-people/post/waiting-for-obamacare/2012/06/12/gJQAEpFNXV_blog.html.

Miner, Horace. 1956. "Body Ritual Among the Nacirema." *American Anthropologist* 58:3.

Morland, K., S. Wing, A. Diez-Roux, and C. Poole. 2002. "Neighborhood Characteristics Associated with the Location of Food Stores and Food Service Places." *American Journal of Preventive Medicine* 22(1):23–29.

Moseley, W. Henry, and Peter Cowley. 1991. "The Challenge of World Health." *Population Bulletin* 46(4, December). Washington, DC: Population Reference Bureau.

Muennig, P., K. Fiscella, D. Tancredi, and P. Franks. 2010. "The Relative Health Burden of Selected Social and Behavioral Risk Factors in the United States: Implications for Policy." *American Journal of Public Health* 100(9):1758–1764.

Murphy, S., J. Xu, and K. Kochanek. 2012. *Deaths: Preliminary Data for 2010*. National Vital Statistics Reports. 60(4), Jan. 11, Table 2. Retrieved July 2012 from http://www.cdc.gov/nchs/data/nvsr/nvsr60/nvsr60_04.pdf.

National Center for Health Statistics (NCHS). 1997. *Statistical Abstract 1997*, Tables 129, 130.

National Heart, Lung, and Blood Institute (NHLBI). 1998. *Clinical Guidelines on the Identification, Evaluation, and Treatment of Overweight and Obesity in Adults*. NIH Publication 98-4083. National Institutes of Health. Retrieved July 2012 from http://www.nhlbi.nih.gov/guidelines/obesity/ob_gdlns.pdf.

National Highway Traffic Safety Administration (NTSA). 2009. *Traffic Safety Facts: Distracted Driving 2009*. Washington, DC: US Department of Transportation, National Highway Traffic Safety Administration, September 2010. Publication no. DOT-HS-811-379. Retrieved July 2012 from http://www.distraction.gov/.

National Institute on Drug Abuse (NIDA). 2010. *National Survey on Drug Use and Health, 2010*. Retrieved July 2012 from http://www.drugabuse.gov/related-topics/trends-statistics/infographics/prescription-drug-abuse-young-people-risk.

National Institutes of Health (NIH). 1998. *NIH, NHLBI Obesity Education Initiative. Clinical Guidelines on the Identification, Evaluation, and Treatment of Overweight and Obesity in Adults*. Retrieved July 2012 from http://www.nhlbi.nih.gov/guidelines/obesity/ob_gdlns.pdf.

National Institute of Mental Health (NIMH). 2012. *Eating Disorders Among Adults*. Retrieved July 2012 from http://www.nimh.nih.gov/statistics/1EAT_ADULT_RB.shtml.

Naumann, R. B., A. M. Dellinger, E. Zaloshnja, B. A. Lawrence, and T. R. Miller. 2005. "Incidence and Total Lifetime Costs of Motor Vehicle-Related Fatal and Nonfatal Injury by Road User Type, United States, 2005." *Traffic Injury Prevention* 11:353–60.

New York State Health Department. 2012. *Anabolic Steroids and Sports: Winning at Any Cost*. Retrieved July 2012 from http://www.health.ny.gov/publications/1210/1210.pdf.

The New York Times. 1993a. "Clinton Considers Plan to Vaccinate All U.S. Children," February 1, pp. A1, A10.

The New York Times. 1993b. "Rise in Health-Care Costs is Linked to Social Behavior." February 23, p. B7.

The New York Times. 1993c. "U.S. Labor Department Study of Work-Related Deaths." October 3, p. 13.

NewsHour with Jim Lehrer/Kaiser Family Foundation National Survey on the Uninsured. 2003, April 6. Retrieved July 2012 from http://www.pbs.org/newshour/indepth_coverage/health/uninsured/whoaretheuninsured.html.

Novelli, P. 2010. *HealthStyles 2010 Survey*. Unpublished raw data. Washington, DC: Adam Burns. Retrieved July 2012 from http://www.cdc.gov/Motorvehiclesafety/Distracted_Driving/index.html.

Ogden, C., M. Carroll, B. Kit, and K. Flegal. 2012. *Prevalence of Obesity in the United States, 2009–2010*. NCHS Data Brief No. 82. Jan, 2012. Retrieved July 2012 from http://www.cdc.gov/nchs/data/databriefs/db82.pdf.

Olshansky, S., et al. 2012. "Differences in Life Expectancy Due to Race and Educational Differences Are Widening, and Many May Not Catch Up." *Health Affairs* 31(8):1803–1813. Retrieved August 2012 from http://content.healthaffairs.org/content/31/8/1803.short.

Organization for Economic Cooperation and Development (OECD). 2010. *StatExtracts*. Retrieved August 2012 from http://stats.oecd.org/Index.aspx?DataSetCode=SHA.

Palfreman, J., and T. Reid. 2008. *Around the World*. PBS Documentary. Retrieved August 2012 from http://www.pbs.org/wgbh/pages/frontline/sickaroundtheworld/.

Palmer, K. 1999. *A Brief History: Universal Health Care Efforts in the US.* Talk given at Physicians for a National Health Program, San Francisco, Spring meeting. Retrieved August 2012 from http://www.pnhp.org/facts/a-brief-history-universal-health-care-efforts-in-the-us.

Parens, E., and J. Johnston. 2009. "Facts, Values, and Attention-Deficit Hyperactivity Disorder (ADHD): An Update on the Controversies." *Child and Adolescent Psychiatry and Mental Health* 3(1):1. Retrieved July 2012 from http://www.ncbi.nlm.nih.gov/pmc/articles/PMC2637252/?tool=pmcentrez.

Park, A. 2012. "HIV Continues to Spread among Gay Men, Studies Show." *Time: Healthland.* July 20, 2012. Retrieved July 2012 from http://healthland.time.com/2012/07/20/hiv-continues-to-spread-among-gay-men-studies-show/?hpt=hp_bn16.

Parsons, Talcott. 1951. *The Social System.* New York: Free Press.

Pope, H. G., A. J. Gruber, P. Choi, R. Olivardi, and K. A. Phillips. 1997. "Muscle Dysmorphia: An Underrecognized Form of Body Dysmorphic Disorder." *Psychosomatics* 38:548–557.

Porter, E. 2012. "Rationing Health Care More Fairly." *The New York Times.* Aug. 21, 2012. Retrieved August 2012 from http://www.nytimes.com/2012/08/22/business/economy/rationing-health-care-more-fairly.html?pagewanted=all.

Prince, Raymond. 1985. "The Concept of Culture-Bound Syndromes: Anorexia Nervosa and Brain-Fog." *Social Science and Medicine* 21(2):197–203.

Rampell, C. 2009. "Suicide Rates, around the World." *The New York Times.* Dec. 9, 2009. Retrieved August 2012 from http://economix.blogs.nytimes.com/2009/12/09/suicide-rates-around-the-world/.

Remini, Robert V. 1984. *Andrew Jackson and the Course of American Democracy, 1833–1845.* 1984. New York: Harper & Row.

Ritenbaugh, C. 1982. "Obesity as a Culture-Bound Syndrome." *Culture, Medicine and Psychiatry* 6(4):347–361. Retrieved August 2012 from http://www.springerlink.com/content/r2434r5278261km7/.

Rockett, Ian R. H. 1994. "Population and Health: An Introduction to Epidemiology." *Population Bulletin* 49(3, November). Washington, DC: Population Reference Bureau.

Roetzheim, R., et al. 2000. "Effects of Health Insurance and Race on Colorectal Cancer Treatments and Outcomes." *American Journal of Public Health* 90(11):1746–54.

Roter, D., and J. Hall. 2006. *Doctors Talking with Patients/Patients Talking with Doctors.* Westport, CT: Auburn House.

Salcido, D. 2012. *Jill-Care: Pre-existing Condition Insurance Plan Keeps Her Running.* Retrieved September 2012 from http://www.healthcare.gov/blog/2012/08/mycare_jill.html.

Singh, I. (2008, December). "Beyond Polemics: Science and Ethics of ADHD." *Nature Reviews Neuroscience* 9(12):957–64.

Squires, David A. 2011. "The U.S. Health System in Perspective: A Comparison of Twelve Industrialized Nations." *Issues in International Health Policy.* The Commonwealth Fund, July, 2011. Retrieved August 2012 from http://www.commonwealthfund.org/~/media/Files/Publications/Issue%20Brief/2011/Jul/1532_Squires_US_hlt_sys_comparison_12_nations_intl_brief_v2.pdf.

Starr, Paul. 1982. *The Social Transformation of American Medicine.* New York: Basic Books.

Szasz, T. 1970. *The Manufacture of Madness: A Comparative Study of the Inquisition and the Mental Health Movement.* New York: Harper & Row.

Szasz, T. 1984 (1975). *The Therapeutic State: Psychiatry in the Mirror of Current Events.* Buffalo, NY: Prometheus Books.

Szasz, T. 2001. *Pharmacracy: Medicine and Politics in America.* New York: Praeger. p. 212.

Thompson, Becky W. 1992. "'A Way Outa No Way': Eating Problems among African-American, Latina, and White Women." *Gender and Society* 6(4): 546–561.

Treatment4Addiction.com. 2011. *"Drunkorexia" Becoming a Problem in Young Women.* October 18. Retrieved July 2012 from http://www.treatment4addiction.com/blog/addiction/drunkorexia-becoming-a-problem-in-young-women/.

Turney, L. 2011. "Designer Drugs: Accidents Will Happen." Do It Now Foundation 159(3):159. Retrieved October 2012 from http://www.doitnow.org/pages/159.html.

UNAIDS. 2012. *UNAIDS Fact Sheet: The Global AIDS Epidemic.* Retrieved July 2012 from http://www.unaids.org/documents/20101123_FS_Global_em_en.pdf.

United Nations Office on Drugs and Crime (UNODC). 2012. *World Drug Report 2012* (United Nations publication, Sales No. E.12.XI.1). Retrieved July 2012 from http://www.unodc.org/documents/data-and-analysis/WDR2012/WDR_2012_web_small.pdf.

US Census. 2012. *The 2012 Statistical Abstract*, Table 1114. Retrieved July 2012 from http://www.census.gov/compendia/statab/2012/tables/12s1114.xls.

US Department of Health and Human Services (DHHS). 2012. *Hispanic/Latino Profile.* The Office of Minority Health. Retrieved Sept. 2012 from http://minorityhealth.hhs.gov/templates/browse.aspx?lvl=2&lvlID=54.

US Department of Justice Disability Rights Division. 2009. *A Guide to Disability Rights Laws.* Retrieved July 2012 from http://www.ada.gov/cguide.htm.

US Department of Justice Disability Rights Division. 2012. *Questions and Answers: The Americans with Disabilities Act and Persons with HIV/AIDS.* Retrieved July 2012 from http://www.ada.gov/archive/hivqanda.txt.

US Department of Veterans Affairs. 2012a. *History—VA History.* Retrieved August 2012 from http://www.va.gov/about_va/vahistory.asp.

US Department of Veterans Affairs. 2012b. *VA History in Brief.* Retrieved August 2012 from http://www.va.gov/opa/publications/archives/docs/history_in_brief.pdf.

Vastag, B. 2012. "'Radical' Bill Seeks to Reduce Costs of AIDS Drugs by Awarding Prizes Instead of Patents." *Washington Post.* May 19. Retrieved August 2012 from http://www.washingtonpost.com/national/health-science/radical-bill-seeks-to-reduce-cost-of-aids-drugs-by-awarding-prizes-instead-of-patents/2012/05/19/gIQAFGfahU_story.html.

Vrangbaek, K., I. Durand-Zaleski, R. Busse, N. Klazinga, S. Boyle, and A. Anell. 2008. *Health Care System Profiles.* The Commonwealth Fund, 2008. Retrieved August 2012 from http://www.commonwealthfund.org/Resources/2008/Mar/Health-Care-System-Profiles.aspx.

Waananen, L. 2012. "How the Number of Uninsured May Change With and Without the Health Care Law." *The New York Times.* June 27, 2012. Retrieved July 2012 from http://www.nytimes.com/interactive/2012/06/27/us/how-the-number-of-uninsured-may-change-with-and-without-the-health-care-law.html.

Waldron, Hilary. 2007. *Trends in Mortality Differentials and Life Expectancy for Male Social Security–covered Workers, by Average Relative Earnings.* U.S. Social Security Administration, ORES Working Paper No. 108. Oct., 2007. Retrieved August 2012 from http://www.ssa.gov/policy/docs/workingpapers/wp108.html.

Wiseman, N., and A. Ellis. 1996. *Fundamentals of Chinese Medicine.* Brookline, MA: Paradigm Publications.

Woodside, D. B., P. E. Garfinkel, E. Lin, P. Goering, A. S. Kaplan, D. S. Goldbloom, and S. H. Kennedy. 2001. "Comparisons of Men with Full or Partial Eating Disorders, Men without Eating Disorders, and Women with Eating Disorders in the Community." *American Journal of Psychiatry* 158(4):570–4.

World Health Organization (WHO). 1946. *Constitution of the World Health Organization.* New York: World Health Organization Interim Commission.

World Health Organization (WHO). 2004. *The World Health Report 2004: Changing History, Annex Table 3: Burden of Disease in QALYs by Cause, Sex, and Mortality Stratum in WHO Regions, Estimates for 2002.* Geneva: WHO.

World Health Organization (WHO). 2008. *Commission on Social Determinants of Health.* Retrieved Oct. 2012 from http://whqlibdoc.who.int/hq/2008/WHO_IER_CSDH_08.1_eng.pdf.

World Health Organization (WHO). 2010. *World Health Statistics 2010.* Retrieved August 2012 from http://www.who.int/whosis/whostat/2010/en/index.html.

World Health Organization (WHO). 2011a. *The Top 10 Causes of Death.* WHO Fact Sheets. Retrieved August 2012 from http://www.who.int/mediacentre/factsheets/fs310/en/index2.html.

World Health Organization (WHO). 2011b. *Malaria: Elimination and Eradication.* Retrieved August 2012 from http://www.who.int/mediacentre/factsheets/fs094/en/index.html.

© Medioimages/Photodisc/Thinkstock

Chapter Overview ▼

16 Population and Urbanization

Learning Objectives ▼

16.1
- Explain how demographers use the balancing equation to predict population change from births, deaths, and net migration.
- Discuss the use of population pyramids to examine population structures.

16.2
- Compare and contrast theories and perspectives of population growth.

16.3
- Analyze the processes that shape the growth of cities.
- Illustrate theories of urban growth.
- Describe general trends in urbanization.

16.4
- Discuss sociological theories of the role of community.

16.5
- Examine the role of new technology in population distribution.
- Discuss how social life is changing in rural areas.
- Analyze how population increases and increased consumption affect the environment.

© Atomazul/Shutterstock, Inc.

A tale of two cities. The first time I visited Detroit it was during the 1980s. The population of Detroit had declined more than 2% in the 1970s and would drop 2% more during the 1980s. There was a lot of crime. Whole neighborhoods were run down, with boarded-up houses, trash on the streets, bars on the doors, and broken windows. Hardly anyone could be seen walking on the street, and those who were looked surprised to see a family driving in this neighborhood. Driving to the hotel, I began to wonder whether the decision to build this huge, expensive modern hotel here to help turn the area around had not gone terribly wrong.

I was driving with my family to attend a meeting of the American Sociological Association. My son and daughter were preteens then, and I became increasingly worried about what they could do and where they could go safely while I attended the meetings. My wife and I quickly decided to keep them near us at all times and to stay in the hotel most of the time.

Later, we were able to get away for most of a day, and we took a day trip to Windsor, Canada, just across the Detroit River. When we drove into Windsor, it was like night and day. The streets were clean. The buildings were well kept. There were lots of people, including families, walking around. The people were friendly and welcoming. We just felt safer, and we were able to relax and enjoy our family time together.

How could these two cities so close to one another be so different? While Detroit at that time had one of the higher crime rates in the United States, Windsor had one of the lower crime rates in Canada—a country with lower crime rates than the United States in general. Both Detroit and Windsor had lost population in the 1970s. Both cities were racially and ethnically diverse. The difference is not just a United States versus Canada difference. We could have compared Detroit to more successful US cities like Minneapolis or Omaha. What causes some cities to succeed so well and others to struggle?

These two cities pose some of the issues we will discuss in this chapter. How are communities affected by population size, growth or declines in population, and racial and ethnic composition? How do cities grow over time? How does land use in specific areas change? What can cities do to rejuvenate themselves when things start to go wrong? What can be done by individuals? These are issues faced by every community.

16.1 Sociological Study of Population: Demography

Rapid increases in global population highlight the need for understanding factors that affect population growth as well as consequences of the age and sex distribution of populations.

- Explain how demographers use the balancing equation to predict population change from births, deaths, and net migration.
- Discuss the use of population pyramids to examine population structures.

Demography The scientific study of human populations.

Population The people who inhabit a country or geographic region.

Census A survey of the entire population of a country or region counting the number of people and their characteristics.

Census undercount The number of people missed in a census and includes illegal immigrants, the homeless, and vagrants, as well as people who, for some reason, did not want to be counted.

Demography is the scientific study of human populations. Demography is concerned with the size and composition of populations as well as with their rate of growth and the movement of people from one location to another. When demographers speak of a **population**, they are referring to the people who inhabit a country or geographic region.

Most demographic research focuses on social facts in the form of statistics describing populations. Those statistics are usually obtained using a combination of questionnaires or social surveys and a census. A **census** is a survey of the entire population of a country or region counting the number of people and their characteristics. A census is taken in the United States every 10 years as required by the US Constitution. Many other countries also conduct censuses on a regular basis to monitor population changes and plan social policy. The census is the major method used to gather population data. However, there are other sources, such as birth records and death records, which are often used by researchers to identify causes of death and study factors influencing mortality rates. Like any other research method, the census is not perfect. The **census undercount** is the number of people missed in a census and includes illegal immigrants, the homeless, and vagrants, as well as people who, for some reason, did not want to be counted. The Bureau of the Census estimates there were about 36,000 people (0.01%) who were overcounted by the census (counted twice), while 2.1% of the black population and 1.5% of the Hispanic population was undercounted in the 2010 US Census (US Census Bureau 2012b). Undercounts of minorities can occur when those groups are more likely to be homeless, illegal, or recently moved.

Population Changes

Over most of recorded human history, the world population remained fairly stable and small at roughly a half million people. However, beginning between 200 and 300 years ago, population began to grow rapidly. Today there are more than seven billion people in the world, and that number is projected to grow to 9.3 billion by 2050 and to 10.1 billion people by the end of the century (Gillis and Dugger 2011). This rapid increase in population has made clear the need to understand population growth.

The key to understanding population growth lies in what demographers call the **balancing equation** (sometimes called the basic demographic equation)—a simple equation that expresses population growth as a function of four factors. Population changes over time can be expressed as the result of these four factors in the balancing equation, shown here with the US figures for 2012 (in thousands).

$$\text{Population } (t_2) = \text{Population } (t_1) + \text{Births} - \text{Deaths} + \text{Net Migration}$$
$$316,643 = 313,847 + 4,293 - 2,633 + 1,136$$

In words, this equation says that the population at time 2 (t_2) is determined by the population at time 1 (t_1) plus the number of births minus the number of deaths plus the **net migration**—the number of people moving into the geographic area minus the number of people leaving the area. Thus, the population of the United States in 2013 can be estimated from the population in 2012 (almost 314 million) plus births (more than 4 million) minus more than 2 million deaths plus more than 1 million in net migration (US Census Bureau 2012b). The net change in population is 316,643 – 313,847 or 2,796—slightly less than 3 million. The annual change in population divided by the midyear population produces the rate of increase in the population. Here, this is 2,796/313,847 or 0.89%. The **natural rate of increase** is the rate of increase in a population due to births and deaths ignoring net migration. Adding in migration provides the rate of increase in the population.

The US population is increasing at a rate of 0.89%, or less than 1% a year. Demographers often compute one more statistic to make this growth rate meaningful: They compute the doubling time for the population. The **doubling time** for a population is the number of years it would take for the population to double in size if it were to continue to grow at its current rate. This is approximately 70 divided by the growth rate. Some doubling times for the United States, Africa, and the world as a whole are shown in FIGURE 16-1. For the United States between 2012 and 2013, the doubling time is 78 years. That is, if the population in the United States continued to grow at

Balancing equation (sometimes called the basic demographic equation) A simple equation that expresses population growth as a function of four factors.

Net migration The number of people moving into the geographic area minus the number of people leaving the area.

Natural rate of increase The rate of increase in a population due to births and deaths.

Doubling time The number of years it would take for the population to double in size if it were to continue to grow at its current rate.

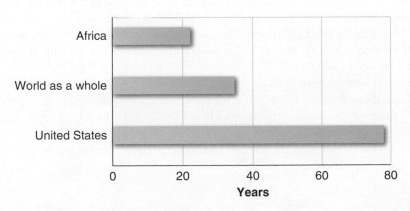

FIGURE 16-1 Doubling times for different regions in years.
Source: Data from Population Reference Bureau. 2012. 2012 World Population Data Sheet. Accessed November 2012 (http://www.prb.org/pdf12/2012-population-data-sheet_eng.pdf).

that rate, it would double every 78 years. The world as a whole was growing at a rate of 1.2% annually in 2012 for a projected doubling time of 35 years. Africa was doubling every 23 years.

There is, of course, much more to demography than this simple equation. Let us consider each of the key factors that lead to population change (fertility, mortality, and migration) and, using the sociological imagination, how public issues might affect these population changes.

Fertility

In theory, during a woman's childbearing years (the years during which it is biologically possible for her to bear children), a woman could have as many as 20 or more children. This maximum possible childbearing is called **fecundity**. However, most women do not even begin to give birth to that number of children, either in the United States or in any other country. The actual rate of births is the **fertility rate**—the average number of children born per woman over her lifetime. In 2012, the fertility rate in the United States was 2.1 (US Census Bureau 2012b), which is roughly equal to the **replacement-level fertility**—the average number of births per woman required to replace the population in most industrialized countries (Espenshaade, Guzman, and Westoff 2003). In contrast, in 2012, the fertility rate for the world as a whole was 2.4 and ranged from a low of 1.1 in Latvia and Taiwan to a high of 7.1 in Niger (Population Reference Bureau 2012). Women in Niger have six more children on the average than do women in Latvia and five more children than women in the United States! Higher birth rates are often found in poorer countries depending more on agriculture because the entire household often participates in agricultural production, providing an economic incentive to have more children. In contrast, in richer countries with complex divisions of labor and jobs requiring greater skills, children are more of an economic burden than an economic advantage, encouraging lower birth rates. These countries reflect general trends for developing countries (like Niger) to have high fertility and growing populations, European countries (like Latvia) to have low fertility and shrinking populations, and other developed countries (like the United States) to have moderate fertility and slow population growth.

It is also possible to look at birth rates—the number of births per year. The **total birth rate** is the average number of live births per year per thousand women in the population. Less accurate but often the only statistic that can be computed from data available for many countries is the **crude birth rate**—the average number of live births per year per thousand people in the population. In the United States for 2012, the estimated crude birth rate is 13.7 per thousand (US Census Bureau 2012b).

The US Postwar Baby Boom

Fertility rates sometimes change dramatically over time. The best known example of a dramatic but temporary change in birth rates in the United States began just after World War II, when the United States experienced a **baby boom**—a period of time in which the birth rate was elevated for several years. During this time, there was a decrease in childless and one-child families but little increase in couples having three or more children. The baby boom peaked in 1957, but the elevated birth rate, of more than 20 live births per 1,000 population, continued until 1964. The baby boom can clearly be seen in FIGURE 16-2, in which birth and death rates in the United States are plotted between 1900 and 2005.

Several reasons have been suggested for the baby boom. In the language of the sociological imagination, these constitute public issues that affected large numbers of people during those times. Returning soldiers from World War II were eager to get on with their lives by getting married and starting households. High wages and prosperity, along with the GI Bill, gave them access to affordable house mortgages, which encouraged family formation. Huge suburbs providing mass-produced housing were being

Fecundity The maximum possible number of children a woman can have during her lifetime.

Fertility rate The average number of children born per woman over her lifetime.

Replacement-level fertility The average number of births per woman required to replace the population.

Total birth rate The average number of live births per year per thousand women in the population.

Crude birth rate The average number of live births per year per thousand people in the population.

Baby boom A period of time in which the birth rate was elevated for several years.

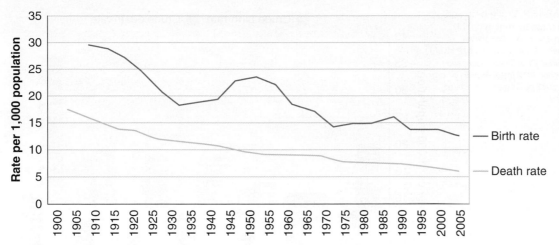

FIGURE 16-2 US crude birth and death rates (1900 to 2005)
Source: Data from National Center for Health Statistics. 2007, August 21. National Vital Statistics Reports 54(20). Accessed November 2012 (http://www.cdc.gov/nchs/births.htm; http://www.infoplease.com/ipa/A0005067.html; http://www.infoplease.com/ipa/A0005131.html).

constructed in places like Levittown. At the same time women, who were no longer welcome in factories where they had worked during World War II, faced many social pressures on them to marry and have children (Coontz 2000). As a result, the age of marriage declined and rates of marriage and the birth rate went up dramatically.

Global Birth Rates

Birth rates vary dramatically from country to country. This can be seen in FIGURE 16-3. Highest birth rates are found in low-income countries such as in Africa, where the average birth rate is 36 per thousand. Medium birth rates (18 to 19 per thousand) are found in Asia, Oceania, and Latin America and Caribbean. Low birth rates are found in North America (13 per thousand) and Europe (11 per thousand; Population Reference Bureau 2012). The crude birth rate in the United States is now about 13.7 births per thousand people annually. China has instituted tough policies to reduce its birth rate by penalizing families with more than one child, encouraging the use of birth-control measures, and, in some cases, even resorting to forced sterilization or forced abortions.

Mortality

Another factor that obviously affects population is **mortality**—the incidence of death in a population. A commonly used measure of mortality is the **crude death rate**—the number of deaths per year for every thousand people in a population. For example, in the United States for 2012, the projected number of deaths is 2.633 million for a midyear population of nearly 314 million, so the estimated crude death rate for that year is 2.633/314 or 8.4 per thousand (US Census Bureau 2012b).

Death rates vary considerably around the globe, but not nearly as much as birth rates. Looking at FIGURE 16-3 again, the lowest death rates are in Latin America and the Caribbean (6 deaths per thousand annually), while the highest death rates are found in Africa and Europe (11 deaths per thousand).

For more than a century, death rates have dropped substantially in most countries around the world. While those drops have been greatest in industrialized nations, there have also been significant drops in death rates in less developed countries as well. As a result of decreased death rates, the **life expectancy**—the average number of years people are expected to live—has increased substantially. In the United States, the average life span increased from 40 years in 1900 to 79 years in 2012 (Population Reference Bureau 2012) FIGURE 16-4. Generally, global life expectancies are inversely related to death rates, with countries having greater wealth and resources able to use resources to lower death rates and increase life expectancy. As a result, the lowest life expectancy is found in Africa (58), next lowest but much higher life expectancy in Asia (70), and highest life expectancies in North America, Europe, and Oceania.

Mortality The incidence of death in a population.

Crude death rate The number of deaths per year for every thousand people in a population.

Life expectancy The average number of years people are expected to live.

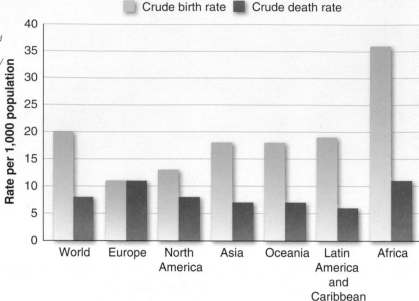

FIGURE 16-3 Crude birth and death rates by region (2011). *Source: Data from Population Reference Bureau. 2012. 2012 World Population Data Sheet. Accessed November 2012 (http://www.prb.org/pdf12/2012-population-data-sheet_eng.pdf).*

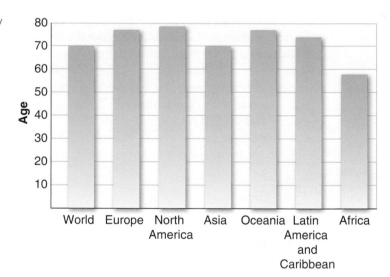

FIGURE 16-4 Life expectancy by region. *Source: Data from Population Reference Bureau. 2012. 2012 World Population Data Sheet. Accessed November 2012 (http://www.prb.org/pdf12/2012-population-data-sheet_eng.pdf).*

Migration

Migration The movement of people from one geographic area to another.

Immigration People moving into a geographic area.

Emigration People moving out of a geographic area.

Net migration The difference between immigration and emigration.

Net migration rate The rate of increase in a population due to net migration.

The last factor affecting population is **migration**—the movement of people from one geographic area to another. When people move into a geographic area, it is called **immigration**. When they move out of a geographic area, it is called **emigration**. Since both of these occur at the same time, demographers usually focus on the **net migration**—the difference between immigration and emigration. Migration rates, like birth and death rates, are usually expressed as some number per thousand people in a population. For example, in the United States for 2012, the projected net immigration is 1.136 million for a midyear population of 313.847 million, so the estimated **net migration rate** for that year is 1.136/313.847 times 1,000, or 3.6 per thousand (US Census Bureau 2012b).

Voluntary immigration is another example of a public issue that influences all of us. Voluntary immigration is influenced by push factors that encourage people to leave an area (such as a poor economy or political turmoil) and pull factors that encourage people to move to an area (such as a strong economy and a stable political system). Push and pull factors generally lead to immigration becoming strong sources of population growth for affluent countries, while the population of poor countries tends to increase almost exclusively from natural growth (births and deaths within the country) and is diminished as people emigrate to more desirable countries. For most of its 220-plus years, migration has played a large role in population growth in the United States. In FIGURE 16-5 are displayed the number of legal immigrants entering the United States annually from 1820 to 2011. Immigration varied dramatically but generally increased between 1820 and 1907, peaking in 1907 at 1.28 million. Then it dropped generally over the next 38 years until the end of World War II, taking a huge drop in World War I and again beginning in the 1930s during the Great Depression. Since World War II, immigration has generally increased, exceeding one million every year since 2005. In 2011, immigrants made up 13.0% of the US population, the largest percentage since 1920 (Migration Policy Institute 2012).

The country of origin of US immigrants changed dramatically between 1820 to 2010, as displayed in FIGURE 16-6. Throughout the 19th century, 80 to 90% of immigration to the United States was from Europe. However, this plummeted over the 20th century, dropping to around 10% by 2000, while immigration increased dramatically among Hispanics from the Americas, approaching 50% by 1960. Then from 1960 to today, immigration from Asia rose from less than 10% to nearly 40% by 2010. So immigration is not only changing the size of our population, it is also increasing our racial and ethnic diversity (US Department of Homeland Security 2010).

The United States has also experienced a great deal of **internal migration**—migration from one place to another within a larger geographic area. A dramatic example of internal migration was the movement after the end of the Civil War of large numbers of blacks seeking escape from racial discrimination in the South by moving to large urban centers such as Chicago, New York, Cleveland, and St. Louis in the Northeast

> **Internal migration** Migration from one place to another within a larger geographic area.

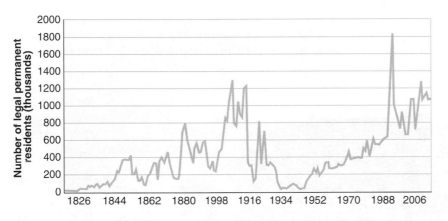

FIGURE 16-5 Annual legal immigration to the United States (fiscal years 1820 to 2011).
Source: Data from Department of Homeland Security. 2011. 2011 Yearbook of Immigration Statistics. Office of Immigration Statistics. Accessed November 2012 (http://www.dhs.gov/sites/default/files/publications/immigration-statistics/yearbook/2011/ois_yb_2011.pdf).

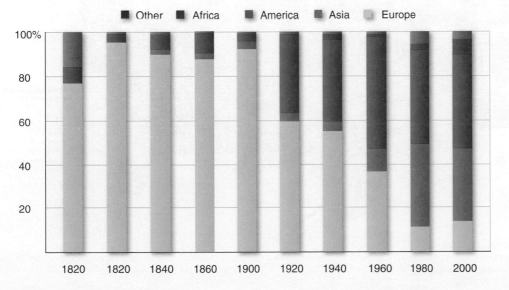

FIGURE 16-6 Percent immigration by region (1820–2010).
Source: Data from Department of Homeland Security. 2011. 2011 Yearbook of Immigration Statistics. Office of Immigration Statistics. Accessed November 2012 (http://www.dhs.gov/sites/default/files/publications/immigration-statistics/yearbook/2011/ois_yb_2011.pdf).

and Northern Midwest. The largest internal migration trends since the latter part of the 20th century have been migration from the Northeast and North Central regions to the South and West. The map in FIGURE 16-7 displays the net migration for each US county between 2000 and 2010. Much of the in-migration in this figure is to urban counties. Much of the out-migration is from rural areas, the northern Midwest, and some areas in the Old South.

Population Structure

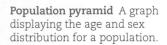

Population pyramid A graph displaying the age and sex distribution for a population.

Age cohort A subpopulation of people all born within a narrow age range.

The structure of a population refers to its distribution of people based on age, sex, and other characteristics. The most common way to examine and describe a population structure is a **population pyramid**—a graph displaying the age and sex distribution for a population. In FIGURE 16-8 are two population pyramids. Each population pyramid displays successive **age cohorts**—subpopulations of people all born within a narrow age range—with the youngest age cohort on the bottom and the oldest on the top, and with males on the left and females on the right. The width of the population pyramid at its base is a direct result of the birth rate of a population. The rate at which each successive cohort decreases in size reflects any changes in birth rates between age cohorts, along with the effects of death rates and net migration.

The structure of a population tells us a lot about the public social issues facing a population and the need for various goods and services. These issues have consequences for both the society and individuals within the society. In Figure 16-8 are two population pyramids, one for the United States and one for Nigeria. The population pyramid for Nigeria was selected because it illustrates the problems faced by many less affluent countries. Nigeria has a high crude birth rate of 39 per thousand, leading to a large proportion of the population in the younger age cohorts and higher crude death rate of 13 per thousand with virtually no net migration, leading to a sharp drop-off in population among the older age cohorts. As a result, Nigeria and countries like it have many children to support (44% of its population is less than 16 years old) and a

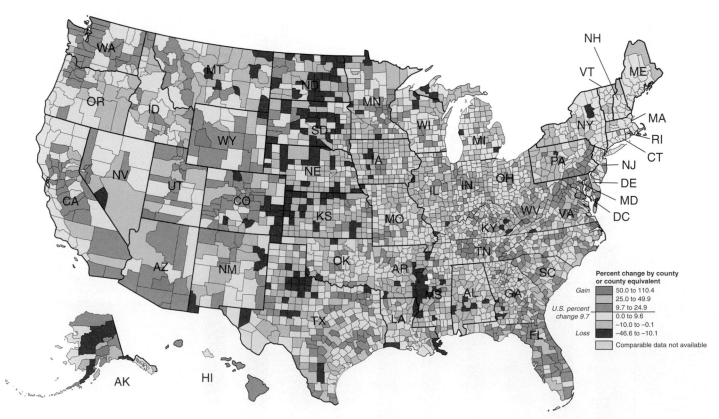

FIGURE 16-7 Percent change in population (2000–2010).
Source: US Census Bureau. 2011. Percent Change in Population: 2000 to 2010. US Census Bureau, Geography Division, June 13, 2011. Accessed November 2012 (http://www.census.gov/geo/www/maps/2010pop/us_perchange_2010map.jpg).

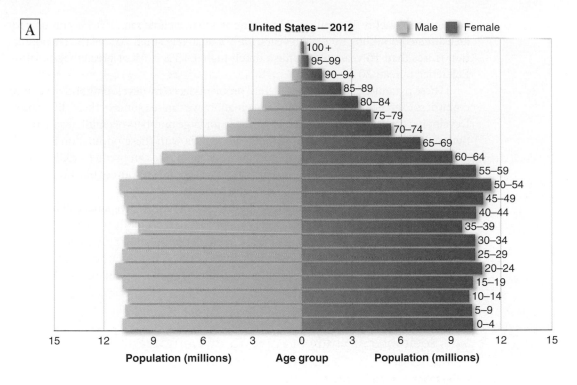

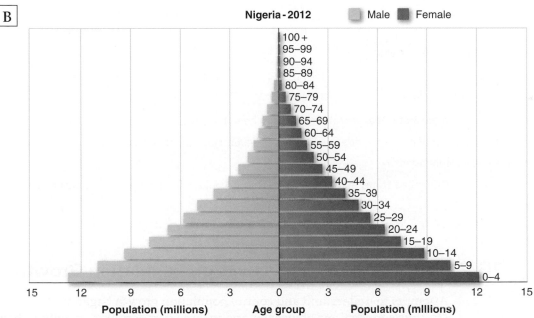

FIGURE 16-8 Population pyramids: (A) United States (2012) and (B) Nigeria (2012)
Source: (A) Central Intelligence Agency. 2012. The World Factbook. Accessed November 2012 (https://www.cia.gov/library/publications/the-world-factbook/index.html); (B) Central Intelligence Agency. 2012. The World Factbook. Accessed November 2012 (https://www.cia.gov/library/publications/the-world-factbook/index.html).

relatively small 3% of its population 65 and older. Nigeria, with a population of 170.1 million in 2012, is growing at a rate of 2.6% annually for an estimated doubling time of 27 years (Population Reference Bureau 2012).

In contrast, the US population pyramid looks much like those of many relatively affluent industrialized countries. A lower crude birth rate of 14 per thousand reduces the width of the younger age cohorts, and the lower crude death rate of 8 per thousand and a net migration rate of 4 per thousand permits a longer life expectancy of 78, producing a modest drop in size as cohorts become older. The population pyramid becomes much more box shaped. The bulge between ages 40 and 60 is the result of the baby boom experienced in the United States between 1945 and 1970, when birth rates were temporarily much higher. As a result of these dynamics, the US population, currently at roughly 314 million, is growing at a manageable rate of 0.9% annually for an estimated doubling time of 78 years. Only a relatively small 20% of the US population is less than 16 years old, while a much higher 13% is 65 or greater (Population Reference Bureau 2012).

These pyramids highlight the different problems faced by developing and developed countries. Exercising our sociological imagination, we can see some of these differences. Developing countries like Nigeria must provide for large numbers of children and infants but few elderly. It is a difficult time to live in Nigeria with these population demands outstripping the country's ability to keep up with them. We can predict a difficult time for individuals and their families as they compete for scarce resources like housing and food, and later education and social services, to survive.

In contrast, developed countries like the United States have small, manageable numbers of infants and children but a growing population of elderly who will eventually need more health care and other services. The slower population growth of developed countries makes their task much easier than that of developing countries. In this case, in the 78 years it will take the US population to double, Nigeria's population will increase by a factor of seven!

CONCEPT LEARNING CHECK 16.1	Sociological Study of Population: Demography

Use the equation to respond true or false to the following questions.

Population changes over time can be expressed as the result of four factors in the balancing equation, shown here with the US figures for 2012 (in thousands).

Population (t_2) = Population (t_1) + Births – Deaths + Net Migration

$$316{,}643 = 313{,}847 + 4{,}293 - 2{,}633 + 1{,}136$$

_____ **1.** The population is increasing over time.

_____ **2.** More people migrated to the United States that year than were born here that year.

_____ **3.** Net migration is the total number of people moving in and out of the country during that year.

_____ **4.** Net migration is the same as emigration.

_____ **5.** Even if no babies were born in the United States that year, the population would have increased overall due to net migration.

16.2 Theories and Perspectives on Population Growth

Attempts to understand and control population growth began with Malthus's predictions of disaster and include demographic transition theory that predicts declines in population growth.

■ Compare and contrast theories and perspectives of population growth.

Because of the importance of population growth, a number of social theorists have attempted to understand that growth in hopes of controlling it, beginning with the work of an English clergyman at the end of the 18th century.

Malthusian Perspective

Thomas Malthus (1766–1834), an English clergyman, was the first to argue the world was becoming overpopulated (Malthus 1798). Malthus recognized that the number of births is directly proportional to the number of women of childbearing age in a population. So the more potential mothers available, the more births result. This means that population increases exponentially rather than linearly. Malthus argued that population was growing exponentially, doubling every few years, while the food supply was increasing at a linear rate. The problem is exponential growth, like compound interest at a bank, keeps growing faster and faster. If, for example, it takes 10 years for something to double, then in the next 10 years it becomes four times larger, in the next 10 years it becomes eight times larger, and on and on in the geometric progression (1, 2, 4, 8, 16, 32, 64, 128, 256, . . .). At some point, the accelerated population growth was bound to overtake the food supply, leading to catastrophic starvation and disorder, as illustrated in FIGURE 16-9. Malthus argued that population should be controlled through postponing marriage but rejected artificial measures of birth control because they were not sanctioned by the church.

There is some support for the argument put forth by Malthus. World population growth for the past few hundred years has increased exponentially, as can be seen in FIGURE 16-10. This has been particularly true in developing countries but far less true in developed countries. The great majority of growth in world population has been and continues to be in developing countries.

Fortunately, things are not as simple as Malthus made them out to be. The food supply has grown much faster than he expected thanks to modern agricultural technologies. Rates of population growth have diminished in some parts of the world to the point where some countries are actually losing population or in fear of doing so. However, population growth continues to challenge many developing countries even today.

Marxist Perspective

Karl Marx (1867) objected to Malthus's argument that blames overpopulation for human misery. In particular, Marx objected to characterizing human suffering as a "law of

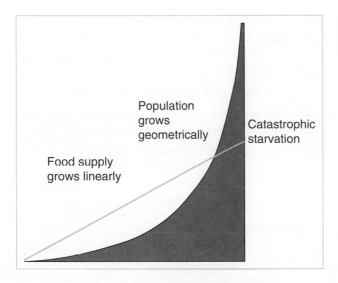

FIGURE 16-9 The Malthusian perspective on population growth.

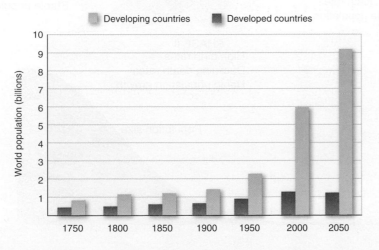

FIGURE 16-10 World population (1750–2050)
Source: Data from World Bank. 2004. World Population Growth. The World Bank Group. Accessed November 2012 (http://www.worldbank.org/depweb/english/beyond/beyondco/beg_03.pdf).

nature" when Marx believed suffering was more clearly the consequence of capitalism and the social inequality that it encourages. Contrary to Malthus, Marx argued, there were sufficient resources to sustain the world population of that time (approximately 1 billion people) if those resources were just distributed more equitably. Capitalism and the great inequalities it created were the problem, argued Marx, not overpopulation. Marx's argument is supported by the fact that we now have seven billion people on the earth, and if resources were more equitably distributed, we could successfully sustain that many and more with today's technologies.

However, while Marx made a good case arguing that inequality leads to great human suffering, New Malthusians (the intellectual heirs of the Malthusian argument) remind us that Marx did not offer a solution to rapid population growth. In 2012, according to the Population Reference Bureau (2012), there were an estimated 267 births every minute globally, more than 385,000 people per day, and more than 140 million new births annually. At its present rate of growth, the global population will double every 35 years.

Demographic Transition Theory

When Thomas Malthus was writing his pessimistic predictions regarding population growth, Europe and England were in the midst of a period of rapid population growth unknown before in the history of humanity. It is no wonder he was so pessimistic. However, since then, a dramatic change has taken place. Today, most Western industrialized countries in Europe and North America are no longer experiencing such rapid population growth. Instead, they are experiencing manageable, modest growth, no growth, and in some cases even a decline in population. For example, Europe's population is expected to decrease from 740 million in 2012 to 732 million by 2050 (Population Reference Bureau 2012). What happened in these countries during the 19th and 20th centuries is the demographic transition (first described by Thompson 1929).

The **demographic transition** occurs when countries change from high birth rates and death rates to low birth rates and death rates. The demographic transition has three phases, as shown in FIGURE 16-11:

I   High birth rates and death rates, with little population growth

II   Declining death rates due largely to reductions in infant mortality, with little or no reduction in birth rates, resulting in high population growth

III Low birth rates and death rates, with little population growth

Demographic transition The shift that occurs when countries change from high birth rates and death rates to low birth rates and death rates.

FIGURE 16-11 The demographic transition.

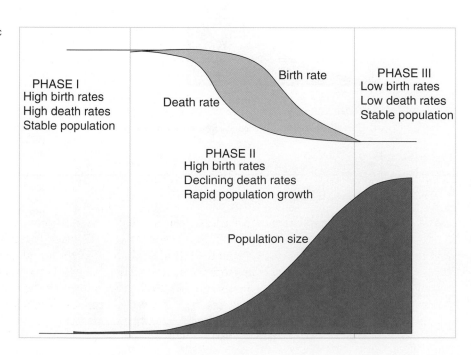

The crucial question becomes whether developing nations that are still in Phase II and experiencing rapid population growth will also transition to Phase III, and how soon. The demographic transition describes the history of industrialized nations, but it is not a "law" that must necessarily describe population transitions in other countries now or in the future. In fact, this transition has been made more difficult for developing nations today because their death rates often plummet rapidly due to technology transfers from industrialized countries, while reductions in birth rates require cultural changes in attitudes regarding the size of the family that require much more time. For countries that became industrialized early, reductions in death rates took much longer, giving those countries greater opportunity to reduce birth rates more gradually. Even when reaching Phase III, countries will continue to experience population growth for a time due to the large number of people of childbearing age.

In 2012, the countries in both North America and Europe have clearly entered Phase III. Dozens of industrialized countries, most of them in Europe, have achieved **zero population growth (ZPG)**, in which the population is expected to change little or none over time, or even population decline in which their population is now dropping. As long ago as 1972, the US fertility rate dropped below the replacement level fertility rate of 2.12, the fertility rate required to keep the population constant (this number is more than 2.0 to adjust for women who do not live to reach childbearing age).

In 2012, North America had an average rate of increase of 0.8%, including net immigration and a doubling time of 88 years, while Europe has gone even further with an average rate of increase of 0.2%, including net immigration. As a result, Europe is projected to lose population between now and 2050 (Population Reference Bureau 2012). Asia (growth rate of 1.1%), Latin America, and the Caribbean (growth rates of 1.2%) are each showing some decline in population growth, suggesting they are entering Phase III. Oceania continues to have a higher 1.5% growth rate with significant net immigration. African countries, on average, continue in Phase II with an average growth rate of 2.4%, meaning the population of Africa is doubling roughly every 29 years.

A number of demographers argue that Phase III of the demographic transition is now being followed in some countries by a Phase IV in which countries are experiencing modest population declines (Haub 2004). Some even predict that declines will become larger and that the world population as a whole might shrink significantly over the long run. For example, fertility rates have fallen below the replacement level, resulting in population declines, in some of the most highly developed nations in the world, including South Korea, Japan, Germany, Spain, and Italy (Stein 2009). Yet more recent data suggest that fertility rates are rising again in some highly developed countries (Myrskyla, Kohler, and Billari 2009). The authors suggest that, in moderate levels of development, birth rates decline because of the costs of raising children in developed societies, but when societies pass a threshold of development, more people have resources to afford children despite their economic drain on the household (Myrskyla, Kohler, and Billari 2009). Of course, it is difficult to know whether population shrinkage or population growth will dominate in the future. But at this point, world population is still increasing rapidly, doubling roughly every 35 years.

> **Zero population growth (ZPG)** A state in which the population size is expected to change little or none over time.

THE SOCIOLOGICAL IMAGINATION   World Population Growth and the Demographic Transition

Fortunately, there is some evidence that at least many developing countries, too, are in earlier phases of the demographic transition. This can be seen in data from the World Bank in FIGURE 16-12. In this figure, we see two separate demographic transitions: one for developed countries and one for developing countries. The demographic transition for developed countries began earlier and has had more time to moderate population in those countries. The transition for developing countries began later but is leading to a more rapid change than occurred for developed countries. If this transition continues to occur, and rapidly, in developing countries, then there is hope we can get the population explosion under control. But what if it does not?

(Continues)

THE SOCIOLOGICAL IMAGINATION (Continued)

The sociological imagination encourages us to consider how our individual biographies intersect with history and how our individual problems reflect broad social issues. Let us extend this a bit now and consider future histories and biographies and alternative social contexts and social issues. Consider the huge population growth in developing countries relative to developed countries in Figure 16-10 and the birth and death rates for developing and developed countries shown in Figure 16-3.

What if countries are unable to persuade their people of the need to manage population growth? Countries that continue to encourage childbearing in an effort to gain political strength or prevent and/or limit access to birth-control methods as part of family planning might continue to accelerate out-of-control population growth. How different will the possible futures be for people in developing and developed countries with population growth under control versus population growth out of control?

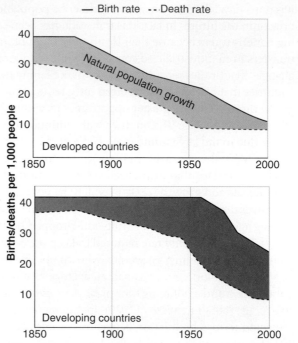

Note: Developed countries include high-income countries and present-day transition economies.

FIGURE 16-12 Two demographic transitions.
Source: Data from World Bank. 2004. World Population Growth. The World Bank Group. Accessed November 2012 (http://www.worldbank.org/depweb/english/beyond/beyondco/beg_03.pdf).

EVALUATE

1. If you are in a developed country such as in Europe or North America, how does this public issue of population growth affect private problems you face or might face in the future? What kind of public issues does your country face related to population growth today and how might these create private problems for you now and in the future? Consider Figure 16-8 as an example.

2. In contrast, what types of public and private issues related to population growth do developing countries and citizens face and what possible future consequences do you foresee? Is it likely to matter to you whether population growth slows or continues to be high? If the consequences are manageable for you, will they also be manageable for your children and your grandchildren?

3. How do cultural differences affect population growth policies? What kind of political issues such as those related to human rights violations might surface when developing countries attempt to control population growth—for example, China's one-child policy?

Current Analysis of Population Growth

The demographic factors discussed here, including rapid population growth, immigration, changing age composition, and even transient phenomena like the US baby boom, can produce important social changes in a society and require governments to develop policies regarding demographic issues. Sometimes population policies reflect ethnic conflict. Many countries have immigration policies that exclude certain groups from entering the country. Singapore initially had policies rewarding few children and sterilization during the 1970s to halt the population boom, then switched to policies encouraging children once births fell below replacement levels in the 1980s. In 1984, Singapore had a policy that favored children of educated mothers over others (Chadwick

1992). In 1994 in Rwanda, the Rwandan military made a systematic effort to slaughter as many Tutsis and pro-peace Hutus as possible, regardless of age or sex (Lemarchand 2002). We even have a term now, **ethnic cleansing**, which refers to the practice of killing people from some ethnic groups and encouraging the surviving members to emigrate to another country. Many countries, such as the People's Republic of China, have population policies designed to reduce their rapid population growth. Ironically, some countries, including a number of Islamic countries, are encouraging larger families in an effort to increase their populations, presumably to increase their political and military strength in their regions.

In the United States, we can trace the impact of the post-WWII baby boom as those babies grew older. Initially, they produced increased needs for baby products and housing. Next, they increased enrollments in schools, requiring communities to build new buildings and hire new teachers. By the 1960s and 1970s, they produced rapid increases in enrollments in colleges and universities and increased demand for automobiles. Then they flooded the workplace, requiring dramatic increases in the number of jobs. Over the next few decades, they will be placing increased demands on Social Security, nursing homes, hospitals, and the other facilities required as they age, retire, experience declining health, and die.

Internationally, the impact of population varies dramatically depending on the phase of the demographic transition a country is currently in. Using the sociological imagination to consider the intersection of history and biography as it affects individuals in societies with different population concerns and to understand how the broad public issues raised by population pressures influence the lives of individuals, we can better understand the effects of population. Countries in phase II are experiencing rapid population growth and fighting to maintain or improve the standard of living in the face of that tremendous burden. Countries already well into phase III, on the other hand, face stable or even declining populations and an aging population. Their economies need to shift away from goods and services aimed at the young and toward those aimed at the elderly. Rising healthcare costs become a significant social policy issue, as does maintaining the social security of the increasing number of elderly as the number of workers contributing to those programs declines.

China's one-child policy is designed to reduce population growth.

© iStockphoto/Thinkstock

Ethnic cleansing The practice of killing people from some ethnic groups and encouraging the surviving members to emigrate to another country.

CONCEPT LEARNING CHECK 16.2   Theories and Perspectives on Population Growth

Here are two diagrams summarizing the demographic transition and Malthus's view of population growth. Match the following items with the letters marking where each of the numbered items is most likely to be found in the two figures.

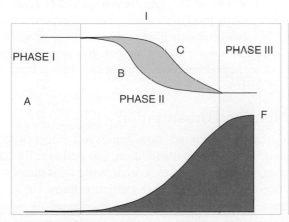

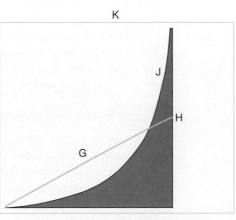

_____ **1.** Demographic transition theory

_____ **2.** The Malthusian perspective on population growth

_____ **3.** Growth of food supply

_____ **4.** Exponential growth of the population

_____ **5.** Moderate increase in population or stability

_____ **6.** Point at which catastrophic starvation is predicted to occur

_____ **7.** Birth rates

_____ **8.** Death rates

Match the following items with the phases in the diagrams.

_____ **9.** High birth rates and low death rates

_____ **10.** Low birth rates and low death rates

_____ **11.** High birth rates and high death rates

_____ **12.** Rapid increase in population

_____ **13.** The most likely phase for many African countries

16.3 Urbanization: The Growth of Cities

Urbanization is occurring worldwide, with its earliest effects among developed countries but with developing countries rapidly catching up. Cities are not static but continue to change and grow, as reflected in theories of urban growth.

- Analyze the processes that shape the growth of cities.
- Illustrate theories of urban growth.
- Describe general trends in urbanization.

Cities are both loved and hated. On the one hand, the poet Percy Shelley said, "Hell is a city much like London—A populous and a smoky city." As this passage reminds us, some people think of cities as crowded, dirty places where people face and often succumb to temptations. On the other hand, the English author Samuel Johnson said, "when a man is tired of London, he is tired of life." This latter view suggests a favorable view of cities with opportunities for all manner of work and entertainment.

In this chapter, we examine issues faced by cities today, including the deteriorating infrastructure in aging US Rust Belt cities, the declining tax bases of inner cities, the flight to the suburbs by affluent whites and corporations, the rising numbers of homeless people, pollution, and crime. However, cities are also places of great art, commerce, industry, and opportunity where most of us work, play, and experience the diverse rewards of modern life. While cities certainly have problems, the predominant view of cities is one of satisfaction. In national surveys, more than 90% of respondents repeatedly indicate that they get either high or medium levels of satisfaction from the city in which they live (Smith et al. 2010).

The Link between Demography and Urbanization

There is more to population than change and composition. Population cannot be fully understood without understanding its geographic distribution. For well over the past century, in both the United States and globally, the most consistent and most important trend in the geographic distribution of population has been **urbanization**—the large-scale movement of people from less populated areas to more populated areas. We cannot understand the major trends in population without also examining urbanization, nor

Urbanization The large-scale movement of people from less populated areas to more populated areas.

can we understand cities without considering their populations. Here we consider how cities are influenced by changes (either increases or decreases) in population, by the age and sex distributions, and by racial and ethnic composition. Later, we will consider how changing population often plays a role in how cities change through processes such as ecological succession.

Population Growth and Decline

In 2010, the Phoenix, Arizona, and Detroit, Michigan, metropolitan areas had nearly the same population. But they face huge differences, because one is growing rapidly while the other struggles. The Phoenix-Mesa-Glendale, Arizona, metropolitan area is one of the fastest-growing urban areas in recent years. Phoenix alone added 70,349 people between April 1, 2010, and July 1, 2011 (US Census Bureau 2012b). The entire metro-area population increased steadily from 726,183 in 1960 to 3,251,876 in 2000 to 4,192,887 in 2010 (CensusScope 2012c). During that same period, Hispanics in the population increased even more rapidly, from 14% in 1980 to 29.5% in 2010. In contrast, the Detroit, Michigan, metropolitan statistical area grew rapidly through the 1960s, increasing by 12%, then declined more than 2% each in the 1970s and 1980s, increasing by 4% in the 1990s (CensusScope 2012b), declining again by about 3% to a population of 4,296,250 in 2010 (US Census Bureau 2012f). The population in Detroit in 2000 was 23% black, 70% white, 3% Hispanic, and 2% Asian. Thus, these two cities face very different prospects. Detroit is fighting off population decline along with older infrastructure issues and aging housing stock as the tax base declines and jobs and affluent households have left. In contrast, Phoenix faces rapid growth requiring new construction, which stimulates more jobs and still more people moving to the city. Much of the new population in Phoenix is Hispanics and younger families, leading to a younger demographic mix and increasing ethnic diversity (CensusScope, 2012c).

Population Structures of Urban Areas

The age and gender distribution of the population in a community also has important implications for the issues faced by communities. In FIGURE 16-13 are population pyramids for three different communities in the author's home state of Missouri. Pulaski County has a clear bulge of 15- to 24-year-old males because it contains a large military training base, Fort Leonard Wood. Columbia, Missouri, the college town in which the main campus of the University of Missouri is located, has a similar bulge in the same age range, except there it is evenly split between males and females. Finally, Taney County has a surprisingly top-heavy population distribution, with nearly 20% of its population 65 and over. That fact is less surprising once we realize that the largest population center in Taney County is Branson, Missouri, with many country-western entertainment establishments that attract elderly retirees. Clearly, these three communities are likely to have very different characters and to face different issues.

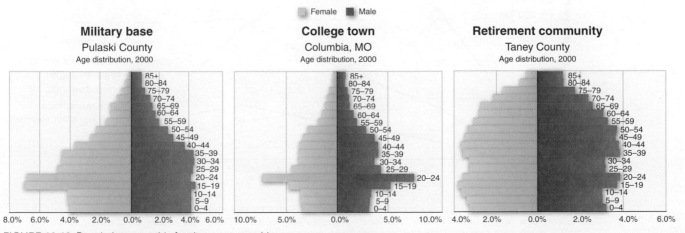

FIGURE 16-13 Population pyramids for three communities.
Source: www.CensusScope.org. Social Science Data Analysis Network, University of Michigan. Accessed November 2012 (www.ssdan.net).

In FIGURE 16-14 are displayed average annual expenditures for selected categories of expenses by age of householder. There are substantial differences in the amount and kind of goods and services for which people expend money on the average. The elderly, for example, see increased costs for health care, lower transportation costs, lower costs for rent (until they are 75 and older), and lower costs for entertainment and food away from home. Because of these differences, the age distribution of a community suggests a lot about which kinds of business would be most viable there. A military base has an excess of young adult males and often attracts adult stores, bars, and similar businesses. College towns, with an excess of both male and female young adults, of course attract education-related businesses such as bookstores, lots of rental dwellings, few repair and insurance businesses, and fewer hospitals and drugstores. Retirement communities attract less rental housing and fewer businesses aimed at entertainment or food away from the home but more healthcare services and drugstores.

A Brief History of Cities

Cities are a relatively new development. Cities are only 7,000 to 9,000 years old. Cities were not possible before efficient agriculture was available. People in cities cannot produce their own food. Hence, cities could not be sustained until farmers could produce a food surplus. Large, modern cities were not possible until the Industrial Revolution, which provided job opportunities in urban areas, more efficient production and transportation, permitting more people to subsist with fewer farmers. Only 10% or less of the entire population could live in preindustrial cities, and the size of those cities was restricted by poor transportation, the limited ability to preserve perishable goods, and health problems related to sanitation.

England was the first country to have more than half of its population living in cities; it passed the 50% mark well over 100 years ago. It was not until 1950 that more than half of the US population lived in cities. By 2000, that figure had reached 80.3% FIGURE 16-15. In 2010, there were 486 urbanized areas with populations of 50,000 or more. Forty-two of them had one million or more people, and the largest, New York City, exceed 18 million in population (US Census Bureau 2012c).

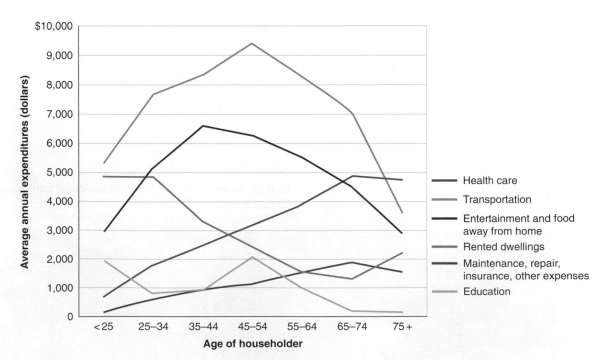

FIGURE 16-14 Average annual expenditures in the United States for selected categories by age (2009).
Source: Data from US Census Bureau. 2012. The 2012 Statistical Abstract. Table 686. Average Annual Expenditures by Age of Householder 2009. Accessed December 2012 (http://www.census.gov/compendia/statab/cats/income_expenditures_poverty_wealth/consumer_expenditures.html).

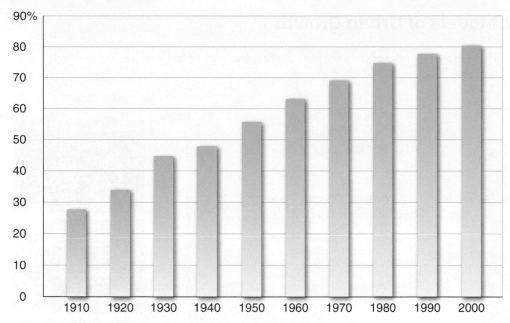

FIGURE 16-15 Percent of US population living in urban areas (1910–2000).
Source: Data from Hobbs, Frank and Nicole Stoops. 2002. U.S. Census Bureau, Census 2000 Special Reports, Series CENSR-4, Demographic Trends in the 20th Century. Washington, DC: U.S. Government Printing Office. Accessed November 2012 (www.census. gov/prod/2002pubs/censr-4.pdf).

The entire world has become urbanized. In 2011, 52.1% of the entire world population lived in urban areas. In more developed countries, 77.7% of the population is urban, compared with 46.5% in less developed nations, and 36.7% in sub-Saharan Africa. Each of those is becoming more urbanized, however, and by 2050, those numbers are predicted to increase to 67.2% for the world as a whole, 85.9% for more developed regions, 64.1% for less developed regions, and 56.5% for sub-Saharan Africa (United Nations 2012). There are more than 100 cities of more than three million around the world. The size of cities is also growing. In 2010, the three largest cities in the world were Tokyo with more than 32 million, Seoul, South Korea, with more than 20 million, and Mexico City, Mexico, with more than 20 million (Worldatlas 2010).

The Dynamics of Cities

Cities are fascinating sociologically for many reasons. One of the most interesting aspects of cities is how they grow and change over time. If you think about it for a minute, you quickly realize it is a very complex problem. Some cities have been in the same place for thousands of years. During that time, their population has often grown far beyond what could have been imagined when the city was young. Buildings are built, grow old, are torn down, and new buildings are constructed. At different times, the same area is occupied by different populations of people from different cultures and different racial and ethnic groups. Areas that were once residential may become commercial, or vice versa. London grew from more than one million to more than seven million residents in the space of a single century. Chicago grew from a town of about 100,000 in 1860 to nearly 2 million only 40 years later in 1900. It was at the University of Chicago that several sociologists developed an approach we now call **human ecology**—the study of people and their environment. That approach offers three competing theories of urban growth.

Human ecology The study of people and their environment.

Models of Urban Growth

There are three well-known theories of urban growth: concentric zone theory, sector theory, and multiple nuclei theory.

Concentric zone theory. In this view, cities grow as a series of concentric circles radiating from the center, looking much like a dartboard or target. Ernest W. Burgess

Visual Overview Models of Urban Growth

Each of these theories offers some insight into urban growth and land use, but no single theory accounts for all aspects of urban growth.

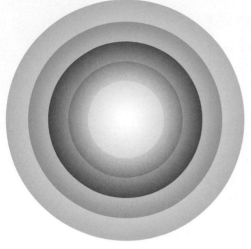

Concentric Zone Theory
Park, Burgess, and McKenzie, 1925

In this view, cities grow as a series of concentric circles radiating from the center, looking much like a dartboard or target.

Sector Theory
Hoyt, 1939, 1964

In this view, growth tends to expand outward along transportation routes to form "wedges" along major streets or highways. As a result, cities tend to be star shaped, growing farther and faster along these routes.

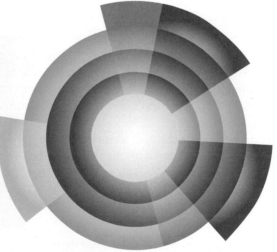

Multiple Nuclei Theory
Harris and Ulman, 1945

In this view, cities do not necessarily follow any particular pattern of growth but may have several centers or nuclei that are the focus of different specialized activities. Nuclei are influenced by history, geography, and other factors, which are unique to each city and therefore result in different patterns of growth.

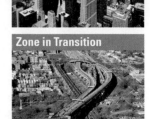
Central Business District

Zone in Transition

Zone of Working Class Homes

Residential Zone

Commuter Zone

Residential Suburb

Industrial Suburb

Outlying Business District

(1925) at the University of Chicago proposed the concentric zone theory to explain the tendency for cities to radiate outward from the central business district. This is an ideal-type model, and not all cities can be expected to fit this model. For example, cities bounded by a physical barrier such as a river or mountain will not expand as quickly in that direction. Burgess's own city, Chicago, for example, is bounded on the east by Lake Michigan, so the concentric zones stop at the water's edge.

In this theory, Zone 1 is the central business district and forms the center of the city. Zone 2 is a zone of transition containing deteriorating housing that, in a growing city, is being progressively replaced by businesses expanding out from Zone 1. Zone 3 contains inexpensive housing in which lower-income workers live and remain close to their work in Zones 1 and 2. Zone 4 includes more expensive apartments, single-family homes, and some exclusive housing for the more affluent. Zone 5 includes even more exclusive areas and expensive homes of the more affluent in commuter communities and suburbs or satellite cities.

Aerial view of Chicago showing Lake Michigan on the east.

© Comstock/Thinkstock

Sector theory. Homer Hoyt (1939) modified Burgess's concentric zone theory of city growth. He argued that cities do not grow in perfect circles, though that can be one element of their growth. Growth tends to occur along major transportation routes. Inner circles tend to expand outward along transportation routes to form "wedges"—that is, neon strips along major streets or highways. As a result, this theory predicts cities will tend to be star shaped, growing farther and faster along major transportation routes. In some cities, this pattern can be seen as it developed over time, first following streetcar routes, then later following highways, and now in cities like Washington, DC, in which urban mass-transportation systems were developed in the '60s and '70s, following those new mass transit lines.

Multiple nuclei theory. Chauncy Harris and Edward Ullman (1945) argue that cities do not necessarily follow any particular pattern of growth but may have several centers or nuclei. Different nuclei may be the focus of different specialized activities—for example, restaurants may cluster in one area, banks in another, residences in yet another. A combination of push and pull factors influence this clustering. Incompatible activities such as manufacturing and residences or schools and red-light districts push one another apart. In contrast, many types of businesses seem to do better when around other similar businesses, encouraging the development of a retail district, a garment district, a manufacturing district, a financial district, and so on. Nuclei are influenced by history, geography, and so on. Factors influencing each city are different, so different patterns of growth are expected.

Evaluating urban growth theories. Each of these theories offers some insight into urban growth and land use, but no single theory accounts for all aspects of urban growth. Concentric zone theory highlights the tendency of cities to grow outward as population expands. Sector theory highlights the importance of transportation routes. Multiple nuclei theory de-emphasizes the role of central cities in future growth. However, these theories each tend to focus on the macro level, highlighting overall patterns of growth in cities but telling us much less about the underlying micro-level processes that produce that growth. In a sense, they offer the view from 30,000 feet as though we were flying over in a plane. To understand how these changes take place over time, we must turn our attention to what goes on in the streets as people interact. For this, we need to examine important processes of ecological succession, including urban decline, urban renewal, and gentrification.

Ecological Succession

The growth and evolution of cities can be described as a process of **ecological succession** in which a new social group or type of land use first "invades" territory and then becomes the dominant social group or dominant land use for the territory. Thus, ecological

Ecological succession
A new social group or type of land use first "invades" territory and then becomes the dominant social group or dominant land use for the territory.

Invasion The intrusion of one group or activity into an area occupied by another.

Succession The replacement of activities or people by others.

White flight The large-scale migration of whites out of areas increasingly occupied by minorities.

Concentrated poverty A tendency for people who are poor to be located in focused geographic areas where most of the residents are also poor.

Gated communities Communities that erect walls or other barriers around a neighborhood and erect gates on streets entering the neighborhood, restricting traffic to local residents.

Urban decline Ecological succession in an urban environment that results in increased crime, flight of affluent residents, or an exodus of businesses.

succession involves first invasion and then succession. **Invasion** is the intrusion of one group or activity into an area occupied by another. This might include a gas station being built in a residential neighborhood or Asian immigrants moving into what had once been a primarily Jewish neighborhood. **Succession** is the replacement of activities or people by others. Succession might occur as more and more gas stations and other businesses are built in an area until eventually there are no longer any residences and it has become a business district. Succession might also occur when the predominant ethnic, racial, and cultural heritage of people in an area shifts from one category to another, as when neighborhoods that were once predominantly white become predominantly African American.

History is full of violent examples of invasion and succession in which one group of people conquer another by force and occupy their territories, only to be conquered in turn by someone else. In cities today, this invasion and succession rarely involves violence but still occurs with great regularity. In most cases today, ecological succession is driven by economic and social concerns as more affluent people drive up prices and force out the less affluent, as more lucrative commercial uses replace other uses of land, and as people sharing one or more social characteristics occupy a neighborhood, leading other groups of people to leave. Even without direct violence, this ecological succession can cause considerable social upheaval, anger, resentment, and protest.

Sociologist William Julius Wilson, an award-winning author of many books on urban, racial, and class issues, argues in *The Truly Disadvantaged: The Inner City, the Underclass, and Public Policy* (1987) that the changing geography of large urban areas has often led to the disappearance of industrial jobs in cities, leading to increases in unemployment for urban blacks trapped there. His work provides an example of how public issues of cities can create private troubles for individuals. As urban areas deteriorate, affluent whites who are able to leave move to the suburbs in what has come to be called **white flight**—the large-scale migration of whites out of areas increasingly occupied by minorities. The exodus of whites and affluent people able to move leaves an inner city with fewer job opportunities and an increasingly higher concentration of the poor. **Concentrated poverty** refers to a tendency for people who are poor to be located in focused geographic areas where most of the residents are also poor. As an urban area becomes occupied almost exclusively by the poor, opportunities become even more scarce and community breaks down, trapping many blacks and poor people with few opportunities for improvement.

Resistance to invasion of other populations or other uses of land is common. Such resistance can range from political battles in zoning boards to the organization of neighborhood groups to help protect the quality of life in a neighborhood to even erecting physical walls or barriers to keep others out. Ironically, one of the most recent efforts to protect neighborhoods mirrors the centuries-old strategy of walled cities. Today, in large urban communities across the United States, in increasing numbers, affluent residential communities are becoming **gated communities** that erect walls or other barriers around a neighborhood and erect gates on streets entering the neighborhood, restricting traffic to local residents. While gated communities are ostensibly efforts to reduce crime for their residents, critics often argue that their primary consequence is to provide a way for rich people to separate themselves from the poor and to declare their superiority, in the process engendering hostility and resentment by those living outside the gates (Davis 1990).

Within ecological succession are three common forms—urban decline, urban renewal, and gentrification—along with a persistent consequence—residential segregation.

Urban Decline

Urban decline is ecological succession in an urban environment that results in increased crime, flight of affluent residents, or an exodus of businesses. An example of urban decline found in many older cities occurs when entire neighborhoods of once-exclusive houses deteriorate as the affluent residents move to the suburbs, while the more needy such as the mentally ill, unemployed, and recent immigrants remain or move into the city. Urban decline also occurs when businesses leave the city and its tax base erodes. As a result, social service needs increase and the tax base declines, creating a need for outside financial support. Another common form of urban decline occurs when there is a deteriorating infrastructure. By **infrastructure**, we mean the roads, bridges, subways, storm water and sewer systems, communications lines, power lines, and other physical structures necessary for the continued operation of industrialized societies. As cities age and grow, this basic infrastructure must be maintained and expanded to meet new needs. Unfortunately, many of the cities in the United States have been around for decades or even hundreds of years. A number of those older cities, particularly some of the older industrial cities in the North and East, are well over a hundred years old and have deteriorating infrastructures. This problem gets worse over time. Bridges have actually collapsed due to structural deterioration, with the loss of life in several states. The water-treatment systems of half the communities in the United States are at or near capacity.

Urban Renewal

Urban renewal includes efforts to improve the urban environment intended to reduce crime, attract more affluent residents, or improve the tax base by attracting new business or industry. A typical example of urban renewal would be a project razing slums to build a new sports complex and convention center, intended to eliminate the undesirable slums while attracting a sports team and related businesses. Urban-renewal projects often involve massive amounts of public funds and major projects such as sports stadiums, convention centers, airports, or commercial projects such as office complexes to attract business. In this respect, they tend to be unlike gentrification, which typically does not require massive amounts of public funding. Ironically, urban renewal projects have contributed to the number of homeless found in American cities. Urban renewal projects frequently demolish some of the most decayed areas of a city and often result in a loss of **skid rows**—old, decaying housing where many of the poor and unemployed once found homes.

Gentrification

Gentrification is the resettlement of a low-income, inner-city neighborhood by affluent residents and businesses, often forcing out the low-income residents who once lived there. Gentrification and other forms of urban renewal take place when inner cities lose sufficient population and experience enough deterioration to cause a drastic drop in property values. Once property values are low enough, they offer an opportunity for developers to invest large amounts of money and transform the neighborhood. This reinvestment tends to occur because the location in the inner city makes the land valuable for new uses due to its proximity to other parts of cities. Resentment of the displacement gentrification causes is compounded when—as is often the case—one ethnic group is displaced by another. For example, Betancur (2011) studied the negative impacts on Latinos of gentrification in five Chicago neighborhoods, while Murdie and Teixeira (2011) examined negative consequences on Portuguese residents in Toronto.

Residential Segregation

A recurring outcome of ecological succession is **residential segregation**—the separation of categories of people into different geographic areas of residence. A form of residential segregation that has been a part of the United States since well before the Civil War is **racial segregation**—the geographic separation of people based on race or ethnicity. Sociologists John Logan and Brian Stults (2011) analyzed the 2010 Census data to identify long-term trends in residential segregation. They found that black–white segregation peaked around 1960 or 1970, and since then,

Infrastructure The roads, bridges, subways, storm water and sewer systems, communications lines, power lines, and other physical structures necessary for the continued operation of industrialized societies.

Urban renewal Includes efforts to improve the urban environment intended to reduce crime, attract more affluent residents, or improve the tax base by attracting new business or industry.

Skid rows Old, decaying housing where many of the poor and unemployed once found homes.

Gentrification The resettlement of a low-income inner-city neighborhood by affluent residents and businesses, often forcing out the low-income residents who once lived there.

Residential segregation The separation of categories of people into different geographic areas of residence.

Racial segregation The geographic separation of people based on race or ethnicity.

Urban decay.
© iStockphoto/Thinkstock

there has been a continued steady but slow reduction in black–white segregation. They also report that Hispanics and Asians are less segregated than African Americans but still tend to live in ethnic enclaves. Since both Hispanic and Asian populations are growing rapidly, those ethnic enclaves are actually becoming more homogeneous, making them further isolated from other racial and ethnic groups.

FIGURE 16-16 displays the racial and ethnic distributions of neighborhoods in which different groups typically live. Note that in each case, people tend to live in neighborhoods with other people more like themselves than the population in general. For example, whites typically live in neighborhoods that are 75% white, blacks in neighborhoods that are 45% black, Hispanics in neighborhoods that are 46% Hispanic, and Asians in neighborhoods that are 22% Asian.

Decentralization: Suburbs, Exurbs, Edge Cities

US cities come in many shapes and sizes. In order to compute statistics describing cities, the Office of Management and Budget (OMB) distinguishes two core-based statistical areas (CBSAs). A **metropolitan statistical area** is a densely populated area consisting of a county containing a core urban area (specifically, a city with a population of 50,000 or more) as well as adjacent counties having a high degree of social and economic integration. A **micropolitan statistical area** identifies centers of population with smaller population cores with populations of 10,000 or more but less than 50,000. Currently, more than 80% of the US population lives in metropolitan statistical areas and roughly 1 in 10 live in micropolitan areas (U.S. Census Bureau, 2012e).

Some of these metropolitan areas have grown together over the years. A **megalopolis** is a densely populated area containing two or more metropolitan areas that have grown until they overlap one another (the rural areas between them have themselves

Metropolitan statistical area A densely populated area consisting of a county containing a core urban area (specifically, a city with a population of 50,000 or more) as well as adjacent counties having a high degree of social and economic integration.

Micropolitan statistical area Centers of population with smaller population cores with populations of 10,000 or more but less than 50,000.

Megalopolis A densely populated area containing two or more metropolitan areas that have grown until they overlap one another.

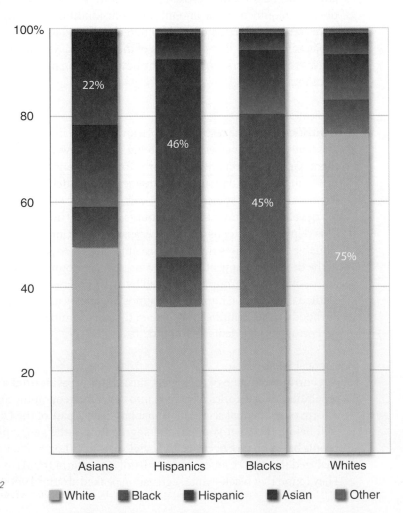

FIGURE 16-16 Diversity experienced in each group's typical neighborhood in the United States.
Source: John R. Logan and Brian Stults. 2011. "The Persistence of Segregation in the Metropolis: New Findings from the 2010 Census" Census Brief prepared for Project US2010. Accessed December 2012 (http://www.s4.brown.edu/us2010).

become urban). An example of a megalopolis can be found in the Boston-to-Washington, DC, corridor where one can travel through several states between these two cities and be consistently surrounded by urban sprawl.

But this does not begin to capture the rich variation in cities. For that, we need to examine some of the variety as expressed in terms like *central cities*, *suburbs*, and *exurbs*.

Central Cities

Central cities are the original cities in metropolitan areas, often surrounded by suburbs. Often, central cities contain older facilities and many have a deteriorating infrastructure. Central cities often contain many varieties of urban dwellers, including less affluent, working class, poor, and minorities who may not be able to move from the central city to the suburbs. Many central cities face a dilemma as their tax bases erode due to the exodus of many affluent residents and industries, while those left behind are often people most in need of social services.

> **Central cities** The original cities in metropolitan areas, often surrounded by suburbs.
>
> **Suburb** Any territory in a metropolitan area not included in the central city.

The Suburbs

A **suburb** is any territory in a metropolitan area not included in the central city. Compared to inner cities, suburbs are often cleaner and less crowded, have newer infrastructure, are more homogeneous in the lifecycle-stage of families (e.g., retired couples and young families tend to live in different areas, and families in suburbs tend to grow old together), and have less crime FIGURE 16-17. Suburbs do have some problems. These include high rates of juvenile delinquency and little for adolescents to do, obsolete structures from poor planning, and inadequate resources for the elderly and other more needy groups.

For more than 100 years, as transportation improved, and particularly after the development of the automobile, people have been moving to towns near cities in which they work. Suburbs grew more slowly during the Depression and World War II when gasoline was rationed, making transportation more expensive and difficult. Suburbs began to grow much more rapidly during the 1950s and later, as the automobile replaced trains and trolley cars, making further expansion easier. Guaranteed mortgages for veterans after World War II contributed to the growth of the suburbs. Suburbanization also increased rapidly after the civil rights movement of the 1960s. In 1960, there were

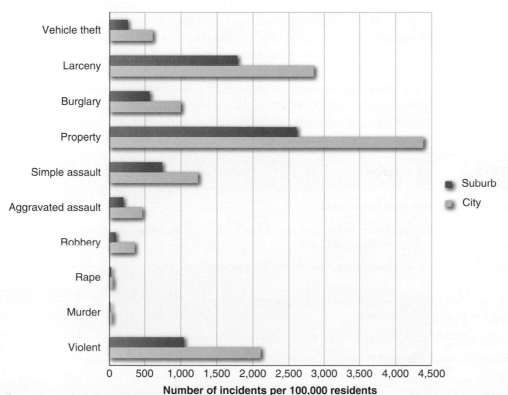

FIGURE 16-17 Violent and property crime rates for the 100 largest US metropolitan areas by city and suburb.
Source: Data from Kneebone, Elizabeth, and Steven Raphael. 2011. "City and Suburban Crime Trends in Metropolitan America." Metropolitan Policy Program at Brookings. Accessed November 2012 (http://www.brookings.edu/-~/media/research/files/papers/2011/5/26%20 metropolitan%20crime%20 kneebone%20raphael/0526_ metropolitan_crime_kneebone_ raphael.pdf).

roughly 60 million people living in suburbs. By 1970, it was 74 million, and by 1980 it was 100 million. Today, more people living in metropolitan areas live in suburbs than live in central cities.

Families are not the only ones moving to the suburbs. Industries and commerce are moving to the suburbs as well. As a result of the exodus of people and industries to the suburbs, many inner cities are experiencing declining populations and declining tax bases. Detroit lost more than 50% of its population since 1950. Cleveland, St. Louis, and Pittsburgh lost 13% or more of their populations in the 1970s. Some cities began to gain population again in the 1980s. Along with shrinking populations, inner cities have experienced shrinking tax bases as jobs and higher-income residents left. Yet those same cities often face an increased burden in crime prevention and social services as more needy and less wealthy residents stay or move in. Suburbanites often resist efforts by city governments to join together to address regional problems by sharing revenues or control with the central city. This typically leaves the central city to address these problems on its own. The net result is a "doughnut structure," with a decaying inner city having an older infrastructure at the core, surrounded by more affluent and rapidly growing suburbs. But even the suburbs are now beginning to feel some of the pressures of central cities with the rise of yet another type of city: the exurbs.

The Exurbs

Exurbs The area beyond the old suburbs, forming a second ring farther out from the central city.

Edge cities Less compact than older cities, have no clear center, and tend to grow up near major transportation routes.

Exurbs are the area beyond the old suburbs, forming a second ring farther out from the central city. Exurbs have been the fastest-growing areas during the past 20 years. Exurbs differ from suburbs and the inner city in many respects. Development is much less dense. Exurbs often have their own economic base in shopping malls rather than being dependent upon the central city. Residents of exurbs may be anticity and are mostly highly educated, wealthy, white professionals. Common reasons people move to exurbs include retirement, a nearby job, friends or family in the area, and wanting to get out of the city (Fuguitt 1984). An example of exurbs is provided by the state of North Carolina, which decentralized its state university into 16 campuses, improved roads throughout the state, and is a major manufacturing state yet has no city larger than 350,000 (Herbers 1986).

One form exurbs are taking has been called **edge cities** (Garreau 1991; Suro 1990). These new edge cities are less compact than older cities and have no clear center. They tend to grow up near major transportation routes such as freeways and around intersections of major routes. Their growth is facilitated by new technology, permitting easier communication and transportation over long distances. They rival older central cities in size, investment, population, construction, and stores; but they lack some of the community life and institutions characteristic of older cities. Examples of edge cities can be found around the Washington, DC, area, along Route 128 and the Massachusetts Turnpike in the Boston area, and around major transportation routes encircling many metropolitan areas.

CONCEPT LEARNING CHECK 16.3   Urbanization: The Growth of Cities

For each item below, identify the concept that best describes it.

_____ **1.** This section of older, three-story brick houses includes many that have been purchased by young families and renovated.

_____ **2.** This is the original larger city in the metro area, now almost surrounded by newer, smaller cities.

_____ **3.** The new football stadium was built with state and local government funding and replaced a rundown section of town.

_____ **4.** Where there had once been farms, a huge housing project has been built.

_____ **5.** The neighborhood had many dilapidated houses, abandoned houses, and even empty lots.

A. Urban decline

B. Urban renewal

C. Gentrification

D. Ecological succession

E. Central city

F. Suburb

G. Exurb

16.4 Urbanism and City Life

Several sociologists have examined ways in which community changes in cities when compared to small towns and rural areas and the diverse circumstances of different urban residents.

- Discuss sociological theories of the role of community.

What is it like to live in an urban area? How is it different from life in a smaller town? To what extent do people in large urban areas share a sense of community and have a sense of belonging? Several different sociologists have attempted to understand just what is meant by a sense of community in rural and urban areas, small towns and large cities, beginning as far back as the 19th century. The term **community** is meant as a collection of people who share a common geographic territory, most of the daily interactions of members take place within the territory, and members have a sense of belonging.

Ferdinand Tönnies: Gemeinschaft and Gesellschaft

Well over a century ago, German sociologist Ferdinand Tönnies (1887) described urbanization as moving away from strong, long-term personal bonds and a shared culture to more impersonal, short-lived interactions based on individual interests. **Gemeinschaft** describes the relationships among people in small, close-knit rural communities where social cohesion is achieved by strong personal bonds uniting members based on primary relationships, shared life experiences, and a shared culture. Thus, gemeinschaft is experienced by people living in a small town where they grew up and where they have known most people for years and are similar to most other people, having similar values and aspirations. A **primary relationship** is a relationship involving multiple roles for each participant that is often emotional, personal, and not easily transferred to other people. It is often valued for its own sake, endures over time, and involves many aspects of a person's life.

Gesellschaft describes the relationships found in large and impersonal communities where many members do not know one another personally and cohesion is based on a complex division of labor and secondary relationships, where individuals have little identification with the group and little commitment to shared values. Gesellschaft relationships are typical of large urban communities. For example, residents of a new suburb, most of whom only recently moved there, who hold a wide range of different jobs in a nearby city, and who rarely see one another or share experiences in common are probably experiencing gesellschaft. A **secondary relationship** is a relationship that is specialized, lacks emotional intensity, often ends once specific goals are achieved, and can be reestablished with other participants with relative ease (as distinguished from a primary relationship). The relationship between you and the sales clerk who sold you this textbook, for example, is probably a secondary relationship.

Emile Durkheim: Mechanical and Organic Solidarity

French sociologist Emile Durkheim (1893) took a view similar in many respects to that of Tönnies. Durkheim believed that traditional rural and small-town life was based on **mechanical solidarity** in which people are held together by shared moral sentiments and tradition. In contrast, larger urban communities were more diverse and could not rely on shared moral sentiment to provide solidarity. However, urban life was also characterized by increasing **division of labor**—the allocation of different roles to different social statuses. This created a new form of social solidarity based on interdependence. In **organic solidarity**, people are mutually dependent on one another due to a complex division of labor, and most relationships are neither intimate nor personal. Thus, in urban communities, people depend on skilled specialists to perform needed tasks such as car repairs, plumbing, and so on.

Community A collection of people who share a common geographic territory, most of the daily interactions of members take place within the territory, and members have a sense of belonging.

Gemeinschaft Describes the relationships among people in small, close-knit rural communities where social cohesion is achieved by strong personal bonds uniting members based on primary relationships, shared life experiences, and a shared culture.

Primary relationship A relationship involving multiple roles for each participant; often emotional, personal, and not easily transferred to other people; often valued for its own sake, endures over time, and involves many aspects of a person's life.

Gesellschaft Describes the relationships found in large and impersonal communities where many members do not know one another personally and cohesion is based on a complex division of labor and secondary relationships, where individuals have little identification with the group and little commitment to shared values.

Gemeinschaft is experienced by people living in a small town where they grew up and have known people for years and have similar values and aspirations to other people.

© iStockphoto/Thinkstock

Secondary relationship A relationship that is specialized, lacks emotional intensity, often ends once specific goals are achieved, and can be reestablished with other participants with relative ease.

Mechanical solidarity People are held together by shared moral sentiments and tradition.

Division of labor The allocation of different roles to different social statuses.

Organic solidarity People are mutually dependent on one another due to a complex division of labor, and most relationships are neither intimate nor personal.

Urban overload People are exposed to more stimuli than they can respond to each day.

Norm of noninvolvement Expectation that people will not become involved in the affairs of others to help preserve their privacy, typical of urban settings.

Studied nonobservance Polite behavior in which someone strives to appear not to notice someone else, often employed in an attempt to help the other person save face.

Urban villages Areas of a city that people know well and in which they live, play, shop, and work.

FIGURE 16-18 Robert Park argued that cities are, in many respects, collections of small communities nestled up against one another.

Courtesy of The American Sociological Association.

These two concepts are similar to the gemeinschaft and gesellschaft concepts of Tönnies. However, Durkheim is more optimistic about these changes than Tönnies. Where Tönnies bemoaned the loss of primary relationships as a result of the Industrial Revolution and urbanization, Durkheim saw the replacement of mechanical solidarity with a new social order forged by organic solidarity leading to greater moral tolerance, independence, and privacy.

Georg Simmel: The Blasé Urbanite

Urban dwellers often experience what is sometimes called **urban overload**, in which they are exposed to more stimuli than they can respond to each day. To protect themselves from unwanted intrusions, they often develop a blasé attitude and a detachment from others, making them sometimes appear cold and heartless (Simmel 1905). They often follow a **norm of noninvolvement**—the expectation that people will not become involved in the affairs of others to help preserve their privacy, typical of urban settings. They use various means to convey the message they do not want to be disturbed. These include using newspapers as props to shield themselves from eye contact with others, listening to music or browsing the Internet with their smartphones to avoid engaging in unwanted conversations, unlisted telephone numbers, post office boxes to avoid revealing their home address, and locks. Sociologist Erving Goffman describes such efforts as **studied nonobservance**—polite behavior in which someone strives to appear not to notice someone else, often employed in an attempt to help the other person save face. Ignoring someone arguing on a cell phone or making a conscious attempt to not appear to be peering over someone's shoulder while he reads are but two examples of studied nonobservance. Thankfully, studied nonobservance often breaks down when people really need help. When natural disasters such as Hurricane Katrina hit New Orleans or Hurricane Sandy hit New York and New Jersey, thousands of people stepped up to help strangers (Medna 2012).

Louis Wirth: Anonymity and Self-Interest

Louis Wirth (1938) argued that cities undermine kinship and a sense of neighborhood, which are the traditional bases of social control. Urban dwellers live in relative anonymity, with only transitory interactions with others rather than lasting intimate relationships. Often, their only relationship with someone else is as someone who performs a particular task, such as bus driver or landlord, and in that relationship, each person pursues his or her own self-interest. As a result, people become indifferent to one another. Where rural communities are quite willing to impose rigid norms for behavior, in urban areas, people are more heterogeneous, usually know much less about one another, and rarely have shared norms of moral conduct (Wilson 1985). It matters little whether the butcher shares your traditions and values so long as he provides a good-quality product at a reasonable price. But urban dwellers pay a price for this self-interested autonomy in alienation and loneliness.

Robert Park: Urban Villages

Sociologist Robert Park FIGURE 16-18, one of the leaders of the first major sociology program in the United States at the University of Chicago, argued that cities are, in many respects, collections of small communities nestled up against one another (Park 1950). Many sociologists call these small communities "urban villages." **Urban villages** are areas of a city that people know well and in which they live, play, shop, and work (Leinberger and Lockwood 1986). Urban people create a sense of intimacy for themselves by personalizing their interactions. They regularly shop in the same stores and get to know the shopkeepers. They meet friends and become acquainted with people in neighborhood taverns, restaurants, and laundromats. Those places become meeting places in which people build social relationships. Even areas that appear to be slums to outsiders can achieve this sense of community as people see one another often, become familiar with each other, and develop lasting relationships (Gans 1962, 1970).

Herbert Gans: Diversity of Urban Dwellers

It would be a mistake to believe that all people respond to the city in the same way or enjoy the same benefits of the city. Ours is a diverse society, and this diversity is found in cities as much as anywhere else. In what has become a classic work, sociologist Herbert Gans (1962, 1968, 1970) identified five types of urban dwellers: cosmopolites, singles, ethnic villagers, the deprived, and the trapped.

Cosmopolites are well-educated, high-income people who choose to live in the city to take advantage of its convenience and cultural resources such as museums, theaters, and symphony orchestras. Cosmopolites enjoy many of the benefits of cities by virtue of their wealth and, likewise, are protected from many of its drawbacks by that same wealth. **Singles** are young, unmarried people who live in the city by choice for its convenience and to meet people, seek jobs, and enjoy entertainment. They stay in the city during this stage of their life cycle but may not develop strong attachments and are likely to move to the suburbs after they marry. **Ethnic villagers** are people living in tight-knit inner-city neighborhoods united by race and social class and resembling small towns. (Notice, ethnic villages are essentially urban villages in which ethnic group membership plays an important role, such as Chinatown, Little Italy, and other ethnic neighborhoods found in many large cities.) Ethnic villagers often develop intimate, enduring relationships within the neighborhood. They often try to isolate themselves from the harmful aspects of city life and participate little in activities of the city as a whole.

Where these first three types of urban residents live in the city by choice, the last two types often have no choice. **The deprived** include the very poor, emotionally disturbed, handicapped individuals living at the bottom of society. Their poverty gives them little or no choice where they live, and they have few prospects for a good future. **The trapped** are people who cannot afford to leave the city who may identify with their neighborhood but dislike the city and what it has become. Trapped people include: (a) those who cannot afford to move after their neighborhood is invaded by another ethnic group, (b) elderly people on a downward slide who drifted into the city because they cannot afford to live elsewhere, (c) alcoholics and drug addicts, and (d) downwardly mobile people. Like the deprived, the trapped are often victims of street crime. As we noted in the discussion of ecological succession, there is often a racial element to this, too, as poor blacks are disproportionately the ones who are often trapped in the inner city, unable to move to the suburbs where many jobs have moved, argues William Julius Wilson (2009) in *More Than Just Race: Being Black and Poor in the Inner City*.

Urban dwellers protect themselves from unwanted intrusions.

© Darrin Klimek/Thinkstock

Cosmopolites Well-educated, high-income people who choose to live in the city to take advantage of its convenience and cultural resources.

Singles Young, unmarried people who live in the city by choice for its convenience and opportunities.

Ethnic villagers People living in tight-knit inner-city neighborhoods united by race and social class and resembling small towns.

The deprived Include the very poor, emotionally disturbed, handicapped individuals living at the bottom of society.

The trapped People who cannot afford to leave the city who may identify with their neighborhood but dislike the city and what is has become.

CONCEPT LEARNING CHECK　16.4　　Urbanism and City Life

Match the following statements with concepts they best represent.

_____ **1.** Donald Trump

_____ **2.** Walking on by without acknowledging a beggar

_____ **3.** A homeless person who appears to be mentally ill

_____ **4.** Purchasing groceries at a big-box store from a clerk you have never seen before

_____ **5.** A second-generation Pole living in a Polish neighborhood in Chicago

A. Cosmopolite

B. Urban village

C. Ethnic villager

D. The deprived

E. Norm of noninvolvement

F. Organic solidarity

G. Secondary relationship

16.5 The Future: Population, Cities, and the Environment

Three trends appear particularly important for the future: communities without walls, changes in rural life, and the impact of increasing population and consumption on the environment.

- Examine the role of new technology in population distribution.
- Discuss how social life is changing in rural areas.
- Analyze how population increases and increased consumption affect the environment.

Attempting to foresee the future is always fraught with error. But there are at least three ongoing changes that will clearly continue to be important for understanding population and urbanization for decades to come. First, our notion of what it means to be in a community is continuing to evolve, and it has been changed considerably by urbanization. New technologies raise the possibility that much of what we gain from community will be less tied to geography in the future as people find new communities without borders as collections of like-minded individuals are able to interact with one another through the Internet and other technologies. Second, rural life appears likely to continue to be transformed and provides an important point of contrast for understanding continued urbanization. Third and finally, the growth of population and—even more importantly—the growth of consumption continue to strain the capacity of our environment. It seems likely that sometime during this century, we will have to face the ecological consequences of rapid population growth, urbanization, and the depletion of natural resources. Let us begin with communities without walls.

Communities without Walls

One of the interesting dilemmas we face early in the 21st century is the notion of community as a geographic location in which most of our daily interactions take place. Frankly, for most residents of industrialized societies, this just does not describe reality. If this notion was weakened by telephones and fax machines, then it has certainly been dealt a death blow by the Internet. People today commonly interact on a daily basis with friends and collaborate with colleagues hundreds or thousands of miles away. Mail-order business accounts for a larger proportion of economic activity each year. We can conduct business over the Internet. You can order flowers, books, computers, cars, and even sex over the Internet. People belong to various networks of like-minded individuals throughout the world who share their interests in a particular hobby, profession, or element of popular culture. Community in the sense of a single geographic location where we do most everything of interest and meaning in our lives simply no longer exists for many people. Instead, we have overlapping communities that are not restricted by geographic space—communities of friends, communities of professional colleagues, communities of fellow Star Trek fans, or whatever. Each day, our reliance upon the community in which we are geographically located becomes incrementally less than it was the day before, as new opportunities become available for us to interact in communities in cyberspace. If these trends continue, we should expect continued dramatic growth of such communities without walls and a progressive reduction in the central role of geographic community.

Rural Life

In the United States, we often have idealized images of rural life. Throughout the 20th century, many urban residents had fond memories of growing up on the farm or visiting grandparents who still lived on farms. However, as long ago as 1920, more of the US population lived in cities than in rural areas. The agricultural basis for the rural economy disappeared as family farms were replaced with commercial agricultural enterprises. New technologies permit people to interact, conduct business, and work over long distances, making it more feasible to live in rural America while participating in the urban economy. The communities without walls just discussed above are part of this trend. However, at this point, those new economic opportunities for rural residents are still not keeping pace with the loss of population and loss of jobs that have dominated rural life over the last 50 years or more.

A look at some of the statistics helps tell this story. In the United States, for statistical purposes, **rural areas** are defined by the Census Bureau as communities having fewer than 2,500 residents along with areas in open country outside of any city. Rural areas have 19.3% of the US population and 75% of the land mass (US Census Bureau 2011b). This is down immensely from the 60% of the population that lived in rural areas in 1900. The exodus of people and economic opportunities from rural areas has had a profound impact on rural life. In FIGURE 16-19 are displayed urbanized areas and urban clusters in 2010. The white area comprising most of the map represents rural areas that are not urbanized.

To illustrate what life is like in rural America, consider one rural county. In FIGURE 16-20 is a population pyramid for Shelby County, Missouri, a rural county only a few miles from Hannibal, Missouri, and the Mississippi River where Samuel Clemens grew up as a boy. This graph is top heavy with large numbers of people 35 years old and older, while people between 20 and 34 are much less numerous. This pattern is the **aging-in-place** pattern typical of many rural areas, where the young adults leave for job and educational opportunities in more urban areas, leaving a region with more older adults. Eventually, the lack of younger adults also leads to a lack of young children and further erosion of jobs and economic opportunities, while the average age of the population continues to increase. This particular county declined in population by 25% between 1960 and 2000. Even in 2000, it had a high unemployment rate of 46%, with roughly half of those with jobs employed in transportation or construction. The poverty rate was 16.3% and the median household income was roughly $30,000. Seventy percent have no college and roughly 10% are college graduates. Most grew up in Shelby County, with 95% living in the same state 5 years ago, more than 80% in the same county, and 60% in the same house (CensusScope 2012a).

Rural areas Defined by the Census Bureau as communities having fewer than 2,500 residents along with areas in open country outside of any city.

Aging in place Pattern typical of many rural areas where the young adults leave for job and educational opportunities in more urban areas, leaving a region with more older adults.

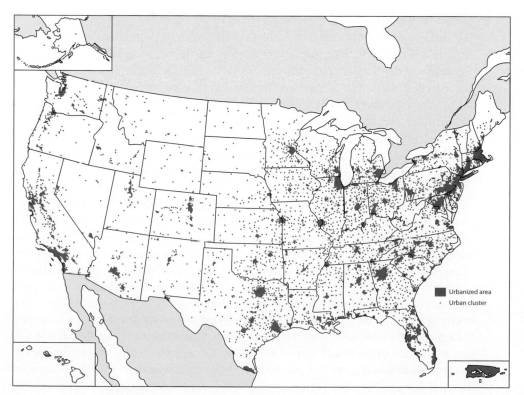

FIGURE 16-19 Urbanized areas and urban clusters (2010).
Source: US Census Bureau. 2010. "Urban Areas and Urban Clusters: 2010." 2010 Urban Area Thematic Maps. Accessed November 2012 (http://www.census.gov/geo/www/maps/2010_census_UA_maps/imgs/UA2010_UAs_and_UCs_Map.pdf).

■ Urbanized area
· Urban cluster

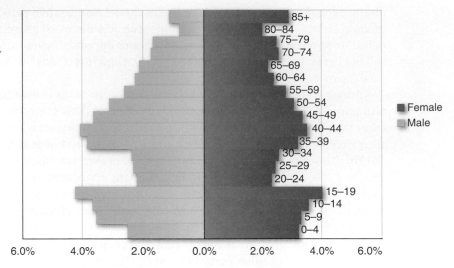

FIGURE 16-20 Population pyramid for Shelby County, MO. *Source: www.CensusScope.org. Social Science Data Analysis Network, University of Michigan. Accessed November 2012 (www.ssdan.net).*

Not all rural areas display this same pattern, however. Throughout the rural Midwest, many rural areas have packing plants or other manufacturing facilities that have attracted Hispanic immigrants. Counties nearer metropolitan areas often turn into bedroom communities, with residents driving 50 or more miles to work in nearby cities while still living in their long-term homes. But the pattern displayed in Shelby County is relatively common.

The deep divide between life in rural areas and life in urban cities is also reflected in political voting patterns. As Josh Kron (2012) points out, the political divide in the United States is no longer regional differences such as a Republican South and a Democratic Northeast and West Coast. Instead, it is a rural–urban divide, with only four major cities voting Republican in the 2012 presidential election. Even in one of the reddest states, every one of Texas's major cities voted Democratic. Kron goes on to argue that "the voting data suggest that people do not make cities liberal—cities make people liberal" (Kron 2012:231).

Ecological Limits to Population and Urbanization

The third trend that appears to be central to the future is population growth and its impact on the environment. Rapid population growth places incredible strain on the economies of developing countries, forcing them to devote scarce economic resources just to feed, shelter, and clothe people. In more affluent, industrialized countries, population growth is slower and hence more manageable, and their stronger economies can handle the growth well. However, even in these countries, increasing population leads to another danger—the risk of an ecological disaster. These countries may be able to afford the economic resources to sustain the increased populations, but they are not capable of sustaining the increasing drain on nonrenewable natural resources such as oil, gas, fresh water, and clean air.

In 1972, a distinguished group of scientists published the results of a large-scale computer model of the world, taking into account population growth, land available for cultivation, rates of food production and industrial production, and pollutants released into the atmosphere and the water supply. That book, *The Limits to Growth*, by Meadows and colleagues (1972a), as the title implies, argued that there are natural limits to growth that can be sustained by our planet. The authors chart changes since 1900 and then use their computer model to predict how those same variables will continue to change through the 21st century. The results are reproduced with permission from their book in FIGURE 16-21. Those authors believe that increasing population size will lead to declining supplies of natural resources that will eventually lead to declines in food production and industrial production along with deterioration of the ecosystem due to pollution. Their predictions were greeted with some skepticism, but mounting

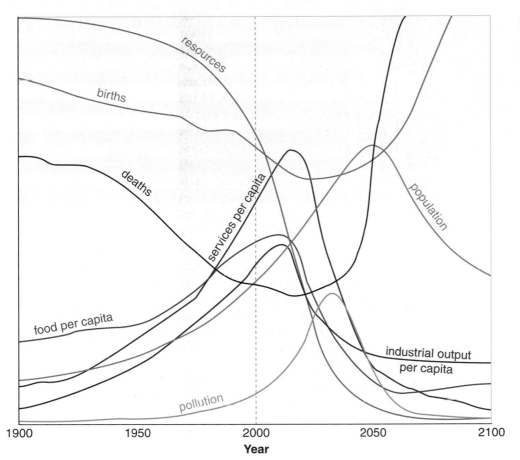

FIGURE 16-21 Projections from *The Limits to Growth* (1972). *Source. Meadows, D. H., et al. 1972. The Limits to Growth. P. 124, fig. 35, World Model Standard Run. New York: Universe Books.*

evidence of global warming, the bulldozing of much of the natural rain forests, declines in water quality, mountains of hazardous waste, and other measures of ecological decline may eventually prove them to be right. An updated version in 2004 (Meadows, Randers, and Meadows 2004) and a separate analysis by Graham Turner (Turner 2008) compared the predictions in *The Limits to Growth* with changes in the ensuing 30 years and concluded that the ensuing changes in food production and industrial production and the resulting pollution were generally consistent with predictions from the book. These authors make arguments similar to but more complex than those of Malthus and are sometimes called New Malthusians.

Stopping or slowing development is unlikely to be politically feasible in most countries, and development brings with it advantages as well. So international bodies, beginning with a United Nations report in 1987, *Our Common Future*, have called for **sustainable development**—constrained economic growth that recycles instead of depletes natural resources while protecting clean air, water, land, and biodiversity. This approach encourages moderating consumption in high-consumption countries and less extreme inequalities in consumption globally. Critics of this approach worry that it goes too far to promote an agenda of globalization and distribution of wealth from the developed world to the underdeveloped world.

High-income countries and low-income countries contribute to the ecological problems caused by rising populations in distinctly different ways. True, low-income countries are still in Phase II of the demographic transition and are experiencing rapid population growth. However, the amount of resources consumed (and often the amount of pollution that results) for each person in low-income countries is far less than the amount consumed for individuals in high-income countries. The latest global study comparing per-capita consumption on many dimensions was a study by the United Nations Development Program in 1998. This study found dramatic inequalities in consumption between the richest and poorest countries as seen in FIGURE 16-22.

Sustainable development Constrained economic growth that recycles instead of depletes natural resources while protecting clean air, water, land, and biodiversity.

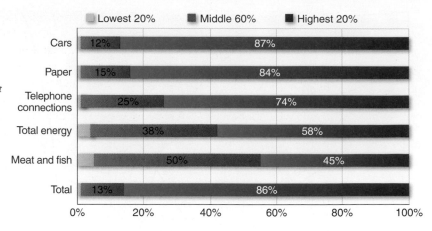

FIGURE 16-22 Share of world consumption for the richest and poorest 20% (1995). *Source: Data from United Nations Development Program (UNDP). 1998. "Consumption for Human Development." Human Development Report 1998. Accessed November 2012 (http://hdr.undp.org/en/media/hdr_1998_en_overview.pdf).*

Human Development Index (HDI) A simple composite measure including health, schooling, and income.

Overall, the 20% of the world's people in the highest-income countries accounted for 86% of all total private consumption expenditures globally, 87% of all cars, 84% of all paper, 74% of all telephone connections, 58% of total energy, and 45% of all meat and fish.

Runaway growth in consumption among the most affluent countries in the world continues today to threaten the global environment. Dramatic inequalities persist. In the United States, for example, there are more than 900 cars per 1,000 people of driving age, while in India there are fewer than 10 per 1,000. The average US household has more than two televisions, while in Liberia and Uganda fewer than 1 in 10 households has a television. To compare nations, the United Nations uses a summary measure of development, the **Human Development Index (HDI)**—a simple composite measure including health, schooling, and income (United Nations Development Program 2011:23). Domestic per-capita water consumption averages only 67 liters a day in low–HDI countries, compared to 425 liters a day in very high–HDI countries (United Nations Development Program 2011:27). The United Nations estimates that 870 million people (12.5% of the global population) were undernourished between 2010 and 2012, with the most affected people in Southern Asia, sub–Saharan Africa, and Eastern Asia, in that order (FAO 2012).

Efforts to create sustainable growth in very high–HDI countries have been unable to keep up with economic growth. While those countries have reduced the carbon intensity of production by 52%, consumption continues to increase due to economic growth, with total emissions and emissions per capita more than doubling to 112% higher now than 40 years ago (United Nations Development Program [UNDP] 2011:32). Environmental consequences of increased consumption can be seen in consequences as diverse as air pollution in China, global warming, and rising sea levels.

Air pollution in China is particularly high in urban areas and the north, with nearly 20% of cities failing to meet China's own governmental standards, which are lower than those of the World Health Organization (WHO) air-quality standards. Outdoor pollution in China is estimated to be associated with 300,000 deaths and 20 million cases of respiratory illness a year, costing roughly 3% GDP per year (UNDP 2011:52).

Global temperatures have risen an average of 0.75°C since 1900, and the rate of increase is accelerating. Most scientists (e.g., see Stern and Taylor 2007) and many international bodies accept that this warming is at least in part due to human activities driven primarily by population increases but also by increasing per-capita consumption (UNDP 2011:32). One serious side effect of global warming is rising sea levels, which have already risen 20 centimeters since 1870 and are projected to be 31 centimeters higher in 2100 than in 1990. By one estimate, a half-meter rise in sea level by 2050 would flood an area the size of France and Italy combined, affecting 170 million people (UNDP 2011:35). We do not have to accept the conclusion that global warming is due to effects of humankind to recognize that rising sea levels could affect coastal regions. Here in the United States, more than half the American population lives within 50 miles of the coast, placing millions of Americans at risk to rising sea levels (National Oceanic and Atmospheric Administration [NOAA] 2012). Damages done by Hurricane Sandy in New York and New Jersey in November of 2012 illustrate how serious hurricanes can be.

To sum up, population changes in both numbers of people and kinds of people are the basis for many of the problems and opportunities faced by countries today. The effects of population can also be felt on cities. Cities are a big part of our past and will be an even bigger part of our future. Roughly four of every five Americans lives in an urban area, and in developed countries throughout the world, the great majority of people live in urban areas. Developing countries are urbanizing at astounding rates and, undoubtedly, most people in the world will be spending the next century living in large urban areas.

Sea-level rise caused by global warming affects all coastal regions and likely played a role in the damage done by Hurricane Sandy.

© Anton Oparin/Shutterstock, Inc.

CONCEPT LEARNING CHECK 16.5   The Future: Population, Cities, and the Environment

Which of the following statements are true and which are false?

_____ **1.** A rural area, according to the US Census Bureau, is an area in open country outside of any city.

_____ **2.** Rural areas in the United States that are not near a major urban center are generally declining in population or are growing more slowly than urban areas.

_____ **3.** The aging-in-place pattern is a pattern typical of many rural areas, where the young adults leave for job and educational opportunities in more urban areas, leaving a region with more older adults.

_____ **4.** New technologies such as the Internet have all but eliminated disadvantages faced by rural residents, giving them economic and educational opportunities comparable to those of people in urban areas.

Visual Summary Population and Urbanization

16.1 Sociological Study of Population: Demography

- Demography is the scientific study of human populations with a census to count people and their characteristics, though the census is not perfect and can have an overcount or undercount.

- Population changes are consequences of initial population, birth rates, death rates, and net migration into a geographic area as expressed in the balancing equation.

- The doubling time is the number of years it would take for a population to double in size at its current rate of growth. For the United States, the doubling rate is 78 years.

- The fertility rate is the average number of children born per woman over her lifetime. The replacement-level fertility rate is the rate required to have births keep pace with deaths in a population.

- The crude birth rate is the average number of births per year per thousand people, while the total birth rate is the average number of births per year per thousand women.

- The baby boom was a period of elevated birth rates in the United States that lasted for several years, hitting a peak around 1957.

- Birth rates vary dramatically from country to country, with highest rates in low-income countries such as in Africa.

- Some countries such as China have instituted tough policies to reduce their birth rate by penalizing families with more than one child.

- Mortality rates are measured by the crude death rate—the number of deaths per year for every thousand people in a population.

- Mortality rates also vary around the globe, with highest mortality rates in Africa and Europe and lowest rates in Asian and Oceanian countries.

- Life expectancy—the average number of years people are expected to live—has increased substantially, rising to 79 in the United States, and highest expectancies are in North America, Europe, and Oceania.

- Migration—the movement of people from one geographic area to another—includes both immigration (moving into an area) and emigration (moving out of an area) and is summarized by net migration (immigration – emigration).

- Immigration rates have in many years been a large factor in population growth in the United States, increasing regularly since World War II.

- Immigrants made up 13% of the US population in 2011.

- Internal migration— for instance, migration from one place to another within the United States—included the movement of large numbers of blacks out of the South after the Civil War, movement from rural areas to urban areas, and movement from the Northeast and North Central regions to the South and West.

- Population pyramids graph the age and sex distribution for a population, displaying successive age cohorts—subpopulations of people all born within a narrow age range.

- Population pyramids for countries with rapidly increasing populations look pyramidal in shape, while population pyramids for countries with stable populations or moderate growth look more box-like, with little change in population from one year to the next.

- Developing countries with rapid population growth must provide for large numbers of dependent children, while more stable populations in developed countries are aging and must provide services to an increasing proportion of elderly.

- World population is growing at a rapid rate. The world as a whole is growing at a rate that would double every 35 years, Africa every 29 years, and the United States every 78 years. Most of the new population growth during the next decades will be in developing countries.

Visual Summary Population and Urbanization, continued

16.2 Theories and Perspectives on Population Growth

- Malthus's theory of population growth predicts catastrophic starvation due to the population growing too large for the available food supply. He argues food supply grows linearly (e.g., 1, 2, 3, 4, 5, . . .), while population grows exponentially (e.g., 2, 4, 8, 16, 32, . . .). Hence, population will outstrip food supply.

- Marx argues the problem is not too little food or too large a population but inequitable distribution of resources.

- Demographic transition theory describes a shift in developed countries from a period of high birth and death rates (Phase I) to a period of reduced death rates but still high birth rates, leading to rapid population growth (Phase II) and then to a final Phase III in which birth rates drop to produce stable or moderate population growth.

- Zero population growth (ZPG) occurs when a country's fertility rate approaches the replacement level of fertility required to keep the population constant. Many European countries have reached ZPG and are actually decreasing in population.

- Developed countries generally appear to be in Phase III of the demographic transition with moderate population growth, while developing countries in Africa and, to some extent, other regions are showing some slowing of population growth.

- Some demographers suggest there is a Phase IV in which countries experience population decline.

- Some countries pursue a policy of ethnic cleansing in which they deliberately reduce the size of the population of some ethnic groups, often through horrific acts of warfare.

- Changes in population, such as the baby boom in the United States, have consequences for the economy and social policies countries must adapt to address problems created by those population changes. Countries in different phases of the demographic transition face very different population-related problems.

16.3 Urbanization: The Growth of Cities

- Cities simultaneously are places of great opportunity and are facing major problems.

- Urbanization—the large-scale movement of people from less populated areas to more populated areas—is a major social process involving the geographic distribution of populations.

- Understanding the population structure, composition, and trends in cities helps us to understand the problems they face. Factors to consider include the size of the population, whether population is increasing or decreasing and at what rate, the age and sex distribution of the population, and the ethnic and racial mix. This is illustrated by comparing metropolitan Detroit, Michigan, with metropolitan Phoenix, Arizona. Detroit faces declining population while Phoenix faces rapid increases in population and a changing ethnic mix due to rapid increases in the Hispanic population.

- The population structure of a community, as reflected in population pyramids, helps us understand the issues faced by those communities. This is illustrated by a military base, a college town, and a retirement community.

- Urbanization is a relatively new development, with developed countries becoming urbanized first, followed by developing countries. Globally, more than half of the world population lives in cities, with developed countries highly urbanized and developing countries undergoing rapid urbanization. More than 80% of the US population lives in cities.

- The size of cities is also increasing. The three largest cities are Tokyo with more than 32 million, Seoul, South Korea, with more than 20 million, and Mexico City with more than 20 million.

- The growth of cities has been described at the macro level by concentric zone theory that sees growth as a series of concentric circles, sector theory that sees growth focusing on transportation routes, and multiple nuclei theory that focuses on the development of multiple cities that grow together. Each predicts different activities such as business, manufacturing, and residential growth will occur in specific regions of the city.

- On a more micro level, the growth of cities can be understood as a process of ecological succession in which new categories of people or new uses for space first invade a territory and then take it over. Urban decline is often fought with large-scale urban-renewal projects or more individualistic efforts at gentrification.

- Residents resist invasion in many ways, including zoning regulations and even gated communities that restrict access to local residents.

- Aging physical structures and economic obsolescence are markers of urban decline, while massive urban-renewal projects based on public funding and gentrification of neighborhoods by affluent residents rejuvenate old areas.

- A metropolitan statistical area is a densely populated area including a city with a population of 50,000 or more, and a micropolitan statistical area identifies a smaller population core having a largest city of 10,000 but not more than 50,000. A megalopolis is two or more metropolitan areas that have grown together.

- Central cities are the original cities in metropolitan areas and are typically surrounded by suburbs that make up the balance of the metropolitan area.

- Cities themselves have evolved with central cities coming first, followed by suburbs and then exurbs. Large numbers of affluent residents have moved from the central cities to the suburbs and now the exurbs—a second ring of communities beyond the old suburbs—during the 20th century. This has reduced the tax base of the older central cities, while aging and decaying infrastructure strains their financial resources. Edge cities tend to spring up along major transportation routes and often have no clear center.

16.4 Urbanism and City Life

© Darrin Klimek/Thinkstock

- The movement of people to cities and the expanding size of cities have transformed what we mean by community.

- Tönnies argues urbanization replaces the gemeinschaft relationships of small towns, where people often know one another for years and have strong primary relationships, with the gesellschaft relationships of cities, where people are largely strangers relating to one another in specific, secondary relationships such as store clerk and customer.

- Durkheim sees urbanization as transforming community from mechanical solidarity based on shared moral sentiments to organic solidarity based on mutual dependence. Durkheim saw the replacement of mechanical solidarity with a new social order forged by organic solidarity leading to greater moral tolerance, independence, and privacy.

- Urban dwellers experience urban overload in which they are exposed to more stimuli than they can respond to each day and, as a result, according to Simmel, often adopt a blasé attitude. They often follow a norm of noninvolvement—the expectation that people will not become involved in the affairs of others to help preserve their privacy, typical of urban settings, and use strategies such as studied nonobservance—polite behavior in which someone strives to appear not to notice someone else, often employed in an attempt to help the other person save face.

- Louis Wirth argued cities undermine kinship and a sense of neighborhood and relationships are often based on self-interest, which provides relative autonomy but also alienation and loneliness.

Visual Summary Population and Urbanization, continued

- Robert Park argued urban residents sometimes regain a sense of community through urban villages—areas of a city that people know well and in which they live, play, shop, and work.

- Cities contain diverse populations, including people who are trapped there and the very poor, as well as others who seek out the city as a place where they want to live, including wealthy, highly educated cosmopolites, singles, and ethnic villagers living in tight-knit inner-city neighborhoods united by race and social class.

16.5 The Future: Population, Cities, and the Environment

- Three trends appear particularly important for the future: communities without walls, changes in rural life, and the impact of increasing population and consumption on the environment.

- The Internet and related technologies make it possible for people to find and form communities of people with similar interests largely independent of geographic location (communities without walls). This may make geographic-based community less important in the future.

- While we often have romantic images of rural life, declining populations and loss of economic opportunity make many rural areas unattractive to young adults, who often leave to find education and jobs elsewhere.

- For more than 40 years, academics have been attempting to model and predict the ecological consequences of increasing populations and increasing consumption in books such as *The Limits to Growth*.

- International agencies such as the United Nations have called for sustainable development—constrained economic growth that recycles instead of depletes natural resources while protecting clean air, water, land, and biodiversity.

- However, continued increases in population and continued inequalities in consumption are leading to measurable changes in our environment including global warming and rising sea levels.

16.1 Sociological Study of Population: Demography

1. What information is *not* provided in a population pyramid?
  A. The gender distribution
  B. The age distribution
  C. The amount of immigration
  D. All of the above are provided

2. The maximum possible number of children a woman can have is:
  A. replacement-level fertility.
  B. the fertility rate.
  C. the crude birth rate.
  D. fecundity.

3. Which is not a part of the balancing equation?
  A. Births
  B. Deaths
  C. Net immigration
  D. Life expectancy

16.2 Theories and Perspectives on Population Growth

6. Modest or slow population growth is most consistent with:
  A. the Malthusian perspective on population growth.
  B. Marx's perspective on population.
  C. the demographic transition phase III.
  D. high birth rates and low death rates.

16.3 Urbanization: The Growth of Cities

8. Which of the following is not true of ecological succession?
  A. It involves both invasion and succession.
  B. It refers to the environmental consequences of growth.
  C. It can involve a change in the land use of an area.
  D. It can involve a new dominant social group for an area.

9. Which theory of urban growth assumes cities grow out from the center, expanding fairly evenly in all directions?
  A. Sector theory
  B. Radial arm theory
  C. Concentric zone theory
  D. Multiple nuclei theory

10. Which type of city is decentralized and tends to occur along major transportation routes or intersections of major highways?
  A. Suburbs
  B. Central cities
  C. Exurbs
  D. Edge cities

16.4 Urbanism and City Life

12. Gemeinschaft is:
  A. where people are exposed to more stimuli than they can respond to each day.
  B. where people are mutually dependent due to a complex division of labor.
  C. relationships among people based on strong personal bonds based on primary relationships and a shared culture.
  D. the expectation that people will not become involved in the affairs of others.

4. Doubling time is the time required for:
  A. an age cohort to double its age.
  B. a population to double in size.
  C. mortality to be double fecundity.
  D. the birth rate during the Baby Boom to equal twice the birth rate before the boom.

5. What does the balancing equation do?
  A. It provides the age and sex distribution of a population.
  B. It permits us to predict future population size.
  C. It permits us to predict life expectancy.
  D. It permits us to predict life span.

7. Which of the following is predicted by the Malthusian perspective on population growth?
  A. Food supply grows linearly.
  B. Population grows linearly.
  C. Food supply will outstrip population.
  D. Population will be stable.

11. Leveling several city blocks of outdated manufacturing plants to replace them with a new retail mall paid for largely with financing from the state and city government is an example of:
  A. gentrification.
  B. urban renewal.
  C. suburbs.
  D. edge cities.

13. Which of the following is not one of the types of urban residents identified by Herbert Gans?
  A. Cosmopolites
  B. Village people
  C. Trapped
  D. Deprived

16.5 The Future: Population, Cities, and the Environment

14. Which of the following is not part of sustainable development?
   A. Uses recycling where possible
   B. Applies in rural communities only
   C. Avoids depleting natural resources
   D. Protects clean air, water, and biodiversity

15. A rural area is likely to:
   A. have a smaller percentage of young adults than in urban communities.
   B. be more diverse ethnically and racially than most urban areas.
   C. be experiencing rapid population growth.
   D. have more highly educated people than are found in most urban areas.

CHAPTER ESSAY QUESTIONS

1. How do you read the information in this population pyramid from Nigeria in Figure 16-8B: Population Pyramid, Nigeria, 2012? Be sure to indicate what is represented by each row and what the length of each level or row means. What is the difference between the left and right sides of the pyramid? What does this pyramid shape tell you about the population change over time—is it increasing, decreasing, or staying about the same?

2. Describe the three phases predicted by demographic transition theory. For each phase, indicate what is predicted for its birth and death rates as well as its rate of population growth. Also indicate which phase you think best describes a European country like Spain and an African country like Nigeria.

3. Read this brief description of a city, then identify at least three of the following concepts or theories illustrated in the text and include a brief quotation from the text in which each concept is illustrated.

Rockmount, California, is a city of 320,000. It has always been the largest city in the county but is now surrounded by other cities and no longer able to expand. It boasts a new hockey arena that was just constructed with a city bond issue in a low-lying area that used to be filled with inexpensive apartments that frequently flooded. The oldest part of town is occupied by retail businesses along with a number of regional corporate headquarters. To the north of downtown is an area with large brick homes. Those homes were once very nice, but over several decades, many have been converted into apartments or become vacant. But in the past 5 years, several have been purchased by young professional families who often totally restore them. Most of the growth in Rockmount for the past decade has occurred along the I-67 corridor, including several new malls and large housing developments.

CONCEPTS AND THEORIES
   A. Urban decline
   B. Urban renewal
   C. Gentrification
   D. Central city
   E. Suburb
   F. Central business district
   G. Sector theory

4. Jared has lived in the city for several months now. He hoped to find a girlfriend to date, but he still finds it to be kind of lonely and the people seem aloof and unfriendly. He hates the way he only seems to interact with strangers he has nothing in common with who are trying to sell him something or asking him for money. He tries to counteract that by deliberately visiting many of the same places most days so that he has begun to recognize some people and even carries on conversations with the clerk in the local deli, talking about her son his age and how she fears crime in the neighborhood but cannot afford to move away. Sometimes, though, he just gets overwhelmed by so much going on and even when he has to go somewhere on the subway, he will pretend to be looking up something on the phone to avoid having to talk to someone who looks like he might ask him for money.

Identify at least three concepts from the following list and indicate a quotation from the text that illustrates each concept.
   A. Gesellschaft
   B. Studied indifference
   C. Urban village
   D. Trapped
   E. Singles
   F. Urban overload

CHAPTER DISCUSSION QUESTIONS

1. Immigrants make up 13% of our total population, and roughly one million immigrants become legal residents each year. No doubt some immigrants take jobs that might have otherwise been available to US citizens. However, it is also true that many international students come to the United States to get advanced degrees in science and engineering where we have a shortage of trained people, and yet we usually require them to leave the country after their education visa expires. Should we reduce the number of immigrants admitted to the United States every year? Should we increase it? Who gets hurt by immigration? Who gets helped? Is the country as a whole better or worse off with so many immigrants?

2. Is demographic transition theory likely to apply to developing countries and lead to slower population growth there? Why or why not? What barriers must be faced? Why has it not happened already? Can you imagine some countries where it is less likely to occur? Why?

3. Review the population pyramids for the military base, college town, and retirement community in Figure 16-13. Which community do you think would be the best place to open:

A. An adult-related business.

B. A fast-food restaurant.

C. New residential rental property.

D. A drugstore.

What kinds of public issues do you think would be most important in each community (e.g., tax rates, crime rates, schools)?

4. Much of the literature suggests that our global environment is at risk because of both increasing population and increasing per-capita consumption. Developing countries are contributing to the problem primarily through rapid population growth, while developed countries contribute more based on inequalities and their far greater consumption per capita than people in developing countries. Which of these is worse? Who is more to blame for the environmental consequences? Many people argue that greater equality in the world with the wealth and benefits of development spread more evenly will lead to a better world. But what happens when developing countries with huge populations such as China begin dramatically increasing their per-capita consumption?

CHAPTER PROJECTS

INDIVIDUAL PROJECTS

1. Choose a country and find population data for it over many decades. Plot both its birth rate and its death rate over that time. Also plot its population over the same time period. Does the pattern you get look at all like the demographic transition? Which theory best accounts for population growth in this country?

GROUP PROJECTS

1. Take the city where you grew up or the city in which you currently live and analyze it in terms of population growth and its current population pyramid along with its ethnic and racial mix. You should be able to find nearly current data online. If you cannot find recent data, check for data from 2000 at http://www.censusscope.org/.

2. Take the city where you grew up or the city in which you currently live and analyze it to see how well the theories of urban growth work. Which theory do you think best describes your city? Look in the news for that city and identify a controversial rezoning application or building project. Does that have elements of ecological succession? Can you find evidence of urban decline? What examples can you identify of gentrification or urban renewal?

2. Select a rural county and obtain census data describing it, including recent population changes, the population pyramid, and other social factors such as the ethnic and racial mix, income, educational status, employment status, and types of jobs. If you cannot find recent data, check for data from 2000 at http://www.censusscope.org/. How does the population pyramid relate to the economic opportunities available there?

KEY TERMS

Age cohort	Fertility rate	Population pyramid
Aging in place	Gated communities	Primary relationship
Baby boom	Gemeinschaft	Racial segregation
Balancing equation	Gentrification	Replacement level fertility
Census	Gesellschaft	Residential segregation
Census undercount	Human Development Index (HDI)	Rural areas
Central cities	Human ecology	Secondary relationship
Community	Immigration	Singles
Concentrated poverty	Infrastructure	Skid rows
Cosmopolites	Internal migration	Studied nonobservance
Crude birth rate	Invasion	Suburb
Crude death rate	Life expectancy	Succession
Demographic transition	Mechanical solidarity	Sustainable development
Demography	Megalopolis	Total birth rate
The deprived	Metropolitan statistical area	The trapped
Division of labor	Micropolitan statistical area	Urban decline
Doubling time	Migration	Urban overload
Ecological succession	Mortality	Urban renewal
Edge cities	Natural rate of increase	Urban villages
Emigration	Net migration	Urbanization
Ethnic cleansing	Net migration rate	White flight
Ethnic villagers	Norm of noninvolvement	Zero population growth (ZPG)
Exurbs	Organic solidarity	
Fecundity	Population	

16.1 Sociological Study of Population: Demography

1. [T] The population at time t_2 is greater than the population at time t_1.
2. [F] Net migration of 1,136 is less than the 4,293 born here.
3. [F] Net migration is the number moving in minus the number moving out, not the total moving.
4. [F] Net migration is immigration minus emigration.
5. [F] More people died that year (2,633) than net migration (1,136).

16.2 Theories and Perspectives on Population Growth

1. Demographic transition theory [I]
2. The Malthusian perspective on population growth [K]
3. Growth of food supply [G]
4. Exponential growth of the population [J]
5. Moderate increase in population or stability [F]
6. Point at which catastrophic starvation is predicted to occur [H]
7. Birth rates [C]
8. Death rates [B]
9. High birth rates and low death rates [Phase II]
10. Low birth rates and low death rates [Phase III]
11. High birth rates and high death rates [Phase I]
12. Rapid increase in population [Phase II]
13. The most likely phase for many African countries [Phase II]

16.3 Urbanization: The Growth of Cities

1. This section of older, three-story brick houses includes many that have been purchased by young families and renovated. [C. Gentrification]
2. This is the original larger city in the metro area, now almost surrounded by newer smaller cities. [E. Central city]
3. The new football stadium was built with state and local government funding and replaced a rundown section of town. [B. Urban renewal]
4. Where there had once been farms, a huge housing project has been built. [D. Ecological succession]
5. The neighborhood had many dilapidated houses, abandoned houses, and even empty lots. [A. Urban decline]

16.4 Urbanism and City Life

1. [A, Trump is a well-educated and very wealthy city resident.]
2. [E, Not acknowledging someone seeking help is consistent with the norm of noninvolvement.]
3. [D, The deprived are often emotionally disturbed and handicapped.]
4. [G, Interacting with a stranger to fulfill your own self-interest while having little in common with him or her is an example of a secondary relationship.]
5. [C, Someone belonging to an ethnic group who lives in a community of people of that ethnicity is an ethnic villager.]

16.5 The Future: Population, Cities, and the Environment

1. [F] A rural area is a community having fewer than 2,500 residents along with areas in open country outside of any city.
2. [T] Many rural areas are losing population, particularly those far from a major city.
3. [T] Aging in place involves older people continuing to stay in the same community as they grow older.
4. [F] While new technologies have increased opportunities in rural areas, many rural areas lack infrastructure such as high-speed Internet and are still at a disadvantage compared to urban communities.

16.1 Sociological Study of Population: Demography

1. C. The population pyramid provides the age and sex distribution of a population.

2. D. Fecundity is the maximum possible number of children a woman can have during her lifetime.

3. D. Life expectancy is not a part of the balancing equation.

4. B. Doubling time is the time required for a population to double in size.

5. B. The balancing equation predicts future population size from current size, births, deaths, and net migration.

16.2 Theories and Perspectives on Population Growth

6. C. Phase III of the demographic transition has low birth rates that match the low death rates to produce modest population growth or stability.

7. A. Malthus expected the food supply to increase linearly.

16.3 Urbanization: The Growth of Cities

8. B. Ecological succession, despite its name, does not refer to the environment.

9. C. Concentric zone theory assumes cities grow as a series of concentric circles, much like on a dart board.

10. D. Edge cities grow up along major transportation routes and are decentralized.

11. B. Urban renewal is typically paid for with public funding.

16.4 Urbanism and City Life

12. C. Gemeinschaft is the cohesion found in small communities based on strong personal bonds, primary relationships, shared life experiences, and a shared culture.

13. B. Village People is a band from the 1980s.

16.5 The Future: Population, Cities, and the Environment

14. B. Sustainable development applies to urban areas as well as rural ones.

15. A. Young adults often leave for urban areas to get educations or find jobs.

1. Good answers should indicate each row represents an age cohort consisting of people about the same age. The length of each row represents the number or proportion of the population for that age cohort. Males are represented on the left and females on the right. The pyramid shape suggests the population is increasing rapidly.

2. Good answers should indicate Phase I would have high birth rates and high death rates and low population growth; Phase II would have high birth rates but low death rates and high population growth; and Phase III would have low birth rates and low death rates. Spain is most likely to be in Phase III and Nigeria is most likely to be in Phase I.

3. Good answers should identify at least three concepts and should link them to appropriate quotations or paraphrases as follows:

   A. Urban decline is illustrated by "Those homes were once very nice, but over several decades many have been converted into apartments or become vacant."

   B. Urban renewal is illustrated by "boasts a new hockey arena that was just constructed with a city bond issue."

   C. Gentrification is illustrated by "been purchased by young professional families who often totally restore them."

   D. Central city is illustrated by "has always been the largest city in the county."

   E. Suburb is illustrated by "but is now surrounded by other newer cities."

   F. Central business district is illustrated by "The oldest part of town is occupied by retail businesses along with a number of regional corporate headquarters."

   G. Sector theory is illustrated by "Most of the growth in Rockmount for the past decade has occurred along the I67 corridor, including several new malls and large housing developments."

4. Good answers should include three or more of the following linking the appropriate concept to an appropriate quotation that illustrates it.

A. Gesellschaft is illustrated by "He hates the way he only seems to interact with strangers he has nothing in common with who are trying to sell him something or asking him for money."

B. Studied indifference is illustrated by "pretend to be looking up something on the phone to avoid having to talk to someone."

C. Urban village is illustrated by "deliberately visiting many of the same places most days so that he has begun to recognize some people."

D. Trapped is illustrated by "how she fears crime in the neighborhood but cannot afford to move away."

E. Singles is illustrated by "He hoped to find a girlfriend to date."

F. Urban overload is illustrated by "Sometimes, though, he just gets overwhelmed by so much going on."

REFERENCES

Betancur, John. 2011. Gentrification and Community Fabric in Chicago. *Urban Studies* 48(2):383–406.

Burgess, Ernest W. 1925. "The Growth of the City." Pp. 47–62 in *The City*, edited by R. E. Park and E. W. Burgess. Chicago, IL: University of Chicago Press.

CensusScope. 2012a Age Distribution. *Social Science Data Analysis Network*. Accessed November 2012 at http://www.censusscope.org/us/chart_age.html.

CensusScope. 2012b. Population Growth for Detroit, MI. *Social Science Data Analysis Network*. Accessed November 2012 at http://www.censusscope.org/us/m2160/chart_popl.html.

CensusScope. 2012c. Population Growth for Phoenix-Mesa, AZ. *Social Science Data Analysis Network*. Accessed November 2012 at http://www.censusscope.org/us/m6200/chart_popl.html.

Chadwick, Ruth F. 1992. *Ethics, Reproduction, and Genetic Control*, Revised edition. London: Routledge.

Coontz, Stephanie. 2000. *The Way We Never Were*. New York: Basic Books.

Davis, Mike. 1990. *City of Quartz: Excavating the Future of Los Angeles*. Los Angeles: Vintage.

Department of Homeland Security. 2011. *2011 Yearbook of Immigration Statistics*. Office of Immigration Statistics. Accessed November 2012 at http://www.dhs.gov/files/statistics/publications/yearbook.shtm.

Durkheim, Emile. 1893(1964). *The Division of Labor in Society*. New York: Free Press.

Espenshade, T. J., J. C. Guzman, and C. F. Westoff. 2003. "The Surprising Global Variation in Replacement Fertility." *Population Research and Policy Review* 22(5/6):575.

Food and Agriculture Organization of the United Nations (FAO). 2012. The State of Food Insecurity in the World. *Executive Summary 2012*. Accessed November 2012 at http://www.fao.org/docrep/016/i2845e/i2845e00.pdf.

Fuguitt, Glenn V. 1984. "The Nonmetropolitan Population Turnaround." *Annual Review of Sociology* 11:259–80.

Gans, Herbert J. 1962. *The Urban Villagers*. New York: Free Press.

Gans, Herbert J. 1968. *People and Plans: Essays on Urban Problems and Basic Solutions*. New York: Basic Books.

Gans, Herbert J. 1970. "Urbanism and Suburbanism." Pp. 157–164 in *Urban Man and Society: A Reader in Urban Ecology*, edited by Albert N. Cousins and Hans Nagpaul. New York: Knopf.

Garreau, Joel. 1991. "Life on the Edge." *The Washington Post*. Sept 8:C1.

Gillis, Justin, and Dugger, Celia W. 2011, May 3. "U.N. Forecasts 10.1 billion people by century's end." *The New York Times*. Accessed November 2012 at http://www.nytimes.com/2011/05/04/world/04population.html?_r=0.

Goffman, Erving. 1963. *Stigma: Notes on the Management of Spoiled Identity*. New York: Prentice-Hall

Harris, Chauncey, and Edward Ullman. 1945. "The Nature of Cities." *Annals of the American Academy of Political and Social Science* 242(November):7–17.

Haub, Carl, 2004. *2003 World Population Data Sheet*. Washington, DC: Population Reference Bureau.

Herbers, John. 1986. *The New Heartland: America's Flight Beyond the Suburbs and How It Is Changing Our Future*. New York: Times Books.

Hoyt, Homer. 1939. *The Structure and Growth of Residential Neighborhoods in American Cities*. U.S. Federal Housing Administration. Washington, DC: US Government Printing Office.

Johnson, Samuel. 1791. Quoted in Boswell, James. *The Life of Samuel Johnson, LL.D.* Reprinted in Everyman's Library.

Kneebone, Elizabeth, and Steven Raphael. 2011. "City and Suburban Crime Trends in Metropolitan America." Metropolitan Policy Program at Brookings. Accessed November 2012 at http://www.brookings.edu/~/media/research/files/papers/2011/5/26%20metropolitan%20crime%20kneebone%20raphael/0526_metropolitan_crime_kneebone_raphael.pdf.

Kron, Josh. 2012, November 30. "Red State, Red State, Blue City: How the Urban-Rural Divide Is Splitting America." *The Atlantic Monthly*. Accessed December 2012 at http://www.theatlantic.com/politics/archive/2012/11/red-state-blue-city-how-the-urban-rural-divide-is-splitting-america/265686/.

Leinberger, Christopher B., and Charles Lockwood. 1986, October. "How Business is Reshaping America." *The Atlantic Monthly* 258(10):34–38.

Lemarchand, René. 2002, March 29. "Disconnecting the Threads: Rwanda and the Holocaust Reconsidered." *Idea Journal* 7(1). Accessed December 2012 at http://www.ideajournal.com/articles.php?sup=11.

Logan, John R. and Brian Stults. 2011. "The Persistence of Segregation in the Metropolis: New Findings from the 2010 Census" Census Brief prepared for Project US2010. Accessed December 2012 at http://www.s4.brown.edu/us2010.

Malthus, Thomas Robert. 1798(1926). *First Essay on Population 1798*. London: Macmillan.

Marx, Karl and Engels, Friedrich. 1867. *Capital: Critique of Political Economy*. Germany: Verlag von Otto Meisner.

Meadows, Donella H., Dennis L. Meadows, Jorgan Randers, and William W. Behrens III. 1972a. *The Limits to Growth: A Report on the Club of Rome's Project on the Predicament of Mankind*. New York: Universe.

Meadows, Donella H., et al. 1972b. Accessed November 2012 at http://gailtheactuary.files.wordpress.com/2011/10/limits-to-growth-forecast.png.

Meadows, Donella H., Jorgen Randers, and Dennis L. Meadows. 2004. *Limits to Growth: The 30-Year Update*. White River Junction, VT: Chelsea Green.

Medna, Sarah. 2012, November 2. "Random Acts of Kindness after Hurricane Sandy (slideshow)." *Huffington Post*. Accessed December 2012 at http://www.huffingtonpost.com/2012/11/02/hurricane-sandy-random-ac_n_2061005.html.

Migration Policy Institute. 2012. *US Historical Immigration Trends: Number and Share of the Total US Population, 1850 to 2011*. Accessed November 2012 at http://www.migrationinformation.org/datahub/charts/final.fb.shtml.

Murdie, Robert, and Teixeira, Carlos. 2011. "The Impact of Gentrification on Ethnic Neighbourhoods in Toronto: A Case Study of Little Portugal." *Urban Studies* 48(1):61–83.

Myrskyla, M., H. Kohler, Francesco C. Billari. 2009. "Advances in Development Reverse Fertility Declines." *Nature* 460:741–43. Accessed December 2012 at http://www.nature.com/nature/journal/v460/n7256/abs/nature08230.html.

National Center for Health Statistics. 2007, August 21. *National Vital Statistics Reports* 54(20). Accessed November 2012 at http://www.cdc.gov/nchs/births.htm, http://www.infoplease.com/ipa/A0005067.html, and http://www.infoplease.com/ipa/A0005131.html.

National Oceanic and Atmospheric Administration (NOAA). 2012. *Over Half of the American Population Lives within 50 Miles of the Coast*. Accessed December 2012 at http://oceanservice.noaa.gov/facts/population.html.

Nigeria National Population Commission. 2009. "2006 Census Priority Tables Volume I. Abuja." http://www.population.gov.ng/index.php?id=3. Accessed November 2012 at http://www.census.gov/population/international/data/idb/region.php?N=%20Results%20&T=12&A=separate&RT=0&Y=2012&R=-1&C=NI.

Park, Robert E. 1950. *Race and Culture*. Glencoe, IL: Free Press.

Population Reference Bureau. 2012. *2012 World Population Data Sheet*. Accessed November 2012 at http://www.prb.org/pdf12/2012-population-data-sheet_eng.pdf.

Shelley, Percy. 1839(1994). "Peter Bell the Third." In *The Collected Poems of Percy Bysshe Shelley*, edited by Mary Shelley. New York: Modern Library.

Simmel, George. 1905(1964). "The Metropolis and Mental Life." Pp. 409–424 in *The Sociology of Georg Simmel*, edited by Kurt Wolff. New York: Free Press.

Smith, Tom W., Peter V. Marsden, Michael Hout, and Jibum Kim. 2010. *GSS 1972-2010 Cumulative Codebook*. Storrs, CT: Roper Center.

Stein, Rob. 2009, August 10. "Some Highly Developed Countries See Increased Fertility." *The Washington Post*. Accessed December 2012 at http://www.washingtonpost.com/wp-dyn/content/article/2009/08/09/AR2009080902294.html?hpid=moreheadlines.

Stern, N., and C. Taylor. 2007. "Climate Change: Risk, Ethics and the Stern Review." *Science* 317:203–4.

Suro, Roberto. 1990. "Courts Ordering Financing Changes in Public Schools." *The New York Times*. June 18. 1, 16.

Thompson, Warren S. 1929. "Population." *American Journal of Sociology* 34:959–75.

Tönnies, Ferdinand. 1887(1963). *Community and Society (Gemeinschaft and Gesellschaft)*. New York: Harper and Row.

Turner, Graham. 2008. "A Comparison of 'The Limits to Growth' with Thirty Years of Reality." Commonwealth Scientific and Industrial Research Organisation (CSIRO).

United Nations. 1987. *Our Common Future*. Report of the World Commission on Environment and Development, World Commission on Environment and Development. Published as Annex to General Assembly document A/42/427, Development and International Co-operation: Environment August 2, 1987. Accessed November 2012 at http://conspect.nl/pdf/Our_Common_Future-Brundtland_Report_1987.pdf.

United Nations. 2012. "Urban and Rural Areas 2011." *World Urbanization Prospects, the 2011 Revision*. United Nations, Department of Economic and Social Affairs, Population Division: New York 2012. Accessed November 2012 at http://esa.un.org/unup/Wallcharts/urban-rural-areas.pdf.

United Nations Development Program (UNDP). 1998. "Consumption for Human Development." *Human Development Report 1998*. Accessed November 2012 at http://hdr.undp.org/en/media/hdr_1998_en_overview.pdf.

United Nations Development Program (UNDP). 2011. "Sustainability and Equity: A Better Future for All." *Human Development Report 2011*. Accessed November 2012 at http://hdr.undp.org/en/media/HDR_2011_EN_Complete.pdf.

US Census Bureau. 2010. "Urban Areas and Urban Clusters: 2010." *2010 Urban Area Thematic Maps*. Accessed November 2012 at http://www.census.gov/geo/www/maps/2010_census_UA_maps/imgs/UA2010_UAs_and_UCs_Map.pdf.

US Census Bureau. 2011a. *2010 Census Urban and Rural Classification and Urban Area Criteria*. Accessed November 2012 at http://www.census.gov/geo/reference/urban-rural-2010.html.

US Census Bureau. 2011b *Percent Change in Population: 2000 to 2010*. US Census Bureau, Geography Division, June 13, 2011. Accessed November 2012 at http://www.census.gov/geo/www/maps/2010pop/us_perchange_2010map.jpg.

US Census Bureau. 2012a. *Census Bureau Releases Estimates of Undercount and Overcount in the 2010 Census*. Press Release May 22, 2012. Accessed November 2012 at http://2010.census.gov/news/releases/operations/cb12-95.html.

US Census Bureau. 2012b. *Census Estimates Show New Patterns of Growth Nationwide*. US Census Bureau Press Release April 5, 2012. Accessed November 2012 at http://www.census.gov/newsroom/releases/archives/population/cb12-55.html.

US Census Bureau. 2012c. *Growth in Urban Population Outpaces Rest of Nation, Census Bureau Reports*. US Census Bureau press release March 26, 2012. Accessed November 2012 at http://www.census.gov/newsroom/releases/archives/2010_census/cb12-50.html.

US Census Bureau. 2012d. *International Database*. Accessed November 2012 at http://www.census.gov/population/international/data/idb/region.php?N=%20Results%20&T=12&A=separate&RT=0&Y=2012&R=-1&C=US.

U.S. Census Bureau. 2012e. Metropolitan and micropolitan. U.S. Census Bureau. Accessed December 2012 at http://www.census.gov/population/metro/about/.

US Census Bureau. 2012f. *Table 2. Annual Estimates of the Population of Combined Statistical Areas: April 1, 2010 to July 1, 2011*. US Census Bureau. Accessed September 2012 at www.census.gov/popest/data/metro/totals/2011/tables/CBSA-EST2011-02.csv.

US Census Bureau. 2012g. *The 2012 Statistical Abstract*. Table 686. Average Annual Expenditures by Age of Householder 2009. Accessed December 2012 at http://www.census.gov/compendia/statab/cats/income_expenditures_poverty_wealth/consumer_expenditures.html.

US Department of Homeland Security. 2010. *Yearbook of Immigration Statistics 2010*. Table 2. Accessed November 2012 at http://www.dhs.gov/yearbook-immigration-statistics-2010-3.

Wilson, Thomas C. 1985. "Urbanism and Tolerance: A Test of Some Hypotheses Drawn from Wirth and Stouffer." *American Sociological Review* 50(1):117–23.

Wilson, William Julius. 1987. *The Truly Disadvantaged: The Inner City, the Underclass, and Public Policy*. Chicago: University of Chicago Press.

Wilson, William Julius. 2009. *More Than Just Race: Being Black and Poor in the Inner City (Issues of Our Time)*. New York: W. W. Norton & Company.

Wirth, Louis. 1938. "Urbanism as a Way of Life." *American Journal of Sociology* 44:1–24.

Worldatlas. 2010. *Largest Cities of the World (by Metro Population)*. Accessed November 2012 at http://www.worldatlas.com/citypops.htm.

World Bank. 2004. *World Population Growth*. The World Bank Group. Accessed November 2012 at http://www.worldbank.org/depweb/english/beyond/beyondco/beg_03.pdf.

Chapter Overview ▼

17 Collective Behavior, Social Movements, and Social Change

Learning Objectives ▼

17.1
- Define collective behavior and explain its challenges to sociologists.
- Compare and contrast types of collectivity.
- Examine examples of mass behavior.

17.2
- Illustrate the various types of social movements.

17.3
- Describe the stages of a social movement.

17.4
- Analyze key social movements in the United States.

17.5
- Explain the main theories of social movements.

17.6
- Illustrate the theories of social change.

© iStockphoto/Thinkstock

Before graduate school, my job as a welfare eligibility specialist put me in contact with a wide variety of people. Some were disabled and unable to work. Some had criminal records and could not find jobs. Others had families and were desperately trying to make ends meet. They were white, Hispanic, and African American. They were from Mexico, Russia, and Puerto Rico. They were Christian, Jewish, Muslim, and even Sikh. Despite this considerable diversity, however, they all had one thing in common. All of them needed help. All of them could have benefited from social reforms that would have improved their quality of life and made their lives easier. Yet none of them—not one—tried to help themselves. Not one worked to change society in such a way that it would actually benefit them. Instead, they hunted for work, hunted for peace of mind, and filled out their paperwork to receive public assistance to get by for another month.

As I began studying sociology, I remembered these people and their struggles. I asked myself why these people—poor, desperate, and dispossessed—did not react with anger and violence to the situation they found themselves in. I asked myself, and then I asked my professor. He paused for a moment, and then bit his bottom lip.

"Hmmmm," he said. "Consider it this way. If you are poor, you are either working a low-wage job—maybe two—or you are looking for work. Either way, you are so busy with trying to get by that you don't really have time to think about how bad things are. And even if you do know, what can you do about it? If you are so busy trying to make sure that the rent is paid, the lights stay on, and there is food in the fridge, you are not going to have time to think about making the world a better place."

The answer made sense. Sometimes the people who need help are in the least advantageous position to fight for it. As I learned more, I realized that the problem went even deeper. People who struggle to get by on a day-to-day basis also have to contend with a social structure that limits their educational opportunities, limits their occupational choices, and limits their voice in society. Social movements, I came to realize, are the knights in shining armor that challenge the kings for the damsel in distress. They are the voices of those who want to make a better society. Even though social movements sometimes set goals they cannot possibly achieve, they cut small chinks in the armor and weaken the status quo until it changes. At the same time, social movements shape our history and experience as we develop our sociological imaginations. Social movements influence history as they seek to change society. They influence our experiences both through the ways in which we think about the issues that social movements address and through our participation in them.

17.1 Collective Behavior

Collective behavior forms a cornerstone of study for sociologists.

- Define collective behavior and explain its challenges to sociologists.
- Compare and contrast types of collectivity.
- Examine examples of mass behavior.

Studying human social behavior is what sociologists do. Much of that social behavior is predictable within reasonable limits. However, sometimes spontaneous social behavior emerges from a specific event or set of events that challenge and excite sociologists. **Collective behavior** refers to behaviors involving a large number of individuals that are usually unplanned, often controversial, and sometimes even dangerous (such as staging a revolution). Studying these unplanned social behaviors provides unique challenges to sociologists but also provides interesting opportunities to study important aspects of human behavior.

Studying collective behavior poses significant difficulties for sociologists to study for several reasons. First, much collective behavior does not exist for long, especially when compared to more enduring social institutions such as the family. Second, collective behavior is diverse. It encompasses a wide range of possible behaviors. Often, the

Collective behavior Behaviors involving a large number of individuals that are usually unplanned, often controversial, and sometimes even dangerous.

direct causes of these behaviors are difficult to see and even more difficult to study scientifically. It is often difficult to see how the specific behaviors emerge from the identified causes. Finally, collective behavior is highly variable. Because such a wide array of social circumstances can lead to a wide array of possible behaviors, it is often very difficult to make generalizations about how people will behave in the future given similar circumstances. While it is hard enough to accurately predict the actions of individuals, it is even more difficult to predict the actions of many people acting in a collective way.

Despite these issues, sociologists have been able to learn a lot about collective behavior. The cornerstone of all of our knowledge rests on the seemingly obvious point that all collective behavior involves the actions of a collectivity. We define a **collectivity** as a large number of individuals whose minimal interaction occurs without the benefit of conventional norms. Collectivities come in two general types. *Localized collectivities* are collectivities that emerge among people who share close physical proximity. An example of a localized collectivity would be a riot. By contrast, a *dispersed collectivity* involves people who influence one another even though they are spread over a large area. Fashion offers an excellent example of a dispersed collectivity because unlike people who are close together congregated at the same beach, fashion can be shared by people all over the world who do not necessarily even know that the others exist.

It is important to understand how collectivities differ from social groups. First, unlike social groups in which individual members have considerable interaction with one another, members of collectivities have only minimal interaction with other individuals in the collectivity. In fact, members of a collectivity need not even interact at all—such as when people follow a fashion or engage in a fad. Second, collectivities have no clear social boundaries. While members of a group share a sense of identity, members of a collectivity do not. For example, members of a political party constitute a social group because there is a shared sense of identity that accompanies membership in a political party. In contrast, people who like the same television show do not establish a strong sense of identity from that show. They would form a collectivity. Finally, collectivities are characterized by the emergence of weak and often unconventional social norms. Group norms are typically strong and have the goal of regulating the behavior of members of the group. In contrast, the weaker norms of collectivities are often insufficient to properly regulate the actions of individuals.

Let us look in more depth at each of the main types of collectivities and their relation to social life.

Because collective behavior takes so many forms, it provides interesting opportunities for sociologists to study human behavior.

© CREATISTA/Shutterstock, Inc.

Collectivity A large number of individuals whose minimal interaction occurs without the benefit of conventional norms.

Crowd A temporary gathering of people who share a common focus of attention and who influence one another.

Localized Collectivities

As already noted, localized collectivities are characterized by the close proximity of individuals. One of the main ways this occurs is through crowds. A **crowd** is a temporary gathering of people who share a common focus of attention and who influence one another. Crowds can gather for a variety of reasons, some planned and some unplanned. Planned crowds include people at a concert or sporting event. Unplanned crowds might emerge during a disaster or other event that occurs spontaneously.

Crowds differ in their social dynamics depending on the kind of crowd and its origins. Sociologist Herbert Blumer (1969) identified four types of crowds. A *casual crowd* is defined as people who share the same proximity but interact very little. People lying on a crowded beach or people who gather in a park to watch fireworks are examples of casual crowds. Casual crowds rarely develop social norms. *Conventional crowds* are crowds that form from deliberate planning. A lecture or concert is a planned event that draws a conventional crowd. In such cases, a clear set of norms dictates the behavior of the collectivity. An *expressive crowd* emerges from an event that has a strong emotional component. A church revival is one example of an expressive crowd. Another example might be a concert in which the performers get an emotional reaction from the audience. Finally, an *acting crowd* is a collectivity that has a single purpose, usually

A casual crowd is defined as people who share the same proximity, but interact very little.
© Jennifer King/Shutterstock, Inc.

Conventional crowds are crowds that form from deliberate planning.
© iStockphoto/Thinkstock

Expressive crowds have a strong emotional component.
© Design Pics/Thinkstock

fueled by strong emotions. As an example, consider the crowds that form outside of a department store on Black Friday—the day after Thanksgiving. These crowds mill about the doors waiting for the store to open. When the doors open, the crowd surges forth with a single purpose: to get the best deals for Christmas. Often, fights occur as people compete for items. Some researchers have added a new category to Blumer's typology (McPhail and Wohlstein 1983). *Protest crowds* are crowds that form specifically to hold demonstrations for political purposes. An anti-abortion protest is an example of a protest crowd.

It is important to keep in mind that crowds may change from one kind to another fairly easily. For example, when a conventional crowd forms, it may quickly become an expressive crowd, which may in turn become an acting crowd. As an example, consider the many examples of riots that have occurred after championship sporting events. The conventional crowd that comes to the championship game quickly gets emotional as one team scores, then another. The crowd gradually becomes an expressive crowd as the excitement of the competition grows. When the game is over, fans of the winning (or losing) team sometimes riot, pouring into the streets. Sometimes this results in property damage such as overturned cars and broken street signs. It may also result in injuries or looting. For example, in 1989, the city of Miami, Florida, hosted the Super Bowl between the Cincinnati Bengals and the San Francisco 49ers. After the game, spectators overturned cars, started fires, and looted across the city in celebration of their team's victory or out of anger from their team's defeat. All in all, 11 people were injured, 400 were arrested, and the city incurred more than $1 million in damage. The expressive crowd became an acting crowd.

Riots and Mobs

When crowds become violent or destructive, the result is a mob. A **mob** is defined as a highly emotional crowd that pursues a destructive or violent goal. Mobs often form spontaneously and are usually short-lived, disbanding as quickly as they form. Mobs will tend to last longer if a clear leader emerges during the fray.

A **riot**, by contrast, is an eruption of social activity that is highly emotional, undirected, and violent. It differs from a mob in that while a mob has a specific goal of being destructive, a riot has no clear goal. Riots often emerge out of a long-standing feeling of dissatisfaction that simmers underneath the prevailing social order before erupting. Many riots are the result of some perceived social injustice or in response to undesired social change. For example, the Haymarket riot in 1886 occurred after industrial workers in a variety of fields united under the emerging Federation of Organized Trades and Labor Unions and protested peacefully for better working conditions and an eight-hour work day. Conflicts between law enforcement and protesters erupted in a violent riot that claimed 11 lives and caused dozens of injuries.

Crowds and Social Change

Riots are often exhilarating for those who participate in them and frightening for the victims. Riots give the participants—usually ordinary people—considerable power. Acting in a spontaneous situation with other people offers the perception of legitimation and protection from wrongdoing. Sometimes, however, riots can be a force for social change. Shootings of unarmed citizens in several cities such as New York, Los Angeles, and Cincinnati at various times in history caused rioting and drew attention to claims of racial bias in policing that have helped to change police procedures.

Riots and mobs, therefore, can be both good and bad. They can cause unimaginable harm, such as in the Miami Super Bowl riot, or significant social change, such as improving working conditions for vast numbers of employed Americans and making police procedures safer for everyone. For this reason, riots and mobs are often feared by people who have a stake in keeping things the way they are. At the same time, mobs and riots are sometimes defended by individuals who seek to change society, especially when there is a perception that individuals are desperate or disenfranchised.

Theories of Crowd Behavior

There are several theories that attempt to account for the behavior of individuals in crowds. Contagion theory was developed by French sociologist Gustav LeBon FIGURE 17-1 in 1865. According to LeBon, crowds have an almost hypnotic effect on their members. In large groups, there is anonymity that makes people abandon reason and personal responsibility. Like a contagion spreading through a population, behaviors spread through the crowds, causing people to act in ways that they would not ordinarily act. The crowd assumes a life of its own, and people act within its wake. The run on banks that ushered in the Great Depression is one example of a contagion. At first, only select customers—businesses trying to shore up their failing investments—withdrew money from the bank. However, their actions caused many people to overstate the danger of keeping their money in the bank. As more and more people began to withdraw their savings from the bank, a panic ensued, causing a run on the cash reserves of many large banks, effectively bankrupting the banks and bringing about the exact tragedy that many people feared.

In contrast to contagion theory, which states that crowd behavior is a result of the crowds, convergence theory argues that crowd behavior comes from the people who join crowds, not the crowds themselves. In other words, the behavior of the crowds occurs from the convergence of many people who are all thinking alike. So while contagion theory believes that crowds cause people to think in a certain way, convergence theory argues that people thinking in a certain way cause crowds. The Occupy Wall Street protests, for example, were caused by the convergence of many like-minded people rather than the other way around. While the bank runs described above caused people to be like minded, convergence theory hypothesizes that people who already think alike will form social movements.

Ralph Turner and Lewis Killiam (1987) developed emergent norm theory as yet another way of explaining the emergence of crowd behavior. Emergent norm theory admits that predicting human social behavior is never perfect. However, in collectivities, it may be possible to observe patterns that help predict the behaviors of individuals within that collectivity. Emergent norm theory argues that individuals in crowds may have different motives or interests. However, their behavior may become consistent with the behavior of others as collective norms emerge. While these norms may be vague and changing, they do serve to guide the behavior of the people in the crowd and serve as a starting point for analysis of crowd behavior. For example, while some people who join environmental movements seek to lessen the impact of human consumerism on global climate change, others in the same movement seek more specific goals of reducing energy consumption, encourage community gardening, or even promote veganism as a way of life. Over time, these different ideals and goals will converge through the lens of the social movement and become part of the broader message of the movement itself.

Dispersed Collectivities

As we already learned, collectivities need not be clustered together. Collective behavior can occur among people who are dispersed over a wide geographic area.

Acting crowds have a single purpose, usually fueled by strong emotions.
© Joshua Bickel/Corbis

Mobs are defined as highly emotional crowds that pursue a destructive goal.
© Gideon Mendel/CORBIS

FIGURE 17 1 Gustav LeBon argued that crowds can have an almost hypnotic effect on people.
Public domain

Mob A highly emotional crowd that pursues a destructive or violent goal.

Riot An eruption of social activity that is highly emotional, undirected, and violent.

Sociologists refer to this as **mass behavior**. One of the most common examples of mass behavior is rumor.

Rumors

Rumors refer to unconfirmed information that people spread, often by word of mouth. While traditionally rumors spread through face-to-face communication, modern technologies have facilitated the spread of rumors. Through the use of these technologies, rumors spread faster and farther than ever before. Despite this, the characteristics of rumors have remained fundamentally the same. Rumors have three main characteristics.

First, rumors occur in situations in which there are large degrees of uncertainty and in which facts are difficult to authenticate. Second, rumors are unstable and change frequently. As rumors spread, they change to fit the preconceived notions of the people who are spreading them. Finally, rumors are difficult to stop. As noted, rumors thrive in environments in which facts are difficult to determine. Because rumors spread quickly, they are difficult to intercept even when the facts are known.

Gossip refers to rumors about the personal affairs of a person. While rumors tend to have broad social appeal, gossip typically has a much smaller audience that is limited to a small group of people. For this reason, rumors spread widely, but gossip tends to be localized. Gossip acts as a means of social control by encouraging the victim of gossip to adhere to social norms. Nicholson (2001) also argues that gossip functions as means by which individuals raise their own status. When an individual spreads gossip, it is usually denigrating to the victim, which lowers the victim's social status relative to the person spreading the gossip. Additionally, the person spreading gossip may get an increase in status by being perceived by others as a social insider. At the same time, spreading too much gossip can backfire, as society may see the person as a busybody.

Propaganda and Public Opinion

Everybody has opinions about something. Sometimes, opinions act as polarizing forces to divide people into in-groups and out-groups. Conversely, opinions can act as cohesive forces as well. Although people sharing an opinion may be geographically dispersed, they may in fact engage in collective behavior because they share a common view on a particular issue. For example, people all over the United States have opinions about global warming. Although people who have similar opinions may never meet, they may still engage in similar, coordinated actions that center around their opinion.

Sociologists use the term **public opinion** to refer to widespread attitudes or beliefs about a particular issue. While almost everybody has an opinion about major social issues, most people indicate that they do not have strong opinions about most issues. Clearly, not everyone's opinions are given the same weight. For example, society often gives more weight to the opinions of educated people over uneducated people. How many average Americans are invited onto television to weigh in on the economy, foreign policy, or even sports predictions? The weight of opinions may also vary by race, socioeconomic status, or gender. Expertise in a particular area may also influence how much clout a person's opinion carries. For example, the opinions of teachers or principals about the state of public education may carry more weight than the opinions of a professional golfer on the same topic. By the same token, few people would ask a high school principal for putting tips.

Advocacy groups, politicians, and others may all try to influence public opinion. To do this, they often use **propaganda**, which is information given with the intention of shaping public opinion. This differs from information, which is designed to educate. Swaying opinions can be done in several ways. First, propaganda may appeal to facts or evidence in order to persuade people to change their opinions. It may also appeal to emotions. Finally, propaganda can appeal to religious or other authority as a means to

Gossip refers to rumors about the personal affairs of a person.

© Jupiterimages/Thinkstock

Mass behavior Collective behavior can occur among people who are dispersed over a wide geographic area.

Rumors Unconfirmed information that people spread, often by word of mouth.

Gossip Rumors about the personal affairs of a person.

Public opinion Widespread attitudes or beliefs about a particular issue.

Propaganda information given with the intention of shaping public opinion.

convince people of the propagandist's point of view. Hitler's Nazi party members were masters of propaganda. Writings that blamed the economic crisis and defeat in World War I on the Jews were based on the writings of historian Houston Stewart Chamberlain, giving them a sense of authenticity and credibility. Early Nazi leaders, such as Alfred Rosenberg, were highly educated individuals who wrote their own treatises on Aryan superiority, placing their theories in every school, church, and public institution in Germany.

Fads and Fashions

Other dispersed collectivities are fashions and fads. A **fashion** is a social pattern that is adopted or followed by a large number of people. Fashions include taste in clothing, art, music, and other aspects of culture that may change rapidly in modern society. Fashions are used to distinguish groups of people from others. Traditionally, this distinction would usually be determined by social class, as the wealthy would seek to display their wealth through brightly colored, ostentatious clothing or furnishings (Simmel 1904). As the middle class developed and gained wealth, it mimicked the tastes of the wealthy, often buying objects not out of necessity but rather to increase their status (Veblen 1953). Social critic Thorsten Veblen called this phenomenon **conspicuous consumption**.

Because individuals in the lower classes seek to mimic the fashion of the higher classes, often seeking out more affordable copies of high-end merchandise, fashion tends to move downward in the socioeconomic structure. As more and more people adopt the fashion, it tends to gradually lose its appeal. Often, this precipitates the wealthy to seek out new ways to distinguish themselves. Thus, fashion is constantly changing.

On occasion, fashions remain relatively stable. In some cases, fashions even move from the lower socioeconomic status to the higher socioeconomic statuses. For example, denim jeans began as a durable item of clothing favored by the working class. During the civil rights movement, blue jeans were often worn by college students and professors who wanted to show their identification with the working class. Today, it is not unusual to see celebrities or the wealthy elite wearing brand-name, expensive blue jeans.

Sometimes, elements of fashions are embraced very enthusiastically by members of a society. Often, these elements are unconventional or unique, which tends to contribute to their popularity. When a unique or unconventional social pattern is embraced briefly and enthusiastically by members of a social group or society, it is called a **fad**. Fads appear most often in high-income societies because individuals in high-income societies have the money to spend on nonessential items. In the early 1990s, pogs became a national craze. Using brightly colored collectible cardboard discs adapted from bottle caps used by a Hawaiian juice company, people competed to slam the pogs into a face down position with a much heavier disk. The game gained popularity when it was promoted by the World POG Federation, gaining popularity until the mid 1990s, when its popularity rapidly faded. Other examples of fads include Beanie Babies and Pokémon.

Fads are different from fashions because fads catch on more quickly with the general population but also fade out more quickly. Traces of these fads can now be seen by searching Internet buying sites, which often offer these objects quite inexpensively. While many elements of fashion become long-lasting and even permanent features of society, fads rarely make a lasting impact.

Panic and Mass Hysteria

Imagine being in a crowded room. People are milling about, talking and having a good time. Suddenly, a loud explosion shakes the walls of the room. After the initial shock wears off, people begin scrambling toward the only door, pushing and shoving one

Fashion A social pattern that is adopted or followed by a large number of people.

Conspicuous consumption Spending money on things that advertise status and prestige.

Fad A unique or unconventional social pattern that is adopted briefly and enthusiastically by members of a social group or society.

Fads are unconventional social patterns that people embrace briefly but enthusiastically.
© Gamma-Rapho/Getty Images

Panic A form of collective behavior in which people react to a perceived threat in a frantic and irrational way.

Moral panic A form of dispersed collective behavior in which people react to a perceived threatening event with an irrational fear.

Disaster An event that causes extensive harm to people and property.

another in a mad attempt to get out of the room. As you fight to get closer to the door, you are kicked and punched by the increasingly frantic mob. You are experiencing a **panic**—a form of collective behavior in which people react to a perceived threat in a frantic and irrational way.

Relatedly, a **moral panic** is a form of dispersed collective behavior in which people react to a perceived threatening event with an irrational fear. A moral panic is also called *mass hysteria*. An early example of a moral panic in America is the temperance movement, which irrationally blamed alcohol for what was perceived as a deteriorating society. Anti-alcohol protestors claimed that alcohol resulted in starving women and children because men drank away all of their wages. Some also claimed that alcohol was a direct cause of spousal and child abuse, as well as many other actions considered morally degenerate. Temperance advocates used fear and selective examples to spread their dislike of alcohol, culminating in a Constitutional amendment banning the sale and distribution of alcohol in the United States. A more modern example of a moral panic is the fear generated around the AIDS epidemic. When the first cases of AIDS were announced to the public, there was broad fear of the deadly contagion. Despite very little actual risk of contracting the disease through casual interaction, many people refused to even speak with anyone suspected of having AIDS. This irrational fear of AIDS resulted in numerous hate crimes that targeted people suspected of having AIDS.

Moral panics are often fueled by the mass media, which disseminate information very quickly. A classic example of a moral panic being fueled by the media occurred in 1938. As part of a radio drama series, actors adapted the novel *War of the Worlds* by H.G. Wells and performed it on the air the day before Halloween. The novel depicts the invasion of Earth by aggressive aliens from Mars. The broadcast took the form of simulated news bulletins and interviews. Hearing this caused many people to believe that the invasion was actually occurring! Some people took to the streets with whatever weapons they could find to defend their planet from nonexistent aliens. It took several days and many additional broadcasts to convince people that Earth was safe from alien invasion.

In 1938, a radio broadcast of a reading of the popular novel War of the Worlds *incited a panic.*

© Forrest J. Ackerman Collection/CORBIS

Disasters

A **disaster** is an event that causes extensive harm to people and property. Generally, three kinds of disasters are recognized. *Natural disasters* include such incidents as floods, hurricanes, earthquakes, and tornados. Disasters also occur when humans fail to adequately regulate and control technology, resulting in a *technological disaster*. The Deepwater Horizon oil spill—more popularly known as the BP oil spill—occurred in 2010 when an underwater drill exploded, causing oil to gush into the Gulf of Mexico. Oil flowed freely for nearly three months before the well was finally plugged. Today, nearly three years later, the effects of this technological disaster are still being felt. Finally, *intentional disasters* are disasters caused deliberately, with the intent to harm others. War, terrorist attacks, and genocide are all examples of intentional disasters.

Disasters often happen suddenly and swiftly, though the effects of disasters can last for years. For this reason, among others, disasters are inherently social events (Erikson 1994). Aside from the direct harm that disasters can cause to the environment, disasters also damage human communities. Even after the immediate damage of a disaster is gone, the emotional and psychological scars of a disaster may linger. For example, the city of New Orleans is still recovering from the devastation of Hurricane Katrina, which struck in 2005. Some research shows that the type of disaster influences the way in which people recover from it (Erikson 1994). For example, recovery from natural disasters tends to be shorter than the recovery time from technological disasters or intentional disasters. This is because it is easier to understand disasters that occur naturally than intentionally at the hands of other humans.

Natural disasters can cause extensive harm to people and property.

© Dustie/Shutterstock, Inc.

CONCEPT LEARNING CHECK 17.1   Collective Behavior

Fill in the blank.

1. A(n) _____ is a highly emotional crowd that pursues a destructive or violent goal.

2. Unconfirmed information that people spread is called _____.

3. Sociologists use the term _____ to refer to widespread attitudes or beliefs about a particular issue.

4. A(n) _____ is a manmade event that causes extensive harm to people and property.

5. A large number of individuals whose minimal interaction occurs without the benefit of conventional norms is called a(n) _____.

17.2   Social Movements

Social movements are any organized activity that encourages or discourages social change.

- Illustrate the various types of social movements.

> **Social movement** Any organized activity that encourages or discourages social change.

Social movements are one of the most important kinds of collective behavior. They are widely studied by sociologists. Indeed, entire courses are frequently devoted to in-depth analysis of social movements. Sociologists define **social movements** as any organized activity that encourages or discourages social change. Social movements are important because they have lasting and significant effects on our society. In fact, C. Wright Mills (1959), who developed the idea of the sociological imagination, considered social movements an integral part of that development. Mills began with the assumption that how a person thinks sociologically is shaped by the social and historical structure that the person is in. Social movements shape the social structure by influencing the way in which we think about and experience issues in society. Social movements shape the social structure as they push social institutions to change.

Historically, social movements are a relatively recent phenomenon. Pre-industrial societies are strongly rooted in tradition, making social movements generally unnecessary and very rare. Conversely, the cultural variety that accompanies industrial and postindustrial societies makes social conflict more likely. The clash of norms that accompanies the proliferation of countercultures means that a wide range of public issues come into the public rhetoric. For example, a rising gay rights movement has emerged in the past two decades, winning numerous legal battles and creating a moral backlash that has led to the creation of countermovements led by moral traditionalists who seek to limit the social and legal recognition of homosexuality. Most recently, this backlash has led to a growing advocacy of the Defense of Marriage Act, a federal law that would define marriage as between one man and one woman—thereby effectively prohibiting gay marriage at the federal level.

Alternative social movements seek to change only limited aspects of society.
© Michael S. Lewis/CORBIS

Types of Social Movements

Each social movement is different, though they share similar patterns. Social movements may differ in the kinds of people they target or the kinds of changes they advocate. Despite the wide variation among social movements, sociologists have been able to categorize them into four general types.

Redemptive social movements target specific groups.
© John Van Hasselt/Corbis

Reformative social movements target everyone, but seek change that is limited in scope.

© Rick D'Elia/Corbis

Alternative social movement A social movement that seeks to change only very limited aspects of society.

Redemptive social movement A social movement that seeks radical change for a specific, targeted group of people.

Reformative social movement A social movement that targets a broad group of people but whose changes are limited in scope.

Revolutionary social movement A social movement that seeks radical change of an entire society.

Claims making The process of trying to convince people that the cause of a social movement is so important that they should join the movement.

Revolutionary social movements seek radical change to the entire society.

© Getty Images

All social movements are some threat to the status quo. Some social movements, however, are more threatening to the prevailing social order than others. **Alternative social movements** are usually the least threatening to the status quo. Alternative social movements seek to change only very limited aspects of society. The aim of such movements is to help certain people alter their lives. One example of an alternative social movement is the Promise Keepers, a religiously based group that encourages men to support their families through traditional family values.

Redemptive social movements also target specific people or groups. However, as compared to alternative social movements, redemptive social movements seek radical change. For example, Narcotics Anonymous is an organization that helps people make the radical change of overcoming addiction to drugs. The goal of Narcotics Anonymous is to help members redeem themselves and lead healthy lives. Religious groups that seek to radically reform a person's character through being "born again" are other examples of redemptive social movements.

The third category of social movements is **reformative social movements**. These types of social movements target everyone, but the change they seek is limited in scope. Usually, reformative social movements work within the law and the existing political system to affect their social change. The multiculturalism movement is a good example of a reformative movement. The multiculturalism movement seeks to increase social equality for people of all ethnic and racial groups.

Finally, **revolutionary social movements** are the most radical and extreme type of social movements. Revolutionary social movements seek to transform entire societies. They reject existing social institutions as fundamentally flawed and propose radical alternatives to these existing institutions. For example, the American Communist Party seeks a radical overthrow of the capitalist economy in favor of the abolition of private property.

Revolutionary social movements can be further subdivided into two types. Progressive movements promote new social patterns—they advocate for change. Reactionary movements oppose movements that seek change or try to return to previously existing ways of life. The American Communist Party mentioned earlier is an example of a progressive social movement. In contrast, the Tea Party movement may be seen as a reactionary movement because its members want to return to an era of smaller government and fewer government controls.

Why Do People Join Social Movements?

People join social movements for a variety of reasons. It is important to know that not everyone joins social movements for the same reason. Additionally, the same person may join different social movements for entirely different reasons. Generally speaking, sociologists have identified four main reasons that people join movements. It is important to understand that these reasons may work singularly or in combination. People often join social movements for multiple reasons that are often connected.

People may join social movements for personal advantage. Usually, this means material advantage, such as better wages or benefits. People may also join social movements because of principled commitment. Individuals sometimes have strong moral views and join social movements because they believe in the cause the movement is fighting for. Joining a social movement connects the person with others who share the same moral commitment. This brings us to the third reason that people join social movements. Developing a sense of group solidarity is important to a person's sense of identity. By joining a social movement, an individual may feel like part of a group. This is often because movements connect people with similar principled commitments. Relatedly, people join social movements out of a desire to part of a group.

Individuals sometimes join social movements without prompting. However, sometimes people need to be persuaded that the cause addressed by a social movement is important enough to join. **Claims making** is the process of trying to convince people that the cause of a social movement is so important that the person should join the movement. This is usually done by first convincing society that the cause is important and demands public attention. Claims making is often started by a select small group of people who have a strong commitment to a particular issue. For example, Mothers Against Drunk Driving was started by one person—Candice Lightner—whose daughter had been struck and killed by a young intoxicated driver. Lightner used the emotional appeal of her tragic life event to convince many people that the drinking age needed to be raised from 18 to 21. Lightner's claims making resulted in a national movement that resulted in a significant policy shift.

Candice Lightener convinced people that the legal drinking age in America needed to be changed.

© Bettmann/CORBIS

THE SOCIOLOGICAL IMAGINATION Social Movements

As we have learned, social movements are important for the development of the sociological imagination because they allow us to take our personal troubles public. Social movements shape our experiences as well as social history and help make us who we are.

EVALUATE

1. Think about a social movement that you would be inclined to join. What claims making process has convinced you that this issue needs attention?

2. How has the social movement influenced the way in which you view your life? How has the social movement shaped history? How has the social movement influenced the construction of your sociological imagination?

CONCEPT LEARNING CHECK 17.2 Social Movements

Match the description to the kind of social movement.

_____ **1.** A trade union is seeking to improve workers' rights.

_____ **2.** The new People's Popular Party wants to overthrow the government and replace it with a socialist utopia.

_____ **3.** The New Church of the Better Individual seeks to convince people to lead a morally pure life style by forsaking all material possessions.

_____ **4.** Mothers Against Drunk Driving

A. Revolutionary social movement

B. Redemptive social movement

C. Reformative social movement

D. Alternative social movement

17.3 Stages of Social Movements

All social movements go through a series of similar stages.

■ Describe the stages of a social movement.

As we have already learned, social movements come in many varieties. Despite the significant differences, sociologists studying social movements have discovered that all social movements emerge, grow, and atrophy in the same way (Tilly 1978). All social movements go through four identifiable stages.

Emergence The tendency for social movements to form to address a perceived social problem.

Coalescence A stage of social movements in which the social movement begins to mobilize resources to achieve its goal.

Bureaucratization The tendency for a social movement to adopt the characteristics of a bureaucratic organization to achieve its goals.

Decline The tendency for all social movements to fade in power and significance.

In the first social movement stage, termed **emergence**, the claims making process convinces people that there is something that needs to be changed about society. As social awareness of the problem grows, the social movement gains momentum. Sometimes the momentum of a social movement is rapid, such as with the Occupy Wall Street movement. In other cases, the momentum of the social movement builds slowly over time. Emergence is key to the development of the sociological imagination because it helps to show people how their personal issues are embedded in the larger social structure.

After it emerges, the social movement solidifies its message and goals and develops a strategy for accomplishing those goals. Leaders emerge and develop strategies for improving morale and growing the movement. During this **coalescence** *stage*, the movement will begin to acquire and mobilize resources. The social movement will begin to engage in social action designed to attract the attention of the media, government, or other movements that might have a stake in the issue or in a related issue.

As social movements grow and coalesce, they become more and more involved in the political process as a means of advancing the cause. People in the social movement begin to link their personal issues with the public events. They begin to realize, as Mills pointed out, that their personal troubles are public issues. As the social movement becomes more political, it also tends to become more bureaucratic. To navigate the complexities of the political landscape, social movements have to adapt their tactics and resources to the political climate. This often results in the formalization of the leadership structure and tactics of the movement. In other words, during the stage of **bureaucratization**, social movements become bureaucratic entities. The strength of the movement relies increasingly on the competency of the bureaucratic process and the staff that implements it rather than the charisma of leaders. Social movements that fail to bureaucratize risk dissolving, particularly if the leader leaves or exhibits weakness. By contrast, social movements that move through the process of bureaucratization tend to become well established. At the same time, bureaucratization can have negative consequences for a social movement as well. Research by Piven and Cloward (1977) showed that when social movements become bureaucratized, leaders often begin to neglect the emotional nature of the social movements that keep members motivated in favor of the more technical aspects of leadership required by bureaucracies.

Although some social movements last longer than others, all social movements eventually enter a period of **decline**. There are several reasons social movements decline. First, they may decline because they accomplish their goals. For example, the women's suffrage movement faded away after women won the right to vote. Second, social movements may fail because of poor leadership. Sometimes, as noted, leaders may become more bureaucratic and less charismatic. At other times, leaders may be lured away from the movement by offers of power, prestige, or money. For example, a leader of the National Urban League, an activist group that advocates on behalf of African Americans and against racial discrimination in the United States, left the organization after President Clinton gave him a high-paying job. The movement itself may also go mainstream. That is, some social movements may eventually become part of the established system after realizing some of their goals.

Social movements may also fail because members of the movement lose interest or as the demands of real life get in the way of participation in the movement. Consider, for example, that no matter how committed people might be to the success of a particular movement, they still have to pay bills, care for their children, and see to other responsibilities that take precedence over participation in the movement. Finally, social movements might fail because they are taken down by outside forces. Opposition to the social movement may mobilize against the movement, defeating it through public opinion, law, or even overt resistance. Generally speaking, the more radical or revolutionary the movement is, the more likely it is to meet resistance.

Social Movements and Social Change

The purpose of social movements is to encourage or resist social change. American political life is increasingly based upon claims about what problems exist in society and how society should respond to those problems. Social movements are an integral part of deciding which problems will be addressed and how they will be seen. In Western society, social movements have had a significant impact on how we see social issues and how we live. Social movements addressing issues of workers' rights have led to improved wages, hours, and benefits for many Americans. Social movements have also won the right to vote for minority groups, improving the democratic process and giving more Americans a voice in government. The green movement has raised awareness of many environmental issues and has already led to several changes in policy to improve pollution controls and regulate harmful substances in the environment.

The proliferation of social movements has also had the latent function of polarizing segments of the population. For instance, the environmental movement has spurred a backlash, leading many people to angrily deny claims of global climate change. Over time, the two movements have become increasingly polarized in their views, both sides making claims and competing for public attention. Similarly, social movements advocating amnesty for illegal immigrants have spawned a backlash of groups like the Minutemen who oppose illegal immigration and patrol America's borders to help stem the tide of illegal immigration.

CONCEPT LEARNING CHECK 17.3 Stages of Social Movements

For the following scenarios, identify which stage of social movements is represented.

_____ **1.** The Brotherhood of Pens and Pencils just rented its first office space. It hired a secretary to take phone calls and created a public relations division.

_____ **2.** Bill and Joe are angry that lots of cities prohibit chickens as yard pets. They have gathered a group of people to begin a petition drive in their neighborhood.

_____ **3.** At a regional meeting of the Hesperus Alliance, leaders have just laid out plans for their first press conference. They hope this will increase membership and get people excited about their movement.

_____ **4.** The Patsy Petunia Club achieved its goal of promoting petunias for the public city gardens; membership dropped 60%.

A. Coalescence

B. Decline

C. Emergence

D. Bureaucratization

17.4 Social Movements in the United States

Social movements in the United States offer important examples of social movements.

- Analyze key social movements in the United States.

As we have learned, social movements are an important force for social change. Taking a deeper look into some of America's most influential social movements will provide insight into the development of the sociological imagination. We will explore six important social movements: the American civil rights movement, the feminist movement, the environmental movement (also known as the green movement), the gay rights movement, the Occupy Wall Street movement, and the Tea Party movement.

The American Civil Rights Movement

Although the passage of the 13th Amendment outlawed slavery in America, free blacks still faced significant discrimination and even continued slavery. Largely relegated to low-paying, menial jobs with little opportunity for upward advancement, African Americans remained trapped in a cycle of oppression. Segregation forced blacks to attend separate schools, eat at separate restaurants, ride in the back of the bus, and even drink from separate water fountains. The United States Supreme Court even ruled that segregation was legal as long as the separate facilities were equal to those enjoyed by whites. However, while things remained separate, they were certainly not equal. Facilities for African Americans were grossly inferior to those that existed for whites, even nearly a century after slavery was abolished. Dilapidated buildings used as schools for African-American children, warm water fountains, and poor housing were all routine for African Americans well into the 1960s. Limitations of voting rights were also put in place to limit the participation of blacks in the democratic process.

The National Association for the Advancement of Colored People (NAACP) was co-founded in 1909 by sociologist W. E. B. Du Bois to help promote the interests of African Americans in society. The organization fought to end racial discrimination through litigation, education, and lobbying efforts. Initially, these efforts had little effect. Gradually, public action replaced attempts at litigation and lobbying as the dominant means of achieving racial equality. Although the Supreme Court desegregated schools in 1954, many aspects of society remained racially segregated.

Although violent protests still occurred, the crux of the movement was centered around peaceful—but forceful—motivation. Organized by many people, but most notably by the Reverend Dr. Martin Luther King, Jr., the Montgomery bus boycott, sit-ins, and other peaceful protests gradually led to changes in public opinion. However, public opinion did not always translate into government action.

The movement changed tone with the emergence of more radical groups, such as the Black Panthers. Called the Black Power movement, these groups advocated—and sometimes used—violence to achieve their goals when all else failed. Generally, the Black Power movement had the latent effect of giving blacks a sense of pride and purpose in a society that sought to systematically oppress them.

Although most people associate the civil rights movement with Martin Luther King, many civil rights heroes worked behind the scenes to make the movement successful. One such person was Charles Hamilton Houston. A Harvard-educated lawyer, Houston was the architect behind *Brown v. Board of Education*—the Supreme Court decision that legally, if not practically, ended racially segregated schools. Houston demonstrated the flaws of the separate-but-equal doctrine by successfully arguing that African-American schools were vastly inferior to white schools. Houston died in 1950, four years before *Brown v. Board*. Thus, he never got to see the final result of his long struggle toward equality. Nevertheless, Houston remains an important figure in the American civil rights movement.

Since the 1970s, African Americans have made remarkable progress in many areas. Although African Americans, on average, earn less than whites, the gap is slowly closing. In education, progress for African Americans has made even greater strides. The percentage of blacks graduating from high school is more than 84%, drastically reducing the gap between races. The number of African Americans in college has risen to more than 19%.

In politics, African Americans have also made significant progress. As a result of migrations to the city that followed the end of slavery, the political power of urban blacks has increased substantially. Many of the nation's biggest cities now have African-American mayors and predominantly minority councils. Additionally, an increasing number of state representatives are African American. At the federal level, the election of President Barack Obama followed an increasing representation of African Americans in Congress.

Charles Hamilton Houston worked behind the scenes to end segregation.
© Bettmann/CORBIS

The Women's Movement

The women's movement—also known as the feminist movement—really refers to a series of movements occurring over many years that have been committed to achieving equal rights for women. Through its long history, the movement has focused on a variety of women's issues, from voting to reproductive rights to domestic violence. The feminist movement can be generally divided into three distinct phases.

Phase one feminism dates back to the 1800s. The first wave of feminism was concerned with the basic rights of women, such as voting. Women at the time were unable to hold public office and had to forfeit their rights to own property after they got married. Harriet Martineau (1837) FIGURE 17-2, the first woman sociologist, travelled to America to observe its social institutions. Martineau was appalled by slavery. She also criticized the state of women's education. Martineau likened the treatment of women to the treatment of slaves, noting that such discriminatory policies were antithetical to the Declaration of Independence, which holds that all men are created equal. Martineau called for the abolition of slavery as well as for greater social power for women.

Martineau's work was controversial for a variety of reasons. First, writing at that time was a very gendered activity. That is, it was considered poor taste for a woman to write. Martineau not only wrote, however, she wrote about politics, and her views were considered radical. Still, her writings influenced many later social thinkers and were influential in developing sociology as a discipline as well as later feminist thought in America.

In Chicago, Jane Addams co-founded the Hull House, a settlement house for recent European immigrants. The purpose of Hull House was to provide education, skills, and support to working-class immigrants. Immigrants were given lessons in art, literature, current events, and many other subjects in an effort to increase civic engagement by women in the community. Addams and other workers at Hull House also acted as emergency doctors and social workers for the immigrants in the communities, often providing them with food or even delivering their babies. Hull House attracted many female residents who went on to become prominent leaders and advocates for women's issues.

More influentially, Margaret Sanger was an early champion for women's reproductive rights. Sanger coined the term *birth control* and opened America's first birth-control clinic. At the time, birth control was illegal in most of the United States. Sanger was distraught at such restrictions and witnessed numerous self-induced abortions, stillbirths, and unwanted pregnancies that negatively impacted the quality of life of poor women. Sanger believed that women had a right to use birth control, and she began illegally importing birth-control devices from Europe. Sanger was arrested and convicted of distributing birth control. She was sentenced to 30 days in a workhouse. News of the trial spread, spurring the birth-control movement forward. Eventually, laws prohibiting birth control were overturned by the Supreme Court, due in large part to Sanger's efforts.

During World War II, women flocked to the factories to replace men who were fighting overseas. For many of these women, this was their first paid labor. After the war, these women were expected to relinquish their jobs to men. Dutifully, these women returned to domestic lives, forming families and raising them in a stubbornly patriarchal society. Second-wave feminism spanned the period from the 1960s through the 1990s as a delayed reaction to this imposed domesticity. In contrast to first-wave feminism, which focused on overturning legal barriers to gender equality, second-wave feminism focused more on issues of sexuality, family, and the workplace.

In 1963, Betty Friedan wrote an influential book, *The Feminine Mystique*. Friedan objected to stereotypical portrayals of women, particularly by the mainstream media. She argued that portraying women as merely domestic servants limited their potential and wasted their talents. The image of the nuclear family as an ideal is illusory, she

FIGURE 17-2 The first woman sociologist, Harriet Martineau, likened the treatment of women to the treatment of slaves.

© Hulton-Deutsch Collection/CORBIS

Jane Addams was the first woman to win the Nobel Peace Prize for her work at Hull House.

© Underwood & Underwood/Corbis

Margaret Sanger was influential in changing American norms and laws about birth control.

Courtesy of Library of Congress, Prints and Photographs Division (LC-USZ62-29808)

Betty Friedan's book, The Feminine Mystique, *helped launch second-wave feminism.*

© WireImage/Getty Images

Mission drift The changing of goals within a social movement.

argued, and does not equate to happiness for women. In the same year, President John F. Kennedy's Commission on the Status of Women released a report that documented systemic and pervasive discrimination against women. These revelations led to the formation of women's groups at the local, state, and national levels, all advocating for the rights of women. These many fragmented movements were united in cause under the newly formed National Organization of Women—NOW. The movement gained momentum, which led to several legal victories, including the Equal Pay Act of 1963, which abolished wage discrimination based on sex, and the Pregnancy Discrimination Act, which prohibited sex discrimination on the basis of pregnancy.

The movement also achieved legal victories aimed at reducing domestic violence and increasing women's reproductive choices. Aside from those already mentioned, some of the most important victories were the passage of laws that made marital rape illegal and a Supreme Court decision that legalized abortion for women. Perhaps the movement's most enduring legacy, however, was success in changing social attitudes toward women. Gradually, the movement changed the way society thinks about women and the roles they play in society. Second-wave feminism criticized the way culture viewed women. Feminists argued that the way in which popular culture portrayed women was sexist and demeaning. The movement tirelessly fought to change the images of women in society. In large part, the movement was successful.

Third-wave feminism began in the 1990s and continues to this day. The movement arose largely in response to a perceived social backlash against the major ideas of second-wave feminism. As the economy gradually improved after a recession in the 1970s, women began making conscious decisions to stay home and raise children rather than go to work. This return to the family was seen by many feminists as a step backward. Many feminist leaders recognized that this trend was more prominent among white, middle-class women, and they began to bring their feminist ideals to women of different racial and ethnic origins. This significantly diversified the feminist movement.

Because of this diversification, third-wave feminism evolved to criticize social definitions of what it meant to be a woman. The roles and expectations of womanhood were built around the dominant social group and did not necessarily reflect the beliefs, values, or behaviors of all women. Third-wave feminism sought to change the way in which women were defined in the media, politics, and social discourse. In this way, third-wave feminism seeks to broaden the definition of womanhood, which, unlike the previous two waves, is not centered around a single goal or theme.

As you can see, the feminist movement is a complex, evolving movement that has adapted to historical circumstances. Part of this adaptation is mission drift. **Mission drift** refers to the changing of goals within a social movement. Goals may change for a variety of reasons, including new leadership, new membership, and, as in the case of feminism, changing historical context. Sometimes, movements may even change their mission because the movement is successful in making significant change. Rather than simply disband, the movement seeks to accomplish another goal of social change.

Despite their different approaches, the civil rights movement and the feminist movement often intertwined, and not always harmoniously. For example, feminist black women often found themselves fighting on two fronts. Being both black and female, they had a profound stake in the outcome of both movements. However, the civil rights movement was heavily patriarchal, often excluding women from leadership roles. On the other hand, the feminist movement pressured black women to see themselves as a female first while neglecting the African-American part of their identity. In other words, feminist approaches neglected the importance of racism. This frequently caused role conflict among black feminists. The response was the birth of black feminism, a movement that sought to define the uniqueness of experience of the black woman. By integrating issues of racism and sexism, black feminism spoke directly to the special challenges that accompany multiple layers of disadvantage in society.

The Environmental Movement

The environmental movement is generally seen to encompass two main parts. The first part is the conservation movement, which is concerned with preserving the world's natural resources and species. Green politics has the broader goal of creating social policies that will lead to environmental sustainability.

The movement has its origins in the industrialization of Europe. As the factory system expanded, it created the latent consequence of significantly increasing pollution, particularly in the air and water supplies. Early environmentalists recognized the damage that was being done to the environment, and various independent organizations emerged to raise awareness of the effects of environmental degradation. One such organization was the Sierra Club, founded by John Muir in 1892. However, it was not until after World War II that the various movements began to build significant membership and solidify their message to the public.

While initially, the movement focused on the preservation of natural resources and the reduction of pollution, in recent years the environmental movement has focused increasing energy on raising awareness of global climate change. Environmentalists argue that global climate change is a significant environmental concern because global temperature changes exacerbated by the expulsion of greenhouse gases will impact the habitats of many species, perhaps driving them to extinction. Perhaps the most widely known attempt to bring the concerns of global climate change to the public was the release of the film *An Inconvenient Truth* by former Vice President Al Gore in 2006. However, while this film did increase public debate on the subject of global climate change, not all of the debate focused on ways in which climate change could be averted. Rather, as occurs with most social movements, the film caused a backlash and was criticized as being overtly political, antiscientific, and unnecessarily alarmist.

As a direct result of the environmental movement, governments have begun to adopt policies that seek to balance quality of life with sustainability. For example, in some states, paper and plastic bags have been outlawed and replaced by reusable grocery bags. On the federal level, Congress has taken steps to phase out traditional incandescent light bulbs in favor of the more efficient compact fluorescent (CFL) and LED bulbs. On the community level, many cities and municipalities encourage recycling and backyard composting to reduce the amount of trash in landfills.

The environmental movement has also spawned profitable enterprises. As people become more aware of the benefits of environmental efficiency and sustainability, they desire products that reflect those values. Biodegradable packaging, organic foods, and houses built solely from recycled materials are all examples of the ways in which the marketplace has responded to the increasing demand for sustainable products. No doubt in the future, these demands will continue to increase despite continued criticism of the movement.

John Muir founded the Sierra Club in 1892, which helped usher in the environmental movement.
© CORBIS

The Gay Rights Movement

Properly known as the LGBT (lesbian, gay, bisexual, and transgendered) movement, the gay rights movement remains one of the most controversial social movements in American history. Although the movement has deep historical roots, the American gay rights movement found its voice after the Stonewall Inn in New York's Greenwich Village was raided by police in 1969. The Inn had been converted to a gay bar by its new owners. The establishment was considered the premier gay bar in the city and became a prominent target for law enforcement, who were told to enforce the illegality of homosexuality. Of particular concern to law enforcement were male patrons dressed as females, under the suspicion that they were soliciting sex. The raid turned violent and led to a riot that lasted more than two days. Today, the movement is largely concerned with achieving acceptance and equal rights for people of all sexual orientations and sexualities. This has been done in a variety of ways.

A police raid at the Stonewall Inn set the stage for the LGBT movement in America.

© Emily Anne Epstein/Corbis

Mainstream aspects of the movement have been primarily concerned with achieving social justice through gaining acceptance for LGBT people in society by increasing their presence in media, as well as through legal victories on issues such as marriage equality and the rights of same-sex partners to make medical decisions for one another. Indeed, this aspect of the movement has had considerable success. A growing number of primetime television shows feature gay characters, and LGBT people have been featured increasingly prominently on reality television as well. However, some people have grown increasingly concerned that these representations are strongly stereotypical and do not reflect an accurate picture of homosexuals in society. They fear that such portrayals will result in a backlash against gay people in the real world.

More importantly, the gay rights movement has achieved significant legal victories that have increased the rights of LGBT people in society. Despite some states passing Constitutional amendments defining marriage as being between one man and one woman, same-sex partners have achieved the right to marry in other states FIGURE 17-3. For example, Massachusetts became the first state to legalize marriage for homosexuals in 2004. Six other states followed: Iowa, Vermont, New York, Connecticut, Washington, and New Hampshire. Washington, D.C., has also passed legislation allowing homosexuals to marry. Some states, such as New Jersey, Rhode Island, Colorado, Maine, Nevada, Delaware, Hawaii, Illinois, Oregon, and Wisconsin, have legalized civil unions for same-sex partners, which offer some—but not all—of the legal rights and privileges of a traditional marriage.

Other states have met with considerable resistance to the idea of gay marriage. California legalized gay marriage, only to have it rejected by voters in 2008 with the passing of Proposition 8. The state of Maryland legalized gay marriage as well, but legal challenges have meant that no actual marriages have taken place in the state. States with Constitutional amendments banning gay marriage, such as Ohio, will have to see the amendment repealed prior to any legislation allowing gays to marry.

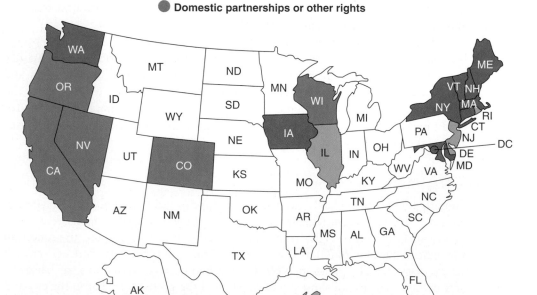

FIGURE 17-3 Gay marriage is gradually becoming more accepted in society (2012).
Source: Adapted from KQED. 2012. The Lowdown. Accessed October 2012 (http://blogs.kqed.org/lowdown/2012/05/10/obamas-evolving-stance-on-gay-marriage-and-the-art-of-the-political-waffle/).

The patchwork differences in the handling of gay marriage have led to considerable controversy over the recognition of marriage between states. For example, if a homosexual couple marries in Vermont but then moves to Ohio, because Ohio does not recognize the validity of the marriage, the couple is not considered married and cannot receive the same rights and privileges as other married couples. It is likely that these kinds of issues will have to be settled by the United States Supreme Court.

As already noted, the LGBT rights movement has met with strong resistance. Many groups rooted in traditional Christian values have sought to vilify homosexuality as sinful or abnormal. However, scientific studies on homosexuality and homosexual relationships have helped to temper the influence of such groups. For example, contrary to the claims of many socially conservative groups, a child raised by gay parents is no more likely to be gay than any other child (Gottman 1989; Patterson 1992). There is also mounting evidence that homosexuality and bisexuality have a strong biological component, largely silencing the claims that homosexuality is a choice or a disease that can be cured (Roughgarden 2009). Rather, as biosociologists like to point out, homosexuality is simply a type of human variation, such as skin color or height. It is part of the biological heritage of the human species (Roughgarden 2009).

The Occupy Wall Street Movement

The Occupy Wall Street movement began in 2011 in New York City after financial markets and housing markets tumbled. The movement centered on issues of corporate profit, economic inequality, and the influence of large corporations on politics. The movement argued that financial greed led to questionable business practices that directly led to the collapse of several large corporations. Deemed "too big to fail," these corporations were bailed out by the government using American tax dollars.

The movement spread to cities across the country, attempting to raise awareness of growing income inequality and corporate influence. Adopting the phrase "We are the 99%," the movement sought to identify itself with the average American by illustrating the separation between the few wealthy individuals who own and influence major segments of the American economy and the rest of Americans, who work for the profit of those few.

Unlike other social movements that have a clear and solid leadership, the Occupy Wall Street movement relied on consensus-based decisions made in large assemblies. As the movement grew, the democratic nature of the movement made focused action increasingly difficult. Additionally, the movement expanded its demands to include jobs, forgiveness of debt, and other financial incentives that were seen by opponents as excessive and irresponsible. The confusion about the actual goals of the movement led some critics to contend that the Occupy Wall Street movement had no real focused demands at all but rather simply adopted the ideas of whoever yelled the loudest.

The Occupy Wall Street movement differs from many social movements in its lack of formal leadership and clear goals.

© Glynnis Jones/Shutterstock,Inc.

Although the movement officially continues, it lost steam after a protest in New York led to the arrest of 700 people who blocked traffic on the Brooklyn Bridge in October 2011. Although many people remain sympathetic to the movement, it has failed to achieve any of its many stated goals.

The Tea Party Movement

The Tea Party Movement is named after the historic Boston Tea Party, in which colonial Americans tossed tea into Boston Harbor to protest an English tax. The modern Tea Party movement arose in protest of increasing government intervention in the lives of citizens, increased government spending, and perceived abandonment of Constitutional provisions.

Unlike the Occupy Wall Street movement, the Tea Party movement articulated a clear set of demands since its inception. Among them is a drastic reduction

The Tea Party movement seeks
a return to constitutionally
limited government.
© Cheryl Casey/Shutterstock, Inc.

in the federal deficit through a decrease in federal spending; a return to Constitutional principles of limited government; and a reduction of taxes. The Tea Party movement seeks to accomplish these goals through peaceful protest, increasing awareness of the issues, and the election of sympathetic politicians. Through this last strategy, the Tea Party has managed to influence the direction of American politics.

However, the Tea Party has faced considerable opposition and even backlash. Using media outlets, Tea Party opponents have managed to associate the movement with evangelical Christians and social conservatives. Many of the political candidates supported by the Tea Party have not been as effective as legislators as anticipated. However, the fiscal conservatism of the Tea Party platform has tended to resonate with large segments of the population concerned about the state of the economy, and the movement has remained politically relevant at the state and local levels.

CONCEPT LEARNING CHECK 17.4   Social Movements in the United States

Match the social movement to the description or event.

_____ 1. The American civil rights movement

_____ 2. The women's movement

_____ 3. The environmental movement

_____ 4. The gay rights movement

_____ 5. The Occupy Wall Street movement

_____ 6. The Tea Party movement

A. Also known as the LGBT movement

B. Advocates for less government and a balanced budget

C. Differs from other social movements in that the leadership is consensus based

D. Occurred in three phases

E. Charles Hamilton Houston was one of the unsung heroes of the movement.

F. Advocates for social policies to combat climate change

17.5 Theories of Social Movements

There are many theories to explain social movements.

■ Explain the main theories of social movements.

As we have already learned, social movements appear only relatively recently in human history. For that reason, it is challenging to understand the circumstances of their emergence in human society. On the other hand, because social movements are intentional and generally longer lasting than other forms of collective behavior, they are somewhat easier to study. A number of theories have been proposed to explain and understand the emergence of social movements.

Mass Society Theory

Mass society theory A theory that suggests that people join social movements because it gives them a sense of belonging to something larger than themselves.

Developed by sociologist William Kornhuaser in 1959, **mass society theory** argues that people join social movements because it gives them a sense of belonging to something larger than themselves. It gives them, in other words, a sense of importance. Whereas people in traditional societies gain a sense of belonging from conformity to society, people in industrial and postindustrial societies gain a sense of belonging from the groups they belong to. The sense of belonging that comes from joining a social movement occurs not only on the personal level but also on the political level in that it is perceived as changing society for the better. That is why, according to Kornhauser, social movements occur only in large-scale, impersonal societies. When people are strongly integrated into society, they have no need to join a social movement. However, as their sense of anomie increases, so does the likelihood of people joining social movements as a means of gaining a connection to society. People join social movements to achieve a sense of belonging and fill a void in their sense of self that is left by an increasingly impersonal society.

Mass society theory has been heavily criticized. Several studies, including one done by McAdam, McCarthy, and Zald (1988), have found that, contrary to the predictions of mass society theory, individuals who had actively participated in social movements had strong family and community ties. They participated in social movements not to overcome isolation but rather to overcome perceived injustices. Similarly, it should be noted that the most marginalized citizens in modern society—the poor and the homeless, for example—rarely join social movements because they are often too worried about day-to-day living to engage in social movements. In fact, most people who join social movements are well adjusted, strongly integrated members of society.

Deprivation Theory

An alternative theory of social movements is deprivation theory. According to this theory, people join social movements because they feel deprived by society in some way. This deprivation could be monetary, but it also could be in terms of status, justice, or privilege. People who feel deprived join social movements to overcome their deprivation. For example, deprivation theory would suggest that the thousands of African Americans who participated in the civil rights movement fought to overcome the material, social, and legal deprivation that segregation imposed.

While this theory may explain some social movements, it still leaves much unexplained. For example, while it is clear that some people join social movements because they feel in some way deprived, clearly not everyone who is deprived will join social movements. In fact, as already noted, the vast majority of people who join social movements are relatively well off in terms of social status, privilege, and money. Additionally, it is clear that while deprivation occurs in every society, not all societies see the emergence of social movements. For example, a century and half ago, French writer Alexis de Tocqueville (1835/1955) noted that while peasants in both French society and German society were living in horribly bad conditions, only the French revolted and overthrew their government. De Tocqueville argued that the French Revolution occurred because, while the conditions of the Germans were remaining poor, the conditions of the French were actually improving.

Why would improving conditions facilitate a social movement? De Tocqueville argued that the reason was **relative deprivation**. As conditions improved for the French, they realized exactly what they lacked relative to the wealthiest classes. French peasants realized they could have much more, and they sought to get for themselves all of the things that they believed they could have. Conversely, the Germans peasants believed that things would never improve and thus never formed a movement to improve their conditions. In other words, when people's expectations exceed their experiences, the perception of deprivation is stronger, making the emergence of a social movement more likely.

Resource Mobilization Theory

Resource mobilization theory argues that for a social movement to be successful, it has to accumulate and mobilize substantial resources. Resources may be tangible, such as money or equipment, or intangible, such as commitments of participants (Freeman 1979). Through the accumulation and distribution of resources, the social movement articulates and clarifies its goals and gains momentum.

Alexis de Tocqueville noticed that relative deprivation can explain some social movements.
© adoc-photos/Corbis

Relative deprivation The feeling of dissatisfaction upon realizing that while conditions are improving, they are improving more for other people than for you.

Resource mobilization theory A theory that suggests for a social movement to be successful, it has to accumulate and mobilize substantial resources.

Proper mobilization of resources is important for the success of a social movement for a couple of reasons. First, resources are important to provide funding for the social movement. In the modern world, money can be used to buy air time on various media outlets, influence people in power, and provide essential equipment for the movement. Money can also help provide intangible resources such as human labor or a positive public image.

Resources also help the movement to achieve an identity and define its agenda. Research by Staggenborg (1988) suggests that social movements that develop formalized bureaucratic structures are better able to sustain movements over time. However, at the same time, social movements that are more informal tend to be more innovative in their tactics and in the use of their resources.

Political Process Theory

Political process theory extends traditional resource mobilization theory by including external forces in understanding the factors that allow a social movement to succeed or fail. The political process approach emphasizes the role of the political structure and public opinion in the outcomes of social movements (Staggenborg 2011). In other words, the ability of a social movement to mobilize resources and the way in which it distributes those resources are dependent upon the social and political climate. For example, when the political climate is hostile to the goals of a social movement, leaders of the social movement may need to devote more resources to combat that hostility than when the political climate is amenable to the goals of the social movement.

Culture Theory

Culture theory is a relatively recently developed theory of social movements. **Culture theory** argues that mobilization of a social movement is dependent upon factors discussed in other theories, such as deprivation theory, but that these theories do not go far enough in understanding how social movements are formed. Culture theory recognizes that social movements do rely on the mobilization of resources. However, it also suggests that cultural symbols are also important to the success of social movements. That is, people will join and participate in a social movement to the degree that they develop shared understandings of the world that lend legitimacy to social movements (Williams 2002). The ways in which a society defines justice and opportunity influence the way in which people perceive the necessity and effectiveness of a social movement. People who perceive that social justice is unattainable through individual action come to see social movements as means to achieving justice. As the social movement gains strength, it develops its own understandings, symbols, and definitions that help build a connection between the movement and its members and that frame its appearance and actions in the larger society.

As an example, consider some of the symbols that represent social movements. The LGBT movement that was discussed earlier in the chapter represents itself with a rainbow to represent the diversity of human sexuality. The black power movement used the symbol of a fist to represent the goal of racial power. The environmental movement uses symbols such as the recycling logo to make the goals they advocate visible and identifiable to people in society. Some symbols remind us to recycle. Others try to move our emotions toward environmental issues, such as pictures of polar bears trapped on an ice floe. Thus, symbols can have a powerful effect on influencing members of a society and shaping their beliefs, values, and behaviors.

New Social Movement Theory

So far, all of the theories of social movements that we have discussed assume that social movements are fundamentally the same. However, **new social movement theory** suggests that social movements in postindustrial societies are substantially different from social movements that occurred in industrial societies (McAdam, McCarthy, and Zald 1988). In industrial Europe, early social movements were focused primarily on

Political process theory A theory of social movements that emphasizes the role of the political structure and public opinion in the outcomes of social movements.

Culture theory A theory that argues that cultural symbols are important for the development of a social movement.

New social movement theory A theory that suggests that social movements in postindustrial societies are substantially different from social movements that occurred in industrial societies.

economic issues such as wages and hours worked. Current social movements are generally focused more on improving social and physical surroundings. For example, the green movement has focused more on environmental policy and sustainability than on economic reform.

Additionally, most modern social movements are international rather than regional. New forms of social media and increasing globalization allow social movements to reach across national boundaries to create international social movements. Again, consider the green movement. Members of Greenpeace, a radical faction of the environmental movement, have lobbied for international bans on whaling, even going to the extreme of attacking foreign whaling ships.

Finally, while traditional social movements were supported primarily by the working class and the poor, modern social movements draw more support from the middle class and the upper middle class. While more affluent people tend to be conservative on economic issues, they tend to be more liberal on social issues. Thus, modern social movements appeal to their sense of social justice. Also, while working-class people have less time to devote to social movements because of the demands of working, more affluent people have more leisure time to devote to social movements.

Marxist Theory

Although less well known as a theory of social movements, **Marxist theory** has nonetheless been highly influential in helping us understand the emergence and development of social movements. The writings of Karl Marx have offered a general model of how to transform the dominant social structure. In fact, Marx's writings (1848/1988) have laid the foundation for many of the early social movements that resulted in improved working conditions and greater social justice.

Of particular importance is the concept of the dialectic FIGURE 17-4. Borrowing from philosopher Friedrich Hegel, Marx discussed how social movements result in a new kind of society. The dialectic begins with the *thesis*—the way things already are. Individuals or groups dislike the thesis for one reason or another and wish to change the status quo. As the idea of change is promoted, it is clarified and refined. It then becomes an *antithesis*—an alternative to the thesis. Eventually, through the process of social change, political upheaval, revolution, or pressure from citizens, a new position emerges that is no longer the thesis but does not meet all the demands of the antithesis. This new position is neither the thesis nor the antithesis but something in the middle. This is called the *synthesis*. The synthesis then becomes the new thesis, and the process is repeated.

Marx saw social change as occurring through this dialectic. However, Marx believed that the dialectic changed little except who was in charge of society. Marx advocated for a revolution of the working class to overthrow the wealthy. Through this revolution, the dialectic would end in a perfect society in which private property was abolished. The need for further social change—for further social movements— would vanish.

Marxist theory A theory of social movements that suggests that societies change through a dialectical process.

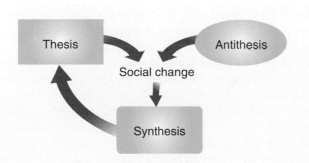

FIGURE 17-4 Marx used the dialectic process to explain social change.

CONCEPT LEARNING CHECK 17.5   Theories of Social Movements

Identify the appropriate theory of social movements.

_____ 1. Social movements are caused by the realization that as social conditions improve, the improvements do not affect all groups equally.

_____ 2. A social movement needs to appropriately accumulate and mobilize substantial resources in order to be successful.

_____ 3. Social movements need to develop shared understandings with the larger society in order to get and maintain members.

_____ 4. External factors such as the political and social climate are important for the success of a social movement.

_____ 5. People join social movements to gain a sense of belonging to something larger than themselves.

_____ 6. Social movements in the modern era are different than social movements in the industrial era.

_____ 7. Social movements are part of a larger dialectic that models how societies change.

A. Political process theory

B. Relative deprivation theory

C. Marxist theory

D. Resource mobilization theory

E. New social movement theory

F. Mass society theory

G. Culture theory

17.6 Social Change

There are several convenient models to explain how societies change over time.

- Illustrate the theories of social change.

All societies change. Of course, some societies change faster than others. Sometimes the change is predictable; often, however, changes in society are unpredictable. For example, the terrorist attacks that occurred on September 11, 2001, were unexpected, yet they changed the course of history and affected many aspects of society.

Sociologists have been fascinated by social change. As we already learned, Karl Marx discussed social change as a process of dialectics. Nearly every prominent social theorist has developed a theory of social change. Generally, these theories can be grouped into four major categorizations: natural cycles, evolution, conflict over power, and technology.

Natural Cycles

Natural cycle theories attempt to explain the rise and fall of entire civilizations. For example, what forces led to the successful expansion of the Roman Empire? What forces led to its decline? In general, natural cycle theories approach civilizations as if they were organisms, complete with birth, growth, decline, and senescence. There is evidence that supports this cycle. The deeper question is why the cycle seems to be universal, regardless of the civilization's place in history or its geography.

Historian Arnold Toynbee (1946) offered one explanation. Toynbee suggested that every civilization faces challenges to its existence. Groups within the society develop solutions to those challenges, which often conflict with the ruling class. For a while, the ruling class is able to deal effectively with these challenges. However, as the empire grows, external challenges consume more and more of the ruling elite's energy and time. The ruling class becomes less and less able to deal with internal challenges. Eventually, the ruling elite must turn to force to keep the masses under control. This leads to a fracturing of society that eventually causes the decline of the empire. This decline is rarely sudden. In fact, the decline may occur over many generations. However, Toynbee notes that this decline is inevitable.

Evolution

So-called evolutionary theories of how societies change are more akin to development than to evolution. Generally speaking, these theories suggest that societies develop from lower forms to higher forms. At first, these theories were unilinear. That is, they supposed that all societies develop along the same linear trajectory that begins from the simplest and progresses to the more complex. Although there are many ways in which this linear process may be categorized, the most influential has come from Lewis Morgan. Morgan suggested that all societies proceed through three stages: savagery, barbarism, and civilization.

Later evolutionary theories of social change rejected the unilinear view and opted instead for a multilinear view. Rather than assuming that all societies follow the same sequence of change, multilinear theories propose that there are many developmental routes that lead to the same outcome. For example, although all paths eventually lead to industrialization, there are many ways to get there. Regardless of whether development is perceived of as unilinear or multilinear, all evolutionary theories assume that societies go through phases of cultural progress. As they develop, cultures become more complex, more sophisticated. That is, they will all eventually advance to a higher state.

Critics of evolutionary theories point out that such approaches are ethnocentric because they presume that more advanced cultures are superior to less advanced ones. For example, Lewis Morgan, being British, naturally assumed that British culture was the pinnacle of civilization and that all other societies aspire to the British ideal. As sociologists gain an appreciation for the diversity and richness of all cultures, the ideas of the evolutionary theorists become increasingly less palatable. In fact, there is mounting evidence that all societies are equally complex. Many critics also contend that Western culture is in decline, with high rates of violence, poverty, and war.

Conflict over Power

The conflict-over-power approach to social change has its origins in the dialectic of Karl Marx. With each thesis, the seeds of its own destruction are sown through the development of the antithesis and the creation of the synthesis. According to the conflict-over-power theory, many of the antitheses are conflicts over who will gain or maintain power in society. This process occurs both between groups within societies as well as between societies. For example, as relative deprivation theory points out, people who see social progress desire to get what they perceive as their fair share and will often act in direct conflict with the status quo to get it. Between societies, conflicts over power often occur in violent clashes or as indirect competition. For instance, when one nation in a region gets nuclear weapons, other nations in the same region feel the need to also possess nuclear weapons, not just as a means of defense but also to assert their power in the region.

Technology and Social Change

No one can dispute the notion that technology affects the ways in which societies change. The first person to formally develop the ways in which technology affects social change was William Ogburn (1922) FIGURE 17-5. Ogburn said that technology changes society by three main processes.

Ogburn defined *invention* as the combining of existing materials to form new ones. Although most people think of inventions as material items, Ogburn believed that inventions could also be ideas or social interactions as well. As an example, Ogburn offers the idea of democracy, which could be considered an invention of Greek civilization. Such an invention, though immaterial, has been exceptionally influential in human history, changing people's relationships with one another for centuries.

FIGURE 17-5 William Ogburn argued that technology can strongly influence social change.

© Bettmann/CORBIS

Diffusion The spread of invention or discovery from one culture to another.

Cultural lag The phenomenon of some elements of a culture changing faster than others.

The second way in which technology influences social change is through *discovery*. Ogburn defined this as a new way to see reality. This differs from invention in that while invention is created, discovery is found. The reality already exists; it is just seen for the first time. As one example, when Christopher Columbus landed on North America, it was always there—it just had not been found by that part of the world yet.

Finally, Ogburn stressed that diffusion is a strong force of social change. **Diffusion** is defined as the spread of discovery or invention from one area to another. Diffusion can have a significant impact on society. There are numerous examples of diffusion in history. As the Roman empire was in its ascent, it borrowed religious ideas from the declining Greek city-states. Pasta, invented by the Chinese, was brought by explorer Marco Polo from the Orient to Italy, where it established itself as the cornerstone of Italian cuisine. Democracy, too, diffused from the Greek Isles to other parts of the globe, forming the foundational structure of many contemporary civilizations.

Of course, not all elements of society are affected by invention, diffusion, and discovery in the same way. Sometimes only certain parts of society are affected. Sometimes different social institutions change at different rates. Ogburn coined the term **cultural lag** to refer to how some elements of culture change faster than others. Technology, for example, often changes faster than a society's ability to ethically grasp the meaning of technological change. For instance, although it is now possible to clone animals, society has largely failed to develop new moral understandings that incorporate cloning into the value system of society. As the pace of technological change accelerates, cultural lag will doubtless continue to occur as we struggle to adapt our lives to rapidly changing technologies.

Ogburn's theory has been criticized as being one directional. In other words, while Ogden showed how technology affects social change, he failed to acknowledge how social change affects technology. As just one of many possible examples, consider how the graying of America—the fact that the average population of America is getting older—is driving the need for new medical technologies. Thus, at best, Ogburn's theory can be considered incomplete. It should be noted that Ogburn never indicated that technology was the only force for social change, nor did Ogburn suggest that people or societies are at the mercy of technology. However, he did argue that material culture usually changes before symbolic culture. It appears that most of the time, this directional rule holds true.

CONCEPT LEARNING CHECK 17.6   Social Change

Fill in the blank.

1. According to _____, societies change through a process of development that proceeds from lower forms to higher forms.

2. Ogburn argued that some areas of society change faster than others. Ogburn called this _____.

3. The _____ approach to social change has its roots in the dialectic of Karl Marx.

4. According to _____, the rise and fall of civilizations can be explained in a way that is analogous to the way in which an organism grows and dies.

Visual Overview Stages of Social Movements

Despite great variance in the scope and method of social movements, sociologists have noticed that all social movements progress through a series of stages. These stages track the birth, development, and death of social movements in society.

Stage 1: Emergence

The claims making process convinces people that there is something that needs to be changed about society.

Stage 4: Decline

Although some social movements last longer than others, all social movements eventually enter a period of decline.

Stage 2: Coalescence

The movement's message and goals are solidified; leadership emerges; a strategy is developed to improve morale and grow the movement.

Stage 3: Bureaucratization

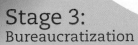

The movement adapts their tactics and resources to the political climate, which often results in the formalization of the leadership structure and tactics of the movement.

Visual Summary Collective Behavior, Social Movements, and Social Change

17.1 Collective Behavior

- Collective behavior refers to behaviors involving a large number of individuals that are usually unplanned, often controversial, and sometimes even dangerous.
- Collectivities are defined as large numbers of individuals whose minimal interaction occurs without the benefit of conventional norms.

- There are two general kinds of collectivities: localized collectivities and dispersed collectivities.
- Localized collectivities are characterized by the close proximity of individuals and include riots, mobs, and crowds.
- Dispersed collectivities are spread out over a large geographic area and include rumors, fads, and gossip.

17.2 Social Movements

- Social movements include any organized activity that encourages or discourages social change.

- There are four general kinds of social movements: Alternative, redemptive, reformatory, and revolutionary.
- People join social movements for a variety of reasons.

17.3 Stages of Social Movements

- All social movements go through four identifiable stages: emergence, coalescence, bureaucratization, and decline.

- The purpose of social movements is to encourage or resist social change.

17.4 Social Movements in the United States

- Social movements in the United States offer examples of key aspects of social movements.
- The American civil rights movement has helped to reduce discrimination against African Americans in society.
- The women's movement occurred in three stages, each with its own goals to advance the rights of women.
- The environmental movement has evolved to cover both the conservation movement and green politics.

- The gay rights movement remains one of the most controversial social movements in American history.
- The Occupy Wall Street movement is a recent social movement that differs from other social movements in that it has no formal leadership structure.
- The Tea Party movement is an American countermovement that seeks governmental fiscal responsibility and accountability.

17.5 Theories of Social Movements

- Mass society theory argues that people join social movements because it gives them a sense of belonging to something larger than themselves.
- Deprivation theory suggests that people join social movements because they feel deprived by society in some way.
- Resource mobilization theory argues that for a social movement to be successful, it has to accumulate and mobilize substantial resources.
- Political process theory expands resource mobilization theory by suggesting that external forces also matter in determining whether a social movement succeeds or fails.

- Culture theory argues that the success of a social movement is dependent upon the cultural symbols that help to define the social movement.
- New social movement theory suggests that social movements in the contemporary world are fundamentally different than social movements during the Industrial Revolution.
- Marxist theory describes the process of the dialectic as a way that societies change.

17.6 Social Change

- There are four general theories to describe the ways in which societies change.
- Natural cycle theory believes that all societies follow the same cycle of growth, zenith, and death.
- Evolution theory suggests that societies proceed from lower to higher forms.

- Conflict-over-power theory suggests that social change occurs because of competition over power in society.
- Technology theory suggests that technology acts as a strong force for social change.

17.1 Collective Behavior

1. Pete just began running down the street with a bunch of people with torches who are looting the Kwik-E-Mart. Pete has just joined a:
   A. mob.
   B. crowd.
   C. aggregate.
   D. collectivity.

2. Bella likes to spread unconfirmed information about the company she works for. Bella is involved in a:
   A. mob.
   B. rumor.
   C. crowd.
   D. mass behavior.

3. Bella also likes to spread rumors about her coworkers, suggesting that some of them are stealing from the company or having extramarital affairs. Bella is involved in:
   A. public opinion.
   B. collective behavior.
   C. mob.
   D. gossip.

4. Cletus developed a pamphlet that seeks to change people's mind about capital punishment by appealing to their feelings about killing people. Cletus has developed:
   A. rumor.
   B. gossip.
   C. propaganda.
   D. public opinion.

5. Desiree and her friends just started buying Pop-n-Go cards, a new game sweeping schools across the country. Desiree is engaged in:
   A. fad.
   B. fashion.
   C. rumor.
   D. propaganda.

17.2 Social Movements

6. Kianna has been talking to all of her friends, trying to convince them to join her social movement to save Wels catfish from extinction. Kianna argues that her movement is important because not only is the Wels catfish a majestic beast, but it is also an integral part of the local ecosystem. Kianna is involved in the process of:
   A. propaganda.
   B. claims making.
   C. fashion.
   D. rumor.

7. Kellen is a member of a social movement designed to completely change the way people are compensated for their work. Kellen is involved in what kind of a social movement?
   A. Reformative
   B. Redemptive
   C. Revolutionary
   D. Alternative

8. Gomer just joined a group to help him recover from his addiction to comic books. Gomer has joined what kind of a social movement?
   A. Revolutionary
   B. Redemptive
   C. Reformative
   D. Alternative

9. Arturo joined a social movement to promote perfect attendance among college students. What kind of social movement best describes the one Arturo joined?
   A. Reformative
   B. Redemptive
   C. Alternative
   D. Revolutionary

17.3 Stages of Social Movements

10. Glendon has worked tirelessly to promote his new social movement and increase membership. What social movement stage is Glendon's social movement in?
   A. Emergence
   B. Coalescence
   C. Bureaucratization
   D. Decline

11. Pascal's social movement has just used donations it collected to buy some television time. The members also started a website via which people can make donations to the movement. This social movement is in what stage?
   A. Emergence
   B. Coalescence
   C. Bureaucratization
   D. Decline

12. Ivana has just retired from her position as the director of her social movement after having accomplished her main goal of improving worker conditions in coal mines. Her movement is likely in what stage of development?
   A. Emergence
   B. Coalescence
   C. Bureaucratization
   D. Decline

17.4 Social Movements in the United States

13. Charles Hamilton Houston was one of many people working behind the scenes in this important social movement.
   A. Tea Party movement
   B. Women's movement
   C. Civil rights movement
   D. Occupy Wall Street movement

14. Along with Harriet Martineau, Charlotte Perkins Gillman was an influential writer who advocated for basic women's rights. These two authors were instrumental in what wave of the women's movement?
   A. First-wave feminism
   B. Second-wave feminism
   C. Third-wave feminism
   D. Fourth-wave feminism

15. Rachel was reading a book by one of the founders of second-wave feminism. In this book, the author objected to the portrayal of women by the mainstream media. Rachel is reading a book by:
   A. Harriet Martineau.
   B. Charles Hamilton Houston.
   C. Margaret Sanger.
   D. Betty Friedan.

16. Kennedy just joined a social movement that has no formal, structured leadership. She most likely joined which social movement?
   A. Tea Party
   B. Women's movement
   C. Occupy Wall Street
   D. Environmental movement

17.5 Theories of Social Movements

17. Darnell is working as a volunteer for a social movement. His job is to get supplies and donations for the movement to expand. What social movement theory should Darnell become familiar with to help his task?
   A. Deprivation theory
   B. Resource mobilization theory
   C. Culture theory
   D. New social movement theory

18. Clem and Mia have mobilized the residents of their neighborhood who are angry that a new park on the other side of town included a playground, while a park newly built in their neighborhood did not. Which social movement theory explains the anger of the neighborhood?
   A. Political process theory
   B. Culture theory
   C. Mass society theory
   D. Relative deprivation theory

19. Pascal has been working on developing a logo for the social movement he joined. He needs to develop a logo that will communicate the intent of the movement to the general public. What theory of social movements might aid Pascal in his task?
   A. Culture theory
   B. New social movement theory
   C. Relative deprivation theory
   D. Mass society theory

17.6 Social Change

20. Petula has been analyzing how Eastern empires have risen and fallen throughout history. She is particularly interested in what social forces allowed these empires to expand. What theory of social change best explains Petula's focus?
   A. Evolution
   B. Conflict over power
   C. Natural cycles
   D. Technology

21. Boris has just written a book that argues that societies move from a period of simplicity into a period of complexity and then into a period of complementarity. What theory of social change is Boris using?
   A. Evolution
   B. Conflict over power
   C. Natural cycles
   D. Technology

22. Kevin just wrote a book that argues that the discovery of cheese was the single most important event in European history. What theory of social change is Kevin using?
   A. Conflict over power
   B. Evolution
   C. Natural cycles
   D. Technology

23. Mervin was reading how the fork was invented in China but spread throughout the rest of the world as the principal utensil in the world. This is an example of:
   A. cultural lag.
   B. invention.
   C. diffusion.
   D. discovery.

CHAPTER ESSAY QUESTIONS

1. List and describe three ways in which social movements shape public opinion.

2. List and describe three ways in which public opinion can shape social movements.

3. Discuss why the wealthy and powerful may want to support a social movement.

CHAPTER PROJECTS

INDIVIDUAL PROJECTS

1. Choose a societal topic of interest and then go online to search for organizations that are working toward social change regarding this topic. Analyze their efforts using chapter information.

2. Write an analysis paper making societal predictions 50 years from now. Use the chapter models for social change to guide your analysis.

3. Choose some item of material culture. Research the history of the item. Then prepare a presentation that shows where the item came from, how it diffused to other cultures, and how it has changed over time.

GROUP PROJECTS

1. Create a social movement! Consider what problem you would like to solve, what group you would like to target, how you would target them, and what your goals would be. Then create a pamphlet or flyer that convinces people to join your social movement.

2. Go online to learn about flash mobs. Analyze what you have learned using chapter information and key terms. Present your group's analysis to the class.

3. Choose one of the social movements in the United States. and go online to learn about the global effects and influence of this movement. Write a summary of your findings.

CHAPTER DISCUSSION QUESTIONS

1. Discuss how social media technology is changing how social movements recruit members and resources.

2. What factors are necessary for the formation of a mob? What forces are necessary for the formation of a riot? Discuss how the social structure influences which form of social action will emerge.

3. Share with the class examples of collective behavior that reflect collectivity including the different types of crowds that can form.

4. Discuss how celebrity rumors and gossip serve the function of maintaining social solidarity in an impersonal society.

5. What kind of propaganda emerged in the last election and do you think it was successful in swaying public opinion? Why or why not?

6. Share with the class examples of fashion trends or fads that did not follow the usual patterns but instead moved from lower socioeconomic groups upward. In what ways can social media affect the usual patterns related to fashion?

7. Discuss how recent natural, technological, or intentional disasters may have been catalysts for new or existing social movements.

8. Share with the class a social movement that you might be inclined to join. What claims making processes may have convinced you that this social movement needs public attention? What patterns emerged in the class? Do you notice any examples of mission drift?

9. Vote on the top three current successful social movements and discuss which theory best explains their successes including mass society theory, relative deprivation, resource mobilization, or culture theory among others.

10. How does the Internet encourage or limit social change in terms of both diffusion and cultural lag?

Alternative social movement
Bureaucratization
Claims making
Coalescence
Collective behavior
Collectivity
Conspicuous consumption
Crowd
Cultural lag
Culture theory
Decline
Diffusion

Disaster
Emergence
Fad
Fashion
Gossip
Marxist theory
Mass behavior
Mass society theory
Mission drift
Mob
Moral panic
New social movement theory

Panic
Political process theory
Propaganda
Public opinion
Redemptive social movement
Reformative social movement
Relative deprivation
Resource mobilization theory
Revolutionary social movement
Riot
Rumors
Social movement

ANSWERS TO CONCEPT LEARNING CHECKS

17.1 Collective Behavior

1. A [mob] is a highly emotional crowd that pursues a destructive or violent goal.

2. Unconfirmed information that people spread is called [rumor].

3. Sociologists use the term [public opinion] to refer to widespread attitudes or beliefs about a particular issue.

4. An [intentional disaster] is a manmade event that causes extensive harm to people and property.

5. A large number of individuals whose minimal interaction occurs without the benefit of conventional norms is called a [collectivity].

17.2 Social Movements

1. A trade union is seeking to improve workers' rights. [C. Reformative social movement]

2. The new People's Popular Party wants to overthrow the government and replace it with a socialist utopia. [A. Revolutionary social movement]

3. The New Church of the Better Individual seeks to convince people to lead a morally pure life style by forsaking all material possessions. [D. Alternative social movement]

4. Mothers Against Drunk Driving [B. Redemptive social movement]

17.3 Stages of Social Movements

1. The Brotherhood of Pens and Pencils just rented its first office space. It hired a secretary to take phone calls and created a public relations division. [D. Bureaucratization]

2. Bill and Joe are angry that lots of cities prohibit chickens as yard pets. They have gathered a group of people to begin a petition drive in their neighborhood. [C. Emergence]

3. At a regional meeting of the Hesperus Alliance, leaders have just laid out plans for their first press conference. They hope that this will increase membership and get people excited about their movement. [A. Coalescence]

4. The Patsy Petunia Club achieved their goal of promoting petunias for the public city gardens; membership dropped 60%. [B. Decline]

17.4 Social Movements in the United States

1. The American civil rights movement [E. Charles Hamilton Houston was one of unsung heroes of the movement.]

2. The women's movement [D. Occurred in three phases]

3. The environmental movement [F. Advocates for social policies to combat climate change]

4. The gay rights movement [A. Also known as the LGBT movement]

5. The Occupy Wall Street movement [C. Differs from other social movements in that the leadership is consensus based]

6. The Tea Party movement [B. Advocates for less government and a balanced budget]

17.5 Theories of Social Movements

1. Social movements are caused by the realization that as social conditions improve, the improvements do not affect all groups equally. [B. Relative deprivation theory]

2. A social movements needs to appropriately accumulate and mobilize substantial resources in order to be successful. [D. Resource mobilization theory]

3. Social movements need to develop shared understandings with the larger society in order to get and maintain members. [G. Culture theory]

4. External factors such as the political and social climate are important for the success of a social movement. [A. Political process theory]

5. People join social movements to gain a sense of belonging to something larger than themselves. [F. Mass society theory]

6. Social movements in the modern era are different than social movements in the industrial era. [E. New social movement theory]

7. Social movements are part of a larger dialectic that models how societies change. [C. Marxist theory]

17.6 Social Change

1. According to [evolutionary theory], societies change through a process of development that proceeds from lower forms to higher forms.

2. Ogburn argued that some areas of society change faster than others. Ogburn called this [cultural lag].

3. The [conflict over power] approach to social change has its roots in the dialectic of Karl Marx.

4. According to [natural cycles theory], the rise and fall of civilizations can be explained in a way that is analogous to the way in which an organism grows and dies.

ANSWERS TO CHAPTER REVIEW TEST

17.1 Collective Behavior

1. A. A mob is defined as a highly emotional crowd that pursues a destructive or violent goal.

2. B. Rumors refer to unconfirmed information that people spread, usually by word of mouth.

3. D. Gossip refers to rumors about the personal affairs of a person.

4. C. Information given with the intention of shaping public opinion is called propaganda.

5. A. An unconventional social pattern embraced briefly and enthusiastically by members of a society is called a fad.

17.2 Social Movements

6. B. Claims making is the process of trying to convince people that the cause of a social movement is important so that people will join the movement.

7. C. Revolutionary social movements seek to radically reform entire societies.

8. B. Redemptive social movements target specific groups or people to make radical changes to their lives, such as overcoming addiction.

9. C. Alternative social movements seek to change only a very limited aspect of society.

17.3 Stages of Social Movements

10. A. During the emergence stage, the process of claims making convinces people that there is something that needs to be changed about society.

11. B. During the coalescence stage, social movements begin to acquire and mobilize resources.

12. D. When social movements accomplish their goals, they enter a period of decline.

17.4 Social Movements in the United States

13. C. Charles Hamilton Houston was the architect behind the successful Supreme Court case to end racial segregation in America's schools.

14. A. First-wave feminism had the goal of advocating for the basic rights of women.

15. D. Betty Friedan wrote *The Feminine Mystique* and is generally considered the founder of second-wave feminism.

16. C. The Occupy Wall Street movement is unique in its lack of formal, structured leadership.

17.5 Theories of Social Movements

17. B. Resource mobilization theory argues that for a social movement to be successful, it has to accumulate and mobilize substantial resources.

18. D. Relative deprivation theory suggests that as people's lives improve, they often get angry because they realize that they could have so much more.

19. A. Culture theory suggests that cultural symbols are important to the success of a social movement.

17.6 Social Change

20. C. Natural cycles theory seeks to understand how social forces lead to the rise and fall of societies.

21. A. Evolution theories of social change argue that societies develop from lower to higher states.

22. D. The technology theory of social change suggests that technology is an important source of social change.

23. C. Diffusion is defined as the spread of discovery or invention from one culture to another.

ANSWERS TO CHAPTER ESSAY QUESTIONS

1. Social movements can shape public opinion in several ways. First, social movements need to convince people that a problem exists in society that needs fixing. This means that society will be shaped by the perception of the problem. Social movements also have to convince society that the problem is more important than other problems. Thus, social movements influence the competition for ideas that occur in society. When this influence occurs, social movements also have to influence the way in which society addresses the problem—how many resources are necessary and appropriate to solve the problem. Finally, social movements can influence public opinion in the ways in which they shape public views of government. Whether or not the government responds to social movement—and the way in which it responds—may influence the way in which society views the effectiveness and responsiveness of government.

2. Public opinion may shape social movements in a number of ways. First, as society socializes an individual, it influences how that individual identifies and interprets the problems in society. For example, a person socialized toward traditional family values may feel that gay marriage is a problem in society, whereas a person socialized toward more liberal social values may not. Second, socioeconomic status may influence whether people join

social movements. As we have learned, most of the people who join social movements are middle class. Therefore, even if a poor person were to benefit from the success of a social movement, he or she is less likely to join.

3. The wealthy and powerful might benefit from social movements more indirectly than directly. However, they definitely benefit. It is often in their interest to support social movements—even ones that might cost them money or power in the short run—because their support of social movements may increase their power or wealth in the long run. The popularity that a wealthy or powerful individual might gain from supporting a social movement actually increases that person's social power because it makes it more likely that people will reciprocate support. Conversely, a person who dismisses or opposes a powerful social movement may find his or her company disliked or even boycotted. The monetary damage aside, the damage to the reputation of the individual may negatively affect the person's social power and long-term interests.

REFERENCES

Blumer, H. 1969. "Collective Behavior." Pp. 65–121 in *Principles of Sociology*. Third edition, edited by Alfred McClung Lee. New York: Barnes and Noble Books.

de Tocqueville, A. 1835(1955). *Democracy in America*. Edited by J. P. Mayer and Max Lerner. New York: Harper & Row.

Erikson, K. 1994. *A New Species of Trouble: Explorations in Disaster, Trauma, and Community*. New York: Norton.

Freeman, J. 1979. "Resource Mobilization and Strategy: A Model for Analyzing Social Movement Organization Actions." Pp. 167–189 in *The Dynamics of Social Movements: Resource Mobilization, Social Control, and Tactics*, edited by Morris N. Zald and John D. McCarthy. Cambridge, MA: Winthrop.

Friedan, B. 1963. *The Feminine Mystique*. New York: Dell.

Gottman, J. S. 1989. "Children of Gay and Lesbian Parents." *Marriage and Family Review* 14(3–4):177–196.

Kornhauser, W. 1959. *The Politics of Mass Society*. New York: Free Press.

LeBon, G. 1865. *The Crowd: A Study of the Popular Mind*. New York: Viking Press.

Martineau, H. 1837. *Society in America*. London: Sauders and Otley.

Marx, K. 1848(1988). *The Communist Manifesto*. New York: Norton.

McAdam, D., J. D. McCarthy, and M. N. Zald. 1988. "Social Movements." Pp. 695–737 in *The Handbook of Sociology*, edited by Neil Smelser. Newbury Park, CA: Sage.

McPhail, C., and R. T. Wohlstein. 1983. "Individual and Collective Behaviors within Gatherings, Demonstrations, and Riots." *Annual Review of Sociology* 9:579–600.

Mills, C. W. 1959. *The Sociological Imagination*. New York: Holt.

Morgan, L. 1877. *Ancient Society*. New York: Holt.

Nicholson, N. 2001. "Evolved to Chat: The New World of Social Gossip." *Psychology Today* (May/June):41–45.

Ogburn, W. F. 1922. *Social Change with Respect to Culture and Human Nature*. New York: W. B. Heubsch.

Patterson, C. 1992. "Children of Lesbian and Gay Parents." *Child Development* 63(5):1025–1042.

Piven, F. F., and R. A. Cloward. 1977. *Poor People's Movements: Why They Succeed, How They Fail*. New York: Pantheon Books.

Roughgarden, J. 2009. *Evolution's Rainbow: Diversity, Gender, and Sexuality in Nature and People*. Los Angeles: University of California Press.

Simmel, G. 1904(1971). "Fashion." In *Georg Simmel: On Individuality and Social Forms*, edited by Donald N. Levine. Chicago: University of Chicago Press.

Staggenborg, S. 1988. "The Consequences of Professionalism and Formalization in the Pro-Choice Movement." *American Sociological Review* 53:585–605.

Staggenborg, S. 2011. *Social Movements*. New York: Oxford University Press.

Tilly, C. 1978. *From Mobilization to Revolution*. Reading, MA: Addison-Wesley.

Toynbee, A. 1946. *A Study of History*. New York: Oxford University Press.

Turner, R., and L. Killiam. 1987. *Collective Behavior*. Third edition. Englewood Cliffs, NJ: Prentice Hall.

Veblen, T. 1899(1953). *The Theory of the Leisure Class*. New York: New American Library.

Williams, J. E. 2002. "Linking Belief to Collective Action: Politicized Religious Beliefs and the Civil Rights Movement." *Sociological Forum* 17(2):203–222.

Glossary

Absolute monarchs Claim a monopoly on power based on divine right.

Absolute poverty A condition of deprivation in which people have too little money or other resources to obtain all they need for basic survival.

Achieved status A status earned through some effort or activity within your control and facilitated by opportunity.

Adult socialization Socialization that occurs as the individual takes on adult roles.

Advance directive (AD) A statement by an individual communicating preferences for his or her own health care under possible future circumstances that might make it impossible for the patient to make those decisions.

Affirmative action Policies that mandates preferential hiring, promotion, and college admission of historically disadvantaged groups.

Age cohort A subpopulation born within the same time frame who experience different ages as they grow older together.

Age dependency ratio for the elderly The ratio of people 65 and older to the working-age population.

Ageism Prejudice and discrimination against the elderly, usually based on negative stereotypes.

Agency The capacity for people to act to change their own lives and to influence others.

Agents of socialization Groups, individuals, or circumstances that socialize the individual.

Aggregate People who occupy the same space and time but who have no common goals, purpose, or sense of belonging.

Aging in place Pattern typical of many rural areas where the young adults leave for job and educational opportunities in more urban areas, leaving a region with more older adults.

Agnosticism Doubt or skepticism about the existence of God.

Agricultural economies Economies in which agricultural production is efficient, leading to a food surplus, permitting a more complex division of labor and making it possible to settle permanently in one place.

Agricultural societies Societies made possible by the invention of the plow drawn by animals, making agricultural production vastly more efficient, leading to an even greater food surplus, permitting a much more complex division of labor.

Agriculture Farming using machinery powered by engines.

AIDS (acquired immune deficiency syndrome) The final stage of HIV infection in which people have badly weakened immune systems.

Alienation Marx's term for the limitations in life choices that accompany low social status.

Alienation from work The breakdown of the natural connections people have with their work and with other people through their work.

Alternative medicine Several approaches to medicine that fall outside scientific medicine.

Alternative social movement A social movement that seeks to change only very limited aspects of society.

Alzheimer's disease An incurable degeneration of the brain leading to a progressive loss of mental capacity.

Angel investors Affluent individuals who provide initial capital for a business startup, usually in return for a share of ownership.

Anomie A feeling of normlessness caused by a disconnect from the dominant norms of society.

Anorexia nervosa An intense fear of becoming fat and a distorted image of one's own body, leading someone to drastically reduce body weight through starving.

Anticipatory socialization Learning to play a role before entering it.

Antiracism Ideologies or practices that seek to eliminate or ameliorate racism.

Ascribed status A status that a person takes on involuntarily, either through birth or through other circumstances.

Ascribed social statuses The categories into which one is born.

Asexual A person who has no sexual attraction to other people regardless of their sex.

Assembly line A mode of production in which a complex task is broken into individual tasks, with each worker performing only one or a few of the tasks repeatedly.

Assimilation The adopting of the values, beliefs, and practices of the dominant culture.

Associated When the values of one variable depend on or can be predicted from the values of the other variable.

Asymmetric warfare War between opponents with significantly different military power and, consequently, significantly different tactics.

Atheism The absence of a belief in God or the denial of belief in God.

Authoritarian governments Concentrated power in the hands of a strong leader who often rules for life and may exercise absolute power.

Authoritarian leaders Leaders who take personal charge of the task, dictate the jobs of other group members, and expect them to follow orders.

Authoritarian parenting A dictatorial style of parenting in which unquestioning obedience is expected from children.

Authoritarian personality theory Authoritarianism is a personality trait of individuals that is the result of a poor upbringing.

Authoritative parenting A democratic style of parenting in which parents give guidance and encouragement with limited freedom.

Authority Power that has been institutionalized and is recognized as legitimate by the people over whom it is exercised.

Authority ranking One of Fiske's four elementary forms of social action, in which one person has more status or authority than another and can thus dictate the terms of interaction.

Baby boom A period of years during which the birth rate is elevated.

Back stage behavior Behaviors that are not part of the role being played.

Background assumptions Understandings of the way the world works that are deeply embedded in our social understanding.

Balancing equation (sometimes called the basic demographic equation) A simple equation that expresses population growth as a function of four factors.

Biased Results that are systematically different from those of the population in a specific direction.

Bilateral descent A System by which members of ociety trace kinship from both the mother's and father's side.

Binge drinking Widely recognized as consuming four or more alcoholic drinks per occasion for women or five or more for men.

Binge eating disorder Occurs when the person engages in recurrent binge eating (eating too much at a sitting).

Biological age Changes in physical characteristics such as graying hair, wrinkles, declining health, reduced strength, and greater susceptibility to injuries.

Bisexual Person is attracted to members of either sex.

Blended family A family created when people with children from previous relationships remarry. Also known as a stepfamily.

Blue-collar jobs Manual-labor occupations often having relatively low status, such as machinist, assembly-line worker, truck driver, or auto mechanic.

Bonded labor An exploitive arrangement in which the victim becomes indebted to undefined or exploitative terms, making it impossible to pay off the debt.

Bourgeoisie (capitalists) Those owning the means of production, including land, raw materials, forests, factories, and machines in a capitalist economy.

Brain drain/bright flight The emigration of highly skilled people from a country.

Brutalization effect The idea that executions increase the rate of violence in society.

Bulimia nervosa Binge-eating followed by self-induced vomiting.

Bullying Repeatedly being mean to another child.

Bureaucracy The primary design principle of modern formal organizations, based on a hierarchical structure of authority, codified rules and regulations, and principles of fairness and efficiency.

Bureaucratic inertia The tendency of a bureaucracy to perpetuate itself over time.

Bureaucratic ritualism A focus on rules and regulations to the point of undermining the goals of the organization.

Bureaucratization The tendency for a social movement to adopt the characteristics of a bureaucratic organization to achieve its goals.

Capitalism An economy based on private ownership of wealth, competition, profit, and noninterference by the government.

Capitalists Marx's term for the owners of the means of production; people who own large businesses employing many workers.

Case studies Participant observation studies of a single setting, usually constituting an intensive analysis of a single unit or case.

Caste system A system of social stratification based on birth.

Causes of death are categories of reasons attributed for deaths on birth certificates.

Census A survey of the entire population of a country or region counting the number of people and their characteristics.

Census undercount The number of people missed in a census and includes illegal immigrants, the homeless, and vagrants, as well as people who, for some reason, did not want to be counted.

Central cities The original cities in metropolitan areas, often surrounded by suburbs.

Charisma Personal qualities that make people want to follow you.

Charismatic authority Power made legitimate by a leader's exceptional personal characteristics and emotional appeal to his or her followers.

Charter school A school that is run by private individuals or corporations but funded with public tax dollars.

Chronological age The number of years since birth.

Church A type of religious organization that is formally recognized and is well integrated into society.

City-states Small centers of power restricted to cities in which a monarch ruled the city surrounding a castle.

Claims making The process of trying to convince people that the cause of a social movement is so important that they should join the movement.

Clan system A stratification system in which social standing is based on membership in an extended network of relatives.

Class (social class) Ranking in a stratification system based on either one's level of wealth and income (Max Weber) or one's relationship to the means of production (Karl Marx).

Class system A stratification system in which social standing is based primarily on individual achievement.

Clique A small group of people who are part of a larger group and who interact with one another as a group in and of themselves.

Closed-ended questions Questions that require respondents to select from a list of available responses.

Coalescence A stage of social movements in which the social movement begins to mobilize resources to achieve its goal.

Coalition The formation of preferential interaction in a group.

Code blue A hospital emergency code indicating a patient is in need of resuscitation.

Coercion Occurs when one person or group forces its will on another, based on the threat of physical force or violence.

Cohabitation Two people living together in a sexual relationship without being married.

Collective behavior Behaviors involving a large number of individuals that are usually unplanned, often controversial, and sometimes even dangerous.

Collectivity A large number of individuals whose minimal interaction occurs without the benefit of conventional norms.

Colonialism A world stratification system in which powerful nations forced weaker nations to become colonies, thereby securing them as sources of raw materials and markets for goods produced by the stronger nations.

Communal sharing One of Fiske's four elementary forms of social action, in which the group is more important than the individual and in which all members of the group work for a common interest.

Communism As envisioned by Karl Marx, an extreme form of socialist economic and political system in which all members of the society are equal.

Community A collection of people who share a common geographic territory, most of the daily interactions of members take place within the territory, and members have a sense of belonging.

Community-based corrections Correctional programs operating outside traditional prisons in the community at large.

Comparable worth The principle that jobs requiring similar levels of education and training should be paid at similar levels regardless of whether they are predominately female or predominately male occupations.

Competitive capitalism The capitalism of Marx's day in which no single capitalist or small group of capitalists could dominate a market.

Complete observer Does not take part in the interaction at all and hence is less likely to cause the people studied to modify their actions.

Complete participant Someone who participates in the setting fully and engages in unobtrusive research.

Compulsory education The legal requirement that all children attend school.

Concentrated poverty A tendency for people who are poor to be located in focused geographic areas where most of the residents are also poor.

Concept An abstract idea or theoretical construct usually represented by a word or brief phrase summarizing some meaningful aspect of the real world.

Conformity When an individual both subscribes to the cultural goals of society and has access to legitimate means for achieving them.

Conspicuous consumption Spending money on items, such as expensive cars or clothes, that advertise status and prestige.

Constitutional monarchies Members of royalty serve as symbolic rulers while elected officials actually govern.

Content analysis A commonly used procedure for studying text by identifying specific characteristics of the text such as the frequency of occurrence of specific key words or phrases.

Control group A group not exposed to the treatment.

Control theory A theory which argues that people have an inner control system supported by a conscience, internalized morality, a desire to be good, religious principles, fear of punishment, and a sense of integrity.

Core countries The high-income countries that dominate the world economic system.

Corporate capitalism Capitalism dominated by public corporations owned by many stockholders.

Corporate crime Illegal acts conducted by or on behalf of a corporation.

Corporation A legal entity separate from its owners.

Corridor curriculum Lessons that children teach one another at school while not in class.

Cosmopolites Well-educated, high-income people who choose to live in the city to take advantage of its convenience and cultural resources.

Cost/benefit analysis The comparison of the costs and benefits of remaining in a relationship.

Counterculture A subculture that challenges important elements of the dominant culture such as beliefs, attitudes, or values and seeks to create an alternative life style.

Coup d'état The abrupt replacement of government leaders illegally, often relying upon coercive force or the use of violence.

Credentialism The tendency to emphasize a diploma or academic degree rather than experience, skill, or subject knowledge.

Crime A violation of criminal law.

Crimes against persons Crimes involving the threat of injury or force against people.

Crimes against property Crimes involving stealing or damaging property.

Criminal justice system The social institution whose primary purpose is to exert formal social control in a society.

Criminology The scientific study of crime and its causes.

Critical period hypothesis Hypothesis that suggests there is a window of time for primary socialization to operate.

Critical race theory A theory that examines the intersection of race, law, and power.

Crowd A temporary gathering of people who share a common focus of attention and who influence one another.

Crowdfunding A process in which entrepreneurs post their idea and proposal on a website asking for people to contribute small amounts either to purchase a product in advance or to gain equity in the business.

Crude birth rate The average number of live births per year per thousand people in the population.

Crude death rate The number of deaths per year for every thousand people in a population.

Cult A religious organization that is completely outside a society's cultural traditions.

Cultural capital The tastes, language, attitudes, and general ways of thinking that influence our interactions with one another.

Cultural diffusion The spread of cultural elements, including objects and ideas, from one culture to another.

Cultural goals Widely shared objectives such as achieving financial success.

Cultural integration The coherence and consistency typically found among elements of a single culture.

Cultural lag The phenomenon that some elements of culture change faster than others.

Cultural lag theory A theory that argues technological change is the driving force for much change and that changes in other elements of culture often lag behind technology.

Cultural leveling The reduction of differences (both good and bad) between cultures, resulting in a loss of cultural uniqueness and the loss of cultural heritage.

Cultural relativism A view that judges other cultures not by standards of the observer's culture but by the standards of the other culture itself.

Cultural transmission The passing of culture from one generation to the next.

Cultural universals Cultural elements found in all cultures.

Culture A combination of ideas, behaviors, and material objects that members of a society have created and adopted for carrying out necessary tasks of daily life and that are passed on from one generation to the next.

Culture-bound syndrome A conception of disease or ill health that is limited to a small number of cultures and is shaped by culture.

Culture of poverty A subculture associated with people in lower social classes thought to encourage them to become resigned to their fate and to discourage personal achievement.

Culture shock Disorientation when first experiencing a new culture.

Culture theory A theory that argues that cultural symbols are important for the development of a social movement.

Cybercrime Crime executed with the use of a computer and usually over the Internet.

Cyber sex Virtual sex using computers over the Internet.

Cyberwarfare A form of information warfare using digital software and hardware to conduct sabotage and espionage.

Cyclical unemployment Unemployment resulting from lower production rates during recessions.

Data Empirically obtained information.

Dating scripts Culturally guided rules and expectations about dating practices.

De facto segregation Segregation that is part of social practice.

De jure segregation Segregation that is allowed by law.

Decline The tendency for all social movements to fade in power and significance.

Deep integration Most large corporations are multinationals that both produce and sell their products and services around the world.

Definition of the situation A statement or action that explicitly or implicitly suggests the meaning the actor would like others to attribute to his or her actions.

Definitions of acceptable acts Views of which acts are tolerable and which are unacceptable.

Degradation ceremony A public ritual in which one's stigmatized status is made known.

Deindustrialization The systematic withdrawal of private investment from manufacturing and the decline of industry through plant shutdowns, layoffs, and downsizing.

Democracy Government in which the people governed elect those who govern and, in some cases, to participate directly in governance themselves.

Democratic leaders Leaders who seek input from all members of the group before accomplishing a task.

Democratic republics A form of representative democracy in which chief executive sale chosen by popular election.

Demographic characteristics Characteristics of populations such as age, sex, race, and ethnicity.

Demographic transition The shift that occurs when countries change from high birth rates and death rates to low birth rates and death rates.

Demography The scientific study of human populations.

Denomination A church, independent of the state, that recognizes religious pluralism.

Dependent variable A variable thought to be influenced by an independent variable.

The deprived Include the very poor, emotionally disturbed, handicapped individuals living at the bottom of society.

Descent A system by which members of society trace kinship through generations.

Designer drugs Lab-made versions of drugs similar to designated controlled substances under US law.

Deskilling A reduction in expertise, training, and experience required to perform a job.

Deterrence The attempt to discourage criminal behavior through punishment; preventing war from occurring.

Deviance The violation of norms of a group, society, or one's peers.

Dictatorship Rule by a single person.

Differential association The tendency of someone to spend more time with some individuals and less with others.

Differential association theory A theory which argues that people are more likely to be deviant to the extent they are exposed to deviants.

Differential reinforcement The selective reward of some acts and punishment of others.

Differential reinforcement theory A theory which argues that individuals learn criminal behavior through differential association, differential reinforcement, definitions of acceptable acts, and imitation.

Diffuse characteristics Status characteristics that are presumed to always matter in determining a person's relative position in the group.

Diffusion The spread of invention or discovery from one culture to another.

Digital divide Inequalities in access to technologies such as the Internet and computers.

Direct democracy A democracy in which all members come together to make decisions.

Disability A reduced ability to perform tasks expected of a normal person at that stage in life.

Disaster An event that causes extensive harm to people and property.

Discovery When something that was unknown becomes known.

Discrimination Actions against a group that are designed to deny access to the same rights, privilege, and opportunities as the dominant group.

Displacement The process of individual feelings of hostility, inadequacy, or anger are directed against groups that are not the origins of those feelings.

Division of labor The allocation of different roles to different social statuses.

Dominant culture The culture that takes precedence over other cultures in activities or events involving people from many categories of the population.

Dominant group A group that has greater power, privilege, and prestige than other groups.

Double standard Different standards of sexual behavior for men and women.

Doubling time The number of years it would take for the population to double in size if it were to continue to grow at its current rate.

Downsizing Reducing the size of companies to cut costs by laying off workers or even selling parts of the company.

Dowry deaths The murder of brides for failing to provide adequate dowry payments.

Dramaturgy A microsociological approach that analyzes social life in terms of the stage.

Drive to technological maturity The third stage of development theory, in which the country adopts the cultural values that support a modern complex society, reinvests in industry, and begins to mature.

Drone warfare The use of remotely controlled airplanes to conduct surveillance and to kill suspected militants with laser-guided rockets and other armaments.

Dropping out Leaving school prior to graduation.

Dual labor market One in which there is a relatively advantaged primary form of employment and a relatively disadvantaged secondary form of employment.

Due process The stipulation that the criminal justice system must operate within the bounds of law.

Dyad A group consisting of two people.

Dysfunctions The negative consequences of a social structure.

Eating disorder An extreme effort to control weight through unhealthy means.

Ecological succession A new social group or type of land use first "invades" territory and then becomes the dominant social group or dominant land use for the territory.

Economic sectors Large segments of the economy representing fundamentally different kinds of production.

Economy Consists of the organizations and processes that produce and distribute goods and services.

Edge cities Less compact than older cities, have no clear center, and tend to grow up near major transportation routes.

Egalitarian system A system in which both sexes have equal authority.

Ego Freud's term for the conscious part of the personality that seeks to balance instinctual desires with the demands of society.

Elections Formal decision processes in which citizens vote for their favorite option.

Emergence The tendency for social movements to form to address a perceived social problem.

Emergent properties Important characteristics that cannot be reduced to a simple combination of characteristics of individuals or other components; properties of a group that emerge through the process of interaction.

Emigration The movement of people out of a given country or geographic area.

Emotion regulation The idea that businesses try to regulate the emotions of their workers.

Empirical generalizations Summary statements about the data that highlight important findings.

Empty nest syndrome A myth that parents mourn after the last child leaves the home.

Endogamous Marriage within one's own social group.

Entrepreneur Someone who takes an innovative idea and, through financing and business savvy, turns it into a viable business.

Epidemiology is related to the term *epidemic*, which refers to an outbreak of a disease within a population.

Equality matching One of Fiske's four elementary forms of social action, in which individuals are presumed to be equal in status and authority but seek individual goals.

Estate system A system with three strata or estates: the nobility, the church, and peasants; position is determined largely by inheritance.

Ethnic cleansing The practice of killing people from some ethnic groups and encouraging the surviving members to emigrate to another country.

Ethnic villagers People living in tight-knit inner-city neighborhoods united by race and social class and resembling small towns.

Ethnic work The process by which a person identifies with and constructs their identity.

Ethnicity Cultural practices that distinguish one group of people from another.

Ethnocentrism The view that your own culture is the standard against which other cultures can be judged right or wrong.

Ethnography A typically detailed descriptive account summarizing and interpreting a culture or a collection of people studied.

Ethnomethodology A type of symbolic interactionism that seeks to understand how individuals make sense of their everyday surroundings.

Exogamous Marriage outside of one's own social group.

Experimental group A group exposed to a treatment.

Export jobs to low-wage countries To move production from high-wage countries to low-wage countries, resulting a net loss of jobs in high-wage countries and a net increase of jobs in low-wage countries.

Expressive leader Also called a socioemotional leader; a person who is responsible for maintaining group morale and smoothing tensions in a group.

Expressive leadership Leadership that focuses on the well-being and morale of group members.

Extended family A family consisting of more than two generations or relatives living within the same household.

Exurbs The area beyond the old suburbs, forming a second ring farther out from the central city.

Face-saving behavior Actions that seek to salvage a performance that is going wrong.

Fad A unique or unconventional social pattern that is adopted briefly and enthusiastically by members of a social group or society.

Faith Belief based on conviction rather than on empirical evidence.

False consciousness A lack of awareness of the severity of class differences by members of the proletariat.

Family A group of individuals related to one another by blood, marriage, adoption, or social convention.

Fashion A social pattern that is adopted or followed by a large number of people.

Fecundity The maximum possible number of children a woman can have during her lifetime.

Fee-for-service A method of payment in which providers are paid for each visit, each operation, and so on.

Feminism A perspective that argues men and women are essentially equal and should be treated equally in social life.

Feminist theory A theory which looks closely at ways in which men and women are treated regarding deviance and crime and how those differences are influenced by gender.

Feminization of poverty A tendency for women to be poor much more frequently than men.

Feral children Children raised by wild animals or without appropriate socialization.

Fertility rate The average number of children born per woman over her lifetime.

Fictive kin Unrelated people who are regarded as family.

Field experiment A study conducted in a natural setting such as a classroom where the researcher cannot control everything that happens.

Filiarchy Emphasis on the power of children in the family.

First World Industrialized nations allied with the United States and NATO, including many nations in Western Europe and North America, along with Japan, Australia, and New Zealand.

Folkways Rules governing everyday conduct that are not considered to be morally important and are not strictly enforced.

Forced labor People who are physically coerced to work.

Formal norms Norms that are written down and enforced.

Formal organization An organization that is rationally structured to efficiently achieve specific goals using rules and regulations.

Formal sanctions Explicit punishments written into regulations or laws.

Front stage behavior Behaviors that are part of the role being played.

Frustration-aggression hypothesis The idea that discrimination is the result of displaced anger for an individual's inability to achieve highly desired goals.

Function The consequence or effect of a social structure for the society as a whole.

Functionally illiterate The absence of basic reading and writing skills necessary for everyday living.

Fundamentalism The literal and rigid interpretation of a sacred text.

Game stage Mead's third stage in the development of the self, in which the child adopts roles that are dependent upon other roles for their structure and meaning.

Gated communities Communities that erect walls or other barriers around a neighborhood and erect gates on streets entering the neighborhood, restricting traffic to local residents.

Gemeinschaft Describes the relationships among people in small, close-knit rural communities where social cohesion is achieved by strong personal bonds uniting members based on primary relationships, shared life experiences, and a shared culture.

Gender The social status associated with a person's sex.

Gender gap A tendency for women and men to have different political preferences on many issues.

Gender pay gap The difference between average pay for men and women.

Gender reassignment Usually surgery and hormone treatment to make a person's body conform to his or her self-identity.

Gender roles Expected behaviors associated with males or females.

Gender stratification The distribution of wealth, power, and social prestige among men and women.

Generalized other The collective attitudes of the entire community regarding how they are expected to behave.

Generational equity The concept of a balance in costs and benefits going to each generation.

Gentrification The resettlement of a low-income inner-city neighborhood by affluent residents and businesses, often forcing out the low-income residents who once lived there.

Geronticide The killing of the aged.

Gerontocracy A society in which the elderly have the most wealth, power, and prestige; rule by the aged.

Gerontology Study of aging and the elderly.

Gesellschaft Describes the relationships found in large and impersonal communities where many members do not know one another personally and cohesion is based on a complex division of labor and secondary relationships, where individuals have little identification with the group and little commitment to shared values.

Gini coefficient The extent to which the distribution of income differs from an equal distribution.

Glass ceiling A barrier that, while not obvious or easily visible, blocks women's movement into the top ranks of management.

Global commodity chains Worldwide networks of production activities are required to produce the finished product for sale.

Globalization Increasing interdependence throughout the world.

Gossip Rumors about the personal affairs of a person.

Government The formal organization that acts on behalf of the state to regulate interactions with other states and among citizens of the state.

Governmental gridlock An inability to resolve important issues when neither party has sufficient votes to determine government policy.

Grade inflation The trend of giving everyone higher grades for mediocre work.

Graying of America The increasing proportion of the population over the age of 65.

Group Individuals who share common beliefs and values and who regularly interact with one another.

Group dynamics How the individual influences the group and how the group influences the individual.

Group position theory When groups interact, the dominant group will promote social policies and attitudes that advantage themselves over other groups.

Groupthink The tendency for groups to develop a rigid way of thinking.

Hate crime A crime against persons or property when the offender is motivated by bias.

Hawthorne effect The unintended effects on behavior produced when people are aware they are being studied.

Health Defined by the World Health Organization (1946) as a state of complete mental, physical, and social well-being.

Health maintenance organization (HMO) A prepaid healthcare plan delivering comprehensive care to members through designated providers.

Heterogeneity Diversity in groups.

Heterogeneous societies Societies with members from diverse ethnic, racial, and religious backgrounds.

Heterosexism A view that labels anyone who is not heterosexual (including homosexuals, lesbians, bisexuals, and transsexuals) as "queer."

Heterosexual Someone attracted to members of the opposite sex.

Hidden curriculum Values that are taught through the presentation of standard curriculum that are not an explicit part of that curriculum.

High culture The artifacts, values, knowledge, beliefs, and other cultural elements that elites in a society use to distinguish themselves from the masses.

High-income nations Nations with a GNI of $12,276 or more.

High mass consumption The fourth and final stage of development theory, in which people in the country enjoy a high standard of living based on the mass consumption of goods and services.

Historical-comparative research A study examining the ways in which social life changes across cultures and over time.

HIV (human immunodeficiency virus) A lentivirus that weakens the immune system, leading to acquired immunodeficiency syndrome (AIDS).

Holistic medicine Medicine that considers the whole person, including physical, mental, and spiritual needs, and is an alternative to scientific medicine.

Homogamy The tendency of people with similar characteristics to marry one another.

Homogeneous A group in which all people are similar.

Homogeneous societies Societies in which members are generally from the same ethnic, racial, and religious backgrounds and share a common culture.

Homophobia Prejudice and discrimination against homosexuals driven by an aversion to or even hatred of homosexuals and their life styles.

Homosexual Someone attracted to members of the same sex.

Hookups Casual, usually one-time encounters with others that may lead to sexual activity but often stop short of intercourse.

Horticultural societies Societies in which people plant crops in small gardens without the use of plows or more advanced technology for subsistence.

Horticulture Farming using simple hand tools to raise crops.

Hospice care Care designed to help people have a "good" death experience by relieving pain and discomfort for the patient and providing emotional and spiritual support to both the patient and the patient's family.

HPV (human papillomavirus) The most commonly sexually transmitted infection, including more than 40 types.

Human Development Index (HDI) The composite measure of well-being that includes life expectancy, literacy rates, education, and other measures of standard of living.

Human ecology The study of people and their environment.

Human trafficking The smuggling of humans, in which a victim relies on a smuggler to help him or her enter a country illegally.

Hunting and gathering societies The simplest societies, in which people rely on readily available vegetation and hunt game for subsistence.

Hypothesis A testable statement about the relationship between two or more concepts that is not known to be true but can be tested in research.

"I" The self as subject who makes decisions and takes actions based on his or her desires.

Id Freud's terms for the most basic part of the human personality, geared toward satisfaction of the basic instincts.

Ideal types A pure form of a concept usually used for the purpose of categorization.

Illegitimate opportunity structures Having ready access to illegal means.

Imitation Mead's first stage in the development of the self, in which the child imitates the behaviors of adults without understanding the actions.

Immigration The movement of people into a given country or geographic area.

Impression management The ways in which an individual playing a role will try to control the performance such that others are convinced by the performance.

In-groups Groups to which we belong or identify with.

Income The money people receive as rents, royalties, wages, or profits.

Independent variable A variable expected to cause changes in a second variable.

Industrial Revolution A dramatic change in the nature of production in which machines replaced tools, steam and other energy sources replaced human or animal power, and skilled workers were replaced with mostly unskilled workers.

Industrial societies These societies emphasize manufacturing and mass production in which machines replace much human labor and craftsmen are replaced by less skilled laborers.

Industry A means of subsistence that relies on the production of goods using machinery driven by advanced sources of energy.

Infant mortality The number of deaths per 1,000 infants born live in a year.

Infant mortality rate An age-specific death rate, the number of deaths of infants under 1 year of age per 1,000 live births in a given year.

Influence The exercise of power through the process of persuasion.

Informal economy Unpaid labor such as doing housework, repairing one's own car, or performing voluntary charity work.

Informal norms Norms that are often expressed only informally and never written down.

Information economy An economy based on the product of skilled professionals, which is the information or knowledge they provide.

Information revolution A change that began during the last half of the 20th century in which service jobs become more common than jobs in manufacturing or agriculture.

Infrastructure The roads, bridges, subways, storm water and sewer systems, communications lines, power lines, and other physical structures necessary for the continued operation of industrialized societies.

Innovation The idea of accepting cultural goals (e.g., wealth) but rejecting accepted means in favor of unconventional ways of achieving those goals (e.g., crime).

Institutional capitalism Capitalism in which large shares of corporations are owned by institutional investors such as pension, insurance, or trust funds.

Institutional racism The belief that racism is built into the structure of society, and that society is structured to favor the dominant group.

Institutional sexism Discrimination against one sex that results from the day-to-day operations, rules, and policies of organizations and institutions.

Institutionalized means Legitimate means, such as job opportunities and education, for achieving goals.

Instrumental leader Also known as a task leader, a person who is responsible for leading a group toward the completion of a task.

Instrumental leadership Leadership that focuses on the completion of tasks.

Interest groups Groups that consist of a voluntary association of citizens who attempt to influence public policy.

Intergenerational social mobility An upward or downward change in social standing or social status of children relative to their parents.

Intergenerational transmission of violence The tendency for people who are victims of abuse or who witness abuse to be perpetrators of violence at a later stage of the life course.

Internal migration Migration from one place to another within a larger geographic area.

International division of labor theory A theory that argues that multinational corporations split production into tasks that are then performed in whatever part of the world can provide the most profitable combination of labor and technology.

Intersexual people People whose bodies have the characteristics of both sexes.

Interviews Surveys in which the researcher interacts in person with the respondent, asking him or her questions.

Intimate partner violence Physical, emotional, or psychological abuse toward an intimate partner.

Intragenerational social mobility An upward or downward change in social standing for an individual over the course of his or her lifetime.

Invasion The intrusion of one group or activity into an area occupied by another.

Invention A new combination of cultural elements.

Iron cage of bureaucracy Limitations on creativity and flexibility that are placed on workers by the bureaucratic process that causes alienation.

Iron law of oligarchy An idea, developed by Robert Michels, that suggests that bureaucracy always means the rule of the many by the few.

Jargon Specialized language that indicates the authenticity of the person in the role.

Just-world hypothesis A tendency for people to want to believe the world is predictable, orderly, and fair.

Juvenile delinquency All of the usual crimes that might be committed by adults but are committed by minors, such as theft, arson, and murder.

Kinship The linking of people through blood, marriage, adoption, or social convention.

Labeling theory A theory which argues that an act becomes deviant only when it is labeled as deviant by others.

Labor unions Groups of workers who unite to engage in collective bargaining with corporations.

Laboratory experiment An experiment conducted in a controlled setting.

Laissez-faire leader A leader who lets the group function more or less on its own, offering guidance only when necessary.

Language An abstract system of symbols and rules for their usage permitting people to represent abstract thoughts and experiences and communicate them to others.

Latent dysfunction A negative consequence of a social structure that is not immediately obvious.

Latent functions The less obvious and often unintended consequences of actions.

Law A formal norm that has been enacted by a legislature and is enforced by formal sanctions.

Leader A person who influences the beliefs, values, and behaviors of others.

Legal-rational authority Derived from written rules and regulations of political systems.

Life chances The likelihood of realizing a certain quality of life or the probability of experiencing certain positive or negative outcomes in life such as material goods and favorable life experiences.

Life expectancy The average number of years people are expected to live.

Life styles Activities, behaviors, possessions, and other, often visible characteristics of how an individual spends her or his time and money.

Living will A written document in which a patient expresses his or her wishes regarding use of life support measures in the event of a life-threatening illness or injury.

Lobbyist Someone who represents an interest group and meets with public officials to try to influence their decisions by providing information supporting the interest group's goals.

Lockout An action in which the company is locked up and workers are not permitted to work or draw pay until the conflict is resolved.

Looking-glass self Cooley's process of the development of the self, in which individuals interpret how they think others see them and adjust their behavior accordingly.

Low-income nations Nations with a GNI of $1005 or less.

Lumpenproletariat Marx's term for the dispossessed, criminals, mentally ill, and disabled in society.

Macro-level studies Studies that focus on social structures that influence individuals, such as groups, organizations, cultures, or even societies.

Macrosociology Analysis of social life that focuses on broad features of society, such as social institutions.

Magnet school A publicly funded school that concentrates its curriculum on a particular subject area.

Managed care A program in which physicians no longer have complete freedom to decide what services are provided to patients but must first approve those services for payment with a third-party payer.

Managerial capitalism Occurs where managers, through both their day-to-day involvement in the corporation and their ownership of large blocks of stock as part of their compensation, often dominate the corporation.

Managers People who sell their own labor but exercise authority over other employees.

Manifest functions The obvious and usually intended consequences of actions.

Market economy An economy in which consumers are the key decision makers, the market drives the economy, and transactions are based on the profit motive and competition.

Market pricing One of Fiske's four elementary forms of social action, in which the terms of exchange are dictated by market forces.

Marriage A socially approved union between individuals.

Marxist theory A theory of social movements that suggests that societies change through a dialectical process.

Mass behavior Collective behavior can occur among people who are dispersed over a wide geographic area.

Mass media Means of delivering impersonal communication to large audiences.

Mass production A process of production in which products are standardized, parts are interchangeable, precision tools fit parts together precisely, and the production is mechanized to produce a continuous high volume.

Mass society theory A theory that suggests that people join social movements because it gives them a sense of belonging to something larger than themselves.

Master status characteristic A status characteristic that is so important that it overshadows all other status characteristics.

Material culture All of the art, architecture, technological artifacts, and material objects that are created by a society and that reflect the ideologies of the culture.

Matriarchy A society in which women maintain the majority of social power.

Matrilineal A type of society in which kinship and sometimes property is passed from mothers to their children.

Matrilocal A family system in which the new family lives near the wife's parents.

"Me" The self as object as the person is regarded by others.

Means of production The technologies and resources required for producing goods or services in an economy, such as factories, raw materials, and machines.

Means test A qualification procedure to determine whether someone's wealth and income are sufficiently low to qualify them for some form of federal support.

Mechanical solidarity Durkheim's term for societies based on strong moral values and a deep sense of community among members; people are held together by shared moral sentiments and tradition.

Medical sociology The special area within sociology focusing on "the phenomena of health and illness, the social organization of health care delivery, and differential access to medical resources."

Medicine The social institution that focuses on maintaining health and preventing or treating disease.

Megalopolis A densely populated area containing two or more metropolitan areas that have grown until they overlap one another.

Melting pot A blending of ethnic traditions in a society.

Mental illness See *psychological disorder*.

Meritocracy A system of social stratification based entirely on personal merit.

Meso-level studies Studies that either focus on intermediate-level structures, such as the family or small organizations, or may try to bridge the micro and macro levels to show how one influences the other.

Mesosociology Analysis of social life that falls between the microsociological and macrosociological levels.

Metropolitan statistical area A densely populated area consisting of a county containing a core urban area (specifically, a city with a population of 50,000 or more) as well as adjacent counties having a high degree of social and economic integration.

Micro-level studies Research focusing on individuals, thoughts, actions, and individual behaviors.

Micropolitan statistical area Centers of population with smaller population cores with populations of 10,000 or more but less than 50,000.

Microsociology Analysis of social life that focuses on the specific aspects of interactions.

Middle-income nations Nations with a GNI between $1,006 and $12,275.

Migration The movement of people from one geographic area to another.

Military-industrial complex The conjunction of interests of the combination of the federal government, the military, and the defense industry.

Military junta A group of military leaders who have seized power from the prior government.

Minority groups Groups that society sets apart in some way and disadvantages due to the traits that set them apart.

Mission drift The tendency of formal organizations to shift their goals for their own survival.

Mixed-methods research Research that combines both qualitative and quantitative research in the same study.

Mob A highly emotional crowd that pursues a destructive or violent goal.

Modernization theory A theory that argues that progress can be made in poor countries through the greater economic and social development that comes from adopting modern technologies, cultural values, and economic institutions.

Monarchy A government in which the right to rule is passed from one generation to the next by inheritance.

Monogamy Marriage to only one partner at a time.

Monopoly Occurs when a single firm dominates an industry.

Monopoly capitalism Occurs when one or only a few capitalists control a sector of the economy.

Monotheism The belief in one god.

Moral holidays Times or places in which the usual norms are suspended and can be violated without punishment.

Moral panic A form of dispersed collective behavior in which people react to a perceived threatening event with an irrational fear.

Mores Serious norms for important activities that have a strong moral imperative and are strictly enforced.

Mortality The incidence of death in a population.

Multiculturalism A perspective that recognizes the contributions of diverse groups to our society and holds that no single culture is any better than all the rest.

Multinational corporations (transnational corporations) Commercial organizations whose operations span international boundaries, typically both producing and selling goods and services in multiple countries.

Muscle dysmorphia A condition in which males see themselves as smaller than they are and work very hard to gain muscle mass.

Nation-states Political entities extending throughout a relatively large geographic region.

Natural rate of increase The rate of increase in a population due to births and deaths.

Negative sanctions Actions directed against a person or persons in response to an act of deviance.

Neglectful parenting Parenting in which the parents neglect the child, or act as though the child does not exist.

Negotiated order A shared meaning for the situation agreed upon by all participants.

Neocolonialism Former colonies often continue to be dominated by more powerful nations in the world economy.

Neolocal A society in which the new family lives apart from both sets of parents.

Net financial assets Household wealth after equity in homes has been deducted.

Net migration (rate) The number of people moving into a country (immigration) minus the number of people moving out of the country (emigration).

Network A small society of one or two family groupings that are related.

Net worth Household wealth based on the difference between assets and liabilities.

New social movement theory A theory that suggests that social movements in postindustrial societies are substantially different from social movements that occurred in industrial societies.

No code order; do not resuscitate (DNR) order A written order from a doctor directing that resuscitation not be attempted if the patient goes into cardiac or respiratory arrest.

Nomadic People who do not live in one place but move from place to place as conditions require for survival.

Nonmaterial culture Intangible creations of people expressing everything from fundamental religious beliefs to abstract scientific knowledge to proscriptions for behavior; symbols and ideologies that define a culture.

Nonviolent resistance Political actions relying on nonviolent acts to protest particular policies or regimes.

Norm of noninvolvement Expectation that people will not become involved in the affairs of others to help preserve their privacy, typical of urban settings.

Normative crisis The struggle people go through between what society expects them to do and what they actually accomplish.

Norms Expectations for behavior.

Nuclear family A family consisting of two parents and children.

Observer as participant Research in which the observer has only minimal participation in the setting and is not a natural or normal participant.

Occupational structure In the United States, refers to the number and types of jobs available—experienced major shifts during the 20th century.

Oldest old People 85 and older.

Old old People between 75 and 84.

Oligarchies Authoritarian governments ruled by a select few.

Oligopoly Occurs when a few firms dominate an industry.

Open-ended questions Questions that permit people to use their own words to answer.

Operational definition A description of procedures used to measure a concept in sufficient detail so that someone else could perform the same procedure and get a similar result.

Optimum foraging strategy A pattern of foraging that leaves enough flora and fauna in a foraged area for the land to recover in a reasonable amount of time.

Organic solidarity People are mutually dependent on one another due to a complex division of labor, and most relationships are neither intimate nor personal.

Organization A group that is deliberately constructed to achieve a purpose common to its members.

Organizational environment Outside forces that influence the structure and performance of an organization.

Organized crime Crime committed by collections of criminals who coordinate activities much like a business.

Ostracism Excluding someone from the normal activities of a group.

Out-groups Groups toward which we feel a sense of competition or antagonism.

Outsource To discontinue production and contract with another company to supply those goods or services.

Panic A form of collective behavior in which people react to a perceived threat in a frantic and irrational way.

Pan-Indianism The idea that all Native Americans share a common identity that is rooted in the experiences of past prejudice and discrimination.

Parliamentary systems Representative democracies in which candidates for the national legislature (parliament) represent political parties.

Parole Release of a prisoner to serve the remainder of his or her sentence in the community supervised by the court.

Participant as observer Research in which the researcher has a nonresearch reason for participating in the setting and decides to conduct research.

Participant observation or field work Research in which the researcher participates in and is directly involved in the lives of those he or she is studying.

Pastoralism A means of subsistence that relies on the domestication of animals as the primary food supply.

Pastoral societies Societies in which animals are domesticated and raised for food in pastures.

Patriarchy A society in which males maintain the majority of social power.

Patrilineal Describes a system of descent that considers only the father's side.

Patrilocal A family system in which the new family lives near the husband's parents.

Peer group A group of people, usually of similar age, background, and social status.

Peer-reviewed scientific journal A journal in which other researchers who know the topic examine an article before it is published to make sure it meets the standards of science.

Peripheral countries The most dependent countries in world systems theory, having low levels of industrialization.

Permissive parenting A style of parenting in which parents make few demands on their children, imposing few rules and offering little guidance.

Personal space Space surrounding a person that, when violated, causes discomfort.

Personality stabilization The role that family plays in the cognitive and emotional development of the individual.

Petty bourgeoisie People who own small businesses.

Pink-collar jobs Female-dominated occupations.

Play stage Mead's second stage in the development of the self, in which the child adopts and acts out a specific role.

Plea bargaining A formal negotiation in which defendants agree to plead guilty rather than appear in court.

Pluralist models Argue that many groups within a community or country have access to government officials and compete with one another in an effort to influence policy decisions.

Police discretion The power of police to exercise judgment in their interactions with suspects.

Political action committees (PACs) Interest groups formed to campaign for or against political candidates, legislation, and ballot initiatives.

Political crimes Crimes committed within or directed against a political system.

Political parties Organizations whose major purpose is to gain legitimate control of the government.

Political process theory A theory of social movements that emphasizes the role of the

political structure and public opinion in the outcomes of social movements.

Political revolution The replacement of one political system with another through violent means.

Polyandry A form of marriage in which a woman has more than one husband.

Polygamy Marriage that unites more than two partners.

Polygyny A form of marriage in which a man may have more than one wife.

Polytheism The belief in more than one god.

Popular culture All of the artifacts, values, knowledge, beliefs, and other cultural elements that appeal to the masses.

Population The people who inhabit a country or geographic region; everyone of interest for a study.

Population pyramid A graph displaying the age and sex distribution for a population.

Pornography The portrayal of sexual subject matter for the purpose of sexual arousal.

Positive sanction An action aimed at a person that seeks to reward good behavior and encourage the person and others to continue such acts.

Positivism An approach to sociology that assumes the methods of the natural sciences such as physics can be applied successfully to the study of social life and the scientific principles learned can be applied to solving social problems.

Postindustrialism A means of subsistence that relies on the production of services and information.

Postindustrial society A society dominated by information, services, and high technology more than the production of goods.

Poverty line (poverty threshold) Roughly three times the amount of money required for a family to spend for food.

Power The ability to realize one's goals and interests, even in the face of resistance; the capacity to influence or control behavior of others.

Power elite Leaders of dominant institutions, including the military, corporations, and political institutions.

Prejudice Beliefs or attitudes about a particular group.

Prestige The respect and admiration accorded a social position or occupation and people in those positions by others.

Primary deviance Occasional minor deviance that does not affect an individual's reputation or self-image.

Primary groups Groups that are characterized by small, intimate relationships and that have a strong influence over your socialization.

Primary labor market Enjoys relatively good working conditions, reasonably high pay, opportunity for advancement, and—most important—job security.

Primary relationship A relationship involving multiple roles for each participant; often emotional, personal, and not easily transferred to other people; often valued for its own sake, endures over time, and involves many aspects of a person's life.

Primary sector Agricultural production; the major resources are raw materials and the technology employed is labor intensive.

Primary sex characteristics A person's genitalia and a woman's ability to bear children and nurse.

Primary socialization The basic and fundamental aspects of interaction that help an individual develop self-awareness; the main process by which children learn the values and norms of their society.

Private equity Investors contribute funds in exchange for a share of ownership or equity in a company.

Probability sampling Procedures for which each case in the population has some known probability of being included in the sample and all segments of the population are represented in the sample.

Probation Allows a convicted offender to be supervised in the community under conditions imposed by the court instead of going to prison.

Profane Part of the realm of ordinary experience.

Profession A high-status occupation based on abstract knowledge, enjoying considerable autonomy and authority and, in turn, serving the public good and regulating its members.

Professionalization A process of defining a type of work as a profession.

Projection The process whereby a person unconsciously projects their own characteristics on others.

Proletariat Marx's term for the working class who provide labor for the capitalists.

Propaganda information given with the intention of shaping public opinion.

Proportional representation A system in which seats in a legislature are divided among parties in proportion to the number of popular votes received by each party.

Proselytizing Actively attempting to recruit members to a particular religious view.

Prostitution Paid sex.

Protestant work ethic A disciplined work ethic, rational approach to life, and an emphasis on this world.

Psychological disorder A psychological condition that is deviant, may cause harm to oneself or others, and may cause psychological distress.

Public opinion Widespread attitudes or beliefs about a particular issue.

Qualitative research Research emphasizing verbal descriptions and avoiding counting items or the use of mathematics.

Quality-adjusted life year (QALY) Would be 1 for one additional year of life at optimal health, but between 0 and 1 for an additional year of life with an adverse condition causing pain or reducing participation in activities.

Quantitative research Emphasizes numerical descriptions of data, counting, and the use of mathematics and statistics to describe and analyze data.

Questionnaires Surveys in which the respondent completes a form mailed to her or perhaps accessed on the Internet.

Race A socially constructed category of people who share some biologically transmitted traits that society considers important.

Racial segregation The geographic separation of people based on race or ethnicity.

Racialization The process by which people are placed into racial categories.

Racism Discrimination that is directed at a particular race.

Random assignment Assigning people at random to different conditions to avoid bias and to make sure the conditions are comparable.

Rape Forced, nonconsensual vaginal, oral, or anal intercourse.

Rationalization A process in which traditional methods and standards of social organization based on tradition, belief, and even magic are replaced with new methods and standards of social organization based on objectively calculable scientific criteria.

Rationalization of society The transition from a society dominated by tradition to one dominated by reason and rationally calculable scientific criteria.

Reactivity The extent to which humans being studied "react" or respond to the research process or the researcher by changing their behavior, either unintentionally or intentionally.

Realistic group conflict theory Discrimination is the result of competition between groups for limited societal resources.

Rebellion When someone rejects these goals and accepted means and actively offers an alternative.

Recidivism rate The rate at which former prisoners are rearrested, reconvicted, and re-imprisoned.

Redemptive social movement A social movement that seeks radical change for a specific, targeted group of people.

Reference groups Groups by which we gauge ourselves and that act as reference points for future behavior.

Reformative social movement A social movement that targets a broad group of people but whose changes are limited in scope.

Refugee Someone who was forced to leave his or her country of origin to avoid violence and bloodshed in civil wars, regional conflicts, and other disputes.

Rehabilitation The process of helping criminals become productive citizens.

Relative deprivation The feeling of dissatisfaction upon realizing that while conditions are improving, they are improving more for other people than for you.

Relative poverty Deprivation experienced by some people in contrast to others who have more.

Reliability The extent to which a measure or scale produces consistent results for different times, different people, and different research methods.

Religion A social institution involving beliefs, values, and behaviors based on the sacred.

Religiosity The importance that religion plays in a person's life.

Remittance Money sent home to households by migrants.

Replacement-level fertility The average number of births per woman required to replace the population.

Representative democracy A democracy in which representatives of the people are elected to govern on their behalf.

Residential patterns Culturally determined patterns that dictate where new families will live.

Residential segregation The separation of categories of people into different geographic areas of residence.

Resilience The degree to which a person can endure changes in his or her environment.

Resocialization The process of changing a person's personality through careful control of that person's environment.

Resource mobilization theory A theory that suggests for a social movement to be successful, it has to accumulate and mobilize substantial resources.

Respondent Someone who answers questions in a social survey.

Response rates The proportion of people asked to participate in the study who actually did so.

Retreatism When a person drops out of society, participating only minimally.

Retribution Punishment to seek vengeance.

Revolutionary social movement A social movement that seeks radical change of an entire society.

Riot An eruption of social activity that is highly emotional, undirected, and violent.

Ritualism When someone rejects cultural goals while continuing to pursue legitimate means.

Role Expected behaviors that accompany a status.

Role conflict Tension between roles connected to two or more statuses.

Role exit Disengaging from a status and the social roles attached to it.

Role performance The way in which a person plays a particular role within a given framework.

Role set More than one role associated with a single status.

Role strain Tension between roles connected to a single status.

Romantic love People being sexually attractive to one another and often idealizing one another.

Routine personal service workers Workers who perform repetitive tasks for providing a service.

Rumors Unconfirmed information that people spread, often by word of mouth.

Rural areas Defined by the Census Bureau as communities having fewer than 2,500 residents along with areas in open country outside of any city.

Sacred Things that are set apart as inspiring awe or reverence.

Salient characteristics Characteristics that distinguish between members of a group.

Sample A subset of members of the population rather than the entire population.

Sanctions Punishments or rewards designed to encourage behaviors conforming to norm and discourage behaviors that violate norms.

Sapir-Whorf hypothesis Argues that language shapes thought.

Scaffolding Socialization whereby a parent or other person helps a child bridge a gap between the child's current skill level or knowledge and a more advanced state of knowledge or skill.

Scapegoats Groups that are blamed for the problems of society that are not their fault.

Scientific management (Taylorism) Applies scientific and engineering principles to human labor by breaking a complex task into simple components and using time-and-motion studies to specify every detail of the job to maximize efficiency.

Seasonal unemployment Unemployment due to seasonal variations, such as school teachers on summer vacation, or variations in weather, which often affect agriculture, construction, and tourism jobs.

Second shift The extra hours women often spend performing child care duties, cooking, and cleaning after a full shift of work outside the home.

Second World Communist and socialist nations allied with the former Soviet Union, including many nations in Eastern Europe and Asia.

Secondary analysis The analysis of data for purposes other than the primary reason the information was originally collected.

Secondary deviance When an individual is labeled a deviant by others and comes to see himself as a deviant.

Secondary groups Large and impersonal groups whose members share a specific goal or activity.

Secondary labor market Employees routinely experience high turnover, low job security, few or no benefits, low wages, and little opportunity for advancement.

Secondary relationship A relationship that is specialized, lacks emotional intensity, often ends once specific goals are achieved, and can be reestablished with other participants with relative ease.

Secondary sector Manufacturing; its activity is goods producing, the key resource is energy, and the technology employed is capital-intensive machine production.

Secondary sex characteristics Physical characteristics not directly related to reproduction, such as general body shape, the amount and distribution of body fat, height, weight, muscular strength, the amount of body hair, and the tone of one's voice.

Secondary socialization Social influences that extend beyond the family.

Sect A religious organization that sets itself apart from mainstream religious beliefs.

Secular trend The increasingly early onset of puberty seen in children.

Secularization The declining importance of religion in society.

Segregation The physical or social isolation of a group of people from the rest of society.

Self-fulfilling prophecy A prediction that leads, directly or indirectly, to becoming true.

Semiperipheral countries The middle-income countries between the core countries and peripheral countries, having intermediate levels of industrialization, some manufacturing and services, and greater autonomy than peripheral countries.

Sex The biological distinction between males and females.

Sexism A belief that one sex is superior to the other.

Sexting The transmission of sexually explicit photographs, videos, or messages by cell phone.

Sex trafficking Victims are forced to work against their will in the sex industry.

Sexual harassment Unwanted attention based on someone's sex or sexuality that interferes with job performance or causes discomfort.

Sexual orientation A person's preference for sexual partners of a particular sex.

Sexuality A person's sexual orientation, sexual behavior, and attitudes about sexual behavior.

Shallow integration Occurs when most products were produced in a single country and then sold in that country and abroad.

Shaming Using status symbols to identify those who have violated societal expectations.

Sick role A set of societal expectations for the behavior and attitudes of someone who is ill.

Sign-vehicles Elements that communicate the message of a performance, comprised of the social setting, scenery, and appearance.

Significant other Mead's term for family and other intimate or close agents of socialization.

Single-payer system A healthcare system in which the government pays all bills.

Singles Young, unmarried people who live in the city by choice for its convenience and opportunities.

Singularity The point in time at which computer intelligence will equal human intelligence.

Skid rows Old, decaying housing where many of the poor and unemployed once found homes.

Social age Changes in the social and/or economic roles the person can competently perform.

Social bond theory A theory which argues that everyone is tempted by opportunities for deviant behavior, but deviant acts are less likely when the individual's bonds to society are strong.

Social class A broad measure of the location that a person occupies in the social structure.

Social conflict perspective A theory which emphasizes competing interests of groups of people having different amounts of power and how those having more power use it to exploit those with less power.

Social construction of reality We as individuals do not directly experience reality but are influenced in our perception of it by social interaction and meanings other people attribute to that reality.

Social control Efforts by society to regulate people's behavior and thoughts.

Social determinants of health The circumstances in which people are born, grow up, live, work, an age, and the systems put in place to deal with illness. These circumstances are in turn shaped by a wider set of forces: economics, social policies, and politics."

Social epidemiology The study of the distribution of mortality (death) and morbidity (disease) in a population.

Social facts Regular patterns of behavior characterizing a society that exist independent of individuals and are beyond the control of individuals.

Social group Two or more people who have something in common.

Social identity theory People desire a positive social identity, and will discriminate to elevate their own identity.

Social institutions The ways in which a society meets it basic needs.

Social learning theory People engage in prejudice and discrimination because they have been socialized to feel and behave in those ways.

Social mobility Changing one's social status and thereby changing one's social ranking in the stratification system.

Social movement Any organized activity that encourages or discourages social change.

Social networks Links that connect people to one another in a web of connections.

Social order A level of social organization based on institutions, customs, and patterns of interaction capable of providing the conditions for their continuing survival.

Social promotion Passing a student through grades as a result of age rather than academic ability.

Social stratification Patterns of inequality in a society.

Social stratification system The structured ranking of people in a society based upon selected social statuses.

Social structure Enduring, relatively stable patterns of social behavior.

Socialist economies Economic systems in which the means of production are collectively owned and the economy is government regulated.

Socialization The process by which an individual learns the beliefs, values, and behaviors that are appropriate for his or her society.

Socialized medicine A healthcare system in which the government owns most of the medical facilities and employs most of the physicians.

Societal protection Seeking to remove offenders from society to make them incapable of further crimes.

Society People living in a specific geographic region who share a common culture.

Sociocultural evolution Development in human societies resulting from cumulative change in cultural information from inventions, diffusion, and discoveries.

Socioeconomic status (SES) A composite index of social status based on occupational prestige, income, and educational attainment.

Sociological imagination The capacity for individuals to understand the relationship between their individual lives and broad social forces that influence them.

Sociology The scientific study of social life.

Sociology of the body The study of how our bodies are shaped by our social experiences, values, and culture, as well as ways in which our bodies affect those experiences.

Sole-parent family A family composed of one parent and children.

Specific characteristics Status characteristics that matter in determining a person's relative position in the group only if they are shown to be relevant to the circumstance of the group.

State The political entity having a monopoly over the use of force in a specific geographic territory.

State capitalism Capitalism in which capitalistic enterprises exist side by side with state-owned production enterprises and the state regulates and manages the economy.

State church A church that is sanctioned by or allied with the government.

Statistics Mathematical measures summarizing important characteristics found in data.

Status The position that a person holds in a group.

Status consistency The tendency for people having high status in one area of their lives to also have high status in other areas.

Status inconsistencies Statuses that contradict one another.

Status symbols Signs that identify a particular status.

Stereotypes Generalizations that are applied to a group of people.

Stigma A distinctive, strongly negative label that marks the person as socially unacceptable or disgraced.

Street crime Crime that often occurs in public settings.

Strikes Temporary work stoppages by a group of workers to seek changes in working conditions.

Strong ties Ties that link people in a close fashion.

Structural-functional theory The theory that society can be viewed as a system of parts, each of which contributes to the whole.

Structural mobility Mobility resulting from changes in a society's occupational structure or stratification system rather than from individual achievement.

Structural unemployment Unemployment that results when the skill set of unemployed workers does not match the skills required for available jobs or when the unemployed are in a different location than available jobs.

Studied nonobservance Polite behavior in which someone strives to appear not to notice someone else, often employed in an attempt to help the other person save face.

Subculture A culture containing many elements of the dominant culture but having unique features that distinguish its members from the rest of the population.

Subjects People participating in the study.

Suburb Any territory in a metropolitan area not included in the central city.

Succession The replacement of activities or people by others.

Superego Freud's term for the expression of internalized cultural values that reinforces the conscious understanding of the ego.

Surplus value The difference between what manufacturers are paid for goods or services and what they pay workers to produce them.

Sustainable development Constrained economic growth that recycles instead of depletes natural resources while protecting clean air, water, land, and biodiversity.

Symbolic analysts People who manipulate information: data, words, and oral and visual symbols.

Symbols The words, gestures, and objects that communicate meaning between people who share a culture.

Symmetrical family A family that is equal in the distribution of responsibilities.

Taboo A norm considered so important that to violate it is seen as reprehensible and even to speak of violating a taboo is frowned upon.

Take-off stage The second stage in development theory, a period of accelerating economic growth, a decline in the influence of tradition, the beginnings of a modern market economy, the growth of trade, increased individualism, risk taking, materialism, and saving for the future.

Take the role of the other To understand how others view the situation and what it means from their perspective.

Teamwork Two or more people working together to make a performance more realistic or appropriate.

Techniques of neutralization Strategies often used by individuals to excuse or justify actions that might otherwise be viewed negatively.

Technology Consists of the knowledge, tools, and machines used to produce artifacts or manipulate the environment.

Telecommuting Occurs when workers work from their homes and communicate with their workplace through communications technologies like Skype, including interactive voice, video, and data conferencing.

Terrorism The use of violence and threats to intimidate or coerce a government or civilian population to further some political or social objective; a form of asymmetric warfare.

Tertiary deviance When people attempt to redefine stigmatizing acts, characteristics, or identities as normal or even virtuous.

Tertiary sector Dominated by services ranging from high-wage professional advice based on knowledge to low-wage menial services.

Tests of significance Statistical procedures used to determine whether observed results could have occurred by chance.

Theoretical sampling A procedure that selects new cases different from already sampled ones to provide a basis for comparison.

Theory An organized set of concepts and relationships among those concepts offered as an explanation or account of some phenomenon.

Third-party payer Someone other than the healthcare provider or the patient who pays for the service.

Third World Nations that did not fall into the Western or Eastern blocs.

Thomas theorem If something is perceived as real, it becomes real in its consequences.

Total birth rate The average number of live births per year per thousand women in the population.

Total institution A place where a person is set apart from the rest of society and controlled by an authority within a structured environment.

Totalitarian government An authoritarian government having complete control over all aspects of people's lives—even aspects having little or nothing to do with politics.

Totem An object in the material world that a society collectively defines as sacred.

Tracking Assigning students into different types of educational programs based on their perceived aptitude.

Traditional authority Power conferred by custom and accepted practice.

Traditional stage The first stage in development theory, characterized by fatalism, an emphasis on traditional values, little or no investment or saving for the future, little work ethic, and little or no change.

Transferable If the results are likely to apply in other settings and circumstances.

Transgendered People of one sex who live as a members of the opposite sex, with which they identify.

Transsexuals People who have the biological characteristics of one sex but identify with the other sex.

The trapped People who cannot afford to leave the city who may identify with their neighborhood but dislike the city and what is has become.

Triad A group consisting of three people.

Two-tier medical system Provides one level of care for the rich and a lesser level of care for the poor.

Underclass The most impoverished segment of American society, for whom poverty is relatively permanent.

Underemployed People working at part-time jobs or self-employed and working less than desired because they cannot get a full-time job.

Underground economy All economic transactions involving income that is not reported to the government as required by law.

Unemployment rate In the United States, it is measured by the percentage of unemployed workers in the labor force actively seeking jobs.

Universal health care Health care is regarded as a right of citizens and available to all.

Unobtrusive research Research in which those studied are not aware they are being studied.

Urban decline Ecological succession in an urban environment that results in increased crime, flight of affluent residents, or an exodus of businesses.

Urbanization The large-scale movement of people from less populated areas to more populated areas.

Urban overload People are exposed to more stimuli than they can respond to each day.

Urban renewal Includes efforts to improve the urban environment intended to reduce crime, attract more affluent residents, or improve the tax base by attracting new business or industry.

Urban villages Areas of a city that people know well and in which they live, play, shop, and work.

Validity The extent to which a measure or scale measures what we think it measures.

Values Standards of desirability, rightness, or importance in a society.

Variable A measurable trait or characteristic that can vary and that is used to measure a concept.

Venture capital Companies in business to loan money to high-risk, high-potential, early-stage growth startup companies.

Verstehen The subjective understanding of individual participants anchored in a context of shared cultural ideas.

Vertical social mobility A significant increase or decrease in social standing as measured by social status, class, or power.

Veto groups Interest groups that have the capacity to prevent the exercise of power by others.

Victimless crimes Violations of the law that have no obvious victims.

Violent crime Crime that attempts to harm a person.

Virtual sex When two or more people use some form of communications technology such as text, photos, or videos to arouse each other sexually by transmitting sexually explicit messages.

War Organized conflict between nations.

Weak ties Links to people with whom we do not interact often, or with whom we have weak social relationships.

Wealth The property or economic resources owned by someone and not required for immediate consumption, such as buildings, factories, cars, stocks, and bank accounts.

Wealthfare Government policies and programs that primarily benefit the wealthy and large corporations.

Wedge issues Issues about which people have strong opinions and the position of their party receives greater public support than the other party.

White-collar crime Crime committed by relatively affluent white-collar workers, usually in the course of conducting their daily business activities.

White flight The large-scale migration of whites out of areas increasingly occupied by minorities.

Winner-take-all elections Those in which the party receiving the most votes in each district wins the whole district.

Work ethic A respect for and appreciation of people who work hard and a sense that hard work should be rewarded.

Work to rule The slowdown of work by meticulously following all regulations and doing only the minimum work legally required.

Workers People who sell their labor.

Working poor Working people whose incomes fall below the poverty line.

World systems theory A theory that argues that globalization unites countries into a single worldwide political and economic system of interrelationships.

Young old People between 65 and 74 years of age.

Zero population growth (ZPG) A state in which the population size is expected to change little or none over time.

Index

Figures and tables are indicated by *f* and *t* following page numbers.

M

Machines increasing productivity, 575
Macro-level studies, 21
Macrosociology, 137, 138–144
MAD (mutually assured destruction), 573
Magnet schools, 515
Male genital mutilation, 396
Malthus population perspective, 670–671, 671*f*
Malware, 225
Managed care programs, 636
Managerial capitalism, 578
Managers and management, 263, 591–592
Manifest functions, 18
Manufacturing and mass production, 575, 576*f*
Maquiladora plants, 326
Market economy, 577
Market pricing, 180, 180*t*
Marriage. *See also* Family; Intimate relationships
    Defense of Marriage Act (1996), 541, 717
    defined, 473
    divorce and dissolution, 488–489*f*, 488–490
    happiness and, 491, 492*f*
    marital status of elderly, 441, 442*f*
    patterns, 473–474, 474*f*
    racially mixed, 494–495, 494*f*
    same-sex partners, 726–727, 726*f*
Martineau, Harriet, 15, 723, 723*f*
Marx, Karl
    biographical information, 12
    conflict views, 262–263
    photograph, 147*f*, 530*f*
    population growth, 671–672
    religion and social change, 530
    social conflict, 149–151
    social science role, 22
    workers, view of, 12
Marxist (socialist) feminism, 415
Marxist theory, 731, 731*f*
Mass behavior, 713
Mass hysteria, 715–716
Mass media, 116–118, 400–401. *See also* Social media
Mass production, 591
Mass society theory, 728–729
Master status characteristic, 141
Material culture, 61, 145, 146
Matriarchy, 475
Matrilineal societies, 475
Matrilocal families, 474–475
The McDonaldization of Society (Ritzer), 153
The "Me," concept of self, 15, 109
Mead, George Herbert, 15, 108–109
Mean, defined, 29
Means of production, 12, 262, 263
Means test, 643
Measurement, research data, 26–27
Measures of association, 30
Mechanical solidarity, 154, 687–688
Median, defined, 29
Medicaid, 643
Medical savings accounts, 641
Medical schools, 631
Medical sociology, 611
Medications
    illegal drugs, 625–626
    over-the-counter, 626, 626*f*
    prescription drugs, 626, 626*f*, 640
    targeted to African Americans, 344–345
Medicine, 631–632
Megalopolis, 684
Melting pot, 349
Mental illness, 619, 644
Men who have sex with men (MSM), 628–629
Meritocracy, 259–260, 260*f*
Merton, Robert, 175, 176*f*, 213
Meso-level studies, 21
Mesosociology, 137–138
Metaphysical stage of sociology, 12

Metropolitan statistical area, 684
Miami Super Bowl riot (1989), 712
Micro-level studies, 21
Micropolitan statistical area, 684
Microsociology
    defined, 137
    family, 478
    social interaction, 137, 156–161
    society's development and maintenance, 149–155
Middle-income nations, 307
Migration, 318–322, 319*f*, 321*f*, 329–330, 666–668
Milgram experiment, 187–189, 188*f*
Military
    gender inequality, 411
    personnel make up, 572–573
    war and, 570–573
Military-industrial complex, 572
Military juntas, 558, 559
Mills' sociological imagination process, 99, 99*f*
Mind guards, 190
Minority groups, 347–349, 536, 589. *See also* Ethnicity; *specific minority group (e.g., African Americans, Hispanic Americans)*
Mission drift, 153, 724
Mixed economies, 578–579
Mixed-methods research, 24
Mobs, 712–713
Mode, defined, 29
Modernization theory of aging, 323–324, 330, 437
Monarchy, 557
Mongoloid, 344, 345*f*
Monkeys, social isolation, 99–100, 100*f*
Monogamy, 474
Monopoly, 594
Monopoly capitalism, 578
Monopoly of medical care, 631–632, 646
Monotheism, 531
Moore, Wilbert, 261, 261*f*
Moral boundaries, 212
Moral development, 106, 107*t*
Moral holidays, 70
Moral panic, 716
Mores, 68–69
More Than Just Race: Being Black and Poor in the Inner City (Wilson), 689
Mortality, 665, 666*f*. *See also* Death and dying
Motor vehicle accidents, 630–631, 630*f*, 635
Movies, 117–118
MSM (men who have sex with men), 628–629
Multiculturalism, 80
Multinational corporations, 330–331, 580, 582
Multiple nuclei theory, 681
Muscle dysmorphia, 624
Mutually assured destruction (MAD), 573

N

NAACP (National Association for the Advancement of Colored People), 722
National Defense Education Act of 1958 (NDEA), 523
National Health and Social Life Survey, 33–35, 385–386, 386*f*
National Organization of Women (NOW), 724
Nation-states, 330–331, 557
Native Americans
    age distribution, 441–442, 442*f*
    European settlers and, 364
    family structure, 497
    health among elderly, 451
    health and life expectancy, 614
    infant mortality rate, 643
    intimate partner homicide, 411
    socialization, 114
Natural cycle theory, 732–733
Natural disasters, 716
Naturalization Act (1790), 359
Natural rate of increase (population), 663

Nature vs. nurture, 398–399
NDEA (National Defense Education Act of 1958), 523
Negative sanctions, 210
Neglectful parenting, 485, 485*t*
Negotiated order, 20
Negroid, 344, 345*f*
Neocolonialism, 324–325
Neolocal, defined, 475
Net financial assets, 268
Netherlands, healthcare system, 640
Net migration, 318, 319*f*, 663, 666
Networks, defined, 145, 146
Net worth, 268
New social movement theory, 730–731
No Child Left Behind Act (2001), 514
No code order, 449
Nomadic people, 72
Nonmaterial cultures
    components of, 62, 62*f*
    defined, 145, 146
    ideal and real culture, 69–70
    language, 64–66, 65–66*f*, 75, 75–76*f*
    norms, 68–69, 212
    symbols, 19, 63
    values and beliefs, 66–68, 68*f*
Nonverbal gestures, 63
Nonviolent resistance, 559, 560
Normative crisis, 104
Normative organizations, 193, 193*t*
Norm of noninvolvement, 688
Norms, 68–69, 212
NOW (National Organization of Women), 724
Nuclear family, 473
Nursing homes, 454
Nurture vs nature, 398–399

O

Obesity, 622–623, 623*t*
Observer as participant, 36
Occupational inheritance, 272
Occupations and occupational structure, 585, 587, 588*t*. *See also* Workers
Occupy Wall Street movement, 330, 727
OECD (Organization for Economic and Cooperative Development), 310–311, 311*f*
Ogburn, William, 733–734, 734*f*
Old age. *See* Elderly population
Oldest old and old old people, defined, 434
Oligarchies, 558, 559
Oligopoly, 594
Online groups, 177–178. *See also* Social media
Open-ended questions, 33
Operational definition, 26
Opinions, 714–715
Opportunity, social mobility and, 275, 275*f*
Opportunity theory, 214
Optimum foraging strategy, 145, 146
Organic solidarity, 13–14, 154, 580, 687–688
Organization, defined, 192
Organizational environment, 151, 194–195
Organization for Economic and Cooperative Development (OECD), 310–311, 311*f*
Organizations
    bureaucracies, 14, 151, 193–196
    formal, 192–196, 193*t*
    future opportunities for, 197–198
Organized crime, 224–226
Ostracism, 210
Our Common Future (UN report), 693
Out-groups, 175, 190
Outsource, 580–581
Over-the-counter medications, 626, 626*f*

P

Pacific Islanders, 361, 361*f*, 441, 442*f*
PACs (political action committees), 565